# NOT THINKIN'...

## JUST
## REMEMBERIN'...

### The Making
### of John Wayne's

## THE ALAMO

## ALSO BY JOHN FARKIS

*Alamo Village: How a Texas Cattleman*
*Brought Hollywood to the Old West*

# Table of Contents

# Acknowledgments

PRIOR TO BECOMING AN AUTHOR, I WAS AN EXECUTIVE IN A FORTUNE 100 company, where *kaizen*, or the art of continuous improvement, is almost a religion. We were taught to borrow ruthlessly— take the best from the best and improve upon it. Therefore, it goes without saying that this book would not have been possible without the previous work of my illustrious compatriots. I have attempted to tell a story in the words of Messieurs. Wayne, Ford, Hawks, Widmark, Harvey et. al but obviously, to do so, it was necessary to interview each of the aforementioned individuals. However, as the research for this project began only a few years ago, many of these previously mentioned luminaries had unfortunately already passed away. As a result, in many cases, it was necessary to utilize interviews conducted by others in the past, whether they were included in books, tapes, DVDs, interview notes, newspapers, magazine articles, cassettes, or unpublished manuscripts.

I am thus grateful to Peter Bogdanovich, Harry Carey Jr., Dan Ford, Tag Gallagher, Des Hickey, Emanuel Levy, Tim Lilley, Joseph McBride, Todd McCarthy, Richard McGhee, Carolyn McGiven, Maureen O'Hara, Lee Pfeiffer, Robert Relyea, Chuck Roberson, Donald Shepherd, Anne Sinai, Andrew Sinclair, Robert Slatzer, Dean Smith, Gus Smith, George Stevens, Jr., Frank Thompson, Maurice Zolotow, and, of course, Aissa and Pilar Wayne for all their ground-breaking efforts. This book would not have been possible without their involvement, deliberate or otherwise. They had the fortunate opportunity to interview John Wayne, John Ford, Richard Widmark, Laurence Harvey and all the others who were involved in this magnificent film. I had the good fortune to benefit from their work.

For those readers interested in further pursuing the careers of Wayne, Ford, Hawks and others, I would strongly suggest you browse through the bibliographical section of this book. I would, however, like to highly recommend the following for their in-depth and insightful efforts on John Wayne: *Duke: The Life and Image of John Wayne*, by Ronald L. Davis; *John Wayne: The Life and Legend*, by Scott Eyman; *Duke: We're Glad We Knew You*, by Herb Fagen; *The John Wayne Filmography*, by Fred Landesman; *John Wayne: The Man Behind the Myth*, by Michael Munn; *John Wayne–American*, by Randy Roberts and James Olson; and last, but certainly not least, *John Wayne's The Alamo: The Making of the Epic Film*, by Donald Clark and Christopher Andersen.

Several individuals and organizations have been instrumental in providing invaluable research and materials for this project. Therefore, I would like to thank the following for all their hard work and effort: The Academy of Motion Picture Arts and Sciences, Margaret Herrick, Library; Sally Phillips and Treva Schroeder–Alamo Village, Brackettville, Texas; Gayla Cloud, Alex Frye, Rebecca Goksever and Lee Hilyer–M.D. Anderson Library, University of Houston; Jill McCleary and Christine Seliga–Arizona Historical Society, Southern Division, Library and Archives; Shanna O'Brien and Gretchen Wayne–Batjac; Lucy Carr–Bonhams; Leigh Volcsko–The Brackett News; Ellen Keith–Chicago History Museum; Kristen Lafollette–Columbia University Center for Oral History; John Rumble–Country Music Hall of Fame and Museum; Elaine Davis, Leslie Sitz Stapleton, and Warren Strickler–The Daughters of the Republic of Texas Library; Jane Elder, Cynthia Franco, and Russell L. Martin III–DeGolyer Library, Southern Methodist University; Noel Kalenian–Denver Public Library; Laura Heller and Gerrianne Schaad–Donald C. & Elizabeth M. Dickinson Research Center, National Cowboy & Western Heritage Museum; Danielle Salway–Guardian/Observer; Mahnaz Ghaznavi and Melanie Hubbard–William H. Hannon Library, Loyola Marymount University; Lisa Driscoll–Historic Newspapers; James V. D'Arc–Harold B. Lee Library, Brigham Young University; Zach Downey, David K. Fraiser and Michael Taylor–The Lilley Library, Indiana University; Cynthia McNaughton–Los Angeles Public Library; Bill Kemp–McLean County Museum of History, Bloomington, Ill; Maurice Klapwald–New York Public Library; Harry Ransom Humanities Research Center–University of Texas; Beth Standifird–San Antonio Conservation Society; Edward "Ned" Comstock, Sandy Garcia-Myers and Yesenia Martinez–University of Southern California Libraries; Mathew Martin–Southwestern Oblate Historical Archives, Oblate School of Theology; Laura Cantu–University of Texas Institute of Texan Cultures Tom Shelton–University of Texas San Antonio Libraries; Anna

Zanardo–Toronto Reference Library; Katherine Haskins, Sherry Laysen and Amy Shepherd–Wayne Enterprises; Patricia Pedersen and Judith Ann Schiff–Yale University Library.

The following research assistants located and provided the documentation necessary to enhance the quality of my work: Lisa Baehr, Tim Hommey, Margaret Kadziel, Pat Lofthouse, Ann Waters and, in particular Leisa Johnson-Kalin. Without their efforts, this book would not be possible.

In addition, I owe a special thank you to the following individuals: June Parker Beck, Daisy Jo Birchard, Mike Boldt, Bob Bryden, Richard Crawford, Alyce Davidson, Randy Dorman, Brian Downes, Cindy Edwards, Pat Faar, Jim Grieco, Jeff Grant, Jacqui Hairston, Robert Harris, Richard Hatch, Chris Hearn, John Helm, John Hinnant, Erlinda Huizar, Ned Huthmacher, Bill Jweid, Myra Mackay, Kipp Martin, Cynthia McNaughton, David Mocniak, Chris Nolan, Robert Oliver, Chuck Schoenfeld, Jim Scott, Patrick Saunders, Wylie Simmons, Debby Smith, Ann Snuggs, Phil Spangenberger, Marti Vallee, Mario Vazquez, Trey Ware, Mike Waters, Murray Weissman, Bob Williams, Bruce Winders, Nancy Wilcox and Joe Zuckschwerdt as well as members of the Shahan family including, Jamie Rains, Tulisha Wardlaw and Tully and Virginia Shahan. Although too numerous to mention, I would also like to specifically thank all the individuals who were gracious enough to share their stories with me. Their names are listed in the interview sections. Without their wonderful stories and anecdotes, there wouldn't even be a book. I sincerely apologize if I have omitted anyone. It certainly wasn't my intention.

In particular, I would like to thank Franz Karl Brown and the Daughters of the Republic of Texas for allowing me to use Reynold Brown's painting on the cover of my book. I'd also like to thank Mike Boldt for not only designing the cover but also for sharing his Bruce Minnex interview tape with me; To Craig Covner and Frank Thompson for their advice, encouragement and the Happy Shahan/Al Ybarra interview transcripts; To Jeffrey Dane for his invaluable assistance in not only offering me the names of several possible publishers in addition to reviewing my eventual contract, but also for his insightful thoughts and comments on Dimitri Tiomkin; To Ashley Ward, I can't begin to describe the innumerable conversations we had on his tremendous *Alamo* photographic collection. To Bill Chemerka and the collective members of The Alamo Society, thanks for constantly asking when this book would be published. You all gave me the needed drive and excitement to finally finish it. To James D'Arc and BYU for allowing me to view the Patrick Ford "Alamo" script written in 1948. This is what started it all. To Brian Huberman for allowing me to view the raw interview tapes of his wonderful documentary. And to my very dear friend, Maurice Jones, owner of John Wayne-The Alamo.com, and an Alamo historian, for keeping the dream alive. Too bad we live so far apart.

I would also like to thank three individuals without whom this book would not have been possible. To Rick Hassler, thanks for not only providing the back cover photograph but also for performing the difficult chore of copy editor. I'm sure when you agreed to do this you had no idea what a long, strange trip it would be. Your suggestions, comments, and recommendations significantly added to the quality of this work. I owe you a tremendous debt. To Richard Curilla. Long-time friend, mentor and confident. Your advice, technical and otherwise, significantly improved this book. I hope this is worthy of your expectations. I thoroughly enjoyed all our discussions, even the Houston camp site one! You really, really need to finish your book on Alamo Village. And finally, but most importantly, I want to thank my beautiful wife Jean. Thanks for your constant source of encouragement. They wouldn't have put all the keys in the keyboard if they didn't want me to use them and you reigned me in when necessary. Advisor, critic, and walking thesaurus, your suggestions took an otherwise pedestrian book and turned it into something I'm extremely proud of. You're the best, kiddo!

# Foreword

"HEY, JOHN. HOW'S THE STEAK?"

"Not bad, Jim. Not too bad at all."

"Want another beer?"

"Naturally."

"Say, why don't we go up to Brackettville tomorrow?"

"Why? What's in Brackettville?"

"Shoot! That's where John Wayne filmed *The Alamo*."

And so, I began a journey that culminated in the publication of the book you now hold. It was January 1996, and Jim and I were at the Cripple Creek restaurant in Del Rio, Texas. At the time, I was vice-president of operations for an automotive supply company and was looking for a new location for a maquiladora facility. I had flown into Phoenix several weeks earlier, rented a car, and driven down to Douglas, Arizona, to check out a site. It didn't meet my requirements so I started to drive back and forth across the border, checking out any and all possible locations. Along the way, I picked up Jim, one of my plant managers, and we were hard at it. After a few weeks with no luck, we took a break and found ourselves in Del Rio.

"Yeah. Back in 1959, Wayne built the set, and it's still there. Let's take a look."

"Well, do you know where it's at?"

"Not really. But it can't be that hard to find. Brackettville isn't all that big."

After a few more beers, this idea sounded pretty good, and, as we didn't have anything scheduled for the next morning, we decided to head up there to see what there was to see. As Jim said, Brackettville wasn't all that big, and we really didn't have any problem finding the set; it was only about seven miles outside of town. But, when we reached the main gate, we were disappointed to find the place closed. A tall, lanky, grizzled old cowpoke told us that Happy Shahan, the owner of the ranch and Alamo Village, had just passed away and they were having a funeral for him that day. What bad luck! So, after offering condolences, all we could do was drive back to Del Rio, cross over into Acuña, and continue our site search. Upon my return home, though, I started researching Wayne's movie set to see what it was all about. Jim was right! The set was still there, and you could even visit it, so I vowed that, as soon as I was back in the area, I'd make it a point to visit again. Six months later, I did just that.

I still vividly recall that first visit to the Village. Like thousands before me, I paid an admission fee, was handed a map of the set, and started to drive down a dusty, rutted, rock-strewn road toward the Village. Actually, to call it a road is an insult to roads. I saw a sign: "Welcome to Alamo Village. Home of John Wayne's 'The Alamo.' Lonesome Dove, Bad Girls, and over 100 Other Productions. Roam the streets that John Wayne, Jimmy Stewart, Raquel Welch, Matt Damon, Drew Barrymore, Tommy Lee Jones and Robert Duvall have walked." Another sign read "Shahan HV Ranches and Alamo Village welcome you to the largest outdoor movie set in the world." It was but a short trip; as I drove over the last rise, there it was. The Alamo. Strange, it was smaller than I expected, but, really, I didn't know what to expect. This was a movie set, not the real thing. And where should I go first, to the town or to the fort? That was easy–I parked my car by the main gate, entered the Alamo compound, and started looking around. I began to pick out where scenes were filmed in Wayne's movie. A sign said not to climb the stairs over the gate. OK. I'm a law-abiding citizen, so I just wandered around. And wandered and wandered. After a time, I decided to visit the village. As I drove toward town, I noticed the absence of other cars and realized I hadn't seen anyone in the Alamo, either. Where was everyone? I saw a sign: "Alamo Village, pop 2. We Think." Where were they? As I parked behind the "hotel," I noticed yet another sign: "No Parking. This space reserved for Happy. Violators, please notify next of kin." Discretion being the better part of valor, I decided to move over one more space. As I got out of my car, I heard strangely familiar music. Was it from *The Alamo*? So, naturally, I tried to find the source; it was coming from the Cantina. As I entered the bat-wing door, it took a moment for my eyes to adjust to the lack of light. There it was, exactly as it appeared in Wayne's film. Well, almost. But where were all the people? I returned to the street and started exploring. The jail, San Fernando church, the John Wayne Museum, Bowie's room. I had the whole village to myself. Not another soul was to be seen all day. Eventually, I entered one of the gift shops to look for a brochure or perhaps a book on the history of the Village. Nada!

After walking around for several hours and taking literally hundreds of photos, I decided to head back to the Alamo. Except this time, I ignored the sign and climbed the stairs over the main gate. How cool!!! I knew this was just a movie set but now, oddly, it had a developed a strange hold over me. I visualized what it must have been like for the Alamo's defenders on the evening of March 5, 1836, as they gazed at the massive Mexican army camped outside the walls. Surrounded, with no hope of reinforcements, all they could do was wait for their inevitable demise. I knew then I would have to write something about this movie set. But what? Then, it struck me. Using my architectural and engineering background, I would write a spec magazine article on Hollywood movie set construction techniques, using the Alamo Village as a case study. I contacted Sally Phillips at Alamo Village and pitched my idea. Once she received approval from Virginia Shahan, owner of the HV Ranch and Alamo Village, Sally began sending me dozens of set construction photos. She also put me in contact with a man named Richard Curilla, who turned out to be the Alamo Village sheriff and historian extraordinaire! Rich was instrumental in assisting me throughout the project. Eventually, my prospective article turned into a small book, *Alamo Village: How a Texas Cattleman Brought Hollywood to the Old West*. A tour guide, if you will, on Alamo Village. In its pages, I not only compared the historic Alamo with the John Wayne film, I also identified where specific scenes were filmed in the area and addressed a variety of topics that included the local history of Brackettville and Ft. Clark, John Ford's involvement in Wayne's film, a list of scenes filmed and never used, and dozens of movie-set photographs. I was privileged to interview many people who'd been involved in Wayne's film, and their anecdotes were priceless. Unfortunately, much of what they shared was never included in my book as their conversations didn't really address the topic I was writing about.

After my first book was published, I began to think about my next project. It was a shame I couldn't share the stories from all those wonderful interviews. Wait! Why not write a book about the making of John Wayne's film, but told in the words of those who'd actually been there? In many cases, the people I interviewed had never been asked to ever share their stories before. Soon, the book began to write itself. Every time I interviewed someone new, they shared the names of others who had been involved in the film; my list of interviewees eventually numbered into the hundreds. Actors, extras, crewmembers, stuntmen, and wranglers–they all had stories to share. The results of those interviews–and countless trips to Alamo Village—spawned the book you now hold in your hands. I hope you enjoy reading it as much as I did writing it.

# Introduction

WEDNESDAY, SEPTEMBER 9, 1959. AFTER ALL THE TIME, ALL THE RESEARCH and the preproduction activity, all the costume designs and the set construction, all the interviews and casting, all the begging and pleading for financing, all the discussions and endless nights, all the script revisions, all the EVERYTHING—this day had finally arrived. Duke would fulfill his dream, a dream that had its inception as far back as 1946. He would no longer be just John Wayne the *actor*. He would *produce*, *star*, and, most importantly, *direct* a major motion picture. His first! Not Howard Hawks or Raoul Walsh, not Victor Fleming or Henry Hathaway, not Herb Yates (heaven forbid) or even Pappy Ford. No, this was Wayne's picture, and he was totally in charge. How could he fail?

He had surrounded himself with the best of the best: Jimmy Grant, his favorite writer who knew exactly how he thought; Bill Clothier, an absolutely outstanding director of photography who had already been with Wayne on most of his films; Cliff Lyons, who probably had forgotten more about movie stunts than most professionals ever knew. And what about the actors! Laurence Harvey, on a tour of the United States with the Old Vic Company after filming *Room at the Top*, would add taste and elegance to the production; Richard Widmark, not of the same political persuasion as Duke but a professional nonetheless; Chill

Wills, Ken Curtis, and Denver Pyle–the latter two had just appeared with Wayne in *The Horse Soldiers*; Joan O'Brien, a talented, gorgeous young actress; Linda Cristal, a beautiful Latina actress as Crockett's love interest; Frankie Avalon, to attract the teenagers. Add Olive Carey, Jack Pennick, and Danny Borzage, and, for crying out loud, you almost had the entire John Ford Stock Company. Except it wasn't Ford's, it was Wayne's–his show, his rules, his risk. Rise or fall, succeed or fail, the responsibility was entirely his.

Early that morning, Wayne left the Wainwright house at Ft. Clark in Brackettville, where he was staying with his family: wife Pilar and daughter Aissa, along with son Michael and his wife Gretchen, daughter Toni and her husband Don LaCava, and headed out of town on a seven-mile drive to Happy Shahan's ranch where the Alamo set was located. Bill Clothier mused, "Wayne was always on the set. He was the first on the set in the morning and the last one to leave in the evening. I've come on the set many times, and John Wayne was already there, in a chair, by his motor coach. He devoted every minute of his time to the picture." And today was no exception. Although anxious to start directing his very first principal production scene, Wayne had decided to commemorate the occasion with a prayer–something not usually done when starting to shoot a movie. In fact, veterans in the film industry said they had never even heard of such a thing.[1]

Wayne had first met that day with Father Peter Rogers O.M.I. in Duke's production office on the village of San Antonio set. Father Pete, as his congregation knew the good padre, had traveled that morning from St. Mary's Catholic Church in San Antonio, bearing a prayer he had written on the way to Brackettville. Rancher Bill Moody flew Father Peter down in his private plane. Marshall Jones, Duke's lighting stand-in also aboard the plane, recalls the adventure: "Bill said, 'Marshall, I'm fixin' to take Peter Rogers down, and he's gonna bless the set. I'll be over there to get you in just a few minutes,' and we took off." Rogers was taking flying lessons at the time, and "That's what he was doing," Jones adds. "He was flying and asking questions of Bill. As we were starting down (to Brackettville), we all smelt a (burning) wire. An electrical wire somehow had done it. Both me and Bill said, 'Father, say a real good prayer for us.'"[2]

Fortunately, they landed safely. After a brief conversation with Rogers, Wayne, wearing his *Red River* Double D belt buckle, donned his "lucky" cavalry hat he had worn in numerous films in his career and, along with Richard Boone, Grant, Michael and Patrick Wayne, started the long walk up a dusty, unpaved, winding road to the Alamo compound set. There, 321 members of the cast and crew had assembled in work clothes and costumes, on foot and on horseback, awaiting the reading of the invocation. It was 8:00 a.m. As Duke stood in front of the Alamo chapel with his son Michael on his left side and Richard Boone on his right, surrounded by the rest of the company all with heads bared and bowed, Father Peter said:

"O, Almighty God, centuries ago, Thou raised a magnificent mission–a harbor, for all, of peace and freedom. This was the Alamo. Today we ask Thy blessing, Thy help, and Thy protection as, once again, history is relived in this production.

During these weeks and months that follow, keep safe, we beseech Thee, all engaged in the film. Bless it with good weather and superlative effort on the part of all.

We ask these things so that the film, *The Alamo*, will not only be the world's outstanding production, but will also be a tribute to the men who first built it, who lived in it, who died in it. We ask these things in the name of our Lord, Jesus Christ, who lived, and reigns, world without end, Amen."[3]

Clothier, Lyons on horseback, Bob Relyea, Jack Pennick, Ken Curtis, John Dierkes, Bill Daniel, and Jester Hairston, along with many, many others, listened to the invocation. Rudy Robbins, a first-time actor as a member of Crockett's band of Tennesseans, had fond memories of that morning. "I was there the first day of filming on the Alamo village set," he recalled. "It was real touching that a prayer… (they) prayed that everything would go well and no one would be hurt. And asked God's blessing on the film, and I thought that was, that was something. I was impressed." Ken Curtis, who played the part of Capt. Dickenson, agreed: "I'm not sure why Duke decided to do that. I guess he felt making *The Alamo* was his kind of divine mission, and he might just as well get the good Lord on his side from the outset. If it were anyone but Duke, I would have said the prayer was a gimmick. But you didn't get gimmicks with Duke–especially when it involved God."[4]

After the invocation, Wayne was ready to direct his first scene. It was 8:20 a.m. The Master Shooting Schedule called for filming scenes #4 and 5 that morning: the arrival of Sam Houston's column into Bexar, as well as Houston and Travis entering the headquarters building. Fifty mounted soldiers along with Texicans, Travis, Dickinson, Bonham, and extras were included in the shot.

As Joyce Bacon, *San Antonio Light* correspondent, reported, "Wayne is probably the busiest man on the set, showing actors and extras the motions he wants, expressions or the exact place to stand or walk. Frequently, he peers through the camera to check out each detail of a scene. Huge lights are raised or lowered to correct defects of the natural outdoor lighting, and the lights themselves are supplemented with big, foil covered reflectors, tilted around the fringes of the action."

To show the effect of a long, hard ride, actors' costumes were splattered with mud. Large dowser vehicles sprayed water on the dirt streets to recreate a recent "rainstorm" and keep dust to a minimum. Widmark, a costumed Harvey, and Patrick Wayne came by to watch the action, though none participated in that particular scene. Bacon wrote, "When all was ready, the actors ran through their lines and motions. Then, from a loudspeaker, came the call for quiet." Complete silence reigned, and with photographer Phil Stern, Michael Wayne, and others closely watching, Wayne, standing high above the ground on a scaffold, softly said, "Action."[5]

The scene started with a tracking shot from left to right across the screen. Boone, as Sam Houston riding a white stallion, led a column of mounted soldiers across the plain and into San Antonio. Many of the soldiers wore serapes, ponchos, and yellow or blue rain slickers. Muddy horsemen–wearing a motley collection of homespun or buckskin pants and wide-brimmed flat hats–rode in a ragged column of fours. At the front of the column, to Boone's left, were Bill Daniel as Col. Neill, Curtis as Captain Dickinson, and Bill Moody (uncredited). Bringing up the rear of the column were a caisson and limber, followed by a mule-drawn covered wagon. Animal wranglers released a small herd of goats as the first horsemen passed.

Scene #4 as revised on August 3, 1959, was written as follows: "EXT. ALAMO PLAIN–DAY. We are Shooting across a corner of the Alamo when it is (sic) the state of disrepair. Beyond the Alamo we see Houston and perhaps fifty horsemen come over the hill at a canter. They are dressed in improvised uniforms. We PAN with them as they come down onto the plain toward the town of Bexar. As we center on Bexar we can see that a column of infantry is already entering Bexar. Houston's outfit rapidly catches up with the infantry and starts to enter Bexar." (According to the Master Schedule, both Dickinson and Bonham are to be included in this scene.)

Subtle differences appear between the intended scene and the one in the final version. The Alamo itself does not appear in the scene, nor do the caissons and wagons. The infantry column referenced in the scene was never filmed in its entirety; instead, it was represented as foot soldiers marching around the corner of the Cantina. Patrick Wayne's Bonham does not appear in the scene either. This was not the only time the scene would be shot. There would be multiple takes from various angles or for just the right effect of gesture or action. Between takes, make-up and costume adjustments were made on the spot. The ground in and around the center of action was hosed down constantly to settle the dust. Under the broiling Southwest Texas sun, with the temperature over 100 °, actors spent much of their time made up and in costume, awaiting their turn in front of the camera. Several takes were necessary before Wayne was satisfied.

Initially, several covered wagons, artillery limbers and caissons were filmed as a part of the scene but were cut from the final version. This was not unusual as Wayne shot a tremendous amount of footage in making this movie. The film's continuity, pace and overall length dictated in the editing room what scenes would be included or excluded. Virginia Shahan said that when she, Wayne, and Happy watched a rough cut of the film one day, it lasted over six hours. Hard to believe, but with all the scenes filmed but never used and all the extended scenes that were eventually shortened, it was possible. (In all probability, however, she may have been referring to the dailies as she recalled seeing slate numbers and hearing Wayne swearing in the background after the scene was finished, or it could possibly even be the "first assembly." In a first assembly, the editor and director have already selected the take they will use for each scene. The editor strings them together end to end, but each shot is edited in "from camera start to camera finish," not just the segment they will ultimately trim it down to. This at first even includes the scene identification slates. A "first assembly" can be twice as long as the final edited motion picture.)

(Originally, Scene #4 included dialog. Daniel would have had the distinction of delivering the first spoken line in the film. He would be at the head of a column of cavalry that Houston brought to San Antonio. Riding alongside Boone, Daniel's dialog required him to comment on various places in town. According to those present, Daniel played the scene flawlessly and received a hand from the crew for his efforts. This sequence, though filmed, was not used. Amusingly, the *Dallas Morning News* reported Daniel shouted "Column right: forward march" to a group of ragged *Tennesseans* about to enter San Antonio before the Alamo siege.)[6]

When they finished filming that particular sequence, Wayne began setting up Scene #5. "EXT. BEXAR STREET–ANGLE ON San Antonio HOTEL. As Houston and his men dismount. A few aides enter the hotel with Houston. TRAVIS comes from where he was leading the infantry column and follows Houston. As they enter we see that a man is painting "HEADQUARTERS" on the wall of the doorway." This scene was slightly modified as scripted in that Travis enters the hotel prior to Houston's arrival and the man painting "HEADQUARTERS" is eliminated.

Using a camera mounted on a movable dolly on wooden tracks, this scene as filmed follows Houston and his horsemen as they move down the street, past a column of twenty-five or so foot soldiers, standing at attention. Houston's arrival is a combined pan and tracking shot. As Boone rides around the corner, the camera begins to dolly right (almost backward). Then the camera pans right 180° to follow Boone as he passes and then holds on the hotel as the camera tracking comes to a stop. It is a slightly clumsy move, but it was in the day of a camera crane or truck driving on heavy wooden boards laid on ties. The complicated maneuver kept the camera centered on Boone throughout the shot. The first of several continuity errors in the movie appears in this sequence. In the previous scene, Ken Curtis and others rode into town at the head of Houston's column. In this scene Curtis is absent. In fact, he now appears inside the hotel, awaiting Houston's arrival and greeting. Apparently, they discovered the error during filming and decided not to redo that scene.[7]

After filming these first two scenes, the production company broke for lunch. Surrounded by cast and crewmembers, Wayne was presented with a large rectangular sheet cake congratulating him on the start of his project. The cake had a relief of the Alamo chapel in frosting on its top. With a smile, Duke gladly sliced the cake with Harvey's saber and passed out pieces to happy members of the company. With lunch completed, the crew returned to the set to film another outdoor scene.

Scene #15. "EXT. STREET–As Houston and Travis come out. Houston crosses to his horse. The other men start to mount, when Houston looks off and sees an aged Negro in the group at the foot of the stairs. After a short conversation with the man... He tickles the horse with the spurs and all move off, leaving Travis and Dickinson and their men looking after them. Jethro looks after them a moment, then trots across the courtyard. He goes up a flight of steps." Again, the scene filmed differs from the directions. Dickinson and Travis were not in this scene, as Travis had remained inside the hotel after speaking with Houston, and Dickinson had walked outside when Houston demanded "Clear the room!" In addition, Hairston's Jethro walked through a doorway into Bowie's room, rather than up a flight of stairs.

Marshall Jones, having flown in with Moody, appeared in this scene as a bystander behind Hairston. Marshall recalls this scene fondly: "I never noticed before, but, for some reason, I'm always staring at the ground. Don't know why. They never asked me to audition, just said to stand behind Jester and smile. I guess they wanted to see how I would look." Brackettville resident Chuck Hall recalls another inconsistency in this scene: Dressed in a long-sleeve shirt, dark pants, boots and slouch hat, the youngster stands next to a woman and little girl as Boone walks by to speak with Hairston. Seven seconds later, though, in an over-the-shoulder shot of Boone, Hairston, and Jones, Chuck now is sitting in the crook of a tree, immediately behind Hairston. "Wayne placed me in that tree," says Hall. "He did that personally." He must have really liked the amazingly quick appearance of young Chuck.[8]

After a brief conversation, Houston mounted his horse and rode out of town at the head of his column. Jack Pennick, ex-Marine veteran of the Peking Garrison, World War I, and the John Ford Naval Field Photographic Reserve (Field Photo), appears in the background as Sgt. Lightfoot, leaning against the hotel wall watching the column leave Bexar. Houston's departure is another scene shortened from what was initially filmed. The scene originally continued with the column riding down the street, out onto the plains outside the town, and back across the front of the San Fernando Church—similar to the way it had entered the town in the opening scene. This was eliminated from the final version of the film with the exception of a short sequence as the column starts to ride out of town. In the background, you can hear a voice shouting encouragement to the men. Actor/Extra Jim Brewer says, "...in one of the scenes where Richard Boone and his men ride off in the San Antonio street, you could hear my voice-over saying, 'Take care, men!' I wasn't on camera during that scene. As they rode by, I yelled those lines. I don't think Duke or the assistant director(s) told me to do so. I just improvised it, and the editors left the line in the film."[9]

With a seemingly endless number of extras to draw on, it is interesting that several cast members appeared in a variety of scenes as different individuals. Rudy Robbins (one of Crockett's Tennesseans) and John Dierkes (who played Jocko, one of Bowie's men) both rode out of town as part of Houston's column. When questioned, Rudy replied, "Yes, I forgot about that. They just picked a bunch of guys and dressed them up like that, and, later, most of them wound up working as part of Bowie's men. They put me in there. I forgot about that." (A careful analysis of numerous photos taken this day would suggest two other scenes were also filmed but not included in the finished film: the mounted arrival of Travis, Bonham and Dickenson into San Antonio, and the subsequent entrance of Travis into the hotel (as filmed from outside). The first sequence would explain why the trio was already in the hotel when Houston arrived. This sequence was filmed with the same camera set-up subsequently used to film the arrival of Houston and his troops. It was eventually deleted from the final print either because it was too repetitive or didn't move the story along.)[10]

After they finished filming Houston's departure, the company wrapped for the day. Three scenes and 1½ pages of script had been completed–an excellent beginning. First shooting days for a company are usually planned as fairly light–well within the means of what could normally be expected for a day. The production team is just starting to work together and must form routines–sort of a way to shake things down. *The Alamo* was no different. That evening, as Wayne drove back to Ft. Clark, he must have wondered, *Why had it taken fifteen years to finally reach this point?*[11]

# CHAPTER ONE
# BEGINNINGS

*"This is going to shake hell out of people all over the world. And that is what I want most of all to accomplish. I want to remind the freedom loving people of the world that not to (sp) long ago there were men and women in America who had the guts to stand up and fight for the things they believed in. The people of the Alamo realized that in order to live decently, a man must be prepared to die decently. There were no namby-pamby pussyfoots, malingerers or skedaddle in that brave band. They were rough, lusty, hard-fighting, hard-drinking, hard-loving men who held to one common conviction, that freedom is worth fighting and dying for, and they gave their last drop of blood to be true to it. In San Antonio, Texas, the Alamo is venerated as a sacred shrine, but it does not belong to Texas alone. It belongs to people everywhere who value the priceless treasure that has always been bought with blood; freedom...remind freedom loving people all over the world of the kind of guts my country is built on. You think I'm cornball? Well, I'm not ashamed to be proud of my country!"*[12]

WAYNE REALIZED HIS DREAM WHEN HE DECIDED TO DIRECT, PRODUCE, AND star in the culmination of his lifelong pursuit: *The Alamo*–a movie that celebrated heroism. This project embodied the personal values for which he stood. For Wayne, the heroic defense of a crumbling fortress in 1836 against overwhelming Mexican opposition represented one of the most glorious episodes in American history; it was a moment when, as so eloquently stated in the opening titles, men had to choose "...to endure oppression or to resist." Despite unbelievable odds and the reluctance of major Hollywood studios to finance the project unless he starred in it, *The Alamo* was something Wayne felt passionate about. It was

1

the reaffirmation of the basic goodness of the human spirit, of how people of principle and courage could sacrifice everything they held sacred for the benefit of a greater cause. "This is the big American story that I didn't think anyone could do better than I," he said. "It's the first time in my life that I've been able to express what I feel about people."[13]

Duke's dream to honor the men who died fighting for freedom at the mission fortress in San Antonio came from his lifelong love of American history, particularly the settling of the frontier. Born in Middle America Winterset, Iowa, 1907, only thirty-one years removed from the country's centennial birthday, the West represented for Wayne the ultimate challenge. Said Duke, "The West–the very words go straight to that place of the heart where Americans feel the spirit of pride in their western heritage–the triumph of personal courage over any obstacle, whether nature or man."[14]

John Wayne started in the movie industry in 1925 in order to fund his education at the University of Southern California. Working behind the scenes at Fox, Warner Bros., and MGM, he toiled in the property department. "My first job," he told a reporter in 1953, "was herding geese in *Mother McCrea* (sic). I got nailed with the job of scaring them out in front of the camera to waddle up a hill. To this day, I can't get excited about anything with feathers." While there, he also appeared as a bit player, stand-in, and extra–whatever was necessary or asked of him. "In those days, you could operate in every department of pictures," said Wayne. "You didn't need a union card. I was a carpenter. I was a juicer. I rigged lights. I helped build sets. Carried props. Hauled furniture. I got to know the nuts and bolts of making pictures. That is why I know what a scene is going to look like on film. I don't have to look at the daily rushes. I never do."[15]

In the fall of 1926, a surfing accident prematurely ended his college football career, and the following June, Wayne dropped out of college to pursue full-time employment. He returned to Fox and once again worked in the property department. Over the next eleven years, he was involved in eighty-one movies in one capacity or another: costumed extra, spear-carrying guard, stand-in, corpse, wrangler, stuntman, featured player, and, finally, lead actor. During that period, although he had starred in *The Big Trail*, his career had consisted mainly of low-budget, formula-driven, action-packed, cliché-ridden "B" serials and "oaters." Entertaining certainly but of little substance, those films failed to attract critical acclaim. Wayne's attitude was somewhat laissez-faire: "My main duty was to ride, fight, keep my hat on, and at the end of shooting still have enough strength left to kiss the girl and ride off on my horse, or kiss my horse and ride off on the girl–whichever they wanted." While working at various studios such as Fox, Columbia, Mascot, Monogram, etc., Wayne studied, perfected, and fine-tuned his craft. It was during this "apprenticeship" that he developed his halting cadence, trademark walk, and screen persona.[16]

Pausing in the middle of a sentence, slowing down his delivery, Wayne explained his unique style: "You say, 'I think I'll . . .' Now they're looking at you, and you can stand there for twenty minutes before you say 'go to town.' If you say it normally, 'I think I'll go to town. Umm (pause). Then we can go over and see something,' the audience would have left you. But if you say, 'I think I'll go (pause) to town and I'll (pause) see those three broads,' now they're waiting for you. You can take all the goddamn time you want if you choose your time for the hesitation."[17]

As for Duke's famous rolling walk, his friend, acting coach, and confidant Paul Fix engineered that. For years, he would stand off-camera when Wayne worked a scene. Using hand and facial signals, Fix would give direction to Wayne: how to move, where to stand, when to turn. No one was ever the wiser. "He had trouble with the physical side of acting," said Fix, "like how to move and what to do with your hands. He said he hated watching himself on the screen because he always looked so stiff. I told him to try and point his toes into the ground as he walked, and, when he did that, his shoulders and hips sort of swung. He practiced that walk until it looked so graceful on the screen...." "When I started," said Wayne, "I knew I was no actor, and I went to work on this Wayne thing. It was as deliberate and studied a projection as you'll ever see. I figured I needed a gimmick, so I dreamed up the drawl, the squint, and a way of moving meant to suggest that I wasn't looking for trouble but would just as soon throw a bottle at your head as not. It was a hit-or-miss project for a while, but it began to develop." According to Wayne, the waffled forehead, the cocked eyebrow, and the swiveled-hipped walk were his own inventions. Wayne learned his craft and learned it well.[18]

He learned to ride a horse from Jack Padgin, stunt coordinator and wrangler on *The Big Trail*. "I'd say," Wayne mused, "that Jack Padgin was one hell of a fine horseman. He could ride like a bat out of hell. And he was the guy who went out and got the horses for a picture and got the right kind of horses to do the job. He was more a less ramrod as they say, hiring cowboys and horses for a picture, but not that much of a stuntman in those days." Of course, "Motion picture riding is tough," admitted Wayne. "You can't fake it. I had a bad fall in *Yellow Ribbon*. I was leadin' a bunch of horses through an Indian camp. We were ridin' McClellan saddles, which have no horn. I was supposed to wave a blue coat and start some ruckus to confuse the Indians. Well, the cinch belt came loose, and, when I started waving, the saddle came loose, twisting me out of position, and the horse sensed something wrong, and he panicked and stiff-legged and threw me. I blacked out and damn near had a brain concussion, and there was something like fifty horses behind me, charging in the direction of my body and Mr. Ford's yelling and there's general hysteria. But some wrangler with guts, he just runs out and heads off the stampeding horses. I think that was just about the closest call I've ever had on location. Those horses came within a few feet of trompin' me to death!"[19]

3

*Rugged individualism, self-reliance, patriotism, and loyalty*–these were more than just words to him. He appeared in Westerns and adventures and the character traits of Wayne the actor became the values of Wayne the man. He once told a friend, "If I could choose one person in American history I wish I'd been, I'd choose Sam Houston. He had a philosophy of life I've tried to live by. He always wore a ring, a ring his mother gave him. Just a plain gold ring. When he died, they took it off. It had a word inscribed inside: *honor.*"[20]

In 1937, Republic Studios lured Wayne back from Universal Studios with an offer to play Sam Houston in a large-budget film *if* he signed a five-year contract at less money than previously offered. He also had to work in a series. The only reason he went to Universal in the first place was to try to break out of the "B" picture Western mold he'd found himself in. Tired of being typecast, he was restless for change. Unfortunately, some poorly conceived, low-budget projects resulted in his loss of prominence as a Western star, and failure with the major studios. As a result, he was forced to sign the Republic contract but, when it started filming the Houston story, Herbert Yates, president of Republic, told him he wasn't big enough at the box office and gave the role to Richard Dix (*Man of Conquest*, 1939). In Wayne's words, "I was ambitious and wanted to vary my pictures. I just had to come crawling back to Herbert Yates and beg for money. I didn't want to make these cheapies for Republic, but seemed like there was nothin' else to do. I lost my stature as a western star. I got nothing in return."[21]

Ford had initially suggested Raoul Walsh use Wayne when *The Big Trail* was made back in 1930. "I took one look at him," Walsh said, "and thought, here's my lead. Dammit, the son of a bitch looked like a man. To be a cowboy star, you gotta be six-foot-three or over; you gotta have no hips and a face that looks right under a sombrero." (Interestingly, *The Big Trail* was filmed and released simultaneously in both the Fox Grandeur and standard 35mm version.) Walsh also changed Duke's name from Marion Morrison to John Wayne, a name that has become synonymous with the American hero. In 1938 while at United Artists, John Ford elected to borrow the thirty-two-year-old actor for his movie *Stagecoach* after not being able to afford his first choice: Gary Cooper. Ford described the part to Duke and asked him to recommend an actor; in his naiveté, Wayne recommended Lloyd Nolan. Ford's decision to use Wayne instead was a wise one as glowing reviews of Wayne's performance as the Ringo Kid catapulted Duke to the forefront of the movie-going public and Monument Valley as the place to film Westerns. "John Wayne seemed born for the part he plays," said *The Hollywood Reporter*. "*Stagecoach* was a milestone in film history as well as in John Wayne's history," said Duke's eldest son Michael. "It took my father out of 'B' movies and put him into 'A' movies. Interestingly, it did the same thing for westerns as a film genre." Wayne also had the honor of "discovering" Monument Valley despite Ford legend to the contrary. Years earlier, Duke had been hired as an assistant on a George O'Brien Western. A scrounger, if you will. "One of my jobs," wrote Wayne to the *Saturday Evening Post*, "was to get four hundred head of cattle into Blue Canyon which was 150 miles from any paved road. A preacher who had a little church on the Hopi reservation agreed to help me gather them. In gathering those cattle, we horse-backed into Monument Valley. For ten years I held that back as a possible future location. Finally, when Jack Ford decided to use me for the lead in *Stagecoach*, he said, 'Now, if I could only find a fresh, picturesque area to represent the West of the 1800s.' I promptly suggested Monument Valley. He promptly suggested that I was hired as an actor and not the director, but he took note of what I had said and, upon his return from location hunting, I was standing with some of the crew when he approached and said, 'I have found the most colorful location that could ever be used for a picture.' Then he looked directly at me and said, 'Monument Valley.' I assure you from that moment on, Jack Ford discovered Monument Valley."[22]

Wayne's popularity soared overnight, but unfortunately he was still under contract to Republic and forced to appear in more low-budget Westerns. Yates would not let other studios utilize his services until he fulfilled his obligations, and Yates must have thought Wayne's popularity was fleeting. From February until September 1939, Wayne appeared in five more "oaters." In November, he teamed up once again with Claire Trevor, who had also appeared in *Stagecoach*, and made *The Dark Command*. Receiving favorable reviews, some said it was probably the best film Republic made in its first five years of existence. It was even nominated for three Academy Awards including Best Picture, but failed to win any. "Republic moves definitely into the big leagues," said *The Hollywood Reporter*. "The most pleasant surprise of the movie (though) is the solid performance of John Wayne." Set photographers also must have been fairly impressed with his performance as during a particularly important stunt, in which a wagon pulled by two horses crashed over a cliff into the water below, not only were two movie cameras used to film the sequence, but still photographers preserved the gag for posterity with five additional cameras![23]

It was two more years before he worked again with Ford, this time co-starring in *The Long Voyage Home* at United Artists. The film was a compilation of four Eugene O'Neill's one-act plays: *The Moon of the Caribees*, *In the Zone*, *Bound East for Cardiff*, and *The Long Voyage Home*. A critical success, the film did poorly at the box office in its initial release, but Ford was voted Best Director by the New York Film Critic Circle, and the film received six Academy Award nominations including Best Picture. No longer just a journeyman actor and because of his ensuing success, other studios finally recognized the emerging star. After completing the Ford film, Wayne went to Universal to star with Marlene Dietrich in *Seven Sinners*, and, upon completing that, he worked with Henry Hathaway in *Shepherd of the Hills* at Paramount. Wayne began a torrid affair with Dietrich while filming *Sinners*. According to Hollywood legend, when she first saw Wayne at a studio commissary, she turned to director Tay Garnett and said, "Daddy, buy me that!" Prior to the start of filming, she invited Duke into her dressing room, closed the door, and locked it. As he stood idly by observing the star's luxurious appointments, Dietrich, with a smoldering look, murmured, "I wonder what time it is?" Then, before he had a chance to reply, she "lifted her skirt, revealing the world's most famous legs. Her upper thigh was circled by a black garter with a timepiece attached." She looked at it, dropped her skirt, swayed to Duke's side, and said in a husky voice, "It's very early, darling. We have plenty of time." Once again, he gave a top-notch performance. (In later years, when asked if he ever fell in love with one of his leading ladies, he immediately said, "Yes, Dietrich.") He had played opposite Dietrich, Trevor, Paulette Goddard, Joan Crawford, and Susan Hayward and been directed by Ford, Walsh, and Hathaway. He was finally on his way. Starring in five movies in 1940 and another four in 1941, Wayne rode the crest of the wave of acclaim, demand, and respect. Although not a major attraction like Gary Cooper or Clark Gable, his movies usually were successful and profitable. Completed in September 1941, Wayne starred in Cecil B. DeMille's *Reap the Wild Wind*. Before it was released, however, the Japanese attacked Pearl Harbor.[24]

Hollywood responded by enlisting in droves: Jimmy Stewart, John Ford, Henry Fonda, Robert Montgomery, William Wyler, Frank Capra, and Darryl F. Zanuck. The list was endless. Young or old, popular or not, single or married, director or actor, all responded to the call of patriotism. Former pacifists readied their affairs for early enlistment. Those past draft age volunteered for Home Defense duty. Most active Reservists eagerly stepped back into uniform. Many not called in the draft prepared to enlist; the country was facing its most serious crisis. Everybody in Hollywood wanted to do something—to contribute in some way. Even Wayne's brother, Robert Morrison, had been drafted into the Navy. Wayne, however, struggled with the issue of enlistment. Married with four children and thirty-four years of age, Wayne probably would not be drafted. He was at the peak of his early acting career and the only way he was going to serve in the armed forces was to enlist. The California Selective Service was instructed to issue deferments to individuals vital to the motion picture industry. Many Washington and California officials argued that Gary Cooper was more valuable to the war effort as *Sergeant York* than as Sergeant Cooper.[25]

Later in his career, Wayne stated that Republic would not let him out of his contract. That may have been true as Wayne was the studio's leading money-maker at that time, but negative publicity associated with the studio's decision not to allow Wayne to enlist would have been devastating. In fact, Herb Yates told him he would sue Wayne for breach of contract if he tried to enlist. According to Henry Hathaway, "Frankly, I think the excuse that he didn't enlist because of a shoulder injury was a story the studio put out to justify their own reasons for keeping Wayne to his contract and preventing him from enlisting. I think... he would have enlisted if he were able." Wayne treasured a notion of himself in officer's garb. "But I would have had to go in as a private," Wayne said. "I took a dim view of that. I felt that it would be a waste of time spending two years picking up cigarette butts." But Gable, Stewart, Montgomery and Fonda enlisted. Why didn't Wayne?[26]

Witness the case of Lew Ayres. The thirty-two-year-old actor who had starred in *All Quiet on the Western Front* (1930) was so affected by the character he played that when war broke out, he announced he was a conscientious objector and would not serve. Newspapers questioned his patriotism, his studio dropped him, and his movies were banned by one hundred theatres. That choice "...has ruined him. His film life is dead, because a fellow can't live down the fact that he has refused to bear arms in defense of his country." Stated John Balaban of Balaban & Katz (Illinois theater owners), "We are not in sympathy with Ayres's attitude, and we don't believe the film-going public is either." Why should Wayne risk similar backlash?[27]

An analysis of Wayne's Selective Service records provides an interesting perspective of his relationship with Republic Studios. At various times throughout the war, Wayne was classified as 4-A (deferment on the basis of age); 3-A (deferred for dependency reasons); 2-A (deferred in support of national health, safety, or interest); and 1-A (available for military service). Local draft boards periodically reviewed all classifications, and, depending upon its needs, the government changed some classifications. Although there is no record of Wayne asking for a different classification, authors Randy Roberts and James S. Olsen in their book *John Wayne: American* make a strong case that Republic, in order to protect its moneymaker, filed for a deferment on Wayne's behalf. At least twice during the war, Wayne's classification was revised to a 2-A level. At no time during the war did Wayne appeal any of these deferrals. Close friend Paul Fix also believed that Republic was responsible for Wayne's status. "Duke was anxious to get back to the troops," said Fix, referring to Wayne's tour of the Pacific, "but Yates saw to it that he didn't go. He filed for a 2-A deferment for Duke. Although he did his best, (Wayne) always felt like a fraud for not getting in uniform, but that was never his fault, despite what some have said."[28]

Wayne was no conscientious objector, so the decision not to serve weighed heavily on his mind. According to biographer Maurice Zolotow, Duke tried to enlist three times, going so far as to fly to Washington to request the aid of John Ford, then a naval lieutenant commander, to help him get into the Navy. "I remember a rougher time," said Wayne. "The time when the Army, Navy, and Air Force turned me down, wouldn't let me fight for my country." He said he was rejected because he was unfit due to a bad back, an old shoulder injury, and an inner ear problem. Said George Sherman, who directed Wayne in a number of *Mesquiteer* films early in Wayne's career, "It frustrated Duke like hell that he couldn't join up... I know he felt tremendous guilt about not serving. It's plagued him all his life." Wayne's youngest daughter Aissa states that perhaps her father's fervent passion about *The Alamo* resulted from his lack of service in the armed forces during World War II: "I also suspect that he was eager to make *The Alamo* because of a longtime private regret. To a man who believed that life largely meant testing one's self, this (failure to serve) was an ultimate test untaken." Catalina Solor Lawrence, a script supervisor at Republic during the war who sometimes doubled as Wayne's secretary, remembered writing letters of inquiry to military officials for Wayne, but he never really followed up on them. (She would later be promoted to producer's assistant on *Angel and the Bad Man*.) There is a story that when Wayne met with PT boat commander Lt. Robert Montgomery and Lt. Cmdr. John Ford, both in their naval uniforms, to discuss *They Were Expendable*, he was so overcome with emotion that he had to leave the room to weep over his shame at not fighting for his country.[29]

*(Author's disclaimer: Although information from Maurice Zolotow's biography of John Wayne, "Shooting Star," was used in the development of this book, it should be noted that both Wayne and members of his family vehemently denied the accuracy of Zolotow's book and called it "unauthorized" and "almost fiction." According to Michael, "There's hardly a statement in it about my mother that's correct. I was John Wayne's son for forty-four years and Mary St. John was his secretary for twenty-eight years, and we can recall only two hours that Zolotow ever spent with him." Duke was furious as well. "I have two choices... I could go kick his God damn teeth down his throat or not pay any attention to him. So I decided not to because he'd sue me anyway. That's the type of man he is. (Zolotow) said my mother was carrying me when she was married. If I knocked that guy on his ass, what would you people say? If Zolotow has a broken hip, a broken neck, and he didn't get it in an auto accident, don't blame me. If my mother had been alive I guarantee you she would have horse whipped him down main street.")[30]*

If he was not going to enlist, Wayne decided the best way for him to support the war effort was to make entertaining movies that would promote American ideals and beliefs. For a time, he and Ward Bond were even air-raid wardens, watching the sky over the La Brea district in Los Angeles, every night from midnight to 6:00 a.m. (Bond, an epileptic, was rejected by the draft.) Ford did not miss a chance to taunt Wayne about the civilian clothes. He wrote, "I hear you're doing a hell of a job air wardening. How does Uncle Ward look with a tin hat and a pair of binoculars?" Years later Ford humiliated Duke for his lack of service. Donna Reed, his leading lady in *They Were Expendable*, recalled the vicious manner in which Ford treated Wayne on the set. "In one scene Ford didn't like the way Duke was saluting. He said, 'You don't have the faintest idea how to salute, do you, you clumsy so-and-so? That's because you never joined up. You just stayed home and made money from lousy pictures while your countrymen were giving up their lives.' And he kept on about this, really putting Duke down who said nothing in his own defense, until, finally, Bob (Montgomery) stepped in and shouted at Ford, saying, 'You don't ever talk to Duke like that. You should be ashamed of yourself.' Ford just sat there, stunned into silence, and I think he did feel ashamed. In fact, I'm sure he was crying. Duke went over to him, patted him on the back, and said, 'That's okay, Coach. You just want to make this film the best it can be.'"[31]

Wayne periodically washed dishes and bused tables at the Hollywood Canteen, an entertainment venue manned by celebrities. He even carved a turkey on Thanksgiving, 1943. Upon his return from a Hollywood Victory Committee-USO tour of Pacific bases, Wayne declared, "Overseas is where I belong. I have some picture commitments that I have to fill, but aside from that, I have told the Hollywood Victory Committee that as long as I can contribute something to the war by visiting our troops, that I shall do." He continued, "What they needed is more letters, cigars, snapshots, needles, and radios. They're fighting a hellva war. It's work and sweat. If it's one hundred and thirty degrees, they call it a cool day. That's when they scrape the flies off."[32]

According to John Ford, Wayne was a member of the O.S.S. (Office of Strategic Services), reporting directly to Ford. "He was doing undercover confidential work. Duke never wore a uniform while he was in the South Pacific. But we saw very little of him during the war. He was always on a mission someplace." One must take what Ford said with a grain of salt, though. With a twinkle in his eye and his typical Irish humor, Ford was a master of sarcasm. In personal correspondence to his wife Mary during the war, Ford constantly belittled Wayne and Bond for their failure to serve in the military. However, in an unpublished portion of Dan Ford's biography of his uncle Jack, it states that it was arranged for Wayne to receive a secret commission as a captain in the Army Reserve. He was given an assignment by William (Wild Bill) Donovan, director of the O.S.S., as a part of Wayne's U.S.O. tour to meet with General Douglas MacArthur and file a report on the effective functioning of MacArthur's headquarters. Although Wayne never did meet the general, he did file a report including observations made during the tour, and, when he returned, he received a plaque indicating that he served in the O.S.S. According to Wayne, "It was a copperhead. Something Jack set up. It didn't mean anything." Paul Fix also recalled the mission: "Duke was over the moon when he got a secret commission from…Donovan to use the tour to collect information about the officers and men serving in the South Pacific. Duke tried to get to meet MacArthur, but it seems he got wise to Duke's mission and avoided meeting him under any circumstances. Duke made his report as best he could, and Donovan sent him a certificate of commendation, although it was sent to Ford's house. Duke got pretty mad when he received a plaque saying he served in the O.S.S. because John Ford had made it out of copper–his way of putting Duke down. So Duke never even bothered to pick up the certificate. He felt he had done his duty, and Ford snubbed him anyway. Ford could be really cruel that way."[33]

However, on August 2, 1943, Wayne did file form SA-1, Application for

9

Employment and Personal History Statement with the O.S.S. In his response to question Sec. 26, part d, qualifications, Wayne replied, "Having a natural inclination and being suited physically and mentally to outdoor activity and having the ability to get along with any class of people (that) might have a particular bearing on the position in which I might be of value to the Service." He also replied that he was "going through a stage of marital misunderstanding." While there is no record Wayne was interviewed for any particular position, there is circumstantial evidence he may have been accepted into the Service. As mentioned, Catalina Lawrence wrote letters to various members of the military on Wayne's behalf inquiring about openings in John Ford's O.S.S. Photo unit. A Navy official responded that although the navy and marine allotments for the unit were filled, there was room under the army allotment. Wayne then submitted the application. In later years, he confessed Donovan approved his request, but the letter was sent to Josephine, his estranged wife, and she never told him about it. His application stated his current address was 312 North Highland, Los Angeles, which was where his family resided. The only issue was that he was staying at the Chateau Marmont Hotel on Sunset Boulevard, so it is possible he may have been accepted. Wayne wrote to Ford, "Finally obtained by hook, crook, threatening phone calls letters and telegrams, the information required for form (number 21, etc.) It's on the way. They took me on location before I could complete the information–Bond and a couple of others tried to finish filling it out but had trouble obtaining some of my in-law data...."[34]

Before Pearl Harbor, Hollywood had produced a number of contemporary combat films. *A Yank in the R.A.F.* was the fourth most popular film of 1941. *Dive Bomber*, *I Wanted Wings*, and *Flight Command* had stressed the importance of military preparedness. But once the war started, the film industry joined hands with the government to produce ultrapatriotic, even blatantly propagandistic entertainments to bolster the war effort. *Reap the Wild Wind*, released in March 1942, was a saga of America's fight for freedom of the sea in the mid-1800s. Part of the proceeds from the world premiere went to the treasury of the Navy Relief Society. After he made *The Spoilers* and *In Old California*, Wayne appeared in his first patriotic war film, *Flying Tigers*, as Squadron Leader Jim Gordon of the American Volunteer Group, fighting over the Chinese mainland on the eve of Pearl Harbor. The movie showed it took a team effort to win the war. He followed this movie with *Pittsburgh*, "(a) carelessly made film but it's pretty good propaganda and it teaches a good lesson–that in working for others is true happiness found." As Charles "Pittsburgh" Markham, Wayne's character throws away his life focusing on greed, power, and pleasure. It was a strong tribute to American factory workers, exhorting them even greater levels of wartime production. After he lost his wife and company, the outbreak of World War II gave Markham a second chance, and he redeemed himself by supporting the war effort. Wayne followed this with *Reunion in France*, in which he played a downed RAF pilot who escaped from a concentration camp. The following year, Wayne appeared in *The Fighting Seabees* as Wedge Donovan, who formed the first construction battalion for the navy. It showed that no matter what you did, whether in uniform or not, it was important to the war effort.[35]

After making two period films, *Tall in the Saddle* and *Flame of Barbary Coast*, during the summer of 1944, Wayne starred in *Back to Bataan*, which was an "honest tribute to Filipino resistance... and a vivid re-enactment of the Corregidor victory." During the filming, executive producer Robert Fellows insisted on a stunt double for Wayne in a scene where the star was blown out of a foxhole. "If you do it yourself," explained Fellows, "no one will believe it is you anyway, so use the double." But director Edward Dymtryk sided with his star, and Wayne did the stunt. Later, Wayne met Fellows and ruefully said, "You were right, Bob. I haven't found anyone who believes it was me and not a double in that scene." Wayne followed that up with *They Were Expendable*. He co-starred with Montgomery as the members of Motor Torpedo Boat Squadron Three chosen to escort MacArthur's evacuation from the Philippines. Wayne was a believable war hero. "When you saw Wayne on-screen," said David Miller, director of *Flying Tigers*, "you caught his sense of patriotism and sincerity." He even collaborated on a screenplay with director Irving Cummings and sold it to Twentieth Century Fox. "But I know it frustrated him being a hero on screen only and not in real life," Miller admitted. "One time he said, 'Jesus, David. What are people going to think when they see me winning the war against the Japs when they know I'm a fake?' I said, 'You're not a fake, Duke. You're the real thing. You act with your heart, you give your character honesty and sincerity, and you're going to make Americans feel safer if they can believe that there are men like you fighting the enemy. So stop beating yourself up.'"[36]

By the end of the war, Wayne was a leading actor. Confident, mature, and dominant, he had developed into a major screen presence. An All-American hero, he embodied all the traits that the country aspired to have. "My father became the symbol of the cowboy," said Michael Wayne. "He wasn't a cowboy, but people saw him that way." And the same could be said when he played the role of the American fighting serviceman. Trading in his chaps for fatigues, strong and silent, a defender of the weak, Wayne exemplified the patriotic beliefs of a nation desperate for a hero. Maureen O'Hara said it best when she testified before a congressional subcommittee: "...John Wayne is not just an actor, and a very fine actor, John Wayne is the United States of America. He is what they believe it to be. He is what they hope it will be. And he is what they hope it will always be. It is every person's dream that the United States will be like John Wayne and always be like him." According to Wayne, "In all my films, I try never to forget that people are seeing me for enjoyment, and, if there is a message to a movie, it is a positive, simple one. I believe the good guys should win, and that, when they don't win personally, the principle of goodness should win out." The war was over and Wayne's career was forever defined.[37]

# CHAPTER TWO
# POLITICAL REFLECTIONS I

*"…now I always thought I was a liberal. I came up terribly surprised one time when I found that I was a right-wing, conservative extremist, when I have listened to everybody's point of view that I ever met and then decided how I should feel."*[38]

WAYNE WAS A SIMPLE MAN WITH SIMPLE IDEALS. HE HAD A VERY CLEAR, elementary outlook on life. When told everything isn't black and white he replied, "Why the hell not?" His traditionalism was a result of his conservative background and a deep, profound belief in what the country stood for. "I am proud of every day in my life I wake up in the United States of America," said Wayne. Loyal, honest, patriotic, and a man of integrity, Wayne wore his beliefs on his sleeve. It was no accident that Wayne the actor became indistinguishable from Wayne the man. Duke was exactly the way you saw him on the screen: no pretense, no ego. He was concerned with the image of America and the film industry. As author Ronald Davis wrote, the development of Wayne's character traits and beliefs mirrored the natural evolution and maturation of the nation.[39]

The decade of the 1930s was one of transition and change. After the stock market collapse in the fall of 1929, the United States faced a crossroads. If you had any money, you pulled it out of the economy to protect its value. Unemployment continued to rise, and the number of bankruptcies increased. There was a run on the banks and a call for government to stop the ever-increasing spiral descent into complete economic chaos. Depositors lost faith in the financial system, and the country was overwhelmed by the sheer impact of the situation. In 1931, world trade and Europe's credit structure failed, deepening

13

economic depressions in Austria, Scandinavia, and Germany. Europeans began withdrawing gold, loans and other investments from the United States, adding to the decline. While many individuals espoused a "hands-off" policy, allowing the marketplace to correct itself naturally, others demanded that the government step in and alleviate the problem. Ex-president Herbert Hoover, with a slow and limited response, indicated, "We are at the end of our string. There is nothing more that we can do." However, when Democrat Franklin Roosevelt was elected president in 1932, he embarked on a one hundred-day blitzkrieg of activities, tailored to stop the bleeding. He believed relief "must be extended by Government, not as a matter of charity, but as a matter of social duty; the State accepts the task cheerfully because it believes that it will help restore that close relationship with its people which is necessary to preserve our democratic form of government." His administration ended the run on banks, bringing confidence back to the economy. It suspended the export of silver and gold and increased the money supply by three billion dollars. It created the Tennessee Valley Authority and enacted the National Industrial Recovery Act, which fixed minimum wages and abolished child labor in various industries. On July 5, 1935, the Wagner-Connery act was signed, creating the National Labor Relations Board (NLRB). This agency had the power to investigate and decide unfair labor practice issues and to conduct elections in which workers could decide if they wanted union representation. It was the view of liberal economists that workers would benefit not only from better working conditions but also that better wages would improve the economy by creating increased purchasing power. Gradually, the economy started to recover.[40]

In Hollywood, the discovery of politics led to a creation of social consciousness. In fact, the city had become one of the two most politically charged centers of internationalism and liberal causes in the country, led by a small but dynamic group of communists, European refugees, and an active, wealthy liberal community. It was estimated that, during the 1930s, the Hollywood film community fluctuated between 50,000 and 60,000 people. Of that number, perhaps 15,000 joined one or another of the many Hollywood political organizations. According to Larry Ceplair and Steven Englund's, *The Inquisition in Hollywood*, most of the activity was the result of "a core group of about two hundred progressives" working "closely with, and following the lead of, fifty to seventy-five committed radical activists." More than half were *screenwriters*.[41]

John Wayne was initially a liberal and supported Roosevelt's policies of the 1930s. When asked if he always voted conservatively, Wayne replied, "I voted for Roosevelt once—just once." In 1938, he even supported the liberal gubernatorial campaign of California Democratic state senator Colbert Olson. "He wasn't a radical; he was liberal. Well, he probably gave us our worse administration we ever had, but he's a fellow I was out proselytizing for and he won." Still, in his later years, he indicated he was not very interested in politics. "I'm not a political

14

figure," said Wayne. "I hate politics and most politicians. But when things get rough and people are saying things that aren't true, I sometimes open my mouth and eventually get in trouble." In an interview in 1962, he stated, "I don't want any handouts from a benevolent government. I think government is naturally the enemy of the individual, but it's a necessary evil like, say, motion picture agents are. I do not want the Government to take away my human dignity and insure me anything more than a normal security. I don't want handouts."[42]

Wayne's stubbornness and independence had started long before–back in grade school. As a child, Duke rode the family's pet horse back and forth to school. The horse was slow and frail but served its purpose. "But it's when the small town 'do-gooders' began sticking their nose in my business that I got mad," he said. "The damn nosey women in that town accused me of not feeding the animal and reported me to the authorities." After that day, Wayne repeatedly said that he was against all "do-gooders," especially those who think they know more on how to run the government than those doing the job. "I was never much of a joiner," Wayne admitted. "Kids do join things, but they also like to consider themselves individuals capable of thinking for themselves. So do I. In the late 1920s, when I was a sophomore at USC, I was a socialist myself–but not when I left. The average college kid idealistically wishes that everyone could have cake and ice cream for every meal. But as he gets older and gives more thought to his and his fellow man's responsibilities, he finds that it can't work out that way–that some people just won't carry their load."[43]

As an actor, Wayne was very interested in the Screen Actors Guild (SAG). Founded in 1933, SAG was created to protect the rights of its members by improving working conditions and wages, reducing hours worked, and enforcing meal breaks: everything a labor union attempts to protect. According to its Mission Statement, the Guild was to negotiate and enforce collective bargaining agreements that establish equitable levels of compensation, benefits, and working conditions for its members. Typically a union created for this expressed purpose is fairly liberal, yet, over time, SAG became more and more conservative.[44]

The Screen Writers Guild (SWG), however, was as liberal as they come. Created in 1921, a strong social organization gradually turned into an extremely powerful political machine. Of course, there was a natural animosity between actors and writers. Writers had little or no control over how their products were to be used; actors were required to read dialogue like trained monkeys. Hard-working and down-to-earth, actors were somewhat resentful of the perceived arrogance of the socially conscious writer. Smug and self-satisfied, writers usually tried to inject liberal views into their screenplays and looked down on the typically conservative actor. As isolationists, writers were the most political, and most leftist, group in the movie capital. A small number of Hollywood figures were members of the Communist Party, and they were chiefly writers.[45]

Prior to the start of the war, movies were a form of escapism, made for entertainment and generally, with a few notable exceptions such as *The Birth of a Nation*, *Wings*, *The Big Parade*, *What Price Glory* and *All Quiet on the Western Front*, were not used as propaganda for the masses. In fact, Hollywood policed itself by adhering to guidelines developed by the Hays Office. Will H. Hays, former Postmaster General and head of the Republican National Committee, was a Presbyterian elder charged by the Hollywood studios to improve their image. The original Production Code was enacted in 1930. A 1934 amendment established the Production Code Administration (PCA), which required all movies receive a seal of approval before being released. The Code addressed such issues as moral standards, drug usage, offensive language, sexual perversions, scenes of passion, and the sanctity of marriage, among others. Only wholesome entertainment was allowed for public consumption. Hollywood studios hoped that voluntary conformance to these guidelines would eliminate the need for government censorship. And for the most part, that is exactly what the studios produced.

As the Nazi scourge spread its ugly stain across Europe, a Special Committee on Un-American Activities was established in 1934 to investigate Nazi propaganda and certain other activities. Its mandate was to get information on how foreign subversive propaganda entered the United States and the organizations spreading it. The committee was established in reaction to the overthrow of a number of established foreign governments in favor of communist or fascist governments. During the 1930s, a great majority of Americans were isolationists. If there was a war, they wanted the Allies to win but were reluctant to get involved in European alliances. They believed America's perspective on the world was different from that of European societies and that America could advance the cause of freedom and democracy by means other than war. Congress passed a series of Neutrality Acts in the mid-1930s with bi-partisan support. The acts addressed embargos on the trading of arms and war materials to belligerents, as well as loans and credit. In 1933, Roosevelt's foreign policy had included the formal recognition of Russia. Given the violent, intense international political situation, the committee was determined to insure that a fascist foothold would not take place in America. At the other end of the debate, interventionists wanted the United States to do all in its power to help its Allies, whoever they might be. Each day, newspapers highlighted German aggression in their headlines, making it impossible not to realize the significance of these reports.[46]

In May 1938, the House Committee on Un-American Activities was established and chaired by Congressman Martin Dies and Representative Samuel Dickstein. Known as the "Dies Committee," it investigated German-American activity in the Nazi and Ku Klux Klan organizations. The previous year, the Hollywood Anti-Nazi League was formed to unite Jewish people and others in the Hollywood movie community to combat Nazism on a local scale. With over 3,000 members, the FBI stated that the organization supported various projects associated with communism and that its influence was clearly discernible in the League. The majority of its officers and many prominent members were associated with communistic activity. However, as the League was financed by individuals who supported the rights of European Jews, Joseph Breen, the head of the PCA, felt the League was conspiring to make propaganda films that would emphasize the plight of Jews and their treatment by the Nazis. During the Spanish Civil War, Liberals and the Left generally supported the Loyalists. Conservatives and the Right, along with elements of the Catholic Church, supported Franco and the Fascists. The Soviet Union supported the Loyalists. Ergo, the Left supported Russia. Left, Right, Interventionist, Liberal, Conservative, Communist and Fascist, for and against–the political lines began to blur in Hollywood and the rest of the nation. Isolationist groups were determined America should remain neutral while Roosevelt wanted to enter the fray and support his European allies. The nation was torn asunder.

The storm brewing over Europe broke on September 1, 1939, when German troops crossed their eastern frontier and invaded Polish soil. Since 1936 when it sent troops into the Rhineland, Germany had executed each step of a carefully calculated plan, the ultimate objective of which was the regaining of its position as one of the world's great powers. Congressman Dies authored a national magazine article accusing Hollywood of being a hotbed of communists' intent on provoking America into war through its propaganda films even though the PCA was in effect. The Code resulted in an interesting paradox in that issues that were freely discussed and debated across the nation were not allowed to be addressed or even mentioned in the movies.[47]

Slowly but surely, that type of censorship began to change. The turning point in political films came with *Confessions of a Nazi Spy* released in April 1939, followed by *The Great Dictator* in October 1940. Although Hollywood released many more films during that period that addressed social and political issues, these two movies shattered the barrier between entertainment and propaganda. By 1940, Hollywood had crossed an important threshold. Studios had begun to make explicitly interventionist films. In a message to the annual Academy Awards banquet in 1941, Roosevelt thanked the industry for its "splendid cooperation with all who are directing the expansion of our defense forces," and appealed for continuing support. Nineteen forty-one also marked the year *Sergeant York* was released. Pacifism, religion, rationalization, inspiration, heroism, and patriotism–this movie had it all. It was a virtual recruiting ad for interventionists. That summer, isolationists and interventionists went at it tooth and nail, casting accusations and aspersions against each other willy-nilly. Isolationists charged that the studios were making blatantly aggressive propaganda and that Roosevelt was trying to glorify war. Interventionists claimed the opposition was anti-Semitic and attempting to censor the industry. The debate became moot when, suddenly, on Sunday, December 7, Japan viciously sneak-attacked the United

17

States without provocation. Four days later, Germany and Italy declared war against the United States, and America began to energize itself for war.[48]

During the war, officials of the Office of War Information (OWI), the government's propaganda agency, issued a constantly updated manual instructing the studios how to assist the war effort, sat in on story conferences, reviewed screenplays, pressured the studios to change scripts and even wrote dialogue for key speeches. As Clayton Koppes and Gregory Black pointed out in *Hollywood Goes to War*, the result is that the OWI was able to exert considerable influence over the content of movies. The cooperation between the studios and the government helped shape public opinion during the war and resulted in extremely unambiguous political diatribes.[49]

In the war's early years, the Communist party was in a phase where its position was also indistinguishable from that of European social democrats and advanced New Dealers. It was not that the American liberals had moved left; it was more that, owing to the war, the Communist party had temporarily moved right. Slowly but surely, the tone of the American political landscape was changing, supported by a conservative coalition in Congress. Tired, after eleven years of Roosevelt's "New Deal" politics, the Republicans supported laissez-faire capitalism, less government intervention, lower taxes, and conservative social policies. Liberals feared the end of the New Deal in 1943, but hoped Roosevelt would lead a liberal revival once victory was assured. Conservatives seized on the war as a way to cut back on New Deal programs they found abhorrent and to build toward a future takeover of the federal government.[50]

The American public was also torn in its feelings toward Russia. Grateful that the Soviet armies halted the relentless German aggression in Eastern Europe, Americans were nevertheless wary and suspicious of what a strong Russia would mean. Historically anti-Communist, America struggled to accept a new Allied relationship. If Germany was the enemy of the United States and Germany attacked Russia, Russia must be an ally of America. The enemy of my enemy is my friend. In Hollywood, liberals and Communists typically supported Roosevelt's New Deal politics while conservatives espoused lower taxes and less government intervention. The Republican base felt Hollywood had been taken over by liberals and Communists advancing their own agenda.

"In the 1940s, Duke was one of the few stars with the courage to expose the determined bid by a band of Communists to take control of the film industry," said Ronald Reagan. "Through a series of violent strikes and systemic blacklisting, these people were at times dangerously close to reaching their goal. With theatrical employees' union leader Roy Brewer, playright (sic) Morrie Ryskind and others, he (Wayne) formed the Motion Picture Alliance for the Preservation of American Ideals (MPA) to challenge this insidious campaign." The Statement of Principles of the Alliance mirrored Wayne's own beliefs: "We believe in, and like, the American way of life: the liberty and freedom which generations before us have fought to create and preserve; the freedom to speak, to think, to live, to worship, to work, and to govern ourselves as individuals, the right to succeed or fail as free men, according to the measure of our ability and our strength."[51]

The Alliance, formed on February 4, 1944, by over seventy-five film writers, producers, actors, directors and executives at the Beverly-Wilshire Hotel in Los Angeles, was dedicated to fighting Communism and Fascism in the film industry. Over 1,500 individuals representing the craft unions attended the first public meeting and included such top stars as Gary Cooper, Clark Gable, Ward Bond, Robert Montgomery, and many others. Dimitri Tiomkin, Cecil B. DeMille, Victor Fleming, and John Ford also attended. The genesis of the Alliance was a result of the defeat of the right wing portion of the SWG in the attempt to be recognized as an instrument for collective bargaining with the studios. The loss to militant, vocal, labor-minded liberals was interpreted as symptomatic of a malaise embracing all the professional guilds. The coalition of actors, directors, and screenwriters decided that a small group of Communists, under party discipline, would take over the unions and control American movies. The creation of the Alliance would help alert Americans to this subversive element in society.[52]

Wayne recalled the creation of the Alliance: "A group of us comprising Jim McGuinness, MGM Production Head, director Sam Wood, Adolphe Menjou, Ward Bond, writer Morrie Ryskind, director Leo McCarey, and A.F. of L. Leader Roy Brewer decided to form the Motion Picture Alliance for the Preservation of American ideals. It started at a small meeting at McGuinness's house. The next morning a top executive at one of the studios phoned me. 'Duke,' he said. 'You've got to get out of that MPA. You're becoming a controversial figure. It will kill you at the box office. You will hit the skids.' I hit the skids all right. When I became president of the MPA in 1948, I was thirty-third in the rating of box-office leaders. A year later, I skidded right to first place."[53]

Elected the Alliance's first president, director Sam Wood stated that some writers were injecting Communistic propaganda into their film plays. He further declared, "These highly indoctrinated shock units of the totalitarian wrecking crew have shrewdly led the people of the United States to believe that Hollywood is a hotbed of sedition and subversion, and that our industry is a battleground over which Communism is locked in death grips with Fascism." Walt Disney, art director Cedric Gibbons, and director Norman Taurog were elected vice-presidents. Members of the executive committee included Victor Fleming, Rupert Hughes, and King Vidor, among others.[54]

Chastised for being slow to organize, the Alliance was nevertheless lauded for its efforts. "It is high time," The San Antonio Light editorialized, "for patriotic organizations in the motion picture industry to organize and defeat any effort of any GROUP of or INDIVIDUAL to divert the loyalty of the screen from the free America that gave it birth." It was expected that the result would be more wholesome, more popular, more profitable, and more American pictures.

The Alliance was supported by the Los Angeles County American Legion, which refused to allow the SWG use of the Hollywood Legion Stadium to stage a protest against the Alliance. In the Legion's words, they "don't want to get mixed up in any factional fight among motion-picture people." Many felt that "for a good many years now, Hollywood has been functioning as a sounding board for subversive interests, masquerading as liberals and shrieking about their patriotism whenever an investigation of their activities began to grip on the acid of their breeches."[55]

In an interview with reporter Walter Naughton, Congressman Dies shared his views on the motion picture industry and his support of the Alliance. Among other observations, he stated, "Hollywood is the greatest source of revenue in the nation for the Communists and other subversive groups... let's look at the bad side. In my opinion, two elements stand out in this category—that making of pictures which extol a foreign ideology—propaganda for a cause which seeks to spread its ideas to our people and the 'leftists' or radical screenwriters. Many of them, perhaps in the belief they are aiding a cause they could not even give an intelligent explanation of if called on to do so, slyly and cleverly insert the 'leftist' ideas in their screen writings."[56]

Not everyone supported the Alliance. Many considered it a bigoted anti-Semitic organization. In an industry in which many Jewish individuals were studio heads and producers, the anti-Semitic innuendos threatened the Alliance. In a satirical article published by *Time*, February 14, 1944, the magazine compared the Alliance to the Leftist Hollywood Free World Association starring Vice-president Henry Wallace. In a letter to the editor, Orson Welles took umbrage to the comparison. "Hollywood is guilty of deliberate withdrawal from the living world. It seeks to entertain," wrote Welles, "and we suspect that the success of the withdrawal is what makes Hollywood funny. But let *TIME* Magazine view with alarm or point with pride, but not laugh off Hollywood's growing recognition of the fact that every movie expresses, or at least reflects, political opinion." An article written by John T. McManus referred to the Alliance as "Mainly composed of the Know-Nothing bloc among MGM producers" and suggested that the Alliance was directing its aim against the "Hollywood writers Mobilization, an organization of some 1,500 Hollywood screenwriters, publicists, and journalists who have done the most significant job in America of training the attention of the American public on the issues of the war."[57]

According to Wayne, "I didn't attend the first few meetings of the Alliance because I was making *Back to Bataan*, which Edward Dymtryk was directing for RKO. I had been asked by our State Department to make this movie because it was about the Filipino underground. Our technical advisor was an American colonel (Col. George S. Clarke, commander of the 57th Infantry, Philippine Scouts), one of the first to get out of the Philippines. He was a religious man and a very sincere patriot. On days when I wasn't on the set, a few men—

including Edward Dymtryk—were ragging him (Clarke) about God, singing the *Internationale* and making jokes about patriotism. He (Clarke) finally came to me and said, 'Mr. Wayne, I haven't anybody to turn to. These people are doing everything in their power to belittle me.'" When confronted by Wayne, however, Dymtryk said it was all a joke. He (Dymtryk) said, "No, I'm not a Commie. My father was a Russian. I was born in Canada. But if the masses of the American people want Communism, I think it'd be good for our country." "The only guy that ever fooled me was…Dymtryk," said Wayne. "He started talking about the masses, and as soon as he started using that word—which is from their book, not ours—I knew he was a Commie."[58]

That incident must have had a profound impact on Duke, though. Earlier that year, Wayne had taken part in a three-month tour of Pacific bases and battle lines from Brisbane, Australia, to the front lines of New Britain. Though he played the role of an American fighting man on the movie screen, he entertained real soldiers, not Hollywood make-believe patriots. He heard their stories, saw their living conditions, and slogged through the same mud they did, visited their hospitals, and heard their good wishes. He gained a real appreciation of what these men were and what they were fighting for. There was no way he was going to stand idly by and watch someone make fun of a true patriot.

In a proposed autobiography, Wayne discussed his reason for joining the MPA: "Despite all the complications and pressures of my personal and professional life, I found myself drawn into the anti-Communist fight in Hollywood. An actor has to (be) more than a part of a self-contained group. We're part of a bigger world. We've got to have a sense of responsibility about that world. I had been conscious of an infiltration of Communists and fellow travelers in the picture business since about 1937. This was an important target for the Communist Party because the movies are an important medium of mass-communication. I could see these enemies of my country infiltrating into unions like the Screen actors Guild and Screen writers Guild. You'd go to parties and hear that Russia is the hope of the world and the United States is shot to hell, and patriotism is a joke. You'd see the subtly slanting of a script to turn American citizens against the values that had made us great. You'd see motion-picture stars with estates and swimming pools giving large sums of money to Communist-front causes and lending the glamour of their names to those same fronts. Our organization was just a group of motion picture people on the right side, not leftist and not Commies," Wayne added. "There was no black list at that time, as some people said. Later on, when Congress passed some laws making it possible to take a stand against these people, we were asked about Communists in the industry. So we gave them the facts as we knew them. That's all. Many of us were being invited to supposed social functions or house parties—usually at well known Hollywood writers' homes that turned out to be Communist recruitment meetings."[59]

Slowly but surely, Wayne's political beliefs swung more and more to the right. Growing up during the Depression had forced him to become extremely self-reliant. With a father who could not make it as a farmer or druggist, it was entirely up to Wayne to support himself. Working at anything he could get, he gradually not only became more confident but also more experienced in a variety of facets of the motion picture business. Times were tough. Some hotels made out-of-work actors put on performances in lieu of room rent. Many actors, down on their luck, earned eating money by selling perfume, novelties, and greeting cards door-to-door. Hollywood was basically a two-class town. There were those who earned top dollars and all the rest, who scrounged to survive. Fortunately Wayne was employed, albeit in low-budget Westerns. He was down-to-earth and self-sufficient, relying on his own efforts and resources and not depending upon those from others. He had a reputation for being hard-working and hard-drinking. He felt everyone was accountable for his or her own actions and no one should look to the government to bail them out of jams. When Wayne discussed his acting style, he also discussed his values. Duke once told an interviewer, "All I care about is the liberty of the individual." By the end of the war, Wayne was anti-Roosevelt, anti-New Deal, anti-tax, anti-Communist, and essentially conservative. He was also a major leading actor. *(For an in-depth evaluation of Hollywood, politics and World War II, please refer to the following excellent books: "Hollywood Party: How Communism Seduced the American Film Industry in the 1930s and 1940s," by Kenneth Lloyd Billingsley; "The Inquisition of Hollywood," by Larry Ceplair and Steve Englund; "The Hollywood Propaganda of World War II," by Robert Fyne; "Hollywood Goes to War," by Clayton R. Koppes and Gregory D. Black, and "Hollywood Left and Right: How Movie Stars Shaped American Politics," by Steven J. Ross).*[60]

# CHAPTER THREE
## YORK, BRITTLES, AND YORKE

*"They aren't forgotten because they haven't died. They're living, right out there. Collingwood and the rest. They'll keep on living as long as the regiment lives. The pay is thirteen dollars a month; their diet beans and hay. Maybe horses before this campaign is over. Fight over cards or rotgut whiskey but share the last drop in their canteens. The faces may change, the names, but they're there. They're the regiment. The Regular Army. Now, and fifty years from now. They're better men than they used to be. Thursday did that. Made it a command to be proud of."*[61]

THE WAR WAS OVER, AND WAYNE HAD SECURED HIS PLACE IN THE MOTION picture industry. Due to Roosevelt's revised income tax structure, many stars refused to appear in more than two films a year during this time as their incomes would be taxed at an exorbitant rate, and the players chosen for the additional pictures were demanding star salaries. As a result, some actors turned down roles they might have otherwise accepted, but not Wayne. Wanting to capitalize on the opportunity, as well as constantly be in the public's eye, he made thirteen movies from 1942 through the end of the war, more than most of his contemporaries. Cowboy, mine owner, druggist, saloon owner, RAF pilot, construction worker, PT boat commander, resistance fighter—Wayne played them all.[62]

World War II ended with the Japanese surrender on September 2, 1945, and, later that month, Duke finished his newest project, *Dakota*. Another Western, the movie was an inauspicious beginning to Wayne's postwar career. The reviews varied. While the *New York Times* reported that "Republic Studios expended a vast amount of ammunition and set the torch to miles of prairie land for a smashing climax," other reviews were not as forgiving. "John Wayne and Vera Hruba Ralston drift through their roles as if the whole thing would be better off forgotten, and perhaps they have the right idea," said one. Another said, "Until a worse one comes along, *Dakota* can stand as a classic example of how to dress up a Western with character curlicues of comedy until it loses all worth as a Western and gains nothing either in character or comedy." Ralston, a former Olympic figure skater, was Herb Yates's paramour and future wife. A poor actress with limited command of the English language and an Eastern European accent, she also appeared with Wayne in *The Fighting Kentuckian* in 1949. Yates felt by teaming Ralston with Wayne, she might gather the attention of the movie-going public. She did—she was a bad actress. Wayne didn't think much of her, either. "Vera was attractive and she never pushed her weight around just because she was about to marry Yates. As a human being, she was okay. But she was no actress." (A lawsuit brought against Yates by a shareholder in 1956 alleged that of the twenty-one films the actress appeared in, only two, *Dakota* and *The Fighting Kentuckian*, were profitable. The others were "financial failures." By permitting his wife to appear in films after a rule was adopted not to do so without Republic board approval, the suit alleged the defendants were guilty of wasting the firm's assets. Among other charges, the action also protested the hiring of Sterling Hayden at "an excessive salary." Wayne had refused to appear with Ralston because he thought it was a waste of corporate funds.)[63]

Yates knew it was only a matter of time before he lost his star actor and leading moneymaker to another studio as he had heard rumors that others were courting Wayne. He assumed that if he gave Wayne an opportunity to produce his own features, Yates might retain his services. Therefore, on September 24, Wayne signed a seven-picture, non-exclusive contract with Republic in which he received 10% of the gross with a guaranteed minimum of $150,000 per picture. He was only required to appear in one high-budget film per year. Non-exclusive meant he could work for and with anyone he chose. He was already in the midst of the six-picture, six-year contract with RKO he had signed in 1943. The Republic deal would significantly change his financial status and allow him to fund future projects as he saw fit. As an example, in 1946 Wayne worked for three different studios (RKO, Republic, and United Artists) and eventually earned over $643,000 for the films he made that year. This can be compared to the relatively paltry $220,000 he had made the previous year.

*Dakota* also in effect marked the beginning of the John Wayne Stock Company. Similar to John Ford, Wayne felt more comfortable working with the same people over and over; he knew what to expect from them and knew the strengths and weaknesses of each. Not surprisingly, many people who worked for Ford also were friends with Wayne. Fellow USC Trojan actor Ward Bond, stuntman Cliff Lyons, long-time friend Paul Fix, and stuntman/second unit director Yakima Canutt all were involved in *Dakota*. As a part of his agreement with Republic, Wayne became an independent producer and had the right to develop his own projects. The reason he signed the contract was obvious: "The most important thing for me was that I would be able to produce some of my own films. That was a big step for me, to produce. But I felt that if anyone was going to give my career a kick up the rear, it would have to be me." Creation of his own production team was the first step toward complete autonomy.[64]

Wayne immediately hired, as his personal secretary, Mary St. John, whom he remembered from her days in the secretarial pool at Republic. She'd been working for director Joe Kane and Duke had known her for years. On the day in 1939 when she congratulated Wayne for his performance in *Stagecoach*, he told her that if he ever needed an assistant, he wanted her for the job. Once hired, one of the first things Wayne asked of St. John was to order items he had marked in some mail-order catalogues. She chuckled as he left the office, but he turned around and explained the request: "Let me tell you something about myself. When I was a kid, we got the Montgomery Ward catalogue. I used to thumb through it, and there were a hell of a lot of things I wanted. But we were too damn poor to buy any of them. I made up my mind if I ever got rich, I'd order anything that caught my eye."[65]

Next, he brought on board James Edward Grant. Grant was an ex-Chicago newspaperman who had written screenplays for such movies as *Whipsaw*, *Boom Town*, and *Johnny Eager*. His good friend John Ford had introduced him to Wayne prior to the war. The peppery, hard-drinking Irishman took an instant liking to the big, rugged, hard-drinking ex-athlete from California. Wayne went to Grant in the early 1940s and asked for help with the scripts he had received. "I liked his style of writing," said Wayne. "He seemed able, better than any other screenwriter I knew, to write the kind of dialogue that suited me best." For Grant, the feeling was mutual. "Duke was the first man in Hollywood to realize that writers could actually do something for an actor. We worked out a system. We gave as many lines as possible to other guys in these five-day oaters, and usually they were too stupid to realize how bad they were. I had Wayne say as little as possible. But he did things. I added little touches to his parts, to make him stand out and give people the idea he wasn't just another cowboy actor."[66]

According to Michael Wayne, "Jimmy Grant became my dad's favorite movie writer. He not only wrote many screenplays for dad but also did a lot of rewriting on pictures for which he got no credit and did so as a favor to my father. What Jimmy could do was to write short crisp dialogue and put a lot of meaning into it. He would take one line and not only kept the action going, but advance the plot, and reveal the character all at the same time. My dad likes short sentences of dialogue. Now that does not mean that he has to have lines tailored for him. He believes that the lines should fit the character and the character should say the lines that are right for him."[67]

Wayne and Grant were extremely close friends and, predictably, drinking buddies. "All the offices had bars," Grant recalled. "You started drinking when you got to the studio, and you didn't stop until you went to bed. If you went to bed. One writer I knew had a desk with eight drawers. Seven of them had nothing in there except liquor." And of course, Wayne could drink anyone under the table. Paul Lansen, an extra in *The Alamo*, recalls an incident: "There was a little bar right on (Hwy) 90...just across from Ft. Clark. We were sitting in there, having beer one night, just shooting the bull. And in walks Wayne, Chill Wills, and Ward Bond. Now in those days you had to take (in) your own bottle of whiskey or whatever you were drinking and then they'd sell you set-ups. Well, they had a little room in the back of that bar and the three of them went back in. John Wayne had a (sack) and he threw the sack down as he walked in...he had a bottle of vodka. I think he used that quite a bit on the set when he was directing. He had a little cup, you know, with a little water. Ward Bond and Chill Wills each had a bottle of Jack Daniels. But the three of them walked into that little room back there and they were back there for a couple of hours. And you could hear them every once in awhile. Of course, Chill Wills had a voice that everyone could hear. And when they left the place, John Wayne had Chill Wills under his left arm, and Ward Bond under his right and he was taking them both out of the bar. He was still relatively sober and the other two were just plastered."[68]

Later on, Chuck Roberson, Harry Carey Jr., Paul Fix, Grant Withers, Bruce Cabot, Jack Pennick, Victor McLaglen, Ken Curtis, Denver Pyle, and George O'Brien all became part of Wayne's traveling road show. His personal entourage would eventually include: Al Murphy, wardrobe and general handyman; Beverly Barnett, press agent; Ernie Safting, military advisor; J. Hampton Scott, houseboy; Bob Morrison, brother and production assistant; and Webb Overlander, make-up man, gun expert, and toupee protector.[69]

Two weeks after he signed the Republic contract, Wayne started work on *Without Reservations*, an RKO feature with Claudette Colbert. Directed by Mervyn LeRoy in the fashion of *It Happened One Night*, the movie was a typical screwball comedy. An amusing, fun-loving, good-natured farce, the film exhibited Wayne's surprising flair for comedy and received decent reviews.

Upon its completion, Wayne and Grant began to develop a project together, the first in a long series of collaborations. Grant brought an unusual screenplay to Wayne and wanted to direct it. With a working title of *The Gun* or *The Angel and the Outlaw*, it was the story of a gunslinger who turned pacifist under the tutelage of an attractive Quaker woman. Wayne wanted Gary Cooper for the lead role, but Coop declined, so Wayne went after Randolph Scott before taking on the role himself. The film was both Grant's first attempt at directing and Wayne's first attempt at total cinematic responsibility. "I knew that the film was a modest one," said Wayne, "and a good one to start with. But the pressures of producing and acting were more than I'd realized, and I have to admit I gave a tongue-lashing to just about everybody, which was more than was usual for me in those days. I found I was going around apologizing to everyone all the time, and thankfully, because they were my friends, they forgave me." The film was also a bit unusual, not only for its subject matter, but also for Grant's tendency to be loquacious and wordy in his dialogue, interesting, given his reputation as a word-miser. However, not all was in vain as it finally allowed Wayne to utilize his years of experience in front of the camera. Naturally, many aspects of the film are Fordian in their content, such as the climatic showdown, a long tracking shot of Wayne walking down Main Street toward the saloon and calling out the villain. Grant must have learned from this experience that it was better to write succinct dialogue because, in later years, he indicated, "A short story writer has to be a miser with words. A screenwriter has to be a miser with film. Usually, you've got only one hundred minutes to tell a pretty complicated story. You can't waste a foot of that film."[70]

Wayne's reputation as a he-man was difficult to live up to as there was always someone out there trying to prove himself. One day, when Wayne and Grant were in New Mexico scouting locations for *Angel*, they stopped for a drink in a bar in Santa Fe. Wayne left early, but Grant and a few studio pals stayed for another round. After a while, a big, tall, lanky character stepped up to the bar and announced that he was going outside as he had a "date" with Wayne. When he returned inside a few minutes later, he wore a grin and a bandaged right hand. When asked what happened, he replied, "I just wanted to see who was the best man. John Wayne or myself. Now I know. I am!" Grant, concerned for Wayne's well-being, quickly called Wayne's hotel room. "Hello," yawned Wayne. "Are you all right?" Grant anxiously asked. "Of course," replied Duke. "I've been asleep for three hours."[71]

Postproduction work on *Angel and the Badman* lasted the remainder of the year, and the film was released to generally decent reviews in early 1947. Interestingly, Wayne was not very concerned about the critics. "When people say 'A John Wayne picture got bad reviews,' I always wonder if they know it's a redundant sentence. Hell, I don't care. People like my pictures, and that's all that counts." By the time the film was released, Wayne was already involved in a new project, possibly the most important one of his life.[72]

In January 1946, director Howard Hawks purchased a story from pulp fiction writer Borden Chase. Published in installments in the *Saturday Evening Post*, it was called "The Chisholm Trail" and was about the nation's first major cattle drive. Hawks subsequently hired Chase to write a screenplay of the book, which was significantly modified by Hawks with the help of screenwriter Charles Schnee. With its grand theme of how the creation of a cattle empire helped build a nation, its contrast of an old authoritarian ethic with a newer and more democratic one, and its elemental conflict between the older man seeking revenge upon the foster son who took away his herd, Chase's dramatic architecture was sound and full of tremendous potential. Hawks initially wanted Gary Cooper and Cary Grant to star in the movie, but Cooper thought the role was too violent, and Grant didn't want to play second billing to anyone. As a result, Hawks chose the veteran Wayne and rising star Montgomery Clift. Wayne was initially apprehensive about playing a character so much older than he in real life. "I never showed Wayne the screenplay," recalled Hawks. "I just told him the story and he thought it was one of the best he'd ever heard, but he said I don't want to play an old man. I said, 'Duke, you're going to be one pretty soon, so why not get some practice?' He said how the hell am I gonna play one? I was about fifty then, so I said, 'Just watch me getting up. That's the way to play it.'" Hawks even called in Walter Brennan to demonstrate how to play an older man. "Brennan showed me how to walk like a tottery old man," said Wayne. "I went home that night and thought of all the old cattlemen I knew when I was a kid. I was raised in the West. I rode a horse to school. And none of the outdoors-men were tottery." So he played the old rancher as erect and domineering.[73]

And play it he did. Generally regarded as one of the best films of the Western genre, *Red River* was an epic of massive proportions. Filmed in black and white, as Hawks felt at the time that color was "garish," the scenery was absolutely stunning, "a spectacle of sweeping grandeur," with "massive cattle herds moving in panoramic display." Powerful and dramatic, the relationship between Wayne and Clift was a great characterization between blatant authority and moral responsibility. Wayne received outstanding reviews, with comments ranging from "withering good job of acting" to "unforgettable" to "best performance of his career."[74]

Even John Ford seemed impressed. Allegedly, he helped Hawks edit certain portions of the film. When he first viewed Wayne's performance, Ford exclaimed, "Damn, I never knew the sonofabitch could act!" Hawks even told Ford, "Hey, I've made one almost as good as you can do. You better go and see it!" However, he was also confused about Ford's exclamation. "I thought it odd that he never considered Wayne a big enough star to carry a motion picture, despite the fact that he was doing just that at Republic." Wayne thought he deserved an Oscar nomination for his performance. "But Montgomery Clift was in the picture too, you know?" said Wayne. "And they wanted to give that poor kid an Academy Award so bad they simply forgot about me. Clift was *acting*, they said. Duke's only playing himself. I played an *old* man in that. And I was only forty." Ford called Wayne, "a splendid actor who has had very little chance to act." And Hawks was just as effusive in his praise. "Wayne is under-rated. He's a much better actor than he's given credit for. He holds a thing together, he gives it solidity and honestness, and he can make a lot of things believable. If he's kind of grousing around in a scene you know that there's something wrong with the scene. He has a very true sense of cinema."[75]

As a gift, Hawks presented principal actors in the cast with *Red River* "D" belt buckles made by a Nogales, Mexico silversmith; the design was based on the one Wayne's character drew on the ground in the movie. Each buckle was initialed for the intended recipient. Wayne, Clift, Walter Brennan, Russ Harlan, son David Hawks, and a few others received full-size buckles, while Joanne Dru and Hawks's wife Slim (Nancy) and daughter Barbara, among others, received smaller versions. Wayne and Hawks exchanged their buckles in a gesture of friendship, and in subsequent movies, whether Wayne was a cowboy or cavalry officer or sheriff, he always wore it as a sign of respect.[76]

Two weeks after Wayne finished *Red River* for United Artists, he started working on *Tycoon* to fulfill his 1947 obligation to RKO. Initially, Maureen O'Hara was to be his co-star, but as she was cast in another picture, Laraine Day was chosen instead. This proved a huge mistake as the pairing of Wayne and O'Hara was a dream made in heaven. The movie O'Hara was cast in first was called *The Big Heart* and then *It's Only Human* and then, finally, its better-known name, *Miracle on 34th Street*. The American movie-going public would have to wait three more years before it would see this magical pairing onscreen. Wayne recalled, "Some bright spark at RKO decided we were mismatched or something, and so they decided to put another actress in the part. Obviously someone at RKO didn't know dick." Released to generally unfavorable reviews, *Tycoon* lost over $1 million. As *Red River* would not be released for another nine months and not knowing what the reaction would be to his performance, Wayne started having serious misgivings about his profession. That was all to change, however, as he was about to enter the most productive and critically successful period of his career.[77]

In March 1946, producer Merian Cooper and director John Ford joined creative forces and re-established an independent company called Argosy Productions. This partnership had been created in 1940 for the Ford production of *The Long Voyage Home*. Their first project together under the new organization was *The Fugitive*, starring Henry Fonda. While still in preproduction, Ford was forced to fulfill a contractual obligation to Fox Studios, so he turned control over to Cooper and started work on his next film, *My Darling Clementine*, again starring Fonda. Completed in June, Ford returned to Argosy and started filming *The Fugitive*. Although visually impressive and called "a symphony of light and shade, of deafening din and silence, of sweeping movement and repose," it was a commercial disaster. According to author Joseph McBride in *Searching For John Ford*, the box-office failure of Argosy's first production caused the cancellation of *The Quiet Man*, which RKO feared would be another runaway art-house project, and obliged Ford to play it safe by concentrating on Westerns for the next few years.[78]

Earlier that same year, James Warner Bellah had published a series of Western short stories in the *Saturday Evening Post*, the first of which was titled "Massacre." From the first time he read it, Ford was drawn to its emotional impact. As Dan Ford accurately stated in *Pappy: The Life of John Ford*, "Beyond the vigorous prose and its spirit of aristocratic militarism, (the stories) seemed to articulate all (John Ford's) wartime emotions, his fascination with the American military tradition, and the special nobility he felt was born of combat. Before the war, the military had been an avocation, something Ford had played at for his amusement and used as a way of gaining social status. Now it became the centerpiece of his life. The war profoundly changed him, and he developed a virtual obsession with military glory. Ford knew that wars were less about men than about symbols. It was the symbols and timeless rituals that glued men from different ethnic groups, races, religions, and classes together. By the thousands, they had died for the flag, and Ford loved the simple ceremonies that surrounded it. *Fort Apache* (was) a stirring, patriotic reaffirmation of that flag and those military traditions." As it did for Wayne, the West held a special attraction for Ford. "I've always been hooked on Westerns," explained Ford. "I liked the action, the freedom. I like to get out on the desert in Monument Valley and smell the fresh, clean air," adding, "I don't think that there is any aspect of our history that has been as well or completely portrayed on the screen... as the Old West." When he was in high school, Ford even wrote a Western short story and submitted it to a magazine for publication. He received $25 for his effort.[79]

Ford had read the Bellah story on a train trip to San Francisco. At the first available stop, his daughter Barbara wired a telegram to Cooper requesting Argosy buy the rights to the story for $4,500. He then asked Frank Nugent and Lawrence Stallings to develop a screenplay. "The Cavalry. In all the Westerns, the Cavalry rides in to the rescue of the beleaguered wagon train or whatever, and then it rides off again. I've been thinking about it," said Ford. "What it was like at a Cavalry post, remote, people with their own personal problems, over everything the threat of Indians, of death...."[80]

Once again, Ford cast Henry Fonda in the lead role, this time as Col. Owen Thursday. In *Searching for John Ford*, Joseph McBride vividly describes Thursday: "Thursday is an arrogant career officer, an Apache-hating racist and man who lives only for glory. A stickler for regulations, he finally redeems himself in the eyes of his men through his reckless, albeit courageous return to his besieged command just prior to its annihilation." Fonda had already appeared in numerous Ford films including *The Grapes of Wrath* and *Young Mr. Lincoln*. Esteemed by Ford, he was the consummate professional. "Great actor. Plenty of acting on the stage. Lots of experience in pictures. Well educated. All in all, just a fine man. He has a fine war record," said Ford. "He never advertised the fact, but I'm very proud of him; he was in the Navy."[81]

Ford believed Wayne was not yet strong enough to play the demanding role of Thursday but was perfect for Capt. Kirby York. "I could see the writing on the wall," Wayne lamented, "when Ford cast John Agar in the romantic role of Lt. O'Rourke, Hank Fonda in the lead role, and me just trying to make peace with the Indians. All I had to do was quietly, and with whatever dignity I could, display a sense of honor, duty, and service." According to Peter Cowie in *John Ford and the American West*, "York became our alter ego in this absurd campaign against Cochise (who replaces Custer's nemesis Sitting Bull for the sake of convenience). York's is the voice of sweet reason in the confrontations with the Apache. He is the valiant subordinate officer who gallops into the canyon to try and rescue his benighted colonel. Good-natured and a man of his word, York is much more easygoing than his prissy commander. Experienced in the ways of the West, York nevertheless supports Thursday's ill-fated decisions." Honest, loyal, trusted, compassionate, opinionated, and courageous, these traits would continuously appear in the characters Wayne played.[82]

Newlyweds Shirley Temple and John Agar appear in the movie as the young love interest: Philadelphia Thursday and Lt. Michael O'Rourke. For some reason, Ford did not care for Agar and kept him "in the barrel" the whole picture as a designated patsy. Constantly called "Mr. Temple," the lad could do nothing right, whether it was the way he delivered his lines or rode a horse. Stuntman Gil Perkins said, "He ate John Agar alive. There was nothing this poor kid could do that was right. Ford just chewed him up one side and down the other." Ben Johnson, who doubled for Fonda and Wayne, thought, "He just did it for damn meanness." After enduring yet another Fordian embarrassment, Agar packed his bags and prepared to leave the set before Wayne talked him out of it. Mrs. Agar was not spared the sarcasm, either. A scene called for the women of the fort to watch their men ride off to their destiny. After Anna Lee delivered her line, "I can't see them anymore. All I can see is the flags," Shirley observed, "I don't think that's good grammar." "What?" said Ford. "It should be, 'All I can see are the flags.'" *No one* ever dared make suggestions to Ford. With the rest of the cast silent and shying away from an expected explosion, Ford smiled and simply asked, "Where did you go to school, Shirley? And where did you graduate?" Everyone laughed and the line remained unchanged.[83]

Though always a challenge, working with Ford was always rewarding. Walter Pidgeon, who worked for Ford on *How Green Was My Valley*, was profoundly affected by the experience. The director hardly ever removed his pipe from his mouth and tended to mumble when giving instructions. "With most directors, the result…would be helpless confusion," Pidgeon said. "With Ford, no. You go out on the set and find yourself following orders you haven't heard. Readily and naturally, you act exactly what Ford had in mind, and only later, with a perceptible shock, do you ask yourself how you did it." Pidgeon was so taken with the director that on those days when his scenes were finished in the morning, "for the first time in my Hollywood record, I stayed in the studio all afternoon, simply to watch Ford work."[84]

Produced in the desolate magnificence of Monument Valley, *Fort Apache* was the first film in what would be called "The Ford Cavalry Trilogy." Known under the working title of *War Party* during production, the movie was really the story of Gen. Custer laid against an Apache background. It was not intended to be a character study of Custer but rather a portrait of the everyday life of a frontier outpost, complete with military rituals and traditions, formal dances and receptions, class barriers and social differences, military courtesies and rousing songs. Filmed by Archie Stout in black and white, it took advantage of infrared film, which resulted in dark skies and allowed the clouds to dramatically stand out. The scene before the fatal final assault, with the cavalry troop and officers in silhouette against a cloud-filled sky, is artistically resplendent in its brilliance and worthy of a Charles M. Russell painting.

It has been said the creation of the trilogy was not Ford's intent, that the third film of the series, *Rio Grande*, was made to fulfill a requirement by Herb Yates, so Ford could film his dream project: *The Quiet Man*. Ford stated, however, that was not true. "Yes, (I had in mind to do a series of pictures about the cavalry). I wanted a relief. It was a very happy time in my life. I was anxious to get away from Hollywood (...the whole background. Probably, particularly the studio heads), and get out in the great open space, so called. I worked hard; felt better, slept well, and ate well." According to McBride, although cavalry was the unifying factor for all three films, the stories are inevitably about family, tradition, discipline, emotional and moral conflicts, and the effect of advancing civilization on an ever shrinking frontier. Wayne convinced Yates that Ford was an economical director, and managed to persuade Yates to let Ford make *The Quiet Man* by promising to star in it with Maureen O'Hara after they first made a black-and-white Western together for box-office insurance.[85]

Between *Red River* and *Fort Apache*, Hawks and Ford had revitalized Wayne's career and made critics and the public completely forget about *Dakota* and *Tycoon*. A *New York Times* article written by Gladwin Hill commented on Wayne's increasing popularity: "Theatre marquees blazon *Fort Apache* and *Red River*, both and each starring John Wayne. The dailies report that John Wayne, having finished *Three Godfathers* and at the moment engrossed in *Wake of the Red Witch*, is about to start work in *She Wore a Yellow Ribbon*." For an actor "trying to make a living in the movies," Wayne was at a loss to explain why the characters he played were so appealing. "I guess it's my honest blue eyes." But he knew what he looked for in a script. "I think a story has to have basic emotions," he explained. "A kid...a dog...a woman's love...a man's love...those are the things that strike at people's hearts and makes them like a movie. That's why a picture with basic human qualities is better than the fluff of a drawing room picture. Also, I look for a background that will give a picture the bigness that only a motion picture medium can provide." Whatever it was, the public was in love with him. And the reviews were just as loving: "A rootin', tootin' Wild West show, full of Indians and United States cavalry, dust and desert scenery and a nice masculine trace of romance, has been honestly put together under the masterful direction of

John Ford. Folks who are looking for action in the oldest tradition of the screen, observed through a genuine artist's camera, will find plenty of it here. Wayne is powerful as (a) captain, forthright and exquisitely brave." In Ford's mind, it was proof that the public shared his vision of military glory and was ready for more pictures based on the stories of James Warner Bellah.[86]

After Wayne finished *Fort Apache*, he took a well-deserved respite aboard Ford's yacht *Araner*, and traveled with Ford, Fonda, and Ward Bond down to Mazatlan, fishing, relaxing and generally getting drunk. Harry Carey Sr. had passed away one month earlier, and, at his wake, Ford told Carey's widow Olive he was going to remake *Marked Men* as a tribute to Harry. The fishing trip gave Wayne a chance to relax before he embarked on this project. Initially, the movie was to be filmed in Mexico, and, in March 1948, Wayne, Bond, Ford, and Merian Cooper traveled to Mexico City to scout locations. Eventually, it was decided the locations there would not be suitable. Filmed in Death Valley during May and June 1948, *The Three Godfathers* starred Pedro Armendariz, Harry Carey Jr., and Wayne as three cattle rustlers who fail in their first attempt to rob a bank. In their efforts to evade the law, they come upon a pregnant woman who perishes giving birth. Her dying wish is that the "three godfathers" save her son and take him to New Jerusalem.[87]

During preproduction, Armendariz, a major star in the Mexican cinema, had a *slight* problem with the wardrobe selection. Ford asked Mickey Myers, the wardrobe coordinator, to get out the costumes Ford had selected for the principal actors. According to Dobe Carey, "Armendariz says, 'Jack, I want to tell you all about that. I bought the most fantastic outfit. Fantastic leather man in Mexico, I paid a hell of a lot of money for this outfit. I want you to look at it. I think my image in Mexico is much different than up here, and I have to think about my following in Mexico, and this is the outfit I'm going to wear here.' So Jack just looked at him and told him to go and put it on. He comes back in, and he looks like Leo Carillo in the Santa Barbara parade. Jesus, it's all new, and it must have cost him three-hundred, four-hundred dollars. He's got spurs on, sterling silver and rowels on them that big–gut hooks and a great big sombrero. He looks like he's gonna ride in the parade. Jack walks around and says, 'That's a really fantastic outfit. It looks terrific, Pete.' Armendariz says, 'I knew you'd like it. Look at the pants. Jesus Christ, look. You can't tell the belly or anything. They are made so that I can mount easily on the horse. I knew you'd like them.' Jack says, 'I do. Oh, yeah, you can wear them. But not in this picture, in your next picture. Not on my picture.' Well, Armendariz goes into a rage and starts screaming in Mexican. He's screaming to the gods and swearing. Jack finally says, 'Pete, you keep talking about a Mexican. Forget Mexican, you are Guatemalan. In other words, get the idea that you are not playing the hero that you want to play down there in Mexico. You're a bandit. You've got a flock of kids in Mexico. Illegitimate.

You're a rogue, everything you wear you have stolen. So these are the pants that you are going to wear or else you are not in the God damn picture.' So Pete tries on these pants, and they are perfect, they look great, they are beat up, and they have Conchos here and there down the sides and the boots…and Armendariz says, 'The God damn things are too tight. I can't even lift my God damn leg up, Jack.' So Jack said we'll fix them. Now they get back to the wardrobe, and they bring out a gringo shirt. It's a cotton shirt with little kind of flowers on it and looks like a homemade old shirt and then a Mexican vest. A great outfit, and an old Mexican sombrero and he looked terrific. Now Pete is miserable about his wardrobe. Finally when we get him all dolled up, he goes into this tirade. He says, 'Jack, I can't wear this God damn outfit.' He had those low cut Jodhpur boots with the high heel and Mexican spur, and he screams about the wardrobe. Finally, Jack turns to the wardrobe man and says, 'For Christ sakes, dress this guy up in a tuxedo. He's going to play a pimp in my next picture!'" According to Wayne, ". . . the final straw was when he took his good hat away from him and gave him this fucking straw hat with a cord under it, and he has a beard, and the God damn cord would catch in the beard all the time. One day, we are going up the side of a hill, and it's one of those things where we are climbing up the desert and there's–and the whole crew is spread out across the valley and everything and Pete was saying this fucking hat–I don't know. Maybe he couldn't remember his lines or something–but anyway it was the God damn hat's fault, catching in his beard. Finally, Jack calls wardrobe…and Jack says I want you to measure this son-of-a-bitch for a black suit. He's gonna be a mortician in my next film." Ford won the "discussion" and Armendariz never worked for him again.[88]

A thinly veiled version of the story of the Magi, the movie included humor, tenderness, and poignancy. Despite being visually stunning, most reviewers thought the film was boring, lacked depth, and generally ignored it. *Variety*, though, stated, "The performance he (Wayne) delivers does him proud," while the *New York Times* said he was "wonderfully raw and ructious." Even the *New York Herald Tribune* said, "Wayne is better than ever as the leader of the bad men." One month after *Godfathers*, Wayne was back at Republic to begin work on his next project. "I think that was one time Duke would have liked a break," said Paul Fix, who was also part of the production. "Because he was just so exhausted from making the Ford film…but Republic [was] waiting for him." Yet another in a long line of low-budget films, *Wake of the Red Witch*, based on a novel by Garland Roark, starred Gail Russell, Gig Young, and Luther Adler. *Witch* involved extensive underwater sequences for Wayne in a studio tank, and in shooting those sequences, he picked up a fungus infection in his ears from saltwater fish that had been placed in the tank to enhance the ambience. Although it was an "A" production, it suffered from many of the same problems as the more common Republic "B" features: quick, easy, cheap, and action-filled. It did, however, feature the sheriff of Honolulu, better known as Duke Kahanamoku, as a tribal chieftain.

Duke Wayne brought him over from Hawaii to the California lots of Republic as he remembered that Duke "K" was an Olympic swimming champ in 1912.[89]

Bone-tired from so many films in such a short time, Wayne was not allowed even a brief respite. Impressed by his performance in *Red River*, Ford wanted Wayne in his next movie, yet another western. "Jack never respected me as an actor until I made *Red River*," Wayne recalled. "I finally arrived. And I think it's the best thing I've ever done." Afterwards, Ford had given him a birthday cake with one candle to mark his first year of maturity as an actor. Written on the cake was "You're an actor now."

Based on two stories by James Warner Bellah, "War Party" and "The Big Hunt," *She Wore a Yellow Ribbon* is the story of a career military officer trying to come to grips with forced retirement after forty-three years of service. Wayne was required to play a character twenty-three years older than he actually was. *Ribbon* is a reverse take on *Fort Apache*. The earlier film is about a military disaster transmuted into heroism by posterity; *Yellow Ribbon* is about a military success in which bloodshed is averted, but it's overweighed with a melancholy air of reverie and grief. The earlier film is about men in their prime, while the later film is about old men getting ready to retire. Trickery is shown as superior to bravery, intelligence outdoes folly. In June 1948, Argosy brought Bellah to Hollywood to adapt his story into a screenplay. He was good at creating certain kinds of characters and writing at a high emotional pitch, but weak at love interests and at developing complex composition. So when Ford felt Bellah had contributed all he could, he turned the draft over to Laurence Stallings. Upon completion, the script was then turned over to Frank Nugent for final polishing.[90]

Filmed in glorious Technicolor against the backdrop of magnificent Monument Valley, Winton C. Hoch won an Academy Award for his cinematography on this movie. According to Ford, Hoch filmed the celebrated thunderstorm sequence with "under protest" written on the clapperboard. As the story goes, Ford thought the angry clouds would make a dramatic background and wanted to film it. Loud cracks of thunder and a misty rain. You could smell the electricity in the air. Hoch didn't think there was enough light, but Ford insisted he shoot it anyway. Hoch did, but filed a formal protest with the American Society of cinematographers, claiming the scene was not acceptable to him and that he only shot it because he was ordered to do so. According to Ford, Hoch would send written notes to Ford affirming that he was in disagreement with Ford's directives. However, Hoch said that simply wasn't true. The brewing storm made the sky devoid of light except for flashes of lightning. After Ford called a wrap and the crew was walking to the station wagons that would take them back to Goulding's, he looked around and said, "Winnie, what do you think?" Hoch said, "Jack, it's awfully dark, but I'll shoot it. I just can't promise anything." Ford told Hoch to open up the lens aperture, and he would take responsibility if it did not come out. Ben Johnson remembered, "Lightning hit this big butte right beside us. It was pretty scary, and everybody was mad at Ford because he was making them stay out in the rain." Wayne led the cavalry walking along, leading their horses, the saddles and harnesses creaking, canteens rattling, and the horses snorting and coughing under the black, eerie sky. It ended up as one of the most powerful, dramatic sequences in the film and was a main reason why Hoch won the Oscar.[91]

"That lucky son of a bitch," recalled Wayne. "We were on location in Monument Valley. Ford always was lucky, on almost all of his pictures. But he had the entire troop out to shoot a sequence where we were going to an outstation. The sky became overcast, and one of those sudden desert storms broke, lightning, rain. Ford kept on shooting. Just sheer Irish luck."[92]

Before shooting *Yellow Ribbon*, Ford studied Frederic Remington's paintings carefully, noted the artist's groupings and composition, and recreated the painter's imagery with striking accuracy. "I think you can say that the real star of my westerns has always been the land," Ford said. "When I did *She Wore a Yellow Ribbon*, I tried to have the cameras photograph it as Remington would have sketched and painted it. It came out beautifully and was very successful in this respect, I think." Bellah wired Ford after he had seen the completed film, "Bless your heart, Pappy. You sure painted a Remington this time."[93]

Victor McLaglen, a charter member of the Ford Stock Company, appeared in the film, this time as Sgt. Quincannon—a crusty, rough, lovable Irish top sergeant. Victor, an ex-boxer and former heavyweight champion of the British Army whose athletic claim to fame was lasting six rounds in a 1909 exhibition with Jack Johnson, had earlier won an Academy Award for his performance in *The Informer*, as did director Ford. McLaglen had an interesting recollection of the bout: "I do remember how I tried my very best to rattle (Johnson) during the last two rounds," McLaglen recalled, "conscious of the fistic immortality that would be mine were I lucky enough to slip a 'sleeper'... During the first two rounds, he had forced the pace, in a smiling, mechanical way, like a man who has a rush job of work to do and is anxious to get it over. Good luck and a certain ability to slip punishment without springing too serious a leak enable me to weather the attack, and, by the middle of the third round, he had settled down to giving and taking fancy stuff. But his grinning face darted in and out behind the thud of his gloves... my best leads frequently pawed the air altogether, for that amazing supple body of his weaved and pranced around me. We both left the ring as fresh as we went into it. There had not been a single count, even from a slip. Johnson was undoubtedly the hardest man to hit whom I ever met... He was certainly the greatest boxer I ever saw in action." In later years, he condensed the story: "He never knocked me down, lad," he once told Dobe Carey, "but he sure beat the livin' be-Jesus out of me." (According to author Scott Eyman in *Print The Legend*, McLaglen was knocked down in the first round, and Johnson may have carried him the rest of the way.) McLaglen had worked for Ford several times in the past and, at sixty-four years of age, had no reason to fear him. He never remembered his lines and always fell asleep on the set, snoring loudly enough to ruin a scene. "Somebody wake up Vic, for Christsakes," Ford would yell. One day while filming a particular sequence, Ford had an idea he wanted McLaglen to try. Victor was to walk back and forth in front of a group of troopers and make an announcement about a patrol. After he finished, he was to spot a dog lying on the ground, ask who owned it, then pet the dog on the head and say, "Good dog. Irish setter." After a few rehearsals, Ford decided to shoot the scene:

"Victor, do you know your lines?"

"Of course, Jack darlin'. Of course."

"All right, we're rolling."

McLaglen continued, "Men, I want you to pay strict attention to what I gotta say. Now there's going to be women with this column. And I want you men to watch them words. Watch them words!" He looked around and spied the dog. "Whose dog is this? Whose dog is this? Nice dog…Cocker Spaniel!" Ford was beside himself, and Wayne bent over and covered his face with his hands, so Ford wouldn't see him laughing. "Oh, Christ! Oh, my god!" Wayne just about had a stroke and filming was delayed for hours because each time the shot was set up Duke would collapse in laughter.[94]

Wayne's performance as Capt. Nathan Brittles was perhaps one of the most dynamic and compelling of his career. Quiet, powerful, and a man of action, his older character dominated the film and firmly established Wayne as a mature leading man. Even his co-stars felt his portrayal was worthy of recognition. "I feel strongly that Duke should have been nominated for an Academy Award for his role in *She Wore a Yellow Ribbon*," said John Agar. "He was just brilliant. Remember, too, I have a lot of scenes with him. He played a guy twenty years older. To me, *Yellow Ribbon* was the best thing Duke ever did." And the public felt the same way. From the moment the film was released, it was a success. Called a "sure fire hit" and "one of the best efforts in John Ford's distinguished career," it grossed $9.15 million worldwide in its first year of release. Wayne felt very satisfied with his performance. "For the first time, Pappy was treating me like an actor, and he showed me great respect, which I appreciated. I felt that I'd worked hard and long to reach that stage of my career, having been thinking of giving it up." But he was also discouraged that he did not receive the recognition he felt he deserved. "I was disappointed at not even being nominated for *Yellow Ribbon*," Wayne admitted. "I had played a man sixty-years old, which was seventeen-years older than I was. I have always believed that this was my best achievement in pictures."[95]

Wayne took time off for the Christmas and New Year holidays and then began work on his next project at Republic. He still owed Yates another film and figured, if he worked for him again, the studio would support him in his efforts to make his own films. As a result, he was forced to star with Yates's girl friend Vera Ralston in *The Fighting Kentuckian*. Furious that Yates insisted he use her again, Wayne told him, "Damn it, Herbert, I know you love the gal, but she just can't act." Wayne played a Kentucky rifleman returning home after five years of soldiering. He falls in love with a French mademoiselle and tries to protect French refugees who settled in Alabama. Fortunately, most movie-goers remembered the film for its action sequences and comic interludes with Oliver Hardy and not for Ralston's atrocious acting and poor accent. Years later, Wayne still seethed about using Ralston. "I was producing and acting," he recalled. "I wanted to have some say in who was going to play the French girl. I wanted a girl who was French. Simone Simon or Danielle Darrieux, but no. Yates made me use Vera Hruba. She talked with this heavy Czech accent. It hurt the picture, because now we had to hire other Czech and Austrian actors to play French characters, so her accent would be matched. I've always been mad at Yates about this because we lost the chance to make one damn fine movie."[96]

Not only did Wayne produce the film, it was also the first time that Chuck Roberson would double for Wayne. Over the years, Roberson appeared in numerous Wayne projects as both stuntman and actor. He doubled both Wayne and Grant Withers in *Kentuckian*. At six-foot-four, he was the same height as Wayne, and, although his hair was curlier in the back, he was a perfect double. "I had to practice that pigeon-toed walk of his for days before I finally got it right," said Roberson. "But riding like him was no trouble at all. He rode tall in the saddle and rested his hand on the saddle horn. That much was easy." Grant Withers? Well, that is another story. Withers was as big as Wayne but lacked his horsemanship skills. When the director requested that Withers ride into town in the middle of a shootout, he refused. Wayne yelled, "Hell, Grant, there's nothing to it. Go on! You can't get hurt." Withers replied, "That's easy for you to say. Damned stuntman turned actor, that's what you are." Nevertheless, he tried his best but fell off the horse when it half-heartedly reared. As he sat in the middle of the dust, his horse ran away, and the director asked which one was his so that the wrangler could get it. Grant replied, "Hell, I don't know. Look for the one with the shit in the saddle."[97]

Two months later, Wayne gave a memorable performance in *Sands of Iwo Jima*. As Ronald Davis stated in *Duke, The Life and Image of John Wayne*, "The picture would be Duke's quintessential war movie; it earned him his first Academy Award nomination, increased his power as a Hollywood star and helped make him a national legend." Wayne spent a great deal of time associating with local Marines at Camp Pendleton, San Diego, to get a handle on his character, Sgt. John M. Stryker, a ruthless, no-nonsense squad leader responsible for turning raw recruits into tough fighting men. An exceptionally realistic film, the Marine Corps contributed 1,200 off-duty soldiers as extras in the battle scenes. It also supplied Sherman tanks, planes, Jeeps, trucks, artillery, weapons, flame throwers, and walkie-talkies. For the beach-landing segments, two squadrons of Corsairs from Marine Air Station at El Toro and thirty amtracs were used. Official combat film clips were also included.[98]

The film had its inception with producer Edmund Grainger but was approved by Herb Yates only if it could be produced for the ridiculous amount of $200,000. Grainger had run across the phrase "sands of Iwo Jima" in a newspaper and felt it worthy of development. In desperation, Grainger went to his father Jim, head of sales at Republic. After considerable pressure, Yates agreed to the project and approved a $937,000 budget if Wayne would star and a name director would be involved. It was estimated that the involvement of the Marine Corps saved in excess of $1 million.

Grainger initially wanted Kirk Douglas for the lead role but claimed Wayne approached him about starring. However, Wayne's son Michael said his father was reluctant and uncertain. It was only after the Marine Corps contacted him directly and personally asked him to play Stryker that he agreed to do it. Written by Harry Brown, Wayne asked Jimmy Grant to polish his dialogue in Grant's unique way. "The script was perfect for Wayne," remembered veteran director Allan Dwan, "except that he wanted to say things in a certain way, and a writer sometimes writes a phrase a little differently. Wayne was very simple and very plain, and he seemed to think that Grant was the only man who could put words the way he ought to say them." Wayne wanted dialogue that was direct, without rhetoric and verbal decorations, lines that revealed his character, opened up his emotions, and advanced the story.[99]

The film's high point was the recreation of the iconic flag-raising atop Mount Suribachi. Ira Hayes, Rene Gagnon, and John Bradley, three surviving participants of the actual event, appeared in the movie just before the recreation. First Lt. Harold Schrier, who led the flag-raising patrol on Iwo, also played himself. The flag in the film was the actual one raised, on loan from the Marine Corps Museum. The Marine Corps Memorial design was based on Joe Rosenthal's actual photo of this historic moment. Rumors persist that the massive bronze memorial contains thirteen hands: two for each of the individuals depicted and one symbolizing either all the other Marines who made the flag-raising possible, or the hand of God. When questioned about this, sculptor Felix de Weldon exclaimed, "Thirteen hands. Who needed thirteen hands? Twelve were enough."[100]

Nominated for four Academy Awards (Best Actor–Leading Role, Best Writing–Motion Picture Story, Best Film Editing, and Best Sound Recording), the film failed to win any. Wayne unfortunately lost to Broderick Crawford's performance as Willie Stark, a character based on Louisiana politician Huey Long, in *All the King's Men*. Said Duke, "I guess that I am never chosen because the kind of acting which I do is not considered acting by anybody. They would say, 'Well, it is only John Wayne being John Wayne. He is not acting.'" In later years, he would tell his wife Pilar, "I wouldn't have minded losing so much if anyone else had won." Duke had turned down *King's Men* on the grounds that it was un-American. He refused to make movies that showed the United States' faults or portrayed debauched U.S. citizens. Wayne thought the film "smears the machinery of government for no purpose of humor or enlightenment...degrades all relationships...and threw acid on the American way of life." Although he lost the Oscar, he did receive the 1950 *Photoplay* Magazine Gold Medal Award for most popular performer of the year in addition to similar recognition from *Showman's Trade Review*, *Box Office Magazine*, and the Independent Theater Owners of America. He also won the accolades of movie-goers who felt Wayne symbolized America and represented the epitome of military champions. Even though he didn't serve, his presence was felt; in the armed forces a flat instrument used to open "C" rations, and worn attached to dog tags, was called a "John Wayne." Wayne felt the character fit him to a "T". "The role itself was such a good one—a great one for me. The picture was made with much more realism than many other war films, and Grainger had managed to get real marines to play marines, so there was none of the phoniness you sometimes get with extras trying to play soldiers." "Not until John Wayne created the role of Sgt. Stryker," said author and military historian Laurence Suid, "and then merged his own personality with the character did Americans find a man who personified the ideal soldier, sailor, or Marine."[101]

After *Sands of Iwo Jima*, Wayne rode a wave of popularity and critical acclaim and was at the pinnacle of his career. With signed contracts at RKO, Republic, and Warner Bros., he could pretty much write his own ticket and pick projects that suited him. Money was no longer an issue. He had earned over $1.3 million for the five movies he starred in between 1948 and 1949. On January 25, 1949, Wayne was immortalized in the concrete forecourt of Grauman's Chinese Theatre where filmland's most illustrious members had for years recorded their existence by placing their hands and shoes in wet cement. Assisted by Sid Grauman and a uniformed Inga Boberg, and with several Marines in dress blues in the background, Wayne made an impression of his fist in the cement, which was made with Iwo Jima sand.[102]

Unfortunately, though, he was still stuck at Republic. Herb Yates was a businessman, not a filmmaker. Content to roll out an endless series of "B" movies, he was only concerned with the bottom line. A former speculator and investor on Wall Street, he wanted only to make movies quickly and cheaply. Wayne spoke to Ford about Republic and Jack worked out his own deal with Yates. It required Ford and Argosy Pictures to deliver to Republic up to three films over the next two years. The studio would own and finance the movies, and Argosy would receive 50% of the net profits. Yates retained approval of the story, shooting script, budget, cast, and start date of each picture. Either party to the agreement was allowed to cancel it after the first film, so, if the first one was profitable, Ford could film his pet project.[103]

Yates requested that Ford, once again, select another James Warner Bellah story for this first Argosy-Republic project. "Mission with No Record" concluded the cavalry trilogy. It was the story of a soldier whose son enlists in the regular army after he flunks out of West Point and turns up in his father's regiment. Alternately known as *Rio Bravo* and *Rio Grande Command* during production, Bellah's story was modified and expanded by James McGuiness. The least impressive and significant of the three trilogy films, it almost appeared that Ford did not take this movie seriously. Filmed again in black and white by Archie Stout, Yates did not want to incur the cost to shoot it in color. Ford rode Yates about it every time he saw him, though. He also used several of the same character names he had used in previous films, such as Quincannon and Yorke. Ford must have loved the lyrical quality of the names as Dick Foran had played Quincannon in *Fort Apache*, the first film of the cavalry trilogy. Despite the fact that he used the same names in both films, the characters are not supposed to be the same. Even Trooper Tyree's name was carried over from *Yellow Ribbon*.

Falling back on a tried-and-true formula, Ford used the Bellah short story and cast Wayne and most of the Ford Stock Company regulars in the movie. Similar to *Fort Apache* and *She Wore A Yellow Ribbon*, it was as if Ford had so little respect for Yates and Republic that he felt no compulsion to make a classic. *Rio Grande*, his attitude said, was a money picture—nothing more, nothing less. And according to Wayne's leading lady Maureen O'Hara, "Neither John Ford or Duke really wanted to make this picture. To them it was just a path to *The Quiet Man*. It was understood by all of us that this was the only reason we were doing it." Ben Johnson recalled, "It seemed to me that Ford wasn't taking the film as seriously as he normally did. He seemed to be sort of easier to work with. Not much shouting and abuse."[104]

Ever the businessman, even with an all-star cast, Yates continued to look for ways to justify the costs he incurred in bringing this movie to fruition. An internal communication clearly reflected his mindset: "Please advise me what justification Argosy has in paying (Ben) Johnson $20,000 and (Harry) Carey Jr. $10,000. Neither one of them will sell a ticket at the box office." A telegram from Yates to Ford later appeared to rescind this demand:

"Dear Jack I am in sympathy with you in respect to budget however we must all understand what the market is and govern our cost accordingly especially (sic) when we're are facing a declining market that continues to go down and not up. However being a good gambler I will say this–if you will limit (Johnson's) salary to $10,000 and Carey's salary to $5,000.00 for picture we can save $7500.00 plus 15% overhead will reduce the budget $8,625.00. Also, in order for you to have Chill Wills I would approve adding to (the) budget an additional $4,000, (p)lus overhead as I understand this character in the screenplay was budgeted at $10,000.00. Chill Wills will be of great value to us in connection with exploitation campaign for *Rio Braoo* (sic) I have in mind.

"This of course is all predicated on your stated effort to bring the pix in at a cost less than budget. In (phoning) Baker this morning he advised me that he had a practical suggestion to make to you on your arrival at the studio that would reduce the budget an (additional) $28,000.00. However on the basis I have been trading with you, that (it) is that you should have a free hand and without annoyances, I have instructed Baker that whatever the budget totals after his conference with you to anticipate my approval and to proceed without further delay regardless of anything I have stated herein. In other words, Jack, you are elected to pitch the entire nine innings. Warm personal regards, Herb."

He was also concerned about the title *Rio Bravo* as it "is not a box office title, nor does it lend itself to universal exploitation." In that Yates felt that 65% of the motion picture attendance was made up by the younger generation, he also felt that the screenplay lacked "some moderate love interest" and suggested that Ford "resolve the post Civil war North-South conflict in a manner acceptable to the South." Ford regarded these suggestions in his usual positive, receptive manner. He ignored them.[105]

Ever the penny-pincher, Yates showed up one morning and complained to Ford, "It's almost ten o'clock. When are you going to start shooting?" Ford answered sarcastically, "Just as soon as you get the hell off of my set." Yates left, Ford went back to work. After the film was complete, Ford, with his tongue firmly planted in cheek, replied, "Dear Herbert: I've had a peaceful quiet summer free from annoyance and nuisance. Nevertheless, I'm frank to say I'm glad you're back. Affection. Jack Ford."[106]

According to Harry Carey Jr., who played Pvt. Daniel "Sandy" Boone, his time on the set was very pleasant, and the filming was extremely easy for Ford. He did not go in for close-ups too much and used a loose shot, which allowed room on either side of the frame of the lens for a margin of error. That way peripheral activity was always in the shot. Carey had previously worked for Ford in *Wagonmaster* and basically played the same type of character, except, this time, he was in the Union cavalry. Years earlier on *Yellow Ribbon*, Victor McLaglen had warned Carey about Ford.

"Tell me, lad," he'd said. "You've worked for him, have ya?"

"Yesssir," replied Carey. "Last summer."

"Mean to ya, was he?"

"Oh, God, yes. Very mean."

"Yeah, yeah, yeah. I know, lad. I know. He's a sadist, he is. A sadist. A big part in this one, have ya?"

"Oh, yes. I'm Lt. Pennell."

"Ah, yes. I haven't read it yet, lad, but he's a bad one. A fucking sadist, he is. But ya can't let it bother you, lad. Ya mustn't let it bother ya."[107]

Carey did not have to worry about that now, but Ben Johnson did. Each evening after filming was completed, *Rio Grande*'s cast and crew would gather for dinner. Ford, O'Hara, and Wayne were at the head table, Carey and Johnson at another. During a lull in the conversation one night, Johnson said to Carey, "Well, there was a lot of shootin' going on today, but not too many Indians bit the dust," and Ford heard it. After Ford asked Johnson several times to repeat it, and was refused, he finally said, "Hey, stupid! I asked you a question. What did you say?" Johnson stood up, left the tent, but, on his way out, stopped and quietly spoke to Ford. "I wasn't very smart," Ben recalled, "but I told him what he could do with his damn picture." Although they appeared to get along relatively well for the remainder of the shoot, Johnson did not work for Ford for another thirteen years.

Of course, it wasn't all hard work on the set, either. There was always time for fun and games. "When we went to places like Moab, Utah," Wayne remembered, "we'd put on entertainment for the kids. Actors who would love histrionics would do recitations. Victor McLaglen and I worked up an act in which we managed boxers, who were stunt men. We'd meet in the center of the ring and start punching, showing the things they weren't supposed to do. The thing became a free-for-all. I broke it up throwing a bucket of water on the fighters, and another bucket, full of confetti, at the kids."[108]

Ken Curtis was a part of the singing group Sons of the Pioneers and sang two songs on location: "My Gal is Purple" and "I'll Take You Home Again, Kathleen." He had fond memories of his time on the set. "Cliff Lyons was the ramrod on *Rio Grande*," recalled Curtis. "He had a covered wagon with a four-up or a six-up coming across the sand dunes. We were riding in behind him, and we're supposed to stay behind the wagon. After we shot it, Cliff said, 'Pioneers! Come over here. I thought you guys could ride. Now I want you to do it again and ride like hell!' I was riding a green horse, and it had this little tiny McClellan saddle, and I lost my stirrups as we upped and went riding ahead of this wagon. I don't know how I stayed on the horse. After we shot it, Cliff just shook his head and said, 'Why don't you guys get your banjos and go home.'"[109]

If *Rio Grande* is memorable at all, at the least, it is because it is the first time Wayne was paired with Maureen O'Hara. An absolutely inspired bit of casting, O'Hara was unbelievably attractive, with beautiful red hair, brilliant hazel-green eyes and a fair complexion. She described herself as an Irishwoman who was "strong and feisty. She has guts and stands up for what she believes in. She believes that she is the best at whatever she does and proceeds through life with that knowledge. She can face any hazard that life throws her way and stays with it until she wins. She is loyal to her kinsmen and accepting of others. She's not above a sock in the jaw if you have it coming. She is only on her knees before God."[110]

Although not yet best friends, the two loved working together. As a couple on the screen, they seemed right for each other, projecting quiet dignity, tempered with humor, and an inner core of strength. O'Hara played Kathleen, the estranged wife of Wayne's Kirby Yorke. Wayne's "real" life son Michael summed up their onscreen relationship perfectly: "I think Maureen was just as much a woman as my father was a man. She was very feminine and just illegally beautiful, but Maureen could be a steamroller. She was just as strong as any guy, although still a lad. But boy, she'd throw the overhand right if things weren't going right, just like a guy would." Friends observed that she seemed to embody many qualities that the director idealized in a woman, and O'Hara confirmed that Ford had a fantastical crush on her.[111]

During the 1940s, Wayne's stature in the industry rose from a "B" level cowboy to one of the most popular leading men. Starring in thirty-three movies, he single-handedly won World War II, subdued the savage Indian, and sailed the Seven Seas. *Rio Grande*'s review was typically effusive: "Outdoor action at its best, delivered in the John Ford manner...It features big, brawling mass action clashes... Wayne is very good as the male star, and Miss O'Hara gives one of her best performances." During the next ten years, Wayne would further define his screen character, as well as his own persona. He would become an active member of Hollywood's political machine and complete a journey that would culminate in his production of an epic masterpiece. *(Although this book is about the story of John Wayne and The Alamo, an exploration of the relationship between Wayne and Ford is necessary if one is to understand Wayne's complexity. In that regard, the following works were both invaluable and highly recommended: "John Ford: Hollywood's Old Master," by Ronald L. Davis; "Print the Legend: The Life and Times of John Ford," by Scott Eyman; "Pappy: The Life of John Ford," by Dan Ford; "John Ford: The Man and His Films," by Tag Gallagher; "Searching for John Ford," by Joseph McBride, and "John Ford," by Andrew Sinclair.)*[112]

# CHAPTER FOUR
## POLITICAL REFLECTIONS II

*"I first thought of doing Alamo in 1946 and went down there to research," Wayne said. "I was at Republic at the time and when I left there they tried to steal the idea. They came up with Last Command which was a quickie. Nuff' said. Instead of five thousand Mexican soldiers, they had 150-spaced 180 feet apart," he chuckled.*[113]

OVER THE YEARS, WAYNE HAD MENTIONED NUMEROUS TIMES THAT HE FELT a movie about the Alamo was important but had never fully explained why he chose that particular subject. He could have made a film about Bunker Hill, Gettysburg, or even Pearl Harbor. Each would have been exciting; each could have told a story about a fight for freedom; each was a classic tale of patriotism and determination. Instead, he chose to film the fight for Texas independence. A journey begins with but a single step. Wayne's long journey toward the Alamo may have begun when he was enticed back to Republic Studios from Universal by an offer to play Sam Houston, a man he very much admired. Then again, maybe it was his failure to serve in the armed forces during World War II. Perhaps he felt he owed something to the men and women who did: something to glorify their sacrifices, something to honor those who gave their last full measure of devotion to their country.

In 1926, when Wayne was still a teenager, Robert Bradbury, father of his best friends Bob and Bill, made a short film, *Davy Crockett at the Fall of the Alamo.* "I'd read up on the history of our country," said Wayne. "And I'd become fascinated with the story of the Alamo. To me, it represented the fight for freedom, not just in America, but in all countries. Seeing Robert Bradbury's film was a real inspiration to me, and I guess it stuck with me until it became a passion of mine to make *The Alamo*. It's a story of freedom, and courage, and doing right in the face of adversity." According to Ronald Davis, Wayne had dreamed of making this film since 1944; it was a subject he often talked about over supper. He used every spare minute to plan and research the project. In an interview shortly before his death, Wayne said, "I had been working on *The Alamo* since I think '44 or '45. I finally did it in '59, so that many years I had been working on it, off and on." He said he started thinking about doing the film after he read Travis's letter of appeal that was sent from the Alamo during the siege.[114]

During the next several years, Wayne laid the groundwork for this project. He created his own production team in 1945/46 when he hired Mary St. John and James Edward Grant. Between wrapping up *Without Reservations* and working on *Angel and the Badman* and *Red River*, 1946 was an extremely busy year for Wayne, yet he still found time to search for suitable locations for his project. He would produce and direct the film but would not star. Oh, *maybe* he would do a small cameo as Sam Houston, but that would be it.

He attacked the project with unbelievably focused passion. Wayne flew thousands of miles and visited multiple sites, seeking a location that would suit his purpose. From South America to Panama to Mexico City, he always looked for property that would match his vision. No matter what project he was involved in at the moment, be it *The Three Godfathers*, *The Quiet Man*, *The Horse Soldiers*, or any of the other numerous films he made during the late 1940s and early- to mid-1950s, he always had *The Alamo* in the back of his mind. How to finance it, where to film it, which actors should be involved and all the countless details that needed resolution before his project could get off the ground.

Wayne divulged his idea to do a film about the Alamo to Grant before they began work on *Badman*. As early as 1947, Wayne and Grant visited San Antonio and hired a research group to pull together all the information they could find in preparation for an eventual movie. "It was Duke who got me interested in it," Grant said frankly. "But once I started, I couldn't let the idea go. In the next two years, I must have read one hundred books on it." Later that year, Wayne, Pat Ford, and D.L. (Tex) Hill visited San Antonio mayor Alfred Callaghan, as well as San Antonioian David Lee Hill, a former fighter pilot in the 1st American Volunteer Group or "Flying Tigers" who'd earned his "triple ace" status during the war. Predictably, their presence in the mayor's office brought work to a screaming halt, as secretaries and clerks stared admiringly at the trio.[115]

On March 9, 1948, just two months before production began on *The Three Godfathers*, John Ford, Wayne, Ward Bond, Tex Hill, and Merian C. Cooper visited San Antonio while scouting locations for Ford's next movie. Cooper, a pilot in the First World War, served as Gen. Claire Chennault's chief of staff in China before the United States entered World War II. Cooper was a good friend and frequent collaborator with Ford, and, in 1947, they had created Argosy Productions. Wayne stayed at the Gunter Hotel and took time to get a shave and haircut. Said barber Lennie Baugh, "He wouldn't let me use the clippers. Said he didn't want it to look like a new haircut." In San Antonio, Ford, who liked to get away from customary locations, visited the Alamo along with Wayne. They spent several hours in the museum gathering historical information. Standing next to Ford, Wayne was photographed holding David Crockett's rifle, "Old Betsy." During this visit, he spoke about the possibility of a movie.[116]

"Some pretty good men wrote the beginning and end of that one," said Wayne when asked who was writing the script. Ford indicated Duke would play David Crockett, and he (Ford) would be involved in the project. "It may be a year before we start shooting scenes of the Alamo picture," said Ford. The film would be confined to the actual battle and the events leading up to it. Pat Ford, John's son, recently discharged from the Navy, was already writing the script with the thought it would be filmed in San Antonio. Gossip columnist Sheilah Graham even announced that Duke's co-star would be a *well-known Mexican film star*, his wife Esperanza, who decided the best way to spend more time with her hubby, was to share his business interests.[117]

Later that week, Hill escorted Wayne and Ford to Richard Freiderich's Bear Creek Ranch on the North Fork of the Guadalupe to look at Texas Longhorn cattle. After he left San Antonio, Wayne continued on to El Paso where he met with Juarez officials and discussed plans to film at Los Mendanos (The Sands), forty miles south of Juarez. He asked for aid from the Juarez American Consulate in arranging entry of technicians and equipment.[118]

Wayne decided it would be to his advantage to get John Ford over to Republic Studios. To entice Ford, Wayne's strategy was to influence the hiring of Ford's son Pat, who was unemployed at the time. Wayne went to Yates and said, "You know, this kid's a bright guy–work on things I'm going to be in–charge him to me." A little later, Yates called both Fords into his office and announced, unbeknown to either, "I want this boy–he takes good care of Wayne." As the meeting adjourned, Pappy turned to Duke and, with condescending reassurance, said, "Well, you're going to be okay now. You got a Ford watching your stuff!" Duke was convinced Pappy never knew Wayne pulled off that charade. Starting in March, for the next ten weeks, Pat Ford was paid $250 a week as a staff writer at Republic and worked on *The Alamo*. In a letter to Brigham Young University in 1980, Ford stated, albeit inaccurately, that he took the characters and general course of events in his treatment from David Crockett's autobiography: "During the siege, (Crockett) continued making notes in his diary. The day before the fall of the Fortress one of his men chose to desert—this man, Moses Rose, carried Crockett's diary and Travis's formal report with him. (The diary) was the property of the Rose family until sometime in the early 1940s when it was given to J. Frank Dobie...he loaned the original to me...the final Alamo battle was reconstructed for Sam Houston by Mrs. Dickinson—Gen'l Santa Anna himself filled in some of the details while a prisoner of war following the battle of San Jacinto—in other words, the battle as I have outlined it is historically as accurate as anyone could make it."[119]

Ford's intent was a semi-documentary, but, by his own admission, the treatment was jingoistic and a bit racist. "I had served with Marines on a few occasions and knew something about the silent, deadly riflemen of my generation—all of this is reflected in the script." By September 1948, a preliminary draft had been developed. The industry rumor at that time was that Wayne would play Travis with Gail Russell as his co-star. Once he finished *She Wore a Yellow Ribbon*, the film would be made for Republic in Mexico. Unfortunately, when Republic announced several studio cuts, all Wayne's films were put on indefinite hold, including his pet *Alamo* project.[120]

While Pat Ford polished the treatment, Wayne continued to work. In January 1949, he took a break from the silver screen and agreed to star in the John Ford stage version of *What Price Glory*. The Motion Picture Relief Fund board asked Ford to help replenish its depleted funds and what better way to do it than to put on a star-studded show. It played up and down the West Coast at twice the usual ticket price. After the first show on February 21 in Hollywood, it continued to San Francisco, San Jose, Oakland, Long Beach, and Los Angeles. Duke was not the only big name in the cast—Pat O'Brien played Sgt. Quirt, Ward Bond was Capt. Flagg, and Maureen O'Hara played Charmaine. Gregory Peck, George O'Brien, Forrest Tucker, Harry Carey Jr., Robert Armstrong, Wallace Ford, Oliver Hardy, and Herbert Rawlinson filled out the cast, many of whom would appear in Wayne's next two films: *The Fighting Kentuckian* and *Sands of Iwo Jima*. On February 22, it played at the Long Beach Strand Theater to benefit the combat wounded of the Military Order of the Purple Heart.[121]

John Ford commented on the production with his usual no-nonsense unflappability. "If I had $5 million to wave at these stars, I doubt if they'd had come to work," he said. "But when I told 'em it was for free, they came running. Not only have the veterans in wheelchairs inspired these famous actors to work for free, but they are doing so at the sacrifice of their sleep. Many of them have to report to the sound stage at 6:30 in the morning, and despite that they are rehearsing with me on this play until 1 or 2 a.m." After Wayne finished his "tour of duty," he was asked if it whet his appetite for the stage. "Heck no," he asserted. "It makes me laugh when I hear these characters talk about how they would like to return to the stage. All they remember are the hits. They forget about the flops they starved through." "No, that's completely out for me," Wayne told Hedda Hopper. "It's a different racket altogether, I think. I think it may be good for newcomers, but only because it gives them a certain confidence and poise. But, to me, screen acting is reacting. You come on the screen in a given situation, and the audience wants to see how you handle yourself. I think I work best in front of a camera." According to Marilyn Carey, Paul Fix's daughter, this was not the first time Wayne appeared on stage: "Duke was in one and was terrified. I'm not sure they ever did more than the dress rehearsal."[122]

Once finished with *What Price Glory*, Wayne immediately started working on *The Fighting Kentuckian*. In April, Hedda Hopper announced that Wayne wanted Ford to direct his independent production of *The Alamo*. He knew if he had the name of the famous director attached to his project, he would have a much better chance of seeing it go into production. Wayne was a proven commodity as an actor but still an unknown when it came to directing. Although wanting to direct eventually, he was less than enthusiastic about it at this point. Before starring in *Tycoon* in 1947, he said, "I wouldn't mind directing if I washed up as an actor. I do believe, however, that one man should serve as producer and director. Making a film is like painting a picture. If you have your portrait painted, you wouldn't have one artist do your eyes, another your nose, and still another your mouth. But that's what often happens in the motion-picture business. Consequently, instead of harmony in the finished product, you get mixture, or even distortion. That's why I think production control should be centered as nearly as possible in the talents of a single individual…I learned to look for things that could hurt actors, and I'm lucky to have survived the dozens of 'B' pictures in which I've played. They've killed off many a fine actor."[123]

Wayne continued to discuss his theory on making movies: "The camera should tell the story—not the actor. When an actor has to pause and explain what's going on, you have a cheap picture. That's what happens to most 'Bs'. But if you're trying to tell four different stories in ninety minutes—as many films propose to do—you've got a problem on your hands. There's not time enough for that much action. So I say keep the yarn simple. I've discovered that short stories, by their very brevity, can be turned into the best pictures."[124]

By the following January, Wayne's *Alamo* message became a bit clearer: filmed in Technicolor, he would have Ford as a sort of foster-father for the enterprise. Wayne would star, but Ford would take over the directorial reins for those sequences in which Wayne would appear. It was a reasonable compromise for those who felt Wayne was yet a bit inexperienced for such an endeavor. Wayne was not shy about touting the relationship, either. "I've got a finished script for a story I'd like to do," he said. "It's called *Alamo*, and I hope to make it next year. I'll play in it, too. Jack Ford has offered to help me with it and to direct the scenes in which I appear. What more help could a man ask?" Hedda Hopper, never one to ignore a rumor, indicated that Johnny Weissmuller would shed his loin cloth and play the part of Davy Crockett. Wayne would star in the picture, and, according to some reporters, the film would be made at Camp Bullis, a U.S. Army training reservation just north of San Antonio. Hollywood columnist Harrison Carroll revealed Wayne had won permission to also film in a small below-the-border town later identified as... Mexico City. Neither rumor was true.[125]

Reluctant to rest on his laurels, Wayne chose for his next project an abysmal movie, *Jet Pilot*. Filmed between October 1949 and February 1950, with additional sequences shot throughout 1951, 1952 and 1953, it was not released until 1957. A tale of espionage and counter-espionage, its single redeeming feature, other than Janet Leigh, was its innovative aerial sequences, which, when released, were woefully out of date. Chuck Yeager, a technical adviser on the project, actually piloted a supersonic plane, the X-1, for the first time in this film. The first of a three-picture deal Wayne signed with RKO and Howard Hughes, he played an Air Force colonel who falls in love with a Soviet pilot who pretended to defect. They fly to Russia and then escape back to freedom. "I'm a character lead, not a leading man. I'm old enough to be Janet Leigh's father and in this picture, she looks about fifteen years old. It's a pretty dramatic role," he said sarcastically. "I say 'Yes,' 'No,' and 'Do you think so?' I keep saying things like that all through the picture. The only scene I'm not in is the one in the ladies' washroom. Don't get me wrong, I can be mistaken. I think the picture itself will be okay...Also, I have a contract to fulfill. I've never welched on a contract and I never will. If I make a bad deal, I'll go through with it. But Mrs. Morrison so far hasn't raised a boy who makes the same mistake twice." Upon further reflection though, Wayne stated, "That is without doubt one of the worst films I ever made. The script was too silly to get the message across, and to make things worse, the director, Josef von Sternberg, insisted on making us rehearse over and over, and he kept making remarks which I didn't take kindly to. I'd take them from Pappy but not from him. I was ready to punch the son-of-a-bitch in the mouth, but Janet kept calming me down." Wayne even told Leigh, "Honey, if I ever let loose, if I ever started on him, I'd kill the son-of-a-bitch."[126]

Leigh learned how to smoke for the film. "I had never smoked before," recalled Leigh, "but a cigarette case played an important part in the story, and I'm sure it probably could've been changed, but who knew at that time the dangers of smoking. And because I was one of the few who didn't smoke, I actually felt sophisticated, if you can imagine how funny that sounds. And I remember trying to learn to take a puff, and I didn't want to inhale, because I thought that would have looked phony. I mean, I knew Bette Davis could get away with it, but I didn't think that I could. And I remember doing a scene and being so dizzy from smoking." Leigh seemed to enjoy the love scenes with Wayne, though. Ribbed on the set that Wayne didn't look very expert in his lovemaking, she replied, "Maybe not. But he's very thorough."[127]

Ostensibly a film about the evils of Communism, *Jet Pilot* was outrageously ridiculous, with outmoded airplanes and a lead actor playing a character much younger than his actual age. Had Hughes released it in 1950 when first made,

50

audiences would have been enthralled by the supersonic aerial aerobatics. By 1957, though, it only served to show how Wayne had aged over the past several years. "As for Hughes," Wayne said derisively, "he was obsessed with filming hours and hours of jets flying, and he spent the next eight years doing that. That's why the film didn't get released until 1957. The final budget was something like four million. It was just too stupid for words." Years later, when it was finally released, Janet Leigh attempted to justify the project. "Look," she exclaimed. "I saw the jet planes when we were making the picture and I've seen the latest ones. I couldn't tell the difference and I defy the average moviegoer to spot any changes." She also quipped, "I'm wondering if Hughes will advertise it: See the YOUNG John Wayne. I can hardly wait to see how I looked when I was a child." Wayne concurred. Hughes held *Jet* back because by the time it was ready for release the Korean War was raging, and the picture's treatment of Communism would have rendered it inappropriate. "The general trade suspicion that new advances in airplane design might have outdated the film was not justified," according to Wayne.[128]

Bill Clothier, the fifth cameraman hired for the movie, recalled the instructions he received from Hughes. "Hughes and I only met once. It was in the dark projection room. The cutter who was there said, 'Mr. Hughes, this is Bill Clothier, the cameraman.' He said, 'Glad to meet you. Roll the film.' What he showed me was *Hell's Angels*. After the aerial scenes were over, he turned to me and said, 'Unless you have clouds that good, don't shoot.' Sometimes I would have arguments with the front office, but I said Mr. Hughes says he wants clouds and I will give him clouds. Each foot I made had beautiful clouds. Now Duke never was up in the air. We shot around him in these aerial sequences and then went into the studio and shot it in process, using my aerial sequences as background and having close-ups of Duke in a plane. It looked real."[129]

Both Wayne and Hughes were fervent anti-Communists and the film served as the medium to get their message across. In *The Cold War: A New History*, John Lewis Gaddis explains that after the end of World War II, in the minds of virtually all Americans, the image of the Soviet Union changed from reluctant ally to passionate adversary. A fundamental incongruity in how the postwar world would be configured led to this difference. Each side held dissimilar ideas regarding the establishment and maintenance of postwar security. The Western Allies desired a system in which democratic governments were established as widely as possible, permitting countries to peacefully resolve differences through international organizations while the Soviets sought to increase security by controlling the internal affairs of countries that bordered it. Failure to reach agreement at the Yalta Conference of 1945 resulted in postwar Europe effectively being divided in two with the Western region occupied by the U.S. and its allies while the Soviets controlled the Eastern region.[130]

Early in its existence, Wayne rarely attended Motion Picture Alliance meetings. In fact, he played no active role whatsoever. When asked to read a stock address by James McGuinness, head of the Alliance Executive Committee, Wayne declined and indicated he attended the meeting as an American, not an actor. If he spoke at all, it would be based on what he thought, and not the words of others. "I said now whoa," recalled Wayne. "Wait a minute. Jim, now you know, you hire me as an actor is one thing, but you know I'll use your help and if these ideas are my ideas, I'll read them. But I just don't jump in and join the hysteria." Instead, Ward Bond gave the speech as written. "It wasn't a bad speech," said Wayne, "but it was just the idea of not just talking about it beforehand but just coming to a meeting and saying 'Here, read this,' Christ, I wouldn't have done it for anything."[131]

If Wayne was not yet active in his defiance of Communism, the Alliance certainly was. It sponsored a series of meetings to discuss the specter of Communist infiltration. Guest speaker Dr. Sidney Hook, professor of philosophy at New York University, indicated that an effective way to combat Communism was to enforce existing laws against proven secret agents. The issue, he stated, was that "there is a great deal of confusion about (Communism.) It is caused...by the...trick of using our democratic terminology with reversed meanings. If you criticize Russia, people will say, 'but we have faults too.' Yes, we have many grave faults in America, but the point is that we have the institutions, the mechanisms to abolish them. The Russian Communist party is not really a political party. It is an organized conspiracy that has religious-nationalistic inspirations which arise from one source. To have a democracy, you must have at least two political parties, and the parties must have some similar ideals." Ayn Rand, novelist, playwright and screenwriter, declared in the MPA's *Screen Guide for Americans*, the influence of Communists in Hollywood "is due, not to their own power but to the unthinking carelessness of those who profess to oppose them. Red propaganda has been put over in some films produced by innocent men, often by loyal Americans who deplore the spread of Communism throughout the world and wonder why it is spreading." The purpose of the Communists in Hollywood "is not the production of political movies openly advocating Communism. Their purpose is to *corrupt our moral premises by corrupting non-political movies*–by introducing small, casual bits of propaganda into innocent stories–thus making people absorb the basic premises of Collectivism *by indirection and implication*."[132]

A Russian magazine writer alleged Hollywood subordinated profits to an underhanded campaign intended to portray the American way of life as more desirable than other ways, particularly communistic ways. In a weekly publication *Culture and Life*, Yuri Zhukov accused the movie industry of making productions that served the policy of monopolistic capital. "Hollywood companies...are flooding the market with films which correspond to the social order dictated by representative of the State Department and the head of the motion picture industry," he wrote. "The industry has now put the making of dollar profits second to this new program. An analysis of statistics shows that the number of films devoted to social programs has sharply decreased and that biographical and historical films are almost never produced. Instead the number of thoughtless musical comedies, revues, and melodramas has doubled and from under cover they propagandize the notorious 'American way of life' giving a distorted and sweetened picture of life in the United States, advertising American capitalists as noble and successful people who must be imitated and who should be obeyed. American films also depict labor leaders as 'dangerous and thoughtful groups of suspicious persons who incite workers to act against employers and the employers are pictured as worrying only about the interests of their employees.' The stink of race propaganda is smelled miles away from the Hollywood pictures."[133]

As expected, Hollywood ignored this criticism although McGuinness, executive producer at MGM, replied, "I know of no definite policy of propaganda within the motion picture industry. We have made pictures like *The Grapes of Wrath* and *I Am a Fugitive from a Chain Gang* that point out the wrong things in America. But primarily we believe the screen is a medium for entertainment."[134]

The House Un-American Activities Committee (HUAC) was created to investigate disloyalty and subversive activities on the part of private citizens, corporations, and those organizations suspected of having Communist ties. In 1947, HUAC raised the specter of Communism within the movie industry. Kenneth Lloyd Billingsley wrote that some industry moguls feared their private lives would be aired publicly as the newsreel cameras rolled. The idea of hearings provoked a backlash against friendly and unfriendly witnesses alike, both of which were seen as bringing a plague upon Hollywood. Hollywood's response was immediate. On October 16 the Republican and Democratic Joint Committee of Hollywood (For the Preservation of Civil Liberties, and the Defense of the People of the Motion Picture Industry) developed a pronouncement declaring in part "...we are not making this statement in the belief that there are no Communists in Hollywood. We assume that there are some here as there are everywhere, but if so they constitute an insignificant minority, the parallel of which is to be found in every American industry and in every American medium. We see no reason. Other than the political capital and headlines which are to be secured from the seemingly easy target of Hollywood and its people, for singling out the motion picture industry... Further, we resent the careless hurling of the word "Communist" at every left-wing member of the Democratic party or its more radical splinter groups... We hope, and we have confidence, that we shall be but the first of countless Republicans and Democrats to recognize that it is our duty and obligation as Americans to defend the rights of Americans of political faiths different from our own... We are tired of our industry, and of our profession, and of our families and friends, eternally being placed in a defensive position by every group seeking notoriety at Hollywood's expense."[135]

Four days later, an equally august group of individuals from the Screen directors Guild, including George Stevens, John Ford, Merian Cooper, John Huston, George Sidney, and William Wyler, stated, "… we firmly believe that an American citizen should not have his reputation attacked by anyone without the rights which we believe were the intention of the Constitution to give… We believe these rights of defense should include the right to make a statement in his own behalf, to be represented by counsel, and to have the privilege of cross-examination of witnesses against him. We petition that the present congressional investigation…be so conducted, and we make this petition directly to Congress."[136]

Even the Motion Picture Chapter #1898, Military Order of the Purple Heart, condemned the investigation for "Gestapo methods used by such members of Congress" for their "unethical tactics" and "selfish interests" and "repeated Communist witchhunts (sic) which have been defamatory and slanderous to the entire Motion Picture Industry."[137]

HUAC selected forty-five industry individuals to appear before it. Nineteen, who later became known as the *unfriendly nineteen*, refused to cooperate. Director Billy Wilder later quipped that only a few in this group were talented, the rest were just unfriendly. The nineteen were later reduced to ten and became forever known as the *Hollywood Ten*: screenwriters Herb Biberman, John Howard Lawson, Ring Lardner Jr., Samuel Ortiz, Alvah Bessie, Lester Cole, Albert Maltz, and Dalton Trumbo, producer Adrian Scott and director Edward Dmytryk.[138]

The movie industry united behind the unfortunate ten. Marsha Hunt, a young actress who flew to Washington to support her fellow industry employees, summed up Hollywood's position: "We were all fired up with our mission, to defend our industry's good name and to defend, not Communism or Communists, but all Americans' right to privacy of opinion and freedom of advocacy. We were flying to keep the First Amendment alive. In that year, after weeks of a headline circus that was nationwide, all Hollywood seemed to be outraged at the charges against our industry that were coming from the HUAC hearings. And they were rallying behind the nineteen talented film people who were now being called the *unfriendly witnesses*." Hollywood luminary Gene Kelly declared, "I think it is not only the freedom of the movie industry and the professional integrity of its workers that is at stake but the whole future of cultural and civil liberties in America." Close to thirty filmmakers, actors, directors, writers, and other celebrities such as Danny Kaye, John Huston, Ira Gershwin, Humphrey Bogart, and Lauren Bacall, flew to Washington to express their outrage at the hearings.[139]

The hearings began with the testimony of friendly witnesses like Jack Warner, Louis B. Mayer, Ayn Rand, Adolphe Menjou, Robert Taylor, Robert Montgomery, Gary Cooper, Ronald Reagan, and Walt Disney. Each individual gave testimony regarding the insidious nature of Communism and its effect on the movie industry. Disney testified that Herbert K. Sorrell, head of the

Conference of Studio Unions, admitted using Communist money to finance a 1937 walkout. He also mentioned he was troubled by individuals he thought were planted in his studio by Communists. The committee received a detailed explanation of the way subversive factions infiltrated the film industry.[140]

With the advice of Communist Party-affiliated lawyers, the Hollywood Ten adopted a common front and defied the committee by refusing to admit or deny they were Communists. Each of the Ten arrived with prepared statements, denounced the committee, and challenged its right to ask questions relating to political affiliations. They based their stand—after much preliminary discussion—on the First Amendment's guarantee against incursions on free speech, rather than the Fifth Amendment's protection against self-incrimination. Rather than admit they were card-carrying members in good standing of the American Communist Party or, at least, Communist sympathizers, they posed as pseudo libertarians and wrapped themselves in a blanket of individual freedoms. Some refused to answer even the most rudimentary questions, and, when they did, they stoked the flames of the committee's anger by responding with pugnacious defiance.[141]

Morrie Ryskind, an original founder of the MPA, commented on the Hollywood stars who defended the Ten: "They got a billion dollars' worth of stars to defend Hollywood. And they came to Washington in a burst of publicity and they made speeches and had a lovely fanfare. When the Unfriendly Ten showed their true colors—well that billion dollars' worth of talent looked like thirty cents."[142]

The defendants refused to name names or cooperate with the committee in any manner and, as a result, were held in contempt and sentenced to between six months and one year in confinement. A lengthy appeal process ended in April 1950 when the Supreme Court refused to review John Howard Lawson and Dalton Trumbo's contempt convictions and sentenced the Hollywood Ten to federal detention. Trumbo tried to rationalize their defiance: "Another thing, the Ten were virgins. We went into an unpredictable situation which had results we could not predict. As a matter of fact, we felt that we were going to win on the constitutional issue. So we could not be certain we would lose our jobs; neither could we have been certain we would go to jail; neither could we have been certain we would become so notorious that there would be no way we could clean ourselves up for a decade."

Perhaps had they known the consequences of their actions, they might have been more responsive. Of course, if you were a Communist in Hollywood, you weren't anything if you weren't flexible in your position. In the late 1930s, to be Communist was to be anti-Nazi. However, after the signing of the Nazi-Soviet Pact on August 23, 1939, in which the Baltic States were ceded to Russia, Poland was divided, and the subsequent Soviet invasion of Finland, Communist sympathizers needed to rationalize a position they previously condemned. Their position again reversed on June 22, 1941, when Germany invaded Russia. No longer an ally after the war ended, American Communists were told to stop cooperation with capitalism and get on with the business of class struggle and revolution. Whew! It's a wonder the sympathizers didn't fall over from spinning around so much.[143]

Immediately after the Hollywood Ten were cited for contempt, the association for Motion Picture producers condemned the defendants' actions and stated: "We will forthwith discharge and suspend without compensation those in our employ, and will not reemploy any of the Ten until such time as he is acquitted or has purged himself of contempt and declares under oath that he is not a Communist." Further, "We will not knowingly employ a Communist or a member of any party or group which advocated the overthrow of the government...." Although not specifically mentioned, "blacklist" now officially entered Hollywood's vernacular. Columnist George E. Sokolsky commented that those personalities who testified against the Communists were also chastised: "...the bankers, lawyers and press agents of this industry, thinking only of box-office, feared the power of the Communists and their allies and sympathizers; they feared strikes and picket lines outside of theaters. They feared the gossip columnists and the critics of new pictures. They counseled a hush-hush policy. They hoped that the public would soon forget the hearings. They assumed that most Americans would go to see pictures even if made by those whom they regard as enemies of their country. The result is that the Communists, their allies, sympathizers, and friends are working while many of those who oppose the Communists, who went to Washington to testify against Stalin's stooges, are not working. They are boycotted. They are penalized for being Americans."[144]

In 1948, Wayne and Ward Bond were elected to the Alliance's executive board and the next year Wayne followed Robert Taylor as its president. Taylor, whose private testimony to HUAC was unexpectedly revealed by the media, was asked by MGM executives to step down from that position. Taylor had been a reluctant witness, and his testimony was brief yet not particularly coherent. Although he hated Communism, he was hesitant to identify Hollywood colleagues as Communists. Through studio and government coordination, Taylor became the face to blame for the Hollywood Ten imprisonment and blacklisting. Wayne took over from Taylor at the March 30, 1949, Alliance meeting at the Hollywood American Legion Stadium after Taylor presented the annual report. (Sam Wood was the first MPA president, followed by Clark Gable and then Taylor.) Robert Stripling, former chief investigator of the HUAC, was the guest speaker that evening. Wayne was in favor of "alerting Hollywood to the danger that a small group of Communists, under Party discipline, would take over the unions and control American movies." A victim of a mud-slinging campaign by Communist sympathizers after he made a speech at a previous MPA meeting,

Wayne was tenacious in his resistance. "I was called a drunk, a pervert, a woman-chaser, a lousy 'B' picture western bit player, an unfaithful husband, an uneducated jerk, a tool of the studio heads," Wayne recalled. "Well, that just made me determined to be the president of MPA if the members wanted me. Charlie Feldman advised me not to stick my neck out. Bo Roos told me to stay out of it and Herb Yates told me, 'Duke, you're a goddam fool. You are crazy to get mixed up in this. It'll put you on the skids in Hollywood.'"[145]

Wayne had a history of antagonism with Hollywood Communists. In 1976, longtime friend Yakima Canutt said, "John stood for what we like to think of as good old American freedom. He was becoming more hostile toward the Communists in the business, and he got criticized a lot for his politics later on. But Wayne was standing up for what was right, and he knew it..." One time, Wayne received a threatening letter from someone in the Communist party. "When Wayne told me about this letter, I said, "Sounds to me like you better watch out,"" said Canutt. "He said, 'No goddamn Commie's gonna frighten me.' I said, 'Duke, why don't you let me look into this? See if I can find out who's behind all this?' He just said, 'Nah! It probably won't come to anything.' So I let it rest."

Canutt remembered, "The Communists in Hollywood that were being given full support by the Stalinists were really gunning for Wayne. Why they singled him out, I don't know for sure, but my guess is that they thought him an easier target than anyone who was a part of a great body like the Motion Picture Alliance. Duke kind of stood out." Canutt even volunteered the use of his fellow stuntmen as 'undercover' investigators to find out what was going on with the threats. Duke reluctantly agreed but nothing ever came of it. According to Orson Welles, Joseph Stalin and Mao Tse-tung even conspired together to have Wayne assassinated due to his popularity and his fervent anti-Communist position.[146]

Ward Bond, Robert Montgomery and many others had asked Wayne to assume the presidency in 1949, but he had turned it down. They kept at him. They told him his increased stature within the industry demanded that he take a stand and assume a public profile. In his brief acceptance speech, Wayne stated, "We don't want a political party here that any bully boy in a foreign country can make dance to his tune. I never felt I needed to apologize for my patriotism. I felt that if there were Communists in the business—and I knew there were—then they ought to go over to Russia and try enjoying freedom there. We were just good Americans and we demanded the right to speak our minds. After all, the Communists in Hollywood were speaking theirs. If you're in a fight, you must fight to win, and in those early years of the Cold War I strongly believed that our country's fundamental values were in jeopardy. I think that the Communists proved my point over the years."[147]

Explaining his position a few years later to Maurice Zolotow, Wayne said Communists "were rotten and corrupt and poisoned the air of our community by creating suspicion, distrust, hatred. We (members of the Alliance) were called anti-Semite, even though Ryskind was one of our leaders. We were called anti-labor even though Roy Brewer and three other AFL leaders were in with us. Actually, we were the real liberals. We believed in freedom. We believed in the individual and his rights. We hated Soviet Communism because it was against all religion, because it trampled on the individual, because it was a slave society."[148]

Wayne served as Alliance president for four one-year terms; the longer he served, the more politically involved he became. Of course, as he became increasingly popular, his income significantly increased, which also increased his taxes. A life-long believer of Thomas Jefferson's maxim, "government is best which governs least," Wayne constantly condemned excessive Federal involvement. Joe De Franco, one of Wayne's closest friends, remembered that Wayne "hated politicians and big government. They wasted too much money, including too much of his money. For the rest of his life, he supported political candidates who believed in reducing tax burdens and the cost of government." In his later years, Wayne discussed the reason behind his passion: "It's been proven that Communism is foreign to the American way of life," he insisted. "If you'd read the official Communist doctrine and then listened to the arguments of these people we were opposing, you'd find they were reciting propaganda by rote. Besides, these Communist sympathizers ran a lot of our people out of the business. Suddenly, everybody from make-up men to stagehands found themselves in seminars on Marxism." It didn't hurt that other Hollywood actors supported Wayne's position. "(Ronald) Reagan, who was supposed to be so violently opposed to me politically, called up and said, 'These commies are going to take over the SAG. They're loaded. And I can't stand by and see this happen to our industry. I need your help.'" At the time, Reagan was a militant Democrat, but that didn't faze Wayne. "Ronnie was a liberal in those days," said Duke, "but he was an American first."[149]

The willingness of people to testify and the evident failure of the 1947 hearings prompted, in 1951, a new series of congressional inquires in Hollywood. In 1947, the unfriendly witnesses relied on the protection of the First Amendment and the right of freedom of expression. In 1951, they instead depended on the Fifth Amendment and protection against self-incrimination. Most witnesses either denied they were Communists and refused to answer other questions, or denied they were party members and failed to have independent recollection of the issues. The committee demanded that the "unfriendlies" identify others who were members of the Communist party. As they knew the result would be prosecution and incarceration if they didn't comply, the witnesses were then placed in the unenviable position of turning in their friends or standing by their principles.[150]

Actor Larry Parks' testimony was typical. His reply to the request to name Communists in the industry was both indignant and entreating: "I think my career has been ruined because of this, and I would appreciate not having to... Don't present me with the choice of either being in contempt of this Committee and going to jail or forcing me to really crawl through the mud to be an informer, for what purpose? I don't think this is a choice at all. I think it is not befitting for this committee to force me to make this kind of choice... As I told you I think this is probably the most difficult thing I have done... There was another choice open to me. I did not choose to use it. I chose to come and tell the truth...so I beg of you not to force me to do this."[151]

Parks repeatedly implored the HUAC not to force him to name specific individuals, but, once he admitted he had been a former member of the Communist party, his fate was sealed. Parks later met with the committee in private and revealed four or five names but named no one the committee didn't already know about. Others like writer Paul Jarrico defiantly stood their ground. After Jarrico learned that he was to be subpoenaed, he telephoned the U.S. Marshals office to notify officers where he worked, and even offered to leave a pass at the RKO gate for the federal officer. Said Jarrico, "I certainly won't become a stool pigeon in order to save myself from a contempt charge. If I have to choose between crawling through the mud with Larry Parks or going to jail like my courageous friends, the Hollywood Ten, you can be sure I'll choose the latter." Betty Garrett, Parks' actress-wife, collapsed when she heard he had admitted being a Communist.[152]

Wayne was never one to hold a grudge. Or, at least, for very long. He believed people deserved a second chance if *he* felt they deserved it. The fervent anti-Communist said that Parks' long silence on his Communist connections was "not to his credit," but declared "We hate no one. We hope that those who have changed their views will cooperate to the fullest extent. By that I mean give names and places so that they can come back to the fellowship of loyal Americans. I think I can speak for the alliance when I say that his courage in speaking the truth is to be commended." He also declared, "Let no one say a Communist can be tolerated in American society and particularly in our industry. We do not want to associate with traitors. I'm sure they'll give him a second chance. The American public is pretty quick to forgive a person who is willing to admit his mistake. I think it's fine that he had the courage to answer the questions and declare himself."[153]

But there were some in Hollywood who thought Parks should be punished for his admission. At a MPA meeting on March 22, Hedda Hopper expressed outrage that Wayne would choose to speak on behalf of all Alliance members. "She berated me for an hour!" Duke exclaimed. "In she came, very dramatic," he recalled. "Oh, I love her, but...She gave me fifteen minutes of the roughest go—our boys dying in Korea and the whole thing. Real rough, and I had to take it. I wanted to say something good about him (Parks). I realized this was a crucial issue. Parks was breaking, not just with the Party but all of his friends. He needed our moral support, so other witnesses would be encouraged to break." Wayne admitted he spoke about his own beliefs and not that of the MPA.[154]

Hopper contended that Wayne deserved the chastisement. "Duke is a little dumb about these things," she told a friend. She asked to speak before the Alliance, and Duke graciously introduced her and proceeded to return to his seat. Hopper asked him to remain standing and proceeded to lambaste him for his comments on Parks.[155]

"I feel impelled to say some things that I believe would speak the minds of the mothers of the 55,000 casualties in Korea...I have read the papers. I've listened to the radio. And I was shocked as I read the statement of our president, John Wayne, which would imply that he voiced the opinion of our alliance. If it did—we should so express ourselves. It is not my opinion. I wish to be impersonal from now on. I, too, have sympathy for anyone who sees the light. But Mr. and Mrs. Larry Parks were visited by a member of the FBI four years ago—who pleaded with them to give up their membership in the Communist party. If they had listened, Larry Parks' appearance in Washington yesterday would not have been necessary. And this man was practically thrown out of their house. Larry Parks read the best script of his career yesterday—but he gave no news. All the data was already in the committee's possession. One, two, or ten careers in Hollywood aren't worth a dime unless we're willing to lose them for our country. Why so much emphasis on one career? Do we know what the careers of those 55,000 would have been if they had not been caught short by the refusal of information in our country? And I, for one, believe that the life of one soldier fighting for our freedom is worth more than all the careers in Hollywood. How can anyone expect to hold his position in public life who withholds valuable information until put under pressure? I suggest that before we let the traditional theatrical charity govern our reason that we consider whether the mud of an informer is worse than the mud of Korea mixed with the blood of our 55,000 boys whose luck ran out before they came to fame in Hollywood or anywhere else...Larry Parks says he felt he'd done nothing wrong. I feel sorry for him... And I'm wondering if the mothers and families of those who died and the wounded who are still living will be happy to know that their money at the box office has supported and may continue to support those who have been so late in the defense of our country?"[156]

At the conclusion of her tirade, the meeting turned into a donnybrook. While many members took umbrage with her comments, others commended her on her stance against Wayne. Hopper received a standing ovation lasting for several minutes.[157]

The problem was that Hopper never heard Wayne's remarks. She was scheduled to speak that evening, but Wayne received word she couldn't make it. When he found out that she had shown up at the last, he introduced her to the audience, and the tirade began. "She didn't know what the hell I said," reflected Duke. "I'd said nothing about the MPA and what I said should have been helpful…she had already put it into her column and the same things she was saying to me was in the column the next day. This poor guy (Parks) did it and neither side would take him in or talk to him and he never did sing, he never told anybody a single thing."[158]

One week later, after a great deal of discussion, the Alliance declined to take a stand on the issue and declared "that the gravity of the Parks case merits a submission of the entire record" and voted to withhold comment "until the complete facts are known." Charles Ralls, commander-in-chief of the Veterans of Foreign Wars, called for a nationwide boycott of movies made by Parks. "He was carrying a Red card while we were overseas and made a million dollars doing it," Ralls declared. "(The) VFW is certainly going to hold it against him." Under contract by Columbia Pictures, Parks was immediately dropped from the cast of the film *Small Wonder*.[159]

The Alliance, however, wasn't afraid to voice its opinion when it came to the Red menace:

"WHEREAS, American blood is being shed and American boys tortured and killed resisting the wanton aggression of Communists in Korea, and

WHEREAS, it has been shown beyond doubt that American Communists and their sympathizers are militant allies of Korean, Russian and all other Communists everywhere in the world, and are pledged to serve them, even to the end of betraying the United States in this foul service, and

WHEREAS, the second largest concentration of Communists in our country exist in the Los Angeles area, and

WHEREAS, the grave threat of sabotage in our community and the existence of a shooting war against Communists constitutes the clear and present danger which the United States Supreme Court recognizes as justifying action for the protection of our lives and our institutions, now, therefore,

BE IT RESOLVED, that the Motion Picture Alliance for the Preservation of American Ideals calls on the city of Los Angeles City Council to adopt measures compelling Communists in this community to register, so that our enemies may be identified and our citizens afforded full measure of protection against sabotage and treason, and

BE IT FURTHER RESOLVED that the Motion Picture Alliance urges all organizations within the motion picture industry and all civic organizations in our community to adopt similar resolutions."[160]

Wayne also had the dubious honor of running Carl Foreman out of Hollywood. *High Noon*, with screenplay by Foreman and co-produced by Stanley Kramer, is the story about a retiring marshal (Gary Cooper) who, on his wedding day, is forced to defend an unsupportive town from three gunmen and a paroled murderer. The film tried to assay the mettle of men who live by violence, die by violence, or run away from it. It then becomes somewhat of a commentary on men and social behavior. The film is a powerful allegory of its time, condemned by some as "un-American" and praised by *Pravda* for its depiction of "the grandeur of the individual." Almost as soon as the film was released, audiences questioned whether they were watching Marshall Will Kane facing his enemies in the main street of Hadleyville, or screenplay writer Carl Foreman, standing alone under interrogation by the House Un-American Activities Commission (HUAC) in relation to his Communist sympathies.[161]

Midway through the filming, Foreman was subpoenaed by the commission, appeared as an "unfriendly witness" and took the "diminished" Fifth Amendment when questioned. He denied present Communist party membership but refused to name names from the past. When he returned to the set, he rewrote several scenes to reflect his protest against HUAC. "I became the Cooper character," Foreman later stated. Foreman called the film a "parable about Hollywood and McCarthyism." He described Hollywood as a "community beginning to crumble around the edges as these high-powered politicians came in...putting the community through an inquisition that was getting more and more painful for a lot of people, and people were falling to the wayside one way or another. They were either capitulating to these gangsters—political gangsters from out of town—or they were being executed by them here. And I could see that my time was coming sooner or later—it was just being delayed by a couple years or so—and I wanted to write about that. I wanted to write about the death of Hollywood. So all that shaped the writing of *High Noon*. That was very conscious, see."[162]

Communist sympathizers, real and imagined, were being investigated by the Committee. When *High Noon* premiered, some even considered the film un-American. "We were picketed by every kind of group in the world," said Kramer, "from the Klu-Klux-Klan to the All American Activities Committee, whatever they call it. I think you stand for what you are. The picture is there. Is it moral? Yes. The Marshall leaves the town because the people did not stand behind him against the people that entered. So it's moral. Is it American? I think so. It's a part of the Old West. Is it, is it something that you can truthfully back with your feelings, your emotions, your morals? I did and I believe it." There were those, however, who rightly believed they were watching a classic. "Every five years or so," wrote one reviewer, "somebody—somebody of talent and taste, with a full appreciation of legend and a strong trace of poetry in his soul—scoops up a handful of clichés from the vast lore of western films and turns them into a thrilling and inspiring work of art. This tale of a brave and stubborn sheriff in a town of do-nothings and cowards has the rhythm and roll of a ballad spun in pictorial terms."[163]

Shortly after Foreman testified before the committee, Kramer, who four years earlier had created both the Stanley Kramer Company and Stanley Kramer Productions, Inc. with Foreman, split with the screenwriter and in a written statement declared he was in "total disagreement" with Foreman's refusal to state if he was ever a Communist. A "satisfactory financial agreement" was reached between the two; it cost Kramer $350,000 to let Foreman go.[164]

The Motion Picture Industry Council's (MPIC) stand on the hearing was to urge witnesses to talk and repudiate those who didn't. Art Arthur, executive secretary of the MPIC, further defined the council's position: "A good deal of individual action (among the several studios) probably will be taken within the general framework of this policy." Even Gary Cooper, the star of *High Noon*, was forced to reconsider his position. Immediately after Foreman and Kramer dissolved their partnership, Foreman announced plans to go forward with an independent production company (Carl Foreman Productions) and further stated that Cooper would purchase stock in it. Hollywood was aghast that Cooper, an avowed anti-Communist who voluntarily appeared before the committee and was vociferous in his denunciation, would agree to support Foreman, who hid behind the Fifth Amendment. However, after considerable unfavorable reaction to the potential stock purchase, Coop issued a statement. While hunting and fishing in Idaho, he declared that, although he "was convinced of Foreman's loyalty, Americanism and ability as a picture maker," he felt that it would be better for all parties concerned that he did not purchase any stock.[165]

Foreman was eventually blacklisted, but Wayne again gave him a chance to name names. In a closed-door meeting in the office of Wayne's business manager Bo Roos one Saturday morning, Foreman refused and subsequently left for England. In Wayne's famous or infamous *Playboy* interview, he succinctly expressed his views about *High Noon*: "It's the most un-American thing I've ever seen in my whole life. The last thing in the picture is ole Coop putting the United States marshal badge under his foot and stepping on it. I'll never regret having helped run Foreman out of this country. Running him out of the country is just a figure of speech. But I did tell him I thought he'd hurt Gary Cooper's reputation a great deal. Foreman said, 'Well, what if I went to England?' I said, 'Well, that's your business.' He said, 'Well, that's where I'm going.' And he did." According to Zolotow, Wayne even had the presumption to telephone Foreman and ask him to remove his name from the credits.[166]

Foreman remembered the meeting a bit differently. According to him, the meeting resulted from a conversation between Foreman and a press agent friend. The MPA had seen them talking together in public and, as a result, was going to take away all the agent's clients. Foreman met with Wayne to plead the agent's case. Foreman said, "Duke magnanimously agreed to let my errant friend off the hook." Once that was resolved, they then discussed the matter of Foreman's testimony before the HUAC or lack thereof. According to Wayne, in order to make amends, all Foreman had to do was make "a few public confessions complete with breast-beating and a reasonable amount of informing on old friends. Just a little cooperation..." Foreman refused, and Duke said that was too bad as Foreman wasn't a "Commie bastard, just a dupe." According to Foreman, Wayne then listed numerous other individuals, similarly accused, who would not be able to leave the country as their passports would be revoked. As that came to pass, it convinced Foreman that Wayne must have had inside information.[167]

Even Lloyd Bridges, who had played Cooper's deputy, suffered from the backlash of criticism: "I felt that after I did *High Noon*, my future would be pretty rosy," said Bridges. "But anyone who was sort of liberal in those days, wanting to do anything about improving humanity, kind of suffered. It was a terrible period. And I was a part of a thing called the actors' Lab, and there, apparently, were Communists in that organization. So I supposed that was one of the reasons I was put on that list. Didn't work for several years. Evil was very strong in those days."[168]

Wayne, critical of anything that struck him as un-American, was quick to make his opinion known. In 1949, he lost the Oscar race to Broderick Crawford and *All the King's Men*. Although respectful of Crawford's performance, he thought the film "smeared the machinery of the country's government" and that it would "tear down people's faith in everything that they have been brought up to believe is important in the American way of life." Crawford's portrayal of Willie Stark, a thinly veiled caricature of Huey Long, not only lacked moral fiber but served to prove that corruption was its own reward. Wayne never testified before HUAC and never personally blacklisted anyone, but he felt relieved that Congress was aware of the danger presented by Communist sympathizers in the entertainment industry. When Senator Joe McCarthy began hunting for Communists inside the government...Duke gave him his full and vocal support. Although the Senator was later discredited, his faith in the man never wavered. Wayne believed that McCarthy was a good—though much maligned—American.[169]

According to director John Farrow, who worked with Wayne on the movie *Hondo*, Duke's politics revolved around a single issue: "He felt protective of his country and its way of life." And he was consistent in its application. As a result, he emerged from this turbulent time virtually unscathed. Wayne's liberal peers didn't agree with his involvement with the Alliance, but respected his conservative views and recognized him as a "fair minded individual who was not a reactionary, but a balanced, understanding man." According to some Hollywood columnists, "Wayne's blunt attacks on Communism in and out of Hollywood during his recent tenure as president of the Motion Picture Alliance are models of succinct phrasing and gutty approach. Hollywood would have nothing to fear from Congress if it produced more gents like this one." "I think those blacklisted people should have been sent over to Russia," declared Wayne in his later years. "They'd have been taken care of over there, and if the Commies ever won over here, why hell, those guys would be the first ones they'd take care of—after me." He also began to select projects that more closely reflected his political views. From 1947 to 1949, of the eleven films Wayne would appear in, seven were Westerns. From

1949 to 1956, he would make only one Western. If the 1940s defined Wayne the *Actor*, the 1950s created Wayne the *Patriot*.[170]

# CHAPTER FIVE
# THE NOT SO QUIET MAN

*"I asked a native how they gauged the weather," recalled Wayne while on the set of 'The Quiet Man.' "They overlooked Lake Corrib. Off in the distance were some islands and beyond that the mountains. The fellow pointed across the lake to a range of hills. 'When you can see those hills,' he said, 'it's going to rain. When you can't, it's raining.'"*[171]

AFTER WAYNE WRAPPED *RIO GRANDE* IN LATE JULY 1950, HE TOOK A WELL-deserved break. One of the hottest properties in Hollywood, his film contracts were split among four studios. In 1940, Duke had signed a contract with Howard Hughes and RKO that called for one picture a year for five years. By early 1950, only two were completed, and *Jet Pilot* would be the third. After that, RKO wanted him for *No Place Called Home*. Warner Bros. had *The Traveler* and *Operation Pacific* lined up. Republic had *Fair Wind to Java, China Coast,* and *Devil Birds* ready for his approval. Argosy was waiting in the wings with *Rio Brava* and *The Quiet Man*. Wayne himself had planned to produce *The Alamo* and *Torero,* a movie about bullfighting in Mexico that was later known as *The Bullfighter and the Lady*. An article in the February 19, 1950, edition of *The Cedar Rapids Gazette* summed it up nicely: "John is planning a vacation in 1953."[172]

Wayne's break didn't last because, less than two months later, he started *Operation Pacific*. The second of his "message" films between 1949 and 1952, it was infinitely better than *Jet Pilot*. Produced by Warner Bros., *Operation Pacific* starred Wayne as Lt. Commander Duke Gifford of the submarine *Thunderfish*. By the end of the movie, Wayne rescues nuns and children, woos back his wife from a Navy flyboy, attacks the Japanese Imperial fleet, fixes a defect in torpedoes, and "finds time to instruct Americans about duty and sacrifice, about putting one's enemy and mission above one's happiness." Though staged in World War II, the message was clear: America was in the middle of an ideological war with its archenemy, the Soviet Union. The sacrifices Americans made in the recent war were necessary again if they expected to end up victorious.[173]

To make the submarine sequences as authentic as possible, Vice Admiral Charles Lockwood, U.S. Navy, Ret., commander of all submarines in the Pacific during World War II, served as technical adviser, and the Navy even let Warner Bros. use the submarine *Thunder*. As a result, the submarine sequences were realistic, and reviews reflected this effort. "Submarine warfare," wrote the *LA Times*, "has seldom, if ever, had a finer demonstration on the screen than in *Operation Pacific*... For once a film was proffered which concentrated on essential action, without an intrusive but at the same time a very satisfactory love story. The technical side of the feature was admirably and efficiently carried out with authentic quality." Even the eternally liberal *New York Times* praised Duke. "Our old friend John Wayne as the hero does a good square-jawed, iron man, ship-shape job..." Admiral Chester Nimitz, wartime Commander-in-Chief of the Pacific Naval forces, stated, "The great work of the American submarine service, a magnificent branch of the U.S. Navy, is depicted in the screen production of *Operation Pacific*. Everyone who sees the many dramatic achievements of the submarine *Thunderfish* in this picture will better understand the quality of men who operated these subs and their important and vital function in guaranteeing the freedom and security of America. The picture shows the fine balance and coordination that go to make up a successful submarine operation." Not only did the Navy approve the film, it also showed it on its bases. Although grateful for the praise, Wayne didn't think the film was particularly good. "You hope every film you make will be great," he lamented, "and the reality is that it ain't gonna happen. So you do your best and hope to come out of it with your dignity intact. But the film made money, which is all the studio cared about anyway."[174]

A few weeks later, Wayne changed uniforms—from a Navy lieutenant commander to a Marine fighter squadron major—when he started work on *The Flying Leathernecks*. Same message, different branch of service. The Marine planes and pilots in the film came from Marine Training VMF-232, stationed at El Toro Air Station. Unable to use F4F Wildcat fighter planes due to their unavailability, F6F-5 Hellcats were substituted. Jimmy Grant wrote an uninspired script, and Nicholas Ray directed the picture. The screenplay was a stockpile of war film clichés, devoid of dramatic tension. All the major characters in the movie are motivated by their sense of duty, though they occasionally define duty differently. Throughout the film, officers do their duty and make tough command decisions, soldiers grumble but do their duty and follow, and the wives do their duty and keep the hearth warm. Produced at RKO, Howard Hughes paid Wayne $300,000 for the film. That, at the time, was the highest salary ever paid an actor for a single picture. John Mitchum, actor, friend and songwriter of "America, Why I Love Her," thought Wayne blended in nicely on the set. "So we had quite a time down there and he (Wayne) fit in with almost everybody," Mitchum said. "We had a Marine fighter pilot unit from Georgia which had also been in Korea. In fact, the Korean (War) was going on at the time and these guys from Georgia were the wildest bunch of fliers I had ever seen. They would be drinking until five in the morning, then suck straight oxygen out of tubes, and go straight in the air." Yup, Wayne fit in just fine.[175]

After wrapping *Leathernecks*, Duke needed to catch his breath before his next big project. Hughes's never-end disaster *Jet Pilot* needed a bit more fine-tuning and the month of February and last half of March 1951 were devoted to finally wrapping it up. Wayne wasn't all that happy with *Pilot*, but he'd fulfilled his contract. Once completed, Duke and his second wife Chata flew to Central America on a tentative search for potential locations for the *Alamo* project.

On February 11, 1933, *The Saturday Evening Post* and *Chamber's Journal* each published a short story titled "The Quiet Man." Initially rejected, it was written by Maurice Walsh and told the story of Shawn Kelvin, a young Irish lad who traveled to America to seek his fortune. Disillusioned, he returned home, reticent to discuss his past. "For he was a quiet man, not given to talking about himself and the things he had done." He met a fine bonny lass, married her, and faced a brother-in-law who refused to pay her dowry. With great reluctance, he eventually confronted the brother, fighter that he was, and won the dowry, as well as his wife's love, respect, and admiration. Two years later, Walsh significantly expanded the tale and included it in a five-part collection of stories called *Green Rushes*. The book told the tale of men and women whose lives were caught up in the Irish War of Independence (1919-1921) and what happened to them after the truce.[176]

Born Sean Aloysius O'Feeney, John Ford fancied himself a typical Irishman and immediately recognized the tale's rich opportunities. He optioned the short story from Walsh on February 25, 1936, for $10 with the promise of more if the film was ever made. (Walsh received an additional $2,500 as an advance on the sale of the rights to the film company, and eventually received another $3,500 when Republic purchased the rights for the film version). In May 1937, Ford formed his own independent production company, in collaboration with actor Ronald Colman and producer-director Tay Garnett, and announced that Renowned Artists would start camera work on *The Quiet Man* in December. For production purposes, a subsidiary, Ford Productions, was created, and was jointly owned by Ford and Renowned. This was the first in a series of premature announcements regarding the start of production. The truth was, although Ford had a growing reputation as a director, studios just weren't interested in this quaint little story. There are precious few movies that cleverly spell the idea of r-e-l-e-a-s-e, and this was not one of them. The film was a nonpolitical, romantic adventure, and the studios didn't want to risk their reputations or money on a film that didn't have a built-in audience.[177]

Throughout the 1940s, Ford continued to develop the project. Even after Wayne, O'Hara, and Victor McLaglen agreed in 1944 to appear in the film, he still couldn't attract adequate financing. Ford had contacted O'Hara that fall while she was filming *The Spanish Main* and asked her to be female lead in his movie. While director Frank Borzage stood by as a witness, O'Hara agreed. By February of the following year, unless one of them was working on a film, O'Hara would spend every weekend with Ford and his wife Mary on Ford's 110-foot, double-masted yacht *Araner*, and take dictation in Pittman shorthand. "Then I'd go into the yacht club and type up the notes (for the script) he dictated," said O'Hara.[178]

In March 1945 rumors leaked that Ford and Herb Yates were huddled together to develop a deal similar to the one Borzage had at Republic. Ford would have complete jurisdiction over his productions, including the choice of stories, writers, and actors, but the films would be made on the Republic lot and released as Republic productions. Unfortunately, there wasn't any agreement, and Ford wouldn't make a movie at Republic until *Rio Grande*. One year later, however, it looked like Ford's dream might be realized. In September 1946, after Ford incorporated Argosy as his production company, Merian Cooper, president of the company, put together a financing package with RKO. Argosy would make four pictures for the studio and be allowed to make *The Quiet Man*, with one major provision: the first picture made had to be profitable. Ford chose to make an adaptation of Graham Greene's book *The Power and the Glory*. It was renamed *The Fugitive*. Starring Henry Fonda, it was a morality play that told the story of a disgraced Latin American priest who served God despite self-doubt and trying circumstances. Hounded by a military government intolerant of religion, the priest was torn between faith and fear of capture.[179]

Confident of the movie's success, Ford announced plans to go to Ireland the next summer to produce and direct his dream. Friend Lord Killanin (Michael Morris) was informed and asked to work on the project: "We will wander all around," Ford wrote, "shooting it in color, all over Ireland, but with stress laid on Spiddal." (Ford's ancestral family came from Spiddal, a small village on Galway Bay, north of the port city of Galway, in the county of Connaught). "We will bring the principals there from America and pick up the incidental parts and bits in England and Ireland."

"It's a lovely story," the director wrote, "and I think we should go all over Ireland and get a bit of scenery here and a bit of scenery there and really make the thing a beautiful travelogue, besides a really charming story." Ford indicated that Sir Alexander Korda, chairman of London Films Productions, might finance the film. Unfortunately, after a great deal of negotiations, the deal fell through due to "money, percentages, credits and what not." At least Ford had his RKO agreement to fall back on.[180]

*The Fugitive*, released in November, had been filmed in Mexico in stunning black-and-white, which generated a smoldering, mystical quality. Yet another project long in maturation, Ford had first tried to make this film in 1939. According to Fonda, "It had been rejected all over town because there were too many censorship problems. But Jack felt that if he took out the love affair he could make the story acceptable to them and be left with a beautiful Christ allegory." The *New York Times* called it "a symphony of light and shade, of deafening din and silence, of sweeping movement and repose." Sadly, although a critical success, it was also a box office failure, resulting in the indefinite cancellation of *The Quiet Man*. Ford wondered if he was ever going to bring this project to fruition. But he never lost faith, never gave up.[181]

After the dismal failure of *The Fugitive*, Ford became a little vague on projects details. While he still wanted to make his Irish movie in 1948, he was financially strapped. In a December 8, 1947, letter to Lord Killanin, Ford stated, "The picture…is still on the books, but, as you know, money and production is so tied up here and costs are so excessive that I have to proceed cautiously." As an independent production company, most of Argosy's funds were tied up in *The Fugitive*, and, without reserves for support during lean times, Argosy had to wait for returns from the last film before it could proceed to the next one. That didn't stop the publicity campaign however, as it was announced in June that Victor McLaglen was going to appear in *TQM* the following year. One week later, John Wayne was also said to be a part of the cast. It was rumored that Duke wouldn't set sail for Ireland for several months, as he was supposed to star in *Alamo* and *Eagles in Exile* as soon as he completed *Wake of the Red Witch*. By August, The Abbey Players from Dublin's prestigious Abbey Theatre school, along with Ben Johnson, were announced as having starring roles in the project.[182]

Even Maureen O'Hara was getting frustrated by the constant delays. "Each year we would hold the summer open," she says, "and each year there was no money and we wouldn't make the movie. The script was taken to Fox, RKO, and Warner Bros. and all the studios called it a silly, stupid little Irish story. 'It'll never make a penny, it'll never be any good,' they said. And the years slipped by and John Wayne and I used to go to the studio and say, 'Mr. Ford, if you don't hurry up I'll have to play the widow-woman and Duke will have to play Victor McLaglen's role because we'll be too old.'"[183]

Over the next few years, Ford was involved in several movies at numerous studios. In 1948, he directed *Fort Apache* for RKO and *The Three Godfathers* for MGM. The next year, it was *She Wore A Yellow Ribbon* and RKO. In May, Hedda Hopper announced Ford would finally make *TQM* the following spring.[184]

Republic Studios, generally unconcerned with the socio-economic issues of the day, was only interested in supplying low-cost, prosaic, and unassuming weekly filler, usually shown on the lower half of a double bill—mindless yet entertaining enough to provide a short diversion for the public. Granted, every now and then, it would have the good fortune to showcase "A" quality films such as *Man of Conquest, Dark Command, Wake of the Red Witch,* or *Sands of Iwo Jima,* but more often than not it focused on economically produced (cheap) serials, Westerns, adventure, and gangster movies: *The Three Mesquiteers, The Higgins Family Series, Dick Tracy's G-Men, Zorro's Fighting Legion, Drums of Fu Manchu, Jungle Girl, Captain America, The Purple Monster Strikes, King of the Rocket Men, Rovin' Tumbleweed, Wall Street Cowboy,* ad nauseam. With "B" features, both the formulaic storyline and dependable profits were predictable. Even with this genre, many of Hollywood's recognizable names found themselves in a Republic film or two: Gene Autry, Don Barry, Johnny Mack Brown, Ralph Byrd, Judy Canova, Yakima Canutt, Ray "Crash" Corrigan, Richard Dix, Wild Bill Elliott, Joan Fontaine, Monte Hall, "Gabby" Hayes, Susan Hayward, Robert Livingston, Clayton Moore, Vera Hruba Ralston (???!!!), Roy Rogers, Bob Steele, Peggy Stewart, Gale Storm, etc., etc., etc., and last, but certainly not least, John Wayne.

Wayne remained under contract to Republic for many years even after his breakthrough and resented the studio featuring him in projects he deemed unworthy of a star of his stature. During various tenures there, starting with *Westward Ho!* in 1935, he appeared in thirty-one movies, the vast majority of which were "B" films and extended Western series. Although he didn't mind the studio, he was fed up with the movies he had been asked to make and, by 1950, had had enough. "As long as I was stuck at Republic, I thought I might as well get Jack to come out there too," said Wayne. "I knew that Yates was worried about television taking audiences away from 'B' pictures. I knew he wanted to start making 'A' pictures." Those higher-quality features, while not only prestigious for the studio, also resulted in guaranteed distribution and percentage contracts with significant profits. Wayne knew, having worked at other studios and with other directors, that a director of Ford's stature at Republic would increase the studio's prestige and perhaps change the quality of future Republic projects. Yates, though, hoped to break into the "A" production percentage rental market while remaining active in "B" categories. All through the 1940s and early 1950s, Republic remained profitable with this strategy. While it continued to make "B" Westerns and serials, Republic's plan was to make two "big-scale" films each year. Yates had no desire to use any major actors as "for some reason or other... (they) feel as though they're lowering themselves by working for us," he said. "We'd rather farm out our promising players to other companies and let them do the experimenting. Take John Wayne for example. He's in our Westerns–which are cleaning up doubly because we loaned him out to Warner for *Stagecoach.*" Republic's production development strategy consisted of four classifications: Jubilee productions were standard "B" movies. Anniversary movies were slightly upscale "B"s. A little more expensive but "B" nonetheless. The Deluxe category included major films involving Republic personnel while Premiere films were intended to compete with all the major studios. Featuring prestigious directors, they were the best Republic could offer. To Republic, Wayne was nothing but a cash cow. Reliable and consistent. Predictable at the box office. A guaranteed financial success. As Yates had no intention to develop Wayne any further beyond what he currently had, Duke felt he had nothing to lose.[185]

Appealing to his mercenary side, Wayne told Yates that if he was successful in bringing Ford into the Republic fold, other name directors might follow. He suggested that as Ford was fanatical about *The Quiet Man,* it would probably be a good idea to let him make it. Wayne went to Yates and said, "…you've got to do something for this guy. You've got to give him a deal. He (Yates) said, 'Well, I'd love to talk with him.' Jack was being wined and dined by these other people so he sent (Merian) Cooper over there and Cooper went in and Yates didn't know anybody in the business." When Cooper started to discuss what he wanted, Yates brushed him off and called Ford. "Who the hell is this guy you sent over to talk to me?" he asked Ford. "Talking about what he wants and what he doesn't want." Ford immediately hung up. Yates then called Wayne to ask what had happened. "You stupid son-of-a-bitch," Duke exclaimed. "Here's a war hero from two wars and a helluva fine man, head of RKO, one that has made a lot of money…and you screw it up." Yates said he was willing to go along with Ford, but he wasn't going to turn the studio over to him. What should he do? "Give him 15% of the gross and tell him nobody checks his budgets," recommended Wayne. Yates immediately agreed, and Wayne wrote a three-page contact on yellow legal paper. Yates asked Duke to deliver it to Ford when he was playing bridge with Jimmy Grant and Dick Calhoun that evening, but, when Wayne did, Ford read it, crumbled it up, and threw it into the fireplace without a word. Wayne thought Ford felt he was speaking on his behalf and didn't appreciate it. Shortly thereafter, however, Argosy announced it would move its operation to Republic which would release all future Argosy films.[186]

Ford's long journey had finally ended, but, yet again, there was another qualification. Similar to the deal Argosy had with RKO years earlier, Ford had to make three pictures for Republic and the first had to be profitable before *The Quiet Man* could be produced. Yates said, "Very well, I will finance it on one condition—that you make a western first with the same cast, same director, same everybody to finance and make up for the money I'll lose on *The Quiet Man.*" The result was *Rio Grande.*[187]

Ford now had approval, which meant full speed ahead. So pleased with the results, Yates gave the go ahead even before *Rio Grande* went into general release, and Ford finally, officially, announced the long-planned feature would be made the next spring, on location, in Ireland. One month after *Grande* wrapped, Ford left for Ireland—the first of many trips—to meet with Killanin and discuss the project. While there, he stayed with Maureen O'Hara's parents in Ranelagh,

Dublin. "He sat up for hours," says O'Hara, "trading Irish stories with Daddy, breaking his cigar in half and sharing it." Yates, Ford, and Ward Bond traveled to Europe in November on a preliminary location search. Upon their return, Ford headed off to Korea, but, before he left, he asked Richard Llewellyn to do the screenplay. Llewellyn immediately flew to Ireland to gather some atmosphere—as he said, "the talk and the smell." Later Frank Nugent would significantly modify, polish, and expand on those efforts because rather than a comedy/love story, Llewellyn's screenplay was heavy on violence and politics. In late February, Ford, along with Wayne, went back to London to meet with British exhibitors in a building taken over by Republic in connection with its setup of new distribution facilities in the British Isles. Yates was nothing if not respectful when he described his relationship with Wayne. He believed Duke's success was due to Wayne's honesty and sincerity. "He came to me when he was a young fellow," said Yates, "new in the game, and was having a hard time, and we put him in the *Three Mesquiteers* westerns. I've watched him rise by dint of perseverance. We are great friends, apart from his motion picture career. *(Really?)* He is the kind who makes for solid friendships. He is going with me to England, even though he doesn't like personal appearances, because it helps to build up our prestige abroad, and may pave the way for a picture which I hope to do over there."[188]

By April, cast and crew were ready to leave for the Emerald Isle as soon as Ford was well enough to travel. Due to "too many hours in the air catapulting and landing on carriers, helicopters," he had suffered a double-hernia while shooting a documentary for the Navy. In the meantime, Wayne continued to negotiate with Yates on *his* long-awaited project. When Yates announced in anticipation of the filming of *The Alamo* that Wayne was designated by contract to be a director with Republic, Duke felt he had finally reached his goal. He immediately left for Mexico City on April 14 to meet with president Miguel Aleman and several high-ranking officials to discuss his project. He also inspected a site in Teuacan where preliminary construction was already under way. In a letter to the Motion Picture Service, United States Information Office, Wayne wrote, "I went to the Mexican government in 1951, presented my script to the Censor Board, there under the Cabinet Seat of a Mr. Martinez, who found no fault with our script, after inviting us to meet with top Mexican representatives chosen for their historical knowledge. I went to the Sindicados in Mexico and gained their permission to make it in Mexico, if I wished. At that time financial problems postponed the making of the motion picture." "Actually," said James Edward Grant, his writer, "that was the best thing that ever happened to us. If we had made the picture then, it would have been just another western. A little bigger and better, maybe, but nothing great. For one thing, it was only a one-star picture. We would have had to write the picture around Duke, and end up distorting the facts, probably."[189]

After Ford recuperated, he traveled once again to Ireland, along with

Winton Hoch, director of photography, to meet with unit manager Lee Lukather and work out final details for shooting the film. By the end of May most of the principals had finally arrived in Ireland. Victor McLaglen and Ford left the United States on May 26, and Maureen O'Hara took off on June 2, immediately after finishing *Flame of Araby*. Barry Fitzgerald, who played Michaleen, the matchmaking cabbie, said upon his arrival at the sun-drenched Shannon airport, "A day like this would revive the dead."[190]

As he had numerous financial interests in Venezuela, Wayne took a vacation in Central America in a reconditioned Navy PBY provided by Howard Hughes. "There is a big waterfall in the jungle which has never been explored," Wayne exclaimed excitedly, "and I'd like to try. Also, I hear that the natives dive in the rivers for diamonds. I've done a lot of diving for abalone and other things and I'd like to try for diamonds." Though not finding any jewels, he did have a relaxing time. Flying directly from Caracas, Wayne left New York on June 4, dressed in white tropical trousers and a crimson shirt, and by June 6, the remainder of the cast was on site. Since the film would be made during the summer, Wayne brought his entire family. Many of the cast stayed at Ashford Castle, a battlemented, turreted Victorian fortress that appeared in the opening credits. Several scenes were filmed on and around the castle grounds. Toni Wayne LaCava, Wayne's oldest daughter, recalled their time in Cong: "We've lived in California all our lives with palm trees," she remembered. "All of a sudden there's a huge castle there. There's a great big river there, it was fabulous. It didn't have a lot of modern conveniences. My father had a bathroom, I think Maureen had a bathroom but the rest of the crew and everybody, we had to share one big bathroom area and one big shower area and so we learned very fast, if we wanted to get up in the morning and take a shower, we should not go in there early 'cause it would not do to have the crew waiting for us to get out of the shower."[191]

The citizens of Cong were stopped cold when ten trucks of clothes were moved in for six stars and a private bath was installed for O'Hara. According to Michael Wayne, "Cong got electricity while we were there. I remember they had the lights on the wires all around the kind of, the town square and people were dancing and people were very, very happy. And then they found out they had to pay for this electricity, and they said, 'Well, hey. We don't need it. Get rid of it.' And they really said we don't need the electricity. Ashford Castle had its own generator but the people did not have electricity and this was 1951."[192]

The attraction of Wayne, O'Hara, Ford, et al. was also a boon to Irish tourism. The small borough of Cong enjoyed more visitors than any Irish tourist campaign ever. An average of ten busloads a week came through during 1953, and trains brought an average of five hundred individuals every Thursday during the season. With over 14,000 tourists, no wonder they hoped Ford would do a projected sequel.[193]

To call the film a family affair would be a mild understatement. Not only did

Ford's older brother Francis play the part of Dan Tobin, but Edward O'Fearna, his other brother, was a second assistant director. His daughter Barbara was an assistant editor, his son Pat was a stunt man and second unit director (as was Wayne), and his future son-in-law Ken Curtis played the part of Dermot Fahy. Wingate Smith, Ford's brother-in-law, was also an assistant director. Wayne's children Michael, Toni, Patrick, and Melinda appeared in scenes with Maureen O'Hara at the horse race. O'Hara's brother Charles FitzSimons played the role of Forbes while her youngest brother James Lilburn was Father Paul. Victor McLaglen's son Andrew was another second assistant director; Barry Fitzgerald's brother Arthur Shields played the Rev. Cyril Playfair, and Ward Bond played Father Peter Lonergan. Talk about nepotism. If you weren't related or didn't know someone who knew someone, you weren't in the cast.

*The Quiet Man* was Ford's vision of an idyllic, tranquil, pastoral Ireland, filmed in glorious Technicolor and wrapped in a shawl of emerald green—a green so bright it hurt your eyes just to look at it. "When the picture was shown in Ireland," Ford complained, "all the critics were angry. They didn't like it. Every one of them came up with the same statement—that Mr. Ford used a green filter on his camera to make the hills and the fields green. I really blew my top at them, and I had to laugh. I've never heard of a green filter, and you can't use a filter on a Technicolor camera anyway. So I wrote each one of these critics a nice letter saying, if you would get out of that goddamn apartment and take a bus ride into the country, you would see that the hills of Northern Ireland are green. But these stupid guys, these city-dwellers living in Dublin, saying that I used a green filter—that really got my goat."[194]

The penny-pinching Yates was aghast when Ford insisted the movie be filmed in color. Once the budget was established, he sent Ford a ream of telegrams, endlessly browbeating him about minutia and requesting, nay, demanding, constant cutbacks. At his wit's end, Ford asked Wayne and O'Hara to accept salary cuts just, so the project could continue. Yates further insisted the film run only 120 minutes and not one second more. He also suggested several titles he felt were more acceptable: *Uncharted Voyage*, *The Fabulous Yankee*, *Homeward Bound*, *Hearts Across the Sea*, *The Silent Man*, *The Man Untamed*, and *The Prizefighter and the Colleen*. "I felt that was an awful title," recalled Ford, "because it tipped the story that Duke was a boxer. Well, Yates had said that he received a lot of letters from exhibitors that they preferred his title to *The Quiet Man*. I asked to look at the letters, and he showed them to me. 'What a strange coincidence!' I told him. 'All these letters have the same date and say the same thing.' Obviously, he had sent out a letter that was practically mimeographed and asked the theater men to write in letters. And they did. But I still wouldn't go with his title."[195]

Yates continued to complain to Ford, and Pappy continued to bitch and moan about Yates. Finally, Bond was fed up. He climbed to the top of a ruined tower on the grounds of Ashford Castle and etched a typical Ford epitaph on a piece of slate he had found. Charles FitzSimons recalled it was scraped on an inside wall. No matter. Satisfied with his efforts, Bond climbed back down and found someone to convince Wayne of the spectacular view to be had from the tower. Wayne took the bait and went to check it out. According to FitzSimons, "(Wayne's) face was priceless when he saw the message in such an unlikely spot. He came back roaring and laughing when he realized the joke that had been played on him. He laughed himself silly," for Bond had written a clear, short, simple script: "FUCK HERB YATES."[196]

Many stories describe the miserable weather Ford encountered in the Emerald Isle. Frank Nugent mentioned most of the time was spent in a fine drizzle and "only four days of unbroken sunshine were counted during the six-week period but otherwise, the company was rained out only once." O'Hara took great exception to that, however. In her autobiography *'Tis Herself*, she states, "We had so much sun that we used to ask cameramen Winton Hoch and Archie Stout if they were putting sunshine pills in the camera…the weather was so wonderful that I used to take naps in the tall grass." Jack Murphy, an extra in the movie and current owner of Cohan's Bar, recalled, "The Republic people were very lucky with the dry weather. Had they come in 1950 they would have been swept away by the rain and the summer of 1952 wasn't much better. They actually had to call in the fire brigade to hose down the street for the cattle-fair scene."[197]

Wayne felt right at home in Cong and had little difficulty adapting to the food, drink, and casual atmosphere. With eighteen-year-old whiskey selling for a shilling (14¢) a shot, cast and crew found numerous opportunities to partake of local beverages. Cong villager Robert Foy recalled that Ford and Wayne made a much-publicized pact to eliminate heavy drinking while the cast was in Ireland. Of course, that didn't stop those determined to indulge. "I saw Wayne not able to stand up at times in the village," Foy said, "and Ford would get very annoyed with him…" One day, after a drinking bout with Irish professional heavyweight champion 'Marching' Mairtin Thornton, Foy remembered, "Wayne was footless as he went into Ryan's hotel right opposite my front door here." Andrew McLaglen recalled, "Duke had an afternoon off and went to a local pub. That evening I went with Jack Ford to look for Duke and we walked into that pub, and Duke was as drunk as I've ever seen him. I mean, he was falling down drunk. That night around twelve…he had just the worst-ever hangover. But by the morning he was perfectly okay." Apparently, good times were had by all.[198]

Of course, a wee bit of whisky didn't affect Wayne's acting whatsoever. Not only did Duke look forward to this role, he was grateful it wasn't a western. Admitting he always wanted to direct ever since he got into pictures, Wayne said, "I also want to get out of the saddle and away from the uniform. When I do *The Quiet Man* for John Ford in Ireland that will be different. I play a prizefighter who has killed a man in the ring and doesn't want to fight any more. He becomes involved in a fight when he goes to Ireland, a fight that goes on in field, town, pub, and everywhere else. The fighters go in and have drinks and start fighting all over again. That should be a riot as Ford will do it. I like the idea of the comedy possibilities." Of course, it wasn't all fun and games either. "You know, *The Quiet Man* was a simple enough story, but that was a goddamn hard script," said Duke. "For nine reels I was just playing a straight man to those wonderful characters that people like Ward Bond, Barry Fitzgerald, and Victor McLaglen got to play and that's really hard." But he had his children with him, and it was as if he was on holiday. He fished with Ward Bond, played rummy with Pappy, and watched McLaglen fall asleep in a high-backed chair by the fireplace at Ashford Castle. Could anything be better than that?[199]

A lovely, light-hearted, romantic romp, *The Quiet Man* was rich in both color and whimsical characters. Wayne thoroughly enjoyed the film, and it showed on the screen. The second of five movies he would make with O'Hara, their chemistry was unmistakable. According to O'Hara, she "was the only leading lady big enough and tough enough for John Wayne. Duke's presence was so strong that when audiences saw him finally meet a woman of equal hell and fire, it was exciting and thrilling. Other actresses looked as though they would cower and break if Duke raised a hand or even hollered. Not me. I always gave as good as I got, and it was believable. So during those moments of tenderness, when the lovemaking was about to begin, audiences saw for a half second that he had finally tamed me—but only for that half second."[200]

Andrew McLaglen seconded that opinion: "They had a special chemistry on the screen. I feel they loved working with one another. They worked great together. They were never romantically linked in their personal lives, but they sure could transmit (romance) on the screen. You can't get better chemistry than in *The Quiet Man*." Michael Wayne was able to watch his father's acting first-hand and recognized his presence: "My father was a major movie star," he declared. "And I think you kind of have to explode off the screen and be larger than life. And I think Maureen was a woman who could match him on the screen and so something happened on the screen. There was an electricity there but she could match John Wayne kiss for kiss, punch for punch, stride for stride."[201]

Wayne also had a mischievous side. In the scene where he dragged O'Hara across the countryside, both actors rehearsed the various movements well in advance: the loss of a shoe, a fall, the swing and duck, a kick in the rear. Although seemingly spontaneous, the motions were carefully choreographed. However, as the scene was filmed on the golf course at Ashford Castle, they used sheep to keep the grass short. Naturally, where you have sheep, you have sheep manure. The actors had their respective posses of co-conspirators: Wayne used Ford and Bond, O'Hara her Irish friends. "There was Duke's gang kicking more and more manure along the path he had to drag me," O'Hara recalls, "and my gang would go in and kick it out. They'd kick it in and we'd kick it out. It went on and on, and finally, right before the scene was shot, they won, getting in the last kick.

The cameras began to roll, and Duke had the time of his life, dragging me on my stomach through that sheep manure, and it just stank!" After the scene was over, Ford gave instructions not to get O'Hara a towel or water to clean herself. She had to wear the aromatic clothes all day. That evening, Neva Burn, her wardrobe mistress, attempted to clean and iron the clothing for the next day's shooting. "She hit that skirt with a steam iron," O'Hara remembers, "and the smell came up with the steam. She took the skirt off the ironing board, opened the window, and dropped the skirt out into the bushes." Fortunately, they had an identical replacement for the next day.[202]

Many locals and extras were disillusioned when they watched the filming of the climactic brawl between Wayne and McLaglen. Reputed to be the longest cinematic fight ever, many were surprised when they discovered nary a punch ever landed. Wayne had long since perfected the long, looping, roundhouse swing without landing a blow and confirmed the deception: "He didn't lay a hand on me and I didn't lay a hand on him," admitted Wayne. "We did not touch each other once, and yet we were punching away as hard as we could. I was no youngster at forty-five, but Victor McLaglen was almost seventy, and he said, 'Don't you worry about me, youngster. I can still give you a good whooping if I had to.'" Foy recalled, "… when you saw it being made close up it really was one big phony. The fists were never nearer than eight or nine inches off the target." He remembered that Andrew McLaglen, Victor's son, told him, "Dad, you're telegraphing your punches." Ford agitated McLaglen by telling him he was too old for the fight. "We'll see about that, you Irish son of a bitch," yelled McLaglen. After numerous takes and endless hours of shooting, Victor was still standing. Wayne said, "You did all right for an old Cockney." Victor replied, "And you did okay for an old Yank!"[203]

The illusion of the fight was better than the real thing. "Back in the thirties," recalled Wayne, "I was one of the originators of the *past your face* style of movie fist-fighting. Before that time, most fight routines just did not look believable. Fighters would always miss their opponent's jaw by a mile and it turned out awful on screen. With our idea the camera can shoot the left side of the person's face receiving the punch, while the opponent's fist passes by the right side. The end result is very convincing. It looks quite real when you see the finished film. It was all a case of camera angles and well-timed reactions from the fighters. The real knockout punch travels about twelve inches or less and is a real delight to boxing fans and sports writers. The only trouble with it is in the movies. It's no good there. It's not just photogenic as far as most of the people are concerned who see movies."[204]

Extra, stand-in, and stuntman Joe Mellotte crashed through the door at Cohan's in place of Victor McLaglen. "It was a nice soft landing," said Mellotte, "because they had cushions on the street. The replacement doors were made of the thinnest plywood. It's amazing the illusions film people can create." Even Ford's son Pat got into the act. He doubled for McLaglen when Victor's character fell into the creek.[205]

Of course, Wayne wouldn't back down from a *real* fight, either. While taking a break from shooting the boxing flashback sequence, he was asked about the last time he was in an actual fight. "You mean really?" Wayne asked. "Not in a picture? About eight years ago. He was a drunk. I tried to get out of it. I agreed that I had long hair and that I was everything he said I was. But he kept after me. Finally, he took a swing at me." The reporter asked, "Well, what happened?" "What do YOU think?" bellowed Wayne. "Like most actors, I'll take a lot of guff to avoid a fight. But when they lay a hand on me, that's different."[206]

One of the legendary stories to come out of this production has to do with the final words between Sean Thornton and Mary Kate Danaher. (Interestingly, Ford's real first name was Sean and the Thorntons were a Ford family relation in Ireland. Mary Kate was named for the two loves of Ford's life: his wife Mary, and Katharine Hepburn. According to O'Hara however, the character was named after two of the names suggested for her on her birth.) In order to get the exact reaction he was looking for, Ford told O'Hara what to whisper in Wayne's ear during the scene. At first she refused, "No, I can't. I can't say that to Duke." But Ford insisted and eventually she agreed, on one condition: None of the three could ever reveal exactly what she said. Ford said "Action" and got the reaction he wanted. Wayne was both shocked and amused, never believing something like that would come out of O'Hara's mouth. "Pappy told Maureen what to say to me," he recalled, "and believe me, coming from the lips of a lady, it was shocking. Pappy wanted me to look shocked, and the look on my face was real. When Pappy told Maureen what to say, she was shocked..." To this day, it has never been revealed what was said, and it never will be. Television personality and interviewer Larry King tried to pin O'Hara down when she guested on his show. "One can imagine it was sexual or cursing or both?" he asked. "Little bit of both," she admitted. One of life's great mysteries, curious fans have gone so far as to hire lip-readers to decipher the words without success.[207]

Shooting wrapped in mid-July, and the crew headed back to Hollywood for interior scenes. By the end of August, it was a wrap. According to Wayne, he was in "a really good fucking mood because I knew we'd made a great picture." Even then, Yates still wasn't convinced they had a winner on their hands. Early in the project, he tried to convince Wayne the role was a serious career mistake; now he was only concerned about the film's length. At 129 minutes, Yates absolutely insisted nine minutes be trimmed but Ford resisted all changes. "My experience has taught me that audiences, no matter how good a picture is," wrote Yates, "do not want any picture to run over two hours. Exhibitor reaction is the same." To gauge their interest, Yates set up a private screening for Republic executives and distributors, but, at exactly the 120-minute mark, Ford halted the film. Yates demanded to know why, and Ford said that to meet the time limit, he cut the fight scene. The audience beseeched him to show the ending, and Ford acquiesced. At the end of the showing, Yates knew he had a classic on his hands.[208]

Moreover, the critics realized it as well. *The Hollywood Reporter* stated: "*The Quiet Man*" is a heart-warming, tender comedy drama of nostalgia which reflects the directorial genius of John Ford. It foams like a glass of Guinness with the classic attributes of the Irish: their brogue, hot tempers, passion of betting, above all their belligerence, which keeps them whacking at each other in a blood-thirsty and utterly charming way for the two hours of film time." Wayne's performance was nothing short of spectacular. Arguably worthy of an Academy Award nomination, he failed to receive one. However, the film received seven: Best Picture, Director, Supporting Actor, Screenplay, Cinematography, Art Direction, and Sound, and won two: Director and Cinematography. On Oscar night, Wayne picked up Ford's award for Best Director and Gary Cooper's for Best Actor in *High Noon* but none for himself. Hollywood, never one to forgive or forget, would not overlook Wayne's presidency of the controversial MPA. According to Mary St. John, "Duke's politics definitely hurt him. *The Quiet Man* was his best performance to date. In a film nominated for a half dozen awards, he was simply ignored." Ironically, when he accepted the award for Cooper, he commented, "Why can't I find me a scriptwriter to write me a part like the one that got you this? Good sportsmanship is okay as far as it goes, but when I leave here I'm going to get hold of my agent and damn well make him find me a writer who can write me a picture like *High Noon*." Did Duke forget that the writer was Carl Foreman?[209]

Wayne was justifiably pleased with his performance and looked forward to his next starring role. According to Pilar, Duke had returned from Ireland in an expansive mood and knew he'd done some of his best work there. While most of Wayne's films were action-packed adventures, this film allowed fans to see him in a good old-fashioned romantic comedy. Upon his return, Ward Bond wanted to rent a boat, and Ford, Wayne, Bond, and Hank Fonda went on a fishing trip to parts unknown. Traveling up and down the Mexican coast, they visited hot spots, fished, and generally got drunk. The following skipper's log was typical:[210]

1:18PM. Went ashore—got the owner, Fonda, Wayne and Bond out of jail. Put up a bond for their behavior.

9:30PM. Got the owner, Fonda, Wayne and Bond out of jail again. Invited by Mexican officials to leave town.[211]

Ford stated that *The Quiet Man* could be his swan song. "This may be my last picture," he said. "I am tired and I want a rest. All the people I like best have been in this film, and this is the kind of film I wanted to be the last one." Little did he know that both his and Wayne's best efforts were yet to come.

# CHAPTER SIX
# FALSE STARTS

*"The man has the soul of an accountant. Sink or swim, (leaving Republic Studios) it had to be better than working with men like Yates...." Wayne discusses his relationship with Herb Yates and Republic.*[212]

WHILE THE WEATHER WAS PLEASANT IN ERIE, A MAELSTROM HAD BEEN brewing back in the United States. Although the publicity mill was in high gear when it announced Robert Clarke, the romantic lead with Sally Forrest in *Hard, Fast and Beautiful,* might be in the cast for *Alamo,* there was considerable disdain that Wayne and Republic Pictures would make the film in Mexico due to economic considerations. R.J. O'Donnell (Vice-President and General Manager of the Interstate Circuit, one of the largest movie chains in Texas), Jesse Jones (Texas politician, publisher of the *Houston Chronicle,* entrepreneur and Secretary of Commerce under FDR) and others contacted Herb Yates to dissuade him from doing so. "To make the story of the Alamo in Mexico," implored O'Donnell, "would be disastrous, in my opinion, and would be like making the story of Bunker Hill or the Liberty Bell in Philadelphia or any other of our patriotic stories in a foreign country. Nothing is closer to the hearts of Texans than the story of the Alamo, and it should make a great picture, and definitely should be made in Texas to insure authenticity and should have its world premiere in Texas. I realize that John has many problems and certainly the Mexicans will resent any angle in the picture that would in any manner belittle Santa Ana(sic) and his soldiers, but certainly Texans would resent anything but an authentic story.

Frankly, I am so concerned that I am afraid that the complications would effect (sic) the picture nationally if it were made in Mexico City–and I definitely know that it would damn it immeasurably in Texas. Won't you please convey to John my thoughts, and if there is anything further that I can do to persuade him to confine the production to the United States definitely, and to Texas if possible, I will consider it a privilege."[213]

Hedda Hopper reported that O'Donnell and Jones might take steps to boycott the film. Jones also enlisted the support of several fellow Texans, including Howard Hughes and his chief of staff, Noah Dietrich. As a result of his intervention, Dietrich contacted Yates. Later, the Sons and Daughters of the Republic of Texas became involved when the president of the San Jacinto chapter wired Yates that they "earnestly protest your filming of the *Alamo* in Mexico City. We suggest San Antonio, Texas, for the picture." A flood of complaints from civic organizations, business and professional clubs, and everyday Joe Publics engulfed Hollywood. Although some say there is no such thing as bad publicity, Wayne must have had second thoughts about filming in Mexico.[214]

To acquaint the public with the motion picture business and celebrate the industry's golden jubilee, Wayne visited San Antonio in early October 1951 as part of a star-studded publicity tour. Known as "It's Movie Time in Texas, U.S.A.," the delegation consisted of fourteen top-flight Hollywood personalities, including Greer Garson, Wendell Corey, Dan Dailey, Keenan Wynn, Chill Wills, director King Vidor, producer Jesse Lasky Sr. and six stars of the future. With one-night visits in several Texas communities, the personalities would give radio and press interviews, sign autographs, pose for photos, and generally enlighten the moving-going masses.[215]

The outrage following the Mexico filming announcement forced Wayne to reconsider his position while in San Antonio. To placate Texas-sized egos, he indicated portions of the movie would be shot in San Antonio if details could be worked out. "We hope to use the interior of the Alamo for some of our shots," said Wayne. "We will use the chapel if they will let us," and added that he had been in contact with San Antonio mayor Jack White. He further mentioned that he felt the current appearance of the Alamo didn't lend itself to the look that he wanted, but he believed that some arrangement could be made to film the chapel scenes there. He also noted shooting the film locally would cost him "a million dollars more" than making it in Mexico or California. Several years' work had gone into the planning of this project and since it was going to be his first big picture, he was "not going to make a cheap job of it." Wayne's remarks were challenged by Ken McClure, former movie consultant to the San Antonio advertising commission. The organization paid McClure more than $5,000 to negotiate with the film's producers. "You wouldn't shoot the Battle of Bunker Hill in Mexico, would you?" he questioned. Wayne replied, "They didn't shoot *Gone with the Wind* in the south." Mayor White indicated a last-ditch effort would be made to film the movie there, but admitted the negotiation efforts with the film's producers were probably in vain. "After all, we spent a lot of money on that deal. It looks like all that money is gone," he declared. Alas, he was correct. William Saal, executive assistant to Herbert Yates, sent a letter to Mayor White coyly skirting around the *Alamo* affair: "If we had known we weren't going to start *Alamo* until spring, we would have made a motion picture named *Golden Herd* which was written by a Texan man and has its locale near San Antonio." Eventually, the whole idea of filming a portion of the movie locally was dropped.[216]

Wayne tried to mend bridges a little later when he told hundreds of spectators in a crowded Alamo Plaza, "I'm not too sure what the purpose of this tour is. I think we're supposed to brag about Hollywood. But when I get back, I'm going to brag about Texas." It appeared Wayne's response may have been a way to potentially deflect criticism of an unpopular decision.

Continuing the tour in Austin the next day, Wayne, who was president of Theatre for Freedom, Inc., defended Hollywood against charges of Communism: "None of our pictures have been shown behind the Iron Curtain, which is proof enough that we are not as communistic as some would have you believe. We're happy to be made guinea pigs in these investigations to show that we believe in America and the American way of life." Wayne declared, "Our community is no better or worse than yours. We are a lot of decent hardworking people. There are twenty-five thousand persons working in the movies in Hollywood, and we have ten percent less than the national average in divorces. There are eighteen thousand married people in Hollywood who have never been divorced."[217]

Unbeknownst to Wayne, Yates had already made a decision to change the film site. Internal memos from Interstate Circuit suggest Republic reconsidered its direction in early August, *before* Wayne went on the publicity tour, and decided to film the movie in San Antonio, no matter how impractical. In fact, at the *Rio Grande* premiere the previous year, Yates had received a scroll from the city just because he planned to make a movie about the Alamo. Obviously, the feelings were he would do it locally.[218]

Wayne was fed up. In a four-page letter to Yates, he stated his position in no uncertain terms: "I repeat I am not going to work my butt off for this studio and be belittled and argued with when I am doing something, and then have it turn out well, and not even so goddamned much as be thanked. This happened on *The Bullfighter and the Lady*. I am not going to plan a picture, work and worry my head off, to have it stopped because you have made up your mind—without looking into the facts—what should be done. I've spent the last two weeks with my head buzzing with a lot of negative thinking that would have been unnecessary had you not double-crossed me. I can't spend all my time at the studio fighting with people who do not understand or recognize the needs of class A pictures. I have my health to think of, and so I repeat I know you like me very much, but you have not appreciated or understood the hard work I have put in for this studio, and I am not going to do it anymore until I am certain everyone is behind me... Perhaps we can make it next October. All I know is that I am not up to the worry and pressure it would take to get it underway now. I've left my fight in the locker room."[219]

Filming was tentatively scheduled to start in October 1951. The initial script had been revised numerous times and was modified by Paul Fix and further polished by James Edward Grant. Fix, who later played Marshal Micah Torrance in the TV series *The Rifleman*, was a close friend of Wayne's and appeared in over two dozen films with him. Marilyn Carey, Fix's daughter, recalled her father's writing: "He wrote many plays and produced them in Hollywood and directed some of them," she said. "He was a 'script doctor' for Duke in the forties, and wrote a lot. It wasn't just a hobby...."[220]

Throughout the late 1940s and early 1950s, Wayne constantly searched for a suitable location to film his dream. During one trip, he finally found one. "I was all set to make *The Alamo* in Panama," said Wayne, "where I'd spent weeks scouting locations. There was a perfect area outside Panama City that looked like the San Antonio area in Texas of the time. Panama was having a depression right then that would have made the whole operation cheaper." As an added bonus, Wayne noted, "There was a two-mile airstrip nearby that the Americans had built so transport would have been easy." Even though the movie would have been made in a foreign country, Wayne had the financial backing of several influential Texans, as long as Republic would be involved in the distribution of the film.[221]

Suddenly, though, his financing began to mysteriously dry up. Investors who heretofore were going to support the project now backed out. Believing that Wayne was going to make the epic in Texas, they were furious when told he was still considering filming outside the country. Wayne believed that Yates "deliberately told some folks that I was shooting it in Texas...but now the Texans were angry with me. I had to go down there and square it with my Texas friends." Wayne was due back in Hollywood by October 20, to have it out with Yates once and for all. Once again, Wayne's project was on hold.[222]

In the mid-1940s while at Republic, Wayne had donned a producer's hat and was involved in several films in that capacity. He utilized his accumulated cinematic knowledge acquired over the years, both from behind and in front of the camera, and was finally in a position to share in the profits from those endeavors. He had worked with some of the best directors and actors in the business and was frustrated by his lack of control over his career. Cary Grant had made a bold move by going "freelance" in the 1940s by refusing to sign exclusive multi-picture contracts; now, Wayne took charge of his own projects. He'd cut his teeth on *Angel and the Badman* and *The Fighting Kentuckian*....Now he wanted more: script control and development. Actor and director selection. Which projects to accept, which to decline? Just as John Ford, James Cagney, Burt Lancaster, Humphrey Bogart, and many others realized the benefits of independent production, so would Wayne. Andrew J. Fenady recalled, "The first picture that he did was *Angel and the Badman*. Well, after that, part of Duke's deal in staying with Republic, not exclusively, guaranteed that he would make so many pictures. He would produce those pictures, and that was how some of those others came about; *The Bullfighter and The Lady* and some of the other pictures that he made over there because he was their cash cow."[223]

In 1950, former bullfighter Budd Boetticher required financial backing for a potential project. He gave a script to his friend Andrew McLaglen, who after soliciting an agreement that he would be the "associate producer and first assistant," handed it to Jimmy Grant. Grant liked it so much he convinced Wayne to meet with Boetticher at the Hotel Reforma in Mexico City. After several hours of drink and talk, Wayne agreed to produce the film, and they both flew back to Hollywood where Wayne insisted that Yates and Republic finance the film. *The Bullfighter and the Lady* is the story of an American Broadway producer and sportsman who, while visiting Mexico, learned the art of bullfighting to impress the *señoritas*, but eventually came to respect the sport. Wayne and Robert Fellows collaborated on the film, which Wayne produced. He had first worked with Fellows at Universal in 1942 when Fellows was an assistant producer on *Pittsburgh*. The following year, Fellows produced *Tall in the Saddle* and in 1944 brought together the various talents that would combine for *Back to Bataan*.

For bringing the script to Wayne's attention, McLaglen ended up as the First Assistant Director. "I didn't get the Associate Producer credit," remembered McLaglen, "but I was responsible for that movie being made." Boetticher recalled, "The best way to describe my relationship with Wayne was that he was my best friend or deadliest enemy according to how he woke up in the morning..." On the first day of filming, Robert Stack and several other actors stood on a porch. "Duke came around right in the middle of the first scene and grabbed Bob around the lapel and said, 'Jeeze, if you're gonna play the part, play it like a man! If you're gonna say the line, say it with some balls!' Well, Duke did that about five straight times. I told Duke I wanted to talk to him. I said, 'Do you think you can direct the picture better than I can? You walked right in front of the camera, and I'm the director. I'm nobody yet, but I am going to be big one day. And if you think you can do the picture better than I can, considering I've been a bullfighter and have really written the script'—Duke cut me off. 'Or?' he said. 'Or I'll go home.'" Wayne stood in front of the camera and to his credit said, "Ladies and gentlemen, I have implicit faith in my young director here and what he says goes! He suggested that I go home and I'm going home. And I'll be back when we give a party for you after the picture."[224]

During filming, Grant, who was rewriting the script, was conspicuously absent. At the wrap party, Wayne was so drunk he fell over a veranda railing into some bushes. After the party, the company attended a bullfight. "...there were eleven seats to our right in the front row in Plaza, Mexico. All of a sudden, just before the opening parade, there is a hustle and bustle behind us and here comes Grant with ten hookers, and he had been living in a whorehouse. Chata (Duke's second wife) turned to Wayne and said, 'If you even smile at one of those women, I'm going to hit you!'"[225]

Robert Fellows and Wayne had been friends ever since they had met on the set of *Seven Sinners* in 1940. Fellows grew up in the movie industry, just like Wayne. When Wayne was an assistant prop man at Fox, Bob worked as a "chair boy" for Cecil B. DeMille at Pathe Studios in 1926 on *King of Kings*. "He always had a dozen people around him," recalled Fellows of DeMille. "You know, with scripts, pencils, megaphones and such. And when he got tired, he'd just sit down. It was my job to see that there was a chair under him every time he looked as if he was going to relax." As Wayne grew into his acting persona, Fellows graduated to assistant director and unit manager at Warner Bros. and Universal. While at Warner's Fellows produced such hits as *Virginia City* (1940), *Knute Rockne—All American* (1940) and *They Died with Their Boots On* (1941). Eventually, he moved over to Paramount and continued with *A Connecticut Yankee in King Arthur's Court (1949)*, and *Streets of Laredo (1949)*, among many others. As Wayne said, "What Bob doesn't know about the business isn't worth knowing. He's been a stage manager, actor, assistant cutter, prop man, writer, and director—just name it." They had kicked around the idea of forming a production company for years, and, when Wayne decided to branch out on his own, he couldn't have picked a better partner.[226]

Wayne already had a multi-picture contract with Warner's, and, on March 5, 1952, the partnership modified the arrangement whereby in addition to producing one more film per year starring Duke, Wayne-Fellows would also participate in the profits generated by that picture. The revised contract troubled Wayne, though. Fellows had signed an exclusive seven-picture contract that would prevent Wayne from making movies for other studios, which basically negated the freedom he realized as an independent. After a heated discussion, Wayne agreed to a five-picture non-exclusive contract. Warner's agreed to finance and distribute Wayne-Fellows productions and pay Duke $150,000 per film and 10% of gross receipts. Left out of the arrangement, however, was *The Alamo*. Warner's was not going to finance the film at all, so Wayne reluctantly put the project on hold while he filled his contractual obligations. Immediately after the agreement was signed, Wayne headed off to Honolulu to scout locations for his next movie, *Big Jim McLain*. Loosely based on a *Saturday Evening Post* article entitled "We Almost Lost Hawaii to the Reds," it was a modern adventure yarn based on a screenplay by Grant that dealt with a Texas cattle buyer who followed a trail of excitement to Hawaii. Eventually, the direction of the project changed focus as it followed the exploits of two investigators from the House Un-American

Activities Committee who undertake a mission to Hawaii where Communists are scheming to hamper shipping. Hollywood speculated that Warner Bros. agreed to release the film after the studio and Wayne failed to agree on a project to fulfill Wayne's one-picture-a-year contract. Interestingly, company records indicated that *McLain* was produced by the Fifth Corp. This company was created by Wayne and Fellows on November 26, 1951, and was named after the approach Communists used when accused of subversion. Taking refuge behind the Fifth Amendment was constantly referred to in the movie. Wayne-Fellows Production Inc. was subsequently formed on April 22, 1952, as a subsidiary of the Fifth Corp. Wayne would be responsible for all production creative activity while Fellows would be in charge of finances. Wayne recalled that, "When I first started it with Fellows, Bob was supposed to work on television shows and then, if you had five reels of film, you could sell it but he never really got into it. He wasn't hungry, I guess. We had a beautiful opportunity. Now, there is cutthroat competition but then, it was simple. You didn't have to be very smart to make five reels of film."[227]

As author Emanuel Levy noted in "Wayne Tribute: Big Jim McLain-Anti-Communism Propaganda," although commendable in concept, the film treated the subject of subversive activity rather casually and without substance. Blatantly propagandistic, it was no coincidence that Jim McLain's initials were the same as Senator Joe McCarthy's. A ninety-minute paid political announcement with romance, comedy, and tropical scenery, it only scratched the surface of an otherwise serious subject but served to enhance Wayne's image as a right-wing anti-Communist. Wayne did the voice-over in a fashion similar to Jack Webb on *Dragnet.* The cast included James Arness and Nancy Olson, with Hans Conreid and blonde, brassy Veda Ann Borg for comic relief. *McLain* was the first major post-war contemporary film made in the Hawaiian Islands using local color and talent. Wayne learned that co-star Arness was a surfer and arranged for temporary membership at the Outrigger Canoe Club on Waikiki. Arness had nothing but kind words about his time with Duke. "Working with Wayne was terrific," he said. "*Big Jim McLain* was the first picture I did with him, and I was blessed with his friendship. During the entire location shoot, I came to realize just how special a person he was…" Citing a scene filmed at the Arizona Memorial, Arness recalled, "The beautiful memorial as we know it today had not yet been built; there was just a crude quarterdeck and a flagpole. Standing on the platform, we looked down right beneath our feet and saw the buckled hull. There was a big plaque mounted there, and someone starting reading it aloud. Work just stopped on the set, and it was so quiet. Then John Wayne began reading the plaque to all of us, and everyone, including Duke, was very moved."[228]

Armed now with his own production company, Wayne was anxious to start his Alamo project once again. He and Fellows went to Yates, indicated he was ready to commence pre-production, and had set the budget at $3 million. Yates waffled as usual; the budget alone made him apoplectic. He demanded Duke give up Wayne-Fellows and make the picture for Republic. Not only that, he further requested they postpone the starting date and cut the budget. Film it in black & white, reduce the scope, cut costs wherever possible. "I was in high spirits," recalled Wayne, "and I went to see Robert Fellows, my partner in our own production company, and together we went over to talk over *The Alamo* with Yates. It turned into a real battle of words although I'd like to...! Anyway, the long and the short of it was that Yates wasn't going to let me make *The Alamo* at Republic...and when he said, 'I'd still like us to work together. How about signing a new contract?' I said, 'You know where you can put your contract. I'll never work here again.' And I didn't." He went on, "Yates said I should give up my company and make the picture for Republic. He said I owed it to Republic. How do you like that? I don't owe Republic anything. I've made a lot of money for the studio. I've brought Frank Borzage and John Ford to the studio. And Jimmy Grant, who wrote *Sands of Iwo Jima*, one of the biggest hits Republic ever had."[229]

After yet another fruitless conversation with Yates regarding approval of the project, Wayne delivered an ultimatum. "You go through with this, Herb, or I won't be on the set when you get back." Calling his bluff, Yates indicated they would discuss it again in two weeks after Yates returned from a trip and stated, "Well, I'll have to figure it all out again." Replied Wayne once more, "Come on, I've done plenty of favors for you. I've done all the figuring that has to be done, the locations are set up, we're sending men down there, and suddenly you stop them. I want the okay right now or I won't be here when you get back." Yates refused to answer and just laughed. A shouting match ensued, and Yates stormed out of the office. He was on his way to New York, come hell or high water.

Less than half an hour later, Wayne phoned Mary St. John and told her to start packing. He had called a moving company and said the van would be there shortly to pick up their files, personal belongings, etc. Eventually Yates got word of the impending departure and marched into Duke's office. He demanded to know where Wayne was, and St. John replied, "He's not here." After he realized Wayne was serious and was really leaving, Yates lost his composure and yelled at St. John, insisting she stop packing. She refused. He screamed, "Who are you working for, him or me?" She replied with one simple word, "Wayne," picked up her purse and left the studio, never to return. "It sure shook Herb," said Wayne, "but that picture had been a dream of mine for years, and I was determined to make it. I felt he was belittling my efforts by refusing to do it. Yates will have to make me a darned good offer to get me to make another picture with him. I'm fed up." All that stood between Wayne, Yates, and the project was $750,000. That's what it would cost extra to shoot in Texas. Yates was adamant about not making it in Mexico but wouldn't pay the extra cost for San Antonio. Wayne had given Yates an ultimatum: put *The Alamo* back on the prepping skid within ten days, or else. Yates didn't; Wayne walked.[230]

(According to an item posted by Sheilah Graham, the real reason behind the disagreement was that Yates insisted Wayne use Vera Ralston as his leading lady. Four days later, Graham retracted the statement.)[231]

The feud between Yates and Wayne over ownership of *The Alamo* project began almost immediately upon their split. Yates said it belonged to Republic because development started while Wayne was still under contract there. Wayne said arrangements were made before he ever started it to make it as an independent venture. The entire project was to be filmed in Mexico, and he planned to leave for there after Thanksgiving to set up production. Wayne lost the rights to the script, and he was furious. "Yates is saying he built me as a star!" Wayne growled. "Why, I built his studio! He said before I can make *The Alamo* for myself, he'll see the Wayne-Fellows company dissolved. After all these years at Republic, I didn't expect this…" Once again, Wayne's efforts to make *The Alamo* were thwarted.[232]

Wayne explained his decision in an October 29, 1952, letter to Ford: "Regarding my past (and I mean pluperfect past) association with Republic; As I told you over the phone, Herb called me in—gave me a friendship kick—and then kicked my teeth out by saying that his Sales Department was upset, and he was personally upset, over my going into business for myself—said that you were against it, and explained to me how wonderful he had been to me… He then put out a story that I had left Republic because he wanted to make *The Alamo* in Texas and was being loyal to the Texans, and that I insisted on doing it in Panama. He knows, you know, and I know that the reason we are not making it in Texas is that he wouldn't put out the money, and that the reason he caused a hassle at this time is that he wants to make a picture called *The Golden Tide* to follow the last abortion he made with Vera… I hated to move out of the studio, and it's damn irritating. The things that are good at the studio that I have been a party to helping build, like the crews, and the attitude of the crews on pictures— the things that his horrible front office gets, not because they're worth a goddam, but because of the people who make the pictures—these things I hated to leave, and have that smug old bastard sit back and tell me what he had done for me and you and the motion picture business in general. I know I can't get any security his way. I see no reason why he should begrudge me doing it another."[233]

Failure to receive approval wasn't the only reason Wayne left Republic; Duke justifiably felt Yates had taken financial advantage of John Ford through spurious, unethical, and "creative accounting" practices. In a July 8, 1952, letter to Republic, Lee Van Hoozer, the Argosy treasurer, questioned the accounting of revenue associated with *Rio Grande*. "Our experience tends to indicate we should expect approximately $250,000 to have been yielded by this gross figure. (With a fifty-fifty split of over $700,000 in foreign receipts, Argosy only had received $82,425.90.) Both Mr. Ford and Mr. Cooper are deeply concerned with the financial reports for this picture."[234]

Yates replied with a classic non-denial denial. "Your letter is insulting to me and highly objectionable. In all the years I have been in this business and have never had anyone question our honesty and integrity in any of our dealings. I cannot believe that Mr. Ford requested you to write your letter...as I see Mr. Ford every day, and if he or Mr. Cooper has any doubt about our method of release and its obvious quality, multiple bookings in conjunction with other pictures and so forth, it seems to me either Mr. Ford or Mr. Cooper would discuss the matter with me...we do not interfere with Argosy in the production of pictures they make for Republic, and we will not permit Argosy to interfere with the distribution of these pictures, which both Mr. Ford and Mr. Cooper can rest assured will be distributed strictly in accordance with our contract, and on a basis of honesty and integrity."[235]

At the same time, he protested his innocence, Yates continued to pull financial shenanigans when he changed the wording in Ford's contract, and increased the overhead charge from 15 to 35 %. He included costs for props, wardrobe, and musicians that were used elsewhere and also deducted foreign costs and distribution fees against American receipts, a procedure that virtually guaranteed an absence of net profits. Ford's contract called for a fifty-fifty split of the profits on *The Quiet Man*, which was enormously successful, yet Republic's financial records didn't indicate anywhere near that type of revenue.[236]

Ford and Yates's relationship had stretched beyond the breaking point. Pappy wired Lord Killanin: "Having acrimonious legal business complications with M. de la Republique. Suing in process. Just won't pay up his obligations. This could happen to us. So stall, procrastinate, linger on our deal. Absolutely impossible for me personally to do business with him until settled." Nevertheless, Ford fulfilled his obligation to Republic for his third and final movie when he made *The Sun Shines Bright*, a remake of *Judge Priest*. A personal favorite, Ford said, "The only trouble was that when I left the studio, old man Yates didn't know what to do with it. The picture had comedy, drama, pathos, but he didn't understand it. His kind of picture had to have plenty of sex or violence. This one had neither; it was just a good picture. Yates fooled around with it when I left and almost ruined it."[237]

Ford consulted the Donovan, Leisure, Newton, and Irvine law firm, which in turn arranged for Price Waterhouse to audit Republic's records. Evidence of an enormous fraud had been discovered and Republic offered a cash settlement: Eventually, in 1956, Ford and Cooper were paid $546,000 in compensation due to shoddy accounting. Ford felt Wayne was responsible for getting him involved with Republic in the first place, told him that "he had worked too hard to put up with this cheap poverty-row bullshit," and refused to speak with him for months. He also blamed Argosy co-owner Merian Cooper for failing to protect their best interests. Shortly before the release of *The Quiet Man*, Cooper signed a contract with Cinerama to be their general manager and sold his Argosy stock.[238]

In August 1952, after *McLain* was released to the public, Wayne made a trip to Peru, accompanied by long-time friend and Wayne-Fellows production assistant Ernie Saftig. While there, in addition to accepting a vacation gift from Howard Hughes, he searched for both potential *Alamo* locations and possible investments. According to Noah Dietrich, Hughes's business manager, there was a less obvious reason for the trip: "...Howard feared that Wayne would make another movie that would reach the screens before *Jet Pilot*. So Howard devised an intricate scheme which would keep Wayne away from alien cameras. He proposed a goodwill trip of South America, to be paid for by RKO. Glen Odekirk flew Wayne in a PBY and they visited major capitals and stopped to fish and hunt along the way. Wayne had a great vacation, but he didn't realize that it was simply designed to keep him from working for other producers." RKO Studios and Panagra (Pan-American Grace Airways) arranged the trip, and Wayne visited Brazil, Chile, Argentina, and Venezuela. In addition to swimming, scuba diving, soaking up the sun, and sampling the nightlife, he also made goodwill visits to distributors of American films in South America. Although he found no location that suited his purpose, he did meet an attractive twenty-three-year-old Peruvian woman, with luxurious black hair and ravishing figure, who would eventually become his third wife.[239]

Richard Weldy, a director of Amazon Adventure Tours and Panagra executive, was Wayne's long-time friend and assigned host. After Duke finished his commitment of a formal dinner in Lima, Weldy drove him to Tango Maria, a tropical tourist resort in Central Peru for a bit of R & R. *Sabotage in the Jungle*, a remake of *Green Hell* that included Weldy's actress wife Pilar, was filming there. He introduced Wayne to her and that, as they say, was that. "I was dancing barefoot by firelight, wearing a low-cut gypsy costume," says Pilar, "my skirts whirling around my body as I swayed and turned...I'd never been so immediately and powerfully affected by a casual meeting with a man the way I was by my meeting with John Wayne...I couldn't believe anyone's eyes could be so turquoise, so piercing. He was the handsomest man I've ever seen."[240]

To refer to Pilar as an actor was an overstatement. "She never had much of a career," Wayne once explained. "Once Sol Lesser sent a crew to Peru to make a picture about hunting Inca gold, and they needed a girl to walk in front of the camera with bare feet and long hair. She did it. Then an independent producer went down there to make a picture, using amateur actors, and she was in it. But I don't think the picture was ever released here." Nevertheless, it was infatuation at first sight, and, upon Wayne's return, he stopped at Churubusco Studios in Mexico City where they were filming *Plunder of the Sun* and conducted a screen test with Pilar. She followed him to Hollywood to dub dialogue for an English version of *Green Hell*, and eventually signed a contract with Wayne-Fellows in December, never to return to Peru. (Later, while Wayne was filming *Hondo*, Pilar slipped quietly out of town to divorce Weldy. Her former employer found

Pilar's good fortune unbelievable. She once worked in the offices of a U.S. airline located in Lima, happily married and pounding away on a typewriter with no idea of a career. "Then she quit to work in a movie in Brazil," said one executive, "and the next thing we heard she was divorced and running around Mexico with Wayne.")[241]

In 1956, *Confidential* magazine published an article claiming Wayne stole Pilar from Weldy. Weldy took exception to the statement and, in the Jaraboacoa mountain wilds of the Dominican Republic, accidentally shot and wounded its publisher, Robert Harrison. "I never had any intention of hurting Harrison," stated Weldy, "although I was sore because of the story in the magazine." When asked if he could have killed him if he wanted to, Weldy replied, "Naturally. I am a good shot. But it's not my nature to hurt anybody. I don't even kill animals." He further indicated, "A big argument came up. He called me a lot of names. In the heat of the argument, my rifle fell and went off accidentally." Harrison was on a hunting expedition with A.P. Govani, managing editor of *Confidential*, and nightclub singer Geene Courtney. Weldy had had an argument with Harrison the previous weekend at El Embajadoe Hotel in Ciudad Trujillo and somehow encountered the hunting party again in the mountains. A sudden discharge from Weldy's rifle struck Harrision's left arm. Barely injured, Harrison and Courtney were admitted to a local hospital suffering from exhaustion, exposure, and a slight flesh wound.[242]

When Wayne found out, he commented on Weldy: "I think he is a nice enough fellow and I hope he's not in trouble. But I deplore the fact he's such a poor shot." Unfortunately, Harrison's wound wasn't his only problem. When his wife found out that he and Courtney were alone in the jungle, she yelled angrily, "Why that old hag! I just don't like her. Are you sure she was with him?" She went on, "She's (Courtney) nothing but a fifth-rate performer. The papers say she is thirty. She's forty-five if she's a day...I wish she would stay away from my darling husband." Harrison said he didn't hold a grudge, and Weldy was exonerated of all charges. When Harrison returned home to New York, he wasn't so lucky. After Mrs. Harrison heard what had transpired in the tropical jungles, she wasn't sure if she would forgive him. "First I want to hear what he has to say in private," she said.[243]

Although it had been announced earlier that James Arness would star in the next Wayne-Fellows feature, by the time filming of *Plunder* started on October 1, Glenn Ford had taken over the assignment. Rhonda Fleming was also slated for the movie, but as Ford had injured his back in a fall on the set of *The Man From the Alamo* and was laid up for a month, she wasn't available when filming began. Wayne was also supposed to be in the movie, but eventually backed out. Instead, on October 13, he starred as divorced football coach Steve Aloysius Williams ("Winning isn't everything, it's the only thing.") in *Trouble Along the Way* (aka

*Alma Mater*), a light-hearted, sentimental, romantic comedy based on a story in *The Saturday Evening Post*. The picture was screenwriter Melville Shavelson's first opportunity to produce, but Wayne felt the script was weak and asked Grant to polish it. The result was so atrocious they ended up with two scripts. Wayne was given Grant's, and when Wayne wasn't on the set, they shot one script; when he was there they shot Grant's. Unfortunately, Wayne showed up one day when he wasn't supposed to and found out. "Ordinarily Wayne is one of the most kindest and levelheaded of men," said Shavelson. "But when crossed, and particularly when double-crossed, he can make an underground nuclear explosion seem like (a) baby's sigh." Beyond furious, Wayne grabbed the producer and had a serious conversation. "To be grabbed by a guy who is six-foot-four, who is running the goddamn picture, was a terrible moment," confessed Shavelson. No longer on speaking terms with the producer, the film was completed, *Wayne's* way.[244]

According to another source, Wayne initially requested Grant to rewrite the script, and director William A. Wellman refused to let him do so. It wasn't until Wayne started to "improvise" dialogue that Wellman realized Grant was working behind the scenes. Shavelson was said to have countered by bringing in phony revisions, which Grant would then rewrite, and he would shoot from the original script instead, making Grant's lines, which Wayne had memorized, useless. In either case, it was not a very supportive environment to find one's self in.[245]

Wayne injured himself on the set while foolishly attempting to "take out" an actor who just happened to be a college football player. Oh, he took him out all right—flattened him like a pancake—but in the process Wayne re-injured his shoulder so badly that it left his right arm temporarily paralyzed. The next day, in a key scene in which he threw a football through a church window, he couldn't even hold the ball with his right hand and was forced to throw left-handed the remainder of the movie.[246]

Although it received decent reviews from *Variety* and *The New York Times* ("It gracefully displays such virtues as delightful dialogue, astute and swiftly paced direction..." and "Chuckles and laughs are rampant... [Wayne] leans toward a humorous lightness and delivers it that way"), it proved one of Wayne's lowest-grossing films. Shavelson admitted, "The picture never made any money because people didn't want to see John Wayne in something other than a Western or an action picture." Or maybe because it really wasn't very good. Wrote the *Morning Herald*, "Even a second trip to *Trouble Along the Way* fails to shake us from our disappointment and our conviction that it misses fire on every point where *Going My Way* scored so beautifully... It seems to us that the tenderness and spiritual quality which Barry Fitzgerald and Bing Crosby bring out into their picture is entirely missing from the Charles Coburn–John Wayne movie." The experience wasn't a total loss as during production, Wayne and director Michael Curtis filmed a short promo supporting the American Red Cross.[247]

In March 1953, Warner Bros. announced a four-year extension of its agreement with Wayne-Fellows. Wayne would also star in some of the features: *Island in the Sky* would be the first and plans were in place for a 3-D Western spectacle. *Island*, written by Ernest K. Gann, a pilot who flew in both World Wars, was based on Gann's own experiences in searching for a downed flyer on February 3, 1943. Originally written in 1944, Gann, who was hired by United Artists producer Robert Stillman, collaborated with Seton Miller on the screenplay in June 1950. Robert Stillman Productions and Stanley Kramer had purchased the rights to the novel that January. In April 1951, Stillman announced that Frank Rosenberg would produce the movie, starring Richard Widmark. However, Stillman dropped plans to produce the project and Twentieth Century-Fox then paid Gann $5,000 for the rights but dropped the option after a year. In November 1952, Wayne-Fellows bought the treatment from Gann, and he received yet another $5,000 check from Warner's. At this rate, he could retire without ever having his script filmed.[248]

Wellman immediately fell in love with the project. "I hadn't met Ernie Gann," he remembered, "but they got hold of the story...they sent it to me to read. Wonderful. His writing about anything to do with the air is absolutely tops to me. And so we worked on the script together. The only thing I can tell you is that it's a true story and every one of the characters was really true. There was a flier down, and they all left everything; they left their wives, they left their kids. You saw the story; I can't tell it any better than it was done. And they went up in there, and they found him. That's the whole story. They gave everything up to find a pal. And that was fliers." Directed by Wellman who also did the narration, production began on February 4, 1953, and wrapped on March 2.[249]

Filmed on location at Truckee, Donner Lake, northern California and Burbank studios, the actors faced tremendous cold, wind, ice, and snowy conditions. In one scene set up on Stages 4 and 5 at Goldwyn, liquid snow was tossed in front of a wind machine as cold air was piped in. It wasn't very hard to act chilly. A secluded valley with six-foot drifts in Donner Pass served as the crash site. Cast and crew stayed at Donner Lake Lodge and the Gateway Motel, and each morning, after riding chartered buses, army weasels towing sleds would take them to the film site. Located 7,000 feet above sea level, severe snowstorms and gales interrupted filming numerous times. Due to the extreme cold, sperm oil and kerosene were used in place of grease and oil to keep lubricants from congealing. Heating plates kept the cameras warm while film magazines were wrapped in padding until they were required.[250]

Wellman was a gruff, old-school director who focused on action, and Wayne got along exceedingly well with him. "He's a wonderful old son-of-a-bitch," Duke said of the filmmaker. "He had a metal plate in his head from some accident... and all the actors we had would never get into an argument with him...and he'd go around belting all these big, tough guys and they'd be afraid to hit him back for fear they'd kill him." Wayne continued, "(He was a) fine director. He didn't delve into characters as much as some. I'll tell you the difference between directors: Hawks has tremendous patience with people. He'll keep working with a fellow, even if he's not cutting the mustard. Ford won't hire you unless he knows he can get it out of you. Wellman figures you're a pro and doesn't bother you much as an actor. If you don't deliver, he'll simply cut the part down. It's that simple."[251]

Filmed in penetrating black-and-white, Archie Stout, who handled the land-based scenes, and Bill Clothier, who focused on the aerial ones, perfectly captured the vast expanses of snow-covered solitude. A Douglas C-47 Skytrain transport plane (the military version of a DC-3) crash-landed in the frozen tundra of the Quebec/Labrador border, and the plane's pilot fought to keep his crew alive until rescued. Gann served as technical director adviser and piloted a plane for the second unit.

In addition to the normal standbys, the movie included Arness, Andy Devine, Dobe Carey, Paul Fix, Darryl Hickman, Touch (Mike) Connors, and Fess Parker, who would soon don buckskins in Disney's *Davy Crockett: King of the Wild Frontier*. Two former child actors, Carl *Alfalfa* Switzer of the *Our Gang* comedies and James Lydon, once widely known as *Henry Aldrich*, were also in the cast.

Wayne's performance exuded the quiet confidence of an ordinary individual in extraordinary circumstances. Modest, yet able, heroism fit him like a glove. "John Wayne plays perfectly, the clean and leathery hero," wrote *Time*, "that has made him a top box-office attraction for years." *The Hollywood Reporter* wrote that the movie "...is that rare combination of expert writing, acting and directing that holds an audience enthralled from the opening shot to the close 108 minutes later. John Wayne lends marquee strength and contributes a fine performance," while the *Los Angeles Examiner* stated, "Wayne, looking and acting the part every inch of the way, is plain great and gives one of his finest performances in his distinguished career."[252]

Although Wayne had received favorable reviews, strain was beginning to show in his business life. Warner Bros. failed to advertise his film properly, and though financially successful, the beginning of a separation between Wayne and the studio started to manifest itself. Friends for over eleven years, Fellows and Wayne's business relationship also began to fray at the edges. At a party after the opening of *Island*, Bo Roos, Wayne's business manager, drunkenly accused Fellows of outright incompetence and deceit. In later years, Duke confided to Pappy, "I built Bob Fellows into such an important character that I can't do anything with him. I find him incompetent. Even when he's trying…I'm afraid if I just fired Fellows and moved someone else in, number one, I'd wreck Fellows's (sic) career—and I might have just as many headaches with someone else."[253]

On April 14, 1953, Wayne and John Farrow left for Mexico City to set up advance arrangements for their next project. While there, they undertook technical research and scouted locations. One month later, Wayne started *Hondo*, his first and only 3-D movie. As television, "the magic box," became more attractive and available to millions of consumers, Hollywood needed a gimmick to halt its dwindling attendance, and 3-D seemed just the trick. A concept that provided the illusion of depth through the use of special projection hardware and/or eyeglasses, it was *the thing* in the1950s. It was the device studios used to offset the increasing popularity of television.[254]

"Depthies," as they were known in the industry, held out the possibility of a sustainable success in the struggle against the growing popularity of television. As Vincent Di Fate wrote in *3-D Cinema: Yesterday, Today and Tomorrow*, since no cost-effective video technology existed at the time to make the airing of 3-D programming practical on TV, the stereoscopic process offered new and persuasive evidence of cinema's inevitable ascendancy. A special camera or cameras recorded the image from different perspectives, and theaters needed dual projectors to coordinate the two strips of film with Polaroid filters. Because the features utilized twin projectors, a capacity limit of film loaded on each projector meant an intermission was necessary for each film. And since there was a specific print for each eye, they had to be synchronized in the projection booth. (The left eye negative was used for conventional 2-D release.) Theaters had to project the print on silver or reflective screen as polarized light wouldn't register on the typical matte white screen, which resulted in improper separation of images. Even a slight disruption between the two created a viewing experience that would "hurt the eyes."[255]

The Golden Era of 3-D films occurred between 1952 and 1955 with the release of movies such as *Bwana Devil, Melody, It Came from Outer Space, Man in the Dark*, and *The House of Wax*, which was the first 3-D feature with stereophonic sound. Warner Bros. was so gratified by its reception they announced twenty-two additional 3-D movies would be released, each with WarnerColor, WarnerPhonic sound and WarnerScopic wide screen.[256]

Although a unique, entertaining, eye-opening experience, 3-D films were fraught with technical problems, and their attraction started to decline by late fall 1953 which, unfortunately, is exactly when *Hondo* was released. "In the early 1950s there was a whole rash of 3-D films," recalled Michael Wayne, "and the audience was quite excited about it. When we started filming *Hondo*, 3-D was the rage. However, it takes a year to complete a film, and by that time the interest in 3-D had died down...Dad wanted 3-D because that was the way things were going."[257]

Factors reducing the popularity of 3-D included: the simultaneous projection of multiple prints, multiple projectionists, dual repair of prints to insure synchronization, reflective silver projection screens, and the requirement of reusable Polaroid glasses. Shooting in 3-D also was a laborious, time-consuming process. Not only were the cameras large and cumbersome, they tended to frequently break down resulting in a waste of time and money. Rain, wind, and sun all wreaked havoc on the cameras' mechanisms and lugging them hither and yon over remote Mexican locations was no easy task, either.

Arguably the best Wayne Western not directed by Ford or Hawks, the film was based on a Louis L'Amour short story, *The Gift of Cochise*, published in the July 5, 1952, edition of *Collier's*. *Hondo* depicted a conflict of interest rather than a battle of good vs. evil. The story dealt with the relationship of individuals set against a backdrop of skirmishes, gunfights, and Indian attacks. Hondo Lane, a half-breed civilian scout for the U.S. Cavalry and perpetual wanderer along with his raggedy dog Sam, developed a romantic interest in the wife of a man he had killed in self-defense. Sam was played by Pal, the son and stand-in for Lassie. The canine star's owner and trainer, Rudd Weatherwax, gave Pal a makeover for the role with a hairpiece, false scar on the forehead and a shave to disguise the collie. Pal won the Patsy, an animal equivalent of the Oscar, for top animal performance in 1953.[258]

Practically abandoned by her ne'er-do-well husband, Angie Lowe was forced to do ranch chores by herself, tasks with which Lane assists. Lane was described as "a big man, wide shouldered, with the lean hard boned face of the desert rider. There was no softness in him. His toughness was ingrained and deep. Without cruelty, yet quick, hard and dangerous. Whatever wells of goodness might lie within him were guarded and deep." The role fit Wayne like a glove, and it was a character he was to play repeatedly. He had lost some weight and came into the project fit and trim. "I think he really liked the way he looked," said his son Michael. "Because it was so hot and he was wearing those buckskins throughout, he went down to about 210 pounds. Not a lot of weight for a man over six-feet-four." In later years, it was suggested to Wayne that he always played the same type role. "They're absolutely right," Wayne replied. "Years ago I used to ache to play different kinds of roles until one smart man told me folks came to theatres to see John Wayne, not John Wayne impersonating someone else."[259]

Duke was a last-minute replacement for Glenn Ford, who turned down the role when he learned John Farrow was to direct. Ford had previously worked with Farrow on *Plunder* and found it a difficult experience. Wayne refused to fire Farrow and decided to play the role himself. According to Ford's son Peter, "(Wayne) thought my father did such a good job (in *Plunder*) that he asked him to appear in another film...but Dad was stuck on the ill-fated *Americano* project in Brazil." So Wayne took the role himself. Jimmy Grant again adapted the story for the screen and received an Oscar nomination for Best Screenplay Adaptation.[260]

Though rumored a potential co-star, Katharine Hepburn's indignation at Wayne's activities while Alliance president and his subsequent treatment of alleged Communist sympathizers resulted in her rejecting an offer to co-star in the project. "Politically, he is a reactionary," wrote Hepburn. "He suffers from a point of view based entirely on his own experience. He was surrounded in his early years in the motion picture business by people like himself. Self-made. Hard-working. Independent. Of the style of man who blazed the trails across our country. Reached out into the unknown. People who were willing to live or die entirely on their own independent judgment. Jack Ford…was cut from the same block of wood. Fiercely independent. They seemed to have no patience and no understanding of the more timid and dependent type of person. Pull your own weight. This is their slogan. Sometimes, I don't think that they realize that their own load was attached to a very powerful engine. They don't need or want protection. Total personal responsibility. They dish it out. They take it." (Hepburn would later star with Wayne in *Rooster Cogburn*.)[261]

As a result, Broadway actor Geraldine Page appeared in her first starring role. Described as "tall and reedy with a bony, expressive face and long fingers," she had burst upon the New York theater scene the previous year, garnering rave reviews for her portrayal of a southern spinster in a revival of a Tennessee Williams play called *Summer and Smoke*. According to Paul Fix, Wayne "wanted a woman with a more hardened look, but still sort of handsome–not ugly." Fellows had tested Page, who was also represented by Wayne's agent, Charles Feldman, on Duke's recommendation, but after having worked with her for a while, he had a decidedly different opinion. When Pilar visited the set, Duke confided, "She (Page) may have been great on Broadway, but she didn't know a damn thing about making movies. I don't know where some of these arty New York theater people get their manners. Would you believe she sat down at dinner one night and ate her mashed potatoes with her fingers?" One evening, he was so disgusted with her table manners, Wayne dumped his dinner plate over her head. Fellows had sent her to a dentist to have her teeth fixed prior to the start of filming, and according to Wayne, Page didn't care for makeup or soap and water. "She had a rather bad aroma. I think it was her way," said Fix, "as a New York stage actress, of getting into the part of a realistic frontierswoman." Mary St. John remembered it as well. "Do you know how bad she smelled? Page did not have the best morals in the world, and hard-up stuntmen were seen stumbling out of her room every morning, but even Ward Bond wouldn't take advantage of her availability. That's how bad she smelled."[262]

While not a classical beauty, Page was nevertheless handsome and it must have pained her a great deal when Farrow changed Grant's script to comment on her beauty. "I know I'm a homely woman," she was forced to say, "but I love you." John Ford had visited the set and exclaimed that no one would believe Duke would fall for such an unattractive woman. How cruel. You can only imagine Wayne's surprise when Andrew McLaglen told him Page had been nominated for Best Actress. "There was silence on the other end of the phone," McLaglen recalled. "Duke couldn't understand it."[263]

Page wasn't the only actor with whom Wayne lost his temper. "Every morning," Page recalled, "he (Wayne) would just scream and destroy somebody, like the time he lost his temper with Lee Aaker, who played my son Johnny. Lee was just a kid and made mistakes in several scenes, blowing his lines or opening a door at the wrong time, and Wayne would walk around the set saying, 'What are we going to do about that goddamn kid?' Then Wayne would calm down and apologize, but poor Lee became quite terrified."[264]

Ford directed two shots of a line of cavalrymen that Hondo sees when he visits the army post. When asked what Ford contributed to the movie, Wayne snapped, "Jesus Christ, don't you people ever give me credit for anything?" Page recalled that Ford, "affects army fatigues as a way of dress with a hat cocked way over on one side, and he has a habit of having a very used handkerchief in his pocket, which he takes out and twists, and puts in the corner of his mouth and sucks on while he's talking. He sits way down, and he has quite a big belly that sticks up and he sorts of pats himself. The visual image of him is so revolting that you have to remember the wonderful things that he's done."[265]

The 3-D camera filming also gave Duke fits. The process required two cameras mounted side by side. Warner Bros. demanded that one of the cameras on loan be returned and be replaced by an "all-media camera." However, even when the camera worked, it caused problems. "For instance," Wayne reported to Warner's, "this morning for a two shot, because we're being so careful of this first picture with your new camera, it took us an hour and a half. It would probably save us three hours a day to have two cameras here. At this rate, our picture will take us forty-five days, at least a third longer. I feel that this is very unfair to us, particularly when this camera was not completely practical mechanically... Please, Daddy, send more money or camera."[266]

Wayne brought along sons Patrick and Michael for company and the production crew stayed at the Motel Baca in Camargo, Mexico, "a one-horse border town—not much more than a cantina, a store, and a few houses." When filming was completed for the day, there was little to do except drink, play poker, and discuss politics. Hot and dusty, it contributed to his miserable demeanor.[267]

It was in *Hondo* that Wayne lost his beloved cavalry hat for the third time. (He had lost it previously on the sets of *The Three Godfathers* and *Rio Grande*.) After it disappeared, hours were spent looking before a local radio station was asked to broadcast news of its loss. Three more hours passed before a local peasant and his son sheepishly appeared on the set with hat in hand. They admitted they had wandered onto the set when the crew was away, saw the hat, assumed that someone must have abandoned it, and "liberated" it. Once they heard on the radio that it was Wayne's, they immediately brought it back. Wayne was so grateful to retrieve his lucky chapeau, he rewarded them with a pocket full of pesos.[268]

Advertised as *Hondo, In Natural Vision, A New 3-D Process That Explodes Off Your Screen!* The 3-D version was released in only three theaters. New lamps were installed in projection rooms, and new and improved 3-D glasses were made available; clip-on for people who already wore glasses, plastic frames instead of paper framed ones and child-sized glasses were also available. Although accepted by the public, theater owners felt the cost of specialized equipment wasn't justified by the potential of increased box-office receipts, and, as a result, general release prints were manufactured in a traditional 2-D ratio. The public loved it. Wayne again received kudos for his performance, and the movie was praised for its photography, excitement, and special effects.[269]

Unfortunately, *Hondo* was released the same year as another adventure film, *Shane*. Both were Westerns, and both involved lone, solitary men who came out of the wilderness to protect blond females with small tow-headed sons. Shane was the arch-typical Western hero; Hondo the loner, unattached to women, family, and civilization. "*Hondo* was a fine film," recalled St. John, "but *Shane* was better. *Hondo* got lost in the shuffle." Fortunately, the film caught on and repaid its negative costs in about eight weeks.[270]

Wayne enjoyed working with Farrow so much that, as soon as *Hondo* was completed, he announced that they would re-team for *The Sea Chase*, a story by Andrew Greer, in which Wayne played a sea captain. Wayne-Fellows was on a roll and even attempted to purchase the rights to Charles Shaw's novel *Heaven Knows, Mr. Allison* but lost out to the partnership of Eugene Frenke and Rene Williams, who had previously relinquished his rights. Wayne planned to star in the film, and it was rumored his co-star would be Deborah Kerr. Frenke announced Kirk Douglas would take over for Wayne, and his co-star would still be Deborah Kerr.[271]

# CHAPTER SEVEN
# "AN RKO RADIOACTIVE
# PICTURE"

*"You wouldn't have been there for twenty-seven trillion dollars if you had known that." Jack Williams discussing nuclear fallout on the set of The Conqueror.*[272]

BY THE TIME WAYNE FINISHED *HONDO*, HE WAS EMOTIONALLY EXHAUSTED. TWO months later, his divorce trial from second wife Esperanza (Chata) Bauer began, and by then claims and counterclaims were flying fast and loose. Wayne had married her one month after the interlocutory decree on his divorce from first wife and mother of his four children—Josephine Saenz—became final in 1946. His marriage to Chata was volatile from the get-go. Tall, dark, and unattractive, she had been *involved* with Ray Milland until introduced to Wayne. Not a typical Latina beauty, she refused to shave her legs or bathe on a regular basis, and heavy make-up covered her poor complexion. Rumored to be either a well-known Mexican actress or a high-paid Mexico City call girl, John Ford, Bo Roos, and even Ward Bond warned Wayne not to marry her. But love is blind, so after a short honeymoon in Hawaii, they moved into Wayne's Van Nuys address.[273]

Mean, foul-mouthed, and belligerent when drunk, Chata was unbearable, and her mother was as much an alcoholic as she. As might be expected, there were more good times than bad, but the years rolled by, and they became fewer and farther between. Declaring "Our marriage was like shaking two volatile chemicals in a jar," the end came swiftly after Wayne discovered Chata had entertained Nicky Hilton as a houseguest when he was away on location. By the time he started filming *Hondo*, enough was enough. An extremely acrimonious divorce was inevitable; Chata and her noted criminal lawyer Jerry Giesler accused Wayne of assault, infidelity, drunkenness, and dragging her around by her hair. Duke claimed, "The only time I raised a hand to her was in self-defense. In fact, I was woman-handled. On many occasions I had to protect myself from her temper. I never at any time during my marriage struck my wife... I had to hold her arms and grab her foot when she was trying to strike me or kick me." (At a press preview for *Hondo*, after Wayne's character took one beating after another, one wag said, "Who wrote the script for this, Esperanza?")[274]

Romantically linked to Gail Russell, with whom he had co-starred in *Angel and the Badman* and *Wake of the Red Witch*, Wayne vehemently denied any involvement. Chata even hired two Hollywood investigators to bug Wayne's hotel room in Mexico, but they inadvertently placed microphones in the suite of Gov. Soto Maynard of Chihuahua instead, and were unceremoniously thrown in jail. One investigator reportedly became ill, and Wayne interceded on his behalf. He was flown back under guard to the United States for medical treatment. His co-conspirator was left in jail. This wasn't the first time Duke bumped heads with Chata's detectives. While Wayne filmed *Trouble Along the Way*, she set private dicks on his tail. "One day he shook the detective," recalled producer Melvin Shavelson, "and didn't show up for a week... This affected his work on the picture."[275]

Wayne's deposition in the divorce trial took so long he had to push back the start of *The High and the Mighty* to mid-November. Deeply wounded by his wife's insinuations against Russell, Wayne declared, "The damage has been done. I want to fight it to the end. If the trial should end now, what chance would I have to refute the outrageous accusations that have been leveled at me? She can hit me with anything but why drag in the name of innocent people, like Gail Russell...?" (Russell decided to sue Chata for a mere $130,000 worth of slander to teach her a thing or two.) Duke even left a sick bed to testify about his wife's alleged affair with Hilton.[276]

While Wayne was on location in Honolulu, Hilton was her Van Nuys houseguest. Wayne's butler gave him samples of Chata's doodling on paper. The doodling contained the words "Chata and Nick," "Mrs. Nick Hilton" and "Esperanza Hilton," repeated several times. Wayne explained how, early in their marriage, he often collected her doodling. "Only then," he said, "it was 'Chata and Duke.' Then I used to think it was real romantic the way she would leave those doodling around. That's how I knew the significance of these new doodling with Hilton's name substituted for mine. That's what made me disgustedly sick."[277]

Chata testified she almost shot Wayne one evening when he came home late from a party and tried to break their front door down. "I thought it was a burglar until my mother shouted, 'Don't shoot, it's your husband,'" she said. "He was very intoxicated. He was flopped on the living room couch, and I was very frightened. I asked him if he had broken in and he could hardly answer. He was disheveled and quite intoxicated. I tried to help him to bed but he couldn't get up." Wayne replied he broke down the door because it was locked.[278]

Wayne had proposed a property settlement that would have given his ex-wife an annual payment of $80,000 for the first two years and up to $40,000 for each of the next eight years of the divorce plus "a home and other property." But after she rejected the offer, Wayne became steadfast in his refusal to pay anything. "She is sure going away with less money if I can help it," he declared. He recalled that once, he was "stupidly in love" with his wife, but "I assure you, I am not in love with her now."[279]

Eventually the court declared the marriage a draw and granted each party a divorce under California's law of "humane principle" or double-decree. This little-used law was reserved for cases where cruelty charges fly fiercely between both parties with no sign of concession. Fortunately, he wasn't required to pay the $800 per month Esperanza requested to support his mother-in-law in Mexico City. Wayne had his day in court, successfully defended the allegations, and was now free to take a few well-deserved days of rest before he started *High and Mighty*. "It was an embarrassing ordeal to live through," he lamented. "I think I tried to live a dignified, respectable way. My life was almost ruined."[280]

Esperanza played the role of poor, innocent victim, and rationalized her situation. "It is a disadvantage being married to a film star," she lamented. "It is even worse when a thing like this happens. He is a hero—one of the most popular stars who ever lived. And it is difficult for anyone to believe that Duke could be anything but one hundred percent right. But it is Duke who wants the divorce. I have never wanted a divorce… I tried for a long time to keep our problems to myself …The only place I ever said things that might have hurt was in the courtroom. And I said what I had to say there because it is necessary to stand up for your rights… I washed dishes and did laundry when there was no maid. Anything he wanted was fine… Because I knew this and wanted it, I gave up my career. Now there is no career and no security."[281]

For a while, Chata had a relationship with actor Steven Cochran, but, after the "pepper left the romantic enchilada," she abandoned the relationship, left Hollywood with her $150,000 settlement, and returned to her mother in Mexico. Cochran was kind in his parting comments, though. "She's a wonderful person," he said gallantly. "She has the biggest heart in Hollywood." He must have not known her all that well. In June 1954, she tried to re-open her settlement and get a hefty increase in alimony, to no avail. Two months later, she signed a contract to appear in a bi-lingual movie made in Mexico City where she was billed as Esperanza *Wayne*. Less than one year later, after wasting her cash settlement, she died of a heart attack, surrounded by liquor bottles, broke and alone in a hotel.[282]

In business together only a year and a half, Wayne-Fellows prepared to produce its sixth feature film. Asked why he succeeded when so many other independents failed, Wayne confessed, "Because we have the best deal in town. I went into this thing with my eyes open. I spent a lot of years at Republic apprenticing for production. And I've profited by the mistakes that friends of mine–stars, directors and producers–have made with their own companies. Other companies have failed because they haven't been able to buck the big companies. They make deals that look swell on paper. But when they finish up, they're taken for all kinds of hidden charges. You can't make a go of it unless you can keep the companies from piling up the costs on you. That's what is great about our deal with Warners." *(Interesting that six months earlier, he had complained about Warner's lack of support for Island in the Sky.)* "We agree to bring in a picture for a certain cost, and they put up the money. They are limited to a certain figure for charges on distribution, advertising and prints. The deal has worked out well for both parties. Warner got back thirty-three and one third percent on its investment on our first picture, *Big Jim McLain*, which wasn't my idea of a very good movie. They also made money on *Plunder in the Sun*. *Island in the Sky* has done well for a Wayne picture, but it would have done better if they had sold it properly. Our latest one is *Hondo* and it appears set to make a fistful. I went down to Texas to see that it got a good sendoff."[283]

While at the film's premiere, to Wayne's frustration and Texas photographers' dissatisfaction, the first photos of Wayne and Pilar, his wife-to-be, were published. He had asked them not to photograph her during the festivities with the arrangement that no one else would get the first pictures of the couple until his divorce was final. Apparently, not everyone agreed.[284]

Ernest Gann's 1953 novel *The High and the Mighty* was based on an actual flight he made as a commercial pilot for American Airlines between Honolulu and Portland. Purchased by Wayne-Fellows on William Wellman's recommendation before the novel was even finished, the movie was to be filmed in 3-D, and it reunited the successful actor/director/writer trio from *Island in the Sky*. Gann received $55,000 plus 10% of the profits for the story and screenplay while Wellman got 30% to direct. Set on a commercial flight from Hawaii to San Francisco, the picture included a veritable rogue's gallery of characters: Lydia—who was as low as high society could get; Childs—a wealthy collector of other men's wives; May—strictly a night-time woman; Sally—who lived in a world of whistles; and Dan—who had used up his nine lives and was starting on ten! The story was told in a series of flashbacks and monologues, with characters developing and tension mounting as the plane began to experience mechanical problems. Although it earned mixed reviews, the public loved it, and it was in the top ten for 1954.[285]

Gann wrote the script with Wellman's input. The director commented, "If I bought a book or a story and I loved it, I wanted to do the book, but Ernie kept wanting to change it because he said, 'I can improve on it.' I said, 'Look, Ernie, let's just stick to the book. That's all I want,' and we almost had a fistfight about it on one occasion. 'Look,' I said, 'I am going to get hold of Gann who wrote this novel and tell him what this silly son of a bitch who is writing the script is trying to do.' It worked." After the screenplay was finished, Wellman shunted Gann aside.[286]

When Wellman tried to cast *The High and the Mighty*, several name actors turned him down because their parts were insignificant. One of the first ensemble productions, many of the roles were of equal small size. "I asked Joan Crawford, Ida Lupino, Barbara Stanwyck, Ginger Rogers, Dorothy McGuire," confessed Wellman. "Two of those I had helped in the past, too. They all turned me down. Why, some were insulted when I offered them the roles." Even Spencer Tracy turned down the opportunity after the deal was set because he needed a rest in Europe, or because he heard that Wellman was going to direct, or...take your pick. "We had lunch," recalled the director, "and shook on the deal and then (Tracy) changed his mind. Didn't think the role was good enough for him, I guess." Spence told Wellman the script was lousy.[287]

Duke's choice to play the part of co-pilot Dan Roman was Gary Cooper or Randolph Scott. After Tracy turned it down, Wayne called upon his old friend Henry Fonda, sent him the script, and asked him to play the lead. When Fonda turned it down, and Warner's threatened to pull out of the deal, Duke was forced once again to take the part himself. He had initially declined to play the role as he had too many commitments elsewhere. Wayne underestimated the impact this role would have on his career, though. He was a pilot in both *Island in the Sky* and the unreleased *Jet Pilot*, and wished there was more of a time interval between them and *High and Mighty*. "I think that part's good for the picture," he said wryly, "but I don't know what the hell it will do for me." Little did he realize. Wellman had a different opinion. "It turned out to be a great part for him," the director said, "and it would have been great for Tracy."[288]

Wellman then decided 'to hell with those other big stars.' "They think they know so much," decried Wellman. "I decided we could do without 'em. I decided to get competent, fine actors and actresses." Pedro Gonzales-Gonzales was picked up from the Groucho Marx show and put under contract by Wayne-Fellows. He played Manuel Aboitis (aka Gonzales), a radio operator on the ocean freighter who first contacted the disabled plane. He was the second actor (after Wayne) signed to the production. John Howard was hired to play Laraine Day's husband. Before World War II he worked almost constantly but volunteered to go into service and spent the entire war in the dangerous waters of the Mediterranean. Upon his return, he was forgotten by Hollywood and had to go to Broadway where he appeared in *Hazel Flagg* and was "re-discovered."[289]

Wellman had initially hired Walter Reed for the part Howard played, but Bob Fellows didn't like him. "Walter Reed. I don't want some damn stock boy doing this part," recalled Reed. "Wellman put me in a smaller part for two days... (he) took a liking to me. He went over to Wayne, and he said, 'Why did I let that ass, Bob Fellows, talk me into that? I like him better for Howard's part. I think Howard's stiff.'"[290]

Wayne-Fellows also signed former New York high fashion model Doe Avedon. Previously married to photographer Richard Avedon, she lost her second husband, actor Dan Matthews, in a car crash earlier that year. Tommy Irish, the singing boy in the Paper-Mate pen jingle, also attracted Wayne's attention. He put him in *Hondo* and liked him so much he signed him to a five-year contract and gave him a role in *The High and the Mighty*. J. Carrol Naish was considered for the role of Jose Locate, which John Qualen eventually played. Karen Sharpe, part-time bakery sales girl and ice skater, made her professional debut as Nell Buck, a bride on her honeymoon.[291]

Glamorous blonde Jan Sterling chose a path to becoming a dramatic actress by wiping off her eyebrows and makeup to look gruesome on the screen. "I figured if you're going to look bad," said the shapely actress, "you might as well look the worst. The cutter told me it was the most gruesome thing he's ever seen on the screen. And I have to do it in Technicolor yet, and Cinemascope so they can spread it all over the side of the theater." (*High and M*ighty was only the fourth movie made in both color and Cinemascope.) She played a high-living blonde who covered her dissipated face with heavy makeup. Near the end of the film, she decides to wipe it off and reveal her face for what it is. "I wiped off the lipstick and the yellowish makeup," she admitted. "In Cinemascope the natural skin looks pinkish so you'll see this through the yellow make-up and it looks awful. Then I wipe off the lips, two layers of false eyelashes and the eyebrows."[292]

"And it took daring guts for Jan Sterling to do that part," admired Wellman. "Stanwyck turned it down. She did a small role in *Executive Suite*. But it was the same Stanwyck stuff, always going to commit suicide and having hysterics. My picture would have been different for her." Ann Sheridan, Jack Carson, James Arness and Andy Devine were also considered and shortly before filming began, Lionel Barrymore and Keenan Wynn were replaced by Sidney Blackmer and Paul Fix.[293]

Wayne even gave the director's five-year-old son Michael a part in the film. He was paid $350 per week applied against his college education. Wellman only received $150 a week when he directed *Wings*! Wellman said tongue-in-cheek, "Mike is the greatest actor I have ever used in my whole life. I'd say, 'All right, Mike, you go to your spot now and you go to sleep.' He said, 'Do you want me to sleep or do you want me to play sleep?' He went to sleep, and I'd shoot all around him. At lunchtime we had to waken him. He had a lot of fun. I've often said that if some of the actors had a little more of Mike in them they'd be much better."[294]

Laraine Day, happily married to New York Giants manager Leo Durocher, had a month off after she returned from Japan and decided to "sandwich in a picture" before she moved into her new house. "I've never done anything like this before," she said of her role as an heiress with a nasty disposition. "If there'd been a nurse in this picture, I figure that's what I would have drawn. But that would have been no fun. This role is a challenge and Leo is very pleased I'm doing it."[295]

As for the role of pilot John Sullivan, Wayne offered it to his friend Bob Cummings at a movie premiere on nationwide TV. Cummings also happened to be a licensed pilot, which was what Wayne wanted. Unbeknownst to Wayne, Wellman had also offered the role to Robert Stack. Andrew McLaglen said, "I think Bob (Stack) really enjoyed doing the part which was a different role for Bob. That had an interesting sidelight to it. William A. Wellman was a terrific director—an icon of the Golden Age of films. He would wake me up at 5:30 a.m. and I really was his assistant director. Every day for two weeks, he received a telegram from Bob Stack's agent saying (Stack) would work for nothing if he were cast. We'd talked about casting everyone, including Ronald Reagan (as the pilot). Finally, Wellman said, 'Oh, what the hell. If he wants the part that badly, let's give it to him.' That's how he got the part."[296]

According to Stack, he attributed it to his performance in *War Paint*. "You have no idea of how much trouble I had in getting that part," he said. "The role was that of a tough cavalry sergeant...and the first person a producer thinks of is someone like Richard Widmark or Jim Whitmore. It's tough on an actor when he walks into a producer's office, well dressed and clean-shaven, and tries to persuade him he can play a hardboiled sergeant. I've pleaded with producers to at least give me a screen test and see what I can do. But it's usually the same old story, 'Come back when you get experience.' *War Paint* got me the part of a young pilot in *The High and the Mighty* which will be the real break of my career. Wellman finally saw me, probably to get rid of me." Wellman then acted out all the scenes the way he thought they should be played and the director asked Stack why he wanted the part. "I told him one reason was that I would be co-starring with John Wayne," said Stack, "and that meant everybody would be seeing the picture." Sounds logical. Wayne personally signed Stack for the role of Captain Sullivan. Years earlier, when Spencer Tracy heard that Stack, a former national champion skeet shooter, had given up athletics to become an actor, he commented sarcastically, "We've lost a good shot and probably gained a lousy actor." When Stack, resplendent in his captain's uniform, finally walked onto the set for the first time, Wayne wrinkled his forehead, shook Stack's hand, and said, "Mr. Cummings. I believe."[297]

"He did a smart thing," said Wayne about Wellman's direction. "The first thing he shot was with these two inexperienced kids. So everybody on the set was pullin' for them. Smart, huh? We all wanted them to look good. Without makin' any speeches. Or givin' us orders, Bill Wellman, with one scene, made us work together as a group, gave us this *esprit de corps.*" Wayne thoroughly enjoyed working on *The High and the Mighty* and expressed his pleasure in an interview he gave to the papers. "As far as I am concerned," he said, "it's a tossup between the horse and the airplane for the best means of getting real action into a picture. To me, motion pictures mean what it says—motion. That's why I like stories that take place out of doors and that offer a chance for movement. In actual flight, a passenger frequently loses all sense of motion, because of the height above the earth, but on film a plane flying against a background of mountains or cumulus clouds, can create terrific suspense. In *The High and the Mighty* for instance," he pointed out, "almost all of the action takes place in the air. As far as the scenes themselves are concerned, they could have taken place anywhere. But the exterior shots, cut in with the panic of the passengers and the frantic work of the crew, with the plane photographed against storm clouds, and slowly settling down to the Pacific, provide mounting excitement and suspense for the audience."[298]

Wellman was just as enthusiastic. "It has Eastman Color too. The works!" he exclaimed. "If we're gonna make 'em bad, we wanna make 'em bad with everything there is. We're shooting the book just as we did with *Island in the Sky.* To me Cinemascope is no mystery. I never did resort to many close-ups, anyway; and the tests we have made of all the characters in the plane are absolutely amazing. When I saw them, I threw out the notes I'd been making for three months and started over. We have a new four-inch lens which brings all the people closer than ever. We can't cut as often, but we don't have to. What I was most worried about was the things I want to see would be well lit; and Archie Stout, my cameraman, has licked that problem beautifully."[299]

However, the work for the actors wasn't as exciting. Sitting in your assigned seat in a mock airplane hour after hour, day after day, proved extremely tedious. The actors had to battle boredom, as well as the cold as the soundstage wasn't heated. Some did puzzles; others stayed in character, but everyone ended up getting sick. Before filming had even begun, tragedy struck the unfortunate set. William Word, a stunt pilot on *Island in the Sky,* was hired as a technical adviser for *High and Mighty.* Wayne wrote him a bonus check for $1,000 which was never cashed. On his last flight before reporting to the set, Word disappeared in the Pacific, never to be found. Wayne sent the grieving widow another check.[300]

The backgrounds for the epic were authentic as camera crews traveled to the Royal Hawaiian Hotel and Waikiki Beach in Honolulu, Fisherman's Wharf and the Coast Guard station in San Francisco and Oakland. One special crew flew five hundred miles to keep a date with a storm. Scenes with an electrical storm were needed, and, with the emphasis on realism, Wellman dispatched a camera crew when the weather bureau notified him of a particularly photogenic group of cumulonimbus storm clouds. And the results were worth it. Most interior scenes were filmed at the Goldwyn and Warner soundstages in Hollywood. They were even granted permission to film the flight of a guided missile at the U.S. Naval

Testing station at Inyokern. Bill Clothier asked how he could ever film a missile traveling over 1,000 miles per hour. A government official quipped, "You might fasten your camera to another rocket!"[301]

As producer, Wayne reverted to form, making suggestions, giving directions, telling other actors what to do. Wellman recalled, "I made three pictures with him…and in *The High and the Mighty* he suddenly wanted to become a director." In front of the entire crew, Wellman told him, "Look, you come back here behind the camera and do my job, and you're going to be just as ridiculous doing it as I would be out there with that screwy voice of yours and that fairy walk being Duke Wayne." Wayne offered no more interference. Wellman could be tough, too. According to Wayne, "He wasn't helping you one bit—you were to help him. He'd say, 'So and so, you come out that door.' You'd be sitting here. 'All right, we'll line this up for this shot.' Now maybe he would rehearse or maybe he wouldn't, but you said the lines as they were written. And he'd be saying, 'All right we're finished with that one over here.' That kind of enthusiasm—great for the crew. A little tough on the actors. You were through if you weren't the character."[302]

In an extensive interview before he started *Blood Alley*, Wellman was very open about working with Wayne: "I like working for Duke and I like to have him working for me. When we're on the set, I'm the boss, and he goes along with it. We fight plenty when we're making a picture, but never on the set in front of other people. We spend hours arguing about dialog and bits of dramatic business—and I listen to him, too. Duke's made a lot of pictures and knows what he can do. But when the cameras are rolling, he takes orders as meekly as a lamb. One thing Duke and I don't agree on is his ability to act. He tells people he's no actor and that he's limited. Well, he's all wet. I think he's a great actor and someday the right guy will get a hold of him and the two of 'em will turn out a job that'll be unbelievable. When it comes to the finer points of acting I've tricked him a couple of times into doing stuff he swore he couldn't do. But he's a hard man to fool because he's been in pictures so long. Duke works like a horse on a picture. When he isn't acting he strolls around fixing lights and scenery or helping out with a boom. If all actors were as hard-working as he is, I wouldn't have as many gray hairs as I do."[303]

When finally released, the reviews were extremely flattering. Accolades from the *Los Angeles Times* were typical: "…a great story of human reactions and emotions. It is an enormously vital picture, amazingly associated with life's panorama today, and thus filled with a rare kind of tingling excitement, especially for a modern air-minded public. The picture above everything else remarkably blends human, technical, dramatic and all other values so they constitute a finely perfected screen accomplishment." Columnist Philip Scheuer said, "…it bears this veteran's individual stamp, even to the Wellman touches of "hoke." But it is always lively hoke, and it adds up to the year's best "big" entertainment to date… let us say that is the kind of rattling good movie for which, when the industry was really rolling, we used to crowd the theaters automatically every couple of weeks." The *Los Angeles Examiner* wrote, "Wayne turns in the finest performance of his career. He has a scene telling the passengers of the trouble they're in for that has seldom been topped for emotional restraint," while *Cue* stated the movie was "a successful combination of tight script, masterful direction and production, skillful editing...plus well-nigh perfect performances by a distinguished multi-star cast."[304]

All the reviews weren't as positive, though. *Stars and Stripes* called the film "...nothing but a star-studded CinemaScopic blunder that could easily set commercial flying back a good twenty years. Everybody from the pilot on down is a potential straightjacket case with a shaky past, a shaky present, and a puzzling future... It's very doubtful if a bigger collection of trite, contrived and potentially neurotic characters have ever before been assembled in one movie. Adding another problem to the already endless string of soap opera trials and tribulations is like adding insult to injury, rubbing salt into the wounds and strapping Little Nell to the railroad tracks at the end of Chapter 6. If nothing else, the unemployment situation was aided considerably... just about every old face in Hollywood appears...at one time or another. We highly suggest: *The High and the Mighty Uncalled For*."[305]

Wayne-Fellows had contracted to make ten pictures in five years for Warner Bros. but, by the end of 1954, it had already completed nine. Moreover, Cinemascope proved extremely popular. Projected on a wide, curved screen, it used directional sound that followed action across the screen as did other formats such as Cinerama. By mid-1954, 4,800 theaters in the United States and 1,500 theaters abroad were already equipped with the appropriate equipment with over 10,000 theaters projected by the end of the year. A film such as *High and Mighty* was born for this type of projection.[306]

The next year, to no one's surprise, Dimitri Tiomkin, who worked on the film, won an Academy Award for Best Score for a comedy or dramatic picture. His acceptance speech was the talk of the town for years to come. Unintentionally humorous, he said, "Ladies and gentlemen, because I am working in this town for twenty-five years, I like to make some kind of appreciation to very important factor which makes me successful and adds to quality of this town. I like to thank Johannes Brahms, Johann Strauss, Richard Strauss, Richard Wagner... Beethoven, Rimsky-Korsakov..." Laughter drowned out the rest of the acceptance speech. In later years, Tiomkin confessed he wasn't trying to be funny, but rather he wanted to express homage to the heroes of the musical past. What greater recognition could a musician give than to the masters who developed the art of music and created the traditions that their successors follow? After the ceremony, Tiomkin visited his eighty-year-old grandmother. "Look what I won, Grandma," he announced proudly, holding out the statuette. "Oh," she said. "Where were you...Ocean Park?"[307]

As usual, Wayne didn't win an Oscar. Of course, he knew ahead of time that he wouldn't as he wasn't even nominated, although theater owners had voted him top box-office star of 1954. Having been among the "Golden Ten" for six straight years, he topped the list three times, a record only exceeded by Bing Crosby (five) and Shirley Temple (four). Nevertheless, Duke was dismayed that an Oscar had eluded him. "Sure, I'd like to win one," he rationalized. "The Academy Awards are important. They've help given size to our industry. They hand us back a little of the dignity I feel we deserve. As a group, motion picture people have proved pretty fair citizens." Yet he was annoyed he didn't receive the recognition he felt he deserved. "I wonder what they think acting is?" he questioned. "I've been earning a living as an actor for more than twenty-five years. I don't go in for chi-chi or the dirty shirt school of acting. Perhaps nobody but another actor knows how difficult it is to play a straight character part." In an interview with Zolotow, he admitted, "I never won an Academy Award. It's getting to be a Tinkers or Evans or Chance for me. And I'm always Tinkers. The toughest thing to do is nothing. Where you're standing by. And they see it's only as playing myself—not acting."[308]

Wayne so enjoyed working with Wellman and Gann he even considered a third "high-flying" film with the duo. Jimmy Angel, pilot and great friend of Wellman, planned an aerial survey trip of South America. He requested the author go along with him with the hope that Gann would write yet another novel about the problems of flying over the southern continent, where air transportation had meant so much for development.[309]

In January 1954, Fellows and Wayne dissolved their partnership. According to William Wellman, "Robert Fellows got involved with one of his secretaries and he told his wife Eleanor that he wanted to leave her." "Fellows was a friend of mine who came in and didn't quite do the job," said Wayne. "Besides, I didn't like the idea of my name being on it (the Wayne-Fellows company.) I wanted the company to have a proper name, and this was a good chance to have something other than 'A Wayne-Fellows Production' on the marquee, or 'A John Wayne Production.' I didn't care much if audiences knew whether I'd produced the film or not. The only thing that mattered to them was whether I was in it." An amiable separation, Fellows was not averse to dissolving the partnership. Wayne's obsession with his *Alamo* project, and the ever-increasing proposed budget, gave Fellows great concern. Even John Ford suggested this wasn't the right project to cut directorial teeth on, but Wayne was adamant. Fellows was reportedly against the idea and didn't want to be around when it materialized.[310]

Before the project could be accomplished, Wayne began prepping for his next feature, *The Conqueror*, a Chinese Western as he called it. An ill-conceived project written for Marlon Brando, Wayne portrayed Temujin, a young Mongol antagonist, complete with cheesy mustache and stilted dialogue. In an attempt to break out of the Western typecast mold, Wayne wanted to stretch his acting abilities. Second only to *Jet Pilot* in poor choices, the movie is astonishingly laughable with bad characters, bad acting, and bad script. Howard Hughes and RKO invested over $6 million in a film billed as the most expensive epic ever. Complete with dancing girls, battle scenes, Navajo Indians dressed as Tartar warriors, and authentic Mongol huts built from burlap and blankets, Wayne and love interest Susan Hayward struggled to find romance in the 12th century.[311]

Filmed in the remote Escalante Desert of southern Utah, the film company had to bulldoze an eight-mile road so equipment could be brought to the location. With temperatures exceeding 120°, the country was so wild, locations had to be scouted by air. (Texas, New Mexico, and Arizona were also scouted as possible locations.) The cameras were draped with wet towels to keep the color film from melting. When producer-director Dick Powell was asked if it was really so rugged, he replied, "Just to give you an idea, we'll probably have to take the oxen in by helicopter." They had a bit of trouble finding the correct locations, though. "The story takes place in the Gobi desert," Powell explained, "but it isn't the large desert most people think it is. Parts of it are quite green and there is much cattle raising. We asked the Air Force what part of the United States most resembles the Gobi desert. Through them we found a location in southern Utah."[312]

After initially being refused permission by husband Jess Barker to bring her twin nine-year-old sons on location, Susan Hayward, who was going through a divorce, brought them along with a nurse. And they all went fishing in a trout stream. Pilar showed up with Michael and Patrick. Twenty top magazine and newspaper syndicate writers flew into St. George to cover the filming. In fact, an army of 243 men and twenty women took over half the town's twenty-two motels, one of the movie houses, the school, and several gas stations. Stuntman Gil Perkins recalled, "Sometimes we'd be Cossacks, sometimes we'd be Mongols, and we'd have these fur jackets on, sometimes steel helmets, sometimes fur helmets, and hot flannel pants and high boots. We were working in Snow Canyon for about four or five days, and it was 128° in the shade. You'd come in at night, and you weren't fit to talk to until you'd had three gins and tonics. The only two locations I was glad to leave were *Virginia City* in 1939 and *The Conqueror* in 1954."[313]

Fellow actor Gregg Barton remembered, "One day, we were all going crazy. I think it was 120, 125° in a place facetiously called Snow Canyon...they used oxen to draw the carts, those big heavy things that looked like a house on wheels...the oxen would put their feet in that hot sand—you've seen a cat walk through water, how it shakes its feet—with their toes spread, the sand would burn them. Finally the humane society stepped in and when the animals weren't being used, they would have lean-tos made of canvas so the animals could keep cool."[314]

Although willing to fulfill his contract, Wayne was upset with the constant delays in kicking off the project. "There's no beef right now," he commented, regarding his relationship with Hughes, "but I'll admit I was pretty put out. I set aside three whole months for my commitment to RKO in (January) 1952, and another three months in 1953. Neither of those periods was used. I have also been sitting here and waiting for this picture to start since January 4 of this year. Now it won't finish until mid-summer. I could have been making two pictures in that time." Wayne vented his frustration in a letter to Hughes:

"My racket isn't writing letters any more than answering them promptly is yours…" he wrote sarcastically. "I must get some serious beefs off my chest… they are very simple. At the other studios and for my own company…I seldom get involved on a picture for more than eight or ten weeks over-all. I am paid top terms for that time. At RKO, I wind up giving six months of my time…and it's hectic, uncomfortable and unpleasant time…for a fraction of the compensation paid me by other studios. You can resolve this by paying me what the others do for the two pictures I owe you.

"It is very obvious to me why RKO has always gotten into trouble from the standpoint of time. No forethought has really ever been given by your studio executives to the proper selection for properties for me at the right time. Frankly…none of them have enough ability or experience to decide upon what represents real showmanship. Their efforts have been devoted to coercing me into pictures that are not ready…and not even suitable for me.

"Are you aware that I completed my services on *Flying Leathernecks* for RKO in 1951? Under my contract, I should have had my next suitable material ready for March 1952. Any stories I suggested were frowned on. I have had to hold months open. After five months, I took a job with another studio.

"For three years, I have had your two commitments hanging over my head. Both should have been finished a year ago.

"One after another, I have lost pictures because of the great length of time you tie me up… I am speaking of outstanding quality pictures…the very essence and lifeblood of an actor's existence.

"I guess I've run out of words concerning the situation, but certainly not of feeling."[315]

Due to lost income, Wayne was forced to borrow $100,000 from Hughes to pay his income tax and expense obligations. "When the picture is over," Wayne rationalized, "we can see how much I have lost and we can get together and make a settlement. But they didn't give it to me free, as a bonus or anything. I borrowed it. And I'll have to pay it back, half this year and half next." Wayne was glad that the movie would eventually be finished. "I owe RKO only one more picture," he said as he breathed a sigh of relief. "Then I'm completely free to work for my own company. No, I don't have ulcers now. I don't have so much frustration. No one tells me what to do or what to say. I'm not so much of a pawn in the hands of a guy who doesn't know my limits." (One reason for the delay was indecision regarding whether or not to film in Cinemascope.)[316]

Pedro Armendariz, who played Wayne's "blood brother" Jamuga, suffered an injury on the set when thrown over a horse's head while leading another. Believed to be a broken back, it proved only to be a severe bruise though he sustained bad cuts, several loosened teeth, and a gash that required twelve stitches. Armendariz took absolutely no responsibility for the accident. "Horse lovers may hate me," he confessed, "but I don't think the horse is a very smart animal. In Mexico we have a saying, 'The horse is very fast at learning the wrong things; the right things take a very long time.'"[317]

The *Conqueror* did afford Wayne one big thrill: he played a scene with his nineteen-year-old son Mike, who played a Mongol who fell asleep on guard duty. He was dragged in before Khan, who thundered, "Hang him!" "He looked more scared of me than he ever did in real life," laughed Wayne. "My kids may become actors in spite of themselves." Michael had a slightly different memory of the experience. "I made my acting debut on the film," he recalled, "in the summer, wearing a suit of armor, and almost burned up...began and ended my acting career."[318]

Wearing fur caps, leather jackets, short quilted coats, leather boots, and brocaded coats, the cast not only endured excruciating temperatures, it also dealt with dirt and dust. Ah, yes. The dirt. Dirt in their clothes, in their mouths, up their noses, in their ears, in their food...in their *lungs*. It was everywhere. Director Powell often wore a surgical mask on set due to severe dust storms. Pedro Armendariz Jr. remembered his father's role as a hard-riding Mongol soldier: "He did take an awful lot of falls and was constantly having to be hosed down due to the heavy dust." Large fans blew the dust during filming to give scenes a special realism. The problem was that the dirt and dust were *radioactive!* Filmed near nuclear testing grounds, the entire region was contaminated with fallout. To make matters worse, more than sixty tons of the radioactive dirt was shipped to soundstages in Hollywood for retakes. Scores of cast and crewmembers developed various forms of cancer in the decades following filming, and it was alleged the radioactive fallout caused the abnormally high incident rate.[319]

On May 19, 1953, the Atomic Energy Commission (AEC) set off a thirty-two-kiloton device atop a tower at the Nevada Nuclear Test site in Yucca Flats. The code name was *Harry*; people downwind now bitterly remember it as *"dirty" Harry*. Though 145 miles away from populated areas, prevailing winds blew the radioactive fallout directly over Cedar City and St. George where filming took place two years later. The cities had been exposed to over 1,200 times the permissible fallout rate and stayed that way for two weeks. Local prospectors reported finding evidence of caches of uranium with Geiger counters but couldn't find the source. Ranchers suffered numerous mysterious, unexplainable livestock deaths. According to some testimony, Snow Canyon, where much of the movie was filmed, glowed red at night from radioactivity. AEC monitors picked up readings of 6,000 mill roentgens. Residents were warned to stay indoors, cars were washed down in an attempt at decontamination, and locals noted a metallic taste in the air. In La Verkin, twenty miles northeast of St. George, goats turned blue after clouds of fallout wafted through their grazing area.[320]

Even before filming began, Powell, Hughes, and others were well aware of possible safety concerns. They questioned the appropriate government departments and were assured their concerns were unfounded. Radiation levels were within acceptable ranges. Yet official minutes of a secret meeting at Los Alamos, New Mexico, on August 1, 1950, acknowledged, "the probability that people will receive perhaps a little more radiation (from the explosions) than medical authorities say is absolutely safe." In 1979, the Justice Department stated in answer to interrogations and admissions filed in U. S. District Court, "The public was warned during the 1950s that there was some risk from exposure to radioactive fallout, and some claims were paid." There was even a publicity photo of Wayne walking around the set with a Geiger counter, but not everyone was aware of the concern. Asked about the danger of working on that movie, stuntman Jack Williams said, "If they gave you a trillion dollars, you wouldn't (have) been around. Nobody would have (been) involved in that stuff (had we known). For six weeks, where the ambient temperature was 120, those sand dunes were 140 (degrees) and absolutely alive with that radioactive ash with wind machines blowing it at you." Regrettably, Williams, who had undergone thirty-five radiation treatments and the removal of 100 percent of his right vocal cord and a third of his left, died of cancer in 2007.[321]

Those charges infuriated citizens who produced numerous proclamations distributed by the federal government throughout the 1950s claiming the radioactive fallout posed no danger. One widely posted statement, dated January 1951 and signed by AEC project manager Ralph P. Johnson, read: "Health and safety authorities have determined that no danger from or as a result of AEC activities may be expected... All necessary precautions, including radiological surveys and patrolling the surrounding territory, will be undertaken to insure that safety conditions are maintained." In 1957, the AEC published a booklet assuring readers, "all such findings have confirmed that Nevada test fallout has not caused illness or injured the health of anyone living near the test site."[322]

In 1979, three London newspapers including *The Sun* and *The Daily Express*, published articles that indicated individuals associated with the movie were dying of cancer at an abnormal rate and suggested that several of the actors' deaths may be related to fallout from an atom bomb exploded in 1953. In 1964, Armendariz committed suicide at the UCLA Medical Center after learning he had kidney cancer and terminal cancer of the lymphatic system. Six months earlier, Powell had died of lymph cancer when it spread to his lungs. Agnes Moorehead, who played Hunlun, Tenujin's mother, died of uterine cancer in 1974, and Hayward succumbed to skin, breast, and uterine cancer in 1975. Wayne died of lung, stomach, and throat cancer four years later. Admittedly heavy smokers, nevertheless, the deaths were disturbing. A 1980 report in *People* magazine revealed ninety-one crew members had contracted some form of cancer out of a total crew complement of 220, an astonishing 41 percent! Even Chivwit Indians, who portrayed Mongol and Tartar horsemen, were not immune. What was even more startling was that no bombs were exploded in Nevada the year the movie was filmed. The cast and crew were exposed to residual radioactivity left by atomic tests in previous years. "With these numbers, this case could qualify as an epidemic," remarked University of Utah Radiological Health director Dr. Robert C. Pendleton. What in the world were Hughes and Powell thinking when they decided to film in such a hostile environment? "I knew the picture was a bomb," recalled Lyn Unkefer, the film's publicist, "but I don't think it was that kind of a bomb."[323]

An absolute bomb, pardon the pun. The *New York Times* review summed it up nicely. "The forward to *The Conqueror*," it stated, "which invaded the Criterion yesterday, somewhat apologetically states that this is fiction based on fact. The facts appeared to have been lost in a Technicolor cloud of charging horsemen, childish dialogue and rudimentary romance—'Dance for me, Tatar woman!'" Wayne concurred. "*The Conqueror* is one of the worst films I ever made," he reflected, "and it was a massive success. I think it was only because epic films were in vogue at the time, and although I thought the film was a sort of Mongolian Western, it was a historical epic, and I guess people liked those films. I began to wonder if they'd like Westerns anymore."[324]

On June 1, 1954, Wayne-Fellows changed its title to Batjac Productions, Inc., a name already being used with other aspects of the partnership. Originally a limited operation, the title was changed because it was deemed unsatisfactory to have such a personalized name for an operation, which had grown beyond its initial conception. Wayne recalled, "I got Batjac out of a picture I'd done, *Wake of the Red Witch*, in which there was a big Dutch company called Batjak. I told my partner and he thought it was a good idea, so we went ahead and changed the spelling." According to producer Andrew Fenady, "Wayne said, 'You know what? How about we call it Batjack? I always liked to say Batjack.' So Duke said to Michael, 'Go out and have some stationary made.' It came back and found they had spelled it *Batjac*. They left out the *k*. So Duke said, 'How much will it cost to have that done over?' and they said, 'Well, it will cost $700.' and he said, 'Ta hell with it. Leave it Batjac.'" Others believed Michael suggested the name. Mary St. John recalled a legal secretary questioned the spelling of Batjack on the incorporation documents and called Fellows for confirmation. "Was a *c* missing from the title of the company?" she inquired. Fellows replied, "No c." But she thought he meant, "No, c." So she typed it Batjac. When the documents came back and everyone noticed the error, Wayne responded, "I like it better with a *k*, but it's no big deal. Leave it alone." Regardless, somewhere between the stationary and the incorporation documents, the *k* vanished.[325]

Wayne explained Batjac was originally formed with the idea it would be a production unit which would function for independent producers, supplying them with all the production personnel necessary to make a picture.[326]

Once the company became successful, it was inundated with calls from writers and agents, all trying to pitch scripts for John Wayne films. Bob Fellows would talk with everyone—at least listen to their pitch—and if interested, run it past Wayne. "But if Wayne says 'no soap,'" said Fellows, "I don't argue with him. He knows too well. We don't have any rules for picking stories. You use your accumulated experiences. Something told Wayne and me that *Island in the Sky* was right. The same goes for *Hondo* and *The High and the Mighty*. The last two will make an awful lot of money."[327]

Even after two years, the Wayne-Yates feud showed no sign of letting up. Wayne still couldn't get rights to his Alamo script. When he learned that Yates was rushing to make an Alamo film of his own (*The Last Command*), Wayne was furious. "*The Alamo* was my idea. I invested $10,000 of my own money in it plus two or three years of my own time," he exclaimed. "Then Yates failed me once we were ready to start production. If we don't come to terms, I'll never do another picture for him." They didn't and he didn't. Initially called *The Unconquered Territory*, Yates's film was scheduled to go before cameras the last of February in Brackettville and Del Rio, Texas, according to Louella Parsons. Director Frank Lloyd was not enamored with the proposed name or *Texas Legionaires* either, and decided to call it *Men of Texas*. Also referred to as *San Antonio de Bexar*, *Men who Dared*, *Texas*, and *Alamo*, the project included Richard Carlson as Travis, Sterling Hayden as Bowie, Arthur Hunnicut as Crockett, with Ernest Borgnine, J. Carrol Naish, and Anna Maria Alberghetti.[328]

On November 1, 1954, Wayne married his third wife, Pilar Palette, during a sunset ceremony in Kailua, Hawaii, at the former home of King Kamehameha III. One hundred fifty people attended, including members of the cast and crew of the movie *The Sea Chase*, on which Wayne had been working. Overlooking Keakoa Bay, the bride wore a pink organdy cocktail dress and was given in marriage by John Farrow. Mary St. John served as matron of honor while Francis Brown, a wealthy friend of Duke's from Pebble Beach, served as best man. District Magistrate Norman Olds flew from Hilo to perform the ceremony. Olds brought along license clerk Francis Weber to fill out the legal forms and waive the usual three-day waiting period, making it possible for the couple to be married immediately after signing the license application. Duke had been released from a hospital in Honolulu the previous week after treatment for an ear condition. "For four weeks I have been unable to clamp my jaw shut," he lamented. "I've been eating milk and eggs and other soft foods. I haven't had a steak in weeks. That's hell for a guy that likes meat three meals a day." Doctors took three different cultures of the ear infection but were unable to find an antibiotic to cure it. He spent agonizing days and nights in Hawaii with only an occasional painkiller to give him rest. The infection was dangerously close to his facial muscles, and he lived in fear that his career as an actor might be in jeopardy. Wayne even felt too miserable to have a drink. That's how bad it was.[329]

Duke married Pilar just a few hours after his divorce from Chata became final. As she didn't want to wait until his divorce was official, Pilar pressed him for a "Mexicanning" but Duke refused to break his promise to the California courts not to marry before he was legally able to do so. In order to throw off the press, Wayne denied he would be married in the islands. "Listen, honey," he told a reporter. "I've had a nerve-shattering earache for a month. I'm in agony. They can't do anything for it in the hospitals here. It's so bad I probably wouldn't be able to hear a judge asking me to repeat 'I do.' We should wind up *The Sea Chase* here in four days, then home and marriage later." He told another, " ...you may be sure that I am going to sign the (divorce) papers and have that final decree picked up the minute I can... I've been trying to settle down for the last couple of years. Troubles? I've had enough of those." Their vows only took ninety seconds to repeat and didn't include the word *obey*. "None of the others ever obeyed me anyway," Wayne laughed. Pilar had secured an annulment from former husband Richard Weldy just two days earlier.[330]

Pilar was Wayne's third Latina wife, not that there was anything wrong with that. "I certainly don't have anything against American women," he confessed. "As a matter of fact, my wives have been as much American as they have been Latin. None of them speaks with an accent. I've never been conscious of going for a particular type. They say a man follows a pattern, but I haven't been aware of it myself. Each of the women I married has been entirely different. My first wife had a French and Spanish mother and father, but she was brought up in Texas. Esperanza spent a lot of time in this country, not here, but in Florida and elsewhere. And Pilar has been here a great deal and speaks English perfectly." When asked why he always married Latinas, Wayne laughed, "Some men collect stamps, I happened to like Latins. I was a married man at breakfast, single at lunch, and married again by dinner!" No sense wasting any time.[331]

Nineteen fifty-four proved to be a productive year for Wayne; he finished *The High and the Mighty* in January, filmed *The Conqueror* in the spring and summer, renamed Wayne-Fellows as Batjac, filmed The *Sea Chase* in the fall, and wrapped up the year by marrying Pilar. But the best was yet to come. Nineteen fifty-five would show the world what a fine actor Wayne truly was.

# CHAPTER EIGHT
# "LET'S GO HOME, DEBBIE."

*"What makes a man to wander? What makes a man to roam? What makes a man leave bed and board and turn his back on home? Ride away, ride away, ride away."* The Searchers title song.[332]

THE NEW YEAR PROVED EXCITING FOR WAYNE AND HIS FILM COMPANY. IN EARLY January, Batjac, in association with Warner Bros., signed Robert Mitchum to appear in *Blood Alley*. (Under contract to RKO, Mitchum had previously worked for Wayne in *Track of the Cat*.) Lamentably, this arrangement didn't last long as Wayne cut his honeymoon short and took over the role after he relieved the star because of reports of Mitchum's disagreements with director William Wellman. (Wayne initially wanted the part for himself but had to bow out due the constant delays with *The Conqueror*.) Wellman had asked Mitchum to go to San Francisco to shoot preproduction footage. There, in a hotel room right above the director, Mitchum and a friend had a few drinks and the racket kept Wellman awake all night. According to witness Andrew McLaglen, assistant director on the movie, a conversation between production manager Nate Edwards, transportation coordinator George Coleman, and Mitchum escalated into an argument the next day. Mitchum grabbed Coleman, spun him around, and yelled, "Don't walk away from me like that! I'm a partner in this picture. Where do you get off acting like that?" Wellman gave Wayne an ultimatum: either Mitchum or the director but one way or another, someone would have to go. Wayne had also heard Mitchum pushed the unit's transportation manager into the water. According to McLaglen, "…it never happened. I was standing right next to them." When

121

neither man reacted, Mitchum turned to Wellman and "...said some things that he shouldn't have said...one thing led to another," and Mitchum was gone. Mitchum's dismissal was announced by Warner Bros. at the film's location site near San Rafael, California, and called it "action detrimental to the making of the film."[333]

The participants shrugged off the argument as just horseplay. According to Mitchum, a ferry boat used in the film was lost in heavy fog off Angel Island. After waiting several hours, Mitchum suggested taking a bus into San Francisco, so some workers could "go and buy shaving blades and other little things they needed." Coleman declined because it would cost $25, so Mitchum volunteered to pay the cost. "He objected," explained Mitchum. "Said it would require an additional driver and the money to do this. I think he was wrong. I have principles. A man can talk about his principles. Okay. But when he is put to the test, he should live up to them." As the party boarded a launch (via a gangplank) for the trip to shore, Mitchum, a healthy 215-pounder, began bouncing on the plank, causing Coleman to teeter. Witnesses said Mitchum then ran back and shoved Coleman into the bay. Both parties denied the shove. Coleman said, "Nobody shoved me," while Mitchum's denial was less specific. "Me? Push anybody? Who told you that?" Bob Fellows flew in the next day after a letter from Wellman cited "creating disagreements between the production staff" and requested a "disciplinary action." After a forty-five-minute closed-door meeting, Mitchum refused to apologize and was fired by Fellows.[334]

It was later suggested Wellman drove Mitchum to quit. The TV show *This is Your Life* once profiled Wellman and asked the director for a list of individuals to interview. Wellman included Mitchum whom he had directed in the 1946 movie *The Story of GI Joe*. The actor refused and said he didn't have time to chat with the producers. When Wellman found out, he was livid, and, when the two worked together on *Blood Alley*, he got his revenge by badgering Mitchum around the clock.[335]

Once Mitchum was dismissed, the production company was forced to find a replacement. Humphrey Bogart reluctantly turned down an offer due to "previous film commitments" (*The Left Hand of God*). It would have been a dream pairing as his wife Lauren Bacall was already in the film. Others mentioned for the part were Wayne's first choice, William Holden, as well as Gregory Peck, Gary Cooper, Alan Ladd, Fred MacMurray, Kirk Douglas, and Robert Ryan before Duke decided to take it. According to Wayne, he was forced to fill the role when it became apparent no other actor had the physical requirements the role demanded. He had to also temporarily assume the role of director when Wellman came down with a case of influenza. "I'm just about the only producer who would trust me with a directing job," Wayne laughed. John Ford was a little more positive about Duke's abilities, however. "He'll make a top director.

Duke knows immediately what's wrong with a script—but more important, how to fix it."[336]

Now that Wayne was officially in the movie, he became apprehensive about a fight scene with Mike Mazurki. Years earlier, both actors had appeared in *Dakota*, where Wayne was supposed to pull Mazurki's hat over his head and throw a haymaker, thus felling him. Unfortunately, Wayne didn't pull his punch. "You know," he confessed, "I've apparently slugged hundreds of villains before and since, but never actually hit one of them." Mike said there were no hard feelings, but Wayne was still a little leery. Later during filming, he suffered a severe muscle strain when he slipped while walking the gangplank between a ferry boat and dock and injured his back. Shades of Mitchum. Talk about bad luck. The location was sarcastically called *Pneumonia Alley* and not only was everybody on the set sick, they also had the worst weather known there in fifty-six years. Wayne bailed out five members of the trouble-plagued company after they were arrested following a barroom brawl. The pugilists were given thirty-day suspended sentences, two-year probations and fines for interfering with an officer in the performance of his duties. The police found a local resident unconscious in a corridor outside a hotel bar.[337]

Of course, it wasn't all aches and pains, either. Wellman ordered the set closed to all women when Wayne pulled a classic switch and did a beefcake bathing scene. "You always notice they close the set when the beautiful girls are doing the bathing scenes," Wellman rationalized, tongue-in-cheek, "and I just thought it was high time someone returned the dirty trick." Bacall didn't seem to mind though: "I tell you, on Wayne it looks better."[338]

*Blood Alley* was filmed in Northern California, including China camp, located five miles north of San Rafael and thirty miles north of San Francisco. Its buildings offered authentic Chinese flavor, a colony of Chinese lived there, and the area was hailed as one of the richest shrimp beds in the world. "When I flew up to look it over, I was sold instantaneously," Wellman said. "The coast could have been any of a thousand spots in China. And all we had to do at China camp was to paint a few Chinese slogans on the shacks, and add a touch here and there—and we were in business. The locations we have chosen seem to have everything. The story concerns 180 villagers, who tire of Communism, steal a ferry boat and make a break to Hong Kong and freedom. Wayne is the interned American sea captain, who pilots them to liberty."[339]

A fervent anti-Communist, Wellman wasn't afraid to redo a scene if required. In one instance, a squad of communist soldiers dashed menacingly across the screen, hot on the trail of Wayne and Bacall. "No good," said Wellman. "It looked swell to me," said the cameraman. "Not to me," responded the director. "One Communist was smiling. There will be no smiling Communist in any movie I direct." If Wellman didn't have bad luck he wouldn't have any luck at all. He struggled with laryngitis over a public-address system as he directed the deployment of 130 coolies to precise positions in a Great Wall sequence in which they were to climb down. It took over two hours to set up the scene by which time his voice was almost gone. "Shoot!" he croaked. Down marched the coolies as the cameras rolled. Unfortunately, an unperturbed stranger, oblivious to his surroundings, aimlessly wandered directly toward the camera and ruined the take. Wellman was figuratively and literally speechless.[340]

Immediately after he finished *Alley*, Wayne met with Warner Bros. to discuss a new arrangement. As a result, he had to delay a vacation to Mexico with his new wife. Wayne admitted the double job of acting and handling the many affairs of Batjac was a heavy load. He wanted to make fewer pictures and shed some responsibility. Like that was going to happen. "We plan to release other independent pictures besides Wayne-Fellows Productions," explained Wayne, "so it's very likely that my partner in Wayne-Fellows Company, Bob Fellows, will head our new releasing service. The Wayne-Fellows Company made five million dollars on one picture last year and seven million on another. Not bad when you think two of our pictures are in the top ten." Not bad indeed![341]

While Wayne was shooting his movie, John Ford gave the first inkling of a project he had in mind. Just back from Ireland after a six-week rest, he was anxious to direct a film based on a new Alan Le May novel. *The Searchers* was the title of a book that followed a serial version in the November and December 1954 issues of the *Saturday Evening Post* called *The Avenging Texans*. According to Ford's daughter Barbara, "Daddy was trying to get Warner's to buy it and they goofed around and goofed around so... (C.V.) Sonny Whitney hears about it, reads the book, calls up Daddy and says, 'What can I do?'" Ford told him to purchase the rights so Whitney, after getting some cash, bought the rights even though someone else was already negotiating for them. Whitney announced *The Searchers* would be the first in a series of movies called *The American Series*, which would tell the history of the United States. Initially, he wanted to launch the series with a Civil War project called *The Valiant Virginians*, but placed it on hold as he felt a Western would be a bigger draw.[342]

Behind the scenes, Wayne also applied pressure on Warner's to close the deal. "Jack Warner was enthusiastic about a John Ford-John Wayne Western," said Wayne, "but when Ford told him it would cost nearly $4 million to make, Warner nearly burst a blood vessel and wanted to back out. Pappy was not in the best of health back then. He'd had something of a breakdown while making *Mister Roberts* and he really wasn't up to bartering with Jack Warner. So I wrote to Warner and said that if he didn't agree to Ford's terms, I'd terminate my relationship with Warner Bros. So Jack Warner agreed. Anyway, I was pretty damn mad with the way Warner had treated Pappy, so I decided I'd end my relationship with Warner Bros. anyway. After *The Searchers*, it was a long time before I went to work at that studio again."[343]

Frank Nugent, Ford's son-in-law, developed the screenplay. Although the film wasn't scheduled until that summer, Ford hoped that Wayne, as usual, might be available. Ford told Nugent to write parts in it for Dobe Carey and Ken Curtis, but as he didn't like Curtis, "Don't make it too good." Interesting, considering Curtis had married Barbara Ford just three years earlier. "We are working on the script of *The Searchers*," Ford wrote Michael Killanin. "It is a tough, arduous job as I want it to be good. I've been longing to do a Western for quite some time. It's good for my health, spirit, and morale and also good for the physical health of my numerous Feeney Peasantry, by whom I am surrounded." By March, Ford and C.V. Whitney were seeking locations in Colorado and were still trying to pry Wayne loose from his Batjac commitments. Upon completion of *Blood Alley*, Wayne flew to Texas for a quick appearance with Bob O'Donnell and then traveled to New York for two days of business conferences. "Maybe," confessed Duke, "Pilar and I will be able to get to Mexico before I start *The Searchers* for John Ford. For the time being, I think I had better attend to business." Finally, on April 26, it was announced that Wayne would star and the film would go before the cameras in June. Pat Ford, the project's associate producer, began to film early sequences in March in the stark white snow of Gunnison, Colorado. Stuntmen Terry Wilson and Chuck Hayward respectively doubled Wayne and Jeffrey Hunter.[344]

Monument Valley beckoned Wayne and Ford once again, like a captivating siren. Unforgiving but full of promise. Sunny, dusty, hot, dry. They say it's not the heat, it's the humidity. But when it's 120° in the shade, it's hot. You leave the pavement a few miles north of Tuba, Arizona. Then it's nothing but dirt and gravel until you reach Blanding, Utah, 167 miles later. To call it a road is an insult to roads. Tonalea, Elephant's Feet, Cow Springs, Calamity Flats, through Marsh Pass into Kayenta and then north. Sandy in spots, easy unless it's raining. Then watch out. The Indian Service keeps a road grader constantly at work. Spires, buttes, monuments. Colors that change with the sun, the seasons, the clouds. Red cliffs, sparse brush. Goats, sheep, horses, silhouetted against the sky. Supplies had to be hauled in. This wasn't *like* the old west, it *was* the Old West. If you're a star, you stay at Goulding's Lodge. Modern conveniences with heat and refrigeration. Otherwise, you're out of luck. Pitch a tent on the valley floor and hope the winds are forgiving.

"In the early days of the new West," wrote *The Laredo Times*, "this location was one of the most picturesque and one of the most hazardous in the long trek from the Mississippi Valley to the California gold mines and the scene of the last Indian uprising, several thousand feet above sea-level. The Monument Valley desert with its sharp natural obelisks of red and orange granite and sandstone, its many miles of uninhabited, uncultivated alkali-whitened sand and clay, is extremely hot in daylight and usually cold at night."[345]

Goulding's Trading Post sat at the base of Big Rock Door Mesa, a few hundred yards from the entrance to Rock Door Canyon. (The Mesa had been given that name by the Navajos because of a narrow defile that went south between Tsay-Kizzi Mesa and Old Baldy Mesa, into the Navajo Reservation just two miles away. A trail through the canyon provided the Indians with convenient entrance and exit.) Constructed in 1927, the two-story trading post was built with large sandstone blocks, supplies stored on the first floor and living quarters on the second. A one-room stone cabin was constructed the same year and provided extra space for guests. A second cottage was added several years later, followed by a dining room and kitchen. John Ford and the main actors were housed in the lodge while the remaining cast and crew roughed it in tents on the valley floor. Ford always stayed in the last room at the end of the building, farthest away from the Trading Post. "By then, we knew how Ford wanted his room," declared Mike Goulding. "He wanted one double bed in his quarters, and he liked to have a refrigerator with different kind of juices." Everyone, though, had the same view of this magnificent vista: Train Mesa, Eagle Mesa, Brigham's Tomb, King on his Throne, Bear and Rabbit, Castle Butte, Big Chief, Sentinel Mesa, and Mitchell Mesa.[346]

The Valley was Ford's and Ford's alone. He may not have discovered it or been the first to film there, but it was his nonetheless. Monument Valley not only was virtually unspoiled land for Westerns when Ford first went there to shoot, enabling him to make the landscape seem his own, but it largely remained so during Ford's lifetime; with occasional exceptions, other filmmakers tended to avoid the place out of deference to the master.[347]

When a *Los Angeles Examiner* reporter asked him to compare the limitations of the stage versus an outdoor film, Ford replied, "I like outdoor dramas best. On the stage, there is a voice to carry the large share of the drama. In pictures, there is no opportunity for the tonal graduations that convey such meaning on the stage. The compensating thrill comes in what the stage lacks–the 'long shots' that bring in a herd of cattle, massive mountain peaks, a chain of waterfalls, or a huge mob of men and women." The reporter suggested that Ford believed a successful motion picture capitalized on the limitations of the stage. The reply sounded like "Exactly," but perhaps it was "Bologna."

When Ford filmed *The Searchers*, he admitted he tried to photograph it as Charles Russell had sketched and painted. Ford felt that... "the thing most accurately portrayed in the Western is the land. I think you can say that the real star of my westerns has always been the land. I have always taken pride in the photography of my films, and the photography of Westerns in general has often been outstanding, yet rarely draws credit. It is as if the visual effect itself was not important, which would make no sense at all. (Monument Valley) has rivers, mountains, plains, and desert, everything the land can offer. I feel at peace there. I have been all over the world, but I consider this the most complete, beautiful, and peaceful place on earth."[348]

A half million dollars were spent just to travel to the location. Two hundred and sixty miles of roads were constructed or improved in the Valley. Nearly three hundred Navajos were employed as actors, extras, and laborers including Away Luna, Billy Yellow, Bob Many Mules, Percy Shooting Star, Pete Grey Eyes, and Smile White Sheep. Pat Ford admitted that his father was a perfectionist. "He wouldn't get a Hollywood extra if he could do otherwise," said Pat. "He wouldn't use a Hollywood Indian when there was still a real Indian alive. His term was 'I want stone-age faces.' I want faces of men and woman who have seen people die of snake bite, whose women and babies die in childbirth, and whose men die from being bucked off horses, just the life of primitive people."[349]

The trading post airstrip buzzed with planes moving personnel and film to and from the location. Wayne, Ford and others arrived in Flagstaff via the Santa Fe Chief before heading out to the set. Many members of the crew had arrived earlier but due to heavy rains, were advised to wait a day or so until the roads dried out. And as usual, whenever Ford filmed at Monument Valley, Navajo medicine man Hosteen Tso served as professional weatherman. While on the set of *Stagecoach*, Goulding claimed the medicine man could create any type weather Ford required. "I've got an old Indian," said Harry, "...and when it gets too dry out there, he makes it rain; he has some ceremonies. I just wouldn't worry about the weather. You let me know what you want about four o'clock in the evening, and he'll fix you up with the weather the next day. If he's not right there, he can do it from quite a ways off even. We can get a smoke signal off to the medicine man if you let me know what you might want with the weather." Ford accepted the challenge and asked for a few theatrical clouds hanging around in the sky. Goulding said, "I can't send that to him. I don't know what a theatrical cloud is." "Just pretty, fluffy clouds," replied Ford. Sure enough, the next day the clouds were there. Ford was convinced, and Tso was on the payroll.[350]

Known as "Old Fat" to the crew, the medicine man had a large belly and wore a khaki shirt, work pants, and a hat with a feather in it. He loved whiskey, and Pappy used him on every movie filmed in the Valley. According to Dobe Carey, the day after Ford shot the fantastic, famous lightning scene in the rain in *Yellow Ribbon*, "they went to Old Fat and asked him what the weather was going to be like the next day. After ten years of relying on his predictions, (the medicine man) said, 'I don't know.' Ford said, 'What do you mean you don't know what the weather is going to be like, you are a medicine man.' Fat replied, 'The radio's broke.'"[351]

The role of Rev. Captain Samuel Johnston Clayton was played by stock player Ward Bond. The publicity mill was in high gear when it announced seventeen-year-old Natalie Wood would be Wayne's leading lady, but there would be no romance between them in the picture. "At my age and hers," Wayne laughed. Natalie's five-year-old sister Lana played Natalie as a young child. "It's the first time both of us had one part," Lana said proudly. Natalie had started her film career at the tender age of four. "I guess I was lucky," she confessed. "I was always skinny when I was young. So when I was eleven, I could play a nine-year-old. When I was thirteen, I could seem eleven. When I got to be a teen-age type, I was in a TV series, *Pride of the Family*. The show was pretty bad but it kept me busy for a year. By the time it was over, I was ready for leading roles." Warner Bros. recognized her talent and placed her in *Rebel Without a Cause*. Once completed, she immediately started on *The Searchers*.[352]

Pilar flew out to visit Duke in Monument Valley. With his family there, Wayne was proud that son Pat had a role in the film. "And acting comes easy to him," said Duke. "Shucks, he had a scene in *The Searchers* that was a terror. He had to come bursting in and tell me and Ward Bond the whole story. We interrupted him with questions but he kept going. Ford let it run and the kid did the scene perfectly." Just sixteen, Pat had already appeared in three Ford films: *The Quiet Man*, *The Long Gray Line*, and *Mister Roberts*. Wayne offered pretty simple advice for his son. "...know (your) lines, get to the set on time and take direction." Duke explained the advice he gave his son: "He's got the teen-age gals dropping like flies since *Mr. Roberts*. He can be a big star if he wants it. But I still don't know whether he wants it. But it would be so easy for him if he does want to act. You should see the fan mail he's getting already. Stacks of it! Pat was up for Gary Cooper's son in William Wyler's *Friendly Persuasion* (a role Anthony Perkins eventually played.) It was a fine role but I didn't want him to take it. He would have had to miss the football season at Loyola High as he did last year. I think it's more important for him to play ball. If he's going to be an actor, it's important for him to learn athletics. By playing a good American game like football, he'll learn how to move, how to get along with other men. Pat's in no hurry. I don't want him to be a child actor. And a man can't really get ahead in this business until he's thirty. I can't practice lines with him, because I think it's a mistake to get too set in a role. You might get on the set and find the director has an entirely different conception of the scene." Even brother Michael got into the act as second assistant director to William Wellman on *Goodbye, My Lady*. But the most important advice he gave both sons was this: "Be a man first and an actor second."[353]

Young Wayne developed a crush on Natalie Wood while on the set. "I had a friend who was my age," recalled Pat, "so that I wasn't completely dependent upon my father or an adult for my entertainment. There was a pretty girl, a super gal, with us on location. So *The Searchers* was great for me in the daytime as well as the nighttime." The attraction was mutual. "Duke's son Patrick had a part in the film," recalled Wood. "He was really handsome. Didn't look a lot like his father, I thought. Duke had a real rugged kind of handsomeness, but Patrick, who was the same age as me, had a really boyish face. Just my type. I had a deep crush on him." Wood's younger sister Lana accompanied the couple everywhere and Pilar recalled what a gorgeous couple the two made. "I'm lucky," said Natalie, "I have a lot of boyfriends, but I don't expect to get serious about anyone until I'm at least twenty-three or twenty-four years old. Right now, I don't think I'm one of those girls who will put her career before her marriage. When I meet the right boy," she laughed, "well, I'll tackle that problem when I have to."[354]

Even Bond got into a romantic mood. According to Carey, Bond "thought he was God's gift to the women…and Vera Miles was the leading lady and she was—I don't think I've even seen a more beautifully proportioned woman in my life. Oh, God, was she built. And Ward, of course, was out of his bird and he thought she wanted his body so bad and she didn't even know he existed. She happened to be married to a Texan at the time…and she couldn't have cared less about Ward Bond. So we had these pen windows naturally so you looked upon Monument Valley and Ward would always walk around naked waiting for Vera to go by. He wanted Vera to see him naked. He would pound his chest and barge up and down in front of the window hoping Vera would look in and see him in the nude and it would turn her on. And that didn't work so then he'd time it—Vera was rooming with Ollie (Carey) and they had Ollie in there to protect her because otherwise—he'd be breaking the door down and my mom would say, 'Get out of here, you dumb son of a bitch.' But what he would do is wait and time it until he thought Vera was just taking her blouse off and then he'd zoom out the door. They were right next door and then he'd open it real quick and say, 'Oh, Ollie, I just wanted to see you,' and try and catch Vera in half undressed." Dobe Carey remembered that "In a lot of ways, Ward really was a horse's ass. He thought he was God's gift to women. He thought that the way to impress a woman was to be as crude as possible, to say the dirtiest things. He was always saying to some big star like Maureen O'Hara, 'Jesus Christ. Maureen, but you've got great tits,' or 'Why don't you put your ass down on old Uncle Ward's lap.' He thought that was being really sexy."[355]

Five-foot-four-inch blonde, blue-eyed Vera Miles, Miss Kansas 1948, had been signed and dropped by three major studios—RKO, 20th Century-Fox, and Warner Bros.—before C.V. Whitney and Merian C. Cooper picked up her contract. "…I didn't let it get me down," she said thankfully. "I just squared my shoulders and determined to learn to act. I received my reward making *The Searchers* when John Ford told me after my big scene, 'Kid, you're okay.'" Two years earlier, Miles had plodded through a factitious jungle on RKO's Pathe's back lot with Tarzan and a trained chimpanzee. When she couldn't get any movie parts, she played a variety of characters on TV, which gave her confidence to tackle new roles. "It pays to keep plugging," she confessed. "I never thought I'd be struck by lightning, but it has happened." Years earlier, she had a small bit part and a single line of dialogue in *When Willie Comes Marching Home*, but Ford remembered her and asked Wingate Smith to search through the roster of extras to find her name. "There was something about her that I discerned," said Ford. "I said this girl has talent…It's a great American face." He told her she had to change her name from

Ruta Ralston to something else, so as not to be confused with the *legendary* Vera Hruba Ralston. "Do you have any suggestions?" Ford asked. "She said she had a grandmother named Vera Miles and I said I think that's great. So, from now on you are Vera Miles, period." She agreed in order to get the part.[356]

Besides being an actress, Miles also was a science non-fiction enthusiast. Interested in the power of thought projections, she felt that concept would eliminate the need for space travel. She even expounded her theories to Wayne and Hunter. "I told them how reasonable the whole thing should be," she explained. "I think interplanetary travel in a rocket ship is a long way off. It follows that if this is so, it follows (that) an alternate method should be attractive. And I think the quickest and simplest way to explore space would be through thought projection... This would take an extensive overhaul of our mental habits, I admit. Dogs seem able to transmit messages through sheer brain power. Now in view of all this, I don't think it's madness to suppose someone can project his intelligence for great distances and still maintain telepathic communication with his brain. There'd be no need of actual physical eyesight as sight is only a translation of light vibrations. I'd call something like this an intelligent balloon." *You're traveling through another dimension: a dimension of sound, a dimension of sight, a dimension of mind. You're moving into a land of both shadow and substance, of things and ideas. You've just crossed over into... the Twilight Zone.*[357]

Many actors auditioned for the role Jeffrey Hunter eventually played, including John Agar and Robert Wagner. After a bit of idle chitchat, Wagner recalled that Ford asked him if he wanted to play the part. "Yes," replied Wagner. Told he wasn't going to get it, he stood up and dejectedly headed for the door. Ford asked, "Boob? (Yes, he actually called Wagner Boob.) You really want to play the part?" "Very much," replied Wagner. "Well, you're still not going to get it," he said viciously. Ford also contacted Walt Disney and requested the services of Fess Parker but was rejected. In a 2002 interview, Parker admitted that was the reason he left Disney. "Actually, it was what happened after that...I wasn't consulted about *The Searchers.* I was en route with Jeffrey Hunter, who played the role of Martin Pawley in *The Searchers,* and Walt Disney, on the way to Clayton, Georgia, for our locations for *The Great Locomotive Chase.* The conversation turned to Jeff's greatest experiences of his life, which he described as (working in) *The Searchers.* Walt turned to me—we were sitting in the back seat—and he said, 'They wanted you for that.' I was a newcomer, but I realized even then that you don't get too many shots, and I'd already been heavily exposed in one dimension. Then the movie I was cast in, *The Great Locomotive Chase*—there was more tender loving care of the locomotives than of their live assets."[358]

Nineteen-year-old Pippa Scott, who'd played Juliet in a UCLA production of *Romeo and Juliet,* caught the eye of a local talent scout and appeared as Wayne's niece. Walter Coy appeared on Broadway opposite Gertrude Lawrence in

*Lady in the Dark*, and Shirley Booth in *Land's End*, before he was signed as Ethan's brother, Aaron.[359]

At sixty years of age, Ford, though not yet in the twilight of his career, approached *The Searchers* more somber and reflective than he had in the past. From 1939 to 1941, Ford had filmed some of the most important, dramatic and successful movies of his career: *Stagecoach, Young Mr. Lincoln, Drums Along the Mohawk, The Grapes of Wrath, The Long Voyage Home*, and *How Green Was My Valley*. Talk about a Murderer's Row! No other director had ever been involved in so many classic films in such a short period! Crusty, cantankerous, intimidating, and sadistic. Always sadistic. Yet on the set of *The Searchers*, he was very serious, a mood which seemed to pervade the entire cast and crew.[360]

Perhaps it was the story itself: Three years after the end of the Civil War, a Confederate veteran returns home from Mexico. Money in his bag and a medal in his pocket. With longing eyes for his sister-in-law, he greets his brother's family's open arms. Unfortunately, a clever Indian ruse leaves the homestead unprotected, and the family is massacred, save the two young daughters. The ex-soldier then begins a five-year odyssey, searching for his young nieces, knowing if they aren't found, they will never be the same. According to Ford, "what interested me most were the consequences of one tragic moment and how Ethan reacts to that moment, his search for the naked truth and the brutality of that action. He endures everything the desert offers and in such a hostile landscape, it was his own brute strength that determined his own, and finally Debbie's survival. We largely dispense with language. Ethan was a man of strength and few words."[361]

Perhaps Ford's actions were a result of personal misfortune. The decade had not been kind to Pappy, and his career was on the decline. Years earlier while filming *Mogambo* in Tanganyika, he came down with amoebic dysentery and during *Mister Roberts*, suffered a ruptured gall bladder. Drunk and unable to finish the picture, Ford was replaced by Mervyn LeRoy. Ford's perpetual stubbornness resulted in his near-blindness. Impatient after cataract surgery, he removed his bandages too soon and left his vision permanently blurred in his left eye. Pappy and his wife lost their home in Los Angeles under the laws of eminent domain, and even his beloved yacht Araner began to suffer from dry rot. According to grandson Dan, Ford began "a long, slow professional decline. Although his reputation within the industry had never been higher...cracks were already beginning to show. Things that he could have dealt with only a few years before—demanding stars, an intransigent front office, or a too-tight shooting schedule—now posed real problems for the nearly sixty-year-old director... For the first time in his life, he realized that the number of his working years was finite." But all was not lost. As one of his soundmen observed, "The Old Man can't hear, he can't see. All he can do is make good pictures." He had to remind Hollywood what he was capable of.[362]

## TALES FROM THE SET

While filming an emotional, intense confrontation between Wayne and Dobe Carey, Bond inadvertently or deliberately caused a retake. Carey's character learned that the Indians had murdered his girlfriend Lucy. Overcome with grief, he loses his grasp on reality, grabs a gun, and races to take revenge on the Indian camp. Filmed in a single take, Ford approved the scene and said, "Right." Unfortunately, a cameraman noticed the cameras weren't operating as an electric cable had been disconnected. Sitting on a chair behind a hill, Bond had innocently unplugged the cable, so he could use his electric razor. Obviously, the scene needed to be re-done. Mad as hell, Dobe could do little but grin and bear it. "Ford apologized to Duke and me," related Carey, "and said, 'Let's do it just the same way—if you guys can do that the same way, you'll make me happy. I don't think you can,' but—a lot of crap. And I ran in, we did it again, and it was perfect. He went, 'Right!' and that was it."[363]

But the tables could be turned on Bond as well. One day on location, Bond arrived later for dinner and sat at a table with an attractive young blonde-haired woman. She told him that more than anything, she wanted his autograph. Bond warmed to the request and after awhile, decided to make his move. She said her husband, who worked for the railroad, was out of town, so, if Bond wanted to visit that evening around 11:30, she would be waiting for him. And oh, by the way, bring a six-pack of beer and a watermelon. Bond eagerly showed up at the appointed time and was let into the room. Wayne, cast members, and stuntmen were all in on the gag, as was the blonde, and after a minute, began to shoot off their guns. Fearing the husband's retribution, Bond dropped the beer and scampered "au natural" into the desert, watermelon in tow. Coincidentally, he didn't know but his first scene the next day was with a young pioneer woman, the same young blonde from the evening before. He entered the room to say his lines, looked at the woman and almost fainted.[364]

According to Ken Curtis, his role in "*The Searchers* was to have been a straight part. It came out of a character I used to do called Dink Sweet when I was with the Pioneers. I used the dryland accent. When we were rehearsing my first scene in the picture, which was when I come courting at the Jorgenson farm, he (Ford) said to me, 'Do it in dryland.' I thought it was just to give the crew a laugh. We ran through it and he said, 'That's the way you're going to play it.' The accent made the part. Otherwise, it would have been a real nothing part. A Ralph Bellamy part." Initially, Curtis was resistant to the suggestion. He told Carey, "I don't want to do that in the picture. I'll make an ass of myself." Wayne set him straight though. "What in the hell is this crap I hear about you not wanting to do the accent that Pappy asked you to do!" he screamed at Curtis. "Bullshit! Listen, you're a nice looking fella', but ya' ain't as good lookin' as this Jeff kid, an' on toppa' that, yer playing the second lead and there's nothing more thankless than a second fuckin' lead! Dobe here can attest to that! Play it like the Old Man says, fer Christ sake, an' you'll be noticed in the goddamned picture!"[365]

John Ford was an inveterate alcoholic but absolutely forbade drinking on location. Rumors had it that while filming *The Quiet Man,* Maureen O'Hara rebuffed his advances. Overcome with grief and despair, he turned to alcohol. According to second assistant Andrew McLaglen, "We knew why he was under the weather. I think Maureen had turned him down the night before." But, O'Hara vehemently denied it. While on *Mister Roberts,* Ford ordered the prop-men to have iced beer on the set. How strange then that he acted the way he did when faced with the aroma of liquor on an actor's breath. Yet another of his idiosyncrasies, Ford would instantly terminate anyone who dared test his will when it came to liquor. Stuntmen were notorious for their hard-working, hard-drinking ways and wetting down a dry throat after a long day only seemed natural. Diminutive Frank McGrath, who would go on to play Charlie Wooster on *Wagon Train,* was no different. Rough and tough, he was a hard drinker, and no rule from Pappy was going to stop that. One evening, ostensibly to scare up participants for a game of pitch, Ford wandered into McGrath's tent. McGrath wasn't there, so Ford asked which bed was Frank's. After pulling back the covers, Pappy dropped trouser, and pissed all over the bed. "If a man can drink it," he said, "he can lie in it, and if any of you bastards ever tell him who did it...."[366]

Ford was stung by a scorpion on location. Whitney, who was on the set that day, was understandably concerned and asked Wayne to check on the director's health. After a few minutes, Wayne reported back. "It's OK," he explained. "John's fine; it's the scorpion that died."[367]

Filmed in Technicolor, *The Searchers* was photographed in VistaVision, a wide-screen process utilizing a dual 35mm negative. The process included wider-angle lenses to give greater scope on the screen, with the negative traveling horizontally resulting in an image with an area nearly three times the area of a standard negative image. The result for the theater patron was improved picture resolution, clarity, sharpness, and a greater depth of field. As only two theaters in the country were able to utilize the new technology, the film was also printed in conventional 35mm format.[368]

Ruth Clifford, a veteran actress of silent films, played a rescued Comanche captive who goes berserk when she sees a doll. Ford confided in her almost off-handedly, "You know, I'd also whisper it (the dialogue). She's...just...lost her...No English." Clifford had lost her own child, and Ford sensed that she was thinking of it. He put a piece of wood in her arms and told her to let go of her emotions. A very powerful scene. "They ain't white...anymore. They're Comanch." "I'm proud of you," Ford whispered afterward.[369]

The Mexican man who takes Edwards and Pawley to meet Chief Scar was played by actor Antonio Moreno. His character's name, Emilio Gabriel Fernandez y Figueroa, is a combination of the names of Mexican actor and director Emilio Fernandez and his cinematographer Gabriel Figueroa.[370]

After the film was completed, the movie company proceeded to tear down two ranch houses built for the production lest some other company used them to make a quickie film or television movie. Either one would have ruined the originality of the scenery. Harry Goulding asked Ford to allow the Navajos to have them. The lumber built good-sized chicken-houses. More importantly, it provided windows, which was the dream of every Navajo.[371]

During a Fourth of July party that included barbecues, horse and foot races, songs and fireworks, in appreciation for all Ford had done for the Navajo during his many visits to the Valley, the tribe presented him with a ceremonial deer hide, including ears, legs, and tail. Written on the hide was the inscription: "We present this deer hide to our fellow tribesman Natani Nez, (Tall Leader) as a token of appreciation for the generosity and friendship he has extended to us in his many activities in our valley. In your travels may there be beauty behind you, beauty on both sides of you, and beauty ahead of you. From your friends, the Navajos of Monument Valley, Utah-Arizona."

Ford wasn't the only Hollywood individual honored with a Navajo name. Fred Libby was a member of the John Ford Stock Players and appeared in several Wayne films including *Fort Apache, Three Godfathers, Wake of the Red Witch*, and *Yellow Ribbon*. One time when working on location, he was given the name Hostene Nez, which means "big inside and tall outside." "They told me they couldn't give me that name immediately," he remembered. "The medicine man had to go up into the mountains and contemplate in solitude before he came up with a name. His name was Nez Chilly Be Gay. I ended up having part of his name in mine when he came up with Hostene Nez. It was amazing how that information travels around a reservation like that. I remember going into places where the Indian children were playing and they would come up to me and say 'Hostene Nez.'" Wayne was given a name as well. According to Charles John Keiskalt, author of *The Official John Wayne Reference Book*, during filming a two-year-old Navajo girl became critically ill with double pneumonia and an advanced case of measles. The nearest doctor was the crew location doctor, but the only thing that could save the girl was an oxygen tank at a hospital one hundred miles away. When Duke heard this, he offered his plane as transport, so the girl could enter the hospital. She arrived in time, and Wayne had a new name, "The Man with the Big Eagle."[372]

Filmed in the late afternoon of July 3, 1955, the final scene in *The Searchers* was homage to Harry Carey Sr., according to Wayne. Early in his career when he filmed *Shepherd of the Hills*, Duke decided he was tired of playing goody-goody characters. He wanted to be a "rough-tough heavy" and told others on location about that. Olive and Harry Carey were there and after the set was cleared, with Harry standing next to the door, Olive gave Duke a piece of her mind. "Ollie said, 'You big stupid son-of-a-bitch,'" remembered Wayne. "'Would you like to see Harry doing all these things you were telling these people?' And I said, 'Well, no. Of course not.' And I looked over there and that's when Harry was giving it that (holding his arm across his front). And she said, 'You know, people have accepted you, they've taken you into their homes and their hearts now and they like you as a certain kind of man and it's like sitting in the room talking to somebody. If you get overboard with histrionics, a fellow can say, 'Pardon me. I've got to get a drink,' and never come back. But if it's in the theater and he's sitting in the middle of the aisle and he's been with you and all of a sudden he sees you do some silly things that are petty and small or not you, then he starts looking at you instead of being with you and he can't get up and go get a drink so he'll start to resent you.' And I thought that this was (a) great observation about our business and I loved the two of them."[373]

Wayne had a hangover when they shot the film's final scene. Olive Carey always carried a bottle of Dexamyls for those who needed the "hair of the dog." Dobe related that morning: "...the old man heard that Duke had been drinking and man, he got on him, and Duke has never been a person that ever takes pills, ever. And he still doesn't. And Ollie says, 'You can't make it,' and she gave him one of these green pills this morning because old Duke was—and the old man was on him for drinking on the job and he picked on Duke... He was using the hangover; I think he was glad he had a hangover. Ollie gave Duke the green pill in the morning. It kept him alive and just got him even." The scene was rehearsed but just twice. Olive and Dobe were watching in the shadows behind the camera. As the wind was blowing on him, all Duke had to do was stand in the doorway, look, and then walk away. But, at the last moment, he noticed Olive. "She and I had talked about Harry in that stance on other occasions," recalled Wayne, "and I saw her looking at me and I just did it." He raised his left hand, reached across his chest and grabbed his right arm at the elbow. A gesture he'd seen Harry Carey do numerous times, in countless films. He stared at Olive for a moment, then finally turned and walked into the desert. "Goddamn, tears just came to her eyes," said Wayne. "I was playing the scene for Olive Carey." If it was up to Dobe, a sign should have been put up on the door of Duke's room at Goulding's Lodge: "In this room John Wayne got drunk before he shot one of the most famous scenes in motion picture history."[374]

The door set-up that opens and closes *The Searchers*, a powerful symbolic motif referred to often as the film goes on, comments on the central conflict of family versus the wandering hero. Ford projected emotions through images. In scenes poignant in their simplicity, Edwards gradually becomes more and more isolated and is finally shut out from the others surrounding him. Not content to stand on the porch and merely look in, his only choice is to go back to the desert from where he came. He'll never be a part of society, and, once again, as he was in the beginning, he was alone. *(An insightful analysis of this scene can be found in "The Cinema of John Ford," by John Baxter, as well as "'They ain't White. Not anymore. They're Comanche.' Race, Racism and Miscegenation in The Searchers," by Brenton Priestley.)*[375]

Ford was an artist, an impressionist. His canvas was the landscape, the actor his paint, and music his brush. He could convey more with a glance, a shadow, a stroke of the hand, than other directors with pages of dialogue. Routinely criticized as just another John Ford western, albeit with magnificent photograph and scenery, it was only in later years that *The Searchers* was recognized as a cinematic masterpiece. Not only was it Wayne's best performance ever, the film was recognized as one of the best Westerns, nay, one of the best films ever produced. Ford knew what he wanted to display before he ever even filmed a scene. He cut it in the camera, in his head. It was the reason he filmed so few takes. The actors had to be up, had to be fresh for they never knew if a take was the *one* or not. Ford explained, "I don't give them a lot of film to play with. In fact, Eastman used to complain that I exposed so little film. But I did cut in the camera. When I take a scene, I figure that's the only shot there is. Otherwise, if you give them a lot of film, when you leave the lot the committee takes over. They're all picture makers; they know exactly how to put a picture together and they start juggling scenes around and taking out this and putting in that. Hey can't do it with my pictures. I cut in the camera and that's it. There's not a lot of film left on the floor when I'm finished."[376]

According to Ken Curtis, preparation was the key. "Too many directors are too concerned with the camera angles," he recalled, "and don't worry about anything else. Ford worried about his actors. He would get them together in the morning and run through the scene before he put it on camera. He would have his stand-ins on the set lighting. We'd run through the scene while they were lighting. We'd get it exactly the way it seemed to work best. He always knew what he wanted and when he got it, he would print the take. He never shot more than he needed, he never shot less."[377]

Wayne confirmed this approach. "He (Ford) required that you be there at 9:00 and then when everybody came he would say, 'Let's have some coffee.'

He'd say. 'Pardon me, fellow,' and go over and look at the set. And he'd say, 'Hey, Duke—come over here, Duke. Why don't you sit? Just read the lines.' So now you read the lines and you're not hampered by having to go here or to go there. You're free to do anything you want. Well naturally, there's always a tendency in conversation to get close together and so you do the normal thing that's good for the picture. Now he'd say, 'Jesus, that was nice,' if he liked the way it was playing and you get a chance to get the other fellow's timing for that scene. Now he'd call the cameraman over, nobody else was there. No lights or anything—just a work light. He'd say, 'What do you think about this? Run through it again, fellows.' So you'd run through it again. He talked to the cameraman and say, 'Duke, let's try it once more. Could you get on—could you cross him and get over to where that lamp is and look back at him from there?' Now you are asked to do that and it is the easiest thing in the world to say 'Sure.' There's the lighting board and you stand there and take the reaction. There's his compensation shot. If he had said when you first came in, 'Read your lines,' and you read them and he says, 'No, let's get over to that thing,' you've got to be over there. Then there would be no, I mean there would be no good feeling about the scene. You allow the scene to develop. Now he would take about an hour to set up that scene. Now somebody comes into the scene and he'd work them. Now you have suited your action for the words… That's the way Jack Ford worked…."[378]

"Jack never used the same lines that were in the script–hardly–the scenes he generally cut half of them out," continued Wayne. "He'd grab the important lines and throw them at you. You had to be ready…(he) would let the words and the character meld and if the words were not exactly right, he'd change the words or give them to somebody else. Jack was very positive about what he was going to do, but he gave you time to relax and catch everything that was in your personality that maybe you hadn't thought of the night before… he was always so far ahead of everybody else. The only thing he was weak on was stunts because he was scared he would hurt people."[379]

According to Dobe Carey, Richard Widmark said Ford knew the details of making movies so thoroughly that it appeared he did everything by instinct. Carey remembered, "Ford would say, 'All right, kids, get some chairs,' and if we were outside in Monument Valley or whatever or wherever, the station wagon would pull up and Danny Borzage would play 'Bringing in the Sheaves' and he'd just sit there in the station wagon looking out across the country. He did the same way for every movie I ever made for him. Like ten minutes, he wouldn't move, they'd hand him a cup of coffee and he'd sit there in the station wagon and just stare off with his cigar and in the older days he used to smoke a pipe and all of a sudden he'd get out of his car and he'd start to walk and everybody would follow him and he'd stop and say, 'Put the camera there,' and still nobody had a scene number, nobody knew what we were going to do. He would start at the beginning, and get an idea and then another, and another. He would have the actors walk through the scene and do it repeatedly until it was just right. It gave the actors an opportunity to immerse themselves into their role; they became the character rather than act the part." That style of direction fit Wayne to a T.

As a result, in Ethan Edwards, Wayne gives his finest and most complex performance. (According to Ford, Whitney, fearful of "Amos and Andy" connotations, changed the character's name from Amos to Ethan.) Filled with troubling moral ambiguity, Edwards will forever be the loner, the outcast, the wanderer. Respected, feared, looked upon with sympathy and disgust, he constantly searches for justification. Deeply racist and contemptuous, he confronts his worst fears. Searching, always searching. Obsessive in his hatred, vindictive in his treatment of the Indian, he struggles with his place in society. Knowledgeable with the savage's traditions, languages and religion, he straddles the line between civilization and barbarism. The quest for Ethan Edwards and the half-breed Martin Pawley...is like all quests, an odyssey of self-discovery. The heroic Ethan learns the truth about himself he has always avoided... Miscegenation is seen—bold for the fifties—and Ethan's acceptance of this saves his sanity and his soul.[380]

Duke struggled with the character as Edwards was the antithesis of Wayne. Notably free of racial prejudice, he looked deep into himself to express a rage that was foreign to him. He was submerged so deep in his character it was frightening. "When I looked at him in rehearsal," Dobe Carey recalled, "it was into the meanest, coldest eyes I had ever seen. I don't know how he molded that character. He was even Ethan at dinner time. He didn't kid around on *The Searchers* like he had done on other shows. Ethan was always in his eyes. That character seemed to be built into him, and no other actor, no matter how great his talent, could have played that part as well." Ken Curtis remembered that, "...(Wayne) wasn't quite so loose. He just didn't seem as relaxed. It was simply his concentration on the part. And that was because Duke was, I felt, reaching down deep inside himself into some dark corner he'd never gone before. Now that's the mark of how good an actor he was." Even Wayne realized he needed to go where he had never gone before as an actor: "I just thought of the Apaches not as Indians but as Communists who'd been trying to kill me. I thought, what if the Commies were the ones who had done this? What if they had managed to burn down my home and kill my family? You see, I can be a method actor, too." Extremely intense. Who said Wayne couldn't act![381]

Pilar Wayne resented Ford when he stated, "Duke cannot escape playing himself. He has to accept playing big, rough men, simply because of his physical size. He isn't a good enough actor to do anything else and he should play to his strengths." But Duke loved the role of Edwards. "A great deal of the work was instinctive," he admitted, "and I loved the fact that I wasn't just a good guy. I was kind of an anti-hero... He (Edwards) had been dedicated to a wrong cause, dedicated to vengeance, but I'm optimistic about the character... Simply, I'm an optimist. I believe in the old thing where a guy looks in his stocking at Christmas and says, 'Goddamn! I got nothin' but horseshit,' but the other guy says, 'Oh, boy, they got me a horse, but it got away.'"[382]

When asked to name his favorite films, Wayne replied, "*Stagecoach*. It was my first role in an 'A' picture that the public went to see. It was also probably one of Jack's (Ford) best pictures. *Red River*. After working with Jack Ford, I'd go back to five-day westerns at Republic, and people in your field of endeavor (the media) decided I was only good when I worked for Ford. But after this picture, Hawks spent a lot of time saying how much help I'd been to him, and that helped change things. *The Quiet Man*. A beautiful picture. I enjoyed it because we went to the wild west coast of Ireland. And we had the Abbey Players, the greatest collection of fine actors I've ever been associated with. Jack Ford put me in a tough spot there. I had to be the straight man for eight reels. That's tough to do. And (finally), *The Searchers*. That was one of the best Westerns ever made, but the public was never informed of how fine it was. Warner Bros. saved money, they lost the picture. It was a great personal story of human behavior, which doesn't change." "We watched some of the rushes together," Mary St. John remembered. "Duke was special in the film, and he knew it. Remember that scene when Ethan's looking at the white women who have spent years with the Indians? You could see sympathy and hate in his eyes at the same time. He was never better."[383]

Now widely recognized as a cinematic masterpiece, *The Searchers* still did not garner a single Oscar nomination. Nor was Wayne acknowledged for undoubtedly his finest performance ever. Though financially successful, with a domestic box-office gross of $10.2 million, it was only in later years that the film became appreciated for its haunting composition and magnificent richness. When released, few critics picked up its dark sub-text, its message, or Wayne's portrayal of the Western anti-hero. Moving ever closer to very edge of evil, Duke forever dashed his good-guy image and moved into a darker, deeper realm, a character he would never play again. *Variety* called *The Searchers* "somewhat disappointing. There is a feeling that it could have been so much more. Overlong and repetitious at 110 minutes, there are subtleties in the basically simple story that are not adequately explained. There are, however, some fine vignettes of frontier life in the early southwest and a realistic presentation of the difficulties faced by the settlers in carving out a homestead in dangerous country."[384]

The *New York Times*, although generous in its praise of Wayne, took exception with Ford to the point of being picky and trivial: "There are only two faults of minor moment that we can find in this slambang Western film. The first is that Mr. Ford, once started, doesn't seem to know when to stop. Episode is piled upon episode, climax upon climax and corpse upon corpse until the whole thing appears to be taking a couple of turns around the course. The justification for it is that it certainly conveys the lengthiness of the hunt, but it leaves one a mite exhausted especially with the speed at which it goes. The other fault is that the director has permitted too many outdoor scenes to be set in the obviously synthetic surrounding of the studio stage. Mr. Ford's scenic stuff, shot in color and VistaVision, in the expanse of Monument Valley that he loves, has his customary beauty and grandeur, but some of those campfire scenes could have been shot in a sporting-goods store window. That isn't like Mr. Ford. And it isn't like most of this picture, which is as scratchy as genuine cockleburrs."[385]

Even the usually effervescent Philip Scheuer of the *Los Angeles Times* seemed confused by what he saw. While he stated "The Western attains new magnificence in...*The Searchers*," he also stated "the production is virtually a virtual guidebook to all that is great and all that is deficient in the work of this 'practical' Ford. As with someone who is respected, admired and even loved, so with John Ford; You take the bad along with the good. The fault is not so much, per se, that the director overshoots; he always does. What matters is how he arranges his material. If Ford had organized his picture as masterfully as he composes each shot, his *Searchers* could itself stand as a monument in the valley of this year's movie scene."[386]

Ignored by critics and film historians alike, it was only in the seventies that the film's influence came to be recognized. Then, as now, the film was a brilliant masterpiece, melding Wayne's outstanding performance with Ford's genius direction. Directors Spielburg, Lucas, Scorsese, and others have all been influenced by and paid homage to *The Searchers* in their work. "The dialogue is like poetry," Scorsese said, "and the changes of expression are so subtle, so magnificent! I see it once or twice a year." Spielberg is said to have watched it a dozen times including twice when he made *Close Encounters*. Both Ford and Wayne gambled in a shrewd career move, and it paid off handsomely.[387]

Wayne signed a seven-picture contract with Warner Bros. on May 2, 1949; *The Searchers* fulfilled the requirement. In June 1957, Warner's attempted to sign him for one additional project and offered three suggestions: *Trouble Marshall, The Marblehead,* and *The Long Highway.* Wayne rejected them all.[388]

# CHAPTER NINE
# LOVE AND MARRIAGE

*"I'm fine, love. I just wanted you here so you could see the sunsets with me." Wayne's explanation to his wife when he asked her to rush to Libya while he was filming* Legend of the Lost.[389]

DUKE ADMITTED FIRST WIFE JOSEPHINE WAS ALWAYS THE LOVE OF HIS LIFE. He was devastated when they divorced, as was she—so much so that she never remarried. In 1960, he confessed to Paul Fix, "I didn't see it then but my divorce from Josie was the stupidest thing I ever did in my life." The mother of his four eldest children, Michael, Mary Antonia "Toni," Patrick, and Melinda, she unfortunately operated in a different social environment than Duke. He was a movie star, a celebrity, used to attending premieres and grand openings, staying out late drinking with his buddies. Josie was much more refined. Always known as Mrs. Morrison, she was a staunch Catholic; he had little belief. She was an elegant lady with ambitions in high society; he was a plainspoken guy more comfortable in jeans than a tuxedo. After a hard day in front of the camera, all he wanted was a long, hot bath and early dinner. Instead, he was welcomed by socialites and clergy. She wanted Duke to dress for dinner, and, in her world, that meant black tie. He drank; she disapproved. Duke recalled, "Josie and I—we were moving in two different channels. I was part of the movie group. She was part of the society group. I found small talk boring. So we went our own ways. Josie didn't like my friends and I didn't like hers. I really didn't ever do anything wrong, except maybe stay away from home too long—but I thought I was doing the right thing then. That's no good for any marriage. Josephine and I simply drifted

141

apart. She's a fine girl, and a really wonderful mother."[390]

His childless second marriage to Chata was more lust than anything. The exact opposite of his life with Josie, this romance flared hot and bright but died just as quickly. Twice married, Wayne vowed the third time would be the charm. "This is my second chance at being a father," confessed Wayne. "It isn't often a man gets a second chance in life. This time, Pilar, I swear I'll do it right." Dressed in her finest attire, with a new coiffure, Pilar shared the joyous news of her pregnancy with Duke. Excited beyond belief, like Rhett Butler, he swept her up in his strong arms and carried her in the house. Conceived while making *The Searchers*, Aissa's impending birth was announced to Hollywood in October by Louella Parsons. How she heard about it was anyone's guess. It wasn't the first time Pilar had been pregnant with Duke's child, though. While Wayne was going through his divorce with Chata, Pilar began to miss her periods. She gained weight, became nauseous and run-down. There was only one possible explanation: a child. Rather than being a joyous occasion, it turned into a heartbreaking ordeal. If Chata found out, Pilar could be called as a co-respondent in the divorce proceedings. Not only that, Duke had a morals clause in every contract he signed. A clause the studios could invoke if it became known he fathered a child out of wedlock. Imagine the publicity. She couldn't even go back home to Peru. Labeled an unwed mother with an illegitimate child, it would break her mother's heart and cause a huge scandal. Though Duke told her, "Do what you have to do and I'll support you all the way," unfortunately, she knew an abortion was the only solution. Bo Roos, Wayne's financial adviser, suggested a gynecologist who recommended an unlicensed doctor on Sunset Boulevard to do the procedure. Afterward, Pilar vowed, "If I was ever lucky enough to have another child, I'd be the best mother in the world. I'd put the baby's needs before everything else. Only, please. God, let me have another baby." In 1955 her prayers were answered.[391]

Duke was ecstatic! Walking around the house with a perpetual smile, he even drew up plans for a proposed nursery. Close friend Maureen O'Hara had a unique perspective of Wayne's family relationship: "His career is very important to him," opined O'Hara, "but not nearly as important as his four children... He talks about them all the time. When we're not in a scene working, Duke is usually curled up in a chair on the set, drinking mugs of coffee, and chats incessantly about the kids. He's tops as a father. He attends every show at the school in which one of his family appears. More than anything he loves to listen to people tell him about something his kids have done." Pilar's introduction to Duke's first family was as positive as it was enjoyable. He was never happier, never more relaxed. "This is what it is all about," he rejoiced. "What I've always wanted. A successful career, a wife I love who loves me back, my family around me." Regrettably, it didn't last. Familial resentment lurked on the horizon.[392]

At a gathering of the clan in early October, Duke announced Pilar's pregnancy. To say he didn't get the reaction he expected is an understatement.

Eldest daughter Toni, eight years younger than Wayne's newest wife, was momentarily speechless, and then let out an anguished wail. "How could you, Dad! You know I'm going to be married next month!" Wayne could only shrug his shoulders and lamely reply, "Don't scream at me. She's the one who's pregnant." When asked why he didn't defend Pilar, he said, "It was the first thing that came into my head. Oh, Jesus, I shouldn't have said that." Already distraught by the announcement, Toni realized that the birth of a Wayne sibling would divert attention from her impending marriage to fiancé Don LaCava. The wedding she and Josie had planned included a social-event-of-the-year reception at the posh Beverly Hills Hotel. Bad enough that Duke had divorced her mother; now he had upstaged her wedding. Wayne was convinced that Michael, Toni, and the others never forgave him for leaving Josie. Reluctant to confront the situation, he told others that "the children of his first family resented his new family." However, Claire Trevor recalled, "Duke adored all his children. He took them everywhere with him. He loved them all with a passion. I never saw him show favoritism. He was always hugging and kissing them. But when Aissa was a baby, I sensed there was some jealousy there among the older four."[393]

During Pilar's pregnancy, Wayne postponed or turned down all acting offers except one. Shortly before Christmas, he played a supporting role to his son Pat in an episode of *Screen Directors Playhouse* called "Rookie of the Year." Directed as usual by John Ford, it also starred Vera Miles and Ward Bond. Duke also looked forward to his next movie, a non-Western. "It'll be nice for a change, to be able to walk straight-legged again," he admitted. He also announced Batjac would temporarily suspend its production activity although it would complete its ten picture financing and distribution agreement with Warner Bros. Rumors had circulated for weeks that Batjac had received offers to affiliate with RKO, Paramount, and United Artists upon expiration of the Warner commitment. MGM also had eyes on John Wayne Productions now that Wayne suspended Batjac activities.

On March 30, 1956, a frantic, nervous and totally lost John Wayne drove his wife to St. Joseph's hospital in Burbank where she gave birth to a seven-pound, eight-ounce daughter. Wayne was such a mess he didn't know whether to pee, whistle, or wind his watch! "I wasn't nervous at all," Pilar recalled, "but he was. Driving me to the hospital he kept singing off-key songs, the kind he used to sing with Ward Bond and John Ford around campfires in places like Utah. They were meant to calm me, I suppose, but they weren't those kind of songs at all!" Forty-nine years old, with four grown children, Duke was anxious to start another family.[394]

Less than two months later, and just a day after *The Searchers* was released in general distribution, Duke escorted Toni down the aisle of the Blessed Sacrament Church. Los Angeles archbishop James Cardinal McIntyre performed the ceremony in front of more than five hundred guests including

Bob Hope, Ward Bond, Ann Blyth, Ray Milland, Loretta Young and other Hollywood personalities. Whether Duke would even attend the wedding had been debatable up to the last minute. Toni was adamant Pilar not attend. She wanted her father to sit in the front pew next to Josie. This wedding was for the first family, not the newest one. Duke pleaded to no avail, stormed around the house, and threatened not to go at all. In the end, he acquiesced, but Pilar was heartbroken. The first family affair and she wasn't invited. Nor did it bode well for her future relationship with Duke's children. Nevertheless, he was as proud as could be. At the wedding, it was very hot inside and Toni almost passed out before the final vows. She slumped, and Wayne was the first at her side, taking her outside the church to get air, hugging and kissing her, giving her words of consolation and walking her back to the altar.[395]

Shortly after the wedding, Wayne signed a new contract with 20th Century-Fox. He would star in three films for a total of $2 million dollars, which would make him the highest-paid actor in the history of movies. Paid out at $200,000 annually over a ten-year period, Duke received a record $666,666 per movie. A fourth feature film was on the agenda to be discussed as well with separate remuneration. Unbelievable, and worth every penny! Though ecstatic, he was also dismayed by the state of the industry. The studios were foolish to pay astronomical salaries and only did so because there were just a handful of top stars in the business. "I'm glad the producers were stupid," grinned Wayne when asked why he was worth so much. "But they should develop new stars. They won't spend any money to make stars. They won't take a chance on these kids. And the new ones who have come along all go in for that mannered acting. They won't take any directing. There can be only one boss on the set, and that has to be the director."[396]

In July, with Pilar's pregnancy over and anxious to get back to work, Wayne filmed a two-day cameo in *I Married a Woman*. Starring George Gobel and British blonde bombshell Diana Dors as an advertising executive and his pregnant wife, the duo attend a movie when she is unable to explain her condition to her husband. (In a case of *reel* life imitating *real* life, Wayne appeared as himself in that movie with twenty-four-year-old screen wife Angie Dickinson. In *Forever and Forever and Forever*, Duke played the part of a man so in love, he bought his wife a diamond necklace and, together they waltzed in the moonlight.) Devastated by poor reviews, Dors sued the studio claiming she was made an object of ridicule and disgrace. Dors's real name was Diana Fluck. "They asked me to change my name," she confessed. "I supposed they were afraid that if my real name Diana Fluck was in lights and one of the lights blew…" In her autobiography Dors related an embarrassing moment when she returned home as a guest of honor. The local vicar had the privilege of introducing the movie star to her adoring fans. But when told her real name, he became flustered and worried he might…oh…accidentally say something else. The time came, however, and he rose magnificently to the challenge. "Ladies and gentlemen, it is with great pleasure that I introduce you to our star guest. We all love her, especially as she is our local girl. I therefore feel it right to introduce her by her right name; Ladies and Gentlemen, please welcome the very lovely Miss Diana Clunt." And, as Jack Paar was so fond of saying, "I kid you not."

Later that same month, Wayne starred in a film about Frank "Spig" Wead, a pioneer in naval aviation. World War I ace and long-time friend of John Ford, Wead fell down a flight of stairs, fractured his neck and was paralyzed in 1926. Producer Charles Schnee recalled the accident: "He was living in a new house in San Diego. He got up in the night to look at one of his daughters and was going back to bed when he slipped and fell downstairs..." Ford claimed to have met Wead as a young deck officer on the battleship *Mississippi* in the period after 1920, when Ford had put aside his reserve naval uniform. Forced out of service due to his physical condition, Wead regained partial use of his limbs through determination, perseverance, and just plain hard work. Following his release from Balboa Naval Hospital, he moved to Santa Monica and while convalescing, at the encouragement of Ford and other Navy comrades, began writing down his military experiences: first in pulp fiction stories and then screenplays. Published in such magazines as *The Saturday Evening Post* and *The American Magazine*, Wead wrote the screenplay for *They Were Expendable* and also received two Academy Award nominations in 1938: one for Best Original Story for *Test Pilot* and a second for Best Screenplay for *The Citadel*. He was accepted back into the Navy the day after the attack on Pearl Harbor when he volunteered his services. Wead was instrumental in the development of the concept of *Jeep carriers*, small aircraft carriers whose sole purpose was to re-supply large carriers with planes lost in combat. Wead's doctor, who helped on the picture, said he would have lived much longer had he not gone into active duty. Several years after the war, Wead passed away, supposedly in Ford's arms.[397]

Based in part on a short story called *We Plaster the Japs*, *The Wings of Eagles*, aka *The Eagle Has Wings*, depicted Wead's life both in the military and out. Initially reluctant to direct the film, Ford relented when told MGM had promised to team Wayne with O'Hara. (Robert Taylor was originally considered for the role.) "I didn't want to do that project because Spig was a great pal of mine," Ford confessed, "but I didn't want anybody else to make it (either)... I was under contract to MGM. They persuaded me to make it. And they had—if I didn't make it they were going to put a young, inexperienced director on it and out of my friendship for Spig, I decided to do it. I didn't want a young lad who never knew Spig to tackle this thing. So that's why I stepped in and did it. I don't want to talk about it." In a letter to Wayne in 1955, Ford conceded, "God knows I want you for the picture, but you mustn't do it as a sacrifice to yourself. You have been doing that for me for too many years. If you have any chance for a great deal with Danny O'Shea, please be assured that I understand perfectly. After all, nothing ain't never going to break up our friendship." Once Ford was on board, though, his goal was to tell the story "as truthfully as possible." Ford admitted, "Everything in the picture was true. The fight in the club—throwing the cake actually happened. I can verify that as an eyewitness. I ducked it. And the plane landing in the swimming pool right in the middle of the Admiral's tea—that really happened." Many extras in the movie were actual Navy flight students and instructors from the Naval Air Station in Pensacola, and despite Navy objections, were paid "extra" wages.[398]

To more closely resemble Wead in his later years, Wayne even went without the use of his traditional toupee. He enjoyed his time on the set: fist fights, cake throwing. In one scene, several individuals hurry to exit a building only to fall fully clothed into a swimming pool. When a reporter asked if he ever did that before, Wayne replied, "Well, let's say it's the first time I ever fell into a swimming pool *sober* with all my clothes on!"[399]

Ward Bond appeared in the film as John Dodge, a thinly disguised version of Ford. "I didn't intend it that way," remembered Ford, "but Ward did. I woke up one morning and my good hat was gone, my pipe and everything else. They'd taken all the Academy Awards and put them in the office set." Ford's wife Mary offered the use of them. Bond even wore tinted glasses and used Ford's hollow cane. Ford and Bond had an interesting relationship. Although respectful of his acting abilities, Ford never held Bond's intellect in high regard. Cruel, with a sadistic streak, Ford recalled, "Duke and I were always spending most of our time thinking up tricks to play on Ward. If we spent half the time, just one quarter of the time, reading the script or trying to help the story, we'd have made better pictures." Former co-star Anna Lee reminisced about the relationship. "I've got a picture of Pappy and John Wayne with three horses standing with their rears to the camera, and Ford's signature underneath saying, 'Guess who?'" Others had the same photo with the comment "Thinking of you," written on it.[400]

Bond stories are legendary. One day he called up Wayne at 9:30 a.m. "The servant told him Mr. Wayne was asleep," recalled Ford's daughter Barbara. "He says, 'What the hell is he doing asleep at this hour? It's 9:30.' So she woke Duke up, and he said, 'What the hell are you doing, Ward? I'm asleep. I'm tired.' Ward says, 'I've been up since 5:30. I took the Danielson kids for a ride, went for a swim, had breakfast, played nine holes of golf, and now I'm going for another ride with the kids.' Duke said, 'That's fine. You go right ahead.' Ward said, 'What are you doing sleeping so late?' Duke said, 'I'm just tired, that's all.' Ward said, 'What's Jack doing?' Duke said, 'I think Jack's asleep too. You better leave him alone.' 'Asleep at this hour. What for? Why is he asleep?' Duke said, 'For the simple reason, you son of a bitch. We were up until four putting you into that alcoholic ward where you are now!'"[401]

Maureen O'Hara played Wead's long-suffering wife Minnie, who slipped into alcoholism late in life. At the request of Minnie's children, Ford left all the dramatic footage of the volatile relationship on the cutting-room floor. Although Wayne was once again in military uniform, this homage to Wead and the Navy lacked sufficient action to keep audiences enthralled. Though full of slapstick and stunts, something was missing. As O'Hara lamented, "The edited picture was good, but not vintage Ford... Perhaps that old magic—the Ford-Wayne-O'Hara-fire was hard to recapture given all that had happened among us." Very inconsistent, the first-half of the film was played for laughs; the second drama. Ford grumbled that MGM executives felt it had *too* many laughs. "How in the hell can a picture have too many laughs, I ask you? Maybe they should take them out and distribute them over the entire MGM program," he said sarcastically. Dan Dailey had received a personal call from Ford to play the other male lead. "I was crazy to accept," said Dailey, "but before I could give an answer I had to get permission from Twentieth to loan me to MGM."[402]

Wayne received decent reviews; some felt his performance was right up there with *The Searchers*. *The Motion Picture Herald* said, "The film is about fifty percent rambunctious slapstick comedy, twenty-five percent heroic drama and twenty-five percent sentimentality. Under less skillful direction, these sometimes-conflicting elements would cancel one another out. Ford, however, has seen to it that they combine to make a generally lusty piece of entertainment." And therein lies the problem—it wasn't supposed to be a comedy! The written prologue after the opening credits clearly stated the reason for the movie: "This motion picture is dedicated to the men who brought Air Power to the United States Navy. One such man was Commander Frank 'Spig' Wead. The flying records he smashed helped him win the lasting respect of his fellow Navy men. The screenplays he wrote helped him win the lasting respect of his fellow writers in Hollywood." Even the MGM publicity campaign struggled to find the correct niche: "This picture has Wings! It lifts you to the skies with its thrilling story, taken from the career of reckless, devil-may-care 'Spig' Wead. A perfect role for John Wayne. Not since *The Quiet Man,* such fun and excitement on the screen—and the same director, John Ford, brings you another really big entertainment!" Confused as to which genre this film belonged, some critics even questioned its necessity. "Like many affectionate tributes, this one comes more from the heart than the head ...The life of Spig Wead, while full of daring and a remarkable fortitude, was not one to delude a Hollywood veteran into thinking it meant for a deep biography." *Wings* had its premiere aboard the aircraft carrier Lexington in Long Beach Harbor. Ford, a rear admiral in the U.S. Navy Reserve, was presented with an admiral's flag. Despite the enthusiasm of all the sailors present, the film wasn't as successful as expected. Budgeted at $2.75 million, with domestic and oversea rentals of $4.65 million, the movie lost $804,000.[403]

Pilar Wayne brought six-month-old Aissa to the *Wings* set but was torn between being a mother and movie star's wife. She wanted a daughter, not a celebrity offspring. However, she also realized there were duties and responsibilities associated with her new station. Somehow, some way, she had to reconcile the two. Once in a while, though, it seemed like they were a real family. Maureen O'Hara recalls once when they were on a set, "I remember (a) time when Duke insisted his wife Pilar and daughter Aissa, who was then about six-months-old, come on location with us. The "Sons of the Pioneers" also on the picture, sang a song to Aissa every night after we finished shooting and every night Duke had tears in his eyes. I found myself with tears in my eye."

But even Pilar had to admit Duke's focus was on his career. "Duke had devoted six months to impending fatherhood," she wrote in her autobiography, "postponing or turning down all offers of new films. Once Aissa made her appearance, his attention quickly returned to making movies." It was a cycle repeated over and over. Perpetually concerned about his finances, Wayne always looked for new opportunities. In 1956, he considered and rejected more movies than ever before: *Unchained, The Sun Also Rises, Adam and Eve, Tigrero, Around the World in 80 Days, The Judge and the Hangman,* and *The Enemy Below.* (His keen sense of selection failed periodically. In years past, he had also turned down or rejected *Knute Rockne, All-American, Duel in the Sun, All the King's Men, High Noon, The Left Hand of God* and *The Tall Men.*)[404]

Restless and anxious to get back in front of a camera, Wayne also longed for the comfort of his family. Prior to Aissa's birth, Pilar, though sometimes bored, would sit patiently on location and endure insufferable heat, intolerable living conditions and long hours while Duke went about the business of being a star. Once she became a mother, however, what was once agreeable now became unacceptable. Air-conditioned rooms, modern conveniences, and a nanny were a must. Living in a hotel room was not a life she wanted to become accustomed to. The more Duke worked, the unhappier she became. To watch Duke's boundless energy was exhausting. His day began before daybreak. After breakfast, he would arrive on the set, coffee cup in hand, well before any of the crew. Not satisfied to just act, he would review camera placements, massage the script, assist the grips, give advice to newcomers and generally do whatever he thought necessary to create a quality product. Again, O'Hara had a unique take on Wayne's work ethic: "Working with Duke was a revelation. This man belies his exterior by being the hardest working actor I know. He worries himself sick with concern for everyone on the picture. He frets and stews and practically goes out of his mind wanting to tell an actor or actress what it is the director is trying to get in a scene. He is so conscientious about his work that he gets furious when an actor doesn't listen to directions. On more than one occasion, I've heard him blow his top with, 'Why don't you listen to the man?' As a result, performers with Duke are quite attentive."[405]

While his persona made for quality pictures, it did little to strengthen the family relationship. All Pilar could do was to wait patiently until the day ended. Exhausted, Duke would return to wherever they were staying that evening, wash off the day's dust, have a bit of dinner and perhaps play some cards with the stuntmen and crew. Totally drained, he would fall into bed only to start it all over again the next day. Admirable, but a brutal schedule.

Pilar's next opportunity to strengthen the relationship would come on the set of *Legend of the Lost*, but unfortunately, a preproduction disagreement hurt any chance of that. Duke would be away on location for three months and wanted his wife to come along. Aissa, too small to receive inoculations, would have to remain behind. Duke was furious when Pilar decided to stay home. "Damn it, Pilar. You're my wife," he exclaimed. "The nurse is perfectly capable of taking care of Aissa, and I need you with me." Pilar held firm in her rejection, and they eventually agreed that she would catch up with Duke when filming moved from the Sahara to Rome.[406]

In October 1956, Wayne reactivated Batjac operations and signed a four-picture production/distribution agreement with United Artists. The agreement did not require Wayne to produce the films within any specific time period nor to star in all of them himself. UA would have distribution rights and would receive 50% of the profits for the first five years following release of the films. Thereafter, all rights would revert back to Batjac. *Legend of the Lost* would be the first movie under the combined Batjac/UA banner. After filming was complete, Wayne expected to return to Hollywood in the spring and produce a feature-length presentation of *Gunsmoke* starring his good friend, James Arness.[407]

*Legend*, produced and directed by Henry Hathaway under a partnership agreement with Wayne, was filmed on location in Tripoli and Libya and Cinecitta Studios in Rome. Originally, Wayne expected to film the project locally. "There's a spot of sand out near Mojave, California," he said, "that would be a great desert if we scooped up some dunes with bulldozers…" Hathaway interrupted. "The script," he said slowly, "says the Sahara Desert." Wayne agreed, "But that's way the hell and gone on the other side of the world. Have you ever seen those Texas deserts? They have more sand in Texas than…" Again Hathaway interrupted. "The sand in the Sahara is golden, yellow gold, and God made the dunes without bulldozers. The people will be able to tell the difference." He was right; the audience could tell the difference. They could also identify a lousy movie. With working titles of *Legend of Timbuktu* and *Man from Timbuctoo*, production ran from January 2 to April 10, 1957. Initially, Wayne wanted Gina Lollobrigida and James Mason as co-stars, but Sophia Loren and Rossano Brazzi eventually filled the roles. Loren, just as hard-working as Wayne, never rested for a moment. "What can you do in daytime?" she asks. "You can see TV and you can read a little. But I am not used to that, I am used to working. I have been working since I am fifteen years old, so I do not know what is a holiday. I just do not know what to do with time. If you're an Italian actress, you can't be bad. I'm twenty-two, but please don't print it—because as I grow older, everyone will know my right age."

149

Asked about her sex-appeal, she shrugged, "You are born with sex, you can't make it up."[408]

When Wayne arrived in Libya, he immediately realized it wasn't going to be business as usual: he couldn't find a bed large enough to suit him. You see, the Libyans were small of stature, and a search was made to find a European bed large enough to fit Duke's *much* taller frame. If it wasn't one thing, it was another. The airstrip nearest the location was so small no one knew if a four-engine aircraft could land. It was only after they did that they realized they could! And the sand: for miles and miles, all you could see was miles and miles...of sand. The weather was unseasonably cold. At night, the rocks in the desert, soaked with moisture, exploded with the staccato rattle of machine guns. Intense heat, cold that chilled to the bone, and a bright relentless sun. Unbelievable. For a key scene, poisonous tarantulas were rented. When one died, the trainer was paid $1,600! They even had to sweep footprints off the sand dunes when additional takes were necessary, and Hathaway worked them from five in the morning to nine each night. Wayne lamented that Libya didn't permit the entry of U.S. magazines or newspapers, so he was forced to keep current with events through the use of a radio—but only when the "Reds" didn't jam the broadcast![409]

Hollywood professionals were not accustomed to working under such conditions. A typical problem was the Case of the Three Skeletons. Plaster props were not available so the production crew was forced to obtain bones from local natives. Twelve hundred dollars changed hands and then the troubles began. The Italian cameramen must have believed the bones were cursed due to the numerous problems they caused. On the first take, film buckled in the camera causing a one-hour delay. On the second take, a wind appeared out of nowhere and blew a protective device off the top of the camera, spoiling the footage. On the third take, the camera jammed, and the entire mechanism had to be taken apart and reassembled. Finally, the fourth take was the charm. Not wasting any time, the crew gave the bones back to local tribesmen for proper burial...again. The problem was...the bones were 100-years-old![410]

Shortly after he arrived on location, Wayne tore two ligaments in his left leg when he fell atop the ancient Roman Forum ruins at Leptis Magna. Initially, it was feared he broke his leg, but X-rays revealed a broken bone in his foot instead. As a result, he had to use crutches. "No more pictures," he declared, "until I've had a long rest." Apparently, the only one who came out of *Legend* with any success at all was a local Arab shoemaker. After crafting a unique pair of shoes that kept sand out of Loren's shoes, Wayne and Hathaway took an interest and ordered pairs as well. Eventually, the cast and crew purchased over four hundred pairs, and the shoemaker was ready to retire. At least someone was glad they decided to film in Libya. During production, Hathaway and Wayne hatched the idea of shooting a French Foreign Legion film when they came across an old Legion fort in their extensive travels through the desert. Unfortunately, or perhaps fortunately for Wayne, it never materialized.[411]

Wayne's marriage wasn't getting any better, either. Shortly after filming began, Pilar received an urgent telegram: "Please hurry here. I need you. I love you. Duke." Fearing the worst, she dropped everything and, along with *Photoplay* magazine editor Ruth Waterbury and columnist Henry McLemore, flew to Wayne's side in the desert, taking the better part of three days, only to find he was suffering from a severe case of loneliness. Duke also requested that, as long as she was coming, could she bring four large cans of frankfurters, so they could make hot dogs while on location? Pilar departed Hollywood and switched planes in New York. While there, Dorothy Kilgallen scooped the rest of the media by obtaining a private conversation with Pilar. "Mrs. John Wayne boarded a TWA plane for Rome yesterday afternoon," wrote Kilgallen, "for the most American reason in the world. Her husband...cabled her he wanted some hot dogs—desperately. So the dutiful Mrs. W. hopped...to New York, the colorful Roosevelt Zanders met her with four large cans of frankfurters, and off she went to the Eternal City, where she was to take a plane for Tripoli and a final change to a jungle plane that will fly her (and the hot dogs) to her true love. (Do hope she remembered the mustard!)" While Wayne wanted to share the gorgeous sunsets with Pilar, she longed for her daughter. He simply couldn't understand the maternal relationship between a mother and daughter. It was rough on Pilar: living in a mud-plastered, thatch-roofed room with a dirt floor, sharing a single bathroom with cast and crew, she ached for Hollywood civilization. Duke described the living conditions in a letter he wrote early in February 1957: "This little village is completely isolated from the rest of the world; no radio, telephone, no modern facilities. We bunk in tents. In the days it's sunburn hot, at sundown the temperature drops to around thirty degrees. We have to sleep in all our clothes bundled in sleeping packs to keep warm, even with kerosene stoves burning full blast all night." Pilar found it difficult to rest and a doctor prescribed sleeping pills for her. As per their previous agreement, Wayne insisted she accompany him to Rome's Cinecitta Studios where interior scenes were filmed. Grudgingly, she accepted, although she did spend much of her time shopping for antiques.[412]

The shoot wrapped in April; after a short vacation in Italy and Switzerland, Wayne winged his way back to England for postproduction work. "I'm going to be a producer this time," rationalized Wayne. "I want to be in on the cutting and scoring..." Wayne felt the movie was too confusing, too jerky and the interaction between he, Loren, and Brazzi without rhythm. "I think music will be very helpful to correct this," suggested Wayne. While in London, John Ford saw a print of *Legend of the Lost* and declared it one of the greatest jobs Wayne ever did. Too bad the audience didn't think so. A weak script, less-than-convincing performances, and a formulaic storyline contributed to its downfall. "The script never worked," admitted Hathaway, "but I told the idea to Wayne and he was fond of it. The picture was a fiasco. Everybody tried to change it from my original concept."

Loren almost died of asphyxiation from a space heater, Brazzi questioned why he was even there, and Hathaway thought Loren was one-dimensional. Wayne summed it up nicely: "It was a long, hard shoot and after all that it wasn't much of a picture." Budgeted at $1.75 million, *Legend* barely made a profit. Combined with the abysmal performance of *Wings of Eagles*, the industry started to question whether Wayne was still a draw. And when Republic finally released the legendary fiasco *Jet Pilot*, Wayne questioned his future as well. In *Motion Picture Herald's* list of top-ten box-office moneymakers, Wayne, who led in 1950, 1951, and 1954, placed second in 1957, but his popularity was on the wane. With back-to-back disappointments, he needed a hit and needed it bad.[413]

By her own admission, Pilar resented her time away from Aissa and blamed Duke for it. He refused to discuss his career problems with his young wife: *She* wanted to stay home and raise their daughter; *He* wanted her at his side on location. A difficult situation at best, she grew more and more frustrated. Annoyed and confused, she took a friend's suggestion to visit a physician "who was noted for dealing with the nervous crises which are an occupational hazard for Hollywood wives." He gave her several prescriptions; Seconals seemed to resolve her anxieties. Unfortunately, Pilar started to take them whenever she felt "nervous, upset, depressed, angry, or inadequate." She later confessed to Aissa that she took them daily "to sleep. To combat depression. Before Hollywood parties. She took them then in lieu of liquor, to try and loosen up, to mask her insecurities, in the face of her husband's hard-drinking, fast-track crowd." Rather than address the underlying issues, she hid behind a veil of drug-induced confidence. Growing more and more dependent on the pills, this temporary relief would come back to haunt her.[414]

While in England, Wayne agreed to a proposal from John Huston to star in *The Townsend Harris Story*, a film about the United States' first consul to Japan. The first of a three-picture contract with Fox, filming would begin in December and, once again, for the third time since Aissa was born, Duke would be on location and away from Pilar. Knowing it was useless to argue, Pilar agreed to join him in Japan in early December. Scenes were filmed in the fishing village of Kawana, at the Temple of Flowers, and the Nijojo Castle in Kyoto, in a village on Lake Biwa and at Eiga Studios.[415]

Desperate for a box-office smash, this would be the fifth non-Western movie Wayne made in a row, In fact, since *Rio Grande* was released in 1950, of the last seventeen films he made, only two were Westerns: *Hondo* (November 1953) and *The Searchers* (May 1956.) Curiously, this was the first time he had an opportunity to work with the legendary Huston. Known for such films as *The Maltese Falcon*, *The Treasure of the Sierra Madre*, *The Asphalt Jungle*, and *The African Queen*, Huston was a man's man and an eccentric of massive proportions. Wayne looked forward to bonding with the director and stretching his acting ability. However, it was not to be. Within days of his arrival in Japan, Duke was furious. He couldn't get a handle on either his character or Huston, and established absolutely no rapport with the director whatsoever. Having worked in the past with Ford, Hawks, etc., the lack of direction from Huston was frustrating. "I have done everything but stand on my head to get near this man's thinking," Wayne wrote Pilar. "Just have to hope and pray that he's good." When Pilar arrived, he took the opportunity to unload his frustration. "I can't work with the son of a bitch… When I tell him I can't memorize the script unless I know what we'll be shooting, the bastard says, 'Don't worry, we'll improvise.' The son of a bitch can't make a good movie without his father or Bogart to carry him… It's a little frustrating trying to arouse the… sleeping talent of our lead, Mr. Huston, who wears the clothes of an Irish country gentleman. Maybe I'm prejudiced, but I'd say without the manner."[416]

They started off on the right foot initially. Huston was downright effusive in his praise for Duke. At a news conference announcing the project, Huston said, "Only one man is right for him (the part of Townsend Harris) and that's Wayne. I want to send Duke's gigantic form into the exotic world that was the Japanese empire in the 1800s. Imagine! The massive figure, with his bluff innocence and naïveté, with his edges rough, moving among these minute people. Who better to symbolize the big, awkward United States of one hundred years ago? Duke's our man." Big was the key word. At six-foot-four inches, he towered head and shoulders over the Japanese. This caused a slight problem for Duke. "I brained myself half a hundred times on the ceiling beams in my hotel room," joked Wayne." Now I've learned to move around like a cave man with my hands dangling somewhere around my knees!"[417]

What started so positive ended as a disaster. While Huston wanted Wayne to glide idyllically through the Japanese pastoral countryside, Duke was more concerned about his image. "Hell," he lamented, "my fans expect me to be tall in the saddle." He argued with Huston about which side was his better side. Huston admitted he deliberately shot Wayne's opposite side. When the film was completed, Huston left to direct *The Roots of Heaven*; Wayne took over and made the film he wanted. By cutting scenes, re-shooting and adding others, Duke finally had a film he could live with. Huston couldn't. "…a man I have no great esteem (for)," said the director, "took over, shot scenes I hadn't planned and took out others I liked, in short completely changed the picture, which I now disown… John Wayne apparently took over after I left. He pulled a lot of weight at Fox, so the studio went along with his demands for changes. When I finally saw it, I was aghast. A number of scenes had been re-shot, at Wayne's insistence, simply because he didn't like the way he looked in the original version. By the time the studio finished hacking up the picture according to Wayne's instructions, it was a complete mess." Duke replied, "Considering he never told me at any point what he did want, I consider his comments a little unfair."[418]

Their animosity had even spilled over into a potential catastrophe. Naturally, they had different opinions as to what had happened. A scene called for dead, cholera-infected bodies to be loaded on a barge and set afire. A barge was set on fire to depict the effect of burning bodies. A line attached to it unfortunately broke free, and the barge drifted toward a fleet of fishing boats anchored in a small cove. Several boats caught fire, and their fuel tanks exploded. Huston recalled, "We got some fine shots (and the fire) started a riot as the local fishermen and the villagers attacked the Japanese crewmen I had. A lot of people were knocked unconscious and thank God no one was hurt." Wayne had a slightly different view on how the problem was resolved. "When I saw the riot begin," he remembered, "I ran down to the docks and began waving my hands and shouting for everyone to calm down... I promised all the fishermen that I would make good their losses out of my own pocket if the studio wouldn't. Well, when Huston saw and heard this, he just walked away and never said a word. He couldn't bear the fact that he'd goofed badly and I was the one who handled the situation."[419]

In early January 1958, Pilar returned to her Encino home from Japan. She and Duke had planned a Hawaiian vacation that would start on January 13 when he would meet her in the islands. Even though she had left her daughter in the care of her grandmother, Pilar had a sense of foreboding. Calling home frequently to reassure herself, she felt anxious, uneasy, and guilty. Eventually, Duke thought it would be best for both of them if she returned home, so, two weeks before Christmas, she did. On the evening of January 14, at 3:30 a.m., shortly after retiring, she woke to the smell of smoke and the sound of a barking dog: a Dachshund named Blackie. Fire!!! With thick black clouds curling halfway down the walls, Pilar rushed to Aissa's bedroom, wrapped her in a blanket and dashed down the stairs to the first floor where she left her in the protection of her maid, Consuelo Saldana. The maid called the fire department, and she and her sister Angelica escaped the blaze along with three dogs. They ran outside screaming, "Fausto! Fausto!" to rouse the Peruvian cook, asleep in separate quarters down the hillside. She grabbed a fire-extinguisher and returned to the second floor in a futile effort to put out the fire, as well as to rescue Wayne's good luck trophy cavalry hat! It was then she suffered a slight burn on her arm. With Blackie at her heals, she went next door for help. "Looking across the lawn," she recalls, "I could see smoke billowing from the roof and the second-story windows of my home."[420]

Seven engine companies fought the blaze for over an hour. The fire was believed to be caused by a faulty gas-jet in the fireplace. Ward Bond, Jim Henaghan and their wives hurried over and took Pilar, Aissa and the dog to the next-door neighbor's house, Duke's friend and make-up artist, Web Overlander. Toni LaCava and husband Don also arrived. A doctor treated Pilar's burn and gave her a sedative for shock. Overlander's wife excitedly told the newspaper reporters, "Flames were shooting out all over the second floor. It was like an explosion. I was afraid they were all trapped in there. Then I saw Mrs. Wayne with the baby and the maids coming out of the kitchen area on the ground floor." Saldana called the fire department, and Pilar reached Wayne in Japan by phone several hours later and notified him of the tragedy. After promising to return as soon as the picture wrapped, he sent her a blank check by special messenger with a note that read: "For the girl who really has nothing to wear." Pilar replied, "How do you like one-story houses?" The entire second floor was gutted and the first damaged by smoke and water. Including the loss of antiques and personal belongings, the fire cost Duke over $500,000, but firemen were able to save Pilar's fur and jewelry. She moved into a Beverly Hills hotel where Mrs. John Ford brought her a mink stole and two pairs of pajamas. Everything a woman needs. Eventually, she moved into Alice Faye's and Phil Harris's home, only a few blocks from hers, to supervise the rebuilding of the one that burned. What a disaster. And when *The Barbarian and the Geisha* (revised title) was released, movie-goers must have thought it was one as well. Budgeted at $3.2 million, the movie took in only $2.5 million in domestic rentals. *(The general rule-of-thumb was that a picture had to generate twice its cost in revenue to breakeven.)*[421]

Now fifty, Wayne could no longer realistically play romantic leads and certainly didn't want to spend the rest of his career playing character roles. His screen presence was such that he couldn't and wouldn't be relegated to the background. Hollywood didn't want old-timers, it needed fresh new faces. Too young to retire, too old to play youngsters. Wayne needed roles befitting his age but the scripts available were few and far between. Four strikes in a row and you're out. The public loved him but wouldn't put up for any more failures. What to do? His house was a shambles, and his career only marginally better. "Proof that times heals all wounds, while in Japan, Wayne had received a phone call from Herbert Yates to discuss filming the screen adaptation of Robert Mirvish's novel, *The Long Watch*. Surprisingly, Duke accepted the call. Early the following year, Yates meet with Wayne for further discussions which were unsuccessful.[422]

Wayne desperately needed another hit and the only solution was to hit the trail once again. The public didn't want to see American diplomats, paraplegic scriptwriters, or desert-dwelling adventurers; it wanted horses and dust, ten-gallon hats and spurs, gunfighters and school marms, cavalry-style tunics, Winchesters and Double D belt buckles. In short, moviegoers wanted to see the Old West. And Wayne would give it to 'em.

# CHAPTER TEN
# IT'S ABOUT TIME!

*"I understand you want to do a picture called The Alamo.... Where are you going to do it?" Wayne replied, "In Mexico or Panama." I said, "Man, you can't do it in Mexico." Wayne said, "I can do it any god-damn place I want to!"* Happy Shahan's first conversation with John Wayne.[423]

THE TALL, LEAN, BESPECTACLED RANCHER STOOD UP AT THE TOWN MEETING and called for silence. He needed to say what was on his mind. As mayor, he was responsible for the well-being of the community but wasn't being too successful. What was once a thriving hamlet now stood on the brink of becoming a ghost town. When troops were stationed at the local army base, things were hopping. In an article for the *New York Herald Tribune*, an enlisted man stationed at the fort in 1889 painted the town as a raucous frontier town: "Adjacent to Ft. Clark, across a narrow stream dignified by the name of Las Moras River, was Brackettville, a nondescript frontier town, ten miles from the railroad. County seat of Kinney County and about the worst place on the map. Everything ever pictured in the 'movies' of the wildest kind was there, and lots more. The population was some 500, mostly Mexicans. Saloons were on every corner and plenty in between. Dance halls, brothels—let your imagination run riot and you may approximate what this town was in those hectic days... there were several kinds of dances indulged in that are not seen on stage or ballroom floor. There was cheap liquor, cards, all kinds of gambling, women and no legal restraint."

157

Expansion of the army post led to the subsequent growth of the town. With more saloons than churches, law enforcement officials had their hands full. Over time, though, peace was restored. In the 1940s, with over 10,000 soldiers stationed there, the army base had influenced life in town. Soldiers on leave would come to town, spend their time and well-deserved dollars at the movie theater or perhaps take their girlfriends to a dance or restaurant. Taverns were available if someone wanted something stronger than soda-pop, and they could always hang out on the corner at McCabe's Drug Store. After the base was decommissioned, however, the town faced its future alone, and the city council was responsible to assure it had a future. The mayor certainly wasn't doing a real great job; in 1943, the town had 3,500 residents, many of Mexican or Seminole-Negro descent. By the mid-1950s, that number would decline to less than half. Even the local lumberyard lost 90% of its business when the base closed. If something wasn't done, the town would end up just a gas stop on a lonely highway.[424]

Stone buildings in town, some more than a century old, provided residences and businesses. With their sharp, angular architecture, these structures attest to the town's past: simple, solid, sturdy. There was no farm crops production in the area. This was strictly ranching country. Beef, it's what America eats. Mohair from goats, wool and mutton from sheep, that's big industry. With over 200,000 acres of farmable soil, what they really needed was water. Without rain, the soil was drier than dry. Guajilla, a drought-resistant yielder of forage, shed its yellow leaves. "In this country, guajilla is the last card in the deck," said a local rancher. "When you draw that, you are through." When brush plays out, if you have one hundred head of cattle you have ninety-nine too many. No rain, no moisture. No forage, no cattle. It was as simple as that. Something needed to be done.[425]

After the crowd quieted down, the mayor made his pitch. "Why don't we try to make Western movies here?" he suggested. "They make them in Monument Valley and around Tucson and the ranchers always make money. Why not here?" He didn't know anything about the film industry, although in the 1940s he had made a few beer commercials. But he knew it would be profitable if the town could attract filmmakers. He said he became interested in films as a kid when he sold popcorn at the silent movie house. "I knew I'd be connected (in movies) when I was in third grade," he said. The town elders threw out a challenge to make it work, and they laughed him out of the meeting. "Who in the world would want to come all the way out here, just to make a movie?" they asked. "I don't know," he replied. "'Who has asked them?' I got it in my craw and decided I'd do it, God willing, or die trying." He then bet he could do it.[426]

Earlier he had had the exact same conversation with a friend while the two were out riding horses. "I asked why they (filmmakers) would come...," recalled the friend, "when they have all this beautiful scenery with streams and pines in Wyoming and Utah?" The mayor was always fond of saying, "I firmly believe that man can achieve whatever the mind can conceive." After the meeting, he returned home and told his wife, "I think I'll go out to Hollywood and tell them that they should come here to make movies." She didn't know why her husband thought the movie industry would save their town. Perhaps someone gave him the idea. She thought a film was made in the area way back in the 1910s but couldn't be sure. (Old-timers around Ft. Clark recalled in 1913-14, the old Vitagraph Company made three pictures there–two Westerns and a Civil War reel. For the most part, all of the extras and many of the minor actors were drawn from the enlisted personnel of the 14th U.S. Cavalry stationed at the fort.) When the woman asked her husband if he had lost his mind, he shrugged and said, "No…I think I'll go out there."[427]

So in the spring of 1950, go he did. James Tullis "Happy" Shahan was that kind of guy. A sportswriter had given him the moniker when he was on the Baylor basketball team because Shahan smiled no matter the circumstances. Upperclassmen treated the freshman to what was then known as hazing. "They whipped my butt, and I laughed at 'em," Happy said with a grin. During summers, the East Texas Irishman worked as a roughneck at Humble Oil Co. and looked forward to a career in the oil business. But his future wife had other ideas.[428]

In 1927, Elisha and Fannie Faye Webb, along with their young daughters Virginia and Sara, traveled from Rocksprings, Texas, to Brackettville and bought land in Kinney County, only forty-five miles from the Mexican border. Ambitious, Elisha was the first to introduce sheep into the county as well as Angus and Longhorn cattle. Happy and Virginia married in Waco in 1939, and the ranch continued to prosper under Fannie even when Elisha passed away later that year, just five days after Happy and Virginia's youngest daughter Jamie was born. Shahan graduated from Baylor the next year and immediately received a request from his mother-in-law to move to Brackettville and take over the ranch duties, which had become too much for her. Though considering an offer from Humble Oil, Happy had to decide. Recognizing he needed time to consider his options, he asked for and received a leave of absence from the oil company. It was a decision he would never regret.[429]

A regular jack-of-all trades, the youthful mayor, only thirty-five when first elected, had a varied, unusual background: boxer, lampshade salesman, singer, drummer, hat blocker, and lumber-feed storeowner. Donating his time, hard work, talent, and finances for civic and community projects, he was a promoter of many things he truly believed in. "When you decide to live in a place, you do what you can about building it," he explained. Honest and a man of his word, he would honor a contract written on a napkin and shake hands. Virginia recalled Happy wanted to become mayor of Brackettville in the mid-1940s when the decommissioned army base was offered to the city for "$1 and other valuable considerations." The government initially offered to sell the property to Kinney County, which wasn't a bad idea as the county thought it could be used for a military academy or possibly a woolen scouring plant. One local commissioner traveled several times to Washington, D.C., to work out the details. Upon his return, however, the county changed its mind. The fort was then offered to the city with the same results: an initial favorable response, but then the city council just changed its mind. After the fort was officially deactivated in 1946, it was sold for salvage to the Texas Railway Equipment Company in Houston, a subsidiary of Brown & Root. Happy knew of rumored injustices that were going on in Brackettville and wanted to put the town on the map. By being mayor, he could lead the community, instead of asking someone who wasn't a visionary to lead.[430]

B.J. Burns, Happy's later secretary, vividly described Shahan's first trip to the West Coast: "...he did his homework, took some pictures, hopped on a plane, and went to Hollywood. (Close friend Bill Moody flew him out in his personal Twin Cessna.) He knocked on doors for eight days, trying to get an appointment to present his proposal. He couldn't even get a door open." Happy never had any training in approaching people. All he knew was to "go after 'em." If you want something, just ask for it. But he found out that the movie industry was a little different. "I got to thinking," he said, "This isn't getting me anywhere." Finally, in frustration "after getting thrown out of every studio," (on his last scheduled day) he visited Disney Studios. "I'd like to talk to the man in charge of making pictures," said Happy. "Well, that's Mr. Disney, but he's not here." "Well, who else can I talk to?" "Well, you can talk to Mr. Lyon, but he's busy." "Discouraged," continued B.J., "(Happy) sat down on the edge of a secretary's desk and said, 'My community is going to die if someone doesn't hear my story. How do you get an appointment with these people? You know, being a rancher and a horse trader and a farmer, it's either a deal or it isn't. You buy my potatoes or you don't; you trade horses or you don't.' Mr. Shahan couldn't understand why he couldn't get an appointment with anybody in power." Luckily the person Happy was chatting with had a fair bit of influence. Alpha Steinman was Walt Disney's executive secretary and had momentarily covered for a Disney Studios receptionist. "Before you say no to anything I ask, I just want to sit down and tell you my story," begged Shahan. "Are you leveling with me?" she asked Happy. "'Cause if you are I know this guy at Paramount who is planning to do a Western." She called her friend and got Happy an appointment. "Okay, I'll tell him to come over, Harry." Burns continued, "A little later he walked into Paramount for his appointment with his hat in hand and said, 'I'm Happy Shahan from Brackettville, Texas. You probably never heard of Happy Shahan or Brackettville.' The man from Paramount looked at him and said, 'Well, I don't know about that. Do you know Colonel Hobbs?' Shahan said, 'Yeah, that's my neighbor rancher!' The man from Paramount Pictures had been to Brackettville and had hunted at Colonel Hobbs's ranch." Shahan had already been to Paramount earlier that week, but he didn't know who to see. He asked to meet location managers but didn't know who."[431]

Shahan continued the story: "The producer (Harry Templeton)... happened to be a World War II pilot with the rank of major. His colonel was named Louis

Hobbs and was from Brackettville. (After thirty minutes) when the producer found out I knew Colonel Hobbs, he reached over to his phone, called the colonel, and told him he was sitting there in Hollywood talking with his friend Happy Shahan. That was my first stroke of luck in Hollywood. You have to be at the right place at the right time with the right product. If I'd been five minutes earlier or later (into Disney's office), I would have missed the opportunity to meet with him." After some discussion, it was agreed that Brackettville was a potential location to film the Western. First known as *Adobe Walls* and later *Arrowhead*, the movie was produced in November 1952 and starred Charlton Heston, Jack Palance, Brian Keith, and Katy Jurado. Filmed at Ft. Clark in Brackettville as well as south of town and on the Hobbs ranch, Happy always gave credit to Hobbs for bringing the project to the community. Perhaps he meant if it wasn't for the relationship between Hobbs and Templeton, he would never have been so fortunate. Interestingly, local newspapers said Bob O'Donnell, Interstate Theaters vice-president and general manager, received the credit for persuading Paramount to make the movie in Texas. Regardless as to who was responsible, Hollywood finally came to Brackettville.[432]

Now successful in attracting a film project, why couldn't he do it again? The region had everything necessary for Westerns: trees, desert, mountains and streams, limitless expanses of flat lands. Livestock. A local lumber mill to construct movie sets, qualified handymen to build them. An abundance of willing citizens to appear as extras (both Texans and Mexicans). Even a local resort complete with a spring-fed, three hundred-foot-long swimming pool and hundreds of rooms and cottages for the cast and crew to call home, at least for a while. What more could one ask for? A real win-win situation. And more importantly, it helped the local economy when it brought in badly needed income. During filming, craftsmen, carpenters, extras, teamsters, plumbers, and common laborers all found work. With actors in town, spectators came from miles around to watch the movie being filmed on location. Cafes, gas stations, hotels, motels, grocery stores, and restaurants generally saw increases in business.

As a result, Happy visited the West Coast every three or four months, or maybe once a month for five to ten days, or maybe five times in three years, or whatever, depending upon what day of the week Happy was telling the story. As they say in Texas, "You should never let a good story get any worse with the telling." On his own, with no partner, he hustled all around town, touched base with old contacts, made new ones, and generally tried to attract Hollywood to come out once again to the wild and woolly west. He wasn't always successful, but he was persistent: "My wife used to get mad at me the way they'd treat me. I couldn't even get in to see a secretary. But I told her, 'That's all right. Someday, they're going to be calling me.'" Having already learned a little more about how to operate, Happy traveled out there so frequently the studio executives picked him up in limousines. Shahan could be pretty stubborn when he wanted something.

And he wasn't afraid of anything. Well, almost anything. "I'm afraid of God, that's all I'm afraid of," said Happy. "I didn't say that there weren't people smarter or people who couldn't whip me or people who weren't just as hardheaded. I'm just saying I wasn't afraid of them (Hollywood executives). I'm not afraid of anybody! And I'm not saying that braggingly." Good thing, too, because that's exactly the type of individual you need when you're fighting for the survival of your town. "I didn't know anything about making movies, but I did know something about putting packages together," Happy admitted. "I found you can sell those Hollywood people if you just keep trying. I was hustling! Hell, from 1950 to 1960 I went to Hollywood every month for five to ten days. This was strictly on my own. I didn't have any partners. There was a time when the old hands of the studios who were there would furnish me with a limousine during my visit—for example, Herbert J. Yates at Republic Pictures. He and I would sit and talk… He was a tough man; he was tougher than tough."[433]

Shahan went to Hollywood "and talked to Yates about a picture they were thinking of doing but it didn't pan out." Persistence paid off, though, when Yates called later and said, "'We're going to do another picture. We're gonna have John Wayne.' I found out that Republic Pictures was thinking about shooting a movie in Texas. It was to be called *Texas and the Alamo* or something like that." In late 1954 it was announced that *The Last Command* would be filmed in Brackettville. According to Happy, "we got ready and everybody thought Wayne was coming…" Republic brought builders to construct the sets and Shahan furnished material from Shaker Feed and Lumber. He didn't want any movies filmed on his ranch at that time. His job was to build sets and hustle. With movie sets constructed of papier-mâché "they didn't spend a whole lot of money on that picture." Local residents got a kick out of telling everyone that a pickup truck could be seen on the horizon when Mexican soldiers charged some mock-up and not-very-authentic Alamo walls. As a result of near-sighted cameramen, the film was exhibited around the world including that vehicle. One London critic editorially wondered how a truck got mixed up in a charge of 1836 troops.[434]

According to Happy, location personnel informed him there had been a falling out between Yates and Wayne, and Sterling Hayden had been selected to play Jim Bowie, a part Wayne was supposed to do. After the Wayne and Yates's parting-of-the-ways, Duke had second thoughts and indicated he would still be willing to do the film even though he wasn't employed at Republic any longer. Yates waffled about the quality of the script, so Duke said, "Well, just give it back to me—I'll pay you whatever you want." Yates refused. He hired Interim Scriptwriter Allen Rivkin to polish the script after Warren Duff was unavailable and asked Wayne to reconsider. Duke analyzed the changes, realized the script direction and content was not to his liking and, once again and for the final time, rejected Yates's offer. But Wayne wasn't finished. He contacted his good friend Robert Newman, who worked at Republic, with a Machiavellian suggestion.

162

*(Bob, usually a man behind the scenes, was president of Batjac while Wayne filmed his Alamo project.)* "I tell you what you do," he told Newman. "Tell Yates to give you that story of Jimmy Grant's for a dollar, and I'll give you twenty thousand dollars for it." Sounded reasonable, but Yates wouldn't go for it. Oh, well, Wayne would pursue the project on his own.[435]

According to Rob Newman, "My father was always sort of that kind of go-between, trying to bridge people who don't necessarily get along. My dad was a fixer; he actually loved being a fixer. My uncle Doc (Irving George Newman, father of composer Randy Newman) was pissed with the Army; he was a medical doctor. My dad said, 'All right. We'll pull you out.' So he called up James Farley, President Roosevelt's Postmaster General, and said, 'Okay, we've got to pull Irving out now. It's over.' And, boom, Doc was home. (My dad) could pull that stuff. That was kind of his specialty. If you were having a problem with a phone, (say) you couldn't get your phone fixed, he'd have it fixed in ten minutes, (in) the old GTE days. People told many stories like that. You need a divorce, he'll have you divorced. In two hours you'll go to the Dominican Republic and sit by the pool. Which he did for my cousin Carol." Unfortunately, he couldn't fix everything. "He was president of Batjac for only a couple of years," adds Rob. "Then my mom got divorced. She sent (him) a divorce letter right in the middle of (*The Alamo*) when he was on location (in Brackettville). He was there the whole time; he got the divorce letter from my mother because she didn't want to face him."[436]

Ernest Borgnine, who co-starred in *The Last Command,* informed Shahan that Duke was going to produce, direct, and star in his own version of the story. "While we were doing (the movie), I heard about a guy named John Wayne who wanted to do a picture called *The Alamo.* I heard that on the set...Yates... who had made millions on his B-Westerns, didn't want to spend the money Wayne wanted to spend...I confirmed the story with some of the head people at the studio." All wasn't lost, though. He did obtain Wayne's phone number while on the set. Happy continued, "Then I called Wayne's office (in the spring of 1955) and got his secretary Mary St. John and told her who I was and said I wanted to talk with Wayne. She put him on. That's when Wayne told me he was planning to film *The Alamo* in Mexico. I called him Mr. Wayne. That's the only time I ever called him Mr. Wayne. I said, 'I understand you want to do a picture called *The Alamo.*' I said, 'Where are you going to do it?' He said, 'In Mexico or Panama.' I said to him, 'Man, you can't shoot *The Alamo* in Mexico.' He said. 'I can shoot it any god damn place I want to.' I told him, 'Hey, look, you've got problems you don't know you've got.' He was just as hardheaded as I was. I finally said, 'We're not getting anywhere with this. Why don't I just get on a plane and come out there and talk with you about your favorite subject–*The Alamo?*' 'Fine,' he said, so I went out, and we visited, had a good time. He gave me sound reasons for shooting it in Mexico. They were sound reasons for *him*, but they really weren't sound reasons for a picture of that type."[437]

Happy traveled to Hollywood once in 1955, and twice in both 1956 and 1957 in an attempt to convince Wayne that Brackettville was the right location for his epic project. Armed with a briefcase of photographs taken by Rural Electrification Administration (REA) manager Tom Hurd, Happy made his case. And he and Wayne argued and argued and argued. Argued until the summer of 1957. They never agreed on anything, according to Shahan, but "we enjoyed each other's arguments. Wayne and I fought like nobody else; it would be hard for someone to believe that we were close friends. He had his convictions and I had mine. We argued more than agreed on anything." Wayne, strong-willed as always, was concerned about his financial situation. Filming the movie in Mexico would cost millions less than if he had to do it in the States. Shahan accepted that fact but told Wayne if he filmed it there, the Daughters of the Republic of Texas (DRT) would never let the movie be shown in Texas. Happy even set up a letter-writing campaign called "Make the *Alamo* in Texas," to try and persuade Wayne to make the right choice. Several weeks later, just as Happy predicted, Wayne received a letter from the DRT. A furious Wayne called Happy and point-blank accused him of being behind it, but Happy pleaded ignorance. "He always thought I had something to do with it," laughed Shahan. "I didn't have anything to do with it. It's just one of those things… He had property down there in Durango, and he had already shot some pictures down there. He just thought he would do *The Alamo* down there. He found out, though, that the politics would eat him up down there. At one point when he'd gotten really serious about building the sets in Mexico, he'd had a million 'dobes made down there for use in the sets. Then he found out they had made them into little houses. The Mexican there had sold them all. They used 'em more than he did. So things just began to snowball on him. I had a lot of respect for Wayne, but we didn't mind arguing. Wayne was like I am, I guess—headstrong and used to getting his own way." When tempers cooled, he eventually convinced Wayne to, at least, visit Brackettville to check out the location before he rejected the suggestion. (In later years, Shahan told B.J. Burns, his office manager, that in fact, he spearheaded the campaign.)[438]

Happy was a self-promoter; he wasn't going to wait for something to happen. A mover and a shaker, if something didn't happen, he'd make it happen! Earlier that year he worked on a fund raising campaign to help build a local hospital. In a community of 1,800 residents, it didn't have a single doctor in the immediate area. Happy recalled once when Yates had some difficulty: "I remember when he sent some of his studio people down here to Texas to set up a world premiere in San Antonio for *The Last Command*. They spent a lot of money, stayed two weeks, and didn't set up anything. When Yates's people reported back to him on their failure, he gave me a phone call. Now you have to understand that at this time, 1955, Yates didn't really know me; we were just acquaintances. He called and

164

asked what was wrong down here and why his people had not been able to set up a premiere in San Antonio. I just called it like it was. I told him, 'In the first place, you don't set up a deal down here with lying drunks! You set up a deal quick and simple with cold sober people!' He said, 'I've only got a week left.' I told him, 'That's all you need. I don't give a damn what they said; it can be done.' 'Can you do it?' he asked. I told him, 'Yeah, I can do it.' And I did it."[439]

As a result, in June 1957, Wayne sent production manager Nate Edwards to Brackettville to check out the area and see if it would be suitable for filming purposes. Happy, delighted that someone was actually coming to follow up on his constant pestering, offered to chauffeur Nate around personally. Edwards also brought his wife and soon he and Happy settled into a routine. Each morning, Nate would leave his wife at Ft. Clark and Happy would pick him up in a ranch truck, having driven eight miles into town from his Shahan-Angus ranch. Then over the course of a single week, they would spend the rest of each day driving all over the four-county area, looking at potential sites. Housing, scenery, climate, local resources, manpower, and accessibility were all critical requirements in the decision-making process. Wayne wanted a location that most resembled the terrain where the actual battle had been fought. They no doubt visited Louis Hobbs's ranch and viewed the remains of *The Last Command* set as well as other potential locations on the Nueces River. Shahan lived in town at the time. "I didn't even bring him to the (Shahan) ranch. I didn't even want him on the ranch. I never hustled a picture for our ranch 'cause I didn't want to make (any) pictures on the ranch. Ranching was my business, by then I'd become successful." He admitted he'd sold over $60,000 worth of materials from Shaker Feed and Lumber when *The Last Command* was filmed. That was sufficient for him.

At around 4:30 p.m. on the last day of Edwards's visit, Happy decided to call it a day. They were hot, tired, and hadn't found anything suitable yet, and there really wasn't anything left to show. Happy mentioned that he wanted to stop at his ranch to cut out a few head of cattle and Nate asked if he could come along as he had been born and raised on a ranch in El Paso. Later that evening, the two men planned to cross the border at Acuña and have dinner with their wives. No doubt discussing where to eat, they drove past a "bull trap" pasture on their way to "Ten-Mile," a loading pen and house located about three miles from Shahan's office. Nate's head rapidly turned left and right as they drove over the pasture. He challenged Happy as to why he hadn't suggested this location. "You know, this is the prettiest spot there is," said Edwards. Using his hands as a viewfinder, he exclaimed, "I think this is what we're looking for." He then got out of the truck and, surrounded by mesquite, prickly pear cactus, blackbrush, postoak, and guillo chaparral, took some photos. Nate was going to leave the next day but canceled his flight and came back to take another look at the site. Impressed, he shot one hundred or so more photos and then returned to California. There, he enlarged them and showed them to Wayne. Duke liked what he saw.[440]

In the summer of 1957, Shahan, tired of local politics, wrote a resignation letter as mayor of Brackettville. It wasn't anything in particular; the pressure of trying to satisfy everyone just was tiring. Happy was the type of mayor who would do anything for you and the citizens of Brackettville took advantage of his good nature: calling all hours of the day and night, asking Happy to address issues that had nothing to do with being a mayor. But he tried to resolve them nonetheless. Eventually, he tired of it and resigned. On July 2, he grabbed Virginia and the kids, got in his car, and drove to Canada for a vacation. It lasted almost two months, and, at the end of August, he drove from Lake Louise, Alberta, down the West Coast and stopped to see Wayne at his Batjac office. According to Mary St. John, she had called Happy and indicated Duke wanted to see him. Shahan hadn't heard anything after Edwards's visit in June and wondered what Wayne was going to do. No surprise there; that summer Wayne was in London and Rome completing the final edit on *Legend of the Lost*. In early September, Duke attended a sneak preview of the film, hosted by ballerina Margot Fonteyn.[441]

While Shahan was busy trying to convince Wayne to at least come *visit* Texas, Wayne was busy trying to re-energize his career. *Jet Pilot*, *Legend of the Lost*, and *The Barbarian and the Geisha*, although not losing money, brought in significantly less revenue than many of the other movies Wayne had made during the 1950s. It was time, once again, for a box-office smash. Getting a little long in the tooth for an action hero or romantic lead, Wayne needed to find his niche.

# CHAPTER ELEVEN
## A BULL BY THE TAIL

*"I thought you were never going to say it."*
*"Say what?"*
*"That you loved me."*
*"I said I'd arrest you."*
*"It means the same thing. You know that. You just won't say it." Sheriff John T. Chance and Feathers discuss their relationship in* Rio Bravo.[442]

DUKE HARBORED A LIFELONG DISLIKE OF *HIGH NOON*. "WHAT A PIECE OF SHIT," he once said in an interview. "I think it was popular because of the music. Think about it this way. Here's a town full of people who have ridden in covered wagons all the way across the plains, fightin' off Indians, and drought and wild animals in order to settle down and make themselves a homestead. And then when three no-good bad guys walk into town and the marshal asks for a little help, everybody in town gets shy. If I'd been the marshal, I would have been so goddamned disgusted with those chicken-livered yellow sons of bitches that I would have just taken my wife and saddled up and rode out of there." The film, an allegory about the impact of the Red Scare on community values, bothered Howard Hawks as well. "I didn't like (the) picture," he admitted. "I didn't think a good sheriff was going to go running around town like a chicken with his head off asking for help, and finally his Quaker wife had to save him. That isn't my idea of a good Western sheriff."[443]

Hawks hadn't made a film since the abysmal *Land of the Pharaohs* in 1955. Starring Jack Hawkins and Joan Collins (perhaps because of them), *Pharaohs* was an absolutely terrible movie. The worst of Hawks's illustrious career. He admitted the only reason he made the film was because of its Cinemascope format. He found it clumsy and "good only for showing great masses of movement. We have spent a lifetime learning how to compel the public to focus on a single thing," he explained. "Now we have something that works in exactly the opposite way, and I don't like it very much." He never used the wide-screen format again. Even though assisted by several historians in the Egypt Department of Antiquities, he only paid attention to the suggestions that best suited the picture. "I didn't know how a Pharaoh talked... I should have had somebody in there that you were rooting for. Everybody was a son of a bitch... We thought it would be an interesting story, the building of a pyramid, but then we had to have a plot, and we really didn't feel close to any of it." Hawks's art was based on dialogue, gesture, and behavioral exchanges and his not knowing how a given character would react in a specific context deprived the film of the kind of spontaneity and nuance that can be found in his best work. With brutal acting and stilted dialogue, the film was little more than sand and sex.[444]

Thoroughly discouraged, Hawks went to Europe to reflect on his life's direction. He remembered how pictures used to be made and how they were now being made. He reviewed the making of pictures he liked and "determined to go back and try to get a little of the spirit we used to make pictures with. We used to do comedy whenever we could and then we got too serious about it. I also decided that audiences were getting tired of plots... People seemed to like it better. I don't mean that if a story comes along you shouldn't do it, but I think the average plot is pretty time-worn. They're a little too inclined to say 'Oh, I've seen this before.' But, if you can keep them from knowing what the plot is, you have a chance to hold their interest." Hawks believed characterization—what a character felt and thought—motivated the story and situation. He and John Ford often discussed how everything they had done had been done before, and that the only chance they now had was to do it differently. With only a finite number of plots, the successful artist changes the story and character elements and presents to audiences a heretofore unthought-of variation. In an interview with author Michael Munn, Hawks stated, "I always feel that there are about thirty plots in all, and they've all been done. If you can think of a new way to tell a plot, that's fine. My only criteria is that I like to start a picture with a dramatic sequence and then find the place in the story where we start to get some laughs out of it." Asked if he saw any change in Hollywood since he had been away, Hawks replied, "Yes, the most startling seems to be that the fun has gone out of picture making. They're producing sad, unhappy stories. We get enough of those is real life."[445]

Licking his wounds, Hawks pursued several projects to no avail: producer Sam Spiegel even approached him to direct *The Bridge on the River Kwai*. Writing to his agent, Hawks observed, "I don't believe I'll do it. First, I think it's a good story, probably get great reviews as a picture but I don't think it will make money. It's a war story, no dames, too expensive and too damn much work for no gain." Lawsuits from both his ex-wife and Warner Bros. and a broken leg from a skiing accident combined to make his European sojourn a bittersweet event.[446]

Hawks liked to make movies: comedy, drama, musicals, and action adventures. And he loved Westerns. "There's a lot of great stories about the West that haven't been told," he said. "There are three kinds of stories. The story of the founding of the West–the historical thing of which *Red River* was a fairly good example. Then when law and order came to the West–your bad sheriff, your good sheriff. I've done that: your bad sheriff, your good sheriff." So when Hawks decided to make another film, a Western was a logical choice. Jack Warner asked him after he came back from Europe, "What are you going to do?" "A Western," he replied. "Oh, no! You don't want to do a Western, Howard." Hawks replied, "Okay, I'll go someplace else…it's about time for a good one. There's been nothing decent made for about two or three years, and I'd like to make the kind of money that that made." "No, make it here," Warner conceded. "I thought I would quit, and I did for awhile. But I got bored and decided I might as well be doing what I know best," Hawks admitted.[447]

A typical Western could be pretty boring: good guys, bad guys, heroines, cattlemen, and sheep herders, bank robberies, robber barons, etc. But to make it interesting, you must mix up elements and change it in a way audiences don't expect. Hawks wanted to shake it up, do the exact opposite of what one would expect. With a career equally divided between action films and comedies, he emphasized the dramatic or comedic aspect of an individual's character. As Hawks explained, "…a comedy is virtually the same as an adventure story. The difference is the situation—dangerous in an adventure story, embarrassing in a comedy…The only difference between comedy and tragedy is the point of view."

Wayne hadn't made a film with Hawks since *Red River* in 1946 so when the director called, Duke didn't hesitate for a moment. "I never read a script for one of Hawks's films," Duke said. "Mostly he'd say, 'Duke, do you want to make a Western?' and I'd say, 'Let's do it.' I'd get around to asking what the story was later. He'd start telling me the story, and I'd say, 'Don't tell me. I never like your stories, but they always turn out to be good.' I didn't need to see his script. We'd get to a scene, and I'd say, 'What do I do?' and he'd tell me what he wanted. Then I'd take the script, read the lines, and learn 'em, and we'd do the scene. It makes working real easy that way. But you can't work with most directors that way. I don't always trust directors if I haven't worked with them before. But Hawks I trust with my life." In fact, Hawks never seriously considered anyone but Wayne for the film's starring role. But if for some reason he declined, a list was made of eleven possible choices including Gregory Peck, Kirk Douglas, Burt Lancaster, and Sterling Hayden. With a role perfectly suited to his larger-than-life persona, the sheriff's character in the initial treatment was actually called John Wayne.[448]

First announced in preproduction as *El Paso Red*, then *Bull by the Tail*, and finally *Rio Bravo*, the film had little to do with a gunfight between the forces of good and evil. More than anything, it is an interrelationship study wrapped around a non-traditional Western. Although including classical elements such as singing cowboys, elderly comic relief, a woman of questionably ill-repute, and a strong, silent hero, the film focused instead on the relationship between Wayne and his deputies, and how they react in each specific situation. Duke, as sheriff of a small town, enlists the aid of a recovering alcoholic, an old wise-cracking cripple and a young gunslinger after he arrests the brother of a powerful local rancher for murder. The rancher's men cut off the town in preparation of breaking the brother out of jail. The unlikely foursome are all that stand between confinement and freedom. A female gambler who refuses to leave town provides a romantic relationship for the unsuspecting sheriff.[449]

The kinship between Sheriff John T. Chance and the alcoholic deputy Dude, however, defined the film. One of platonic support, Chance never failed to offer assistance when needed, criticism when warranted, and advice when required. Dude, a friend who has fallen from grace, redeemed himself only to fail yet again before finally shaking off the shackles of rye whiskey. As author Robin Wood so eloquently stated, "The expository first few minutes, where the situation from which all the action develops, and the film's central relationship, are established without a word being spoken, constitute, whether intentionally or not, a homage to the silent cinema which takes us back to Hawks's roots."[450]

According to Hawks, "Wayne represents more force, more power, than anybody else on the screen. John Ford and I often discussed how tough it was to make a good Western without Wayne... His persona provided the perfect foil for all the rest of the characters; because of his well-developed image as the toughest son-of-a-bitch on the range, he does not have to win every fight, or dominate every scene. His mere presence, even offstage, is enough... People for a long time thought of Wayne as just being a personality and not an actor. I always thought he was a good actor, and I think he's proved that he's one of the best. He carries a picture. And unless you get somebody strong with him, why, he just blows them right off the screen." As strong an actor as Wayne was, he needed to play off of an individual who, as deputy, would elicit compassion and sympathy. Someone who could draw the audience into his struggle with psychological demons. Someone to root for, and, just as important, someone who could be a convincing drunk. Wayne had a magnetic presence so powerful, he would overshadow other actors. Just as he had with Wayne, Hawks developed a list of possible co-stars: Montgomery Clift was his first choice, reuniting the trio that was so successful in *Red River*. Clift was even announced in the papers as was Frank Sinatra's name. For whatever reason, though, Clift turned down the role. Maybe he didn't want to work with Wayne, maybe Hawks was too domineering or maybe Clift saw something in Dude that he didn't want to recognize in himself. Sinatra had many talks with Hawks, liked the story and wanted to work with Wayne but that didn't work out, either. The director's list was a veritable who's who in Hollywood: James Cagney, Richard Widmark, John Cassavetes, Edmund O'Brien, Rod Steiger, John Ireland, Robert Mitchum, Tony Curtis, Spencer Tracy, Burt Lancaster, Henry Fonda, Glenn Ford, William Holden, Van Johnson, Ray Milland and Cary Grant. Jack Warner wanted James Cagney, but Hawks was still undecided.[451]

After breaking up with comic partner Jerry Lewis several years earlier, Dean Martin had appeared in several movies, including *The Young Lions* and *Some Came Running*. While garnering decent reviews, there was little to suggest that Martin had the required depth or strength to play the deputy. Martin's agent at MCA suggested Hawks might want to speak with the singer and, for some unknown reason, the director felt he could be suitable. So Dean was asked to meet with Hawks first thing the following morning. The agent didn't think that was possible, but Hawks set him straight: "Look, if he wants to get here at all, have him get here at nine-thirty." As Martin was appearing in Las Vegas at the time, he had to finish a midnight show, get up early and charter a plane just to make the meeting. This effort impressed Hawks. "You went to all that trouble to get here at nine-thirty?" Hawks asked. "Yes," Martin replied. After chatting a few minutes, Hawks told Martin, "Well, you better go up and get your wardrobe." Dean asked, "What do you mean?" Hawks replied, "Well, you're going to do it—go get your wardrobe." "I knew that, if he'd do all that," recalled Hawks, "he'd work hard, and, if he'd work hard, we'd have no trouble because he's such a personality." Confessed Martin, "I'm not lazy. Never was. That was a misconception circulated by a certain fella. Here I am, making two pictures a year, doing four or five shows for my own company on television, playing eight weeks at the Sands in Las Vegas, making twenty-four records a year and running a restaurant. And they call me lazy!"[452]

So impressed with Martin's dedication, Hawks hired him on the spot and sent him to wardrobe to pick out a costume, but Martin came back looking like a singing cowboy. Sent back down to wardrobe, Martin came up with the clothing he ended up wearing in the movie. Marlon Brando offered advice after reading Martin's script. "He didn't tell me how to play the part," confessed Martin. "He just told me what to think about. I play a drunk with DT's. I'm fighting the bottle, the bad guys, and John Wayne." After filming a scene, Dean beamed, "A lot of guys wanted to do this role. Mr. Hawks said it isn't the words that count so much in the role. It's fitting the personality to the part... It's the kind of role you'd play for nothing. I read the script and said to myself, 'Dino, this is where you gotta buckle down. This is it.'"[453]

"Having two good actors like that," admitted Hawks, "means that the dialogue and the events that take place between them are easy to work out. Dean was a great drinker in real life, and we had him play a drunk. We saw Wayne watching his old friend Dean getting rehabilitated. And just as he's getting better, someone tells him, 'You stink,' so we catch him taking a bath. I like that kind of storytelling... When you have people like Wayne and Martin, you don't always have to stick to the script. You can tell them some bit of business, and they'll ad-lib it, and, if it works, I stop there. I don't like to do retakes."[454]

Initially, Hawks envisioned gunslinger Colorado being played by an older actor. Mitchum, Curtis, Lee Marvin, Lloyd Bridges, Jack Lemmon, James Garner, Chuck Conners, and Jack Palance were all under consideration. However, as he calculated his options, he decided it might be better to cast a younger actor to attract the youth market. Michael Landon, Rod Taylor, and Stuart Whitman were all measured and found lacking. Singer Ricky Nelson, not yet eighteen and still in high school, fit the bill. Born to the entertainment business, Nelson had ten years' experience in radio and television in his family's top-rated comedy series, *The Adventures of Ozzie and Harriett*. With four gold singles and a number one album, he was sure to draw a younger audience. According to a period newspaper article, a garage mechanic tipped off Hawks to Nelson's popularity and planted the seed. He told Hawks he saw Nelson at a Los Angeles midget race track. "I've never seen anything like it," the mechanic said. "Clark Gable wouldn't have caused that much fuss. They mobbed him." Hawks paged Nelson and signed him for the role without even a test to see what he would look like in Western clothes. Along with Wayne and Martin, Hawks now had a leading man for every female generation. Fan attention for Nelson was so overwhelming, the young heart-throb had to move from the Tucson Sands hotel to an undisclosed site, just so he could practice his lines and get some rest. Females were constantly pounding on the door of room 228 with autograph books cocked and pencils sharpened yelling, "Ricky! Ricky!" Even Wayne and Martin got into the act. On his 18th birthday, Nelson was held by a bearded Martin while Wayne gave the singer eighteen whacks with a pair of water-soaked chaps. Then they threw him into three hundred pounds of manure. Wayne would be so impressed with Nelson's performance, he wanted him for a *Rio Bravo* sequel.[455]

The role of "Feathers" was a perfect opportunity for Hawks to use an up-and-coming actress. It was a great role: a mysterious dance hall beauty with hands that can shuffle cards faster than a Las Vegas blackjack dealer and with eyes for Wayne. The problem was Hawks didn't have anyone under contract. At a party thrown by producer Harold Hecht, it was suggested Wayne consider brassy, scratchy-voiced Barbara Nichols. Up and around despite a thirty-eight-inch chest cold, the shapely actress looked at Wayne and exclaimed, "But Mr. Wayne doesn't like blondes!" Duke replied quickly," "You're wrong, Barbara—I just don't marry them!"[456]

Overseas for four years, Hawks was out of the loop and so once again, made a list of potential candidates: Rhonda Fleming, Jane Greer, Martha Hyer, Diane Brewster, Beverly Garland, Carolyn Jones, Piper Laurie, Julie London, Sheree North, Janis Paige, and even Donna Reed. None seemed to fit the bill. Then,

Chris Nyby suggested auditioning a young actress Nyby had twice directed on television. He told Hawks he shouldn't cast the role without looking at the girl. Angie Dickinson was a sexy, attractive, twenty-six-year-old beauty with golden-brown hair. Moving from Kulm, North Dakota to California as a youngster, she had studied at Glendale College to be a secretary. However, winning a beauty contest on a local TV station prompted her to pursue an acting career. She attended the Batami Schneider workshop in Hollywood and quickly appeared in numerous television programs, including *Cheyenne*, *Gunsmoke*, *Line Up*, and the *Alcoa-Goodyear Theater*. "I also started to get some small roles in movies," says Dickinson. "A lot of Westerns—I seem to be the Western kind of girl. I didn't want to get ahead too fast. It's no good to have the breaks come too soon. If I got a real break, I wanted to be ready for it. So I worked at the small things and learned all the time... TV is a good stepping-stone for experience, but it can't touch the real movie makers. TV settles for too much mediocrity. The small screen makes it impossible for acting quality to really come through. And TV photography isn't good enough. It is too limited. I turned down a lot of TV series. I think a series over-exposes an actress. And I didn't want to get tagged with a character. Also, I didn't want to wear myself out."[457]

Hawks loved her low, rough, sexy voice. Reminiscent of Lauren Bacall, it was deep-throated and alluring. When he first heard it, he thought she had good tone, but "we can get it lower." According to the actress, "I did not do the yelling routine. I don't think it's such a good idea, because you scar the voice box and can't get as much shading. I did it through voice control with a coach." In addition to having the most beautiful legs in show business, Hawks said, "She has all the qualities for achieving top billing status someday. Like the rest of the great ones, she has, beyond the customary attributes, a certain 'plus' quality setting her apart from the others." And Hawks knew what he was talking about as he was largely responsible for the emergence of actresses such as Carole Lombard, Rita Hayworth, Ella Raines, Joanne Dru, and Joan Collins. One evening, Hawks watched Dickinson in a *Perry Mason* TV episode, then had her drop by his office. Hollywood lore has it that Hawks was so impressed by what he saw, he hired her on the spot without a screen test. However, according to Dickinson, she met with Hawks several times before she had a screen test with Frank Gifford as the sheriff.[458]

Not satisfied with just changing her voice, the director suggested, "You've got a pretty good figure, but it could be better." Dickinson took that as an order and got in even better shape. He also recommended she change her name but as the only suggestion she could come up with was "Anna Rome," he decided he liked her real name better. He also told her, "Now, you picked up some bad habits on TV. We're gonna get rid of those."

Dickinson enjoyed working with Wayne: "Duke was a real man. And I mean a *real* man." And the feeling was mutual. "We were damn lucky to have Angie

Dickinson," recalled Wayne. "She had beauty, sex appeal, and brains. There was none of that, 'Don't mess my hair up,' or 'I'm late because I had to get my hair just right.' She was there on time, she knew what was needed, and she did the job as good as any actress. And with Angie you had someone who was not the female equivalent of me, nor was she fragile, but she was a real woman who could be tough and gentle and sexy, and she didn't have to rough me up to get her way with me. She was the kind of woman in *Rio Bravo* you just couldn't resist."[459]

Rounding out the cast was veteran character actor Walter Brennan. Included on the early list with Arthur Hunnicutt, Gabby Hayes, Burl Ives, William Demarest, Lee Marvin, Buddy Ebsen, and Lee J. Cobb, Brennan was the obvious choice. His character in the film is a man with a limp. In order to get into character, he insisted on having a sharp nail driven up through the heel of one shoe so that it would protrude one-third of an inch above the inner sole. As a result, every time Brennan took a step, he involuntarily jabbed himself into the twitchy limp, and whenever he stood still, the leg is bent forward to keep the painful heel from the nail point. Pretty effective. He also took out his dental plates and was unshaven. "Think of it," he lamented. "After three Oscars and forty years in the business. I'm known for a character I did one season on television! I wanted to get as far away from Grandpa McCoy as I could and still, the visitors on the set always recognize me from the TV show." Veteran television actors Ward Bond, John Russell, Claude Akins, and Pedro Gonzales-Gonzales also were part of Hawks' ensemble.[460]

Hawks planned to film in Old Tucson but wasn't satisfied with its condition or appearance, even though the set could be rented for only $50/day. Time had taken its toll: adobe walls and buildings had deteriorated from the ravages of wind, rain, and the relentless sun. Originally constructed almost twenty years earlier for the movie *Arizona*, most directors only wanted to spruce up the place. Not Hawks. Spending over $100,000, he brought one hundred carpenters and painters from Warner Bros. to build twenty new buildings at ⅞ scale so the characters would look larger than life. Art director Leo Kuter explained, "Some of the buildings are little more than skeletons, others have been superimposed upon the old adobes already here, others are to be used for interior sequences and have been finished, both inside and out. Some have catwalks on the roofs, strong enough to hold the heavy camera and lighting equipment for shots angled from above. On the south end of the town, a large barn and warehouse were built. On the north end, a jail, two saloons, a hotel, and several business buildings were completed. Most of the buildings have covered porches and several are two-storied." All in all, picturesque, authentic, and functional.[461]

Script development started in August 1958 with a thirteen-page treatment by Leigh Brackett and Jules Furthman, two writers Hawks had worked with twelve years earlier on *The Big Sleep*. With drafts completed in September and November, the script was finally taking shape. Hawks' daughter Barbara received screen credit as "B.H. McCampbell" for suggesting the explosive finish. In an interview with author Todd McCarthy, she said her father "came back from Europe with a basic idea for a Western, but he didn't know how to resolve the story, to get them all out of jail." So she and her husband Don worked out a long story with numerous situations for the characters to confront, Warner's legal department never saw the original material and her credit was based on an "unpublished story" without documentation. The script would constantly be tinkered with: add a word here, delete there, even through the actual filming, so much so that the final approved script was significantly different than what was filmed. Sharper, crisper, tighter.[462]

Wayne was a perfectionist on set with little patience for sloppiness or lack of professionalism. But he was quick to offer suggestions and encouragement when needed. Although young master Ricky had a great deal of television experience, he was still a novice to the big screen. "John Wayne took me in hand the first morning I arrived on location at Tucson," he said. "He spent two hours helping me just pick out a cowboy hat that was right for me. I'd never worn any kind of hat before in my life, and I was worried about this Stetson bit. The wrong size or shape could have made me look pretty silly." Even Hawks' daughter Barbara pitched in to help Nelson learn to ride a horse. But Wayne had a tough time on the set—Hawks was rough on him. Not rough like Ford: short, verbally abusive. Rough in the sense that he didn't give Wayne anything to sink his teeth into. Hawks would just say "Oh, well, Duke will get by," and give everybody else everything to do. "I would have been lost in *Rio Bravo* at one point," said Duke. "We took a whole day—when Dean goes in and discovers the blood and shoots the guy down and I stand back as the father image. I was a pain in the ass. You know, I'm just the father image then and that woulda wrecked me. I finally thought me a thing—when we first come in and the guy says, 'Nobody came in here.' So I said, 'Nobody came in here, huh?' Not even the hitting him with the rifle. But Martin says, 'Easy there.' And I said, 'Aw, I'm not gonna hurt him!' Shit, now this puts me back in the picture. But I would have been out of it too long if I couldn't find something for right there."[463]

Hawks was a deliberate, cautious director. As a newcomer, so to speak, Dickinson sometimes found it difficult to understand his direction. "He knew that he wanted something special," she says, "but if he told you what he wanted, it wouldn't be special. He wanted to make you come up with something special. And that was tough. But he had the patience…to say, 'Okay, that's not too bad but let's try it this time with…' whatever. He would sit back and kind of wait for his thinking to filter through to you." As a result, Hawks' approach allowed the actor to "find" the character and develop the individual personality—an approach Wayne fully supported. "I see no reason for running down Westerns or masking them under such phony sub-titles as 'adult' or 'psychological' or 'different,'" he said. "Westerns are our folklore, and they become folklore in less than a hundred years. Folklore is important in every country's history and background. However, I don't condone Westerns that are just an excuse for gunplay and gore. They've got to have a good human story, and, as long as they have a real story, westerns will always make for top entertainment." Martin agreed. In a guest column he wrote for columnist Frank Morris, Dean concurred, "Let me say right now that *Rio Bravo* is not what the Madison Avenue boys call a "psychological Western," an "adult western," or any of that josh you've been hearing about lately. It's a straight, old-line, blood-and-guts Western with believable characters and logical action. It's legitimate American folklore which doesn't need to be jazzed up with sounding adjectives. Remember *Red River*? Then you know what I mean."[464]

## TALES FROM THE SET - PART II

Robert B. Lee was in charge of "mixing" the sound on *Rio Bravo*. It wasn't all fun and games, though. Ambient background noises could be deadly to the soundtrack. One day the filming area seemed overrun with rattlesnakes. A mysterious hissing sound would drown out dialogue. After twisting control panel sound dials in vain, Hawks shut down the set and asked everyone to help the wranglers liquidate the snakes. "We tracked down the noises for two hours and finally found out they were not rattlers after all," Lee said sadly. "Locusts. Packs of them." The production simply moved away from the locusts' area.

Coughing horses also squelched the soundtrack. With throats irritated by desert dust, there was only one solution: cough syrup every morning. Squealing pigs were also a problem. Giving them corn kept them too busy eating at a lower register to bother the recording devices. But the toughest critters were the turkeys. According to Lee, "Their gobble-gobble was apparently actuated by the cameras or something because that's when they'd set up a racket—soon as the cameras rolled. But we solved this one too. We also solved the question of what to eat for dinner for the next three nights."[465]

Both Dean Martin and Ricky Nelson were six-footers but felt like shorties on the set with six-foot-four Wayne and John Russell towering over them. Even Hawks and Ward Bond were six-foot-three. Martin said philosophically, "(Well,) at least they can't sing!"[466]

A horse that objected to music had to be thrown off the set. Every time a certain tune was played, the horse began pawing the dirt, shaking its head and mane, and baring its teeth. The steed was ordered removed after its upstaging distractions ruined a third consecutive take. The horse, standing with two other animals at a hitching rail, was supposed to be minding its own business in the background while Wayne and Nelson listened to the sound of "El Deguello" coming from a saloon. "You can't really blame that horse," said head wrangler

Ace Hudkins. "He's Texas-bred and his name is 'Tex.' He's only doing what any Texan would do about that song." ("El Deguello." A signal of no quarter, it literally translates to the cutting of one's throat. This music was probably played by Mexican buglers prior to the battle of the Alamo.)[467]

Harry Carey Jr. received a screen credit, even though he never appeared in the film. Hired to play Harold, a townsman whose help Wayne rejects, Carey angered Hawks on one of his first days on the set. "I really messed myself up with him," confessed Carey. "I was a full-fledged drinker when they called me over to do *Rio Bravo*. It would have been a ten-week job for me." Carey arrived on the set and met with Hawks and Wayne to do a costume check. Already in cowboy costume, Hawks wanted him dressed as a townsperson in top hat. Carey retired to the hotel, had three or four shots of vodka, and was feeling no pain. When he came back to rehearse with Wayne, he wore a purple cowboy hat. Wayne said, "Where'd you get that hat? It's a good thing we're just rehearsing." Hawks said, "Okay, you get a new hat, and we'll shoot that tomorrow." Carey turned, and as he walked away, he said, "Okay, Howard." Angered by the informal use of his name. Hawks significantly reduced the size of Carey's role. A ten-week stint became just two days. Eventually, Carey's scene was cut, but his contract was honored in full.[468]

One day, during rehearsal, Wayne was supposed to enter the saloon and say to Claude Akins, "You're coming with me." Akins was to reply, "I don't think so. Look around." Wayne looked around and saw several men with guns pointed in his direction. Akins then said, "So what are you going to do now?" At this point, Wayne replied, "Well, the first thing I'm going to do is change the tone of my voice if all you assholes are going to talk just like I do." Hawks asked what he meant. Duke replied, "Well, goddamnit, everybody is playing John Wayne!" Director Budd Boetticher, who was also on the set at that time, recalled, "Wayne had a powerful presence, and he was so perfect in cowboy boots and a cowboy hat that what he did kind of rubbed off on other actors if they weren't careful. It was really funny to hear the other actors start to talk like Duke and they didn't even realize it."[469]

As a publicity stunt, Angie Dickinson's legs were insured by Lloyds of London as well they should be.

The music for the song "My Rifle, My Pony and Me," was originally written by Dimitri Tiomkin as the main theme for *Red River*. According to Hawks, "it didn't get down to the location in time, so we had to use another little cowboy song in that picture. I said we'll use some strains of it there and keep it for a song later on. We remembered it and changed the words and used it in *Rio Bravo*.

Awfully nice song. It was very popular in Europe; he made a lot of money on it." The song's initial title was "Settle Down" with lyrics by Paul Francis Webster. Johnny Cash had written the song "Restless Kid" for Nelson to sing, but Tiomkin insisted instead on "Pony." Criticized as being self-indulgent for adding a musical interlude that added virtually nothing to the plot, Hawks confessed he did it for the sheer pleasure of watching them sing: "When you've got some talent, your job is to use it." Tiomkin also wrote the "Deguello" used in the film. Hawks admitted, "I heard what they *really* played, and I told Dimi, 'You can write something better 'n *that*.' And he did." The instrumental would also be used in Wayne's *The Alamo*. Explained Hawks, "I remember (Wayne) was laughing and he said, 'You son of a bitch—I had to go and buy that from Dimi!" (Previously, Webster and Tiomkin had teamed up on *Giant*, *Friendly Persuasion*, *Old Man and the Sea*, and *The Last Train From Gun Hill*).[470]

In the final action sequence, a large storage barn exploded. Hawks yelled, "Cut!" in mid-explosion. Unfortunately, the barn had to be rebuilt and blown up a second time as multi-colored stacks of paper, stored in the front office of the building, blew into the air like confetti, creating a gay, colored effect. Appropriate for a New Year's celebration but not suited for a hard core Western.[471]

Hawks deliberately distorted the typical Western in *Rio Bravo* and created a new genre all its own. By turning the storyline inside out, he created a deformation of relationship and situation. Traditional ethics and values no longer applied. Characters reacted in ways unexpected to the norm and resulting action drove the story in new and unforeseen directions. For Wayne, this was an ideal situation. He wasn't required to "carry the load." An ensemble cast allowed him to react to the situation rather than create it. Wayne was able to act so well within it that it seemed he wasn't even acting. He glided easily through the complicated character relationships with a skill that was something to behold. Supporting a drunken friend, mentoring the young gunslinger, or being seduced by the dance hall girl, he brought realism, belief, and honesty to the character. Too old to be a romantic lead, Wayne was always better when the woman forced the issue. His relationship with Feathers was more innuendo, implication, and sly asides than consummation.

Contemporary reviews were generally favorable but failed to recognize the film's significant accomplishment. Oh, there were those who thought Wayne was just playing Wayne, as if there were anything the matter with that. *Films in Review* called it a "routine Western that is almost actionless in the first 120 of its 140 minutes. Trite dialogue and stock characterizations make these 120 minutes a soporific bore...The performances lack any distinction." And the *New York Times* wrote "It is hardly likely that anyone will sleep through *Rio Bravo*, but chances are that a wide-awake viewer will not be particularly startled by its random fireworks…despite its slickness, virility, occasional humor, and…authentic professional approach, it is well made but awfully familiar fare." Others, though, gave credit where credit was due. *Variety* admitted "Wayne delivers a faithful portrayal of the peace officer." *Time* wrote, "Wayne, of course, walks off with the show—not by doing anything in particular, but simply by being what he is: at fifty-one, still one of the biggest believable he-men in Hollywood," and the *New York Herald* suggested that "the inventiveness that keeps this picture fresh and flavorsome for nine minutes less than two hours and a half ought to be a lesson in directorial ingenuity to be studied by some directors of Westerns." High praise indeed.[472]

When Duke finished *Rio Bravo*, he felt his career was back on track. Older but wiser, confident and strong, Sheriff John T. Chance would emulate the persona Wayne would play for the rest of his career. Hawks and Wayne so enjoyed working together again, they planned on yet a third project. Supposedly based on a true story, it was to be called *Klondike*; it started out in California as a Western and ended in Alaska's gold rush. So enthralled with the idea, they even considered the Cinerama process. The three-camera technique had been used primarily to film travelogues without much viewer interest. Even the Cinemiracle refinement failed to pique audience interests. Hawks and Wayne decided to change all that. "I think the time is ripe for putting a story on that big screen," the director said. "Wayne and I have a story which I think would work—a kind of Western. It won't be easy. You've got to have a very special kind of story for the big screen, one that gives you a variety of backgrounds, *Red River* would have been ideal because it concerns a long cattle drive. *The Searchers*, which Wayne did with John Ford, would also have been good—if they had carried the search through a lot of different Western backgrounds." *(Second only to John Ford as Wayne's greatest director, the following books on Howard Hawks are worthy of further analysis: "Howard Hawks: The Grey Fox of Hollywood" by Todd McCarthy, "Howard Hawks Interviews" edited by Scott Breivold, and "Howard Hawks" by Robin Wood.)*[473]

# CHAPTER TWELVE
# "HURRAH FOR THE BONNIE
# BLUE FLAG..."

*"I left my love, my love I left a sleepin' in her bed. I turned my back on my true love, when fightin' Johnny Reb. I left my love a letter in the hollar of a tree. I told her she would find me in the US Cavalry. Hi-Yo! Down they go, there's no such word as 'can't.' We're riding down to Hell and Back, for Ulysses Simpson Grant."* Written by Stan Jones for *The Horse Soldiers.*[474]

BORN FEBRUARY 29, 1908, IN ALBERTA, LOUISIANA, DEE BROWN EXHIBITED a life-long intense interest in Native Americans and the old West culminating in his magnificent opus *Bury My Heart at Wounded Knee*. Reporter, librarian, historian, he used books to expand and enhance his imagination. Long before his ground-breaking efforts, though, Brown happened upon the unpublished letters of two brothers who served with the Union army during the War of the Rebellion: Henry and Stephen Forbes of the 7th Illinois volunteer cavalry. Along with the 6th Illinois and 2nd Iowa, they rode on Col. Benjamin Henry Grierson's famous raid from LaGrange, Tennessee, to Baton Rouge, Louisiana, in April/May 1863. Leading his undersized cavalry brigade deep into the heart of Mississippi, utilizing skill and a great deal of luck, Grierson tied up a significant number of Confederate troops while Gen. Ulysses S. Grant continued his Vicksburg offensive. Long fascinated by the Civil War, Brown felt there were elements of the story that were appealing: demolished railroads, freed slaves, destroyed locomotives, diversions, feints, vigorous pursuits, and heroism. What more could a reader ask for? "Only bits and pieces of this dramatic adventure had been published," recalled Brown, "and so I resolved to write the complete history." As a result, in 1954 The University of Illinois published *Grierson's Raid*, which soon became the definitive historical work on the subject.[475]

By then, writer Harold Sinclair had published seven novels with middling success. Recipient of a Guggenheim Fellowship after his first novel *Journey Home* was released in 1926, Sinclair went on to write a trilogy: *American Years, Years of Growth*, and *Years of Illusion*, the partially fictionalized history of Bloomington and McLean County, Illinois. Finishing five books in six years, he was extremely prolific yet commercially vacant. Nineteen fifty-five would change his financial position. Combining historical fact with literary dénouement, Sinclair crafted a Civil War novel worthy of Louis L'Amour. With deep roots in the Bloomington area, it was only natural that he would eventually cross paths with the tale of Benjamin Grierson. Sinclair had apparently puttered with this story off and on for a dozen years and what first attracted him to the raid remains unclear. However, after signing a contract with publisher Harper & Brothers that spring, it would take just six months before he completed his work.[476]

Utilizing Brown's basic story, Sinclair invoked an author's license to modify characters and subject matter (as if the story wasn't already exciting enough.) Grierson became Col. John Francis Marlowe, a civilian drawn into "North-South dissention (that) should have been settled long since by means of the intelligence nature had provided." Marlowe was a reluctant hero who knew his duty and did it. Sinclair also wrote of a skirmish at Newton's Station which never occurred but was used primarily as a backdrop for the interplay of characters. Receiving favorable reviews not only from the general populace but Civil War academia as well, *The Horse Soldiers* became Sinclair's most popular and successful novel to date and placed him on the best-seller list for the first and only time of his career. Dee Brown became so enamored with Sinclair's manuscript he consented to write the forward to the book: "...factual history seldom reaches into the hearts and minds of the characters who made it. The novelist, however, creating a story around a historical event is free to develop character, to invent speech and thought that reveals character. Because of this, a novelist who knows humility often reproduces in his work a picture of the past that is more believable to us than the bare bones of history. Such a book is Harold Sinclair's *The Horse Soldiers*, a masterful recreation of one of the Civil War's most dramatic adventures." However, all is not what it seems. Sinclair informed Brown that Harper's would not publish his book unless it could be shown that there was no pilfering by Sinclair from Brown's previous work. Despite his wife's premonitions, finger-shaking, etc., Brown wrote the introduction.[477]

John Lee Mahin and Martin Rackin were relatively successful screenwriters/

producers, Mahin more so than Rackin: *A Star is Born, Captains Courageous, The Wizard of Oz, Show Boat, Darby's Rangers,* and *Heaven Knows, Mr. Allison.* Mahin was nominated for two Academy Awards. Working together at Warner Bros, they decided to strike out on their own and create an independent production company. Mahin, tall, chunky and soft-spoken, started out as an actor before beginning a career in journalism. A favorite of Clark Gable and Victor Fleming, he contributed dialogue to their projects without screen credit. As a glib, friendly screenwriter, Rackin wrote extensively for Red Skelton as well as Martin and Lewis. As a young lad, he started out as a delivery boy for a men's milliner. He used to deliver hats to Damon Runyon. Feeling sorry for the youngster, Runyon gave him $5 a week to go to school between jobs. From there, he advanced to a copy boy at the *New York Mirror.* Later, he spent several years at RKO and freelanced as a screenwriter/producer throughout the 1950s. With almost a half-century of combined experience, they made a formidable team. In 1957 at Warner's, Mahin-Rackin worked to develop Pearl Buck's book, *Letter From Peking.* Mahin would write the script, and Ms. Buck would help bring it to the screen. Purchasing the story from galley proofs, the duo advertised for a "handsome, tall, Eurasian" who was half-American and "can act," for the starring role. Michael Anderson, who directed *Around the World in 80 Days,* would be at the helm. Unfortunately, the project never got off the ground. Failing that, they decided to develop their own projects. "But we weren't satisfied," they said when asked why they left the studio system. "When you're working for a studio, you never get to roll the dice yourself. You write a picture for Marlon Brando, and you end up with a second-rate actor saying your lines. Or you change a whole script to make it fit Gary Cooper. You never do things the way you want them done."[478]

For their first film, it was announced in April 1958 that Mahin-Rackin Productions would make a movie based on Sinclair's novel, the story of a daring Union cavalry raid deep into Rebel territory. Fox initially had purchased the rights but failed to act on the option. After it kicked around town for a while with no takers, Mahin-Rackin gambled one dollar to option the property. They actually used very little of the book; the Civil War incident, Grierson's Raid, of course, was public domain. Asked why they were interested in the piece, they stated, "To us as writers, it had all the dash and boldness of a commando raid. It had a fresh background for its type of story, and we both felt sympathetically that the War Between the States was the last of the gallant wars. It was the last of the great cavalry charges with guidons flying, colors unfurled, sabres pointed, and horses' hooves-pounding. It was the last time that America would ever war brother against brother. There was a chance in this epic story for a spectacle and an opportunity for warmth. It had the necessary elements for color and large screen. It had reality, which to us is the prime requisite of a great motion picture." With the story and preliminary screenplay in place, the next step was to attract a lucrative investor.[479]

As the development project seemed to be a sure-fire winner, M-R took it to the Mirisch Company, which agreed to provide $3.5 million in financing *if* Rackin could deliver two top-notch stars and an important director. Get the right director; you'll get the right stars; John Ford was the immediate choice. A six-time Academy Award winner, Ford was a Civil War buff but had never directed a film dealing with that period. When asked, Ford was delighted to accept the opportunity. Of course, as Dan Ford wrote in his biography of his grandfather, "baiting his hook by offering John $200,000 plus 10% of the net," didn't hurt. He took it like a hungry fish. "With a good script," Mahin explained, "(a screenwriter) can pick any company he wants. We picked Mirisch; we were promised no interference; it was even put into our contracts. So we were able to promise John Ford the same thing–no front office!" Releasing the movie through Mirisch for United Artists let M-R avoid huge outlays in preproduction costs. They would incur only 2.5% overhead vs. 37% at a large studio like MGM.[480]

Once secured, Walter Mirisch met with Ford to discuss the film. "I think we better start talking about casting," he mentioned to Pappy. "Well, Duke. Duke," Ford replied without hesitation. Mirisch was pleased but concerned about timing. "We really need to make this picture in the spring or summer," he continued, "because it's almost entirely exterior. So we must be able to submit the script to Wayne for his approval as soon as possible, so that we can get an answer from him as to whether he will be available when we're ready to shoot." Ford wasn't worried. "When I'm ready, he'll be there," he replied confidently. Just two hours before he left on a short vacation, a Hawaiian graduation gift for his two grandsons, Ford signed a contract to direct *The Horse Soldiers*. Though touting Wayne, Ford made no secret at the time that Clark Gable was his first choice to play Marlowe. Shortly before he left on a fishing trip to Northern California, Gable had dinner with Mahin and Rackin and received a copy of the script "so that he could get to work on it." He returned to Los Angeles in mid-July, at which time he met with M-R to discuss the picture.[481]

James Stewart's situation was a bit more complicated. Though interested in the role, he had significant concerns about his character's motivation. Stewart felt Keller (Kendall) was insubordinate, too cocky...too feisty...too fresh with Marlowe. He also felt Marlowe's revealing the reason he hated doctors came too late in the script. Consequently, he felt the audience would, by then, be annoyed with Marlowe and no longer be in sympathy with him. M-R agreed; if Stewart insisted on playing the typical Stewart character (quiet, peace-loving, gentleman-like, etc.,) the character, as written, was definitely more Wayne than Stewart. Stewart re-read both the script and Sinclair's book yet still felt the character was wrong for him.[482]

While M-R was in discussions with Gable and Stewart, they were also negotiating with Wayne in case other options fell through. Duke had contacted them, but M-R laughed and hung up after his first proposal. Obviously, though, they were interested in a Gable-Wayne marquee. Stewart remained uncommitted until he met with Ford in early July. Once he turned down the role, Duke was then seriously considered for the role of Dr. Kendall. But, by then, Gabel wasn't available. At one point, Gregory Peck approached Mirisch, told them he was available for a movie in October and wanted to know, "What's going on with *The Horse Soldiers*?" M-R wanted Elizabeth Taylor to play Hannah Hunter, but, with so much of the budget going to the leading actor's salary, little was left for Liz. By the time Ford returned from the islands, Duke was now rumored to star as was Gena Rowlands and the voluptuous former Miss Utah, Carol Ohmart. The director was right, though. When he was ready to start production, Duke was there. On a visit to Ford's home, Rackin met Wayne, who signed a contract even before he read the script. Now the question was, if Wayne was Marlowe, who would be Kendall?[483]

After William Holden starred in the blockbuster *The Bridge on the River Kwai*, he could pretty much pick and choose exactly which projects he preferred. Unfortunately, he had one small problem. He was under contract to Paramount, which wasn't giving him new scripts worth starring in. Not only did the studio not have anything available for him, it hadn't had anything for almost two years. While the studio could afford to wait, Holden couldn't. Also under contract to Columbia, he flew off to London where he filmed *The Key* with Sophia Loren and Trevor Howard in December 1957. With nothing on his schedule, he returned to New York for the premiere of *Bridge*. He wanted to appear in 20th Century-Fox's *Roots of Heaven*, but Paramount wouldn't allow it. Offered *The Counterfeit Traitor*, which wouldn't be ready to start for another year, Holden took off on a whirlwind tour promoting *River Kwai*: London, Paris, Rome, Munich, Berlin, Africa, Tokyo, Hong Kong, and Singapore. He didn't mind the travel, though. With one hundred fifty thousand miles under his belt in the last year, Holden admitted, "(in the past) a star could get by on acting talent and personality. Today, under many profit-sharing deals, he not only has to act in the picture, he has to go out and beat the bushes to sell it, both here and abroad. Most of my traveling hasn't been to location work; it has been in the exploitation and promotion end of the business. But it's necessary because 58% of our gross today is from foreign markets."[484]

While in London, Holden's disagreement with Paramount came to a head. Holding out for scripts, the studio demanded he make a film or go on suspension. Holden chose suspension. "It wasn't a good picture," he said, "and nobody can afford to appear in a bad one these days. People tell me not to worry about good scripts. Then they chide me for playing secondary characters… I'd rather play second lead in a great picture than the lead in a turkey." Holden had previously been suspended eight times; he gave in twice, the studio gave in twice and four times, it was considered a draw. While on suspension, an actor can't work in any other film and does not draw a salary. All he can do is sit and wait. Holden would have had sixteen months of waiting before his contract expired.[485]

Holden and Wayne were two peas in a pod: major movie stars, adored by the public, perpetually on the top ten lists of favorite actors. One evening, Rackin held a party in his Bel Air home, and director Richard Quine wandered into an interesting conversation between the two drunken actors. Lamenting their chosen profession over a bottle of cognac, they complained about the makeup, the hair dye, the costumes, the indignity of exposing emotion before a hundred people, the adoration of strangers. "I'll be damned if it isn't a job for sissies," grumbled Wayne. "I hate being a picture actor," exclaimed Holden. "Goddammit, so do I!" Wayne agreed.[486]

In September 1958, Paramount submitted a request for a preliminary injunction to stop Holden from appearing in *Soldiers*. While the studio claimed it would suffer irreparable harm if he was permitted to make the film, Holden countered he stood to lose $1.5 million if denied the opportunity. Paramount further claimed in an agreement reached with the actor, Holden entered into an oral contract the previous January to star in six films. It also asserted under a disputed 1956 oral agreement, which superseded a 1951 written contract, that Holden was not a free agent. Holden vigorously disagreed. His contention was that he never recognized the 1956 agreement and further declared that the studio had failed, under a pre-emption-of-service clause in the 1951 contract, to object within four days of his notice of intention to appear in *The Horse Soldiers*.[487]

Pending court approval, he looked forward to working with Ford. Approached at a party, Holden liked the sound of the project and came on board. "I can just see Jack Ford telling me to get into the swamps and start sloshing," he said sarcastically. "I haven't worn a business suit or worked in a Hollywood Studio for three years..." In mid-October a Federal judge refused to issue the injunction, and Holden was cleared to accept a co-starring role in the film. Holden felt the legal fracas helped burnish part of his talent. "I've played all kinds of roles," he said, "but I've never felt really ready to portray a lawyer. By the time I get finished with this case though, I'll be ready." And Holden didn't mind that Wayne had a meatier part. "Stories with two good men's parts are difficult to find," he said, "yet they are one of the best of all types for a film. But I've never been interested in the length of a role. You're not playing second-fiddle as long as you're giving the best of your talent. What I look for is a property that is stimulating and exciting for an audience and has something they can identify themselves with. That's the real secret of the fantasy—being able to look and say, 'There, but for the grace of God go I.'"[488]

For the female co-star, Ford chose relative unknown, twenty-five-year-old Constance Towers, a five-foot-ten blonde with a resonant voice. Rackin, who had previously considered her for an Alan Ladd film, remembered and introduced her to Ford. A former nightclub and TV singing partner to Jack Carson and a singer at the St. Regis in New York, she was working the supper-club circuit in

Las Vegas when Columbia brought her out West for a quickie film with Frankie Lane, *Bring Your Smile Along*. Towers, though enamored with Hollywood, asked for her release and went back to the supper clubs. "I had to find out who I was and where I wanted to go," she remarked. Her career started when she sang on the radio while attending high school in Seattle. "For a year and a half, I was on the road, playing the Hilton hotel circuit," she said. "It was a wonderful experience. I discovered what kind of songs I could sing and what kind I couldn't. I met up with all kinds of audiences." But the constant grind wore her down and, once again, she wanted to try her hand in films. She studied dramatics and sang occasionally on TV. When the casting call for actresses went out, over five hundred were considered; she was just one of ten tested for the role. "It didn't hurt that he (Ford) had served with my uncle, who is an admiral in the Navy," Towers said after she won the part, "and that my father was born in Dublin." In order to better play her role, she perfected a southern accent with the help of Virginia Smith, a Jackson, Mississippi native who was a secretary at Columbia studio.[489]

To fill the role of Towers' Negro servant, Ford chose tall, gangly, athletic, thirty-one-year-old tennis sensation Althea Gibson. Ranked No. 1 in the world at the time, Gibson was the first African-American to win a Grand Slam title (the French Open in 1956) and both the U.S. Open and Wimbledon in 1957-8. At the time, she had given up competitive tennis though she played a few exhibitions to keep in shape. She first heard about the role of Lukey when her agent asked her to fly out for a screen test. Not too hopeful since numerous experienced actresses also sought the role, she was ecstatic when she got it. "My goodness, who wouldn't be thrilled working with Wayne and Holden?" she exclaimed. "They're the very best in the business. I've never had a minute's dramatic coaching. Never took a lesson in my life. Come to think of it, I've never been on a stage before except to sing a couple of times on (the) Ed Sullivan television show. But I don't believe I got the part in the picture just because of my tennis fame. I wouldn't be in Hollywood today if director John Ford didn't think I could do the part the way he wants it done. So I'll do the best I can. I've done that all my life. I didn't even know I had the part until a couple of weeks ago. I took a screen test quite a while back, but I didn't have any idea how it would turn out. Before accepting the role I checked very carefully to make certain the job wouldn't interfere with my amateur status as a tennis player. That's the most important thing in my life. I think tennis has prepared me a bit for acting. Through tennis I learned poise and dignity. You stand alone out there on the court and have no one else but yourself to blame for your mistakes. I believe acting is a lot that way, too. The picture might open an entire new career for me. It might be nice to become a full-time actress, but it all depends on how well I perform this time." Her first day on the set, she had a scene with difficult dialogue. "At least Mr. Ford said, 'Cut! Print it!' So I guess it was all right," she said modestly. "He has been very kind to me. It's not much different from playing in a tournament. The camera is the same as the spectators. I just go out there and do the best I can."[490]

As usual, Ford wasn't averse to using veteran cinema stars to round out his supporting cast. Hoot Gibson, rodeo champion, stuntman and cowboy movie star for nearly twenty years, was one of the most popular western stars on the silent screen, second only to Tom Mix. As a teenager, he worked at Owl Drug Co. delivering drugs and packages. "That is where I got the name of Hoot," he recalled. "It came from Owl and later the boys started calling me Hoot Owl, then it got down to Hoot and Hoot has stuck with me ever since." Born in 1892, Gibson was already sixty-six when Ford ran into him at the Golden Nugget in Las Vegas, where he lived with his wife. Asked if he wanted to be in the movie, Gibson worried about an injury he'd incurred two years earlier. "...I was climbing up a ridge on a horse," he remembered. "The horse slipped, and I couldn't get out from under. I smashed all the cartilage in the joint." Hoot hesitated, suggesting his hip wouldn't allow him to climb on a horse. Compassionate individual that he was, Ford replied, "We'll get a couple of cowhands who can throw you up on the horse."[491]

Even songwriters got in the act. Stan Jones, famous for writing *Ghost Riders in the Sky* in 1948, wrote the song *I Left My Love* for the film's title sequence and made an uncredited appearance as Ulysses S. Grant.

Pulling a cast together seemed relatively easy; developing a workable script proved a bit more difficult. Sinclair adapted Brown's story, Mahin modified Sinclair's. And they needed some romance in the script to entertain the mass audiences (read: "women"). Sometimes this was done in the typical hug-and-kiss school of Hollywood, but, according to Mahin, they felt the adult approach to a love story would have greater appeal. As details of the massive production began to take shape, Mahin became concerned. "Poor Marty (Rackin) is dead now, and I don't want to blame him," confessed Mahin. "He was a funny, witty man, and he always had a joke for everything, but he didn't have any warmth. I think that's what the story needed."

"You know, Marty," he once told his partner, "I think we'd better do some more work on the script. It needs fixing." "Oh, the hell with it," replied Rackin. "Don't worry about it. Leave it alone. We've got John Ford, John Wayne and William Holden. That's enough. We're going to make a fortune." Ford didn't agree, though. After he read the first draft, Ford told cinematographer Bill Clothier, "Well, if you think I'm going to make their god damned script you are mistaken." While he and Rackin worked on the script on Ford's yacht in Honolulu, the director asked parenthetically, "Do you know where we ought to make this picture?" "No, where?" Rackin replied. "Lourdes," said Ford sarcastically. "It's going to take a god damn miracle to pull this off." His heart really wasn't in it and according to Rackin, Ford was the reason the script never came together.

"I don't think Jack really liked *The Horse Soldiers*," he confessed. "He never really got into the script. He never really applied himself to it."[492]

If the script had difficulties, they were insignificant compared to the contract negotiations between agents, lawyers, and accountants. With six separate entities involved (Batjac, Argosy, Mahin-Rackin Productions, United Artists, William Holden Productions, and the Mirisch Company), it took six months of haggling over terminology, defining basic contractual terms, and complex legalese before a 250-page contract was agreed upon, twice the length of the actual script. Each leading actor agreed to a fee of $750,000 plus 20% of the profits. Towers received $5,000 and Althea Gibson, who had never appeared in a film, $13,500. With a total budget of $3,599,447, including the costs for bit players and extras, almost $1,990,251 was devoted to salaries. "We don't mind," Rackin said airily. "You gotta give away to get in this business. And even if we don't get, it'll be worth it. We've had the time of our lives." Rackin was pleased with the arrangement and was willing to sign up the pair for six films at that price. "I'll tell you this," Rackin said. "When we bought the book we didn't have the money to make the picture. But, the moment we had the book, the script and John Ford to direct the picture, we could get all the money we needed. It was just a matter of deciding whom we would let loan us the money. Everyone thinks a producer today has to have handmade suits and Cadillacs to attract stars. And, when John and I decided to go into business for ourselves, everyone in Hollywood tried to talk us out of it. But, we believed that today, because stars are no longer under contracts to studios, they can be attracted. And the things that attract them are good stories. No matter how big a star a man is, he knows that people won't come to see him in a bad story." Wayne finalized his contract September 10, 1958, less than two months after he finished *Rio Bravo*. Back in the saddle once again.[493]

As Holden dealt with legal issues and Mahin and Rackin worked on the script, Ford's son Pat headed south to scout locations. After searching through six states, he flew to New Orleans, looked around the swamps of Natchitoches and Clarence, Louisiana, and then drove to Natchez, Mississippi, where he discovered additional potential sites. Twenty-eight shooting days were scheduled on location with another nineteen in the studio. Period slave quarters and shacks were purchased, not duplicated, and moved to the locations. The Prudhomme Plantation, outside of Natchitoches, was also used. Exteriors were filmed at Lot 3, MGM studio, with interiors at Goldwyn.

While on location, John Ford came face-to-face with the hideous segregation issue. According to Mahin, the director had severe problems dealing with it. "Jack found a black church in Louisiana and hired the whole congregation as extras. Then the redneck supervisor of the local board of labor appeared and said, 'Now, Mr. Ford, you can't pay these people more than two dollars a day.'" Jack thought they could do better than that. Mahin continued, "Then the guy had the gall to say to Jack, 'Mr. Ford, I want to warn you of one thing. These colored people; they really resent it if you keep your hat on when you walk into their church. They are liable to get real mad, maybe even violent.' Can you imagine this son of a bitch even presuming that Jack Ford would walk into a church and not take off his hat?" Ford glared at him and walked away. Once he received the minister's permission to speak to the congregation, he was warm and gracious. He said, "I'm paying you people regular Hollywood scale, and I'm serving lunch at twelve noon. It isn't the best food in the world, but it's the best we can do. We would consider it a great honor if you would join us. I don't want any one of you to feel that, because you're portraying slaves, we are putting you down in any way. Everything in this picture actually happened, and you are playing your grandfathers and grandmothers. You are a part of history, and you should be proud of it. We are glad to have you as part of our picture." To shield Althea Gibson from the indignity of separate dining and housing facilities, Ford filmed all her scenes in Los Angeles. A stand-in was used on location.[494]

But that wasn't the only issue Ford faced. The public and media wanted to know if the South was getting a fair break in the film. So he came up with a creative ploy to deflect potential criticism. While filming a battle scene on the Cane River in Louisiana, Ford reversed all roles: Northern extras were dressed in Rebel uniforms, Southerners in Yankee uniforms. Both sides got so mad at his idea that they precipitated a "battle" that nearly became the real thing. In fact, one Johnny Reb broke a leg charging a Rebel redoubt, forgetting it was make-believe and thinking only that he was wearing the hated Yankee uniform while Northerners were dressed in the beloved butternut. Southerners, dressed as Yankees, even insisted on being paid $2 more per day than their compatriots in Confederate gray. That seemed to do the trick.

Harold Sinclair visited the set and seemed impressed with all the activity: 168 craftsmen from Hollywood on location with fifty to sixty trucks, carrying building materials and following cameras. When a fence was needed, they built a fence, or wooden tracks for the cameras. Sinclair was amazed. "Why, they built a 250-foot bridge, just like in *The River Kwai*, and they're gonna blow it up. Why, it's fantastic. Those big pilings and all. And they built railroad cars, duplicating the ones of that time. They built them from scratch. They've got carpenters, electricians and everything right with them. Why, they feed five hundred people every noon, right there in the middle of nowhere. They couldn't find any railroad tracks for their railroad. They hunted all over the country. You know what they finally did? They went to Houston, Texas, where they found some old street car tracks that had been torn up. And they're gonna blow them up, too." He told Ford it looked like confusion, but he said it wasn't. He told Duke it was confusion, but Wayne replied, "Nope. Organized confusion." Wayne didn't mind the new bridge either because he finally got a chance to blow it up! "Holden blew one in *The Bridge on the River Kwai*," he kidded. "In the new picture, he lets me blow it."[495]

*The Horse Soldiers* included one of the most characteristic yet overly sentimental scenes Ford ever filmed. He loved history but wasn't married to it. At a Southern military academy, young cadets were warned Union troops were crossing their property. Any exhibition of force would surely hinder their advance. With flags flying and drums beating, the cadets, ranging in age from nine to sixteen, marched into battle with the dreaded enemy. As they advanced upon the entrenched Union positions, Wayne, as Col. Marlowe, hesitated, reflected upon the age of the Confederates, and sounded recall. The Union cavalry retreated in the face of youthful enthusiasm. This sequence was somewhat reminiscent of the battle of New Market where cadets from Virginia Military Institute, initially deployed as reserves, were attacked by Union forces, and forced to plug a gap in Confederate lines. Veteran Jack Pennick was sent in advance one week earlier to train 150 cadets from Jefferson Military College and the Chamberlain Hunt Academy, which received new uniforms as a reward for being in the movie. These were faithful reproductions of one found stored at "Green Leaves" antebellum house in Natchez. It represented military attire worn in the 1850s. Filmed over a three-day period, the cadets' final assault was shot on a solemn Sunday morning, November 24, 1958. The cadets prepared to charge the dismounted Union cavalry. Firing simultaneously, they crawled over logs, charged full force and, with bayonets held high, screamed the horrendous rebel yell. On horseback, Wayne wheeled about and ordered retreat. Filmed on the first take, Ford said, "Print it." "They damned near outran us!" exclaimed Wayne.[496]

John Ford was an inveterate alcoholic; his binges were legendary. But when he went on the wagon, everybody was on the wagon. No exceptions. Nothing like a reformed alcoholic, gambler or smoker, no matter how temporary the reformation. It was just their luck that Wayne and Holden, known to have a soda pop every now and then, were stuck with Pappy smack-dab in the middle of his proselytizing zeal. Nothing's worse than a mean drunk, but even sober, Ford still was temperamental and unpredictable. Ordered by his physician to refrain from drinking or he would surely die, Ford was subject to constant tantrums. Having no one else to bear the brunt of his humor, he quite naturally took it out on Duke and Holden. Watching the actors like the proverbial hawk, he constantly checked their breath for any hint of liquor. It drove Duke absolutely crazy. At least Holden could get away each evening; he rented accommodations in Shreveport and traveled daily to and from location in his Thunderbird. Wayne, however, was stuck in Natchitoches with Ford. According to Wayne, "The Old Man got us to make a two-drink-a-day pact. I never take two drinks. Twenty, maybe, not two. Two I find a very uninteresting number."[497]

But after a few weeks, he was beside himself with grief and begged Rackin to secure a reprieve from this inhuman punishment. "Jesus, Marty," Duke complained, "the old man is driving me nuts. You gotta get me outa here." Ever clever, the producer informed Ford that Wayne's teeth were starting to appear yellow in the dailies and suggested that both co-stars travel one day to New Orleans to have their teeth cleaned. The ruse worked and shortly thereafter, numerous beverage emporiums in The Big Easy welcomed the trio that night with open arms. But Ford's cadre of spies worked overtime and knew exactly which taverns they visited. The next morning, Rackin rushed to get the two stars back before Ford missed them. Driving at speeds in excess of one hundred mph, Wayne glanced at the speedometer and commented, "You know, Marty, if we all die in a crash, you'll get third billing." Rackin slowed down. Ford then requested both Wayne and Holden stand next to him behind the camera, all day, in full costume under the hot Louisiana sun, just on the off-chance they might be required to appear in a scene. Not trusting Wayne's teeth to once again turn yellow, Ford made a habit of sneaking into Wayne's room searching for bottles. Pappy never found any; Duke would hide them with Bill Clothier. "I always had a jug in my room," confessed Clothier, "and Duke would come down to my room to have a drink or two after work, and we'd be sitting in there and pretty soon—I had the windows open and I would see the Old Man coming across the courtyard and I'd hide the bottle. Put it under the bed or someplace. The Old Man would knock on the door, and he'd come in and look around and he'd walk right through and go to the bathroom looking for bottles, but he never found one. And he used to have a great ga(g)—(Fred) Kennedy, (Slim) Hightower, Bobby Ray—he used to line them up every morning, and he'd say 'Fall in,' and these guys would line up, and he'd walk by and smell their breath. And one day he came by Bobby Ray and he smelled Bob's breath, and Bob said, 'Is it okay?' And (Ford) said, 'Yes.' And he said to Ford, 'Your breath doesn't smell very good!'" *(For an outstanding analysis of the actual raid, Sinclair's book and Ford's film, please refer to "Fiction as Fact: The Horse Soldiers & Popular Memory" by Neil Longley York.)*[498]

While Pappy was trying to minimize Wayne's attraction to alcohol, Duke had issues of his own. When he returned home after filming *Rio Bravo*, Pilar was at wit's end. She wanted a husband and family; Duke wanted a career. When she lost her home and almost lost Aissa to the fire, she had had enough. She announced they were separated. "Unfortunately, business is sometimes more important to a man than his wife," she explained. "How can a woman live with a man who, after four years of marriage, spends two-and-one-half-years on location? When he does get back from his movie-making, he spends all his time on business affairs." Wayne couldn't find any fault with her comments. "We are not separated yet," Wayne told reporters, "but I guess we're going to be. I don't know what it is unless it's the fact that my business is so rough. I talk about it all the time, I have to, and then when I make a picture I'm gone for three or four months at a stretch. Pilar and I can't seem to get any warmth and understanding between us anymore. It's been coming for some time. I don't know whether Pilar will get a divorce or not. It's too soon to tell." According to Duke, Pilar intended to move into an apartment in Beverly Hills. "I really don't know," he admitted, "but it is true she's moving out." By the next day, they reconciled and all was bliss once more. Pilar attributed their disagreement to the weather. "It was a hot day and we were moving," she rationalized. "Well, I'm Latin, and sometimes I explode, you know? It was just a small argument. We're back together now and in our new house." Wayne concurred, "We had a tiff and it looked like we were going to separate…but we've reconciled and everything is okay between us now and I'm glad."

Wayne said he was reluctant to discuss his personal affairs but added, "I guess it's news." According to Paul Fix, "Duke was shaken by what could have happened. It was an experience that seemed to stir up the deepest, darkest emotions in both Duke and Pilar, and Pilar suddenly told Duke she wanted a divorce. She said she couldn't bear Duke's long absences from home, and she just couldn't cope with the kind of life a wife of John Wayne was expected to lead… so they lived apart for a bit, but they loved each other so much they decided they had to try and make their marriage work." Fix added, "He was so damned relieved when she moved back in with him. And he'd missed Aissa. For a time there, his life was so bleak. He got to drinking a lot more than usual, and he seemed to lose interest in work." And, to top it off, Duke's daughter Melinda had been involved in a car crash during the holidays. She was driving a brand-new car she had been given as a Christmas present for the first time, and the vehicle was demolished. Fortunately, she escaped with only a few bruises.[499]

Earlier that year, the tragic fire had virtually destroyed his home. While he was in Tucson filming *Rio Bravo*, Pilar was in charge of the re-modeling. By the time he returned, she was finished and in September a house-warming party was in order. Ward and Maisie Bond, James and Josephine Grant, and other friends were invited to watch a movie in the new screening room. For years, in order to help get her through anxious and stressful situations, Pilar would need the assistance of mother's little helper. However, she had run out of pills the previous day, so, midway through the evening, she started to feel the effects of withdrawal: clammy sweat, lack of concentration, nausea. Excusing herself, she hurried upstairs, followed by Duke. In a fit of panic, she admitted her pill reliance to Wayne and begged him to get the prescription refilled immediately. Furious, Duke refused and forced Pilar to struggle through the remainder of the evening. The next day, her physician admitted she was sick and suffered from an addiction to pills. "Your wife needs to be under constant supervision until she's over this crisis," he counseled.

Incredulous but sympathetic, Wayne replied, "Pilar and I will conquer this ourselves." If he couldn't help Pilar get through this experience, no one could. He would leave for location in Louisiana in a few days and wanted her to join him. "I'll be with you every minute, every step of the way," he promised. "As soon as the picture wraps, we can go down to Mexico for a vacation. All you need is a little rest, a little good food." But it wasn't to be. Pilar was in no shape to travel,

193

and, when he left for location, Duke had to leave her behind in Mary St. John's care. A few days later, Pilar, Aissa, and the maids followed Duke to Louisiana. Despite his promises, Duke was the consummate professional on the set. He lived, breathed, and dreamed the movie. Whether studying a script, rehearsing lines, or discussing a scene with Holden and Ford, he was consumed with filming the project. Regardless of his good intentions, he just didn't have time for his wife. Alone with Aissa, Pilar became more and more depressed. Daughter Toni was back home after recently giving birth to her first child. Son Patrick was off at Loyola taking freshman classes. No one to comfort her, no one to support her. Only two days after her arrival on location, she started hallucinating and attempted suicide by slashing her wrists. Fortunately, St. John was with her and called an ambulance. Duke knew her condition was critical; she couldn't remain on location, and he couldn't leave. So he chartered a plane and Pilar, two nurses, and a maid departed for California where she was admitted to an Encino hospital. With Pilar under a doctor's care, it would be safer for Aissa to remain with Duke. Distraught, Wayne called hourly to ask about his wife.[500]

Lamentably, that wasn't the only catastrophe to beset the production. A veteran character actor and stuntman for over twenty-five years, Fred Kennedy had appeared in numerous classic Westerns during the golden age of Hollywood: *Red River*, *Yellow Ribbon*, *Wagon Master*, *Hondo*, and *The Searchers*. In the classic *Rio Grande*, he played Trooper Heinze, his only speaking role. Claude Jarman Jr. as Trooper Jefferson Yorke, Victor McLaglen as Sgt. Major Timothy Quincannon, Ben Johnson as Trooper Travis Tyree and Harry Carey Jr. as Trooper Daniel "Sandy" Boone. Yorke was involved in some fisticuffs with Heinze, defending his father's honor. Quincannon broke it up and asked some questions:

Tyree: "This fella here spoke real derogatory about the boy's pappy." Boone: "Yeah. He also said he was the teacher's pet of a chowder-headed mick sergeant. What's that mean, Doc?"

Quincannon: "Did ya say that?"
Heinze: "Yes, I did."
Quincannon: "Ya did, did ya?"
Heinze: "Yes, I did."
Quincannon: "Did ya mean it, did ya?"
Heinze: "Yes, I did."
Quincannon: (Pause). "We'll settle this tonight. Behind the picket line. Soldier fashion. Marquis of Queensbury rules. Chowder-headed...what was it he said?"
Boone: "Chowder-headed mick sergeant."
Quincannon: "Chowder-headed mick...and ya meant it, did ya?
Heinze: "Yes, I did."
Quincannon: "Nine o'clock tonight, boys."[501]

194

Kennedy, an expert in saddle falls, pioneered the training of falling horses. As he had worked for Ford in the past, it was no problem to play a small part in the director's newest film. Chuck Roberson remembered that Kennedy told him he was going to retire after one last picture with Ford. During the film, for most of the time, he played one of the two troopers assigned to guard Miss Hannah Hunter of Greenbriar. As Fred needed a little extra money, Ford agreed to let him perform a simple saddle fall. "A Christmas present for Fred," said Pappy. Filmed on what was to be the last day of shooting near Natchitoches, the script called for Kennedy (doubling Holden), to fall and feign injury, which would elicit sympathy from Constance Towers. According to Wayne, who witnessed the stunt, "Pappy wouldn't let him do any tough stuff." (Kennedy was forty-nine at the time.) "But there was this one shot...all Fred had to do was just fall in front of the camera. They were at a gallop, a lope, yes. But there wasn't any speed. No...nothing deadly about it. Well, he made the fall, turned over, moaned, and jerked a bit. I could see that he was doing something odd. Then Pappy said to Constance Towers, 'Go in and kiss him.' He meant it as a gag, because you know how bashful Fred was. I felt like saying, 'Jesus, I think he might be hurt,' but I didn't say it, and I'm sorry I didn't." Towers ran over the Kennedy and leaned down to kiss him. Then she leaned back and let out a scream. "He's hurt," she cried, which wasn't in the script. Kennedy, who gasped for breath and couldn't speak, broke his neck and died. He didn't use a stirrup step and had nothing solid from which to leap.[502]

Some accounts indicated he died instantly, others said it happened in an ambulance on the way to a hospital. Regardless, Ford was devastated. It was his fault; he allowed Kennedy to do the gag knowing full well Fred was too old. No excuses. Sure, it was simple; sure, Kennedy had already done it hundreds of times. But this time was different. Ford was shocked. He went back to the hotel and didn't work for days. Blaming himself for the accident, he started to drink heavily and lost interest in the film. As a result, production was shut down and final scenes were shot on a soundstage in Hollywood. Frank Sinatra, dressing room neighbor on the Goldwyn lot, sent a bottle of Jack Daniels apiece to Wayne and Holden with a card that read, "Welcome back to civilization and have yourself a snort of booze—there's a virus floating around."[503]

As Pilar said, "The final product didn't live up to Ford's high standards and was poorly received by the critics." Duke agreed, "Ford just doesn't seem to care anymore. Hell, he looks and acts like a beaten man."[504]

Though it appeared Ford didn't care, Duke still did and he wanted to promote the film. United Artists paid ABC $100,000 for the rights for Wayne and Holden to be heard on the radio between rounds of the June 6, 1959, Floyd Patterson/Ingemar Johansson heavyweight fight. The Hollywood duo would assist Howard Cosell with color commentary. "I'm pretty nervous about doing this," Wayne said surprisingly. "I could use somebody to hand me some notes describing the action like an expert. But that's out. All I'll be sure about is what I would have done in the same spot. If they'd put it out on the pavement, I'd know more about it." Great idea. Ironically, Johansson knocked Patterson down seven times by the third round, and referee Rudy Goldstein stopped the fight. (Patterson would go on to defeat Johansson in a rematch one year later and regain the undisputed world heavyweight title.)[505]

Reviews for *The Horse Soldiers* were mixed. Typical was the following: "It is a credible film, not another *GWTW* and not Ford's masterpiece, though he has not directed a better one in years… On the spectacular side Ford's at his most vivid in the depiction of the burning of 'contraband' at Newton Station and the Rebs counterattack. But the noblest, most inspiring sequence of all is that in which all the boys, little and littler, of Jefferson Military Academy march scores abreast in their proud school uniforms to repulse the invading Yanks.""…a saber-rattling good picture. Ford brings to it the immense gusto that has remained undiminished in his film-making these many years. Melodrama, suspense, scenic spectacle, even the Ford brand of take-'em comedy (but not too much of it, really) are all present in this familiar 'Western.' Wayne dominates with a generally excellent portrayal, although Holden resists being submerged and makes his few good scenes count."[506]

Having made one movie after another for the last three years, Duke, along with Pilar and Aissa took off to Acapulco in mid-January for a well-deserved four-week vacation. They even discussed continuing on to Peru, so Pilar could visit her mother. But the financially judicious Wayne ordered business manager Bo Roos not to send him more than $200 a week spending money. Grant tagged along to work on the *Alamo* script.[507]

After a short losing streak, Wayne now had two relatively successful movies in a row. More importantly, he revived his sagging career and most importantly, he augmented the funds necessary to complete his dream project: *The Alamo*. Duke admitted, "Ever since the idea first came to me, my determination to make it a reality has been paramount in my career." Now, all he had to do was pull it all together. Easier said than done.[508]

## CHAPTER THIRTEEN
## IT'S ABOUT DAMN TIME!

*"Another advantage to a deal like ours is that there's no room for temperament or star complexes; we're all partners. If someone acts up we can sit down quietly with him and say, 'Do you know what we spent today?' That usually does it. Too, we have no major studio overhead; ours is REALLY a $4 to $5 million picture. What we spent you're going to see on the screen." Mahin-Rackin discussing financial arrangements on The Horse Solders.*

SHAHAN WAS ECSTATIC AFTER HE VISITED BATJAC. WHEN HE ENTERED WAYNE'S office, he was surrounded by enlarged photos sitting on easels: shots Nate Edwards had taken weeks earlier at Happy's ranch. Three hundred sixty-degree views from every possible angle. Very impressive! And Wayne couldn't have been more agreeable. Happy listened with great interest: Wayne wanted to make the movie, Happy wanted it made. What more could you ask for? When Herb Yates continued to let people believe Wayne's project would be filmed in Texas, not Mexico as initially planned, Duke had no choice but to change direction, even though it would cost significantly more. And Happy's ranch fit the bill: hill, valleys, and rolling plains, scenic Pinto Mountain as a background. Streams and creeks. A decommissioned army base to serve as base camp. The Mexican border just a half-hour away, close enough to attract the numerous extras needed. All that was left was for Wayne to give the location his blessing. According to Shahan, "Wayne said 'I like it. I like the place. But I don't know for sure.' Still trying to leverage the situation, Duke added 'I've got a million 'dobes made in

197

Mexico and I'll make it down there.' But after he made 'em the Mexicans used 'em more than he did. They made little houses or something." After additional discussion, Shahan left the office, but a week after he returned home, Wayne called him; Duke wanted to fly down to check out the location himself. "When?" asked Happy. "Tomorrow," Wayne replied.[509]

*(Author's note: It should be mentioned there is a great deal of conflicting information regarding the number and dates of Shahan and Wayne's various meetings, what was actually said, the actual sequence of events leading up to these meetings, etc. Wherever possible, primary sources were used, including travel records and contemporary newspaper and magazine articles to support interview comments. However, stories changed over the years. As a result, the meetings, conversations, dates, and locations described in this chapter are the best compilation based on available information.)*

During the week of September 2, 1957, Wayne, along with son Michael, traveled to Texas and flew over portions of the state, looking for potential filming sites. He had just returned from England where he had sneak-previewed *Legend of the Lost*. After Texas, he would be off to Japan to start *The Barbarian and the Geisha*. His base of operations while in Dallas was at the University Club. He even enjoyed a Giants-Bears game at the Cotton Bowl. Sharing very little of his plans, he indicated, "I love this town, and I'm really looking forward to spending a lot of time here if we decide on a Dallas location for our next picture." While at the U-Club, Wayne was coerced into singing but halfway through "Red River Valley" he froze. "I overheard somebody say I sounded like Dizzy Dean, so I quit," he chuckled. The following week, Ward Bond joined Wayne in his search.[510]

Wayne eventually reached Brackettville and met with Shahan, who was at a neighbor's ranch at the time. Duke seemed pleased with the potential location but apprehensive when it came to set construction. Even though he and Happy had had numerous meetings and discussions over the past two years, he was still skeptical as to how the set actually would be built. "There was a doubt in their mind because, who was I?" said Shahan. "They just knew me to argue and maybe go have dinner with." Shahan told Wayne, "Fourteen years you've been trying to make this picture. All I want is an architect, your art director, and that's all. I can do the rest." When Happy insisted that his construction firm's workmen could build a permanent set instead of Hollywood crews building it, Wayne still wanted reassurance it was possible, so Happy sent a man to town to bring his foreman out to the ranch. As the foreman stepped from the pickup truck, Wayne just shook his head with an expression that said, "You gotta be kidding!" Short, forty-year-old Jose "Chato" Alvarez Hernandez, Jr. wasn't an imposing figure. But he knew his trade. Skilled in carpentry, bricklaying, roofing, framing, and foundations, he had honed his proficiency through the Works Progress Administration program. As he had previously completed work for numerous ranchers in the area, he was well-known for his carpentry skills, but not to

Wayne. Shahan recalled, "He (Chato) was about five-foot-three, about that wide also, didn't finish the third grade in Mexico, could speak English very little but understood English, understood anything you said." So Duke decided to have him questioned...for almost two hours! Hernandez was asked to identify various architectural drafting symbols that Ybarra drew: concealed wiring or center lines, property lines, compacted earth fill, framing lumber, electrical lines, etc., etc., etc.

Finally satisfied with Chato's background, experience and knowledge, Wayne asked one last question:

"Chato, do you really think you can build the Alamo?"

"Mr. Wayne," Chato replied, "do you think you can make a picture?"

Well, that was good enough for Duke. He laughed so hard he fell on the ground. Laughed until tears came to his eyes.

"That's good enough for me," he said.

"He would have done his picture somewhere, sometime," recalled Happy, "but what caused him to do his picture here was my saying that all I needed was his art director, and I would see to the construction of his sets. I said, 'We'll do the picture the way you want it done. It's your picture.' In other words, I would see to it that he got his sets the way he wanted them for the picture. All I needed was a blueprint. I owned a building company here that could supply everything he required in the way of sets for the picture. All I needed from him was a 'Yes.'"[511]

Obviously, the availability of water was going to be a huge issue: water for livestock moved into the area, water for irrigation, water for domestic use for production groups and technicians, and water to manufacture adobe blocks. Wayne wanted to know where it would come from. According to Shahan, the conversation went something like this:

Wayne: "Where's your water?"

Shahan: "Underground."

Wayne: "How do you know there's water underground?"

Shahan: "Look, I said there's water underground."

Wayne: "You're not God!"

Shahan: "Hey, I didn't say that, but I know there's water underground because I know the formations here."[512]

Wayne suggested they drill for water on the crest of a gentle nearby hill. "It looked like the worst place on my ranch to drill for water," said Shahan. "Still, we humored John. And the other day, we got a regular water gusher. Thousands of gallons! The well driller said we tapped an underground lake at 135 feet. Gosh! If I could have just had John Wayne here during the drought telling me where to drill for water!" Hoping to get fifty gallons per minute, the well tested 350 gallons per minute for three hours without noticeably lowering the level of the water. Happy later exaggerated that amount to "one thousand gallons per minute!" A large concrete 25,200-gallon reservoir was built at a cost of $5,000 for storage, with an electric pump to keep the water flowing. Open the floodgates and Pinto

Creek became the San Antonio River! Later, Happy substantially changed the story. Wayne planned to put the well inside the Alamo compound, which wouldn't work since noise from the generators would be heard on the soundtrack. Happy said it would be better on top of a nearby hill, but Wayne scoffed at the idea because it would mean drilling farther to get to the water. Happy told him no, it didn't. He then brought Charles Dolstrum out from Ft. Clark, who arrived complete with a willow wand and started witching. Happy drew a ten-foot circle and told Charlie water could be found in there somewhere. Immediately, the wand went down. "Gimme that!" Wayne said, grabbing the stick. He also felt the tug. "Fine, Shahan. We'll drill it here," relented Wayne, "but if there's no water, you'll pay for the well." They did and there was. The next day, according to Happy, there was a headline in a Dallas newspaper: "John Wayne Witches for Water on Shahan Ranch." Happy said he knew Wayne needed publicity and he got it for him. Wayne had a slightly different recollection of the event. When he returned to San Antonio, Duke told local restaurateur Big John Hamilton that *he* discovered the well. Apparently Wayne was one of those few lucky souls who possess "hidden powers." Armed with a "fresh Y-shaped willow branch," he wandered over Shahan's ranch, looking for a spot to drill a well. With the bottom of the "Y" pointed downward, the branch suddenly "came alive," beginning to twist away from him until it pointed directly at the ground. Shahan started digging a well at that location. Either way, water was discovered.[513]

Whatever the real story, they somehow found the necessary water. "It served two purposes," related Ybarra, "'cause we piped water in from the church itself down to the village, in the event of fire. And we put a five hundred-gallon tank down in the soil with pumps on it to provide water for ...to prevent fire. We kept fire hoses and everything there. Up in the main tank, it served a dual purpose 'cause we had five hundred to six hundred horses up there. We had two dump trucks going constantly to and from the corrals. 'Cause five or six hundred horses, they eat a lot of hay! They make a mess!" A second well was located in the village in addition to Ybarra's five hundred-gallon tank. Through a three-inch line, it fed three fire hydrant access points strategically located around the village, covered by three-foot by three-foot iron plate trapdoors.[514]

While Wayne negotiated construction details with Shahan, Ybarra evaluated the proposed location: "...regarding a spot for the village in relation to the Alamo church/mission itself: The distance between the two," recalled Ybarra, "is approximately a quarter of a mile downhill. In order to determine how big I wanted to make the village, I had a man go down into the area where we were going to build the set. And I would stop and sit from the position of the Alamo and motion to him. 'Left' and he stopped and waved a flag and I'd say, 'That's right.' Then I'd go 'Right, this way,' about a quarter of a mile. And that's it. We put up two telephone poles. That was the extent of the village proper." Then, Ybarra took two wide-angle photographs of the terrain, one of the countryside as it looked from the town of San Antonio. Four hundred yards away he placed a marker for the site where the Alamo would be. From there he took another photo looking back at "San Antonio" where the first marker had been placed. On those two photos, he painted complete perspective drawings of the Alamo and the village as they would look when construction was completed.[515]

Although now satisfied with the capabilities of the construction crew, Wayne was concerned about the quality of material used. He didn't want the set to appear fake, didn't want a sham as it was to be filmed in Todd-AO which showed every flaw, every nuance. It was his picture and he was determined to make it look right. During preliminary investigation and research one major problem popped up several times. He insisted real adobe blocks be used where adobe should be used. But until those arrangements could be made, no definite agreement or schedules were to be made. No adobe, no go. But Happy was optimistic. There was no way he wasn't going to pull this off. "I made a deal…in 1957 in September and started building the next day," said Shahan. Happy would also be the first to admit that buying Wayne the best Stetson hat he could find in San Antonio didn't hurt the negotiations. Now he only had to guarantee delivery.[516]

Henry Fuentes, of Rio Grande Electric Co-op, explains how difficult it was to run power to the set. "I was with Rio Grande Electric," recalls Fuentes, "when Happy came by with Mr. Wayne. I was a part of the engineering department. Happy and Mr. Wayne came by and, of course, Happy had always, always been a big supporter of Rio Grande Electric Co-op. So we were tickled to death to do whatever it was that was needed. Just, shortly after that, why, they both came in and Mr. Wayne had a couple of architects and some of his engineers there. They told us what they needed out there and we said, 'Well, let us study it a little bit.' So, based on the proposed load that they had quoted, we did a quick "power requirements study." And, of course, we had a line serving Happy's house. That line was a typical rural single-phase line. A single-phase line is a line that's got one hot wire and one neutral wire. The capacity of that line was at 7,200 volts. Well, based on what they told us, we concluded that that wouldn't do the job. So, we went in there and we rebuilt about fifty spans or fifty poles of line. We took that single-phase line and converted it from 7,200 volts; we added cross-arms to every pole; we added two additional conductors, and we converted that 7,200 to 12,500 volts, which gave the line the capacity. To serve the load in that immediate area, we talked to Mr. Wayne, and we said, 'Look. We don't guarantee anything unless we can build a small sub-station up there.' So we met up there with Happy and Mr. Wayne and they picked the site behind a small hill. We wanted the sub-station on the ground so it wouldn't be seen. But we built that sub-station behind a small hill and out of sight of the proposed Alamo structure. And got him what he needed up there in the way of capacity. As a matter of fact, I remember after we concluded our study, we started one weekend and we worked, just about overnight for a couple of days, but we got that line in there, and we built the substation. The substation took a little while longer, but by now we had a line with capacity. And, of course, that tickled Mr. Wayne and Happy was always warm to progress."[517]

After Duke flew back to Hollywood, Happy knew, to pull this off, he needed support from the entire community. So, with the cooperation of "Big" John Hamilton, Kinney County Judge Charles Veltmann, and the Commissioners Court, Happy and local businessmen A.H. Kreiger, C.C. Belcher, W.L. Moody IV, Tom Hurd and W.Z. Conoly formed a civic organization called Brackettville Enterprises (BE). Shahan, Belcher, Moody, and Conoly were also members of the Rio Grande Co-op, which was charged with supplying power for construction and the movie location. Created as a focal point for all activities connected with construction of facilities for filming of the movie, BE would be involved in obtaining electrical power, inducting long-distance telephone arrangements, installing two-way radio communication and private telephone lines on location, planning for patrolling the area, and many, many other small but very important phases of production. Power lines and other discordant items had to be camouflaged and/or buried. Totally free from the markings of a jet-age civilization, "No fences, utility poles or paved roads (were apparent)," Ybarra noted happily. Once final arrangements were made, Batjac turned over plans to BE for construction but only after a guarantee that more than 500,000 homemade adobe blocks would be furnished for construction. Publicity at the time stated that that approximately one mile of adobe walls of uniform shape, ten feet high and three feet thick, would be required. (According to Kreiger's son Alan, BE was just a sham organization. When Hurd was questioned about it, he was said to reply, "Well, it doesn't matter if you stretch the facts a little." There may have been a consortium of local businessmen that coordinated activities, but Alan was sure that his father didn't have anything to do with it.)[518]

From October 1957 through the end of the year, BE obtained a water supply, finalized temporary living quarters for the workmen, and graded the location. The site selected for the Alamo set rested on top of a small rise, so the land had to be graded to maintain a gradual slope over one thousand feet to permit better filming of the various assaults on the Alamo. The terrain, characterized by hilly, rolling country, was flattened and leveled. Giant dirt-moving machines sliced away from four to eight feet of soil in the process. Shahan seeded the newly level area with a number of grasses including buffel, blue panic, and bluestem to provide a natural look.[519]

Once the well was drilled, they took the next step. "We scoured the border country for first-rate adobe-making practitioners," said Shahan. An average of twenty-two makers were capable of mass-producing between 3,500 and 4,000 blocks daily. "We had to get Mexicans to make the adobe bricks," admitted Ybarra. "Adobe weighs forty pounds per brick, as against the eight pounds of our own bricks and is made by traditional methods strange to us. At one point we had fifty acres of bricks drying in the sun. You couldn't build a set like this out of plaster. Wind and rain would tear it apart. When we're finished with the movie, this set will stay here permanently. I'm told it will be a museum." Laborers were brought across the border at Del Rio, taken to the ranch each morning and taken back at night.

However, Brackettville resident Ralph Gonzales took exception to several of the above comments. "A local sixty-five-year-old gentleman was in charge of making the adobes. The adobe mixing was done with local people only, not with people from Mexico. When they had openings (for) labor, they made it a point to hire from Brackettville, to give the locals work. Myself and a lot of my friends, we made the adobe brick, but there was no one from Mexico." As for how many bricks were lying in the sun, well, that was another slight exaggeration. According to Ralph, "First of all, there were ten of us and we would nail two by fours and make all these squares on the ground. And we would pour the adobe mixture in each square. We had a total of six hundred squares, and we would cover all six hundred squares and then the next day we would (remove the squares and) do another six hundred. By the time they needed them, about four or five days later, they were dry enough to put them together and make walls out of them. That's what we had to look forward to every day. If I remember, they paid us $2.50 an hour." Once all the blocks were made, Gonzales was out of a job. But not for long. "Happy Shahan called me and asked me if I was working. I said, 'Not anymore.' He said, 'Well, you come out here. I need you to help me park vehicles.' So, I did that for awhile. There were a lot of people out there because they wanted to see the movie and they kept (them) at a certain distance because of the noise."[520]

Adobe was made the old-fashioned way: a combination of caliche, black dirt, straw, and water. Four giant plaster-mixing or cement-mixing machines were converted into adobe mixers. Straw was sprinkled in by hand. The blend was dumped into wheelbarrows, then pulled from the barrels and pushed by hand into wooden forms. Once the thick oatmeal-type mixture set for awhile, the forms were removed, and the adobe was left to dry in the hot Southwest Texas sun for five days. After they had dried, excess straw was shaved from the blocks with the blade of a hatchet. They then had to be used in construction within ten to fifteen days or the blocks would start to crumble. "If you use black dirt, you have to use a little manure in the recipe to make the abode breathe," explained Happy. "Using the caliche, you can omit the manure. Horse manure is an important ingredient in making an adobe wall. If you can't get horse manure, then cow manure will have to do. It's pulverized and yet it makes the adobe wall 'breathe,' expand and contract with changing temperatures. If you don't put some kind of manure in there, the walls will sweat."[521]

Clay for the adobe came from a quarry one-quarter mile from the replica of the Alamo. Publicists indicated the pit would be all of two acres in size and fifteen feet deep. Hardly. At 120x240x140x350 feet, the pit was barely three-quarters of an acre.[522]

In mid-January 1958, Nate Edwards arrived to formally announce Batjac would spend $5 million to produce *The Alamo*. The previous December, Shahan had let the cat out of the bag by prematurely notifying friends in San Antonio of Wayne's plan to film in Brackettville. Edwards also announced Wayne would play the role of David Crockett, and although other stars had not yet been selected, local restaurateur "Big" John Hamilton had been promised an important role. A.V. Bonnet, manager of the Texas Employment Commission, Eagle Pass branch, heard Brackettville was the official location and contacted BE's Tom Roselle to inquire about the truth of the rumor. Informed what he had heard was true but "unofficial," Bonnet was promised to be contacted after the announcement was made.

Later that same month, a meeting was held to discuss future employment requirements. In attendance at the Shahan ranch were Ybarra, Shahan, Roselle, Bonnet, and Augustin Estrada, placement interviewer from the Eagle Pass office. A consensus was reached in that as the branch office had responsibility for Brackettville, it would coordinate the hiring of extras and laborers in the area. Almost 150 local workers were hired...after Wayne agreed to increase their wages to insure the project wasn't delayed by a work stoppage. (Local wranglers were forced to join the Teamsters union before they were allowed to work on location.)[523]

BE had hopes for future use of the facilities it was building on the Shahan ranch. In addition to potential construction of a western street to be used in television productions, BE also contemplated an insulated, air-conditioned sound stage building approximately eighty by one hundred foot building with a thirty-foot ceiling. In addition, *Dallas Morning News* columnist Frank X. Tolbert suggested that before filming, Wayne should read *13 Days to Glory* (at that time the definitive book on the siege) by SMU professor and *News* book critic Lon Tinkle to determine what the compound looked like.[524]

In the early days of construction, the set was inundated with visitors: Grant, Ybarra, Edwards, and even Duke's son Michael, who stopped by after a hunting trip with Big John Hamilton. All things considered, though, construction was progressing smoothly: the land was graded, electrical and water lines laid and buried, telephone poles put up to support phone lines, wells drilled, water pumps and tanks installed, roads graded and tarred, unwanted objects camouflaged, and concrete foundation footings poured and laid. In an attempt to be somewhat historically correct, Ybarra also dug an acequia or aqueduct that wound its way from the base of the hill facing the "North Wall," under the parapet where the breach was made, down two-thirds the length of the plaza and then out a port in the "West Wall" next to Bowie's room. (In all likelihood, the acequia was created for Scene 322 in the May 19, 1959, shooting script and the August 21, 1959, shooting schedule in which reads as follows: "This is the small duct which brings water into the Alamo through the Mission wall. Some defenders stand about and with them are a couple of dripping men. As we watch, we see why they are wet. A man suddenly pops up from the water. The bystanders fish him out. Then another man pops up and then another... We see a man grab his nose and dive into the aqueduct. Obviously he passes through. Inside the wall, as the man we saw on the other side emerges." A defender explains what was going on: "Some fellows sneaked in from *Goliad*...there's maybe a couple dozen more outside." This scene, as written, remained in the script until mid-October. Interestingly, scene 165 from the earlier script described Juan Seguin's nocturnal arrival with fifteen Charros. No mention is made from where they came. Grant eventually changed the acequia to correctly reflect the arrival of volunteers from Gonzales.)

**S**hahan hired between three and four hundred laborers to augment his local crew. Wayne had already sent a core team of twenty individuals to expedite material and manpower for the project. Alan Kreiger even sold Batjac a workmen's compensation insurance policy for the construction of the set that his son thought was from the Commercial Union Insurance Company. This turned out to be a less than satisfactory experience because the company told Kreiger it would never again be involved in the film industry as "somebody was always fabricating a work comp claim everyday; falling down or something like that."[525]

Because of the remote location, the construction site presented unique, expensive transportation problems. It was said to cost over $800,000 to transport cast, crew, and equipment to and from Brackettville. Each day during filming, Batjac's sixty-four drivers, supervised by Transportation director George Coleman, averaged more than 1,500 miles between the location and Ft. Clark. Twenty cars and station wagons, as well as thirty-four passenger buses were leased to accomplish this. Duke, who visited the set in mid-April after stopping in Dallas, told friends there he had already invested $80,000 on construction and wanted to see what he was getting for his money. Pilar flew to Dallas to spend some time with her husband, and they both flew back home to enjoy Easter with the family before Duke was off, once again: this time, to Tucson where he would star in *Rio Bravo*. (Duke had an interesting story about Coleman: "At Republic Pictures, sixteen years ago, there was a nice, hard-working, efficient guy, George Coleman, who told me about an idea he had to make the first movie on the Seabees. Three days later, Al Cohen, a Republic boss, told me he had a wonderful new idea, *The Seabees*, and was going to talk to the big boss, Herb Yates, about it. Two days later Yates tells me of his great new idea. Yeah–*The Seabees*; five days later, Coleman is fired. Typical of Yates. Typical of Wayne, he hired Coleman to work at Batjac.)[526]

Early on, about 15,000 adobes had already been manufactured—not nearly enough to begin construction but a start nonetheless. It was a good thing adobe bricks were so easy to make. *It was a dark and stormy night...* From June 16 to17, 1958, torrential rains washed away thousands and thousands of blocks drying in the sun, literally dissolving them in the downpour. Furious thunderstorms caused a flash-flood on the West Nueces River, near Uvalde. Ranchers were advised to remove their livestock from bottom land, warned of low water crossings and notified that highways leading into the county would be closed. Las Moras Creek roared out of its banks on the morning of the seventeenth and sent almost five feet of muddy water racing through Brackettville. In addition to the Gateway Hotel, over sixty homes and twenty-five businesses were damaged by the flooding, with losses estimated at over $100,000. Highway 90 east of town was closed down as well as Highways 674 and 344, north and northeast of Brackettville, and Highway 1572 at Spofford. A fifteen-foot wall of water rolled down the Nueces River. Just the day before, it was a dry river-bed. At least three deaths were blamed on the flooding in the Brackettville-Utopia-Sabinal area.[527]

According to Ybarra, "The next morning the adobes were mush. Well, the day after the rain I went down and took a look at the telephone poles; the high water mark was six feet. If we'd built the set down here, it would've been..." One could only imagine. Belatedly, Shahan directed construction of a one-half-mile-long dike to reroute excess rainfall; a ridge of earth separating the creek from the village. Again, Ybarra commented on the damage: "Well, Happy had a bulldozer on the ranch, and he channeled the water away from where the set was gonna be. He worked for a couple of weeks, bulldozing dirt way, way away from it and building embankments to channel the water. And then, of course, we finally got started."[528]

Shahan said they lost over 36,000 'dobes as fourteen and a half inches of rain hit the ranch within a twenty-four-hour period; normal annual rainfall for Kinney County was only twenty-two inches. "First time I've ever felt sad when it rained," said Shahan. "The Alamo wasn't washed away. That was one consolation. Part of the walls of the quadrangle and part of the walls of the chapel were already up. Stone work on the front of the chapel was going to start the next week. The Alamo was set on higher ground and wasn't affected by the incredible downpour." Shahan continued almost philosophically, "1836 was a year of floods in Texas. So maybe nature is cooperating with us. I sure wish, though, that nature had spared me all those thousands and thousands of adobes." The following week, much of the rain-damaged compound and chapel had been restored, but heavy rains left the area too wet to resume adobe-making activities. Concrete foundations had already been poured and adobe dwellings were being built when the rains came. Everything but the foundations was swept away by a creek that roared all but out of bounds during the hard storm. Rain damaged portions of the walls and about sixty percent of the chapel, as well as the face of the arch leading into the compound. "The arches in the chapel held, but the walls swelled and gave way, bringing everything down with them," Happy lamented.[529]

Usually, ninety men were at work when the construction crew was at full strength, but it was temporarily reduced to only fifty because of the rains. When the ground dried out completely, the making of adobe began again. Men were hired based on their ability and construction requirements. Day labor made $1 an hour, the foreman $2.50. Once they started to make bricks again, another problem raised its smelly head. Believe it or not, they were running out of a key ingredient: manure! Too bad Dallas was so far away. During the Texas State Fair, it was estimated that over 4 million pounds of it would be removed from the fairgrounds. With forty men and four to six tractors pushing manure and loading it onto fifty dump trucks all day, well, that's a shitload of manure. During construction, delegates to a convention in Brackettville were taken to the set, where one woman asked Shahan how many adobe blocks had been made. "About 750,000 so far," replied Happy, "but there will be more than a million." When she asked what they were made of, he explained, "The first 250,000 were made of hay, water, mud, manure and such." "What about the rest?" she asked. "Well," said Shahan, "we encountered certain shortages." Replied the woman, "You being a Texan, it must have been hay, water, or mud."[530]

"The rains did a lot of damage," Happy remarked, "but didn't set us back too much. We'll be ready in plenty of time for the production date, which isn't definite but will probably be about the first of the year (1959)." Many of the adobe walls had already been plastered and whitewashed. According to Shahan, research on the design and construction of the Alamo and compound had been going on since 1951. "In making their research," he explained, "they travelled all over, even to Mexico City, to make the Alamo, the quadrangle and the little village as authentic as possible." While still working at Republic in March 1951, Ybarra developed a set of blueprints for the Alamo. Fairly correct and, in his words, "This is a measured drawing. The detail is accurate as of the era of the 'Battle of the Alamo' 1836." While the façade was close in measurement of both height and width, he noted, "Height of (side) wall to be determined by art director." When the set was finally constructed, it was just a tad bit narrower than his drawing of six years earlier.[531]

In late September, Wayne inspected the set after, once again, stopping in Dallas where he conferred with Interstate Theaters officials concerning the promotion of his latest flick, *The Barbarian and the Geisha*. He was accompanied by several associates, including production manager Edwards, art director Ybarra, script writer Grant, and son Michael. Construction of the buildings was now almost complete with trees and plants yet to be planted. With telephone poles in place for structural support, the Alamo church was only lacking its stone façade, and cannon ramps on the outer walls were being prepared. White-washed walls gleamed in the sunlight and down in the village, the San Fernando church was finished. Initially, plans for start of filming were scheduled for early 1959, but

Wayne's commitment to *The Horse Soldiers* forced the date to be pushed off. But Wayne was also anxious to get started on his own film. "After all," he admitted, "I've already got $230,000 tied up in the *Alamo* set."[532]

As they strolled around the compound, Wayne argued with his compatriots. Reporter Bill Allert was on hand to record the conversations:

Said Wayne as he studied a windowed wall, "This is fine. We'll shoot that scene here. The men can be lying here...just getting up in the morning...rubbing their eyes. And we can have the sun streaming through that lattice work for effect."

Said Grant, "Say, Duke, why not shoot the dying scene right here...it's just right."

Roared Wayne, "Wait a minute. Look how the sun hits this side. It's 9:30 now and if we shoot this scene any later the sun will be too high. Make a note of that."

As the group moved to the south wall, Wayne, sleeves rolled to the elbows and non-filtered cigarette in hand, motioned for a light, eyeballed the layout, squinted and said, "We'll have the Mexicans tearing down that wall and coming in right through here. And that barricade...I want it in flames when that happens. It'll pop right at you in color."

When Michael said of his dad, "He's a stickler for authenticity," he knew whereof he spoke. Edwards somehow wanted to use the song "The Yellow Rose of Texas" in the script and started to argue with Duke. Wayne replied no, the song was too new for a story that happened over one hundred years ago. Wayne's personality shone through as he roamed the set. When he saw laborers taking too much time mixing adobe, he smiled and said, "Lady, that's costing me so damn much money." But he was pretty pleased with what he saw. "We're building a lot of the stuff complete," he explained, "not just a front. We've been building the set for the past two years, and we don't start shooting before next September. I want the vegetation to look right, not like something out of props, so we're growing it. We transplanted an oak tree the other day as big as Toots' (Shore) fireplace."[533]

Since Happy's wife, Virginia, had horticultural aspirations, Wayne enlisted her help landscaping the set. "In the yards and houses in the village supplementing the main set of the Alamo," she explained, "we want to have colorful blooming plants—bright yellows and reds and blues. This during September, October and November, when the camera crews will be shooting." She requested that the community pitch in to help landscape Old San Antone. "We also wish to have some kind of vine growing on the walls of the Alamo compound. If people want to send seeds, I shall be very grateful. But their advice on what to plant and when, will be welcome too." All submissions were to be sent to Mrs. J.T. "Happy" Shahan at Brackettville. No other address was necessary. Usually, a member of the set decoration department called a "greensman" was responsible for selecting, purchasing, and placing all appropriate greenery. Obviously, the land was stripped naked in order to build the various sets, but vegetation would have grown back by the start of production. Virginia's efforts and those of the local community helped augment nature.[534]

The set's adobe walls varied in height from nine to twelve feet and were a minimum of thirteen inches thick in a quadrangle enclosure that measured 350 feet long, 268 feet wide at one end and 162 feet at the other. An assistant saw the walls and suggested to Ybarra they be built slightly higher. Wayne said no, "I want to see thousands behind every wall." As the walls required a certain amount of stability, they were strengthened with buttresses. Most of the Ybarra/Hernandez adobe bricks measure 4x12x17 inches. Sometimes Ybarra had Chato lay them lengthwise, giving a wall with a thickness of thirteen or fourteen inches. But the Alamo "south" and "west" walls were laid perpendicular to the length of the wall, rendering a wall eighteen or nineteen inches thick. Long Barrack walls were laid lengthwise, making the walls thirteen to fourteen inches thick as is the back walls of the rear courtyard.[535]

And while Wayne's Alamo church was built virtually full-scale, the compound was deliberately constructed at seventy-five percent scale to accommodate the wide-angle dynamics of the Todd-AO camera. The lens would give proper depth perspective when viewed on film, so for that reason, all distances could be foreshortened, including the distance between the village and the Alamo. Nails used in construction were artificially rusted so the heads didn't shine and reflect on the screen. There were other touches. Here and there, cactus grew out of the walls, corn-cribs were placed strategically around the compound to give it a sense of authenticity, and tree trunks were hollowed out to serve as water troughs. Much of the wood used for doors, windows, shelves and wheels was said to come from native timber found on the Shahan ranch. To obtain age-appropriate fixtures, Ybarra traveled to Mexico and brought back old handmade iron hardware. On one of Duke's frequent visits, he noticed the walls were bare and white, so he instructed Ybarra to "Put something in the walls." Designs were added "to give it character, for the sake of the camera."[536]

Working from measurements, photographs, and molds, Ybarra tried to make the Alamo church as accurate as possible. "We have to know where and how the action took place before we can make the place for it to happen in the film," Ybarra explained. "We have built them (the Alamo buildings) from measured drawings of the original Alamo. They are as faithfully and accurately reproduced, inch by inch, as any replica could be." The Alamo church was constructed around a framework of telephone poles. Used to assure structural integrity, they were also a visual part of the building, and guaranteed a straight line as well as correct perpendicularity. Living at Ft. Clark, he enjoyed close proximity to the set, roamed endlessly around Brackettville and the surrounding area, and thus kept busy, not only supervising the masons, adobe-makers, and other crew members, but also looking for material that could be used in construction. Costumes, artillery–no detail was too small. Ybarra had been an art director and designer for over twenty-three years and had served in that capacity for every picture Wayne had made as an independent: *Hondo*, *The High and the Mighty*, and *Blood Alley*.[537]

Trained as an architect, he had worked on the Empire State Building. A resident of California, he naturally gravitated toward the movie industry, and, in 1946, RKO sent him to Mexico City to work at Churubusco Studio. While there, not only did Ybarra design a few rooms for the Mexican White House, he also worked on President Aleman's private residence. At Churubusco, he represented Hollywood construction, set design, and was supervising art director, as well as being in charge of all technical departments. It was during this time that he worked on *The Fugitive* for John Ford and developed a special fade-out scene. The director liked it so much, he showed the rough cut to his cronies, including Ward Bond, Henry Fonda, and Wayne. Duke told Ybarra, "I saw it and Ford told me you did it, you designed it." Ybarra replied in the affirmative. Wayne continued, "Look, one day I'm gonna do a story on the Alamo. I want you to be my art director. As soon as you get back to Hollywood, don't see anybody else. Come see me first." When Ybarra returned to California, Fox Studios called and wanted him on *Viva Zapata* (1952). So he talked to Wayne and said, "Fox wants me to start tomorrow." "To hell with that," yelled Wayne. "I want you to get started on *The Alamo*." So he went to Yates and insisted Ybarra be put on the payroll. "From then on," remembered Ybarra, "I sat around Hollywood not doing anything but taking naps in the office. So Wayne had to do the Irish picture (*The Quiet Man*) with Maureen O'Hara. I piddled around and made some drawings and some models for *The Alamo*. And by the time he got back I'm flying over with the production manager to Texas to look over the location that he proposed."[538]

Ybarra continued, "John Wayne started me off on the project about ten years ago. We were about to start the project in Mexico about six years ago, but the Mexican government had raised a fuss—they'd just as soon forget the Alamo and we had to give it up for awhile. Then, two years ago, John gave me the signal to get going again. There were several old illustrations available to show what the place looked like, as well as accounts and descriptions. Then I came across some drawings made by a Mexican officer after the battle. He was a trained engineer, and his measurements differed somewhat for the Texas ones, but I decided I'd better follow the Texan version. For missing details, I went to Spain and dug up architectural drawings of the type of Spanish missions built in the new world."[539]

By mid-October, the stone façade on the church was finished. It was one of the last structures completed. The only building that wasn't entirely made of adobe, its façade was built from quarried limestone. Ybarra indicated, while traveling one day to Brackettville, he noticed a road construction crew with several dump trucks loaded with rock that had been blasted out of a nearby hill where a road was being constructed. Close enough in appearance to match the original façade in San Antonio, he negotiated with the road crew to use the material. He then sent over his own men to haul it away for free. "I sat in front of the chapel," he said, "and supervised the placing of each stone. It was the most important building on the set, and I wanted to make sure it was perfect." Shahan, however, thought the stones came from a building razed at Ft. Clark. Regardless, irregular in form and massive in size, they were a perfect match to the original appearance.[540]

At the time of the actual battle in 1836, the church facade had four niches thought to hold statues of San Francisco and Santo Domingo on the lower level, and San Antonio and San Fernando on the upper level. To represent the saints, Ybarra painted silhouettes of the statues in the niches. The scrollwork around the mission door and niches, as well as the four columns that adorn the face of the building, was molded by Redondo Manufacturing, a San Antonio firm. The company had been allowed to make plaster castings of the (Alamo's actual) columns in 1936, and the molds were still available. The columns were made of concrete, but, when set in place, they were inadvertently reversed. The spirals in the columns rotated in the opposite direction from the original church. By the time it was noticed, filming was already under way. According to Ybarra, he didn't think anyone would catch it. Interestingly, Ybarra's original 1951 blueprint also showed reversed spirals on the columns.[541]

It appeared Ybarra may have developed most of the layout for the Alamo compound from information derived from R.M. Potter's 1860 plat and, perhaps, Alamo engineer Green B. Jameson's map as well. The latter was reproduced from a previous copy and was available at the time in Amelia Williams's 1931 thesis, as well as a *San Antonio Light* article dated July 5, 1936. The original map was lost and had yet to be re-discovered. Publicist Russell Birdwell confirmed in his massive news release that "sketches" by Jameson were located in Texan archives along with an architectural plat made by an "un-named Mexican officer," in the Mexico City Museum. However, everything mentioned by Birdwell needs to be taken with a massive dose of salt because Birdwell's press release also stated, "Every physical aspect of San Antonio de Bexar and the Alamo itself (were) established and faithfully recreated. The adobe buildings...are directly out of the context and fabric of actuality. The discovery of a location site exactly duplicate(d) the Alamo battlefield... Ybarra even made a quick trip to Spain to unearth the original plans of the Alamo...the plans (however) had been long lost or destroyed," though he was able to discover mission architectural designs in musty archives. Even Wayne wasn't averse to blatant publicity falsehoods; during the one-hour ABC Television special *Spirit of the Alamo*, broadcast on November 14, 1960, he stated, "That town down there; this wonderful old mission. We know we got them pretty close to right. We took the measurements from the old and original drawings and plans." None of this was factually correct. Ybarra did, though, make several trips to San Antonio to physically measure the Alamo and, along with Nate Edwards and Big John Hamilton, take advantage of the research materials available in the Daughters of the Republic of Texas Library.[542]

Although Ybarra went to some length to insure the compound was historically correct, inaccuracies nevertheless are present. The most obvious one was that Wayne's Alamo faced in a different geographic direction than the one in San Antonio. The actual church faces due west, but the cinematic church faced the rising sun. As a result, dramatic dawn and dusk shots, with the church in profile before a magnificent orb, were now possible. The entire Alamo compound in essence was rotated 180 degrees from the historical layout. Even though Pinto Mountain appeared in the background, there were two reasons why the set faced the wrong direction. According to Shahan, "One is we just shouldn't have faced it east. And the other...I just can't think of the other reason."[543]

Initially, Ybarra designed the top ridgeline of the Alamo chapel in a flat configuration, similar to the historic Alamo of 1836. However, Wayne asked that it be changed to add the iconic pediment, so people would be more familiar with the structure.

Another example of artistic license is the construction and size of the palisade. At 116 feet in length from the front corner of the church to the end of the Low Barracks, the historical palisade is now believed to be built of two rows of cedar logs, seven to eight feet in height, packed with fill, with a ditch and berm on the outside face. It had been suggested there may have also been "an earthen firing step almost two feet high (with) loopholes cut about four and one-half feet from the step." Other plats indicated it was protected on the outside with an abatis in addition to the trench. But, such a configuration would be unsuitable for the set. As the compound had been reduced in size, so must be the palisade wall. At sixty-five feet in length and three to four feet in height, the wall consisted of a single row of posts, without trench or outer works. Its height had to accommodate the needs of the movie company. The right center of the palisade was constructed with gabions–large baskets made from woven sticks and filled with rocks and dirt. Functional and artistic, they filled gaps and when moved by forklifts, allowed heavy machinery to be brought onto the film set. Ybarra's original blueprints showed two rows of cedar posts, eight to ten inches in diameter, separated by five feet of fill dirt but, but by the time the set was constructed that concept proved ill-conceived. During one of Wayne's frequent inspections, he noticed Ybarra had already built the palisade and yelled, "What the hell were you thinking of? You know we can't have that wall up yet—the first scene doesn't call for it. Take the damn thing down." Ybarra patiently explained that, rather than having a stationary structure, it was designed so it could be moved when necessary to allow large movie equipment trucks to enter and exit the compound during shooting. A shallow trench was excavated, and palisade stakes were set in place; if the palisade wasn't needed, the stakes were pulled, the ditch covered with boards, and the boards with dirt. Quick, convenient, and efficient. Wayne just smiled.[544]

A San Antonio newspaper article detailed material used in constructing the movie set: 500,000 feet of lumber, six carloads of cement, 3,000 sacks of plaster, 200 gallons of paint, forty kegs of nails, 15,000 square feet of corrugated iron roofing and 5,000 square feet of tile roofing. In addition, it took fifty truckloads of limestone rock to build the mission church and 450 truckloads of gravel were spread over the streets. Who keeps track of this stuff? An onsite evaluation of the set would suggest that the aforementioned numbers were *slightly* exaggerated for publicity purposes. Nineteen completed buildings sat in the village with many of the doors and windows salvaged from buildings at Ft. Clark. In fact, as the salvaged doors were not of standard size, doorways had to be custom-made to accommodate them. Several structures consisted only of four walls with unfinished interiors. Reworking the script necessitated the completion of several adobe buildings on the street behind the Cantina as the layout of the set is always designed as a direct response to the needs of specific scenes. Some of the buildings would be finished in a way not readily apparent in the film, though, thus allowing them to be used as dressing rooms, medical facilities and commissary. They were also used to temporarily house the harness for caissons and bridles, saddles and reins.

Dirt piled on top of adobe walls streaked the sides whenever it rained, which gave it an authentic appearance. "Adobe is actually fine construction," Ybarra pointed out. "It is naturally insulated and when kept properly, will last forever." He noted there was a tremendous amount of painting that needed to be done. "What the hell. If I paint this whole set, I'll need $5,000 worth of paint. So I talked with my Mexican foreman about whitewashing the whole thing. In other words, we put pigment in the washtub. I had fifty gallon sacks of it, mixed in with water, and I get the colors I want. I don't think I spent $150 on pigments. The buildings were finished so close to the start of shooting that we didn't have time to go around and spray them for antiquity. And I put dirt on the top of all the buildings, washed it down, and it looked natural."[545]

In addition, chemicals from a hose were sprayed on various structures to give them a streaked appearance. Local resident and extra Tim Cumiskey recalls, "When they first built the structures out there, they were so white you couldn't even look at them; the sun was so bright that you couldn't even see. When the special effects guys came in, they all had a sledge hammer in one hand and a spray, backpack-type, water canister-type thing, like a bug sprayer-type thing, and they would come along, and they would put an adobe brick on top of the wall, and then they'd go around and slam that hammer into the wall and then make the adobe run down the side there to make it look old. By the time they got done, it looked like it had been sitting there for two hundred years."[546]

The village structures, painted pale blue, white, and pink, represent typical Mexican dwellings of the 1830s. According to Ybarra, the authenticity of the layout was omitted purposely (as) most of the shooting would be of close shots of building fronts, street scenes, entrances, and exits. Said he, "I have built so many of these 'Mexican towns,' I know exactly how and where they placed everything." The use of individual buildings determined how they would be finished inside. On an early visit to the set, Wayne read the script and decided specific action should be moved around behind the main street—this required finishing several adobe structures. Peppered with names such as "Escuela para Ninos," (School for Children), "Huevos frescos," (Fresh eggs), and "Cantina," the village buildings served an entirely different but functional purpose. The Children's School was used as an air-conditioned make-up room, filled with dressing tables and brightly lighted mirrors. Wayne's office, the "Comanderia de Policia" or police station, had telecommunication capabilities and housed a plush lounge for the stars. The two-story Hotel de San Antonio was a dining room for the cast and crew; the lower level filled with row after row of costume storage. Also equipped with air-conditioning, the "Correo" (post office) was located next to the police station. (Wayne installed ten, three-ton A/C units in the mess and recreation halls, so cast and crew could relax in comfort). The village included a hardware store (Tlapaleria), grocery store (Abarroles), pharmacy (Botica), coal shed (Carboneria), warehouse (Almacenes), bakery (Panaderia), two inns (Hosteria and Fonda Noche), barber shop (Barberia), and blacksmith shop (Herrero). (Speaking of a post office, in order to promote and publicize the film, Batjac would eventually purchase 18,000 commemorative 9¢ Alamo airmail stamps to use on all its mail, and the U.S. post office realized a bonus in unexpected revenue!). During a tour of the village, Wayne told a reporter, "When we built these houses and decided to make them solid, we also made up our minds to make practical use of them. So we installed air-conditioning and moved in all our production departments. This way the prop section, costumes, makeup, the kitchen, and even the hospital are right where we are working. It saves us hours."[547]

Individual restroom buildings for men and women also were constructed as was a medical first aid facility. Ybarra explained, "Around 2,000 people will participate in the fighting. It's very likely some casualties will occur. Somebody usually gets hurt in falls from horses. Others get cut by bayonets, powder burns, etc." Two emergency rooms were set up to take care of the injuries. And a helicopter was also on hand to transport the seriously "wounded" to local hospitals. As for the restrooms, it was publicized that five miles of sewage lines were laid into massive leach fields. Just 'tain't so. Three septic tanks were strategically located around the set; one behind the village restrooms, one behind Wayne's office, and one behind the Alamo compound restrooms. (Prior to the construction of Duke's office down in the village, whenever he was checking on construction, Wayne would stay out at Happy's ranch in what was known as the "white house," the original Webb family residence.)[548]

Grant was effusive in his praise of Ybarra's efforts; "This set is tremendous, just great. There is no cheating here—no false fronts or painted backgrounds— but you don't need anything in this area. This is the greatest area for movies I've seen. You can find everything here. Sand dunes, real rough country, timbered areas, and that sky. I've never seen such a perfect sky in my life. This area is definitely bound to figure in more movies. It has a terrific potential." Stunt coordinator Cliff Lyons called it the "most fantastic set I've seen in twenty-five years in the movies. If you pull out all the cameras and cables and dumped some movie men in here, they'd never believe it was a movie set. It's just too real. I've never seen anything like this street. There's no worrying about angles; you just shoot every side of it. There's no doubt this area has a big future waiting. I told Duke, 'Duke, if you don't take advantage of this and make another movie here real quick, you're really missing out.'" Michael Wayne agreed: "The Alamo was constructed in its entirety, so we could film anywhere in it. All the rooms were designed so you could be outside; go through the door, and you were in a room designed, so filming could take place. It was actually cheaper than renting space at a studio." Publicist Henaghan, as usual, went a bit overboard: "The entire town has been constructed to scale. When we are through, we'll leave it to Mr. Shahan. What else can we do with it? But first we're going to blow the dickens out of it." Wayne may have had an ulterior motive when he decided to take that approach. Reportedly, he was unhappy it would be used for television shows after his film was complete and one way to prevent that was to destroy the set.[549]

Just as Wayne played a bit fast and loose with factual accuracy and the chapel, so did Henaghan when it came to the village: "It is a practical livable set," he stated. "Six or seven thousand people could live there." Well, with only nineteen buildings in the village, that would equate to a minimum of three hundred inhabitants in each structure. Probably not. With a set rumored to cost between $500,000 and $1,500,000 to construct, Wayne even had to spend $70,000 to revamp some of the quarters at Ft. Clark where cast and crew were staying, which made Batjac tight-fisted comptroller Al Podlasky none-too-happy. Sparing no expense, Duke also built an airstrip large enough to handle twin-engine planes a half mile from the set to accommodate visitors and facilitate transporting daily rushes back and forth to California.[550]

By late 1958, the movie set was well on its way to completion. While construction progressed, Wayne was off making movies but kept in constant contact with Ybarra, overseeing every aspect of the preproduction work. On February 14, on his way back home from vacation, Duke stopped in Brackettville for a few days to inspect the set. Once again, he was accompanied by his usual entourage: Edwards, Grant, Bill and Paul Clothier, electrical engineer Ralph

Owen with son Bill and, of course, Michael Wayne. By then, the set was complete except for some interior work and background scenes and only required weathering through the summer to achieve the necessary appearance. He even found time to attend a local high school basketball game. En route back to San Antonio, he stopped in Uvalde to visit with former vice-president John Nance Garner. "It was the biggest thrill I ever had," admitted Wayne. "I was really impressed. Boy, that guy's the greatest." Later, when asked if he discussed politics with the veep, Duke sipped his coffee, thought a moment, puffed his cigarette, raised an eyebrow and said, "Heck no. We swapped stories. But you couldn't print most of 'em." Travelling to San Antonio, he attended a rodeo and chatted with its star, Dale Robertson. Later, they attended a party held in their honor by John Hamilton at his restaurant. Before taking off for Hollywood, he even dropped in at Lucchese's store to be fitted for a pair of boots. What a world-wind tour. While in town, he indicated William Holden would be in the film, and he hoped to have Robert Mitchum, Maria Felix, the Mexican star, and Constance Towers for other roles. Interestingly, he also indicated he had one more film commitment to fulfill before *The Alamo*. In all probability, this was *The Alaskans* which was subsequently deferred until his Texan project was completed.[551]

When not on the set, he devoted all his waking moments to the project: checking on the progress of the script with Grant, reviewing production schedules, projecting possible casting choices, approving contracts and design. And constantly monitoring the costs he was racking up. He was forever sending representatives all over Texas to raise more capital. Publicizing the project as the most expensive movie ever was one thing. Having to pay for it was quite another. And to be honest, Duke was broke.

# CHAPTER FOURTEEN
## "BUDDY, CAN YOU SPARE A DIME?"

*"When I say we spent $12 million, I'm leveling. I've got everything I own in it. I borrowed from banks and friends. Take a look at one scene and you'll never be able to count the thousands of people."* Wayne commenting on his investment in *The Alamo.*[552]

BY THE END OF 1957, WAYNE HAD BEEN IN THE FILM INDUSTRY IN ONE FASHION or another for thirty-two years, appeared in 135 movies that grossed well in excess of $245 million in revenue, and earned, at least, $6 million, not including his percentage of the profits on several films. (By the time *The Alamo* was released, it was estimated Wayne's films had grossed in excess of $300 million). By all measures, Wayne was considered extremely successful. As luck would have it, truth was stranger than fiction. Although involved in numerous extracurricular activities, Wayne's business acumen was less than stellar. Or maybe it was just plain bad luck; financial statements laced with red ink for years with many business ventures losing money. With $500,000 tied up in a shrimp operation in Panama, Duke lamented, "God. At one time we controlled seventy percent of the business there, but it's been going down and down. Broke? Yeah... But that was my fault, I made a lot of bad outside investments. Beach clubs. Country clubs. Restaurants. Hell, I've owned more restaurants than you've eaten in. Gold mines. Oil wells. I was known as Dry-Hole Wayne in the oil industry. The only thing I've ever made money on was the California Country Club. We sold when

217

the property became valuable." Wayne manned-up and accepted responsibility. "I should have known better," he admitted. A paperback publishing venture in New York, cotton farms and cattle in Arizona, office buildings in Long Beach, land and oil wells in Oklahoma. He was even part-owner of Sea Service Corporation, which sold oil to yachts. Along with Johnny Weissmuller, he jointly owned Los Flamingos resort, a hideaway for Hollywood stars like Errol Flynn, Cary Grant, Richard Widmark, Fred MacMurray, and Red Skelton. He had a large financial chunk of a J. Paul Getty hotel built in Acapulco. He maintained an active interest in a fishing fleet in Panama, apartment houses, the West Side Tennis Club in Los Angeles, the popular Pantry in Brentwood, a hunting lodge in San Joaquin Valley, a Colorado beer company, the Culver City Hotel, and a Mexico cab company. He even owned stock in Cinerama. Whew!!![553]

Of course, the law of averages meant some investments had to be successful. Wayne, MacMurray, Frank Borzage, and Bo Roos signed a leasing agreement with Signal Oil for 104 acres of land that a California geological survey called the largest undeveloped oil basin in the state. Though not owning the land, they did own the oil rights. Risking $150,000 during the war years, they grossed $1.3 million in later sales. Signal Oil paid $30,000 a year plus 16 ⅔% royalties on gross distribution. But our benevolent government in its infinite wisdom saw to it that most of the stars' income was taxed in the 90% bracket, which was why personalities like Wayne got into income property sidelines that were taxed at a significantly lower rate. "If the land goes up in value, you show a profit. If you lose, especially if you're in high tax brackets, the government recognized the losses as a principle of deduction," advised Roos.[554]

So with all the investments, profitable films, glory and accolades, why was Wayne struggling? "I keep working because I need the money," admitted Wayne. "I've been acting almost thirty years and never came close to amassing a fortune. I'd like to take it easy for a while, but I can't. I have to work to keep my head above water. By the time I pay off alimony, my business agent and manager, and raise five kids, I'm lucky if I break even." Wayne borrowed almost a quarter of a million dollars from RKO and Warner Bros. to pay off former spouses, not including alimony and child support. "Because of high taxes, I'll have to earn a million and a half dollars to pay off those loans. Under normal conditions, I'd be a millionaire, but right now I figure it will take five million dollars to get myself out of debt. Kind of funny," he mused, "when you realize I've earned eight million dollars during my career, and lord knows how much money my pictures have made. I'm conservative. I don't throw big parties. I don't have expensive hobbies. I came along too late to make good investments before taxes. I've made a few investments—in a boat company and a couple of hotels—but so far, there's no money coming in. So I have to make movies. It takes time to work out financial problems, and I can't afford time either. I start for the studio at 6 a.m. and seldom get home before 7 in the evening. Then, after a shower and dinner, I'm ready to hit the sack. But I'm not worried about the situation. I enjoy my work. Every four or five years, I figure I've got my money troubles licked. Then, something pops up to set me back. The way I'm going now I'll never be able to take a rest. I've got to work to keep Uncle Sam off my back. To be honest, I really need the money. I need it bad."[555]

Wayne had started out as a stand-in for Francis X. Bushman, Jr. in the 1926 film *Brown of Harvard*. By 1929, along with football players from USC, Duke was earning $50 a week participating in *Salute*, a West Point-Annapolis rivalry film. In 1939, his pay jumped to $600 a week for *Stagecoach*, though most of his films in the 1930s paid in the $3,000 to $6,000 range. He finally came into his own financially in the 1940s with a string of successes: 1941 (*Reap the Wild Wind* $30,839); 1942 (*Pittsburgh* $50,000); 1943 (*In Old Oklahoma* $43,229), (*A Lady Takes a Chance* $55,115), (*The Fighting Seabees* $31,770); 1944 (*Tall in the Saddle* $50,000), (*Flame of the Barbary Coast* $50,000); 1945 (*Back to Bataan* $87,500), (*Dakota* $144,869), (*They Were Expendable* $75,000); 1946 (*Angel and the Badman* $179,460), (*Red River* $165,000); 1947 (*Tycoon* $101,000), (*Fort Apache* $100,000); 1948 (*Three Godfathers* $207,800), (*Wake of the Red Witch* $283,617), (*She Wore a Yellow Ribbon* $175,000); 1949 (*The Fighting Kentuckian* $175,052), (*Sands of Iwo Jima* $480,000).

Modifying and/or augmenting contracts with profit participation generated an absolute windfall for Wayne. When Duke left Republic in the early 1950s and formed Wayne-Fellows, he created the opportunity to not only star but also direct and produce his own projects. In 1952 *Big Jim McLain* earned Wayne $150,000 plus a substantial percentage of the profits as co-producer. *Island in the Sky, Hondo,* and *The High and the Mighty* garnered him $175,000 each plus a percentage of each film's profits and ownership of the film negatives after seven years. In *The Searchers,* he reaped $250,000 against 10% of gross receipts after Warner Bros. recouped the first $2.5 million in rentals. With profit participation, Wayne realized over $350,000 from this single film. And finally, the piece de resistance: a $2 million contact to star in three films for Fox, each paying him $666,667! He would earn $200,000 each and every year for the next ten years. What more could one ask?[556]

Indeed, that was the question most major studios asked themselves. With the creation of independent production companies by stars like Brando, Cooper, Stewart, Douglas, Holden, Peck, Lancaster, Wayne, and many others, the balance of power shifted from Hollywood's pioneering producers to top-draw stars. The producers claimed that the movie stars priced themselves out of the business. Confided one, "You've practically got to give away 125% of the picture to line up the stars. By the time the talents' demands are met, there's no profit left for anyone." Paramount gave Brando all the profits on *One-Eyed Jacks,* deducting only studio and distribution costs. Mirisch paid Wayne and Holden $750,000 each plus 20% of the profit on *The Horse Soldiers*. Holden received 10% of the gross on *Bridge on the River Kwai*, which generated over $2.5 million for him. Marilyn Monroe received 10% of every box-office dollar for *Some Like it Hot*, and Liz earned $500,000 plus 10% of the gross for *Two for the Seesaw*. Cary Grant requested a Rolls Royce, complete with chauffeur, to tour Scotland for the promotion of *Indiscreet*. Warner promptly agreed. And Burt Lancaster wanted his wife and four children to accompany him to England for the making of *The Devil's Disciple*. United Artists said, why not? Wow! Were they worth it? With one of the above names on a contract, studios had no problem lining up money needed to make a film. Without the stars, studios couldn't remain in business.[557]

Major stars were like a warm, comfortable blanket. You knew what you were going to get: a certain quality, a certain style, a certain *je ne sais quoi*. Why take a chance on something you're not familiar with? Jimmy Stewart summed it up nicely. "After the glamour and glitter is stripped away, you've got to realize that movies are pretty much like any other business," he admitted. "We exist on supply and demand, too. The demand now is for solid, reliable performers who can get people out of the homes and into the theaters. People don't have the movie habit anymore. They won't go to the theater unless they're pretty sure of getting their money's worth. When they know that Duke Wayne or Gary Cooper is in the picture, they can judge from past performance that it ought to be pretty good." And demand was greater than supply.[558]

Creation of one's own production company not only allowed a "Star" to earn and keep more money, but also gave them something no other arrangement could: artistic control of their product. No longer would a corporate weasel have final cut control or determine which projects an actor had to star in to fulfill a contract. Actors could now pick and choose, rise and fall on their own merits.

With a 90% tax bracket, only 10% was left to cover living expenses. Wayne and others used their production companies and other methods to minimize tax liabilities on salaried income, utilizing such techniques as co-production deals, sharing a percentage of profits based on gross receipts and limiting the amount of income they generated annually by deferring earnings to future years. All perfectly legal ways to pay as little tax as possible.

When television came into play, studios panicked and tried to reduce expenses by cutting back on their contract players. Right after the war, there were 750 to 800 actors under contract. By the late 1950s, there were 175 and virtually none of them were big names. According to one actor, "As soon as the picture business started getting tough, the studios dropped the actors. The producers argued, why should they pay an actor $2,500 or $5,000 a week when they can let him go and hire him back at $100,000 a picture." As a result, the remaining players, usually well-established with long-standing value, became even bigger box-office draws. Realizing there were few replacements, these stars refused to renew their contracts as they expired, and once contractually free, formed their own production companies, thereby becoming more expensive and less available to the studios. The studios argued the deals the stars were asking for were unrealistic, that the stars were pricing themselves out of the industry, and granting them would drive the studios into bankruptcy. Wayne had no sympathy for the studio's situation. "After thirty years in this business, the pendulum has finally swung to the actors and everybody hollars," Wayne retorted. "We're only getting the money that used to go to the relatives of the studio bosses. At least we work for what we get. And that's more than you can say for a lot of nephews around this town. If I can help our country beat the Russians for control of outer space, then I'm all for it. At least my money is going for something constructive. When I used to turn out those old westerns you see on television every day, I was getting $75 a week and doing my own stunts. The pictures cost about $11,000 and made big profits. Those same profits built Beverly Hills mansions for a lot of people who would be on relief if their uncles hadn't been movie moguls." Not all studios felt the actors were solely responsible for outrageous salaries, though. Harold Mirisch of Mirisch Bros. Co. stated, "We independents can get any personality, provided we have the right story and a good director. But, of course, we have to pay those stars what they have been getting." He further stated that everyone wasn't forced to make "outrageous deals" and that, if he chose to pay a player a large sum in lieu of a percentage "that's just taking a calculated risk."[559]

Wayne was absolutely obsessed with making *The Alamo*. Every waking moment, every dollar he had, would be invested in the project. But it wouldn't be enough. Both the scope and costs were rapidly escalating out of control. One man, even one as successful as Wayne, couldn't be expected to fund everything. He needed help, and he needed it now. Over the past several years, he had gone to extraordinary lengths to increase the Wayne coffer: co-production arrangements, mega-million multi-picture deals, percentage of the gross. Film after film after film, and still it wasn't nearly enough. Though he continued to be in demand, major studios were reluctant to financially back Wayne's project for one very simple reason: he wanted to direct it himself. He insisted upon it. This obsession, more than anything, was a major factor in the dissolution of his partnership with Robert Fellows in 1954. Duke desperately wanted to bring this project to fruition; Fellows couldn't see the need. In order to buy Fellows out, they agreed the payoff would occur over several years. And it was one reason he needed more funding.

Wayne admitted, "I've gambled everything I own on this picture; all my money and my soul… everything I own (is) in this picture—except my necktie. I went to every studio in town, tried calling in favors, reminded the studio heads how much money I made for them, but they all turned me down unless I got John Ford to direct. But this was my dream. I didn't want anyone else to direct it—not even my dear friend Jack Ford. United Artists only agreed to put up part of the money if I played a part, so I said I'd play Sam Houston, which was really a cameo kind of role. But they said I had to play a major role and said if I didn't play Davy Crockett, they wouldn't be interested." (Wayne later said that if it wasn't for his death in a plane crash, his good friend producer Mike Todd would have been involved in the project.)[560]

The fly in the buttermilk was...he didn't want to play Crockett. As director/producer, all of Wayne's time and efforts would be focused on bringing the project to fruition: casting, financing, set construction, budget development, script revisions. To wear yet a third hat would be inconceivable. In the past, Wayne had acted as unofficial director when required, or more succinctly, when he felt he and the actual director weren't on the same page. In many cases, with Duke's extensive cinematic background, he was more qualified to take charge than the real director. "Before I became an actor, I was a prop man, electrician, stunt man, and assistant director," recalled Wayne. "I've wanted to be a director since I entered the business; in fact, that's why I came into it. But they paid me so much as an actor that I couldn't afford to direct." Had this been a life-long ambition? "How long have I wanted to direct?" he retorted. "Just since the day when I started as a prop-man with John Ford on a picture called *Mother Machree*." Wayne's long-term plan not only addressed his aspirations but also his considerable talent. "I intend to be around motion pictures for a while yet," he admitted. "When I begin to creak at the hinges and take on the appearance of a tired water buffalo I'll play character parts. And, because I know my trade as well as the next man in Hollywood, I'll direct. But no matter what, I'll always be part of the motion picture industry, for it has been good to me. It has been my life and I love it." Unwilling to compromise his beliefs, all he needed now was funding.[561]

He hawked his project all over town. According to Aissa, "He cajoled, argued, seduced, and called in old markers," but all anyone wanted to hear was, "What character will you play? Yes, we know you're a tremendously popular actor. Yes, we know you have a great deal of experience. But Duke, this would be your first official time behind the camera with no one to help you. No one to guide you. You're asking us to take a huge chance here. What happens if this is a box-office failure? Then what? We'd feel more comfortable lending you money if we knew you'd be in the picture. And not just a cameo role. It's got to be a starring role. And let's get a name director to run the show. You know how much we appreciate you, Duke. You know what you mean to this studio. But we just can't take the chance..." It was the same story wherever he went: "If you're not going to star..."

At Republic, Wayne not only had the backing of a major studio, well, the backing of a studio, he also had commitments from several independent investors; as long as Republic put up its share and covered distribution costs, the investors were willing to commit to the *Alamo* project. Wining and dining wealthy Texans, at this time the anticipated budget was about $3 million.

Undeservedly, when Wayne and Yates had their falling out, the expected arrangements disappeared. Ironic, considering that during the world premiere of *Rio Grande*, the city of San Antonio presented Yates with a scroll because of his plans to produce *The Alamo* early the following year. "Who the hell is going to pay to see a picture where all the heroes die?" Yates scoffed. According to Maurice Zolotow, Universal said it would be interested if Frank Lloyd, John Ford, or Howard Hawks directed. Paramount would co-produce if DeMille or Hathaway were involved. Warner Bros. agreed to support Wayne but purposely left his pet project out of his most recent contract. (All films were to be produced within a specific budget that precluded a high-budget film such as *The Alamo*.) Jack Warner pointedly told him, "It'll be too god-damn expensive, and I don't think the fans want to see this kind of picture anymore, Duke. Forget it." When his relationship with that studio started to deteriorate, he looked elsewhere. "I made ten pictures at Warner Brothers that made a great deal of money for them," he admitted, "and a great deal for me, too. Finally other people there started saying I was getting all the breaks, making too much money. They were going to start changing the terms of the deal. So I left and went to United Artists. It was a lesser deal, but one that gave me more freedom as a producer." If he was going to pull this off, he needed to start beating the bushes for additional investors.[562]

He finally secured studio funding from UA, but it was only partial and he would have to raise several million more from private sources, as well as invest heavily himself. Fundraising affected the film's strategic planning since Duke had intended to only play a cameo as Sam Houston, devoting most of his time to directing and producing. But contributors wanted assurance that Wayne, a top box-office attraction, would play a leading role. His agreement with UA addressed both those issues; in order to receive funding from the studio, Batjac had to match UA's investment, which meant Wayne had to come up with $2.5 million. In addition, the studio insisted Duke play a starring role. Wayne agreed to the terms as he believed he could come up with the necessary funds. Hadn't he worked in films for almost thirty years? He was a major star with big-time films, and big-time contracts. He could afford to finance the project. Couldn't he? But in late 1958 he contacted Bo Christian Roos, his business manager, only to find the proverbial cupboard was bare.[563]

Duke had first become acquainted with Roos in 1940 in the midst of his short affair with Marlene Dietrich while they filmed *Seven Sinners*. Roos was tall and heavy, dark hair and mustache, flamboyant in both clothes and mannerisms. Dietrich convinced Wayne he needed someone to manage his money and introduced him to Roos, her business manager. She also pressured Roos, who persuaded Charles Feldman, Wayne's agent, to renegotiate Duke's contract with Republic. As a result, Herbert Yates agreed to give Wayne a percentage of the profits on the pictures he made for the studio. (According to Carolyn Roos Olsen, Roos's daughter, Wayne was a client long before Dietrich joined Roos.) The business manager, though successful, was, according to some, "the sort of man that, once you shook his hand, you wanted to take a shower." Manager to the stars, his clientele included Joan Crawford, Red Skelton, Johnny Weissmuller, June Haver, and Frank Borzage, among many others. "He showed me," Wayne explained, "that an actor like me can gross more'n most businesses and corporations. I had tax problems like any business. And I had to bring my expenses into line with how much I made. He wanted to put me on a strict budget, something ridiculous like fifty bucks a week, but I wouldn't go for that. However, I listened to him. He made a lot of sense." Roos was a combination adviser, friend, and father confessor. As business manager, he controlled and disbursed the star's earnings, and they didn't make a single financial decision, no matter how small, without his permission. Roos took a very systematic approach to his client's financial responsibility. "First, we take three or four months to survey the star's financial structure," Roos explained. "Then we try to get his living expenses down. Usually a star is spending $2,000 a month when he should be spending $1,000. But that's not because stars are spendthrifts. Living is automatically higher for them. For instance, they can't buy $50 suits; they'd be called cheapskates—and they have to look the part of movie stars. They can't tip 10 or 15%, as we can. They have to give $5 for every $1 that we give—or they'd automatically lose a fan." Wayne agreed. "An actor has to put up a good front," he said. "If you went into a barbershop and didn't tip the barber a few dollars, he'd tell his friends you were a heel and the news would get around."[564]

After paring expenses, Roos looked for other opportunities. "I've always believed in methodical gambling," explained Roos, "10% down on real estate and let it mature. Nowadays, there are a lot of sharp promoters who try to make faster money for actors by getting them into businesses. But you've got to watch secondary things like bowling alleys and other businesses. It takes hours away from acting, which is what actors should be doing. Trouble is, so many stars have their own producing firms now, they think they know a lot more. A little knowledge is dangerous. I've been called a gambler for one reason—I'm only good for the client who wants action for his money. A lot of business managers never stick their necks out, and so they're never wrong. But I know my kids only have so long to get well in, so somebody has to carry the ball."[565]

Initially, Duke was successful. In August 1955, Wayne, along with MacMurray and Roos, purchased an 18% interest in the Lyle Guslander Island Holiday Hotel chain, which included the Maui Palms on Maui, the Coco Palms on Kauai and the Kona Palms on Hawaii. Duke, MacMurray, Roos, and Fellows had previously bankrolled Phil Silvers's Broadway play *Top Banana* in 1951, and had also owned interest in the California Country Club, which was sold in 1950. Graham-Michaelis Oil leases, Ione Ingle Oil, Polar Pantry, Insurance Service

Bureau and Beverly Wilshire Construction were only a few of the ventures Duke and Roos were invested in.[566]

Roos can take credit, or more likely accept blame, for indirectly introducing Wayne to his second wife. In 1944, Duke, Roos, Ward Bond, MacMurray, and Ray Milland traveled to Mexico on a business-pleasure junket to potentially invest in Churubusco Studio in Mexico City, and set it up as an independent film company. While there, though unsuccessful in their efforts, Wayne encountered Chata. A supposed high-class call girl, Milland was one of her clients.[567]

Duke had his first inkling that his finances were not what they seemed when he started getting past-due notices on $3,200 worth of purchases he and Pilar had made at Saks Fifth Avenue in New York. Normally, all bills would be sent to Roos for payment, but now Duke was getting daily reminders that they were still unsettled. Eventually, he called his business manager. "Jesus Christ, Bo," Duke screamed. "Would you please pay the bills? I look like a goddamn deadbeat!" Roos promised to take care of them immediately. Duke admitted he hadn't seen his paychecks in years. They were handled by his business manager. But rumors had circulated about Roos's shenanigans and Wayne became suspicious. According to others, Roos would borrow money on his client's life insurance policies and invest the money in short-term, high-interest paying investments. Supposedly, when the money came due, he'd return the principal to the client's policy and bank the interest earned in his own account. No one was the wiser. Checks had already started to bounce on Clari Land before the cotton harvest. "I'd been hearing people saying that Bo Roos had screwed them," said Wayne, "but I thought they were joking. Then I started wondering about it, so I asked my secretary Mary to take a look at my files in Roos's office. It should have been packed with papers about my investments. But all Mary found were mortgage papers on property in Culver City and the Flamingo Hotel in Acapulco." (The Los Flamingos Hotel was initially purchased in 1939 by Roos, MacMurray, Rex Allen, Weissmuller, Frank Belcher, Frank Borzage, and Wayne. As there were limits on Americans owning property in Mexico, the hotel was purchased by using a Mexican citizen, Carlos Reyes, as a participant. Eventually Roos bought out Allen and Belcher.)[568] Not at all pleased with what he had heard, a conference was scheduled to determine precisely what was going on. And Wayne didn't beat around the bush:

"Bo," he asked, "exactly how much money do I have?"

"Well, Duke," Roos admitted, "not a great deal of cash. Your money isn't sitting in a bank somewhere. It's all invested: real estate, various business ventures…"

"I know that," Wayne said exasperatedly. "Just tell me how much money I could raise if I had to."

Roos delayed replying by asking for a few more weeks to pull everything together. Wayne knew he was stalling, but what could he do? Uncomfortable, he left the meeting but vowed to give Roos the benefit of the doubt. After all, hadn't he given the manager millions and millions of dollars to invest over the years? Roos was the business manager for the stars: MacMurray, Skelton. Hell, they were rich, so was he. Yeah, it just took time to pull it together. Two weeks later, they met again.

"Well, Bo," asked Wayne, "how much am I worth?"

Stalling yet again, Bo was evasive. "It isn't that simple, Duke."

Wayne blew his stack. Rearing up to his full six-foot-four-inch height, he slammed his fist on the desk and demanded, "For chrissake, I've given you a goddamn fortune over the years. It's a simple question. Where is it, goddamn it?"

Roos melted in his chair. "It's all gone," he admitted with despair. "You've got the house, personal possessions, and Batjac. That's all I could save."

Wayne was aghast. Everything he'd worked for, everything he'd earned—was gone! Wayne stormed from the office to call his lawyer. A subsequent investigation showed no malfeasance or criminal negligence by Roos, just incompetence and gross mismanagement; countless poor investments, throwing good money after bad, one after another, after another. According to Pilar, "There'd been deals such as an Acapulco hotel which stayed so full of non-paying friends that it never made a profit or the Culver City property that had been carried on the books in the red for years." Mary St. John was even more explicit. "Roos had a passion for business trips," she recalled. "If Wayne were at home for six or eight weeks, Roos would not even call him, but as soon as he was on location, Roos would invent some a reason for a visit, and they would talk about nothing of consequence. In 1957, when Duke was in Japan filming *The Barbarian and the Geisha*, Roos spent more than a month in a high-rise Kyoto penthouse, having sex with geisha girls, eating in the finest sushi, and charging it all to Duke's account." Roos, along with Fellows, Ford, and others, had advised against the Alamo project, calling it extreme, extravagant, and ill-advised. Perhaps Roos already knew Wayne didn't have adequate resources to finance the project and was attempting to divert this showdown.[569]

"It was a hard time," Duke remembered. "Before then, on paper, I was supposed to be worth four or five million, and suddenly I found I didn't have a damned thing. If I'd sold everything, then I'd have just about broken even, that means broke... Bo Roos cost me the first twenty years of my career. I'd worked for twenty years for nothing." And, of course, it didn't help that he had to pay $150,000 each and every year in alimony to his ex-wives.[570]

Told if he took the case to court it would make him look like a complete fool. Duke agreed, knew it was time to forget about it and move on. Wayne was beside himself and absolutely positive Roos had stolen his fortune. "I'll be goddamned," he exclaimed. "I was sure he stole it, nobody's stupid enough to lose that much money." Apparently Roos was. Duke had to be convinced not to sue for damages. "I wanted to sue the living shit out of that son-of-a-bitch!" said Duke. But when asked, "How the hell could you give a guy millions and not ask any questions, never follow up on him?" Wayne knew the battle was lost. It was pointless to sue his manager as, according to Wayne, Roos was penniless.[571]

*In all fairness, it should be noted, Carolyn Roos Olsen stated, rather than her father's lack of financial expertise, Wayne's economic situation was a result of Duke's largess and communication skills. She suggested that his two previous divorces, lack of written communication on the part of each business partner, and an attempt to create new systems to preserve income, caused Duke's cash-flow problems. Howard S. Meaghan, arbitrator in the dispute between Wayne and Roos, further claimed a power struggle between Wayne's "inside" staff (Fellows, Newman, LaCava, and Wisner) and "outside" staff (Roos) resulted in multiple opportunities for friction and rivalry. The result was "During 1958 Wayne permitted the responsibility for his affairs to become subtly bifurcated, setting his inside organization and his outside organization in competition for his favor and esteem. The extraordinary services demanded by those who were not previously familiar with the complex background of Wayne's affairs were costly." On December 27, 1958, Wayne terminated Roos's employment as business manager effective December 31.*

Red Skelton, who severed his ties with Boos in 1959, said this about business managers in general: "I'll tell you what business managers do—not all of them, but some of them in the Hollywood group. Whenever a business manager walks up to you and says, 'You've had a great year, a sensational year, but we can't pay the tax yet,' I'll tell you what they've done. I knew a guy who used to manage about nine stars and pay their income tax, and, of course, he had power of attorney. He would have 'em sign checks for the tax, which came to about two million dollars. Then he'd ask the government for an extension, maybe for six months, maybe for a year. He'd deposit the two million in various banks, collect the interest for himself, then eventually pay the government. In addition to this, he takes 10% for management fees, and 10% for accountancy fees. And he gets a cut on all the purchases. I think I've lost close to $10 million by not managing my own affairs."[572]

Sadly, this wasn't the first time Wayne had issues trying to finance his *Alamo* project. By mid-1958, the movie set was well on its way to completion. Construction workers had been hired, material purchased. Ground had been graded; wells dug and compound and village walls were being erected. It was starting to look like old San Antone. And then disaster struck. Wayne ran out of money. Well, that's not quite right; he had the money but couldn't use it for the film. Duke had formed a partnership with Bob Fellows in February 1952 and joint productions of *Big Jim McLain*, *Plunder of the Sun*, *Island in the Sky*, *Hondo*, *The High and the Mighty* and *Ring of Fear* quickly followed. By early January 1954, however, the partnership began to fall apart. Fellows had entered into a liaison with one of his secretaries and notified his wife Eleanor that he wanted a divorce. She asked Wayne, as a friend of her husband, to mediate a reconciliation meeting. Reluctantly, he agreed. However, the discussion quickly deteriorated into shouting, threats, and accusations. Wayne, uneasy to begin with, found himself in an awkward situation. Suddenly, he arose and left the discordant couple. "I am very uncomfortable here," he admitted. "This is none of my business. Settle it yourselves." Convinced that he would need to liquidate his assets as a result of the divorce, Fellows requested Wayne buy him out and Duke agreed. The monies would be paid out over time.[573]

"But it wasn't all smooth sailing," recalled Happy Shahan. "I remember one time in 1958 that Wayne called me and said, 'Stop building.' I said, 'Why?' 'Because I don't have any money.' I said, 'Are you going to shoot this picture?' He used a few choice words saying, 'You know we're going to shoot this picture!' I said, 'Well, if you're going to shoot the picture, we better not stop building.' He said, 'I told you; I don't have any money!' 'Hey,' I said, 'we got to keep building. I'm coming to Hollywood.' 'Well, it won't make any difference,' he said. 'I don't have any money to continue.' I told him I would be out there the next day which I was. Before I left, I went to the bank and got me a ($100,000) note. I told them at the bank to make it out to John Wayne and Happy Shahan, John Wayne's name first, and I'd sign it at the bottom. Then I went out to Hollywood and told Wayne, 'Hey, we're going to keep building, you sign this note. When we get the money, we'll pay them. You'll be better off and I'll be better off, and you won't have to worry about anything.'" Happy reminded Duke that by laying off three hundred to four hundred workers then, it would result in a major problem in the future because "you can't just re-hire them at the drop of a hat." They had to find other employment somewhere, and chances are they wouldn't be available when "you" needed them again.

"I went out and ate with him that night," continued Shahan, "and, in fact, he took me to his home. We argued a good part of the evening, which was not unusual for us. But, you know, after he got to thinking about it, he realized it wasn't a bad deal. We just kept building the sets. And it wasn't a bad deal for me. He had money coming in; he just didn't have enough right then to keep them working on *The Alamo*. You know, Wayne was plenty smart about the way he was paid in his movie deals. Let's say he was to be paid a million dollars for a picture. He might take a quarter of a million up front and the rest over a long period of time, and he was making several movies a year. I knew that, so I said, 'Here's what we'll do. I'm going to complete this town set for *The Alamo* and that will be my money. You have to agree not to destroy the town. *The Alamo* set is your money; you can destroy anything you want there.' So everything worked out. I got a town, and he got his picture. *The Alamo* sets weren't intact, of course. He blew the hell out of them at the end of the picture. It cost me a million dollars to put the *Alamo* set back together again." In exchange for allowing Wayne to build the village set with four-sided wall, a roof and foundation thus creating "practical" buildings instead of two-sided sets, continuing this concept into the construction of the

Alamo and, not damaging any structures in the village, Happy agreed to take out a loan. He may have set up a consortium to do so; Wayne co-signed the note and agreed to repay the cash as soon as he could.[574]

Whenever Wayne ran out of money, Happy took care of it. He would cover the payroll, bills, whatever was needed. "He was good for it, and Wayne would repay it," related Shahan's wife Virginia. "I tell you why he was out of money," recalled Happy. "Bob Fellows, who was his business partner, wanted three million dollars cash to get out of his deal; he wanted to separate from Wayne. So Wayne had to hock everything he had; I mean he hocked everything to pay off Bob Fellows." (Shahan was a bit mistaken. It was only the remaining portion of the $3 million payout that Wayne owed. Nevertheless, after he met Fellows's demand for payment, he didn't have the necessary remaining funds to support his Alamo project. With salary paid out over time, Duke was suffering a cash-flow timing issue). According to Aissa, her father mortgaged everything he owned: their house, Batjac, family cars, anything with capital value—as collateral for loans. As Duke admitted, "I have everything I own in this picture…except my necktie." (During the final days of filming, Wayne needed another $700,000 to complete production. He asked UA but was told by a studio executive, "You won't get it, Duke. They're short of money themselves right now. And you and I know they can't borrow on your movie." So he had to come up with it himself. He took out a second mortgage on his house, sold his Mexican property, and borrowed the rest against his personal possessions. Later, he was told UA really had had the funds but thought it had risked enough and didn't want to make a further commitment. UA also knew Duke would move heaven and hell to finish the film. Predictably, Wayne was annoyed: "That's what happens when the little accountants who want to make a name for themselves in a company interfere with the creators.")[575]

Unbelievably, Wayne experienced funding issues on this project yet another time. On April 23, 1959, newspaper headlines across the country screamed "John Wayne Linked to Rebellion Plot Leader in Panama." Sources close to the Panamanian government stated that captured documents and personal effects from accused revolutionary leader Robert (Tito) Arias indicated Wayne may have been involved in a plot to overthrow the government. A letter containing Wayne's name and address was discovered inside Arias's confiscated suitcase. Inside the envelope was an interoffice memorandum to Wayne from his attorney, Robert D. Weesner, dated April 9, 1959, outlining a "schedule of funds totaling $682,850 given to or drawn by Tito Arias in connection with his Panamanian operations in which you are involved." The suitcase also allegedly contained a notebook with an itemized list of arms and ammunition, a map of Panama's Pacific coast, a tide table, and several round military-type patches. A letter from Wayne to Arias signed "Duke" was also uncovered, but the contents were not disclosed. Although Wayne was not accused directly, officials were concerned that "the memorandum mentions $525,000 turned over to Arias personally, apparently without supporting documents to satisfy Mr. Weesner." The implication was that Wayne, either knowingly or unknowingly, financed a potential revolution through funds advanced to Arias without proper justification.

Wayne was quick to deny any responsibility. He indicated he was shocked to hear that Arias and his ballerina wife, Dame Margot Fonteyn, were involved. "I have been in business with the Arias family for a long time," he stated. "A group of us are in several business ventures, including a shrimp company. Roberto never talked politics, and I never heard him saying anything about overthrowing the Panamanian government. I've got business in Panama with him and without him," he admitted. "I also know other members of his family. His father is a well respected lawyer in Panama." He indicated further, "Some (newspaper) writers have been trying to link me to the rebellion in Panama, but the only revolution I'm planning is a picture called *The Alamo*, which I plan to start this summer." He had first been introduced to the Arias family in the early 1940s by Bo Roos. Long-time friends, Duke once lent his yacht to Arias when Tito was courting Fonteyn while she appeared in Los Angeles. The couple returned the favor by throwing a party for Duke while he was in London. Wayne along with Roos and Tony, Arias's brother, had invested heavily in the Trivoli Shrimp company. A close friend of the family, Tony was asked to be Aissa's godfather. With their numerous joint financial investments in the country, Wayne periodically took the opportunity to scout potential locations for his *Alamo* film while down there. Duke had even established Batjac Productions Panama Inc., which he used to produce *Legend of the Lost*.[576]

An official Wayne spokesman stated it was ridiculous to think Wayne was involved in any plot. Supposedly, Arias and ten other rebels landed in the beach resort of Santa Clara, seventy-three miles from Panama City. Their hideout was uncovered by the National Guard, but Arias had already fled. They also found military-type shoulder patches that consisted of a green "22" on a white background. It was assumed the rebels were trying to start a "May 22" revolutionary movement, taking the name from a clash that had occurred one year earlier between students and the government. Arias was charged with trying to start a revolution against president Ernest de la Guardia. Ironically, Arias's father was the former president of Panama who, one year earlier, had broken from the de la Guardia administration. Evidence from a second captured cache of weapons suggested Dame Margot, who had earlier been expelled from Panama, was aware of her husband's plot to overthrow the government. However, from her exile in Britain, Fonteyn declared, "Mr. Wayne had nothing to do with it." Documents received by the FBI suggested Arias set out on a fishing trip aboard the Nola, planned to transfer to a shrimp boat, and then storm the National Guard barracks at La Chorrera. Eventually, eighty-seven Cuban invaders supporting the revolution were captured after temporarily seizing the small coastal town of Nombre de Dios. Arias had already fled to safety in the Brazilian embassy in the capital city. He was sought by the government while his wife was in New York where she had been temporarily jailed overnight.[577]

The $525,000 mentioned in the captured documents referred to investment capital needed to start a variety of operations including a ship-repair business in the Panama Canal. The memo was dated March 5, 1959, and was headed "Subject funds given to Roberto E. Arias." In an accompanying letter, Wayne wrote as follows: "Since I...am trying to get my affairs straightened out and a decent bookkeeping and accounting system set up, I am enclosing a memorandum that Bob Weesner made up for me on the things about which he would really like to have some information." The Weesner memo indicated that Wayne had invested funds with Arias beginning in 1953 through a Wayne subsidiary, Batjac Productions, Panama, Inc. Starting in November 1957, Arias began to draw unaccounted monies against the investment. They included: "$10,000 for stock in Ocean Products, Inc., $101,600 advanced in connection with shrimp boat operations, that you loaned Ocean Products, Inc., $31,250, that you advanced Panama Cooperative Fisheries, Inc., $15,000, and that you have loaned in or has been drawn by "Tito" Arias $525,000."[578]

Eventually, the FBI investigated allegations against Wayne but concluded there wasn't sufficient evidence to implicate him in anything. President de la Guardia fostered an interesting opinion on the matter. He stated he was convinced the invasion had been staged by Arias because he was pressed for an accounting of a large sum on money advanced to Arias by Wayne. He did emphasize, though, that he felt Wayne was not involved. Nevertheless, over $500,000 was now lost to Wayne, money that he would desperately need later in production.[579]

Signing the UA contract began to free other monies that had been pledged by Wayne's Texan contacts. And it was a good thing as the budget had now begun to spiral out of control. While Wayne was still at Republic, the epic was budgeted for $4 million. By December 11, 1957, that increased to $5 million. In mid-May 1959, it was pegged at $6 million. And with six weeks to go before the start of production, it increased to $6.5 million. The cost of the sets alone was said to range between $500,000 and $1.5 million. (However, Schedule A of a supplemental loan agreement with Bank of America dated March 22, 1960, stated Batjac only spent $184,678.89 on set construction.) Duke didn't want to risk all of Batjac's financial resources, so the more he raised outside, the less risk to his company. Having the support of UA helped get his foot in the door, so to speak, with other investors. Texans supported him before...why wouldn't they do it again? A personal request to Texas Governor Price Daniel resulted in a list of potential investors. Duke insisted on doing all the legwork himself. Armed with a personal introduction from Daniel, he worked night and day, traveling the length and width of Texas, utilizing his immense charm to entice wealthy contributors by begging, pleading, knocking on doors, day after day, week after week. Every revision of the script increased the total cost. The longer it took, the more the cost increased. And he was successful! Checks poured in from land, cattle, and oil barons. Some didn't even care if they were ever repaid; just as long as the film was made in Texas. The closer he was to the start of production, the more money he required.[580]

In mid-July, a meeting in Houston took place in a back room of Club Maxim, hosted by brothers O.J. and I.J. McCullough. The cream of Texas entrepreneurs—Glenn McCarthy, Frank Waters, Claude Hamill, Temple Hargrove, Dr. Hampton Robinson, Ralph McCullough, Sid Adger, Veron Frost, Grover Geiselman, A. W. Larkin and Dave Wallace—were there. Representing over one billion dollars in capital, their various business holdings included banks, oil companies, bars, newspapers, radio stations, hotels and ranches, just to name a few. At that time, with $3.5 million already raised, Wayne needed, at least, $3 million more. So what did he do? They were Texans, right? Wasn't the battle at the Alamo a quintessential event in the history of the Republic? Appeal to their patriotism and sell the value of the investment. So Wayne told them in so many words that freedom and liberty do not come cheap. That sometimes you may have to fight and die for what you believe in. That such a message needed to be shared with the world. Come and join me by supporting this film and share in the glory. Both Jim Henaghan and Don LaCava attended this meeting, and Henaghan and Wayne admitted they weren't trying to "promote" the money. They just wanted to let some Texans in on the deal. "We just want to get something going in Texas," claimed Jim, "and a movie about the Alamo seems to be the way to do it."[581]

And join they did. Clint Murchison started the ball rolling with a check for $1 million. Additional funding was forthcoming. Along with UA's $2.5 million and Batjac's $750,000, Texans anted up the following: O.J. and I.J. McCullough, $1.1 million; Texas businessmen Clinton and John Dabney Murchison, $1 million. To make up the difference in total requirements Wayne agreed to have $700,000 of his salary for *McLintock!*, which was to be filmed in late 1962, held in abeyance until the film turned a profit. Interestingly, an article dated July 18, 1958, stated Texas millionaires headed by Murchison already had backed Wayne to the tune of $6 million. Perhaps the announcement was a bit inflated and somewhat premature, but it did help publicize the project's success. At a press conference to exploit the film's premiere in 1960, Wayne once again disclosed his financial backers: United Artists, $2.5 million; the McCulloughs, $3 million; Murchison, $2.5 million; the Yale Foundation, $1.5 million; with the rest coming from Wayne. According to Duke, he invested somewhere between $1.2 and $1.5 million of his own money—everything he could scrape up. One can see how the budget and investment details were both elusive and ethereal.[582]

Wayne and Murchison actually had been in financial negotiations as early as mid-1958. In a July 8 letter to Duke, Clint had laid out the necessary details of the proposed loan: "We have agreed to raise for you $1,500,000 to be loaned to you for the purpose of making your picture, "The Alamo." We agree that this loan will be subject to $2,000,000 first mortgage against your picture. We want to have the same rights that you give the first mortgage holder. After the $2,000,000 is repaid to the holder of the first mortgage, we expect to get liquidation out of all proceeds. If the holder of the first mortgage does not require that you furnish them with monthly audit accounts of your expenditure, we would require that. We would also require that you receive no personal funds during the time the picture is being made, and we want your position in a third position until we receive our $1,500,000 plus 6% interest. If this is agreeable to you, I would appreciate it if you would get a commitment out of some bank to furnish the $2,000,000. After we have read that commitment, we will draw up a firm contract with you, furnishing you with the $1,500,000. We, of course, expect you to spend our $1,500,000 before you require the first mortgage holder to spend his $2,000,000."[583]

Duke was eternally grateful to Murchison and addressed him as "Boss" in an October 3, 1959, letter: "Regarding our venture, I know how tight money is. I can't tell you how much I appreciate your backing up your word, though there were many reasonable excuses you could have used to back out." After the film was finished, he further expressed his gratitude in a letter he wrote June 10, 1960: "I really appreciate what you did for me, and want you to know it had a lot to do with the integrity and hard work that went into the picture. I couldn't let such confidence down. It may sound a little stilted, but I really mean it." One may wonder what Wayne meant by "though there were many reasonable excuses...." Murchison had initially agreed to increase his loan to Wayne to $2 million in return for a larger profit percentage (7½% to15%). But then he reconsidered. In June 1959, Wayne had received a letter from the Dallas law firm of Jenkens, Anson & Spradley that stated Murchison intended to withdraw funding for the film: "Mr. Murchison earlier in the week requested that I write to you and advise that he does not desire to pursue further the matter of any proposed participation by him with you in the picture "The Alamo," and since he has made this decision he felt that he should let you know as soon as possible in order that you might make other arrangements with respect to the financial requirements regarding such picture." Duke was devastated and wrote Robert Thompson, Clint's best friend, that "Almost a year ago Mr. Murchison gave me his word that he would put up a million five hundred thousand dollars at 6% interest for the production of THE ALAMO... Because of my faith in Mr. Murchison's word and the letter he signed to back it up, I have spent $677,823.50 in actual cash and have given commitments of twice that amount... I would never have obligated myself to the extent I have, had I not been assured of this money by a man of Mr. Murchison's stature. If Mr. Murchison were he to withdraw at this time, eight weeks prior to the actual shooting, I don't have to point out to you the effect it would have... Now I find myself in a terrible bind. As a result of this situation, I do not know how I can raise the $250,000 I will need in the next six weeks... I reiterate I would not be in this predicament had I not accepted Mr. Murchison's word and confirmation." Wayne also worried that, if word on this got out, the Todd-AO commitment might also be rescinded. That, combined with Wayne's renegotiated contract with Twentieth Century-Fox on *North to Alaska*, "Cost me an earned position of $700,000 in April, May, and June and also a re-arrangement of my salary percentage position with them on the balance of my contract... The cumulative effect of all of the above will force me into a bankrupt or near bankrupt position."[584]

To convince Murchison of Wayne's financial status, Loeb & Loeb's Roger Davis sent a copy of Batjac's balance sheet to Clint's attorney, Walter Spradley. On the surface, Batjac seemed relatively solvent: $707,344 in assets, $464,401 in liabilities with a net surplus of $242,943. However, once the data was unpacked, it wasn't all that it seemed. Of the total assets, $456,581 were advances for *The Alamo*. Conversely, Batjac also carried a note of $350,000 to Todd-AO. Eliminating *Alamo* related-monies showed that Batjac's net worth was really $136,362 of which $20,000 was stock. Not nearly enough to run an independent studio. Davis tried to paint a rosier picture when he stated Batjac expected to have additional cash-on-hand of $365,000 by the time the film was finished. In addition, it also wrote down over $500,000 of film residuals for *Hondo*, *Island in the Sky*, *High and the Mighty*, *Ring of Fear*, and *Big Jim McLain* to the paltry sum of only $27,655. (Batjac would subsequently use its interest in those films to also cover a Bank of America loan.) Finally, Davis stated, "Batjac owns a number of developed and undeveloped story properties worth conservatively $250,000. It was obvious that Davis tried to show that Batjac was a viable operation worthy of Murchison's investment.[585]

Fortunately, the two parties resolved their issues: Duke would receive Murchison's $1.5 million spread out in biweekly increments starting August 15, 1959, and Murchison would be paid back immediately after monies owed United Artists were paid. Further, he'd receive 5% interest in the net profits of the film. Once again, he also insisted payments to Wayne on his 7½% personal interest be deferred until Murchison received all of his $1.5 million, plus interest.[586]

Wayne also was rightly concerned about Todd-AO's commitment; in fact, he was fortunate to have received it at all. On July 8, 1959, George P. Skouras, president of Todd-AO, had received a letter from Duke that requested permission to use the unique high-resolution widescreen film format for *The Alamo*. Skouras had replied that "different interests of the board of directors" would have to read the script before they would grant a license. But apparently, in anticipation of approval, Wayne had already purchased the raw film stock. Skouras was less than pleased: "I was disturbed by the last paragraph of your letter in which you state that you ordered the raw stock as if a commitment was given to you. No commitment for a license was made to you directly or indirectly by any person who represents THE TODD-AO CORPORATION and any action you take or expenditures you make at this time which assume that this will be a Todd-AO film are at your own risk and responsibility." Skouras even told Wayne's agent Charles Feldman that if Wayne persisted with Grant's script, the film would be a fiasco.[587]

Trying to sooth Skouras's fears, Wayne replied, "...Mr. Ford read it, and we just finished our first conference with him. His comment was: quote—It's thrilling—unquote. Mr. Howard Hawks has worked with us and given us worthy suggestions." Duke then went on to explain some of the more interesting aspects of the film:

"...take the sequence of the second night raid. In it we will have El Greco and his Flamenco troupe re-enact in motion the painting "El Jaleo" by (John Singer) Sargent. Picture that being used just as a background to a sequence in which a group of our men are sneaking through enemy lines, and you will realize the scope of our artistic planning in this picture.

"Follow that with a stampede of the last remaining herd of true Longhorn cattle—not just a stampede, but a stampede through a camp of 5,000 Mexican soldiers and camp followers, and you will begin to realize our change of pace and our value to your medium."

Duke then laid out his plans for promotion: Carl Sandburg, J. Frank Dobie, Dr. Frank Baxter from USC, a special *Life* magazine supplement and the $300,000 Pontiac television special including "such notables as our beloved Ex-Vice president James Garner, Jose Greco, and his troupe, Frank Sinatra or Dean Martin, Sammy Davis, Jr., and all the top columnists, headed by Considine and Lyons." Obviously, Duke tried to persuade Skouras that he was pulling out all the big guns to promote this film. Further, by accident or not, he definitely gave him the impression that Ford was intimately involved in the project.[588]

Skouras took the bait because, a week later, he was even more direct in his concern: "To be frank, I am not enthusiastic over the script. I find the first 112 pages more or less anemic, and I would be afraid if the script was followed that I would lose the audience by the time of the night raid by Bowie and Crockett. If the director (and of course I have the greatest admiration for John Ford) were to take liberties with the script and show in the beginning of the story that the characters are moved by more idealistic principles rather than being just soldiers of fortune as they are apparently depicted, that might give the basis of arousing the sympathy of the audience and hold their interest. I don't believe, however, even in the hands of John Ford, that the story incorporated in the script has the ingredients of a road show Todd-AO picture."[589]

While Wayne and Skouras were in negotiations, Feldman tried a different approach. He contacted George's brother Spyros, president of 20th Century-Fox. On April 28, 1959, Wayne had attempted to make a deal with the studio for its pre-emptive rights with Todd-AO, but, according to George, "there is no such provision as 'pre-emptive' rights in our contract with Twentieth Century." Nevertheless, Feldman was able to convince Spyros of the marketability of the project. As a result, Spyros called his brother twice from Paris and encouraged George to support the film. "(Spyros) tried to make me believe that a great picture can be made from this script," wrote George. "He also, like you, believes that John Ford can implement and enhance the action and the scenes and thus make a great picture." Feldman subsequently wrote a memo that outlined the status of Wayne's request in which he stated that George hated the script, but Spyros finally convinced him and said Fox would even pay half of the guarantee that Todd-AO demanded. Wrote Feldman, "If Spyros didn't put it in a personal basis—brother to brother—George would have said no." Spyros even offered to have Fox take over the film from UA if necessary.[590]

However, George wasn't finished yet. He wanted a guarantee that Ford would direct key scenes. No doubt, both Wayne and Spyros planted that suggestion in his ear. Feldman had earlier written Spyros that "in all probability there will be a co-director who may not get credit for the personal scenes and of course a second-unit director for the big battle scenes." Given the personal relationship between student and mentor, as well as the constant barrage of newspaper articles confirming his involvement, there is no doubt that both Skouras brothers thought, and rightly so, that Ford would be heavily involved in the film.[591]

While dealing with Murchison and Skouras, Duke also was trying to reinforce investor confidence in his project. In letters to I.J. McCullough and Roger Lewis, he first detailed the approximate cost to reach the break-even point on a production the size of *The Alamo*:

Production costs $4.5 million
Interest (6% at one and one half years) $405,000
Advertising and Publicity $1 million
Distribution $1.5 million
Checking $60,000
Miscellaneous $50,000
Cast $1.5 million
Todd-AO prints $500,000
Total $9.515 million.

Wayne also detailed the domestic and foreign distributor's gross on the last three Todd-AO features: *Oklahoma* $11 million, *Around the World in 80 Days* $40 million, and finally *South Pacific* $25 million. Wrote Wayne, "These figures certainly prove in the worst case the investor would get their money back plus 6% interest plus a profit. In the instance of *South Pacific*, it would mean a profit of around $600,000. If we get a real smash like *80 Days Around the World* (sic), my adding machine's broken down. (Our picture is currently budgeted at $4,100,000.

At this date and before actual production, it is hard to estimate to the exact penny. I am taking a leeway of $400,000 that may or may not be used)." As a point of interest, Wayne added that the decision on who would play "Cotton" (either Frankie Avalon or Ricky Nelson) would be made on August 1. And finally, he projected future expenditures: "Before turning a camera on the picture, we will have spent $1,100,000. On that day, we will have a tremendous increase in crew, transportation, and housing costs, plus heavy rental charges for equipment, etc. on the picture. We will then have a weekly charge varying from $200,000 to $350,000." Wayne's analysis did the trick—the investor's nerves were calmed.[592]

The project was progressing. At the end of the day he had a location, construction was coming along, and he finally had the funding. All he needed now was a cast and script. And he had literally been working on those for years.

*The Alamo*, starring John Wayne as Davy Crockett . . .

. . . Richard Widmark as Jim Bowie . . .

. . . and Laurence Harvey as Col. William Barrett Travis.

Also co-starring Chill Wills as Beekeeper
(with Danny Borzage on accordion) . . .

. . . Denver Pyle as the Gambler . . .

Ken Curtis as Capt. Dickinson . . .

Hank Worden as the Parson and Frankie Avalon as Smitty . . .

. . . Linda Cristal as Flaca . . .

. . . Joan O'Brien as Sue Dickinson . . .

. . . and guest starring Richard Boone as Genl. Sam Houston.

. . . With Pat Wayne as Jim Bonham . . .

. . . Aissa Wayne as Lisa Dickinson
and John Henry Daniels as Happy Sam.

John Ford and stuntmen. (L to R) First row: Ed Juaregui, Bill Shannon,
Chuck Roberson, Dean Smith, Jack Williams, W.B. Stevens, Buff Brady.
Man in white shirt behind Brady is Bob Rose. Second row: Joe Canutt,
Bob Morgan, Jim Burk, Rudy Robbins, Bill Williams, Leroy Johnson,
John "Bear" Hudkins, Mickey Finn, Chuck Hayward, Red Morgan
and John Dierkes.

Virginia and "Happy" Shahan. (From the Shahan family collection).

Jamie, Tulisha and Tully Shahan.
(From the Shahan family collection).

Alamo compound with white-washed walls. Travis' headquarters is located immediately behind the telephone pole in the center of the photograph. The Main Gate is on the far right. Alamo Village archives.

Alamo chuch façade being constructed from native limestone rock.

Village of San Antonio de Bexar; the Cantina is located left-center
on the photograph.

An aerial view of the Alamo set. An arched adobe wall and jacales are
seen on the plain between the Alamo and the village buildings.

Village of San Antonio de Bexar, the Hotel de San Antonio is located
right-center on the photograph and the San Fernando church
is left of center.

Original painting of blocks on the face of Alamo church. This was initially planned as background for the opening introduction. "In the year of our Lord, 1836, Texas, which has known many flags, was then under the colours of Mexico."

Opening scene; Houston/troops riding towards San Antonio. (l to r) Phil Stern with camera, James Edward Grant on ladder, John Wayne with cowboy hat, Bill Clothier holding hat while sitting in front of camera, Bob Relyea kneeling with sunglasses, first four horsemen (r to l) Richard Boone, Bill Daniel, Bill Moody, Ken Curtis.

Houston's entrance into San Antonio. Artillery limber/cannon
and covered wagon are not seen in film.

Houston's arrival. Note the camera crane/movable dolly
and wooden tracks.

256

"I've been given command of the armies of Texas. But the fly
in the buttermilk is, there ain't no armies in Texas!"
Houston's officer call. Airport hangar soundstage.

"But, I've been a temperate and God-fearing man all my life."
Jester Hairston as Bowie's man servant. Wayne's double, Marshall
Jones on right. Chuck Hall in fork of tree.

"Back to one." Boone et. al. return to plain outside of village to film scene again.

Filming raising the cannon. Laurence Harvey and Karl Flenn on top of Alamo.

Richard Widmark waiting to be called to the set.

"No boy, that's how you learn; asking." Hank Worden and Frankie Avalon. John Wayne in buckskins directs the scene being filmed.

"Them guns don't give it no mission look to me." (l to r) Chuck Roberson, Gil Perkins, Tom Hennesey, John "Bear" Hudkins and Ted White.

Arriving in San Antonio wearing "foo-faw-raws." Filmed but not included in the movie. (l to r) Hank Worden, Frankie Avalon, Denver Pyle, John Wayne, Chill Wills.

Cantina dancers.

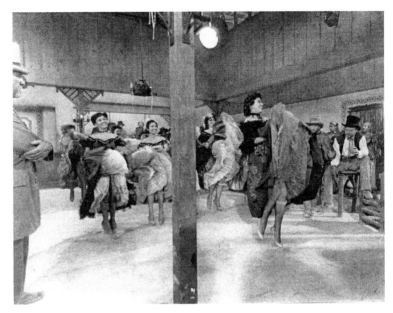

Can-can dance, filmed but not used.

(l to r) John Ford, Laurence Harvey, John Wayne.

"Kind of a game the boys play back in Tennessee." Scene 295, take 1. Feather fight. One of the rare photographs showing a specific scene number.

Teresa Champion in Cantina table-top dance.

"Pray to the North Star. Ten minutes every night. Long line of star-wor-shippers. It keeps the rheumatiz away." Rehearsal. Note there are two men in the buggy; only one appears in the movie.

John Ford, Linda Cristal and bird. Filmed but not included in movie.
Alamo Village archives.

Outside "Flaca's" room, airport hangar set. Wesley Lau (Emil Sand) can be seen in window.

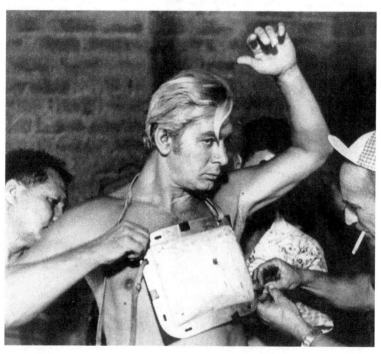

Wesley Lau wears protective device to receive the Bowie knife that would be shot along a wire from off-camera.

Continuation of the scene in which Mexican dragoons led by
Carlos Arruza meet peasants. Filmed but not included in movie.

Caisson crossing, smashed camera. Filmed on a small creek near the
West Nueces River.

Davy Crockett watches departing villagers on Back Street in advance of Mexican army.

John Wayne directs Linda Cristal and LaJean Ethridge. This scene was trimmed from the roadshow version of the film.

"Every size they get to, seems to be the most loveable." Aissa Wayne, Joan O'Brien and John Wayne.

"Pyrotechnics. What does that mean?" "Why, it means, uh . . . Ah! You know what it means as well as I do!" Rehearsal for "Pyrotechnics" scene. Dave Marshall and Marshall Jones, Richard Widmark's and John Wayne's stand-ins look on.

Scene 61, take 1. Crockett instructs the Parson to gather up Flaca's
belongings. Filmed but not included in movie.

John Wayne, Henry Garcia, Joseph Calleia and Linda Cristal. Filmed but not included in movie.

"Cut, slash and run." Cost Santa Anna fifty or a hundred troops at every
creek crossing between here and the north." Crockett
and his Tennesseans along with Bowie ride towards the Alamo.

"You shook hands with me." "Oh, I'll do her again!" "He didn't vote for you though. Other fella gave him four bits." (l to r) Denver Pyle, Frankie Avalon, John Wayne, Chill Wills, John Dierkes and Veda Ann Borg.

Stand-ins, Dave Marshall (Widmark), Marshall Jones (Wayne), and Ray Everson (Harvey). Photo taken on "Faux" Alamo top, 750 yards from main set.

(l to r) Carol Baxter, Frankie Avalon and Olive Carey in scene filmed but not included in the movie.

"Here comes Bowie, quarrel written all over him." "I expected that." (l to r) Ken Curtis, Laurence Harvey and John Wayne (sans toupee).

Stuntmen Bill Williams (Widmark) and Dean Smith (Avalon) execute a horse fall in front of Alamo.

"Well, Davy. It looks like you've done it again." The morning after.
Carol Baxter and Frankie Avalon.

## CHAPTER FIFTEEN
## OUR PLAYERS

WHEN PATRICK FORD FINALLY COMPLETED THE INITIAL SCRIPT FOR *THE ALAMO* in 1948, it was shaped to fit Republic contract players, members of the John Ford Stock Company and, generally, Wayne's friends and hangers-on. In a letter written on June 30, 1980, Ford indicated that the following actors were slated to fill the roles:

Crockett – John Wayne
Bowie – Ward Bond
Travis – Laurence Harvey (sic)
Parson – Chill Wills
Thimblerig the Gambler – John Carroll
"Bub" – Harry Carey Jr.
"Bee Hunter" or "Fat Man" – Burl Ives
Lupita – Estrellita Rodriguez
Sam – Blue Washington
Young Messenger – Ben Johnson
Antonio – Alfonso Bedoya

Of course, Wayne, Bond, Carey, and Johnson all were honorary members of John Ford's *traveling medicine show*. Interestingly, at the time Harvey was being considered for Travis, he was only twenty years old; too young, considering the historical Travis was twenty-six in March 1836. In fact, up to that point, Harvey had only appeared in a single film: *House of Darkness*. It was released in the United Kingdom in June 1948, only three months before Ford completed his script. No doubt Ford had selective recall when he indicated he wrote the script with Harvey in mind. Chill Wills was a character actor, mainly in Westerns. He had previously appeared with Wayne in *Alleghany Uprising*. John Carroll had appeared with Wayne in *Flying Tigers* as Woodrow "Woody" Jason. Burl Ives, actor, writer and ballad singer, debuted on Broadway in 1938 in *The Boys From Syracuse*, although his first feature film wasn't until 1946 when he appeared in *Smokey* as a singing troubadour. Although Ives had his own radio show in the early 1940s, it's doubtful Ford would have crafted that role for him, despite comments to the contrary. In all probability, "Estrellita" was Estelita Rodriguez, a tiny, black-haired Cuban actress briefly married to Chu-Chu Martinez, a rumba band leader. Singing and dancing in New York nightclubs such as the Copacabana, she moved to Hollywood with an MGM contract at the tender age of fifteen. A hot Latin-American tamale, her screen characters had a tendency to break out in song at a moment's notice. Republic gave her a seven-year contract after her dancing in *Mexicana* and immediately followed that with a dancing/acting role in *Along the Navaho Trail*. Wayne served as best man when Grant Withers married the dancer in 1953, and she would later appear with Duke in *Rio Bravo*. Blue Washington was an American character actor who personified Hollywood's characterization of blacks in the 1930s: unskilled, passive, compliant, and wide-eyed. Alfonso Bedoya was the Mexican character actor and director John Huston hired to play "Gold Hat" in the classic *The Treasure of the Sierra Madre*. Filmed between April and July, 1948, Bedoya had the honor of delivering the iconic line: "Badges? We ain't got no badges! We don't need no badges! I don't have to show you any stinking badges!" Most of the actors on Ford's list were from Republic's stable, so the characters were modeled after their screen persona and unique personalities. When the film didn't materialize, they went on to other projects, other studios. Carey was offered a part in Wayne's movie but didn't want to have anything to do with it. He said some of the "political stuff was a little heavy-handed."[593]

During the late 1940s and early 1950s, although there was continuous publicity on Wayne's impending epic and where it would be filmed, little was said about who would actually star in it. Every time Duke went on vacation or location, he would scope out the site to see if his film could be made there. "He was looking for locations when I was making B*ullfighter and the Lady* in 1950," recalled director Budd Boetticher. "And all those years he was working for *The Alamo*. We'd stop. He'd go, 'Oh, there's a great spot there, you know? And here's a great spot here.' He was dedicated to make that picture. And, damnit, he did it." Wayne was the producer on *Bullfighter*, and they searched in Mexico City, Queretaro and Xayai, trying to find an ideal location for Wayne's pet project. A 1951 article discussing the latest trend of actors shifting positions behind the camera and becoming directors mentioned that Wayne would star, produce, and direct *The Alamo* in Tuacana, Mexico, upon his return from his South American tour. Or it was Panama or Durango or Mexico City or wherever he happened to be at that moment.[594]

Wherever Duke went, his PR mill was in high gear, pumping up the project, keeping it in front of everyone:

"Movie producer Seeks San Antonio Scenery." March 9, 1948.

"…John Wayne to co-star with wife Esperanza in *The Alamo*." April 6, 1948.

"*Alamo* Set as Rep's film Wayne Starrer." August 11, 1948.

"…Wayne is supposed to do *Alamo* as soon as his current film, *Wake of the Red Witch*, is finished." August 30, 1948.

"…Wayne was set for several films including *Alamo*…not sure when they'll be made." September 15, 1948.

"Wayne Will Play Role in *Alamo*." November 19, 1948.

"…Wayne wants Ford to direct…the *Alamo*." April 20, 1949.

"…Wayne plans to direct *The Alamo*…except own scenes…" January 24, 1950.

"Johnny Weissmuller…to play…Crockett in *The Alamo*…with John Wayne starring." August 8, 1950.

"John Wayne will shoot *Alamo* in Mexico…" August 8, 1950.

"…Republic will also sponsor *The Alamo* which John Wayne will direct and star in on Mexican locations…" January 22, 1951.

"John Wayne to Direct *Alamo* in Fall." February 21, 1951.

"Wayne…to inspect the site at Teuacan (Mexico) where the Alamo will be duplicated in construction now under way." April 16, 1951.

"Texas Ready to Wage New Battle of Alamo If Wayne Does Pic in Mex." July 4, 1951.

"John Wayne and Republic have plans to produce it (*Alamo*) in Mexico." July 10, 1951.

"Movie-Men Shoot *Alamo* Film In Mexico City." July 18, 1951.

"*Alamo* Picture Moves To Texas." August 26, 1951.

"Chapel of Alamo May Be Used for Forthcoming Film." October 8, 1951.

"Shooting of *Alamo* in S.A. Unlikely." October 9, 1951.

"John Wayne to Direct *Alamo* in Fall." February 21, 1952.

"To Oblige the Mexican government (Wayne) has dropped *The Alamo*…at least until after the elections." February 26, 1952.

"*Alamo* is shelved until next year." July 14, 1952.

"Wayne is thinking of shooting the *Alamo* in Panama." October 2, 1952.

"Wayne Severs Connection with Republic (over *Alamo*.)" November 13, 1952.

"John Wayne to Make *Alamo* In Mexico as Result of Dispute." November 21, 1952.

"There's a St. Bernard-sized bone of contention between John Wayne and

Herbert Yates...over a film property titled *The Alamo*." June 18, 1954.

"Those talks between John Wayne and...Herbert Yates about *The Alamo* must have come to naught." August 13, 1954.

"John Wayne...is finalizing the deal with Cinerama to do *The Alamo* for them." April 27, 1956.

Etc., etc., etc.[595]

The closer Wayne got to actual production, the greater the need for publicity. Early in the project, though, a few names were sporadically mentioned as possible candidates for the feature film. Walter Brennan admitted that, as much as he wanted to, he had to turn down a role in the project as his television series *The Real McCoys* was taking up too much of his time. In mid-November 1948, Louella Parsons indicated Wayne planned to play William Barret Travis and was attempting to get Gail Russell to co-star. The actress had already appeared in several movies with Duke, including *Angel and the Badman* and *Wake of the Red Witch*. Young, attractive. "When I was first discovered for the movies," she once recalled, "I was sleeping on the living room floor on newspapers. I went for my first interview with paint all over my face—I'd been helping paint a room at the technical school." But the paint could never hide her beauty. With hair black as night, and large blue eyes, she was devastatingly attractive. Unfortunately, a painful shyness combined with brutal stage-fright drove her to drink. Tragically, she died August 27, 1961, from an alcohol-induced heart attack at the age of 36.[596]

On August 8, 1950, Hedda Hopper wrote in her daily column that Johnny Weissmuller would play Davy Crockett in Wayne's film. She also said Wayne would star and the picture would be made in Mexico City. The former five-time Olympic swimming champion had appeared in *Tarzan, the Ape Man*, and would go on to make eleven more of the genre before being replaced by Lex Barker. Weissmuller followed *Tarzan* with thirteen *Jungle Jim* films between 1948 and 1954. When looking for an individual to play to the simian humanoid, MGM director William S. Van Dyke indicated, "What I want is a man who is young, strong, well-built, reasonably attractive, but not necessarily handsome, and a competent actor. The most important thing is that he have a good physique. And I can't find him." Weissmuller seemed to fit the bill, and he loved the part: "It was up my alley. There was swimming in it and I didn't have much to say." And he made over $2 million doing the series. One of Hollywood's original action-heroes at six-foot-three and 190 lbs, Weissmuller complemented Wayne in both size and stature. He would later join Duke and others when they invested in the Los Flamingos Hotel in Acapulco. Unfortunately, Weissmuller never appeared together with Wayne in any feature film.

The following year, there was conjecture Robert Clarke might star in Wayne's film. A yeoman supporting actor, Clarke appeared in dozens of features over the years, ranging from sci-fi to comedy to adventure to crime mysteries, appearing as a bartender, orchestra leader, reporter or uncredited announcer/narrator. At the time of this rumor, Clarke had just played the romantic lead in *Hard, Fast, and Beautiful* with Sally Forrest, and was scheduled to appear opposite Estrellita Rodriguez in *Girl from Panama* (aka *The Fabulous Senorita*.) According to *Variety*, Wayne called Clarke personally from Acapulco to hire the young actor. But like Weissmuller, Clarke would never appear with Wayne.[597]

After Wayne and Yates parted ways at Republic, Duke's project was relegated to the back burner, simmering but not yet ready to serve. Once he settled on his location in the fall of 1957, stories started to come out faster than a speeding bullet.

Dorothy Manners, substituting for vacationing Louella Parsons, broke the news in October 1957 that Wayne, who held his contract, had bought the rights to the "Steve Canyon" comic strip for decathlon champion Bob Mathias. Duke's intention was to promote the Olympian in both television and film. The columnist indicated Michael Wayne would produce the feature *after* the athlete starred in *The Alamo*. Unfortunately, the series never materialized, but Mathias did appear in a Batjac production, *China Doll,* the following year. After a short stint in construction, Mathias would co-star with Keenan Wynn in the *Troubleshooters* television series.[598]

By the start of 1958, San Antonio restaurateur Big John Hamilton's name was mentioned in connection with the proposed film. Born October 29, 1916, in Ashville, North Carolina, Hamilton, a long-time Bexar resident, would appear in numerous Wayne-related projects. His father ran movie theaters in their home town, and it was then that the acting bug first bit young John. In a 1977 interview, Hamilton recalled his start in acting. While working as San Antonio assistant mayor in 1950, it was his duty to act as the city's official greeter. At the time, some thought Hamilton a likely mayoral candidate, but he never ran for office. "I met all kinds of famous people," he said. "That's really how I got started in the movies. I wined and dined a lot of stars. John Wayne came here, and I got to know him quite well along with Maureen O'Hara and all those kinds of people. I became friends with them." Wayne recalled Hamilton affectionately: "He's a wonderful person and friend, but a lousy actor." In 1954 *Gunsmoke* producer Bob Stabler became friends with Hamilton and suggested if Big John could get into the Screen Actors Guild, Stabler would get him a part in the TV series. John was able to get a card for $200. And it was worth the money as Stabler kept his promise. Hamilton received $500 for being on the Western. John appeared in several TV series in the 1950s, including *Blondie*, and had a memorable appearance with Groucho Marx on *You Bet Your Life.* In early 1957, he appeared on the nationally televised *It Could Be You*. Hosted by Bill Leyden, *ICBY* was an elaborate participation game show that "framed" audience members in advance by discreetly acquiring humorous or poignant anecdotal information about them before the show. After appearing in *The Alamo* as Mr. Dennison, Hamilton would work the following year on *Two Rode Together*, also filmed in Brackettville. According to fellow thespian Denver Pyle, "Big John wanted to be a movie star in the worst way!" Quite the entrepreneur, Hamilton owned Big John's Steak House on Harry Wurzbach Road in San Antonio as well as two bars, which was a good thing. At six-foot-five, 240 lbs, it took a heap of food to fill him up. Though not yet signed to the part at that time, Hamilton had been promised the role. Later that spring, it was stated that other than Wayne, Big John, who signed a fourteen-week contract, was the first definite member of the cast. (Interestingly, in the aforementioned January newspaper article, Hamilton indicated filming of *The Alamo* would start in late *August or early September, 1958*.)[599]

Native Texan Audie Murphy was only seventeen when he first tried to enlist in the military, immediately after Pearl Harbor. Rejected by the Marines, Navy, and paratroopers due to his short stature and slight weight, he was finally accepted into the Army. "A (Marine) sergeant glanced over my skinny physique," recalled Murphy. "It was evident that my weight did not measure to Leatherneck standards... The (paratrooper) recruiting sergeant was more sympathetic. He did not turn me down cold. He advised me to put on some thirty pounds and then try again." Entering the service at the lowest rank possible, he was discharged three years later as First Lieutenant and the most decorated American soldier ever. An expert marksman who as a lad had to hunt to feed his family, he took his unique skill and put it to good use in the war against Germany. Wounded numerous times, he eventually received over three dozen medals and awards for meritorious service, including every possible honor awarded by the Army: Medal of Honor, Distinguished Service Cross, Purple Heart with Second Oak Leaf Cluster, Silver Star with First Oak Leaf Cluster, Bronze Star with "V" device and First Oak Leaf Cluster and Legion of Merit. When the Korean War broke out, he joined the Texas National Guard and attained the rank of Major. After Murphy's photo appeared on the cover of *Life* magazine, James Cagney invited him to Hollywood for a shot in the movies. Starting with *Texas, Brooklyn & Heaven* in 1948, he appeared in over twenty Westerns by the late 1950s in addition to the critical success, *The Red Badge of Courage*.[600]

In December 1958, a group of Texas theater owners began a campaign for Murphy to be cast in Wayne's film. Officials from Interstate Theaters were instrumental in assisting Murphy in getting his first appearance and felt it was only proper that a hero of Texas play a part in the epic. Suggesting that he might be cast in the role of John W. Smith, a messenger from the real Alamo, they were not alone in their desire. Appearing in 1955 at an opening of his new film *To*

*Hell and Back*, Murphy stepped off a plane in San Antonio and was greeted by a cheering crowd. A youngster wearing a coonskin cap looked up at his father and asked, "Is that Davy Crockett, Dad?" "No," said his father. "It's Audie Murphy. But they're made of the same kind of stuff."[601]

Author Lon Tinkle of *13 Days to Glory* fame, felt Murphy would be perfect for either Smith or defender Daniel William Cloud. Cloud's outcome, suggested Tinkle, "is lost to history," so his character could be subject to whatever liberties the scriptwriter chose. "His letter (to his mother) makes his personality stand out so clear," he suggested. "One can see him in the imagination as the very man Travis and Bowie would pick out at the last public dance and fandango in San Antonio on February 22, to stand guard in the church tower the next morning..." If not Cloud, then Smith, a courier from the Alamo, Tinkle mentioned, "was a horseman, loved adventure, loved land, and had a genius for friendship—for him the fall of the Alamo was a symbol that such courage was not only a legacy but an obligation and a philosophy." *Dallas Morning News* columnist John Rosenfield wrote a passionate article in mid-December unsuccessfully imploring Wayne to use Murphy in his production and recommending all concerned readers write R. J. O'Donnell of the Interstate Circuit with their fervent requests, which would be forwarded to Wayne. Batjac Production manager Nate Edwards indicated, "We don't know about him although there is a lot of interest. He doesn't fit one of the top three parts, although the final script may have a part he would fit well, if he is available." The campaign reached its crescendo the following June when it was announced Murphy would probably not be in the production. While Wayne was sympathetic to the feelings of the masses, with the three main roles almost cast, there wasn't a part left for the soldier to play, except one of the minor characters, which would have been considerably beneath the stature of an actor of his magnitude, contrary to Edward's statement.[602]

While the Audie Murphy-*Alamo* circus was taking center stage, Michael Wayne had other ideas. "I knew we needed someone to bring in a young audience, especially someone who would appeal to teenage girls," recalled Michael. "So I suggested we give the part to Frankie Avalon. Well, my father wasn't keen on that idea, but I convinced him, and we all agreed that Frankie did a good job." *Variety* announced Avalon's role on August 5, 1959. It made perfect sense. After all, hadn't Ricky Nelson drawn the teeny-boppers for *Rio Bravo*? Of course, Duke was a bit older, no longer the leading man-heart throb he may have been earlier. Perhaps a gradual transition to an appropriately mature persona would be in order. "My father had looked forward to that picture for so long. In fact, the joke was when he initially wanted to do *The Alamo* he was right for the part that Frankie Avalon played. That's an obvious exaggeration, but he ate, slept, and dreamed that picture," said Patrick.[603]

Francis Thomas Avallone was born September 18, 1940, in Philadelphia.

At age ten, he saw a young man with a horn, decided he liked what he saw, and began to practice. "It seems like every young kid in Philadelphia wanted to be a singer," recalled Avalon. "I started as a musician...a trumpet player in the beginning. But, when I picked up a paper one day and read about Jimmy Darrin who was from my own neighborhood and school, making a successful career for himself, I decided I could do it just as well." Tutored by a volunteer from the Philadelphia Symphony Orchestra, at eleven, Avalon was talented enough to make an appearance on the *Jackie Gleason* TV show, in addition to *The Garry Moore Show*, *Perry Como*, and even *Pinky Lee*. He eventually became part of a local music combo for a few years, and then signed to record on the *Chancellor* label. By 1958, he had already placed four songs on the charts with "De De Dinah" reaching number seven. But the best was yet to come. His next record, *Venus*, became his first number one hit, where it spent five weeks atop the Billboard Hot 100. Not satisfied with just recording, Avalon also appeared in the movie *Jamboree* in 1958 and *Guns of the Timberland* the following year with Alan Ladd, Jeanne Crain, and Gilbert Roland. Duke chose Avalon to play Cotton, a young messenger sent with the Alamo's last desperate plea to Sam Houston, who returned too late to aid his fellow defenders. Cotton's name was eventually changed to Smitty due to Avalon's obvious lack of white hair.[604]

Even as Texans campaigned for a native son, others campaigned for themselves. According to a Parsons column in late December 1958, Sammy Davis Jr.'s dream to play a role with no singing or dancing would come true if he co-starred with Wayne in *Alamo*. Sammy wanted the dramatic role of a slave owned by Bowie who is freed by Bowie just before the Alamo falls, and refuses to leave. Rather, he stays behind, meets his death with the rest of the fort's defenders, and becomes a hero instead. Sammy Davis Jr.: singer, dancer, musician, recording artist, comedian and actor. If you look up *entertainer extraordinaire* in the dictionary, you'll find a photo of Sammy. Dynamic, versatile, graceful, he was a consummate professional. A mere lad of three when he first joined his father and Will Mastin on the vaudeville circuit, he quickly proved his mettle and at seven made his film debut opposite Ethel Waters in *Rufus Jones For President*. After serving in the army during the war, where twice he had his nose broken in fights with white soldiers, he re-joined the Will Mastin Trio as a headliner. Nightclub and television appearances quickly followed, and, in 1951, he signed with Decca records. In November 1954, Davis had a near-fatal car accident and lost the use of his left eye, but even that didn't slow him down. Davis first became interested in Judaism while convalescing from his accident and converted several years later. In 1955, he once again appeared on film as Fletcher Henderson in *The Benny Goodman Story*. He debuted on Broadway in 1956 in *Mr. Wonderful*, a semi-autobiographical musical, and overcame many hardships throughout his career: religion, flamboyant lifestyle, the color of his skin. Once, while playing golf with Jack Benny, he was asked what his handicap was. "My handicap?" he replied. "I'm a one-eyed black Jew. That's my handicap!" When he heard there was a part for a black in Duke's film, he managed to get a look at the script and was amazed. Sammy wanted to be an actor, not an acting entertainer. And this was the part. "Man, this Negro slave has dignity and integrity," he thought. "Usually Negro slaves were portrayed as stereotypes, but this was different. It was unlike anything I'd done before. I wanted to take a chance and play a straight role instead of always being the song-and-dance comedian." So he went to see Duke to personally ask if he could be considered. Wayne was confused. "Sammy," he said, "This is the role of a slave. It's a straight part." When Davis agreed and said that's exactly why he wanted to do it, Duke said he would think about it. The issue wasn't Wayne, though—Duke could see beyond the color of a man's skin. But he had influential Texan investors who may not have been quite so liberal, quite so agreeable to Sammy's situation. Sammy, who had previously been involved with Kim Novak, was seeing Swedish actress May Britt. Not everyone agreed that it was proper. Davis was convinced he was going to get the part, but Wayne "had a lot of influential Texans investing in the film, and they didn't like the idea that I was seeing May Britt at the time," said Sammy. "They disapproved of a man of color going out with a girl who was white. Duke was upfront with me about it. I respected him for being upfront, but I was damned disappointed not to get the gig."[605]

Instead, Wayne selected noted choral director, songwriter, singer, and composer Jester Hairston. Born July 9, 1901, in Belews Creek, North Carolina, Hairston, grandson of a slave, was educated at the University of Massachusetts and Tufts University, where he majored in music. Upon graduation he went into the theater in New York in 1929. Hairston sang in several groups and quartets, including the Hal Johnson choir. "I sang in any group that wanted to sing," he recalled, "and pick up a few dollars. And I lived from hand to mouth all those years." Through a stroke of good fortune, he wound up on the *Maxwell House Coffee Hour* radio show where he conducted the choir for thirteen weeks. "I liked the Negro spirituals, and working with the Johnson singers made me more aware of the rich music that came from the slaves," Hairston once told a reporter. "It came out the same basic feelings that the classical composers had—pain, joy, suffering—and there was no reason not to know more about that music." Two years later, Hairston graduated from Julliard where he had continued his musical education. After *Green Pastures* completed a three-year run on Broadway, Warner Bros. asked Hairston to come to Hollywood and fulfill the role of the assistant choral conductor when the play was made into a feature film in 1936. Hairston would continue in that position on innumerable films in the 1940s and 1950s, including *Duel in the Sun, Red River, She Wore a Yellow Ribbon, Land of the Pharaohs,* and *Lost Horizon,* where he first worked with Dimitri Tiomkin. Appearing as LeRoy Smith, Kingfish's brother-in-law, as well as Henry Van

285

Porter, the multi-talented Hairston was also a regular on the *Amos and Andy Show*, as well as several *Tarzan* films. Later in his career, he would appear in *To Kill a Mockingbird*, *In the Heat of the Night*, and *Lady Sings the Blues*, among many other films.[606]

By the time Wayne interviewed Joan O'Brien for a part in his film, she had already experienced an extremely successful entertainment career. Born Feb 14, 1936, in Cambridge, Massachusetts, she relocated to southern California at a very young age. When she was eight, she began taking dancing lessons, but her beautiful singing voice was discovered while doing recitals and community shows. "The first time they heard me open my mouth to sing, they wouldn't let me dance anymore," she remembers. Impressed by her talent, Lawrence Welk asked her to be his Champagne Lady. "The negotiations fell through," recalls Joan, "when he found out I was only fourteen years old." While at Chaffey Union High School in, Ontario, California, she was discovered by local celebrity Cliffie Stone. Stone hosted *Hometown Jamboree*, a country-western variety program, where Joan appeared along with Tennessee Ernie Ford. That led to a successful four-year run, starting in 1954, on the *Bob Crosby Show*. "I didn't think I had a chance of getting the job," she recalls of the audition. "There were, at least, six girls who were older and more experienced than me. In fact, I had so little confidence in getting the job that I left the next day on a vacation in Pennsylvania." A week later, though, she received a telegram asking her to report immediately. With the show's cancellation in 1958 due to slipping ratings, Joan suddenly became available and her MCA agents suggested she might give acting a try. She subsequently signed a multi-picture deal at MGM. "I was very young and loved the excitement," she says. "But like so many other giddy gals had no particular goal. Then I decided to become an actress. So I quit singing. That was a mistake."[607]

Working at MGM was an ideal arrangement for O'Brien as it had to use her in three films within a certain period of time. But she also had loan-out rights to work at any other major Hollywood studio if she chose to. She quickly starred with Dean Jones in the drama *Handle With Care*. That film was followed in January 1959 with the hit comedy *Operation Petticoat*. Her eye-appealing 38-24-36 dimensions gave O'Brien an advantage over a dozen other hopefuls in winning the opportunity to star opposite Cary Grant and Tony Curtis. Joan admits, "I don't care what won the role for me. The main thing is that I got it." Chosen because of her impressive physical endowments, she portrayed a submarine passenger whose personal measurements exceed the dimensions of the narrow confines of a submarine. In fact, the replica submarine was redesigned to take into account O'Brien's curvaceous physique. The narrower passageways made it impossible for her to pass a crewmember without contact and longer ladder steps displayed her legs to great advantage. When told Tina Louise had turned down the role of Nurse Crandell because of the numerous jokes alluding to her physical attributes, O'Brien was incredulous. "I can't even imagine a young actress at the stage of her career or mine at that particular time refusing a role opposite Cary Grant." Directed by Blake Edwards, *Petticoat* was an immediate hit.[608]

As a result of her loan-out clause, O'Brien's agents arranged an interview with Wayne. At the time, O'Brien rationalized, "I thought it would be a nice thing to play an historic character, and this role had the big dramatic ending as she and two children are the sole survivors of the massacre. I could envision that whoever portrayed Sue would get a big play on the screen." O'Brien was summoned to Duke's office alone, without representation. "I was terrified when I went to meet him," recalls Joan, "because he was bigger than life to me. You know, I admired him like the rest of the world. I'd seen him on film and I thought, 'Oh, my God. I can't believe I'm going to go in there and have an interview with John Wayne.'" Suddenly, Duke walked in. "Wayne was a huge guy—a giant. But he made me feel very much at home. I remember he put his feet up on his desk and looked down at me from his big leather chair. And he said, 'You know what? You remind me of a young Lana Turner.' He just talked to me like a regular person. I thought, 'Gee, he's not hard to take.' Then he told me that Loretta Young had offered to do the part for free. Right away he had me because I thought, 'If Loretta Young offered to do it for nothing, I should be so happy to do this and get paid.' He thought I was right for the part, and I knew I had nothing to lose by taking it." At one point, Wayne even mentioned he had considered Constance Towers for the role after her performance in *The Horse Soldiers*. "I was thrilled when John Wayne suggested the role," O'Brien says. "But I was even more excited about playing Mrs. Dickinson when I read the last great scene in James Edwards Grant's screenplay. Even if I only had a few lines in the story, I'd have taken the part just to play the final scene in which I walk out of the Alamo proudly, with my head held high, through the whole mass of Santa Anna's victorious army. It's a scene that will be remembered forever." It was a fortuitous fourteen-week guaranteed offer from Wayne; O'Brien was just about to sign a contract to be a regular on the Pat Boone television show that fall.[609]

Later, Pilar Wayne told Joan that Duke came home one night and said, "You know what? I have this beautiful girl in this film, and I've got to put dirt all over her face. I'm going to have to dirt on her face, and I don't feel good about that—but I have to do it, because she should be bloody coming out of there, you know?" By August 20, 1959, O'Brien was on-board. She played Sue Dickinson, wife of Captain Almeron Dickinson, and, along with daughter Lisa, Smitty, and the young boy Happy Sam, were the film's only defending survivors. (On October 13, 1959, *Variety* announced that Wayne wanted Hillary Brooke to play the last woman out of Alamo, which didn't make any sense as O'Brien had previously been inked for the role in August.)[610]

"Uh, Miss, Miss Cristal?" It was crowded at the Coconut Grove nightclub that evening. Linda had to weave her way through the room, passing tables on either side. She was attending some sort of director's dinner or something or other. No matter. When she heard a voice calling her name she turned around. It was a big man; it was John Wayne. He said, "I want you to know that I'm going to make a picture in the future, and, when I do, you're going to be my star." Reflects Linda, "Now, how unusual, you know? I guess someone else would have gone to him and said hello and introduce myself, and how grateful that I am that you think of me, blah, blah, blah. But instead of that I smiled like Queen Elizabeth walking into a crowd. You know what I mean?" She didn't take it seriously as she knew Wayne drank a bit, and, as she walked away, she thought, "Maybe he didn't know what he was saying."

Cristal, born in Buenos Aires of Italian and French parents, was christened Marta Victoria Moya Burges. Tragically, at age thirteen, she lost her parents in a head-on collision with another vehicle. Linda was in the back seat at the time and fortunately was unhurt. The family, returning from the seaside resort of Plata del Mar, collided with a truck that had lost its brakes. A different version of the story indicated that her parents died in a suicide pact. Years earlier, her family had fled to Uruguay after her father became involved in a political dispute with the Argentine ruling party. Returning from the coast, Cristal believed her diabetic mother became comatose from lack of insulin. Her father thought his wife was dead or dying and, humiliated for failure to support his family while in exile, accelerated their vehicle into the path of an oncoming truck. Consoled by a family friend more than twice her age, she married at sixteen, then realized four days later it was a mistake. Linda recalls the tragedy, "A terrible thing happened. It burned into my mind. I was unhappy for years. Then I tried to learn to be happy. And now I am happy. Peaceful. Happy."

Raised by her brothers Miguel and Antonio, she decided to go abroad for further education. In Mexico City a few days before she was to go to Vera Cruz and then to Spain, she and a friend were walking through a movie studio, looking at the sights. A man spotted her and came over to introduce himself. Miguelito Aleman, son of then-president Miguel Aleman, was a producer-director in search of someone to fill a role in a film he was making. He noticed the young raven-haired, brown-eyed teenager and thought she would be perfect for the part of a society debutante. Offered the role, Linda politely declined as she was going to Spain to become a nun and join her father's five sisters, also nuns. "I believe I have but one friend," admitted Cristal. "That friend is God. I would like to become even more friendly with Him." The producer asked if perhaps God wouldn't want her to become friendly with the world rather than running away from it. That evening, alone in her room, shades drawn, she reflected on the producer's words. An hour later, she had made her decision. "I always planned to live a life of peace. I always thought I would become a nun. Never did I think of becoming an actress. But I found I was too selfish. The life of a nun is one of selflessness. I was not strong enough to do that, strong enough spiritually."[611]

Cristal would go on to appear in eight films over the next four years. After several Spanish-speaking roles, she noticed an ad in a Mexican paper for an actress who spoke English. Linda recalls, "When they asked me if I spoke English to make the film, because I only spoke Spanish, I said 'Yes, I can learn it in one week.' I speak Italian and French and…Spanish, so I can learn English… and they believed me." Hired by Independent producer Carl Krueger for her first American film *Comanche*, the curvaceous actress had a unique clause in her contract: lose twenty pounds. "I guess there is more refined taste here," said Linda then in her halting English. "In Mexico and Italy, the men are thin. So they like the contrary. If you are plump, they like it much better. All the girls in this country are thin and tall. Audrey Hepburn, Joan Crawford. I like to see this on the other girls. But not on me!" Co-starring with Dana Andrews, she went on to work opposite Gilbert Roland and Lorne Green in *Last of the Fast Guns*. She followed that with a series of films by European producers in France, Italy, and Yugoslavia. Finally, in 1958, she signed a Hollywood contract with Universal.[612]

In an interview later that year, Cristal factiously said the price of movie success must be a good soaking. "I've been in two films in Hollywood so far, and, in both of them, I've been thoroughly soaked," she explained. "I think sometimes that some of the boys plan these things—that they just don't happen." The plot of each film (*Last of the Fast Guns* and *The Perfect Furlough*) somehow has been so constructed that she wound up wearing a dress in which she got soaked to the skin. "Let's be realists," she said. "Before I was soaked for the screens, the dresses were tested. This means that each dress first was checked carefully for the proper measurements. Then I had to put it on wringing wet. This was so the cameraman and directors could decide if the material was behaving correctly. That's what they told me, anyhow. I guess maybe they were right, too, because not all kinds of dresses worked out. I liked one particularly, but it wasn't much good for our purposes—looked great dry but terrible wet." In *The Perfect Furlough*, she fell into a wine vat, and, in *Fast Guns*, she fell into a river. "I guess you just can't get wet in any old dress," she said. "We gave ours dry and wet runs first. The scenes turned out fine, but I didn't understand one remark someone made about soaking the rich. Or does 'endowed' mean rich?"[613]

A year or so after the encounter at the Coconut Grove, her phone rang. It was Wayne. "'Linda, this is Duke.' And I said, 'Duke?' 'Remember, I told you when I make this film, you were going to be the star in it with me? We're going to start filming, so can you come and play the part I promised you.' And I said, 'Oh, my goodness, and you remember?' He said that he was aware of when I came into the country, and he saw the pictures because it was a big thing because United Artists brought me from Mexico. I was making films there for my country. In Argentina. And so he followed my career and he was impressed and he said that he convinced his mind that he would like to work with me. He remembered and he gave me the film." Referring to film studios, she admitted, "They have faith in me, but they don't know what to do with me. They think me only an exotic because of my odd accent and 'torrid' looks, and they farm me out. John Wayne is the first American director who sensed that I am not what I seem on the surface...I am not a 'pepper-pot' Latin. I'm much more complicated than that. I am very dignified, very philosophical, very sophisticated. I am like a little child, and yet I am eighty-years-old in the experiences of life. I like playing the kind of woman who influences the important men in history. All of the really successful men had the gentling hand of a good woman to guide them." Cristal's involvement was announced on August 13, 1959. She would fulfill the other major female role in Wayne's film: Graciela Carmela Maria de Lopez y Vejar, aka Flaca, Crockett's love interest and Wayne's mechanism to expound on patriotism, freedom, and liberty.[614]

Concerned about the needs of a female box-office, three other minor female roles would be filled by a veteran, a bubbly model, and a relative newcomer. Cast as pioneer woman Mrs. Dennison, Olive Carey had already appeared in numerous Westerns, as well as *The Wings of Eagles* and *The Searchers* with Wayne. Her first motion picture, *The Vintage of Fate*, was made when she was fourteen, just two years after she arrived in California from New York. In Hollywood, she was a member of D. W. Griffith's repertory company that included Mary Pickford, Lillian and Dorothy Gish, and western film star Harry Carey. She would appear in dozens of silent films only to retire four years later after she married Carey. She was also instrumental in introducing her husband to John Ford, creating a partnership that would continue for years. After a fifteen year-hiatus, Olive successfully made the transition to "talkies" when she returned to the screen in *Trader Horn* in 1931. Four years later, she retired once again. But after the death of her husband, she returned to the screen in 1951 with *The Whip Hand*. A life-long friend of Duke's, Carey would appear in countless television programs in the 1950s and 1960s.[615]

At age twenty-one, Veda Ann Borg, a fiery Boston red-head and former department store mannequin model, traveled to New York and applied for a job. Her mother read in a film magazine of the unceasing search by talent agents for new faces. Veda mailed letters to five studios, enclosing her photo in each. Four of the studios failed to reply, but the fifth instructed her to go to the Big Apple and meet with talent scout Oscar Serlin. She was placed in acting school, and, after six weeks, was given a successful screen test. She was immediately hired by Paramount and cast as Consuelo Dormant in the musical *Three Cheers for Love*. It was suggested she change her name to something more conventional, perhaps Ann Noble. Miss Borg contended that her name was more descriptive of her personality than Noble, and, with a convincing argument, she would be evermore billed as Veda Ann Borg. Regrettably, after appearing in fourteen films for Warner Bros., she was involved in a horrific automobile accident with boyfriend and fellow actor Richard Purcell. "On the way home at about midnight," she recalled, "we had a head-on collision, and I went right through the windshield. It was old-fashioned plain glass. It cut my face into millions of little pieces. When I woke up in the hospital, I asked for the mirror. The nurse shuddered and ran out. She couldn't stand to tell me." Thinking she was through as an actress, she had numerous reconstructive surgeries; a rib was used to rebuild her nose, cartilage came from her ear lobes, and a piece of glass removed from her left eye. After two years and twenty-two operations, funds were getting tight, so she arranged to work in a department store. But in a final casting call at Metro, she was selected to replace an actress who was ill. "Sometimes you read stories about people coming back from the grave," she reflected. "I feel that way. More so, maybe. A woman without a face is better off dead. Now I've got a face. Now I'm glad to be alive." Just a year later, she had almost experienced another disaster. Due to the carelessness of smoking while cleaning a dress, a spark ignited the cleaning fluid and the actress's dress went up in flames. Fortunately, while visions of her horrible car accident raced through her mind, she escaped with only a slightly burned shoulder and singed eyelashes. Changing her red hair to blond, Borg would go on to make over one hundred films, including *Big Jim McLain* and *The Wings of Eagles* with Wayne. Once married to Victor McLaglen's son Andy, she would appear in thirty-two television series, but *The Alamo* would be her final feature film. Borg appeared as Blind Nell, the wife of Alamo defender Jocko. [616]

Carol Baxter aka Carol Berlin was born in Dallas but moved to California with her family when only four. It was there she started school and grew up. Electing to forgo college after graduating from Marymount High School, she was befriended by actress Irene Dunne, who was impressed by her talent. "I've always been acting crazy," said Baxter. "What girl from Texas who goes to Hollywood isn't?" She subsequently enrolled in the American Academy of Dramatic Arts in New York. Appearing in several television episodes including *Father Knows Best*, *Highway Patrol*, and *The Bob Cummings Show*, her first feature film would be Wayne's epic "…who could have dreamed that anything as important and great as *The Alamo* would come along to kick off my career," she said enthusiastically. She would play the role of Melinda, Frankie Avalon's teenage love interest. Interestingly, on July 16, Jim Henaghan announced that Greek actress Maria Demas was signed to appear in the film. One wonders what part she would have played. Four days later, it was also announced that Sondra Osborne, a Miss USA contestant from Oklahoma, was also offered a part in the film. [617]

Born July 18, 1902, in Seagoville, Texas, on what was supposedly the hottest day of the year, Theodore Wills was forever known as Chill, humorously named for the polarity of the day's temperature. A different version of the story, but no less true, said he was named for the physician who delivered him, Dr. Childress or Dr. Chillin. Wills said he was the seventh child in a family that "had run out of common names. So they picked Chill Theodore for me. I dropped Theodore in a hurry." An entertainer at an early age, his characteristic voice as a falsetto tenor in the church choir earned him jobs at local parties. Wills joined Dr. Pryor's Medicine Show in Chicago at age fifteen, doubling as a performer and hustler. He also performed in New York vaudeville shows doing monologues as a master of ceremonies and later formed the singing group The Avalon Boys in the mid-1930s. The ensemble appeared in numerous Western films for Paramount and the Hal Roach Studios until Wills broke out on his own in 1938. Discovered by an RKO executive at a restaurant where the group was playing, Wills would go on to sign with MGM where he first appeared in *Boom Town*, written by John Lee Mahin and James Edward Grant. Famous as the voice of Francis, the talking mule, he performed in the series of films including *Francis, Francis Goes to the Races, Francis Goes to West Point, Francis Covers the Big Town, Francis Joins the WACS*, and *Francis in the Navy*. His voice was distinctive—deep and expressive. Wills once jokingly said his voice degenerated as his salary rose. The leathery-faced, gravel-toned Wills was also a character actor and had already appeared in over forty films, including *Giant*, with Rock Hudson, James Dean, and Elizabeth Taylor, before being cast in *The Alamo*. However, Wayne's film was not the first Alamo film Wills was involved in. In 1953, he played one-armed shopkeeper John Gage in Budd Boetticher's *The Man From the Alamo* with Glenn Ford, and had previously appeared with Wayne in *Alleghany Uprising* and *Rio Grande*. Wills would be one of the first actors named to appear in Wayne's film. The role for which he was announced was not the part he would eventually play. On a trip to Austin shortly before the start of production, Wayne indicated, "Chill plays an unusual part in this picture, a character called the Parson. He's not a real parson, but a sort of conscience for Crockett. He changes Davy from Crockett the Liar to Crockett the Truthful." Later, Wayne had a change of heart as Wills eventually played Beekeeper, comic relief to Crockett. As for the Parson, Duke would turn to old friend and veteran character actor Hank Worden.[618]

Taxi-driver, Western Union messenger, real estate salesman, singer, polo player, waiter, truck driver, steer rider and wrangler, jack-of-all-trades Norton Earl Worden was born in Rolfe, Iowa, but grew up on a cattle ranch in eastern Montana. He first became interested in acting while attending the University of Nevada in the mid-1920s where he studied engineering. He tried out for the campus players but didn't make the grade. Nevertheless, he was bitten by the entertainment bug. Escorting a divorcee and her young children across country, he found himself on the East Coast. Starting out as a bronc rider in New York, he and roommate Tex Ritter were appearing at a rodeo in Madison Square Garden when they were chosen to play cowhands in the 1931 Broadway show, *Green*

*Grow the Lilacs*, the play on which Rodgers and Hammerstein's *Oklahoma!* is based. Following the show's run, Worden was forced to travel west in 1933 when jobs started to dry up during the Depression. After a detour through the Bobcat Ranch in Cody, Wyoming, Hank found himself in Arizona and decided that being a guide on Bright Angel trail on the South rim of the Grand Canyon wasn't that bad a job. At least, he could sing and dance around a campfire in the evening, entertaining the campers, and he would be closer to Hollywood where he could resume his career. Worden recalled, "People used to tell me 'Why don't you go over to Hollywood? You'd be a good character actor or something like that.'" A chance encounter with actress Billie Burke at the Smoke Creek dude ranch in Palm Springs led to recommendations at several movie studios. "(She) invited two of us over to her place for dinner one night, and I told her I certainly would like to work in pictures," said Worden. "So she called up Bert McKay who was casting extras in *The Plainsman*," and he was hired. Following that with appearances in *The Three Mesquiteers* series, as well as dozens of other Westerns, Worden solidified his career as a veteran character actor: tall, thin, lanky, bald, and laconic, but wise beyond his years. Burt Kennedy once commented on Worden's unique appearance: "He looks like he's been dead about three weeks." Over time, Hank appeared in countless feature films utilizing a variety of stage names including Worton Norton, Henry Snow, Heber Snow, Hank Warden, and Norton Worden, his real name. The actor's credits were impressive: *Stagecoach, Duel in the Sun, Angel and the Badman, Fort Apache, Red River, 3 Godfathers*, and *The Fighting Kentuckian* and dozens of others, working with Buck Jones, Johnny Mac Brown, Hoot Gibson, Tex Ritter, George O'Brien, Gary Cooper, and, of course, John Wayne.

When Worden graduated from high school in 1921, he made the rodeo or roundup as they called it back then. Some broncs he rode, and some he fell off, but that was his start in rodeoing. According to stuntman Dean Smith, "A lot of people don't know it, but Hank was probably one of the finest horsemen in the picture business. Hank could ride the hair off of any horse I ever saw." Though he had previously worked for Ford on *Stagecoach*, it was his appearance in Hawks's *Red River* that caught Pappy's attention. Worden had already worked with Wayne in *Angel and the Badman*, and Duke had put in a good word for him when Hawks was casting *Red River*. As a result of that performance, Hank followed up that film with several other collaborations with Ford, culminating with his paradigmatic role, Mose Harper in *The Searchers*. The insightful, spectral simpleton who doled out pearls of information buried under incessant ramblings, Hank spoke in short, clipped, half-sentences. Mose only longed for "a roof over my head and a rockin' chair by the fire." "Playing the character Old Mose Harper," recalled Worden, "…is probably one (of) my best; at least, I only can tell when I'm around someplace, in a restaurant or somewhere like that, somebody comes over and says, 'I recognized you when I heard you talking,' because everyone remembers your voice, and that was very nice and I liked it very much." Hank and Duke became fast friends on that project and would go on to make several films together, including *The Horse Soldiers* in early 1959 where Worden would play Deacon Clump, a distant relative of the character Hank would play in *The Alamo*. "Follow me brother Colonel through the swamps, all the way to the river Amite."[619]

"My parents named me Denver because they were fond of that city," said Pyle. "I'm glad it wasn't Chattanooga." Actually, Pyle maintained he wasn't named after the Mile High City. "I was named after a guy who was named after the city!" Born in the eastern Colorado town of Bethune, population forty, Pyle enjoyed a long, illustrious acting career portraying individuals of Southern or Western descent. His tall, scraggy frame bode well for the veteran character actor and brought a Western authenticity to his performances. After high school, Pyle tried the world of higher academics but quickly dropped out of the University of Colorado to pursue a career in show business. After a short stint as a musician didn't pan out, he worked in Oklahoma oil fields and on Galveston, Texas shrimp boats. He even harvested wheat and cleaned out petroleum stills in an effort to find his niche. Desiring to see his brother and sister in California in 1940, Pyle hitchhiked from Oklahoma to Hollywood where he worked at NBC as a page and car-parker. He worked there during the day and at Lockheed as a riveter at night. Pyle drifted from job to job, but settled on none. During World War II, he enlisted in the Merchant Marine. It was also suggested that he enlisted in the Navy and was discharged in 1943 after being wounded at Guadalcanal, but evidence of that is lacking. In a 1993 interview, he stated, "I went down to join up, and I got a 4F from the Army. But I had figured out what I had done wrong. I had flat feet, and I learned how to hold my feet so that I could pass the physical. I became a cadet midshipman in the Navy. I was a maritime cadet. And then they took the top 5 percent of the graduating class and made them midshipmen. Anyway, I sailed all through the South Pacific with a 4F card in my pocket!"

Upon his discharge, he started his acting career, appearing in numerous films and such television shows as *The Cisco Kid, The Roy Rogers Show, The Adventures of Wild Bill Hickok, Hopalong Cassidy, Annie Oakley, The Gene Autry Show, The Adventures of Kit Carson, The Lone Ranger,* and *The Adventures of Jim Bowie.* Acting in a California theater production, he was spotted by a talent scout; his first film, *The Guilt of Janet Ames,* co-starred Rosalind Russell, Melvyn Douglas, and Sid Caesar. Pyle was an uncredited extra. One evening, director Charles Vidor stopped by to investigate Pyle's acting skills. "I couldn't believe it when Vidor said he wanted to test me for a picture which Melvyn Douglas had trouble testing for," recalled Pyle. "Vidor said, 'You're a good actor. Sit down.' He got me my guild card, and he said, 'This is just a small part, but I'm going to be doing a western in about six weeks, and it will be a big part.'" True to his word, Vidor followed that up with *The Man From Colorado* with William Holden and Glenn Ford. Pyle would go on to appear in seventy-one features between 1947 and 1959, including *The Horse Soldiers*. As a result of his performance in that film, Wayne cast him as Thimblerig the gambler in *The Alamo*.[620]

"I knew John Wayne long before I started to work for him," recalled Pyle. "I first really got to know him in *The Alamo*. I guess I got that job because I was hanging out with his brother, Bob Morrison, up at Batjac. Bob had me looking for properties for Duke, you know, stuff to produce of one kind or another. I thought I was a whizzer at that; of course, I wasn't. But through Batjac and his brother Bob, I got to know Duke." In a scene in *The Horse Soldiers*, Pyle and Strother Martin played Confederate deserters, and Denver wore an eye-patch. "Remember, I had that little patch that Mr. Ford put on me. He always had a patch on somebody because he had to wear one. 'If I had to wear one of these, you might as well wear one.' I sent a telegram to Duke, and I said, 'Have patch– will travel.' And that's why he put a patch on me when I first got to *The Alamo*. The first day of shooting, he said, 'Where's your patch?' And I said, 'Oh, I got it. I got it. And I ran and found a prop guy real fast and said, 'Jesus Christ, give me a patch!' And I got to wear one that first day." Batjac contacted Pyle's agent and said they wanted to speak with him. "There really wasn't an audition per se," remembered Denver. "I think they just cast it 'cause they knew anybody in town would work with him or for him (Wayne.) I think he just called these guys and said, 'Hey, I need you for a part,' and they made their deals and did it. I don't think anybody got rich off of his picture. But it went a long time, and everybody made a lot of money only because it was a long time in the making."[621]

Ken Curtis. Gifted character actor, talented singer, horseman, John Ford's son-in-law. Born Curtis Wain Gates on July 2, 1916, in the southeastern Colorado town of Las Animas, his father was sheriff of Bent County. Curtis worked on the family ranch and the town jail and was even a substitute jailer when his father was out of town. "I was twelve when Dad was elected," recalled Curtis. "Our living quarters were on the ground floor, and the cells were upstairs. Mother used to cook the meals for the prisoners, and I took them up (to) the cells while she held a shotgun in her hands in case any of them got frisky." He studied music and played saxophone in high school but still entered a pre-med program at Colorado College. He wanted to be a doctor but was so successful as a songwriter in school productions that he left college and headed for Hollywood to ply his trade. After joining a small band, one night Cecil B. DeMille's secretary heard him sing. So taken by his melodic voice, MGM hired him to sing on its lot. Eventually he recorded a song heard by Tommy Dorsey, who hated the tune but loved the voice. Dorsey then hired young Gates and changed the crooner's name to Ken Curtis. As Frank Sinatra had just left Dorsey, the bandleader wired Curtis funds to take the train to New York and join the band at the Paramount

Theater as a replacement. (However, on the night of Sinatra's last performance with the band, he introduced Dick Haymes to the audience as his replacement.) Later, Curtis joined the Shep Fields Orchestra before enlisting in the Army in 1942 where he served in the Pacific.

Discharged, Curtis once again picked up where he'd left off. Columbia Studios hired Ken as a singing cowboy after he'd appeared on a radio program hosted by Johnny Mercer where Curtis sang "Tumbling Tumbleweeds." He would go on to make over a dozen films between 1945 and 1949, playing characters creatively known as Curt Walker, Curt Chambers, Curt Durant, Curt Stanton, Curt Norton, Curt Mason, and, of course, the ever-present Curt Benson. His comic sidekick, more often than not, was Guinn "Big Boy" Williams. From 1949 to 1952, Curtis was a member of the Sons of the Pioneers, a musical ensemble created by Bob Nolan, Tim Spencer, and Roy Rogers in 1934. Known for their soaring harmonies and impeccable musicianship, Curtis was a perfect Sons replacement for Rogers, who went on to become a Western star. Nineteen fifty-two also marked the year he would marry Barbara Ford, the director's only daughter. Because of this connection, Ken would appear in several John Ford/John Wayne collaborations: *Rio Grande*, *The Quiet Man*, *The Long Gray Line*, *Mister Roberts*, *The Searchers*, *The Wings of Eagles*, *The Last Hurrah*, and *The Horse Soldiers*. Curtis eventually divorced the director's daughter in 1964, and Ford would recall sarcastically, "Yes, he has a nice singing voice, except for the day I punched his face because he beat my daughter. It's hard to sing without teeth." Wayne would cast Curtis as Capt. Dickinson, but he was not Duke's first choice. An announcement had been made on August 14, 1959, less than three weeks before start of production, that John Gavin would play the role. Gavin had previously appeared in *A Time to Love and a Time to Die*, *Imitation of Life*, and had just played Julius Caesar in *Spartacus*. Unfortunately, Universal-International and Batjac were unable to agree to contract terms on Gavin's proposed loan-out. As a result, Curtis was hired to replace him, literally at the last minute. Gavin would go on to appear in *Psycho*.[622]

Born February 20, 1920, of a middle-class family in Mexico City, Carlos Ruiz Camino Arruza was the son of immigrant Spaniards; his mother, a successful businesswoman who owned several children's clothing stores; his father, a custom tailor. At age thirteen, Arruza entered a bullfighting academy. A natural *torero* and successful beyond his instructor's wildest dreams, Carlos eventually became one of the greatest *banderilleros* of all time. Fighting in Portugal and all provinces of Mexico, Arruza took his *alternativa* in 1940 from the veteran Armillita and became a full-fledged *matador*. Mentioned in the same breath as Manolete, Silverio, and Belmonte, Arruza, better known as *El Ciclon*, was considered one of bullfighting's most complete and dominating *matadors*. It was suggested that he could hypnotize a bull with his skill. Starting young at thirteen, Arruza would eventually record over 1,200 kills. *Matador de toros* will fight at least one *corrida*, killing two bulls per *corrida* each and every day for two to three months each season. One day in Mexico, Arruza and Manolo Dos Santos made history by killing twenty bulls between them, fighting in Morelia in the morning, Mexico City in the afternoon and Acapulco in the evening. When a matador provides an exemplary performance in the bull ring, the *presidente* will wave a handkerchief to signify an award: once for a bull's ear, a second time for another ear, etc. One afternoon after a particularly outstanding display by Arruza, the *presidente* waved his handkerchief for one ear, again for two ears, again for the tail, again for a hoof–and still again for another hoof. But the crowds kept chanting, "Mas y mas y mas! (More, more, more!) Finally, as the crowd kept up and kept up, the *presidente* shrugged and said, "Take the whole bull."

A multi-millionaire at twenty-six, Carlos had achieved it all, so he decided to retire and live life to its fullest. And live he did: traveling, bad investments, fast cars, and faster women. In two years, he was flat broke, so he returned to the ring. Three years later, now married and once again a multi-millionaire, he retired for the second time. The recent death of Manolete, a close friend and fierce rival, had affected him greatly. Arruza became a *ganadero* and purchased a bull-breeding ranch, formerly a fortress for Pancho Villa and Emiliano Zapata in the Mexican Revolution. However, he was not yet finished. Feeling he had reached the pinnacle of success, he was persuaded to return yet one more time—not on the ground as a *matador* but on horseback as a *rejoneador*. Usually taking a lifetime of training, Arruza's unique passion, drive, and ability allowed him to master the very specialized maneuvers required of this profession. A great *matador*, Arruza would also become one of the great horsemen in the world; as good on horseback as he was on the sand. Arruza's ranch was located in Pasteje, Mexico, and was used as background for the Batjac production, *The Bullfighter and the Lady*. According to Robert Quinones, son of the famous Mexican General Jesus Jaime Quinones, Wayne and the general were at a bullfight in Acuña where Arruza was the featured attraction. After watching Carlos's performance, Wayne said, "'I could probably use this individual in my movie.' And the general said, 'Well, I'll get you together,' and he made a meeting possible between (Ruben) Padilla (Arruza's manager) and Arruza and his crew with John Wayne. (Jesus) stepped aside and let them talk and whatever agreement they came to. Then, Wayne said, 'Well, I wonder how we can get them across (the border)?' (Quinones) said, 'I have friends at U.S. Immigration, and I'll see what we can do.' And apparently something worked out, and (Padilla and Arruza) were able to do the movie." Arruza would be cast in the role of Lt. Reyes, aide to Santa Anna, although in the film, he would clearly be called Lt. Rodriguez. (*Torero*: bullfighter. *Banderilleros*: a bullfighter who sticks barbed darts into the bull's back or nape. *Alternativa*: a ceremony in which a bullfighter shares the kill with his novice, accepting him as a professional. *El Ciclon*: The Cyclone. *Corrida*: a bull fight. *Presidente*: judge of the bull ring. *Ganadero*: bull rancher. *Rejoneador*: a bullfighter on horseback who uses a lance or spear.)[623]

Eternally described as tall and dark with craggy face and characteristic deep, hollow voice, John Dierkes was a prominent character actor who appeared in such cinematic features as *The Red Badge of Courage*, *The Thing*, *Shane*, *Friendly Persuasion*, *The Buccaneer*, and *The Hanging Tree*. But it had not been his intention to become an actor. Born in Cincinnati in 1905, he grew up in the local area and eventually attended both Brown University and the University of Chicago, where he was an economics major. Upon graduation, he worked at the U.S. State Department as…an economist. When war broke out in 1941, he joined the American Red Cross and served in England where he met John Huston, who suggested Dierkes try his luck in Hollywood. Huston had taken a liking to the lanky man and thought his scraggy looks and husky voice could serve him well. After the war, Dierkes represented the Treasury Department at the Nuremberg trials. When he returned stateside, Dierkes was assigned as a technical adviser for *To the Ends of the Earth*, a film based on the files of the Treasury Department. Taking almost two years to complete, filming extended to the far corners of the earth: China, Egypt, Cuba, the Caribbean, and the Panama Canal. While on location, a talent scout noticed him and suggested he audition for Orson Welles, then casting the film *Macbeth*. Dierkes won the role, his film debut. He returned to government employment upon completion of the film, but, two years later, after appearing as an unaccredited night court judge in *Three Husbands*, Huston cast him in *The Red Badge of Courage*. After Huston's recommendation to Howard Hawks, Dierkes appeared in *The Thing* and then took a leave of absence from his governmental position, a leave that lasted the rest of his life. He went on to appear in numerous television series in the 1950s, including *Death Valley Days*, *The Adventures of Rin Tin Tin*, *My Little Margie*, *Casey Jones*, *Wanted: Dead or Alive*, *The Rifleman*, and *Wagon Train* before appearing in Wayne's film as Jocko Robertson, a Scot named after Dierkes's maternal grandfather.[624]

Supporting cast announcements for *The Alamo* were made throughout the spring and summer of 1959, and, with each, excitement over the epic increased. Some announcements were accurate, others not so. A September 1959 *Hollywood Reporter* news item stated that Diahann Carroll was offered a role, but she didn't appear in the film. There remained one announcement, though, that everyone waited for. Who would play Crockett, Bowie, and Travis? Obviously, this was a Wayne film. Surely he would play one of the leads, most likely Crockett. Maybe just a cameo. But what of the others? Who would play James Bowie, the reckless adventurer, landowner, slave trader, and renowned knife-fighter? And what of William Barret Travis, lawyer, soldier, and Texas patriot? The story of their selection was a soap opera in its own right.

# CHAPTER SIXTEEN
# THE HOLY TRINITY

DUKE DID NOT WANT TO STAR IN *THE ALAMO*. IN CHARGE OF A MILLION DETAILS, he was both the producer and director and thus didn't need to appear in front of the camera as well. The potential issues associated with that decision could be catastrophic. God forbid he fell ill while filming. Not only couldn't he shoot his own scenes, he couldn't even direct the film. If Wayne goes down, the show goes down. Everything was on the line, and the conditions he would face while shooting were absolutely ridiculous: weather ranging from freezing cold to brutally hot, night-time filming, inexperienced extras, the enormous pressure of all the stunts, working six and seven days a week. He needed to devote full attention to the countless details and not worry about whether he could remember his lines or where his mark should be. And over and above everything else, the budget. Always the budget. How much each scene would cost, costume and prop rentals, set construction, catering and transportation, horses and cattle—the list was endless.

The problem was as simple as this: if he wasn't in the film, no one would finance it. Why waste money on a project that wouldn't draw the necessary audience? As much as Wayne wanted to only direct and produce, he knew the project wouldn't get off the ground if he didn't appear onscreen. People wanted to see John Wayne in a John Wayne movie. So…if that's the case, maybe a cameo would suffice. That way he could film his part, get it out of the way, and then focus his attention on the rest of the film. Unfortunately, that suggestion just didn't work. The studios told him point-blank: either play one of the leading roles or look elsewhere for funds. No Wayne, no money. If that was the case, he might as well go all in. Play the role he was meant to play—Davy Crockett: folk hero, adventurer, soldier, politician, King of the Wild Frontier.

When he died at the Alamo, Crockett was forty-nine years old. Wayne was fifty-two when he started to film his project. He had played a variety of larger-than-life roles; he could certainly fill Crockett's shoes. Earlier in Wayne's career, he was slated to play Jim Bowie in Warner's *The Iron Mistress*, but, according to Duke, "it was too theatrical for me." Finally, after almost a decade of false starts, it was announced mid-December 1957 that Wayne would play Crockett with four (?) other stars set for major parts in what was described "as the first definitive treatment" of the historic battle, a slight barb against *The Last Command*. By agreeing to star, he also assured creative control would not be taken away from him, and he would receive $175,000 to boot.[625]

With Crockett's casting settled, the question became, "Who would play Travis and Bowie?" His co-stars needed to be of equal cinematic stature and physical size as Duke. At six-foot-four, he towered over other actors, with a formidable screen presence. He had to make sure the other actors would not be intimidated by his size and persona. While casting of supporting roles continued, several names floated in the media. As copies of the script had been given to numerous actors, it wasn't a surprise that each would have his name associated with the film as a definite possibility: Clark Gable as Travis, Burt Lancaster as Bowie or Houston. When Fess Parker heard that Wayne would play Crockett, Parker "volunteered to play one of the other top roles." He even sent Wayne a coonskin cap with the following inscription: "I hope this does you as much good as it did me." Ironically, when George Montgomery met Wayne, he jokingly asked him if he played Fess Parker in the film. (Wayne amusingly related a story about the furry headwear to Louella Parsons after filming of *The Alamo* was complete: "A funny thing happened. A firm manufactured thousands of coonskin caps, and, when Fess Parker's role as Crockett waned, they tried to sell us these caps. But I figured we couldn't hope to revive Fess's popularity by doing so. I wonder why Fess hasn't done more work, because I think he's a good actor.")[626]

Less than a week after Wayne made his Crockett announcement, *Variety* published the earliest *unofficial* announcement—William Holden had been lined up to play Bowie. At that time, though, the film had been planned for the summer of 1958. (Batjac would take out a January 8, 1958 full-page ad stating *The Alamo* was in preparation for that year.) Although desirous of teaming up, Holden and Wayne had never appeared together in a film, and it would be almost a year before they would do so in *The Horse Soldiers*. Their pairing for that film would be announced Christmas Day 1957.[627]

By summer 1958, Duke said both Rock Hudson and Holden had reacted favorably to the *possibility* of starring in his project. Newspapers and trade journals took it as a given that the trio would work together. In fact, they also reported that over $3 million would be dropped on their salaries. Except now, Holden would play Travis. Other papers said Hudson would be Travis. The only fact everyone agreed on was that Wayne would play Crockett. Typical was this definitive statement from the *San Antonio Light*: "Shooting of the movie—which William Holden will star as Travis, Wayne as Crockett, and Rock Hudson as Bowie—will begin next September." Even Wayne confirmed the rumors. While on location for *The Horse Soldiers*, he expressed his admiration for Holden: "I'm trying to sign him for one of the leads in *The Alamo*, which we'll make down in Texas next September. I want him to play Travis. I'll do Davy Crockett—yeah, with a coonskin cap—and I'd like to see Rock Hudson as Bowie." Names were thrown around willy-nilly; some were approached; others were used strictly for publicity. Some thought Duke's old friend Jim Arness might be in the running for a top spot. Louella Parsons suggested Robert Stack would do anything he could, even rearrange his schedule, so he could co-star in the feature. *The Hollywood Reporter* even said Stack and actress Dorothy Malone had signed firm contracts for the film, only to issue a retraction the next day. Wayne categorically denied either had been approached and stated that neither had been considered for any parts in his project. At six-foot-five and a half inches, Chuck Connors was approached numerous times by Batjac to play Bowie. Wayne unsuccessfully called five times to arrange enough free time for Connors to be in the film. Supposedly, even Western actor Don "Red" Barry of *Adventures of Red Ryder* fame, was approached to play Travis. According to Barry, Wayne had promised him the part of Travis but, upon further reflection, rescinded the offer and gave it to Harvey. "Horseshit!" Wayne exclaimed. "It just isn't true! Barry's a fuckin' liar! I like Don; he's a nice guy, and I've known him since the 1930s. But his temper and his lies have always gotten him in trouble. That statement he made to you just isn't true. At no time did I ever consider him for the part. But use your head. Don Barry is no Laurence Harvey. Don is always trying to ruin my career, and I have often told him to worry about his own career—it needs tending to."[628]

Strange as it may sound, Wayne actually was in negotiations with Frank Sinatra to play Travis. At five-foot-eight and 140 pounds, Sinatra would have been comically small compared to Wayne. The historical Travis was six feet tall and weighed 175 pounds. Sinatra was woefully undersized to pull it off. Yet Wayne still pursued him. Frank was definitely interested, but, as he was deep in preproduction with his own project, *Never So Few*, he requested Wayne delay his project until Sinatra was finished with his. It was a favor Wayne couldn't grant. "But I had (already) waited a year," explained Duke, "and I had all this money out at a high interest, and they wanted to go, and Frank came over. He talked to me about the Travis part—he knew Travis as well as I do—and says, 'Well, I got this thing, and I couldn't do it until next year.' I couldn't wait." Deep in debt, Duke had to get *The Alamo* out and in distribution as quick as possible. It was also rumored Wayne was courting James Stewart to fill the role of Travis. In early July, Charlton Heston also received a copy of the script and a firm offer from Wayne. "I wanted Heston to play Bowie," admitted Wayne. "He could have played Travis. Either part." But three days later Heston declined the offer. "There seemed to be good reasons for me not to do the film," he admitted. Asked if one of the reasons could be that Wayne would direct, Heston replied, "It might be."[629]

In late February 1959, Wayne stopped in San Antonio after a quick visit to Brackettville and mentioned his dream pairing: Holden would definitely play Travis, and he hoped to sign Robert Mitchum for Bowie. Ever since he had seen them co-star in the 1948 RKO feature *Rachel and the Stranger*, he knew they were perfect for the parts. Nate Edwards suggested, "Mitchum may not be available, or may not accept the part. The cast isn't final, but this is the planning if stars' commitments let them fit in." Duke and Holden had become good friends in the early 1950s and wanted to work together. However, that was not to be the case. At the time of the proposed start of production, Holden was already under contract and neither Batjac nor William Holden Productions could manipulate the shooting schedule and other matters. If Duke couldn't get Holden, at least he could have Mitchum. The two were well matched: tall, powerful screen presences. According to Howard Hawks, "If you get somebody who's not pretty strong, he (Wayne) blows them right off the screen. He doesn't do it purposely; that's just what happens." Wayne and Mitchum would complement each other. The problem was that United Artists, a partial investor and distributor for the project, insisted on Richard Widmark, whom it already had under contract. Although a more than worthy choice, UA felt Mitchum would appeal to the exact same demographic group as Wayne; it wanted someone who could appeal to the feminine audience and generate larger box-office receipts. A graduate of the *film noir* school, Widmark was intelligent, versatile, and much respected.[630]

Wayne was adamant; he wanted Mitchum for Bowie. UA was equally adamant; Widmark was its choice. But it was willing to negotiate. If Wayne could convince Widmark to play Travis, Duke could ask Mitchum to play Bowie. "John Wayne didn't want me," Widmark admitted, "but UA pushed him into it. Then, he wanted me to play Travis, and I didn't want to play him. I said, 'I'll play Bowie.' Wayne said, 'You're not big enough.' I told him, 'I'll be big enough.' Wayne liked big guys; everyone was a midget to him." Widmark confided, "I had to turn Travis down twice and get into a heck of an argument with Wayne before I convinced him I was the man for Bowie. Wayne wanted a great big guy for Bowie, and he wanted me to play Travis with an elegant flair...an elegant flair I don't have, and I'm glad. Wayne finally took my word for it and let me play Bowie. Besides, I needed the work."[631]

If Pilar had anything to say about it, it was probably a good thing that Wayne didn't hire Mitchum. Still fuming over the premature termination of her honeymoon due to Mitchum's antics on *Blood Alley*, she held a grudge against the actor. Eventually, though, the ice somewhat thawed, and Robert and Dorothy Mitchum were invited to a dinner party at Wayne's house after the release of the movie. Dressed in a low-cut gown, Pilar greeted the couple at the front door with a smile on her face. Mitchum had already had a few belts, and, peering down her dress, exclaimed, "Boy, do you need a new bra!" Furious, Pilar demanded they leave that instant; Duke hadn't even met them yet. When told later of the incident, Wayne was careful not to crack a smile.[632]

Resigned to the fact that he had to accept Widmark as Bowie, Hollywood legend has it that Wayne took out a one-page advertisement in the *Hollywood Reporter* saying, "Welcome aboard, Dick." The next time Widmark saw Wayne he allegedly stated, "You tell your press agent…that I didn't like that ad. The name is *Richard*." Duke stared him down, lit a cigarette, waited, and then replied, "If I ever take out another ad I'll remember that, Richard." Great story, but the problem was that it wasn't true. The trade papers had already published on July 20, 1959, that Widmark would play Bowie and Ford would direct Wayne in his scenes. One week later, an ad *was* taken out and placed on the back cover of the July 27, 1959, issue of the *Hollywood Reporter*, but it read, "Welcome Richard Widmark to the *ALAMO*. We at BATJAC are proud that you will portray Jim Bowie in our motion picture which we hope will be the greatest outdoor spectacle ever produced." In addition, Widmark always referred to himself as Dick and signed correspondence that way as well. Said Widmark, "I doubt that Wayne ever told that story; he wasn't that petty. In the first place, I never saw an ad welcoming me. In the second place, I would never say to anybody, 'The name is Richard,' because everyone calls me Dick. Wayne had a publicity guy (Henaghan?) who I didn't like. He used to plant terrible stories about me and Wayne that just weren't true." Wayne admitted, "United Artists insisted on Richard Widmark. I thought he was wrong for the part. I was wrong. He was magnificent. We didn't always see eye to eye, but he was just great as Bowie."[633]

Born December 26, 1914, in the small Scandinavian community of Sunrise, Minnesota, Widmark was frequently taken to the local cinema by his maternal grandmother. Moving frequently as his father was a traveling salesman, Widmark grew up in small Midwestern towns. When he found out he could eloquently express himself, he decided to become a lawyer. "I always loved movies and had a feeling I'd like to do them," recalled Widmark, "but, when I found out I could talk, I thought I'd like to be a lawyer. Theater and movies were a million miles away, totally removed from my ken." Widmark enrolled at Lake Forest College, just a short distance from Princeton, Illinois, where he lived, and entered the pre-law program. However, once the head of the drama department got him involved in acting, he appeared in over thirty plays, graduated with degrees in speech and political science and spent the next two years as an instructor at the college in both disciplines. In 1938, Widmark left academia and moved to New York where he began a successful ten-year career as a radio actor. Five years later, he made his Broadway debut in *Kiss and Tell* but shortly thereafter left the production (Kirk Douglas replaced him) and appeared in another play, *Get Away Old Man*. In 1943, he received an offer from MGM to test for a role in the film *Bataan*, but declined the opportunity as he didn't want a seven-year contract. Rather, he went on to appear in numerous Broadway plays.

Widmark's big break came in 1947 with his screen debut in *Kiss of Death* as the maniacal, sinister, disturbing giggler Tommy Udo, a role for which he would be forever known. However, Widmark almost didn't appear in the film as his screen test was rejected by director Henry Hathaway. But the test was surreptitiously sent to 20th Century-Fox Studio Head Darryl F. Zanuck, who loved what he saw and immediately signed the actor to the film. When Widmark's character pushed a woman in a wheelchair down a flight of stairs, he created an iconic cinematic moment. Laughing throughout the film, Widmark admitted he was nervous. "I don't know whether (the scriptwriter) had indicated the laugh or whether I did it out of nervousness," he said. "I think it was probably a combination. (Hathaway) liked it and said, 'we could use a little more of that.'" Whatever the reason, Widmark's performance was outstanding, and he received both a Golden Globe Award as Most Promising Newcomer and an Academy Award nomination as Best Supporting Actor. He also signed a contract from Fox and went on to appear in over twenty films during the next seven years, including *Yellow Sky, Panic in the Streets, No Way Out, Halls of Montezuma, My Pal Gus, Road House, Down to the Sea in Ships*, and *Night and the City*. Asked how he felt about the Udo role, he said he at first had been afraid he'd "be typed as a nut villain." But as he gradually proved he could play altogether different roles, this fear subsided and "no longer worries me." Widmark failed to re-sign with Fox in 1954 because "I was tired of being shot from one movie to another—finishing one on a Saturday and starting another on Monday. I could get more money on the outside and get a wider variety of stuff." As a result, like Wayne, Holden, Brando, and so many others before him, he decided to go freelance and sell his wares to the highest bidder. Appearing on television's *I Love Lucy*, he promoted his next film, *A Prize of Gold*. After several more features, in 1957, he finally created his own production company, Heath Productions. Several more films followed at MGM and Fox before Wayne approached him in the summer of 1959. Upon the announcement, Widmark immediately flew to Brackettville for five days of preproduction conferences. "By the time he came to Texas," said Widmark, "Bowie was a man seeking peace. He had lost his wife and two children to cholera. He had become a respected leader of his community. But he was also, in many ways, a jealous and petty man. I'd like to get all of these sides of the man into the portrayal of Bowie in this film."[634]

Once discussions with Widmark were resolved, an even larger problem presented itself: who would play Travis? Since Widmark insisted on playing Bowie, Mitchum was out of the picture. And if Wayne couldn't have him, then he needed to find someone to fill the role of Travis—fast. He initially wanted Lancaster, but he was committed to *Elmer Gantry*. With two of the three major roles filled, the situation was no less dire than it had been initially. Time was running short; start of production was the first week in September. Enter Zvi Mosheh Skikne.

Zvi Mosheh Skikne was born October 1, 1928, in Joniskelis, Lithuania. With his family, he immigrated to South Africa in 1934 at the age of five where he took on the anglicized name Harry. In his early days his mother would give him sixpence to go to the cinema once a week, and with such favorite movie stars as Clark Gable, Mickey Rooney, and Shirley Temple on the screen, he wanted to go three and four times. At age ten, he was sent off to a private boarding school for discipline as he had misbehaved. At fourteen, he ran away to join the Navy, but his mother brought him back home. After completing secondary schooling at a private college, he joined a semi-professional theatrical group in Johannesburg and became known as Larry. At seventeen, he ran away yet again and enlisted in the South African army during World War II. A sign of things to come, he was assigned to the Union Defence Forces Entertainment Unit. Traveling throughout Italy, Austria, and Egypt during the war, he moved to London upon his discharge and enrolled in the Royal Academy of Dramatic Art. During a mid-term production of an Oscar Wilde play, he caught the attention of a scout searching for new talent. Subsequently signed to a management contract, Larry Skikne, as he was known at the time, also got an interview and screen test by MGM. After appearing the next season with the newly formed Manchester Intimate Theater, he was signed to a seven-year contract with Associated British Pictures.

Skikne's screen debut was the 1947 low-budget melodrama *House of Darkness* in which he performed under his new stage name: Laurence Harvey. Changed because the film company and distributor felt that Skikne wasn't a proper name for an English actor, Harvey was suitably disenchanted. He wrote his brother Nahum: "Another regrettable thing happened over which I have no control: this time it is something more personal—they have changed my name because it was suddenly decided by the distributors that it wasn't commercial, so I am now known as 'Laurence Harvey.' O, this too, too unfortunate society!" Although he appeared in a baker's dozen of films between 1947 and 1953, it wasn't until *King Richard and the Crusaders*, with Rex Harrison and George Sanders, that he firmly established himself in British cinema. Earlier, Associated had dropped the third-year option on his contract when his profitability to the company was unsatisfactory relative to his cost. Quite simply, Harvey had extravagant tastes: Saville Row suits, expensive wines, all billed back to the company through his agent. By his own admission, he wasn't satisfied with the direction his career was going. "I hate these messy little films," he once confided.

Though he received decent notices, Harvey was always looking for work. After a stint at the Shakespeare Memorial Theater at Stratford-Upon-Avon, where he met his future wife Margaret Leighton, he flew to Hollywood where he did another screen test for MGM. And once again, nothing came of it. Dejected, he flew back to London where he appeared in a screen version of *Romeo and Juliet*. After *The Good Die Young* premiered, Hollywood accepted him, and he appeared in *King Richard*.

After yet another season in Stratford, he returned to the screen with *Storm Over the Nile*, followed by several other films, capped off with one that made him famous: *Room at the Top*. As Joe Lampton, a working-class lad who wanted to get the hell out of the working class, Harvey's performance was a tour-de-force. Immediately following the filming of the final scene, Harvey flew to San Francisco to join the Old Vic Company on opening night. Midway through a six-month tour, he received notification he had been nominated for Best Actor in a Leading Role. BAFTA also nominated him for Best British Actor as well: quite an accomplishment for a Lithuanian South African.[635]

While working on the television series *Alfred Hitchcock Presents*, Harvey was approached by Wayne for a part in his new film. Although interested, he was incensed they were questioning his credentials. "It's hideous to think they are asking me about my experience," he railed. "Don't they know I've made all these films? Don't they know I've emerged from a sweatshop of theatrical experience? Is all the work I've done lost to them? Or are they just idiots and morons?" Still, he went to the dinner meeting with Wayne only to find John Ford there as well. It was Harvey's impression that Ford just muscled in. It really wasn't a screen test; there really wasn't an audition. Familiar with Harvey's work, as was Ford, Wayne asked Harvey to tell him about his approach to acting. As he detailed his extensive experience on stage and with the Old Vic, Wayne impatiently interrupted, "Don't give me all that shit about art. I'm up to my ass trying to get this picture together. Can you do a Texas accent?" Harvey continued the story, "So I said to Ford, 'Can I have a cigar?' He looked puzzled, but he gave one to me, and I lit it, and as I puffed on it, I said with a soft Texas accent, 'But soft, what light through yonder window breaks. It is the east, and Juliet is the sun...' And I went on, and that just cracked Wayne up." Ford grunted, turned to Wayne and said, "Don't bother telling him about the part, Duke. *We* haven't got much time. Just sign the bastard up." Harvey confided in Hedda Hopper that he had spoken to Wayne and Ford that day, and they wanted him for the film but "check with the boys before you print it." She did, they did, and she announced it in her column on July15, 1959.[636]

There were two main reasons Wayne chose Harvey for the role: One, many American actors just did not want to be directed by John Wayne. Simple as that, so that whittled down the available talent pool. Two, Duke felt Harvey was a hell of an actor. Jealous because Kirk Douglas was able to attract Olivier, Ustinov and Laughton for *Spartacus*, Wayne wanted *The Alamo* to have the same prestige. "So when I couldn't get a good American actor to play Travis," he admitted, "I thought, The hell with it. Let's get some British class. And that's what we had in Laurence Harvey. I mean this was a guy who could play the part of an aristocrat, which Travis was. He could do a Texas accent that was just subtle enough not to sound fake. And when he had to be a son of a bitch, he could do it, and, when he had to get the sympathy vote from the audience, he could do that." Later, when a fan asked why he chose the Crockett role for himself, Duke replied, "Well, that isn't the biggest role. The main part is of Col. Travis. And since I was producer and director, I, naturally, could have had it. But I got Laurence Harvey for the role. Anyhow, Harvey plays it better than I could have. Travis might have been better for me, but I didn't think I ought to be hogging the whole picture."[637]

With the last major role filled, Wayne still had one final open casting issue—who would play the cameo of Sam Houston? He realized he couldn't play the part but needed someone of similar stature. At six-foot-seven, James Arness more than fit the bill. When Wayne was offered the lead in a new type of television Western (*Gunsmoke*), he declined as it would interfere with his cinematic commitments. However, he did suggest Arness for the part as he was already under contract to Wayne. "It'd ruin my Hollywood career to get tied up with television," Arness rationalized. "What career?" chuckled Wayne. "You haven't made a picture yet."

At that time, Andrew McLaglen, son of Victor, was directing episodes of *Gunsmoke* and *Have Gun Will Travel*, having directed the pilot for both. Duke called him up and said, "Andy, if I come over at the end of the shooting one day, can you get Jim available for me? I want to talk to Arness. I'll bring my people over. I want to talk to him about playing Sam Houston in *The Alamo*." Assured that it was OK, they arranged for Wayne to show up at 5:30, just as they were done shooting. Arness had been told and said he would be there. But when Wayne and his entourage showed up at the appointed time, Arness was nowhere to be found. According to McLaglen, "For some reason or other, and to this day I've never found out why, Jim took a powder. He absolutely did not show up for the meeting. He totally powdered. And he was never able to say why he did that." Wayne, extremely upset, didn't wait for an excuse. "The hell with him," he said. "Who's that other guy you work with?" Told it was Richard Boone, Duke replied, "Yeah, I want to meet Boone." The trade papers weren't aware that Arness blew off the meeting. Appropriately, they published a blurb on April Fool's day that the actor would star with Wayne in *The Alamo*.[638]

McLaglen went to see Boone, a seventh-generation descendent of Daniel Boone, and said, "Listen. Wayne wants you to play Sam Houston in *The Alamo*." Boone jumped all over with excitement. So, one day after finishing up some business at Western Costume, Duke walked across the street to the studio where

Boone was working and currently having lunch. Wayne ordered some coffee and got down to brass tacks. "Listen," he proposed, "there's a part in this picture we're going to do. The picture's called *The Alamo*, and the part's called Sam Houston. It isn't written yet, but we think it's going to be a good part. You want to do it?" Boone agreed, and that was the end of it. No contract, no nothing. The conversation was that long. "I never had a contract until about the time I was going to the premiere," explained Boone. As compensation, Boone didn't want any money. Boone's wife Claire recalled, "…we were paying so much in taxes, 50% at the time. So he said, 'I'll just do it for nothing.'" Grateful, but honorable nonetheless, Duke said, "I'll tell you what. I'll give you a Rolls Royce." And so he did. Boone worked a total of six hours, and the pay came out to $4,000 an hour. "When I got back to town," said Boone, "Duke called up the Rolls Royce dealer and told him to give me whatever I wanted. I went down and picked out a $24,000 Rolls. It was like a dream." Boone loved sport cars but felt that everyone should have a Rolls, at least, once in their lives, so he accepted the offer and had special carpeting and bar installed in the vehicle. Two months later, as he didn't think it went fast enough, he sold the Rolls and bought a Maserati. "I decided I just wasn't rich enough to own that car," admitted Boone. "The Rolls is dull to drive—great if you can sit in the back seat." Boone was so grateful to McLaglen for getting him the part, he gave Andy a three-foot high bronze statue of bare-knuckled fighters as a present.[639]

## CHAPTER SEVENTEEN
## GAGS, NAGS AND RAGS

WHEN WORD OF WAYNE'S PROJECT STARTED TO MAKE THE ROUNDS, ANY stuntman worth his salt wanted to be involved. Cliff Lyons bragged, "Nobody's ever been able to get that many top boys together before, but when word got around what a big stunt film this was, everybody wanted to work on it." The basic salary for stuntmen was $325 a week, and each stunt increased the amount. Falling a horse could pay over $200. Naturally, stuntmen wanted to be there. Some were contacted directly, some just assumed they would be in the show, and others got in touch with whomever they could, looking to get asked. Over the years, Duke had worked with the best of the best and naturally wanted them on this one. While Bob Morgan had been with Duke in *The Quiet Man* and *The Wings of Eagles* and Jackie Williams in six films including *Red River*, *Fort Apache* and *Rio Bravo*, Dean Smith, a relative rookie, had appeared only in *Rio Bravo*. Tom Hennessey was in *The High and the Mighty*, *Trouble Along the Way*, *Blood Alley*, and *The Horse Soldiers*. John "Bear" Hudkins was a veteran of seven films including *Angel and the Badman*, *Apache*, *Yellow Ribbon*, *Rio Grande*, and *The Searchers*. Bob Rose appeared in four Wayne films. Bill Hart's first film was *The Alamo*; Gil Perkins's last. Ted White was in *Rio Bravo* and *Horse Soldiers* while Yak Canutt's boys, Joe and Tap Canutt, would work with Duke for the first time. Rounding out a baker's dozen were Good Chuck Hayward and Bad Chuck Roberson. Between them, these two had appeared in over half the films Wayne had made since 1948, including *The Wake of the Red Witch*, *Yellow Ribbon*,

*The Fighting Kentuckian, Rio Grande, Hondo, Conqueror, Searchers, Eagles, The Barbarian and the Geisha, Legend of the Lost, Rio Bravo,* and *The Horse Soldiers.* Whew! Add Ed Jauregui, Red Morgan, Billy Shannon, Bill Williams, and LeRoy Johnson, and you had the greatest collection of stuntmen ever!

You've probably never heard many of those names, but you've seen them on the screen a thousand times—they are the men who do high-dives and crash cars and brawl in saloons, jump from airplanes and swim through raging rivers, leap through plate-glass windows and ride bucking broncos. They do headers and transfers, vaults and cable jerks, saddle falls and horse jumps, and they die a thousand deaths. In fact, they do the dangerous things high-priced stars are not allowed to do. "We're not supposed to get credit," rationalized stuntman Joe Canutt. "It's our job. This business is about doubling somebody and making sure the audience believes that it was the actors themselves who did it." Cheating death on a daily basis was a stuntman's way of life. Veteran stuntman Bob Rose expressed these thoughts in an article he wrote for *Popular Mechanics*: "After all mechanical preparations, a stuntman has about seven chances in ten to perform a stunt safely and successfully. Consequently, he always inspects and makes sure of his equipment. His most necessary assets to overcome the remaining three points of hazard are experience and mental balance. A mistaken idea is that a trained athlete has all the qualifications to make a stuntman. Overtraining and routine slow the mental faculties. Where the athlete practices one thing until he is perfect in it, the stuntman must never fall into the habit of doing things mechanically. Though great muscular development is not important, perfect physical condition is. Successful stuntmen are credited with having great nerve. They have. But it is not the nerve of a short-lived fool who is merely inviting death. It is the controlled nerve that steadies the mind while the feat is being executed."

They're incredibly ingenious at devising ways to make it look as if they've pulled off something far more painful and dangerous than it actually was. Yakima Canutt put it best: "What is a stuntman? He's an insurance policy to the picture in production... He's an unsung actor, who by his sheer nerve and ability, is able to execute a hazardous stunt and walk away with his body and limbs intact... He's a man who can put a star's wardrobe on and transpose the author's wildest dream into reality... He's a man who can bring audiences to their feet and give out *ooh's* and *ah's*."[640]

According to Neil Summers, "Being a top stuntman not only means you can do the required stunts, you have to be knowledgeable of camera angles, different camera speeds, and how to make a shot sell for the camera and director. The more intricate the stunt, the more you have to absorb the rigging techniques. You have to know what is safe, what is feasible, and what the director and cameraman envision, so everyone is on the same wave length and the shot can be accomplished safely and to everyone's satisfaction." Sounds complicated, doesn't it? Stuntmen wear bruises like a badge of honor: broken bones, cuts, scrapes, separated shoulders. "Most people like to think they treat their bodies like a temple," confessed Terry Leonard. "I treated mine like a South Tucson beer bar." But an accident-prone individual wouldn't last long in the business. Constant training is their weapon of choice. They wear protective gear designed to cover sensitive parts of the body: Knee pads, breast pads, girdles, drag-pads, and breastplates are just a few of the necessary accoutrements. Elbow pads, removable saddle horns and even bowl-shaped safety helmets worn under ten-gallon hats are tricks of the trade.[641]

Just because you were available didn't mean you'd be in the show, though. Hal Needham, a former 82nd Airborne paratrooper, wanted on the film in the worst way. He had already worked as stunt coordinator on *Have Gun Will Travel* for six years in addition to doubling Richard Boone, and was a good friend of Chuck Roberson. But Cliff Lyons, stunt coordinator and a second unit director on *The Alamo*, wasn't familiar with Needham's work, and, after making him wait outside of his office for half an hour, told him, "Sorry." Lyons wanted people he already knew. Discouraged, Needham stood in the front yard of his house on La Tuna Canyon Road (also known as Stuntman Canyon because so many lived there) and waved as each stuntman left for Brackettville. This turned out to be probably the best thing that ever happened because with all the top stuntmen leaving town, Needham received more phone calls than ever asking about his availability. Needham did have a tangential connection to the film though. When Roberson left for *The Alamo* location, he took along two horses, Cocaine and Hondo. Roberson had brought the latter horse home from the *Hondo* location and was training him. After *The Alamo*, he brought home a third local horse from Brackettville that had appeared in the movie's background. Told that the no-name horse had the traits to be a good stunt horse, Needham bought him from Roberson. Chuck threw in Hondo for nothing to close the deal. No Name was later christened Alamo.[642]

Cliff Lyons was born on the 4th of July, 1901, in South Dakota, the oldest son of Wilhelmina and Garrett Lyons. Living for a short time in Tennessee where he attended business school, he returned to South Dakota in 1921 where, after his father's death, he rode in the rodeo circuit with his uncle. An expert horseman, Lyons was attracted to Hollywood during the Roaring Twenties where he tried his hand as an actor and stuntman in oaters. At five-feet-eleven, 185 pounds, he was a bit awkward but, according to Yakima Canutt, "had a lot of guts." Lyons appeared in several Westerns with the likes of Tom Mix, Johnny Mack Brown, Ken Maynard, William Boyd, and Al Hoxie, and doubled Richard Dix, Henry Fonda, and Tyrone Power. Although he starred in two Western series with Hoxie, Lyons's voice wasn't suited to talkies, and he was regulated to minor roles. But as his acting career faded, his career as a stunt double flourished. Child star Dick Jones once said it seemed on every movie set it was either Lyons or Yakima

Canutt doing the stunts. Often the two of them worked together. Lyons's name rarely found its way into the credits, but, when it did, he was listed as technical adviser, stunt coordinator, or stunt double. In 1936, after filling a variety of roles in over 164 movies, Lyons finally had the opportunity to work with John Wayne. In *The Lawless Nineties*, he not only appeared as a local henchman, he also doubled for Duke. Thus began a fruitful relationship, both business and personal, that would span over thirty-six years. In 1939 Wayne was influential in getting Lyons his first work as an unaccredited Second-Unit Director on the picture *Dark Command*. Cliff would also double Wayne in this film as well as perform stunts for supporting actor George "Gabby" Hayes. In 1945, after fifty-nine more films, he would again work with Wayne, this time in *Dakota*.[643]

Finally, in 1947, he would once more hold the reins of second unit director when he worked with both Wayne and John Ford in the classic *Fort Apache*. Duke had introduced Lyons to Pappy, and Cliff soon became a card-carrying member of Ford's Stock Company. *Three Godfathers*, *The Fighting Kentuckian*, *Yellow Ribbon*, *When Willie Comes Marching Home*, *Wagon Master*, *Rio Grande*, *Hondo*, *The Conqueror*, *The Searchers*, and *The Wings of Eagles* quickly followed, along with many others. In several films, Lyons not only filled the role of stuntman, but stunt coordinator, second-unit director and technical adviser as well. In addition, he usually had a small acting part. Though uncomfortable with dialogue, Lyons would dutifully speak his lines. According to Dobe Carey, Ford gave him lines on purpose, and "(Lyons) was God-awful when he did it; and if Cliff were still with us, he would not take exception to that statement."[644]

Ford also used Lyons in a touching tribute to his old friend, silent western film star Harry Carey. Though he had already appeared in three films, most notably *Red River*, Harry Carey Jr. was "officially" introduced in *Three Godfathers*. Dobe was surprised at the end of the film when, Lyons, dressed as Harry Carey Sr., rode Carey's old buckskin horse, Sunny, to the crest of a hill, pushed his hat back on his head, then leaned back with one hand on the horse's rump and looked off into the sunset. The tune "Goodbye, Old Paint" played quietly in the background. On screen appeared the words TO THE MEMORY OF HARRY CAREY, BRIGHT STAR OF THE EARLY WESTERN SKY.[645]

Lyons came in handy off-camera as well. At the end of *Yellow Ribbon's* "picnicking" scene between Carey, John Agar and Joanne Dru, Dobe yelled "Yaaaaaaa!" and let the horses, attached to the buggy he was driving, have their head. Unbeknownst to Carey, Wayne, standing off-camera, threw a huge rock at the horses just as Carey let them go. "You don't see that in the movie," said Dobe. "I'm here to tell you we were on our way to kingdom-come. Outside the gate, there was about one hundred yards of level ground, and then it dropped off at a 45° angle all the way to the floor of the Valley. I had runaways on my hands, and I saw where they were headed. There was nothing to pull because the hack was running up their heels. No brakes, just me, standing straight up 'sawing' the lines and pulling with all my strength. Those horses were flat out! I was a goner! 'You bastards!' I yelled. Then, out of the blue came a rider scorching across the rocky hillside. He was at the team's head in seconds. He practically jerked their heads off, and he grabbed the right wheeler's headstall, and stopped them dead still, like they had hit a wall. It was Cliff Lyons, good old Cliff. He literally saved me from the hospital...."[646]

Cliff would be assigned second-unit director duties on *The Alamo* as well as stunt coordinator. Famous as the man who plunged on horseback over a cliff in *Jesse James*, for which he was paid the princely sum of $2,350 (Cliff made it; the horse died of a broken back), Lyons had a strange habit, a sort of a facial tic with grinning. According to Jackie Williams, "He always had a twitch after that experience. The twitch increased. Quite an action there. The boys would call him 'Smiley.'" And he wasn't the most articulate individual, stumble and stammer. It was usually necessary for someone to interpret his directions.

"One morning (on the *Alamo* set), he gathered all of us on a hill," recalled Roberson. "'Bad Chuck,' he pointed at me. 'You lead out.' Then he squinted his eyes like he was envisioning a terrific action shot. 'The rest of you guys follow Bad Chuck here, and I want you to come down this gawdam hill, dammit, and I want you to, DAMN! I mean I really want to see you, *Damn*! I mean GAWDAMMIT, I want you to, DAMN!' He smacked his hands together and rode off. Everyone in the group was puzzled. 'What's he want us to do? What did he say? He said he wants us to just DAMN! What's that mean,' they grumbled as I smiled and watched Mother's retreating back." Dean Smith told them that Roberson was the only one who could understand Lyons. Mother hollered "ACTION DAMmit!" "Follow me, boy!" said Roberson as he took off at a slow walk, down the hill and into the gates of the mission followed by the rest of the riders. That's all Cliff wanted. Pleased with the results, Lyons's "DAM, DAMmit"-ed like it was the greatest thing he'd ever seen. Roberson explained, "Eventually I got so I could understand what (Lyons) was trying to say simply by listening to the inflections in his phrases. Watching a horsefall, you might hear Mother say, 'DAMN! DAMmit!' and you knew it was a good horsefall. If he said, 'DAMN! DamMIT!' the horse broke his leg. 'DAM-MIT! DAMN! DAMmit!' meant the fall was the best he'd seen in some time, and, 'DAMN! DamMIT! DamMIT! DamMIT!' meant the horse had fallen on the director."[647]

Lyons, known affectionately as *Mother* to the other stuntmen, was tough as nails, grouchy, real old-school, often surly, hard to get to know, and hard to get along with. Roberson said he was the "toughest, roughest son-of-a buck who ever directed a stunt. I don't know if he was always mean, but, by the time I got to know him, he was able to yell himself into a blue-faced fit." But when he was around, he commanded respect. Duke used to say, "God, I'd hate ta' hafta fight that son-of-a-bitch." Other stuntmen said, "To whip him, you'd have to kill him." Dean Smith said, "Cliff Lyons was gruff but as well as gruff he had a big heart. He would take care of the stuntmen, as well as give them grief. Sorta like a mother. I know he liked me, and I would do anything for Cliff. There was something I felt about him like I do my family. He was a father figure for me. If you worked for Cliff, you felt like you had accomplished a lot. Working for him meant you were at the top of your game."[648]

When Lyons was given the job of putting together a top-notch group of stuntmen, he wanted only those he was familiar with, those he could trust, veteran or not. On the set of *The Horse Soldiers,* word was out that he was assembling a small army of stuntmen to take to Brackettville. According to Roberson, "With the making of *The Alamo*, the stuntmen were hired without knowing exact stunts (in advance of production). Basically, whatever action came up, whoever was the best man for the job got it." Jim Burk, who as a teenager trained horses and competed on the rodeo circuit, started his career in Hollywood by doubling for Max "Buddy" Baer, Jr. on the film *Flame of Araby* in 1951. He quickly followed that with work on *Arrowhead, The Big Country,* and *Pork Chop Hill.* Burk had purchased a thoroughbred gelding named Detonator for $200 and with the assistance of Les Hilton (trainer of Mister Ed and Francis the Talking Mule) trained him to be an extremely capable falling horse. Lyons was the second-unit director on *Hell Bent Kid* and needed a steed with just such talent. "Cliff had been so impressed," recalled Burk, "with the way the horse had acted at Lone Pine that he asked my dad if he could take him for the (*Alamo*) project. Dad told him that he would have to take his kid too, because it was his horse, and he didn't want anyone else falling him. The next day I received a call from Mr. Lyons asking if I could come over to the studio to see him. He was all business. I was scared to death. He was a legend. He asked me questions, looked me over, and I got a call from the studio saying, 'Mr. Lyons, would like you to come in.' The rest is history. I was going to do a film with the best men and horses in the industry. A dream come true! And it included my introduction to John Wayne!"[649]

Although a relative newcomer to the ranks of stuntmen, Dean Smith was a veteran athlete. Born and raised in Texas, Smith excelled in track and field, won an AAU national championship in the 100-meter-dash, and ran first leg on the University of Texas world record relay team. He also won a gold medal in the 4x100 relay in the 1952 Helsinki Olympics after placing fourth in the 100 meters. "Fastest white boy I ever saw," said long-time local resident Ray Herring. The next year, Smith's Olympic roommate, J.W. Mashburn, introduced him to a twenty-five-old friend from Oklahoma, Jim Bumgarner. Upon graduation from UT, Smith enlisted in the Army. After his discharge, he played pro football with the Los Angeles Rams but was traded to Pittsburgh at the end of the exhibition season. One Sunday morning, Dean saw his friend's face on the cover of *Parade* magazine, except the friend had changed his name to Garner and was about

314

to star in a television Western pilot called *Maverick*. As Garner was in Dallas, Smith drove over and asked for help in trying to start a career in the movies. Jim contracted Warner Bros. studio, and, shortly thereafter, Smith joined the Screen Actors Guild. Before long Dean was at work in his first film, *Born Reckless*. With the abundance of Westerns on television, Smith had no trouble finding work. Between *Cimarron City* and *Laramie*, he worked on *Rio Bravo* with Wayne. (Dean was to double Ricky Nelson, but it turned out he wasn't needed.) Smith recalled, "The way I got on the (*Alamo*) picture was through Bob Mathias who was under contract to Wayne at Batjac. Mathias introduced me to Bob Morrison, Duke's brother. Through Morrison, I met Cliff Lyons, and that's what enabled me to work on *The Alamo*." Mathias, Morrison, Lyons, Smith, and Mike Wayne were all in Batjac's Sunset Boulevard office when Duke walked in. "Duke," said Mathias, "this here's Dean Smith. He was on the 1952 Olympic team with me. He's from Texas." Wayne grinned, shook Smith's hand and said, "Well, I can't hold that against you." Then, Smith expressed his interest in being in Wayne's film: "I told them I could ride and jump with anybody and that I wanted to go back to Texas and work on something dealing with Texas history." Duke asked Lyons, "Do you think this boy can hold up?" Replied Cliff, "He's faster than a turpentined cat. He can ride a horse, too." "Sounds to me like he'd be kind of an asset for us," agreed Wayne. "Let's take this kid to Texas. He needs to go back home." And Dean was on the film. While on location, Dean would bunk with Roberson and Jack Williams, which is another story.[650]

Though only thirty-eight years old when *The Alamo* was filmed, Jackie Williams was a veteran of Hollywood. The son of stuntwoman Paris Williams, a one-time world champion trick-rider on the rodeo circuit, Jackie was a champion bronc rider and graduate of USC. Starting out as an actor in the short *Tooth Will Out*, Williams graduated to stuntman in the 1936 film *Daniel Boone*. *The Charge of the Light Brigade* quickly followed, along with *The Adventures of Robin Hood*, *Dodge City*, *Gone with the Wind*, *They Died with their Boots On*, *Fort Apache*, *Red River*, *20,000 Leagues Under the Sea*, *Spartacus* and on and on. Some stuntmen specialized in certain areas: fist fights, falling horse, high falls, etc. Williams specialized in spectacular horse falls, always exclaiming as the horse fell, "Never touched me." Jack's dad found that he could train a horse to fall on cue and taught this technique to fifteen-year-old son. His trademark stunt was training a horse to rear up and fall as if shot. "There was probably no feat I could imagine that was as fascinating as that," admitted Williams. "So I took the technique and perfected it. It's the idea that you don't give horses a script to read and then they fall by themselves. You have to, number one, make the horse fall, and then, if there's any time, you concern yourself with your own safety." Fellow stuntman Bobby Hoy agreed, "Jack drove stagecoaches, he wrecked wagons, he could transfer from the horse to the train—he could do anything pertaining to horse work."[651]

As Jackie had previously worked with Wayne and Lyons, it was only natural that he would be part of the crew that Cliff brought to Brackettville. Lyons and Williams even flew down two weeks before the start of production because Wayne wanted a few shots of Jackie falling a horse to test the new Todd-AO camera lens. "Cliff and I shot some pre-production of the Mexican Army moving north before the picture officially started," remembered Williams. "They had a couple of other falling horses down there that I'd never seen before, so I didn't do shots (with them). Then everybody else came down there two weeks later. The (Batjac) company flew down there on a Monday. I had a commercial to do in town. So I had to fly to Dallas, charter a plane. Fly down to San Antone and charter a plane to fly from San Antone to Brackettville. I...literally just arrived as they were about to holler 'action.'" Williams stepped of out his car, changed into costume, took two falls on a horse, and drove away $500 richer. And the horse made $50.[652]

Joe and Tap had a solid gold pedigree; their father was Yakima Canutt, arguably the greatest stuntman ever. Born five years apart, the brothers entered the stunt arena at an early age. Just seventeen, Harry Joe stunted in his first film, *King Richard and the Crusaders,* in which his father was second-unit director. According to Yak, Joe was "loaded with ability and certainly didn't lack courage." *Crusaders* was followed by *20,000 Leagues Under the Sea, Davy Crockett, King of the Wild Frontier, The Last Command, Old Yeller, Pork Chop Hill,* and others. Older brother Edward, or Tap as he was known, had started a few years earlier when he stunted in *Only the Valiant* in 1951. Yakima was stunt coordinator on the project. Interestingly, Tap was short for *Tapadaro,* the Spanish word for a saddle stirrup covering. Appropriate, as Yak was a former rodeo champion and horseman extraordinaire. Tap was out of school for the summer and was on vacation. As he wanted to be in the film, Yak suited him up him in a cavalry uniform. Later, dressed in an Indian outfit, he performed his first stunt. A star was born, or rather, a stuntman. Tap acted and stunted in several films in the 1950s, including *The Last Command, Friendly Persuasion,* and *Rally 'Round the Flag, Boys!* Several years later, the brothers appeared in the classic *Ben-Hur.* Doubling Charlton Heston, Joe was behind the reins of four white stallions when he jumped the actor's chariot over a pair of damaged chariots. Bam, it went high into the air! Holding onto its front rail, Canutt was thrown in a full somersault, still hanging onto the rail. After landing on the reins which were still tied to the chariot, he grabbed the hitch rail, turned a flip off to the side and hit the spina wall, suffering a cut to his chin. Through careful cutting, the audience never knew it wasn't Heston as Joe wore a mask identical to Charlton's face. Given their experience it was fairly easy for the brothers to be asked to join Lyon's crew in Texas. "Well, I don't know about a crew," corrected Joe. "You know, he had certain people he worked with... I was raised around Cliff. My dad (and Cliff) were good friends, and we did

316

*Ben-Hur*. He was over there on the race with us and the picture came. I believe I called him on it, and then, when I heard about it going, then I got a call to come down when they started."[653]

Along with Lyons, at fifty-eight, Bob Rose was one of the oldest stuntmen on the set. Born at the turn of the century in 1902, Rose in 1919 doubled Harry Houdini in his first film, *The Grim Game*. Rose would double Houdini in five additional films. Silent film stars Francis Ford and Eddie Polo "discovered" Rose as a jockey in Tijuana and suggested that his athletic abilities could be better used in Hollywood. Bob was a jack of all trades: parachutist, pilot, wing-walker, high-diver, and trick rider. By 1935 he had already entered the pantheon of expert stuntman that included Duke Green, Gordon Carveth, Lyons, Yak Canutt, Frank Clark, and Matt Gilman. By his own admission, Rose was "never seriously injured in doing 560 parachute leaps, eighty plane changes in the air, 150 dives from heights above ninety feet, 180 automobile wrecks, riding horses over cliffs sixty-five times and staging fights atop ninety-foot ship masts and making the proper fall into the water so many times I have lost count." He could also transfer from a motorcycle to an airplane by grabbing a rope ladder from the plane as it flew by. In addition to Houdini, Rose doubled for the likes of Mary Pickford, Buck Jones, Tom Mix, Buster Keaton, Jean Harlow, and Fay Wray. In *The Alamo*, Rose would portray an Alamo defender and be involved in numerous "gags" (any unique form of action, such as a stunt). "I worked in most of those (explosion) scenes, where I placed myself close to where the explosions were to go off. You don't want to be too far from the center of the explosion because the concussion would be too great. You don't want to be any further than ten feet when it goes off."[654]

Born in Northern Australia, Gil Perkins ran away from home at eighteen. Actually, he sailed away as a deck hand on a Norwegian freighter. Then, in Perkins's words, he "tooted around the Pacific for four months." Even as a youngster, he had wanted to get into the "theatrical business, mainly films," so it was natural that he would be involved in school plays and pantomimes. In 1928, Perkins and a friend left "Down Under" and arrived in San Francisco, where they opened a garage and car business. The next year found him working as an extra and stuntman in director Frank Lloyd's *The Devine Lady*. Over the next few decades, Perkins would appear in films such as *King Kong, Mutiny on the Bounty, Moby Dick, Captains Courageous, The Adventures of Robin Hood, Dodge City, They Died with Their Boots On, My Darling Clementine, Miracle on 34th Street, Fort Apache, She Wore a Yellow Ribbon, 20,000 Leagues Under the Sea*, and numerous other films, as an actor, stuntman, and double for stars such as Kirk Douglas, Eddie Albert, Edmond O'Brien, Bela Lugosi, and Bruce Cabot. He also doubled Red Skelton in every picture the latter made. Once, he was asked to double for

William "Hopalong Cassidy" Boyd. "I went out and ducked between cars," said Perkins. "Then, I went around…and climbed up a cement lamp post and jumped to a hanging fire escape on the Culver City Hotel, went up over the fire escape, and in through a window, out a window on the other side, and jumped eighteen feet to the pavement." The next day, the morning rushes impressed Boyd. "God, who's this kid?" he cried. "He looks more like me than I do!" Perkins was also in great demand on television during the 1950s when he appeared in literally dozens of Western and adventure series. He could also choreograph action, construct mechanical rigging and, as he had learned to fall and tumble on the football field, control his body as a diver. An excellent horseman and fencer, the latter boded well for him on *The Alamo;* he choreographed Laurence Harvey's death scene.[655]

At six-feet-four, Ted White was a huge stuntman, and Wayne liked to surround himself with tall actors: Chill Wills (six-two), Denver Pyle (six-one), Hank Worden ( six-one and one half), Tom Hennessey (six-five) and Guinn "Big Boy" Williams (six-two). Even Ken Curtis was, at least, six foot tall. Frankie Avalon? A veritable shrimp. In an August 1987 edition of the *Chicago Times,* Avalon said with a laugh, "I'm barely five foot seven. I wear elevator shoes which make me five foot nine!" Widmark hit the nail on the head: "Wayne liked big guys; everyone was a midget to him. Smaller guys annoyed him."[656]

White was a natural athlete; while majoring in aeronautical engineering at the University of Oklahoma, he played football, was on the swimming team, and boxed. He boxed so well he fought in AAU and Golden Gloves: eighty bouts as an undefeated heavyweight. Upon graduation, he moved to California where he worked at Douglas Aircraft for a while. Later, he worked at a Lincoln Mercury dealership: "a guy came in that was an extra in the motion picture business," said White, "and we sold him a new Mercury. He said to me, 'I think maybe you'd make it in the picture business.' I said, 'I don't know anything about it.' And he kept coming in after I sold him a car and finally got me to go to the studio with him one day." White decided to visit Warner Bros., which was shooting a Western. "One of the guys was doing something on horseback and couldn't quite get it done," recalled White. "It was roping. I said to somebody standing by, 'I can do that.' 'Are you sure?' they asked me. And the next thing I knew, I was in wardrobe and doing it. Had to ride a horse in, rope a guy standing on the porch, dolly round his saddle horn and ride off. That got me into the Guild." After several films, he received a call to go to Tucson and get ready to double the star. Not knowing who that might be, he nevertheless agreed. When he walked on the set the first morning he met…John Wayne. The film was *Rio Bravo.* White's first stunt was a running horse mount as he rode down the street to check on Dean Martin. Later, he would double Duke as Wayne ran down a flight of stairs and tripped over a rope. After that, he next appeared in *The Horse Soldiers.* On that set, he knew Duke's next film would be *The Alamo,* "but nobody had told me that

I was going to go. You know, I got a call to go, I don't know, maybe a month and a half before they ever went. And you know, everybody at that time wanted to get on it because it was a big picture and a long picture. Everybody wanted to get on it. Wayne had guys like Chuck Roberson, Chuck Hayward, Bear Hudkins. These were people he had known for years and years and years. And he was very loyal to those guys. He had all those on there. He would go right up to Cliff and tell him, 'These are the people I want,' and Cliff would go ahead."[657]

"Big Chuck,""Little Chuck,""Good Chuck,""Bad Chuck." Chuck Hayward, Chuck Roberson. Born just eight months apart, Hayward was of average height and build while Roberson was a husky six-foot-three. Respected and admired, both were excellent horsemen and stuntmen who would perform numerous memorable gags in *The Alamo*. Hayward was born in Nebraska where his family raised horses that were sold to the U.S. Cavalry. At sixteen, he left home and found work breaking horses. After Hayward graduated from Curtis Agricultural School, he attended business school in Omaha. During the war, he enlisted in the Merchant Marines.

In contrast, Roberson grew up on a cattle ranch in Texas before his family headed west to Roswell, New Mexico, where he learned to drive a four-up and become a real cowboy. Although he quit school when only thirteen, Roberson was a graduate of the school of hard knocks: working on cattle drives, rough-necking in Texas oil fields, and, after moving to California, finding a job as a policeman. Two weeks after he was hired, he was assigned duty at MGM. When the war broke out, he entered the Army and served three years in the Transport division. Wounded at Okinawa during a kamikaze attack, he was laid up for quite some time. Upon discharge Roberson returned to the field of law enforcement and while on duty at Warner Bros. met veteran stuntman Fred Kennedy, who suggested Roberson, with his background and knowledge of horses, try his hand in Westerns. Though he had already appeared in several films including *Angel and the Badman*, Roberson agreed and in 1946 was hired to double John Carroll in *Wyoming*, starring Bill Elliott. Roberson recalled, "I grew up on a cattle ranch in Texas and spent most of my waking hours just trying to stay on a horse. Back then, if (anyone) had tried to tell me I was going to make a living falling off horses... I would have punched the guy in the nose." Three years and sixteen films later, Roberson doubled Duke in *The Fighting Kentuckian*, an arrangement that would last throughout both their careers. Wayne recalled how Roberson was hired: "I had one scene where I play a country guy against a French country background...The butler said the girl wasn't at home, and I start to go out and my rival goes up to the door and goes right in. We wanted to show how goddamn mad I was, and we wanted to show me jumping up on a horse and say, 'You try that, you son-of-a-bitch,' and then I'd ride away. Have you ever tried to stand flatfooted and jump high and straddle a horse? Well, we got a young guy who can do it. So he did it, and we hired Chuck Roberson."[658]

While Roberson was busy stunting in films, Hayward did some rodeoing around the Plains states. Surviving on money earned from cleaning barns and stacking hay, Chuck, with fourteen bucks in his pocket and an old beat-up pickup truck, decided to try his luck in California. Eventually, he found his way onto the set of *Brimstone*, his first Western. Asked how he started his career, he replied, "I knew horses; that's my main thing. It's important to get the right horse to work with. You've got to get good horses and work them to the advantage of the picture." Later that year, he also stunted on *The Fighting Kentuckian* with Roberson; no horse falls, just wagon wrecks. Hayward would go on to make *Yellow Ribbon* in 1948, but it was on *Rio Grande* that the two Chucks received their famous monikers. Known as "Big Chuck" and "Little Chuck" due their different heights, John Ford dubbed Roberson "Bad Chuck" because of Roberson's way with the ladies and his nightlife. That automatically made Hayward "Good Chuck." According to Dobe Carey, "Hayward didn't do too badly with the girlies, either, but Ford had them labeled, so that was that. Besides, their looks fit their labels. (Roberson) had a devil-may-care way about him that Ford loved... Hayward... was more reserved, with a quiet humor." Hayward and Roberson would play two of Crockett's Tennesseans in Wayne's film, as well as Mexican soldiers, Dragoons, Texas defenders, and any other role that needed filling.[659]

Born in 1934 in Red Oak, Texas, near present-day Paris, Bill Hart's parents died when he was just a youth. A fine student-athlete, Hart played several sports in school but suffered a skull fracture his senior year. After graduating from Edinburgh High School, he moved to California in 1958 to investigate both college and employment opportunities. His original plan was to support himself by working in motion pictures while going to school, but he found he enjoyed film work so much he never did finish college. And since he'd married Chuck Roberson's daughter Charlene, his father-in-law took him under his wing, and Hart soon was doing stunt work on various television programs including *Wanted: Dead or Alive* and *Have Gun Will Travel*. "I first met John Wayne in 1959 when I first got into the business," explained Bill. "As a matter of fact, he wrote the letter to get me into the business. At that time, you had to have someone doing a current production to write a letter on your behalf. Actually it was because I knew Chuck Roberson. He introduced me to John Wayne, and that's how I got into the business. My first big Western, my first big movie, as a matter of fact, was *The Alamo*. Cliff Lyons was the second-unit director on the film, and they had taken about eighteen stuntmen down there already. I wanted to go on it, of course, but it was a question of how many (stuntmen) they could afford to take. So Cliff took me down as an interpreter, figuring that once I got there, he would convert me over to the stunt end of it, which he did. It was a good excuse to get me there, but I didn't speak Spanish. I could just say a few words in the language. But it was really his ruse (just) to get me down there to work. Having been taken down as an interpreter, the parts were more or less set before I was converted to doing stunts. The different gangs—I call them 'gangs'—were set like the Tennessean gang and Jim Bowie's gang. I was just there for more or less whenever he needed me."[660]

While Cliff Lyons was pulling together his crew of stuntmen, others were responsible for obtaining equally valuable commodities: horses, cattle, goats, milk cows, and other livestock. Ramrod wrangler Bill Jones was instructed to purchase and train as many horses as required. With the veritable plethora of Westerns filming in Hollywood in the late 1950s, it was virtually impossible to bring TV's livestock from California; they weren't available. Scouring all over Kinney County and the surrounding areas, Jones quickly realized he needed to expand his search. The problem? There just weren't enough horses available at the prices he wanted to pay. Ranchers had the stock but didn't want to sell for peanuts. As a result, Jones fanned out his search to include all of Texas as well as Mexico, but to no avail. Racking up over 35,000 miles, his multi-year quest took him to California, Arizona, New Mexico, Texas, Oklahoma, Arkansas, and Missouri. He bought a few Matador horses, made a deal with E. Paul Waggoner for several 3-D horses, and added several more with the Wine-Glass brand. A few were even purchased at the Ft. Smith (Arkansas) Livestock auction. "Santa Anna" rode the handsome white horse "White Cloud" owned by Sue, Bill Daniel's daughter. Its magnificent saddle was donated by General Quinones. Hand-crafted and commissioned by the general, a label was stamped on the cantle as follows: "La Reyna Del Arte, Fusteria Moderna Por J. Reyes Juarez." Roughly translated, it reads, "The Queen of Art, Modern Craftsmanship by J. Reyes Juarez."

All told, Jones acquired over five hundred work and saddle horses for Batjac's remuda at an average cost of only $200 each. (Publicity at the time indicated the number purchased at closer to 1,800, which seems extremely exaggerated, although Happy said, "We had as many as fourteen hundred head of horses on the ranch for the filming. Nobody had fourteen hundred head of horses, of course, so Wayne bought seven hundred and leased another seven hundred. If you figure a bale of hay for two horses each day, that's seven hundred bales a day. That's thirty-two, thirty-three hundred dollars worth of hay, just hay alone, for horses per day." At the end of the show, these well-fed, well-trained horses were sold at a profit. James Edward Grant bought the two horses ridden by Avalon and Widmark and gave them to his nieces as presents. The horses were then re-named–"Frankie" and "Dickie.")

Naturally, there were a few bumps along the road. Uvalde's Walter Bierschwale Jr. purchased thirty-one horses and mules from Nick Kemp of the Fort Worth Horse and Mule Commission. Bierschwale claimed he had a contract to provide the animals to Batjac as a part of three hundred horses and mules, twenty wagons (most from the Waxahachie area), ten buggies and all the stagecoaches he could find. *(Really? Stagecoaches?)* Unfortunately, his check to Kemp for $2,864 bounced. After an arrest warrant was issued, Bierschwale sent Kemp a telegram saying that he would have the funds in a day or two as he hadn't yet been reimbursed for his stock-buying expenses.[661]

After obtaining the required number, Jones gathered his herd and headed to Brackettville, where five hundred acres of stock corrals had been constructed. (Again, an exaggerated publicity bulletin stated that "more than 5,000 cedar posts were brought in to make stock corrals. Seventeen hundred acres were allotted for pens and pastures." Another article claimed over 10,000 posts were used). Full-time veterinarians and ferriers were hired and all horses vaccinated for pleuropneumonia, aka shipping fever, as soon as they reached the ranch. (Most horses are transported with their heads tied, which prevents them from lowering their muzzles–a motion that regularly allows drainage of the normal respiratory secretions that naturally accumulate in the windpipe. The accumulation of these fluids can result in pneumonia. Hence the term "shipping" fever). Distemper outbreaks were controlled by shots administered by the vet. Six hundred new halters, five hundred hair pads and saddles were purchased to "clothe" the horses. With all the horses, mules and burros, keeping them healthy was a constant issue. Over $30,000 in feed was purchased including 830 tons of alfalfa and other grain rations concentrates.[662]

These horses also had to be broken and conditioned to ignore cannon fire, gunfire and explosions, pull caissons, artillery and wagons, and generally perform everything a trained movie horse is required to do. They also needed to become accustomed to the commotion of a movie set: bright lights, cables, raised weapons, fallen bodies, cameras, and microphone booms along with hundreds of assorted actors, directors, and crew members. "A movie horse is just like a fire horse," said Jones. The latter had to get used to burning buildings, certain noises, and confusion. The movie horses, too, must get used to their surroundings. The only difference between Batjac's *Alamo* horses and other movie horses is that these were getting used to Hollywood-type surroundings in Texas. As a result, the corrals were surrounded by light reflectors and microphones dangling from long poles. Trainers would unexpectedly fire blank pistols and set off dynamite charges near the corrals to get the horses accustomed to the loud noises they would experience in battle scenes.

Employing thirty stuntmen, fifteen of whom were local cowboys, wranglers proceeded to put the steeds through their paces. Roy Kennedy, a wrangler on *The Horse Soldiers*, proved invaluable. So were trainers Bobby Davenport and Billy Allen from Uvalde, Dub Glynn from Del Rio, Al Delamare (who had worked with Dale Robertson on the *Wells-Fargo* television series), Bruce Galbraith (who directed the training of animals for *The Charge of the Light Brigade)*, Corky Randall, Rusty McDonald, and Billy Winn. Each wrangler had his own expertise: Galbraith specialized in training and jumping horses, Kennedy supervised training of horses and mules that pulled wagons and caissons, and Sherwood taught horses the fine points of teamwork. Winn recalled preproduction problems: "Oh, they bought them horses from everywhere. People had them damn old crazy horses, bucking son of a guns. Damn, they'd buy them, and Bill Jones was the head wrangler. And he said, 'You boys break 'em.' And so anyway, we did. And they'd bring them; most of the Mexicans came from Piedras Negras in them big old double deck buses. And they'd get there, hell, before daylight, but we had 2:30, 3 o'clock call to saddle up six or seven hundred of them horses. And they'd come over, they'd get here about daylight. One of the first mornings, damn, I felt sorry for them damn boys. Them Mexican boys that had them old McClellan saddles. And they're just like a piece of...it's like a setting on a damn two by four. The little iron stirrups. And then some of them horses are rank son of a bitches. We'd try an get 'em mounted, and we'd give 'em...course that old sword was already flopping and hitting that horse in the flank. And that was already scaring him to death. And then the poor guys would give him a lance, and they couldn't grab the saddle, they couldn't grab. Well, they looked like popcorn in there."[663]

Plunker Sheedy seconded that opinion: "We rode a lot of horses, fresh horses after they got them in those things, and I was kinda in charge of the caisson deal. We rode them around, and that's really what we did all day long. From the time we got them saddled in the morning and we'd just ride, and make sure somebody was going to be able to handle them. I think at that time they were hauling (extras) from Eagle Pass, Piedres Negras, Coahuila, Mexico, over here to work in that movie, somewhere around 1000 of them because we didn't have enough here to work. A lot of them could ride, but some of them couldn't ride—but they didn't let it bother them. They put them on a horse anyway. They got a lot of free falls out of that deal."[664]

Buddy Sherwood had just completed an assignment in Czechoslovakia training horses to pull chariots in the Roman spectacular *Ben-Hur*. Now he was in Brackettville, tutoring mules and horses to be members of "six-ups," six-animal teams pulling wagons and cannon. He used an East Texas mule, purchased from Po' Boy Morris in Cass County, to quiet down the unschooled horses. While doing so, he rode on a McClellan saddle. "This was the most wonderful saddle ever made for the fighting man," joked Sherwood. "After sitting in it for twenty minutes, the trooper is mad enough to fight his own mother. I've tried for years, and I've never found a comfortable spot to sit in these cavalry saddles." Horses were shod on an assembly line basis. As a result, there were a whole lot of shoes left over and a whole lot of horseshoe pitching going on. The short, cigar-chomping Sherwood had his own unique spin on that sport: "You Texicans play sissy-style horse shoes. Where I come from, they pitch the horseshoes with the horses still nailed to the shoes!" Chill Wills joked some of the horses were so "blue-blooded and sensitive," the cowpokes in charge were feeding them pabulum![665]

A one-time cavalry master sergeant came out of retirement to maintain the saddles and bridles. Master-Sgt. Herman Allen had been stationed at Ft. Clark from 1923-1933 and had recently moved to Brackettville. The 402 saddles sold to the Mexican army when the U.S. Army became mechanized were eventually sold back to Batjac and placed in Allen's charge. They included one hundred for officers and the rest for regular cavalry. In addition, he was also responsible for a number of antique Fork A saddles and thirty wooden ones made in Mexico especially for the film. Western saddles with high cantle and pommel, and narrow swell were literally dug out of old barns and stables, anywhere they could be found. Many of these were in such poor shape they needed to be repaired and rebuilt by Mike Hawks from Uvalde and Jack Allred, who worked full-time on the project. Artillery harnesses were purchased from San Antonio's own Sam Maltzman, who'd purchased those years ago as army surplus. Bob and Estelle Townsend (whose daughter Alyce Maye "Pinni" doubled for Linda Cristal) flew their own plane to Mexico City in search of a charra or side-saddle designed for Mexican ladies.[666]

One of the greatest problems Jones faced was the availability of wagons and buggies. Though the complete vehicles never totally appeared in the film, a critical component of each—the wheel—did. Artillery caissons were assembled on site with wooden wheels scavenged from the wagons. A full-time New Mexican wheelwright was brought on site to keep hundreds of caissons and wheels in working order. As this expertise was virtually a lost art, his presence was essential. Most wheels were found in California, East Texas, and Louisiana. Some oak wheels with mesquite hubs were even fashioned on the set. Covered wagons were assembled on location, wagon beds constructed on Shahan's ranch, bows shipped from Tennessee, and yokes and singletrees from Indiana. Buggies were purchased from Royce Heard, who lived, appropriately, in Crockett, Texas. Heard scoured East Texas and Louisiana for buggies or parts of buggies to recondition. Isolated towns in the Louisiana backwoods where folks were of French ancestry seemed the best hunting grounds. "I deal in hug-me-tight or one-seater buggies," said Heard. "That's mainly because hug-me-tights are the only kind I've found for reasonable prices after I went into the buggy business about a year ago." Batjac bought the sturdy, rebuilt buggies for $75 to $100 each. Bill Daniel would donate thirty-two horse-drawn vehicles, including a Victorian coach and oxen.[667]

If you were an extra who could ride, you'd be paid more than normal. Naturally, when the call went out for extras who could "ride well under trying circumstances," the set was filthy with wannabe cowboys. According to Roberson, Lyons "took a look at the mob of cowboy hats and boots and snorted, 'Wonder how many foot soldiers we got hiding in there? All right, cowboys. Ridin' for a gawdam picture ain't like shooin' a gawdam cow out of the gawdam garden. Let's see how many of you cowboys can cut it.'" He asked the cowboys to ride downhill, ten at a time, as fast as they could. As they started, Lyons would get in the middle of them; whip their horses and "whomp on the cowboys until they fell off." *What the hell!!!* they yelled as they fell off. "Mother made a helluva lot of infantrymen that day and humbled many a cow chaser. Only forty out of a group of several hundred were chosen to backup the stuntmen, and there were so many new guys on the picture who had never worked with Mother before that most of them thought he was a little crazy."[668]

While many horses were used to pull wagons or provide background atmosphere, four stunt and twelve falling horses, the crème de la crème of the stunt world, were brought in from Hollywood. Horses trained to fall on command and respond to verbal and visual cues were absolutely critical. Months of practice, training and preparation were prerequisites; so were marvelous reflexes and inherent talent. Every precaution was taken to assure each gag was as safe as possible: hoofs covered in sponge rubber to soften kicks, mouths taped to prevent biting, landing spots softened with dirt, sand and sawdust to cushion falls. Makeup was sometimes used to create "injury," coats were dyed, stockings and blaze marks changed. Falling horses, the most prized of the specialty performers, were worth their considerable weight in gold. Special tack was required: Leather-covered soft rubber stirrups were worn on the falling side, western or cavalry style stirrups on the other side, shielded at the toe with leather to prevent a stuntman's foot from getting caught. In Petrine Day Mitchum's excellent book, *Hollywood Hoofbeats*, Jack Williams described the perfect fall: "It's a judo throw. But it has to be done in such a way that the horse is not anticipating it, that you catch the horse in the right kind of stride so that as you pull the horse to the right, he follows his head. If he's got a rear in him, he will go up in a pirouette. That was the exciting thing to me, to put something on the screen that looked like the horse exploded: got up on a pirouette, come down and, ideally, go over the top of you." The ground where the horse would fall was checked thoroughly for rocks, glass and sharp objects. Training took place in soft dirt and hay until the horse learned the technique.[669]

The horses were almost as famous as the stuntmen. Cocaine was a blaze-faced, sorrel gelding, seven-eighths thoroughbred out of a quarter horse mare. Purchased by Chuck Roberson from Frosty Royce's stable, the four-year-old was a quick study. Trained to jump, do drags, transfers, and bulldogs, the duo would go on to double Wayne in numerous features. Jackie Williams's sorrel mare Coco was only fifteen hands high but suited the smaller Williams perfectly. Coco could bow, sit, lie down, and, with Jack's training, became the quintessential falling horse. And she loved the camera. He also brought along Goldie. Tap Canutt owned a pair of outstanding stunt horses: Hot Rod, a four-year-old thoroughbred gelding falling horse, and Gypsy, a tall sorrel, both trained as falling horses. Hot Rod was later sold to stuntman Boyd Franklin Morgan, better known as Red.

According to Morgan, the duo "did 1,694 falls in pictures of which 1,687 were prints on the first take. The other seven were pilot errors." Bear Hudkins was a nephew of Ace, Art, Clyde, and Ode Hudkins, collectively known as the Hudkins who provided stunt horses to the industry. Bear rode Jerry Brown Falling Horse, a gelding owned by the brothers but trained by Jerry Brown (hence the name). Chuck Hayward rode Twinkletoes; Bill Hart brought Tadpole, a sound bay. Jim Burk rode Detonator, a thoroughbred gelding. Said stuntman Fred Kennedy, "You can't beat anything into a child, a dog, or a horse. I tell ya, these anumals'll do jest about anything for ya if you treat 'em right. 'Course, it don't hurt to have a smart one to work with, but it don't do no good beatin' hell out of a dumb one."[670]

In the meantime, another Bill rustled up a herd of cattle. Born into a wealthy and prominent family, Bill Daniel was sixth generation Texan. Brother of Texas governor Price Daniel, Bill was a rancher and lawyer who graduated from Baylor in 1938. Owner of the historic Plantation Ranch, Daniel was asked to help create a herd of longhorns. Outside of a few state parks where the cattle were kept as a historical curiosity, additional cattle were few and far between. Perhaps 3,000 were still alive after facing near extinction in the late 1930s. If not for the foresight of a select number of ranchers who valued their appearance and heritage, the handsome beasts would be no more. "The script called for four hundred longhorns," said Daniel. "He wanted them; he needed them. He couldn't get them. He, himself. The big man himself. He could not get them. So anyway, he (Wayne) said take a plane. So I agreed to do it. I knew that (Fayette) Cap Yates, another friend, a dear friend at Marfa, Texas, had some big old steers. Old Cap Yates, Oil field Yates and everything. Sat out on the back porch and talked old times. And he said, 'Well, what in the world can I do for you? What are you doing way out here?' And I said, 'I came to see ya, wanted to talk old times.' I told him then that I needed to borrow some of his steers to be in used in the filming of *The Alamo*. He said, 'I'll let you have all you want provided you do one thing.' I didn't know what in the world he was fixin' to say. I hadn't spent any money. I got 'em all for free. And I knew I was going to get his for free, but I couldn't figure what he's fixin' to say. He said, 'If you'll just spend the night where we can talk tonight. You know I'm so old. There's nobody who can talk steers like you all and longhorns and cattle, and, if you'll spend the night, we'll talk and visit...' And his boy is sitting there and he said, 'Yeah, in the morning, we'll have a good time. We'll rope one. I'll rope one, and you'll rope one.' And my fingers are always itching to rope a steer anyways. So I agreed. And by Saturday, I had those four hundred longhorns, and it didn't cost the company a penny." (The actual number was only 148 and even that small number was extremely difficult to obtain). Cattle were also borrowed from Milby Butler's ranch in League City (twenty-three cows, seven steers, and four calves), the J.D. Phillips's ranch in Columbia, the Graves Peeler ranch near Tilden in McMullen County as well as Daniel's own ranch in Liberty. Dozens of mottled, spotted multi-colored Longhorn and wide-horned steers were selected. The only cost incurred was an insurance policy Duke purchased for each animal; the cows were insured for $1,000 each, the steers $400 and the calves $300. (According to *Variety*, some of the same cattle were used for Wayne's next Western, *The Comancheros*.)[671]

In mid-August, Bill and Price Daniel flew down to Brackettville, the former acting as the governor's personal representative, for a tour of the set. Arriving aboard a twin-engine Lockheed Lodestar belonging to McCullough Tool Company, they were met by a perspiring, slightly sun-burned Wayne. Afterward, Duke, finally convinced of Daniel's passion and enthusiasm for the project, named him the film's coordinator of production and public relations. Bill also served as historian and attorney for Batjac. Wayne explained, "Mr. Daniel has proven himself so thoroughly versed and in and so enthusiastic about the history of Texas and the high point of its glamorous past, the battle of the Alamo, that I became convinced he was the one person best qualified to coordinate the forces needed to make the picture with those elements which will bring *Alamo* to the attention to the world at large. Too, he is the one individual who will get all Texas behind us, which is something we desire as much as to make a great picture." Daniel was equally as positive about the opportunity: "I am grateful to find myself associated with a project that will point up so greatly one of the greatest moments in the history of our state. A moment so important to all of us today, faced with decisions which may affect our free way of life, as it did those who died in the Alamo. I am sure the motion picture *Alamo* will tell a story of which all Texas may be proud, which all theatergoers will enjoy, and from which all mankind can benefit. John Wayne has long been one of my favorites, just as he has been a favorite of most of Texas, and it is gratifying to be connected with him and his, particularly in a project which will provide our State with world wide (sic) recognition in the field of public relations through the medium of high entertainment." In a series of articles written by Daniel the following year, he indicated "I first met John Wayne in Los Angeles when I was out there for the Roy Harris-Floyd Patterson fight (August 18, 1958). In August 1959, O.J. McCullough…flew Wayne and his party to my Plantation ranch where Wayne asked me to have a part in his movie epic." Daniel also served as resident historian and proved worthy of that responsibility when he told Wayne that Sam Houston did not have facial hair. Richard Boone had arrived from the *Have Gun Will* Travel set with a beard and, in order to maintain historical accuracy, was asked to shave before his first scene. In an article Daniel wrote in 1960, he recalled, "The very first day on the set…I noticed that Sam Houston was arrayed with a long and flowing mustache. I told…Wayne I had never seen a picture of Houston wearing a mustache…" Wayne said, "Well, I didn't know that," and the ornament over his upper lip was removed."[672]

The clothes the actors wear, and *how* they wear them, are their chief weapons in characterization. The wardrobe plot detailed their costumes. An actor-by-actor, scene-by-scene inventory of all the clothing in a production, with detailed breakdown into every separate item in each costume, it is extremely specific in both content and description, and would include a photo of the actor in costume and possibly a swatch of fabric. The following description was typical:

Colonel Travis, Change #1 – Semi Uniform. INT. OFFICE Sc. 14-20, EXT. GALLERY Sc. 15.

"Brown M.O. Square Top Boots, Cal. Spurs-Brown Straps, Beige Diagonal Twill Breeches, Dark Gray DB Tailcoat-Stand & Fall Collar, Coat Buttoned Except Top Button, Shawl Collar-S.B.-Vest Same Cloth-2" Below Coat In Front, Ruffle Front White Tee Shirt W/Long Pointed Collar Which Is Folded Down Over Tie, Black 1½ String Tie In Bow-Ends Tucked Under-Do Not Show, Straw Hat-Low Crown Flat Top-Straw 5" Brim Shaped At Sides, 1" Black Band, Red Tasseled Silk Officers Sash Civil War Type, Black Officers Belt W/Sword Sling, First Aid Pouch, Faked Up Holster For Cap & Ball Pistol, And Officers Sword."

In addition to the aforementioned, *The Alamo* wardrobe plot included a list of actors and characters they played (including extras and stuntmen), a typed description of each actor's wardrobe, and detailed descriptions of Mexican army uniforms and photos. Wardrobe plots filled the basic need of turning shooting script scene numbers and descriptions into breakdowns, providing each production department with the necessary information to execute their particular activities. In some instances, the unique requirements and design of the wardrobe dictated it be manufactured. In other instances, companies specializing in period costumes were utilized.

Established in 1912, Western Costume Company (WCC) had provided attire for some of the greatest films ever made: from Judy Garland's ruby-red slippers in *The Wizard of Oz* to Clark Gable's period couture in *Gone With The Wind*. From *The Jazz Singer* to *Gilda*, the list was endless: *Beau Geste, All Quiet on the Western Front, Goodbye Mr. Chips, How To Marry a Millionaire, Oklahoma!, The King and I, South Pacific*, and *Some Like It Hot*. According to WCC, they "dressed virtually every major star film has known." Lavish musicals and period pieces as well as Westerns. If a studio produced a film, in all likelihood, Western provided the costumes. Batjac, as an independent, had no costumer on the payroll, nor a wardrobe department. Naturally, Wayne would look to Western to fill his needs. "You have to remember that everything in a movie is visual," said Paul Abramowitz, one-time president of Western. "And costumes are one of the things you see first and remember most." Elois Jennsen, Oscar-winning costume designer and former president of the Costume Designer's Guild, echoed, "Western set the standard for magnificent costumes for the whole industry. I've always felt you can do the most beautiful sketch in the world, but it's the cutter and fitter and tailor who breathe life into it that makes the difference."[673]

Western had previously conducted Mexican uniform research for the 1939 Republic feature *Man of Conquest* in Mexico City at the Chapultepec and National History museums. It had established a branch there which, in 1945, was later housed at Churubusco Studios (currently Azteca studios). RKO had established this complex in conjunction with the Mexican government. Wayne had spent quite a bit of time there when John Ford was filming *The Fugitive*, and it was during that period Duke met and told Al Ybarra he would use him on *The Alamo*. WCC had acquired Joseph Hefter's 1958 booklet, *El Sodado Mexicano*, which recreated Mexican Army uniforms from 1835 through 1848. Hefter tried to offer his services to Wayne, but was rejected. Duke, Ybarra, and John Jensen had compared Hefter's recreations to WCC's primary source research, and believed Hefter fabricated some of his details. (Winged vs. fringeless scale epaulets for rank and file soldiers, absence of green, white, red "target" on top of shakos, etc. Wayne and Jensen correctly knew how the soldiers had been attired and decided not to consult with Hefter any further). Hired by Cecil B. DeMille to work on *The Ten Commandments*, Jensen became a part of the director's permanent staff. He was sent to Egypt to storyboard and do concept illustrations on the spectacular scenes as well as to research and design Egyptian military uniforms. While assigned to *The Buccaneer*, he went on to design and research military uniforms and pirate costumes and also do concept illustrations. For these films, he received two Academy Award nominations. Wayne had viewed Jensen's *Buccaneer* sketches and suggested perhaps Jensen "could help me out." And, since DeMille had passed away on January 21, 1959, Wayne became Jensen's new employer. WCC purchased many of the uniforms used in previous Alamo films including *Man of Conquest* and *The Last Command*. Some of those uniforms had been made by the Sol Frank Uniform Company of San Antonio and were the property of Republic. After *The Last Command,* Western purchased the costumes, hence both WCC and Republic identification stamps on the inside of each garment. The wardrobe was accumulated from a variety of sources: Avalon's fringed shirt previously had been worn by Alan Ladd in *Shane* (1953) while Michael Rennie's costume from *King of the Khyber Rifles*, also released in 1953, showed up as a Mexican officer's uniform. Light tan trousers from *Bengal Brigade* were also utilized.[674]

While in Mexico, Western had access to original uniforms, shakos, and helmets from the 1820-30s and had a shako block custom-made to make up correctly proportioned shakos, as well as the correct tall cavalry helmets used in Wayne's film. This research had been done by Republic, Western, Wayne, and

Ybarra before Hefter and Jensen came onto the scene. They constructed their shakos out of felt, instead of historically correct leather because felt was "camera friendly" and didn't reflect as much as glazed leather. While the "reel" shakos had red, white, and green circles glued on their tops, the "real" shakos had a tri-colored target, consisting of pigment mixed with shellac, painted on top. The entire shako was glazed with a type of varnish for weather/water proofing protection and durability. Both the diamond shako plate and the Mexican eagle plate were cast off originals. The artillery shako plate was similar but not quite as detailed as the original.

Most of the Mexican cavalry helmets were fiberglass and heavily padded for horse falls. For camera purposes only, they also made a few metal ones by modifying 1810 Napoleonic carbineer cavalry helmets that were accurate in size and shape to the originals. In addition to original French metal and fiberglass helmets, they also modified Austrian 1905 cavalry helmets with large black curved crests. The skull of the helmet was boiled hard leather with a metal crest, both originally lacquered black. The top metal center section of the crested comb is "tombak," a yellow metal, and was originally issued in its yellow color. However, for the Wayne film this yellow metal was also lacquered black to blend in with the rest of the helmet and the pot metal, gold-painted Mexican eagle replaced the original Austrian double eagle tombak helmet plate on the front.

Though Jensen's research for different units contained correct uniform details such as the 1832 cavalry tunic, some of his efforts were not as successful. Joseph Musso, historian, author, conceptual illustrator and storyboard artist, noted, "Jensen confused the red tunics for the light infantry, when in reality, they were Mexican band uniforms. This was a misinterpretation of the orders that the light infantry shall be dressed like the light cavalry. The Mexican heavy cavalry was red, hence Jensen's red tuniced light infantry, when in reality, the Mexican light cavalry was blue (like the British Army). At the same time, historically, the Mexican band uniforms were red with blue facings (and blue wings). They were the reverse of the infantry uniforms, which were blue with red facings. So the scenes…showing the red tunic units marching and playing the drums are visually historically accurate." According to Jensen, many Mexican army horse trappings—bridles, saddles, etc.—were located at the Paramount Studio Research Library, created for earlier films.[675]

Many of the costumes used were military khaki jackets found through a Japanese army surplus. With a variety of physical sizes, it would be impossible to create the thousands of wardrobes required by extras. The khaki color of the World War II uniforms was almost a perfect match to those used by the Mexican Army of 1836. The cost of zippers and belts was saved when drawstrings were utilized to eliminate individual fittings. Buttons were sewn inside waistbands so suspenders could be worn, if necessary. Extras were told to wear black shoes or boots to complete their outfits. Not all understood the necessity of this request as white socks and loafers can be readily identified in several scenes. While the costume department made every effort to make sure the correct hat, tunic, and pants were worn together, mistakes did happen. As a result, it was not uncommon to see infantry shakos worn with band member outfits, or identical unit members wearing gray pants with green stripes in one scene and gray pants and red stripes in another. Though it is difficult to determine exactly how many Mexican uniforms were required, an analysis of Jensen's sketches would indicate the amount to be in excess of 1,100.

The first meeting between an actor and his wardrobe is called a costume fitting, and enables the wardrobe staff to ensure a correct fit and enables an actor to see if all necessary movement is possible. The coat in stock at Western wasn't exactly what Boone and Wayne had in mind for Houston's attire later in the film, particularly after they saw period photos of authentic Cherokee Indian styles provided by the research department. So, as Boone recalled, they worked with Jensen as he sketched on a clipboard. The design was based on Houston's 1855 memoirs in which he stated he wore buckskins at San Jacinto as an homage to the Cherokees who adopted him and called him the Raven. "It should have a few more beads," said Wayne. "On the sleeves," clarified Boone. "A raven wing pattern should start at the shoulder," continued Wayne. Boone took another look at himself in the full length mirror. "I think it needs a little more color," suggested Boone. "Right," agreed Wayne. "Do you think we need a red or green sash?" "Red," Boone responded. Wayne then backed away, squinted, and said, "Turn around slowly, Dick." Boone twirled, and Wayne beamed, "With that army saber, you'll look great." Jensen initially designed the wings to be beaded, but Frank Beetson, the film's credited costume director, saved both money and time by burning/embossing the wings on the leather and dying them. Uniforms and costumes for *The Alamo* were all made on-site at Western's original location on Melrose Avenue, in Hollywood. Also involved was Ron Talsky, at the time a twenty-five-year-old trainee at WCC, who earned a dollar an hour and also parked cars on Sunset Boulevard to make ends meet. "I was working for Frank Beetson," said Talsky, "and learning my trade at Western Costume Company when Mr. Beetson was preparing a film called *The Alamo*. He asked me how I would like to go out and work on it as a trainee. So I went to work on the set of *The Alamo*, and that is where I met John Wayne. So I got to meet Duke when I went to Brackettville, Texas, to do the film. Mr. Ford came out there, too, to help Duke with the second unit. Of course, *The Alamo* was Duke's pet project. He financed it; he put it together, and he busted his butt for it. I was there, and we worked hard. We would leave Fort Clark Guest Ranch at one o'clock in the morning with five wardrobe people. We'd go to the Alamo and dress six thousand as Santa Anna's army. At 1:30 a.m. they would start to bring them out in waves and trucks. So at lunchtime we would all lie down in the dirt, no matter where we were. Duke would come up and say, 'Wardrobe!' And we'd just open our eyes and say, 'Working on it!' He just loved it. Whenever he called us, or whatever he said, we said, 'Working on it!' and he just loved that. We didn't even know what he wanted. He just beamed." Costumer Frank Beetson had WCC make up costumes based on Jensen's main costume illustrations. Beetson then oversaw their construction. Ann Peck oversaw the women's costumes. (In an admission that has nothing to do with *The Alamo*, when asked about Wayne's prototypical Western shirt, blue flannel double-breasted front and all, Beetson chuckled, "It's just an old-fashioned fireman's shirt."[676]

Although the percussion-detonating principle was patented in 1807 and percussion-cap guns were in general use by 1825, the weapon most readily available in 1836 was the standard muzzle-loading flintlock. Its firing mechanism was an ingenious combination of flint, steel, and gunpowder. The gun used an ignition system that produced sparks to ignite a pan of priming powder on the outside of the gun and thereby fire the gun's main powder charge inside the barrel. When the trigger was pulled, the flint moved at high speed and struck the steel frizzen in such a way that it shaved off bits and created sparks. The hammer blow also snapped the frizzen back and exposed the gunpowder in the pan. The pan's gunpowder ignited and flashed through a small hole in the side of the barrel to ignite the gunpowder inside the barrel. Unfortunately, in 1959, period-correct flintlocks were no longer available in the required quantities, so Batjac military adviser George Ross was charged with providing weapons to arm both Alamo defenders and Mexican soldiers. Although some of the principle actors used authentic firearms in close-ups, given the number of individuals involved, it was impossible to locate the literally thousands of rifles necessary for background action. However, in searching Hollywood prop departments, Ross came up with the next best thing. Many .45-.70-caliber Trapdoor Springfield rifles had been modified years earlier with brass hammers, frizzens, and springs by Stembridge Gun Rentals, a company created by Cecil B. DeMille and James Stembridge. Unable to obtain enough weapons to arm all the extras, Wayne also purchased all the 1867-88 Remington Rolling Block rifles he could find from Stembridge, Ellis Mercantile, and other prop shops. These he also modified with faux lockplates and frizzens, thereby replicating flintlock rifles. Although not historically correct, they fired blank cartridges and looked real enough for cinematic purposes. These modified rifles were used in close-ups, the unmodified versions were generally used for long shots. "BATJAC" was stamped on the buttstocks of the Remingtons Wayne purchased to keep them separate from the rifles he'd rented. Generally, the Texas defenders used the Springfields while the Mexican army used the Remingtons. In some instances, molded rubber rifles, complete with hammers and frizzens, were also used.

The Remington's faux lockplates were made in two ways: 1) With a metal lockplate that included the frizzen cast in one piece and a separate metal cast hammer that screwed onto the lockplate, or, 2) With a 7¾-inch long metal lockplate with both a separate cast metal frizzen and hammer that screwed onto the lockplate. If desired, the hammer could be attached to the real hammer, but the frizzen, even though screwed on separately, had no real function. The Springfield conversion consisted of a hammer and combination frizzen/spring screwed separately onto the lockplate. (After *The Alamo* was complete, Wayne returned the Springfields to the various studios prop departments and, in 1967, sold many of the remaining Remingtons to producer Ray Pierson and actor Tom Hennesey ["Bull" in the movie]. They planned to sell the rifles as *Alamo* souvenirs at the 1968 San Antonio HemisFair but with the nation torn apart with civil strife, it was not an opportune time. Hennesey stored the rifles in a barn on his ranch in Malibu until a fire destroyed a good portion of them in 1971).[677]

In the film, most of the Tennesseans used original early 19th century flintlocks or 1870 U.S. Springfield and Remington Rolling Block rifles, while Wayne used a 20th century reproduction. However, he did fire an original flintlock in one scene. Extras fired blank cartridges while the original flintlocks and Wayne's percussion rifle were loaded selectively with black powder under controlled conditions. Duke's rifle fired a cap on nipple; the flintlock mechanisms were modified for safety purposes in that each hammer was fitted with a small block of wood painted black to resemble a flint. A small hole was drilled in the block to hold a match stick. When the hammer fell, it would strike the match against the frizzen, creating a flame that suggested a spark, all in lieu of using black powder.[678]

Stembridge provided many of the original weapons used by both main and supporting actors: Nine assorted original flintlock pistols, one pair of English silver-inlay flintlock pistols, one double-barrel flintlock pistol, eleven original flintlock Kentucky rifles, seven converted .45-.70-caliber flintlock Kentucky rifles, twelve converted flintlock muskets, five .38-caliber converted flintlock pistols, 100 converted flintlock rifles (fifty with white leather slings, fifty carbines), a hundred bayonets and scabbards, assorted powder horns, bullet molds, and 20,000 flash and black blanks. While Stembridge provided a multitude of small arms and rifles, it wasn't able to fill an order for cannon, which was where Alamo Planing Mills came in. Forty-two wooden cannon were made for the film: two large balsa wood Long Toms (each thirteen feet, four inches long with seven-foot wheels), and forty smaller redwood cannon. These ranged from an eight-footer to a four-foot-long mortar with an eleven-inch bore. Each had a steel inner casing with electrical firing mechanism. Alamo Planing Mills GM Jim Cummins said the two large cannon were "fashioned in the manner of a French gun the

Mexicans used against the Alamo." One would explode, one as backup just in case. Happy recalled, "The barrels were steel, and everything else was molded wood and fiberglass."[679]

# CHAPTER EIGHTEEN
# ROOM AND BOARD INCLUDED

*"Applications for those interested in extra parts in the John Wayne production will be taken in Del Rio after the first of August,"* announced Nate Edwards, production manager for the project. *"The film will need fifty to 1,300 extras with 1,300 to be employed during the peak shooting time in October. Most of the time the picture will make use of between 300 and 400 extras."*[680]

RUDY ROBBINS, *IT DO*, TENNESSEAN: "WELL, I GOT OUT OF COLLEGE (TEXAS Baptist College) and got drafted immediately into the Army in 1956. I ended up teaching general supply, camouflage, things like that. Well, I met a fellow in the Army whose father was a movie producer, and I figured that, by gollee, that's what I wanted to do—work in the movies. I decided I wanted to be a stuntman, a cowboy stuntman. So as soon as I got out of the Army, I got a job on a dude ranch here in Bandera to kind of tune up my cowboy skills...a few months later Wayne came to the Alamo to film. I was working on a dude ranch as a wrangler at the time. Then I went right into the *Alamo* movie. They were advertising all over this part of Texas for extras. So my idea was just to go to be an extra. And ask questions and find out how does one get to be a stuntman. I went down to Alamo Village, and they had a local test guy; he hired extras. 'Can you ride, can you drive a wagon, blah, blah, blah.' So I went in there and told him I wanted to be an extra and he looked at me and he said, 'Can you ride a horse? Well, we're looking for some tall guys like you that can ride a horse for some special roles, so can you grow your hair and beard, come back in two weeks and we'll see if you're chosen?'"[681]

"When I came back, we were informed that some special guys would be picked for parts, so about fifty or sixty of us–big, tall, cowboy types–were all standing in a line at Ft. Clark. John Wayne came out with an entourage and told us that (he) was going to pick out, I think, seventeen of us for a special part. He said that those who were not selected would still be used in the movie as extras. One day, wardrobe suited me up for an outfit on some backstreet in Alamo Village and here comes Duke. By the way, he was called Duke, never the Duke. Well, he said, 'I've got some good news and some bad news. The bad news is that the parts I had picked out for you are too important, so they'll be going to the actors. The good news is that you'll all still work in the movie.' Then he looked at me and said, 'All but you.' And he selected two other guys, Lee Allison who was from Rock Springs, and Slim Stevens from Bandera. We ended up as Crockett's Tennesseans."[682]

"Little" John Hamilton, Houston sentry: "In the winter of '47 is when (Wayne) came to my grandfather's ranch in Cuero (Texas). Wayne was in *The Flying Tigers*, and he (modeled his part after) Tex Hill. Hill was married to Dr. Sale's daughter in Victoria, and Dr. Sale and my grandfather Thornton were very close friends. So, when Tex went down to Victoria, Dr. Sale called my grandfather (and asked if they could visit). He said, 'Sure,' so they all came over; John Wayne and his two assistants. I met him when I was twelve-years-old. I was in the seventh-grade and let some of my friends in to meet him; they were all hypnotized. Wayne was a very close friend of ours for over thirty years. (When) I was twenty-four, he called me and said, 'I'm making this movie here in Texas in Brackettville. Why don't you come on out and maybe we can find a part for you?' He didn't even have anything planned for me or anything special. So he worked me in."[683]

*"Filming of the $10 million dollar Alamo movie starring John Wayne is due to start the first of next month and at least 300 extras are needed from Uvalde."*[684]

Robert Harris, extra: "It just so happens we had a farm out there (Brackettville). We raised vegetables. We had irrigation farms out there. And I heard that they were building the Alamo, so I went over there one day and saw these people, and they were building a fort and building a town down there, and this is way out in the middle of a ranch. I couldn't believe it. And they said, you know they're going to do pre-production. So I got a job doing pre-production (for six or seven months). My dad told me...I was out there driving a tractor, and he went out there where the guys were and said, 'Where's Robert?' (laughs.) And then he said, 'He said he's going to go over and work in a movie. He gave up the vegetable business.'"[685]

Robert Relyea, assistant director: "Around noon, the phone rang. 'Bob Relyea?' 'Yeah…' 'Hello,' the voice said. 'This is John Wayne.' 'Yeah. And I'm Attila the Hun,'" said Relyea as he slammed down the telephone. A moment later, the phone rang again. "'If you're done fucking around…I'm about to start the biggest picture ever attempted outside of Hollywood,' said Wayne. 'I understand that you're available. I'd like to talk to you about working with me.' 'Yes, sir,' Bob answered. 'When?' 'Now.'" The next day, Relyea left for Brackettville.[686]

*"Wanted. 300 Males, Mexican or Latin decent. Fine facial features. At least six feet tall, well built, confident. Must be able to ride well under trying circumstances. Thoroughly familiar with horses."*[687]

Marshall Jones, John Wayne's lighting stand-in: "I went out there, and, at that particular time, they weren't stopping you there at the entrance. You just went right on in. They were still actually working on (building) the Alamo at that time. Parked the car up there and walked around, fixin' to walk into the Cantina and here comes an old black Cadillac. It pulled around us and went on up there and the guy got out, and, for some reason, I had in my mind, Charlton Heston, but then I heard the Duke's voice. 'Hello there, pilgrim.' He suddenly walked towards us by himself, and he said, 'Howdy. How are you doing?' and I said, 'I'm down here to help ya, trying to get a job.' And he said, 'I'm going to need about two or three thousand more just like ya. Come on.' I went down there and just went in to where you sign up for being an extra and nothing had happened. I went down there actually about two or three weeks before the picture was actually going to be there, but I wanted to go down there. And that was it…they called me in there, and they said, 'How would you like to be John Wayne's stand-in?'"

"They had another fella; he had the Duke's clothes for the part he would wear, and I forget what the hell his name was. He was taller than the Duke. Duke was six-foot-four; I was six-foot-three, and this old boy was about six-foot-five or six-foot-six. Something like that. You had 'Boy's Town' in Acuña. And all the different whores from all over Mexico would come up to that town. This was a block of whore houses. I mean there was nothing like it. Anyway, this old boy loved it over there. Sometimes, it would take thirty minutes to go find him. He was asleep, and, a big picture like that, sometimes it takes an hour or more to set up the scene. I said, 'Hell, Duke, I'll do this.' 'Go ahead and do it,' said Duke. I didn't have a script at all. And I (replaced Duke's stand-in) two or three times, and it didn't take but about three times, and Wayne said, 'That's your job now, Marshall.' And they gave me all of Duke's clothes, and Wayne threw me the script and said, 'You learn my part.' And it was really that simple. At first, we did it with a little talking and doing the actual script, but that took too long. So I just went through the motions, and Duke would look through the camera (to see) how he was gonna look. 'Cause I would imitate his walk and all that sort of thing. And so I went through the scenes with the other actors, with Richard Widmark and Laurence Harvey and Denver Pyle. Denver (and I) became real close friends, and later on Denver said, 'Marshall, do you know how much money you're saving that man? Hell, you're on the ball all the time. You do an excellent job. You've probably saved Duke two to three hundred thousand dollars.'"[688]

Tommy Worrell, extra: "I went to Trinity University (on) an athletic scholarship. Big John Hamilton owned a Big John steakhouse there in San Antonio. And, of course, John Wayne was always visiting him there when he was in town. And we always ate at his steakhouse after our football games, the team did. And he (Hamilton) hired me and two or three other guys to do some landscaping for him and then he had, what we call an "ice house" which is a convenience store. In the back room, he had a couple of pool tables. We shot pool with him all the time. He always said, 'Well, you know, I'm going to get you boys in a movie, goin' to get you boys in a movie with John Wayne, you know?' When I got back to Texas, *The Alamo* had already started. So I went to Brackettville and went to the casting place, and, of course, they didn't have anything. Everything kind of (had) been cast. I asked about Big John if he was there and how to get a hold of him. So they made a couple phone calls, and anyway, they got me on. And I don't know how that came about. I don't know if Big John called John Wayne or talked to John Wayne or what the deal was, but, after telling me there were no positions, well, there were. They got me on as one of Jim Bowie's men. And so, that's how I got on."[689]

Jim Brewer, Travis man: "In August of 1959, I drove to downtown Austin to meet my boxing manager at the Red River Boxing Gym. We were going to Houston to watch the Roy Harris-Sonny Liston fight. As I approached the gym, I saw this extremely tall man leaning against a car. His profile looked like Karl Flenn. As I approached him, I realized it was Karl. I hadn't seen him in two years. He didn't have an Austin address, but he remembered that I was a boxer. He visited several gyms until he found the one in which I worked out in. Karl had a part in *The Alamo*, and he suggested that I meet him in Brackettville when I returned from Houston. I arrived in Brackettville about 1:00 a.m., drove into Ft. Clark, and slept in my car. The next day, I met Karl at the Gateway Hotel Café, and he took me over to meet Frank Leyva. Mr. Leyva told me to start growing a beard. In the meantime, Mr. Leyva had me meet John Wayne, and I suited out in a Mexican uniform. After my beard grew, Duke made me a Travis gun captain, gave me some lines, and that's how I began an acting career that is now going on fifty years."[690]

*"Wanted. Forty Anglos, males, unkempt in appearance; must be willing to let hair grow. Must be expert horsemen and familiar with the handling of rifles."[691]*

John Henry Daniels, *Happy Sam:* "(I) got involved with this movie because of my dad. He heard about the casting call and took us there about 4:00 a.m. My dad took me and my brother to Ft. Clark. I think it was the building across the street from the horse stables. I remember going upstairs, and there was Duke sitting behind a long desk. There were about twenty or thirty people in front of me in line, and I went to see Wayne by myself. He was sitting behind a large desk with the American flag and Texas flag behind him. 'What's your name?' he said. 'My name is John Henry Daniels.'" Duke raised his arm and jerked his thumb back to the flags. "'Well, John Henry. Do you see that?' 'Yes.' I replied. 'John Henry, can you say the pledge to the flag?' I recited the Pledge of Allegiance, and he said, 'John Henry, do you always smile like that?' 'I guess so,' I replied. Wayne said, 'Well, John Henry, you're going to be in the movies. We're going to change your name. Do you smile all the time?' I said. 'Yes.' There was another man in the office, and he took me outside and told everyone that the audition was over and that I got the part. He said, 'Go with that man, and he has the papers for you to sign.' I said, 'My brother is outside waiting for me.' Duke told the person that was there to go and get my brother. And have him sign papers also and that he would be a stand-in for me if I were to get sick or couldn't do my scene. This was after he saw that we looked alike, but my brother was a little taller than me. He called me *Happy Sam* because I smiled all the time." John Henry, second baseman on the Star Little League team, was forever known as Happy Sam in real life.[692]

David Kuykendall, extra: "In the summer of 1959, I was working in an oil field…and I was looking at the San Angelo paper, and it had an article, said they would have tryouts for Tennesseans on a particular (day) in August. It was at Ft. Clark guest ranch at Brackettville, and it was going to start at like one o'clock or two o'clock on Sunday afternoon. Well, I had a sister down in Laredo, and we were planning to be down there, and I told my mother, 'Well, we'll just come back by there.' I had been growing a beard all that spring, just for the fun of it, and we went to Laredo and we got back up there (Brackettville). It was just like one minute after time for that, and I got out of the car, walked around the building. And walked…just as soon as I went around the building, well, John Wayne was up on a porch with some of the others. He hollered, he said, 'Come right on up here. Yeah, you.' Scared me to death. So I came up to the porch. Well, I was picked number three."[693]

After the January 1958 meeting between the Texas Employment

Commission and Brackettville Enterprises, A.V. Bonnet and his staff began creating a card file on those who might be potential applicants. Quickly realizing that they would not be able to fill all employment demands from the local talent pool, they expanded their search to surrounding areas. In June 1959, after a two-week fact-finding trip by Frank Leyva and Tom Roselle, Batjac placed, at its own expense, bilingual representatives in Uvalde, Eagle Pass, and Del Rio to assist in the process. These individuals would also help in the transportation of extras to the film site. Word of the work opportunity quickly spread across the border to Mexico. When they learned the film company would pay extremely favorable wages to extras, hundreds of day-laborers would show up each day at the border, hoping to be selected. Buses would carry the lucky ones to the film site each morning, only to return to the border at the end of the day. Due to the high number of illegal "extras" looking for employment, it was necessary for the U.S. Border Patrol to increase its surveillance in and around the set. Batjac decided it was necessary to add additional security to assure the extras would perform as required.

Kuykendall: "...the time we wondered if things would get outta hand was when they brought all those braceros across the border. And brought them through the hills, and a bunch of us were hired as directors. We were hiding in different places, making sure those guys would go where they were supposed to go. Very few (of our) people could speak Spanish, so keeping them in line and keeping them moving and going like they're supposed to have gone...it was wild, man, it was really wild."[694]

Brackettville city councilman Tom Roselle served as the local personnel manager, with Nate Edwards responsible for Kinney County and Pat Paterson, located in Del Rio, responsible for Val Verde County. A separate list of applicants was made up of Laughlin Air Force personnel for a specific time when they would be available. Airman John Quinn recalled how he was able to be a part of the project: "Well, at the time I was assigned at the Air Force base down the road about thirty miles and one of my fellow airmen was a college classmate of Mike Wayne's. So we went out to see Mike one day, and Mike says, 'Why don't you guys get into costume? We need more Americans.' He and I took some leave from the Air Force, which John (Wayne) had asked the base commander if he could spare any guys; he needed more Americans on the set 'cause they had plenty of Mexicans. They had no way to house extras from Hollywood to start with, so they were relying on the local population pretty much. So we took Mike up on his invitation."[695]

Many individuals weren't really sure what roles they would play when they arrived on the set. For the most part, all the required extras were men but several women were called as were a few children. "I haven't heard any mention of the women who will be cast in the picture," said Shahan, "but I'm sure there'll be a number of them—it might be a little dull without any woman at all." Residents of Del Rio and Val Verde County were anxious to get into the act and arrangements for interviews with them were announced by Bonnet. The first order for 1,300 extras was placed by Nate Edwards in July 1959. Four hundred men were needed as cavalrymen and nine hundred as foot soldiers or in other roles. Bonnet and his staff sent out 1,140 call-in cards, of which 111 were for individuals who had already appeared in other films. Extras were not supposed to be interviewed on the set; in fact, individuals interested in appearing in the film were instructed to not even try and apply there. With production scheduled to begin the first week in September, it was imperative that the casting of extras be completed as soon as practicable. Each relatively sizable local community had been given a hiring quota including Del Rio, Eagle Pass, Carrizo Springs, and Uvalde, whose target was three hundred individuals. By late August, only 165 individuals had been identified, but Uvalde local Travis Kuykendall, who was taking applications, indicated that registrations were going strong and would continue until all positions were filled. Temporary offices were set up in the Tejas Theater as well as at Slade's Saddle Shop. Kuykendall took several applicants to Brackettville for consideration as Mexican officers. Other applicants were interviewed for the parts of Tennessee soldiers. In Del Rio, 275 individuals had applied by August 14. Of the seventeen "Tennessee types" needed, five had already been selected. Casting director Frank Leyva, son of Pancho Villa's minister of finance Con Leyva, interviewed quite a number of those registered. "I've got fifteen beautiful girls from San Antonio," he related, "who will appear in the cantina scene in the *Alamo*. Some of the cast will stay at the Ft. Clark guest ranch; some will stay at a motel near Brackettville, and some will be housed in Del Rio." However, most San Antonian applications weren't accepted. Leyva stated that, except for specialty parts, he was only interested in people from the surrounding areas. It wasn't a reflection on one's acting ability but rather a question of logistics. Local residents could go home in the evening, but San Antonians would have difficulty in finding a place to stay. And it really wasn't a lucrative profession; temporary at best, regular extras were paid $10 a day; those who could ride horseback made $12.50.[696]

> *"Wanted. Ten young females, good looking; flirtatious manner. Hurry."*[697]

Hilda Stillwater, extra: "I was about ten years old when they started recruiting townspeople. (The announcement for extras) was posted at the Post Office, I believe, and anybody that was interested, they needed men, women, children, and my dad took me, and they just looked at you, and they tell you, 'Okay, we need this little girl.' I think we took my brother but...he was not selected. (Nor were

her parents.) They would take us up in the morning at (the Gateway Hotel)...
and everybody would meet there. We had to be there by six in the morning...and
then by seven or so, we would leave to the Alamo Village, and then they would
serve us breakfast...but when we'd get there, we'd go to this area which was the
dressing room and they had this outfit, this wardrobe room that we were assigned
to, and I would go in there and put on my long dress and my bonnet, and there
were ladies that would tell you what clothes you were going to wear."[698]

*"Wanted. Twelve to eighteen Mexican women; long black hair. Must
weight over 160 pounds."*[699]

Maydelle Anderson, townsfolk: "At the time I was living in Eagle Pass. And,
and we heard about it (advertised) over there. And probably in the paper, the
local paper. The lady that was my age, she was probably a movie buff because
her family owned the, the movie picture business there... 'Cause she might have
heard. I really don't know how we found out, but I just remember her name was
Eve Schwartz, and she was the one that said, 'Let's go.' And the other ladies
said, 'Look, we wanna go too,' and so we just pooled our resources. We were in
our early thirties. (There were) two younger and two kinda little older. But they
were probably (in) their forties maybe. They were just older then Edith and I.
We drove back and forth (to and from the set.) Sometimes we drove early in
the morning and stay all day till dark. They had us sitting around doing all kinds
of stuff. So we were in different scenes, but we were just kinda hanging around.
That's what extras do mostly."[700]

Lucky as well, were Bud and Margenia Whistler of Del Rio. Married for
over sixty years, Bud had been a Val Verde County sheriff before he retired due to
failing eyesight. The pioneer couple decided to audition for roles in Wayne's film
as...pioneers. "We went to Brackettville before noon," recalled Margenia, "and
then about 2 p.m. we saw Wayne, since the casting people wanted his approval.
He talked to us, just as nice as anybody would want, and then those in charge of
casting told us they would notify us when to report."[701]

Stockton Briggle, later co-executive producer of the NBC miniseries *The
Alamo: 13 Days to Glory*, with Alec Baldwin, Raul Julia, James Arness, Brian
Keith, Lorne Greene, David Ogden Stiers, and Ethan Wayne, was also an extra.
According to Briggle, "(I) literally ran away from home" to act in the film. Of
course, he was twenty-four at the time he "ran away."

Jack Spain and Ron Lee, members of the Point Theater staff in Kerrville,
were signed as extras. They didn't know what their duties would be but were
told to report on September 7. "We hope to promote this into another film
job," they said. "Our chance may be pretty good since studios usually want to
see something you have done. This will be something for us to show them. The
professional experience we have gotten here in the Hill Country this summer will

also increase our chances in California. What we would really like to do is to get on permanently with Blackjack (sic). And all fan mail can be addressed to us in care of General Delivery, Brackettville." They even brought along their dog, Guy, who would appear in the street scenes.[702]

By August 22, while there were still plenty of roles for males yet to be filled, the full quota of sixty women had already been signed.[703]

*"WANTED: Girls with typing and knowledge of general office work. No dictation. John Wayne Motion Picture Company, Brackettville. Apply at BATJAC Administration building."[704]*

Bill Moody, Happy's close friend, owned Silver Lake Ranch in central Kinney County where some of the film's scenes were shot. The ranch stretched for thirty miles along the Rio Grande from Del Rio to Eagle Pass. "I thought (the film) was an excellent portrayal (of the battle)," said Moody. "I was one of Sam Houston's two aides. I had two lines, and they were cut." Local rancher Elmo Jones, a rider in Santa Anna's army, was also fortunate to be in the film. "Happy invited us to go to a barn dance," explained Jones. "During the dance, Michael Wayne asked if I knew how to drive a wagon." As he was just an old cowboy, Jones replied affirmatively. "We had a ball. They had great people (on the set). We got acquainted with all of them."[705]

Jerry Dickens was another extra in the film, but it took him longer to get there. Dickens read a newspaper article about Duke's planned film and the fact they were hiring locals to be extras. He immediately quit his Dallas job, packed his car, and headed off to Brackettville. Once there, he went to the casting office at Ft. Clark. Naturally, he was asked if he could ride. Once he learned regular extras made $8 a day while riders made $12, he replied, "I can ride." He was signed up as a riding extra and told it might be a few days before he got the callback, so just stay close to a phone. So, he waited, and waited, and waited. A week went by; he slept in his car, ate at a restaurant, and soon ran out of both money and gas. He would call the casting office each day, and each day got the same answer; "Nothing today. Maybe next week we'll have something." Finally, he hitchhiked a few hundred miles to visit his brother in Baytown, Texas. He stayed for three days, ate his fill, and left with $20 in his pocket to keep him in candy bars and Cokes for another week. Eventually, he received the callback he was waiting for and was hired as a Bowie man—except when he wore Mexican army uniforms for the large scenes.[706]

Susan Raney Stone, extra: "I was (a) ten-year-old and in the fifth-grade. That was when I got my Social Security number…and I think we got like $25 a day. And the bus would be at the school. It was not a school bus. I think it was something like a charter bus. But they would pick us up and take us out to the village. We would be out in front of the school at 7:45, and they would pick us up. I remember they would take us to the village, and I was so disturbed because we had to put on these old clothes, and I took my own shoes because I wasn't going to wear the shoes that they had. We got there in the morning, and we got dressed. I think the prerequisite was they wanted little girls with long hair. And I had one or two braids. Whenever they needed a child, they would come over the intercom and say, 'We need ten boys and ten girls on the street scene,' or 'six boys and six girls in the wagon.'"[707]

Once the cast and extras were identified, the next problem Wayne faced was the matter of lodging. In a town of less than 2,000 inhabitants, Brackettville just didn't have that many places where out-of-towners could stay. As a result, 342 permanent production members were housed at the 4,000-acre Ft. Clark Guest ranch. At one time, it was a self-contained town with its own power and water facilities, firehouse, theater, machine shop, garages, air strip, stables, offices, restaurant, and dining rooms. "Its barracks once housed hundreds of cavalrymen," Shahan boasted. "This fort is home of the largest natural spring-fed swimming pool in Texas." Two two-story cavalry barracks there were renovated, but, as they couldn't possibly hold enough members, Batjac funded the cost of additional rooms. According to reports, Batjac had to spend over $70,000 to revamp the fort's quarters, which didn't make comptroller Al Podlasky the happiest man in Texas. Numerous bungalows surrounding the parade grounds were also utilized. Extra Jerry Carlsen and three other individuals rented a house near Shahan's granary west of Brackettville, and many extras found housing in the surrounding area, including Spofford, which was only ten miles south of Brackettville. Wayne and his family stayed at the ten-bedroom Wainwright house along with daughter Toni, granddaughter Anita, and son-in-law Don LaCava. Michael, Gretchen Wayne, and their young daughter Alicia had their own living quarters at the fort as did Linda Cristal and Laurence Harvey and...John Ford, while Richard Widmark was a houseguest at the Shahan ranch. Ft. Clark's relatively spartan accommodations offered little in the way of luxury features. Wild deer and turkey roamed freely over the grounds. The scrub land outside of town was home to scorpions, tarantulas, and snakes. Extremely hot during the day, freezing cold at night, Southwest Texas could be brutal to those not accustomed to such climate.[708]

Tommy Worrell, extra: "There was no place to stay in Brackettville, Fort Clark, Del Rio, Uvalde, Hondo, anywhere. Some people were driving from San Antonio. From Eagle Pass, a hundred miles or so. The guy I was with, we ended up going and buying some crackers and chili, 'cause we had a little bit to eat at the commissary, but then we went out to a roadside park and spent the night. We were just laughing. Here, we were going to star in a John Wayne Western, and the next day we were sleeping in the park. But, anyway, we started the next day."

Joan O'Brien: "This dusty little town had one gas pump, one little café where they only spoke Spanish, and one movie house that only showed Spanish films. There was nothing to do in that town, and I went stir crazy. This shoot was long, laborious, and exhausting."[709]

Pilar Wayne: "...we were in the worst spot in the world in Brackettville, Texas...we lived there for four months. We had a real falling down house, and Duke was in the most nervous state of his whole career. There was nothing there but a square with a bunch of old rooms. But it was a fun picture in many ways with the whole family there together. I have nothing but happy memories of filming in Brackettville. My daughter was with me, my husband was finally seeing his dream come true, and all the Waynes seemed to be growing closer. Toni LaCava came to stay with us for a few days during the filming, and she and I were becoming friends. I got pretty bored. I looked after Aissa and got interested in photography. Duke's daughter Toni and I were the best of friends, so we used to go to San Antonio or Dallas once in a while. Brackettville was nothing, but the beauty of the setting and the horses and the pageantry were very rewarding."[710]

Hank Worden: "I had never been down to that part of Texas, and it was real interesting. We were out of Happy Shahan's ranch, where they had built a duplicate of the film. I never saw so many rattlesnakes in my life. I don't know what the official count was but maybe it was 9,880 per square mile."[711]

Frankie Avalon: "Oh, man. It was like I was in another planet. I was a street kid. I'm from the neighborhoods of South Philadelphia. When I got to the wide-open spaces of Texas, I didn't know where I was. I didn't know what to do. I'd never seen anything like that place. I had no idea. To be exposed to the elements of scorpions and skunks and rattlesnakes. I knew about rats. When we first got here, I thought this place was the dullest—one pool table, one ping pong set, and only one good radio station that you can barely get. You know, I think I'm beginning to understand what it's like to live in the country. It isn't so bad at all." Of course, maybe he was a bit confused as to where he was. In 1959, Avalon had two No. 1 songs: *Venus* and *Why*. While *Why* was generating increased sales, he said he couldn't take full advantage of its success: "While it was riding the chart, I was on location for four months in the middle of *Rackettville*, Texas, riding a horse."[712]

Linda Cristal: "So it was a little, it was, all there was, no entertainment, no place to go. There was a little cantina kind of place the men went to play billiards and I remember I had a rented car. We needed transportation because (of) the distances, you know? It was a huge place. I would go on the weekends sometimes, and have a little bit to eat all by myself. It was a very long time on the location. It was fun. It was like a visit to another planet. Pilar used to go, fly every weekend to San Antonio shopping and so forth, and she invited me several times, but it wasn't something I would have enjoyed...(it) was too social, you know?" To fill spare time, Linda would swim, play tennis, horseback ride, and play ping pong in the evening.[713]

Duke knew Pilar longed for companionship. When San Antonio native Karen Sharpe (amorous bride Nell Buck in *The High and the Mighty*) visited the set with her father, Duke asked if she would accompany Pilar shopping. "You know how they treat Hispanics," said Wayne. Sharpe agreed: "I said I certainly did understand. I could never stand Texas because it's such a reactionary place."[714]

Robert Relyea: "Wayne lived in the commander's house; the stunt guys had their own barracks. We all ate in the mess hall. But Ft. Clark was also a bit like a prison: the structure and its grounds practically made up our entire world for a year. The crew, which numbered over 480 during the height of filming, became so tired of seeing each other across the table three times a day, seven days a week, that nearly every night became 'fight night' in the mess hall."[715]

Chuck Roberson, Tennessean: "Most of the cast and crew stayed at the Fort Clark Guest ranch. It used to be an actual fort, and the rooms were like large dormitories. I kind of liked my privacy, so Jackie (Williams) and I rented a house in Brackettville with a young stuntman named Dean Smith. The new guys pretty much followed us older guys around to learn the ropes, but there were some things we just didn't see eye-to-eye on, like living arrangements and after-work relaxation. Most of us older guys felt that bringing wives on location was sort of like bringing a ham sandwich to a banquet. Dean Smith was a nice, clean-cut, All-American, Texas Baptist, and Jackie and I soon found out that though he shared our house, he would have no part of guests of the female variety that we brought home for supper. Of course, Jackie and I respected his privacy and let him go into the back bedroom and close the door, but even so, Dean was looking for a gracious way to bow out of the living arrangement."[716]

The publicity department's Tom Carlisle said most of the staff had to go to Mexico or San Antonio for entertainment because there was hardly anything to do in a town the size of Brackettville.[717]

Since extra Jim Brewer had no assigned place to stay, he spent the first week on location either sleeping in his car or under a bridge on Hwy 90 just outside town. Eventually he was given a temporary room at Ft. Clark next to Wayne, staying there two or three weeks. Brewer roomed with several electricians, grips, etc. He later moved to a small ranch house owned by Happy Shahan's brother-in-law, Frank Higgins, where he stayed until production ended.[718]

Linda Cristal: "They had rented a huge house for me. A big house, like thirteen rooms. I had thirteen rooms myself. But it didn't matter (to) me, just that it was so big. Thirteen rooms but it was okay. And, I was at one. I went to learn my lines, work on my accent, so it wouldn't be confusing, and rest because I needed to look, what I thought was important then. I needed to look beautiful. So that takes good sleep. I was alone in that house and one night, in the middle of the night, there was a strange smell, very strong, penetrating. And I thought, 'My goodness, there must be gas somewhere escaping.' So I ran in my nightgown out screaming, 'Help! Help!' And some of the people that had smaller areas to live in came out. And I said, 'There must be gas. It's going to explode. The house, blah, blah, blah.' And you know what it was? A skunk...a skunk had walked in. And the smell was unbelievable! I never smelled anything like that. I was so scared. But immediately I had to move out that night because it was impossible to sleep there."[719]

In addition to housing, obtaining, preparing, and delivering food to a crew of almost two thousand people can be a monumental logistical problem. On some film locations, suitable local food only occasionally may be found. But with a community the size of Brackettville, located in the southwest portion of Texas, providing thousands of meals was easier said than done. So Batjac relied on a catering company that specialized in offering the best food in a quick, efficient manner: Enter Rolly Harper.

Harper, ex-police lieutenant and native of Savannah, Georgia, created a million-dollar enterprise from an initial investment of only $125. After only ten years, he would provide more than 65% of all the food served to motion picture and television companies on location. Though some might think otherwise, the quality of food prepared was equal to what you could find in any fine restaurant. "I won't serve a bite that I wouldn't be glad to eat myself," said Harper proudly. He arrived in Brackettville on July 13 along with the advance production crew. With twenty-two waiters, five chefs, thirteen kitchen helpers and five drivers, they served over 160,000 meals! The grocery list would stun the average shopper: 349,000 eggs, 510,000 cups of coffee, 71,000 cups of bouillon, nine hundred gallons of ice cream, 980,000 slices of bread and rolls, 493,000 sweet rolls and donuts, 342,000 bottles of milk, 53,000 steaks, 24,000 pounds of roast beef, 18,000 pounds of ham, 6,800 pounds of bacon and sausage, and 12,500 pounds of chicken, turkey and pork. Four types of steak, veal cutlets, Mexican food, beef stew, fried shrimp, fish, Chinese dishes, and other delicacies filled out the daily menu. Exaggerating publicists said that caterers would provide up to 5,200 box lunches nightly, with as little as twenty-four hours' notice. Virginia Shahan swore she saw 3,300 box lunches being prepared every day for weeks. Not likely as there weren't anywhere near that number of people on location at any one time. Much of the food provided by local suppliers, bread came from San Antonio and dairy products from San Angelo. San Antonio's own Red Barefield, owner of the Select Meat Co., landed a juicy contract to supply the meat. Large walk-in refrigerator/freezers were shipped to Brackettville and erected near the mess tents. It was estimated it cost over $3,000 per day just to feed the cast and crew. According to Happy, "They fixed the food right on the ranch–mobile cooking. That was for cast, crew and extras on the set. For the cast and crew staying in Brackettville, the caterers fixed a kitchen at Ft. Clark where they fed them breakfast in the morning and dinner late at night when they got back."[720]

Of course to some, Harper's epicurean delights were less than satisfactory. Joan O'Brien: "The first day I arrived…in that place, they gave me officer's quarters, and I had two bedrooms and a kitchen and all this stuff. The first thing I did was walk down to the Olympic-sized swimming pool, and Laurence Harvey was down there. We introduced each other to each other, and the first thing he said to me was, 'Can you cook?' And I said, 'Yes, I can cook.' And he said, 'Well, the food here is terrible. Would you do some cooking for us?'" Of course, Wayne wasn't as particular. When asked where Duke's favorite eating places were, Happy replied, "where anybody was serving food."[721]

Harper's wasn't the only company providing food to the location. San Antonio's Martin Bakery delivered over 200,000 pastry items to cast and crew, and, as a special tribute, Martin also presented Wayne with a four-by-six-foot Alamo cake—an authentic replica of the original Alamo sculptured in Styrofoam and frosted with adobe-colored icing with caramel accents. This unique confection duplicated the mission and compound in minute detail complete with mounted cannons, covered wagons (!), hay troughs and even lizards and scorpions.[722]

# CHAPTER NINETEEN
# THE PEN IS MIGHTIER
# THAN THE SWORD

*In 1820 Moses Austin had requested permission from Spanish authorities to bring three hundred American families into Mexican territory. A vast land with unlimited opportunities, the country afforded colonists a second chance, a chance to leave behind whatever issues they may have had, a chance to fulfill their dreams. Rich soil, dense forests, and natural harbors drew adventurers and frontiersmen like bees to honey. Upon Austin's death the following year, his son Stephen continued his efforts under the empresario system, which allowed agents under contract the right to bring in American settlers. Mexico had encouraged immigration of colonists willing to become citizens under the constitution of 1824, which gave power to the individual states and provided for an elected president and congress. It also united Texas with the state of Coahuila under a provision that Texas could eventually become an independent state as its population increased. There were some, though, lawyers and land speculators, who realized profit could be made from a free Texas. As a result, colonists crossed the border in droves and concerns in Mexico about increased American influence grew in direct proportion to the rising population. In 1830, in an effort to stem this tide, Mexico passed the Decree of the Congreso General, which made it illegal for immigrants in adjacent border nations (read, the United States) to enter Mexico. In addition, it also assessed heavy custom duties on all U.S. goods to discourage trade, suspended existing empresario contracts and established Mexican garrisons to enforce the edicts. Although some of the more restricted provisions were later relaxed, this was a turning point in relations between American colonists and the Mexican government. But over time, fences were mended, so to speak. Laws were repealed that prohibited only native-born Mexicans from retail merchandising; Texan representation in the twelve-man state congress increased from one to three individuals; the English language was recognized for official purposes; trial by jury was established; and land was made easier to acquire. At a convention held on April 1, 1833, Texan delegates petitioned the Mexican government to repeal the previously established prohibition of immigration, extend the tariff exemption on necessities for an additional three years, and grant the right to establish Texas as an independent state in the Mexican confederation. Austin was sent to Mexico City to deliver the petitions and a newly drafted constitution. Santa Anna was initially receptive to many of the Texans' concerns, but personal correspondence confiscated from Austin suggested he was attempting to incite a revolution. As a result, he was subsequently incarcerated for almost a year, paroled, and then permitted to leave Mexico in July 1835.*

*After Santa Anna was elected, he promised to uphold the provisions of the 1824 constitution. The colonists then adopted the Turtle Bayou resolutions, repudiated president Anastasio Bustamante and declared their loyalty to Santa Anna and a federalist government. Federalists defended states rights, the right to bear arms, unlimited immigration into the country, and, to a limited extent, slavery. Centralists supported a stronger national government, unencumbered by state limitations. However, after he took office, Santa Anna immediately changed from Federalist to Centralist. He then packed the Mexican Congress with members of the military and clergy. When Zacatecas and Coahuila y Tejas challenged his authority to disarm their militias and disband the legislature, Santa Anna sent troops to quell the uprising.*

*Texan colonists were protesting taxation without representation, the quartering of troops, civil law enforced by the military, trial by military tribunal rather than jury, and a lack of religious freedom. They were rugged, self-reliant, independent individuals, accustomed to self-government and thus resented the heavy-handed authority wielded by a centralist regime. From a Mexican perspective, the colonists were invaders who settled on Mexican land and swore allegiance to Mexico but refused to abide by its rules. Each side considered the other inferior. There also is no doubt some came to Texas solely for the promise of land grants. The Texas revolution "officially" began October 2, 1835, with a skirmish in Gonzales between local townspeople and Mexican soldados intent on seizing the town's cannon. The following day, the Mexican congress stripped the states of authority, voided the constitution of 1824, and created a centralist dictatorship. A skirmish at Goliad (in which the volunteer Texas army captured a small Mexican garrison) and the battle of Concepcion (in which Jim Bowie and a ninety-two-man scouting party were attacked by four hundred Mexican troops) quickly followed. In November 1835, a declaration of causes explained that Texans did not initiate revolution for the purpose of seeking independence but rather as Mexican citizens fighting to restore the provisions of the 1824 constitution voided by Santa Anna. A provisional Texan government had been established and a regular army created with Sam Houston in command. Although Texas supported the constitution, it reserved the right to secede if constitutional rules could not be restored with Mexico.*

*Santa Anna's brother-in-law, General Martin Perfecto de Cos, arrived in San Antonio to restore order and fortify the Alamo. In early December 1835, after a prolonged siege, Texan militia and regular army soldiers assaulted Bexar. Five days later, the Mexican forces surrendered, and Cos and his troops were paroled, promising never to fight again against Texans or interfere with the restoration of the 1824 Mexican constitution. Col. James Neill was placed in command of the retaken fortress, although Jim Bowie and William Barret Travis eventually assumed joint command following Neill's departure.*[723]

PATRICK FORD COMPLETED HIS VERSION OF THE *ALAMO* SCRIPT IN SEPTEMBER 1948, but, regrettably, the power struggle between Wayne and Yates precluded its filming at the time. Over subsequent years, others would fine-tune the script, Yates would dangle a carrot in front of Wayne, and Duke would continue to crank out films and search for possible locations to film his dream. Announcements were made, timing revised, delays incurred, and behind it all, Yates's machinations: scheming, cajoling, promising but never delivering. His reluctance to finance the project was partially due to Wayne's grandiose expectations: elaborate sets and a cast of thousands. In leading Wayne to believe Republic would raise the necessary funds, Yates bought precious time—time to utilize Wayne's talent, time to cash in on his popularity, time for an endless stream of B-features.

Wayne brought James Edward Grant on board the project in the mid-1940s. After he arranged to have Republic hire Patrick Ford in 1948, Wayne assigned the young writer the task of reviewing Alamo-related material Grant had previously amassed. Sent to Texas to interview J. Frank Dobie, Ford was asked to write a synopsis on the Alamo. After a time, Ford felt his efforts were fruitless as none of his research was showing up in Grant's script. Yates tried time and again to fire Ford, but Wayne always stopped him. Taking advantage of a six-week, out of town trip by Duke, Yates finally was successful, telling Wayne he did it because the writer "wasn't doing anything." Ford was livid; when Wayne offered him screen credit on another film, Patrick turned him down flat: "No, you got me fired once." "What? I got you fired?" Wayne replied incredulously. "You goddamn idiot! I kept you working for three years and never told you the truth!" In later years, Ford still resented both Wayne and Yates, referring to Wayne's *Alamo* film as "very bad, much overwritten and over-produced." He alleged he was promised sole screenplay credit, appointment as an associate producer, and $15,000 if Wayne ever made the film. However, in a letter Dan Ford (Patrick's son) wrote to this author, he stated, "I'm sure he would have gone to the writer's guild if he felt he deserved a screen credit." Patrick never did, but apparently thought he wrote a treatment of what he believed the *Alamo* should be.[724]

By late 1952, Duke had had enough and split with Republic after an extremely acrimonious meeting with Yates; their feud would continue over the next two years. Wayne felt he owned the *Alamo* script as he had paid Ford's salary while Pat was employed by Republic. But Yates considered the script his intellectual property as it was created when Ford and Grant were under contract to the studio. Wayne offered to buy the script; Republic rebuffed him. Bob Newman, future Batjac president, offered to accept the script as a bonus while working at Republic. Knowing Newman was a friend of Wayne's, Yates refused and even hired another writer to massage the script in an attempt to entice Wayne back to Republic. After reading the new version, Duke flatly rejected it. Eventually, Yates produced the Alamo project just for spite.[725]

After Wayne left the studio, he was virtually back to square one on *The Alamo*. Independent but desperately needing funds, Duke began to work at a feverish pace. While Wayne traveled the globe, Grant began to work on the script yet again. All the work, all the research, all the revisions, lost to Yates, but not the vision. "By now our ideas about it had begun to grow," confessed Grant. "We saw it as more than a one-star picture. Historically, it had three major parts in it—Travis, the aristocratic South Carolina gentleman who commanded the garrison; Bowie, the tough, hard-drinking, knife fighter who hated Travis; and Crockett, older than both, and already a legend. Each one of these parts had meat in it for a big star." So, yet another script was developed. "I think it was my fourth full-length version," he continued. Taking advantage of the opportunity to start fresh, he significantly modified his approach. An earlier version of the script consisted of only 277 scenes on 107 pages. Long on humor and short on content, the characters spoke like country bumpkins; backwoods witticisms peppered the dialog for no appreciable purpose other than an attempt to show the characters were "common men." As it was lacking in Ford's previous treatment, so was an explanation for the battle missing in Grant's. A lengthy 310-word preamble attempted to explain the reasons but was eliminated in later versions. Supporting characters' names were changed: Bub became Cotton; Lupita became Graciela Lopez (Chela); Bee-Hunter became Beekeeper; and Thimblerig simply became the Gambler. Without the benefit of a back-story, we see Crockett and his twenty-two Tennesseans view the Alamo for the first time as Juan Seguin and his son Rafael approach the main gate with news of Santa Anna's approach. Later, the Tennesseans visit the Cantina, and Crockett confronts Emil Strauss. Informed by Chela that there is gunpowder in the church bell tower, Crockett et al. kill Strauss, liberate the munitions, and deliver them to the Alamo. Also in this version, Crockett romanced Chela and asked her to write a letter. The next morning, the Tennesseans convinced Crockett they should defend the Alamo. Bowie and Travis continued their disagreement. The Mexican Army arrived and presented the defenders with an ultimatum. Travis responded with a cannon shot.

With an epic the size Wayne contemplated, three major roles meant three major stars. And even more funds. Slowly, but surely, the project began to generate its own momentum.[726]

Wayne was particularly struck by Grant's writing, which combined colorful Western language with a good dose of moralizing. But he could also be erratic, full of clichés, with stock characters devoid of emotion and interminably long proselytizing passages. Despite those flaws, Wayne was convinced Grant wrote his best dialogue and understood exactly what his fans expected. In fact, one could say Grant created, in large part, Wayne's screen persona. Of course, he had a skewed view of what that meant. According to Grant, all Wayne needed was a "hoity-toity dame with big tits that Duke can throw over his knee and spank, and a couple of jerks he can smash in the face every five minutes." But Grant also had a very succinct view of the whole Alamo story: "It was an American land grab, pure and simple," he said. Liberated from Grant's scripts, however, Wayne could deliver extraordinary performances as evidenced in *The Searchers*.

Sadly, at this time, Grant believed Wayne was involved in several projects Grant passionately disapproved of. So much so that he sold out his partnership in Batjac and parted ways with Wayne. Wayne, his longtime, card-playing, chain-smoking, drinking buddy. Grant never disclosed what the disagreements were over, but, concurrently, he joined Alcoholics Anonymous. Many were the nights when the two had gotten absolutely hammered, with no memory the next morning. But Duke felt a man who couldn't hold his liquor wasn't worth a damn. And when Grant joined AA, just as Pappy Ford had shunned Wayne years earlier for no apparent reason, so did Wayne shun Grant. It would be years before the two reconciled. An actor brought to his first AA meeting by Grant recalled, "I have never seen AA affect a man as it did Jimmy. When he was drinking, he was a noisy, overbearing, brash Irishman. When he became sober and changed his ways, he became the total opposite. Now he was soft-speaking. He was kind. He was considerate of your feelings. Hell, he became an all-around decent guy. But I think Duke missed his drinking company. It's hard to be around a guy who isn't drinking when drinking is still an important part of your life."[727]

In the interim, Grant remained busy by developing scripts: *Ring of Fear*, *The Last Wagon*, *Three Violent People*, and *The Proud Rebel*. He spent much of his time on his J–Tumbling–J ranch in Winton, California, in the San Joaquin Valley, and, in 1958, received an Academy Award nomination for *The Sheepman*, starring Glenn Ford and Shirley MacLaine. Though temporarily estranged, so to speak, Wayne still sought his advice and, in 1958, welcomed Grant back from his journey through the desert with a telegram: "Come Home Immediately. Ready To Start *Alamo*." At the time, Grant was in Spain trying to convince Ava Gardner to appear with Errol Flynn, Tyrone Power, and Mel Ferrer in *The Sun Also Rises*. Instead, Grant hopped the next plane back to the States. Dusting off his previous work, Grant began anew: "We spent ten years research on this film, and I personally spent $25,000 of Batjac money with research teams. We combed the

Library of Congress, the Mexican National Archives, everything we could find. Duke and I bought every book available on the Alamo. This thing is bound to be authentic."[728]

Movies mirror the traits society values and reflect the culture of their times, as they see it. Not only do they reflect, they also effect cultural change. By its very nature, every movie conveys a message through the mere act of telling a story; some subtle, others, not so. The significance of which can vary depending upon the genre. Movies are viewed as unconsciously reinforcing basic cultural patterns and influencing and directing these patterns through films that affect audience behavior.[729]

Films about the Alamo, while having little to do with historical facts, do shape the way we view the encounter. *The Immortal Alamo*, released May 25, 1911, was the earliest film version of events surrounding the famous battle. Little more than a melodramatic tale about the relationship between Almaron and Lucy (Susannah) Dickenson played against a background of the historic battle, the ten-minute silent film was advertised as "1,000 feet of realism." In this version, Lt. Dickenson, assuming the role usually associated with Jim Bonham, departs the Alamo to deliver a plea for aid to Gen. Houston, leaving his wife Lucy behind. After the fall of the Alamo, Navarre, a Mexican spy, lusts after the beautiful Lucy and plans to possess her. Dickenson appears in the nick of time and kills the would-be usurper. Francis Ford, older brother of John Ford, was cast in the role of Señor Navarre.[730]

In 1914, *The Siege and Fall of the Alamo* was released, in addition to *The Fall of the Alamo*. Unfortunately, little is known about either film, and they have been lost to the ages, though a synopsis of *Siege* written for copyright registration suggests the film was a fairly decent attempt at historical accuracy. Consisting of five reels, it qualifies as the first full-length Alamo film. The following year, D.W. Griffith was credited with releasing *The Martyrs of the Alamo*, a/k/a *The Birth of Texas*, a thinly veiled attempt to capitalize on his previous extremely controversial yet cinematically brilliant, *The Birth of a Nation*. *Nation*, blatantly racist, reflected "widely-held and generally acceptable white views." The film represented how racist a white American could be in 1915 without even realizing it. In *Martyrs*, the message was similar. Mexican troops are shown in stereotypical fashion, displaying disrespect toward white men and mindless lust for white women with only a single goal: total destruction. Women's bodies often allegorically stand in for territory, and the integrity of both must be protected from invaders. Mexicans and Americans are depicted on the opposite ends of the spectrum morally and temperamentally. Santa Anna is portrayed as a dictator, ignoring the 1824 constitution. Texans are shown as liberty-loving Americans who, denied their rights, fight for independence. As in previous films, the main focus is on

Dickenson and his wife. A second couple, Silent Smith and his girlfriend, serve to nicely tie up loose ends. Hidden passages, a buckskin-clad Travis and a "shameful orgy" are added for effect. The film does include a fairly exciting extended battle sequence and is the first film to show survivors being brought before Santa Anna to be executed. (It could be said the Mexican army even symbolizes the German aggressors we would soon face in World War I). A review in the *Waterloo Evening Courier and Reporter* stated, "(Griffith) has made careful research into the history of the Mexican revolution and has followed in the working out of every historical detail available." Although the following comments from pioneering social worker Jane Addams refer to *Nation*, they also equally apply to *Alamo*: "(you) can use history to demonstrate anything when you take certain of its facts and emphasize them to the exclusion of others."[731]

Anthony J. Xydias's Sunset Productions twice attempted to tell the story of the Alamo: *With Davy Crockett at the Fall of the Alamo* (1926) and *Heroes of the Alamo* (1937). Author Frank Thompson correctly noted the Crockett film was "slipshod and superficial," and "aimed at the lowest standards of a juvenile action audience." Part of a series of small-budget dramas based on historical characters, the film focused on the frontiersman's life, culminating in his death at the Alamo. With the story couched in a narrative by a grandfather to a young boy, the following tells all you need to know about the film: "Gee, Grandpa, they didn't give up, did they?" Grandpa turns toward the camera and replies, "No, son. They didn't. For they were AMERICANS!" One reviewer wrote at the time, "In all my years of reviewing and passing on the merit of pictures, I have never seen any role more ably handled, nor any historical character more accurately portrayed. It is a stupendous production...." Another reviewer claimed "A complete reproduction was made of the Alamo for filming and is authentic in every detail." One wonders what film this reviewer actually saw.

Eleven years later, Xydias remade the silent film as *Heroes of the Alamo*. Constrained with a limited budget, he interspersed action scenes from his previous film with new footage. Nevertheless, combined with inadequate direction and amateurish acting, the miserly attempt failed to improve the film's quality. Rather than focus on Crockett, attention now centered on the Dickinsons, Almerian and Anne, and their attempts to preserve home and family. Observed Thompson, "this attitude...had a lot to do with the prevailing mood of the country. The United States had not entirely emerged from the disastrous Great Depression when the film was produced and released... The Dickinsons, like a Depression-era family, personify the hopes and fears of the greater society. Sadly, this message was lost in the low-budget, clumsy production."[732]

A recently discovered, heretofore lost film, *The Alamo, Shrine of Liberty* (1938), was barely fifteen minutes long. The two-reeler was almost certainly filmed for educational purposes with an interesting combination of fact and fiction. Numerous historical characters were present though the Dickensons are called Dickersons. In addition to the final assault, the film included Santa Anna's offer to adopt Angelina Dickerson and the execution of five Texians.[733]

Though devoting a mere five minutes to the battle of the Alamo, Republic Studio's treatment in *Man of Conquest* (1939) was fairly accurate. The film was the studio's costliest effort to date, with an extensive/expensive advertising campaign: a million-dollar effort to find its way out of the shadow of B-picture mediocrity and into the majors. An impressive effort for such a small studio; stock footage of action sequences would show up in other Republic features for years. *Conquest* dealt with the career of Sam Houston from early stages of his life to the governorship of Tennessee and his ill-fated marriage to Eliza Allen, Cherokees, the Alamo and the battle of San Jacinto. Guinn Williams, who would later appear in Wayne's project, was initially slated to play Deaf Smith, but was replaced by Max Terhune. Frank Nugent of the *New York Times* wrote the film "cunningly justifies the revolution in Texas and its subsequent annexation by the United States as a victory of democracy over dictatorship...good old homespun philosophy which sanctifies a cleverly staged land-grab and charitably ignores— or blames on white renegades—the bilking of the Cherokees and the scrapping of their treaties." Sam Woolford of the *San Antonio Light* was a bit more pointed: "...history in spots is warped for plot purposes. The reason for this finally came out when I learned that one of the mainstays of the staff in preparing the film story was a book by George Creel (*Sam Houston: Colossus in Buckskin*) who was a Democrat of some sort whose job it was at one time to keep the truth out of the newspapers. He is still succeeding in films. May I suggest that the next time a historic picture of Texas is made that part of the million dollars be spent for another book...Amelia Williams's thesis contains practically all that is known about our mission and its tragic day."

(Williams? Really? At one time, her doctorial dissertation *A Critical Study of the Siege of the Alamo and of the Personnel of Its Defenders* was probably the most cited secondary source found in articles and books on the Alamo. However, although extensively researched, it has been found to be fraught with inaccuracies, distortions, and fabrications.)[734]

The 1950s saw a veritable torrent of films about the Alamo: *The Man from the Alamo* (1953), *Walt Disney's Davy Crockett at the Alamo*, and *The Last Command* (1955). Each took a different approach to the subject; each was successful in its own way. Starring Julie Adams, Hugh O'Brien, Chill Wills, and Glenn Ford as John Stroud, the 1953 film told the story of a man, chosen by lot, who left the Alamo to defend his friends' families only to be branded a coward. Director Budd Boetticher did an admirable job capturing the chaos inside the Alamo, but the back-story was just a mechanism to move the story along. Ford's son Peter suggested that the film was "based on a true story about a man who leaves the legendary Texas fort...in order to warn his family and other townspeople about an imminent attack." Sadly, that wasn't true. It is true that Wayne and John

Ford protested Universal's use of the word *Alamo* in the title as they had already registered the title *The Alamo*. After the matter went to arbitration, they conceded they did not have exclusive right to the word.[735]

Broadcast on February 23, 1955, *Davy Crockett at the Alamo* was the third in a series of five television programs about the famous adventurer. Aired on Walt Disney's *Disneyland,* Crockett and friend Georgie Russel search for adventure and eventually find it at the Alamo, defending freedom and liberty. Carefully avoiding the true reason for the conflict, the duo is instead shown traveling to Texas to help "Americans in trouble." Stephanie Blackburn, daughter of producer Tom Blackburn, stated that while a stickler for accuracy, her father would bend the truth if need be: "It had to be a good story first! Beyond that he wanted things to be as authentic as they could be. He took basic historical facts—the Indian war, Congress, the Andy Jackson relationship, the Alamo—and then probably made the decision to distort them a little to make it a good story." Disney did more than anyone to mythologize the legend of Crockett. In an interview on the two-disc DVD *Davy Crockett* collection, popular culture historian Paul F. Anderson suspects that "the Crockett show was perfectly timed to capture Cold War ideology: the character's ability to traverse cultural borders (as an "explorer" figure), the parallel between Crockett's restlessness and Americans' desire for social mobility, and the growing need for consumer gratification (the "fad" as a means to show one's affluence). But perhaps most of all, the Crockett craze satisfied our communal need in the 1950s for an American mythos. An extreme simplification of the battle, *Davy Crockett at the Alamo* was a reaffirmation of American values: life, liberty, independence."[736]

Filmed in color, the program was originally broadcast in black and white. Although different Peter Ellenshaw matte paintings combined with constructed set pieces gave the impression of a much larger compound, only two walls were actually built: the South and West Walls. Gathering information from the Disney Studio research library, the Los Angeles library, the American Institute of Architecture and the DRT Library, art director Marvin Davis recalled how the set was constructed: "It was as close as I could make it. A few alterations were required because we didn't have the size and space of the actual Alamo to do it in, but, as far as the details and the feeling of it, it was quite accurate. The fort was built all the way around, so we could shoot it in any direction. We built the upper level of the fort, the interior cells and the offices, the commander's office—everything—where they would be in the actual fort. That way, when you were filming someone coming down the steps, you could actually follow them all the way down and right into the commander's office, or jail cell, or whatever. This gave it a pretty good sense of realism rather than separating it as they usually do on a motion picture." As the structure was built on a sound stage, painted backdrops were used to simulate the surrounding countryside. Davis continued: "The challenge was to make it realistic, because it was only twenty-five feet from the fortress wall. In some places, we had perspectives where a particular scene might not hold for very long. So we would have maybe a caravan of mules or something painted on the background. Then for the next scene, we would put some shrubbery in front of it. That's how we were able to get some variety." Ironically, footage of a nighttime artillery barrage from *The Man from the Alamo* was edited into the final program. Given a limited budget ($700,000 for three television episodes was outrageously expensive at that time), Davis was forced to use various techniques to simulate both the compound and the attack; he succeeded admirably.[737]

At six-feet-five, Sterling Hayden was significantly taller than the average actor; at that height, he was even taller than the average basketball player. Signing with Paramount in 1940, he broke his contract and enlisted in the Marines under the pseudonym "John Hamilton." After graduation from Officers Candidate School, he was commissioned a second lieutenant and transferred into the OSS as an undercover agent. During World War II, he assisted Yugoslavian partisans in their fight against the Wehrmacht. Running guns, rescuing downed Allied pilots, and smuggling supplies into occupied territory as well as parachuting into Croatia to conduct guerilla activities earned him a Silver Star as well as a citation from Marshal Tito. Tito's greatest accomplishment during the war was the organization of perhaps the most effective resistance movement in the history of communism. While resisting the Axis forces, he embarked on a communist revolution. His forces proceeded to destroy the class structure, destroy the old social and economic order, and lay the foundation for a postwar communist state system. Enamored by their passion, Hayden briefly joined the Communist party in 1946, only to resign after six months. He admitted, "It seems to me the people in the Party not only know what's going on in the world but they have the guts to determine a course of action, and furthermore they're able and willing to implement this action...In Yugoslavia...when the going got rough and it was time to be counted, it was the Communists who stood up and fought." Hayden later revealed in sworn congressional testimony he had been a covert agent for the Communist Party with the specific mission to swing the Screen Actors Guild to join up with the painters union. (Undercover Communists had seized control of a painters union, formed a larger umbrella group with cartoonists, readers, secretaries, and publicists and called a jurisdictional strike, with the goal of taking over other unions. He admitted, "You know, I don't know why I got out of the Party any more that I know why I joined. I could say a lot of things about those people I knew in the Party—and you know something? It would all be good. I never heard anything that was subversive.") Because of this prior affiliation, Hayden was blacklisted in 1950 and was unable to work in Hollywood for six months. Wanting to make a private statement regarding his communistic ties, he privately contacted the FBI but was subsequently forced to testify in public before the HUAC, naming names with great reluctance and guilt. He later recalled, "I don't think you have the foggiest notion of the contempt I have had for myself since the day I did that thing."[738]

In *The Last Command*, Hayden filled the role of Bowie, a larger than life character. Hayden hoped that this "flag-waver" would placate Hollywood for his earlier brush with Communism. Interestingly, his co-star was Richard Carlson who played Travis. A journeyman actor in both film and television, Carlson at that time was starring in *I Lead 3 Lives* as a pacifist who, in 1939 joined an anti-war group and agreed to spy on the Communists for the FBI; hence, he was a Communist, FBI agent, and Communist counter-spy. Carlson/Travis would constantly demand that Hayden/Bowie make up his mind and take a stand.[739]

Rushed into production and filmed in just forty-two days between March 1 and April 11, 1955, *The Last Command* was a partial remake of *Man of Conquest*. Where the earlier film focused on the exploits of Sam Houston, *The Last Command* concentrated on Jim Bowie, the struggle for Texas independence and the fall of the Alamo. In the film's publicity material, director Frank Lloyd stated his view concerning the use of fiction in the making of films based on fact: "The addition of fiction to fact is permissible and often dramatically desirable so long as the fiction does not contradict the fact, but is presented as a logical and reasonable development. It is the perversion of facts, not their augmentation that destroys authenticity."

This Alamo set was constructed on the Louis Hobbs ranch five miles south of Brackettville. Its $50,000 pre-fab walls were manufactured in six-foot sections at an abandoned fire station at Ft. Clark. Made of wood, chicken-wire and plaster (all supplied by Shahan's Shaker Feed and Lumber), the hollow structures were built to simulate mortared limestone. However, the compound only consisted of two walls (the South Wall and about 150 feet of the West Wall), a false front representing the southernmost end of the Long Barracks complete with "a peculiar tower", a low wall connecting the Long Barrack section to the Low Barrack, and a twelve-foot high palisade with cannon port. Rather than include the church, a part of the façade of the church and the ruined interiors were painted backdrops. The upper half of the church is a poorly executed matte painting. In addition to the matte painting, a part of the facade was "constructed" on the soundstage later. This was the doorway entrance piece immediately framing the shot of the interior "painted backdrop." While a decent attempt was made to explain the reason for the Texas rebellion, *Command* ended up nothing more than a good B-western: better than most but not what Wayne had in mind. Chuck Roberson, who was also in *Command*, gave a less than rousing endorsement, "I was on the picture, and it was just like any other quickie Western Yates made." Cast member Ernest Borgnine seconded Roberson comments, "No, you never thought of it as an 'A' film if Republic was doing it. They mostly did Westerns and such. Frankly, we were paid our money and didn't care if it was A, B, C, or D. But that's how it was in those days." (*Last Command was Republic's most expensive picture ever at a negative cost of $2,193,939. For additional information on any of the aforementioned Alamo films, Frank Thompson's excellent book "Alamo Movies" is highly recommended.)*[740]

The story of the Alamo has a universality that transcends geographic boundaries. Films about that subject reinforce traditional values. Courage, heroism, and self-sacrifice are traits known and admired by individuals in all societies. Moviegoers are generally given the type of films they come to expect and accept. At Republic, these were action-packed, unpretentious melodramas, heavy on entertainment, and light on character or plot development; the studio's credo was speed, economy, and profits. Pat Ford's treatment of the story for Wayne fit the bill precisely. Condensing a thirteen-day siege into six days, he spent little time developing character personalities or rationalizing their actions. He assumed audiences already knew the story as well as the underlying reasons for the conflict and were only waiting for action sequences before the final, heroic ending.

Historical accuracy was sacrificed for plot development: "Crockett and eleven fellow Tennesseans are chased into the Alamo by a Mexican patrol. Travis and Bowie exhibit intense animosity toward each other, including an accusation of cowardice, but Crockett intervenes. Secondary characters are introduced with little, if any, background. A continual cannonade bombardment results in defenders capturing enemy cannon. Lupita, Crockett's eventual love interest, is introduced. Numerous vignettes of life inside the Alamo are presented. Defenders respond to cannonade and run out of powder. Miraculously, buried barrels of powder are uncovered in the compound. The following day, defenders raid camp, steal horses, and stampede cattle through village. After being accused of insubordination, Bowie decides to leave. That evening, all get drunk, Crockett talks Bowie out of departure. Day four, birthday party, thirty-two men from Gonzales arrive. After wild dance, Mexican musician and defender get into a fight over Lupita, Crockett escorts her from the Alamo. That evening, Crockett and several Tennesseans enter the Cantina in San Antonio, drink, play piano, and dance. Cantina dancers donate petticoats for bandages. The following day, after a messenger arrives with news that Fannin is not coming, Travis scratches a line in the sand and asks all to cross. Day 6, the final battle. Three assaults, all the defenders die. Mrs. Dickinson leaves with children. "The Eyes of Texas" play [sic] loudly in the background." Episodic with stereotypical Mexican womanhood portrayed as flirtatious vixens, Ford wrote of hellcats, men's primordial passion, Tennessee sipping whiskey and selfishness. Very little of the aforementioned historical rational appeared in Ford's treatment.[741]

Though several verifiable individuals are found in the treatment—Robert Evans, master of ordnance; Green B. Jameson, chief engineer; and Amos Pollard, chief surgeon—Ford paid scant attention to historical detail. Fictitious romantic relationships, multiple cannon and cattle raids, surreptitious nocturnal adventures and a distortion of events led to nothing more than a "B" Western. In a letter to Brigham Young University in 1980, Ford stated that he took the characters and general course of events in his treatment from David Crockett's autobiography: "During the siege, (Crockett) continued making notes in his diary. The day before the fall of the Fortress one of his men chose to desert—this man, Moses Rose, carried Crockett's diary and Travis's formal report with him. (The) diary was the property of the Rose family until sometime in the early 1940s when it was given to J. Frank Dobie... He loaned the original to me."[742]

This purported diary, published in 1836 as *Col. Crockett's Exploits and Adventures in Texas*, was actually a compilation of letters, newspaper accounts, and the vivid imagination of Richard Penn Smith, who crafted the document. Supposedly, the journal was confiscated by Mexican Genl. Castrillon after the frontiersman perished, and was subsequently liberated by Charles T. Beale, a Texas soldier at San Jacinto. Beale, recuperating from his wounds, urged Alex J. Dumas, Esq. to see the manuscript into print. Dumas would later write a preface in the 1845 reprinting. In reality, the work was commissioned by Philadelphia publishers Edward L. Carey and A. Hart to capitalize on the nation's interest in Texas and help sell their overstock of Crockett's ghostwritten *An Account of Colonel Crockett's Tour to the North and Down East*. Though few episodes from the "diary" appeared in Ford's treatment, it did allow for the introduction of several fictional characters, including Thimblerig the gambler, and Bee-Hunter. They would later appear in Walt Disney's *Davy Crockett at the Alamo* and Wayne's film but in slightly different persona.[743]

Ford's work was identified as #1746. This number was assigned once a project was green-lighted by the studio and followed it throughout all periods of preproduction, production and post-production. Ford truly believed that all of Crockett's volunteers, as well as the ex-slave Sam, were actual historical characters—after all, they had appeared in Crockett's journal. However, he also theorized Crockett could have invented them for convenience. Nevertheless, he chose to include them in his treatment. A *screenplay* is a general term for what a screenwriter writes. A *synopsis* is an eight-, ten- or twenty-page description of the story. A *treatment* is an expanded version of a *synopsis*, but without much dialogue and no scene division (usually). Still, this script reads, feels, and is scene-divided like a shooting script that hasn't been numbered yet. It is almost as if Ford wrote it as a production script on his typewriter in linear form but was leaving it to the secretary to transform into proper and specific script format.[744]

Neither a historian nor versed in the ways of academia, Ford wasn't particularly familiar with the state of Alamo research when he developed his treatment. Obviously, he took certain liberties with the story in order to elicit proper audience response. "I didn't go out and write an original script," confessed Ford. "I mean, we went out and wrote a story, like the thing…on 'The Alamo.'" Ybarra felt the original story of *The Alamo* was written by Ford: "…a typical Republic Pictures script, you know. That isn't what Wayne wanted. Wayne wanted the basics of the actual happening, which in the original script, was there." In all probability, Ford worked with the research, Grant wrote the script. But Ford did try to explain why the defenders were there with the following dialog:

"Mind if I ask you a question?"

"Go ahead."

"Why are you here?"

"Oh…I dunno. To fight, I guess. For liberty. Texas. Right of man. You know.…"

"Yeah, that's not it."

"Sure it is."

"No. You're here because you're running away from something. Don't get sore. You're not the only one. It's the same with all of us. Some of us are running from liquor, or women, or boredom, or old age. Or ourselves. War's just a good excuse."[745]

Since Wayne had hired Ford to write a synopsis on the Alamo based on the information Grant had already compiled, the question remains: did Ford create the treatment based on Grant's efforts, or did Grant subsequently develop the script based on Ford's ideas? Popular myth stated that, after Wayne left Republic, Yates filmed *The Last Command* based on the script Grant was forced to leave behind. An analysis of the Ford synopsis indicates many aspects of the treatment found their way into Grant's final *Alamo* script:

1) Mexican troops arrive in San Antonio. An officer and guidon bearer ride to the Alamo. Travis takes a lit cigar and fires cannon during the reading of an ultimatum.

2) Crockett and Bowie "Cut and run" discussion. Travis calls Bowie a coward, Bowie challenges Travis and then leaves, Crockett/Travis conversation: "A commander doesn't have to explain his decisions."

362

3) A Mexican sneaks into the compound with a message for Bowie.

4) Raid for cattle: Tennesseans race away from Alamo, crawl through a ditch to the river. They float downriver past Mexican soldiers singing around a campfire on river bank. Two Mexican soldiers are on a bridge while the defenders huddle underneath. They steal horses, stampede the herd through the village and drive cattle into the Alamo. Travis congratulates Crockett and Bowie then charges both with insubordination. Bowie decides to leave in the morning with his men and proceeds to get drunk.

5) The next morning, while Bowie lies in bed, Crockett throws pan of water at him then takes him to visit an injured man in hospital. Bowie leaves, "Unpack that, we're staying."

6) Lisa's birthday party. Crockett dances with her.

7) After the final assault, a Mexican bugler blows recall. An officer enters a choir loft and finds Mrs. Dickinson and children on floor. She walks out into the sunlight, passes Santa Anna as music plays "Eyes of Texas." She then passes down line and out into prairie. Music swells.

By 1946 the world was in a state of relative calm; the Second War to end all Wars had been successfully concluded, while freedom and serenity reigned supreme. The next several years would see the first meeting of the United Nations, Vietnam would be recognized as an autonomous state, Hungary and Indonesia recognized as republics, Jordan and Syria would become independent nations while British troops would leave Lebanon. The Marshall Plan was developed to aid reconstruction in Europe, and the Truman Doctrine was proclaimed to help stem the spread of communism.

Wayne had strong patriotic beliefs and wanted to include them in a movie, a movie that would depict unbelievable sacrifice. And that's when he thought of *The Alamo*. He would pay tribute to the men and women who fought for freedom in World War II. He didn't serve in the armed forces, although he made numerous trips overseas to entertain the troops. He was an air-raid warden, worked at the Hollywood Canteen, and even applied for service with the OSS. Along with movies such as *Flying Tigers, Fighting Seabees, Back to Bataan, They Were Expendable*, and *Sands of Iwo Jima*. *The Alamo* (an analogy for the fight for freedom) would pay tribute to all the men and women who served.

However, by the time Grant finalized the script in 1959, the world had changed significantly. Outbreaks of rebellion and revolution were erupting all over the globe: Fidel Castro and Che Guevara had entered Havana, and Castro became premier; there was an attempted revolution in the Dominican Republic; martial law had been declared in Laos and Indonesia; riots broke out in the Belgium Congo; Khrushchev became premier of the Soviet Union; French-Algerian protesters seized government offices in Algiers leading to a military coup; Vice-President Richard Nixon's car was attacked by anti-American demonstrators in Caracas, Venezuela, and a Tibetan uprising against ten years of Chinese rule erupted in Lhasa.

Wayne needed a mechanism to support and inspire those who were fighting for freedom. "These are perilous times," he said with conviction. "The eyes of the world are on us. We must sell America to countries threatened with Communist domination. Our picture is also important to Americans who should appreciate the struggle our ancestors made for the precious freedom we now enjoy." Grant's script was intended to do just that.

## CHAPTER TWENTY
## PREPARATIONS

*"I was a lamb, I was so sure I could do it. Then all of a sudden one night I woke up and got the shivers. What if my cast resented my direction; what if I couldn't get their cooperation?"* John Wayne discussing his directorial abilities after the film was completed.[746]

IT WAS MID-AUGUST: WHILE GRANT WAS BUSY DEVELOPING A REVISED SCRIPT, Wayne arrived in Brackettville and began addressing the thousands of last-minute details before start of production. The advance production team had arrived July 13. According to Duke, he now was there for the duration and wouldn't leave until the last scene was filmed. With Pilar and Aissa safely encamped in the Wainwright house at Ft. Clark, he headed out to survey the movie set. While he had been looking forward to this moment with great anticipation, sadly, Pilar was still feeling the aftereffects of a recent miscarriage. In May, Wayne had announced he would be a father again as Pilar was pregnant. "Of course, I'm tickled," he confided to Hedda Hopper. "And, no I don't care whether it's a boy, girl, or triplets. Just healthy." Unfortunately, on May 26, it was announced Pilar miscarried and lost the expected baby. She had been warned by her doctor for several weeks that complications could arise. By June 3, she was home from the hospital recuperating from the loss of their baby. When Wayne arrived in Brackettville, he threw himself into his work.[747]

Remaining principal actors would arrive over the next several weeks, but the first real day of filming wasn't scheduled until early September. So Wayne had a great opportunity to make preparations and begin filming a few opening shots:

Mexican troops traveling over hills and valleys, caissons, and artillery, etc.[748]

Earlier that month, Wayne, along with son Pat and Jimmy Grant, arrived in Houston on Continental flight 950 to do a bit of "coon" hunting before Duke would head off to Austin to meet Gov. Price Daniel. Bill Daniel, the governor's brother, had invited Duke to spend the night at his ranch near Liberty to do a little "tree-scouting" for raccoons. During a break between flights, Wayne shared, "We'll start filming in Brackettville, Texas, around September 10. After our little excursion to Liberty and our luncheon engagement with the Governor Thursday, we'll visit the location and see how the sets have weathered. The story about the Alamo will be told in a different way. We want to give it a more adult angle than is usually found in the film versions—especially in the case of Crockett. In most cases, the story of the last days of the Alamo has been told to entertain children. We want to show why those men stayed, fought, and died, and why they regarded liberty as being so important."

Grant explained he had already been working on the script for ten years, with each year bringing new insight about the battle as additional material was discovered. "But actually we've been waiting until Wayne decided the time was ripe to screen the story," he continued, "and now we felt that, unless we go ahead, production cost will be so high it will be impossible to do it. Our production figure has climbed to $11 million as it is." After Wayne received a large white Stetson, the party left to test its shooting skills.[749]

The next day, Duke dined with Gov. Daniel at the executive mansion in Austin where he received a piece of stonework from the historic Alamo. Maj. Gen. Paul Wakefield, president of the Texas Heritage Foundation, indicated that Wayne's chunk was similar to those placed in each of Texas' 254 county courthouses. That weekend, Duke and Chill Wills visited Lackland AFB in San Antonio to highlight recruiting activities surrounding "Aviation Cadet Month." While there, they also visited the base hospital ward and made a personal appearance at the airmen's service club. Michael Wayne, an Air Force reservist, had expressed interest in the recruiting program, and Duke subsequently offered his assistance to the base.

According to Lt. John Quinn, who was stationed at Laughlin Strategic Air Command base in Del Rio, "Michael had to do two days a month for his AF Reserve duty. They had him working at the Information/PR Office at Randolph AFB, San Antonio. He made that trip up there and would arrange for various 'brass' to come to the set to meet his dad. I tried to get his Long Beach, CA. unit to let him transfer to Del Rio for that duty, but Mike was satisfied with the arrangement of having to drive two hours up and back to San Antonio. It was beneficial for his dad's purposes to have good connections with the Air Force Headquarters."[750]

Later that month in the presence of his sons and Laughlin's base commander, Col. Harvey, Wayne was named "Wing Commander for the Day." His entourage, including Cols. Bratton, Harvey, their wives and Mr. and Mrs. Bill Moody IV, were guests of the NCO Club. After lunch, Duke continued the tour of the base, chatting with airmen and their families, posing for photos and signing autographs. He wrapped up the day's activities with a punch party given by the Officer's Wives Club and "appeared to have a gay time…surrounded by attractive and attentive women." No wonder, according to those present, "while the ladies drank tea, Duke replaced his with gin." At the Menger Hotel in San Antonio, Pilar helped promote the film by appearing with Mrs. Moody at a luncheon fashion show saluting Wool Week.[751]

Wayne was more than satisfied as he performed a final walk through the set. All buildings aged effectively, props and set dressing staged correctly. Authentic adobe blocks were used for the walls and buildings—no false fronts for Duke. It was as if he had been transported back to 1836 San Antonio. As he walked with his entourage through the compound, he stopped momentarily and studied the church. Something wasn't right. Suddenly, it came to him. Ybarra had placed a small white cross on top of the church. "Take that down," he ordered. A construction worker immediately did so. Duke paused, and then gave Ybarra direction. "That was Wayne's idea," said Al. "We were looking at the set with the cameraman and he said, 'Gimme something on top of the set. Something allegorical.' His exact words. He said, 'Get a cross up there.' I said, 'No problem.' And put a cross up there. The thing didn't belong. It was all out of scale and everything. No one could say it wasn't there originally. No one knew and no one cared. So I put it up there. Fortunately I put a platform up on top of the Alamo just in case there was some action he might require that was not in the script. I got it, reinforced it, and finally shot some action up there. Shot the cannon…" The cross, built out of a shipping pallet and placed at an angle to represent a fallen cross, was attached to a stand, so it could be positioned correctly. Two cannon were placed on the gun platform; a small one just beneath the cross and a larger one pointing toward the town. Photos suggest the cross was braced against the back of the Alamo "hump" by the cedar gun platform. It was just the final touch the set needed. Ybarra admitted, "Duke had a very good eye for small details like that—for film composition—he has never been recognized for that."[752]

The size of the cross wasn't the only change Wayne had requested. Initially, Ybarra designed the ridgeline of the Alamo chapel to look relatively flat.

Duke would take every opportunity to be involved in local events; on August 27, he spoke at a South Texas Chamber of Commerce meeting in Brackettville, followed by a tour of the set prior to a barbecue at Ft. Clark. He was also invited to attend the Diez y Seis dance and celebration at La Villita in San Antonio, where the queen of the Charro Association was chosen. Lunch in Eagle Pass, bullfights in Acuña, high-school basketball games in Brackettville, Wayne and family were here, there, and everywhere.[753]

Earlier, stuntman Jack Williams had arrived on the set where Wayne and Bill Clothier shot footage of Williams falling a horse to test the new camera lens. Every production must run a series of film tests before principle photography begins. These are for lenses, color blend of costumes and background, make-up under local lighting, etc. Duke then drove to San Antonio one morning and, along with a few "technicians," slipped quietly into the Broadway theater to review the test shots; he was pleased with the results. This was important because at one time Wayne considered shooting the film in Cinerama as the battle action would look tremendous. However, there were numerous issues with three separate reels of film running behind three lenses in a special camera: close-ups were impractical as you couldn't get closer than a shot from the waist up; you couldn't change lenses; and you could see the three films intersect on the screen. Clothier explained the decision: "At the time, CinemaScope looked just awful because it distorted people. You couldn't get good close-ups without it looking like the people had the mumps. But there were a number of good 70mm processes around then which not only eliminated the distortion but gave greater depth. So I was alarmed when Duke said he was thinking about shooting *The Alamo* in Cinerama, which I thought would be a terrible mistake… (Duke) was actually a little ahead of his time in his thinking because, up until then, all the films shot in Cinerama had been travelogues. There hadn't been a dramatic film made in Cinerama."

Clothier continued, "I said to Duke, 'If you shoot in Cinerama, you're going to have to also shoot a version in CinemaScope,' because only a few theatres in the world were equipped to show Cinerama. So you'd have to make a second version of the film shot in CinemaScope for general release, and then you had a film shot from a slightly different angle, and it would have the distortions… I said to Duke, 'Look, Mike Todd created Todd-AO as his version of Cinerama.' Todd-AO was meant to be a single-camera version of Cinerama, shot on 65mm film and intended to be shown on a big curved screen. Like Cinerama, that problem was that there were not enough theatres equipped with a big curved screen. But there were a lot of premier theatres with 70mm projectors, a big screen, and stereophonic sound, and any one of them could show the film. Further, the 70mm negative could easily be transferred into ordinary 35mm anamorphic, or CinemaScope, prints. So we shot it in Todd-AO, and it was breathtaking. And thank God, Panavision refined the anamorphic process, so we didn't lose quality when it was transferred to 35mm." Batjac had to shell out a guarantee of $350,000 to use the special cameras. Wayne agreed, "It was my ambition to make a major spectacular picture…and more than ten years ago, I began formulating its concept. The decision was made to film the story in Todd-AO and color to bring the battle to the screen in all its sweeping dimension and beauty."[754]

Clothier was fortunate to even be on location. "I'm doing *The Alamo* and the Old Man was making *Wagonmaster*. I'm under contract to John Wayne, and we have been down to location two or three times; we are ready to start in September—the Old Man called me and said, 'I'm going to make *Wagonmaster*, and I want you to do the picture.' (I replied,) 'Jack, I'm committed to Duke Wayne.' (Ford) said, 'Let me talk to Duke.' He got Duke on the phone and said, 'Why can't Bill come down and shoot the exteriors? He will be through in time for him to start *The Alamo* with you, and I'll get somebody else to do the interiors.' Duke answered, 'No. (Bill's) got a lot of preparing to do in this picture.' So the Old Man said ok."[755]

Jack Williams also helped Clothier identify locations where various scenes were to be filmed. Robert Harris recalled, "Jackie Williams came down. He's the one that hired me on pre-production. All we had were these stake marks and what I'd do, he said, 'Just follow me on your horse.' And I'd just follow him around and drive stakes up in those mountains. That's where Santy Anna was; their troops would be coming down. So we was flagging it off for the cameramen to set their cameras and stuff by." Wayne and assistant director Robert Relyea would ride out on their horses to check out the potential sites. One day as they were discussing logistical issues, a little old lady drove up, got out of her car, waddled over to the two and proceeded to ask Wayne to autograph her handkerchief. Duke exploded and told the woman what he thought of her. "You think I'm just standing here for my health?" he screamed. "How the fuck would you like it if I interrupted you at your job for no good reason? Sign your handkerchief? How 'bout I sign your fat ass, you little..." The woman was reduced to tears, and wranglers helped her back to her car. Duke and Relyea resumed their discussions.

At that moment, Wayne's horse took the opportunity to bite him in the rear. Relyea continued the story: "He turned to face (the horse), pulled his right shoulder back...and delivered a punch that exploded squarely between the animal's eyes. Unbelievably, the horse's front legs collapsed and its head lowered slowly to the ground. The hind legs stiffened, causing the animal's butt to stubbornly point skyward. Duke then kneeled in front of his horse, put his large hands under its shoulders and helped (it) back up, all the while staring into the eyes of the horse as if to say *don't fuck with me*."[756]

On Wednesday, September 2, Wayne had been rushed to San Antonio to receive treatment for an ear infection; as word raced through the office corridors, employees crowded the hallways to glimpse the movie star. By Friday, though, Duke had already returned to the set and was ready to work. Seventy-five Del Rio extras had already been notified to report for preproduction activities. Costumed as cavalrymen, artillerymen, and those who man caissons, they would represent part of the Mexican army on its way to San Antonio. Required on location at 5:00 a.m. to get ready for wardrobe and make-up, the shooting was planned to "test" later large-scale action. Several women, including Bess Huebner, Daisy

Boyd, Dorothy Baker, and Alice Cromwell, had already traveled to Brackettville the previous day to receive their costumes as pioneer women.[757]

The first pre-production scene filmed involved numerous runaway horses, out-of-control caissons, injured soldados and a drowned camera. Filmed on West Nueces River on the L.L. Davis ranch, next door to Bill Moody's ranch, the plan was to capture galloping horses with thundering hooves, majestically pulling cannons and caissons across a stream. A remote-controlled Mitchell camera was positioned on a grip-flat in the middle of the stream so that its lens was slightly above water level. The horses were supposed to "split the cameras," alternating on either side. With Widmark atop a twenty-foot-high camera platform and Pat Wayne also looking on, Duke called "Action!" and the scene began. Artillerymen are seen roaring down Old Silver Lake Road at full gallop with caissons in tow. In front were two riders leading four horses pulling a limber attached to cannon. Two men rode on the limber. Quickly, the team made a sharp right turn, headed down the bank of the stream and galloped across. One, two, three teams successfully negotiated the stunt although one rider was bucked off one horse and landed on another. Relyea only slightly exaggerated what happened next: "As the caisson hit the stream, the wood beams harnessing its four horses snapped, sending the two animals head over hooves into the water and pinning their riders below. The next caisson slammed into the timber of the first, and a massive pile-up was under way. The poor animals were sprawling and rolling everywhere, their riders flying helplessly through the air or getting pitched into the ground."

Local wrangler Plunker Sheedy rode one of the runaway horses: "Yes, sir. I was riding the horse that ran over it (the camera). We had other people ride the horses that weren't the best horses. (The stream's bank) had a drop off, and they didn't put any sand or grade it with a grader or anything... They came back there at the start and asked me how fast I thought they'd go, and I said, 'Well, you can't go too fast because there are too many wheels and too many horses and especially those big cameras there.' Rusty McDonald was riding one of the lead horses on my right side, and he give him a signal to go and there we were—when we hit that water, it was all over. Broke my girth and...that saddle of mine went all the way back up the horse, and I just held on to the neck of the horse, so I was just straddling in between the horses."[758]

One caisson broke loose as the team rounded the turn and started to slide down the bank; the out-of-control horses split and ran over the camera. Robert Harris was one of the artillerymen on the unfortunate caisson: "They had these guys on the horses up front. And then the caisson guys, we just sat back there and you've only got one handle...and that thing was wagging down...we had went right down a steep divide. About six or seven caissons was all running down. And the stuntmen had told me, 'Don't get on it.' I was pretty good friends with the stuntmen. And they said, 'Don't get on that damn caisson.' They said, 'None of our guys would do it.' 'Cause they weren't paying them enough. I said, 'Hell, I want to be in the movie.' I'd never been in a movie. I'd never been on a caisson, either. Shit, once that thing started down that slope, I'm going to tell you what, there was no turning back. That thing started turning over and the caisson behind me was coming. And the guy that was sitting next to me, he fell off. I was falling fast and looking for a soft spot to land on, and (the other guy) looked good, so I dropped on him for my own protection. And when I jumped he had his foot hung in this wheel in the caisson. Every time it's going around. So when I hit him, I got his leg out from the spinning wheel, and it actually saved his life. He got up, everyone was cheering me thinking I was a hero for saving the man. Because all these other caissons were coming behind us. And those things would have cut your head off 'cause those things were terribly heavy with that big cannon on the back. There (were) several of the guys behind me (who had) their bridles broke, and they were holding on to the horses with just their arms wrapped around the horse's neck. It was about the biggest mess you ever saw. Wayne was sick over this, but he couldn't bitch at me too much because everyone rushed over to me, praising me as a hero for pulling my partner out of the wheel. Wayne's stuntmen buddies Cliff Lyons and Red Morgan were backslapping me ,and they became my friends throughout the picture."

Once the horses ran over the grip-flat, the camera flipped and settled upside down at the bottom of the stream. The injured extra was taken to the hospital where he remained for several weeks. Sheedy was in sad shape as well: ",,,the night before that I was getting ready to get married and had a big party, a bachelor party. So I never did get to bed that night. I just came in from the bachelor party…I had the worse hangover of my life—they picked the worse day in the world to do it as far as I am concerned." After the riders and horses were taken care of, a technician ran into the stream, trying to salvage the camera. Though submerged, it was still running. Before anyone had a chance to cut the power, the well-intentioned tech picked up the camera; the hair on his head stood straight up when he clutched it. When the film magazine was unloaded it was found that the film was in perfect condition. Wayne turned to Relyea with a grin and said, "Well, that takes care of the first shot."[759]

After that shot was complete, Wayne and crew headed downstream on the West Nueces to film another sequence: Mexican dragoons crossing a stream in front of several impressive bluffs. Several takes were necessary as in one an extra fell off his horse during filming. Widmark, present once again, was in full costume. But the question begs itself: why was he even there? Perhaps Wayne requested his presence so Duke could approve his wardrobe or, like Pappy, maybe Wayne wanted costumed actors nearby in case he needed to improvise. Relyea remembered, "Like John Ford, Duke insisted that all the principal actors get into wardrobe and make-up each morning, whether their scenes were on the schedule or not. He made them sit nearby, in case he suddenly decided to add another character that wasn't originally scripted in the scene, or, if they couldn't shoot the scene initially planned. Richard Widmark, Laurence Harvey, Richard Boone, Chill Wills, Denver Pyle, Frankie Avalon, and Duke's son Patrick would all sit nearby on his film. 'I want you here, ready,' he'd tell them. 'If I don't use you today, keep your mouth shut and don't complain. You're still getting paid.'" Stuntmen and extras weren't immune, either. Improvisation may have been more prevalent than one would think: Rudy Robbins and Jim Brewer recalled that scripts were an optional accessory. "I was given a script to read for various parts before I was actually cast," says Brewer. "However, it was a waste of time… I was told what to say and when to say it by either Duke or John Ford." At least, Brewer saw a script. "As for my script," Robbins maintained, "I never had one. Myself, Chuck Roberson, and most of the other minor characters with speaking roles never got a script on any of our movies with Duke. He would simply tell us what he wanted us to say prior to shooting the scenes."[760]

*(Backup: For every day of shooting on a major motion picture, the day's schedule is finalized the night before, and a "call sheet" provided to all cast and crew before wrap. This sheet tells who is needed at what time the next day and what scene numbers or parts of scene numbers will be filmed in what order. Actors would arrive at a specific time, go through make-up and wardrobe…and then wait. At the bottom of the call sheet is a section called "Cover Sets" that lists scenes that will be shot IF they can't shoot the ones planned. They always have a cover set or two lit and ready to go INSIDE a practical set or on a sound stage in case it rains or due to other unscheduled variables. (The airplane hangar at Ft. Clark served as the soundstage). All actors for those alternate scenes are on a "HOLD" day. They can stay in the motel or can come out to the set, whatever. Just as long as they are available to come if needed. Paying the actors to be available is less expensive than losing a day's shooting when nothing can be done.)[761]*

As for Widmark, a photo taken at the "bluffs" shows him wearing brown rough-cut boots; leather britches; two-inch black waist belt with brass buckle and knife with scabbard on right hip; white period shirt with long pointed collar; low crown, narrow-brimmed, tan, felt semi-western hat; and dark leather coat. Every production must run a series of film tests prior to principal photography. As he had just recently arrived on location, Wayne may have not yet had a chance to see Widmark in costume and wanted to okay his appearance. Or, maybe Richard was just trying to break the clothes in, so to speak. Wayne claimed he wore his Crockett buckskins just to give them the correct distressed look: "I want these buckskins to look lived in when the shooting starts. And I've got to get used to this coonskin cap. There will be many more (hot) days like this." (Widmark's "real" wardrobe photo with that particular ensemble wouldn't be taken until September 9, the first "official" day of shooting, which makes sense as those photos are typically taken just before or after the first scene in which they appear.)[762]

Members of the Davis clan were on hand watching this sequence being filmed—it was taking place on Lloyd Davis's property. Along with Ray and Winnie Davis who lived in a house on the ranch, Zack, Diane, Paul, Nan, Helen, and Lloyd Lee, their mother Eloise, and Carol and Bobby Davis and their mother Lydia also looked on. Cousin Alan Krieger Jr. rounded out the group. Ever cordial, Wayne took time out of his busy schedule to pose for several photographs with the children. It was the first time Alan ever saw Duke. "I was an eight-year-old, and I had never heard of John Wayne," says Alan. "I would go to the movies just to see Dean Martin and Jerry Lewis. But I remember seeing him (Wayne) there, and I was noticing, 'What a strange way of talking.' This strange speech. Then, they ran John Wayne movies every weekend here at the Palance Theater when the movie was being filmed, and I remember, 'Wow. He talks exactly the same way in the movies.'" A woman was spotted hiding behind some shrubbery, taking pictures of the action. Zack recalls "they had to scare her out of the bushes" because she was interrupting filming.[763]

According to the August 21, 1959 Master Shooting Schedule, Wayne would shoot the aforementioned countryside sequences on September 4/5. Two additional scenes were also scheduled that weekend: Jim Bonham (Pat Wayne) chased by Mexican cavalry, and Cotton (Frankie Avalon) stopped by sentries as he approaches Houston's camp. (Avalon's character's name Cotton wasn't changed to Smitty until September 14). Pat didn't arrive until the sixth, though, and there is no evidence that the chase scene was filmed. As Avalon didn't arrive on location until the sixteenth, his double was supposed to be used instead. The sentries would have been played by Ron Gast, Ricci Ware, and "Little" John Hamilton, but this shot was canceled as well.

Interviewed shortly after shooting the aforementioned countryside scenes, you can still hear the excitement in Wayne's voice when he said, "On the last day's shooting of my very first picture, *The Big Trail*, back in 1929, I said to Raoul Walsh, the director, 'Mr. Walsh, some day I'm going to direct a picture myself.' He smiled indulgently, and said, 'Duke, *all* actors someday want to direct.' I think that's true, all right, but I don't think most of them have to wait around as long as I did before realizing their ambition. As you are reading this, I will be right smack in the middle of starring in, producing, and directing *The Alamo* in Brackettville, Texas. Believe me, it has been a long haul. Almost twenty years got by, following *The Big Trail*, before I even found a story that I thought I'd like to direct. In 1948, after a thorough study of the Battle of the Alamo, I knew that here was my baby. The story of those thirteen days to glory by those 186 valiant men, one woman, and a child—against impossible odds—had everything. Suspense. Pathos. Heartaches. Humor. Action. You name the dramatic element you like, and this had it. For eleven long years now, I've dreamed, worked, and hoped for *The Alamo*, as I saw it, to become a reality on screen. And now it's getting there. By the end of November, and the grace of God, we'll have it in the can, and come next spring, it will be in your theaters. And, ladies and gentlemen, when you see those scenes—more than 4,000 of Santa Anna's troops, storming that little bastion and its magnificent defenders—your hearts are going to jump. I promise you. When I started out on this piece, I intended to give you a lot of statistics about the number of hours that had gone into pre-production, the number of extras we're using, how many people are necessary to make the picture, and a lot of other stuff. But I've changed my mind. All I want to say is, it's going to be a good picture. A wonderful picture. Go see it. I've made around two hundred pictures, good, bad, and indifferent, in the past thirty years, and I wouldn't give you a bum steer. I'm truly the voice of experience. So—'Remember the Alamo.'"[764]

While Duke was off filming, various actors began to arrive in Brackettville. Most would be housed at Ft. Clark, and those who hadn't previously worked with each other started getting acquainted. Jim Brewer recalls, "The Gateway Hotel was full, Spain's Café on Hwy 90 was always bustling with actors, extras, etc., who congregated to listen to the juke box. There was a band on the weekend at Ft. Clark, and Dave Marshal, an actor in *The Alamo*, sang a few songs. The streets were crowded, and busloads of tourists visited the set daily." (Marshall, a 1953 graduate of Harlandale High School, sang at local San Antonio night clubs before being hired as one of Travis's men. Reporting to the set with long sideburns, he eventually became Widmark's stand-in.)[765]

Pat, Tim, and Dan Cumiskey are three brothers who were fortunate enough to live at Ft. Clark at that time. (Their father was stationed at the Air Force base in Del Rio.) Cavalry officer's quarters had been turned into duplexes that were occupied mostly by Air Force folks, as well as residents from Austin, San Antonio, and Houston who used them as summer homes. Tim recalls, "There (were) about twenty of these duplex-type houses all along this one street which surrounded a parade ground. All of the stars stayed in those homes. My parents and a bunch of other people decided they wanted to have a party and invited some of those people before shooting started. They wanted to invite some of those people for cocktails and just a get-together-type thing." Pat continues, "Well, John Wayne had a cocktail party. At that time, he lived in the Wainwright house. And there was just a series of cocktail parties. Mom and Dad had their turn—it kinda came down the row, and it was their turn." So, one evening both kids were playing in the front yard when "...here comes Richard Boone down the walkway," recalls Tim. "I just stopped and looked up at him and I went, 'You're Paladin.' He didn't even say a word; he just reached into his pocket, pulled out a *Have Gun Will Travel* card, and I wish I still had it. My mother was famous for throwing things away."[766]

Most of the cast and crew stayed at Ft. Clark; actors had their own houses, stuntmen their own barracks, and everyone enjoyed a communal mess hall. A large spring-fed, three hundred-foot-long swimming pool at the fort became a natural gathering place. "An Olympic-size swimming pool—thank God," Joan O'Brien fondly remembers. She and Laurence Harvey would hit the pool every chance they got. "He used to jump in the pool—he had his valet with him, and he'd jump in the pool. They had a big float out in the middle, like a barge float, and he'd jump into the pool, and he'd say, 'Oh, I feel just like a French tart!'" With a constant temperature of only 68°, the pool was a bit chilly, though. Most of the cast and crew would assemble there after a hard day's work and dinner. From August through October, the evening air was warm. Widmark, Harvey, and Brewer were all fairly good swimmers. Brewer started swimming at a young age, competed in the Junior Olympics, and swam at the Austin Aquatic club for three seasons; Widmark and Harvey both swam in college. Brewer remembers, "We would race each other just for fun. There were Widmark, Harvey, me, and other actors who could swim, and we would race. Harvey was the fastest. He was over six-feet-tall, thin, and long limbed, and glided through the water. He had a long freestyle stroke that gave him an advantage over Mr. Widmark and myself. Mr. Widmark and I were approximately the same height. We would participate in individual freestyle races and relay races. It was fun. There were no money bets or losers buying drinks for the winners. These swim events were impromptu. They were not scheduled every evening, just when the participants were available and willing."[767]

On most weekends, Duke, the diminutive Pilar, and cute-as-a-button Aissa would find themselves walking hand-in-hand along Brackettville's Main Street, enjoying the ambiance of small-town Texas. However, on September 5, Wayne took a last opportunity to get away and headed back to San Antonio. Mike, Pat, Pilar, and Aissa came along to help unwind, relax, and prepare for the most important event in Wayne's career. They stayed at the Menger in a lovely suite on the 2nd floor, either #2074 or #2076. As the kids splashed around in the Patio Club pool, Pilar and Duke proudly looked on.[768]

Ernesto Malacara, current director of public relations for the Menger Hotel, recalls, "There was a gentleman here that was in the hotel. At that time, I believe that he worked for Sunbeam. He was a salesman, and he and a group of men were in the patio room, restaurant or the bar. And he said that he looked toward the back of the bar and John Wayne was sitting there with some men." The man in question had a bottle of Chivas. (In those days, you couldn't buy liquor by the glass, but you could bring in your own bottle, hide it in a paper bag under the table, mix your drinks and hide the bottle again.) Wayne's discussion broke up, the other men left, and Duke started walking toward the front door. But he stopped at the other men's table, looked down, and noticed a pack of Pall Mall cigarettes. Malacara continued, "'Hey,' Wayne said, 'my brand of cigarettes.' So he grabs one, lights it up, looks at the bottle of scotch in the paper bag and says, 'Hey, my brand of Scotch.' So they get him a glass, he mixed a drink, and they began to talk."

"After a while, the conversation gave out, and the group began to leave the bar," said Malacara. "An old night cleaner stopped Wayne and wanting to impress him, said, 'Mr. Wayne, I saw this movie of yours. I forget the name, but I thought you were great.' Wayne looked down at the man and said, 'Okay, you saw that one but did you see this one?' and names another movie. The old man indicated he hadn't seen that one, so Wayne picked him up by his collar and said, 'Well, partner. You better see that one too,' and gently set him back down. One of his sons came up, as Wayne was going to take the group of men up to his suite, and said, 'Dad, Mom's already asleep, and I don't think she wants to be bothered by a lot of noise up there.'" Wayne, knowing who the boss was, agreed and the party broke up.[769]

While the set remained open, numerous organizations took an opportunity to visit: The Del Rio Gardenia Junior Garden Club called on the set in late August while the Old Trail Drivers Association of Texas made advance reservations for September 19. Earlier, Cub Scouts had visited the set prior to a picnic at Ft. Clark. Two hundred Scouts of the Rio Grande District participated in a Camporee on Shahan's ranch and visited the set as well. In June, the third quarterly meeting of the Texas Sheep & Goat Ranchers Association and Auxiliary was held at Ft. Clark, a two-day affair, a tour of the set wrapped up the second day. On July 12, the cast of Ramsey Yelvington's *A Cloud of Witnesses: The Drama of the Alamo*, along with members of the press, television and radio fields, visited the set. Later, ten *Odessa American* newspaper carriers visited after winning the paper's subscription contest. Trying to ingratiate himself into the community, Wayne spoke at a South Texas Chamber of Commerce meeting prior to inviting the members out to the film set. A barbecue followed attended by over four hundred people where Wayne boasted he would make the Brackettville address better known than the IRS. Wayne and Shahan would also take time to watch the Brackettville Tigerettes play basketball. As Happy explained the fine points of the game to Wayne, locals would chat with such members of Duke's entourage as Grant, Clothier, and Nate Edwards. Over 1,000 tourists visited the set every day. After filming started on September 9, visitors were permitted to enter only if they had a special pass. (A Batjac representative pointed out that one day in Louisiana, they had let in a crowd to watch filming of *The Horse Soldiers*; the wind shifted, and it carried crowd noise to the sound equipment. $40,000 worth of filming was ruined.) Those wishing to visit the set had to contact Link Widder, who was in charge of issuing passes and making arrangements for a limited number of visits to the set.[770]

As cast and crew tried to settle in, Grant continued pounding out a script. He wasn't above asking for help, though. An August 4, 1959, inter-office memo to all personnel said, "The character of Bull in *Alamo* which will be played by Tom Hennessey, will have with him a big, rough, mastive (sp) type hunting dog. Will you please re-read the script of *Alamo* and if you can think of any bits of business, either comedic or dramatic, involving this dog, please write me a memo on same."

Others just volunteered their services. Howard Hawks recalled, "I tried to help him (Wayne) on *The Alamo*, and I wrote a whole bunch of scenes for him. He read them, and he said, 'They're great scenes, but I couldn't do it. I couldn't do it.' I (Hawks) was going to have the girl in the Alamo raped by twenty or thirty people and want revenge. It would have been a hell of a good story. 'That's a good scene,' Duke said, 'but I don't know how to do those things.' And he did a corny girl."[771]

In his earlier work on the script, Grant had difficulties wrapping his arms around the concept. He struggled: What was the message? What did Wayne want him to say? The opening scene was both difficult and key to telling the tale. Grant would generate a backstory and develop the reason why the Alamo saga was so important. Initially, he just used a written forward, explaining very little about Mexico of the 1830s and Santa Anna. Strong on patriotism, long on heroics, he attempted to set up the story with the arrival of Crockett and his Tennesseans in San Antonio. By mid-May, he scrapped the idea. Instead, behind the opening credits, a short series of out-of-continuity scenes from the film were presented. They began with Travis lighting a cigar and a blast from a cannon and ended with a view of the burning Alamo. "The Eyes of Texas" swelled in the background. Fade out. Fade in to the aftermath of the battle of Bexar. Cos had been paroled; Houston was present, and Dickinson explained the struggle had only just begun. An earlier draft contained 107 pages and 277 scenes. By May 19, after twelve revisions, it had expanded to 155 pages and 563 scenes.

The script was taking shape; most of the vignettes and memorable lines from the finished film would find their genesis in these early versions:

*"Travis—I would trust Jim Bowie with my life—more than that, I would trust him with the lives of my family. And even more than the family I hold dear, I would trust Jim Bowie with the life of Texas."*

*"Travis, I've never been able to like you—but you're another one of the very few men I would trust with the life of Texas. And it could be possible that that life rests in your hands now."*

*"Colonel, the Indians of San Blas have sent couriers to the vaqueros of my properties along the Sangre de Christo—they say that large numbers of soldiers crossed the Baje (sic) Diablo two days ago—The Indians guessed the number of troops at over five thousand—there are also large numbers of mounted horses and supply trains—Also lower down on the Baja Diablo another party of Indians saw signs of large numbers of shod horses crossing at a ford there..."*

*"Some Indians told some vaqueros..."*

*"I give thanks for the time and place. A time to live and a place to die. It's all any man gets. No more, no less. Fire the signal. Boy."*

*"Republic. I like the sound of the word. It means people can talk free and live free. That they can go or come, buy or sell, be drunk or sober, however they choose. I like the sound of some words. Republic is one of the words that makes me tight in the throat.*

*The same tightness of throat a man gets when his baby takes its first step, or when his first baby shaves and makes his first sound like a man. Some words can give a man the feeling of making his heart warm."*

*"Promised mother. Pray to the North Star ten minutes every night. Long line of star worshippers."*

*"Gratuity for the boy."*

*"I'd admire to buy you a drink or eight or ten."*

*"Say, I'm a stranger in these parts. What do you Texicans use for drinking whiskey?"*

*"Please, Colonel Bowie, let us dispense with the fire-eating pyrotechnics."*

*"Blasted lie! One of them stories loose-mouthed people tell around. Me and Mike quit at sundown, and it wouldn't have been the fourth day till the next morning."*

*"But I wrote the letter!"*

*"This may sound like a Bible-beater yelling up a revival at a river-crossing-camp meeting, but that don't change its truth. There's right and there's wrong and you've got to do one or the other...and when you do the one you're living, and when you do the other you may be walking around, but you're as dead as a beaver hat."*

*"Cut, slash and run away."*

*"I hate to say anything good about that long-winded jackanapes, but he does know the short way to start a war."*

*"I wouldn't take Travis's word that night's dark and day's bright."*

*"Well, boys, I'm glad I seen that there cannon out there on the prairie. For a minute I was worried they was shooting at us all the way from one of them old countries in Europe."*

*"Travis, you can't help being you and I can't help being me."*

*"See did any of our boys get hurt. I'll be below getting washed on the outside and wet down inside."*

*"I wonder if Texas will remember these men! I wonder if the world will!"*

*"So, sir, if your stick should float that way and you could see it clear to let these men live past this battle, I'd be thankful. Because they are good men. All."*

*"Men, Jim Bonham has just died. He brought the news that we can expect no help. Fannin has been ambushed. I stay here with my command, but any of you who wish to may leave with all honor. Those who wish to stay with me will step over the line. Failing reinforcement, the Alamo cannot hold..."*

Grant seemed to take a very systemic approach to script development. After he completed his draft, he would go back to the beginning and fine-tune the dialog page by page, scene by scene, completing the entire draft once again before he would start over. During the process, earlier specific dialogue was reassigned to different characters as their personalities developed. Characters became stronger or weaker; they were there to express specific messages or simply move the story along.

In the June 8 version of the script, Flaca and Seguin discuss the evacuation of San Antonio's townspeople and the cost of a burro in scene 123. Crockett excuses himself to speak with Parson, and, although no dialog is used, it implies that he directs Parson to load her belongings into a cart. This scene, though filmed, was not used. To create additional tension after the Mexican troops arrive, scenes 137 through 139 were added to further explain the acrimonious relationship between local residents and Santa Anna. Father Espinosa briefly appears to request sanctuary for the citizens of Bexar but is refused. Again, this is yet another sequence that may have been filmed but did not appear in the final version. This version also has a ridiculous sequence where Beekeeper and Gambler lasciviously watch a young girl hanging clothes in the courtyard. Bull tries to impress the lass by vaulting into his saddle without the assistance of a stirrup, to no avail.

Such scenes irritated Ybarra. "I think (Wayne) made mistakes on two or three different scenes in that picture," he opined. "They did not contribute one damn thing to the picture. One of them was when he was sending his wife, that is, the girl, home. When they were in the woods and he was explaining it to her…he should have done more cutting, eliminating that (feather) scene, and also eliminating that scene in the Cantina. That didn't mean a damn thing. That was just something he thought would contribute to amusement. Well, when guys were down there on that kind of hardship and with a potential war on their hands, they don't mess around with feathers on their noses. That's my feeling. His writer, Jimmy Grant, talked him into that. And he talked him into the love scene, which should never have been left in the final cut. Wayne wanted the basics of the actual happening, which in the original script, were there. Then they started fooling with the romantic part of it. There were no romantic stuff in the actual Alamo. In order to lengthen the picture, I suppose, he felt you oughta get those episodes in there. I think Grant was responsible, as a writer, for injecting some of that stuff in the story. Of course, Wayne went along with it. (Why?) I don't know except that Grant was able to talk him into a lot of things. You know, Grant was a part of the company for a long time. He'd written a lot of stories for Wayne, and he'd also been a director himself. I guess he felt these things enhanced the story and talked Wayne into it. Of course, Wayne never asked my opinion about it 'cause then I would have had a conflict with the writer. I had been in conflict with writers before." Gretchen Wayne agreed, "The script was way too wordy. They never shut up. No wonder they lost—the Mexicans could have come over the walls while they were all talking. But Granddaddy wanted to get his points across, and it was his picture and he could do what he wanted." Shahan was equally adamant. "I have to defend Wayne. It definitely wasn't Wayne's fault as much as it was his writer's…."[772]

Grant's June 15 version included the "European Cannon" sequence, Cotton's saving Bowie when his horse fell, and the recovery of cannon and limber into the compound. It also contained Bowie being charged with insubordination, Crockett tricking him into staying by talking to Cotton, and Cotton being sent for help. (Author and historian Lon Tinkle didn't have much good to say about Grant. In a 1967 letter he confessed, "...(Wayne's) scriptwriter (who had big money invested in the movie and therefore had a lot of power) would not listen to any advice or make one single correction. I have rarely met a more cynical man, with more scorn for the general public and what it can be induced to accept as reality.")[773]

By June 19, Grant expanded the remainder of the script: a raid for cattle, a birthday party, reinforcements from Goliad, notification of the death of Bowie's wife, evacuation of non-combatants, Cotton's arrival at Houston's camp, Parson's death, Cotton and Bonham's deaths as they try to return to the Alamo, Dickinson's line in the sand, Jethro's freedom, and the first and final assault. For all intents and purposes, the script was now complete. Most of the nonsense from earlier versions had thankfully, mercifully, been eliminated: constant references to gambling, ice-skating horses, Parson's sanctimonious attitude, Crockett's long-distance romance with Chela, Crockett's backwoods dialect, the raid for petticoats, and Bowie strapped to a swivel chair. All changes after this were fine-tuning and a strengthening of message.

Still, Grant struggled with the ending. In an extremely early script version, Travis, commanding a cannon, is killed when a squad of Mexican infantrymen roll over him like thunderous waves on a beach; Bowie, slashing and stabbing after running out of pistol ammunition, is bayoneted; and Crockett, while swinging his rifle (shades of Fess Parker), is shot by a half-dozen muskets. The scene dissolves, and Mrs. Dickinson, with children on her knee and Happy Sam at her feet, is asked by an officer to deliver a message to all of Texas. She and Santa Anna exchange glares; he orders a bugler to sound dress parade. As she exits the Alamo on a mule led by Sam, her children held in front of her (in this draft she had two children), Santa Anna barks "Present Arms." The little entourage walks between drawn-up ranks of Mexican troops while a chorus of male voices on the soundtrack begins to sing "The Eyes of Texas." As she passes out of camera only the shattered ruins of the Alamo remain. Patriotic, heart-warming, it might even bring a tear to the eye. But it wasn't quite as effective as it needed to be.

The June 19 version attempted to expand on the deaths of the principals as well as simplify Mrs. Dickinson's responsibility. Bowie, armed with a nock-volley gun, is the first to succumb, while Travis now dies on a parapet, saber in hand. Crockett, out of weapons, turns in front of a flock of troops, runs toward the powder magazine, grabs a torch and flings it onto the stacked powder kegs. Once again, the scene dissolves to Mrs. Dickinson riding a mule led by Sam, with Lisa in her arms. While Mexican music plays in the background, all previous interaction between Santa Anna and Dickinson is eliminated, thereby minimizing the relationship between benevolent victor and fallen-but-proud Alamo widow.

By July 21, Grant had made significant changes to the script—Cotton no longer dies trying to return to the Alamo. Drawn up in parade, the Mexican army watches quietly as Mrs. Dickinson passes by. Santa Anna and an officer discuss the battle's outcome: "A few such victories could lose a war." Dickinson is offered transportation but refuses. As she leaves the Alamo, Cotton rides over a rise and looks down at the small party. With the male chorus still singing in the background, he reaches down, swings Sam onto the horse behind him, grabs the mule's lead rope and leads them toward the camera.

On August 3, just over a month before start of filming, Grant began to take a scalpel to his work. Scenes 1-14 (including Cos's parole) were eliminated and replaced with Houston's arrival into San Antonio and Travis's promotion. Scenes 19-44 were excised. (Travis notifies Bowie that Houston has given him command; columns of troops under Travis and irregulars under Bowie march toward the Alamo; Dickinson and two soldiers run up a flag; Bowie and Travis discuss defending the fort; and Indians are seen counting the number of encamped Mexican troops and subsequently delivering a message to Seguin. However, some of these deleted scenes would later be filmed in a somewhat modified manner). He would also modify scene 49-A by adding dialog between Irish and Bowie: "Say, Jim, how come we got to work like this? I volunteered up to fight, not to build no fort. How come we got to work like this?" "Because old General Sam Houston told Travis and Travis told me, and I'm telling you." Scene 57 was expanded to reflect the increasing animosity between Travis and Bowie: "We have often discussed the fact your men are militia and like all volunteers, undisciplined." Scene 216 was expanded to further explain why it was necessary to defend the Alamo: "It's as simple as this…."

No one wanted to go into production without a finalized script, and Grant was making a valiant attempt at wrapping it up. Director Raoul Walsh offered Duke some good advice. "Read in the trade papers that you are going to direct *The Alamo* and also play in it. This is a pretty tough assignment, but, with all the experience you have had, I know of nobody better qualified to become a director. So I'll be rooting for you. And if you take the advice of an old wrangler, do not start the picture until you have a finished script to your liking."[774]

Upon what he thought was completion, Grant submitted a copy of the script to the Motion Picture Association of America (MPAA) for review and approval. In 1930, the MPAA had adopted the Motion Picture Production Code, which governed content and censorship guidelines in the industry. In 1934, the Production Code Administration (PCA) was created and required all motion pictures to receive a seal of approval before they were released. The PCA evaluated film content in five specific areas: General, including title, footage, location, type, distributor, etc.; Portrayal of professions including role and characteristics;

Portrayal of "Races" and Nationals including role and characterization; Crime including types of crimes and fate of criminals; and Miscellaneous Sociological Factors such as type of violence, inclusion of prayers, divorce and adultery, illicit sex and drinking. Geoffrey Shurlock, director of the PCA, replied to Wayne on August 13, 1959, that "this material seems to meet the requirements of the Production Code with the following exceptions:

Page 46: The business of Crockett kicking the other man is unacceptable. We request that you be very careful in staging the fight sequences in this story, in order that there be no excessive brutality.

Page 47: The scene in which the man's skull is fractured, should be indicated out of frame."

Other than a standard statement to submit all lyrics and consult with the American Humane Association regarding the treatment of animals, the PCA was extremely satisfied with Grant's script. All requirements were addressed in subsequent script revisions.[775]

Grant wasn't the only person to work on the script. Future director Burt Kennedy was a screenwriter on Batjac's payroll in 1953-54. He wrote *Seven Men From Now*, *The Tall T*, and numerous other screen plays and television scripts. Grant had told him, "Burt, if you're going to be in this business, why compete with all the big writers when there are hardly any good western writers as such?" Said Kennedy, "Some good writers have written westerns, but there were very few genuine western writers in this town that were really good writers. (Grant) said that the competition was easier that way, and if you write a good western, you're apt to go further faster." In 1959 Kennedy lived in Royal Oaks, California, and while Burt re-wrote portions of Widmark's part, the actor would go over to his house and rehearse. Kennedy recalled one time during pre-production as he flew back from Brackettville, "We got into one of those horrendous thunderstorms coming out of San Antonio. I was sitting with Richard Widmark, who hates to fly—he's a white-knuckler. I guess he had an ulcer besides, because he drank milk while we were bouncing around in the sky. John Wayne was sitting up front playing poker with some guys, and he wasn't paying any attention to it. I'd look down the aisle while we were bouncing around, and the plane was corkscrewing. Then there was this loud bang as the plane was struck by lightning, and so help me, I saw this blue whatever-it-was come right down the aisle, heading toward the back of the plane. There was an explosion, and then everything was fine. I was told later we were struck by lightning. What happens is that when it hits the plane, because the plane isn't grounded, it eventually jumps off the plane into the clouds, and when it does, it burns a hole in the tail of the plane. It was pretty hairy."[776]

By this time, Grant had made a fairly decent attempt at explaining the complex relationship between the principals as well as detailing the necessity for defending the Alamo in the face of overwhelming odds. Wayne's message of patriotism, freedom, liberty, and self-sacrifice was verbalized through constant repetition and reinforcement. Hokey, Ford-esque sketches had been somewhat minimized, albeit not entirely. The Master Shooting Schedule was now locked in—566 scenes filmed over sixty-six days, including each and every Saturday. Tuesday, November 4, was a scheduled lost production day resulting from the night-to-day transition. The cast was ready; the crew was ready: all Wayne had to do was shout, "Action!"

## CHAPTER TWENTY-ONE
## THURSDAY, SEPTEMBER 10, 1959

*After they finished filming Houston's departure, the company wrapped for the day. Three scenes and 1½ pages of script had been completed—an excellent beginning. That evening, as Wayne drove back to Ft. Clark, he must have wondered, Why had it taken fifteen years to finally reach this point?*

THE NEXT MORNING, CAST AND CREW VENTURED TO A SPOT IN THE FAR southwest corner of Ft. Clark, where Ybarra had discovered the perfect sound stage. An old corrugated metal airplane hangar, not terribly large but big enough to accommodate cast, crew, various walls, lights, etc. At seventy-five feet by one hundred twenty, the building was said to be the second-oldest hangar in the country. Cheaper than paying outrageous studio rental fees, it was convenient, functional, and available. While Wayne was busy filming the opening scene the previous day, his gaffers, grips, electricians, carpenters, and other assorted tradesmen were constructing interior sets. Unfortunately, it wasn't air-conditioned and weather down there in early September can be brutal. Wednesday, it had hit 94º; Thursday would be a bit cooler at 89º but still oppressive. Scattered showers but not enough to cool it down. Crewmembers would bolt from the building at the end of each scene just to get fresh air. Wayne, dressed in a short-sleeve polo shirt, Western pants, cowboy boots, and battered cavalry hat, was absolutely drenched in sweat as he blocked out each scene; changing shirts throughout the day didn't help. Imagine how hot it must have been for fully-costumed actors, many wearing wool or leather. Heavy wooden beams simulated a room's ceiling structure but also supported overhead lighting and technicians. Mounted on

385

wooden scaffolding, these lights poured out tremendous heat; fans and air-conditioners couldn't be used—their noise could be picked up by microphones. The hangar doors were closed to muffle outside sounds. Everyone had to make do.

Two interior sets were created on the sound stage: a hotel lobby that represented Travis's headquarters in San Antonio, and a hallway, vestibule, and hotel room for lovely Flaca. In all probability, the sets were constructed facing each other across the hangar, so the same lighting equipment could be used for both with a minimum of re-rigging. As both sets were three-sided with no parallel walls, elements such as a window (more on that later) were placed in the foreground to create depth. The hotel lobby was located on one of the long sides of the hangar and Flaca's room on the other. The floor of the hanger was a poured concrete pad; one can clearly see expansion joints in the scenes filmed at this location.[777]

The first scene filmed was INT. BEXAR STREET HEADQUARTERS: Houston gives Travis command. Present were Boone, Harvey, Pat Wayne, Ken Curtis, Bill Daniel, Jack Pennick as "Sgt. Lightfoot," Bill Henry as "Dr. Sutherland," and other individuals. As this was the first interior scene filmed, Wayne was particularly intense as he gave out instructions. The first ten pages of a script are the most important: main characters must be established, a location and mood created—a *raison d'*être, if you will. Wayne gestured emphatically, making it crystal clear what he expected of everyone.[778]

While acceptable to Calleia, Henry, and others, veteran professional Boone didn't need to be micro-managed. "Duke was kind of funny because he would liked to have played Houston," Boone recalled, "and he'd say to me, 'I think Houston might have done this,' or 'Houston would have said it like this.' And I'd say, 'Duke, you hired me to act, not to listen to how you'd play the part. Now just tell me where to hit my marks.' And he'd go, 'You're damn right.' Houston was a man of tremendous ambition, and so am I, so I understand this in him. He was a natural born director, and my impulse takes me in that direction. I don't think anybody exists who doesn't have some sorrow. So I have a hinge to go on there. But I think it would be hazardous to play Sam Houston without knowing a lot about him."[779]

"I respected Duke as an actor, and came to respect him as a director because, although he didn't always know the right words to use in directing you, he by God did the job, and it was a helluva good job. He funneled a great deal of energy into his work. He knew what he was doing and expected everybody else to be-have likewise. With a $5.5 million budget balanced on his head, he's the coolest, calmest, and best director I've ever had in a movie. He knows exactly what he wants, and he's articulate in explaining what he wants."[780]

Extra David Kuykendall had the task of delivering one of the first lines of dialog in the film, and it only took three takes. Outfitted as a Travis sentry, David wore a composite uniform of "Travis pants," red canvas shirt, brown leather belt, and white leather canteen strap. He was easily recognizable due to his big straw hat with coonskin tail! Avid collector Hedda Hopper, so intrigued after receiving a photograph, gladly accepted the chapeau after filming was completed. Boone said, "In addition to that big budget and a cast and crew of something like 185 men to handle, he has his son Pat playing a big role in the picture. In the scene Pat started blowing his lines, and we all expected the roof to fall in. But he talked to the kid like a catcher calming a baseball pitcher. There's a gentleness and kindness about him I didn't expect." When asked if he was nervous appearing in this scene, Bill Daniel (Col. Neil) said, "Nothing to it. After you have been a trial lawyer for twenty years, you get used to speaking under a great many different conditions." Oh, really? Kuykendall remembered Daniel appeared to struggle: "I thought they were going to have to literally talk for him because he was pitiful. Probably couldn't remember (the lines.) There were two or three outtakes on that, and each time we'd see Richard Boone was eating tamales. He almost got sick. Each (take) he'd have to eat another one, and it kept going on and on and on." Eventually, Wayne was satisfied; Boone was full, and activity was wrapped for the day.[781]

The Master Shooting Schedule was usually prepared by the first assistant director and gave all necessary information about actors, locations, technicians, special effects, vehicles, animals, props, the sequence of and how many pages of script were to be filmed day by day, etc. The schedule changed as needed in pre-production, but, once established, it was relatively fixed. Created on August 21, it included all script changes through August 3.[782]

But while Wayne was off filming at Ft. Clark, Grant had already started to change scenes that would be shot this first weekend. Whether Wayne was dissatisfied with the earlier approach or Grant just wanted to massage them a bit, previously finalized scenes were subtly changed. In an earlier version, both Bowie and Travis's rooms were on a hotel's upper floor. The open inner courtyard was surrounded by a gallery or a balcony running around the inside wall of the upper floor. When Houston departed San Antonio, Bowie slept the day away, awoke, spoke to Jethro, walked across the courtyard, and went *upstairs* to Travis's office where a meeting was being held. Houston had previously given command to Travis while outside this building. In the revised September 8 version, all of the aforementioned activity took place on ground level in separate buildings. Perhaps Wayne recognized that the hangar/sound stage could not be modified to accommodate this configuration. Further, Bill Daniel's dialog was modified; he would recite some of Ken Curtis's lines, Pat Wayne would recite Daniel's, and Curtis was odd man out. On September 9, Grant revised the sequence of specific scenes. Previously, the delivery of gunpowder, Crockett's introduction to Mrs. Dickinson and her daughter Lisa, Travis and Bowie's pyrotechnic discussion, and

Crockett's fable about Mike Fink all occurred at night, immediately after Emil Sand's death. Only then would Crockett notify Flaca of Sand's demise. The revised script brought Crockett's confession forward into the evening and all the subsequent aforementioned activity occurred the next morning.[783]

Perhaps too much script activity was scheduled for one evening or maybe the sequence would have been too difficult to film at night. Due to the tremendous amount of light necessary to expose negative film stock, most nighttime scenes were usually filmed during the day with a technique called "day-for-night." Underexposure and special filtration generated the effect of moonlight or darkness without all the problems associated with nighttime shooting. Fortunately, new, faster film stock was developed during *The Alamo's* production shoot, reducing by half the amount of light needed to film at night. Going forward, Wayne decided to shoot "night-for-night" for added realism. Grant's script change did show that Sand's murder weighted heavily on Crockett's mind and only an immediate confession would clear his conscience. Whatever the reason, the sequence of events was changed.

On Friday, September 11, production returned to the village set where Widmark would film his first scene. A continuation of a sequence filmed on Wednesday (scenes 16-18) depicted Jethro's conversation with Bowie immediately after Houston's departure. (Sharp-eyed observers will note that two different buildings were used to film this scene. As Jethro walks toward the entrance to Bowie's room, the green wooden lattice and flower pot are missing. Cut to his entrance into the room, and the lattice and pot are present behind him.) Wayne appeared satisfied with the results, but Widmark definitely was not. According to Pilar, he'd challenged Duke's authority from the day he arrived on the set. "Duke tried patience and understanding because he respected Widmark's talent," she explained. "Widmark seemed to interpret Duke's patience as a sign of weakness." That evening, as Wayne dined with his family in the Wainwright house at Ft. Clark, Widmark burst in and shouted that he was quitting the film as he felt miscast. Duke, quietly, patiently, replied, "Richard, I want to have dinner with my family. We can discuss this later." Refusing to take the hint, Widmark insisted they discuss it then and there. Eventually, Wayne lost his patience, stood up to his full six-foot-four-inch height, slammed his hands on the table, and ordered Widmark out. Discretion being the better part of valor, Richard complied. After dinner, Wayne headed to Widmark's house to finish the conversation. Too late to replace him and too expensive to try, both actors screamed at each other until Wayne had enough and threatened to take legal action. Widmark backed down, but their confrontations weren't over.[784]

"We didn't start off too well," confessed Widmark. "The fact is, I thought Duke, who's a really nice man, was not an actor's director. He was great with working with William Clothier to get some good shots, both the action scenes and the intimate scenes. But he couldn't help actors. I already had an idea how I wanted to play Bowie, but Duke would show me what he wanted me to do, and it would have been Bowie as played by John Wayne. (*Shades of Richard Boone.*) So we had some friction to start with." Interesting that Widmark said he had an idea how he wanted to play Bowie; he never researched the role. "I stuck with the script," admitted Widmark. "I'm against too much research because it becomes binding and academic, you're not able to move. In my opinion, once you've learned the fundamentals of voice and movement, so much of acting is instinctive and imaginative. That's what I did with Jim Bowie, I imagined Jim Bowie."[785]

On Saturday, September 12, Wayne had initially planned to film several scenes: 50-53, which showed the Seguins' ride through San Antonio; scenes 69-70, Crockett and the Tennesseans' arrival in San Antonio; and scenes 127-128, Tennesseans' departure toward the Alamo with townspeople following. Grant had earlier eliminated the Seguins' mad dash from the script, so that sequence wasn't filmed. The Tennesseans' arrival in their *foo-faw-raws* was filmed but not used. Their departure was filmed as well. All in all, the first week was fairly productive: eleven scenes filmed (ten and five-eighth pages of script). Good weather, no mishaps. What more could Wayne ask? After shooting wrapped that day, Happy threw an old-fashioned Texas barbecue for the cast and crew. Relyea argued against having the party as it might get out of hand but was overruled. A good time was had by all, and the beer flowed...well, like beer. While the party was going on, Happy's youngest daughter Tulisha was on a date with Cody Wardlaw III. Son of a wealthy West Texas family, Wardlaw was scheduled to leave for college the following Monday, as was Tulisha. Cody's mother had called Virginia Shahan seeking permission for her son to take Virginia's seventeen-year-old daughter to a party the Wardlaws were having for the kids.[786]

Later that evening, Happy Shahan received the phone call no father ever wants to get. Tulisha had been involved in a car accident and was in critical condition. He asked repeatedly, "How is she?" but the caller either didn't know or wouldn't say, so he rushed to the Del Rio hospital. Not saying a word, he entered her room, and she sensed he was there. "Daddy?" she cried. "I walked over," said Happy. "Well, you wouldn't of recognized her. She was torn apart, torn apart. She said, 'Daddy? Am I going to die?' I never thought about it. I know I'm going to die, you're going to die, but that kinda hit me. I said 'No,' but I said, 'If you do, don't worry about it.' I told her like that." The Shahans were deeply religious. No one wanted to die, but no one was afraid of it, either.[787]

She had been injured in a head-on collision on U.S. 90 eleven miles east of Del Rio that killed three people: her date Cody Wardlaw III from Del Rio, Charles Gregory Bryne from Houston, and Arthur Lopez from Burbank, California. Wardlaw and Tulisha were in one car, while the other vehicle was driven by Chester Thomas, also severely injured. Donald McLendon and Alton

Applewhite Jr., members of the Batjac crew, were also in Thomas's vehicle. The cars collided when Thomas pulled to the left to pass a truck. Relyea: "Four of our (crew) who had drank too much and then got in a car and were heading for Del Rio to get another drink. They hit his daughter's car head-on. Besides the disaster aspect, that put a lot of pressure on everybody, including Hap, who thinks I (was responsible) because I had the party."[788]

Tulisha suffered multiple fractures of both jaws, the pelvis, a fractured leg, fractured right ankle, fractured right hand, and a dislocated left ankle. By the following Thursday, September 17, she had been transferred from Del Rio to Nix Memorial in San Antonio where surgery was performed to repair the damage. Her face was so badly disfigured that the surgeon used her older sister Jamie as a model to reconstruct her features. The operations went "right well," according to a hospital spokesman, although she was still on the critical list. Jamie says, "Tulisha stood the operation well, and her blood pressure returned to normal more quickly after surgery than the physicians had thought possible." Unfortunately, Tulisha faced a long, difficult recovery.

When notified, Wayne was shaken. A production that had started out so promisingly was now covered by a black cloud. Wayne was very close to the Shahan family. He had attended Tulisha's basketball games in the Brackettville High School gym; it greatly bothered him that Happy's daughter was injured. Though he would visit Tulisha in the hospital, Virginia fondly recalled a different Wayne: "I think the most interesting thing, and what he did that I'll always remember him about, was when she came home, right after she was in the hospital and taken to San Antonio, Wayne had prayer on the set. Every morning at ten o'clock until she got out of danger. To me, that is one of the most wonderful things, and, I think, one of the most greatest things that ever happened to us, to have that happen." When Tulisha returned home from San Antonio, she was forced to use a wheel chair. Wayne made sure she was set up behind the camera. Virginia added, "And they carried her everywhere; wherever they went, and they changed scenes and everything like that, he carried her and put her right there behind everything. And then when she came in crutches, he saw that she was taken care of."

Many of the cast and crew signed a large twenty by thirty-one inch get-well card for Tulisha: *Dear Tulisha, Our Deepest Regards And Best Wishes For A Speedy Recovery. Sincerely, Your Friends Of The "Alamo."* Like her family, this Texas ranch girl was tough, determined, and believed in the power of prayer. "The accident was a real blow to my family," admits Jamie. "Dad was really devastated. But he had the ranch, the movie, and our Father to keep him busy. Mom was the rock. She never left Tulisha for any time at length. All of us felt we were so blessed with the doctors, the new procedures like grinding up bone and putting it in the cavity of the knee just hoping it would ossify. It did! And the doctors gave God the glory because it had never been done. All because of prayer from all over the area and the far-out realms of people that knew Dad and Mom." Happy even gave the production company a specially baked cake in Tulisha's name for all their thoughts and prayers. (She eventually recovered sufficiently to attend Baylor during the second semester although she faced additional surgery.)[789]

Kuykendall recalled the experience with astonishment: "After about six or eight weeks, they brought her back to the ranch, and she stayed out there. The bugler (Roy Ackland) and I would go out there quite often and visit with her. And we kidded her, she'd never walk. She'd be a cripple the rest of her life. But she was an all-state basketball player, and the idea of her being down was impossible anyway. And she said, 'I tell you what. Within a year, I'll be playing basketball again.' We said, 'Nah, you wouldn't.' Well, after the movie, about a year later, I was working at a filling station in Laredo, and one day a car pulls up. Girl gets out, opens the truck, takes out a basketball, and comes dribbling around and says, 'See!'"[790]

The tragedy didn't make things easy for others there, either. Jim Brewer had the unfortunate luck to be roommates with one of the Batjac victims: "I had several roommates at Ft. Clark. One was a young man about my age. He was one of the many electricians and grips from Houston that had been hired to work *The Alamo*. Approximately two weeks into filming, there was a horrible wreck on Hwy 90, a head-on collision involving two cars, one driven by Cody Wardlaw and the other driven by one of the crew members from *The Alamo*. I got the news that night, and, by the next morning, our roommate had not shown up. The set had shut down, and I walked over to the Gateway Hotel Café, and met one of the (other) roommates there. He had a sad look on his face, and I knew that our roommate had been killed in an accident. Later, news was out that Cody Wardlaw had been killed and that Tulisha Shahan had serious injuries and was in critical condition. (Relyea and Nate Edwards spent the day notifying all the relatives). Several weeks later, my deceased roommate's mother and father visited the set. I was introduced to them, and they asked questions about their dead son. I could only tell them that none of us really had time to spend forming friendships, that the demands of production kept us working many hours into the night and arising early in the mornings. I did tell them that he was a very nice individual, that he seemed honest and looked like a person of integrity. I had a lot of respect for him as did I have with most of the people I worked with during the film. They thanked me, and we said good-bye."[791]

Fortunately, Tulisha would survive the horrific accident. Would Wayne survive the arrival of a famous visitor?

A ghostly voice seared the night like a hot dagger. "You didn't film that right. Duke, you can do better than that." Wayne immediately recognized the voice: his mentor, counselor, sage. Holding back his temper, Duke grimaced, turned, and then with no apparent expression, politely asked, "Well, Pappy. What do you think I ought to do?" "Do it again!" barked the voice. "Why, Coach?" asked Duke. "Because it was no damn good!" yelled Pappy.[792]

John Ford took great pride in the fact that neither actor nor beast was ever seriously injured while working on one of his films. However, after the death of Fred Kennedy on *The Horse Soldiers*, it was something he could no longer claim. It was the director's fault, his responsibility. Sure, Kennedy was old and out of shape. Sure, Fred had broken his neck two years earlier. Sure, Kennedy had begged him, pleaded he needed extra money for Christmas. But Ford was the one who'd agreed. Ford was the one who'd set up the gag to surprise Constance Towers. "We were all right there," said Hank Worden, "and I can remember Ford walking away, blaming himself for Kennedy's death." What little enthusiasm Ford had for the film quickly drained. Wayne admitted to Pilar that Pappy couldn't seem to forget the accident and get on with work. He began drinking heavily again and lost interest in finishing the film. "Ford just doesn't seem to care anymore," confessed Duke. "Hell, he looks and acts like a beaten man." Bad Chuck concurred. Duke confided upon returning from Louisiana, "It really knocked him (Ford) out. He just went back to the hotel, and he couldn't work or think for days. It was a shocking thing." Sickened by the tragedy, Ford quickly headed back to Hollywood, wrapped up the film and took off to Honolulu for a much-needed vacation.[793]

Each day there was the same: in the mornings, he would swim in the warm waters of the Pacific; the afternoons were for reading and relaxing on his yacht *Araner*. Along with wife Mary and daughter Barbara, he drifted aimlessly around the islands for weeks. Depressed, worried about his future, Ford admitted, "The old enthusiasm has gone, maybe. But don't quote that—oh, hell, you can quote it." On March 26, John Bellah and Willis Goldbeck arrived in Honolulu with a script for Ford's next project, *Sergeant Rutledge*. Enthusiastic, he returned to Hollywood to arrange a deal, but initial passion quickly burned out, and he lost interest in the project even before he started it. In mid-April George O'Brien stopped by to assist Ford in a Department of Defense documentary. Traveling overseas to film *Korea: Battleground for Liberty*, evidence suggests Pappy may have engaged in a brief three-day affair with Korean model Hunan Moon.[794]

July found Pappy in a familiar and comfortable place (Monument Valley) to begin *Rutledge* with Woody Strode. Staying just ten days, he quickly wrapped up location shooting and returned to Hollywood to continue filming. But his heart wasn't in it. "He had always been growly with us," admitted Roberson, "but now there was a(n) edge of bitterness to him that seemed to dominate his personality." Happy only when working, Ford became depressed when facing the specter of unemployment. No directing offers on the horizon, no projects in development. Worried about his future, he fell into the proverbial rut: refusing to exercise, he wore the same clothes day after day. Smoking cigarette after cigarette, his teeth and hands stained yellow from nicotine; he refused to cut his beard and fingernails and spent all day in bed. He even feigned deafness to avoid questions he didn't want to answer.[795]

Ford always was an arrogant old bastard, but this was different. Scathing, pretentious, lonely, "He was an extremely sensitive man," said producer Martin Jurow, who had worked with Ford on *The Last Hurrah*, "and he was conscious of his physical ailments, so he retreated. He always carried a handkerchief because there was saliva that came from his mouth. He never looked into the camera because his eyes were bad. He was no longer physically able to do the pictures we wanted to do, yet he wanted to keep active."[796]

Unfortunately, no one called. Not even that "sonofabitch" Wayne. It must have been extremely maddening for Ford that Duke was able to pull off the seemingly impossible. While Jack was busy directing *Horse Soldiers*, Wayne not only acted in the film, but was also actively interviewing possible co-stars for *The Alamo*, pigeon-holing influential Texans in further fund-raising efforts, pounding out script revisions with Grant, and constantly calling Ybarra for updates on the set's status. Wayne was about to pull off something Pappy never even dreamed of. Ford must have begrudged Wayne's success. Not only was Wayne getting paid an enormous sum to act, almost five times what Ford would get to direct, Pappy's bankability increasingly depended upon Wayne's willingness to star in his films. Ford thought it seemed "out of the natural order of things" for an actor (and particularly for "that big oaf Wayne") to produce, direct, and star in his own picture. Though he tried to put these feelings aside, Jack couldn't help but resent Wayne's ability.... It's been said Wayne was the person Ford aspired to be: strong, commanding, a real man's man. Said Ford, "Boys and men admire him, and women love him, because he's a clean-cut, good looking, virile, typically American type. They'd like to have him for a pal, a brother or a husband. When you watch him on the screen, he's not something out of a book, acting according to the rules. He's John Wayne, a rugged American guy. He's real." And Wayne was equally admiring of Ford: "Well, there are times when a man is born and there is a relationship with another man. It is not a father-son, but you listen to him and you want to copy them; you want to be like them. That's the relationship I have with John Ford. There are times when I failed him I'm quite sure, but he directed my life. I tried to pattern my life after his—so not only did he direct my successful pictures, he directed my personal life as well."[797]

But Wayne was an actor; why did actors want to create their own production companies; why did they *always* want to *direct*???!!! Of course he had mixed feelings about the idea. Naturally, he wanted Wayne to succeed. But he had taken a *prop man*, for crying out loud, and transformed him into a screen legend. And now that Wayne wanted to flex his muscles, Ford felt betrayed. "Wayne had been trying to get *The Alamo* off the ground for twelve years," said Widmark. "He talked about it to Ford, who said, 'Go on, make it! You're ready for it.' In fact, he was expecting Wayne to ask him to direct the movie, but Duke didn't." Ford wasn't the only one who thought Wayne would ask. For years, every Hollywood rag worth its salt printed blurbs stating Ford would direct Wayne's epic. According to *Variety*, Wayne said Ford, Hawks and Hathaway all offered to direct the scenes in which Wayne appeared. *The Los Angeles Times* even suggested Ford would direct not for money, but for friendship. But, perhaps not. One week later, *Variety* announced Wayne had hired Ford to direct his scenes, but Ford claimed, "No one ever talked to me about it." Not true. During Duke's 1960 *Alamo* publicity tour, he confided, "I have wanted to make this picture since 1946...and at first I tried to get my favorite director, John Ford, to work on it. But he turned me down. He said it was my picture and my story and that I should tackle it. I decided then and there I'd only make the picture if I could direct it, too."[798]

Bob Relyea felt that Wayne waited too long to inform Ford that he wouldn't be directing the film. As a result, Pappy was irritated. Quite simply, "he was angry because he wasn't directing. Like so many of us, sometimes there are things you don't directly attack head-on; you beat around the bush because attacking it head-on is difficult. And probably Duke had a very difficult time over those many years of saying, 'Is this the right time for me to go to Ford and say 'Oh, by the way." And like he, just like all of us, didn't want to face the music of saying to Ford, and when he did say it to Ford, my reading was that Ford was in shock, and then, when he got over that, he was angry that he wasn't going to direct it. It was a strange love/hate relationship. I think Ford wanted Duke to succeed with the picture, but he couldn't quite forgive him for not wanting him to direct. Or perhaps Ford genuinely didn't think the picture could succeed without him."[799]

Duke had asked Pappy for advice during pre-production, traveled with him to scout locations, even interviewed prospective co-stars. And now, not to be even asked! Well, it was more than Ford could bear. In a September letter to friend Lord Killanin (Michael Morris), Ford wrote, "I hope to go to Texas and cast a paternal eye on Duke Wayne. This young and ambitious lad of fifty-six years is writing, producing, acting, and *directing The Alamo* with the excessive budget of five million bucks." A follow-up letter in February 1960 stated, "I've got to help Duke out with *The Alamo*. This is a picture that actually cost $5,000,000. It's a helluva picture...a real spectacular...but, as I said, I've got to help him." It's plain not only did Ford assume his presence was necessary to assure the film's success, he also felt the project's expected costs were inordinately extravagant. There was only one way to get this under control, so Ford invited himself to the set. Once there, he would make denigrating remarks about the crew or production; "The waste," he muttered. Jim Henaghan remarked to Hedda Hopper that Ford arrived and *asked* for a job.[800]

Makeup man Monty Westmore saw Ford's car pull up in a cloud of dust and followed along to see what would happen. Wayne was directing a scene with Harvey and Widmark inside the Alamo, and when Duke called, "Cut—I think that's a print," Ford's voice was heard saying, "No, it's not." After a pause, Wayne ordered the actors to do the scene again. They did. This time, when Wayne called "Cut," everyone looked at Ford. "Print it," ordered Pappy, who proceeded to take a seat in Wayne's director's chair. Another time, Wayne and Widmark were doing a scene together. Upon completion, Wayne said to Widmark, "Is that OK with you?" Widmark replied, "Yes, is it OK with you?" Ford growled, "Do it again!" Wayne asked, "Why, Coach?" Ford replied in his usual diplomatic manner, "'Cause it was no damn good!" Photographer Sam Shaw said Ford showed up one day, walked in on a scene, and said to Duke, "'Your walk there...' and made Wayne go back. Wayne had walked in his natural manner. But Ford, who had created a rolling gait for him years ago, stopped him and said, 'Now you walk like that.'" Bill Clothier recalled, "A week or two after we started, John Ford arrives on the set. He wasn't invited. He didn't ask if he could come down. He just turned up. Now, that would have been okay if he hadn't brought his director's chair with him and set it up next to me. He'd sit there watching Duke direct, and this intimidated Duke, which didn't help his concentration. Ford would say loudly, 'Jesus Christ, Duke, that's not the way to do it.' Duke was very patient with Ford who began telling him how to make the film." Clothier believed Duke was surprised when Ford showed up as Pappy hadn't been invited, but, in all probability, Wayne must have known Ford would be down.[801]

According to his travel records, Pappy arrived in Brackettville on September 19, two weeks after start of production, and stayed at Ft. Clark. Denver Pyle laughed when he recalled, "Ken Curtis and I, we roomed together. We had one of those officer's quarters along the parade ground at Ft. Clark. Ken and I had one of those little cottages; we had one side, and Old Man Ford had the other side. They were designed to have two quarters in each. So Ken and I stayed together. Ford, at that time, was Ken's father-in-law. That's why Ford wanted to be in the same building as Ken and I, so that we could look after him, take care of him. We'd go to dinner with him; he'd have a little wine before dinner. The doctor told him he shouldn't drink too much, and he'd have a little wine before dinner, which would be about a gallon!"[802]

Wayne provided him with a personalized director's chair, complete with Ford's name identified on the arm. Placing this next to the camera, Pappy, wearing slouch hat and red socks, sat down, sucked on his ratty old handkerchief, and started barking orders. Since most of Wayne's crew were charter members of the John Ford Repertory Company, they immediately bowed to his wishes, which posed a huge problem for Wayne. Just whose film was this? Wayne confessed to Pilar that "he felt a little like a young man who goes into the family business, only to have his father supervising every move." His authority and credibility started slipping. Filling the roles of actor, director and producer already was an all-consuming task. Even the most experienced individual would have had trouble juggling all the balls. Wayne naturally assumed Ford would show up on the set with advice and suggestions. Wayne wanted and needed "backup" to a degree, but the more he directed the greater his comfort level. Wayne had watched Ford direct Towers in *Horse Soldiers*, and his eyes had seldom left Pappy. "I'm never five seconds away from him on set, and I am studying him," Wayne confided. "I plan to direct a movie myself, and I will also produce and star in it. After thirty years, I am ready to see how much I've learned." Wayne grinned. "Listen, you bum," hollered Ford. "Why are you always around, staring at me like that?" Always the student, Wayne replied mischievously, "Just want to make sure you're not slipping a marked deck up your sleeve." Duke later admitted, "I'm physically exhausted because I'm knocking myself out, learning the art of direction from one of the greatest, John Ford." Pappy even allowed Wayne to direct a few scenes while on *Soldiers* location.[803]

Ford wasn't as gracious, however, on the *Alamo* set. Slowly, surely, he began to take over. Many crewmembers had previously worked for Pappy in the past, so it came as no surprise when he started to order them around. Roberson reflected on that association: "One thing that didn't change was his relationship with the rest of us. He was still bullying me around like he might send me home if I didn't straighten up. When my now grown-up little girl Charlene came to visit, the Old Man growled at me, 'Straighten up! You're a family man now.' Then, he looked Charlene over and said to me, 'It's nice to know you hit the mark once in your life, anyway,' and he growled and walked away. 'What did he mean by that, Daddy?' asked Charlene. 'It's a long story, darling,' I said. 'One of these days I'll tell you all about it.'" But he didn't confine this behavior to Bad Chuck alone. According to Widmark, "He (Ford) was a difficult little guy—I hear he was just terrible when he was younger and vile. But he resented that Duke was directing. So he'd drive Wayne crazy. It was like a little kid with his father. Ford would holler at him. Wayne was absolutely subservient—it was terrible. But Wayne took it because he figured Ford had made him, which he had, and made him in Ford's image." One of Ford's associates said, "If he's gently swearing you know everything is all right. But watch out when he's polite. It means he's mad as hell." Jim Henaghan theorized, "Ford is a genius as a director, but a rotten human being. He is sadistic. He kept Duke squirming just for the pleasure of watching him suffer. I never knew why Duke always took insults from him. Duke always worshiped him. Even when he was in the million-dollar-a-picture class, Duke would come running if Ford whistled and work for whatever Ford wanted to pay him."[804]

In the evenings, Ford would command everybody to play poker, tell jokes, and drink until two or three in the morning. The cast would then show up on set around 7:00 a.m.; Ford wouldn't roll in until ten or eleven. Wayne couldn't refuse. He didn't want to hurt the Old Man's feelings, but he knew he couldn't burn the candle at both ends. It was a brutal schedule: work all day, play all night.

Duke was literally exhausted. What he really wanted to do was spend time with his family, have some dinner, a nice massage, review the previous day's rushes, work on the script with Grant, and call it a day. But he couldn't turn Pappy down. Wayne grew weak, weary. And worst of all, Pilar was angered. Ford had begun to monopolize her husband.[805]

Ford's presence even affected Wayne's co-stars. There was no doubt, if Pappy was present, he directed. As Ford once explained, "…you've got to tell your story through the people who portray it. You can have a weak, utterly bad script, and a good cast will turn it into a good picture. I've thwarted more than one handicap of that kind with the aid of two or three really fine actors… In the first place, I can talk to my people while a scene is filming and give them suggestions about expression or movement; as a result, I don't have to make so many takes. I've discovered that, if you rehearse a scene too much, it looks artificial and—well, *rehearsed*… Lighting…is my strong point. I can take a thoroughly mediocre bit of acting, and build points of shadow around a ray of strong light centered on the principals, and finish with something plausible… ." He once said he considered himself a cameraman rather than a director. Ford also could coerce, trick, command, cajole, demand, and thus pull absolutely brilliant performances from his actors. He would dare the actors to do it right. Browbeat them into giving good performances on the first take where they could be spontaneous. But he didn't have a relaxed set; everyone was on edge. Tension was in the air, and he brooked no interference on the set. Wayne admiringly reflected on his relationship with Ford, "He lets the camera tell the story and not the dialogue. Old Pappy started in the business when pictures moved instead of talked. He's never forgotten it, and that's why his pictures are so great. He can be mean as hell, though." Wayne had studied under the best of the best: Hawks, Wellman, Walsh, DeMille, Dmytryk, etc. But Duke was no Ford. Hank Worden, who had worked extensively with both, astutely compared their respective techniques: "The difference between Ford and Wayne as a director," he said, "was that while Ford knew when to yell at actors and treat them roughly, Wayne did so indiscriminately. I think Duke made a mistake…when he didn't let Ford direct it. There are places where there's an awful lot of dialogue, and Jimmy Grant kept adding dialogue here and there. I think Ford would have devised more action."[806]

Linda Cristal agrees. "(Wayne) really wasn't a director," she says. "A director directs. (Ford) directed and if the actor didn't have it in him to give him what he wanted, he would do it in front of you. 'This is what I expect you to show me.' He would do it, you know? Ford was a very cerebral man with a great ego. But, because of his talent one didn't resent that." For example, in the scene where Crockett leaves Flaca's hotel room, "John Wayne had a scene in her room in the hotel, and he is very romantic and flowery in his words and how he admires her beauty, and this and that, and she dignifiedly says, 'Well,' with tongue in check, 'if I were…not a widow, da-da-da, I would certainly listen to your words, but since I da-da-da' she lets him go. But as she walks out she says, 'Oh, by the way, Mr. Tall American...' I remember that phrase. And she was supposed to say something like that, not those words. (Ford) wanted to get something from me that he didn't get, and he told me, 'When he goes, you put your hand on (the side of) your face as you hang onto the door, and then you simply let the fingers (slide down until they) come to the chin while you're saying the words.' I thought, 'Oh, it's going to be so forced; it's going to be mechanical, because it isn't coming out what I'm thinking.' But, when I saw it on the screen it was there, the feeling was there, that he wanted. He directed. He couldn't get the feeling from me that he wanted, so he showed me what he wanted to see. He came and told me in my ear what he wanted and held my hand and then back to his chair and put that dirty handkerchief in his mouth. It was always dirty, and he hung it from, the tip of the handkerchief, when I was doing my scene. Was hard not to laugh, you know? He was wonderful. I saw him be very tough with many people, but, with me, he treated me like I was a little, delicate rose petal. Sweet and gentle. There was sweetness and tenderness; he was gentlemanly."[807]

Reflecting on his time with Pappy, Widmark observed, "Ford had an amazing method of directing. He didn't get everybody around the table and say, 'Now, here, this is this scene, and you're so-and-so.' He left it up to you as an actor to have worked on the scene and to have pretty much worked out your idea of what it should be. Ford would sit there and say, 'All right. Try it out.' He gave you a chance to do it. Then he would say, 'Maybe if you waited before you crossed, see how that works.' You have the script; you know the story; you know the scene, and he's set up the scene visually. Then, he lets you move around in the scene, whether it's on a horse or in a bar, whatever it is. He'd say to the stuntmen, 'This is what I want, and I want it to be rough. I want you to get the scene so that it's quite a shock to everybody.' I think this is good." Ford would rehearse and rehearse until the cast got it right. In the meantime, the crew would light and arrange the set. When finished, the cast would come over, run through it again a few times and, once Ford was satisfied, finally shoot the scene.[808]

Still, Frankie Avalon, young as he was, thought Duke gave excellent direction. "Ford wasn't talkative at all," he says, "but Wayne was a very knowledgeable director. He knew exactly what he wanted. He would never give line readings. He would discuss the scene and talk about it. I remember him directing Widmark, taking him off to the side, talking to him, getting him to relax. He was a real good actor and sensitive man. (Ford) was there a lot of the time. Ford didn't talk to us much at all. Wayne would discuss the scenes, and he always knew what he wanted. He was very sensitive."[809]

Duke had the pleasure of Ford's company for almost ten days. Upon Ford's departure, Widmark wrote a brief thank-you note: "I'm sorry I wasn't there to say goodbye to you, but I want to thank you for the help you gave me while you were here. It was a thrill for me to be directed by a man I've long admired. I hope you can make it back and have another go at this ace location food." Widmark also admired the man's sense of humor and couldn't wait for Ford to get on the set: "I loved Jack Ford. I got him in his later days, and he was a total tyrant and a total autocrat and an Irish drunk. But I had a great time." In all likelihood, Ford may have directed Widmark in scene 49A, Bowie and Finn talk while working on Alamo; scenes 54-57, Seguins arrive at the Alamo and Travis doesn't let them in; and/or possibly scenes 93-94, Bowie helps when Crockett is attacked by Emil Sand's thugs.[810]

Now armed with comfort and verification of his own directing ability, Duke looked for a reason to minimize Ford's involvement. Patrick Wayne confided, "My father had looked forward to that picture for a long, long time. He ate, slept, and dreamed it, and nobody was going to take one frame of it away from him." Ironically, rumors were floating around Wayne was trying to keep it quiet that Ford was even helping him. According to Rudy Robbins, "Ford thought he was contributing, but he made Duke nervous having one of the greatest directors in the world, especially the one who had directed Duke and made him a star... it made him nervous having such a great director sitting there watching him direct a picture, and he just couldn't work with that. He wanted to get rid of him." He correctly believed, if the industry felt Pappy had more than a cursory involvement, Wayne wouldn't receive credit if the film was successful. He knew Ford would come down; he didn't realize he would direct the whole freaking picture! Duke didn't want to hurt the Old Man's feelings, but he didn't have a solution to the problem, either, so he asked Clothier for advice: "'He's gonna take over the whole goddamn picture. What the hell am I gonna do?' (Clothier) said, 'Look, I've got a big crew here and an extra first cameraman who's not doing a damn thing. Let's give the Old Man a second unit. See how he likes that.' Duke said, 'Why didn't I think of that?' (Clothier) replied, 'Because you've got enough to worry about.'" Wayne instructed Michael: shepherd Ford around the set and keep him away from me. "Look," he said, "let him do anything he wants, I'll pay. I don't care what it costs; I'm not going to let him feel rejected. I'd rather spend another a million dollars than hurt his feelings." However, according to Zolotow, after Clothier conceived the idea of a second unit camera crew, Wayne confronted Ford and proposed he film second-unit work as a favor to Duke. Ford objected but eventually agreed.[811]

Michael had mixed emotions about this assignment: "When JW decided Ford could direct a second unit, he gave me the job of watching over him. That was a pretty rough situation to be put in, trying to keep John Ford in line. My father said to me, 'Look, let him do whatever he wants, but whatever you do, don't let him near any of the principal actors.' I said, 'Why me?' He said, 'You're not afraid of him.' So we did stuff with extras and stock shots, shots of the Mexican army charging and retreating. I worked with Ford every single day, and we had a lot of run-ins. Well, there still were some rough moments between Ford and myself because he'd keep asking if I could bring over Richard Widmark or Laurence Harvey, and I'd have to think of excuses for them not being available. He always wanted to get them into the scene and do something with them, so there were rubs between Mr. Ford and myself. One day, Mr. Ford was shooting some vignette scenes and Father asked me to help him. When it came time to shoot, I yelled, 'Quiet, everybody! Second unit is shooting.' I can't repeat what Mr. Ford said about that crack." Pilar indicated Duke had asked Grant to write new action scenes for Pappy as, supposedly, Lyons was too overworked to complete all the second-unit work. It seemed like a workable solution.[812]

That wasn't the only time Ford took umbrage at being called "second." Bernie Abramson, a respected still photographer, got his first important film job on *The Alamo*. Taking an assignment for a magazine spread on the picture, he was eventually hired as the official still photographer. Abramson spent a lot of time setting up publicity shots with the principal cast members, shooting behind-the-scene stills to go along with the hundreds of shots he took while the film cameras were rolling. Using a camera which was muffled to prevent audible shutter clicks, he was able to freeze the moving images of action into memorable photographs. "So I spent a lot of time with Duke," said Bernie. "I have fond memories of working with him in Brackettville. He was a very gracious employer, and I remained with him after *The Alamo* for quite a few years. Duke would ask for me by name; in fact, when I wasn't working for Warner Brothers, I was employed by his own company." Recalled Bernie, "(Duke) was particularly thoughtful and gracious to John Ford." Duke put Ford in charge of a second unit to film various action scenes, and Bernie spent time on these assignments. "When I'd come up and inform him I was shooting stills for the second unit, Ford was quick to correct me. 'Not the second unit, the other unit.' There was nothing second unit about John Ford."[813]

But eventually Mike got even with Ford. Recalled Relyea, "Duke had a very strong admiration for Mike, who was a lot like he was—bright, hardnosed, and short-tempered. And Pat was an actor with his SAG card tattooed on his chest." After awhile, Ford started mimicking what he thought Mike sounded like around his father: "Dad, can we put the horses here? Dad, how about the cannons?" Mike responded by pulling out a handkerchief out of his pocket and tearing at it with his teeth just to mock his godfather. "At that point, Ford went ape shit and started screaming bloody," said Relyea. "You little dumbbell!" Ford was assigned another assistant.[814]

In a letter to Ford upon his departure, Wayne stated that a camera and crew would await his return: "After I put 'Ward' Thompson and guests on the plane, came back to the Robert E. Lee Memorial to find you had made an early exit for the Sunset Limited. Thank God they went home. I've had a helluva cold. If you had stayed, I'd have gone to bed for a night. Am good for about four hours, then start folding. Well, anyway, I can make it until Saturday, then I'll sleep for thirty hours. Saw the cuts you made on the wall. They turned out great, as you knew. There's a light and a camera in the window waiting for your return. Sure appreciate having your shoulder to lean on. Jimmy says hurry back—and 'Up the Texans.'" Obviously, Wayne was trying to mend bridges with Ford, but he also sent a subtle message: while you are here to help, this is still my film. Pappy would return to the set in just five days.[815]

Wayne called all the stuntmen together after Ford left and, knowing full well his mentor would be back, announced: "Gentlemen, I want to tell you something. Old Man Ford's coming to visit, and I know he's going to ask for a camera. And I'm going to give it to him. And I know that he's going to ask for you guys to do stunts. And you're gonna do them. But, whatever he shoots, I'm telling you now, none of that will be in the picture. So do what you want, it makes no difference, but it's not going to be in the picture because all they have to do is find out in Hollywood that Old Man Ford shot a scene or something, they'll say, 'Well, he shot *The Alamo.*' And this is not going to happen."[816]

Through sly manipulation and deceit, Wayne had averted one crisis, but an earlier confrontation with Widmark now threatened to spiral completely out of control.

# CHAPTER TWENTY-TWO
# CLASH OF THE TITANS

*"I know, I know. I'm going to use good judgment. I haven't lost my temper in forty years. But, pilgrim, you caused a lot of trouble this morning. Mighta got somebody killed. And somebody ought to belt you in the mouth. But I won't…I won't…The hell I won't!"*[817]

IN ENGLAND, LAURENCE HARVEY COMPLETED HIS ROLE IN *EXPRESSO BONGO* ON Friday, September 4, and immediately departed for the "colonies." He wrote his brother Robert that he had to fly to Texas "to start work on Monday on *The Alamo* with John Wayne and Richard Widmark and *director John Ford.*" One wonders if he knew something Wayne wasn't aware of. He also wrote that the movie would take all of twenty weeks to complete at a cost of $10 million. "I only hope the quality matches its extravagance," he lamented. Passing through Dallas, Harvey arrived on location September 7 and immediately began enjoying himself. The very next day, Governor Daniel officially proclaimed Harvey a Texan, whereupon Harvey remarked, "I am probably the only Lithuanian-South African from England who ever played a South Carolinian as an honorary citizen of Texas." On Wednesday he was sworn in as a Kinney County deputy sheriff, the first of many honorary decrees. On Friday, September 11, he was made a Bexar County marshal. Enamored with these accolades, he vowed to collect as many as he could. By the end of the shoot he had received a grand total of seven.[818]

He had spent weeks researching Travis and the history of Texas. Harvey realized Travis was a man of such principles and ideals that he gave his life for the cause of freedom. He knew, to honor the story of the Alamo, he needed to honor the memory of Travis. "The story of the Alamo is known around the world, especially in England," said Harvey. "The Travis on the screen must be a convincing characterization of the man who has become almost a legend. (He) was a strange man to become one of this nation's bravest heroes. He was also a vain, self-important young man with a hot temper. But he also believed passionately in the cause of liberty and died valiantly trying to defend it. I'm glad that James Edward Grant's script presented him as the complex kind of man he really was. The character was really something for an actor to dig into. I liked the part I had...there was quality in the script, at least, as far as my part was concerned. It had many layers to it. Although every schoolboy in America knows the facts of the battle for the freedom of Texas, most people abroad will find the story completely fresh and still be able to identify themselves with the fight for human liberty. Travis was a clothes-horse and something of a fop. He was jealous of James Bowie's wealth and David Crockett's easy command of men, but he was also brave and dedicated to the fight for Texas liberty. I suppose that, with his death, he truly found his manhood."[819]

Unfortunately, backlash against Harvey had begun almost immediately upon announcing he would play Travis. How dare Wayne hire an *Englishman* to play a Texan? *What the hell was the matter with him???* Travis was from South Carolina, not South Africa! Wondering what Texans might think of a *European* taking on this most important role, Harvey was assured they would accept his portrayal as long as it included the historical significance of the struggle for independence. He downplayed the issue. "Some wondered why an Englishman was picked to play the part of a Texan. They shouldn't have. If they'll check their history, they'll find that Travis had a European background. We're trying to make an international character out of him, instead of just state-wide. I read a copy of his diary and numerous history books on the man...even made a trip over to San Antonio to see the real Alamo." Harvey later stated, "You didn't see a lot of British actors getting to play Americans in American movies. I must have been one of the first."[820]

Wayne, uncertain of reaction to the news, had delayed announcing to the press he had signed Harvey. When he finally did, he attempted to pre-empt any negative feedback by issuing a press release: "All Texans were concerned over the fact that Harvey, an Englishman, would be playing Travis," he claimed. "But all Texans, in fairness, were taking a let's wait and see attitude." Wayne further explained, "During the first few weeks, I had some criticism about using an Englishman in the story of Texas' proudest chapter of history. But that subsided, when I reminded them that Travis was a South Carolina gentleman, a well-educated lawyer, and probably greatly influenced by British culture and manners. Certainly, his famed letter shows a great feeling for polished rhetoric." Harvey wasn't quite that patient: "People all over town screamed when they heard an actor with an English background was being put into a picture about United States history. How dare they!" he roared. "Those who complained don't know a damn thing about United States history. Inscribed on a plaque at the Alamo site are the names of Englishmen, Irishmen, and Scotsmen who took part in the battle. So you see, that's settled. I have every right to be in the picture. Wayne was really brave to put me into the film with all those people screaming. There's another type of film that Americans shouldn't think is all theirs. Do you know that somebody had to bring a lot of cattle to this country from abroad? It just so happens that Englishmen were among the first to come to America."[821]

Linda Cristal arrived on location in early September, weighted down with both luggage and emotional baggage. Appearing in three films in 1958 and three more in 1959, the attractive actress was versatile, exciting, and exotic. Less than two weeks earlier, she had performed a belly dance in *Legions of the Nile* that would have trouble passing the censors. "I wouldn't have done it if it hadn't been a part of history," she explained. "Cleopatra did that sort of thing to keep Marc Antony's mind off of the ugly problems of state and war." But while her acting career was moving right along, her personal life was less than perfect.

In 1958, Cristal had married Venezuelan oil company executive Robert W. Champion, half-brother to dancer Gower Champion. But the marriage was doomed from the start as he belittled her cooking attempts and objected to her acting career. Shortly after the wedding, Champion was slated to make a business trip to Venezuela. "I asked to accompany him as this would be a honeymoon trip for us," she said, "and he told me that he couldn't be bothered with a wife on the trip, and I stayed home." Later that year, she denied rumors they were going to divorce, but, by March 1959, they announced they had consulted their respective attorneys with a view to separation. Estranged but living under the same roof, they blamed the breakup on her career and his job in Venezuela, which kept them apart. "We are separated in our minds, though," she explained, "and I will move out of the house as soon as I find a place I like." As neither was an official resident of California, they couldn't file for divorce until one of them became eligible.[822]

During her separation, Linda continued to date such celebrities as actor William Campbell and Argentine film director Hugo Fregonese, ex-husband of American actress Faith Domergue. Shortly before she arrived in Brackettville, Champion officially filed for divorce; Cristal immediately cross-filed, charging cruelty. She testified Champion criticized her cooking in front of her friends and insisted she go sailing even though he knew it made her seasick. "He is a good sailor," she admitted, "but I got seasick. He would make me take seasick pills, and they made me sicker. Then, I'd have to go below deck and cook for his friends. They'd all laugh when I got sick." While she was in Brackettville, her friends predicted she would marry multi-talented musical arranger, composer, and record producer Buddy Bregman, ex-fiancé of Anna Maria Alberghetti. He agreed: "Her divorce has almost a year to go, but we both feel it is a good idea to be engaged and to be perfectly sure before we marry." (Cristal divorced Champion on December 8, 1959 and declined to accept any alimony. Married for less than a year, she rationalized, "I don't think that, being married for such a short time, I should have any.") According to Louella Parsons, Buddy Bregman and Linda Cristal had discovered each other. But, while on location, it was rumored she had lost her heart to Avalon and, in fact, there are photos of the two, hand-in-hand, on a picnic at Ft. Clark. A bearded Bregman arrived in Brackettville to film a few days work, but Cristal left for Hollywood upon his arrival. He had expected she would have waited until he was finished. Crushed, he returned to Hollywood after just two days. Apparently, Avalon wasn't the only one Cristal felt affection for. Pat Cumiskey recalled that Bill Moody called his father and "asked him if he would mind picking Linda Cristal up and driving her somewhere where they could rendezvous, shall we say."[823]

Most of the cast was there for the duration, but others, like Patrick Wayne, were on location only when needed. "If Dad hadn't been the director and producer of this whole project, I never could've made it," admitted Patrick, "because I'm carrying almost sixteen units this semester plus nine hours of laboratory work (pre-med at Loyola University of California in Los Angeles)... I was still in school at the time. In fact, I hadn't decided that I was going to pursue a career in motion pictures. My goal was to finish college and try and figure out what I wanted to do with my life. Up until this time, I had worked in several films and television shows but always with my father or godfather, John Ford. The experience was always rewarding and gratifying, but there was a gnawing question to me: Was it the work I enjoyed or being with my father or godfather? I have a seven-year contract, and I receive $250 a week, fifty-two weeks a year. I've been acting for eight years, since 1950. I started with my father in Ireland when he was in *The Quiet Man* with John Ford directing. I was visiting Pop, and he said, 'How'd you like to be in a picture?' He paid me $6 a day. I did two lines. He's always wanted me to be an actor. It's been a terrific life for him and he'd like me to have the same. He doesn't give me too much advice. Just, 'Do what your director tells you to do.' And, 'Don't act, just react.'" After appearing in *Mr. Roberts*, *The Long Grey Line*, and *The Searchers*, Pat signed a contract with C.V. Whitney, for one picture a year until 1963.[824]

Boone appeared in the first scene filmed, not because it was the beginning of the film but because it was the only time Boone was free to leave his television series *Have Gun Will Travel*. It had been announced August 31 that Boone would begin to direct his first episode of *HGWT* the next day. Upon its completion, he'd be free to travel to Brackettville. Along with actress Jeanne Crain, Boone had arrived in Dallas on September 7. Passing out *HGWT* calling cards, he stopped every few steps to sign autographs for his fans. As a result of a sty, he was forced to wear sunglasses to protect his eye. "I hate these," he admitted. "They make me look like a movie star."[825]

Though excited to be in *The Alamo*, like Wayne, Boone's desire was to direct. "It's the director who has all the fun," explained Boone. "Anytime a camera is involved it's the director who tells the story, more than the writer, producer or anybody else. And that's what I want to do. Of course, there's a whole chunk of acting I haven't been able to work clear of *Have Gun*. And I like the theater and want very much to be free to do it. It is here that all the intruders on the craft of acting are shoved aside. When the curtain goes up, you're on your own." In *The Alamo*, Boone would appear on screen for less than ten minutes, but it was the role he wanted. Already tired of Paladin, he was anxious to expand his career. Unfortunately, in order to play Houston, he had to turn down *What Makes Sammy Run*, an NBC presentation on its weekly *Sunday Showcase*, as *HGWT* couldn't spare him for both projects. As Wayne, Harvey and Widmark would get top billings, Boone would be listed as a "special guest star." "I think you have to be terribly cold and analytical about your position," admitted Boone. "With that cast, I figured, 'Just set me up my own card and acknowledge that I have an audience.' As for top billing, I don't figure I rate it yet."[826]

Frankie Avalon also gave up a series of lucrative engagements, so he could act with Wayne. Canceling several months of state fair appearances to accept the assignment, Avalon was replaced on tour by singing sensation Fabian. Appearing at numerous events like the National Dairy Cattle Congress Exposition in Iowa, Fabian picked up a cool $200,000 that summer. Avalon's last official engagement before leaving for Texas was on August 30, where along with Freddy Cannon, Jan and Dean, Bobby Rydell, Annette Funicello, Anita Bryant, Lou Rawls, and many others, he appeared at "A Salute to Dick Clark" at the Hollywood Bowl.[827]

Avalon had arrived on location in early September shortly before his birthday and within days had appeared in his first scene. Duke must have been pleased because after shooting finished, he placed his immense hands on the youngster's shoulders and said, "You'll do fine, son. You'll do just fine." Avalon gave all credit to his co-star: "Well, when it came time to work on the scene, Hank Worden to me was almost a grandfather figure and so gentle and so nice that he would come to me at times and say, 'Would you like to work on the scene a little bit?' which really gave me a lot of confidence because I needed as much work as possible because I was really brand new. By the time we got around to doing that very important scene for me, because it was my introduction to the picture, really, I felt very much at home and almost like talking to my grandfather. So, with all the rehearsals that he and I would do, whether it would be just the commissary or sitting around the set, he would, all of a sudden, throw me a line. 'You gonna pray?' You know, whatever my lines were at the time, so, by the time I did get in front of the camera to do that particular scene, I felt very comfortable. I just don't know exactly what was in the mind of John Wayne at the time, but I know the relationship on the screen should have been, and worked out to be, that kind of the older man, with the knowledge and the wisdom, handing it down to the new generation. And it came across very much like that. I think the most important thing that Hank Worden gave me as a young actor at the time was self-confidence, which he would always pay to me just after our little rehearsals. 'It's sounding good; it's feeling good. You're doing so good.' So he really gave me a lot of confidence."[828]

In addition to rehearsing lines, Philadelphia-raised Avalon had to learn to ride a horse. "Knees and legs tight, toes forward in the stirrups. That's what the wranglers taught me to keep from bouncing up and down in the saddle," says Avalon. "And, man, am I ever anxious to learn that." Wayne gave the kid some advice as well. Avalon recalled, "He wanted me to ride, to sit up tall in the saddle. The way he explained it to me, he said, 'Feel as though you have a coat hanger in your outfit, and feel like it's pulling you with the movement of the horse.'" After practicing for hours on a big bay horse named Skeeter, Avalon was beat. To kill time between riding and rehearsing, extras Kuykendall and Roy Ackland would look after him. Says extra Jerry Carlsen, "I was the same age as Frankie. And something I'll always remember, it reminds me of Frankie is when we were sitting, waiting for scenes or going out in the morning, and we'd get dressed and so forth. We'd sit where they had the cafeteria, and Frankie and I would sit there. He'd run out of cigarettes every day, and I'd buy him Chesterfield Long's non-filters. Added Kuykendall, "One night we took (Avalon) to a football game; several of us ganged up and took him with us, because he didn't have anyone there his age. So we took him, and got up into the stands on the Brackettville side about halfway up, and at halftime, somebody got the word out that he was over there, and, boy, as soon as they blew that whistle, the whole stands cleared and headed across the field. So, we kind of went down through the stadium, kind of crawled through and got outta there, because there would have been a mob. We took him over to Old Mexico, and he bought a bunch of junk, you know how they always want to go across and get stuff. And we ran around with him some." Others felt Avalon wasn't that friendly.[829]

On September 18, Avalon celebrated his nineteenth birthday. Not on call that day, he spent the afternoon lounging poolside with Linda Cristal. Only six years apart in age, they had much in common: acting, music, the opposite sex. There even were unsubstantiated rumors the two were having an affair on location. At 36½-22-36, Linda was voluptuous and shapely. But Avalon didn't have time for a special girl friend. Occasional dates as he toured. Usually he would pick out girls from those introduced to him backstage after concerts. When asked what kind of girls he liked, he simply replies, "Female. I like a girl that I can have a lot of fun with and be at ease with—one that's kind of quiet and doesn't talk too much."[830]

As evening approached, they both left the pool to dress for dinner. In black slacks and checkered short-sleeved shirt, Avalon had a Texas-sized steak for the tenth straight evening; tasty but boring. After leaving the commissary, agent Bob Marcucci (who also represented Fabian) suggested they visit the pool again as it sounded like a square dance was going on. Sure enough, the closer they came, the louder the music. As they approached the pool, a large crowd parted, and with a little girl sitting on Duke's knee, everyone sang "Happy Birthday, Frankie." Kuykendall recalled, "It was a big deal. We went out to the swimming pool, and there were probably two, three hundred people there. As I remember now, there may not have been that many. But you know how you're kinda glassy-eyed when you see all those people." Ever beautiful, Linda led him to a bandstand where Wayne and the cast were waiting with nineteen birthday cakes baked by Martin Bakery lined up in a row. Overcome with emotion, Avalon finally managed to say, "This is the biggest and best birthday I've ever had." And the best was yet to come! One by one, forty local schoolgirls filed by and gave Frankie a birthday kiss. Though not as entertaining, Duke and Pilar presented him with a gift certificate for a pair of expensive hand-made cowboy boots. "Thought you had better get yourself outfitted completely," laughed Wayne. "You can't be a Texan even for three months without a pair of boots." As the local girls screamed with excitement, Avalon wrapped up the evening by singing his best-seller "Venus." Afterward, he was mobbed for autographs. (Widmark wasn't on hand to enjoy the activities; he had taken a short trip back to Hollywood to move his company, Heath Productions, to the Universal-International Studios lot.)[831]

While Avalon was enjoying himself at the party, different entertainment was going on in Brackettville. Jim Henaghan had been a crime reporter, Hollywood columnist and screenwriter before Wayne hired him as a Batjac executive vice-president. Working as a story developer for Charles Feldman when Duke met him, Henaghan now would focus almost exclusively on *The Alamo*, creating presentations and acting as Wayne's personal representative. For assisting in persuading Texas millionaires to invest in Duke's project, Wayne agreed to give Henaghan 2.5% of the profits up to $100,000—a finder's fee, if you will. Henaghan met with United Artists in July to formalize the publicity organization: pre-production, production, pre-release promotion and publicity. He envisioned a staff of twenty-four individuals, fifteen in Texas alone. The unit publicity promotion crew would consist of ten men including photographers. Press representatives would be assigned to New York, Los Angeles, and Paris. On August 11, flamboyant press agent Russell Birdwell, famous for the notorious *Gone With the Wind* publicity campaign, joined the team as vice-president and publicity/advertising consultant at $25,000 a year. Three days later, Joe Hyams, former West Coast director of publicity for Hecht-Hill-Lancaster, also signed on. Batjac unit publicist Milton Weiss remained in Los Angeles while Hank Fine, in a similar position, traveled to Brackettville. (Fine, Frank Phillips, and Emily Stevens would later be fired by Henaghan while on location and subsequently file a lawsuit for unlawful dismissal. Henaghan claimed the three had been doing work on Sundays on location and that this unfairly increased the budget. Charging they had been summarily fired without sufficient reason or notice, their representation insisted when a union member was hired to work on location, they were to remain on the job as long as the local filming continued. The union further claimed that while three union members were dismissed, a non-union publicist was being kept on the payroll...Elena DaVinci. A settlement was arranged in 1960 where each individual received $223/week ($892 each) for four weeks pay).[832]

Once in Brackettville, Henaghan quickly set up shop since writers, publicists, and agents were flying in from all over the country to check out Wayne's film. Henaghan needed to entertain them, keep them occupied, and assure positive press. In charge of press junkets, he would hand out slides and information kits to the writers. Wayne, busy acting, directing, and producing, didn't have time to supervise Henaghan. Soon, though, many media visitors started showing up late on the set, or not at all, hung over from the previous night's *entertainment*. Mary St. John claimed Henaghan had supplied them with liquor, parties, and companionship. Even Wayne had noticed strange women coming out of cabins in the morning, and he wasn't going to put up with such shenanigans. Once he discovered these nocturnal visits, he was determined to put an immediate end to it.

Duke was led to believe that Da Vinci, a woman on Henaghan's payroll, was engaged in some unsavory behavior. Young and attractive, the Italian actress had appeared in such 1950s movies as *Hell on Devil's Island*, *Girl in the Kremlin*, and *Escape from Red River*. Gregarious and engaging, she also had hosted a radio interview program, *Magazine of the Air*. But as a result of her alleged activities, Wayne banished her from the site. She went to San Antonio where she then set up house, so to speak, at the Menger. Tom Carlisle (publicity) heard that "she is meeting planes and getting people bottles of liquor on her accounts, as well as shopping for people of the company." According to Duke's son-in-law Don LaCava, "I remember there was a kind of friction going on about her. Insisting on using her or something. Wayne didn't like you confusing playing with working. He liked to see people concentrating on their jobs and not getting off track. I remember her, and I know she was sort of agitating something."[833]

By the end of the first few weeks of shooting, Wayne began to hit his stride and fell into a routine. He gave his agent an update later that month. "We are working like hell," he wrote, "but the cast is wonderful, and the backgrounds are magnificent. Boone did a beautiful job as Houston, and we have found an exciting manner for opening the picture to take advantage of Todd-AO. I can't tell you how beautiful the weather is here. We haven't had one unusually hot day—beautiful mornings and evenings." But Pilar grew concerned about his passion and dedication to the project, fearing her husband's wearing the multiple hats of director, producer and star was too much. "He was driving himself and all his associates very hard, reaching for an impossible standard of perfection," she recalls. "He wasn't making a movie; he was on a crusade." According to Duke, it was necessary. "I sure keep my nose to the grindstone. Every time I pulled it up even for a minute, I smelled another Wayne in the neighborhood, usually led by Pilar." His routine? Up each morning at the crack of dawn, then off to the set to set up the day's activity. Always the first one there, no matter how early others showed up. First one there, last one to leave. Clothier was impressed as well: "Every morning, Duke and I would get up early and have breakfast, and then we'd go out on the set or to a location, and we'd discuss and plan every shot we were going to use that day. Duke knew the entire script, and we were able to plan each shot, so when we began to work with the cast and crew, we knew exactly what we were going to do. Is Duke not an *augenmensch*? This was the first time I worked with Duke as a director. He took charge even of photography, it was his picture. Duke would even tell me what kind of natural light he wanted, so we were able to plan which shots to start with to get the morning light, and which shots we'd do in the afternoon, so the light would be right. He learned that from Ford. And he knew in his head what he wanted. It is sometimes hard for Duke to visualize things, I have to call him over and say, 'Through the lens. See it through the lens,' and he would see it, but he cannot stand back and visualize a specific scene how it would look on film. (We) came down to see *The Alamo* set inside the fort. The whole city we built down there. He said to me, 'There are no angles.' 'What do you mean?' I said. He said, 'How the hell you gonna compose on? Nothing to compose on.' (I said,) 'We will have carts, animals, the set has not been dressed yet. Lots of things.' He was still not convinced, but, once we started the picture and we started placing things, (he was). If you have foreground with nothing, it looks bad, but you get a couple of pigs, a well, you put a horse there, a few wagons, horse with reins on the ground, and you fill up the space. It did not take him long to find this out. We never had trouble. The little trouble I had, I always got him to look through the camera. Sometimes he got mad at me. I said, 'Okay, tomorrow morning, when I line up the shots, you look through the camera.' After a while he said, 'I don't want to look through the camera anymore.' He accepted it. I am not talking about looking through a finder, right through the camera, not a viewfinder. You see what you are going to get on the picture. You see exactly what is going to be on the screen, some people cannot visualize it so easily, for we have many tricks. I will drop a viewing glass on the lens, so it will increase the contrast. We shot eighty-nine days on *Alamo*, and he would say, 'I will start with this setup,' and I would say that it would be better in the afternoon, and he would say, 'Fine. We will go someplace else.' Lighting is left entirely to me—we photograph the light on the people, not the people. A director's prerogative is to say a close up or a two shot, but I will suggest try a close up; let us take one. Now John Ford is different. He will say, 'If I shoot it, they will use it. I'm not going to shoot it.'"[834]

Pilar was quite amazed. "Never once during the entire three and a half months of shooting did he have to refer to the script while on the set. Like Ford, Duke carried in his mind a detailed version of every shot. He figured out every camera setup, every possible take in advance. At night, we reviewed the rushes together. I was so proud of Duke's work and ability as a director." But she was also worried, "I felt very frightened for Duke. He had put every penny he had on the line for this film and wanted to do it so badly. But I saw him going through such anguish." Mary St. John could only sympathize with Pilar's plight: "I had to leave my husband behind for those four months, but everything was Duke's total responsibility and that meant he had to have me with him. Everything about it took on epic proportions, and we did so much night work we often had dinner at midnight. All the others would be out fighting the war, and I don't think anyone but me and Duke knew what had to be done, so they all could eat. He was so considerate of the crew."[835]

"He knew his script so completely; he was never seen to refer to it," added Clothier. "Quite the contrary, he was seen mouthing the dialog of other actors, which necessitated numerous re-takes. I'd say the biggest problem he had was that during a take, he'd mouth the other actor's lines, like he was willing them to get it right first take. And I'd make a motion to him, and he suddenly realize(d) what he'd been doing, and he'd get mad at himself." Clothier apparently wasn't the only one to notice this faux pas. Denver Pyle recalled, "Duke was doing a scene...I was watching. I was looking over the cameraman's shoulder watching him, and he was mouthing the other actor's lines. I don't know who he was working with, but he wasn't sure of the actor, and he wanted to make sure he was saying his lines and saying it right. (Wayne) was totally involved in this thing, immersed in it. So, when he finished this scene, I went to the cameraman who was watching him (Clothier), and I said, 'Hey, Bill. He was mouthing the other actor's lines all through that scene.' Wayne was kinda depending on Bill when he wasn't in back of the camera. Bill said, 'He was?' And I said, 'Yeah.' He said, 'Well, tell him." I said, 'You tell him. I'm not going to tell him.' So he went to Duke. 'Denver says you were mouthing the other actor's lines. He didn't want (to tell you.)' Duke says, 'I was? Get him over here.' Bill came to me and says, 'Duke wants to talk to ya.' So I went over, and he said, 'Was I mouthing the lines?' and I said, 'Yeah.' He said, 'God damn.' So he turned to Bill and said, 'Print that. Let's do another one.' And then he said to me, 'I want you right back there.' From then on, whenever he was working, I would be in back of the camera watching him."[836]

"Although there were days when he used as many as twenty-six or twenty-seven different camera setups," Pilar says, "nothing escaped his watchful eye. He seemed to be everywhere at once correcting the way an extra sat his horse or carried his gun, rearranging his props, working with the actors, praising his crew."

Wearing his battered cavalry hat, rarely sitting in his personalized director's chair, he would constantly plan his next shot. Surrounded by friends, admired by co-workers, Duke flourished in this environment. Long-time co-worker Hank Worden recalled Wayne coming up to him, putting an arm around his shoulder and saying, "'Hank, you old son-of-a-bitch.' If Duke called you a son of a bitch, you knew you were in. One day on location when nobody else was around, I said, 'Duke, you ever get tired of sweating it out while working on a picture?' He replied, 'Hell, no, Hank, when I'm sweating and working, I love it.'"[837]

When the crew finished shooting at the end of the day, Wayne's work was just beginning. There were script revision meetings with Grant, discussions about the set with Ybarra, and a million other details to take care of. A 1,000-foot-long airstrip was built about a quarter-mile from the compound, so small aircraft could land and take off. The day's rushes were flown to Dallas by Ad-Air Academy, developed and flown back to Brackettville where Wayne viewed them in the Post Theater. Character actor Strother Martin (who would later appear with Wayne in *McLintock!*) commented on Duke's work ethic: "He's ready to bust his ass. And he expects everybody else to bust his ass." Most actors of Wayne's stature wouldn't even think of reciting off-camera dialog, but Duke would; anything to help the film.

His work habits impressed Luster Bayless, costume supervisor, owner of United-American Costume Company, and one of Wayne's long-time friends. "Immediately you knew he was on top of every area of film-making. His work habits (as an actor) were remarkable. He was always on the set on time. He was out there because he wanted to see where the damn camera was, where the director was going to set up the camera before the first scene. He wanted to get the feel. So he never walked in a little late or just in time. He was there early so he could feel he was on top of things." Wayne carried that same attitude into his role of director and producer.[838]

On the set of *Chisum*, veteran character actor John Mitchum saw proof of Wayne's knowledge first-hand. (Mitchum would later pen the John Wayne record album *America, Why I Love Her*). "Wayne was a very bright man and a very alert man," said John, "and he absorbed things wisely. He knew the film game from the ground up. When he was working on a picture, he would listen and pay attention to what the cameraman was saying. So Wayne knew every angle, and I mean every angle, of the picture business." He had one singular purpose, and only one: to make the best possible movie he could. His intensity was such that extraneous disturbances only served to irritate him. However, there was one area in which he lacked the appropriate expertise: he couldn't adequately express the way he wanted his cast to perform. And he recognized this. "I can watch the other actors in rehearsal and tell them what to do," he admitted, "but, when I'm in the scene myself, I can't see what's going on. I realized what happens to actors who direct themselves after seeing a picture Burt Lancaster did (*The*

*Kentuckian*). Everything in the picture was too pat, too perfect. There was none of the spontaneous things that a director can stop and keep, as when a boy forgets his lines and the other actor has to ad lib a sentence or two. These are the things that make a picture come alive."[839]

Others also recognized this. "Wayne worked differently," explains Linda Cristal. "He worked for results. He didn't go for the complicated... He wanted the result, 'This is the way I want it to look.' And the problem with that is that it's hard to touch someone's heart if you don't know how it ticks. You have to understand the function of the heart to know why...a kind of tick-tick-tick, that's a clock, that's a pendulum clock, it's not a heart. But he was terrific, a nice man." Ken Curtis concurred, "Duke didn't know how to motivate an actor with just a word or two. He'd say, 'Do it this way.' If you watch the scene where Pat Wayne rides into the Alamo, gets off his horse, takes a drink, and throws the ladle away, he does it just the way his father would do it. He'd always say, 'Be graceful...like me, goddammit.' Well, guess whose action that was? It was Wayne's. Duke was great for directing action, these rough battle scenes and stuff. But, for directing actors, I wasn't all that pleased with him because everything he told you to do was with all his mannerisms, which nobody else could do. He had the corner on that situation."[840]

*(Both Scott Eyman and I had the unique opportunity to speak with Bob Relyea about his experience on the set. Although many Relyea quotes from Eyman's biography on Wayne appear in this book, the following best summarized Bob's feelings.)*

"The picture was hard," said Relyea. "The nature of the piece was a couple of thousand extras. And we shot forever. People died of old age. And I must say, Duke never went off on me. He did get joy out of calling me 'Bobby.' Somebody had told him I hated being called Bobby, so of course, he had to do that. The shooting was efficient. Some of the picture was storyboarded, but not much. All of it was storyboarded in Duke's mind, and we didn't vary from that much. He would never argue about practicality or logistics. If I told him we were getting deep into gold (overtime), he'd say okay. His preferred method was to do his master shot, then move in. He didn't do a lot of takes, but he wasn't a one-and-out kind of guy. He would stay with a shot until it was right. He wasn't difficult. It was the picture that was difficult. After it was all over, I liked Duke. It was hard not to. Being an assistant director on a picture like *The Alamo*, you worry about everything—shooting, what people do when they're not shooting, everything else. But I could always count on Duke being prepared. Sometimes hung over, but always prepared. And definite. It was always, 'Yes,' or 'No.' Everybody took direction from him. You can tell when a director is organized and has a point of view. If he's got that, unless you're totally opposed to that approach, it's a relief. The cameraman knows where to put the camera, the actor knows where to stand. And you could tell he knew what he was doing. If Duke looked at a set and said, 'We'd better go with the 75mm lens,' he was always exactly right. People pick that up quickly and say to themselves, 'Right or wrong, at least, we have leadership.' A film set is mainly about leadership, and Duke had that."[841]

All that effort took its toll on Wayne, manifested by a brutal smoking habit. From the moment he arose until he went to bed, Duke always had a cigarette in his hand. He'd started smoking as a young adult and, in 1952, even filmed a commercial for Camel: "Mild and good-tasting pack after pack. And I know, I've been smoking 'em for twenty years." Indulging well beyond his customary five or six packs a day, Duke would light a new one before the old one was finished—pack after pack after pack—a chain-smoker with a constant cough. Since Jack Pennick and others were charged with the responsibility of feeding him one after another, Wayne probably lit up as many as two hundred per day! Pilar was concerned with the effect it was having: "…before he went off to start shooting, I listened to his barking cough. I was worried for him. He sounded like he was tearing himself up. I pleaded with him to see a doctor." He wouldn't even take the cough syrup she offered as he said it made him tired. Fatefully, Duke justified, "So maybe it's six months off the end of my life, but they're not going to kill me." Stuntman Dean Smith once remembered a photo taken with Wayne: "He was wearing a bracelet from an elephant's tusk on his wrist. He smoked so many of those cigarettes that he had nicotine all over his hand. He used to smoke the hell out of those Camel cigarettes." Extra Kuykendall used to carry around a pack of Camels for him: "And he'd call me, I don't care where it was. I'd be standing off to the side, and he'd holler at me, 'Come here. I need a cigarette!'" Others complained quietly. After a publicist lent Wayne a cigarette, he whined, "If he don't want to buy his smokes, he shouldn't gripe if you don't happen to have his favorite brand."[842]

None of this stress should have surprised Wayne; he'd faced it before. Dedicated to his craft and an absolute perfectionist, Wayne's wicked temper would once again flare up during *The Alamo*. Late one evening, Wayne and Bob Relyea were walking out of a building after a midnight "lunch break" when Widmark came alongside.

"John, can I talk to you about the next scene?" he inquired.

"Not now, you little son of a bitch," Duke replied as he continued walking away with Relyea.

Widmark quickly caught up with the duo. "What did you say?" he asked incredulously.

"Don't interrupt us, you little shit," growled Duke, as he continued walking.

Widmark quickly planted himself in front of Wayne, fists weaving in and out like a boxer. Wayne walked past the agitated thespian but innocently asked of Relyea, "What's the matter with him?"

Again Widmark caught up and again struck a fighter's pose.

"What's he doing now?" asked Duke.

"I think he's upset," countered Relyea. "I think he wants to fight you." A crowd began to gather.

"Why would he want to fight me?"

"Because you called him a crazy little shit?" offered Bob.

"I did not!"

"Yeah, you did."

Again, Duke denied the accusation. "When?"

"Just now," Relyea explained. "A few steps back there. You said 'you little shit.'"

"I did not!"

Widmark was inching ever closer, breathing heavily, working himself into a furor. "You did. Look at him!" Relyea moved in between the two as if to separate the warriors. "Richard, please put your hands down. You're going to get hurt."

Removing his hat and scratching his head, Wayne questioned his own motives: "Why would I call him a little shit?"

"I don't know, but you did."

Wayne still wasn't convinced: "I don't believe you. I had no reason to call him a little shit."

Relyea attempted to resolve the situation. Turning to the fuming Widmark, he explained, "See, he doesn't really know how to say he's sorry, so let's take that as an apology and forget it. Why don't you grab some food, and I'll meet you in the mess hall, so we can talk about the next scene." While Widmark knew it wasn't a real apology, he also knew there was no way in hell he could beat Wayne in a fight.

Widmark turned away and walked back to the mess hall. Duke and Relyea began walking again and in a loud voice—loud enough for Widmark and the entire crew to hear—Wayne said, "Fucking crazy little shit, isn't he?"[843]

"Fucking crazy little shit." That neatly describes the relationship between the two: Republican vs. Democrat; conservative vs. liberal; professional while on the set and distant toward each other off; anti-social vs. gregarious. One evening, Duke, Pilar, Denver Pyle, Widmark, and many others were at the Maderno Mexican café in Piedras Negras, across from Eagle Pass. One side enclosed a bar area, the other dining and dancing. Four or five tables were lined up to hold the diners. Marshall Jones was there and witnessed an example of the difference between the two actors: "If you knew anything about Duke, you knew he was very, very super friendly. Women in the audience loved him and would come over and grab him, and he got up and danced with them. All the gals would come over—older women, it didn't make any difference. That's how nice he was and all. Not Widmark. Oh, no. He wouldn't. He just sat there. And (in a nutshell) that was the difference between the two."[844]

Pilar describes Widmark's personality as scratchy; "not unlike a tweed jacket, serviceable but uncomfortable." Cristal described him as, "Introverted. He was a maze. Talented, but always within himself." Widmark had earned a reputation for being a bit difficult on location. Edward Dmytryk, who had earlier directed Widmark in *Broken Lance* and *Warlock*, accounted for that behavior: "Dick is an extremely conscientious workman, a study in concentration and creative irritability, and has a very short fuse." Don Siegel, who would later direct Widmark in *Madigan*, concurred. "Widmark is very explosive and doesn't hesitate to show his displeasure." Often described as a loner, he was abrupt and distant while on set with co-workers. Andy Devine, who appeared with Widmark in *Two Rode Together*, warned of the short-tempered actor, "Nobody sits with Widmark in the morning." Recalls Marshall Jones, "He always had a script, and he would always be looking at what was going on, when they were actually shooting a scene. But, if anyone wanted to talk to him, he wouldn't say anything at all to that person. He would just take his folding chair, and he would move on. He would just look at them with a hard look and walk off and sit someplace else." That may very well be, but he also was deaf in one ear, so his aloofness and unresponsiveness could be attributed to the fact that he just couldn't hear when spoken to. Thrice rejected for military duty because of a perforated eardrum, Widmark recalled, "Actually, it's more than perforated. I have a hole in my head. I go every three months to have it drained." Because of this little-known secret, most co-workers just assumed that in his silence, he was ignoring them. In 1960, Widmark would co-star with Jimmy Stewart in John Ford's *Two Rode Together*. "I'm a little deaf in this ear," he said, "and Ford's a little deaf in the other, and Jimmy's hard of hearing in both!" Widmark cupped his ear. "So all through the picture, all three of us are goin' 'What? What? What?'"[845]

Linda Cristal found it difficult to work with Widmark. "He was so cold," she explains. "So withdrawn. He didn't mix with anybody. He finished his scenes and went to his dressing room and never came out. Very hard to establish any conversation. Actually, in a way, I was like him too because I was a loner. But he was like very protective. And he had a shield around him. An excellent actor, but very remote."[846]

In an attempt to explain Widmark's behavior, John Quinn says, "It's a funny thing. He tried to stay in that surly mood, and you'd find him lying on the ground over by the wall somewhere in his buckskins. He would just wait around until his scene came up, and then he'd go to work. I guess a lot of people were scared to approach him because he had that aura. He was protecting his deafness, he didn't want to embarrass anybody by letting them talk to him and not hearing what they were saying."[847]

Widmark's first contact with Wayne portended volumes about their ongoing relationship on *The Alamo* set. One evening, shortly after Widmark had appeared as giggling killer Tommy Udo in *Kiss of Death*, he was invited to a dinner party at Olive Carey's home. Wayne was there as well and already deep in his cups by the time Widmark arrived. As Widmark walked through the front door, Wayne, standing in a corner, drink in hand, hollered, "Well, here comes that laughing son of a bitch!" Each respected the other as an actor, but there was no love lost between them. "Wayne and I were never friends," he admitted. "Chemically, we were two guys who didn't like each other. We were so politically far apart that it made for a breach. He was no Mr. America during the McCarthy days; he was a bad apple. I didn't like what he stood for. Wayne and I got along great professionally, but we weren't friends socially. He was like Mitchum in the sense that he liked the booze." In later years, Widmark still spoke of those times with distaste: "Those idiots (referring to the HUAC witch hunt). Those men were afflicted with the worst period in American history, a period we should be very ashamed of...I had total sympathy with all of them, because I was so against what had happened. (Wayne) was on a different side of the political spectrum— and I was from New York. He didn't like people from New York." In a 1997 interview, he expanded on his comments: "Well, we never got along personally. I respected him for what he did, his work, and, to this day, I love to see him in a Western; he's terrific. But as people, we didn't get along... from that point on, we weren't exactly friendly. We tolerated each other, and, when we worked, we were very professional, got along fine, never had any trouble. But we didn't like each other, politically or personally."[848]

Still, there were those on the set like Rudy Robbins, Avalon, and Western Costume employee Ron Talsky, who claimed never to have seen any animosity between the two. "People made a lot about the difficulties he had with Richard Widmark," said Talsky. "But you can step on that. I never saw it. I admire and respect Widmark, whom I have worked with six times. Duke had a lot of pressure on the film, and Widmark appreciated that point. He was acting and directing, with six hundred extras sitting out there, some half drunk, in the field. So you really couldn't expect Duke to be of good cheer every moment of the day. Duke had a big undertaking, and Widmark didn't want to give any leeway for abuse, whether it was directed at him or anybody. Without (my having) any discussion with Dick, I thought he just wanted to see that things didn't get out of hand. But I can also see how people could have thought otherwise."[849]

Avalon felt the same way: "First of all, you've got to recognize the fact that not only did he star in it, he produced it, directed it and put about a million of his own bucks in there. It was really a lot of pressure. And this was his baby, too. He really wanted to tell his story the way he saw the story, and it was very important to him. You know, I didn't see any of that (friction). I know that Duke was really adamant about doing what he wanted to do, and there may have been some conflict with Widmark portraying the role that he did, but I didn't see any of that. All I know is he was tough to work for without a doubt because he wanted it his way and he wanted professionalism. He wanted everybody to know their lines and be on their mark and do what he wanted them to do."[850]

So did Robbins: "I never did witness it, but I heard that there was some," he said. "But Widmark, for lack of a better word…he was kind of a prick. I worked with Widmark in this picture. Then I worked with him in *Two Rode Together*, and he would never even so much as acknowledged me there or said hello or anything. And then the third picture I did with him was *Cheyenne Autumn*. We filmed it out in Monument Valley, and I got there a day before him, and he came driving in, in a chauffeured car, and he stepped out, and saw me right there and he says, 'Hey, 'It Do', how ya doing?' came over and shook my hand. From then on, we were friends. But for the first two movies, he acted like I was a non-existent person. And he didn't like to sign autographs, or pose for pictures. He was kind of a jerk. So I could see that maybe he and Duke had a falling out, and I heard that they did, but I never personally witnessed that."[851]

As did Happy: "We did two pictures with (Widmark)–*The Alamo* and *Two Rode Together*. He came in my house and left just like it was his own. He was like family. Many time I would go into my living room and find him reading the newspaper, and I'd say. 'Hi, Rich.' Never had an argument with him in my life; never had a bad word with him in my life. My daughter came home one time from college with her sorority sisters—fifteen to twenty girls. They asked Widmark to go to Mexico with them one night. He said, 'If you'd asked anyone else, I'd be mad at you.' He went with them and had a ball; they had a ball. This was during the filming of *Two Rode Together*. I think Widmark is very intelligent, and I think that the people who don't like him don't know him."[852]

Harvey felt Duke and Widmark reached an eventual accommodation: "I liked working with Wayne, and I liked Widmark, although things started a bit strained between Wayne and Widmark. But they sorted themselves out and got on with working together in, shall we say, a professional manner." But others have suggested the two fought like cats and dogs. For instance, there was talk around the set regarding professional jealousy among the cast, as well as Widmark's lack of respect for Wayne's directorial ability. There were numerous stories where either by accident or intentionally, the two stars almost came to blows. Once, one such tale goes, Duke snapped at some extras standing behind Widmark. Dick said, "Don't talk to me like that!" Duke said, "I wasn't talking to you." But it may have looked like he was. On another occasion Duke flipped a cigarette that happened to land at Widmark's foot, which ticked him off. During the filming of *Two Rode Together*, Widmark's close friend Harry Carey Jr. would learn quite a lot about Widmark's ordeal on *The Alamo* shoot: "God, everybody knows there was animosity between Duke and Widmark on the set of *The Alamo*. That's not even a secret. Widmark…is highly intelligent, but he also has a very short fuse. And Wayne could get excited. They had one big run-in, I'm told. Duke was using bad language, and there was a bunch of kids and nuns on top of the hill. According to Kenny Curtis, Duke yelled to Widmark, 'Let's see if you can come down those goddamn stairs.' And Widmark grabbed an axe handle and said, 'I want you to apologize to everybody on the set. Don't ever yell at me again. Apologize to all those people!' Duke just kind of looked around and said, 'What did I say?' But then again, I got this all secondhand."[853]

Widmark expanded on the explanation: "In a big scene—granted, he was tired—he screamed things to me in front of all these people. I told him: 'You no-talent sonofabitch, don't ever talk to me that way.' But I didn't say it before I had an iron bar in my hand, because if he had come at me, I was a goner. I didn't really think he had no talent, but I knew that would set him off." After that, "We got along fine. He's like any bully. If you call a bully, it's over." Marshall Jones was standing to the side, taking it all in: "I don't think he meant it, anything personal, but he was hollering. That little banty rooster. He said, 'Hey! Don't you ever holler at me again. Don't ever holler at me again. You can holler at all these other people anyway you please, but, damn it, you're not going to holler at me!' And Duke went up the stairs, and Lord knows I'm telling you the truth here, he got up there, he walked up there and, speaking in a very low voice, apologized to him and then turned around to go back down. I'm going to tell you what. Mr. Widmark almost kicked him right in the ass! Raised his boot. And I thought, 'God, don't do that.' He woulda done it. He would've kicked his ass down them steps, but he thought better of it."[854]

Gene DeRuelle was one of the crew who seemed to like Widmark: "As an example, one day, Richard Widmark came up to me and said that he had checked the schedule for the next week, and he wasn't involved. He said that if I could get it OK'd, he'd like to go to San Antonio for a few days. It was only up the road, and, if things went bad, he could be back in a couple of hours. I didn't heed Relyea's warning, and when there was a quiet moment I asked Wayne about Widmark. I had also checked the schedule and I asked him if a trip to San Antonio for Dick would be OK. He said he didn't see why not as long as we had a phone number on him. I had the phone number of the hotel, so I told Dick to take off and I'd call him. I thought everything was fine. Boy, was I wrong. The very next morning, Wayne got out of his car, walked to a spot near the Alamo wall and looked directly at me. 'The camera goes right here,' as he pointed to a spot, 'On Richard Widmark. Where is he?' A lot of very nasty things went through my mind, but I remembered that my help was needed. 'Probably in that San Antonio hotel you said it was all right to send him to, I guess.' 'Well, I guess I'll have to think of something else to do,' and he picked another setup. From that day on I stayed away from Mr. Wonderful."[855]

Wayne could swear like a sailor's sailor, and wasn't afraid to hold it back. Joe Canutt said, "Bill Moody was down there working, flying an Apache and landed it out in a field at Shahan's place, and he'd go to work for $7 a day. I mean you had some pretty classy people out there doing actual work. And God, Wayne's calling them names, and one day a guy came up and told him, said, 'Look, my wife's working out here. I'd appreciate it if you wouldn't use that kind of language.' Wayne said, 'Well, if you're unhappy with your job, well then you can just go someplace else.' He's treating them like a bunch of Hollywood extras." Marshall Jones concurs. "(The cast and crew) were just working and doing different things. You'd hear some racket, and (Wayne) climbed up on that damned twelve-foot step ladder with a portable squawk box, whatever the hell you call them, a microphone, and he challenged everybody on that damn set, and I mean we're talking about where you had, at least, five or six hundred men there or more and he said, 'You don't like it, we'll get it on right now!' (No one accepted the offer.) You know that he's making a movie, and he may holler this and he may holler that, but he invited anybody there to come up and they'd get it on right then, but they'd still have a job. And did you know that? Not one did."[856]

Canutt was present once when it got out of control: "Duke could be pretty foul. You know, talking to a lot of people, swearing at them, calling them names and all that. It got to be a habit. Widmark had him by the throat and had him by the collar and bent over. And Wayne was bent over, and he's nose to nose with (Widmark). He said, 'Don't ever talk to me like that, you son-of-a-bitch! You hear me. Don't ever say that to me.' Wayne said, 'Well, it isn't exactly the way I meant it, Dick.' He wasn't afraid to fight Wayne." Fellow stuntman Ted White had worked with Wayne long enough to know that's just the way Duke was: "Well, you know, these are pressures that he had on him, and consequently, with all that pressure, he was yelling. But his yelling didn't mean that he was upset with you personally. That was just the way...that was his mannerisms. I think some of the actors took it to heart and thought it was aimed at them, and they started feeling like Wayne was jumping on them, and they weren't going to take it. They just hadn't worked with Wayne. They didn't know his mannerisms. His yelling didn't mean anything. That's just the way he was."[857]

Extra Jim Brewer noticed things, too: "I do remember when Widmark called Duke a 'son-of-a-bitch' and walked off the set. Duke set up a scene with Widmark outside the Cantina one night. The Travis regiment was standing on the outer perimeter, and, all of a sudden, Widmark shouted at Duke and walked toward the street. Duke ran after him with a smile on his face and apologized to Widmark and asked him to come back and do the scene."[858]

Extra Robert Harris: "It's hard to get to know (Widmark). We used to get where we'd go to work and we'd say, we'd hold our arm in front of our face just to aggravate him and say, 'Good morning, Mr. Widmark.' Kind of like ducking. Most of the time, he wouldn't even look up. You'd ask him to get a picture with him, he wouldn't even look up, or take his, or turn his head toward the camera. He didn't socialize with hardly anybody really, you know? He studied most of his lines all the time. He had a script in front of him." Extra Jerry Carlsen remembers, "I had to go up to the Shahan ranch one day and get him. Widmark would disappear on the sets. He'd be resting or something, and he was always... we always found him on Virginia's couch." Happy recalled, "Widmark was a different sort. In my house, he'd look at a paper or sit down and read a magazine just to get away from people." Extra Tommy Worrell got a taste of the Widmark personality: "(Widmark) had the reputation of not being a very cordial individual. In fact, some people say—an asshole. I was out at 4:00 clock by the pool, early one morning. It was a Sunday, and we weren't filming. He came walking by, and I thought, Well, I'm not going to bother him. I'm just going to say 'Good morning.' I said, 'Good morning, Mr. Richard Widmark.' He ignored me. And I said, well, you know, maybe that's all true. A couple of days later, we were on the bus, they were taking us out to the set, and he was standing there talking to somebody in the road. And the bus driver kind of hollered out the window, 'Hey, Mr. Widmark. Can we get by?' And he just ignored him. So he honked the horn a few times, and he got out of the way. He just kind of had a reputation like that."[859]

Even newspaper columnists were warned to tread lightly. Ed Castillo from the *San Antonio Express and News* warned, "We don't talk to Widmark, he's deep in thought, and reporters never know which way he is going to jump—straight up, or down your throat!" Constant dissension and challenging of Wayne's directorial authority naturally led to violent outbursts, some reasonable, others downright hilarious. Stuntman Red Morgan recalled once, "Wayne had some Mexicans, they were supposed to be shot, and they were falling, but they were looking up. And Wayne yelled, 'You son-of-a-bitch! When I tell you to die, you die!'" According to Linda Cristal, Wayne "was working for results, and he didn't go in for diplomacy. When he exploded, his fury scorched many. He and Richard Widmark had some thunderous confrontations." Arguments in front of cast and crew, day after day, scene after scene. After three weeks of such treatment, Duke, who had been trying his best to remain calm, finally blew his top. He chased Widmark across the set, grabbed him by the shoulders, threw him up against a wall, and with Widmark's feet dangling in the breeze, promised he would literally beat the shit out of him. Phil Stern was present at the altercation and indicated Wayne said, "I don't care what you think about me, but you're my employee, and I'm the director and you're going to do what I say from now on." His outburst had the effect of calming them both for awhile, though no one could have ever described them as best friends.[860]

Widmark finally got the message. They were both professionals, and they both had a job to do. "We needed to get on because we needed certain chemistry on screen," he reasoned. "Crockett and Bowie liked each other, and we had to make the audience believe that. We had some nice scenes together, and, once we'd made it clear where we both stood, we got on with the work, which is all that matters. And we had some good times. We laughed a lot." One year later, though, while back in Brackettville filming *Two Rode Together*, he was a bit more truthful about his relationship with Wayne. John Ford had asked a small favor of

Widmark. "I know what (Ford) wants," yelled Widmark. "I know exactly what the old bastard wants! Wayne has called him, and he wants me to go to that goddamned premiere of *The Alamo* in San Antonio! Well, screw it! I'm not going to that goddamned terrible movie. It was enough grief working on it!"[861]

And, according to Relyea, "The sad part about it was that Duke's respect for Widmark as an actor was enormous. Duke admired him. But Dick thought Duke was a big bag of wind, and he was bored with him and the picture."[862]

Widmark wasn't the only one to feel Wayne's wrath. Stories were flying all over Hollywood about Wayne's temperamental behavior. Early in filming Wayne posted a note in the commissary and thanked cast members for their cooperation, but added, "I still reserve the right to holler at you!" After the film was completed, Harvey admitted, "It wasn't always fun, but it was never dull. John Wayne treated me very well. I found him to be most amiable, although as time went by his fuse burned ever shorter and quicker. But he never lost his temper with me. I think he thought I was *Sir* Larry Harvey because I came from the British theater." However, while filming the movie, Harvey had an entirely different recollection: "Sure, we had our differences. We had a set-to one day that made me very angry, and I stewed about it all evening. Finally, at eleven o'clock, I called up his house and told him I wanted to have it out with him. I went over to see him with a bottle of wine. He brought out his bottle of whiskey, and we argued until 4:30 in the morning. We ended up with an excellent understanding."[863]

That understanding came in handy when Harvey and Abramson once spent an evening drinking. "When we were coming back to Texas," said Bernie, "the border guard stopped (Harvey) and asked, 'Are you bringing anything back?' 'God forbid,' answered Larry. Harvey was about an hour late in reporting to the set next morning. And Duke, who was always on time, was upset. He began chewing Harvey out in front of the cast and crew for being inconsiderate and holding up everyone's schedule. Harvey nursed his hangover in silence while Duke continued his lecture until he finally interrupted the director. 'Well, Marion, can we begin filming?' Duke paused a beat and then announced, 'If you promise you'll never call me 'Marion' again, we can begin filming.'"[864]

But there may have been a method to Wayne's madness. During a scene between Wayne, Harvey and Widmark, Duke egged on his co-stars until a shouting match ensued. The scene was a real rouser and afterwards, Wayne grinned; "Now I've got them fighting each other. That's what I want!"[865]

Mike Wayne: "The arguments were on an hourly basis. We were always at it. It's just a natural thing, nothing to do with being father and son; it had to do with being a star and a producer. It was always combat over whether we could spend money or not. My father would ask me what I was doing, and I would answer, 'I'm producing this film.'"[866]

And on rare occasions even bystanders were privileged to witness Duke's temperament. Once, during an early morning lunch, Duke in full costume and Relyea were walking across the compound when they were accosted by a small, round tourist who had sneaked through security. "Oh, my God, John Wayne, John Wayne, John Wayne!" the woman cried as she picked up a handful of pebbles and flicked them at Duke's face. "John Wayne, John Wayne, John Wayne...!!!" Duke stopped, put hands on hips, and glared at her while Relyea laughed so hard he fell to the ground. After a few seconds, Wayne had enough and demanded of Relyea, "Are you finished?" Bob apologized and jumped to his feet. The excited woman was still bouncing up and down, throwing pebbles willy-nilly. "John Wayne, John Wayne...!" Angrily, he said to Relyea, "If you're finished, I'd like to continue our discussion." Turning to the woman, he lowered his head, removed his hat and excused himself. She bounced one last pebble off his face and moved on. Duke was so upset with Relyea for the next three days; he only spoke to him when absolutely necessary.[867]

A demon for perfection, Wayne would bawl out crewmembers for inefficiency and mistakes. Widmark admitted he saw Wayne throw rocks at crewmen who didn't response fast enough to his commands. It was a cold and rainy day, the electricians were having problems and couldn't seem to fix them. Suddenly, fed up with the delay, Wayne started throwing rocks at them. Relyea was there when it happened: "They were standing on ladders at the time, and he picked them off like he was Sandy Koufax. (Duke) had a hell of an arm." Too bad as the next day Wayne was forced to replace twenty electricians who quit the day before. Clothier said adamantly, "Duke hasn't any patience with anybody. His own family, other actors. Duke's only problem as a director is that he feels every actor should be able to do a scene the way he can do a scene. He'd be pushing and screaming; I must have told him fifty times, 'You don't know how lucky you are; relax and be patient. Other people can't do what you do.'" Intolerant of shortfalls, he expected everyone to give their absolute best. With the area's unbearable heat and humidity, it's no wonder he would lose his temper. Up at 4:30, making sure everything is ready for that day's shooting, work all day, review rushes, and turn in by midnight. Ever-increasing pressure, constant worries and problems. Wearing his buckskin costume, he'd sweat away eight to ten pounds a day. He would lose over thirty pounds by the time filming was complete. Forced to constantly drink water to sooth a dry throat, he also suffered from dehydration and leg cramps. He eventually had to minimize wearing his coonskin hat as it rubbed his forehead raw, and his sweat loosened his toupee. Members of the cast and crew knew to tread lightly. "John Wayne used to scare the daylights out of me when I was around him at the beginning," confessed Dean Smith. "We all wanted so hard to please him because it was such an honor to work with him. Because of this, you always wanted to do your best." Try as they may, though, sooner or later, it had to come to a head. Directing a complicated scene one afternoon, he was distracted by voices behind the camera. Wayne exploded, "JesusfuckingChrist! Shut up back there!" Turning to continue his tirade, he came face-to-face with a group of Roman Catholic nuns visiting the set. Immediately recognizing their unique attire and extremely embarrassed, he quickly apologized and continued the scene. Rudy Robbins recalled a slightly modified, PG-rated version of the incident: "While we were filming, there were four ladies, and they started talking," Rudy said. "And you could hear them talking while the filming was going on. Well, Duke blew his stack, they were behind him and he blurted out a string of 'By-blasted, dam-gum GD's, SOB's women! Ruining my scene!' And when he turned around to look, it was four Catholic nuns in their habits that was doing the talking. And when he saw who it was, it got so quiet you could of heard a rat coughing in the Alamo. And Duke got the funniest look on his face and said, 'Well, excuse me sisters, but, you know, we're making a movie here.'"[868]

But according to Happy Shahan, it was no surprise to Duke that the nuns were on location because Wayne invited them! They were all brought out from the Santa Rosa Hospital in San Antonio. "And (Wayne) got all the crew together," recalled Shahan. "(Duke) said, 'I don't want anybody saying anything bad or wrong. I want everybody doing the right thing. When those nuns get on the set, I want you to be ladies and gentlemen.'" Apparently, Wayne forgot his words of wisdom as, "they'd been shooting a couple of hours and Wayne (lost it.) After the seventeenth take of one of his scenes that he was directing himself, he blew his stack. Then, he happened to think. He walked over to the nuns and said, 'I don't know why I did that. I want to tell you how sorry I am.' One of the sisters said, 'That's all right, Mr Wayne. We'll light a candle for you.'"[869]

Wayne expected professionalism from even the lowliest extra. Kuykendall admitted, "(Wayne) used to have a lot of trouble with some of the extras. You'd see a scene, and here's one particular guy and then the next scene you'd turn around over to another area and there he'd be again. He just, literally, scalded one guy–he was a student at the University of Texas, and he thought he was going to become the next star. And that didn't work. I mean, he walked up to that guy and got him bad, bad, bad and said, "We're going to have to redo all these scenes that you move around (in)!" A mean old son-of-a-bitch one second, Duke could turn into a real pussycat the next. After chewing out a technician in front of the whole production company for not doing his job correctly, Duke subsequently learned that the man's wife was ill back in California. He called the tech into his office, asked him to fly the daily rushes back to Hollywood, and, "Don't come back until your wife is well." He also told Mary St. John to cover all the bills.[870]

Linda Cristal was a bit more philosophical about Wayne's temper: "He went through fights, fires, jealousies, crimes, but he kept his head. He was acting, producing, directing, everything. I would have gone mad if I had his troubles. He is kinder with girls than men. He gets irritated with men—he wants them to know their job and go."[871]

Duke had previously contacted the Air Force and requested it limit its flyovers when production was filming. John Quinn remembers, "One day, while I was visiting with my Base Information Officer, in AF uniform, Duke was having a problem with a 'shot' he wanted of the Alamo Mission. He came over to us and asked my Lieutenant friend if he could ask the Generals at HQ to rearrange some bomber flight patterns. He was getting contrails in the sky above the Chapel. There were many airbases in Texas, so it was unknown which unit was flying those skies. The IO said he would pass the request up to the HQ. Duke had that kind of influence in high places." But planes still buzzed across the sky. Once, Wayne looked up, grinned, and said, "That's my boy, showing the General this outfit." However, he wasn't able to restrict sightseers and over seventy wealthy Texans in their Beechcrafts, Lockheed Lodestars, and Cessna Skylanes. After a scene was ruined by low-flying tourists, Wayne threw rocks in frustration, grabbed a rifle and started shooting at the planes. Told it was no use as the rifle contained blanks, he shrugged his shoulders and replied, "I know, but it makes me feel better."[872]

While Wayne protected his Alamo from aerial attack, Grant continued to fine-tune the script. After numerous revisions, re-writes, eliminations, and expansions, he was just about finished.

# CHAPTER TWENTY-THREE
# HERE WE GO AGAIN

By late September, Grant had polished his script to a high sheen. Superfluous scenes, extraneous dialog, and unnecessary character development all had been fine-tuned and/or eliminated. Upon Avalon's arrival, his character's name finally was changed in the script to "Smitty." With his shiny black locks, you couldn't very well call him "Cotton." Interestingly, several unchanged scenes still referred to the character's old name.

Small vignettes were added; some remained in future script iterations, and others just as quickly were eliminated. Instead of riding through a creek and up its bank to meet Parson and Smitty, Crockett and his Tennesseans ride through tall grass to a hilltop to gaze upon San Antonio. Crockett trips over a drunken compatriot as he leaves the Cantina. The delivery of the powder wagon, the Travis/Bowie "pyrotechnics" confrontation, and the Mike Fink fable all are changed from night to day. Also, an entire sequence that included Father Espinosa and his request to allow refugees to enter the Alamo is eliminated; all subsequent references to Espinosa also are eliminated. Scene 171—a totally useless sequence that included Bull and Pete trying to impress a young señorita by vaulting over a horse—was replaced by an equally ridiculous scene where Blind Nell chops off the fringe on Bull's shoes. He subsequently faints. Travis's "Jeffersonian" speech is expanded, Blind Nell and Jocko meet Crockett, and, in an effort to let Avalon flex his voice, Scene 165A is added in which he and other Tennesseans sit around a campfire at night while Smitty breaks out in song. This

427

scene then segues into a morning flag-raising ceremony. Scene 170C is added in which Smitty accidentally hits young Melinda in the head with a log after she douses him with a bucket of water. Scenes 171A and 171B were added in which Travis identifies the "Sixth Vera Cruzano Fuseliers," and Scene 182A was added to include Travis's "Is your gun ready" question and Jim Brewer's "Primed and ready" response.

By this time, the script looked like a veritable rainbow. Each revision is usually printed on a different color paper to help actors immediately see which pages were changed from the last revision. These colors and script-revisions were: White (05/19/59, 06/08/59, 06/15/59 & 06/19/59); Blue (07/21/59 & 08/03/59); Pink (09/08/59, 09/09/59 & 09/14/59); first and second set of Yellow revisions (09/21/59 & 09/23/59); and the first set of Green revisions (10/05/59). Most productions distribute all new script pages to key production personnel, that is, all those initially assigned a script. Some bit players would only receive those pages that applied to their parts. These pages were called "sides." Some companies would print corresponding serial numbers on the scripts and revisions to assure distribution control. Besides the producer, director and main cast, other key individuals would include assistant directors, production manager, editors, director of photography, key grip, production designer/art director, costume designer, special effects director, construction coordinator, head of make-up, illustrator/storyboard artist, set decorator, property master, technical advisers, sound engineer, stunt coordinators/second unit director, and other individuals at the discretion of the producers and department heads.[873]

Eventually, Grant would eliminate the extended opening sequence and start the film with the arrival of Houston and his troops. Neil would arrive with Houston and be given Dickinson's dialog; Bonham would be given Neil's. Also, Crockett's arrival in Bexar along with his Tennesseans in their "foo-faw-raws" would be eliminated along with an extended scene where Crockett first meets Señor Seguin and his son Silverio. A can-can dance in the Cantina was filmed but never used. The cache of gunpowder in the church tower got moved to the church basement. Rather than bring a captured cannon into the compound, nighttime raiders spike the barrel with mud and destroy it. Volunteers from Goliad arrive via horse and wagon rather than by swimming through the Alamo's aqueduct. Instead of both Smitty and Bonham dying in their attempt to return to the Alamo, Bonham arrives safely, Smitty after the battle is over. Dickinson doesn't scratch a line in the dirt with his sword. Interestingly, the last *official* change to the script was dated October 5, 1959. However, a detailed analysis of that iteration showed that numerous changes, additions, and deletions to the film were added subsequent to that date. How was that possible? In 1959, the Writers Guild of America went on strike for six months over residuals from theatrical films shown on the relatively new medium of television. A union spokesman said the key issue in the dispute involved a demand by writers for payment of post-1948 films released for view. About thirty-eight workers that were currently working on projects were affected by the strike order, but all of the union's 3,000 members were involved in the strike, so how did this affect *The Alamo*? In April 1959, the Writers Guild met independently to discuss how to proceed with negotiations with the Motion Picture Producers Association of America regarding a new contract. Wages, censorship, and affiliation with British writers were key points of the meeting. Negotiations began falling apart in mid-1959, first with the major studios and then with independent producers. Talks with the major studios were called off, and the contract that was set to expire on May 15 was extended to November. But talks with some fifty independent producers on royalties for post-1948 films on television and payments for pay-TV were going nowhere, so the Guild authorized its negotiating team to call a strike in August with a unanimous vote. The strike was called for October 10, and, after continuing negotiations failed, the Guild struck against fifty-six independent producers. The luminaries included such names as Stanley Kramer, John Wayne, Otto Preminger, Frank Sinatra, and Bob Hope productions. After a late-night conversation on October 10, Grant sent Wayne the following letter:

Dear Duke,

This is official notification verifying our conversation of last night. The writer's Guild is on strike against various independents, including Batjac. In view of this development, I will not function any longer as a writer. At this stage of the picture, with the script in as finished shape as it is, and, with nothing much but action sequences left, I cannot see that this will matter much. I hate to add to your burden of overwork, but should you need a line, just write it yourself. All the fans tell me they love you because you say such honest, straightforward things right out of your own balding, pointed head. Yours for better relations or, at least, for more money in the budget for writers."

Grant must have warned Duke what was going on and told him of the strike plans during their conversations. No wonder there aren't any official script changes made after this date. Maybe Wayne did write a few lines of dialogue, but it sounds like Grant didn't. Burt Kennedy was down there unofficially to re-work Widmark's dialogue; perhaps he assisted on the QT, although he said, "There really weren't any rewrites on that script." But, perhaps there should have been. "The problem I always had with the script," confessed Kennedy, "was that it's a big historical picture, and they brought in a romance that didn't make any sense at all. I thought we should spend more time on the backstories of the men at the Alamo, so you'd feel some loss when they were killed.[874]

429

It's also possible Grant worked on changes the week before the strike, but, if so, they weren't officially incorporated into the script before the strike. According to Relyea, "Duke gave me the impression that Grant would not make changes in the script that Duke needed or thought he needed. Duke would say things like, 'I need a scene here,' and Grant would say, 'Sure' and do nothing about it." But Grant struggled mightily with the film's ending. Although the basic content never changed, he constantly added and deleted dialogue between Santa Anna and a Mexican officer in an attempt to explain the battle and portray the general as a compassionate victor. Failing to find the right touch, Grant eventually eliminated all dialogue.[875]

In addition to the aforementioned changes, on September 15, 1959, Grant added Scene 122A—the introduction of Mrs. Guy. Referred to as blonde, brunette, or brownette, LaJean Ethridge was a young, attractive aspiring actress who for over ten years had tried to break into the movie business. After graduating from Lemoore High School in Fresno, California, in 1947, she attended Mt. San Antonio Junior College where she studied theatrics and occasionally worked in films as an extra. Earning high grades in play production, theater arts, and art appreciation, Ethridge wanted to teach dramatics and speech art but left college after one year for financial reasons. Known professionally as LaJean Guye, she took her stage name from her father's middle name. Over the next several years, she worked in stock theater groups in many parts of the country and, in April 1959, signed with the Names-Townsend Players for a cross-country tour that was supposed to last until the end of the year. That summer, she and the repertory group worked at a dude ranch in Bandera, Texas. When the group heard that Wayne was looking for extras, the members ended their engagement and traveled to Brackettville to try to get hired.[876]

The Names-Townsend Players consisted of five California members along with Ethridge: Jim Kinney, Norman Andrews, Ron Lee, Arthur Names, and Chester Smith. To save costs, they rented an old house in Spofford, just nine miles south of Brackettville. While the men were hired as unaccredited extras, Ethridge's talent so impressed Wayne and casting director Frank Leyva, they decided to put her on a $350 weekly salary and give her an entire page of dialogue. (Prior to that, she was making $20 per day with just a single line of dialogue.) Hired just after Labor Day, Wayne liked her so much he applied to the Screen Actors Guild for a membership card on her behalf and cast her as the wife of a soldier in Houston's army. She was ecstatic. Ethridge's mother indicated it was a small part but one her daughter had been struggling for all her professional life. It was her big break. According to her friend Elizabeth Gilliland, "LaJean was strictly dedicated to her art and wanted to be the greatest actress in the world." An eyewitness indicated, "Duke had set up the scene between LaJean and Linda Cristal. LaJean got it the first take, and then Duke called for close ups. LaJean did an excellent job, and she took it in stride. She was a professional actress, very good at her craft." According to Happy, "Once the camera was turned on her, she lit up." That part could be a major stepping-stone in her career. But she needed to be on call at a moment's notice, so it was necessary she move to Brackettville.[877]

By late September Wayne was behind schedule, albeit slightly but behind nonetheless. Yet he had already filmed an amazing number of scenes: On the eleventh, Wayne completed the scenes in which Jethro looks in on Bowie, and Bowie encounters Travis (*"Now that you've told me, I'm aware."*). The following day, in a scene that was never used, Crockett and his Tennesseans were filmed entering San Antonio. Later, they were filmed leaving the town for the Alamo. On the fourteenth, Wayne finished the scene where Bowie encounters Thimblerig (*"Nobody's seen Davy. He ain't about." "First lie you told today."*) in addition to Bowie's arrival in the Alamo. On the fifteenth, the Tennesseans/tamale sequence was completed (*"Have some breakfast." "Breakfast! Tortillas?" "Tamale."*) as well as Parson and Smitty's first view of the Alamo. On the seventeenth, the scene in which Bowie speaks with a bearded volunteer (Fred Graham) was filmed (*"'Cause old Sam told Travis, Travis told me, and I'm tellin' you"*) and on the eighteenth, Carlos Arruza filmed his first scene: the arrival of Mexican troops into San Antonio. According to Dan Ford, his grandfather filmed a wide shot of Santa Anna's army making its initial approach on the Alamo mission. Perhaps this was the shot to which he referred.

Two young brothers, Pat and Dan Cumiskey, were fortunate to play key roles in this scene: they would have the privilege of being personally directed by Wayne. "We were the only people in the scene, basically," recalls Pat. "What happened was…this guy that was the wrangler came in and said, 'Tim, Dan. Come on.' He took us over to the wardrobe area, and they took our outfits and gave us these white linen outfits, and gave us serapes and a little straw hat and then took us over, put makeup on us and everything else and walked us down the street. We were walking down there, and we saw the camera set up and the lights. We were kinda, 'What's going on?' type of thing. All of a sudden, here comes John Wayne out of his chair and gets us in a little huddle with him and he says, 'Now, this is what I want you to do.' He pointed at me, and he said, 'I want you to turn around…I want you to point down the street first, then I want you to turn around. I want you to run up and jump in that window and close the shutters off. Can you do that?' So I showed him I could do it. He said, 'Great.' He told my brother, 'Now, all I want you to do is run toward that gate over there to your left. I want you to go through the gate, and there'll be some people to shut the gate behind you.' So we practiced, and everything went well. The scene was set where the lancers were first riding down the street of San Antonio, coming into the city for the first time. They were high-tailing it down the street. All of a sudden, we're supposed to be young Mexican kids that are afraid, so we took off running away from them. He said, 'Okay. Ready, guys?' We said, 'Yes.' He said, 'Lights, camera, action.' Well, when I turned, my brother, instead of turning to his left, he turned right, into me. So we bumped, and it knocked my hat off. So I started toward the window, went back, grabbed my hat, and took off into the window with my hat in one hand, jumped up into the window, shut the shutters. My mother was watching this from across the street; she didn't know where we were at that point. Nor did she recognize us because we had changed outfits, and they had this real dark make-up on us. She didn't even know it was us. (Wayne) comes out of his chair because it took one take, and that's what he wanted because he was saving money with that. He came over and grabbed us both, picked us up, told us how good we did. We went back and found our mom." (In the previous scene, a donkey is seen serenely standing in the dusty street, oblivious to the commotion. "Bonita," a gray jack (despite the name), was provided to the production company by local Brackettville school teacher Else Sauer. Sauer would also tutor some of the school-aged children on the set.)[878]

In a continuation of this sequence, dance hall girls and patrons were hustled out of the Cantina and cordoned off behind a human barricade of soldiers. Buckskinned extra Jim Brewer appeared in that scene with a beard. Previously, Brewer had been clean-shaven, but Frank Leyva requested he grow facial hair to look a bit more rustic. In a letter to the author, Brewer indicated he had filmed other scenes before that one: "The scenes...were filmed at the beginning of the shoot, sometime in September. We just charged in and bayoneted Bowie after the first run of Mexicans were killed by Bowie. The scenes were done in stages, not all at once. After my beard grew, I was removed from the Mexican unit and placed in the Travis group."[879]

On September 19, Wayne filmed the scene in which Crockett encounters Flaca and Seguin after delivering powder to the Alamo; on the twenty-first, Mexican troops were filmed starting to arrive in town, and Joan O'Brien arrived that day to shoot her first scene. In addition, Crockett and the Tennesseans were filmed overlooking San Antonio (*"Colonel, what do C-A-N-T-I-N-A spell?"*). That scene jump-started Rudy Robbins's career: "My big lines were, 'It do.' I really didn't know it was coming until (Roberson and I) worked together in our first scene. When it came time for the lines, the Tennesseans were riding up a little hill above San Antonio. Frankie Avalon gets out the spy glass, and he sees the cantina and spells that out 'C-A-N-T-I-N-A, cantina.' Just one day (Wayne said,) 'Look', he told Chuck, he said, 'Chuck, you ask him. 'Cantina, do it mean what I think it do?" And he says, 'I want you to say 'It do." And that's all there was to it. Duke never said he would team us up, but then he told me to (be) next to Chuck. And so, that's how that got started. I think that's just something Duke thought of at the spur of the moment. And he liked it and went on with it. He even started to say, 'It do' himself in some of the scenes. Duke thought that was very amusing, the way I said 'It do.' There wasn't any preparing to it. How much preparation do you need to say 'It do'? I didn't have to rehearse my lines at all. So, all through *The Alamo*, he began to come up with little scenes where I could say, 'It do.' At first, the 'It do' lines were just lines—comedy lines. But they became the phrase on the set; everybody was saying 'It do!' Wayne even gave me a coffee mug with the *Alamo* on one side and 'It do' on the other. Of course, Chuck Roberson stood out. He was such a friendly, friendly person. Duke had our characters team up, so that when you'd see one, you'd see the other. It was always Chuck turning to me and saying, 'Do that mean what I think it do?' And I'd get to do my 'It do' thing." Roberson also had fond memories of the ongoing skit: "At first I thought those lines were corny, I really did. But they worked out rather well. In fact, those lines turned out to be quite talked about—both during the film and after."[880]

Rudy continued, "John Ford was very good at that. He'd make up lines as he went along. In fact, he was very notorious for re-writing the script. He would dream up something 'cause he thought it fit in better than the scripted line. And I think Duke learned that from John Ford that there's sometimes, something comes to your mind while you're doing the picture that is better than what the writer put in, or it's an addition to what the screenwriter should have put in."

"(Duke) noticed that I was an excellent horseman, so I got to meet the other stuntmen. They signed me to a contract to do the picture, you know, you're on a weekly contract, like most everyone else that was on contract, except the big stars. So this was a door-opener for me. All of a sudden, I was out of the ranks of the extras to become an actor. I was placed on a SAG (Screen Actors Guild) daily rate, but I was soon switched to the weekly rate—actually because it was cheaper for the production company. But I was so ignorant of the acting profession, I was just glad to be in it—and say something, too!"[881]

On the twenty-second, Juan and Silverio Seguin, along with Juan's body-guard, were filmed arriving at the Alamo *("Some Indian told some vaqueros!")*. Juan Seguin was played by Maltese-born Giuseppe Maria Spurrin-Calleja, better known as Joseph Calleia. Actor, singer, screenwriter, and character actor, Calleia had appeared on Broadway and in over fifty films, usually as a gangster or in ethnic roles. *The Alamo* would be his second-to-last film. All it took for this role was a long-distance call from his agent, Jimmy McHugh Jr. (Calleia had an earlier connection to the Alamo story when he played Juan Moreno, Bowie's ill-fated Sandbar adversary in *The Iron Mistress*). Julian Trevino (Silverio Seguin) was a nineteen-year-old graduate of Central Catholic High school in San Antonio. Listening to a radio, his aunt heard that Wayne was looking for a particular type of individual. He applied for the part, was interviewed by three individuals from Batjac and told Duke would make the final decision. "I was really surprised when he picked me," admitted Trevino. "I would like to continue in movies if all goes well and with the help of God." Once he knew he'd received the part, he went straight to the Alamo library and read all he could on Seguin, the Alamo, and San Antonio. After the film was finished, Wayne said the young man showed "much promise." Trevino would return to Brackettville the following year to appear in *Two Rode Together*. At forty-two, Seguin's bodyguard, jet mechanic Edmundo Trevino (no relation to Julian) filled the role of the Seguin's trusty compadre. In rehearsals, he had been riding at the head of a troop of dragoons in a bright uniform with horsehair plumes on his helmet. "I'm happy I'm getting transferred when the real shooting starts, though," confessed Edmundo. "I'm going to get to die in the Alamo." When it came time to film the scene, Duke didn't hesitate to indicate exactly what he wanted. "Come right up to here," commanded Wayne to Calleia, drawing a line with his toe. "So your horse's head is right here, the horse's head, not (your) hat. Now you, Seguin, look Travis in the eye while you're speaking with him." To say that Calleia couldn't ride a horse is an understatement. If one views the previous scene, it's extremely apparent a stuntman was used to double Seguin's arrival. Low-crown, wide-brimmed sombrero pulled down over his head, fringed serape over left shoulder, hand raised in greeting, the camera never gets a clear view of Seguin's face. But the Girl Scouts present at the time did.[882]

(In fairness, it should be noted that some of the aforementioned dates are approximations based on the Master Shooting Schedule, newspaper articles, clapboards, and wardrobe stills. The clapboard, also known as clapperboard, clapper or slate, is a device used to aid the synchronizing of picture and sound; additionally, it provides scene and take number, date shot and camera crew used to film a specific scene. The sharp "clap" noise the clapboard makes is easily identifiable on the audio track, and the shutting of the clapstick can be seen on the separate picture roll. The audio track and the picture can then be exactly synchronized by matching the noise and movement. In the early days of film, one person would hold a slate for the camera with the scene information, while another clapped two hinged sticks together in front of the camera. Combining the two into one unit made it much easier for one person to handle both jobs. (The Director of Photography's name was also there because he was responsible for the image–and any questions about it in the laboratory: i.e. color timing, brightness, day or night look, focus problems, etc). Wardrobe shots generally are taken on or about the first day in which an actor will wear a particular costume. It thus seems reasonable that the scene in which the costume first appears was probably filmed on or near the date in which the wardrobe photo was taken. Unfortunately, the "official" shooting schedule or log was lost in a fire during production.)[883]

With the inclusion of additional scenes, revisions and expanded dialogue, it was necessary to modify the shooting schedule by pushing out several sequences. Many believe the sequence in which a film appears on screen mimics the chronological development in which the film's scenes were shot. 'Tain't so. Numerous factors are considered when determining when specific scenes should be filmed: location, day/night shooting, interior/exterior shooting, shooting in sequence, child actors, change in time period, time of year, weather conditions, special effects, stunts, special equipment requirements and availability, second camera and/or second units, and last but not least, actor availability. For example, as per the Master Shooting Schedule, the following is the order in which they shot the first few months:

Exterior Countryside/Village-Day
Interior Soundstage-Day (due to Boone's availability)
Exterior Village/Alamo/Wall/Courtyard and Surrounding Areas-Day
Interior Soundstage-Night/Day
Exterior/Interior Village/Cantina-Night
Interior/Exterior Alamo/Gate/Walls/Courtyard-Night/Day/Dawn
Exterior Alamo Plains/Houston Camp-Day
RiverBank/Interior/Gate/Walls/Courtyard- Night/Day
MexicanCamp/Village-Night/Day
TV Show-Day
Hilltop/Plain/Alamo Walls/Hospital/Church/Burial Ground/Courtyard-Day.

As can be seen, Wayne attempted to effectively use, as much as possible, common locations for sequential day and night shooting so as to minimize schedule disruption.[884]

Fortunately, a limited supply of new negative film stock had just become available, which helped solve the scheduling problem. A stickler for realism, Wayne wanted to shoot on location whenever possible rather than use sound stages, and wanted to film night scenes at night. Heretofore, directors would use a concept called "day for night." Utilizing specialized film stock, under-exposing the negative with special polarizing filters, and keeping the camera angle high enough to avoid showing the bright sky, one could simulate "night" scenes actually filmed during the day. In order to work effectively though, it was necessary to shoot early in the morning or late in the afternoon when the low angle of the sun created hard shadows. When filming began in September, the old, slower Eastman Color Negative film required 300 to 350 footcandles–the new stock only 150. (A measurement of light intensity, footcandles are used to calculate adequate lighting levels; the lower the level, the less lighting necessary. One of Clothier's main issues was to determine the proper placement of lighting and camera for the most effective composition. Low ceilings restricted mounting key lights at required levels. Less lighting–a key advantage when space is at a minimum.) Now, a director could truly shoot night scenes at night–what a novel idea. (Resident Alamo Village historian Richard Curilla explains the product/process: "Technicolor demanded visual sharpness throughout the photographic frame. In order for a production company to make a deal with Technicolor

Corporation to use their color lab, they had to agree to include a Technicolor adviser on the principal crew. This person could dictate any details that enhanced the color process—whether or not they supported the art director's and cinematographer's plan. The advisers were very intrusive, and it had nothing to do with overall color. It had to do with an art director having already chosen the color pallet for the production (i.e. limiting the range of colors, like no bright reds, no stunning greens—every art director determines a color pallet for the artistic unity of the film) and then the Technicolor Adviser walking onto the set in the morning and saying something like, 'Change that drab brown vest to a bright green one.' This was to literally show off the color process by dazzling the viewer at the expense of the art form.")[885]

Russell Harlan, director of photography on *Rio Bravo*, expounded on issues associated with night-time filming: "I don't like to fake night scenes. They never have the authenticity that there is in real light, nor the flavor. For instance, we are getting some wonderful effects with the buildings' lights shining through windows onto the street. We'd have lost all that in daytime shooting." He continued, "There's a lot more work at night. We have to keep moving the big lights as the action changes from one place to another. Then, when we take a scene, we have to remember precisely the highlights and shadows. Little things like that are what people notice, and we'd hear about it from all around the world if there was variation in the takes." Filming in color created additional problems. "Even though it's in color, we're keeping it pretty much in monotone with just a touch of bright color here and there for highlights—such as John Wayne's bright red shirt. You have to be careful with color. A combination of bright shades that look effective in life, seem to literally jump at you from the screen, creating a feeling of tension. Too much red and bright blue can kill a scene dramatically."[886]

As a result, Wayne began to schedule night scenes: two weeks on, five weeks off, then back to nighttime shooting. Thirty nights in all. Wayne returned to the airplane hangar set at Ft. Clark and began filming interior hotel sequences. Would-be playwright Wesley Lau had already appeared in several dozen television programs. Explaining his career change to *TV Guide*, he said, "It was a matter of expediency. I'd been playing everything from cowboys to killers on TV. Then I saw that more and more hour and hour-and-a-half shows were coming along. That would mean fewer jobs for actors." Lau already had a copy of the *Alamo* script, but, when they were ready to film his scenes, the dialogue had been changed. As a result, he inked in the new words in phonetically-spelled-out Spanish for his character: arrogant, manipulative, war-profiteer Emil Sand. Similarly, Cristal's dialogue had been modified to express her distain for Lau's character: "*Usted es descendiente de una ligna de puercos... Usted es uno de los mas bajos cobardes... Usted es uno de los mas grande cucarachas!*" ("*You are descended from pigs...you are one of the lowest cowards...you are a big cockroach!*") Another eventually cut scene was filmed during this period as well. Photographic stills suggest,

436

as originally shot, Flaca had a pet bird in the scene where Sand tries to coerce her into marriage. Playing with the bird, she maintains a studied indifference to Sand. No evidence is available to indicate this scene was ever scripted. However, as another photo showed, Cristal and Ford cooing over the bird in a doorway of the hangar where her room's interior set was constructed, it's not unreasonable to assume Ford may well have crafted this scene.[887]

At this time, Wayne also filmed Crockett's offer to assist Flaca, the letter-writing sequence, Crockett's confrontation with Emil Sand (*"Gratuity for the boy"*) and Flaca's notification of Sand's death. Then he moved filming back to the village. (If one looks closely during the Cristal/Wayne aforementioned scene, you can see expansion joints on the floor of the hangar set.)[888]

On the evening of September 26, filming resumed at the village with various scenes outside the Cantina (Travis's arrival with Dickinson, Sand attempts to stop Flaca from leaving/Crockett prays to the North Star, and the Crockett/Bowie/Emil's thugs street fight). Four huge 10K carbon arc lamps with night-blues were mounted on scaffolds or atop buildings to provide required light. Whether they were brutes, goons, Century Lights, Cubans, broads, emilys, silver-bullets, or just a plain old BFLs, they all required power. Two 1500-amp generators had been brought from Hollywood, and a special, giant 4500-amp had been built to order at enormous cost to provide necessary electricity.

Bob Morgan would double Wayne during some of the fight sequence with Chuck Roberson and Joe Canutt. "I was a much better double for him than Robertson," Morgan said. "I was bigger. Before my accident, I was six-foot-four and three-quarters in my stocking feet, weighted about 210." Extra John Quinn recalls, "I remember watching Richard Widmark tapping himself on the head with a 'dummy Bowie Knife' to make sure it would not hurt the stuntman he was fighting. That was late one night, when he and Duke were fighting the gang in the street. He was to hit the man in the head with the knife and was testing to see just how hard the hit could be, safely."

Ford left Brackettville on the twenty-ninth; the next night, Wayne began filming inside the Cantina—drunken Tennessean on table top, Crockett/Travis backroom conversation, Tennessean in the fireplace, feather fight sequence—all filmed in one night. (Wayne even flubbed a line or two several times during those takes, cussing himself out.) Tom Hennesey played Bull, Crockett's friendly adversary. Wearing a veneer device over his natural teeth to create an irregular, decayed, broken appearance, Hennesey already was a fairly large individual. "When I went on *The Alamo*, I was at my normal weight at the time, which was about 230-235," said Hennesey. "Duke asked me to get much bigger. He wanted me around him, and he wanted me to kind of overshadow him physically. So I started putting on a lot of weight down there; we had a really good caterer, Rolly Harper, so, hell, before I knew it, I didn't even weigh myself till I came home, and I was 285! Boy, I carried that weight for a long, long time. It was really bad for me. I recall Duke spent quite a lot of time on that (feather fight). I know that, in rehearsals, he'd go all out. He didn't pull (punches, but) you didn't dare lay a hand on him, you know? Nobody would." Of course, Duke didn't get away unscathed. According the Wayne, the punch that floored him was "the real thing." During a conversation with *Citizen News* reporter Lowell Redelings, he confessed, "It caught me flush on the chin—and you know where I land!" In order to "balance" the feathers in the fight, a dab of putty was placed on each actor's nose with the stem of the feather stuck into it. The remaining interior Cantina scenes, including a can-can dance sequence and Crockett's "Republic" speech, would be filmed over the next two evenings. Amusingly, due to the difference in height between Harvey and Avalon, the Cantina bat-wing doors were lowered for Avalon's scenes so as not to hide his head when he looked into the room.[889]

Frank Leyva had searched high and low for dancers, musicians, and assorted extras. A typical hire was San Antonian Mario Mandujano, who had played violin and trombone in a Latin dance band. Frustrated because he couldn't grow any facial hair, he lamented, "All I could do is grow this short one, even though I started growing it six weeks ago. I'll still be in the picture, however. They said the make-up department would fix me up."[890]

To fill the Cantina with lovely senoritas, Leyva auditioned and then hired dancers Yolanda Almaguer, Ann Barrera-Morse, Madga Carreno, Rosita Fernandez, sisters Maria Nela Garcia and Theresa Ada Garcia, Emma Hernandez, Hilda Jimenez, Alma Reyes, and Mary "Maruca" Vidal. All of their dancing thoroughly impressed him. Leyva had previously contacted Raul Cortez, owner of KCOR, and asked him to find qualified candidates. According to Hernandez, "Raul then called all the singers and dancers he knew to KCOR (now KWEX) for an audition. Once he picked whom he felt was right for the part, they took the finalists to Brackettville to audition for Wayne." Cortez was also instrumental in getting increased wages for the dancers. "At first, they wanted to pay us $60 per week," recalled Hernandez. Through Cortez's excellent negotiation skills, they instead received "$90 per week, plus hotel, transportation and meals and the privilege of being in a movie with John Wayne!" Peggy Ponder, model, actress and singer, was chosen by Wayne himself to portray the owner of the cantina: "The morning he chose me, he was very drunk. He was practically falling down. I wasn't sure about the whole situation. He said, 'Is this the young lady that wants to play (the part)?' I think he would have chosen a chimpanzee at that moment." Ponder said her part was later cut, but she wasn't disappointed as, according to lifelong friend Lula Hatch, Peggy "met and mixed with all the big stars, so that was fun."[891]

Willie Champion, better known as "El Curro," a colloquialism for flamboyant or dandy, always liked playing Mexican and Spanish folk songs on his guitar. In 1955 while with the Los Cristales Trio, he met his future bride, Teresa Martinez, who had another idea: combining Spanish guitar and Flamenco dancing.

Known professionally as "La Chavalida," she had performed the intense, rhythmic, expressive dance form since she was eight years old. Born in San Antonio, she studied that particular dance style in Mexico under the renowned maestro Tarriba. Recalled Willie, "Teresita said to learn flamenco. I said no. Guess who won?" Encouraged by both Teresa and her mother, Wille changed directions. Said Willie, "I saved up all I could and hocked a few things and went to Mexico and took flamenco guitar lessons from a real pro." He later visited Spain for additional experience. Self-taught in the tradition of Sabica, his playing was described as fiery and exciting. He was able to create—with a guitar alone—the sound of a company of drums and bugles with an amazing similarity of tone.[892]

For Wayne's film, Champion was contacted and asked if he wanted to audition as a guitarist. "They (also) were auditioning dancers," remembers Teresa, "but I didn't audition, because they didn't ask for me—they asked for my husband. They had a note, and the note said that they needed the guitarist, not me." At Willie's audition, Wayne noticed Teresa and asked what she did. "I'm a dancer," she replied. "Why aren't you auditioning?" he persisted. "Because you already had all the dancers," she recalls, "and he goes, 'Huh–OK' and that was it." The selected entertainers were then asked to go to Brackettville for follow-up interviews and testing. Teresa assumed that the other dancers already had their parts and were just going to try on costumes for a screen test. Willie asked her to accompany him to Brackettville and confessed, "Well, I'm not going if you don't go." As the young couple and their two children were living with Teresa's mother, they needed the money and couldn't afford to let this opportunity pass by. So, borrowing her father's borrowed car, they left for Brackettville. There, Wayne separated the dancers from the musicians. "We're going to test you," they told Willie. "Who do you play for? Do you play for dancers?" Willie replied that his wife (who was outside) was a dancer, so they asked to see her.

When she entered the Cantina, Wayne saw her, took a second look, and asked, "Did you audition?"

Teresa replied (again), "No, because you already have the dancers."

"But you're perfect for what I want."

(According to Teresa, "The girl that they had picked (Yolanda Almaguer) was real tall, too–she's Mexican but real white complexion. Now, I'm dark complexion and very little).

Wayne continued, "Well, let me see you dance. Do you have any skirt?"

"Well, I have my (size five) shoes and my skirt in the car." So, I put (on) my skirt and my shoes, and I went and I danced," said Teresa.

"This is what I want—this is perfect."

Both Willie and Teresa signed a contract and practiced their routine over and over for two months until it was perfect. Staying at Ft. Clark, Teresa would leave for the set each evening around 6 o'clock, have her make-up applied, hair combed, dress in full costume, and then wait. And wait. Night after night after night.

Unfortunately, on the evening they were ready to film her scene, it started to rain. And rain. And rain. According to Alan Kreiger Jr., who was there that evening with his parents, "It was raining cats and dogs that night, and they had to delay filming because of the noise of the rain and thunder." Given the Cantina's tin roof, the racket was so loud, you couldn't hear the dialogue. Alan and his parents sat in their car while it rained but "finally gave up before they started filming and went home because I was eight-years-old; it was past my bed-time." Eventually, they were ready to film their scene. Teresa had fallen asleep on a bench, as it was around 2 a.m. and she said, "They're not going to call me again. It's too late. My husband woke me up, so I ran over there, and they put (on) my makeup again...and combed my hair. I wasn't that big, and they wanted me to look big, (so) they put...a lot of petticoats on me. And then she goes, 'OK, get up on top of the table,' and I looked at my husband, and I said, 'What? Que?' They teach me the dance. But they didn't tell me I was going to be on top of a table. 'No,' I told my husband, 'There's no way. I'm afraid of heights. I will not dance on the table.' And I remember these words. My husband turns, he goes, 'Do you want to buy a house, or do you want to live with your mom?' And I said, 'No, I want to buy me a house,' and he goes, 'Well, get up on the table.' And I got up on the table, and I danced, and the director told someone, 'She's afraid of heights,' and they go, 'Well, just do it, and we'll see if we can take it in one,' and I did my dance. When I finished the scene, (the choreographer Antonia Morales) said, 'That's it. Perfect. You don't have to do it again.' I was crying by then...so they wanted to give me a drink—some wine. John Wayne carried me down, and he said, 'Do you want a drink?' and I said, 'I don't drink, but I would have a glass of water,' and they gave me a glass because I was so nervous I was ready to pass out." She even wrote her initials, "T. C." under the table she danced on. In the film, after Teresa finished her dance, Chuck Roberson rises as if to grab her. She stamps her foot down on the table top, and he falls backward to the laughter of the actors. Though planned by Wayne, neither Roberson nor Teresa were told what the other was going to do. A completely spontaneous reaction on the part of both—and in character! (After filming was finished, Wille and Teresa Champion, Rosita Fernandez, Hilda Jimenez, Yolanda Alamaguer, and a few other singers and dancers toured Texas as an entertainment troupe. The Champions were asked by Wayne if they would consider moving west: "John Wayne told my husband and me, 'Theresa, go to Hollywood—to California, because you have that kind of face and you can be Spanish, you can be Mexican, and you can be Indian, and, if you go, I'll put you in a lot of my movies.' But you know what? We went to California for about seven days, and it was too busy. My little daughter was...she was about four, and my son was one or a year and a half, and it was too busy, and we saw the children smoking and drinking; it was like too wild for us)." Teresa wasn't the only one to search for fame and fortune in Hollywood. "A bunch of us went (out there)," said Robbins. I only stayed a month or so because of the writer's strike. I went to a few interviews and then came back to Texas."[893]

The Champions, however, had nothing but fond memories of Duke: "John Wayne was down to earth. He was a beautiful, beautiful person They had this big room with long tables, and it was only for the movie stars like for him, his wife, Pilar, and Richard Widmark, and all of them…all the movie stars. Linda Cristal, the old man…what's his name? The very old, old man…Chill Wills. Everybody would eat there, but you know what? They always ate dinner with us. With the soldiers, with the cantina girls, with me, with my husband. All the time."[894]

Teresa wasn't the only girl to catch the eye of a Wayne. Alma Reyes, cast as a cantina dancer, immediately formed a lasting friendship with Duke. He thought so much of her, he introduced her to his son Patrick. The two dated for a short time until Reyes married the boy next door, Arthur Guerra. *(Reyes later performed an on-camera narrative in Wayne's "Spirit of the Alamo" television special.)*[895]

After several weeks on location, the cast and crew began to feel a bit lonely and thus asked their respective spouses and significant others to come to glorious Brackettville to enjoy the ambiance. Thursday, October 1 was a particularly busy day: Michael Wayne's wife Gretchen and young daughter Alicia arrived as did Don LaCava's beautiful wife Toni and daughter Anita. (Toni would have a one-word speaking part in the noncombatant departure scene along with her daughter Toni, Anita, and Don would stay in the Wainwright house with Duke and Pilar; Michael and Gretchen had their own quarters. Gretchen's sister Kathryn Deibel married Frankie Avalon in 1963). Stuntman Bob Morgan's actress wife Yvonne De Carlo, who had recently finished a nightclub engagement at the Coconut Grove, also arrived that day and in the evenings entertained the cast in the mess hall with her new act. Local wags suggested Bob needed to perform a few gags for her as she seemed in a sour mood. Others, like Chill Wills, would head up to San Antonio to Freddy Serur's Swank Key Club or Big John Hamilton's Steak House. (When filming started, Wills chose to spend weekends in Brackettville as San Antonio artist Art Pugh came to paint his portrait.) Mike Wayne would hit the Holiday club, while others frequented Ma Crosby's in Acuna or El Moderno in Piedras Negras. In addition to playing golf with Linda Cristal, Pilar Wayne and Jimmy Grant's wife Josephine attended an American Cancer Society meeting in Del Rio to pass the time. To be honest, there really wasn't much for Pilar to do otherwise. "Usually when I went on location, I didn't like to go on the set," she confessed. "If they give you a chair, there are usually cables under it and someone who have to say, 'Mrs. Wayne, would you mind moving?' I always felt kind of in the way and decided I'd rather be at home with the kids. Doing my painting or cooking something for Duke, because he liked to eat at home." But she enjoyed her time in Texas. On October 3, Laurence Harvey was asked to serve as master of ceremonies at the Dallas Civic Opera Guild Jewel Ball. Said to be as convincing with his Carolina accent as he was with his lyrical Shakespearean, he commented inappropriately that if someone had built a back door to the Alamo, it would have saved a lot of trouble. Probably not a good observation to make as he was in Texas![896]

Even so, many cast and crew found Brackettville quaint and enjoyed its local flavor. Merchants, however, were not always of the same opinion. Brackettville mayor V.G. Deason Jr., who owned a gas station on Highway 90, said the filming hurt hunting, a vital business for the county: "The movie company occupied Fort Clark ranch all during hunting season, and if that happens often it's going to discourage hunters from coming here." He complained about the prevalence of worthless checks received by businesses, while some locals were put off by the caliber of some of the "hangers-on" the filming attracted. Sounded like sour grapes, though, as Happy Shahan estimated between $3 and $4 million would be spent in the area during filming. Happy was elated with all the activity. During the following year when Ford came back to film *Two Rode Together*, Happy exclaimed, "I can remember not many years ago, our town had lost about 40 percent of its population. The army had closed down Ft. Clark, and people were just moving away. Now, we've got 1,600 people living here, and more are coming in. Wayne and his picture put us on the map. John Ford and his production will keep us there." Happy's brother-in-law Frank Higgens, who owned the town's one and only movie theater, said he was surprised to learn how many movie stars actually went to the movies. He recalled Widmark was a frequent visitor and once, Higgens had to "quiet down" Avalon during a Saturday matinee while Avalon's manager complained that the local teenagers didn't seem sufficiently impressed with Frankie's presence. Vera Nash, owner of the local dry goods store, said the past year was "one of the biggest we've had. We sold a lot of Western clothes." And Chuy Munoz, a partner in two grocery stores, found that movie people weren't finicky eaters, but they ate well and business was good. There were those who took advantage of a good thing, however. "Some places which were renting for $50 a month went for $150 a month while *The Alamo* was being made,' he admitted.[897]

Relyea had a slightly different memory of his time in Texas: "Brackettville had a gas station, a Frosty Freeze, and a liquor store. The liquor store did very well. Fort Clark was an army base where Custer had been the last listed commander. Their mess hall became our mess hall, and Custer's quarters became Wayne's, but there was simply no place to go. San Antonio was hours away." *(Relyea was incorrect. Custer was never posted to Ft. Clark, the last listed post commander was Major General Harry H. Johnson, and Wayne lived in the Wainwright house.)*[898]

On Sundays, when Ford was in town, he would attend services at the Brackettville Catholic church. It had a choir loft with additional seating for any

442

overflow from the main floor. Pappy would always sit in the loft. When it came time to pass the collection plate "people were amazed and their eyes popped out when Ford placed a twenty-dollar bill in the basket."[899]

Early that first week of October, after stopping during the daytime to watch the World Series (Sandy Koufax, Don Drysdale and the Los Angeles Dodgers would beat Early Wynn, Ted Kluszewski and the Chicago White Sox in six games), Ford returned in time to watch Wayne film the church "basement" scene. In the May 19 script version, the liberation of the gunpowder was to be filmed in the church tower. After asking Parson to round up volunteers, Crockett, Bowie, Beekeeper and Cotton/Smitty subdue two Mexican soldiers and throw them down a well. The noise from the altercation alerts Emil Sand, who also rousts his confederates. After Crockett, Bowie et. al. remove the powder from the choir room, they are surprised by Sand and his henchmen. After a brief scuffle, Bowie puts Sand in a headlock, Crockett takes Bowie's knife and bashes Sand's head in, killing him. A previous version attributed Sand's demise to a thrown hatchet. In an even earlier version, the "European cannon" was emplaced in the church bell tower to subsequently be blown up after removal of most of the gunpowder.

The church and lower portion of the bell tower were built with adobe blocks, but the wooden belfry and cupola were built on a wooden floor that rested atop the tower. When Wayne halted construction of the village due to cash-flow issues, Shahan agreed to loan him the necessary funds to continue as long as Duke would build four walls for every building with foundations and roof and agree not to destroy the village set. As a result, the previous scene to blow up the tower was modified and rewritten into a "basement" scenario.

It appears the scene in the basement actually *may* have been filmed during the day. Clothier had the grip department build a twelve by twelve wooden enclosure as an extension of the "basement" for camera and crew. The large double doors on the back of the low part of the church were removed like a "wild wall" to let the camera and crew set up outside the "basement" area seen in the film. Blackout tarps enclosed the plywood room, front church window, and doorway and kept out light. Small doorways to the outside on the front and side walls of the low building were covered with adobe bricks to simulate the look of buttresses in an underground basement. The staircase to the bell tower would serve as stairs to the "basement." Lit with movie lights for a torchlight effect, the set could now be used during the day as day-for-night without going into a more expensive nighttime schedule.

At this time, Clothier also would film the scene where Crockett overhears Flaca and Emil's marriage argument. This entire sequence, including the morning-after conversion between Crockett and Flaca, bears further examination. The hotel was a two-story building with multiple window/door openings on both levels facing the street. A second-story wooden balcony extended across the face of the hotel, enclosing the upper doorway and three center windows with three-foot-high front and side banisters/railings. However, in the film, the hotel's frontage appears "L- shaped" with a window at the end of the balcony facing down the length of the balcony. Through the camera's eye, the doorway on the west end of the hotel balcony opened on to a hallway that led to Flaca's door. Her room had the entrance on one end and a window across the room, which is seen in the movie. A mock-up window element, referred to as a "tie-in" piece, was placed on the east end of the balcony looking west, down the length of the balcony. The window element, a theatrical flat with a window in it, served to connect contiguous sets at different locations; i.e., the airplane hangar sound stage and the village set. The interior of the actual Village building was not used to film any scene, either on the first floor or second floor. All interior scenes in the building—whether in the hallway, inside Flaca's room, or outside looking into the room—were filmed at the off-site sound stage located in a Ft. Clark airplane hangar.[900]

According to Richard Curilla, "It is clear to me how the window scene was shot and faked. The 'window element' was only used for one scene in the day and one at night. It was placed at a 45° angle or slightly closer to perpendicular to the front wall of the building and located maybe eight feet in from the end of the balcony. The camera was on a crane or platform just beyond the balcony aimed toward the church for the night scene and more down the length of the balcony for the day scene. Clothier framed the shot with the inside finished surface of the faux window. He used the curtained windows which opened in to mask the camera-left end of the "flat" and had the bars that formed the outer shutters opening out."

Rich continues, "In the night scene, Duke simply walks up to the open window, listens to Flaca and Emil's dialogue and then walks away. The background is the moonlit church and street (from the lights on the roof. Perhaps a 10K carbon arc brute.) In the day scene looking out through the window flat, Wayne is standing farther away on the balcony watching Cristal stretch. Then he moves closer and stands there as they exchange the first dialogue, then moves up to the window and puts his foot up on the sill.

"The bedroom interior set in the airplane hangar at Fort Clark included a window which had both sides of the flat finished and also a section of the main front wall of the hotel, plus of course the interior of the room. All the rest of the dialogue including his outside angle from behind him was filmed there. The window flat was used only to 'establish' the location by showing the church and balcony. That was the tie-in set element that linked the two sets. They built the window flat in order to give Clothier a 'cheated angle' for a more romantic view."

Curilla also suggests that the Crockett/Flaca "morning after" sequence may have been initially planned for Back Street. He explains, "...the angle of the Bexarenos leaving that we see in the movie immediately after the scenes of Santa Anna's army approaching 'over mountain and plain' was designed to be Crockett's POV (point of view) from the balcony of his room. His window was across the balcony from Flaca's window, as originally planned. This window relationship still exists over the back door of (the) current Cantina kitchen and is clearly dramatized in the screenplay. My conclusion is that the scene, where he sees Flaca stretching and then goes to her window, was originally staged for this set and later actually filmed on the front veranda. When they decided to shoot all this on the front of the building, they built the window flat in order to give Clothier an angle with a more romantic (art-wise) background then looking straight up the road toward the Alamo, as it would have been if they had used one of the real windows on the front of the building. In addition, the structure of the set built in connection with Flaca's bedroom interior in the airplane hangar at Fort Clark (the portion outside the duplicate window) was meant to duplicate this rear window and the roof/balcony above (the) kitchen door and NOT the window on the front veranda. That's why it faces the length of the balcony in the movie rather than straight out from the front of the building."[901]

Brackettville resident Billie Foust had an entirely different view of the departing Bexarenos scene. She was behind the camera watching her eighteen-month-old daughter Tamara, who was being held in the lap of another woman in a wagon. Explains Billie, "(Evelyn Roselle), a friend of mine…had (the) job to get extras, and she knew about Tamara. That was about the age they wanted…so, I agreed to do it. Of course, I wouldn't let them take my baby without me. They sent a car to town to pick us up as it was as hot as could be, (and) we didn't expose her to all the heat. They let us stay in the infirmary where it was cool until they needed her. (But, while I watched the scene being filmed), I had to be in costume, so I would be paid, just like I was in the (film)."[902]

Meanwhile, the Elena Da Vinci situation became increasingly unbearable. On October 3, Phil Stern tendered his resignation, completely fed up with all the nonsense: "Duke, I must leave my work on this location. This DaVinci mess has developed into such a ridiculous crock of shit that I no longer want to be a part of it. Hell, I could actually live with this vile broad and Jim's dedicated sponsorship of her…but it has already affected my personal enthusiasm for this work on *Alamo*. Without enthusiasm and strong personal interest, photography comes up as bland, dull and for me, worthless, and I ain't gonna be just a house guest here. At Wayne's home, I'd love it…but on the job, never." He would go on to say, "P.S. My feelings about the broad are purely my own. If the majority of the cast, publicity, press, and ordinary people of the community feel similarly, it's purely coincidental." Wayne tried to convince him to stay, but to no avail. Stern left the *Alamo* location, leaving behind only three press agents. Subsequent correspondence between Stern and Henaghan indicated there was a great deal of animosity and finger-pointing going on.[903]

"Well, Phil," wrote Stern, "you've finally won your battle; the girl quit... Touché! You have indeed won your weird battle. You've managed with skill and some sort of deftness to associate John Wayne and Batjac with some of the vilest aspects of 'Public Relations.' National and local press reps all over Hollywood are buzzing about Henagen's (sic.) 'expediter' whose pimping and whoring talents have been enlisted to aid John Wayne and the Alamo..." Apparently, Henaghan had previously replied and called Stern a "bitter bastard' who was "spreading poison." Stern had the last word, though. "Remember kiddo, I came on Alamo by choice and left by choice," wrote Phil. "It was more than an ordinary lucrative job...it was exciting...had people I liked and respected. At the last moment, Duke invited me to remain despite all occurrences. I haven't lined up a job yet... but I feel clean. Do you?"[904]

Henaghan may not have been sorry to see Stern's leave, but Widmark was, and he didn't mince any words when he wrote to Stern, "I'm very sorry you left, but you're better out of this miserable production. Things are just as confused and distressing as ever. Hope to see you when I get out of here."[905]

Despite the incident, Stern and Wayne were great friends. "We were like the odd couple, admitted Stern. "I was a lefty and he was right-wing." Phil used to tell Wayne he thought the loyalty oath was a crock, and the infamous blacklist an affront to the Constitution. Wayne would retort that Phil was a "bomb-throwing Bolshevik," and Phil would counter with: "You're a Neanderthal fucking fascist!"[906]

Everyone on the set knew what was going on. Widmark and Henaghan got into it one evening when the actor suggested it would be better if Da Vinci would just "go home and stop bothering people." Henaghan subsequently told her to resign as "she could probably be more effective in Hollywood." Saving what little face she could, she told people her boyfriend was sick and by mid-October was gone. There was even a vicious, unsubstantiated rumor floating around that the Menger management asked her to leave the hotel because of her dark complexion. (Apparently, though not printed, it was common knowledge in Hollywood that Henaghan utilized Da Vinci's *talents* to help publicize Wayne's film. Henaghan was also credited with circulating a story that Duke asked her not to return to Los Angeles but stay in San Antonio. Again, not true.)[907]

Helping to temporarily calm the situation down, Dimitri Tiomkin arrived on location October 5 to deliver a pair of songs for the film: "Here's to the Ladies" and "Tennessee Babe." Tiomkin had been signed on August 21 to compose and conduct the score for *The Alamo*. Paul Francis Webster signed on one month later to write the lyrics to Dimi's score. "Ladies" would be sung twice, once by Chill Wills in the Cantina ("*I want you Texicans to open up your ears and listen to a little pure Tennessee!*") and once by Frankie Avalon during the birthday party scene. Wills had reminded Tiomkin that years earlier, when both were working on *Giant*, Dimitri had promised Chill he could sing the film's title song. But when the film was released, only the instrumental version was heard. "Ladies" would wipe the slate clean. The next day, after spending four hours in rehearsal, Wills pre-recorded the song. It would be re-dubbed for the final print. After he finished, Wills asked Tiomkin, "Will it be a hit?" Tiomkin replied mischievously, "Chillee, you sound like Peter Potter. I only write hits for my friends." There was other music being played as well. Teresa Champion recalls, "My husband would teach Pilar during the day guitar, because she plays guitar—she plays guitar, she plays flamenco, and my husband would give her classes. And you know, John Wayne's daughter and my daughter would play together. They used to play together when my husband went to their cabin to teach Pilar guitar." Too bad Willie didn't give Wills any lessons.[908]

Even though Wayne was making progress, problems started manifesting on the beleaguered set. One night, several crewmembers suffered gunshot wounds from local extras; on another, two actors, including Ken Curtis, "had the shit beat out of them" and were left bleeding in the Acuña streets by border patrolmen. Lawyer Bill Daniel hushed up the incident. Crewmembers were getting fired left and right. By early October, the stress finally caught up with assistant director Relyea. The previous night, he awoke, rolled out of bed and began vomiting blood. The next day, informed by a doctor he had an active ulcer, Relyea requested help to get him though the evening's shooting. "Keep an eye on your watch," said the medic. "Every fifteen minutes, meet me behind one of the trucks, and I'll give you a shot of cream. We'll try to coat your stomach lining long enough to get you through the night. Then, we've got to get you to a hospital." Realizing this was his only option, Relyea received injection after injection after injection. And it worked…for a while. The crew broke for "lunch" at three in the morning; Wayne and Relyea began their customary walk to discuss the rest of the evening's schedule when Relyea suddenly collapsed, blood flowing from his mouth, nose, and ears. The ulcer had burst through his stomach lining and eaten through a main artery. An ambulance rushed him to Del Rio, followed by a pickup truck full of well-lubricated stuntmen, each offering a blood transfusion. Insulin worked well, blood was better. Relyea received more than a dozen transfusions that night—blood mixed with "several pints of tequila, Jack Daniels, and God knows what else, but those thirteen stuntmen saved my life."

The next day Duke visited the hospital, leaned over Relyea's bed and growled, "If you die, I'll kill you." Told he needed two solid months of rest before doctors would even think of letting him return to work, Relyea heard Wayne was having trouble. "You know, they are always very careful about what they say," Bob admitted, "so they said, 'This is the diet, which is milk and pudding that you're going to eat for the rest of your life. And you're going to spend two weeks back at the Fort recuperating.' By the time I got back to the Fort, I heard Duke was eating up assistant directors and he was getting a little short on temper. So I got a good night's sleep, and I went back the set the next day to try to put that fire out."[909]

Although many additional members asked to be hired to the crew, Gene DeRulle was one of the few crewmembers actually invited on location. A cousin of Relyea, DeRulle usually worked in television although he had been in Brackettville the previous year when *Five Bold Women* was filmed. Gene was recovering from a bike accident but called the Director's Guild office to see if any work was available. Told that his cousin was trying to get a hold of him, he immediately called Relyea, and "Bob asked 'You know Mike Messenger?' I said yes. 'Well, we just sent him home with an attending nurse under heavy sedation. Wayne got to him, and I'm alone. Get your ass down here.' I had just purchased a new MGA, so I thought it sounded like fun. I packed the car and went off. Some twenty-eight hours later, I was looking at Ft. Clark, the same damn guest ranch I had stayed in before. The pressure finally got to be too much (for Messenger) and he cracked. (Bob) said he really needed my help. The job was enormous, and he needed someone to be another pair of eyes and legs. He told me that the call was out for another 2nd Assistant, but for now it was me."[910]

The previous second-AD was under constant strain and transferred that pressure to the cast and crew. Extra John Quinn recalls, "...when you're directing hundreds of people, you have to have assistants, and sometimes the assistants don't get the instructions correct, and they go out there, and they get the actors in the wrong place and all that—it's really a magnificent chess game, you might say, moving the people around in the right places, and you be sure you're communicating with everybody. I know one assistant director would come by after John Wayne had set up a scene and he'd change the extras around, and somebody said, 'Hey, you know what? You just told us the opposite of what John Wayne said.' And he'd say, 'Well, do it this way anyhow.' I don't know how long he stayed with the company. People were complaining—we were getting two different sets of instructions on what to do." Eventually it became too much, and the AD left the set.[911]

Apparently, Messenger wasn't the only one affected by the pressure. "Tommy Andre was a nice man," recalls DeRuelle, "but I believe the pressure of the job and his intense fear of John Wayne (had) rendered him almost useless. He used to walk up beside Wayne to ask him a question about something that was very necessary to the company. He would wait and wait for Wayne to notice him there, usually with a little notebook and pencil in his hand, and, when Wayne finally did notice him, would usually say something like, 'So what the hell do you want?' Andre would wait a minute, then put away the notebook, mumble, 'Nothing,' and walk away. He was literally too scared to ask. (One evening) the camera was in the midst of a herd of longhorn cattle that were to be stolen by Crockett's men. Relyea had seen the evening sky and, not liking what he saw, asked Tommy Andre to go to the phone, which was some distance away, and get a weather report. By the time Tommy returned, we were crammed into a Ford station wagon, watching the prop truck sink up to its axles in the mud, when through the downpour, a hand holding his hat onto his head and the other hand clutching the collar of his coat closed against the wind and rain, came Tommy. He slogged his way into the car, opened the door and said, 'There's a high cumulus moving in over New Jersey.' Everyone sat in stunned silence until Bob said, 'No, Tommy, we need the weather for this area.' Tommy looked at him for a minute, and then said, 'Oh, yes, of course.' He closed the door and walked away."

With a relatively light schedule for the weekend, Harvey was told he wouldn't be needed, "but don't go more than four hours away." So he didn't. Four hours was just enough time to fly to New York where his wife, Margaret Leighton, was appearing with Jean Marsh in *Much Ado About Nothing*. While there, Harvey had lunch at the swank Carlton House where the crowd ogled him and his wife. Walter Winchell whimsically observed, "La Leighton's millinery was the biggest slouch hat seen since the silent cinemas." Wayne headed out to Sabinal where he would film scenes with Linda Cristal the following week. Peace and quiet reigned supreme. But tragedy once again rocked the unfortunate production when a cast member was *murdered*.[912]

# CHAPTER TWENTY-FOUR
# MURDER IN SPOFFORD

ON THE FATAL EVENING OF SUNDAY, OCTOBER 11, AFTER SPENDING SOME TIME in Brackettville, LaJean Ethridge, accompanied by a waitress and two other men, returned to Spofford to pack her belongings and move to Ft. Clark. As she had been offered a larger part, the star of the Names-Townsend troupe wanted to take advantage of her good fortune. But while packing, she got into an argument with boyfriend Chester Harvey Smith, who declared she couldn't leave. As Ethridge emerged from her bedroom, Smith suddenly drew her toward him and in a fit of jealous rage, stabbed her with a knife below her left breast. Ethridge collapsed to the living room floor, gasped, "I love you," and died. Found sitting next to her body when the police arrived fifteen minutes later, Smith claimed his memory was blank for several hours before and just after the slaying. He also claimed the last thing he remembered was leaving town with Ethridge and the next thing was coming back to town four hours later.

Wayne, who had left Brackettville early that day to shoot scenes in Sabinal, was unaware of the incident. According to *Reuters*, Wayne didn't learn of the murder for over fifteen hours and only when a horseman rode across the rugged county to tell him. When notified, he was "upset" about the "tragedy" but was not expected back until Tuesday night. Sheriff John Sheedy, who arrested Smith, surmised, "She was getting a better part in the movie and she was moving out on Smith and the others. He thought he was going to lose her." County prosecutor John J. Tobin declared, "One of the witnesses said he (Smith) more or less wanted to ride on her coattails, wanted to get something through her that he couldn't get himself," so he killed her. An immediate trial was ordered, due to concern that many witnesses involved in the production would not be available later. Smith was ordered held without bond and taken to the Val Verde County Jail in Del Rio instead of the Brackettville jail because, "Quite frankly, I think you could get out of there with a can opener," the prosecutor noted.[913]

LaJean's sisters, Sue Stevens and Agnes Ethridge, flew to Brackettville on Monday, October 12, to identify the body and arrange for its return to Los Angeles. Stevens pleaded, "Our mother is seriously ill. We have had to keep the newspapers away from her because of the vicious things and implications that have been printed. It would kill her. No one but her family will ever know how hard she worked. Please let her memory not be tarnished. It's hard to know she died so privately and pointlessly, but it's worse to realize that it's nothing but filth, rather than her ability and character, that is being recognized." They were concerned how their sister's reputation was portrayed in the media, and rightly so. *Extra Stabs actress Lover, Romance is Blamed..., Slain By Lover, Broken Romance, Love Nest Knife Killer, Tottering Love Affair,* and *Rift in Romance* read typical inflammatory headlines. Prosecutor Tobin took the sisters to the house to show them what had been printed generally was correct. He said their sister was living in the same house with five other men but clarified that by saying though she stayed in the same house, he wasn't accusing her of "living" with any of them. "The house was divided into separate rooms," said Tobin, "and I could find no evidence that their conduct was anything but proper." He also noted the state would handle the investigation, but, if it wanted a special prosecutor, it could have one. "But I also told them I would not whitewash any facts in the case." His first investigation of the house revealed clothing belonging to Smith and Ethridge in the same room. "When I got there with the sisters, most of the clothing had been removed, but there were a few things belonging to both of them still there," he noted. Mrs. Stevens asked Tobin to write a letter stating that the investigation failed to show there were any acts of impropriety between the Smith and Ethridge. He complied with the request.[914]

From the very start of the investigation, the witnesses' statements were so contradictory, it looked like a script had been created, but no one could remember their lines. Granted, at every crime scene, people have different recollections of what happened: who said what, the sequence of events, etc. But most witnesses, at least, agree on basic information. Not this time. An analysis of the witnesses' testimony, in addition to statements made by Sheedy and Tobin, reveals the following discrepancies:

1) Number of occupants in house: Numerous newspaper articles indicated Ethridge shared the house with five men. Sheriff Sheedy stated it was four men and two women.

2) Final words: Several witnesses, including Ray Henschel and Elizabeth Gilliland, indicated Ethridge said "I love you" to Smith before she collapsed. Later, Gilliland recanted her earlier statement to reporters and said she was misquoted. Big, redheaded, and freckled, she said she might have misunderstood and what Ethridge may have really said was "Chet, Chet, please don't."

3) Murder weapon: Newspaper articles indicated it was a five-inch hunting knife or kitchen knife or butcher knife.

4) Reason for murder: "Tottering romance. She was getting a better part… thought he was going to lose her." "Ride on coattails." According to Sheedy, "…she had a kinda date with another man connected with the show and she was going to move out." When Sheedy initially described the sequence of events leading up to the slaying, he indicated that Smith thought he was going to lose her. He then said, "Two *other* men and a woman went with her to pick up her belongings," thereby implying Smith was not one of those two men.

5) Witnesses: Six: four members of troupe, Henschel and Gilliland. "Most were asleep." Witnesses only awoke when the argument started. According to Jim Henaghan, Batjac vice-president and director of publicity, "They had a party last night, and apparently an argument developed." Only two individuals saw the actual stabbing. Gilliland stated she was "no more than three feet from" Ethridge as she was stabbed, but later testified she was taking clothes to the car when it happened.

6) Ethridge died a few minutes after the stabbing; she collapsed to the floor and died. Arthur Names stated she lay on the floor for ten minutes before she died.

Columnist Dorothy Kilgallen questioned why the murder wasn't investigated more thoroughly. "Reports on the slaying of the young actress…indicate odd police behavior, to put it gently, and just as peculiar behavior on the part of the journalists covering the tragedy," she wrote. "So little has been done, and so few pertinent questions asked; it almost appears the authorities think the girl killed herself, and nobody's giving them much of an argument." She thought Smith had nothing to worry about, the dumbest lawyer could 'spring' him in short order.[915]

Smith, thirty-two, was three years older than his girl friend. Described as blond, slight of build, and weighing 140 pounds, he appeared somewhat mild-mannered but was also prone to violent rages. A background check verified this sinister behavior. In 1954, he was placed on probation for trying to run down his former wife and her girlfriend with a car. Failing, he exited his car and attacked the friend with a hatchet. For his efforts, he received a 180-day suspended sentence and three-year probation for assault with a deadly weapon. In 1958, he was convicted and fined $50 for attacking a bus driver who asked Smith to get off the bus as it was at the end of the line. He instead hit the driver, broke his glasses, and kicked him. This time, the assault charge was reduced to disturbing the peace. While in Bandera, Smith even got into a violent argument with a local deputy.[916]

Three days after the slaying, Smith's defense attorneys, Fred Seaman and Sam Darden, announced they would call John Wayne as a witness in the examining trial. Darden recalled, "When I was coming back later that night, the police had a roadblock set up for me. And they stopped me. They told me that they'd been searching for me all over south Texas that day. And I asked them, 'Why?' They said, 'Well, Mr. Wayne wants to talk to you.' In addition, I'll never forget my first time to ever see him in person. Very impressive, and he looked very Hollywood. But he also looked very menacing. So he asked me what in the world I was doing subpoenaing him to court. Said he was the director, the star, and the producer of this film, *The Alamo*. And that every hour I took him away from his work it would cost him, I believe he said, $60,000 an hour. Anyway, he was very irate, and he demanded that I withdraw the subpoena. I explained to him my client, Mr. Smith, was facing the death penalty and, as far as I was concerned, if the whole movie *The Alamo* was never made, my client's life was worth more than that."[917]

Although there were no provisions for a closed hearing in such a proceeding, Kinney County Peace Justice Albert Postell decided to exclude the public and press "to preserve the testimony of witnesses who may leave soon." The defense attorneys strenuously objected and even cited court cases as well as Article VI of the U.S. Constitution to no avail. Seaman protested, "I don't know what they have in mind, but I aim to find out. One minute this thing's open, the next thing it's closed tighter than a bank on Sunday. If they're trying to hide anything, I'm going to find out. Maybe there's nothing to it, but I'm going to raise a lot of hell finding out if there isn't." The judge also felt that if the testimony was made public, it would prove difficult to find an impartial jury. He needn't have worried about secrecy; potential witnesses were more than willing share their comments with the press.[918]

According to witnesses, Smith joined Gilliland and companion Ray Henschel that night at the Gateway Café a little after midnight; He asked to borrow her car. While discussing this, Gilliland was called to her room at the hotel where she found Ethridge waiting and crying. "Liz," she said, "I want to move in with you." All four individuals subsequently returned to the Spofford rented house at 1 a.m. to discuss Ethridge's impending departure with the rest of the troupe. Smith twisted LaJean's wrist and kept a tight grip on it at all times. Gilliland said the girl appeared transfixed with fear. She believed the actress had a premonition of what was going to happen and she further felt Smith already had his knife at that time as he was never out of her sight for more than a minute. Once they arrived at the house, the other members were roused and more discussion followed. At one point, Gilliland told Henschel that Ethridge was being hurt. Everyone was reasonably calm but a witness heard Smith say, "I'll kill you" when they argued. Gilliland was taking some of Ethridge's clothes to the car when Smith pulled the actress toward him and stabbed her. Henschel and Gilliland, concerned about her condition, sped to Brackettville to find the doctor retained by Batjac. Arthur Names stated Ethridge did not cry but complained of pain and asked for some water. She died ten minutes later.[919]

Wayne, Gilliland and repertory group members Kinney, Andrews, Lee and Names, all were scheduled to testify. Curiously, Henschel, who supposedly rode in the car and was one of the individuals who actually saw the slaying, was not on the witness list. Duke, wearing a large hat, red shirt, tight-fitting Western trousers and boots, was subpoenaed to testify and requested that his statements be made public. His request was denied. He was escorted into the judge's chambers and almost bumped into Smith. "Is that the guy?" he asked. (A photograph of that encounter taken by the *San Antonio Light's* Gilbert Barrera won an award for the best picture shot in Texas during 1959). Questioned for fifteen to twenty minutes, Wayne lit one cigarette after another and glared at Smith across the room. George Carpozi Jr., a reporter for the *New York Journal-American*, asked why Seaman subpoenaed Wayne when he knew Duke wasn't a witness to the killing. Smith's co-counsel didn't hesitate: "...I wanted him on the stand to tell us that because this girl was dead they were going to have to shoot a lot of scenes over again. And for that reason, either he or his company apparently was putting pressure on the D.A. to push the case harder than he should have." After he was served, Wayne told Seaman he wasn't going to appear. The attorney replied he would then have Wayne thrown in jail. During questioning, Seaman constantly referred to Wayne as John Payne, just to get under his skin. "Now Mr. uh...let's see now. Are you Payne or Wayne, I can't remember." "I'm Wayne!" Duke shouted. After completion of the deposition Wayne spoke to reporters as he left the courthouse: Are you going to keep her part in the movie? "Sure, we'll keep it in." How will publicity affect the picture? "How should I know?" Did you know the parties involved? "I didn't know him from Adam, and I had of course directed Miss Ethridge in that one small part." He summarized his testimony for them: "I didn't see nuthin', I didn't hear nuthin', I didn't say nuthin', I don't know anything about it."[920]

Gilliland recanted her previous statements to reporters and rejected as a "misquote" an earlier line attributed to the actress. She supposedly had murmured, "I love you" to Smith before she died. Big, redheaded and freckled, Gilliland said she may have misunderstood and what the actress may have said was "Chet, Chet, please don't."[921]

The grand jury deliberated for five hours, returned an indictment of murder with malice and scheduled a jury trial for early November. Defense attorney Seaman anticipated requesting a postponement, claiming he didn't have sufficient time to prepare for the case or subpoena witnesses. But he was willing to let Smith plead guilty. "It depends on whether they (the state) make a reasonable trade," he said. Not surprisingly, moments before the trial was to begin on November 9, a deal was struck whereby Smith would receive a thirty-year sentence if he pleaded guilty. Both prosecution and defense magnanimously agreed it was in their best interests to do so as a guilty plea would "save the state money and avoid damaging the reputation of the dead girl." Seaman further stressed a lengthy trial also would have a negative impact on the collective impression of the woman, and if the trial had continued, he would have had to bring out details of the Smith-Ethridge relationship. "My client does not want to damage LaJean Ethridge's reputation...she is dead and gone and nobody regrets it more than my client." The pale, slender actor told the Judge, "I plead guilty, your honor." Smith then was taken back to the Val Verde County jail to await transportation to the state prison in Huntsville.[922]

Rumors ran rampant through *The Alamo* set regarding what actually happened that evening. Ironically, the one individual who may have provided the most accurate description of the evening's events was Jim Henaghan, a Batjac vice-president and director of publicity. In a statement given the day after the slaying, Henaghan stated that Smith was jealous of a company executive with whom the actress kept business appointments. "This suspect seemed to get the mistaken idea that there was something wrong in the relationship of the actress with one of the company executives. This man went out with her several times during the last month since we've been on location here. Saturday night, the suspect went to the executive's office and broke the door down. The executive was not in the office. He and the actress and a third party were in the Gateway Café talking business." Members of the acting troupe specifically identified the individual in question and indicated that Smith accused Ethridge of "sleeping with ... to get the role." It seemed Henaghan knew quite a bit about the evening's activities. Interestingly, he never mentioned the executive's name but stated, "This executive's wife just had a baby and he is flying back to Los Angeles." Another article that same day stated the executive had been rushed back to L.A. for emergency surgery. Other than this initial statement, there weren't any follow-up articles that addressed any of the details mentioned.[923]

In later years, *Alamo* extra Jim Brewer related the following: "Several years ago, when I was visiting Alamo Village, I spent a few hours with Joe Townsend, pastor of the Frontier Baptist Church in Brackettville. I asked him if he knew what became of that fellow that killed LaJean Ethridge. Joe said that after the fellow got out of prison, eight years after his incarceration, he became a born-again Christian and visited Joe in Brackettville. They spent some time together on several occasions and that they had corresponded over the years. Joe indicated that the fellow was very, very sorry for what he had done. Apparently he had turned his life around for the better."[924]

Wayne, Ford and Cristal had been at the Sabinal location to film what is known as the "Flaca Tree" sequence: *"There's right and there's wrong—you gotta do one or the other. You do the one and you're living. You do the other, and you may be walking around, but you're as dead as a beaver hat."* Wayne had previously scouted the location to determine its feasibility—a magnificent setting just eight miles from Utopia with wide stream, large picturesque cypress trees, and large bluffs to provide colorful background. O.J. McCullough had mentioned its possibilities. (Wayne had been headquartered at the McCullough Ranch while filming at Sabinal. With all the comforts of home, the ranch even had a mess hall, staffed by Nell Canion, Frankie Loman, and Annie Dorow, who served up tasty meals to the weary cast and crew). Crystal Harvey Wade recalls when Wayne first arrived: "We had a home in San Antonio…and we had just returned from a vacation to California. Rather than go to San Antonio, we went to our property in Utopia. And the first day after we got back, there was a knock on the door, and it was John Wayne standing on our stoop. I answered the door (as the) others weren't up yet. He was dressed exactly as he looks in his movies—a cowboy. Tan khaki pants, boots, and he had on a cowboy hat and his kerchief around his neck, and I don't believe he had his hair on. At the age of eleven, I had not seen a great, great deal of movies, but the movies that I was allowed to see were Walt Disney movies and John Wayne and things like that. Rock Hudson and Doris Day. *Pillow Talk*, stuff like that. Well, John Wayne and Rock Hudson were well-known movie star men names. I knew who they were when I saw them, but I would often get the names mixed up. And I saw him standing there on the stoop, and I just yelled out, 'Oh! Rock Hudson!' But he was such a gentleman about it. I believe he took his hat off and held it humbly, and that's how I knew. And he was very gracious and said that that was an honor, but he was John Wayne. And I said, 'Oh, yes. I get your names mixed up.'"

Wayne was interested in the location and asked to speak to Crystal's parents Cecil and Betsy, who invited him in to discuss renting the property. Duke was so enamored with the site; he asked if he could buy the land outright. The Harveys declined. Afterward, Betsy told her good friend Gwen Watkins, "We're not selling to any old movie star," which amazed Gwen. "John Wayne isn't just any old star," she replied. "He's John Wayne."[925]

But the property was perfect for Wayne's requirements, and, as a result, several scenes were filmed there: the previously mentioned tree scene, Smitty's encounter with Houston's sentries *("Corporal of the guard, post number three!")* and the morning patrol/cattle sequence (subsequently cut). To create an easement so horses could cross, truckloads of stones were poured into the stream downriver from the dam. (After this scene was finished, Crystal's parents had to pay for a bulldozer to remove the stones). Excited, she was able to obtain both Avalon's and Richard Boone's autographs while they were there.[926]

Boone had declared on the first day of filming he would only be on location for a single week since he had to return to Hollywood to continue shooting *Have*

*Gun Will Travel.* But he would return later to work "some more on *The Alamo.*" True to his word, he came to Brackettville on November 19 to fulfill the rest of his commitment.[927]

Avalon would film several different scenes in Sabinal—crossing a stream with waterfall, meeting a sentry outpost, and approaching the outskirts of Houston's camp. Knowing Avalon was young and still wet behind the ears as an actor, Ford wasn't above telling him exactly how to play a scene. Frankie recalled, "For any important stuff, (Ford) was there on his chair, sucking on his handkerchief. He wasn't there all the time, but he was there a lot of the time. He would help Wayne out on his own scenes, where Wayne had to be directed." If Ford could direct Wayne, he certainly could direct Avalon. But the singer still thinks otherwise: "I hate that scene to this day because he gave me the line reading. Boone's (sic) line was 'You've been riding for days, get some food and water.' And I say, 'No sir, I gotta get back to the Alamo.' And Ford directed me to say it like a kid, all wide-eyed and innocent. I cringe every time I see it. Ron Gast, Little John Hamilton, and San Antonio radio personality Ricci Ware were in the scene where Gast declared, "*Hold up there, bub! You get into dangerous territory, where you heading?*"Avalon replied, "*I'm looking for General Sam Houston. Got a message for him.*" Recalls Little John Hamilton, "Frankie Avalon was the messenger and he's at the Alamo and was riding to Gonzales. And I stopped him there on the river at Gonzales, at the Guadalupe River. I was a guard for General Sam Houston... and I stopped (Avalon) there. I was one of the sentries. It's a small part, but it's better than nothing. The way it happened, he (Duke) was nice enough to do it for me. And I joined the Screen Actors Guild."[928]

Linda Cristal admits, "Working with an icon like John Wayne, well, there's nothing better. I was very proud of *The Alamo* and working with John Wayne. The experience was like climbing Mount Everest. John loved the Alamo as a man loves a woman once in a lifetime—passionately." But, during their scene beneath that statuesque cypress tree, Cristal confessed she struggled reacting to Wayne's dialogue "because he was reciting the scene by himself. If you remember, long, long monologue. And I was there observing him without being able to exchange anything because how do you exchange when the person is reciting more than telling you? And that to me was wrong. It was monotonous. No, he was reciting. He wasn't even directly looking at me. There's no exchange there. I was not happy with it. It was more of a speech, and he really didn't reach me as an actor. Contact was impossible. If you look at my face, you can see I'm not getting it. Part of the problem was that we never discussed the scene before we shot it. If there had been, I would have shot that scene, the two of us leaning on the tree together and maybe he could've put his hands on my shoulders or on my face and said instead, 'I do have this war, but I do have these feelings for you.' I would have written it differently. But I would have shot that scene in a way that would have pulled from

458

the strings of the public's heart. Instead of just reciting. Acting. I would have had him telling me things and even if I didn't say anything, I could have said with my expression if he had said them to me. Duke worked for results. He didn't go into any of the complicated motivation. The problem with that is that it's hard to touch someone's heart if you don't know how it ticks." As a result, the scene took several takes, perhaps as many as six or seven. Cristal contrasted that scene with the one in which her character first met Crockett. "I did (like it) very much," she confesses. "That scene made contact. It had juice to it."[929]

Relyea clearly recalled how difficult it was for Duke to express to Cristal what he wanted: "So, in this scene, you're...fucking going away!" Wayne took his position behind the camera, yelled, "Action!" and left Linda without a clue. Later, after he realized she was confused, he demonstrated how she should speak her line of dialogue, and even how she should turn and walk. "Watching Wayne trying to imitate a lovesick woman, with that rugged voice and hard-ass walk, was one of the funniest visuals I've ever come across," said Relyea, who nearly bit through his lip trying to hold back his laughter. The sight was contagious: crewmembers disguised their laughs with a crouch, or ran and hid behind a bush, so Duke wouldn't see them break up. Cristal was devastated. "That's where Duke was," added Relyea, "less than at his best because he gave orders and wanted people to do it—he didn't communicate well with actors, in my opinion. Now he was a fine director, but he couldn't explain to Linda, but to me, she looked totally confused."[930]

Cristal also clearly recalls her lack of satisfaction with Wayne's performance during their scenes there: "I was very young, and Duke was in his fifties, and he was (so) terrified about our love scenes that he kept putting them off until he found a reason not to do them at all," she says. "So I never got to kiss Duke Wayne even though the characters we played loved each other very much. It's like he was kind of...I don't know...maybe afraid or nervous maybe about the age difference possibly on the screen." Additional love scenes were written in pencil, but Cristal adds, "...they would never film them." She feels Duke was somewhat reserved and reluctant to give in to the scene. "And I was unusually—and I say this without false pride—unusually beautiful then and maybe, he was like armed, but you cannot act that way. You cannot act protecting yourself. You have to be all out. You have to be, you know, take your chances and be honest. Otherwise, there's nothing. There's no reality."

Mary Virginia Pittman Waller was only fifteen when this scene was filmed but clearly remembers her involvement. "There were different rocks and things right there," she says, "and they had reflectors that would give them the light that they needed for the Todd-AO vision. When the light is not quite naturally right, they make it right by using reflectors to create the proper light that they do need. There was a rock that was there that they had...well...they created this rock out of Styrofoam that looked like the real thing: a huge boulder, because they had to put a reflector behind it. I had to hold one of the reflectors for them because the men were too large to hold the reflectors—you could see them from behind the rocks. So, I being younger, and a girl and small, I held the reflector for them behind the Styrofoam rock. That was my big moment!" (Microphones, holders and sound equipment remained in the tree when the crew returned to Brackettville. A flood subsequently washed it away in 1986).[931]

The sequence concluded as Cristal drove away in a buggy. Photographs taken at the time showed baggage accidentally spilling from the back of her carriage as she left. This was not planned and a retake was necessary. As soon as the scene ended, she leapt from the buggy and jumped into the Sabinal River. Warm temperature, standing under lights and reflectors, it seemed both spontaneous and sensible. But Cristal confesses to an ulterior motive. Publicity. "There were many photographers on the set," she admits, "and, as I told you, (I) go for the win, go for the kill in everything in my life. And I told them, 'Would you like me to jump into the water?' And I knew that I would take all the attention from anything else. And it's a way of winning. And so, that's what I was doing. I was merely all wet and removing some clothes, like the blouse and the skirt and whatever. I would never go beyond that. And they took a lot of pictures, and there was my intention."

Despite other crewmembers joining her in the river, Cristal minces no words about her actions: "It's always winning, surviving, going forward, making it happen, never take no for an answer," she says. "And taking those pictures like that was taking all the attention from anyone else." Witnesses were surprised she did something like that, particularly fully clothed. Why did she do something to that beautiful dress? Afterward, full of remorse, Cristal confessed the wardrobe mistress "had to work all night to try and dry those clothes. And I never even stopped to consider that, I didn't. I had no idea."[932]

(According to Cristal, there was another outdoor scene in which she was directed by Ford, but she said, it was not the "Flaca tree" sequence. No specifics were given, but, as it was an outdoor scene, it may have been the reading of Santa Anna's letter to the Tennesseans, or perhaps, the short scene in which Crockett asked Flaca to go for a walk. As for the lack of a love scene between their two characters, a sexual liaison is implied; definitely risqué for the 1950s. In the film, it is strongly implied Crockett spent the night with Flaca after he told her he dispatched her would-be husband, Emil Sand. At the conclusion of scene 116 in the May 19, 1959, version of the script, it states: "She sits down and curls against him, dropping her head in the hollow of his shoulder. We HOLD against them for a moment as the girl wilts against the big man, then DISOLVE TO; DAYBREAK. Scene 120 ANGLE ON CROCKETT–As he stands in his window. He is coatless. He watches the people below and then turns and looking off, smiles. Scene 121, ANGLE ON FLACA–As she stands in the open window, across the rooftop, looking at him. The new sun bathes her and she is radiant–a distinct change from the darkly moody woman we last saw go weeping into Crockett's arms. Crockett walks into the scene. She steps back and Crockett follows her into the room.")

*To be honest, though, there is some question whether the Houston camp site scene was filmed at Sabinal or at Ft. Clark in Brackettville. Selective recall and age all seems to color our memories. There are those who are absolutely adamant that scenes were filmed in particular areas while others' memories equally convince them otherwise. Some eyewitnesses recall the presence of specific individuals in addition to a large number of extras, riders, and horsemen. Along with wrangler Bobby Davenport, Dean Smith was at the Sabinal location to assure there weren't any problems with the mule that pulled Cristal's carriage: "We had nothing to do except be there for protection for Duke and what he was filming there." When asked, Dean recalls, "Richard Boone wasn't there that day during that shoot. They could have (filmed Avalon's arrival in Houston's camp) then but I didn't see that. I can't think of anybody else that might have doubled Frankie except when he was going across that creek crossing. (That) may have been one of the cooks that worked for Rolly Harper." After comparing all accounts and visual information, it is clear that Avalon's stream-crossing scene, in addition to his conversation with camp sentries was filmed at the Sabinal site. This analysis also seems to support Dean's statement that the Houston headquarter tent scene was filmed at Ft. Clark. Through the magic of movies, seamless splicing of the two sequences gives the appearance of a continuous scene filmed at the same location.*

While on location, Duke's personal physician was Mary Virginia's father, Dr. James Pittman. As a young doctor in 1933, he was a part of the first iconological surgical team in the world to successfully perform the removal of cancer from a lung. Mary is proud of the fact that "my family had been participating (in the film) from the financial end, as many others did… Wayne had the opportunity to meet my father. And, of course, my father was from Houston, and we had the ranch there…eight miles south of Utopia, actually, and he knew my father was a surgeon and had a great reputation, so he asked him if he would be his personal physician for him and Pilar, should they required that while they were making this film in Texas. And, of course, my father was delighted to do so. And they remained friends after the *Alamo* filming was completed, and we visited many times over the following years until John Wayne's death."

In addition to being responsible for Wayne and his family, as a general surgeon, Dr. Pittman also helped take care of the various bumps and bruises common on such films. Mary Virginia recalls, "There were several times when they asked Daddy to check on someone, or something like that. Maybe there had been a small cut or something, but no serious injuries during the time of the filming. But Daddy was called several times, just to make sure someone didn't have a broken bone, or sewed up a cut. They were small and minor things that would be normal for any type of action-packed film. And then, a couple times, he needed to check on something for John Wayne and for Pilar, which he did do and everything worked out well."[933]

Fortunately, the Del Rio, Nightingale Memorial (William Buck Burditt) and Val Verde hospitals weren't too far away and were patronized by several people associated with the film, including Alton Applewhite Jr., Frank Austin, Layne Britton, Julia French, Roman Freulich, Fidel Gonzales, Marion Harper, Don McLendon, Albert Podaloski, Bob Relyea, Tulisha Shahan, and Nick Toarilas. By mid-October, at least, twelve stuntmen had been hospitalized after major or minor accidents. However, in an article written after filming was complete, Jerry O. Parker and Fred L. Vinson, managers of the company hospital, reported only six fractures during the battle scenes—one collarbone, one shoulder blade, and four wrists. Fewer than thirty working days were lost from both illness and accident by members of the permanent company. Stuntman Jack Young probably suffered the worst accident. "We were working with the second unit," he recalled, "when we did this stunt. There was no way to practice a gig like this so we all just decided where each of us would try to go. There were thirteen of us to charge the Alamo, dressed as Mexican soldiers. We were supposed to go down in one barrage of gunfire, man and horse. Unfortunately, I was leading the pack. My horse was taught that when I touched her nose with the toe of my boot, she would stagger and then go down, giving me ample time to get my boot of out the stirrup. But, I reined a beat too soon, kicked her nose and she went down like a shot, trapped my foot in the stirrup and all hell broke loose. Now, there are twelve other animals around, threshing to get up with me in the middle of the fray. I was told later that a horse probably kicked me in the head, making me like a rag doll, which most likely saved my life. I was out of work for six months recuperating 'cause it took a while for the bones to mend. The company paid for all the hospital bills and kept me on the payroll until I could work again." Young fractured his skull, broke his back, punctured his lung, fractured a number of bones, and spent seventeen days in a coma. "After I got out (of the hospital), it just wasn't the same; it wasn't fun anymore," he said.[934]

Joe Canutt recalls a scene that wasn't including in the final cut: "(The) Mexicans on their way in on the south side of the fort," explains Canutt. "Where we had lines of probably five hundred Mexicans on horseback behind us. There were columns of four and my brother (Tap) and I were in the middle of the front. Cliff was shooting...and had put the camera in the middle of the road, and (we) were supposed to come down in two columns, a bomb goes off, and Tap and my horses go down, and a couple of saddle falls, and the column splits and go two columns to the left and two to the right of the camera to split the camera. And this is really typical with the Mexican horsemen. They hollered 'go'; they came in, and I threw this horse of mine, and all four columns split and right over the top of Tap and I. I mean, it was a mess; I'm not kidding you. I stayed under the black horse I had; I stayed under him. I wouldn't let him up. And I had a steel helmet on that; I had so many hoof prints on it by the time I finally got up. It's amazing you didn't kill a horse there or something 'cause…Billy Shannon's horse, he was going to do a saddle fall, jumped right over the top of him, and I saw him looking right up at him when he did it. Pile-ups, we called them. Plenty of those in there. In fact, my brother dislocated his arm on it. They put him, took him off to the hospital. I tell you, I remember a hell of a wreck one time when a Mexican fell off the limber. I take it back, he fell off; he was on the caisson, and the limber ran over him. Hurt him real bad."[935]

Still, make-up man Bob Keats related a story about a supposed death on the set. According to Bob, "there were at least two men killed in making *The Alamo*. One was a man who was scaling a ladder and when it was knocked over he missed his mark, a special pad to fall on, and broke his back, and another was a stuntman as a Mexican cavalryman who, when shot, fell off his horse and broke his neck." Bob said he was so close to the man he heard his neck bone crack. The scene went on without anyone knowing that the man was injured, let alone dead. When the director called "cut" and the stunt man didn't get up, Bob said that's when he knew for sure he was gone. The other incident involved the extras. According to him, quite a few actually bayoneted some of the actors in the legs, arm, or foot. These were written off as minor injuries sustained in normal battle scene sequences. The details of these stories cannot be substantiated, and the broken-neck incident sounds suspiciously like the death of Fred Kennedy on *The Horse Soldiers*.[936]

In between state troopers, lawyers, court appearances and depositions, Wayne still had a film to make. So after Boone completed his scene, Wayne returned to Brackettville to face yet another problem. He had to solve the Pappy issue. Clothier had previously suggested Duke lend Ford an extra camera crew and send him out to film whatever he wanted. It sounded like a fine idea. Duke loved Ford so much he said, "Well, he's here, so let him do something." But Ford knew he was being shuffled aside and didn't take kindly to it. If that was the way they would treat him, well, he could be a real son-of-a-bitch. One could hear his sarcastic frustration when he explained, "I was merely down there on vacation *(in Brackettville???)* and Duke said, 'Do you mind going out and getting a shot of so-and-so?' And I did. We got some wonderful scenes—guys swimming rivers, that sort of thing—but they were all cut out." According to Clothier, "Ford went out and shot stuff that couldn't possibly be used. Most of it expensive wastage. It didn't have anything to do with the picture that we were making. I don't think we used three cuts that the Old Man did. It cost Duke over $250,000 to give Ford that second unit. But so much of what he shot wasn't used that he was furious at Duke. For a long time after, he was rough on Duke." Stuntmen Roberson and White agreed. "True to form, the Old Man showed up for a visit on location," said Bad Chuck, "but this was one time in his life he did not take over directing.

This was Duke's show all the way, and Ford was close enough to him to know that. Instead, Duke gave him a camera, and sent him out on second unit for some river crossings. Pappy was content with watching Duke take the reins of directing, almost like a teacher is content when his pupil succeeds him. He was there to help if he was needed, but the truth of it was that we all knew he was not needed on *The Alamo*." When asked about Ford's involvement, White concurred: "Not a hell of a lot. He said, 'You might want to cut to a closer shot,' or something like that, but, as far as camera positions and the lenses and so forth, those were Wayne's. I never heard him say, 'That's not the way to do it.' I don't know whoever said they heard that, but I never heard it." Ted went on to qualify that statement, however. "I never stood that close to the Old Man; we all stood away."[937]

Ybarra said, "The only thing that John Ford shot was an exterior of the Cantina at night. During the fight sequence when all the guys get thrown out, he shot that (another cut scene). I don't recall Ford shooting anything else. Not during my presence anyway. I was there (for) 99% of the photography." Relyea seconded Clothier and Ybarra's opinions: "Duke would tell me to give (Ford) a half a dozen stuntmen and twenty extras and a camera, and let him go play someplace. There is not a shot that Ford made that's in the picture because, by design, by Duke and Ybarra's design, the damned thing...every shot had thousands of people in it. And we'd get two or three shots from Ford one day on each visit that would have two of his favorite stuntmen fighting in the corner with four extras. It looked so strange—you couldn't cut it in." Bill Hart said Ford shot "a scene where they had a guy do a saddle fall, and he rolled down into the water, and you could see his reflection in the water. Ford actually did shoot some stuff, but it may not have made it into the final print. It was very little, though, because it's definitely Wayne's picture." Denver Pyle was always present as Ford's assistant. "He'd shoot scenes of the Mexicans attacking the fort," said Pyle. "There are people, belittlers, who say that Ford directed the picture. He didn't. He directed a second unit, and I don't know that Wayne used much of it. They used clips of his footage, but that's all." Ford described his sojourn on the set as follows: "I walked a lot, worked some, and rested. Also ate steak three times a day. John's got a hell of a picture. Dick Widmark will have a new career. Laurence Harvey gave a fine performance, and we all enjoyed getting to know his lovely wife, Margaret Leighton, who was resting there from a Broadway play...I was the coach," said Coach, "on third base."[938]

Although Wayne, Clothier and others may have struggled with Ford's presence, Happy Shahan didn't put up with any of that nonsense. "Everyone wants to know about Wayne," explained Happy in an interview with former Alamo Village employee Patrick Saunders. "And I'll tell you flat out, I knew Wayne very well. Me and him butted heads a lot...and Wayne was many things to many people, but Ford was the man. Let me tell you, I loved him. Ford was one of the few people in my life I wanted to call friend...he impressed me. When

Ford first came out on the ranch, he was just checking on his boy, ya' know. Well, I didn't get involved in all that between him and Wayne. Sure, it was a big deal when Ford showed up, but after awhile he became a regular on the set like everybody else that was working on the picture."

Each morning after Happy checked on his cattle, he would go to the film set. "Ford was always there ahead of me,' said Happy, "and when he saw that I was close enough he would shout, so everybody could hear, 'Good morning, you ol' son-of-a-bitch.'" Ford's picking on people was legendary but pretty soon such behavior even got on Happy' nerves. He knew he shouldn't take Ford's insult personally but neither could he let himself become a joke on the set. Shahan had a reputation to protect, and "Ford was doing this to me on my land." So one morning, he decided to address the issue head-on. "When I got to the set, there he was in his chair. 'Morning, you old son-of-a-bitch,' and everybody started laughing. Well, I marched right over to where he was sitting, and I looked right at him, and I said, 'Mr. Ford, if you call me that again, I am going to put you on your ass.' Well, Ford just cracked up, and then he looked over at Wayne and said, 'You know, I think the boy is telling the truth!'"[939]

Earlier, although not directing, Ford had been present when Wayne and Clothier filmed Mexican troops marching over hill and valley on the way to San Antonio. It would be one of the rare "composite" shots used in the film. Clothier revealed the process: "We pulled a trick there, too. We had about twelve hundred head of horses. And we had about three thousand extras. We had something like two thousand of them dressed in Mexican uniforms, and we split the screen four ways so when you saw it on the screen, there were sixteen thousand people. And a hell of a lot of horses. We just set the camera up and blocked out a portion of the film. We put all these troops in one quarter of the screen. Then we blocked out that quarter of the screen and opened the second quarter of the screen. We put all of our troops in. We cranked the film back and ran it through the camera again. It took us all day to make this one shot. Then, in the lab, it was put together. As you recall, it looked like the biggest army in the world." Local resident Joe York Jr. was there when they filmed that sequence and remembers it well: "… they hauled in—1,600 might be the number I'm looking for—but it could have been 1,600 in the entire shot and that would be people, horseback… They started a scene across; they set up equipment on top of one of those rolling, rolling hills, and there was a kind of a valley there; it was probably a quarter mile to the other, next hill the other side of this big, kind of a, it wasn't a creek or anything but just a dry draw that the water drained out of. They had probably 1,600 in that shot. And they filmed them on the other hill, as they were coming over the hill, and all you could see was Mexican soldiers coming. Horseback and everything. Paraphernalia and everything that came. Wagons. So then around noon, they started early that morning before daylight, at daybreak, I think, and they shot the bottom of this, they probably had a hundred-foot fall, and then it rose back up another hundred-foot, and they had the camera sit there. In the afternoon, they took the third shot with the same people and laid one on, and the third shot was the same people coming up right in front of the camera. And they marched all of the horses and all the soldiers and all the wagons and cannons and everything they had, and they came right just within a few feet of the camera from all of the way from the bottom up, a thousand feet, maybe it seemed, maybe six, eight hundred feet. And they mounted that three times, they took those shots and laid them one on top of the other, and then it showed three thousand or forty-five hundred coming in. Out of doing it three times in different positions, they put 'em one on top, one on top of the other, and it was a very interesting thing."[940]

(A second "composite" or "matte" shot was used to film a scene before the beginning of the final assault. Mexican troops are seen standing in formation in preparation of the assault on the "north" and "west" walls. Mounted troops line the rim of a hill in the background as smoke from an explosion billows into the sky. Curilla explains how Clothier accomplished it: "The camera is locked down on a tripod, so it can't budge, and the shot is framed. A geographic dividing line is selected between halves of the frame. In this case, it is the road along the 'west' wall of the Alamo. All the extras are staged and rehearsed for their actions in the area beyond the road. Clothier's crew then placed a black card in the 'matte box' of the camera (the black accordion-like affair that houses the lens). When looking through the lens, this 'matte' blacks out the bottom half of the frame and its upper edge would be carefully cut and placed to line up with the road. Then they filmed the scene, thus having film exposed only on the top half of the frame (where the extras are) and unexposed on the bottom half. Next, the film is back-wound in the camera with the lens cap on so as not to double-expose the filmed scene. It is backed up to the beginning point of the shot, using the footage counter to be precise to the frame. All the extras are now moved in to the area between the road by the Alamo and the camera set-up and told what to do. This can take all day. Clothier switches mattes in the matte box to one that blocks out the top half of the frame and has a lower edge that is an exact match for the upper edge of the other matte. Like before, he would line this up with the distant road, thus blocking the light from the top half of the frame (which would double-expose the previous shot). Now he shoots the ten-second scene with the extras performing in the foreground on the same strip of film to complete the composite image and turn 3,000 extras into 6,000 soldiers—flawlessly.")

To correctly position the soldiers, wagons, etc., Batjac hired locals fluent in Spanish, but it was a dicey situation. Extra David Kuykendall admitted, "The time that we wondered if things would get outta hand was when they brought all those braceros across the border. They brought them through the hills and a bunch of us were hired as directors, you know? For a better word—we were hiding in different places, making sure those guys would go where they were supposed to go; keeping them in line, keeping them moving and going like they were supposed to have gone. It was wild, man; it was really wild."[941]

Clothier's analysis of Ford's involvement was incorrect, though. And Wayne confirmed that when he wrote to Ford: "Saw the cuts you made on the wall. They turned out great, as you knew." Despite his protestations, Ford did not come down to "cast a paternal" eye on his protégé, nor to lend advice. He came down for one reason and one reason only: He wanted to direct *The Alamo*. Ford was on location for fifty of the ninety-eight scheduled days (September 19-29, October 5-19, November 17-28 and November 30-December 12). And it wasn't just because he liked Mexican food. Ford confessed his real intentions in a letter to Lord Killanin in February 1960: "I've got to help out Duke with *The Alamo*. This is a picture that actually cost $5,000,000. It's a helluva picture…a real spectacular…but, as I said, I've got to help him." (An analysis of John Ford Production Inc., financial records indicated Ford charged $2,800 to *The Alamo* project during October through December. Interestingly, Wayne was vice-president of Ford's company.) Sources suggest the actual relative participation in the finished film was Wayne 85%, Lyons 10% and Ford 5%. But Ford was always there, always available, always instructing. If one assumes Ford was present when a scene was filmed and Wayne and/or Cliff Lyons were not, then it's logical to believe Ford directed the scene. In many cases, as previously stated, Ford directed Wayne in his own scenes. Widmark, Cristal, Avalon and Worden all commended Ford for his efforts on their behalf. An analysis of still photographs, supported by anecdotal interviews with participants, would suggest that by mid-October Ford was present at and/or directed the following sequences:

- Initial meeting between Crockett and Flaca
- Confrontation between Sand and Flaca including bird distraction
- Flaca's hotel room discussions culminating in Crockett's departure
- Sand's death scene in the church "basement"
- Crockett notifying Flaca of Sand's death
- Smitty crossing stream with small waterfall
- Smitty meets Houston camp sentries
- Smitty delivers message to Houston
- Morning patrol ford stream/Mexican cattle sequence
- Crockett/Bowie "pyrotechnics" scene
- Lt. Reyes/troopers ride up creek bed/interview Mexican peasant family
- Crockett delivers powder and muskets to Alamo.[942]

Upon Wayne's return to Brackettville, he again began to film scenes that focused on the interior of the Alamo and its compound. But first, on Tuesday, October 20, he met with Mr. and Mrs. Elmer Jordon of Lubbock, Texas, the

25,000th and 25,001th visitors to the set; they got to have lunch with Duke. That week also saw Wayne film several scenes inside Travis's headquarters, including his young daughter's screen debut on October 22. Joan O'Brien would enter the room, carry on a short conversation with Wayne, and Aissa would follow, to be picked up by O'Brien. After a short conversation with Duke, she would leave and Aissa would say goodbye. Wayne had perfectly cast Aissa. "One morning I was watching Aissa play on the living-room rug with a doll," recalled Duke, "and I noticed that her focus on the doll was intense. I knew I'd found my little Dickinson girl. We had to have a baby in the picture, and naturally I'm a little prejudiced toward the little girl. She was just beautiful in her three scenes and knew her lines perfectly. One thing I like about Aissa's role was the fact we could write in some of the cute little things she says around home." Added Aissa, "More to the point…he liked being surrounded and supported by his loved ones when he made movies. There were big rewards and steep falls from glory at stake, and even Hollywood royalty have their self-doubts." Pilar wasn't as convinced. Duke worked for three days to change her mind as she didn't want to be a stage mother and didn't want Aissa to be child actress. Wayne promised that after the film was complete, Aissa would retire to a normal childhood. Yet, there still were times when Duke's self-control faltered on the set: When Ford arrived and tried to take over direction; the ongoing confrontations with Widmark; and Aissa's lack of professionalism. Granted, at only three years of age, she wasn't an actress and, although she had been on location with the family before, had never even appeared before a camera. Far too young to comprehend what was expected, she thought she was only play-acting. But Duke the perfectionist demanded professional behavior from everyone, from the lowliest grip to his daughter. He couldn't afford the time and money necessary to coax a decent performance from her, no matter how young she was. Pilar recalled, "…midway through the first take, Aissa stopped the entire take by running to her father's side, asking, 'Did I do right, Daddy?' After staring at her a moment, he bent down to pick her up. 'You did just fine, honey,' Duke said, picking her up, and carrying her back to her place on the set." She had already flubbed her first line. Asked to say hello to Col. Crockett, she said instead, "Hello, Daddy." Every take thereafter, she'd run to her father "for a kiss and a pat on the head." Some of the other actors and stuntmen thought it funnier than hell that Aissa had the big, burly Duke wrapped around her little finger. When they finished their scenes, they would ask, "Did I do right, Daddy?" Wayne failed to see the humor. Rumors were her lines were eventually dubbed. (She was far too young to comprehend what was expected but did receive $250 a week, which was deposited in her own personal savings account. Duke confessed earlier, "I'm going to try to get her as cheaply as I can. I think the lowest salary on the picture is $400. Maybe Aissa will agree on $300." He didn't get off so easily with son Pat. "My other boy Michael, he's twenty-four, works for our Batjac production company. Now, all of a sudden, he's

Pat's agent. That Michael is the sharpest money man around. The boys are still arguing with company executives over Pat's salary. I refuse to deal with them. Michael is a better businessman than I am. I'd be a fool to go up against those two.")[943]

The crew had a regular shuttle service going between Hollywood and Texas—quitting because of the hardships and the driving of their director. Wayne only had so much time and so much money; those who held up the filming were summarily dispatched. Even daughter Aissa was not immune to his temper. According to Henaghan, who may have had a bone to pick with Wayne anyway, some feared Duke was going to throttle her because she couldn't remember her lines. No doubt, Dobie Carey heard the following from close friend Widmark. "During the shooting of the film, Wayne was like a man possessed," explained Carey. "He spared no one, including himself, in getting on film the story he had to tell. I'll tell you something else, too. Duke could have been a hell of a director. He was humble with Ford, but in those other films we did in Durango, Mexico, later in his career, he was a hard guy to talk to on the set. That was because he really did know so much. The only thing stopping him from being a great director was his temper. But he really knew what he was talking about. He knew the film game, and he knew the film business. But he had no tact. So he wasn't so full of camaraderie on the set in these later years."[944]

*(An interesting aspect of Aissa's debut is that her scene was identified as #517. However, in the October 5 revision of the script, that particular scene number was one of one hundred set ups listed in a production department bulletin for the final assault on the Alamo. The total number of scenes in this revision was only 566. In fact, the entire Dickinson/Lisa/Crockett introductory sequence, which was revised on September 14, was first identified as scene #119. Script changes are a writer and director's way of preparing for shooting and can take place overnight, affecting the next day's shooting, all from a discussion held the night before. Perhaps a new number sequence was created to identify new or additional scenes.)*

On October 22, Wayne filmed the first shots fired by a limited number of Mexican troops. Hoping to get effective cloud formations behind a field mortar bombardment of the West Wall, the weather would play havoc with Duke's schedule. Plagued by two persistent issues, every time he got a scene rehearsed letter-perfect, he either had trouble with surrounding noise or the sun would duck behind clouds that were constantly drifting across the sky. Exasperated when the sun failed to come out from behind a cloud at a crucial moment when the camera was ready to roll, Wayne blared out a choice expletive. The sun appeared. The next day, the same problem occurred. Wayne grinned at a local reporter, "If that sun would only shine right now." The reporter replied, "Maybe it would if you'd call it what you did yesterday." Pausing for a moment, Duke replied, "I don't know. I wouldn't want to get in bad with the man up there."[945]

When ready to shoot a scene, the AD would order all motors stopped around the set and on the road. But it was impossible to keep people from talking, making noise or shuffling about. Once, after the AD had repeatedly called for silence through the loudspeakers, Duke started pleading through a soft, begging, ingratiating voice, then abruptly roared, "Shut up! Is that clear enough?" And his eyes swept across the entire courtyard of actors, crew, and visitors. Another time, he explained with mock, labored, gentle patience, "Friends. We can't play music to entertain you while we're shooting scenes; it would interfere with the dialogue; so I'll just have to ask you to be patient and—cut out the god damn noise!" Of course, when a local San Antonio newspaper published the location phone number (Jordan 3-251), leaving off only the last number, it didn't help minimize visitors and interruptions.[946]

By late October, Wayne had also filmed another mishap that appeared in the final print. In an extended sequence, several scouts, chased by Mexican dragoons, ride hell-bent-for-leather into the Alamo compound. Directed by stunt coordinator Cliff Lyons, Rudy Robbins, Big Boy Williams, and two other defenders discover the "European cannon" and ride back to the Alamo to notify the garrison. "As you are coming (on to the set) and you pass the horse corrals on the right," recalled Robbins, "there is a ranch road, mostly grown over by now, that continues on due east from where the corrals are. It goes back a mile or two on the ranch to an old house and a set of ranch working pens. This road was kept well graded at the time of the filming, and the airstrip was on the south side of this road, about a half mile east of the Alamo. Because of this well-graded road, several of the movie scenes were filmed out that way, as it was an easy area to get to. Most of the ranch was grown over in brush, and hard to access. This is the same area where me and Big Boy and the other scouts were when the Mexicans got after us, and we made a dash for the Alamo." As they entered the compound, Williams's horse stopped and reared. Robbins' horse bumped into Big Boy's from the back and Williams fell off; unscripted and unintentional. Rudy admitted it was his fault, but Williams was a professional. Holding onto both his rifle and the reins, he got up, pushed the horse out of the way and continued the scene. ("Doggone it, Beekeeper! I thought you weren't gonna open that corn liquor till nightfall. What's the matter with you?" "It's only a half-hour to dark. Besides, it's my keg, ain't it?" "Well, all right. Give me some of that stuff. I'm so scared I could drink all of it. Maybe I will"). Wayne then yelled "Cut!" "Folks," he said. "You all just witnessed a pro at work. He just saved me a lot of money." Extra Tommy Worrell watched the scene being filmed. "If he had just got up and said, 'Oh, I'm sorry. I got thrown,' it would've wasted all that film," explains Worrell. "They couldn't have used it. He got up and just got up, started mumbling going over there, and they dubbed it later. That was a learning thing for us." Williams slid out of the saddle and injured his back but remained in the film.

The beginning of this scene had Chill Wills rationing out whiskey to weary defenders while reciting various rhymes. Duke told Wills, "Just make up some words." ("*Chicken in the bread pan, pickin' up the corn. That's all! Flies in the buttermilk, shoo fly shoo. That's all! Ants on the sugar bowl, two by two. That's all!*") Slightly more ribald rhymes were used during rehearsal ("*Two old maids in a folding bed....*"). Wills was always looking for more screen time. One day he barged into Michael Wayne's room and asked, "Mike, will you tell your dad to let me get a little more time on camera in that one scene, because I was hardly showing up at all."[947]

The sequence continued when Williams described the type and size cannon to Wayne, Widmark, et al. Although he arrived in the compound carrying a flintlock, he is shown scratching a drawing in the ground with a trapdoor Springfield, and even took time to draw spokes on the wheel, even though he is never shown doing so. After an admonishment from Harvey, Williams sheepishly retreated to the headquarters stairs. Chill Wills commented on Williams's report, and Harvey ridiculed his observation. ("*With a cannon like that, them Santa Anna fellas can just sit up there and give us what fer, can't they?*" "*There's no such cannon in the North American continent. Acting Lieutenant Finn is exaggerating!*"). The Mexicans' cannon discharged a shell in reply and not only blew a hole in the South Wall but took out the whiskey barrel as well. The scene was staged with extras in position and stuntmen closest to the explosion. Wayne had already told the cast, "Now, don't worry—nobody's going to get hurt. It's just going to be a big concussion and then a big flame, but there won't be anybody hurt." "When Duke called, 'Action,' the special effects man set off a flammable 'cocktail,'" says John Quinn, who was also in the scene, "and triggered mechanical rigs that broke the masonry fast. Duke was surprised, I believe, that the concussion was as powerful as it was. He had explained that it would not be harmful, but as you can see... a lot of things were flying through the air very rapidly. That would give you an idea of how much of a 'blow-up' occurred even if some of material was lightweight foam blocks." Fortunately, a shelter had protected the camera. Chill's whiskey barrel was broken up separately and set aflame by special effects. Quinn believes the explosion occurred before Wayne anticipated it. He states that both he (Quinn) and Widmark started to move microseconds before the explosion, but Wayne was still standing erect. What resulted was Wayne's unrehearsed, honest expression of surprise. After the scene was completed, one joker hollered out, "Let's do it over!" One shot, one take. That's all![948]

The following day Wayne planned to film Travis's response to Santa Anna's demand for unconditional surrender ("*From the headquarters of Generalissimo Antonio Lopez de Santa Anna, absolute ruler of Mexico, to the rebel commander who deems himself in command of the rebels occupying the mission. Be it known: the province of Mexico known as Texas has shown itself to be in active and treasonous revolt against the rule of Generalissimo Santa Anna. The Generalissimo in his kindness, issues the following order: All occupants of the mission will leave at once, leaving all*

*arms and ammunition behind them. If this order is not followed with your dispatch,
the Generalissimo will be reducing the mission by assault. There will be no quarter
given. Signed....*"). Ybarra recreated a ten-foot-tall, top-right corner of the Alamo
church facade about a half mile to the east of the main set and included a cannon
platform and portable fallen cross. This structure was primarily constructed for
all close-up scenes involving Wayne, Widmark, and Harvey atop the platform.
It is easy to tell which shots were filmed on each set. All shots from ground level
where the entire church is visible were filmed on the main set. Those where the
camera looks up or is level with the platform were probably shot at the faux chapel. Directly behind this re-creation was the caliche pit where they dug up clay
used to make abode blocks. Just across the road from the church top was a short
runway built, so airplanes could ferry "dailies" back and forth to Hollywood for
development and printing. *(This raw, unedited footage is the first positive print made
by the laboratory from the negative photographed the previous day. The footage is then
viewed by the director and selected members of the production. Hence, the term dailies.)*

Along with John Dierkes, Denver Pyle, and a four-man cannon crew,
Wayne, Widmark, and Harvey were present on the platform for this sequence.
As scripted, Travis was explaining battery emplacements to Crockett and Bowie
when told the Mexican army was investing Bexar. Lt. Reyes was charged with
delivering an ultimatum. Travis would interrupt Santa Anna's demand by taking
a glowing cigar, lighting a fuse, discharging the cannon, turning, and walking
away. (As initially scripted, defender Dean Smith was to shoot Reyes, but it
was cut out of the scene). Carlos Arruza would play the part of Lt. Reyes. "We
bought about three hundred horses," Relyea explained. "Then we broke them—
they were wild. We had electricians there in pre-production with lamps(s) and
cable. Horses hate cable because they think it's a snake. And all these horses,
therefore, became very movie-savvy, if you will. Arruza arrived (to select a horse)
and he said, 'No, no. Not that one, not that one. I want this one.' Of course, it was
one of the misbehavers. And I said, 'Well, he's not one of our pupils who's doing
very well.' And he said, 'No, we'll be fine.' And then, when he did that scene...
his hands weren't anywhere near the reins, and that wild-ass horse was doing
everything except dancing, and his (Arruza's) body never moved. Just incredible.
He just sat on that horse, and the horse did everything, and the cannon went off,
and Arruza never moved. He was holding the reins, and he wrapped it in one
hand and rode off, and all the stuntmen were shaking their heads saying, 'That's
a horseman—that's a real horseman.'"[949]

Marshall Jones, Dave Marshall, and Ray Everson stood in for Wayne,
Widmark, and Harvey, respectively, as the scene was being set up (Everson,
an English actor, flew in from London to stand in for Harvey. During stunt
sequences, Bill Williams doubled Widmark, Tap Canutt doubled Harvey, and it
seemed like almost everybody doubled Wayne, including Chuck Roberson, Ted
White, and Bob Morgan). Harvey stood on an "apple box" and several stacked

two-by-fours in order to appear as tall as Wayne. (An apple box is the device used to even out actors' heights. Literally a flipped-over wooden box, it came in a variety of sizes such as full, half, and quarter-apple. Wayne would also stand on a box.) Two gas canisters were connected to the cannon barrel to ignite a simulated discharge. Photographs suggest there were some sort of clamps or tie-downs attached to the wooden cannon wheels to prevent movement, possibly to make sure it would be correct in frame.[950]

The entire sequence was composed of scenes filmed at both the main set and the mock-up church-top set. Three stand-ins were used to represent Crockett, Travis, and Bowie as the cannon was fired in response to the Mexican demand. Once that part of the scene was completed, cast and crew moved to the offsite location, and, when that set-up was ready, Wayne yelled "Action" and the scene began again. Harvey lit the fuse, but, as the cannon fired, it rolled off its support frame and over his left foot. Not wanting to spoil the shot, Harvey exhibited no reaction whatsoever and continued the scene in character. But when Wayne yelled "Cut!", Harvey cried out in pain. Michael Wayne witnessed this and was amazed at Harvey's fortitude: "...when it came down it came down on his foot. A real cannon came down on his foot and smashed his foot to smithereens. Broke it like you can't believe it, but he didn't do...he didn't grimace in the scene. These were professional men; they knew what they were doing. Harvey was a professional actor. He knew his business." Marshall Jones, standing behind the camera when it happened, said, "I saw that damn thing hit. You know, he didn't even change his expression. He was all man. People think he was a little queerish but...if he was, (he) never did wink at me."[951]

Duke was impressed as well: "...And talk about the show must go on... Travis lights the cannon. When it fired, it recoiled—right over Harvey's foot. And he didn't even flinch. He knew it would ruin the take. When I said, 'Cut!' only then did he cry out in pain. Now that's a professional. He had that foot in plaster for weeks, and I had to keep his damaged foot out of the shot." Duke knew it was serious when he saw Harvey's delayed reaction. "Get him to the goddamn hospital," he ordered, but Harvey refused to leave. "Just bring me a bucket of boiling water and a bucket of ice," he asked. "I'm going to try an old cure." His boot was cut off, and he dipped his foot in hot water until he couldn't take it any longer. Then, he placed it in the bucket of ice. The "hot and cold treatment," he called it. He continued the treatment for the rest of the day, into the evening and the following day. When finished, his foot and ankle were wrapped in bandages. "Sometimes I wonder what I'm doing here myself," said Harvey as he hobbled around his suite. "But here I am, and I've got to make the most of it. This sort of thing has happened to me many times," he explained. "I played soccer, you know?" Costumer trainee Ron Talsky volunteered to help. "I went up to Duke," recalled Talsky, "and said I was the same size and, if he needed a stand-in for Harvey for a while, he should let me know. Duke said, 'Good, I really appreciate it.'"[952]

The actual accident is not apparent in the film, although Harvey can be seen limping toward the rear of the cannon after it had been fired—a static cannon with smoke pouring out the barrel. The cannon is not seen rolling or recoiling as part of the scene. Standing behind the wheel axle, between the barrel and outside left wheel, it's possible the vibration or effect of the cannon discharging caused Harvey to fall off the box and the wheel to roll on his foot. Or instead of recoil, which implies a back-and-forth motion, it may have been an up-and-down motion, and Harvey's foot could have been trapped on the downward motion. Rich Curilla may be closest to the truth when he suggests the accident could even have resulted from the crew rolling the cannon back to reset or check the special-effects charge in the mouth of the tube and rather than explain all that undramatic stuff and point a finger at a crew or individual, somebody just decided to say the accident was the result of cannon recoil. A tongue-in-cheek article written several days after the accident stated, "The latest press dispatch from *The Alamo*, near Brackettville, brings the sad word that 'Col. Travis' has been wounded—by a careless Tennessean, who dropped a heavy cannon barrel on the colonel's foot."[953]

By the end of the month, Wayne would also film the first portion of the birthday party sequence. Subsequently cut from the road-show version, this scene addressed the decoration of a chocolate birthday cake by Mrs. Dickinson, Blind Nell Robertson, Mrs. Dennison (Olive Carey), and Melinda Dennison (Carol Baxter). Veda Ann Borg's character provided the candles from her apron and handed them to Olive Carey. The scene begins with the ladies chatting among themselves and ends with a close-up of "Lisa Angelina Dickinson" written on a cake being frosted. Twenty-two local children, including Lynn and Tommy Dee Seargeant, Barbara and Elaine Wills, Susan Raney, Fran Higgins, Paul Davis, Sharyn Postell, Fourth Coates, Joe York Jr., A. J. Schubach, and the Cumiskey brothers, sat around a large table under the Dickinsons' veranda and wore paper birthday hats and crowns as plates of cake and mugs of milk were passed out. Tim Cumiskey remembers, "There were several scenes when my mother and my brother and I were all in the scene and then in the birthday scene that was cut out, both of us were in that scene. I've got a black and gold jacket on and a black hat and a string tie back in the back there. My brother actually had a speaking part and he said, 'Oh, boy, what a beautiful cake.'" John Henry Daniels also remembers the scene: "I do know that there was a party and a lot of my friends were (there). We had cake, juice, and they made out of grocery bags little hats that we put on our heads." Susan Raney Stone recalls, "We had a birthday cake; it was like pancakes. It was like eight or nine pancakes stacked up. And I remember they brought Aissa out, and we sang 'Happy Birthday.' And we blew out the candles, and then immediately they took her back into an air-conditioned room. And the rest of us had to sit outside in costume." It was at this point where the road-show version of that scene began. Defenders sing 'Happy Birthday' to Aissa Wayne and present her with a birthday gift, a wooden crib (*"My first real bed!"*). Elaine Moody, only four at the time, was Aissa's stand-in: "I asked my mom (why) one time, and she said probably because I was about the same size and same coloring as Aissa, so I was her stand-in. I remember when they were getting ready to film the birthday party scene. I was taking a nap, and they came and got me, and I remember all the actors standing around the little crib, they put me in and singing 'Happy Birthday.' They would come and get me to do the run-through to practice and get the lighting and everything like that right before they actually filmed the scene." Standing in the background, costumed extra John Quinn, complete with black sombrero, recalls, "I was part of the crowd in this scene and enjoyed Duke directing his daughter Aissa. Listening to Ken and Joan sing was an absolute bonus. They harmonized so nicely." According to Birdwell, Wayne admitted he was "over sentimental" about the long birthday party sequence featuring Aissa, but, in the interest of tightening the picture, that segment was eliminated. Ken Curtis agreed: "There's a scene where Joan O'Brien, who played my wife, and I have a song to sing for our daughter, played by Duke's own daughter, Aissa. The song was called 'Tennessee Babe' and it was kind of too sentimental, really. (*"Tennessee babe with a sweet-sounding name, dear little rose of the South. You are so sweet that the neighbors all claim, sugar won't melt in your mouth. Oh, Lisa, our Lisa. Dear little rose of the South. Oh, Lisa, sweet Lisa. Sugar won't melt in your mouth."*) And then Aissa had a line which was 'We are three together,' and I said, 'Always, honey.' Well, Duke told me that Aissa used to say that to him and Pilar, and he'd say, 'Always, honey.' But when he and Pilar separated, he'd think of Aissa as a little girl saying that line, and he'd just break down."[954]

Newspapers began to refer to *The Alamo* as a jinxed set. Shahan's daughter severely injured in a car accident the first week and the deaths of others; a tragic murder of an aspiring actress; Harvey's injured foot; southwest Texas storms blowing down sets that had to be reconstructed at considerable cost; Relyea's perforated ulcer. And sickness. Teresa Champion recalls, "Linda Cristal had pneumonia and was in the hospital. She was in the hospital for a week—she didn't do nothing for a week. Everybody got sick—I got sick; everybody got sick—it was super cold—so cold." A flu virus swept through the production company in October and November, the result of dusty winds and sudden changes in overnight temperatures. It affected eight out of ten members of cast and crew. In addition to his injured foot, Harvey was also bothered by a head cold. "They've been spreading some sort of wild insecticide all over our place down there, and I think that's what caused this miserable thing," he lamented. What else could possibly go wrong?[955]

# CHAPTER TWENTY-FIVE
# "GOOD MORNING, MR. WAYNE."

AISSA WASN'T THE ONLY CHILD ACTOR ON THE SET. JOHN HENRY DANIELS (Happy Sam) recalls his own experiences: "I remember we had our own limo and driver. Our driver's name was Gabby Garcia. He would come and knock on the door (4 a.m.), and we would go to the limo, and he would open the door. My brother would get in, and I would say that I wanted to sit in that seat. He would then open the other door, and I would get in. We would get in and lay down for the seven-mile ride. When we got to the village and went to our rooms (third door along the "West" wall), there was hot chocolate and cinnamon rolls waiting for us. We would drink and eat and lay down (on two sets of bunk beds) until someone came and said, 'Happy Sam, it's time for you to practice your scene.'" Other local children weren't as fortunate as John Henry and Caesar as they might get dropped off at the Gateway Café and then have to wait for a bus to take them to the location, or perhaps they rode along with their parents who worked out there.[956]

Batjac had hired Florrie Wills, a certified teacher, for all school children while on location. As there weren't many teachers available in a community the size of Brackettville, her husband, the local school superintendent, had recommended her for the position. Nineteen juveniles ranging from elementary to high-school age were "enrolled" in the set's one-room school. The state had granted a special waiver to the district, so the students could still be counted as present, and, unless an individual was needed for a particular scene, the schooling generally lasted all day. The classroom occupied one of the storage buildings that surrounded the

Alamo compound, and Wills was there to help students and generally assure lessons received from their home schools were completed. Florrie's daughters, Elaine (Moody) and Barbara (Wills White), came along as part of the package and were cast as extras. Neither recalls being interviewed for their parts, although their mother may have been. But they do remember a skunk. Barbara says, "(We) were just sitting around waiting to be called and (a) skunk just wandered into the classroom." Adds Elaine, "...my mom made all of us get up on these mattresses. They had all these mattresses piled up in the corner to be used for stunts, so all the mattresses were piled up there, and we all had to get up on top of the mattresses to get away from the skunk." One of the extras eventually shooed it out with a broom. The younger kids also took naps atop the mattresses when the mood struck. Aissa even napped in her dad's director's chair but confessed to an ulterior motive. "I think my first crush was Ken Curtis," she admits. "I would fall asleep, I pretended to fall asleep, so Ken Curtis would lift me up and carry me into my parents' trailer."[957]

Most of the time, the kids would just hang out and play at Ft. Clark or on the set. What a great place for a young child to be—it was fun, and you got paid to be there! Danny Borzage, bit player and musician, entertained them with his accordion "and my sister and I and Aissa would play Ring Around the Rosie, musical chairs, and things like that," says Barbara. "Anything to amuse ourselves. I remember Pilar would sing and clap along. There was a hill where the flagpole was in the center...we played on that all the time, running up and down it. Getting skinned knees and stuff." Mike Roselle, ten-year-old son of extras casting director Tom Roselle, recalls, "My folks knew someone in casting and got us jobs. The people in charge were too busy to pay much attention to us kids, so sometimes, when we were not needed, we'd go over the top of the hills and play hooky from school. This was the most fun of all in making the movie." But sometimes they got in trouble. One day John Henry and Aissa were playing and knocked over a rack of rifles stacked against a wall. Loaded with blanks, one accidentally discharged, scaring the children. Both scattered, one in one direction, one in another. John Henry ran up the set of stairs next to the main gate, fell and skinned his knee. But he received more attention over his "injury" than the accident. Constantly telling everyone "I'm not hurt," no one was any worse for wear.[958]

Pat Cumiskey had the intimidating honor of shooting pool one day with Wayne himself: "One of my biggest memories...at that time, it was the office or administrative building (at Ft. Clark) where they had a restaurant and a clubhouse kind of place where you could rent for parties," he says. "Upstairs, they had a pool table, and I would go down there and shoot pool 'cause I was fascinated by it, and I could play by myself. Just be down there for hours. And I was down there one day knocking balls around, and John Wayne came up the stairs. At that time, I was twelve or thirteen years old, and I was just a huge John Wayne fan. Saw every movie he ever made, and (this day) he talked to me and actually shot

478

a little pool with me. Once he got up there, I was shaking so bad I couldn't even hit the ball. It was really neat." Pat's brother Dan was tutored in the fine art of stuntmanship: "It was very, very interesting. We got to meet all the stuntmen… we used to have some home movies; I was with Denver Pyle and Ken Curtis. They were stabbing me and taught me how to stab. Take a hit and all that stuff. It was one of those dream things that you never even think was going to happen to you, and you're living in a little podunk town because of where my dad was stationed. Ft. Clark was probably the best place we lived in all the places that we lived every place we went." All the children loved Jester Hairston; he would sing to them and play the three monkey "see no evil, hear no evil, speak no evil" game. John Henry says they all referred to him as "Uncle Remus." Hairston would entertain others as well. "He had made a little game," says Tommy Worrell. "Hand/ eyes coordinating-type game and we would play it all the time. And John Wayne would come in and play that game with us. He really, really enjoyed it. But he would come into the commissary, not all the time, but a good bit. Play that game and just visit around with the guys."[959]

But some of the youngsters also were afraid or put off by a few of the stars: "The only man I was afraid of was Richard Boone," admits John Henry. "He always looked mad. We used to receive these white boxes for boxed lunch, and one time Boone called me over. I came over and looked up at him, and he gave me a box. I took it and walked away. Then I started to run. But I stopped and looked back, and he had a big smile on his face." John Henry also remembers the kiss Linda Cristal gave him on his check. So impressed with the gesture, he even recalls forty-seven years later the kiss was on his left cheek! Others didn't find Cristal as open, though. Hilda Garcia was ten when they started recruiting extras. "I do remember Linda Cristal," she says, "and I remember us wanting to talk to her and she was a little…maybe she didn't like children, I don't know. She was a little snobbish to the children. Didn't want to talk, not positive. There was a bunch of us that would run up to her; we wanted to say hi or talk to her…the lady that was kind of over the children went up to her and said there's a bunch of children that wanted to talk to her or shake her hand." Cristal supposedly replied, "I don't need to talk to them. I don't want to talk to them." Then she walked into her trailer and slammed the door. Garcia was disappointed, but as she admits, "Maybe (Linda) was in a crummy mood. But I do remember talking to Richard Widmark, John Wayne, and Laurence Harvey…(those) three men would come and talk to us. Sit around and go back whenever there was a break."[960]

Sometimes children were needed for just a single scene or two and thus didn't have to attend school on location. Openings for parts were posted at the Brackettville post office. In her case, Hilda explains, "Anyone that was interested, they needed men, women and children. My dad took me (for an audition), and they just looked at me. 'OK, we need this little girl.' I think we took my brother, but he wasn't selected. They would serve us breakfast (on location), and, when we got there, we'd go to this area which was the dressing room, and they had this wardrobe room we were assigned to. The ladies there would tell you what clothes you were going to wear. I would go in there and put on my long dress and bonnet, and then we would do the takes and break for lunch. After lunch, we would continue." Little Barbara Wills couldn't understand why they made it so difficult: "I remember going to wardrobe in the morning, and it was still dark, and I was like, 'Why can't we just take our dresses home with us? Why do we have to leave them here?' Sitting in front of the big mirrors with the lights, doing all that."[961]

Though hired, many extras really didn't know how long they'd be working since some were brought in for one specific scene; others were there the entire time. "I worked for one week, and it was just one scene; one take of people walking down the town," Hilda adds. "There was a shooting, and there was a lady. I was her little girl. They told me I was going to be walking with this lady and hold her hand. They told us what to do, where to go. (We were walking down the street), and we would run across…and hide in the cemetery area. But it was just one scene, maybe four or five days of doing that same thing, over and over. They would have ladies there that would kinda keep an eye on us and we would just sit around and play. It seemed like there were long periods of time when we weren't doing anything, and we would have to sit there and wait. But there were games, and we'd make up our own games and play tag or hopscotch. As a kid, you make friends with other kids. You don't care what their name is or who they are. We would entertain ourselves, and there would be women there that would (be in charge). There were times when we had to stay dressed because we knew we were going to be called back out. We didn't know how much time, and then, there were times when they said, 'Well, you can take your clothes off for a little bit 'cause we still have enough time.' There were days when we were done by four o'clock, five o'clock. And then there were days where we had to have dinner and do the scene again."

She vividly recalls another young girl on the set. "I do remember very clearly because it makes an impact on young children. She had a birthmark on her face. And I remember that, and it's like that made an impact. I remember seeing her with this birthmark, and, at first, it just startled me. At the time, I didn't know what it was. I talked to my parents about it, and they told me it was a birthmark, and some children are born with birthmarks that are very visible like that. I had no idea what her name was."[962]

While the younger children were having a wonderful time playing on the set, older kids were having their own enjoyment. Although Pat Wayne has denied the incident even occurred, Tulisha Shahan distinctly remembered a wild ride on the back of Pat's motorcycle. "I was extremely nervous," she admitted, "but finally got up enough nerve to ask him a question. 'What's the difference between Texas girls and California girls?' He replied, 'Texas girls drink beer; California girls drink whiskey.' All I could think of was, 'Get me back to my momma!'"

And Carol Baxter, hoping to be the new Mrs. Avalon, hung around Frankie like fleas on a dog. With puppy-dog eyes gazing soulfully at the teenage singer, she constantly followed him around the set, walked hand-in hand, spent all available time together. It had to get on Wayne's nerves. Joan O'Brien said Duke would just as soon throw Baxter down a well than to speak with her. Failing to woo the vocalist, in August 1960, Baxter instead married John Anthony Lester. On November 29 of the same year, she gave birth to a baby girl.[963]

San Antonian Darrell Hansen learned first-hand what it was like to be an actor while on location. A 1959 graduate of Robert E. Lee High School, Hansen played the role of a young Alamo defender. He changed his name to Darryl Deayn because "it's not so blunt, has a good movie sound and is easy to remember." He also acquired a manager—Mickey Finn, a character actor who also had a role in the film. Hansen was philosophical about his choice of career: "It's not an easy business. Someone is always trying to knock you down to see if you can take it. They criticize everything you do. But you can't let it get (to) you. If you do, you're sunk." Hansen became good friends with Avalon and seventeen-year-old Sheila Finn, also in the movie. When boredom set in, the three donned old clothes and went on a skunk hunt for something to do.[964]

Other people hung around just looking for a handout. According to Jim Brewer, "You must understand the hysteria surrounding the production company of all the people who wanted to be part of John Wayne's *The Alamo*. There had never been a movie of this magnitude with a star like John Wayne filming in Texas. Every actor that was looking for a break…showed up. The streets were crowded, and busloads of tourists visited the set daily. A month or so into filming, a tall, dark-haired man showed up at the Gateway Hotel. I was going in to have dinner, and I saw him standing at the doorway. He was dressed in a vintage black suit and was wearing a top hat. As I got closer, I recognized him as Abe Lincoln. He said hello, and I invited him to join me and several others at the table. He said that he was traveling the country as Abe Lincoln. I thought he was an actor looking for work because he hung around the Gateway Hotel for several days. He always had a group of people around him asking questions about his life and how it related to Abe Lincoln. I finally realized he was a huckster when I saw him stem (sic) a few bucks off a couple of tourists. He had been panhandling money all the time. The last time I saw him, he was standing by the main gate of the Shahan ranch as we were driving to the set. I assumed he wasn't allowed in, so he probably hitch-hiked to another unsuspecting town."[965]

With all the activity going on, you couldn't help but have a few humorous episodes. Maydelle Anderson was a thirty-something extra who along with three other ladies from Eagle Pass was in the non-combatant departure scene. One of her favorite stories on location was when she got chastised. After endlessly standing and waiting for her scene to be filmed, she got tired and wanted to sit down. A bench was available, so naturally she used it. "I didn't know any better," she admits. "I was young and dumb. I moved John Wayne's coonskin cap." The property manager went ballistic. "Who moved, who dared move John Wayne's cap?" he screamed. "Don't anybody touch this cap. When he wants it, I've got to give it to him!" Of course, it was Anderson. "I was sitting there where he put it, so I confessed." She also recalls a local shoe salesman who doubled as a dead soldier: "And, every time, every time they would move away, well, he'd put his head up. He wanted to be seen. And they'd come back and push it down again. Despite sitting around and getting full of chiggers, being in *The Alamo* was an experience I'll never forget." San Antonio radio personality Allan Dale suggested to Wayne that, after filming was complete, it might not be a bad idea to donate Crockett's coonskin cap to the Alamo museum. Wayne agreed, and so it was. The DRT, official guardians of the museum, said they didn't consider it a historical relic as it was just a movie prop, but accepted it anyway. Although initially displayed in the museum, today it can be found in a box on a shelf in the museum's storeroom. *(Author's note: It has recently been restored to its proper place in the museum).*[966]

Others also apparently were paranoid about Duke's coonskin hat as Tommy Worrell observed. "We were shooting some scenes, and it was getting dusk," says Tommy, "and I went over and set down on a bench, and this assistant director, an AD, started motioning at me, trying to get my attention. You know, we're new at this, and I thought, 'Oh, I'm going to get to do something.' You know, I was really excited, gonna get to do something special. The AD's hollering at me. But I think I'd better check and make sure. I look around, and there's nobody else near me, and I kind of point at me, and he said, 'Yeah, yeah, you.' Then, he starts coming over to me, so I get up and go to him, and he said, 'Oh, Oh, thank goodness. I thought you sat on John Wayne's hat.' I was sitting next to a black hat. 'That's my job to watch that hat, and I thought you sat on it.'" On-site reporters said it was easy to see which job Wayne was doing by looking at his headgear. If he was wearing his coonskin hat, he was playing Crockett; if he was wearing a battered old cavalry hat, he was directing, and if he wore a wide-brimmed light Texas hat, he was the producer.[967]

Robert Harris recalled that on his first day at work, "Ron Gast and I were dressed as Mexican peasants and were told to walk down the back street. We were carrying these heavy baskets on our backs, and it was hard to walk quietly. Ron was wearing heavy boots, and, when we reached the area where Wayne was filming an intimate scene with Linda Crystal, Wayne burst into a rage. 'Who the hell is making all of that 'clump, clump' noise with their boots?' I was close to him, and he immediately blamed me while Ron snuck off. Wayne looked right at me and yelled, 'Well, if you're that good out there in the middle of the street, let's see how good you are in front of the camera.'" Wayne spouted some Spanish words real fast and demanded that Harris repeat them. He tried but could only choke out something close to what he'd heard. Wayne said, "OK, let's film it." With the cameras rolling, Harris tried the line a few times in his mind but still forgot most of it. Finally, in front of Wayne, Cristal and scores of extras, he ad-libbed, "Santi Ana's a-comin'! Run for your lives!" The entire street, including Wayne, burst into laughter. But Duke had gotten his revenge: "OK, kid," he chided, "You're no actor. Now get back into the crowd and keep those thick boots out of microphone range."[968]

Apparently, a lack of Spanish proficiency affected several individuals. "During my tenure...some of the Mexican extras were friendly," says Jim Brewer. "Sometimes they would pass me in the pickup when I was walking back to the shuttle for my ride to Ft. Clark. They would holler 'Good-bye' to me in Spanish, and I would reply 'Huevos rancheros,' and they would laugh. I thought that meant 'Good-bye, ranchers.' I found out weeks later that Huevos rancheros meant 'eggs ranch-style.'"[969]

Extraneous noise on any set is a major issue, and *The Alamo* was no exception. Don McLendon: "We're doing a scene, a concept scene with Richard Widmark and John Wayne. And Wayne was directing it, plus acting in it also. And Jack Solomon, who was a well-known, award-winning sound mixer, Jack says, 'We... I've got a noise. We can't, we can't shoot yet.' And there was a strange squeaking noise. It was barely audible, but, of course, the mics were going to pick it up. As everybody looked around to find this noise that had shut the company down, so to speak, I realized what the noise was. It was a tiny little 6-inch crescent wrench hanging on my tool belt. It was swinging as I moved slightly, made this very, very tiny squeak. I was scared to death; I was petrified because I knew it was me. The whole company was shut down. Jack immediately (said,) 'It's clear, gone.' And Wayne was furious because somebody had stopped the company for ten seconds, twenty seconds, maybe thirty seconds. Hell, a minute."[970]

There also were pranks, and no one was immune. Al Ybarra wore a hearing aid, so Toni LaCava, Pat and Mike Wayne, and some of the youngsters on the set would gather around and deliberately talk in a loud manner. Then they'd abruptly lower their voices to whispers. Unaware, Ybarra would pull out an old-fashioned transistor radio-type device from his pocket and turn up the volume. Then they'd start talking normally again, and the subsequent blast would hurt his ears. Lousy, rotten kids. But Ybarra would get even. During the 1998 reunion celebration, Virginia Shahan told the following story: "Al Ybarra was deaf as a post. And he wore a hearing aid. So when Duke came (to the set), he saw him walking around and Duke's hands started going like this, talking real fast. Al reached up and turned his hearing aid off. And he kept watching him, and he'd agree with him, just off and on (nodding) all through (the conversation). And when Duke kinda quit throwing his hands around, (Ybarra) reached up and turned his hearing aid back on."[971]

Crewmembers would even play pranks on themselves. Recalled Jack Williams, "There was a guy by the name of Danny Borzage...every time Wayne would arrive on the set, Danny would break in (by playing his accordion) with 'Bringing in the Sheaves.' So the guys pulled a gag on him one day. They had Bob Morgan doubling Wayne in a fight thing, Chuck was doing a part, I think, in the same scene, and they got Danny all excited for Wayne's arrival. So here comes Morgan in costume, and here's Danny 'Bringing in the Sheaves' for Morgan, the stunt double." But Wayne didn't mind. [972]

And the Mexican extras weren't immune from the tomfoolery, either. According to Joe Canutt, "this Mexican (was) holding his rifle, and he had his finger in the barrel of it, and he's leaning on it asleep. And another one came along and saw it, and thought it was funny, and he cocked it, and he pulled the trigger and blew his finger off. Things like that only happened in Mexico, I guess," says Canutt. [973]

As said before, if you rode a horse, you'd get paid more than a foot soldier. So everyone claimed he could ride. But almost everyone lied, as Relyea discovered firsthand how badly the recruited Mexican extras wanted to work. "As I hiked up to the camera position and looked out over the prairie," Relyea recalled, "I saw a thousand Mexicans and a thousand horses—but no single Mexican and horse together. As far as I could see, there was chaos: horses running and bucking with no riders, men writhing in pain holding sprained or broken limbs. Men scrambling out of trees and bushes. Men face down in the dirt. One guy was stuck in the dirt like a dart." [974]

But Dean Smith was one stuntman who could ride. He could also run like greased lightning, and it wasn't long before everyone was betting on just how fast he was and the only way to determine was to set up a race. As he'd run in the Olympics, it wouldn't be fair to race against another man so, finally, someone came up with the bright idea of racing against a horse. Chuck Hayward rode a good old Texas quarter-horse, and Dean won two out of three races over forty yards. Most of the other stuntmen bet on the horse...at first. These weren't the only type races the stuntmen would have. An innocent victim would be talked into riding upside down, tied on the back of a stuntman; his legs wrapped around the shoulder and neck of the runner, his face bouncing off the runner's butt. Spotted a ten-yard head-start, the object was to beat the other runner over forty yards. And, who better to select for this gag than Ben Dorsey, Duke's chauffeur. As Ben was tied onto Ted White's back, White complained he didn't feel so good—maybe something he ate in Mexico. Ben yelled to be let off White; White moaned and groaned, saying he didn't think he could hold it. Finally, it was too much to bear; White dropped his trousers; Ben went crazy trying to get off Ted's back. Everyone watching laughed so much at Ben's predicament, it hurt. [975]

Smith, an outstanding athlete, horseman, and would-be stuntman, also was a rookie, so other stuntmen naturally took advantage of that. Roberson, Jackie Williams, and Smith bunked together in a small frame house in what was known as Tortilla Flats, across from Luna's Grocery Store and just down the street from the movie house. Dean lived in the front room of the house, Roberson and Williams in the back. A nice arrangement, but Dean had a problem with his roommates' extracurricular activities. He once told Michael Wayne, "I can't believe the way those old guys carry on every night. I mean, it just seems like they could get some kind of disease from the sort of women they bring home." Eventually, Smith decided enough was enough, so he called his wife and proceeded to move out the next morning. But as he left, Roberson's outraged landlady appeared. "I want to talk to you!" she screamed at Bad Chuck. "Don't give me any of that Hollywood fancy talk. I want y'all out of here by noon! You carry on like a pack o' drunken savages!" Roberson weaved a web of deceit. "Why, ma'am, you must be mistaken," he sincerely lied. "It ain't us. There's your man, right there." He pointed at Smith, who was climbing into his car. Poor Dean—an innocent victim falsely accused. "You mean that nice-lookin' young fella's been carryin' on so ever' night?" asked the old crow. "Yes, ma'am," Roberson replied. "Why, last night was just the last straw. Me and my friend told him to move out this morning…" Shaking her head as she walked away, she could be heard saying, "The very idea, and him a'claimin' to be a Baptist boy, too." From then on, Dean's nickname was "Troublemaker."[976]

Smith's hazing didn't end there. As Dean recalls in his book *Cowboy Stuntman: from Olympic Gold to the Silver Screen*: "One day I was told to go to wardrobe to pick up a costume for another scene I'd be in. When I reported to wardrobe, they handed me this fancy black outfit that came with a little cap. It was a boy's costume, and I looked pretty silly standing around in it. They didn't even end up calling me for a scene. The next day, I was wearing that costume again, still waiting for someone to call me for a scene, when I began to realize something wasn't right. Too many crew members were laughing their heads off. I guess they thought they were initiating me since I was new to the business. I finally figured out they were having a little fun with me, and I got rid of that costume in a hurry."[977]

Even Happy Shahan had a favorite on-set tale. Duke had just finished filming a scene in the Cantina when his driver pulled up to take him to the Alamo where they were waiting. This probably was the first time the young fellow had worked for a star of Wayne's caliber. Duke walked out of the Cantina and was immediately swamped by a dozen visitors asking for autographs. The driver, figuring Wayne needed help, got out of the car. "Mr. Wayne," he said, "we really need to get you up to the Alamo. They're ready to shoot." Wayne scowled. "Just a minute, kid! Don't ya see I'm talking to these folks?" Tail tucked between his legs, the humiliated driver slunk to the car. On the way to the Alamo, he apologized profusely. "I just thought I was helping you out," he said. "Isn't it costing you sixty-thousand dollars an hour to waste time here?" Duke was gracious. "That's right, kid. Sixty-thou. But I'm not wasting time; I'm spending time. These people, these movie-goers, are my bosses! If I don't spend time with them, they may fire me!"[978]

Apparently, there are other vehicle-related stories. For instance, one stunt-man supposedly built a small, noisy car from a lawn mower. Another tale makes Tommy Worrell chuckle: "There's a good story on Big John Hamilton. We were walking quite often from the Alamo set down to the city of San Antonio set at Brackettville, and this one day we were walking along, just talking, three or four of us with Big John Hamilton, and this Cadillac convertible drives by, and John Wayne and two or three other guys (are in it), and they honk, honk, honk, and wave and, of course, we all wave. Big John kind of ignored it. And I said, 'Hey, you didn't wave at 'em. He said...just mumbles. I said, 'Well, what's the deal, Big John?' He just mumbles. I said, 'What's the deal, you know?' He said, 'That's my car.'" And in yet another story, an extra recalled Wayne exploded prior to the whiskey barrel explosion. "There was a bus," said David Kuykendall. "A tour bus went through one scene and we had to re-shoot it because that tour bus was running right through the background. We were all on top of the (Main gate) watching it."[979]

However, the production's most legendary vehicular yarn involves a vehicle no one may ever have seen—or did they? Supposedly, it was caught on screen during one battle sequence moving left to right. Or was it right to left? It might have been coming in over a rise, or perhaps going out. It may have been seen sneaking into view by the palisade or next to a wall. It was a van full of visitors or extras. Or an ambulance. Or a lunch wagon. Over the years, the story has taken on mythic proportions—everyone saw it; everyone knew about it. It was almost like Woodstock. If everyone who said they were there actually was there, the rest of New York would have been empty! Jim Brewer's recollection of the incident is typical. As dawn breaks the morning of the final assault, a lone sentry stands his post, high atop the chapel. The palisade and low barracks are visible to the right. Freeze the film and focus on the point where the palisade meets the structure. Now, slowly advance the film. For several frames, you can see the silhouette of a vehicle start to drive into frame. A white flash inches out from behind the corner of the building. "The white flash...was a white pickup or catering truck that was driving to the location, the driver not being aware of the filming," says Brewer. "Apparently one of the gate guards failed to stop the truck. (But) I never saw it in the film. The cinematographer questioned whether or not the truck was in view, so I guess the decision was to leave it alone. There was always speculation about an airplane or automobile or truck being accidentally photographed during film-ing. If I recall correctly, the white spot in the film may have been a bus; several hundred Mexican extras were driven to the set each morning after boarding the bus in Mexico."

Brewer is correct—busloads of extras arrived on-site each day. But the bus in question didn't carry extras, crew members or visitors: it carried students. Fourth

Coates should know—he was on the bus! "There was one scene that I was in, and it got cut," says Fourth sadly. "I was in the yellow school bus that was going over the hill. I was in that school bus every day, and, more than likely, I was in it when they filmed it…the movie premiered in San Antonio at the Woodlawn Theater. Then they showed it at Brackettville. A lot of people went to see it at the Woodlawn, and then they came back telling the story of the school bus. So when it showed at Brackettville, we're all waiting for it. And we all clapped when the bus went over the hill. It was probably a mile away (when they filmed the battle), but you could tell it was a school bus. There was an article in the *San Antonio Light* (and) on the inside page there was a question-and-answer type deal where the guy would write stuff and say, 'Has anybody heard about this?' And he mentioned the school bus and wanted people to write in that knew about it. So I wrote in with my description of what happened. And a couple of weeks later, he wrote a little article in there talking about the people that had written in. There were several people that had written in, and he said, 'But the most convincing one was from Fourth Coates, who said he was actually on the school bus.' I think I ended the letter with 'Remember the school bus!'"[980]

Wayne was known for his chess-playing ability, so, in their downtime, stuntmen would instead play hearts with him where, at least, they'd have a fighting chance. According to photographer Sam Shaw, "Wayne's an almost compulsive chess player. He was always playing chess. Between takes, he would always play chess. He played with guys in the crew. They were out to lick him; no chess player throws a game." Except Jimmy Grant. According to Jackie Williams, "the most remarkable thing about (him) was that he played chess with Wayne for over twenty years and managed never to win a game! That was the genius of Jimmy Grant." Actor Chris Mitchum learned the hard way how difficult it was to beat Wayne. "I remember the first couple of days on the set (of *Chisum*)," said Mitchum. "He asked me if I played chess. I had been a pretty avid chess player my whole life. I said, 'Sure, Duke! I love to play chess.' We sat down, and he was cheating. He'd reach over with one hand to move a bishop, and, with his thumb, he'd slide a rook over. I didn't know what to say. Here I am playing chess with a god. He's also kind of my boss on the show, and I didn't know what to say. And, of course, he was creaming me because he was getting two moves to every one of mine with those huge hands. I told (actor) Eddie Faulkner that Duke was cheating in chess. Ed replied, 'Of course, he is! You tell him to knock that crap off. He's just trying to intimidate you. You just tell him to knock it off!' So the next time we're playing, he kind of starts to do something. With a great deal of terror in my heart, I say, 'Excuse me, Duke, you're moving two pieces.' He says, 'I was wondering when you were going to say something.'"[981]

In addition to every Monday being payday, it was also "collect" day. Bear Hudkins was appointed commissioner of the game. "So (on Monday), I go over to (Wayne)," he said. And he says, 'What do you want, Bear?' I say, 'You know, you lost.' He says, 'Well, what did I lose?' 'Three dollars and eighty cents,' I tell him. 'Oh, OK,' he answers. 'I'll get it to you.' 'Oh, no,' I say. 'There's no I'll get it to you.' I want it now. Last week when you won six dollars, you got it, didn't you?' And he'd say, 'OK, OK!'" But you knew Duke wasn't going to let everyone get away with that. The shoot was almost over, and one stuntman (Ted White) left the set a day early to get back to Hollywood. As Ted still owed $4.95 to the game, Bear called the production office to confirm White's departure. And who should pick up the phone but Wayne! "He owes four ninety-five?" yelled Wayne. "I'll call the highway patrol!" Sure enough, White was stopped on his way to San Antonio.

"Ted White?"

"Yeah. What do you want?"

"Come with us."

"What for?"

"Because you owe four ninety-five in the heart game."

So he gave the troopers a five, and they let him go. A little later, Wayne called the set:

"Hey, Bear! We got the money!"

Apparently, Chill Wills just couldn't wait for payday. After working hard all week, he needed to blow off steam in Ciudad Acuña and needed cash. "I was Chill Wills's banker," Happy said amusingly. "Chill used to borrow money from me. Not money to buy anything special; just walking around money. Every Saturday night, Chill would come to me and say, 'Cuz, let me have a couple hundred. I'm going to Mexico tonight; I need two hundred dollars.' Well, he was just as good as gold. He'd pay me back the next day or sometimes a day or two later, but he'd always pay me back." Who knows what he did with the money over in Acuña? But, according to Happy, "(Wills) was always sober on the set."[982]

Even the stars took part in occasional high jinks. After few drinks at dinner, Duke was said to do an unflattering but extremely funny imitation of Harvey's British accent and mannerisms. Harvey entertained the crew by rehearsing with a thick English lilt, then shift into a Southern dialect when a "take" was called; his Travis accent at times floated in and out depending upon dialogue and his enthusiasm. But he was a professional and comfortable with himself; Wayne's jocularity didn't bother him in the least. In fact, Harvey started to play the role with a Texas accent. But he explained, "Wayne talks with a drawl. So does Widmark. It would have been monotonous for me to try to, so I decided to play it with my own English accent, and Wayne agreed it was better. It really is not unreasonable for Travis was a Carolinian, and the Carolinas were settled largely by Englishmen."[983]

There were rumors in the industry about Harvey's sexual preferences, and his behavior on the *Alamo* set did nothing but reinforce those impressions. He sometimes amusingly referred to himself as "Florence of Lithuania." In his book *The Great Movie Stars*, author David Shipman claimed that at one time

Harvey was a male prostitute in the red-light sector of Mayfair (London). Duke suspected Harvey was bi-sexual: his accent, mannerisms, language, and flamboyant behavior all supported Wayne's perception. According to actor John Fraser, British producer James Woolf supposedly was Harvey's longtime paramour, and it didn't help matters when Woolf would periodically show up on set. (In later years, when Woolf would later attempt suicide, Harvey admitted emotionally, "Jimmy's my life and my love"). Harvey's marriage to Margaret Leighton eventually became one of convenience, and she sensed his ambivalence: "Larry had an inadequacy in his make-up. But I can't tell you, or anyone, about it. It's too personal. But he was, oh, yes, he certainly was aware of it. I felt he was concealing a certain amount, but not totally. What he didn't tell me, I guessed, and there were moments when he came clean." Leighton was well aware that Harvey had had affairs with both sexes and, when questioned, didn't bother to deny it. "People love me or hate me," Harvey acknowledged. "I obviously don't foster detached emotions." Linda Cristal felt Harvey's sexuality was ambiguous. "I had the feeling," she said, "this I cannot say for true, but Larry perhaps was not sure whether he liked men or women. Not because of the rumor but because of the way he acted. I could see mentally; he was very mental, very, he was a thinking person and well educated, literate. And he had explored; I had a feeling he had explored in many ways what gave him pleasure."[984]

Still, Harvey was a welcome respite from all the stress and pressure on the set. He had a vicious sense of humor and would tell the filthiest jokes with the foulest mouth; this naturally ingratiated him into the ranks of the rough-and-tumble stuntmen, and he would entertain the crew with hilarious stories. Typical humor was a story involving a company of foreign legionnaires isolated for months in the desert that were eagerly awaiting the arrival of a herd of camels and preparing to compete for the prettiest ones. (The telling of this story on a BBC live talk show resulted in such listener outrage that all subsequent programs had to be prerecorded). Wayne recalled, "What I best remember about Harvey is when things got tense—which they did, and often—he'd just crack us up by going into Shakespeare with a Texas accent." Harvey knew Wayne felt he was effeminate and so would play up those traits. One morning on the parapet of the church, Harvey leaned over and called down to Duke, "Hey, Marion!" Wayne couldn't help but laugh. Relyea confessed, "Duke teased (Harvey) all the time, called him 'the English fag.' *To his face.* And Larry would laugh and say, 'Where do I stand? Tell me where to stand.' They got along fine. Larry was an awfully good actor, and dedicated to doing the best job he could. He couldn't have cared less about the insults."[985]

Joan O'Brien absolutely loved him: "(Harvey) had a sense of humor that was really fun. He was the only one in the cast who could get away with calling the Duke 'Dukie.' Wayne would tell him what to do, and Laurence Harvey would (walk over, tweak his cheeks and) always say, 'OK, Dukie.'" Don LaCava was also aware of Harvey's sexual persuasions. "He's a character," LaCava said laughingly. "He was a lot of fun, and he was just very, very gay. And he wasn't hiding it, and it didn't bother anyone. He just had a really good sense of humor."[986]

A gourmet of great food and drink, Harvey had his own wine, champagne, and imported caviar flown to the location in dry ice containers. While others munched on Ritz crackers and boxed lunches, Harvey dined in style at the commissary tent and made each meal an event. To be brutally honest, it was impossible to find a good restaurant and decent wine in Brackettville. He refused to drink liquor because it made him fat, so one day he sent a plane to Dallas for supplies. When Harvey returned to Ft. Clark that evening, he could barely get into his room. It was piled high with case after case of Louis Latour Pouilly Fuisse, a dry white wine made from Chardonnay. O'Brien recalls, "Every afternoon about three o'clock, you'd see Larry—that's what we called him—walking around (smoking Pall Malls in a long cigarette holder) with a paper cup in his hand. He'd have this French wine flown in by the case while we were on location. And he got me hooked on it! It was really good." According to Kuykendall, before Harvey finally left the set, "he had several of us come out and said, 'Well, I ordered a little bit extra wine, so I'm going to give you all a couple of bottles.'" Harvey told them, "What a super lot of winos you make." But not everyone had the same opinion of the wine as O'Brien. Kuykendall comically opined, "Good grief! I don't know how he drank that stuff."[987]

After a few bottles of wine, though, Harvey could be extremely cruel or hysterically funny. O'Brien recalls: "One night, I had a party in my officer's quarters, and I invited the dancers from the movie and anyone who wanted to come, and I rolled back the rug, so the girls could click their heels on the floor, and served cocktails and hors d'ourves and whatever, and I went in the bedroom to put on some lipstick or something. Larry came in, and he said, 'Do you have a dress I could put on?' And I said, 'What kind of a dress?' I mean, I was stunned. I said, 'What kind of a dress would you like?' And so he went through my closet, and he found one—it was blue dress—I'll never forget it—it was solid blue, and it had little spaghetti straps on the shoulders. His shoulders were big, bigger than mine, and I thought he was going to break those straps off. He couldn't get the dress zipped up all the way because of his broad body. But anyway, he put it on, and he said, 'I'm going to do a ballet for everyone.' And I said, 'You are?' and he said, 'Yes.' So we all watched Larry do a ballet. (He ended it by standing) on his hands, and the dress fell down over his head, and we saw his underpinnings and his whole package. That was the end of the ballet. Oh, my God, I'll never forget it—and he was pretty drunk, you know? Then he said, 'I need to lie down,' and I said, 'Go ahead, take that bedroom over there,' and then I got on the phone, and I called his valet, and I said, 'You'd better come and get him because he's really boxed,' and I said, 'We've got a shoot in the morning, and he's in that bedroom laying down, and he's out cold—you've got to come and get him.'"[988]

Pilar fondly recalls, "The one actor who made it a perfect location was Laurence Harvey. He was quite a character, and Duke was crazy about him. They got along quite well, since he was also quite a disciplined actor." But Harvey had developed a huge attraction for Wayne: his voice, his mannerisms, and his walk. Halfway through shooting, he begged, pleaded with Wayne: "Please, Duke. Tonight, just one time. I'll be the queen if you'll be the king. Duke, thoroughly disgusted, shrugged off the offer and walked away." Wayne later confirmed the story. Asked if Harvey had ever addressed him as "Duchess," Wayne replied, "Yes. Only once!"[989]

Although O'Brien would drink Pouilly Fuisse, she was exposed to another type liquor while on location. "I remember during shooting at night," she says. "I remember Duke introduced me to banana brandy—I'd never tasted it, and he said, 'Have you ever had banana brandy?' And I said, 'No,' and he said, 'Here, try this.' Because it was colder than cold, and we were shooting at night and we had tiki torches lit. And you could see the steam rising up off the water. And I thought, 'Boy, I like that stuff; that's good.' And I got liqueurs a little bit after that, because that banana brandy was something else."

Cast and crew found ingenious ways to entertain themselves during downtime. Some, as previously mentioned, played hearts. Jim Burk figured out, if you can't afford to lose, you can't afford to gamble. "I learned very early," he recalled, "that (hearts) was too rich for my blood. I was not good at cards at all, so I spent most of my time practicing my roping and doing some leatherwork on the side, maybe even catching a little nap once in a while," Tim Cumiskey was a young artist—"so I hung around Al Ybarra, and they had some scene people that would draw scenes out. They would sit around and just start drawing; I was so amazed that they could just sit there and draw circles and ovals for faces. And then, all of a sudden, out of all this scribbling, came these beautiful scenes of battle. In detail what these scene were supposed to look like. I had a lot of time where you just sat around, and the stuntmen were there. Denver Pyle and Ken Curtis and all those guys. They'd show us how to do different things. They let us stab them; it was like sitting around waiting for something to happen is what you did the entire time. You waited and a scene would be shot in probably thirty minutes or forty minutes after it was set up. I mean, a scene could be shot in ten minutes because there wasn't that much dialogue and stuff, but the set-up for it was just incredible—to watch the guys in the background with all the smoke machines, pumping the smoke into the air. All of the...'You need to be here,' and then they'd look at the scene, and then they'd look at it again, and they'd place people where they wanted them just to make things a little more interesting."[990]

The set was literally crawling with varmints—snakes, deer, armadillos and... skunks. Gene DeRuelle recalls one encounter: "In the evening, we were pretty much on our own. Some guys went to Mexico for dinner, others just hit the sack. We had some visitors one day, and one of them happened to be a pretty young lady whose father owned a car agency in Eagle Pass down the road. Janie and I got to like each other a lot, and a couple of times a week, I would take the drive to her place, and spend the evening with her. We had no shortage of two things in Brackettville—work and skunks. They say everything is bigger in Texas. I can't say for sure about everything, but they do raise some championship-size skunks. One night, I was coming back from Janie's along a very dark highway. It was a moonless night, and there was absolutely no traffic, so I was cruising about seventy-five and sort of watching the white line down the middle of the road. All of a sudden, the white line made a right turn! I hit that skunk doing seventy-five, and he was big enough to put a dent in my bumper and a big dent in the valance under the bumper. Of course, the real problem was the smell! The air intakes on my MGA are right behind the grille, and the smell just blasted into the cockpit. It was beyond belief. I got back to Ft. Clark, threw away my clothes, and showered. The next morning, I went to the chow hall and asked for a couple of #10 cans of tomato juice. Rolly (Harper) just laughed and handed me a couple. 'You'll meet Widmark out back with his tomato juice,' said Harper. 'He's trying to de-skunk Sam, the Dalmatian puppy he got last week. Skunks got him last night, too.' He was right. Widmark was washing his dog while I was washing my car. I don't think I ever got the smell all the way out."[991]

Joe Canutt was drafted into the armed forces while on location: "(I) literally took a physical there in Brackettville," he says. "It was funny, too. I was trying my damnedest, you know, for the Army. Keep from being drafted, and they congratulated myself and one other made it from Brackettville. Most of them had tuberculosis. I had to get on a plane and fly back to Los Angeles and join a Naval Reserve unit before I could go back down, you know, and finish the picture. I took off four or five days to do that and came back." Jim Brewer may be the other individual Canutt refers to. "Two months after the completion of the film, I had to go into the Army," says Brewer. "During the filming of *The Alamo*, I was drafted into the Army. Senator Ralph Yarborough got me a deferment, so I could complete my first film."[992]

And there was always time for entertainment. With the melodic voices of O'Brien, Hairston, Curtis, and John Quinn, it was only natural they gathered in the evening to entertain the troupe. With Danny Borzage on accordion, Willie Champion on guitar, and the multi-talented Avalon, a good time was always had by all. Teresa Champion remembers hearing a soon-to-be hit song for the first time: "(Avalon) got to be very good friends with my husband and me, and he said—he invited us to his room—he was only sixteen, and he invited us to his room, and he said, 'I'm going to sing a song that I'm going to record,' and it was 'Venus.' We heard it before anybody else! He wanted to share it with us. And I cried—and he goes, 'Why are you crying?' and I said, 'Because it's beautiful, and it's going to be a hit.' And he goes, 'You think so?' and I said, 'Yes.' He was a good friend of ours at the time we were there." *(Teresa was incorrect in her memory of the song. "Venus" reached number one on the pop charts on March 15, 1959, well before the start of filming. Perhaps instead, the song she recalled was "Why." This song also went to number one on December 28, 1959, making it the last number one single in the 1950s. "While I was riding the charts, I was on location in the middle of Brackettville, Texas, riding a horse," said Avalon to Fred Bronson of The Billboard Book of Number One Hits. "Why" remained at number one for a week until it was dethroned by Marty Robbins's "El Paso.")* To Jerry Dickens, one of the youngest extras there, it seemed only natural he and Avalon would spend time together. "I taught him how to play the lower keys of the piano to 'Heart and Soul,'" brags Dickens. "We also worked up a pretty good rendition of 'Chopsticks.'"[993]

Many actors and crewmembers wanted to preserve their memories of the shooting through film; home movies were the favored method. Harvey, Worden, and even Rubin Padilla wandered the set, shooting whatever struck their fancy.

While there were those who would rather swim or sing in their spare time, others were a bit more creative. During preproduction, Batjac funds were used to renovate numerous buildings at Ft. Clark to house both cast and crew. Given the resort's age and run-down condition, restoration was equally welcome and necessary. All buildings were not refurbished, however, with many left in a state of disrepair. Since John Ford and Jack Pennick previously had served in the military and naturally were interested in the area's history, both spent one late-September Sunday exploring the fort's grounds. The pair eventually came upon a vertical log-constructed, cedar post structure the fort's civilian owners identified as the Robert E. Lee Courthouse. Saddened by its neglect but impressed by its former occupant, Ford spoke to several cast and crewmembers later that evening and all agreed to restore the building. As a result, six men, including Pennick, Ernie Saftig, and Hank Worden, spent their next five Sundays repairing the structure's interior and exterior: broken windows, doors, furniture, etc. The surrounding grounds also were spruced up with a rail fence and gravel pathway. Finally finished, the final touch was to add a commemorative white two-foot by four-foot sign constructed by the Batjac paint shop. Two wooden one-foot by two-foot flags were attached: an 1860 United States flag and a Confederate "Stars and Bars." On the sign, it simply read *Robert E. Lee, Lt. Colonel U.S.A. Last Post Of Command. (A touching tribute, unfortunately misdirected. The refurbished building in fact was "The Palisado Building Kitchen/Messroom." Constructed in 1869-70 by the Buffalo Soldiers of the 25th Infantry, it eventually also served as a company storeroom, tailor shop, and amusement hall. Robert E. Lee never visited Ft. Clark, and the building wasn't constructed until eight years after he'd left Texas.)*[994]

There was another story floating around the set at the time, but, whether it's true or not, who's to say? According to Walter Reed (who wasn't a part of the cast), "(There was) some guy in a big Cadillac who drove through a scene, way in the background. And Wayne got mad and got to his feet and went over, and he leaned in the car and he said, 'What in the hell do you think you're doing?' And this great big Texan gets out of his car and hits Wayne. Duke stumbles and falls back across the street, and he says, 'Let him through! Let him through.' Now I don't think you should report those stories as true; those are things somebody could have made up." Another time, a man from Del Rio was said to have driven into a night-scene with his car's headlights on. Supposedly, Wayne ran over to the car and yelled, "Turn those God damn lights off or get out of here!" Are the stories true? Who knows? Apocryphal, perhaps. But if the stories aren't true, they ought to be.[995]

Stuntman/actor Chuck Roberson was a hound dog, and everyone knew it. If it wore skirts, he chased it. Chuck had dated Yvonne De Carlo before she married Bob Morgan. Even tried to talk her out of it, and he considered Morgan the most jealous man he had ever come across. "Any conversation with him turned bitter and sarcastic as soon as he opened his mouth," confessed Roberson. "Bob never forgot an injury to his pride, and he seemed to enjoy digging at his own scars, at opening old wounds." But he admitted Morgan was a "good fight man. One of the best." Morgan didn't reciprocate. "Listen," he told author Tim Lilley. "You can take Roberson's book and shove it up somebody's... He made himself look good, but he lied about everything. That tells you something about the character of a guy, when he puts down other people to make himself look good. (For whatever reason), he just tried to make me look as bad as he could." It surely didn't please him when Wayne later cast De Carlo opposite Roberson in *McLintock!* Bad Chuck's reputation with the ladies was known far and wide, and the *Alamo* set was no exception. While there, he "developed a hankering for a Mexican gal who play(ed) (a) Cantina dancer in the picture," and invited her for a late-evening candlelight supper in his camper. Once inside, he poured her a drink to help her dance a little better. Suddenly, people heard the truck's door slam and the start of an engine. It seems Roberson's daughter Charlene had borrowed the keys to the pickup, and now she was leaving to visit her relatives. Trapped and moving, Chuck pounded on the camper window to no avail; with the engine running, and the wipers and radio on, there was no way Charlene could hear her father. The farther she drove, the more the señorita cried and the louder Chuck pounded. Finally, Charlene stopped for gas and realized her father was in the camper. Enraged, Roberson jumped out, but Charlene, fearful of his temper, refused to open the door. Despite a hysterical dancer and frightened daughter, Bad Chuck finally calmed down. After the gas tank was filled, the pickup headed back to Brackettville, tension inside so thick you could cut it with a knife. As they pulled into the parking lot, the dancer ran into the Cantina. "Two hours late!" was all she said. Pappy yelled, "BAD CHUCK. YOU SON-OF-A-BITCH!!!"

Needless to say, the dancer wouldn't speak with Roberson again, claiming she had been kidnapped. Even Charlene ran the other way whenever she saw her father. All Duke could do was shake his head and roll his eyes in disgust.[996]

# CHAPTER TWENTY-SIX
## "NOT THAT CLOSE!!!"

Wayne needed to significantly pick up the pace. The initial schedule dictated completion of filming by November 24. However, with the first and second assaults yet to be staged as well as the evacuation sequence, the cattle raid, and, and, and… Well, it just wasn't going to happen. Ford wouldn't return to location until November 17, so now was the time to make hay while the sun shone. And Wayne was just the man to pull it off. Although he couldn't cut a film in the camera like Pappy, he didn't waste time with numerous takes: two or three at the most, and he was off to the next scene. And days with twenty-five set-ups were not out of the question. However, there were times when it was necessary to shoot a scene over and over, such as when Crockett, Bowie, and the mounted Tennesseans ride up to the Alamo to join the garrison and are challenged at the entrance by the sentry from atop the stone wall:

*"Hey, Jim. Halt! Who goes there?"*

*"Bob! I swear I'm going to shoot you off that wall! Are you blind?"*

*"That's what I was to holler every time."*

*"Well, don't holler at me!"*

Wayne wanted stuntman Jack Williams to draw out the "Halt!"—as in "Haaalt!"—but every time the camera rolled, he'd say it with only a few "a's." It ultimately took several more takes before Duke was satisfied.

Efficient use of time would be necessary to complete the film before Christmas, and, with the best actors and the best crew, it was certainly possible.

497

To watch a professional film crew in action is to watch a finely crafted machine: each part in perfectly harmonious synchronization with the others, all individuals comfortable in their knowledge and experience. Once a scene is rehearsed and a director has discussed camera angles with his director of photography, he walks away and the technicians take over. It takes time to light and dress a set, time a director can use to rehearse the scene again with actors. Meanwhile, there is an explosion of feverish activity. Miles of electrical and sound cables snake over, under, around, and across everything. While stand-ins for actors patiently go through their motions over and over again, gaffers aim their lights. The boom man enters the set with a microphone dangling at the end of a long pole attached to a dolly. Just off the set the sound mixer, sitting at his console of blinking lights, tests the sound clarity through his earphones. As the set is being lit, camera assistants check exact positions of actors for each moment in the scene and determine their distances from the camera. The distances are marked on little pieces of tape placed on the floor to ensure precise focusing during shooting. The camera operator rehearses the panning and tilting moves required by action and scrutinizes every square inch of the frame. Camera grip Don McLendon was present as Duke prepared a scene: "The minute John Wayne would look through the finder to set a shot, then the finder shows what lens is going to come out of this. You immediately have a man stepping up with a tape that goes from the level of his eye to the ground. And you throw down a tee marker, so you know precisely, from the second, this is here... Then this vast move of fifty, sixty people, immediately goes into a clockwork move. It's beautiful to watch, and everybody knows exactly what you have to do." Eventually, everything is ready; all actors are in place. The AD calls for silence on the set and cues the sound; the director takes one last look through the viewfinder, approves the set-up, stands, starts the roll, and calls, "Action!"[997]

On November 1, Wayne and Pilar celebrated their fifth wedding anniversary. Harvey had ordered two cases of champagne as a gift and had them delivered to Duke's quarters. Realizing it was a waste on someone who preferred tequila, Harvey told a crewmember to return to Wayne's quarters and bring back one case—the vintage one. It didn't cost him a cent as he charged the bill to production, and he had a free case to boot! O'Brien recalls, "(They celebrated) their wedding anniversary while we were shooting down there, and we used to go over to Piedras Negras or Acuña like it was nothing. Now I wouldn't go there on a bet, but we went out to dinner to some little Mexican place, and there was a little candle burning, and the wax was running down (the) bottle. Duke and Pilar were sitting across from Richard Widmark and an extra, Fred Murphy. I was sitting next to him, right across from Duke. And Duke reached over the candle to pour some more...what were we drinking? I think it was vodka, and he reached over to pour some more vodka in my glass, and some of it caught in the flame, and the flame went 'feeeeuuuu' way up in the air. Duke said, 'Do you see what you're putting in your stomach?' Then he looked at Fred Murphy, who was sitting next to me, and he said, 'Son'—I'll never forget this—because it was just like out of a movie. He looked at Fred, and he looked at me, and he said, 'Son—that is one hell of a woman you're with.' And Pilar is sitting right there, and I thought it was great."[998]

One day several weeks earlier, Carlos Arruza had planned to fight at the Macarena bullring in Ciudad Acuña; a special corrida had been dedicated to Wayne. Performing Portuguese-style on horseback and afoot, Arruza would fight two of his own accredited Spanish-blooded Pasteje bulls, especially shipped in from Mexico City. Widmark, Wayne, O'Brien, Harvey, and other members of the Batjac company who had never before seen him fight would attend. But due to heavy rains, the corrida was postponed until November 15 at which time the first bull was dedicated to Joan O'Brien. A man named Ruben Dario Padilla Colon y Magallanes, former tourist director of Baja California Norte—and Arruza's manager—also was there that day. At a staff meeting early in production, Duke was in a bind. Batjac had been in discussions with Marlon Brando's Pennebaker Productions for the role of Santa Anna. Each would appear in the other's film: Brando would have a two-line role in *The Alamo* while Wayne would do the same in Brando's *The Ugly American* at a later date. Unable to reach an agreement, Wayne had to look elsewhere. He spotted Padilla sitting quietly in a corner during the meeting. At six-foot-four and ruggedly handsome, Ruben struck a distinguished figure. Someone suggested, "Why don't we use Ruben?" Wayne replied, "Ruben? He doesn't look like Santa Anna." To which Padilla replied, "And I suppose you look like Davy Crockett?" Wayne laughed uproariously and said, "Get him to wardrobe." Padilla fit the bill perfectly. (Padilla was also offered a role in Glenn Ford's *Cimarron*, which was being filmed at the same time, but wisely decided to join John Alessio's Caliente public relations staff instead. Padilla had worked for Wayne before in Batjac's 1951 feature *Bullfighter and the Lady* where he'd played the part of Dr. Sierra and also had arranged for the matadors in the film).[999]

In the meantime, to the consternation of some in the student body, Wayne had acquired the rights from the University of Texas to use its alma mater, "The Eyes of Texas," as background music in his movie. Gov. Price Daniel personally asked authorization for free use of the song. Owned by the University Student Association, half of the royalties from broadcast and theater use would have gone to the scholarship fund, but F. Lanier Cox, university vice-president for administrative services, said that university provost Harry Ransom would make $1,500 available from private sources to replace estimated lost revenue. Upon learning of the lost royalties, Duke wired UT officials he would personally contribute $1,500 "in grateful appreciation for your cooperation." As a result, a student protest of Wayne's use of the song was withdrawn, and all royalty rights were waived. (A university student court had previously held the Association's action was null and void as control of the copyright resided with a special university copyright committee, not the student assembly). Forced by George Stevens to include this song in the rousing finale of *Giant*, Tiomkin absolutely hated it. So, when Wayne purchased the rights to use it yet again in *The Alamo*, Dimi resisted at every turn. However, as Duke insisted it be used a specific number of times in the soundtrack, Tiomkin acquiesced, but its treatment is so subtle, one rarely notices it.[1000]

As Duke continued to work on the film, a constant stream of visitors bombarded the location. In early October, filming was temporarily shut down as fifty to sixty planes flew over the set as a part of the Eleventh Annual Texas Air Tour. The tour, including small aircraft and flyers from as many as 18 different states and one foreign country, took in the entire state, going by way of towns near the border. When the group stopped at Ft. Clark, Harvey and Widmark were honored luncheon guests. Eight winners from a "Remember the Alamo" radio contest arrived to tour the set. In November, San Antonio theater owner George Watson and Holiday Club owners Al Pisano, Vito Ponzio and Riley Harris arrived to go quail hunting with Happy. Later, Wayne hosted a luncheon for a team of four New Yorkers, including nationally known investor Stanley Berman, who had visited Dallas to study the city's twenty-four urban renewal areas as a possible site for a multi-million dollar real estate development. Duke was also inducted into the ranks of honorary Kentucky colonels, whose roster included Henry Ford III, Conrad Hilton, Cornelius Vanderbilt, Jack Benny, and Bob Hope. Madeline O'Donnell, a young Hollywood actress who strongly resembled Ingrid Bergman, visited the set, and everyone gathered around to comment on the likeness. Widmark's wife Jean and teen-aged daughter Anne, who would eventually marry baseball great Sandy Koufax, also visited the set. As did Ward Bond who had visited the previous month but had been rushed back to Santa Monica's St. John's Hospital after suffering an apparent heart attack, his second. Bond's publicity agent, in fine form, first indicated the actor had acute bronchitis and then stated it was just a routine checkup. One year earlier, while on vacation, Wayne and Ford heard that Ward Bond had an ulcer. Mischievously, they immediately sent off a telegram to Bond, "Congratulations. We knew you had it in you. Glad to hear you finally made it." Wayne and Ford, with whom Bond started in the movies, got their ulcers years ago. It just took Bond a little longer.[1001]

(Ironically, a year later, Bond would suffer a fatal heart attack while Ford, Widmark, Curtis, and Cristal were filming *Two Rode Together* in...Brackettville. Regrettably, on November 7, Fellow actor Victor McLaglen passed away at his Newport Beach seaside home of congestive heart failure. His son Andy was with him: "He never had a heart attack. It was just a matter of his heart growing old. He never had a pain.")[1002]

Trade rags also got into the publicity act. New York restaurateurs Henry

500

Stampler (Henry Stampler's Filet Mignon Restaurant) and Danny Stradella (Danny's Hideaway) were supposedly asked by Wayne to appear in the film. (Besides operating two of the busiest steakhouses in the city, the Stamplers were credited with inventing the "doggie bag" in 1948. To save the face of customers who wanted to take home leftovers, Dan Stampler designed a bag with the picture of a Scottie on it. They could then take home a bone for the dog without embarrassment).[1003]

And the set was absolutely crawling with photographers, movie critics, television reporters and the press. Flying in from all around the country, each had to be wined, dined, and catered to individually: Fred Hift, *Variety*; Hollis Alpert, *Women's Day*; Ed Miller, *Seventeen*; Sue Solter, *Monitor*; Bob Thomas, *Associated Press*; Adalbert Segonzac, *France Soir*; Mel Heimer, *VPI*; Phyllis Battelle, *Hearst Headline*; Hedda Hopper, etc. The list seemed endless. Joe Hyams, *New York Herald Tribune* syndicated columnist and Batjac director of publicity, was particularly frustrated with the Fourth Estate: "The visiting press, as much as we love having them, are really one big pain in the ass. They are full of enthusiasm; they want to see everything, meet everyone, and do all sorts of things. For three weeks, they wore us out, and we virtually had to stop doing many, many things of great importance. You find yourself working fourteen or sixteen hours a day with these people. They are tireless…. You need an experienced hand who has been on the production for awhile and can walk up to a Richard Widmark and say, 'Dick, speak to so and so.' We had an extremely capable girl with us to act as a tour guide, but even she is handicapped in not being able to push stars around, etc. As far as someone covering the set at all times, this is sort of a luxury, but on a film like this, a necessity. Mr. Wayne is quite adamant about one of us being present during shooting. He has several valid reasons why, and, as hard as we try to explain the need for us to be in the office, we can't persuade him otherwise."[1004]

As a promotional plug, Batjac offered various publications services behind-the-scenes footage of the making of the film. Each three hundred- to five hundred-foot-long newsreel revealed Wayne in the dual role of actor and director. United Artists' Val Coleman had an opportunity to view the footage and was less than complimentary of its content: "I have just watched twenty-eight minutes of 16mm footage, which was shot on the Brackettville location apparently by one Jim Logan of KONO-TV, San Antonio, Texas. The footage is a random perusal of location activity with an occasional but inhibited piece of action. It strikes me (as) utterly worthless and of no value to us particularly at this hour. Conceivably, at some later date, there might be a foot or two in this uninspired dross that could be tacked on to something else. The footage…is in the form of a single twenty-eight minute reel, plus three other reels of scrap…."[1005]

The first two weeks of November were scheduled for night-time shooting, and the production continued battling typical late-fall Southwest Texas weather:

hotter than blazes during the day, and cold, misty, and/or raining in the evening. So cold, Wayne sometimes wore surgical gloves during a scene just to keep his hands warm. Temperatures ranged from 120° down to 21°. With freezing temperatures and fifty-five mph winds blowing out of the North, the crew wrapped equipment and themselves in blankets to keep warm. But the show must go on. Even Happy Shahan would be involved...or not. Late one evening, Wayne stand-in Marshall Jones was told to report to wardrobe and then come to the set. "The assistant directors come and got me and said, 'You're gonna be in the picture, Marshall.' I said, 'What's happening?'" This was unusual in that, as Wayne was only going to direct and wouldn't appear in this particular scene, there really was no reason for Jones to be present. Nevertheless, Marshall did as directed. Once there, he was given a line of dialogue. Originally created especially for Shahan, Jones would play one of the Gonzales reinforcements. Duke's original stand-in would play Jones's partner, George Kimbell. Scene #165 originally only featured Bowie and Juan Seguin but was expanded to include Happy. But for whatever reason, Shahan wasn't in it. Maybe he wasn't available; maybe he just didn't want to do it. But his name is mentioned. After Bowie greets Seguin, he is introduced to the two new arrivals: Bowie, shaking hands: *"I've known these old rascals for years! How are you, Hap?"* Hap: *"Hi, Jim."* Speaking just those two words allowed Jones to get a SAG card.[1006]

Extra Robert Harris recalled another scene filmed during that time. After the Alamo defenders raid and neutralize the "European cannon," they get chased by Mexican dragoons. (Harris played the bearded sentry "killed" by Red Morgan while guarding the cannon. For those interested in inconsistencies, one occurrs during its destruction. As powder charges are rammed through the cannon's muzzle, Chuck Roberson straddles its barrel. Crockett asks, *"Where's the mud?"* A defender replies, *"It's coming. Here it is."* But, when the ramrod is pulled out of the barrel, it's already covered with mud even though none had yet been shoved down the barrel). Roberson complained about the scene: "The mud! I leap atop the cannon barrel, positioned myself in the muzzle and promptly empty buckets of mud down the barrel. Hey, I got as much of the mud on me as went down the cannon barrel. One thing, though—that mud could have been less watery!"

After its destruction, Smitty and Bowie attempt a rear-guard action with Bowie's Nock volley gun (*"Golly! What a gun!"*), leap on a Mexican horse and ride double, hell-bent-for-leather. Used to repel enemies or conduct naval boarding operations, the prototype of Bowie's multi-barreled, shoulder-stocked Nock Volley gun was invented by English inventor James Wilson in 1779 for the British navy. Designed to fire simultaneously from a single spark, the gun, though heavy, cumbersome, and difficult to reload, had awesome firepower, tremendous recoil, and an intense muzzle flash that tended to set a ship's rigging on fire. All barrels were grouped around a central barrel. Radial channels were drilled through each of the outer six barrels from the central barrel, and all were connected via a touchhole chamber. There is no evidence Bowie ever used or was even aware of such a fearsome weapon, but, in the hands of the legendary knife-fighter, well, it just seemed appropriate. Widmark's weapon, serial number S595, was provided by Stembridge Gun Rental at a rate of $25/week. Seven twenty-inch .46 barrels, flintlock smoothbore, lacquered walnut with brass furniture and buttplate, the gun weighed thirteen pounds unloaded with an overall length of thirty-seven inches. A Nock first model, the lockplate bears an Ordnance proofmark and next to the "Tower" stamp with crown, cipher, and broad arrow. Stamped in the stock is the "O B" cartouche, indicating approval from the Ordnance Board inspection. Two weapons were provided for Widmark: the original cited above and a copy prop rifle. The prop had a gas line attached to the stock with electrical tape and was used to simulate discharging the gun. A brass collar was fitted on both rifles just below the muzzle, which housed an electrical device that would detonate the weapon. Merely cosmetic on the original so that both guns would look the same, Widmark carried the original gun in several scenes, but as it was very heavy, only used it in close-ups or in scenes where it was resting on the parapet wall or resting against something. While the original gun had a 2-3-2 barrel configuration, the prop weapon was 1-2-1-2-1.[1007]

As the chase sequence continues, Dickinson's men intervene, hitting the Mexican pursuers with a fusillade of gunfire, then turn and protect the defenders as they are escorted back into the compound. *("Pick 'em up! Pick 'em up! Everybody rides double.")* Bowie's horse folds under him, and both riders are tossed just before they reach the Alamo's main gate (Bill Williams would double Widmark; Dean Smith would double Avalon. The gag took just one take). After the rescue by defenders, Melinda expresses her concern (*"Oh, Mr. Smith. You've been hurt!"*); Beekeeper pours whiskey on the wound, and Smitty passes out. Yet another godawful ending to a fairly exciting sequence. Harris was one of the pursuing Mexican horsemen: "I don't know where they got all those horses from; some were barely broken. This horse I had, I couldn't hold him. Man, he was, he just, I couldn't hold him, man, 'cause I had a musket in one hand and then I had a sword hanging off that, banging this horse. And that horse was going crazy, man. The animal had no idea what pulling back the reins meant, and, when we started the chase, he ran away with me. Pretty quick, he had gotten in front of the Mexican group. I pulled as hard as I could, trying to hold him back, but I couldn't. The next thing I knew, I was right in the middle of Crockett's boys and starting to move in front of them. Wayne was behind the camera, screaming, 'Who is that Mexican rider ruining my shot? Get that son-of-bitch a bicycle. He can't ride a damn horse!' Many of us extras had beards and long hair, and he didn't recognize me luckily, and I didn't want him to catch me again for screwing up, so I rode up the hill to where I had parked my car. I jumped off of this crazy horse and changed clothes into my buckskin pants and jacket. I let the horse run away; I have no idea where he went. I then calmly walked back in my fresh clothes to the camera crew, who had stopped filming. Wayne was scanning the faces of the Mexican soldiers trying to find the fool who couldn't control his horse. Thank God he never learned it was me. I would have been fired that day." Bill Hart was one of the stuntmen in the scene. Said Bill, "The very first thing I did (when I arrived) was when we were escaping from the Mexicans and had to pick up the men in the raiding party. I was nervous, of course, but luckily I was working with a stuntman named Jim Burk. I was to ride by and reach down and pick him up. Jim knew I was nervous, and he said, 'Just ride by, Bill. I'll grab the saddle horn, and I'll get up on him. Don't worry.' And he did. He was a fantastic stuntman."[1008]

Eddy "Donut" Donno would also eventually appear in that scene, but, in the beginning, he wasn't quite ready for it. Why? Because the first project Donno ever worked on was *The Alamo*. Initially on location just to visit Frankie Avalon, Donno—like Avalon, a singer from Philly—already had a hit song ("Philadelphia–USA") and wanted to pursue a career. "I stopped out on location to see him," said Donno, "and a stunt guy put me on a horse, and I went through the scene, and I screwed it up. I was falling off the horse, and John Wayne had to cut it, and he said, 'Who the fuck was that on the horse?' He pointed at me and asked, 'How long have you been riding a horse?' I said, 'About three minutes.' He just looked at me and didn't say anything, but he went to Cliff Lyons, and said, 'Every time we mount up, mount him up.' Within days, I was mounted up for that scene where we steal the cattle on the morning raid. I wore a number of different costumes, in various scenes. By the time I left that show, I was able to ride a horse and do the things that needed to be done like falling: I learned all my horse work on that show, believe it or not." According to veteran Jackie Williams, Donno borrowed some protective pads from Red Morgan and never took them off![1009]

Donno wasn't the only one who had trouble with horses. According to Padilla, "Frankie (Avalon) couldn't ride a horse if his life depended on it." Look who's talking—Ruben had never ridden before either, but Duke didn't know that when he gave Padilla the part. Just before filming the scene where Santa Anna appears at the head of his troops, Michael Wayne told Padilla he'd better mount.

"Mount what? I've never ridden before."

"You'd better tell Dad."

"I'm not going to tell him. You tell him."

When Wayne found out, he was furious. "Get him a goddamned horse and teach him to ride!!!"

Eventually, Padilla became skilled enough so that he didn't look like a complete novice on horseback. Well, almost. In his first scene, "Santa Anna" Padilla was supposed to lead his troops over the top of a hill. As it was a long shot, filming would commence once the actors heard the sound of a cannon blast. The cannon fired, Padilla rode over the top of the hill…and immediately fell off his horse. "All I heard was, 'Cut, cut, cut!!!,'" Padilla said. "And I never heard so much cussing in my life!"[1010]

Additionally, several other night scenes were filmed during those two weeks, including Bowie's notification of his wife's death (*"A message for Jim Bowie. In the sombrero"*) and the subsequent confrontation between Bowie and Travis (*"Travis…you can't help bein' you… and I can't help bein' me"*). John Henry Daniels remembers being praised after filming his evening scene. Curtis, O'Brien, Aissa, and John Henry are seen moving to the sacristy the evening before the final battle. "In the scene where I am stepping over people, you will notice that I have something on my head (a paper hat made out of a grocery bag). That was from the party. Duke told me to wear it during my scene. Me, Joan O'Brien, and Ken Curtis. God, I liked him. He patted me on the head and said, 'That was real good. I'm proud of ya.'" Duke also added his compliments. "Quiet on the set," he said. "If we all did our scene like Happy Sam, I would save a lot of money. So far, he has not had to do a retake."[1011]

The most poignant sequence of the film focused on the defenders' last evening before the final assault. Alone in his thoughts, each man knowing in all probability, tomorrow he would die. Thinking of broken promises, regrets, opportunities lost. Things they did and things they should have done. Wondering why they were there, wondering if anyone would remember them. Was it really worth it? Bowie, finally granting manservant Jethro freedom from the shackles of slavery. Jethro, now fighting for freedom along with the rest of the defenders. Dickinson, knowing he'll never see his young daughter grow up. Travis, fulfilling his destiny. And Crockett (*"Not thinking, just remembering"*). Grant and Wayne would take the opportunity to inject a bit of humor into these scenes along with a profound sense of pathos. God, courage, honesty, apologies, love. Chuck Roberson observed Wayne giving the proper motivation for this scene. "Try and imagine that this is your last night to live," prompted Duke. "You got seven thousand Mexicans outside these walls, and come morning, they're gonna kill you. You're not scared, but you're thinking about your life and what it means. Now, see if you can do it." Roberson further noted, "The lines about the real good things—courage, honesty, love—worked so well because of Wayne's direction." In the background, one can hear the haunting opening measures of Tiomkin's "The Green Leaves of Summer". The melody and lyrics were a beautiful counterpoint to the Mexican *Deguello*, which would be heard the following day.

In an article in *Etude* magazine in 1953, author Dave Epstein explained how Tiomkin developed background music. It starts with the reading of the script: "In this phase, he begins to form his major themes and to write out movements (and) themes which must always be done broadly enough to permit for the pruning, padding, changes, and so forth which are inevitable. Tiomkin has found that, in addition to the timbre of the voice, the pitch of the speaking voice must be very carefully considered and reckoned within his scoring. Tiomkin finds that certain stars' voices rule out dominant brasses, for instance, in the background music. Tiomkin goes to the set and listens to the players doing their lines. He talks to them conversationally, noting the pitch and color of their voice. Sometimes he has the studio get him previous films in which the player's voices are heard." Explained Tiomkin, "It may seem incredible, but many actors' voices, however pleasant in themselves, and regardless of pitch, are incompatible with certain instruments. Clarinets, for instance, get in the way of some voices and magnificently complement others. Further, clarinets may be alien to the spirit of a play, or the characterization of a part. Some actors have voices that are easy to write for. Actors like John Wayne impose almost no burdens on the composer. Wayne's voice happily happens to have a pitch and timbre that fits almost any instrumentation."[1012]

Continued Epstein, "Occasionally (Tiomkin) had the director send him some daily rushes...and projects these in his studio or home projection room. After the picture is completed, Tiomkin makes a detailed study of it and of its timing, sometimes spending days running scenes over and over in order to correlate the countless factors that go into the score. Next he uses a stopwatch to arrange his more-or-less final score, collects his musicians and assembles his orchestra, and, after rehearsing, records the soundtrack, synchronizing it directly with the screening of the picture."[1013]

For "Green Leaves", Tiomkin probably prepared a pre-recorded guitar accompaniment for playback on the set for Hairston to mimic on guitar and sing for a cue track that he would later sing again in the studio. Though filmed, Jester's beautiful rendition unfortunately was never included in the final cut. And if one listens carefully to the music cue that begins immediately after Jocko's "I believe" speech, it's apparent this actually was the introduction to Jester's song, which explains why Jethro carried a guitar when Bowie granted his freedom. Obviously, he had just finished singing his song. John Ford directed that scene. "Oh, yeah, he was there," confirmed Robert Harris. "He set one scene up where we're sitting around at the bonfire, and they're playing the music, and we know it's going to be the last, the last chance. Where it's kind of sad music and stuff. And I'm the one that you'll see, it looks like I'm smiling, but I just had my teeth done, and my teeth are showing. And John Ford set that scene up for us." Jim Brewer's close-up in that scene was lost in the edit.[1014]

The evening breeze seemed to make it cooler than it actually was— heavy mist rose off the creek. It was so thick huge fans were needed to disperse it. Near the bank of the Las Moras Creek at Ft. Clark, Chato Hernandez had built an adobe wall to replicate one seen in John Singer Sargent's famous 1882 painting *El Jaleo*. In fact, Duke had a copy of the print on-site to assure complete accuracy of prop placement and set dressing. (Objects that accessorize a set, look appropriate to the period and contribute to the look of a film are set dressing. Items required in the script are props. Example: If a chair is placed against a wall

506

in a room, it's set dressing. If an actor picks up the chair and smashes it over someone's head, it's a prop.)

Extras often were sent home during these night sequences. Not needed, they therefore could be off the payroll. However, Pilar, Toni Wayne, and Teresa Champion appeared in the background of this particular scene as flamenco dancers; Teresa's husband Willie accompanied them on guitar. According to Teresa, "That scene was going to be me, but I didn't have a big nose. When they dressed me, because it starts with the dancers sideways, and I didn't have a big nose, I have a little nose, so he wanted a big nose. So, guess who did it? The choreographer. Antonia Morales is the old lady; she was old already, but she was a good dancer, so she did the part. I'm in the background. (Wayne) needed people, my mother's in there, because they went to visit me when we were there six months, and (she) was taking care of my children, so they would go some weekends to see me, and (Antonia) said, 'We need ladies, and we'll dress your mom. She'll be in it.' And they paid my mom to be in that scene. And the singers and the ones who are singing on that scene is my dancing partner, Felibe de la Rosa." While Morales practiced her dancing moves, Duke instructed Pilar and Toni in proper hand-clapping cadence.[1015]

The scene's premise was that Crockett, Bowie, and other defenders would sneak down a creek past the Mexican encampment as the soldiers were distracted by dancers. As the creek was relatively deep and Avalon relatively short (5-foot-6), it was necessary to build an underwater platform he could walk on. Marshall Jones was Wayne's stand-in but volunteered to help with the work. "Hell, I'll keep you from drowning," he told Frankie. Eight flour sacks were filled with sand and piled high enough to help Avalon keep his head above water. Extras were huddling around campfires trying to keep warm. "Oh, my God," declared one. "I've never been so cold in my life. Just wish I was home in bed with my wife's cold feet in my back." Rudy Robbins also vividly recalled that evening. "It was 27° the night we did it," he said, "so we wore waders under our clothing to keep us warm and dry since we were going into water. Well, as we did the scene, we stepped in areas that were a little deeper. As a result, water flowed into the waders! After each take, the crew would wrap us in blankets and give us a little brandy. We went through four gallons of brandy! Of course, we were eventually in no shape to do the scene." Since Duke had provided the refreshments to ward off the chill, he really didn't have anyone to blame but himself. Wills and Pyle were absolutely wasted and flubbed their lines; Duke cussed them out for their unprofessional behavior: "If you can't hold your liquor, get out of here!" Rudy was feeling so good he started to laugh. Laughing as he walked right into a camera lens. (Of course, Duke was known to have a bit of who-hit-John every now and then. For example, Jerry Dickens recalls that during the filming of the movie, Mexican soldiers huddled around their campfires and tried to keep warm: "They say Wayne visited every campfire and took a drink at every stop. They had to rearrange the shooting schedule. Duke wobbled so much on dry land that they had to shoot a scene where he was chest-deep in water. This kept him steady." Bobby Gardiner, former U-2, Thunderbirds and test pilot, recalled visiting the set and saw Duke sitting in his director's chair—neatly tucked behind one leg were two bottles of liquor. Or so some folk say).[1016]

Robert Harris had a dark complexion—Wayne thought he was Mexican and gave him Spanish dialogue. "One time I looked up at him, I said, 'You'll have to repeat that. I couldn't understand a damn thing you said,'" explained Harris. Wayne tried to inject a bit of humor in the sequence. Mexican soldados were enjoying some drinking, some dancing girls, and partying around a large campfire. Many were dozing off. Harris, a drunken soldier, was to throw a whisky jug over his shoulder that was to land in front of the Alamo defenders. "I was supposed to be staggering down by the river, and Wayne would get right in front of me," said Harris. "He would start staggering, telling me how to do it. My line was 'Ole, Chicana', 'Hooray, gypsy dancer.' We went through that about three or four times, and I remember his wife. She was sitting there, watching the dancers, and she was laughing up a storm watching Wayne do this. Duke said, 'Here's this damn mug. Now drink out of that mug!' This big old mug like the old Kentuckians, you know where they had a one-finger deal. I took a gulp 'cause it's water, you know? I took a shot of that with a straight scotch or Kentucky water, whiskey, or something. I tell you what…it was strong as a March hare. It was great, 'cause it was about four o'clock in the morning when they were shooting these scenes and everybody's freezing. I staggered up, and then I throw this bottle, and Wayne wanted me to get it real close to him. So I was starting to throw this bottle from over my shoulder into the river. I was supposed to be guarding the camp and Wayne and Chill Wills and all of them are coming down the river, and this bottle would splash right, you know, right pretty close to him. But he wanted it closer. So we'd have to redo it and redo it. 'What's wrong with you, boy?' Wayne screamed."

Wayne climbed out of the freezing creek to walk through Robert's action again. "Do it right this time, please. We're all freezing," cried Wills. "Yeah, get it right," the group chanted. Harris continued, "So the next time (Wayne) said, 'I want it close!' You know Wayne would yell and holler; he was a good guy, but he did a lot of yelling. He'd say, 'Damn it! Throw that son-of-a-bitch closer.' So the next time, I threw that son-of-a-bitch, just barely missed him. Water just splashed all over; it got all over Chill Wills and all of them. Wayne yelled, 'Goddamn! Not that close!'"[1017]

And they had to rehearse it and rehearse it and set the cameras and then rehearse it again. Finally, they were ready for a take. Toni LaCava and Pilar portrayed two women clapping in the background. Toni recalled that evening: "My father and the group of Texans were to wade by us. When they reached a certain point, a crew member was to cue our group at which point the guitar player and dancers would begin, and we would start clapping. When the actors in the water reached the point where we were to be cued, the technician forgot to cue us. As they waded by, we were frozen, still waiting for our cue." Wayne, thinking the scene was finished, climbed out of the cold water, yelled, "Cut!" and asked, "How is it?" About that time somebody yelled, "Let me know when you want me to cue the dancers." Toni continued, "Then, not wanting to call the technician by name, my father said, 'That's OK. We've got a wonderful opportunity to do this again, so everyone please take their places.'" Wayne then gave specific notes to some of the guys moving with him, including the people over on the far shore. He was absolutely furious but suddenly, his manner changed. "And this time," he said, "make goddamn sure that the guitar player is playing, the dancers are dancing, and the clappers are clapping." You can be sure the dancers got their cue the next time Wayne waded by.[1018]

The sequence continued with the raiders wading upstream, then up a bank to a nearby wooden road-bridge. Mexican soldiers, stationed on guard as artillery caissons thunder by, are subsequently pulled backward over its railing into the creek and subdued by the defenders. Brothers Joe and Tap Canutt played the guards. "Cliff (Lyons) still owes me a bottle of Scotch from *The Alamo*," recalls Joe. "Cliff didn't like Ted White (one of the attacking party) and he said, 'I'll buy you a bottle of the best Scotch in the world if you take that son-of-a-bitch off with you.'" So, when White grabbed Canutt from behind and took him over the railing, Joe grabbed Ted and took him right into the creek, fulfilling his end of the bargain. However, "Cliff never paid off."[1019]

Though filmed earlier, this sequence also included one of the most memorable stunts in the film. Slight of build but extremely athletic, Dean Smith was chosen to double Avalon. As Dean loves to say, "I could do three things: run, jump, and ride. I was blessed with athletic ability and horsemanship. I had a beard on *The Alamo*. I had to double Frankie Avalon and still had stubble, so I shaved the stubble off. I came in and sat next to Cliff. He looked at me and took a breath and hit the table with both fists. Bounced the plates." Crockett and his men had left the Alamo to steal some cattle to replenish the Alamo's tainted food supply. Cliff Lyons asked Dean, portraying one of Crockett's men, if he could run fast enough to jump and hurdle a horse. Then, while in the air, take out the horse's rider. Dean said, yes, that he thought he could, and they shot the scene. Bear Hudkins would double the horse's rider. Said Bear, "I'm riding herding the cattle, and Dean comes out of the dark to bulldog me off the horse, to kill me." (The stuntman term "bulldog" comes from the rodeo circuit. A cowboy jumps from a galloping horse, grabs a steer by the horns, and throws it to the ground. In stuntman jargon, a bulldog refers to any time one man leaps from a balcony, a rock, a horse, or an airplane, and hits another man). Dean continues, "They had all these quick little shots of the Tennesseans doing away with these Mexican herdsmen. I ran and jumped over a horse in one of the shots. I jumped over this horse, and I must have jumped seven foot. After the shot was over, it turned out just perfect; I ran and cleared the guy, and they shot it in the first take."

Somebody noticed. Adds Smith, "Up walked an old man wearing a blue blazer, cream-colored trousers, white buck shoes with an old slouch hat on, chewing on a red bandana, and I didn't know who the heck this little fella was. He looked like he slobbered all over the front of his shirt. And I thought maybe he had been out all night drinking or something, and he had a patch over his eye. And he walked up to me, and he pulled that patch up, and he was looking out of that bad eye at me, and he said, 'Son, I've never seen anybody jump over a horse like that.' And I said, 'Well, I think that's probably the first time that's ever been done. I think most of the other guys have used trampolines, but luckily, I have some good legs.' He said, 'My name is John Ford, and, if you ever hear of me working on a picture, would you please come to see me? I'll give you a job.' And I worked on every one of his pictures from then on." Asked about Ford's involvement that evening, Bill Hart explained, "(The only time I had a chance to work with Ford was) when they went down to the river to shoot that scene. I think they may have used just one or two shots of what he did there. I recall a shot where they had a guy do a saddle fall, and he rolled down into the water, and you could see his reflection in the water. Ford actually did shoot some stuff; it may not have made it into the final print."[1020]

While Wayne was busy wrapping up the final few night scenes, the last herd of longhorn cattle left League City for Brackettville. Houston's F.L. Lepper truck line had the honor of transporting twenty-three cows, seven steers, and four calves to the set. Once they arrived on November 8, Duke would begin filming the cattle sequence. After delivering the cattle, or so the story goes, Bill Daniel asked Wayne for a part in the film but was refused, so Daniel rounded up his ranch hands (*waddies,* he called them) and headed back to Liberty County, leaving the wrangling to Wayne and his movie crew. Duke couldn't handle the livestock; he called Daniel and his waddies back to take care of business. The cattle had been culled from larger herds that roamed rough Texas back country, and the wranglers had to spend several days working the cattle before they were tame enough to be used in the film. Walter Osterman and Irvin Brittmecher came in from Liberty to help in that effort along with Daniel's son Bill and Herman "Sleepy" Siegler. Siegler's face had been badly burned in a kerosene stove explosion in their bunkhouse, but he carried on and never missed a day. "Hollywood just really didn't have the know-how to handle the longhorn cattle," admitted Daniel, "so Mr. Wayne asked me to bring my cowboys here and work our cattle. So we did. My son Will, the young boy in the movie is our son, but I got him out of Baylor and brought several of my cowboys; Sleepy was the head of that group and Mac, Will, and some of the other cowboys." Their mettle was tested during a particularly fierce hail and electrical thunderstorm. In a little over an hour, more than two and a half inches of rain pelted down with intermittent sheets of lightning and crashes of thunder. According to Daniel, "One night out here, right at the end of (Front) Street, they stampeded, and it took us two or three days to get all those cattle rounded back up."[1021]

Including longhorns in a film about Texas seemed quite natural but, when asked why he did so, Wayne gave all the credit to someone else. "I looked up J. Frank Dobie, the finest historian of the Southwest," admitted Duke. "He's quite elderly now, but, for over twenty years, he wrote articles and books on the subject. He was an exchange professor at Oxford from Austin. He offered to help in any way when I told him the kind of picture I wanted to make. He suggested we try to find the longhorns since they were the cattle that made this country great. When Dobie finally came on the set, there were tears in his eyes when he said, 'We'll never see this again.'"[1022]

Authors and storytellers Lon Tinkle and Dobie had fortuitously arrived the day Wayne planned to film the cattle stampede sequence. According to Tinkle, Dobie was enamored with a gnarled, magnificent old mesquite that grew outside the commissary. After breakfast that day, he communed a while with the tree. As Wayne was waiting on location and wanted to have a few photographs taken with Dobie in front of the Alamo, a photographer encouraged Dobie to hurry on. Said Dobie, "Here's the thing to photograph. Get some pictures of that old mesquite. It has survived wind and weather for, I guess, several hundred years. You never saw such a big trunk on a mesquite. Now, there's something noble. And send me some of the pictures. I'll pay for them." Properly chastised, the photographer did as ordered, and the troupe headed off to meet Wayne. With Grant at the wheel, Dobie proceeded to identify everything along the way. But then, with twelve cars in line, he suddenly asked Grant to stop, jumped out of the car, and proceeded to identify a juajilla bush, extolling its virtues. Finally, everyone returned to their cars, and the caravan continued until it came to a rise overlooking the set. "How do you like that, Mr. Dobie?" Grant began. "We got a Spanish architect who studied old documents and…" Dobie interrupted. "Look, Jimmy. Here's another juajilla bush." Grant gave up. Wayne came over, sat Dobie in his own director's chair, and explained the upcoming scene to the visitor. Ken Curtis and Chill Wills came over to sing a few songs Tiomkin composed for the film. Dobie was in heaven and regaled the stars, extras, and onlookers about longhorns. He even made a few suggestions to Wayne. "No, Duke," he told him. "What you need is some of the songs the Mexicans really sang. I think you ought to make 'La Paloma' your theme song." Assured by his staff that his advisers would be properly taken care of, Wayne started to set up the scene.[1023]

A portion of the cattle stampede was filmed about nine hundred yards from the village near the airstrip. With wranglers dressed as buckskinned defenders interspersed among the actors and stuntmen, a camera truck raced along the airstrip while the cattle were driven beside it in a running shot. Once this shot was complete, the cattle were herded behind the village set on the far side of Pinto Creek. Wayne, as Crockett, yelled "Let's take 'em," and the cattle began to run across the plain, between Pinto Creek and the scenery flats. Although it appears as a continuous sequence (a product of carefully planned direction of movement on the screen), the remaining portions of the cattle stampede were filmed as four separate actions. In each, the cattle were re-grouped then moved in the appropriate direction, according to the screen direction plan. In the first action, the cattle were driven right to left on the far side of Pinto Creek. After the cameras and necessary equipment were placed in the next position (across the creek behind the village), the cattle were re-staged, then filmed as they moved across the creek. Then those set-ups were struck and moved into the village for further angles of the stampede through Back Street. The cattle then were regrouped in the pasture beyond the left end of the village and held until the action call. In the last action, the herd ran down the length of Back Street and turned toward the Alamo. (The sequence in which Crockett, Bowie, et al., drive the cattle through the Mexican camp, trampling men and tents alike, was filmed but cut. The camp had been located on the plain on the right side of Back Street but on the near side of Pinto Creek).

Although Rudy Robbins thoroughly enjoyed his time on location, the cattle stampede sequence was one he'd rather forget. "I remember many things about the filming," recalled Robbins, "but a couple of incidents stand out in my mind. The raid for cattle is certainly memorable. It took several days to film, primarily because the cattle didn't want to move! Finally, we got them going. I remember a number of riders on green horses, which were always jumping. We were riding, and I saw one guy going lickety-split on a green horse; I thought he looked funny. I changed horse for that scene and ended up riding a small cavalry saddle. Well, my saddle started to slip on the right-hand side. Maybe I wasn't cinched up properly. As it started to slip, I threw my left leg over, but my right foot wouldn't come out of the tiny stirrup. I soon found myself thrown off the horse! But my foot got caught; the horse was scared, and I was dragged along over one hundred yards during the cattle raid face down! I finally got loose some four hundred yards from the chapel. Cattle and horses were riding right by me, but none of them trampled me. Chuck Roberson saw me, jumped off his horse, and remained with me to protect me. Chuck did protect me, but, by the time he arrived at my side, I had already broken my nose, which was filled with rocks and pointed sticks." Duke was ecstatic about the sequence. "The longhorns are sure dramatic on the Todd-AO screen," he enthused. "We have a terrific shot where they're crossing a creek, and one cuts himself out of the herd straight into the camera before he veers off at the last second."[1024]

It took several attempts to drive the cattle through the main gate. Said Bill Daniel, "It's like trying to thread a needle with a rope. Some people seem to think you can just tell cattle to move over somewhere and turn around, like actors." Robbins agreed: "If I remember correctly, it took us forever to get those cattle to go in the compound." A gauntlet of huge vans were parked in parallel lines on either side of the Alamo gate, creating an alley with three cameras mounted on platforms on one side as Wayne had demanded the cattle run past the viewfinders. According to Happy, the wranglers were having a hard time getting the cattle through the gate, so he said, "Give me a Tennessean costume, and I'll get 'em through." He simply did what any wrangler familiar with Texas Longhorns knows. Take the lead steer through the gate and the rest will follow. Unfortunately, three steers were killed during the filming and a calf badly trampled. Their heads were mounted and given back to the respective owners. A gift from Wayne.[1025]

On November 7, after fifty-eight Broadway performances as Beatrice in *Much Ado About Nothing*, for which she won a Tony award, Margaret Leighton planned to travel to Texas to meet her beloved Laurence Harvey before heading back to London. Her plan was to stop in Dallas on November 10 to address the Dallas Civic Opera Guild membership at the Adolphus Hotel, but she had to cancel due to health issues. (Across from the hotel was a strip club called the Carousel. It was owned by a man who would be famous four years later—Jack Ruby.) Eventually, she arrived on location November 12 and was welcomed with a huge sign made by the crew. "I was quite hazy about this Alamo," confessed Leighton, "and, in the beginning, I didn't know whether Mr. Wayne or my husband played him. Then I heard that Texans were very sensitive about this sort of thing, and I started reading. Now, I think I shall be able to cope." Asked where filming was taking place, she replied, "Yes, yes, it's Bracketville (sic), near the Alamo. I've been spelling it every other night to long-distance operators, and, if I have to spell it just once more, I'll be neurotic." No wonder she was having problems. She misspelled it every time she used the name, and Brackettville is only near the Alamo if you use "near" in the Texas sense: 120 miles or so as the crow flies. Upon hearing his wife had arrived and knowing that it would tend to curtail his after-hours entertainment activities, all Harvey could say was, "Oh, hell." Fortunately, she was only on location for two weeks. Pilar and Duke threw a cocktail party for the Harveys at their location home, and Maggie left for London on November 26. Leighton wasn't the only celebrity to visit the location. One day University of Texas football coach Darrell Royal and several other coaches flew in on a privately-owned DC-3 just to see the set.

In early August, NBC producer Joe Cates of Phillip Production, Inc., had contacted Duke with an intriguing proposal. Would Wayne be interested in hosting a taped television program aired in advance of his film's 1960 premiere? Its format would be mapped out, so it didn't look like one long movie trailer and would help spread word about the movie. Receiving $250,000 for the privilege (with a total budget of $305,000), Wayne naturally jumped at the chance. Modifying the Master Shooting Schedule, Duke planned a two-day extravaganza for November 9 and 10. (This was later rescheduled for the weekend of November 14/15). The program would simulate *The Alamo* wrap party and include various segments by individual cast members, an interview with an ex-U.S. vice president, and singing, dancing, and behind-the-scenes footage. When Cates announced the agreement, he stated, "The setting will be in Brackettville, Texas, where Wayne has reproduced in absolute scale the San Antonio of 'The Alamo' days. It's been two years in the building. Sometime around the end of October, I'm going to Brackettville to tape a show in which Wayne will appear as himself. He'll not play a part, so to speak, but he'll be involved throughout the entertainment." To efficiently utilize the scheduled "downtime," extras in the Mexican army would simultaneously be wardrobed and trained to be ready when Wayne resumed actual filming. Sponsored by Pontiac, this would be the first-ever taped TV remote from a movie location. Perry Cross and Seymour Robbie were signed by NBC to co-produce the special, and the latter would also direct. (Cates, who figured prominently in the quiz show scandals, backed out of the production when forced to testify at the Oren Harris committee hearings. Allentown, Pennsylvania storeowner Max Hess informed the committee of a $10,000 payoff to get an employee on a quiz show.) Originally advertised by NBC and scheduled as a 1960 Christmas special, the program would eventually air on ABC at 9:30 p.m. Monday, November 14, 1960. Interestingly, some of the advertising for this special accidentally reversed the negative of the publicity still. The "allegorical" cross requested by Wayne appeared on the wrong side of the iconic Alamo hump![1026]

An eighteen-man KTLA production crew arrived in Brackettville on November 6 and scheduled twelve shooting days. Helmed by program manager Bob Quinlan along with chief engineer John Silva and production supervisor Hal Dasbach, the team used six cameras with mounts, three trucks, two Ampex two-inch, quad videotape recorders, and one audio tape recorder. Rain washed out two or three of the twelve days. Estimated to cost 65% less than Batjac's comparable filming costs ($45,500), Quinlan experienced significant scheduling and coordination problems between TV and motion picture people who had separate and conflicting schedules to meet. The job required fifty different setups and change of locations in the same general area. Buried high-voltage Batjac cables caused mic hum. Said Quinlan, "That was typical of the kind of excellent preparation that Batjac had made for their own work. But it slowed us down a bit." Even nature seemed to be against the production. "Skunks the size of police dogs" and rattlers were crawling all over the place. One cameraman had an odoriferous encounter with a nocturnal visitor. The results were predictable.[1027]

Bruce Minnex, program associate director, recalled the opening shot. Wayne, garbed in typical Western clothing, introduced the audience to the set: "You're standing under more sky here than there is over any of the fifty United States, but one. Welcome to Texas, folks. My name is John Wayne. You're on a ranch in Bexar County, about eight miles from Brackettville. (Yes, that was the way it was scripted—Bexar County). And if you can't exactly place Brackettville, well, that way south about fifty miles is Mexico. And 138 miles east is San Antonio…" Robbie and Minnex were tucked down the hill out of sight so that there could be that continuous pan of the sky. After the scene was completed, Minnex, decked out in new boots, tight trousers fashionable on Madison Avenue at the time, a very chic ski sweater, and carrying an attaché case, came up the hill in the middle of the desert in Texas ("You can take the kid off of Madison Avenue, but you can't take Madison Avenue off of the kid.") and asked Wayne, "'Would you like to see it?' Meaning, come into the tape truck, and we'll show it to you. I think he thought that he was going to hear the sound, so he came with the cloak over his shoulders, which was not in the picture, but he just put it on extra. And he walked down to the truck with us which was back down the hill and went into the tape truck, and we showed him the footage we had just shot. And he was thunderstruck. I don't think he realized it was videotape; I don't think he'd ever seen videotape. And he turned from the television screen to look at his associates who were with him, and he moved with a coterie of people at all times. He said, 'My God. They've got instant rushes. I want one of those things strapped to every camera from now on.' So that he could tape. Well, they were not that available. But they did get them within a number of days. They got videotape machines strapped to each camera, so he could watch the videotape. Black and white, though it was. Small monitor, though it was. He did know exactly what the performance in the cinema in the widescreen frame was, although it wasn't the same picture exactly. But he could watch it that way. And they did start using it, and, as far as I know, that was the first use of video on a major motion picture." (Prior to this photographers would take shots of a scene, then compare placement of the individuals actors, props, etc. According to extra David Kuykendall, "Wayne had a still photographer, and he came out and took pictures of all the stars. So much of it was to make sure the next scene was set up properly. They would enlarge the contact sheets to make sure that people were in the right place. Because that was one of the (most critical) jobs whenever we were in any scene. He'd come up and say, 'OK, you were standing here and doing this. Now, look at yourself and make sure you are in the same position because we're going to move from that scene to the next, and we don't want to have a jerk in the action.'"[1028]

J. Frank Dobie and Lon Tinkle had already arrived to serve as technical advisers in the TV production. Tinkle was so excited to appear with Dobie he even asked Wayne if he planned to pay him. "Dobie is crazy to come," wrote Lon. "Did you plan to pay him? If not, give him half of my allotment. I mean this." Dobie was to be in an outdoor shot, seated on an old wagon in front of a herd of longhorns whose history he was to discuss. Dobie was given a suggested script but rejected it. "Give me a piece of paper," he said. "I couldn't possibly say this stuff." After thinking a bit, Dobie wrote down his lines. "This is what I'll say." Wranglers would bring the herd inside the enclosure, close to the fence, so they could be seen milling around, but the cattle became skittish, very skittish. So much so they knocked a drover off his horse and broke his leg. So much so they broke through the fence by the flatbed and stampeded toward the camera truck. With a camera mounted on its roof, the truck was in a perfect position to film the chaos, resulting in over four minutes of sensational footage. Or so the producers thought. When the crew retired to the taping truck to view the video, it started out fine. Dobie and Tinkle were there, and the cattle came in, and they're getting nervous, and the fence starts to go, and that's the end of the picture. Minnex yelled, "What happened? Where's the rest of the picture? What happened? Did they kill the cable?" The cameraman said, "No, I stopped the tape machine." "What do you mean you stopped the tape machine?" He said, "Well, I knew that wasn't part of the script. And I wanted to save as much tape as I could. This stuff is expensive." Unbelievable, but true.[1029]

While on location, the crew had scheduled a taped interview with John Nance Garner, conservative Southerner and vice-president to Franklin Delano Roosevelt. Democrat, former U. S. Representative and Speaker of the House, Nance was known for colorfully describing the vice-presidency as "not worth a bucket of warm piss." Old and frail with a salty vocabulary, he would sometimes lose his train of thought. But he was still feisty and very opinionated. According to Happy Shahan, Garner would only grant the interview if it would be conducted by Shahan. The interview was scheduled for forty-five minutes or so, and some of his comments were scripted, but only two or three minutes would actually be used. It didn't really start off on the right foot, either. According to Minnex, the producer, writer, director and associate producer, all of whom were Jewish, arrived one hour before the scheduled time and started walking for the porch to speak to Garner. "He came to the door," said Minnex, "and he said, 'Well, of course, I'll talk to you. Now, I'm not talking to none of those bushy-headed New York Jews.' I would probably have turned around and gone home, but (Robbie) just grabbed my coat sleeve and said, 'Relax, Bruce.' And I was the only non-Jew there, but I guess they were more used to it. I was deeply offended, and I was particularly offended to think the vice-president of the United States (would have an attitude like that)."

Even the extras had an opportunity to shine in the special. Wayne asked several youngsters to audition for a particular segment. "They had us try out," recalls Tim Cumiskey. "They had a bunch of kids from the Ft. Clark ranch and a bunch of the kids from the Brackettville school came out and did a reading. I got to read *The 13 Days of Glory*. I got chosen to do that on that show. At the beginning of that show, I was sitting on top of the Alamo wall reading that in English. Then there was a young Mexican guy that came on right after that and read it in Spanish." Others, though, had less fond memories. "I was a dragoon in that particular part of the production there," said extra Jerry Larsen. "I was a dragoon, and I had to take this pennant and drag it past my horse's face, and then he'd throw me for about fifty-five yards. Which was unintentional. He just threw me. I was supposed to get out, but my foot got caught."[1030]

Chill Wills and Frankie Avalon sang "Here's to the Ladies" while Ken Curtis and Joan O'Brien crooned "Tennessee Babe," and a mixed chorus, conducted by Tiomkin, sang a rousing version of "The Ballad of the Alamo" along with "The Green Leaves of Summer." Richard Boone was scheduled to sing "Will You Come to the Bower" but, fortunately, only recited the first verse. With Wayne as the emcee, the film's stars appeared to give brief personal plugs, climaxed by a three-minute clip from the film's action-packed battle scenes. In an interview with reporter Leo Guild, Duke explained the importance of the special: "We could have thrown a lot of clips from the picture together and called it a TV show, but we resisted it. Instead we have an interested kind of Life-Goes-To-A-Party show that I think the public's going to like. What we did was to close down the picture for two days while the ABC boys moved in their technical equipment. Just then some genius—and I'm not being sarcastic—thought of throwing a big party, the site to be outdoor sets, and letting the cameras run wild. We rounded up 3,000 people, and it wasn't hard. During the party, we got people like John Nance Garner—he is ninety-six now—Laurence Harvey, Linda Cristal, Frankie Avalon, Frank Dobie, the world's greatest authority on western lore, and some Texas millionaires before the lenses. You know how dull interviews often are on TV? Well, these are different. The spirit of the land, its depth, seemed to seep through everybody. There's fun, dancing, and sweep in the background. Also wonderful music by Dimitri Tiomkin. And when those cameras get tight on people like Laurence Harvey as he's reading old letters on the Alamo, there's plenty of heart and sentiment. I don't think anyone's ever seen anything exactly like this. There are a couple of battle scenes we took from the movie just to whet viewer's appetites."

Duke was on a roll! "But the bit I like best about the TV show is an opening shot that scans the whole empty horizon of the Alamo," he added. "You know the real Alamo is a mission in the heart of San Antonio. We had to build a replica on the plains. It's a very effective shot. You know, you might marvel at the way we rebuilt the old city of San Antonio. You'll see it on the ABC show. It was a big job. But you know what posed the biggest problem? Horses. We couldn't find enough horses in Texas, and we needed six hundred before we could start shooting. There had been a drought, and the horses were scarce. We sent men with trailers all around the West buying all we could find, but it wasn't easy. You'll also see our herd of 350 Longhorn cattle on the show. Borrowing these valuable beasts created problem after problem, but we got them, and they're a sight to see."

Numerous sequences in the script were modified or eliminated entirely. Prior to Harvey's Shakespearian soliloquy, he was to chat with a man who questioned his accent: "I don't mind telling you, Mr. Harvey...a lot of us folks down here were pretty worried about you taking off the part of Colonel Travis." Later, instead of reading Travis's famous "Victory or Death" letter of February 24, 1836, the script called for Gov. Daniel to make Harvey a naturalized Texan. J. Frank Dobie's speech about longhorns and Alamo defenders was split between he and Lon Tinkle, and it was Tinkle, not Dobie, who would translate a young Mexican boy's speech. Duke's sequence with daughter Aissa, though sounding natural, was entirely scripted. Listen closely and you can actually hear Duke feed Aissa some of her lines:

Wayne: "Say Hello..."

Aissa: "Why?"

Wayne: "You're on television....You know what television is?"

Aissa: "Oh, yes. The little small movies."

Wayne: "Tell about the part you play in the picture."

Aissa: "Why?"

Wayne: "Because you're on...Are you Jim Bowie?"

She shakes her head.

Wayne: "Crockett? Travis?"

Aissa: "You're silly."

Wayne: "Well, you tell who you are in the picture." *(Duke whispered her next line to Aissa.)*

Aissa: "Don't you know, Daddy?"

Wayne (giving up): "Thank you, Aissa Wayne."

Aissa: "You're welcome."

Originally, Mrs. Campbell, great-granddaughter of defender John W. Smith, had a short conversation with Duke before Avalon sang Tiomkin's love song. Now, it was shortened to a simple introduction by Avalon. Ken Curtis wasn't initially scheduled to sing "Tennessee Babe." Instead, it was Joan O'Brien, accompanied by Avalon on trumpet. Jester Hairston's beautiful rendition of "The Green Leaves of Summer" was never included in the film. Rather than be seen in a film clip, Widmark recorded an extensive speech about Bowie; Boone talked about Houston, and Wayne described Crockett's life while holding his rifle "Old Betsy." Instead of showing a two-minute sequence of the final assault, the program would show scene #437, Houston's speech to his officers: "I wonder if Texas will remember these men! I wonder if the world will!" This was followed by scene #453, Dickinson's line in the sand sequence and Travis's speech to the defenders. The program would wrap up with voice-overs and appearances by Grant, Ybarra, Tiomkin, Bill Jones, and Nate Edwards. Shahan would explain how to make adobe blocks, and Wayne would give a few closing remarks: "Thanks for helping celebrate the finish of our movie... One thing about doing a picture on the men of the Alamo...kind of living with them...no matter who you are, or what you believe, some of what they stood for rubs off on you...(Music and pull back from

Wayne to the Alamo chapel). Quite a bit to fit into a short 60-minute special.[1031]

It was too bad the program wouldn't air until mid-November 1960, though. "You know, this is such a good, sweeping picture—and so honestly American. I wish the TV show could have gotten to the public before the elections," Wayne confessed. "I don't think I'm immodest when I say it would have helped bring out the vote. Americans will be prouder of America when they see it." And the Pontiac Motor Division (PMD) must have thought so as well as it offered to build and loan a special Pontiac Bonneville convertible to Wayne for a year. All he had to do was pay for the gas and oil: "We just like to see the best people riding in the best car!" (Had they known, PMD might have had a different opinion of working with Wayne. According to Gene DeRuelle, early in the filming, "Wayne was lining up a shot shooting from the top of the gate wall out to where Santa Ana's army would arrive. He grabbed two extras and told them to stand where he put them. He and Clothier discussed the shot, and then he took one step toward the two extras. They had been told to stand, and that's what they did. When they didn't move, Wayne, in his normal wonderful manner, threw his coffee on them and growled, 'Get out of the way.' We leased all our standby cars from the Pontiac dealer in Bracketville *(mostly likely it was San Antonio as Brackettville was too small for a car dealership)*. Within an hour, all the cars disappeared. Behind that grimy costume and full beard, and now dripping from getting coffee thrown on them, was the owner of the Pontiac agency. He was pissed! It took a day of negotiations to get the cars back.")[1032]

Originally called "The John Wayne Show," the proposed television special had a distinctly different flavor from what eventually aired. The program would be taped in basic black-and-white with the exception of film clips that would appear in color. An August 5, 1959, shooting script showed that, after screening a number of scenes from the film and a panning shot of the set, Wayne would open the show with a greeting to the audience "and Duke goes on to tell us that we will be hearing a lot about the picture in the next hour, and he hopes what we hear will make us go out and buy a Pontiac; get in it, and drive to see *The Alamo*—or words to that effect. This done, he invites us to a bar-b-q which is in full swing. (Never should we get the feeling that the party is being staged)." At the conclusion of the dance, Pedro Vargas (a Mexican singer and actor known as "Nightingale of the Americas") would perform, and then Wayne would take over "and Red Skelton will bust on with a big hat and his own material. We tag the Skelton bit with his gunfight gag with Duke…" Wayne would then introduce J. Frank Dobie, columnist Bob Considine, and possibly Carl Sandburg. Theodore Bikel would play a guitar and sing a few songs before Lawrence Harvey was introduced. (Bikel was included because, when the show was scripted, it was said he had been added to the film's cast). After an extremely long sequence in which Travis's journey from Alabama to Texas was explained, both Avalon and Wills would sing a few songs. Sandburg would interview Wayne, a few more songs would be sung, and then the show would mercifully end. Fortunately, saner heads prevailed, and most of the tomfoolery was eventually eliminated from the program.[1033]

Concurrent with the filming of the special, a scandal was rocking the emerging television game-show phenomena. The popularity of this 1950s genre both fascinated viewers and generated huge interest and excitement. The concept was ridiculously simple: armed guards, isolation booths, and questions stored in safes. The greater the question's difficulty, the higher the stakes. Viewers tuned in each week to see if their favorite contestants would risk their winnings for an even greater reward. In its naivety, the public believed the contestants to be either extremely intelligent, absurdly lucky, or both. Some contestants, such as Dr. Joyce Brothers, were exactly that. Initially a publicity stunt, Brothers appeared on *$64,000 Question* as an expert in the subject of boxing. After the topic was suggested by the sponsors, Brothers, a voracious reader, studied every reference book on boxing that she could find. Her excellent memory allowed her to answer even the most difficult questions, and she won the top prize. With over thirty weekly games shows on, viewers could choose their favorites: *Tic-Tac-Dough, The Big Surprise, $64,000 Question and $64,000 Challenge, Twenty-One, Dotto, Beat the Clock, The Big Payoff, The Big Surprise, Who Do You Trust?, Name That Tune, Dough-Re-Mi,* and so on. Newspapers and magazines would publish weekly tallies of game-show winnings. Though initially on the up and up but under constant pressure from sponsors, producers quickly realized the only way to continue to generate high ratings was to manipulate results. On November 2, Columbia University English professor Charles Van Doren, who had previously won $138,000 on the television quiz-show *Twenty-One,* testified before the House Legislative Oversight committee that he had been given questions and answers in advance while a contestant. Albert Freedman, former producer of the defunct program, who denied coaching Van Doren, had fled to Mexico after the show collapsed under rigging charges. Eventually, over 150 contestants and producers would be called to testify; more than one hundred would commit perjury. Eventually, Van Doren, one producer, and seventeen other contestants were formally charged, arrested, and convicted of lying under oath to the New York grand jury. All pleaded guilty and received suspended sentences. None served time in jail. *Dotto, $64,000 Question,* and *Twenty-One* all were cancelled under a cloud of scandal.[1034]

So how does this relate to *The Alamo*? The television special's director, lighting designer, stage manager and associate producer had all been working on *The $64,000 Question.* According to Minnex, they were called out of the blue to work on the *Alamo* television special. "And it was exactly at the time that the quiz show scandal broke. It was that fall," he said. "And they, the Senate, were scheduling hearings, and we all got this assignment on the Mexican border because they preferred that we not testify if we were called. And we were close enough that we'd just go across the border." Luckily, they never had to evade the authorities.

After the wrap party, Wayne passed out his commemorative coffee cups. Individually hand-painted by California artist Bob Williams, the four-inch tall, three-and-one-quarter-inch diameter personalized mugs had a painting of the Alamo chapel on the front under the film's name, with the recipient's name and "from Duke" on the back. Williams estimated the $2.50 mug took thirty minutes to hand-paint with gold-leaf painstakingly applied to the handle. (Some were also made with no specific name on the back to be used for promotional purposes or given to those inadvertently left off the list). "These mugs are like awards for me," recalls Dean Smith. "You'd probably get them a month, or maybe two or three months after the picture was finished. They would come in the mail, and it would be a nice thing to remember the movie which you worked on." An effort to honor the hard work and efforts of cast and crew, Wayne started the tradition in 1951 after completion of *Flying Leathernecks*, though Jack Williams recalled he may have also received mugs for his work on *Red River* and *Fort Apache*. Author Tim Lilley makes a strong case that Wayne got the idea for the mugs from *Leathernecks*. "The fact that the tradition starts around the time Wayne was working on the film *Flying Leathernecks* is more than a mere coincidence in timing," wrote Lilley. "One of the major props in that film are the ceramic mugs which each member of the Marine Aviation Unit VMF 247 has to identify him. One side of the white, gold-handled mugs is blank, but the front side bears the unit's logo...and the cups are personalized. Above the logo is each flier's first name or nickname, making the cup an important form of identity in the group. In the script, the mugs signify a symbol of unity that the desperate group of fliers need to sustain their efforts in unrelenting combat." Wayne decided the gift of a personalized mug was a token of his appreciation and would represent the collective "combat" cast and crew endured when making a film—a heartfelt gesture on Wayne's part. He never forgot the debt he owed to the talented professionals whose team efforts made his films possible. Mary St. John, the only person to receive a mug for every Wayne film, would compile a list of all recipients and take care of ordering and sending out the gifts. Though he never retained the names, Bob Williams estimated he painted one hundred mugs for *The Alamo*.[1035]

Trouble again plagued the beleaguered set on the early afternoon of November 15 as a building at Ft. Clark burst into flames. Built in 1857, the structure originally had served as the commanding officer's quarters and then post headquarters. Following World War I, the building was expanded, doubling its size with additional office space and a second story added by 1943. The building faced the fort's original parade grounds and sat adjacent to the Duplex Officer's

Quarters (Officer's Mess and Club) and Post Theater. Now serving as Batjac's administrative headquarters, and providing temporary housing for members of the cast and crew, it was quickly engulfed in flames despite everyone's best efforts.[1036]

The payroll, accounting, and casting departments were on the first floor and assistant director Relyea had a room on the second floor along with two second assistants and several script clerks. A Sunday with no work scheduled, many cast and crew members had the day off. Relyea took a late morning nap in his room. Awakened by a sound in the attic, he thought it was the wind and soon fell asleep again. But stuntman Bob Morgan had just finished lunch in the mess hall across the parade ground. As he left, he noticed the flames, raced to the blaze, entered the building, and began searching for occupants. Finding Relyea on the second floor, he woke the AD, yelled at him to get his briefcase as Morgan already had his boots, and led him to safety. By this time, the stairwell was already engulfed in flames, and everything Relyea owned was eventually destroyed, save his car, a brand-new Triumph TR3 parked outside the structure. Four other stuntmen picked it up and carried it to safe ground. Between eight and twenty crewmembers in the living quarters were evacuated without incident, and most of the equipment and supplies stored on the first floor were safely removed. [1037]

Batjac had its own fire truck on site, but, when crewmen jumped into the cab to start it up, they quickly realized the fuel tank was empty. Hoses were hauled by hand to the building, but, by then, the fire was out of control. Firefighters from Brackettville, Del Rio, and Laughlin Air Force Base helped Batjac personnel (actors Ken Curtis and John Dierkes among them) battle the blaze. Glen Tetens, Ft. Clark manager, reported the fire began on the second floor and estimated damage at $75,000. It was believed the fire may have been started due to an oil furnace malfunction or faulty kerosene heater. There even were unsubstantiated rumors it had been deliberately set to destroy second-unit footage shot by John Ford, but Relyea said film was never stored in that building. Fortunately, many personal belongings of the building's residents were salvaged.[1038]

Most importantly, one of the items destroyed was the Master script. "The assistant directors all had various parts of scripts," according to Minnex, "but the Master script, which you always keep one copy of absolutely everything that's been done, or is to be done (was destroyed). And it burned while Wayne, I guess, was in Acuña at the bullfights. Everybody went to the bullfights on Sunday, and the production office burned. The Master script burned, and there was hell to pay. I mean, that night, around there, we could tell that there was trouble. Because there were really people...furious. I understand that somebody called Wayne at dinner after the bullfights and that he really blew his top. And grabbed up the production manager, an older, fat, factotum...high man in his own field, but not a glamour figure or anything, and threatened to slap him around. And did hit him, I was told. They came roaring back to Brackettville, to where we were all staying, and there were all sorts of emergency meetings in the dining hall all night, trying to piece together the complete script. Then somebody was assigned to the viewing rooms to make a new record of everything that had been shot, because that had all been lost. There were bits and pieces but nobody knew for sure if, let's say, the third Thursday when you were out in the meadow, you got all the shots listed, so there was somebody assigned to redo, to re-record all the takes so that they would have a master log of what the footage was. Maybe that's what was lost, the master log, not the shooting script per se. Because there would be lots of copies of that…and he really was beside himself. The payoff to that story is that there is this little accounting-type man…two days later, Wayne gave him a $3,000 watch as an apology." (Relyea explained, "The script supervisor keeps a little report that she gets from the camera assistants as to how much film was used and what takes—this confirms which takes were printed and everything else. Now, that gets built into the production report that the assistant director and production manager put together. If you found Duke's script or mine, you would have known exactly what day what was shot. If you are doing a three-page scene (for example), and you shoot half today, you draw a line down your script, and for a page and a half, you draw further down the page and then you put the date in. You remember you've still got a piece left to do. That's just standard procedure.")[1039]

Relyea's cousin Gene was also there that day. "I searched through the ashes for anything that might be saved," says Gene, "and believe it or not, the only thing I found was Bob's script. It was singed around the edges, but it was OK. That was actually very important, because it contained all his production notes, and we would have been lost without them. That was the good news. The bad news was that Ft. Clark told us they didn't have any insurance to cover personal loss. Why? God only knows. To add insult to injury, neither did Batjac Productions, Wayne's company, which was producing the picture. They said they could give us a pay advance to buy clothes, but that was about it. Shopping for clothes in Brackettville with its one general store and gas station didn't seem ideal. Bob and I both had our personal cars down there, his Triumph and my MGA. Just on a whim, Bob called Brooks-Randall insurance, who carried the policy on both our cars. As luck would have it, some little clause, which we both probably paid $4.00 a year for and bitched about it, covered everything under travel coverage. They wired us a bunch of money, and Sunday we drove to Del Rio and restocked the wardrobe. After that, every location I went on, I checked the insurance policy."

In addition to the master log, payroll records, invoices, correspondence, and employee information were irretrievably lost despite valiant attempts to remove filing cabinets and records from the inferno. Syndicated columnist Joe Hyams discussed the lost records in a letter to Fred Goldberg. Through tear-sheets sent to Batjac from various sources including editors, friends, and UA, they were able to determine that news items appeared in both major and minor newspapers throughout the land. "The entire walls of the publicity department were covered by these tear-sheets," Hyams wrote. "On the day of the fire we tried to salvage them but were not too successful. By the time we removed the desks, files, and other furniture, the office was filled with smoke, and as important as tear-sheets are to a press-agent, we said the hell with it."[1040]

Apparently, the weekend of November 14/15 was very action-packed. Not only was a portion of the "Spirit" television special filmed, but there was also a bullfight, a fire, and a good old-fashioned barroom brawl. No doubt upset about Elena Da Vinci's departure, Henaghan got drunk one evening, as his wont, and started making derogatory comments about Duke. When his remarks were relayed to Wayne, Duke sent for the complaining publicist. Henaghan informed the messenger that if Wayne wanted to see him, he knew where to find him. A confrontation was inevitable. Subsequently, Duke and Pilar were having dinner Saturday evening along with photographer Phil Stern, Don LaCava, Ken Curtis, and a few others. Henaghan was at a nearby table, pounding down drinks as was Wayne. Allegedly, Henaghan voiced several extremely vile comments about Pilar, whereupon an enraged Wayne slugged Henaghan. Harvey attempted to intervene and got thrown into a window or set of venetian blinds. Says LaCava, "I was there the evening that Henaghan got on his high horse and rode off into the dust. Wayne wasn't the kind of guy that got into fisticuffs over nothing." Mike Wayne agreed, "Harvey learned that day there is no time to check I.D.s in a fist fight." Wayne was upset—upset that his wife was insulted, upset that Henaghan would conduct his business in such an unethical manner. He may have even told the publicist he wasn't going to honor their financial agreement. Nevertheless, Henaghan showed up at Relyea's bungalow later that evening, "and looked to me like his nose was broken, and (asked) could he have the keys to a car—it was like three o'clock in the morning and he was going to San Antonio. And I said sure, I'll call down, and I'll have a car brought up for you, and he didn't say anything." Henaghan was furious: "Wayne likes to believe that he is relentlessly honorable and that his word is his bond. This is not true, any more than it is true that any man is entirely honorable. Wayne has been known to pull some pretty strange deals, with the help of business associates who lay no claim to honesty. He would like to be in life a John Wayne character in a movie, but he has never quite made it. His ambition is well-buttressed by an almost egomaniac belief in himself."[1041]

(Henaghan could be less than honorable himself. According to photographer Sam Shaw, Duke and Henaghan had a violent friendship: "(Henaghan) was one of the best press agents in Hollywood. A great Irish character. Perhaps the only guy who'd drink Wayne under the table...one of the few guys who'd stand up to Wayne. One day after a wild drinking spree, they found themselves in Acapulco, on a patio in one of their favorite watering holes. In the distance, divers were jumping off a two hundred-foot precipice. Below, tremendous waves smashed against jutting rocks." Henaghan bet Wayne a round of drinks that he could do that, so Duke accepted the challenge. Henaghan went down the steps, hid behind a cactus and paid a diver to wear Henaghan's red trunks. As the diver dove off the cliffs, it appeared from a distance it was Henaghan. Continued Shaw, "When the diver came out behind the bushes, Henaghan went into the water, got himself wet, took back his trunks, put them on. Then he came back: everybody applauded. Jim said, 'I did it!' Wayne said, 'You son-of-a-bitch! You really did it! The drinks are on me.' And Wayne had to buy drinks for everyone on the patio.")[1042]

Russell Birdwell now appeared. "I got a call from Henaghan that Duke wanted me," recalled the publicist. "I would be a kind of a consultant, and not take it as a contract...And then I got a call from Jimmy Grant one a.m. about six, calling from Brackettville, Texas, that Wayne and Jim had a fight, that Wayne had slapped him, and would I catch a plane and come down. They had been shooting about three weeks, so I flew down, and Duke said will you handle the picture, showed me rushes, and cut films, read the script also. We ran the rushes, and Jack Ford sat in. I was terribly impressed with what I saw and closed the deal then and there. When I finished looking at the rushes, went to Wayne's bungalow, and I asked him to tell me why he wanted to make *The Alamo*. He told me as articulate story I ever heard about why he wanted to do the film. I could have made a whole campaign on Wayne's beautiful explanation of why he was doing it. The gist of it was human individuality, self reliance, being willing to die for your country and its freedoms." Birdwell, formerly in charge of special promotions, would take over Henaghan's position: director of advertising, publicity and exploitation. With a fee in excess of $200,000 and a $1 million budget to cover radio, TV time, and newspaper and magazine space, Birdwell would supervise the work of both Joe Hyams and the Milton Weiss Associates. (Hyams would depart Batjac in January 1960. UA is said to have complained about the fee being charged against the project, but a spokesperson denied any such intention. The studio didn't know what Birdwell would receive but indicated it would pay the amount as soon as it understood the deal made between Wayne and Birdwell).[1043]

Though Henaghan was no longer on the set, the family would still be represented. Jim Henaghan Jr. told his mother (actress/dancer) Gwen Verdon he would appear in *The Alamo*. "It's only one scene, but I do talk." Verdon saw him in his stage debut, playing one of the Wise Men in a Christmas pageant. "His role wasn't much," she beamed, "but he was significant. Offstage, his talk is sheer fantasy, but onstage it has truth." By way of celebrating, his parents gave the sixteen-year-old permission to smoke.[1044]

Even the stuntmen got involved in that weekend's shenanigans. While Wayne was in Acuña watching Arruza perform his magic in the bullring, so were several stuntmen, accompanied by girls from the local cat house in Boy's Town. After the bullfight, Dean Smith, who was also there, went off to buy a few Mexican wedding shirts while Roberson and the others headed to Garcia's Bar, a local watering hole. As Smith had a car, Roberson asked Dean to come and take him back to Brackettville after he was done with his errands. Several hours later, Dean did just that but Roberson was pretty drunk. As the duo left the bar, they were accosted by two Mexican cops who took them to jail, frisked them and relieved them of all their money. Smith, stone-cold sober, was furious but what could he do. After a time, he was taken to meet the resident jailer who told him his fine was $12, exactly the amount of money the cops had taken from him. Imagine that. Eventually, Roberson was freed as well, and the two crossed the border back into Texas. When Dean asked Bad Chuck what had happened, all Roberson could remember was that a bunch of airmen from Del Rio got into a fight, and Chuck and the other stuntmen tried to break it up. Yeah, right. Says Dean, "To this day every time someone wants to go to Mexico, my mind goes back to the one and only time in jail when I hadn't done damn thing but try to help a buddy. Needless to say, I stay the hell out of Mexico."[1045]

While the stuntmen *entertained* local señoritas, Wayne and his party were at a barbeque, hosted by General Quinones. Held on his 20,000-acre Paso de las Mulas ranch about forty miles south of Acuña, the entire cast was invited. While there, Pilar asked Frances, the General's wife, where the jelly glasses were. "Jelly glasses?" she replied. Pilar said, "Yes, when we have parties, at the end of the party, we bring out old glassware that we don't want anymore, and that way the guests know that they can pour their drinks into the jelly glasses and take them home, and (you won't) lose your fine crystal." Frances said, "Well, I don't know, but my mom used to put up a lot of fruit and vegetables and what have you, and she had mason jars. What about these?" Pilar was thrilled. "Oh, that would be perfect!" According the General's son Robert, "They quickly got two or three boxes of mason jars and washed them and put them out for the guests, and sure enough, the guests poured their drinks into the mason jars and off they went."[1046]

Despite all the aforementioned problems, Wayne was thrilled. The film was coming together, his vision crystallized. But enthusiasm may have gotten the better of him because in mid-November he announced his next project. Upon completion of *North to Alaska* in late 1960, Duke would continue the saga of Texas by filming the story of Sam Houston. Scheduled for the end of 1960 and written by Grant based on research from Lon Tinkle, the "sweeping historical drama" would depict Houston's early career as the organizer of the Texas army of independence and founder of the Texas Republic. According to Joe Hyams, the idea for the project came from one of Lon Tinkle's frequent visits to the set. Tinkle's colorful description of Houston fired the interest of both Wayne and Grant, and they decided on the spot that "the famous Texas soldier-statesman's life was not only a stirring chapter of American history, but that, like the story of *The Alamo* cried to be put on film." Once again, Wayne would approach Brando to play the pivotal role. Louella Parsons broke the news that parts of the movie would be filmed in Tennessee, and Wayne would play the part of Andrew Jackson. Coincidentally, Texas oil millionaire Glenn McCarthy also announced development of a new three-dimensional widescreen process that didn't require using viewing glasses. Supposedly an investor in Wayne's film, McCarthy indicated the first film made that utilized the new process would be the *Battle of San Jacinto*. The tycoon, who had previously produced *Five Bold Women*, said he was currently in discussion with Wayne to appear in the 3-D movie.[1047]

Finally completing the nighttime shooting, Wayne again began to schedule day sequences during the week of November 16. Focusing on the size of the Mexican army, he first filmed scene 335: the arrival of Santa Anna, the buildup of Mexican troops and the subsequent departure of all noncombatants from the Alamo. Emotional, passionate, moving, the characters knew this would be the last time they would see their families and each other. As usual, Wayne filmed much more than what eventually appeared on screen: fathers saying goodbye to children, husbands kissing wives one final time. Extra Maydelle Anderson said, "We were the ladies. I'm sure we were stand-ins, but we were supposedly the last ladies that were leaving the Alamo…It was a lot of fun. There were two younger ladies. We were in our thirties. And the other ladies were older ladies… probably in their forties. The four of us came together. The lady that was my age, she was probably a movie buff because her family owned the movie (theater in Eagle Pass.) Her name was Eve Schwartz. We drove back and forth. Sometimes, we drove early in the morning and stayed all day and stayed till dark. We'd get dressed every day and be ready with our shawls in the old-timey dresses that we wore at the time and age but…I can't remember other than they'd say get in the wagon and we'd get in the wagon. Or they'd say come sit over here, go walk over there. Just hanging around…we were in the covered wagon; it was just a wagon that was leaving the Alamo. At the end of the movie, I know the four of us were in that wagon… I remember because it was the last one, so I thought we'll be sure to see each other (in the movie). I want to say we just got paid $10 a day. We got to eat in the commissary. We were there several nights, so we must have worked for a whole week." Young Tim Cumiskey, also, was in that departure scene. "I've got several scenes," says Tim, "(and) one of them is when the noncombatants are leaving the Alamo and there's that wagon train sort of thing. My mother drove a wagon—not a wagon but a buggy. I got put in the back of a wagon, and I go right past the camera, and I'm holding on to this woman's hand that was supposed to be my mother at that point. Everybody is supposed to look sad as you're leaving, and I go right past the camera on that one." Siblings Barbara Wills White and Elaine Moody also were in that scene but sadly, their portion was cut. Ford also filmed a scene of some of the defenders standing motionless as they watch the noncombatants leave the Alamo compound. Said Rudy Robbins, "(Ford) had the camera aimed at me as the central figure, and several others in the scene. The arc light was so close to my face and so hot it made tears fall down my cheeks. I think he thought I was acting!"[1048]

One of the funniest stories that came out of filming this sequence involved Guinn Williams and Toni LaCava. As Lt. "Irish" Finn, Williams approaches a pioneer woman with a small child on her lap who is leaving the Alamo. "Ma'am?" he asks. "I ain't got no woman to say goodbye to. Could I tell you goodbye?" She replies, "Surely." Ford directed the scene, Duke's beautiful daughter Toni played the pioneer woman, her one-year-old daughter Anita was the baby. But Williams and/or Toni continually flubbed their lines and after several unsuccessful attempts to film the scene, the company took a break. Toni related, "We had just finished lunch, venison stew, and we got into the wagons lined up that were leaving. My daughter was sitting on my lap, and we were about ready to shoot, and she threw up on my hand! It was too late to do anything but wipe if off on my dress. Big Boy said his line, and the only line I had was 'Surely', but I couldn't get it out. I couldn't keep from laughing, and, after the second take, JW said, 'What's so God damn funny? Get the God damn thing right this time!' I got it right on the third take." Toni's husband Don seems to remember it took as many as a half-dozen. Anita says her mother told her Williams knew the hand had baby barf on it because Toni had told him before the scene started. She felt horrible. "Oh, my god," Toni said. "The poor guy had just kissed my hand in that scene, you know? I just felt so sorry for him. I have one line in the movie, and they have to dub it because my voice was so low it sounded like a man, saying the word 'Surely.'" According to some, Toni smoked like a chimney. Maybe that's why her voice was so husky and very sexy. Beautiful but self-conscious, she also was very near-sighted. Always squinting. People were constantly asking her to model and she'd reply, "Are you kidding me? I can't see two feet in front of me. I couldn't even walk down the ramp." And, frankly, she was just plain nervous. Of her dad, the director, Toni confessed, "He's…he's, you're afraid. You can't blink because you're afraid that they're going to have to redo the scene because of you. And, you know, he would say, 'Every time we have to redo the scene, that's a million dollars,' or whatever." She would try to do her very best because she didn't want to be the one that was chastised for ruining a scene.

Pilar recalled one day on the set when she and Toni portrayed women who were permitted to leave the Alamo during the siege. Supposedly, Duke directed Patrick, Toni, Aissa and her all in the same scene. However, anecdotal and photographic evidence do not support that claim. First, Patrick, as Bonham, wasn't in the Alamo at that time during the film as he was out searching for reinforcements. Second, both Patrick and Aissa as supporting characters are too readily identifiable to be inserted in a scene as extras. Third, Toni was already in that sequence with her daughter Anita and Guinn Williams. Although Pilar indicated the scene was filmed during the day, perhaps she was referring to the flamenco night scene. Regardless, one wonders what might have been had all family members appeared together in the same scene. Most Wayne family members were on the corporate payroll, but Toni and her daughter played their roles for free. "I'm afraid to look at Michael," Duke confessed. "He might take over there, and we'd be arguing salary for those two!"[1049]

Veda Ann Borg would have her turn in the spotlight as well. Wearing contact lenses so she seemed blind, she would give an inspiring affirmation of her love for her husband and a rousing endorsement of his ability and devotion. *"Shut up, Jim Bowie! And you and Travis listen close. My man ain't going out! He's just as much a man as either one of you, and maybe more! In spite of, he ain't rich like you, Jim, or fancy educated like you, Will Travis. Now, Jocko, you get back up on that wall, 'cause you're as good as any man that ever trod leather, and it's your right! And I can't see, but I'm just as good as any woman in Texas, and it's my right to go and leave you. Now we've cuddled nice and said all our goodbyes, but I'll say it again. We'd be fools not to face it; you're likely to go and get yourself killed in this battle, and I don't know what you're going to say going through the gates of heaven, but I'm gonna say that no woman ever lived had herself a better husband than you've been to me. Now, go on!"*

Bruce Minnex always liked her as an actress and thought this part was one of the best things she'd ever done. He recalled the first time he saw her on the set: "I had always liked her as a kind of brassy broad that I just enjoyed in film, and we had gotten settled into the house the first afternoon, and we were just getting ready to have a drink before going over to the dining hall, and in walked this vision from Madison Avenue: full-skirted, kind of pistachio-green cotton dress, a real garden dress, summer dress. Nice jewelry. Big picture hat with ribbons and clear plastic spike-heel sandals. It was wonderful. And she walked in. And she said, 'You're the New York boys, right?' And we said yes. She said, 'Okay. I figured you gotta have good martinis. I need one, and I don't wanna talk none of this motion picture crap.' And she put her feet up on the coffee table, and we became fast friends. She was just wonderful. She didn't want to talk to any of the Hollywood people for a while. She was just a fun person."[1050]

Veda absolutely relished her part and gave everything she had to make the role come alive. And others wanted a chance to speak on screen. Big John Hamilton had been instrumental in getting Tommy Worrell a part in the film as an extra, so naturally Worrell turned to his friend when he wanted some dialogue. "He's John Wayne's buddy, and he's going to help us out," recalls Worrell. "He kept telling me and my friend that he knows from San Antonio, 'I'm going to get you boys some speaking lines.' Oh, great! And about every third day or so, (Tommy would ask), 'Big John, you got those…' 'I'm going to get 'em.' And every time he'd see me, 'Pretty soon, pretty soon.' And then one day, he said, 'Today's the day.' Boy, were we excited and ready. It was, *'Hip hip hooray, hip hip hooray, hip hip hooray!'* Everybody said it. So he was pulling our leg, but they were speaking lines."[1051]

Speaking of pulling legs, Padilla pulled off a great gag. "One day at lunch," recalled Ruben, "I made a suggestion to a bunch of the Mexican extras working in the picture as Santa Anna's troops. I didn't tell them I was kidding. I said,

'Look. Texas belongs to Mexico. It was literally stolen from us. What I'm going to propose to you is dangerous, so if you want to forget it, OK...I can get live ammunition...' At this point, everyone became very tense. I told them, 'We'll get this tall guy—what's his name? Win? Wino? We kidnap him and contact Washington. We'll give him back if the United States will give us Texas back.' One colonel said he had a family to think of. Another said the U.S. Army was only two hours away and, 'They'll wipe us out.' I said, 'Yes. But we'll die as heroes.' The next day, I had lunch alone."[1052]

On Tuesday, November 17, Pappy returned to Brackettville. For the third time. By now, Ford had been on-site for twenty-six out of forty-one days; everyone was painfully aware he wasn't down there on vacation. He wasn't there to look over Duke's shoulders—he was there to help make a movie. When he was on the set, he directed the scene. It was as simple as that. After he arrived, one of the first things he did was to review scenes previously filmed. Watching the cattle stampede, he told Wayne, "Duke, you haven't got a shot of these four hundred longhorns coming over your camera. Got 'em here. Got 'em there, crossed the river, stampeded 'em. (But) the film's not going to be good if you don't get that (shot)." Wayne acquiesced, "All right. Cliff Lyons, you take Bill Daniel. We'll dig a big hole over here, (place a camera in it) and see if (Daniel) can (herd) them over that hole." Cocking an eyebrow, Daniel explained to Wayne: "I said, 'Duke, these cattle are different from Herefords you got in Arizona and Black Angus that my beloved friend Happy Shahan raised here. They're not going to do that. They're not going to go (there). They like to go (where they want). I can't put them over that hole.' He said, 'Will you do it and try?' And I said, 'Well, certainly I will.' (And, we) used pistols (to direct the stampede). I was a point man 'cause they didn't understand about these longhorns." Joan O'Brien clearly recalls hiding in her dressing room. "I was there," she confesses. "I remember (that) day very well because they said, 'You better get in there and close your door because they're going to stampede a bunch of Texas through here.'" Added Daniel, "... they brought a drag line in here, right east of the church and...we got the cattle, and I drove them through here a time or two to let them get used to this area here. Had my cowboys, and we stampeded them... across this hole." Regrettably, all that work and this sequence would not appear in the final print.[1053]

Earlier, Wayne had filmed Lisa's birthday party and Curtis's schmaltzy rendition of "Tennessee Babe." Now it was time to complete the party sequence, which was scripted to run well into the evening with everyone dancing and generally having a wonderful time. Nineteen-year-old Brackenridge High School graduate Buddy Ochoa recalled he was given a single line of dialogue in that scene. To his dismay, Guinn Williams came out of the Alamo and broke up a dance that Ochoa was participating in. Buddy cried, "Oh, no, Finn. No." He added, "It enabled me to get a Screen Actors Guild card, something you can't get until you have a speaking part. Now, in any other movie in which I appear, they will have to let me speak." Veda Ann Borg and John Dierkes, surrounded by merry defenders, were filmed in an extended sequence where they were shown, dancing, swinging each other around, and enjoying the festivities. Unfortunately, it ended up on the cutting room floor.[1054]

Aissa Wayne says one of her most pleasant memories was dancing with Chill Wills. Duke first rehearsed the scene with her and then turned duties over to Wills. "That was my favorite thing to do," admits Aissa. "It was because Chill Wills…Chill Wills was so sweet, and it was just so cool that my feet were on top of his feet, and I was dancing. No, that was not scary, that was a fun thing. In fact, my dad had a bunch of pictures from *The Alamo* on his walls, and I took (some) out of the house after he passed away, the ones with me in them and one of them I'm looking at it right now. Chill Wills has me on his feet and then dancing with me, and they've got their Davy Crockett hats on, and that, to me, was so much fun. I thought that was really cool that Chill Wills would dance with me, and that was really neat. I loved everything on that movie."

Well, maybe almost everything. "I was afraid of (John Ford), but I never really knew to the extent that my dad was afraid of him," she adds. "I knew that my dad would say, 'Hell, you know, Pappy Ford's the only guy that I'm, that I'm scared of.' And I would always think it was a joke, but, in reading some of these biographies, I realize that was maybe true. I'd watch this old guy on the set with the cigar hanging out of his mouth and the eye patch and everything, and he'd be ordering my dad around, which would be really different." No surprise there. When he was on the set, everybody was afraid of him.[1055]

Recalled Chuck Hayward, "Ford came down when we were doing *The Alamo*, and he shot a segment of it, and I went with him. Well, he had a second unit so to speak, but he also had Cliff Lyons there as a second unit director, and there were things that Duke had set out for the Old Man, and the Old Man would say, 'Oh, hell. I don't want to shoot that. Let Lyons shoot it,' and the Old Man would be shooting the soldiers coming here, something here and there." Ford also directed one of the best stunts in the film. After cattle were driven into the compound and all defenders were safely inside, a lone Mexican dragoon charged the main gate, intent on shooting Travis, who had remained outside directing its defense. Calmly, coolly, Travis took aim, gently squeezed the trigger and fired at the rider. One shot, one kill. The dragoon fell backward, flipped off the horse, spun on the ground, and lay dead. Hayward was the dragoon. "I do a rollover drag on (that). (Ford) shot that," he said. "It was shot right. It's a rollover drag that you are hung up, not by your foot, but by your arm, and you go square over the back end of the horse, and then you drag for a just a little bit and then release. You've got the strap fastened back of the saddle that you can't see, and, when you roll over backwards to keep your head up from driving into the ground, you've got that strap that turns you over on. Then, it goes from your shoulder down to your elbow and then down your wrists, and you hang on for about two strides, and it will have you airborne above the ground, and, when you release it, you go into your tumble. It's a very effective shot. (Ford also directed Harvey in that scene) because it was all one sequence, and he probably shot both of them. Most of the stuff Ford shot was not used because he wouldn't do what they told him—what Duke told him." Nevertheless, it was an extremely effective and exciting scene. (Stills taken that day showed a suited executive in the background observing the scene on the south wall. Fortunately, he isn't seen in the film).[1056]

The closer to Thanksgiving, the greater the pressure Duke felt. He had to work quickly; since battle sequences would be filmed starting November 24, he had to complete all remaining interior scenes by then. By November 20, except for O'Brien, all female actors left the set, their scenes completed and promotional responsibilities fulfilled. The KTLA crew wrapped up filming its television special and left earlier in the week, and, several days later, Tiomkin returned on location, so, while Wayne continued shooting interior scenes, Cliff Lyons focused on upcoming battle sequences.

Tons of gunpowder and gallons of movie blood had previously been purchased; now it was time to put them to use. Sandpits were dug, and the hard Southwest Texas ground was turned over to soften the falls for horses and stuntmen. Paths were cleared of rocks and brush—anything that could potentially cause injury. Removal of debris was absolutely critical for safety of both horse and rider. Hal Needham, though not in the show, described one method in which horses were taught to perform stunts: "Training a horse to fall on cue is, I think, the most difficult horse stunt there is, because it's so much against his nature. To train a 'falling horse,' I have to work with him for, at least, a year, and it isn't until you used him three or four years that he gets really good. First you tie his leg up with a rope on a pulley, pull his head around very easy and get him to lie down. That way you assure him he isn't going to get hurt. You do this over and over and over. Then you do it at a walk; pull his leg with a rope, pull his head around, lay him down. Finally you get to the point where he knows that, when you pull his head around, you want him to fall. Then you try it out. Sometimes you get lucky, and you've got him trained. Other times you wind (up) thirty feet out in front of the others, and they're standing there looking at you. When you train a falling horse, you really hurt him in the mouth. I have to put more pressure on his mouth than he gets when he hits the ground. The only reason he falls is that he knows I'm going to hurt him in the mouth if he doesn't. But people who don't know horses don't see that on the screen. They can't know how much abuse that horse has gone through."[1057]

Previously, trainers would use a technique called the *Running W*. A thin wire or cable would be attached to leg bands on the horse's front fetlocks. It would then be run through slip rings on the saddle cinch underneath the horse. The other end would be solidly attached to a post or stake buried in the ground. The wire was given a great deal of slack to allow the horse to build up a strong, full gallop. When the wire was taut, the horse's leg was pulled out from underneath him, throwing the rider to the ground and resulting in a spectacular though dangerous fall. Fortunately, the American Humane Association outlawed the practice. An AHA inspector had been assigned to the location in Brackettville to assure the safety of any animal used in the production. These field representatives are always animal experts. Their backgrounds might include U.S Cavalry experience, being a former rider on the rodeo circuit, a genuine working cowboy, or a horse breeder. Traveling wherever the movie company shoots its scenes, the AHA inspector brings to the attention of an assistant director or the head wrangler, or anyone concerned with the staging of the animal action, any acts which are not in the best interest of the performing animals. Running W's were not used in *The Alamo*.[1058]

A horse is usually around four years old before training to fall begins. By this time, the bones are strong, and the temperament is established. A horse must be limber of neck since the turning of it is critical in training. Using stirrups specially made so a man's foot wouldn't get hung up, stuntmen would train their horses over and over for various falls. Some stirrups are cut on the outside, so, in the event a rider isn't able to fully remove his foot before the horse hits the ground, at least, it isn't caught in the stirrup. Other stirrups may be made of pliable rubber so as not to injure either horse or rider. In most cases, the saddle horn is taken off before the stunt. Once the drop area is established, the ground is dug and made soft. Some sort of marker, a piece of paper, a twig, etc., is placed on the stop where the fall is to take place. Depending upon the length of the horse's stride, the stuntman then determines when to pull and turn the reins. It must be a stride or two before the fall area to insure he falls on the correct spot. If several stuntmen fall simultaneously in the same area, caution must be taken to assure both horses and riders do not gallop over each other. When explosives are used, they must be timed, so they don't discharge under the horse.[1059]

Just as there is a hierarchy in the acting profession, so is there in the equine profession: *Extras'* horses, of all colors and sizes, have one thing in common—they must be gentle. Frequently, the extras have never ridden before, and the horses must be reliable and not buck off amateur riders; *Stunt* horses are trained to fall, jump, and gallop on command; *Specialty* horses have a special routine or appearance used in a film, and *Star* horses are selected for personality, appearance, and talent. Star horses also have doubles and stand-ins just as their human stars do. Stand-ins are brought in between takes when lights are adjusted and camera exposures set. If the star horse was used instead, they could get fidgety and nervous during the long process. This way, the star horse comes in fresh and willing to concentrate on his cues.[1060]

Training horses to work around arc lights and ignore gunfire took constant practice. The trainer would start by firing blanks some distance from the horse and gradually move closer. If you are on a horse and you fire a gun, most always you are firing forward with your arm stretched out. Add six inches for the gun barrel, and that puts the muzzle almost over the horse's head. It's going to make his ears ring, so the horse's ears are packed with cotton whenever the actor has to shoot. Light loads of powder were also used to only produce muzzle flash. The actual shot would be replaced by sound effects in the editing room.[1061]

While Lyons worked with horses and stuntmen, ex-Marine Sergeant and Navy Chief Petty Officer Jack Pennick trained the extras. "He would drill the soldiers," said artist John Jensen. "He had a real tough face, look like you could strike a match on it. He was in a lot of Ford (movies), used to play sergeants. And he'd have these guys doing close order drill and in three days, they were a crack outfit, let me tell you." Described by "Wild Bill" Donovan as "the most perfect soldier I have ever met," and by Ford as that "big six-foot-four-and-a-half mick," Pennick taught extras a course in basic military indoctrination: how to hold a rifle, how to march. Left face, right face. "Square that hat!" March in formation. He encouraged competition by dividing his troops into twelve drill teams; the most professional teams would get close-ups. Pennick also worked on *The Robe*. After working with "Roman army" extras for several weeks, he was asked by director Howard Koster: "How do you know Romans drilled that way?" Without missing a beat, Pennick replied, "Well, Mr. Koster. I'm positive no one in the audience will stand up and say we're wrong."[1062]

Even Ford got involved with the troops. Denver Pyle observed, "Wayne didn't have the way with actors or people the way Mr. Ford had. He didn't have to speak their language; he could get people to work. Like, he knew a little bit of Spanish to work with all the Spanish soldiers and so forth. He had a way of communicating with them. We'd be going to go out and the old man would say, 'Listen, I want to go out tomorrow and do some attacks on the wall. You're not working tomorrow, so let's get out of here, and we'll get over there and get us some of those Mexicans and form our own unit...Go to the wardrobe man, I want about fifty red patches, just round red patches. about that big around.' I said, 'All right.' So I went to the wardrobe man, and I said, 'Mr. Ford needs fifty red patches this big.' He said, 'All right, does he want them...' 'No, just red patches.' He said, 'Where am I going to get red...' Ford just used to drive the wardrobe man and the prop man nuts."

Pyle continued, "Like when we were shooting on *The Horse Soldiers*. I made some comment about (how) great (the prop men) were. And (Ford) said, 'Oh, they're marvelous. Marvelous. Watch this.' And he called over the...prop man. And he said, 'Charlie. I need an alligator, a stuffed alligator about that long.' And he said, 'Yes, sir,' and he turned and ran. (Ford) looked at me and said, 'He has no idea where he's going to get a stuffed alligator that long, (but) he'll come back with something.' And, sure enough, he came back and he said, 'Mr. Ford. I don't have a stuffed alligator, but would an alligator hide be all right? And Ford said, 'Yeah, that'll be just great. Keep that for me.'"

As for the red patches, the wardrobe man noted, "I got a stamp for (the) seals." So, according to Pyle, "...he got some red bunting, and he stamped out fifty red seals that had a little serration around the thing. And he gave those to me. So I gave them to Mr. Ford, and I didn't know what he was going to do with them. The next morning, Mr. Ford and I went out and looked at all the Mexican extras that were working around the Alamo, and he picked out a little division or a squad (of) fifty guys. And he had them all lined up, and he said, 'Attention!' He said, 'Denver, come with me. You stay on my left shoulder.' So he and I walked down this line. He looked at them, and he examined them all. Fixed a little wardrobe, (and) they all immediately knew they were special. Then, he went back, and I had brought a staple gun. And he said, 'All right, give me the gun.' I gave him the staple gun, and we went back down the line, and he took off their hats, took one of these red patches, put it on, and stapled it up. And put the hat back on and he said, 'Now, you know you're a soldier of Mr. Ford.' And they all stood a little bit taller and a little bit straighter. They were all now somebody now. Nobody else in the whole set, in all the group, had a hat with a patch on it, like a Ford patch. Now, what he did, he had these guys. They were special."[1063]

But it always didn't go as planned. Happy recalled, "I remember one time when I had been gone for three or four days and returned to see (Ford) training the second unit soldiers for the picture. He said, 'Where have you been? Sit down. I've been trying all day to get this marching unit from Mexico trained.' They would show on camera, but there wasn't any sound involved. He said, 'We'll be through in a minute; we're going to wrap it.' They were shooting the picture silent, without sound. Ford yelled, 'Action,' and the camera began rolling. About that time, someone in the next to the last row—somebody who obviously hadn't been listening to Mr. Ford—started hollering to me in Mexican and waving, ruining the scene, of course. Well, Mr. Ford screamed at him, 'You-son-of-a-bitch. Get off this set and don't ever come back!' That was the kind of thing that could really rile him."[1064]

On Saturday, November 21, Hank (Parson) Worden had the honor of being the first major supporting player to die in the film, though the explosion that caused his death would be filmed later. *"I'm glad you come, Davy. I wanted to thank you. From the bottom of my heart, I wanted to thank you. Davy, I've seen the world because of you. Seventy years, I lived in a small settlement, and then you brung me here to see a far country. I always wanted to travel, Davy, but I had to stay home. There was always a child to raise, and it was like a divine gift when you said, 'Come along if you want to, old man, but don't do any praying over me.' That's what you said...I just wanted you to know I was grateful."*

Ted White doubled the actor in the explosion just after we see Worden

535

moving in a crouch along the West Wall, stooped over and carrying a bucket of gunpowder or ammunition. Reaching the top of a room as he climbs two steps, it collapses when a shell explodes under him, throwing Worden to the ground. Forty-four-year-old photographer A.Y. Owen stood behind the camera as Hank's death scene was being filmed. Owen explained his presence on the set: "I covered about the last ten days shooting when most of the death scenes were photographed, Duke's, Widmark's, Chill Wills. Lawrence Harvey. I had just finished a *LIFE* magazine assignment in San Antonio and, as usual, called the news bureau chief in New York City. He said he had received a call from Rus Birdwell asking for a recommendation for a photographer who could shoot *LIFE*-type pictures, and that he had suggested me. I received a phone call from Birdwell and Batjak (sic) productions, then flew (in) a small plane (that) pick(ed) me up at San Antonio and returned to Brackettville." Commissioned by Wayne to shoot stills on location, Owen now found his perfect opportunity. After the Parson dies, Crockett takes off his hat, looks toward the sky, and delivers an emotional appeal: *"We haven't had many conversations, sir. Only time I've ever called on you is when I wanted something, when I was in a tight, like a little boy hollering for his pa. And now, I want something again. I brought these men down here, without askin' 'em did they want a piece of this war. It's a failing of mine—deciding for others. So, if you can find it clear to let these men live through this battle, I'll be forever thankful. But if your stick don't float that way, please to remember, sir, these are good men. All!"* Watching this, Owen noted intensity in Wayne he had never seen before. Using his telephoto lens, he quickly, though deliberately, shot two photos. Owen's personal favorites, Wayne used one of them to promote the film. Three days before he passed away in 1979, Duke personally selected that photo to also be used as his likeness for the Congressional medal struck in is honor. On the back of the medallion is a relief of Wayne on horseback riding through Monument Valley. (Don Clark included the following story in his book on the making of Wayne's film: "Wayne had been complaining about all the still photographers ruining scenes with the 'clicking' of their cameras. He brought them all together after observing the way Owen was shooting with his telescopic lens and told them to, 'Start shooting the way A.Y. does and stay the hell back.'")[1065]

The following week, Wayne would film the iconic line-in-the-sand sequence. In his marvelous book *Alamo Movies*, author/film historian Frank Thompson does a yeoman's job explaining and comparing how Alamo films have treated this concept of self-sacrifice and commitment. First, last and always, the story of the Alamo is a tale of dedication and heroism. In Texas (and elsewhere) the Alamo is viewed as almost a religion: Bowie, Crockett, and Travis are the Holy Trinity, Santa Anna the Devil, martyrs are sacrificed, and the Alamo itself is a shrine of liberty. Wayne expanded on this theology in his advertising campaign: *The Mission that Became a Fortress—The Fortress that Became a Shrine.* The line-in-the-sand, though, has taken on almost mythic proportions.[1066]

536

Disregard the fact that the story of the line came from an individual of dubious reputation. There is no irrefutable supporting document whatsoever that corroborates the fable concocted by Moses Rose, written by William Zuber, and published in the *1873 Texas Almanac*. In fact, Rose's presence at the Alamo prior to the final assault is highly questionable. His name fails to appear on any muster roll, whether it is the siege of San Antonio muster roll, James Neill's roll of December 31, 1835, or the February 1, 1836 Alamo voting list. (It should be noted that "Rose," without a first name, does show up in the March 24, 1836 issue of the *Telegraph and Texas Register*. However, that may very well be James M. Rose, who entered the Alamo with Crockett). Those who believe in the story are convinced beyond reproach, citing the testimony/statements of Moses/Louis/Stephen Rose with corroborating declarations by Susanna (Dickinson) Hannig and the academic support of Walter Lord. Others take umbrage with the statement that defenders needed to be coerced into staying and also suggest the inherent inconsistencies and falsehoods in the highly theatrical tale negate any possibility of truth. Author Susan Prendergast Schoelwer may have best expressed it when she wrote, "The real obstacle to incorporating the Rose story into the Alamo legend, however, has never been its dubious historical provenance or the lack of confirmation by other witnesses, but rather its juxtaposition of selfless patriotism with self-interested pragmatism."[1067]

In all honesty, whether Rose was present or whether Travis drew a sacrificial line of courage or not is completely irrelevant. The fact of the matter is that each defender, in his own way, had to "cross the line" in his own mind and determine his ultimate fate. Options were available: surrender and leave one's life in the hands of a inglorious despot, abandon the protective confines of the Alamo and attack overwhelming forces (thereby accelerating one's demise), remain inside and pray for reinforcements (hoping beyond hope they will eventually arrive in time), or succumb to a basic desire of survival( pack one's belongings, and attempt to escape in the dead of night, forever being branded a coward). But there was one last choice—stay and defend the fortress to the last, wring as much damage as possible out of the opposing forces, and buy precious time for Texas. Each defender had to decide which course to take, which option best aligned itself with one's beliefs and convictions. For some, it was relatively easy. Others no doubt struggled with the decision. Yet all remained. In all likelihood, Travis probably did meet with the men, explained the situation, expressed hope and concern, and shared recently received communications.

*In the Shadow of History*, Dobie writes, "But what makes history, whether authenticated or legendary, live is that part of it that appeals to the imagination. No circumstance has appealed more to popular imagination than the story of how Travis drew the line and invited individuals of the little group to choose between life and immortality. Teachers of children dramatize it in school rooms; orators on holidays silver it and gild it; the tellers of historical anecdotes—and there are many of them in Texas—sitting around hotel lobbies speculate on it and say, 'Well, we'll believe it whether it's true or not.'" If you lose the moment of the line, the story is somehow diminished. For this is the moment of moral choice in which the defenders of the Alamo decide to die together.[1068]

Wayne had ambivalent feelings when it came to filming this sequence. In Patrick Ford's version, Crockett and Travis stand side by side in the compound during Travis's pronouncements. Early drafts of the script reflected Dickinson scratching a mark with his sword while Travis beseeched all defenders who wished to remain to cross the literal line. Later revisions eliminated the mark but included Travis's speech from on high: *"Men. Jim Bonham has just died. He brought the news that we can expect no help. Fannin has been ambushed. I stay here with my command, but any of you who wish to may leave with all honor. Those who wish to stay with me will step over the line. Failing reinforcement, the Alamo cannot hold. But do not go with heads hung low. No man can criticize your behavior. Here on these ramparts you have bought a priceless ten days of time for Houston. You have bled the enemy army. You are brave and noble soldiers. I have ordered the band, what is left of it, to play you out. May God bless you."*

In the 06/19/59 version of the script, Crockett, Bowie, and their men, then mount their horses, and prepare to leave the Alamo through an open gate. After a short walk, Bowie suddenly pulls up, slides off his horse, and walks across the line. His men are puzzled for a moment, then dismount and also cross, followed by Crockett, then his Tennesseans. Yet Wayne still didn't feel comfortable; the scene just didn't feel right. By 1959, whether one believed in the gesture or not, drawing a line in the sand seemed so cliché. Perhaps there might be a different way to dramatize such a complex concept. The evening before they were to film scene #453, Wayne, Grant, and Birdwell met to work on it again. Birdwell was adamant. The scene was too melodramatic, too hokey. The line had to go. Wanting a second opinion, Wayne called Happy Shahan around 11:00 p.m. and asked him to join the discussion. "I want you to come over," said Duke. "I need your help." Happy recalled that Birdwell and Grant were fairly persistent in their position. "Nobody knows that but Texas...." Intent on a dramatic climax, Grant queried, "Who in New York or Hollywood will know what the history books say?" Happy was equally stubborn. "I'll tell you one thing... We argued that from eleven o'clock one night till 3:30 the next morning. (Grant) was an opinionated guy. He wrote a lot of good scripts, but, when he made up his mind that he wanted it this way, he fought to get it, so I went in, and we argued, and, when I left, I said, 'Wait till the day comes when you premiere that picture.' *Newsweek, Life, Look,* they were all big (magazines) at that time; they're gonna remember that, and they're gonna tell you about it. I'll never forget this. Russell said, 'What do you know about publicity?' But I told 'em, I said, 'You wait and see. I'm not going to tell you to draw the line. I'm not going to tell you not to draw it. What I can tell you is that it's such a part of the tradition that, if you don't draw it, everybody in Texas will slaughter you in the press.' And that's exactly what happened. They were changing things. Wayne knew what was right, but he let 'em out-talk him."[1069]

Shahan was correct. Wayne modified the scene by eliminating the line, and there were many who didn't agree. "He did not actually draw a line in the Alamo," said Rudy Robbins, "and I thought that was such a dramatic thing. They should have had him draw a line with his sword and have everybody step over, but he didn't. He simply asked those who wanted to stay to join him. That was the only place I thought the script was weak, and it surprises me that Duke didn't insist on that."[1070]

The following day, they filmed the rewritten scene. For the first time in the film, the snobbish, arrogant, aristocratic Travis levels with his command. Previously deceiving the defenders with promises of help, he finally descends from his perch to address the "rabble" and tell them the truth. Halfway through the scene, Wayne hesitates before climbing off his horse. Robbins questioned that movement. "I noticed that, too. That I started to cross the line before Wayne did, and I did so on their instructions. And you would think that the second person to cross, or the first, would have been Wayne. The only reason that I can think that he waited to get down, if you had to analyze it, was that maybe he was proud to see his Tennessee guys going across without him having to tell them to." When the scene was complete the, bystanders broke into applause. Ever sarcastic, Grant walked over to Harvey and said, "Don't look so smug, Larry. They're applauding the writing, not the acting!" Harvey replied puckishly, "Quiet, James, or I will give you a big kiss and all these Texans will be sure you are a fag."[1071]

Actress Irish McCalla was in the midst of a Texas personal appearance tour and was invited to spend Thanksgiving with Guinn Williams, who had earlier co-starred with her in *Five Bold Women*, also filmed in Brackettville. A friend in Houston offered the use of his plane and pilot, which she gladly accepted. Flying into San Antonio, she spent the night at Williams's ranch near Brackettville. The next morning, after a hearty breakfast of biscuits and gravy, bacon and eggs and baked apples, Guinn's wife Toddy drove them to the location. Known for her role as *Sheena, Queen of the Jungle*, when McCalla arrived on the set she was greeted with a low whistle from above. Looking upward, she saw Pat Wayne standing on the West Wall. As she continued her stroll, stuntmen and actors bombarded her with "jungle-type" calls. While explaining to old friend Richard Widmark how she came to be there, Wayne suddenly walked over. "My heart fell," she said in dismay. "I thought he was going to ask me to leave… no visitors. Instead, he gave me that marvelous grin of his and said, 'You're that jungle girl from TV, aren't you?' When I admitted I was, he continued, 'I was standing up there, trying to figure out why, in the middle of Texas, on a western movie, I was hearing all those jungle sounds. Nice to meet ya.'" She was invited back the next day to watch battle scenes.[1072]

On November 24, Wayne filmed the entire Mexican army for the first time. It was a magnificent sight—1,200 soldados in perfect formation, wearing uniforms of blue, red, white, tan or ecru; band members with polished instruments. Gray and blue-clad lancers mounted on handsome steeds, guidons snapping briskly in the breeze, officers and enlisted men. Dragoons with helmets of silver and black, foot soldiers with shakos, sombreros and straw hats providing little shade from the sun. And lines of cannons positioned exactly as Jensen had sketched them. A sky so blue and bright, it hurt your eyes just to look at it. Strong Texas winds blowing over the land, kicking up dust for atmosphere. When Wayne called for silence, it was so quiet you could hear a pin drop. Worden observed, "I never saw so many people in my life in the background. He had the hills lined up with people." Michael Wayne also was impressed and amazed with his father's logistical coordination abilities. "He did shots with three thousand people," said Michael. "He did about ten different shots of the Mexican army arriving. We had allowed three days for that; he got on a horse with a radio, and he did it in a half a day."[1073]

With multiple Todd-AO cameras strategically positioned all around the set, one couldn't help but film simultaneous action in both foreground and background. To film the beginning of the final assault, a camera was placed high above the main gate where, shooting down the length of the wall, Mexican troops are moving into position in the background. A second camera, located inside the compound, filmed the same activity as seen from behind the palisade. Drummers tapping out a cadence were shot at ground level. For other scenes, a camera was positioned over the main gate looking toward the West Wall. Though not filmed at the same time as other scenes, another stationary camera was placed on the Travis headquarters balcony with the same p.o.v. Mexican dragoons are seen riding in silhouette from the perspective of the long barracks roof as well in a close-up shot. Although the impression in the film is that the Alamo was attacked simultaneously from multiple directions, the actual filming of these attacks took place over an extended number of days. Even though equipped with elaborate electronic communication and walkie-talkies, Clothier preferred to make personal contact with each camera crew before filming a scene. Frequently, because of changing conditions and complicated placement of explosives, he had to make two or three trips to assure everything was correct.[1074]

Duke explained, "For the beginning of the battle, when the Mexican army begins their advance, we had two thousand men who all had to begin moving at the same time, and to get it on film, Bill Clothier had five Todd-AO cameras set up. He and I went to each camera to check the blocking of each shot, and we'd go over the fine details to make sure every cameraman knew what to do. He stayed in contact with each cameraman by walkie-talkie. I had various assistants among the extras to make sure their movements would be coordinated. It was like a military operation. Then, when I gave the cue, the cameras began rolling, and the extras began their advance. It was a most awesome sight." Stuntman

Ted White summed up everyone's feelings perfectly: "When we were standing on the wall, and they had, oh, I don't know how many thousands of Mexican soldiers lined up out there in all their colors, red and white and all, they blew the Deguello. That was the theme the Mexicans played to say that no quarter would be given, and that we'd all be put to the sword. After that, they set off the cannon to indicate the charge. I guess we had between four and five thousand Mexican soldiers, and when they made that initial charge against the Alamo, there was no way in hell that you didn't get goose pimples all over your body. These Mexicans really believed in what they were doing. It was a moment that you could just never forget, that's all. Cliff Lyons was there with me...an even Cliff was overwhelmed. We stood there and said, 'Goddamn it, this is like a moment in history all over again.' It was like we were there when it really happened! It was a hell of a thrill." Irish McCalla was equally impressed. When Duke invited her to watch the filming as it would be something to see, she confessed, "He was right! It was really astounding! Much later, when I was kindly invited to the premiere of *The Alamo*, I had to smile as I recalled how they had used the same Mexican army first on one side, and then on another, making it look even bigger." As row after row of Mexican soldiers stand at attention, cannon in alignment awaiting the command to fire, flags snapping in the wind, Roberson's character views the silence of impending onslaught with prophetic clarity: "It's sure loud." Said Chuck, "(That was) another line that originally seemed awkward; I thought (it) was corny. As a matter of fact, there were a few corny lines that I had, but, again, they all worked. The lines about the real good things—courage, honesty, love—worked so well because of Wayne's direction." Even Wayne was awestruck. "Look at all of those troops," he declared. "That gives you a better description what the men in the Alamo had to look at every morning before breakfast."[1075]

With no work scheduled for the remainder of the week, cast and crew took a short break for Thanksgiving on November 26. The initial Master Shooting Schedule stated the film would be finished by then, but no such luck. Nevertheless, Wayne gave everyone time off for the holiday. Some took advantage to take a short trip home; others drove to Uvalde or Del Rio for dinner. Many decided to prepare a meal in their "homes" at Ft. Clark while those who wanted a non-traditional feast crossed the border into Acuña. As usual, the stuntmen were more free-spirited. Allegedly, Red Morgan "liberated" nine turkeys and delivered them to a Mexican whorehouse. There, fifteen stuntmen enjoyed the fruits of their labors. Dean Smith took off for San Antonio, and, by the time he returned, the stuntmen were already in Mexico.[1076]

In addition to Irish McCalla, Guinn Williams invited Ken Curtis and a few stuntmen to share Thanksgiving dinner with the Williams family, but, first, they would have to emancipate a turkey. While Toddy and Irish slept in, the men went hunting. Irish said she would never forget the sight that greeted her that morning when she stood by the kitchen sink and looked out toward the old barn and corral. "Men were sitting and having a smoke beneath the tree from which hung a deer and the wild turkey we would have with cornbread stuffing at dinner," she recalled. "They wore their buckskins from the movie, and the only modern thing about the scene were the guns and cigarettes. The rest of the picture was strictly last-century. I loved it!" That night, after dinner, Ken Curtis entertained the group by singing old cowboy songs.[1077]

Those who remained on location had the choice of several commissaries at Ft. Clark. Built in 1886, by 1959, there were nine stone mess halls and support buildings available, though one would succumb to fire and be reduced to rubble in the 1980s. Seven of the buildings served as mess halls, while two served as administrative buildings housing offices and supply rooms. A sign hung outside one of the buildings: "*Our forefathers thought nothing of working 16 hours a day. We don't think much of it either!*" Each mess hall contained a kitchen at the back end with one or more large cook stoves. Located in the Officer's Club or in a wing behind one of the cavalry barracks, the crew enjoyed a Thanksgiving feast catered by Rolly Harper and his team. Served buffet-style, white-jacketed waiters and waitresses hovered over the crew as the men sat on folding chairs next to long, linen-covered tables. Harper employed forty waiters, chefs, and kitchen helpers; with 328 members of the Batjac cast and crew, he needed them! A sign in the Ft. Clark Post Headquarters listed a partial menu: "Day Katch—Flounder, Tartar Sauce, New York Steak, Mashed Potatoes, Cabbage and Corn, with a reminder: "D-Day December 24. We Never Tole A Lie Yet!"[1078]

Once everyone was fed and rested, Wayne called the cast and crew back to Brackettville on November 27 for a 7:00 a.m. cast call. With a December deadline, much still needed to be done. He couldn't afford any more delays, and, with a promise to be finished by December 24, by God, he was going to meet it!

542

# CHAPTER TWENTY-SEVEN
# THE OLD MAN AND THE SCENE

(*Author's note: Absent daily production reports, daily call sheets, the script supervisor's end-of-the-day1 report and/or production bulletins, it is virtually impossible to determine the exact sequence or upon which day various battle scenes were filmed. Stuntman Neil Summers described the value of the daily call sheets: "They tell us if we're needed, what scenes we're in, what time we leave…they come out every day, and each cast member and crew member gets one. The make-up people, the drivers, the wranglers all have to know who's working and what's needed to get the shots listed for the day." The shooting schedule had little connection with the chronological development of the story. However, since the Alamo and compound were progressively destroyed as the battle reached its climax, the battle scenes were to be left for last. As all action was filmed continuously, some segments were used in the first assault, others in the final assault, and still others in both. Because of how the film was cut, actors may appear in one location in a certain scene and then seconds later, in an entirely different, logically impossible location. For this reason, unless it can be conclusively verified, dates are not given for specific scenes. Suffice to say, with multiple film crews, many sequences were filmed simultaneously.*)[1079]

BY NOVEMBER 27, JOHN FORD ONLY HAD ONE DAY LEFT ON LOCATION BEFORE he had to leave, and he was going to make the most of it. Jester Hairston and extra Jim Brewer were chatting on the set when they noticed Ford standing nearby. Hairston said, "Come with me, Jim." They approached Ford, Brewer was introduced and all shook hands. As Hairston told Ford of Brewer's acting abilities Pappy looked at Jester and asked in a semi-serious voice, "What are you, Jed? His agent?" After lunch, Brewer was told Ford was looking for him. Hearing his name called, Brewer turned, came face-to-face with Pappy and was told Ford was going to film his death scene. With camera and second-unit crew supplied by Wayne, Pappy moved to the courtyard and began to create the little vignettes for which he was so well known. A large earthen mound topped with cannon and flagpole sat in the middle of the compound. Just "north" of the mound was the cattle stockade fence. Said Brewer, "Mr. Ford blocked the scene where I was to stand in front of the fence with a group of Travis's men, shoot a Mexican soldier; then, as the Mexican soldiers charged toward us, take a shot in my chest and fall backward over the fence. The camera (then would come) in for a close-up of my face. We didn't rehearse the scene, just shot it. All went well; I shot my rifle as I was told, took a bullet in the chest, and fell backward over the fence. Suddenly, Mr. Ford yelled 'Cut'. I looked up at him while I was still lying on the ground and wondered why he stopped the onslaught. He looked at me for a second, had somewhat of a smile on his face, and tapped his left wrist several times. I looked at my left wrist and to my dismay, my gold wristwatch was glaring me in the face. In my embarrassment, I apologized to Mr. Ford, took off my watch, and I asked him if my career was over. He laughed and said 'Let's do another take, but don't screw this one up, son.'" Shot in approximately twenty minutes with only two takes, the scene lasted three seconds on the screen...Brewer's close-up was never used.[1080]

Extra David Kuykendall also had a few lucrative memories of working with Ford. "He got me off to the side at one time," said David, "and had me shot different—that's where I say I got shot a number of times. I'll bet you I was killed twenty times with him. You know, we'd go down to the corral, and I would lay down on the ground, and he'd have me position myself just right, and he'd take some pictures. And he had two or three of us, that we changed uniforms or...especially hats, and he'd take pictures from here and there, and he said, 'They may be used.' They'd throw them in. Well, the deal I had was that, any time I did anything to advance the movie, I'd get paid $25 extra, so there was, I imagine, ten or fifteen times that I got extra money. Because I really made more than the two guys that were Tennesseans. $17.50 a day. If I were standing there firing a cannon, I got $25 for firing the cannon, and then, if the cannon blew up, which they put a fifty-five-gallon barrel in the ground and blow that stuff straight up—well, I'd get another for that, and, if I jumped over that and hit and broke—pushed the ladder over, there was another one. I think on that sequence, I got (paid) about eight different (times)." There was a day rate for actors with lines, as well as a day rate for extras. There also were weekly rates for extras and those who had continuing roles. It depended upon the size of the role and what the individual's agent negotiated.[1081]

Rudy Robbins was another actor who thought working with Ford would make him legendary. "I was sitting over there playing the guitar," recalled Robbins. "Had a bunch of people around me. We were entertaining each other while they were setting up the camera for a different scene. All of a sudden, Duke yells over to me. He says, 'It do!' He always called me that; he couldn't remember 'Rudy.' He said, "Come here." And everybody said, boy, you're fixin' to catch it. He's going to chew you out good. You're making all that noise that they're trying to talk, and you're interfering with it,' so I went walking over there like a hound dog. He said, 'I want to introduce you to John Ford.' Well, I could not believe that I was being introduced to John Ford, so I stuck my hand out…and I said, 'Sir, I'm pleased to meet you.' And he just turned his back on me. Ford wouldn't look at me or shake hands or anything. And I didn't know what was going on, and Duke said, 'Oh, that's OK. Just go sit down.' And about thirty minutes later, I got a call over the loud speaker: 'It Do. Report to John Ford.' Duke made on like he needed him, and I was amazed that Duke wanted him to film me. I couldn't believe it. They had assembled a second unit for Mr. Ford, so, for about three days, he filmed scenes with me being the most heroic fellow you have ever heard of. You know, I could see the movie come out, *The Alamo,* starring John Wayne and Rudy Robbins with Richard Widmark and Joan O'Brien."

Ford was famous for improvising on the fly—taking advantage of the elements, adding a touch here, a glance there. With no particular story line to follow, he decided to create an action sequence involving Robbins, a cannon, and onrushing Mexicans. "Ford filmed me and the cannon from several different angles," said Rudy. "First, he filmed, from ground level, the defenders rolling the cannon from about forty feet away, then up the ramp. Then, he filmed them rolling the cannon up the ramp with the camera on the ramp." Ford took a moment, then told Robbins, "Act like you don't have any ammunition and start loading that cannon with whatever you can get your hands on. Spurs, whatever." Robbins continued, "All of this time, he had me motioning and yelling to the men to hurry and get it in place, just ad-libbing the words as they came to me." So Rudy started grabbing spurs off people's feet. "Hey, gimme your spurs," he yelled. "And we were loading the cannon with spurs and horseshoes. And he did a close-up of my hands putting spurs and horseshoes and chains into the cannon. I was asking the guys for a cannonball. They said, 'We're out of ammunition.' So I said, 'Give me whatever you've got.' He then had us fire the cannon, and he filmed it blasting off of the ramp. Next, he filmed the results of the cannon shot, with about fifty Mexicans falling from the blast, and the cannon is so overcharged—it flies off the parapet. Well, I thought, *Can you imagine putting spurs and horseshoes and chains in a cannon because you were out of ammunition?* But I thought that was a great scene, but they never used it. I went off and spent several days filming with him on *The Alamo,* and it wasn't until years later that I found out they were just using me to get rid of Mr. Ford."

As usual, Jack Pennick and George Ross were there to instruct actors on firearms and explosives and to insure their safety. Although it took a significant portion of the day to block and shoot, the sequence only lasted three seconds on film. Knowing that work wouldn't be scheduled for the weekend, Pappy departed for Chicago on Saturday, November 28, only to return the following Monday. He would stay for the duration of the shoot.[1082]

Jackie Williams admired Pappy's artistic efforts tremendously: "(Although) he really had very little to do with (the film), the shots that Ford did had some of the finest composition. Everything that John Ford ever did was a Charlie Russell painting. The composition was just marvelous. Some of the stuff he did with Mexican soldiers going along, their reflections in the water, and the clouds—well, it would just make tears stream down your face." Williams's comments bring up an interesting point, though. The scene to which he referred is seen shortly after the first assault. The reflections of retreating Mexican soldier are seen as they walk past a pond. Women are seen on the bank as they tend to the wounded. The scene had typical Fordian aspects to it, or did it? In a rough draft of an interview Dan Ford conducted with Wayne, Duke said, "...when the sunlight was such, we would get a reflection. And I had Cliff Lyons, the second unit director, and so Jack went out with Cliff and...they did a retreating scene of the women and the men coming back from the first assault and it was beautifully done." But, according to author Don Clark, Chuck Roberson confirmed the scene was filmed by Michael Wayne. Mike agreed, "I had something like two hundred Mexican extras out there, and I didn't speak Spanish. I would have them come in phalanxes. It made an effective shot and is in the film." And an e-mail from Gretchen Wayne stated, "I was on location and can verify that Michael directed second unit activity—also John Wayne's brother, Bob Morrison...directed second unit.")[1083]

While there were those like Pennick who were extremely loyal to Ford, others, including stuntman Gil Perkins ("Scotty"), harbored nothing but ill will. "I never got along with him," exclaimed Perkins. "One day, he said to me, 'Hey, come here, Scotty. You and Bobby Rose and so and so come with me.' And we shot some stuff inside the Alamo, in the corral where the hay, the feed catches on fire, and the horses panic and start going wild. Just before we shot the scene, Ford says to me, 'Well, your tam is on wrong.' I said, 'It is?' And he said, 'Yeah.' And he came up...and changed it around. And I didn't like him; I never got along with him. And I said, 'Well, Duke put it on me that way, and he's already shot half a dozen scenes, and now you're changing it, and it won't match.' I knew it really didn't matter a damn; I just said it to annoy him. Who the hell would care how my tam was? Wayne was shooting about fifty, sixty yards away from us, and, while they were getting his next shot set, he walked over to Ford and said, 'What are you doing, Coach?' 'Oh', he says, 'I've shot this, Duke. I've shot this stuff where the horses panic. You'll need this to cut away from the main action during the fight.' And then he says, 'Oh, and your Scottish tam was on the wrong way.' And

I said, 'Yes, Duke. I told him you put it on me and that you've already shot half a dozen scenes, but he didn't pay any attention, and he changed it anyway.' Wayne looked at me, and he said, 'Gil, I didn't tell you to put it on that way,' and turned and walked away. After all (Ford) made him, and I guess he wouldn't cross him, but I didn't give a damn about Ford because I wasn't one of his Pennicks."[1084]

During a lull in the shooting one day, a still photographer asked a costumed Robbins to pose for a few photos. Rudy climbed the main gate stairs, held a uniformed extra above his head in outstretched arms, and appeared as if to throw the soldier over the wall. According to Rudy, "The still photographer for the company was another person that thought my little character was significant, and he wanted to take a lot of pictures of me. And he said, 'I'd like to take a picture of you. Grab this Mexican guy and hold him up there like you're about to throw him over.' Well, I didn't throw him because there was nothing for him to land on, but he had me pick him up and hold him over my head like I was going to throw him, but that was all done with just still photography and not for the camera. I was really surprised that the head photographer for the whole company came over and wanted me to pose for those. I don't know if he was going to show them to Duke and say, 'Duke, wouldn't this make a great scene to film,' or what because I don't know why he would want them if it wasn't going to be part of the picture. I have an idea he took them to Duke and said, 'Well, what do you think of this?' but Duke kind of wanted to do everything his own way. But anyway, it wasn't used in publicity, and it wasn't used in the picture."[1085]

Despite Wayne's obvious love for Latin American culture and its people, he suffered from one serious disadvantage—he didn't speak Spanish. Oh, sure. He knew some basic phrases: Buenos dias, Como estas?, Donde es el tequila? But his fluency in directing the Mexican army extras was woefully lacking. To address this inadequacy, he utilized an interpreter to translate his orders into Spanish. A visitor to the set wondered why Duke even needed one because the star's three wives had all been Hispanic. "I guess," said the interpreter, "he didn't pay much attention when they spoke to him." Wayne also strategically placed Batjac personnel, locals, and other actors among these extras to insure they were following directions. Wayne's son-in-law Don LaCava, actually an assistant director, would don a uniform and direct lancers and dragoons. So did Bill Daniel. "I remember getting on a horse one day," recalls Don, "and gathering a thousand Mexican soldiers and moving them around. Watching the shooting and then giving directions to extras and that stuff."[1086]

Denver Pyle also enlisted in Santa Anna's forces, but he had a trick up his sleeve. Not only did he want his troops to follow his directions, he also wanted them to get noticed. "Everybody was trying to help him," said Pyle of Wayne. "When he was shooting the big scene of the attack, Mexicans (are) coming over hill and dale, thousands of them. We're out shooting that shot. I got into an outfit, and got a troop of Mexicans and drilled them. I had them out there marching. And I was in this line of marching soldiers attacking the Alamo, out there with my group. So I went to the first assistant. I said, 'Listen. I want the Ford regiment.' And I'm going to get into costume. I'll go out there and march them. 'Cause I kinda know what Duke's trying to do, and he needs somebody out in the field with these guys that's trying to do what he needs to get done. So, by now, I'm Ford. So what I did, I went back to the prop shop, and I got...they had a bunch of bayonets that were chrome. So I got all these bayonets, and I got fifty rifles, and I put these chrome bayonets on them. I told them, 'You're special.' (I stole this from Mr. Ford). I said, 'You're special troops now. You have the bayonets with the chrome on.' Then, I got this guy who was my interpreter and asked him, 'How do you say rotate?' And he told me it was 'rotado' or something like that. And I said, 'Now, on command, I want these fellows to rotate their rifles.' So that when I march my group over there I would have them revolve the bayonets, revolve their rifles about every fifty paces or so, so you see these flashes off the bayonets. 'Cause there's no sound on the thing, and I can holler. I'd say, I'd point at a guy, and I'd say, 'Revolve your rifle.' He'd go like this, and then, when you saw it in the rushes, you'd see these rifles flaring and the sun coming off them. And you'd see...only one regiment, but they're always lighting up. Sometimes they'd all light up, and sometimes it was individuals that light up, but, hell, it really made it work. I told Duke what I had done. 'God, that's great,' he says. 'And you can see it! It looked deadly!' And it did. You see these guys go through a shadow or something, and they come out, and the guns rotate, and these sparkles come off the bayonets." After the scene was finished, Pyle and his troops were resting when Wayne rode by on horseback. Pausing for a moment, he looked at Pyle and simply said, "Thanks."[1087]

Burnt carbon. Sulfur. Hot metal with a hint of sawdust. The ever-present smell of exploding gunpowder was overwhelming. Special powder magazines were built to house 25,000 pounds of black nitrate powder used in the siege sequence—more than three times the amount used in the actual battle, although how someone would know that fact is debatable. The air even had a metallic taste, a texture, grittiness. In preparation, variable-sized metal mortars or flash pots were placed where explosions were needed, then filled with a measured charge of black powder or flash powder, topped with Fuller's Earth, Bentonite, peat moss, or other soft debris such as cork to create a realistic cloud. Planted just below ground level, they were camouflaged and detonated on cue. Pots were used more for directional charges while mortars or concaved iron plates were used for larger explosions. Underground wires connected the devices to an off-camera central control board with pins and switches that corresponded to each device or group of devices. Once the charges were set and wired to the central board, the special effects personnel would notify the director. The director, stunt coordinator and special effects head then would walk the site and discuss the order and timing of the explosions. While the stunt coordinator and his team were doing a dry run, operators were setting up the camera based on the director of photography's instruction of exact position, lens, and lens height. "Places" then was called, and the scene was again rehearsed, sometimes with horses (which added a new detail to the equation). When all department heads were satisfied with the safety and the DP and director agreed on action and framing, the director then pulled his assistant director into it and cueing was finalized. After yet another dry run, everyone was finally ready to go. In the background you could hear the murmur of the spectators fueled by anticipation and excitement. Then, the call for silence. At the director's orders the effects man would touch his battery to the pin, detonating the charge, which the pot funneled so as not to injure anyone. First aid crews and an ambulance were always standing by, just in case. Timing is everything. The stuntmen must pull their horses down at an exact spot or go totally out of the shot before they fall. The special effects technician must, likewise, throw the switch for the planted explosion at a specific moment. Neither takes his cue from the other, so momentary hesitations or delays may occur. And every time a broadside was fired it cost $1,500![1088]

Dean Smith has a few unpleasant memories of those pots: "I was dressed as a Mexican lancer, riding along, when they blew up one of those pots a little closer to my horse than he liked. That horse jumped out from under me, and I went to the ground hard about the time the next pot blew up. It practically exploded in my face, covering me with dirt. That's about as hard a fall as I took in that movie. I must have looked like I've been splattered all over the ground. It shook me up, but I was ready to go again in a few minutes, and it made a great shot."[1089]

Even today, critics remain very complimentary of the excitement and intensity of the film's action sequences: horses spooked by gunfire throwing riders to the ground; burning smoke pots blanketing the sky with billowing black clouds; explosions blowing Styrofoam bricks and timber sky-high; continuous cannon fire; huge eight-foot fans dispersing accumulated battle smoke; painted canvas tarps strategically placed over holes to camouflage previous damage; five-gallon kerosene cans used for special effects and fires; the piercing sound of dozens of bugles, the pounding of thousands of shoes on bare ground; wide camera sweeps of marching men in bright uniforms; stunning cloud formations of the Alamo in silhouette at dawn; five Todd-AO cameras shooting action simultaneously from different angles. (A December 30, 1959, article in *Variety* indicated eight Todd-AO cameras were used in the production but "...five Todd-AO cameras can just about take in everything," as Clothier laconically observed.) Lucky were the hundreds of spectators perched on rooftops, surrounded by organized confusion, excited by the striking degree of realism. The crowds frequently broke into vigorous applause at the completion of a scene.

Film critics also noticed. The *New York Herald-Tribune*'s Paul V. Beckley wrote, "The battle scenes are remarkable for bodily energy and ingenious marshalling of large number of extras in stubbornly good compositions." Added Bosley Crowther of the *New York Times*, "There are dazzling graphic arrangements of panoramic views of the Mexican Army of Santa Anna, gathering for the attack, arriving in companies and battalions like athletes at the opening of the Olympic Games; bone-crushing sequences showing warm bodies hurtling themselves against the walls; scenes of old-fashioned battle that fairly choke you with their clouds of smoke and dust." Movie critic Dick Williams of the *Los Angeles Mirror* described the action sequences: "The action rises on a furious, undiminishing crescendo throughout the give-no-quarter battle and included some of the most remarkable battle photography ever put on celluloid. One of the reasons it is so lifelike, that one seems to be looking through an open window on actual history in the making, is that the camera moves in close on much of the hand-to-hand action. The varying patterns of battle are kept remarkably in focus. The seething turmoil involving men, horse, and cannon was photographed by William H. Clothier in one of the major cinematography accomplishments of the year."[1090]

Stuart Gilmore did a masterful job editing the film, most notably in the action sequences. And Wayne gave him full credit for it. "Gilmore did a damn fine job," said Wayne. "If you've got good stuff on film, the editor makes it all come together. He can even correct mistakes in the process. So I can't take all the credit for the battle scenes. Shows how much the critics know." At only 3:32 minutes, the first assault included forty-eight individual cuts, many lasting just a second or two. Filming of the final assault featured the same rapid, energetic approach: 13:19 minutes, 190 individual cuts. These action scenes even impressed the actors. "When it came to filming the battle scenes, it was amazing to see," reflected Ken Curtis. "I was up on the battlements, and everyone was in place inside the Alamo, and we watched these thousands of extras marching toward us. We opened fire; explosions were going off. Actors and extras were dropping dead on cue. The coverage that Duke and Bill Clothier got is amazing. Once we had all the master shots, we spent many days covering little episodes of the battle. Cliff Lyon directed second unit, and he had the Mexican cavalry charging forward, and, when the explosions went off, all his riders and horses were trained to fall to the side." Prior to the first frontal assault, several cavalry sorties against the palisade were staged; again, filmed but not used.[1091]

Despite all the rehearsals and preparations, sometimes, the best-laid plans didn't work out. "We had such a monstrous scene when the entire Alamo was shot," said Ted White, "and then we had, I think we had something in the neighborhood of 150 to 200 mounted, or maybe more than that, the mounted Mexicans. The initial charge on the Alamo. Well, when those cannons went off, 90 percent of those Mexicans hit the ground. We had loose horses going in every direction." Tim Cumiskey recalls, "We watched some of the battle scenes…and these things took hours to set up because everybody had to be in place, all these different-colored uniformed soldiers had to be in the same area. They had to be coming from different directions, and everybody had to start on time. So Wayne had a dolly out there where he was on one of these seats that go up and down, the director's chairs. He also had a Mexican director near him, so he could yell out this stuff with a bull horn to tell these guys when to go. When it started, the first scene, everything was going great. All these guys were marching forward, and shooting their guns, and the Alamo was just blasting away at them, and they just kept going, kept going, and kept going. I guess somebody forgot to tell them they were supposed to fall every now and again. So you had the entire force going toward the wall, but nobody was falling. John Wayne is just screaming, 'Cut! Cut! Cut! God Damn! Cut! Cut! Cut!' So they finally cut, and they stopped everybody. Now they have to do all the set-up again, and they're burning daylight while all this is going on. He (wants) to get this shot. So they get them all set back up, and that's another couple of hours. Now, they get back up there, and said, 'Go!' and they start and the first shot out of the Alamo, everybody fell. It was like, 'Man, we were really good shots!' It was really funny to watch. Then they finally had to set them up again, and, by this time, John Wayne was absolutely crazy because (he was losing) the light, and all this was costing him, and he was just livid. He told these guys, 'Get ready. Now when this goes, you fall up here, and this goes...' And you can imagine with thousands of non-English-speaking Mexican soldiers because they all had to be brought in. They finally got it right, except for the fact that they were falling on each other, making this big pile. Because nobody wanted to hit the ground and get their uniform dirty or anything, so they started falling in a pile. Well, they 'cut' the third time, and then they shot the scene right the next time."[1092]

Relates Dean Smith, "I remember for one of the shots on *The Alamo*, I was doing one of the Mexicans. They had all these big explosive pots down there. As I was going along there, fixing to do a fall, they set one of these pots off, and this horse jumped out from under me, and all that stuff blew up in my face, and boy, I hit the ground just like that. I thought I broke every bone in my body."[1093]

There were almost two dozen professional stuntmen on location. Men were hired in advance of production without knowing the exact stunts they would perform. Whomever was the best man for the job got to do it. One minute, they were dressed as Tennesseans, the next as Mexican soldados, dragoons, and lancers. It didn't matter—just grab a tunic, pants, and shako, and hope they matched. Roberson explained it perfectly, "Since I played a Mexican rider and an Alamo defender, I ended up shooting myself." Paid by the gag, the stuntmen would do whatever they were asked. If Wayne didn't like the stunt, he'd have them do it again. "Blown off the walls, we did so many of those, so very many of them," recalled Ted White. "In other words, I was a Mexican climbing up the ladder and had guys shoot me, and fall backward on a ladder. Those things we did all day long, for different angles. Wayne was very good about not trying to shoot stunts over and over again. That's when people get hurt, when you start shooting them over and over again." Similarly, extras were known to wear multiple costumes as well. According to Robert Harris, "I had about five different uniforms. I had a Gray Lancer, a Blue Lancer; these are costumes that they keep in wardrobe for you. The next day, you'd come in, they'd say, 'Get in your Gray Lancer uniform,' or 'Get in your Blue Lancer or Red Lancer' or 'Get in your Dragoon'. They had Dragoon uniforms, too. And they just go by color. They just tell...and eventually I got to be a Bowie man, and I worked strictly inside when the battle started. When they had the real battle going on inside the fort, I became a Bowie man. But most of all the other times I was, I played the Mexican out in the field. I had all kinds of uniforms."[1094]

A lack of fluency in the English language combined with an abundance of liquid refreshments resulted in one particularly memorable incident. Jester Hairston witnessed it: "We had a thousand Mexicans who came over from the Mexican side of the border to work as extras. (Brackettville) was so small hardly anyone in the cast could get rooms. So the Mexicans had to stay outside and sleep on the ground. They made a bunch of little campfires, and they drank a lot of tequila to help them to keep warm. We had a great big podium with a bull horn. These people, this Mexican Infantry, had bayonets on all of their rifles. So Wayne says, 'Now, we're going to use these ammunition pieces so that this war will look natural and real. So when I say, 'Camera, action,' I want action. Damn it, I want you to come running like hell on fire!' So, all right. He gives us the signal. We were inside the Alamo...the Mexicans had punched a big hole in the wall. They were supposed to come through this hole, and we were there trying to keep them from coming. We were shooting at them and Wayne gave the signal, 'CAMERA, ACTION.' When he shouted action, all these Mexicans started screaming and coming at us. They were full of this tequila, and they started screaming and coming at us with these bayonets. We were supposed to be shooting at them, and something went wrong. Then Wayne said, 'CUT, CUT.' Here were these Mexicans all full of that tequila. They kept coming, and Wayne said, 'RUN FOR YOUR LIFE, MEN! RUN FOR YOUR LIFE!' And that's just what we did. Everybody ran in different directions. I must have run about a mile and a half. I don't know where everybody else ran, but I'm telling you, I did my best to get away at my age. I kept in front of those Mexicans, and I don't know how I did it because they were coming and screaming. They would have killed all of us. It took us half of a day because Wayne called lunch after he finally got us back in some kind of order. After lunch, Wayne said, 'Now listen, amigos. We're not going to change history. You're going to win. Picture is over. We've got too much money invested in this picture. So use a little sense now and don't kill us all right at once. Let's try it again.'"[1095]

According to DeRuelle, "The Mexican extras were not a happy bunch. They were trucked from the border at about 2 a.m. each day, finished work about 6 p.m. and then went through getting out of costume and turning in props and were finally trucked back to the border. I don't think they slept much. Now I told you that Bob Relyea was the smartest man I ever met. One particular hot, dry day, when the Mexicans had charged the Alamo walls a number of times, and were like the rest of us, hot, dirty, and tired, one of their spokesmen (only a couple of them spoke any English) came up to me and told me that when the picture was over, they planned to kill Red Ryder (Relyea had red hair) and his chickenshit little brother. I went to Bob and said, 'How do the odds of 2,800 to two grab you?' I told him what had just happened, and his face got that look. He said, 'Get the interpreter, so there is no mistake, and tell those bastards that, if there is any kind of problem, I'm going to take all their paychecks home with me and think about them for six months or so.' There was no problem, but I did leave Texas as soon as I could get out of there, just in case."[1096]

Wayne's sense of humor was being stretched to the breaking point. Recalls Tim Cumiskey, "Now they're going to do a scene, an ambulatory-type scene where the wagons came out and pick up the dead and the wounded. They've got these guys; they've got blood on them and everything else. These guys think it's just as funny as they can be. They were picked to be in this movie, and they're being shot, and now they're supposed to be hurt, and they're over there laughing. Well, I tell you what, John Wayne didn't…he got about six feet off the ground, jumped off that chair, came down, and grabbed one of these guys, and that was the last laugh you heard out of any of them. He was so livid at that point that he had wasted all his time and money, this film and everything, trying to get this shot—he was really mad. But nobody got hurt and scene finally got shot." Wayne would bitch and moan and carry on. Cuss people out, throw stones at Clothier. No one was immune. One day, a rich Texas investor, who also doubled as an extra, came up and told him, "Look, my wife's working out here. I'd appreciate it if you wouldn't use that kind of language." Duke replied, "Well, if you're unhappy with your job, then you can just go someplace else."[1097]

With many exterior attack sequences already in the can, Wayne turned his attention to the interior of the compound. Always safety-conscious, he would have the set cleared of snakes each morning as, rather than leave, the rattlers would curl up and hide in the brush and wood. When the weather got colder, they would crawl on sun-baked asphalt roads to stay warm; cars would run over them. "You could just hear a continuing thump, thump, thump," admitted Michael Wayne. "You couldn't avoid them." Mary St. John recalled how Avalon moved around the set as if he had been personally targeted by the snakes. Even Dean Smith remembers all the varmints. "There were lots of rattlesnakes, crickets, and thousands of deer and skunks," says Smith. "They were on the roads, in the ditches, and on the parking lots." There were so many skunks Wayne hired another guy just to round them up; Web Overlander counted thirty-two one day. And so many crickets you couldn't even see the ground at night.[1098]

Unfortunately, the colder the weather, the less time available to film. In September, with an average high temperature of 95°, the set had over twelve and a half hours of sunshine daily. By December, it had cooled down to 66° degrees with just over ten hours of daylight, which doesn't mean ten hours of filming; at this time of year, there were only six to eight hours of usable light. Not only was Duke running out of time, he was running out of light! And the skies weren't helping, either. Variable cloud formations caused huge continuity issues. They were just never the same! In one scene, the sky might be brilliant blue, in the next, gray and overcast. In fact, one might be able to identify on which days specific scenes were filmed just by looking at the clouds. Perfect examples of this are the final assault battle sequences. Grayish clouds that cover the entire sky, parallel waves of puffy mass, thin, wispy clouds blown by high winds in long streams, cotton balls towering majestically upwards—all in the same sequence! Earlier in the shoot, Wayne could afford to wait for the right aerial composition; now he had to film regardless of the weather, even as shadows changed throughout the day. No matter, the show must go on![1099]

And there were so many *details* to attend to. Squibs, or tiny plaques of explosives, taped or attached to metal plates and embedded in adobe walls; mattresses placed at the base of buildings and walls to cushion falls; walls and structures partially deconstructed and rebuilt with Styrofoam adobe blocks in preparation of explosions; balsa wood wagon wheels and clay pots placed in background; duplicate Styrofoam cannon wheels manufactured in preparation of re-takes. Assistant director Relyea recalled how difficult it was just to begin the day: "The extras got in line to be fitted for wardrobe, then got in line for their props and guns, then got in line for their horse, then went off to find their squad and prepare for shooting. At the end of each day, they had to repeat the process in reverse. The running joke was that once you waited your turn behind the thousand other extras, there was no time to sleep between returning everything at night and picking it up again the next morning."[1100]

Dozens of little segments were filmed; some were used; others were confined to the cutting-room floor. Said David Kuykendall, "They took my hat off and put a bandage around it and put blood on it, because there was one scene in the very far southwest corner—southeast corner of the compound—where I had a cannon crew, and I fired the cannon, and then I jumped over the little divider fence, you know, that they had, and then went over and pushed the ladder of Mexicans over, and then hit another with a gun, and then jumped back over, fired the cannon again, and then the cannon blew up, and one of the other guys and I drug another person all the way back to the chapel." And Robert Harris remembered: "One time, I was up on the wall, and they had all these freshly loaded rifles all lined up real close to me, and (Wayne) told me to get this (plunger). He said, 'When I would say roll, start sticking that plunger in that cannon.' And I started, then he'd yell off-camera, 'Well, pull the damn thing out!' And when I pulled it out, we had our rifles lined up on the wall, and I hit one rifle, and they went down like dominos. Wayne yelled, 'God damn! Did you have to hit those rifles! Cut! Cut! Cut!' He stopped shooting, walked right up to me, looked me straight in the eye, and said, 'I think you did that on purpose.' I was scared and didn't utter a sound, but he let me keep working. I think he liked me." Another scene not used.[1101]

During the first week in December, the set was action-packed. Literally! Since he was a student at Loyola, Patrick Wayne could only afford to fly in on weekends, film his scenes, and then return to classes. Tom Kane, production assistant and the one in charge of scheduling Patrick's appearances, was not aware of the revised, accelerated shooting schedule and had Pat flown to Brackettville for the third and final time. Duke was surprised at his son's two-weeks-early arrival ("*What the hell are you doing here?*"), but decided, as long as he was there, they might as well film the final portion of Pat's death scene. In his role as Jim Bonham, young Wayne, standing on the flagpole mound, notices attacking Mexican dragoons coming into the compound through the main gate. With weapons in hand, he charges the oncoming horsemen, fires his pistol at one, and stabs another with his sword. Defenseless, he is then stabbed by a galloping dragoon and left to die in the dust. Chuck Roberson and Dean Smith performed these gags.

To depict a soldier being shot off his saddle, the stuntman would wear a jerk harness—a wide, heavily padded device extending from just below the ribs down to the lower belly. Usually the harness is made to a particular stuntman's physique as the snatch is so violent that an ill-fitting harness could cause body ruptures. Worn under outer garments, the back is attached to a wire cable. The cable would, in turn, be attached to a rope, and the rope would be secured to a corner post in the gateway or a spring-ratchet machine. As the stuntman rode his horse, the rope would uncoil, and, once it reached its limit, the rider would be snatched off the horse. The length of the rope was measured with great accuracy so that the exact position over which the snatch would take place was known. Dean had never performed this type of gag before; the other stuntmen detailed the stunt but didn't tell him how violent the reaction would be. Says Smith, "Well, as we come in the gateway there, Patrick Wayne is standing there, and he shoots both of us 'cause we're coming in there pretty fast. Roberson falls his horse to the left, and I've got to come through there with a saber, and I'm trying to kill Patrick. Well, Cliff Lyons, being a rough, old codger that he was, tied me off there…at the gate. He tied me off with a rope and put a belt around me (without a shock cord), and they hollered action, and I ran out to the end of that rope, and my eyes crossed; that dragoon helmet hit my nose, and I hit the ground like you'd never believe. And then I got up, dusted myself off. Well, old man Ford asked Clothier,

'How's the shot and everything?' (Lyons) said, 'We're gonna have to do that again 'cause they said they couldn't see the flash in Patrick's gun.' So anyway, I had to get up there and do that again, but I came off that horse so hard that my saber was standing up, and it was on top of my foot there. And I'm gonna tell you—it really did hurt. It liked to have cut me in two both times." A week later, Smith was asked to perform another saddle-jerk but declined. "I let Billy Shannon take it," says Dean. "That turned out to have been a good idea for me, because it knocked him out cold."[1102]

With Smith's dragoon disposed of, young Wayne did his own stunt. As two horses raced by, one on each side of him, he grabbed a saddle and was carried along by their momentum. As he let go of the saddle and fell backward to the ground, the other horsemen carefully galloped by on either side. With the hilt of a sword strapped to his chest under his costume, it appeared that Bonham had been run through with a sword. The prelude to this sequence would not be filmed until later in the week after the North Wall breach explosion.[1103]

Wayne tweaked the shooting schedule during the week to give Harvey a few days off to attend the Second World Film Festival in Mexico—he was a guest of honor in conjunction with his performance in the British entry, *Room at the Top*. The Hollywood delegation included such stars as Linda Cristal, Rhonda Fleming, Hope Lange, Don Murray, Maureen O'Hara, James Stewart, and Otto Preminger. Among the major events was a showing of *Compulsion* starring Orson Welles, as well as Preminger's *Anatomy of a Murder*. As Harvey planned to be there on Friday, December 11, his *Alamo* death scene needed to be filmed before he left. (Regrettably, he had a problem at the border—his papers didn't include a re-entry provision. "It was all due to a foul-up on the visas," said Harvey. He was forced to return to Brackettville but began to refer to himself as the *Piccadilly Wetback*. Others suggested the moniker may have been a result of his frequent trips to the border, typically to his favorite hangout—El Moderno.)[1104]

The death scene for Harvey's Travis would be filmed in segments on different days and assembled into one scene in the editing room. In the film, Travis and others are manning the northwest corner battery when their cannon is hit by a shell and explodes. The blast causes Travis to roll down the ramp, and he calls for reinforcements. *("Battery number three! Come on!")* He then helps defenders pull the cannon up the ramp, but, before it can be brought to bear on the Mexicans, an explosion blows a breach in the North Wall. As Mexican soldiers pour through, he pulls out his sword, discards the scabbard and races down the ramp. After dispatching several soldiers in a sword fight, he is cut, once on his left arm, again on the right side, and then shot twice. He breaks his sword in two, throws the hilt at the Mexicans and falls to the ground. Wayne instructed Lyons how he wanted the scene staged: "Look, when the Mexicans blow a hole in the wall and it makes a sally port through, they're all going to have swords. I want our guys to have some swords too and go into a sword battle. Now I don't want any of the Errol Flynn stuff, but I want Larry Harvey, who'll be up on the parapet, to come down with two single-loaded pistols, fire them as these guys come through. Since he won't have time to reload, he'll just throw the pistols and pull his sword and go into action with these Mexicans. Before he's taken out, I want him to kill ten or twelve Mexicans. But none of that Errol Flynn stuff." Based on Wayne's previous comments, it appears he wanted several sword fights, not just the one involving Harvey.

Since Gil Perkins had considerable experience staging sword fights, Lyons asked him to set it up: "Line up this sword fight that's believable where Harvey takes out ten guys." According to Perkins, "Larry had had a lot of sword instruction, in England, I guess. And he would rehearse and rehearse until he'd almost drop, and he got to be great at it, so, when we actually shot the thing, we shot it with three cameras; Duke was behind one, Cliff Lyons behind one, and Ford behind the other. And Harvey hit everything on the button; he did everything perfectly, and the whole scene looked great. So Duke said, 'All right. Cut. Print. How was it for you, Coach?' Ford said, 'It was great for me.' 'How was it for you, Cliff?' 'Great,' he said. 'OK. One take! That's all we need.'" They then moved in for a close-up over Red Morgan's shoulder as he shoots Harvey.

An analysis of this scene shows several inconsistencies. When Harvey is stationed next to the cannon, he wears a red sash and black belt with a gold buckle and attached scabbard, but, seconds later, when he discards the scabbard, the belt is missing. In addition, although he is "cut" by Perkins during the sword fight, no blood appears on his sash. In the close-up after he gets shot, however, blood flows profusely from the cuts on his jacket, sash, and pants. Also, when he initially rolls down the ramp, the back of his jacket is covered with dirt. When he runs back down the ramp to face the advancing soldiers, his jacket back is still covered with dirt. Yet, during the sword fight and as he lies dead, the jacket back is clean. If one looks at the sky, he would see that these scenes were filmed at two different times.

Joe Canutt also was involved in this sword fight. "To be honest with you," confesses Canutt, "I didn't much care for him (Harvey). That was the second picture that I worked with him. I worked with him on *King Richard and the Crusaders*, one of his first pictures over here, and the working title on it was *The Talisman*. He, uh, well, for example, in the specific scene, I jumped in with a sword. I've done a lot of sword work, and made a couple of cuts at him, and he backed off. And all you should do is just tap the blade lightly. Christ, you get a fag up there to work with. He's afraid he's gonna get cut."[1105]

Extra Ed Riley, from Corsicana, was a member of the Travis cannon crew when a "Mexican mortar shot landed at our cannon and (blew) us up. The cannon and all its parts were made of Styrofoam with a small charge of dynamite serving as the mortal shot. (I am the soldier with) my back to the camera who does a back flip when the shot hits."

That evening, Gil had just finished dinner in the commissary when Ford showed up with two bottles of wine in hand and sat down, uninvited. "Gil," said Ford. "That was a hell of a nice scene you laid out today. Are you a fencing master?" "No," replied Perkins. "I'm not even a good fencer, but I've worked with Fred Cavnes and John Hermans and Ralph Faulkner and the best of the guys in the business, and I know what it takes to make a swordfight look good in a movie scene. I've done enough of them, and I just followed what I learned from them." And, with that, he got up and left the table. Jack Pennick followed him out and said, "Gil, that's an awful thing you did to the Commander. That was an awful snub. He just came and sat down, and you got up and left the table." Perkins told him what he thought of the Commander. "Jack, I don't like him," said Gil. "He doesn't contribute enough to my welfare to kiss his ass like all you guys do, and I'm not going to do it. I don't want a part of the old Irish bastard. He's a deathbed Catholic as far as I'm concerned, and I've seen him crucify guys on the set who couldn't fight back, and I don't like him. You can go tell him what I said if you want." And that was that.[1106]

Sharp-eyed observers have noticed, as Harvey lies "dead" on the ground, he moves his left arm, so extras running by won't step on it. It wasn't the only time in the film that dead actors were miraculously resurrected. For instance, in the sequence of shots immediately after Patrick Wayne's death scene, there's an explosion at the West Wall, and two defenders are killed. As they lie on the ground, several Mexican soldiers pass through the subsequent opening under a blazing ramada and enter the compound. As the roof partially collapses, a dead defender nearest the pole rolls slightly to get away from the flames. And earlier, as Gray Lancers enter the compound through the North Wall breach, another defender lies dead behind a low wall. Suddenly, he raises his head, notices their entry, and lies back down again.

Some stuntmen specialized in acrobatic falls, others in explosions, and still others in sword fights. But there were those who, in addition to all other activities, were extremely skilled with horses—riding, falling, jumping. Some of the most spectacular stunts in the film involved horses, and the most spectacular stunt featured twelve! Never before had so many horses fallen in a single scene. A platoon of Mexican cavalry would charge the defenders, jump the palisade in front of the church, and die in a volley of gunfire. The extremely complicated, dangerous gag took split-second timing, so the stuntmen practiced for days, first individually, then in pairs. During the dry runs, many horses balked at jumping as the top of the palisade was too uneven. "The right horse," said Chuck Hayward, "can make you look like a champ. A bad horse can make you look like a dude. No matter how well you train him, your horse always reserves the right to refuse his first stunt. Every horse is going to do it sometime, but you never know when." Wooden planks laid on top of the palisade solved that problem. Some of the horses couldn't jump as high as others, so a ramp equal to half the height of the jump was built on the off-camera side of the barricade. With the proper camera angle the horses would appear to be jumping higher than they actually were. The bolder horses would jump slightly ahead of the more timid ones to create one continuous leap. At sixty-five feet in length, the palisade was fairly narrow, so Cliff Lyons reduced the number of horses from fourteen to twelve because the minimum safety interval between horses was deemed too tight and dangerous. The riders would be paid extra for the stunt as once the jump was complete they would also fall the horses. ($100 for the jump, $250 for the fall.) Virtually all the major stuntmen and their horses would be involved in this scene: Hayward and Twinkle Toes, Chuck Roberson and Cocaine, Red Morgan and Hot Rod, Bear Hudkins and Jerry Brown, Tap Canutt and Gypsy, Jack Williams and Coco, Jim Burk and Detonator, along with LeRoy Johnson, Bob Morgan, Bill Williams, Joe Canutt, and Dean Smith.[1107]

Finally, on December 4, it was time to film the scene. Early that morning, Lyons did a final check to assure all was ready. Both Wayne and Ford were present, but it would be Lyons's show. Extras behind the palisade were directed to fire their rifles as the horses jumped the barricade. Outside the compound, the stuntmen sat on their horses waiting for their cue while the prop department began to outfit the riders with guns, canteens, and swords. When finished, Lyons yelled, "Roll camera. Action!" After instructing the special-effects department to detonate strategically placed explosives, the stuntmen were cued. Yelling and charging in a ragged formation, they quickly approached the palisade. As was his wont, Roberson was first. "I led the pack in all the horse gags," said Roberson egotistically. "Basically, if the first horse and rider was good, the rest could screw up." At the last moment, they galloped up the ramps and leapt over the crouching defenders. Rudy Robbins, lying flat on the ground and as close to the inside of the palisade as he could get, clearly heard the thunder of approaching horses' hooves. With a loud *whoosh*, the animals cleared the barrier, the ground pounding with the force of their landings. Their hooves were so close you could clearly see the horse shoes. As the horses fell, the stuntmen scrambled to avoid being crushed. According to Jim Burk, "I learned a valuable lesson on that film. After jumping the barricade, I attempted to take Detonator too soon—both feet hadn't hit the ground yet, and he didn't take it. As soon as all four feet were on the ground, I took him, and it worked. I remember too, just as I was going to the ground, I glanced over, and Jackie Williams was five or six horses away from me on that great mare of his. Well, I'm on the ground, and the next thing I know, I have a horse on top of me—it's Jackie Williams's horse! To this day, I don't know how she got there!" Chuck Hayward was a bit cleverer: "Regarding the scene where all the horses fell at the same time…I was closer on the side because Ford had a camera there. Wayne was just letting Ford do his own stuff, and I kind of catered to him because I knew where his camera was, and I played it for that one." Hayward also played a trick on his fellow stuntmen in this scene. After the cameras stopped rolling and the fallen men and horses all got up, one man remained motionless. A moment passed, then another. Fearing the worse, Hayward's fellow stuntmen rushed to his side. Only when he got to his feet did they realize they'd been had.[1108]

Lyons didn't believe in re-takes, but, as the scene was filmed twice for different camera setups, it took all morning to get the master shots. Dean recalls how their take-off point looked like a junkyard: "Horses are running wild in the smoke. They looked back there where we started, it looked like a wardrobe prop department 'cause we left all that stuff *(swords, scabbards, shot bags, etc.)* down there when we took off. You remember things like that. When you're a stuntmen, you don't want anything to hang you up or get tied up." Fortunately, only one stuntman suffered an injury—a minor bump to the head from a hoof. (The same group of horses/riders also performed the stunt where dragoons leapt over a row of disabled cannon.)[1109]

Though Ford was present and may have been behind a camera, Bill Clothier took extreme exception to the notion that Pappy directed the scene. "*The Alamo*, in its entirety, is Wayne's movie," insisted Clothier. "His idea. His directing. Santa Anna's army approaching the Alamo was Duke. Everything was Duke's—except the horse falls. Cliff Lyons directed the horse falls. For instance, when Santa Anna's army comes charging up to the Alamo and Lawrence Harvey says, 'Hold your fire,' and then they fire and a hell of a mess of horses falling and men falling, Cliff directed that. These are typical second-unit operations, which on a Ford or a Hawks picture would always be done by the second-unit director. We had about twenty, twenty-five stuntmen. We put down beds of sand, about two feet of sand, so nobody would be hurt in the falls. That's what Cliff did—working with the stuntmen. Horse falls in the sand. Horses, eight or ten horses and riders, right over the camera. Duke directed that scene. Duke directed horses jumping through cannon fire, rifle fire; all the close-ups of the principles, Duke did that. Why, John Ford wasn't even around, and Cliff was just standing by, when those sixteen horses and riders leap over the wall of the fortress—hell, dammit to hell, John Wayne directed that. Placed the men. Told me how to light it. Told me the effect he wanted. Told the stuntmen how to move and when to move. John Wayne directed *The Alamo*. All the way. Could have been one of the best directors in Hollywood if God had not made him a star. "[1110]

En route from Los Angeles to New York with a layover in San Antonio, Duke's old friend William Randolph Hearst Jr. visited the location just in time to see the historic stunt. Suitably impressed, he stayed Saturday as well. On Sunday, Wayne's film received a resounding endorsement in the Hearst newsprint empire. Comparing the film to President Eisenhower's European/Asian/African trip, Hearst stated in his editor's Notebook column, "The story of the Alamo is a great reminder for all of us of the terrible cost of freedom. It is the story of people who believed up to their certain death that it is important to stand up to anyone who threatens individual liberty. It is a pretty universal idea. Basically, it is what Ike is making his trip for." Equally complimentary to Wayne, he wrote, "This has got to be a great picture… Just to watch for a day or two, the cavalry charges, the individual acts of heroism, the suffering and pain, though make-believe, is a reenactment of American history, is, believe me, very thrilling indeed."[1111]

To wrap up filming by mid-December, it was decided the entire company would work the weekend. Chill Wills and his wife Betty, who had flown in from California, made plans to celebrate their thirty-fifth wedding anniversary Saturday evening in Piedras Negras along with John and Judy Hamilton. Jester Hairston conducted a course on choral singing the same day. Earlier, Hairston, known for his marvelous voice and choral arranging talent, was asked by local school superintendent M.W. Mills if he would put on a Christmas program for the students. Jester, unsure of the shooting schedule, told the superintendent he would be more than happy to oblige—if Wayne would allow him to stay on location a bit longer. Days later, though, Wayne blew into the cast dining room and bellowed, "Jester, what the hell is this? You want me to keep you here after Christmas? You know good and damn well you're not suppose to stay here with me now."

"What are you talking about, Mr. Wayne?"

"Why, you know what I'm talking about. You just want to stay here and make more money out of me."

"Well, the principal wanted me to work with these children and put on a program. He said they never had a Christmas program."

"Why in the hell should they ask you?"

"Well, I told them to get in touch with you."

"Yeah, yeah, I know."

Of course, Wayne was just kidding and kept Hairston on for several additional weeks. Parents, teachers, and students from both black and white local schools attended the program. Said Jester, "The place was packed. We had a wonderful time. The blacks in the town left after the concert, and here I was with all these children and their parents. I stayed for an hour after. I'm sure I wasn't considered as a black."[1112]

That weekend, Wayne filmed several battle scenes that appeared multiple times in the movie. In other words, he would film a scene using several cameras from different angles. Then, the footage would be cut and spliced into both the first and final assaults. For example, as Widmark stood on the parapet above the main gate a gun crew prepared to fire a small cannon. Suddenly, a bearded stuntman was "shot"; he dropped his rifle and fell backward over the wall in a full flip. Using his feet to brace himself, he landed in a sand pit as a shell exploded next to him outside the wall. Several Mitchell BNC 65 conversion cameras were set in place to film this particular sequence. Large carbon arc lights were secured to scaffolding to insure adequate lighting; eight-foot fans blew away the smoke; and a boom mike captured dialog and ambient background noise. The same sequence, filmed simultaneously with a second camera placed to the far right of the first (and shooting a wider angle), would be inserted into the final assault. This sequence also was extended to show a secondary explosion on the wall. According to veteran cameraman Lou Jennings, who manned the main camera, the use of multiple cameras to film the same scene was not only cost-effective because it eliminated the time needed to set it up again, but also spared potential injury for the stuntmen. Widmark appeared in both scenes, yet seconds earlier, in the final assault, he was seen standing next to Wayne at the barricade, firing a rifle (not the nock volley gun). Widmark then appeared over the main gate before he was finally injured in an explosion at the barricade. Continuity, continuity, continuity. A close examination of both scenes also reveals a painted canvas tarp hanging above the main gate. Used to cover a prior explosion, the tarp covered a large U-shaped opening created in a previous scene. Earlier, Wayne had filmed a sequence in which Guinn Williams, flanked by several defenders, stood above the main gate and awaited the final assault. Two fully-costumed, papier-mâché dummies were positioned to represent defenders. As the Mexican army advanced across the plain, Williams turned away; a shell exploded, and the dummies were blasted to smithereens.

Sometimes, a scene was filmed in both wide-angle and close-up, or from variable height, thus simulating a seemingly different sequence. Wayne and Lyons would take advantage of this technique when filming the attack: Mexican horsemen and artillery riding across the plain in front of the main gate prior to the first assault, or White Infantry soldiers attacking the palisade. Seconds later, the same soldiers were filmed attacking the West Wall, followed by a wave of defenders firing in unison from the West Wall.[1113]

On Monday, December 7, Wayne filmed the storming of a hastily improvised barricade in front of the church. Turned-over wagons and buggies, gabions and bell, the flagpole mound cannon—anything to halt the onrushing Mexican soldiers in a last-ditch attempt at defense. With a dozen Tennesseans at the palisade and fewer than that at the barricade, several hundred extras dressed in colorful Mexican uniforms stormed over the barrier as the defenders fell at their places. Numerous attacking units merged as one as they blended into an impressive kaleidoscope of color. Yelling realistically, swarming like locusts, the soldiers overwhelmed the meager opposition. Erupting smoke of black and white poured into the sky and blocked the sun; the sounds of screams and gunfire filled the air. Bugler Roy Ackland attempted to sound one last call before being slain; the cannon fired one final discharge; scores of soldiers fell like dominos. Rehearsed several times, the gag was executed perfectly. Simultaneously filmed by several cameras, the attack was so realistic spectators felt they were witnessing the actual battle. Two Todd-AO cameras were to cover the taking of the barricade, one from the roof of the low barrack at the left end, the other on the ground below, just behind the barricade. Four camera angles covered the same action: two from the cameras mentioned previously and two in the small courtyard shooting squarely at the barricade.

As per Richard Curilla, "The sequence was apparently shot in several actions. The first one early in the day with all cameras looking at the barricade from the plaza. Extras were used around the barricade, at the palisade and in the deep background as soldados on the plain beyond the palisade. The other action (was) shot in the afternoon. All extras were moved in from outside the Alamo and used in the plaza, where the cameras had been earlier. Now the cameras were shooting from inside the barricade, out toward the West Wall. The necessary tie-in action between the two reverse angles is the single Gray Lancer galloping across the scene from "south" to "north." He is used deliberately in both directions of shooting, but notice that the sun is coming from the west by the end of his pass, even though from the east at the beginning."[1114]

Though the assault appears to be continuous, breaks in the action were necessary for additional setups; as the camera filmed the advancing troops, soldiers were seen swarming over the flagpole mound. Cut to the shot of the blond-headed officer in the gray jacket as he is killed and the soldiers were replaced by lancers. Interestingly, a *second* barricade was also constructed *inside* the church. Almost five feet high, it stretched across the width of the interior and was built of large and small barrels, sand bags, rocks, and wooden stools. This barricade was never seen in the film, nor did it appear in any background scene. Perhaps it was to be used in a scene that was eventually cut, or, more likely, Duke and/or Ford may have decided to change the way they wanted the assault to end and eliminated the necessity of the second barricade. Nevertheless, one wonders what might have been. And, in yet another scene filmed but not used, tan-uniformed Mexican soldiers were shown charging up the stairway to Travis's headquarters as defenders hopelessly perished on the stairs and balcony.

Earlier that morning, Wayne filmed the destruction of Travis's headquarters (obviously, after the aforementioned soldiers rushed up the stairs.) With defenders positioned on the roof of the building, explosions were set off in the front and rear. Many stuntmen leapt on the porch roof before continuing to the ground. As mattresses had been placed two stories below, others jumped directly to the ground while subsequent explosions created a second wave of fleeing stuntmen. Crew members or stuntmen threw three "dummy" defenders off the roof into the rear courtyard as extras rushed by below. Bob Morgan was in charge of the gag: "Take a beat here and take a beat there. It's choreography, just like a dance routine. In six seconds, we have to get twenty guys blown off of this building, and the building blows up. One, two, three, four, five, six…well, we'll start up here. Start with Ted White coming off the top of the building, get him out of the way, so he wasn't going to ruin the shot…I'm just joking about that. Then, we'd place different people, and then I was the last one to go off the building because I'm setting it up. We're all going to get the same amount of money, two hundred bucks apiece." Denver Pyle's character is initially seen defending the palisade next to Crockett. Seconds later, though, he somehow appears on the HQ roof just before the building explodes. Perhaps another filmed-and-cut sequence, he may have been ordered by Crockett to help defend the building. Nevertheless, a stuntman in Pyle's costume, complete with top hat and feather, is clearly seen leaping to his death from the porch roof. Joe Canutt was also involved in the gag. "We blew that building up with a bunch of us on top of it," recalls Canutt. "Denver Pyle was supposed to be in it, and he hit the roof of the second porch, and then the whole thing came down. They took a cannon ball in the middle of it." Well, not quite. A cable was attached to a post supporting the porch roof. When the explosion was set off, a Jeep pulled the cable, and the roof collapsed. "There were a few of us on the building's roof," said Roberson. "It was set to explode with three of us, I believe, jumping to the porch roof before hitting the ground. Well, when that building blew we were immediately covered in smoke and dust. The building started to move, and we couldn't even see the roof of the porch below. I just yelled out, 'Let's go!' and we jumped. I admit we were taking quite a chance on that one. It took about three or four minutes for us to be found under all that rubble, but we all got out of it fine."[1115]

Though it seemed the stunt was perfectly executed, it was not to be. Some said one of the stuntmen broke his collar bone, and Duke wasn't satisfied with the take, but David Kuykendall, who was there, begged to differ. Recalled Kuykendall, "We were all up there, watching it—everything blew up, and the front end of the building over there fell over, and some of the guys piled off the top. When they got through, (the cameraman) said, 'Uh-oh. We didn't have any film in the number one camera.' And (Duke) just said, 'OK.' It probably cost him quite a bit of money. It was like a morgue around here. I mean nobody said anything. It was like the most beautiful scene you've ever seen, as far as action. And then, it couldn't be used. Oh, man. It made people sick. That's why he didn't get upset. He was just sick. He was sick." As a result, they had to rebuild the building— porch, roof, and all. Built from adobe, the blocks baked for days in the December sun. Rescheduled, the scene was later shot again. The issue this time was the weather. "You'll be in a scene where it's clear with a beautiful sky," explained Kuykendall. "And the next scene—it's just all kinds of clouds. Well, that was one of the problems they had with that one is they shot that first one on a hot day, but, the second time they shot, it was after a northern had come through, and it was just completely different weather, but, with so much smoke and fire and all that going up, you don't notice it." The scene would be shot again after the final sequence in which Joan O'Brien, Aissa Wayne, and John Henry Daniels leave the Alamo but prior to Wayne's departure on December 15.[1116]

Wayne filmed the "death" scenes of several supporting players. Some appear on screen; others don't. Guinn Williams was no exception. Defending the West Wall, he slams his rifle stock against a blue-uniformed soldier and pushes him backward off the wall. Another soldier starts to scale a ladder in front of him. Williams is next seen with headlocks on two soldiers as an officer runs him through with a sword. Williams then knees the officer (who falls backward), lets out a scream, and, with two soldiers still headlocked, falls off the wall to his death. Joseph Calleia's character Juan Seguin is seen stationed on top of the lower portion of the Long Barracks at the start of the final assault. While his death was not seen, it may have been filmed. Photographic stills show Chuck Hayward dressed in Calleia's costume lying on the ground at the foot of an adobe wall with arms folded around a wooden cross. It appears to have been filmed near the connecting wall between Travis's headquarters and the chapel. Earlier in the film, a cross was in place on a stepped embellishment over the archway on this wall. As Hayward was involved, "Seguin" may have been shot, grabbed the cross as he fell, and embraced it in death. There are also stills of his "son" Julian Trevino in the exact same pose. Wayne may have filmed the sequence twice with two different characters to determine which one worked best. Nevertheless, neither shot appears in the film.

The death scene of Wayne's stand-in Marshall Jones, this time as a nameless defender, occurred near a destroyed portion of the West Wall. Jones is seen lying backward over a jorno, rifle, and officer's chapeau nearby. Earlier, a photo was taken as he lay across a Mexican soldier, perhaps after a violent struggle. Unfortunately, his wristwatch is plainly visible, and the scene was never used. Jocko, John Dierkes's character, is seen manning a cannon at the southwest corner of the compound shortly after the final assault begins. An explosion occurs almost immediately thereafter, dismantling the cannon. Dierkes is later seen lying over the same adobe structure as Marshall Jones did—Joan, Aissa, and John Henry pass by Dierkes's body as they leave the compound. So how did he die at that location if he had earlier manned the SW cannon? The answer again may be found in an unused scene. Ford had filmed a sequence in which Dierkes, Dean Smith, and others defend a portion of the West Wall between the southwest corner and Bowie's room. Though not seen, apparently Jocko may have been killed here and simply fell over the aforementioned jorno. Tom Hennessey's character Bull is seen defending a breach in the north wall of the church. Swinging a large timber, he holds off attackers until he is lanced by a mounted horseman and subsequently trampled. Shown on the screen for only a few seconds, this scene was initially much longer and shot from above.

On Tuesday, December 8, Wayne filmed Crockett getting lanced and pinned to a wooden door by a blue-uniformed Mexican soldier. Crockett, with rifle and torch in hand, had retreated from the barricade to the chapel's open doorway.

He now leaps over a fallen lancer, throws his rifle at two advancing soldiers, and swings his torch at another soldier inside the chapel. (Apparently, the torch had previously been used to ignite the cannon in the temporary barricade sequence.) Defenseless, he then is stabbed by another soldier's lance. Crockett then swipes his torch against the lance, breaks its shaft and staggers from the doorway into the chapel. Numerous soldiers are seen moving inside the church. Staggering back to the doorway one last time, Crockett eventually reels toward the powder magazine and throws the blazing torch at the powder kegs.

The first portion of this sequence was filmed on Tuesday; the actual magazine explosion wasn't filmed until the following day. Carefully rehearsed, Crockett's lancing still took several takes to complete. Conceptual artist John Jensen witnessed this and offered the following, somewhat apocryphal story of the first take: "So John Wayne's swinging this torch, slapping a Mexican here and there with it. And here the four hundred guys come in, and this one guys runs in; he's going to stick him with a lance. And this guy trips and falls, and he knocks himself out, stuns himself. He falls down, and he's stunned. And the rest of these guys, they all stand around, not knowing what to do. And they're standing like this" —holding out his chest— "and John Wayne is saying, 'Stick me! Stick me! Stick me! And he's going like this"—holding out his chest— "Stick me! Stick me! Stick me, dammit! Stick me!" Bob Morgan was the stuntman who allegedly fell down. "It was a timing thing," explained Morgan, "where Duke turns around and I shove a spear right through him. Everybody just jokes me, 'You killed Duke Wayne. You son of a buck.' Yeah, I killed Wayne. That was a great scene."[1117]

Morgan's lance had a retractable tip; as it pushed against the right side of Wayne's chest, it receded into the barrel of the lance. Wayne had a blood squib in his left hand, and, as he pushed the lance away with his right hand, he grabbed his chest with his left hand and squeezed the squib, thereby pouring "blood" all over his costume. Not pleased with the first take, Wayne's costume was cleaned with bleach to remove all evidence of "blood," thus the appearance of a white stain on his buckskin britches. Filmed at least twice, the scene would be stitched together from various takes. Consisting of four identifiable cuts, an analysis of the scene reveals several inconsistencies: First cut, Wayne's dash to the chapel (wearing black socks), possible first take; second cut, Morgan's lance advances to pierce Wayne below his ribcage. Pennant on tip of lance, second or subsequent take based on bleached-out stain on pants, two large, faded red spots on shirt; third cut, Wayne in pain as he is lanced high on chest. No pennant on lance. First take, no stains on shirt; fourth cut, Wayne swings torch, leaves doorway, second or subsequent take, shirt, pants and vest drenched in blood. Additional takes/rehearsals showed that Wayne was lanced on his left side, rather than the right (which appears in the film). In the original roadshow version, Wayne was lanced, staggered out of the chapel doorway out of frame, back into the frame again, then finally out once again toward the powder magazine. Duke must have felt the scene looked too melodramatic as he eliminated the second "stagger" in the revised version.

At 10:00 a.m. on Wednesday, December 9, a large contingent of U.S. Army and Air Force generals arrived on location, escorted by an honor guard of fifty Mexican soldier-extras. As always, Jack Pennick, complete with campaign hat, stood at ramrod-straight attention as a costumed Wayne and four-star Gen. Walter Krueger, former commander of the Sixth Army, inspected the troops. Accompanying Kreuger were Maj. Gen. Alden H. Waitt, former commander of the U.S. Army Chemical Corps; Lt. Gen. George Grunert, former corps commander; Brig. Gen. Charles R. Lehner, Kruger's staff officer during World War II; Lt. Gen. Barney M. Giles, Air Force Maj. Gen. Benjamin F. Giles, and Brig. Gen. N. Dwight Allison (managing editor of the *San Antonio Light*). Wayne escorted the group to the set, pointed out various structures of interest and explained the technical aspects of Crockett's death scene, which had been filmed the previous day. He then filmed the latter portion of this scene, when Crockett moves toward the magazine to ignite the gunpowder. With his back to the camera, Duke, as Crockett, leans for a moment against the doorway to the magazine, tosses his flaming torch onto a stack of powder kegs and falls out of sight into the building. A moment later, the explosion takes place. It seems the vest he wore in the previous scene may have been replaced or bleached again as the "new" one was extremely distressed with much more "blood" streaming down its back. Large light- and dark-colored stains were also visible from previous cleanings. Duke was extremely fortunate when he tossed the torch into the room. Swinging it underhand, he bounced it off the side wall or ceiling; it then landed on one keg and wedged itself vertically between two others, smack dab in the middle of the frame. Wayne couldn't have planned it better if he tried. Jensen watched Wayne film this scene as well. "God damn … and he throws this torch through the Alamo … (it) went bouncing through all these big lights and landed right where these guys were putting these dynamite charges in … and they're all like this," he says, demonstrating bug eyes.[1118]

Frame-by-frame analysis of this sequence suggests it consists of multiple takes; the actual explosion occurs behind and to the left of the torch. And there is a barely noticeable splice immediately preceding the blast. The camera moved ever so slightly to the left; obviously, Wayne moved out of frame, "Cut." Explosives were set in place, the torch was relit and filming began again. Following the explosion, Wayne hosted a hot luncheon for the visiting generals while Rolly Harper catered the gathering, complete with booze. Joining Duke to honor the guests were Widmark, Harvey, Ford, Clothier, Mike Wayne, and Tom Carlisle. Several San Antonio television camera crews were present to record the event as were David Zeitlin from *Life* and Roderick Mann of the *London Sunday Express*. After lunch, the visitors returned to San Antonio.[1119]

Later that day, Wayne filmed the powder magazine explosion from an exterior angle. Holes were drilled, and three powder charges in a triangular pattern were placed inside the exterior adobe wall, and then plastered over. Protective wooden barriers were erected to shield the cameras and the crew from the blast. At least, three cameras were used to film this scene. One was placed alongside the palisade, shooting toward the front of the chapel, and a second was placed on the plain outside the compound off the southwest corner of the chapel. Stills taken at the time show the area inside the compound and in front of the chapel populated with numerous Mexican soldiers. The compound had been cleared of equipment and the wider angle of the third camera covered the whole chapel façade and part of the connecting wall to the Long Barracks. Though action took place in front of the chapel, the third camera's footage, if shot, was never included in the film's final version. Sitting behind the scenes, Worden, with camera in hand, and Avalon, both in costume, watched the explosion. "Dead" bodies, horses, and cannon wheels were strategically placed around the outside wall to duplicate the after-effects of battle. Inside the compound, four 10K carbon arc lights were staged to the far left of the camera frame line. This greatly diffused lighting also provided a soft shadow falling to the right from the columns and niches (deliberately on the camera side) to render some three-dimensional definition to the front of the chapel. As red- and blue-uniformed soldiers advanced toward the chapel door, there was an explosion. Fire, smoke, and debris were set off simultaneously with a single lever by the special effects department. A microsecond after the triangular charges ignited, flames were seen coming out of both the powder magazine window and chapel doorway. The Mexican soldiers then retreated for protection. The explosion consisted of three separate effects: the initial directional triangular explosion resulting in the a hole in the magazine wall, an air-gun or some other device that shot out smoke or dust from the hole, and flames erupting from the magazine window and chapel doorway.[1120]

That afternoon, after the flames from the explosion were doused, Dean Smith would die once again, this time trying to kill Chill Wills. As the Beekeeper, Wills is ordered by Crockett to defend the South Wall. Standing atop a wooden staircase, surrounded by attacking Mexican soldiers, Wills pushes a squad of soldiers down the stairs. A red-uniformed soldier attacks from the side but is knocked out with a rifle butt to the head. Unaware of another attacker behind him, Wills is then stabbed in the back with a sword by Gil Perkins and falls to his death. Wayne took great care in setting up the stunt. An almost invisible trip-wire for the sword tip rig was attached to Wills and the staircase. Large mattresses were laid on scaffolds and placed out of camera frame below the top of the stairs to cushion Wills's fall. Wayne described the scene to Wills and mimicked the gestures he wished him to perform. After a few modifications, they were ready to film. Smith, who played one of the soldiers, describes the action: "Well, Chill Wills was having his death scene up there." He pointed to the staircase. "There were some steps right there. These Mexican infantrymen are coming up there to get Chill. Chill standing on the front step. Well, he kicked a couple of guys off (including Ted White), and here I come to get Chill. Now I have this tall infantry hat on, about this tall. To be sure that he didn't hurt me, they put a rubber stock on the end of the gun. Well, old Chill, he got nervous, and, when I came up there, he didn't hit the hat; he hit me upside the head with that (iron) part of the gun and knocked me crazier than a … and I fell off of there. A lot of times in the movies, the actors get carried away doing an action scene, and you can get yourself hurt. That's what happened this time. Old Chill was acting all over the place, and he knocked the crap out of me, leaving me dizzy. We got the scene the first time, and I saw stars over that shot." That particular take appears in the final cut. An analysis of the scene shows that, when they spliced the various shots together, the sword handle in Wills's back, which was already in his back *before* he was stabbed, is not the same sword with which he was pierced. Perkins's sword had a curved, multi-bar cross guard, almost basket-hilt-like in appearance; the appliance projecting from Wills's back has a utilitarian, almost pedestrian profile. Extra Roy Langston said the blade coming out Wills's back didn't stop in the extend position; instead, it went all the way around. When he landed on the mattresses, Wills started to choke and sputter. The crew ran in to help, thinking that the blade might have hurt him. "Nah …." he grumbled when he could talk again. "I swallowed the damn (blood) capsule."[1121]

Extra Eddy Donno watched this scene being filmed while doing a favor. "When we were doing *The Alamo*," said Donno, "Ted White was doing this scene where he fights with Chill Wills on the steps. Ted gives me his Super-8 movie camera to photograph him. So they're getting the shot; there were a number of cameras involved, and one of them ran out of film. Wayne was really pissed; it took like another hour to get things set up for the scene, but they got everything ready to do the scene again, and (Wayne) said to one guy, 'How many feet do you have?' and he said, 'Fifteen.' And he's going to each camera and asking them, and I'm standing next to this one cameraman with Ted's little camera in my hand, and I said 'Twenty-eight,' like there was twenty-eight feet of film in Ted's camera, you know? He just looked at me and didn't say anything. So then we cut for lunch. So after lunch they return to the shot, and Wayne says, 'Who are you shooting that for?' I said, 'For Ted White. He's doing a fight with Chill Wills.' And Wayne said, 'Well, let me tell you about that. You don't really have the right lens on that for this angle. Why don't you stand over here?' And he puts me up on this wall, about five feet higher, and it makes sense to me. I said, 'OK,' and they said, 'Roll 'em. Action!' And I got blown off the wall. He had effects set up an explosion during lunch. Ted's camera was broken." So much for the favor.[1122]

Now that Wills's scene was finished, it was Worden's turn. Duke had filmed Hank's death just before Thanksgiving; now it was time to film the cause of his demise. Although the Parson was reluctant to brandish a weapon, he had no qualms about assisting those who did in the defense of the Alamo. Worden already had been filmed carrying a rifle, ramrod and two buckets of gunpowder as he made his way from the SW corner along the West Wall rampart. After he left the buckets with extras Jim Brewer, Karl Flenn, and other defenders manning the cannons, Worden climbed up four stairs toward the top of a building. As he loaded a rifle, the room exploded underneath him, collapsed, and he fell to the ground. Ted White would perform this gag for Hank.

The last shot of the day may have involved Avalon. Because he was a costumed spectator during the filming of the magazine explosion, we can assume his scene could have been filmed that afternoon. Another possibility is that he was prepared for a "cover set." Each day's scheduled shooting is backed up with a "cover set" that has been prepared (with set decoration and lighting) in case bad weather or other variables make it impossible to film the planned scenes. Actors normally are kept "on hold" for cover sets, meaning not brought out from the hotel but capable of being "called" at any time to come out for make-up and wardrobe. This might be a situation where, due to the complexity of the previous scenes, it might have been necessary to film a static shot. A camera crew could have been waiting there for all the compound scenes to be completed. If so, it would have been the scene where Smitty rides over the crest of a hill and dismounts. Cut and close-up as he holds his horse's reins and looks upon the ruined Alamo. His shoulders then slump as he realizes the defenders are all dead. Amusingly, the last shot of the day also is known as a "martini" shot as the next shot will be "in a glass" or "out of a glass." Alternately known as a "window" shot because you can see through it to wrap, or just the much anticipated "LFS." (Last f%@*^!! shot of the day.)[1123]

Due to scheduling issues with Harvey, earlier, Duke had filmed the destruction of a cannon in the northwest corner battery manned by Harvey, Curtis, Ackland, Kuykendall, et al. As the cannon was constructed of wood and Styrofoam, wires were attached to critical pieces, so, when the directional explosion occurred, larger parts wouldn't fly out and injure the actors. A replacement cannon was then rolled up the ramp and aimed at the open breach in the North Wall. After its discharge, Curtis fires his rifle at the Mexicans flooding through the gap. On Thursday, December 10, Wayne was ready to film Curtis's death scene. The left-handed actor takes aim with a trapdoor Springfield, fires, and is almost immediately "shot." Ken spins, falls, and hangs backward over the timber post ramp and drops his rifle. The prop department had created a very lifelike dummy of Curtis, and dressed it in a duplicate costume. The intent was to hang the dummy over the stockade wall or perhaps use it in a deep background shot. Though dressed, it appears the dummy was never used. As usual, Cliff Lyons set up the stunt. A rope was tied around Ken's left ankle and attached to a stake driven into the ground with enough slack to allow him to move freely. Said Curtis, "I was wearing spurs all the time which were to catch to the posts around the gun ramp. When I got shot, I had to take the bullet this way, which swung me completely around, and then flop over, catch my spur in between these posts that were sticking up. And then flop down and hit the side of the post. It worked perfectly on the first take—with only a knot on my head when I hit the side of the ramp. It did strain me quite a bit, through the groin." Extra John Quinn was there to see this scene filmed. "That was a tricky stunt," admits Quinn, "and (Curtis) was brave enough to pull it off. I had been shooting my rifle with some others to the right of this fence, but that scene was cut."[1124]

At this time, Wayne also filmed the destruction of the North Wall and its subsequent breach. If one carefully examines the architecture and appearance, it's obvious the wall was initially constructed with a broken pediment in place. (A pediment is a triangular architectural feature resting on a horizontal element. In the broken pediment, the raking cornice is left open at the apex.) That particular combination can be seen in numerous scenes prior to the first assault. A wooden cross of variable height was erected in the center of the pediment at its base. (That is, the height of the cross was different in each scene). At least, four different combinations of wall/pediment appear in the film, which suggests it was constructed and demolished several times. In some scenes, the pediment is present; in others, it's whitewashed, sun-baked adobe, or totally absent. In numerous instances, the plaster configuration on the wall is patchy, irregular, and uniquely different from scene to scene. Though never seen from the interior of the compound, a wooden firing platform was temporarily attached to the inside of the wall, no doubt to support additional defenders. The original wall was built early in the construction phase. When time came to film the final assault, the pediment was removed, and the wall was bulldozed in the area of the anticipated breach. Then, it was rebuilt with adobe and Styrofoam. For some reason, the wall was filmed without a pediment for several scenes *before* the breach explosion (i.e., a medium shot of the compound interior with cannon explosions, demolition of cannon in the northwest corner; replacement cannon wheeled into position in northwest corner.) The non-whitewashed adobe pediment was then placed on top of the wall.

A large crowd of reporters and crew gathered to watch the anticipated explosion. Several lines of infantry were massed on the plain outside the wall, supported by mounted lancers. First, they filmed successive Mexican artillery barrages that obliterated the pediment. Multiple explosives were placed in the wall to replicate this effect. The pediment was first demolished at its base. Then two simultaneous blasts occurred at the wall's base, one on the inside, one on the outside. Since Travis and Dickinson had realized the wall would be destroyed eventually, they already had swung their cannon around to cover the interior of the wall. Too late. After the breach was opened, stuntmen Jim Burk, Gil Perkins, Fred Graham, and other Mexican infantry charged through the gap. The breach was further enlarged as Dickinson fired his cannon against the horde.

Once that sequence was complete, Wayne next filmed Mexican infantry and lancers charging through the breach into the compound. This continuous sequence was filmed with three different Todd-AO cameras: the first located outside the compound halfway down the length of the West Wall and angled toward the breach, the second located between the main gate and the flagpole mound facing the North Wall breach, and the third located inside the compound at ground level facing the West Wall. Camera #1 filmed the soldiers' attack as they charge through the breach and advance down the side of the cattle pen. In the background, several flag-carrying lancers are seen as they ride toward the breach. Fires burn in several places along the West Wall. Cut to camera #2: as the last of the soldiers pass the cattle pen, an officer-led squadron of gray-uniformed horsemen enters the compound. Following the officer are a lancer with a flopping hat brim, two horsemen carrying flags, and eight horsemen. The cannon on the flagpole mound fires toward the West Wall, and the subsequent explosion results in a shower of dirt and debris. Cut to camera #3: with the fallout of the blast still in the background, the lancers are seen riding by at ground level—officer, floppy-brimmed lancer, and flag bearers.

Later that day, two cameras were used to film the entry of additional lancers and dragoons into the compound: the first located in the northwest corner facing down the length of the North Wall and the second located inside the compound next to the cattle pen facing the North Wall. Dozens of horsemen waited patiently in two columns as horses before them raced toward the entrance. The first camera filmed lancers entering the breach from the northwest corner angle. Another squadron of red-coated dragoons is seen in the background, entering the compound through a second breach, leaping over a fallen branch and galloping past a burning tree. White uniformed soldiers are visible climbing over the northeast corner as defenders valiantly struggle to hold them back. The second camera filmed the dragoons racing past the fallen branch, but one stuntmen fails to negotiate the leap. His horse stumbles and falls, and the rider is thrown from his mount. As he scrambles to get clear, additional dragoons gallop past.

Sitting in a chair just outside the camera frame to the right and beyond the fence, Virginia Shahan, watching the scene being shot, recalled seeing a stuntman suddenly scamper out from under the dust and almost run over her. "I saw the same tree burn five or six days straight," said Tulisha Shahan. "They used a chemical that would burn but did not damage the tree. They burned that same tree over and over." To help the horses race into the compound easier, a ramp was built on the outside of the North Wall for them to charge over. The crew prepared the gag by knocking down the top center section of the wall, so it would be level with the cannon ramp. The front section of the corral fence was also removed, so horsemen could proceed unhindered.[1125]

Though some battle scenes were filmed out of sequence, a great many were shot in the same order in which they appeared in the film. For example, with a building in flames in the background, a wave of soldiers scrambles over the West Wall and flows like a waterfall down the scaling ladders. Defenders inside one of the rooms shoot and kill two attackers, but a third tosses a grenade through a window. The subsequent explosion and fire drives the defenders outside where they are killed. To film this gag, a partition was constructed in the room between the window and doorway to contain the "explosion." When Chuck Roberson tosses the "grenade" into the room, the special effects department ignites a previously placed charge. On the other side of the partition, flames simultaneously erupt, and Bob Morgan and another glove-wearing stuntman fall into the compound, smoke pouring from the dry-ice on their gloves. Dressed as Mexican soldiers, stuntmen Jim Burk and Gil Perkins are seen in the background.

With Mexican soldiers pouring into the compound, Crockett helps direct a cannon crew atop the flagpole mound. As the cannon is rolled down the mound and trundled to the temporary barricade in front of the church, a lone dragoon charges up the slope. Wayne rehearsed his movements several times while soldiers/extras waited patiently in the background. Sand was placed on the slopes of the mound to soften the fall of the horse and its rider. Once all was ready, Relyea shouted, "OK! This is picture!" As the dragoon rides up the slope of the mound, Crockett swings a hard rubber rifle at the stuntman (Jack Williams), knocking him off the horse (the rifle's rubber barrel is clearly bent). He drops his rifle to confront another dragoon (Roberson) and dislodges both horse and rider. In a continuation of the sequence (later cut), Wayne had grabbed and broken off a portion of a lance as two gray troopers passed by and thrown that section into the chest of a third who falls his horse. The lance had been sawn partially through, two feet back from the tip. When Wayne grabbed it, it snapped cleanly. This latter sequence was filmed out of order as still photographs clearly show the destruction of the West Wall in the background. In a planned but never filmed stunt, Wayne was to be caught without any protection at all, but, at the last moment, he was to pull out two hidden pistols, shoot several soldiers, and fight his way to the temporary barricade.[1126]

On December 11, Wayne and Clothier filmed the exterior explosion of the chapel's south transept. A massive blast, this scene was a continuation of the powder magazine explosion sequence. Once again, the three Todd-AO cameras were structurally protected. One was manned by an operator; the others remote-controlled. All unnecessary personnel were moved back to the village as a safety precaution. To assure proper continuity, the crew made sure that "dead" bodies, horses, and cannon wheels from the previous explosion were placed in their appropriate positions. Lancers and dragoons lined the hills in silhouette against the West Texas skies. Though not seen in the film, a line of cannons and caissons stretched toward the hills. A huge mortar charge was planted underground outside the south transept, and controlled fires were re-started in the magazine window and doorway. Special effects master Lee Zavitz and his team chipped away plaster on the exterior walls, so explosive charges could be planted. Once rigged with wires to a central control panel, 1st AD Relyea called for detonation switches to be thrown. Several actors and extras witnessed the spectacular effect, including Harvey, John and Michael Wayne, Happy Shahan, Jack Pennick, and Pappy Ford. Even though Harvey had completed his scenes, he was there in costume for publicity stills.

As the scene began, debris started to fall out of a second hole, similar to the earlier triangular detonation. A third hole was created with additional debris seconds before the final explosion. Both holes were much smaller in size than the first. A frame-by-frame analysis of the effect indicates it isn't continuous; in that, the scene was spliced together—examination of the smoke formation, the color of the explosion over the fallen cross as well as the position and number of horsemen in the background all indicate a *jump cut*. A *jump cut* is a transition between two shots that seem to "jump" due to the way the shots are framed in relation to each other. The jump cut in the angle of the explosion was an attempt to bring the two explosions closer together, timing-wise, without cutting away. When the smoke cleared, two of the transept's exterior adobe walls had been knocked down and rubble creatively placed. (This was the opening through which Arruza and his lancers would enter the Alamo). The left half of the apse's back wall was likewise razed. It's possible the transept wall was rigged to collapse simultaneously with the exterior explosion. Charges may have been planted over the entire side of the transept, and both the exterior mortar explosion and interior transept collapse occurred at the same time. In fact, a reddish-orange explosion can be seen *inside* the chapel seconds before the exterior transept blast. Afterward, Michael Wayne turned to Happy and said, "Well, Shahan. There goes your Alamo." Happy smiled and replied, "No sir, that was your Alamo. The town is mine." Though Wayne, Relyea, Clothier, and Lyons were present, it has been suggested that Ford directed second-unit coverage of this scene.[1127]

There have always been questions regarding the extent of Ford's involvement in the film, but what is known is that Pappy *did* direct Rudy Robbins's death scene. Given Ford's penchant for humor, it was only natural that, somehow, Pappy would incorporate the "It do" phrase into this sequence. "If you remember," recalled Robbins, "I was about the only ... I'd guess you'd say comedy, if you could call it comedy ... character. Of the Tennesseans, I was the only one who had a kind of a different personality with that silly line. And so, I guess that may be why it was significant because all the rest of the guys were just ordinary, tough, rough frontiersmen. But I was the dummy just saying 'It do.'" Whether discussing refreshments (*"Cantina...Do it mean what I think it do?"*) or being asked for clarification (*"Do chastise mean what I think it do?"*), Robbins always had the correct answer. *"It do."* Even Wayne got into the act (*"It seems to me you're looking for trouble." "It do?"*) So when it came time to film Robbins's scene, Ford used Rudy's comic response. "It's been said that none of the work Mr. Ford filmed was used, but that's not true," said Robbins. "John Ford filmed … directed the scene where Chuck Roberson and I … were laying against the front of the Alamo to the right of the door." Although you never see how Roberson was wounded or learn why Robbins was sitting against a wall, the two Tennesseans shared one final exchange: *"Does this mean what I think it do? It do."* As Roberson dies, Robbins looks defiantly at the attacking Mexican. Said Robbins, "That was the scene that John Ford directed, and we died there. He did a couple of takes because he was trying to get me to have a particular look on my face, and I don't guess I ever did get it. He told me to thumb my nose at the Mexican putting the rifle at me, and then he said, 'Now do that and don't put your finger up to your nose like that.' Yeah, he dreamed that up and filmed it himself." However, Robbins was mistaken about where the scene was filmed. A careful analysis of the stucco configuration on the wall behind him verified the scene was shot not outside the chapel as he thought but rather inside, along the rear wall. Joan O'Brien, Aissa Wayne, and John Henry Daniels would later film their "tarp discovery" scene in the same general area. Presented with photographic evidence, Rudy reviewed it for a moment, realized his error, and confirmed the correct location.[1128]

In the Clark and Andersen book on Wayne's film, A.Y. Owen shared a gag that Duke attempted to film: "Duke thought it would be great if he had a close-up of a Tennessean's-coonskin hat flying off his head after being shot. Duke positioned the hat loosely on the actor's head, but the hat didn't fly off on the take. On the second attempt that hat came off, but not to Duke's liking. He told the actor to really jerk his head back on the next take. Following instructions, the actor jerked his head back, but still Wayne wasn't satisfied. On the fourth take, Wayne positioned himself behind the actor, out of range of the camera. Holding that tail of the actor's coonskin hat, Duke called 'action' one more time. The actor jerked his head and Duke pulled on the tail. The only trouble was that the actor had placed the hat back firmly on his head. Duke stood up, holding the tail and looking at the actor, who still had the rest of the hat on his head. Duke looked disgusted and said, 'Ah, the hell with it.'"[1129]

At the end of the week, Wayne filmed Widmark's death scene. Bandaged leg splinted with a rifle barrel, Bowie sits upright on a cot, awaiting his inevitable death. Wearing leather gloves, Widmark cradles a prop Nock volley gun in his lap, black electrical tape clearly present on the bottom of the stock, his knife and two pistols nearby on a barrel. As dust clears from the magazine explosion, a quick-to-react Jethro (Jester Hairston) takes aim on the white-uniformed soldiers who enter Bowie's room. Jethro's shot kills the first, Bowie's, the next five. A larger group of red-uniformed soldiers quickly moves in. With no time to reload his seven-barreled gun, Bowie grabs and fires his flintlock pistols. In an effort to protect his former master, Jethro throws his body across Bowie and is killed by three bayonets. In a last act of defiance, Bowie grabs his famous knife, slashes the throat of a soldier, and is bayoneted. To simulate the impact of a gun blast, a special effects technician stationed behind Widmark discharged a shower of "blood" from a wand or tube as Bowie fired the Nock volley gun. A line went from the tube to a pneumatic canister that held the "blood." A large fan was positioned in the nave to draw smoke out of the room or perhaps to enhance the blast by creating a draft in the direction it would be going. Several takes were necessary; in some still photographs, Hairston was present, in others, not. The cot and barrel were moved slightly to the viewer's left for the final scene for better framing. As Hairston fell across Widmark, his hand reached out to grab the barrel the knife lay on. Previously, the blade had been stuck upright into the barrel's top so when Jester rocked it with his momentum, the knife swung back and forth like a metronome. Still photo coverage of the scene suggests Bowie may have initially killed two soldiers with his knife before his death. In one photo, a lone shako rests atop the barrel, replacing the knife. The scene ends with a close-up of Widmark as a bayonet "pierced" his chest.[1130]

The Bowie knife used in *The Alamo* was made at Warner Bros. for the 1952 film *The Iron Mistress* starring Alan Ladd. Designed by art director John Beckman, several versions of the knife were created by prop maker Arthur Rhoades: Two knives manufactured from automotive spring steel. A ten and a half inch blade, two inches wide and 3/8-inch thick, tapering to 3/16 inch, with a brass strip brazed on the blade's back. Lugged German (nickel) silver crossguard, a scalloped brass ferrule encasing a dogbone-shaped wood handle that was lacquered black, and a fancy three-piece brass buttcap. The words "Jim Bowie" were cut out of sheet brass. This was laid over an oval nameplate made of cream-colored Formica to simulate ivory. A strip of brass bordered the nameplate, and the entire ensemble was inlaid in the handle on the reverse side of the knife. Flanking the nameplate were two brass rivet heads, each in the shape of a five-petal rosette. Only two rosette rivet heads appeared on the opposite side of the handle. The handle was 5⅛ inches and the crossguard was 3½ inches for an overall length of 15⅝ inches for the knife. These two knives were used only for close-ups. Duplicate prop knives included three one-piece cast rubber knives for throwing and fighting sequences, and a metal collapsible knife in which half the blade retracted back into itself to create the illusion of stabbing. There was also a lightweight hollow sheet-metal knife in which the blade unscrewed from the handle, so the wooden handle could be screwed to a plate, which in turn could be hidden under clothes to give the illusion that the knife is sticking out of someone's back. The stand-in knives had the brass strip painted on the back of the blade, and "Jim Bowie" was painted on the nameplate in block letters.[1131]

Upon completion of *The Iron Mistress*, the knives were sent back to the Warner Bros. property department and subsequently rented out to other studios, including Walt Disney's *Davy Crockett, King of the Wild Frontier*, Republic

Studio's *The Last Command*, and the pilot episode of Desilu Productions *The Adventures of Jim Bowie* television series. Coincidentally, in *The Iron Mistress*, Ladd used the collapsible knife to stab adversary Juan Moreno (Joseph Calleia) at the historic Sandbar fight. Of course, Calleia later played Juan Seguin in Wayne's film. In *The Alamo*, Widmark used the lightweight rubber knives almost exclusively—the hollow sheet-metal knife and collapsible bladed knife appeared in only a few scenes. In the famous last stand, he used the rubber knife and the retractable bladed knife. In this film, Wayne also carried a version of the famous knife, though its pedigree wasn't nearly as prominent. Withdrawn from its sheath during the Raid for Cattle sequence, it was a standard U.S. Navy World War II issue with a 7-inch clip-point blade, with Model "Mark 2," Camillus, and USN all stamped on the inside of the guard. With a leather-washer handle wrapped in a strip of fur-covered cowhide, it was 12 inches in overall length.[1132]

Bowie's death was the last scene Jester Hairston was involved in. On location for the entire shoot, he appeared onscreen numerous times, and his character was always treated with dignity. Though Hairston would refer to Duke as *Marse* Wayne in private, there were no overt signs of discrimination on the set. As "master of the plantation," Duke was in charge of all aspects of the project and in charge of all employees. In a 1971 *Playboy* interview, though, Wayne suggested that there weren't a sufficient number of qualified black professionals in the film industry. "I've directed two pictures," said Wayne, "and I gave the blacks their proper position. If it's supposed to be a black character, naturally I use a black actor. But I don't go so far as hunting for positions for them. There's no doubt that ten percent of the population is black. I suppose there should be the same percentage of the colored race in films as there is in society. But it can't always be that way. There isn't necessarily going to be ten percent of the grips or sound men who are black, because more than likely, ten percent haven't trained themselves for that type of work." Hairston wasn't so affected; a long, successful career on stage, screen, and radio made him more than qualified. However, that did not exempt him from discrimination *off* the set.[1133]

In his journal, Hairston described two such incidents, both in restaurants. After a bullfight where Arruza exhibited his wondrous skills, Jester and six stuntmen visited a Mexican restaurant. Mostly filled with Americans from Del Rio, it was said to be the best in town. After they waited for over thirty minutes without being served, they flagged down a waiter who said he would be with them in a moment. Fifteen minutes later, with still no service whatsoever, one stuntman talked to the manager. "Well, I'll be damned," he said when he returned. "Don't you know they won't serve us because Jes is with us?" Hairston replied, "Well, you're just being introduced to something that I have been brought up with. It's not the Mexicans. It's the Americans in here. I imagine they told these Mexicans they won't patronize them if they waited on a Negro." The stuntmen were furious and wanted to tear up the place. Jester volunteered to leave, but, since the group would have no part of that, they all left. Hairston wrote in his journal, "The (stuntmen) told John Wayne about it, and John was really embarrassed about that. In fact, everybody in the company was embarrassed about it."

Several weeks later, Arruza was fighting again in a different bull ring, and Hairston, Ed Reilly, and another extra decided to go. Afterward, the three entered a restaurant attached to the bullring. The place was packed; they had to wait and eventually reached the head of the line. But the waiter started to seat people in line behind them. Once again, Jester was being ignored. This time, though, an influential friend intervened. "We had been here for over an hour in that line," wrote Hairston. "He (the waiter) had been taking people behind us, and here he runs and takes my coat. So, while he was in the office with the coat, John Wayne had a party of people who were friends of him and his wife. They had a private room off this big dining room. One of his unit managers came out to me and said, 'Jester, Mr. Wayne sent me out here to see how you were getting along. We're not going to have any of this damn mess that you had the other day.' So I said, 'Well, I was getting the run around until just now. This friend of mine over here is getting me a table.' So he said, 'Well, if you have any trouble, you let me know.'" Shortly thereafter, Arruza entered the restaurant and immediately headed for Jester's table. They hugged, and Carlos asked Jester to buy him a drink. Hairston wrote, "Everybody was awed when he came to my table of all tables, and I was the only black spot in that dining room. I don't know, but they seemed to come up out of the floor. There must have been about six or eight photographers around that table right away. I don't know where they came from. Here they were taking pictures of me, Carlos, and these two white boys. The waiters brought the drinks, and then (Carlos) said, 'I think you're all right now, Jester, and I'll go.'" He then went back to Wayne's dining room. A little later, Jester excused himself for a moment. "I wanted to go to the restroom," he wrote. "As I left my table, all these people from almost every table came and wanted my autograph. They didn't know who the hell I was, and here I was black. I know they wouldn't have wanted me in that dining room at all if it had not been for the fact that I was recognized by this great bullfighter. I started autographing people's programs and so forth. But that shows just how stupid this prejudice is in the United States. We could stop it in a little while, in a twinkle of an eye, if they wanted to. They just don't want to. It's just deceit, real deceit of the white man in this country. I can't understand how we can be so stupid and still declare ourselves Christians. Be a Christian and act like one or denounce Christianity."[1134]

On Saturday, December 12, as many of the principal actors would depart location that afternoon, Wayne gathered the entire cast for a group photograph in front of the burned-out chapel. This should not be mistaken for another similar photograph taken during the "crossing the line" scene; the two are easily confused. Longtime *San Antonio Light* photographer Harvey Belgin was on location to take the iconic image. Arranged by category of defender, all male cast members, extras, and stuntmen gathered in front of the blackened, fire-ravaged chapel. The Trinity—Wayne, cradling a fringed-sheathed long-rifle in his left arm; Widmark, supporting the Nock volley gun; Harvey, resting his hand on his hilt of his sword—stood on a raised wooden platform in front of the group. Immediately behind the commanders, rows of Tennessean/stuntmen were arranged with Bowie's men posed behind them. Bandolier-wearing members of Travis's regular militia stood at the right, Mexican defenders at the left. Conspicuous by their absence were Pat Wayne and Hank Worden, both of whom had already left Brackettville. Even though Avalon's character had yet to return to the Alamo, he was still included in the group shot and stood on a large apple-box. To level out the heights of the various actors, Pyle, Wills, and Curtis also stood on boxes, albeit much smaller ones than Avalon's. (At 12x8x20 inches, these wooden boxes are used to raise and lower furniture, cameras, props, and actors. When actors are of different heights, sometimes the shorter one will be asked to stand on a box. Half-apple boxes are three inches thick; a thin small square of plywood is referred to as a pancake. Boxes are also known as man-makers. The standard box can be placed flat, on its side, or on its edge. Really cool crewmembers refer to these as Texas [flat], California [side], and New York [edge]). There were so many different frames exposed of the group shot, that you will find Wayne holding his rifle every which way. Between the color and black-and-white shots, at least, thirty-two different photos were taken. With the completion of that shot, Wayne only had a few scenes left to finish, most of which included Joan, Aissa, and John Henry.

## CHAPTER TWENTY-EIGHT
## THE ABBY SINGER

*"Normally referred to simply as 'The Abby,' this is always the second-to-last shot of the day. In the early days of television, assistant director Singer realized that a few extra shots could be squeezed out of the day's schedule if the crew began packing up and moving to the next location before a location move took place. Over the course of a day, this could save up to an hour of shooting time." But, according to Bill Gilmore, that wasn't the real explanation of the term: "Abby was the eternal optimist. At the end of the day, the director's trying to finish his scene, and he's had a few more … no one knows how many setups he's got left. You're approaching the end of the day, that, whether if you're working a twelve-hour day or ten-hour day or whatever it is, you're approaching overtime. And the crew gets a little antsy and grumpy and wants to go home. So he devised a way in which, when they would line up on a shot right at closing time, he would say, 'Okay, guys. This, and one more.' And, those were his exact words, 'This, and one more.' This setup, and one more. Five shots later, it was still, 'This, and one more.' So he became famous for his 'This, and one more' bullshit that he was telling the crew to try to keep them going. It had nothing to do with moving equipment or anything like that. This had strictly to do with finishing the day's work. The Abby Singer shot is the second-to-last shot of the day, but it has that history."*[1135]

SEVERAL SEQUENCES ALREADY HAD BEEN FILMED INSIDE THE CHAPEL: Worden's death scene, Robbins's last act of defiance, Duke's demolition of the powder magazine. With the south transept successfully destroyed, the production crew now had easy access to the rear of the chapel where additional scenes would be staged. Still in costume, Wayne directed an extended sequence beginning with lancers entering the chapel and concluding with their discovery of O'Brien and children hidden under a tarp. A costumed Rubin Padilla, later to appear in another scene with O'Brien, stood behind the camera for this interior shot, wearing an incongruous pair of sunglasses. Wayne was tireless in his efforts as he moved relentlessly about the set, checking every detail until satisfied. The ubiquitous Ford doled out unsolicited comments and suggestions while gray-clad Mexican and red-uniformed infantry patiently waited outside the set for their cues. Inside, workmen cleared rubble from the transept opening, so horses and riders could safely enter. Slain hospitalized defenders lay strewn about the area as Ford strategically placed burnt timbers on the set. Several small fires were lit for effect. As actors, extras, and crew listened, Wayne explained his requirements: In the first portion of this sequence, Arruza would lead a group of lancers into the chapel. As they rode toward the doorway, he would stop and turn his horse to the camera. Suddenly, three Mexican soldiers would race forward and eventually be joined by two more; this scene would be cut and edited into two sections of the final sequence. The second portion of the scene included the death of "Doc" Sutherland and the discovery of Susannah Dickenson, daughter Lisa, and young Happy Sam hidden under a tarp. Wayne rehearsed Doc's "death" several times until he was satisfied the stuntman wouldn't accidentally stab actor Bill Henry. Still, despite several rehearsals, the filmed scene looks stilted and artificial. As Sutherland is dispatched, another soldier leaps atop a barrel, pitches off the tarp with the point of his bayonet, and uncovers the hidden trio.

"This isn't real, Aissa," warned Duke. "Remember that. It's only a movie. Men dressed as soldiers, holding guns, are going to pull up the tarp. Pretend like you're afraid, but it's all make believe. It's just a movie." The three-year-old recalled being picked up and put in the back of a cart, but, in reality, Aissa, her make-believe mother Joan O'Brien and playmate John Henry Daniels, behind several barrels, hid in the darkness under a tarp and acted as if they were terrified that they'd be discovered by rampaging soldiers. Young as she was, Aissa still knew everyone would be watching and thus enjoyed the prospect of all the applause and attention. With a group of still photographers behind him, Clothier to his left and Ford to his right, Duke said, "Action!"

Suddenly, the tarp was pulled back. O'Brien quickly covered Daniels's eyes: "They're going to bayonet us, she don't want us to see them doing it," recalls John Henry. "When Joan's hand covers my face, that's when my eyes got big, because I wasn't expecting her to do that. She didn't tell me what was going on with that, but I think they told her, it was like ... if they were going to bayonet us ... we won't see it coming. I can remember John Wayne," he says as he points, "and tell me what he wanted me to do." Daniels said he was told about the bayonets in advance and was surprised at Aissa's reaction. "Unless I hadn't been listening," she criticizes, "no one had mentioned these knife things at the tip of the rifles. No one had said they'd be tilted at my throat. 'Cause that was something really scary that happened with the gun." She let out a three-year-old's blood-curdling scream. "I forgot we were in a movie," admits Aissa. John Henry vividly recalls Aissa's reaction: "Aissa is literally screaming. It scared me. She was screaming, 'I want …' At my age, I'm like, 'Oh, my god. Oh, my god. What's happening with her?' Aissa was terrified. I don't know if they told her or not, but I was told that they were going to do that. I don't know why they told me and didn't tell her. (But) she threw a temper tantrum." "Mad at my mother, the cast and crew and stuntmen—everyone but my dad," Aissa says. Ken Curtis also witnessed the humorous incident: "She gave an ear-piercing scream, and proving she had Wayne blood in her, she flew into a rage, yelling at her mother, the actors, the crew, everyone. But she knew better than to yell at her father." Eventually, to the relief of all, she settled down.[1136]

Everybody rested in place and waited to see if Duke wanted another take. Instead, he called for a "gate check." The 1st. Asst. Cameraman removed the lens and looked at the actual film surface in the gate with a flashlight and magnifying glass to assure a hair or something hadn't flipped in during the take. Finding no such evidence, he reported "clear," and filming of the scene was complete. Once calm was restored, the crew moved outside the chapel to film the final scenes. As previously mentioned, Grant had a difficult time trying to determine exactly how to end the film. Several scenes were written, dialogue inserted, then discarded, but, before he eventually eliminated all dialogue, a sequence was filmed where Arruza speaks to Rubin Padilla just before O'Brien's departure. With flags flying, Santa Anna and his entourage ride toward the Alamo chapel, a herd of stray horses and cattle quickly scurrying out of the way. Lt. Reyes meets him outside the West Wall, and they address the discovery of the woman and children. Each makes various gestures toward the trio, and they discuss what to do with them. Eventually, Grant decided to eliminate all dialogue; he knew the ending of a film was critical, as all aspects must focus on the image and thoughts the director wishes to leave in the audience's mind when they leave the theater.

As Reyes watches, motionless, Susannah Dickinson carries Lisa as they leave the chapel and places her gently on the back of a mule, held by Happy Sam. Aissa Wayne has the last line of dialogue in the film, the poignant question: "Where's Daddy?" as she looks in vain for her slain father. Overcome with grief, and knowing her husband died in defense of the Alamo, Susannah can only gaze up at the Generalissimo with tears in her eyes.

The sequence required a wide-angle shot of the ruined chapel that would fill the screen, so it was necessary to completely level a significant portion of the West Wall from the southwest corner of the compound to a point just north of Bowie's room. *(Just a reminder, all directions identified are Alamo historic correct directions, not set geographic directions; Wayne's Alamo set faces east, the historic Alamo faces west.)* This provided the totally unobstructed view Wayne desired. As Duke and Pappy Ford sat in folding director chairs and watched, O'Brien, Wayne, and

583

Daniels rehearsed the scene numerous times; the latter practiced leading the mule across the compound; Joan held Aissa as she became comfortable riding on the mule's back. (Chato Hernendez's son, Jose Hernandez III, was offered the role of Happy Sam but passed on the opportunity. His parents thought the part might be too dangerous.) Just before they shot the scene, Duke pulled O'Brien aside. "I'll never forget it," recalls Joan. "He said, 'Can you kick a tear here, honey? And if you can, feel free to do that.' I got a kick out of that, and I said, 'Yeah, I think I can do that.' And then he said, 'When you walk outta here, I want you to walk tall. Do you know what that means?' And I said, 'Yes, I think I do.' I got the message right away. He said, 'When you look up at Santa Anna, sitting up on that big white stallion, after he had killed all of these people, including your husband and every living thing that walked in this compound, I want you to look at him, and I want you to say a few choice words in your own mind. You don't have to say them out loud, but just think those words when you look at him, and then look away when he offers you transportation. You don't want it because you're strong; you don't like what he did; you're not giving in to him, and you're going to walk out of here and show him that he doesn't scare you and that the spirit of the Alamo will live on forever.' And even though I'm a little woman, you know, short, I put my shoulders (back) and I walked out tall. The thing that he wanted most for me I think in that part, he wanted (me) to feel the strength of the character."[1137]

In the film, the trio slowly leaves the compound, passing slain defenders and Mexican soldiers who watch in silence as the survivors approach Santa Anna. Bexarenos genuflect in prayer. Filmed in several segments, sharp-eyed viewers can see the dirt smudge on Aissa's nose enlarge as she rides; one soldier's black penny-loafer is clearly seen. The general commands his buglers to blow a signal; all soldiers obediently stand in respect. Stopping for a moment, O'Brien looks at the General with a stare of disdain and continues. Padilla removes his hat with a sweeping gesture as she passes by. Once beyond Padilla, the trio then passes a pond. With a large boom microphone stretching into the scene, Wayne stood off-camera and gave directions to O'Brien. "We look like we're walking up a hill, and we're not looking at each other," says Joan. "I had a hard time keeping my short legs up with that donkey, that burro, because that donkey was walking too fast for me, and I was going up and down hills and little holes in the dirt, and I thought, *Oh, my God, I'm gonna trip on my face any minute*, and I had a hard time holding onto the saddle with my daughter in it, which was Aissa, and keeping up with that donkey."

John Henry has less than fond memories of that burro: "I'm nine years old. I can't deal with this jackass. Because he was stepping on my foot. This damn jackass, it was real pain, and I think that damn thing was doing it purposely. I really do. He was stepping on my damn foot. I'm trying to pull him back, trying to hold him back. John Wayne (told) me, 'You want to go down, and you want

584

to go down slow.' But this dog-gone jackass, and he's pulling me (toward the water), and I'm trying to pull him back. Trying to make him slow up, slow up, slow up, but he wouldn't. Joan kept saying under her breath, 'Slow down, slow down. Keep him straight.' And like I said, almost every third step I would take, he'd step right on my foot. Now, mind you, that hurts, it hurts." (Local resident Else Sauer rented out a jenny named "Maria" for this scene. According to family members, "Maria liked to step on toes. It was her way of showing who was in charge.") John Henry added, "There were these four big giant fans blowing to look like wind blowing, and I thought, *Why do they have these fans when it is cool out here?*" The three eventually reach the crest of the hill where Avalon waits. In earlier versions of the script, Avalon's character died trying to re-enter the Alamo, but, just before filming the final scenes, Wayne announced that "the end of the picture is depressing enough. He lives."[1138]

For all intents and purposes, the film was basically finished, although Wayne had a few more odds and ends he wanted to add. But Christmas greetings taped to the sides of cameras constantly reminded him of his self-imposed deadline. With over eighty days' worth of film already in the can, it was critical he wrap up the project. After the destruction of Travis's headquarters was re-shot due the aforementioned lack of celluloid, Duke filmed several close-ups of defenders firing their rifles en masse from behind the Alamo's palisade. As he carefully positioned actors and stuntmen behind the wooden barrier, a painted canvas tarp was placed over a hole in the chapel's exterior wall, the result of a previous explosion. This footage eventually was spliced into the *first* assault. However, editor Gilmore never noticed the soot-blackened window of the chapel in the background—soot from the magazine explosion that occurred in the *final* assault. No matter, the footage remained in place.

Technical adviser George Ross observed during the scene that Wayne was having trouble with his weapon. "I had to tell him he wasn't firing his rifle right, a muzzle-loading Hacker-Martin," Ross said. "I explained to him that he couldn't cradle it against the crook of his arm but had to fire it from the shoulder. Each time he'd fire the gun, he'd hand it back to me, and I would reload it for him. This went on for several takes. Then one time, after firing the gun—which belonged to me—Duke turned and shouted at me, 'Damn it. This gun didn't fire.'" Ross took the gun and showed Duke the burned powder as proof it had fired. Wayne just grumbled and said, "Well, I didn't feel it." Ross figured if Duke couldn't feel the recoil, he'd make damn sure Wayne would the next time. "I doubled the amount of powder and handed it back," said Ross. "The action started again, and John fired. What a jolt! You could see his eyes blink, but he never said a word. He just handed it back, and I kept putting in a double load. The jolts were really something. I'm sure they left bruises on his shoulder, but his pride wouldn't let him complain. Through the whole scene, he never backed off."

Ross began to suspect that Wayne was harboring ideas of revenge. "He knew how much I prized that gun of mine," Ross admitted, "and I could tell from the look in his eyes what he had in mind. He was going to smash that gun in the next scene, even if it meant paying me $750, the price of the gun. It would be worth it to him to get back to me, but I was one jump ahead of the old boy. Just before the final scene started, I stepped up to him and, with a firm grip, grabbed it out of his hand and gave him a dummy. 'Here, John,' I said. 'Better use this.' He didn't say a word, but I could see the light had gone out of his eyes." (Ross had had extra reproductions of this rifle made in case of breakage or additional takes. He also made a straight wooden mock-up that was inserted in Wayne's fringed scabbard when Duke carried it on horseback or around the compound).[1139]

On Saturday, December 12, Avalon, Wills, O'Brien, and Arruza were released from location and left Brackettville. Wayne took a break from the film that morning to fulfill an earlier commitment he had made to the U.S. Marine Corps. In November, Major Robert E.V. Johnson USMCR, had spoken to Duke about filming a television recruitment ad. Before he took off to Dallas for the weekend, Duke filmed three short spots. Birdwell called Johnson and, for once, didn't exaggerate: "This is going to be even better than you think." So, as extras milled around behind him and black smoke poured from the powder magazine window, a costumed Wayne told the camera, "I'm John Wayne. We're down here in Texas filming a picture called *The Alamo*. Now, this story tells about some rugged, self-reliant men. And there's another picture that tells about rugged, self-reliant men. That's what happened at Iwo Jima. Now, I've worked with the Marines, and I know it's a fact when they say the Marine Corps builds men. So see a Marine recruiter. Thank you." Short, to the point, effective. Wayne had the film developed and sent both the film and negative to the USMC headquarters in Washington. Later that day, Wayne gave a short tour of the set to fifteen Corpus Christi Junior Rangers who had spent the weekend at the Fort Clark guest ranch.[1140]

Sunday night found Wayne at the Cipango Club in Dallas where he had a ringside seat at Don Cherry's performance. Duke swapped ad-libs with the singer, but comedian Leon "Ukie" Sherin stole the show. "Wayne's old movies have been responsible for the sale of thousands of TV sets," he said. With that, everyone in the band stood up and shouted, "I sold mine!" as Wayne roared. On Monday, Duke showed up at the University Club where he demanded Ukie give him a preview of that evening's performance. Sherin obliged and even sang a duet with Wayne to "Dear Old Girl."

On Tuesday, Wayne, exhausted and fifteen pounds lighter, filmed a final battle sequence, took one last look at the crumbling set, said farewell to the remaining cast and crew, and left for California, never to return to Brackettville. A two-hour charter flight took him to Dallas where he boarded an American

586

Airlines flight to Los Angeles. Pilar and Aissa had preceded him by one day to their Encino home.

His on-site work completed, Wayne had made different impressions on, at least, five of his actors. Laurence Harvey had nothing but praise for Wayne as a filmmaker and director: "I think he did a great job. This picture will make John Wayne the richest man in the world." (And Harvey's performance wasn't half-bad either. Director Hal Wallis viewed some rushes from the film and then signed the actor to a four-picture deal. Harvey immediately flew to London to spend the Christmas holidays before he returned to New York on January 15, 1960, and co-starred with Elizabeth Taylor in *Butterfield 8*). Richard Boone was equally exuberant in his praise: "It's exciting the way they've created the Alamo just the way it was. It's a tremendous set, like being in another world. John has (worked on) this project, on and off, for thirteen or fourteen years. He really cares about it, and his feeling is contagious. It's much more than a hunk of film being ground out; it's something Wayne passionately believes in. He funneled a great deal of energy into his work. He knew what he was doing, and he expected everyone else to behave likewise. The only way you could get in trouble with him was if you called him 'Sir' more than about twice a year—that got him crazy." Sons Pat and Mike Wayne reiterated those comments: "Watching my father direct was pretty revealing to me," admits Pat. "I never thought of him as a person with much diplomacy and tact, but I suddenly realized that he had a lot of savoir faire." Michael was amazed as well: "It was a mammoth undertaking for one man. My father knew what he wanted, and he worked really fast. I helped him when I could. He had so many things going at one time; he was busy day and night for four months." Avalon was pleased Wayne gave him the opportunity to display his talent. "I hope to be a big performer in all mediums," admits Frankie. "This includes movies, records, TV, and the like. I am glad I was presented in this picture primarily as an actor rather than a singer. It is a new and very interesting field of work for me. I learned a lot from John Wayne during the filming of this picture. I think he is a great guy." Avalon compared Duke to Pappy and praised Wayne for the time he took to prepare the actors for their scenes: "Ford didn't talk to us much at all. Wayne would discuss the scenes, and he always knew what he wanted. He was very sensitive."

However, the person in a position to give the most fair and balanced opinion of Duke's efforts was assistant director Bob Relyea. As Scott Eyman wrote in *John Wayne: The Life and Legend*, "Technically, Wayne was the best director I ever worked with," said Relyea. "He understood, cameras, he understood editing, he understood lenses. What was wanting was communication with the actors. He was so gruff and short on patience that I don't think he even knew he was gruff. If he had a weakness as a director, it was communication with actors. The rest of the stuff he knew. Certainly, he knew exactly what he wanted. Completely. More so than anybody else I ever worked with. His abruptness was part of his nature. He simply had a short temper."[1141]

Naturally, a bit more biased, Clothier also praised Duke's ability. "You know, one way or another Duke was getting the job done, and it was being done with quality. Duke didn't hog the movie. There are some wonderful scenes. Like when Bowie gets a message in his hat that his wife has died. Duke let Richard go with that scene. He put him in the foreground, and Duke stood back in the shadows while Laurence Harvey as Travis reprimands Bowie for receiving information. Widmark was superb in that scene, and so was Harvey. And Duke just stayed back and let the other actors have the scene, which is as it should be."[1142]

Widmark, though, was less than impressed with Duke's efforts. Asked about the vision Wayne was presenting of America in *The Alamo*, he degraded the effort: "I thought it was ridiculous, you know? Grade-school hogwash and all wrong!" He even found Duke's directions humorous. He used to laugh when Wayne shouted at his actors: "Goddamnit, be graceful—like me!" But, Wayne, like all good leaders, gave credit where credit was due: "I had sole credit as director but I couldn't have done it without Bill Clothier and Cliff Lyons. I'd tell Bill what I wanted, and he got what I wanted. The critics think they know it all and write about how well I directed the big battle scene, but I left Cliff to direct that as second-unit director. So while he was directing the action, I was directing the principal actors in the scenes that were dialogue scenes, and Bill Clothier was correcting my mistakes." But he saved the best for last: "I couldn't have done it all without the help of my son Michael, who was credited as assistant producer, but he did a hellva lot an actual producer would have done. I have so many people to thank for that picture, you'll just have to look down the cast and credits, and every one of them made a priceless contribution."[1143]

*The Alamo* set had been relatively peaceful considering all its various issues: accidents and murder, confrontations between actors, dismissals and resignations, etc., etc., etc. Shahan recalled missing only a half-day of shooting because of the rain. And, apparently, it wasn't all peaches and cream behind the scenes, either. On December 2, 1959, Grant wrote Wayne a letter that expressed frustration over what was going on. Although he didn't go into many specifics, it is apparent there was no love lost between Grant and Batjac president Bob Newman. "I want, in the best interests of *The Alamo* to completely divorce myself from the area of exploitation and publicity," Grant wrote. "It is my considered, careful, and thoughtful opinion that Bob Newman is industriously engaged in a campaign to destroy the effectiveness of Russell Birdwell. This will not save *The Alamo* campaign in the end, because in short order the air will be full of accusations and counter-accusations—a din of 'he said that' and 'I did not but on the contrary ...' (Birdwell) will have collapsed under the barrage of slander and gossip. Instead of thinking of creative ideas in the field of propaganda, he will be busy defending himself. I suppose this attitude of mine could be construed as an admission of failure—suppose, hell, it is exactly that. But I tried, with all my newly discovered philosophy and psychology to find a basis of operation with Bob. It is impossible. Today he announced that I lied about relaying the terms of Birdwell's deal to him."[1144]

Because he felt Wayne obviously had chosen sides, Grant tendered his resignation two days later. "The more I think about the matter of the $50,000 item in Birdwell's budget, the more it disturbs me. I think it comes down to this. Certainly nobody—not Rockerfeller (sic), not Onassis—can forget a $50,000 item. Therefore, there are two possibilities: One, I lied about relaying the item of $50,000 to Newman. Or else, he lied when he stated I did not inform him of the item. One or the other of us lied, and I think you have no choice but to decide which one to believe, and fire the other employe(e). If you take no action either way, it could possibly be that you are so often lied to by the people around you that you have forgotten that no business can succeed if the head of the business is lied to by his employees. But the more reasonable possibility is that you have decided Bob told the truth and I lied. So, if no action is taken in this matter, I have decided to quit." Grant then went on to recite various issues he'd had with Newman in the past: "…almost a year ago you asked me to try hard to find a way of working with Bob for your good… Back in July, he did an infantile thing to me about a check that made me decide to phone you on the *Horse Soldier* picture and call off our agreement, concerning him… You asked me to please not become involved in any of the numerous Batjac factional plots to put Bob's well-groomed head on a pikestaff. I'm not going to rehash any of the other incidents—a good many of which you are acquainted with …" Then, as usual, he touted his talent one last time as he headed out the door. "Don't let this upset you for a moment. I have served my purpose on this picture—and well, I think. I'm proud of the job. And this incident will not affect in the slightest my personal attachment to you. It will not dim the almost sexual joy I have experienced from having my stuff put on the screen by a director who had an instinctive and intuitive understanding of the values." Grant quit; Wayne was able to get him back.[1145]

Upon Wayne's departure, Birdwell, the never subtle Hollywood huckster, the Behemoth of Blurbs, published a 1,389-word telegram (at $20.06) touting the completion of Duke's spectacular. It included bombastic superlatives, outrageous adjectives, and, in the words of *Los Angeles Times* columnist Philip K. Scheuer, circus verbiage:

*"In the chill morning air of a typical mid-December day on the Texas prairie, producer-director-star John Wayne today (15) directed the final battle scene of his epic $12,190,000 Todd-AO production of 'The Alamo.' Weary but genuinely satisfied with the result of three and a half long months of location filming on the monumental story of 182 men's courageous and self-sacrificing battle for liberty, the rugged box-office favorite of more than 250 major films took one last look at the crumbling ruins of his authentic replica of the Alamo and then hurriedly flew home to Hollywood (!)*

*"Wayne's co-star Richard Widmark, who plays Col. Jim Bowie, and Laurence Harvey, who plays aristocratic Col. William Travis, both played their death scene at the end of last week and immediately departed for Hollywood. Frankie Avalon, Chill Wills, Carlos Arruza, and other co-starring members of the cast also left the location over the weekend. Wayne's cameraman William Clothier, and other members of his Batjac crew, eager to be home for the holidays, return to Hollywood this week.*

*"No film in the history of motion-picture making has been approached with such singular dedication and assurance with John Wayne's recreation of the Southwest's proudest contribution to our national tradition of independence and personal liberty. He has dreamed of making this film for fourteen years and has staked his career, his time, and a considerable amount of his own money on the belief that he has just completed one of the potentially great box-office films of all time.*

*"In his debut as a director, Wayne has exposed more than 560,000 ft. of Technicolor film, shooting as many as twenty-seven different camera setups in one day. Using more than 5,500 extras in many of the panoramic scenes of Travis's battle action, he has successfully captured on film the total violence and horror of a defense action fought to the death of every last man. During the past three weeks, as the excitement of the tumultuous action has mounted, he has driven himself and his cast and crew of 300 relentlessly to the completion of this great story that has cost $30,000 per hour to film.*

*"Wayne left (for) home confident that he has fulfilled his dreams."*[1146]

Later, Birdwell exceeded his pomposity when he wrote the following to Roger H. Lewis, publicity and advertising chief at United Artists, with copies to Arthur Krim, Robert Benjamin, Arnold Picker, Max Youngstein, and many others in the UA organization:

*"... if we fail to keep 'The Alamo' in the news, we will be failing to reach the kind of an audience that is necessary for 'The Alamo' to reach the $100,000,000 gross which this film deserves and which I predict it will do.*

*"I recall when I predicted that 'Gone With the Wind' would do a $50,000,000.00 gross, and I was quoted to that effect in Life Magazine. David O. Selznick chided me by saying: 'Don't take your work so seriously. That is an embarrassing prediction, and we will never make it.' Having seen 'The Alamo' before I took on the assignment, I am confident that we now have on our hands the most significant, the most important, and the most exciting motion picture ever made — a picture of raw and savage action interlarded with moments of beauty and tenderness, a picture that will never again be duplicated in any way during the next couple of decades.*

*"Wayne has not only made a monumental motion picture, but he has turned out a milestone by which, in my opinion, all other productions will be judged for many, many years to come.*

*"In the midst of cinema cannibalism, perversions of many sorts including homosexuality, strange nuances of immorality, and other forms of garbage and degradation, John Wayne has after fourteen years of dedicated effort produced and directed an inspiring film document about the greatest single event, perhaps, that has*

*transpired since Christ died on the cross. This, the story of the Alamo—the story of the immortal suicide pact of 182 men fighting for freedom—is no doubt the only great, true event of our civilization which has never before been told on the screen. 'And now we have it.'"*

Throwing down a gauntlet, Birdwell closed with this admonition: *"Thus far, I have found a great deal of sloppiness, careless, and uninspired activity in connection with 'The Alamo' publicity, and I can assure you that this will be eliminated as quickly and suddenly as possible."*[1147]

Not satisfied with just praising Wayne's directorial efforts, Birdwell wasn't pleased until he detailed every mundane statistic possible: filmed over an eighty-two-day span with only two days lost to inclement weather; less than thirty working days were lost from both illness and accident by members of the cast and crew; food and lodging for the permanent company, as well as 75,000 meals to extras, cost over $500,000; a catering service provided more than 210,000 individual meals in addition to more than 150,000 gallons of coffee and 242,000 bottles of milk; in excess of $4.0 million was spent in Texas, including $1.5 million to build the Alamo; 11,582 payroll checks were issued contributing over $300,000 each week to the Brackettville coffers; temperatures ranged from 21° to 120°; transportation leased twenty-eight cars and station wagons and thirty-four passenger buses for three and one half months, traveling 1,500 miles per day between Brackettville and the set, at a cost of $850,000; a chartered air service made 350 round trips to San Antonio, and seventy-eight (1,450 miles) round trips to Dallas, sixty-three members of the national press visited the set; chief wrangler Bill Jones traveled 35,000 miles to find and buy 1,500 saddle and work horses; 150 long-horn cattle were borrowed and insured for $1,500 each; over 100,000 people visited the set, representing forty-one states and sixteen foreign countries. WOW! (Birdwell would substantially increase most of these numbers in subsequent press releases).

Other cast members were slightly less grandiloquent in their personal publicity. Representing Ken Curtis, Jimmy Stanley of the Mitchell Hamilburg Agency placed the following promotion in *Variety*'s December 18, 1959, issue: "Talk about Variety! KEN CURTIS as MONK in "HAVE GUN WILL TRAVEL" Saturday, Dec. 19 KNXT Channel 2 9:30 P.M. AND Just completed CAPT. DICKENSON role in the "THE ALAMO" A Batjac Production.

Frank Cooper Associates plugged the upcoming Alamo television special: "PERRY CROSS producer NATIONAL BROADCASTING CO. John Wayne—'Alamo' Special, Preview '59 NBC, NBC Christmas Special."[1148]

Before Wayne had left for home, though, he'd thrown a party for all his Texas investors. Right in the middle of it, Grant started to tell off a "professional Texan" who, although not an investor, had haunted them throughout the filming. The Texan rushed to Wayne and demanded he fire Grant on the spot for embarrassing him in front of all the other guests. Didn't Grant cause Wayne nothing but trouble with his outspoken ways? Wayne paused a moment, scratched his head, then explained to the pompous blowhard: "Well, I know a lot of people who bother me. But damn few of them have got any talent. You, for instance. It wouldn't even bother me to have you around, if you could write a movie script like Jimmy Grant."[1149]

Clothier, Lyons, several crew-members, and stuntmen remained on location to wrap up shooting as Wayne flew home. After a week of second-unit filming, everyone headed back to Hollywood on December 18, eager to return home before the holidays. Happy said a film crew returned after the first of the year to shoot another few scenes, perhaps some pick-up shots, or re-filming scenes the lab may have ruined. It's possible an actor may have returned for publicity photos, but there is no proof of either. Assistant director Relyea was adamant that no one came back to shoot anything after they left in December. Happy may have been confused as, naturally, there would have been a clean-up period where props were picked up, cannons and caissons carted away, photo lab dismantled, temporary structures razed, and trailers removed, etc. However, evidence does suggest that personnel were present in some fashion as Albert Podlasky, a Batjac employee, was admitted to the Del Rio hospital on January 8, 1960, for injuries suffered on location. Portable air-conditioners were removed from various buildings and shipped to Los Angeles while cattle and horse were sold or sent to stables as the corrals remained empty. W-2's were created and mailed to all the extras as the job is never finished until the paperwork is done. (Many books also erroneously suggest that additional scenes were filmed at the Samuel Goldwyn Studio in August 1960. Again, this is incorrect).

Individuals fortunate enough to visit the set at that time may have seen a few extras still hanging around; otherwise, the set was virtually abandoned. Scorch marks singed the wall of the chapel and compound. Travis's headquarters was in ruins as was the West Wall. The cannon were still there, parked in rows with limbers and caissons outside the wall. Broken rifles, bayonets, and lockplates were scattered across the plain, along with ladders and other props. Styrofoam rocks and pieces of walls were lying about, and one visitor reported finding a flat piece of Styrofoam in the shape of a human head—no doubt the remnants of a stunt gag.

*(In December 1958, Wayne purchased 4,000 acres of land in Stanfield, Arizona, and set up the Clari Land Company to manage a cotton plantation. All the extra props, wagons, cannons, etc. from Brackettville were stored there in two warehouses until 1966 when they were moved to the Old Tucson Studio. According to Studio president Bob Shelton, "The collection is ours under a contractual arrangement with Paramount Pictures. At the end of seven years, the property becomes ours permanently. Meanwhile, we will rent the wagons, buggies, and such to other film companies. Some pieces of the collection will go into an Alamo Museum, a renovated existing building. Wagons, buggies, and caissons will be parked along streets and kept in a long shed we're building*

*to house them. We are spending $15,000 reconditioning this collection. And we have set up a complete depot for the work. As we finish pieces we will begin deploying them throughout the movie location for visitors to see and production companies to use." Sadly, an April 24, 1995, fire destroyed much of the studio buildings. The undamaged Alamo Museum is now called Olsen's Mercantile. Today, only a few items remain of the collection: a small navel gun that may have been stationed over the Alamo main gate and a carriage gun. At one time, even the back-up "European" cannon was displayed there.)[1150]*

San Antonio still experienced a star-studded Alamo Christmas extravaganza even though almost everyone had departed the set. Wayne personally selected many talented Latin-American performers from his film to appear on stage at the Alameda Theatre, including Rosita Fernandez, television and radio vocalist; Lydia Mendoza, singer; Mariachi Michoanano, folklore performer; Sylvia Vargas, rhythm singer; Trio Los Andarines, musical trio; Los Chavalillos, dancing group; and Alex Moore, comedian.[1151]

On December 22, 1959, UA's Roger Lewis sent a letter to Birdwell that outlined the proposed relationship between UA and Batjac as it related to staff, budgets, and publicity. Birdwell would receive $125,000 for the period ending November 24, 1960, while Joe Hyams would receive $10,000 and Milton Weiss $8,000. In addition, offices in Los Angeles and New York, secretaries, office expense, travel, and miscellaneous would account for another $147,600. Prior to the start of production, Jim Henaghan submitted an initial budget of $249,700 of which $125,000 had already been incurred. However, in a revised submission, the president of Batjac, Bob Newman, increased the cost to $415,100. Obviously, Lewis was concerned and requested a detailed explanation of exactly how the monies were to be spent. Birdwell failed to respond but briefly met with his counterpart shortly after Christmas. Each individual attempted to control the budget; neither would allow the other to dictate demands and requirements. It was the start of a long, contentious, volatile relationship. *(For those readers interested in a detailed explanation of the publicity campaign, please refer to Clark and Andersen's excellent book, "John Wayne's The Alamo: The Making of the Epic Film", pgs. 103-121. Much of which follows came directly from that volume. Although specific contributions are not always identified paragraph by paragraph, this chapter would not be possible without their previous research.)[1152]*

Birdwell missed no opportunity to publicize Duke's film; no stone was left unturned, no reference too obscure. (In May 1959, Wayne himself had contacted the New York advertising firm of MacManus, John & Adams, and inquired about television publicity). On New Year's Day, while watching the 1960 Tournament of Roses Parade, he heard actor Ronald Reagan mention both Wayne and *The Alamo*. Wasting no time, Birdwell immediately sent Reagan a note of appreciation. (A lifelong friend, Wayne would reciprocate on Ronnie's behalf when, in 1964, as chairman of the Brothers for Goldwater, Duke approved a $60,000 check to cover the cost of a half-hour televised speech to support Barry Goldwater for president. Reagan's "A Time for Choosing" was broadcast on October 27, 1964, on NBC. An amalgam of hundreds of speeches delivered over several years, Reagan denounced what he believed to be the increasingly liberal/communist direction the country was taking and defended Republican politics. When he reached the end of his discourse, he stated, "You and I have a rendezvous with destiny. We will preserve for our children this, the last best hope of man on earth, or we will sentence them to take the last step into a thousand years of darkness." The impact on the nation was immense; an actor's career was finished—a political star was born).[1153]

Birdwell was reluctant to share the overall plan to publicize the film with Lewis—as a result, in a January 12 letter, Lewis instructed Joe Hyams to coordinate a March 6 "Alamo Day" campaign, tying the film to the anniversary of the battle. (This request would eventually spark the flame of Hyams's dismissal. Independent and resourceful, Hyams was not used to reporting in on a daily basis to Birdwell, having his expense reports approved, being told what to write and when. He chafed at these requirements and, on January 18, requested negatives for the Alamo Day layouts from his boss. Birdwell had no intention of listening to either Hyams or Lewis and sarcastically replied, "It is utterly unnecessary for you to waste money on wires to prompt me concerning our work." Never one to back down, Hyams wrote back, "If I am ever to accomplish anything on this film, it is most necessary for me to prompt you. I have been waiting for negatives for four weeks." Birdwell was furious for this perceived insubordination and, on January 20, fired Hyams: "Your attitude, your lack of work ... your failure to come up with a single idea of any kind whatsoever ... leaves me but one choice, and that is to accept your immediate resignation..." Although Wayne and Lewis supported Birdwell's decision, Hyams was less than satisfied and demanded that Birdwell honor his original agreement with Jim Henaghan of Batjac and Fred Goldberg of United Artists—three months' severance pay. Hollywood trade papers stated on January 29 that Hyams had "departed the organization." On February 9, UA was finally notified that the negatives were available from Graphic Arts Lab in New York City).[1154]

While he was at it, Lewis also took the opportunity to send a not-so-subtle message to Hyams's boss. Not knowing what Birdwell's intentions were, he wrote, "Possibly, you have some plans of your own, but I have no knowledge of what they may be." In a follow-up letter, he further requested specific information. Referring to Birdwell's letter of the fourth, although agreeing in principle, he wrote, "I am somewhat disappointed, however, in its lack of specifics, plans, and budgets, whereby the objectives you set forth might be achieved. The point you raised concerning the 'sloppiness, careless, and uninspired activity' to date needs no comment—you are by now fully familiar with the events and confusion in Brackettville which caused so much wasted time, effort, and money. I am determined that this not be perpetuated, as you know, and I, therefore, think that it is essential that we get the ground rules set as I have suggested since our first meeting."

Birdwell had already instructed his staff to develop such a plan. Providing the team with an eight-page memo, he outlined a proposed publicity campaign. In it, attention was focused on the following areas:

1) Federal, state and local government, United States Information Service (Radio Free Europe), and global Freedom Fighters. "Congress should call upon the president (a Texan) to declare 'Alamo Day' a national holiday."
2) Schools should be sent study guides and film.
3) Churches, civic groups, the American Legion.
4) Newspapers including mailings, direct plants, and wire stories.
5) Trade papers such as *Variety*, *Box Office*, *Hollywood Reporter*, etc.
6) Merchandise and tie-ins.

Birdwell challenged his team to come up with new and innovative ways to publicize the film; no idea was too outlandish, no suggestion too outrageous. Obviously, one staff member took the request really to heart and suggested construction of a well-lit, 175-foot statue of Wayne in the middle of Times Square! They even went so far as to pull together the costs of such a preposterous idea. Fortunately, or unfortunately, as the case may be, the idea was never implemented, but Birdwell still refused to share his ideas with Lewis: "I should like to ask you to cease being 'concerned more than ever' in connection with 'basic arrangements and plans' ... I should like to ask you to discontinue fretting about what I plan to do. It is obvious what we are doing to practically everyone in the country, and I should think it would be equally obvious to your department. We are so busy doing our work that it is a little difficult to stop and discuss routine as often as you suggest... I hardly find it necessary to answer your question how we 'intend to continue the operation back there... Let us work hard together, keeping each other posted whenever it is *feasible*...." Previously, Birdwell had reached out to the DRT and proposed several promotional ideas: awards for Wayne, an "I remember the Alamo because ..." contest resulting in a scholarship, etc. In reply, DRT librarian Marg-Riette Montgomery suggested, as most contestants would probably be teenagers, scholarships would not be of interest. Perhaps a trip to both the real Alamo and Brackettville would be more enticing. "If the contest were set up by states with a possible winner in each state: those within 100 miles of the Alamo not eligible, I believe you'd get a nation-wide response." She stated what the Alamo really needed was a made to scale "diarama (sic) of the battle of the Alamo," placed in the Alamo with Wayne's name on it. "This also would help to create a climate for making him an Honorary Hero (of the Alamo). That has never been done—it would be a unique honor. We already have an artist whose project has been approved by the Daughters. He is a son of the Republic, and will "do" the diarama (sic) practically at cost." Montgomery also put forth the idea of a John Wayne Foundation or Sponsorship Fund to finance projects such as a grand opera of the Alamo, a history of music in Texas and even a biography of Clara Driscoll.[1155]

Ironically, while Birdwell fired Hyams over the 'Alamo Day' issue, on January 18, the publicist contacted Gov. Daniel and solicited his aid in supporting the idea. "We are delighted to hear of Mr. O.J. McCullough's recommendation that March 6 of this year and all years to come, be proclaimed Alamo day," said Birdwell. "I had always been under the impression that there was an Alamo day. As one who grew up on the catechism of the Alamo in grammar schools in Del Rio and San Angelo, high school in Dallas, and university in Austin, I had always assumed, as did others, there was such a day of commemoration for those men who gave their lives at the Alamo. Now I am happy that after all these years and many state administrations that you are going to make right this oversight." In a letter to Buck Hood, managing editor of *The American-Statesman*, Birdwell promised egotistically, "John Wayne and I pledge to Texas, to Governor Price Daniel, to U.S. Senators Lyndon Johnson and Ralph Yarborough, to the Honorable Bill Daniel, and to all the others who are interested in Texas and world freedom that we will, to the best of our abilities, tell the story of the Alamo throughout the world during the years to come."[1156]

(Montgomery set Birdwell straight on his facts in a January 26 letter: "The (DRT) began the observance of 'Texas Heroes Day' on March 6, 1897, with appropriate memorial services in which the school children of San Antonio participated. The service was held in the Alamo starting in 1905. The schools do not have a holiday here on March 6, but there is a city-wide effort to observe this day in classroom exercises." She also gave Birdwell an unsolicited idea. "It has been suggested that if you have not already made use of the saying, Thermopylae had her messenger of defeat, the Alamo had none, that an effective opening for your film would be a background of flames and cannon roar then a fade-in of this so-often quoted 'epitaph.' It would certainly be dramatic—and familiar to MANY."[1157]

While production was still going on, dozens and dozens of magazine reporters crawled all over the set looking for human-interest stories. Once filming was completed, they immediately began to file pieces for their various publications. Though not directly associated with Birdwell's campaign, the articles nevertheless primed the pump of public interest. Typical was Lynn Thomas's piece on Frankie Avalon. Written in early September 1959 and published in the January 1960 issue of *Motion Picture*, it focused on Avalon's nineteenth birthday celebration in Brackettville. Spread over five pages and loaded with photographs, the article attracted both movie-goers and teeny-boppers alike. The January 10, 1960 issue of *Parade,* a Sunday newspaper supplement, featured a cover photo of Duke, Pilar, and Aissa on location, along with a two-page article by Arno Johansen about their time on the set. Local papers weren't immune to the hype, either. The February 1960 issue of *Texas Co-op Power* featured a behind-the-scenes cover photo along with a shot of Wayne chatting with Tom Hurd, general manager of Rio Grande Electric Co-op. A blind plant was placed in the March 1960 of *Teen* about a supposed affair between Avalon and Cristal. Frankie appeared again in a four-page article in May's issue of *Teen* complete with *Alamo* photos, while his alleged paramour appeared in a multi-page pictorial spread in the June issue, *Pageant,* photos taken by Sam Shaw. (In November 1959, she had appeared in *Playboy*.)[1158]

The morning patrol. Filmed crossing Sabinal River about fifty yards from Flaca tree sequence. (l to r) LeRoy Johnson, Ken Curtis, Gil Perkins, Chill Wills and Fred Graham.

The arrival of Gonzales reinforcements. (l to r) Julian Trevino, Joseph Calleia, Edmundo Trevino, unidentified, Marshall Jones and Richard Widmark. The unidentified individual was Wayne's first stand-in, to be later replaced by Marshall Jones.

Frosting the birthday cake. Filmed but not included in the movie.
(l to r) Veda Ann Borg, Carol Baxter, Olive Carey and Joan O'Brien.

The birthday party.

The dance after the birthday party. Filmed but not included in movie.
John Dierkes and Veda Ann Borg. Alamo Village archives.

Travis discusses cattle raid with Crockett and Bowie. (l to r) Richard
Widmark, Laurence Harvey and John Wayne.
Filmed but not included in movie.

Toni Wayne LaCava and Pilar Wayne practice clapping hands
for flamenco scene.

Mexican camp, cattle stampede.

Jack Pennick drills the troops.

Departing non-combatants. Caesar and John Henry Daniels.

Defending the Main Gate. Note the canvas sheet that covers a hole over the top center of the wall.

Hospital inside Alamo church after first assault.

John Wayne directs elderly woman after first assault. The man with the bull horn is his interpreter.

Retreating Mexican lancers, reflective pond scene after first assault.

Crossing the line.

(l to r) Bill Daniel, John Ford, John Wayne, Richard Boone
at Sabinal location…or not.

"I hope they remember. I hope Texas remembers." John Wayne sets up Richard Boone's scene.

"Not Thinkin'…Just Rememberin'…" Denver Pyle and John Wayne.

"Horses? We don't need no stinkin' horses!"

"Everyone take your places."

"Is everyone ready?"

Tennessee defenders man the palisade. Alamo Village archives.

Explosion of Travis' headquarters.

Rudy Robbins' cannon scene, directed by John Ford on West wall.

Preparation for Gambler's (Denver Pyle) death scene.

Attack of Mexican dragoons in front of palisade.

The death of Lt. Finn (Guinn Williams). Note mattress upon which actors will fall.

Epic twelve-horse jump over palisade. Note defenders hiding low behind palisade and flat boards on top of posts and baskets.

Explosion of Travis' cannon in NW corner of compound. Styrofoam pieces fly high into the air.

Death of Capt. Dickinson (Ken Curtis). Bugler Roy Ackland looks on.

John Wayne demonstrates how he wants a grenade thrown into West wall window.

Capt. Bonham (Patrick Wayne) stabs charging dragoon. Dean Smith on ground, Chuck Roberson on horseback.

Crockett (John Wayne) breaks lance. Filmed but not included in the movie.

Mexican lancers and soldiers stage outside of North wall while other
dragoons charge through breech in wall near flaming tree.

Mexican dragoon leaps over fallen tree branch. Virginia Shahan,
out of frame on the far right, watched this scene being filmed.

Rehearsal of Beekeeper's (Chill Wills) death scene.
Wayne demonstrates to Wills how he wants him to act.

Mexican soldiers advance up stairway to Travis headquarters as defender falls over side of stair rail. Filmed but not included in movie.

"Half you men! Throw up a barricade here! Throw up a barricade!"
Wayne checks out arrangement of barricade.

Mexican troops advance on defenders behind barricade.

John Ford places rifle prior to lancers jump over palisade.

"Stick me! Stick me!" The death of Crockett (John Wayne.)
Bob Morgan is the lancer.

Jack Pennick salutes visiting retired military personnel.

Crockett (John Wayne) throws flaming torch into powder magazine.

After magazine explosion, prior to main destruction.

Main explosion.

"Golly! What a gun!" Mexican soldiers charge
into Bowie's (Widmark) room.

Wayne stages Dr. Sutherland's death scene (Bill Henry).

Wayne stages the discovery of Sue Dickinson (Joan O'Brien),
Lisa (Aissa Wayne) and Happy Sam (John Henry Daniels).

The arrival of Santa Anna and his entourage after the battle.

"Can you kick a tear here, honey?" Wayne directs Joan O'Brien
and Aissa Wayne as they depart the Alamo.

The lone survivors.

## CHAPTER TWENTY-NINE
## "THIS, AND ONE MORE."

ONCE BACK IN CALIFORNIA, WAYNE TURNED THE FILM OVER TO HIS POST-production team: film editor Stuart Gilmore, assistant editor Bill Gilmore, music editor Robert Tracy, sound editor Don Hall, Jr., and others such as James Richard, Barbara Sherman, Terrell Morse, and Walter Wormell. Director Francis Ford Coppola once said that one creates a picture three times: First, you write it. Second, you shoot it. Third, you edit it. A film editor is responsible for assembling recorded raw material into a finished product and coordinating the post-production process that includes but isn't limited to the dialogue track, sound effects, music, credit title background and reprints. This is a key role in the post-production process, and the editor's skill can determine the quality and delivery of the final product. The pacing of a film's emotional moments, knowing when to cut a scene, add pauses, wide shots vs. close-ups, take six or take seven, eliminate footage—all these and more are critical to a film's success. The editor and his assistant—in this case, Stuart and son Bill—prepared a first assembly of the film, an editor's "first cut." (Some people call it an assembly, but most editors who are any good rankle at that term because it sounds like they just string it together).

Few people in the film industry realize that famed producer Bill Gilmore (*Jaws*, *Against All Odds*, *Midnight Run*, *A Few Good Men*, etc.) started out in the cutting room. Duke hired Bill's father to cut the film. "I had been in the business a couple of years," explains Bill. "I was working for Desilu in television. (My dad) called me up and said that he'd been hired to cut *The Alamo* in 70mm and that he had to go on location in Brackettville, Texas. 'Look,' he said. 'If you're going to learn anything about this business, you might as well learn the right way. So why

629

don't you come and be my assistant, and I'll teach you the ropes?'" Bill agreed, and, for the first two weeks on location, he roomed with Don LaCava, Duke's son-in-law.

Once a scene was shot, the film, along with the soundtrack, was processed at the Technicolor lab in Los Angeles. The picture came out of the lab silent, sound was transferred onto a separate 35mm magnetic film, and both elements were then sent to Goldwyn Studios where an assistant editor synced the dailies. When you sync dailies, you combine picture and sound, so actors' mouths move at the same time they talk. After they were coded with edge numbers so they could be matched up later, the dailies were returned to Brackettville; in the evenings, Gilmore would screen the 35mm dailies for Wayne and his key staff. "They'd look at the scenes together," recalls Bill, "and, if they had multi-takes, Duke would choose one. 'I like take two better than take one,' or, 'I like the second half of take three and the first half of take two.' We'd take notes, and then my dad would use (Duke's) preferred takes, but, in most cases, the film editor always tries to use most everything that was shot. Basically, it's watching the work and whatever hints Duke would give my dad. Usually, it wasn't much because the scenes were professionally directed, so my dad really just had to put the film together." Based on those discussions and input, Gilmore began to cut the scene.

(Amusingly, Wayne had a completely different approach when he was on the other side of the camera. "Rushes?" he snorted. "I don't look at rushes. I don't have to see rushes. I don't look at what they shoot until I see the rough cut. Sometimes I don't bother about that. I wait for the final print with the score and sound effects. I know exactly what I did in every damn scene. How it played. I know what I look like on the screen without havin' to waste my time on rushes. Let them tell me to play a scene. I know how it will look as soon as I've played it. If I have to see the rushes to know what I'm doin', I better get out of this business. Now, a director—he's got to put it together, the pieces. He's editing in his mind. He's sitting with the cutter. He's got to worry about rushes. Not me. I don't worry about the theme song or the scoring. Let the director decide. I never give an opinion on music. The music is an important part of the film. And it's the director's choice. All I ask is leave me alone to work out my actin' problems. And I'll leave you alone to work out your directin' problems or your musical problems or your publicity problems." Funny how your point-of-view changes when you become the boss).[1159]

Actually, the movie was being cut as it was filmed. Bill's father always said there was no reason why he couldn't cut it as fast as they could shoot it. Stuart Gilmore was a very fast editor and able to stay right up with Duke; he was never more than four or five days behind, based on the lag time of sending the film to California. On location, his cutting room was in a rear room on the ground floor of the commissary. The post theater was converted into a first-class projection room—well, maybe not first class. It was basically a room with a bunch of chairs, but a projector and professional projectionist were flown in from Hollywood. The dailies all were in 1,000-foot segments, so Bill would cut them into individual takes. "Those takes, both picture and track, would be sitting on his bench," Bill recalls. "He would then go ahead and cut (the) scene, as long as he had all the film." Occasionally, Gilmore reviewed the assembled footage with Wayne on Sundays. When principal photography was completed, Gilmore packed up the film and returned to Goldwyn Studio in California to complete editing. Upon their arrival, father and son were inundated with reel after reel after reel of battle action footage. As no sequence could be edited until the entire scene was shot, Gilmore could not cut the battle action until he received all the film. "It took about four weeks to cut the battle," added Bill. "The battle was an enormous undertaking. And you can't cut a battle until you have all the footage. They shoot the first couple of days of the battle, (but) you can't cut that because (of) the scenes of cannon(s) going off and explosion and things that are being done by second unit or sometime later or whatever. So you have to accumulate all the footage for the battle and then go in and cut it in one fell swoop, which took weeks." During an interview with Bill, it was observed that several parts of the same battle action were used repeatedly in various sections of the movie and asked if it was deliberate: "Yes. A shot is a shot, an explosion is an explosion," he admitted. "Somebody firing a gun is somebody firing a gun. So in most battles, you really don't know where everybody is if it's fairly close. Whether it was stolen from another part of the battle or what. That's pretty standard."

Although he had already reviewed the daily rushes, the first cut was Gilmore's preliminary effort to pull the footage together based on Wayne's intent and Clothier's photography. Previously, he had screened all the takes, selected the best ones, and moved them from the order in which they were filmed to the approximate order in which they would appear in the finished version. Every few weeks or so, Gilmore would show the cut footage to Wayne. "Not in order," notes Bill. "It would be whatever (his father) had, whatever he cut. Movies are made scene by scene, and you don't actually see the whole movie, scene 1 through scene 150, until the first cut is shown a few weeks into post-production. You don't withhold the cut footage from the director, you try to show it to him along the way, and he might have comments on that … but basically, it was to show Duke how the film looked in cut form and how the performances were tied to that, scene by scene. Everything was cut and shown to Duke. You would start to build reel one, reel two, reel three. If there was a bunch of scenes missing halfway through reel one, you would put in just a sign saying *scene missing* and go on." Titles, graphics, special effects, and composites were usually represented only by crude place-markers. When those scenes were cut, they were spliced back into the footage in the appropriate location.

In the first assembly, the sound was unfinished and required editing; dialogue, sound effects, and music were incomplete. Colors needed to be adjusted. Dubbing is the post-production process of recording and replacing voices subsequent to the original shooting. An actor's lines spoken during filming can be replaced to improve audio quality or reflect dialogue changes. *(Numerous quotes from Eyman's* John Wayne—The Life and Legend *are included in this text. If the reader has an opportunity to pick up a copy, he should by all means do so. The following is an amusing anecdote relayed by Tom Kane, Batjac story editor, which appeared in Eyman's book.)* Duke was bored. After listening to Harvey dubbing his lines, he had had enough. "Let's go over to Lucey's (Restaurant)." It wasn't long before Wayne was autographing menus, napkins—anything anyone placed in front of him as Harvey was completely ignored. "How come nobody ever asks you for an autograph?" queried Wayne. Harvey's rejoinder was priceless. "If we were in London, it would be just the opposite," said Larry. "They'd be coming after me, and they'd say, 'John Wayne? Eh ...' They're *much* more sophisticated over there." Harvey introduced Duke to the Bullshot—vodka, beef consommé and lime. Kane continued, "They had a great relationship. Larry wasn't afraid of Duke. He'd tell him off, and Duke loved that, instead of people kissing his ass all the time."[1160]

Gilmore further explains the post-production process, "You're telling a story on screen, and you want it to move. If a scene doesn't seem to play very well or it gets in the way of movement of the story, it tends to be dropped. You're constantly looking to streamline the film and not have it bog down." Slower than molasses and estimated to be over four-and-a-half hours long, every scene filmed was included in the first editor's first cut. If a director took the time to film a scene, the editor was obligated to include it in the first cut. Four weeks after filming ended, this cut finally was ready to be shown.

Sitting in the darkened projection room, Wayne was impressed. Because he was so optimistic about the film's possible success, he eventually bought Pilar a diamond necklace! His hard work had paid off: the set was amazing, Clothier's photography outstanding, and the action sequences absolutely fantastic. Ford, also watching this viewing, later told reporter William W. Pigue facetiously and perhaps somewhat sarcastically, "This is the most important motion picture ever made. It's timeless. It's the greatest picture I've ever seen. It will last forever—run forever—for all peoples, all families—everywhere!" (Another film critic would be less effervescent in his eventual praise: "May I humbly suggest to Mr. Ford that the film only seems to last forever.") No doubt, Pappy was a bit jealous of the magnitude of Wayne's efforts and even may have wished failure upon his protégée. Nevertheless, either because of the tone of the comment or just failing to understand the meaning behind the words, Birdwell chose to highlight Ford's comments in the publicity campaign.[1161]

However, in excess of 270 minutes, the film was way, way too long, and Duke knew that. As he'd shot almost 560,000 feet, entire scenes would have to be excised: "lifts," they called them. "(Scenes) that didn't advance the story or advance characterization. I remember some of the things that were taken out," says Gilmore. "What was going on inside the fort with the local soldiers and scenes, atmosphere kind of stuff that didn't advance the story. Didn't advance the characterization of any of the major roles and, therefore, was suspect to be cut if you were interested in reducing the length. The length of a movie is something that … it is hard to understand the impact of a film that is too long. But the audience starts to get tired, and, even though it might have some great stuff in it, it also has some filler-type stuff, it does damage to the great stuff because the audience is tired." Wayne sought advice from several associates, including Howard Hawks and John Ford, who both said, "Cut fifty minutes from the film."

When asked about Avalon's acting abilities, Wayne stated, "In the course of editing, we're not cutting one bit of any scene in which Frankie appears. I believe he is the finest young talent I've seen in a long time." However, one of the "lifts" featured Avalon, Olive Carey, Carol Baxter, and a bucket of water. Others were the Cantina can-can dance, Linda Cristal and her bird, Tennesseans in their foo-faw-raws (fancy duds), decoration of a birthday cake, and numerous battle action sequences. All in all, almost eighty minutes of film were cut in order to reduce the running length to a reasonable amount of time.[1162]

Wayne seems to have known all along exactly how long the film should be. Questioned at a stopover at Carter Field in Fort Worth, he replied, "I say it'll run three hours and fifteen minutes, but we haven't even begun cutting yet. For instance, we've got 75,000 feet of battle film alone that'll have to come down to nine hundred feet." At twenty-four frames per second, 75,000 feet of film equaled over eleven-and-a-half hours of footage. Nine hundred feet would run a mere eight minutes!

While Gilmore worked on the edit, Wayne launched a gloves-off attack on what he termed "a trend in certain quarters of Hollywood to glorify all that is degrading in a small percentage of disreputable human beings. The motion picture is for the family—and you just don't tell dirty stories to the kids." With considerable vehemence, he lambasted both *Suddenly, Last Summer* and *They Came to Cordura*, as examples of his disgust. Released while he filmed *The Alamo*, he adamantly stated, "I don't intend to see (*Last Summer*)." Effusive in his contempt, Wayne minced no words. "The subject matter (of that film) is too distasteful to be put on a screen designed to entertain a family—or any member of a decent family," he said. "I have been in our picture business all my adult life, and I deplore the garbage that is now being splashed on our screens. This degrading pabulum is giving the world a false and nasty impression of us, and it isn't doing our own people any good, either. I don't like to see the Hollywood bloodstream contaminated and diseased with perversion and immoral and amoral nuances. Filthy minds and filthy words and filthy thoughts have no place upon any motion picture screen. The motion picture screen is and should be a universal instrument through which we can make a better world, a freer world, through the priceless and invaluable communication of entertainment and truth."

Wayne didn't limit his outrage to *Last Summer* alone. "I don't see how they got Gary Cooper to do that one," he said, referring to *Cordura*, "which, to me, at least, simply degrades the Medal of Honor. I am not surprised at that Robert Rossen, the director, but the whole story makes a mockery of America's highest award for valor in fighting off this country's enemies. The whole premise of the story was wrong, illogical as regards the Medal of Honor. They don't pick the type of men the movie picked to win the award, and that can be proved by the very history of the medal."

Since Duke had not seen *On the Beach*, he wouldn't "comment on the defeatist aspects of the story, with which I am familiar." However, as he would many times in the coming year, Wayne took the opportunity to explain why he felt so strongly about *his* latest project: "The growing defeatist attitude in the Cold War imposed on us by the Soviets is a disgrace, and it is disgraceful that any Hollywood film would reflect such an attitude. America made the bomb, and Moscow stole the secret. Very well. They have it; we have it. The truth is, we won't hurl it first; they will, when they feel they can conquer us. Meanwhile, they are trying to defeat us by breaking our spirit and morale. America—the true, legendary, heroic America—fears no bullying nation. The real American is ready to die for his freedom and the sovereignty of his country. He certainly isn't going to be beguiled into dropping our guard and forfeiting his freedom to the slave world of the Kremlin."

Wayne didn't beat around the bush in publicizing his film, either: "I just finished making *The Alamo*, and I am not dragging that subject in by the heels at this point. The Alamo was made up of men and women who believed that, in order to live decently, one must be prepared to die decently. They were rowdy and lusty, hard-living, hard-drinking, hard-fighting, and hard-loving people, but they all had one thing in common: they believed in freedom; they believed it was something worth fighting for, dying for. I think the fourteen years that I have put in preparing *The Alamo* is going to pay off. And I don't mean just in money. Some very astute people who have seen a rough cut of *The Alamo* believe it will do $100,000,000 gross, not the first time around, but with the reissues that we feel will occur every so often in the years to come. Experts tell me that there have only been three or four motion pictures in all the history of Hollywood to achieve that status of a classic, with reissue value. They cite the industry's first milestone, *The Birth of a Nation*, *Gone with the Wind*, and one or two DeMille productions. They tell me that *The Alamo* will fall into this class and have a life of twenty or thirty years on the screens. I think it is fine that such high hopes are held out for *The Alamo*. I share this thinking, quite frankly, because I believe we have turned out a motion picture that is going to 'shake the hell' out of theaters all over the country. But I believe there is something much more important than the dividends of money coming in from *The Alamo*. I think it is high time that some agency in public life, or in world communications, do something to remind people in, not only America, but everywhere that once there were men and women who had the guts to stand up for the things in which they believed. Fiction can be interesting, but it's a very poor substitute for the real McCoy. The Alamo is something that happened, and it happened only 124 years ago this coming March 6. It was not a story that belongs only to Texas; it belongs to people everywhere who have an interest in a thing called freedom.

"I think we are all in danger, and have been for a long time, of going soft, of taking things for granted, neglecting to have an objective about the things for which we stand and forgetting the things that made this a great nation. The best reminder that has ever happened in the history of the world in my opinion is what took place at the Alamo in San Antonio, Texas. It was there that 182 Americans holed up in an adobe mission called the Alamo, fought for thirteen days and nights against 5,000 troops of the dictator Santa Anna. These 182 men killed 1,700 of the enemy before they were slaughtered because they didn't think a bully should push people around. If a fiction writer had contrived the story of the Alamo, it might have been unbelievable—because never before nor since, to my knowledge, have that number of men joined in a suicide pact to remain at their posts rather than to surrender or retreat. I'm glad to play a part in the making of a motion picture that is true and real and which I believe will present the most inspiring and entertaining subject matter that has ever been put on the screen. I think *The Alamo* succeeds in doing this. Thousands of men and women have been involved in the making of the picture, and, for them, I can say it was not just another job; it was a dedicated effort.

"I'm very proud to have played a part in bringing this film to the world; I'm glad I spent fourteen years, on and off, working with James Edward Grant on the film, which shows the world the sort of spirit and indomitable will for freedom that I think still dominates the thinking of Americans—despite this contaminated celluloid which is the exception, not the rule of Hollywood. Don't get me wrong. What I rap are the isolated exceptions. I don't want anything to happen to this motion picture business of ours. I don't want to see censorship come in again, but I'm hearing rumbles from all over the country that people are beginning to be a little fed up with trash and filth, and I think it is a good time for all of us, who have been in the business a long time and who believe in it, to fight to make our screen the most vital force of entertaining and enlightening communication that has even been known. Scores of splendid men and women, with great respect for our industry, have made this a wonderful business, and I deplore the very few who are trying to make a fast buck by infiltrating the screen with three- and four-letter thinking and writing. In the past year or so, Hollywood has turned out some of the finest motion pictures ever made, but I'm afraid we run the risk of having this exceptional record marred by the intrusion of those films that bring up subject matter and introduce thoughts that can do nothing to advance our industry but contrarily flirts with the awful danger of bringing about nationwide moral indignation that can only lead to a crippling censorship."

There is no doubt Wayne was passionate in his beliefs; he had the strength of his convictions, but he was equally passionate in getting his film out in front of the public. Mentioning *The Alamo* twelve times in his discourse on freedom, sacrifice, and liberty, Wayne's statement was the opening salvo in an unprecedented publicity campaign.[1163]

Since Wayne had decided early in production that the opening credits would run superimposed over a series of paintings of the Alamo chapel and compound, he personally supervised a special photography session of the set's Alamo's facade, unencumbered by filming equipment or personnel. Only Karl Flenn, a lone sentry, stood on the cannon platform, silhouetted against a spectacular sunset. Numerous photos of the chapel were taken from a variety of angles; items strategically placed in the foreground included cannon, buckets, cannon balls, ox-carts, and gabions. Selected transparencies from this session then were sent to Pacific Title and Art Studio. Pacific was established in 1918 as a film processing plant (Pacific Laboratory) and, in 1924, added title production to its list of services. Artist Russell E. Roberts was assigned to render the required views of the Alamo, painting them on coarse hessian laid down on tempered masonite. The rough weave of the fabric gave the paintings a texture and diffused quality that helped the photographically superimposed, sharp-edged lettering of the titled credits stand out.

Roberts, paid very little for his work, painted nine views of the church, each slightly different from the other and each around twenty-one or twenty-two inches by twenty-nine or thirty inches in size. These views consisted of:

The Alamo church, including Travis headquarters and South Wall;
A full frontal view of church;
A frontal view of church, including South Wall;
A closer frontal view of church and South Wall;
A frontal view of church with ox-cart;
A left-front view of church with short palisade;
A full frontal view of church with short palisade;
A three-quarter exterior view of church;
A full frontal view of the church with Travis's headquarters and cannon.

This last painting also appeared as an inside front-cover foldout in the July 4, 1960 edition of *Life* magazine. Comparing the paintings reveals several minor variations among the stone placement, rubble, and timber. There are also slight variations between some of the paintings and what appears onscreen in the actual film. The three-quarter exterior view of the church is a good example. Usually, a camera test is performed, and any elements of the picture that interfere with the readability of the text laid over them are modified. The grille works in the lower windows of this painting were painted over black, and the brightness of the south wall of the church was toned down. The sky was untouched except for a darkening above the low barracks wall where there was a bright spot and an area over the walls of the church side. An "artistic touch" was applied by a soft smear of light blue over the top of the "connecting wall" where the line of the parapet met the church edge. This isolated the church slightly, and a similar soft smear was added to the edge of the apse on the right, which fades and blends the image into the background, so the eye will not stray to the edge of the frame, drawn by a sharp-focused edge. (Batjac retained ownership of most of the paintings, although the *Life* painting was donated by Wayne to Texas A&M in 1964 where it still resides. Another painting is in private hands.)[1164]

Pacific knew bold graphics symbolized the essence of a film story. Titles were closely linked to the content of the movie that followed, and worked to establish the atmosphere of the story. They often included illustrations or pictures of key objects in the film and planted important narrative seeds in the minds of viewers. Opening credits in the title sequence usually displayed only the major contributors in a production cast and crew, which included the production studio, title, director, editor, writer, etc. The lead actor would be prominent, followed by supporting actors. They could also include the film's version of a preface or foreword, with written or oral text that set the scene for the film to come. Films shot in special locations often included an acknowledgement that thanked landowners for permission to film on their property.[1165]

Billing denotes the amount, size, and order in which film credit information is presented in advertising and on the film itself. The billing sheet clearly set out the order of the entire sequence and dictated which names were to be included on which title card, the spelling of each name, and what size the names should be. Given that the sizes of all the participants' names were dictated by the size of the title, the title was made as large as possible. Artists would hand-letter the title on a clean glass sheet over a piece of tracing paper on which the title had previously been lettered. For a glass plate to be shot over a painted background, the camera operator mounted the title in a stand with adjustable lights to illuminate the background and face of the title simultaneously. The camera operator shot the title/background combination, and then mounted a new set of titles, repeating the process until the sequence was complete, making fades and dissolves in the camera. (In a dissolve, two cards intermingle momentarily as one fades out and the other fades in). The operator knew how long to film each title based on the "counts" supplied by the studio. Counts were a precise indication of how long each title should remain onscreen, calculated in feet and frames: a title card might run for three feet, six frames. The studio calculated its counts based on suggestions for reading footage supplied by Pacific Title (a card with three names needed to remain onscreen longer than a card with one name for audiences to have time to read it, therefore, its "reading footage" would be longer). Usually the music department at the studio had already written the opening song for the title sequence, so the studio would know exactly how much time the whole title sequence should take.[1166]

Screen credits are always a huge issue; who gets credit, in what order do the names appear, how large are the names in size in comparison to others on the screen. Some actors had contractual agreements that dictated how large their names appeared on screen; others left it to the production company's discretion. In *The Alamo*, the names of Wayne, Widmark, Harvey, and Boone all had to appear the same size. The rest of the cast received the following percentages as compared to Wayne's 100% size:

Avalon – 75% (Impressed with his performance, Wayne picked up Avalon's option for two more films).
Cristal, O'Brien, Wills, Arruza, Patrick Wayne – 60%
Calleia – 20%
(Impressed with the performances of Hairston, Dierkes, and Borg, Wayne instructed Birdwell to give Hairston 60% and Dierkes/Borg both 20%).
The Todd-AO logo would be 40% of the size of the title.
Technicolor could be used in any size as long as the trademark "In Technicolor"— with the word "Technicolor" followed by a registered trademark—was used.
Original screen play by James Edward Grant, obligated only to abide by the Screen Writer's Guild contract.[1167]

(In much of the film's advertising and publicity, the red capital "A" in "Alamo" appeared slightly offset and unsymmetrical. It was long felt that Ybarra deliberately had outlined a faded blue "A" around the main gate, with two figures to publicize the film's title. "The two figures are monks with their arms raised," explained Ybarra. "I painted them myself. After finishing the paintings, I broke or chipped away plaster to reveal the adobe to age it." When finished, the design resembled a large "A," similar to that later used in publicity documents. Asked if he did it on purpose, a puzzled Ybarra said he never even noticed, that it was just an unintentional, fortuitous coincidence. Another myth said the publicity department spotted the "A" around the main gate and began using a red "A" in all publicity, which is incorrect. The red "A" began after filming stopped and the department started rough drafts of posters, etc).[1168]

While Birdwell was busy revving up his publicity engine, back in Brackettville, Happy Shahan had a decision to make—what should he do with the movie set? Admitting if he was located closer to a major metropolitan area he probably would've opened a different type attraction, Happy confessed, "I'm not amusement park-minded. I just want to make it the best Western town that there is in the world." Although there had been some conjecture as to when Happy actually decided to open the movie set as a tourist attraction, the idea had always been in the back of his mind. In October 1958, somebody asked Happy what would become of the location after filming was complete: "Well, we won't even start shooting until September of 1959, and I don't know when the picture will be finished," he said, "but, when it is, all this will be mine. All mine!" "But what will you do with it?" he was asked. "I don't know," Happy replied. "But I'll think of something." Later that year, during a television interview with a *San Antonio Light* reporter and station KONO cameraman Bill Allert, Happy confirmed his intention to "convert the movie set into a worldwide tourist attraction with shopping facilities and top-notch entertainment." Because of the Shahan/Wayne loan arrangement, Happy owned the village while Wayne owned the Alamo compound and church. But once filming was over, Duke had a set he really couldn't do anything with. As Wayne said, "We built the sets, then gave the whole thing away. They may make more money from it as a tourist attraction than we will from the picture. If it's a flop, I'll have to change the billing to star, director, producer, bankrupt."

Shahan had to borrow a great deal of money to repair and preserve portions of the Alamo and even planned to add a western street to the village along with a dance hall on the second floor of the hotel, red soda pop served in the Cantina, and fishing tanks. Native American families were to be brought in to give demonstrations in making pottery, jewelry, and weaving. Motor vehicles were to be halted a certain distance away from the village as tourists would travel by stagecoach. At one time, Shahan even contemplated having full-sized wax figures of Crockett, Travis, and Bowie placed in the Alamo, along with the remainder of the defenders in addition to the Mexican army. "All I wanted at first," explained Happy, "was a movie set, because I knew what I could do with it. I didn't conceive the idea of building a town until we had built the fronts. Also, I had been collecting old junk and antiques for years, and I wanted a museum kind of place to put them in. Everything here is as real and true as we could make it," bragged Shahan. "Right on down to the last detail." He pointed to a dry draw near the Alamo compound. "Across the river there—I'm going to doze out the bed and sort of clean it up—I plan to build a real 1870 western town. We'll have a general store, a livery stable, marshal's office, board sidewalks, dance-halls— everything a real frontier town had. The buildings will be board-and-batten and no false fronts. The real thing. Over there'll be the U.S. across the river where the western town will be. This side will be Old Mexico. Maybe there'll be a toll bridge and all. And these buildings will be all furnished. Not just shells like a lot of movie sets have. They'll be as real as we can make them. Of course, that'll be maybe a couple of million dollars and maybe five years away."[1169]

But as his wont, Happy would change this story depending on the audience. In later years, he said the idea of a tourist attraction came to him while he was out mending fences for the third time as a result of curious individuals cutting the wire to sneak in to see where the movie had been filmed. Sightseers wanted to take photos, but there was no place to buy film. They walked down the frontier streets and stopped in the Cantina for a drink, but there was nothing to quench their thirst. They wanted souvenirs to take home, but nothing was for sale. "Wayne blew up part of it during the battle scenes," Happy explained, "and then the property reverted to me as a tourist attraction. This spring we hope to have a grand opening, but just last week—without even a sign on the highway—we had cars from eleven states visiting there." Ever the businessman, if they wanted to get in so bad, hell, let 'em pay. So he started charging $1 per vehicle; open from 9 a.m. to 5 p.m. In the first year almost 150,000 people visited the set. (With the increased number of visitors, Happy was forced to beef up ranch security. Several lads from Ciudad Acuña even decided to steal some of the cannon left over from the film. Fortunately, a few of Happy's cowhands caught the boys trying to steal a six-pound cannon. The thieves confessed to the wild plot).[1170]

Too bad Wayne wasn't involved. Happy recalled, "I tried to get Wayne to go into business with me ... when Wayne and I agreed on building the Alamo here, Wayne paid for the Alamo compound, period. He wanted to just build fronts. I told him not to destroy the village in the film, and I would give him a town, instead of fronts. I had in mind then what I wanted to do with the town after the film was completed. After this, I had a meeting with him and his two sons, Pat and Mike, in my house. I said to them, 'Here's what I want to do. I want to show you that we can make this a movie center. I want you to give me five thousand dollars, and we'll call this location John Wayne's Alamo Village.' We talked it over at great length, and John seemed very interested in the plan. When we were about through talking, Mike said, 'Daddy, why don't we just sleep on this tonight and talk to Happy tomorrow?' Well, I knew right then what Mike's attitude was, and the deal never came to be. I knew I could take Wayne's name and advertise it as John Wayne's Alamo Village. He'd own half of it, and I'd own half of it. I'd own the land, and we'd pay the ranch a dollar a year rental. But they turned me down. John said, 'Five thousand dollars; why should I put up anything?' I said, 'Why shouldn't you? I saw you lose eleven thousand dollars one night in just one throw of the dice in Vegas.'" Pat Wayne's recollection was slightly different. "I don't recall actually being at the meeting, although I know that a discussion took place. I remember that my father did not want to join the venture. He arrived at his decision independently. He did not need counsel from my brother. He was adamant about this. He wanted to destroy the set in the hopes that the village would never happen. To my knowledge, he never recanted on this decision. Knowing how he felt at the time, I would be shocked, in fact, if it turned out that he had." (In a conversation with future Alamo Village employee Patrick Saunders, Happy said he felt that it was actually Ford that deserved much of the credit for what Alamo Village became. "(Ford) had the idea, and wanted to partner with Wayne, but his son cut that off.")

It has been said that once Wayne left Brackettville, he never returned. That may not be the case, however. According to Shahan after the picture opened, Wayne and his two boys came back and said, "Hey, what do you think, could we get together on your idea?" Happy said, "'You turned me down! I've already borrowed money to rebuild your Alamo.' Now I wasn't being smart; I might have been smart-assed, but hey, business is business. Wayne and I would have gotten along great; we could still have gotten along."[1171]

Later, Duke regretted his decision. "I'm sorry to say I didn't keep the rights to the location," Wayne lamented, "because I understand the guy who now controls it is making a good thing out of it charging admission to tourists. I have bad dreams about this." However, in a March 6, 1978 letter to fan Ned Huthmacher, Wayne had a decidedly different take on it: "I spent close to three-quarters of a million dollars bringing the Alamo village to Brackettville, Texas, and did it on inexpensive property at Happy Shahan's and dug him two beautiful water wells, brought electricity, and telephone lines in assuming that we would be doing something together with it after production. I found out I had made one mistake. I didn't have it on a signed paper."[1172]

Although Duke never returned to Brackettville, he still had a tangential connection with the Village. In 1961, the town needed to replace a used ambulance. Said Frank Higgins, Happy's brother-in-law, "I rushed a man stricken with a heart attack to the Del Rio Hospital a few days ago and was lucky to make it. Later, when I stepped on the starter to return home, the ambulance motor wouldn't start." Civic leaders decided to hold a day-long fund-raising program of activities including a barbeque, rodeo, and an auction. Happy even offered free use of his Village as the festivity site. That's where Hollywood stepped in. The list of movie stars who jumped at the opportunity to help a worthy cause was quite impressive: Rock Hudson, Jayne Mansfield, Sandra Dee, Jennifer Jones, Loretta Young, Barbara Stanwyck, Robert Taylor, Jill St. John, Don Murray, Bobby Darin, Cornel Wilde, Linda Cristal, Kim Novak, Jack Lemmon, and John Wayne. Auction items donated by the stars included personal items or articles worn or used in movies. Suffice to say, the auction was a rousing success. According to Happy, "Funds raised in excess of the price of a new ambulance will go to the Kinney County Memorial Clinic fund to help retire the indebtedness."[1173]

(Alamo Village has been for sale numerous times over the past few years. In October 1971, the Alamo and village were offered in the Sakowitz department store's annual Christmas gift catalog. The $3 million price tag included a square mile of ranch land and living quarters behind the cantina, ready for immediate occupancy. "It is paneled, has inside plumbing and air conditioning … very plush," described the catalog. "We'll even equip it with some bourbon and branch water." April 1973, Shahan listed the property with Llano's Johnson and Inks Real Estate. Included in the listing were the Alamo, the Village with all its contents, and 9,000 acres surrounding the set.)[1174]

On January 18, 1960, shortly after Wayne's comments on the state of the film industry, Birdwell planted an announcement stating Wayne would be honored with a special citation from the Headliners Club of Austin, Texas, later that month. Coordinated by Interstate Theater Circuit executive Raymond Willie and written by Birdwell a month earlier, the award was to recognize Wayne's efforts for making the film in Texas. (Thanks to Willie's influence and involvement, Texas soon was inundated with articles about Wayne and *The Alamo*). But, that same day, former Batjac vice-president Jim Henaghan sued Duke for $102,500, claiming he'd been promised $100,000 for helping Wayne obtain financing for the film; he'd only received $9,000. In addition, he also asked for another $11,500 in salary for twenty-three weeks of activities. Henaghan asserted Wayne had agreed to pay him a finder's fee for securing a $1.5 million investment from I.J. and O.J. McCulloch. Wayne's position in the lawsuit was that the payment would come out of the film's profits. At a news conference, Wayne said he would honor the agreement; the suit eventually was settled out of court, the terms not revealed. Wayne said of the fight, "I'm sorry his ego was hurt. It was just too big a job—Birdwell was the guy I wanted." Henaghan claimed it's his pocketbook that was hurt, however. "Wayne and I have a fight every Saturday night. I was as much at fault as he was."[1175]

While Gov. Price Daniel spoke in Dallas/Fort Worth at the American National Cattlemen's Association convention and the TCU Citizenship and Career Conference, on January 29, Duke, Pilar, Grant, Birdwell, Bill Daniel, and O.J. McCullough flew to Austin in McCullough's plane, so Wayne could receive the Headliners award. Earlier that day, Duke had offered his opinion of the defenders at the Alamo: "They were men who didn't like bookkeepers, bankers, or wires (fences). You can't get away from them in this age, but those guys did." He'd also commented on his film: "The thing that set the whole tone of the picture was something that J. Frank Dobie told me back in 1948. He said not to forget that Col. Travis used to say, 'Never eat on an empty stomach or drink on a full stomach.' I decided then to make the defenders of the Alamo rough, hard-living men who became heroes." Previously, Duke had stated Dobie told him it was *Crockett* who said that. No matter, it was a great story. That evening Wayne was guest of honor at a reception at the home of business tycoon H.H. Coffield. The following day, Daniel returned to Austin for a morning coffee at the Governor's mansion honoring Wayne. A stag luncheon was held for five hundred people at the Driskill Hotel where Wayne received a plaque. Senate Majority Leader Lyndon B. Johnson was honored for his success in uniting the country in a time of an international crisis, and Wayne was honored for the power he brought to the screen with his talent and good looks. That evening, the awards were presented at the Municipal Auditorium by Gov. Daniel. Present to receive citations for distinguished achievement were Johnson, Raymond Willie, and Oveta Culp Hobby, president and editor of the *Houston Post*, who was named Texas Publisher of the Year. CBS commentator Douglas Edwards served as master of ceremonies for the awards party. The citation for Wayne's award read: "To John Wayne, Who has made motion picture stardom one of the great professions; Who has made 'The Alamo' an international symbol of man's undying fight for freedom."[1176]

For Wayne, the award was special thanks from a state where he had invested so much time and energy. Introduced as "the man who owns 50 percent of Anita Ekberg," Wayne replied, "That was three or four years ago. I no longer own even that half!" LBJ piqued the interest of the gathering when he said, "I'm going to make an important announcement real soon. In fact, I think I'll make it now." The crowd immediately became quiet, thinking the senator would announce a possible presidential campaign bid. After a moment of silence, Johnson said, "This concludes my remarks."[1177]

Later that evening, Birdwell made his "Alamo Day" pitch to both Gov. Daniel and Johnson. Columnist Ivan Spear clearly identified Birdwell's approach when he wrote: "The Wayne-Birdwell stratagem is as sagacious as it is transparent. Remind the public of the historic significance of the Alamo, and there is sure to be a limitless worldwide ready-made audience for the stratospherically budgeted motion picture which it inspired." Johnson was asked to have the U.S. Congress declare March 6, 1960, a day of remembrance while Daniel was asked to contact the other forty-nine governors requesting them to do the same. Eventually, governors from seven of eighteen states that had defenders at the mission did so. Congress thought otherwise. Along with Georgia, Maryland, Missouri, Louisiana, Tennessee, and Virginia, the governor of Texas proclaimed:

"**Of all the battles fought** on American soil for the cause of democracy, liberty, and freedom, the thirteen-day defense of the Alamo has become one of the brightest beacons of dedication, courage, and self-sacrifice in the history of the United States.

"**Appropriately it has been said**, 'Thermopylae had her messenger of defeat, the Alamo had none.' This was because the 185 heroic defenders, native sons of eighteen present States of the American Union and six foreign countries, pledged themselves to fight until death rather than to live under the tyranny of dictatorship.

"**This important chapter** in mankind's endless fight for freedom began on February 23, 1836, when the small band of citizen-soldiers gathered within the crumbling adobe walls of the Spanish Mission in San Antonio, Texas, known as the Alamo, determined to stop or, at least, delay the Mexican dictator, Santa Anna, whose 7,000 well-trained soldiers were bent upon destroying the growing movement for freedom and independence in Texas.

**"Outnumbered** thirty-five to one, and facing the certainty of defeat and death, the Alamo defenders withstood the enemy for thirteen days until their fortress was overrun on March 6, 1836. Not one man gave up his post, but every man gave up his life. They lost a battle but won a war. They destroyed 1,700 enemy troops and delayed the others long enough for General Sam Houston to assemble an army which forty-six days later defeated Santa Anna on the field of San Jacinto with 'Remember the Alamo' as their most inspiring battle cry.

**"It is appropriate** that lovers of freedom everywhere should honor the memory of William Barret Travis, David Crockett, James Bowie, James Bonham, and all the other gallant heroes of the Alamo, because they fought and sacrificed their lives for a cause which has no geographical boundaries—the cause of democracy and individual liberty. Their number included eleven different national origins: American, Mexican, Spanish, English, Irish, Welsh, Dutch, German, Scotch, French, and Danish. Thus, their heroism has been described as an international symbol of man's undying fight for freedom.

**"Texans have long honored** the memory of the Alamo defenders with special ceremonies on March 6, and this year the Governors of the seventeen other States whose sons gave their lives for freedom within the walls of this historic shrine are being invited to join in commemorating Alamo Day.

"Therefore, I, as Governor of Texas, do hereby proclaim Sunday, March 6, 1960 as Alamo Day in Texas, and urge all of our citizens to join in tribute to the memory of the heroes of the Alamo who died at the hands of tyranny in order that others may live in freedom."[1178]

Birdwell's campaign was off and running, yet he still hadn't resolved one critical issue. United Artists felt the only proper way to publicize the film was through the use of its own fieldmen planting stories and paid advertisements. Running out of patience, Birdwell replied with his usual tact: "Let's get one thing straight: I am not accountable to you ... I believe in using advertising when the message can't be said any other way. But my idea of a truly great campaign is an editorial campaign in every department of all media, flanked by advertising when it is indicated." In a meeting between UA and Birdwell subordinates, it was apparent that, while they attempted to work together, their respective organizations' hierarchy worked hard to make it impossible. Birdwell required that, while layouts, features, and daily releases could be prepared in New York, all material would have to be TWX'd to Hollywood for his specific approval before servicing. UA asked for details on various Birdwell publicity gimmicks, to no avail, and there wasn't any hard plan for the Pontiac-sponsored television special. UA Executive Burt Sloane wrote, "All of this does not represent a complete or fully satisfactory working arrangement from our point of view." But it wasn't all gloom and doom. "On the other hand," he continued, "the air is certainly clearing, and, with more congenial and careful explorations, I think we can shape a more active role for ourselves in the campaign." After additional correspondence failed to resolve the problem, Birdwell and Lewis agreed to meet face-to-face to work out the issue.[1179]

Lewis, however, wasn't the only individual Birdwell would antagonize as he also came to verbal blows with his predecessor, Jim Henaghan. This was only natural as Henaghan had been replaced by the pugilist of pontification—even Wayne stated he wouldn't support the ex-vice president of Batjac. Don LaCava somewhat understated the obvious when he said, "(Birdwell) finally came on (the project) to the consternation of several people. He was a very strong personality, and he ran rough-shod over a few people." After Birdwell's bombastic claim that *The Alamo* would gross in excess of $100 million (a letter photocopied to eighteen industry executives), Henaghan couldn't restrain himself. In a March 9 letter to the editor, he wrote, "I read the excerpted letter in the Feb 10 issue of *Variety*, having to do with Birdwell's astonishing contentions and predictions for *The Alamo* with more than passing interest. As a matter of fact, I feel quite like the fellow who was quoted as saying of Mickey Rooney that he 'was responsible for his career—because he had seen him as a child in vaudeville and didn't kill him.'" (*Variety*'s editors warned their readers: *"Henaghan's comments, an excerpted critique of an excerpted missive, should be read as humor. More seriously, litigation pends between some of the parties to the promotion of the battle celebrated in Texas legend."*)

"I engaged Birdwell as a thumper for *The Alamo* in the hope that his fertile brain might add something to our program of exploitation. In fact, Birdwell did not, as he says, 'accept the assignment after he saw the picture.' He leaped to the challenge at a time when neither he nor I were sure it was going to be anything more worthy of him than "I Was A Teenage Mountebank." During his first five months on *The Alamo*, his literary output pointed to a marked refusal to surface. On the first of each month, he sent me a lot of figures and the simple sentence, 'Please remit.'

"Prodded by the spirit of Munchausen, I lifted the budget of the picture from its actual below-the-line figure of some $2,000,000 to a sparkling $10,440,000—a set of numbers I found in the bottom of a bottle. When I shed my lying ways and Birdwell took my place, I was humbled to discover that his first act was to increase my budget to $12,220,000, a rounder figure I must admit.

"While I was crowding my big lie into a corner, many things deeply concerned me in the honest dark of the nights. Should I chance a capital E in spelling epic? I fretted that so many coonskin caps might remind folks of Jackie Gleason and Art Carney on Lodge nights—and that some clown with an adding machine might count 265 Mexicans in Santa Anna's gallant army, rather than the 7,500 I had promised. I sweated that terror out along with the fear that some sober reporter might look under his bed at the location and find the shoes of the fellow who had played in the same story, shot on the same location, just a couple of years before.

"I dealt too delicately, I suppose, with Wayne's talent as an actor-director. I shied from comparing him with Brando, Gielgud, Guinness, et al as a thesp— and Wyler, Capra, Ford, et al as a director. There is no excuse for that. And I dummied-up like a crooked undertaker when it came to discussing the spiritual elements of the show, because the plot featured a Walt Disney idol debauching himself into certain hell, a more than likely homosexual, tyrannic fop, a specialist in switchblade techniques, and a raucous band of Sunday-school ineligibles who in thirteen days drank Southwest Texas as dry as a burned stew. Fortunately, we had no cannibals.

"I admit I rejected the possibility that the passing of these poor, sick, rustic lushes and misfits might not stir audiences to trauma a whit more than the news that the guest list of a Bowery flophouse had entered Kingdom because someone had neglected to thoroughly strain the Sterno.

"I am afraid I was guilty of the inability to interpret. After all, I did have the same set of facts and circumstances as Birdwell."[1180]

Henaghan does bring up an interesting point, though. Exactly how much money did Wayne spend on this epic? As written previously, the film was budgeted at $4 million while Wayne was still at Republic. Later, Nate Edwards announced in mid-January 1958 that Batjac would spend $5 million to produce the film. In mid-May 1959, the budget was pegged at $6 million, and, with six weeks to go before start of production, it increased to $6.5 million. At the conclusion of a press conference to exploit the film's premiere, Wayne stated he had received commitments for $9.5 million from various sources (United Artists, $2.5 million; the McCullough brothers, $3 million; Murchison, $2.5 million; the Yale Foundation, $1.5 million), and he personally contributed another $1.2 to $1.5 million to make up the difference. (Toward the end of filming, Wayne ran out of funds and asked UA for additional money. They refused and indicated the cupboard was bare. As Wayne had already pledged his salary from the film to cover any shortfall, his only recourse was to dip further into his own pocket. He took out a second mortgage on his home, sold property in Mexico, and borrowed the rest against his personal possessions. When he found out later that UA had the money all along but decided not to use it, he was furious. Wayne explained, "It was never about the money for me. It was about a group of men who believed in liberty enough to die for it. It was about them, and it was about my soul, too. It was right that I gambled everything on it. My whole well-being was at stake."). Harvey wrote his brother the film would cost $10 million while Grant stated the production budget has climbed to $11 million. So the question begs itself: if Wayne already had received over $9.5 million, why would he have to contribute anything if, as Henaghan states, the below-the-line figure was only $2 million?[1181]

The answer is that it depends on how one interprets the various comments. "Above-the-line" costs include monies paid for the story and rights, the producer's unit, direction, and cast, while "below-the-line" costs refer to the cost to shoot the film, including location, props, transportation, crew salaries, editing, music, post-production, and sound. The total sum of both categories is referred to as "bottom-line" cost. Add to that distribution costs and publicity, and you have a final cost. Perhaps, the best explanation comes from Wayne himself. In a July 6, 1977 letter to author Fred Landesman, Duke explained the financing and total costs associated with the film: "The actual cash spent upon 'The Alamo' was as follows: United Artists—$2,500,000; McCullough's—$1,100,000; Murchison's—$1,000,000. Total—$4,600,000. *(If you take Henaghan's $2 million below-the-line cost and add the cast salaries and direction/production costs, you can arrive at a figure not too far off from Wayne's calculation. In addition, an April 3, 1962 letter from the Insurance Service Bureau to Batjac president Robert Newman stated total insurable production costs for the film were $4,212,759.26).*[1182]

"Batjac spent $750,000 that was not charged against the picture, but against Batjac. The picture grossed worldwide $15,000,000 the first time around (equally split between foreign and domestic receipts). United Artists took a little over 35% for distribution, which means they took over $5,250,000. For the money that they had invested, they would have considered it a very successful venture if they had received $3,000,000 for distribution. Therefore, it is quite obvious that UA made an extraordinary profit of $2,000,000 over and above a normal profit expectancy for the amount of their investment. This profit naturally was taken out of distribution and does not show as an end profit to the picture.

"So let us add $5,250,000 for distribution, plus $4,600,000 for actual production, plus an exaggerated $1,000,000 for advertising, plus an exaggerated $1,000,000 for prints, plus an exaggerated $1,000,000 for interest. These are more than adequate figures for the costs at the time of the release. Let us add those *($12,850,000)* and subtract them from the $15,000,000, which means that there was $2,150,000 above and evidently for extraordinary miscellaneous charges, plus added costs imposed by UA's foreign distribution associates, plus interest on delayed refunds of monies to the United Artist Company of U.S.A. At any rate, there was quite a healthy reserve left beyond the profit for UA." Given Wayne's explanation, it is clear the total cost of the project was well in excess of the advertised $12 million, despite *Variety's* claim the film only cost at most $3 million. Associated Press reporter Bob Thomas stated that, while on location, Wayne told him the film would cost $5.5 million to film. His salary and other deferments brought the total to $7 million. Advertising, distribution, and other charges would bring the total to $11million.[1183]

An undated document in the Batjac files titled "Alamo Comparison of Costs & Grosses" further complicates the issue. The negative cost is listed as $6.56

million, $2.5 million for advertising, $1.5 million for prints, $1.235 million for interest, $250,000 for miscellaneous, and $175,000 as a license/royalty fee to Todd-AO. The total UA distribution fee was $4.829 million. Add them all together, and you get $17.049 million! With numbers flying fast and loose like that, it's anyone's guess how much the film really cost.[1184]

Birdwell wasn't the only Batjac employee concerned about UA's perceived lack of effort in publicizing *The Alamo*. As usual, Grant held nothing back when he wrote to Wayne, "I think you'll agree with me that (UA has) no intention of letting the picture ever break even. There is one thing we should consider at this point. That is bringing in some expert to consult with along the lines of an eventual lawsuit against United Artists. One simple instance is that UA did not advertise the picture in most situations in Sunday morning papers." He also recommended attorney C.J. (Tev) Tevlin as the "expert." The following day, Grant expanded on his previous comments: "Tevlin states we would be insane to approve contracts, as all we do is exempt (UA) from any later complaint that they did not put forth best effort. He says, as a result of our man approving all the roadshow contracts, we do not have a leg to stand on except to beef that they did not advertise sufficiently ... 35mm contracts are being made for the first week in March. We are unable to find out if UA intends to accompany these openings with any sort of campaign ... unless these openings are accompanied by an aggressive campaign, the black eye earned in the roadshow will carry over and kill us in general release."[1185]

As the publicity campaign moved into February and March, numerous interesting approaches were taken to insure the film was always on the minds of both the film industry and the general public—some planned, others a fortuitous circumstance. An ad in the February 1 issue of *Box Office* touted Widmark's contribution to the production: "Richard Widmark—the dedicated, heroic cynic who reaches a new height of stardom as James Bowie in John Wayne's *The Alamo* already acclaimed as a coming world event by the Hearst Headline Service." Several Texas millionaires, including H.H. Coffield, John Mecom, Glenn McCarthy, Frank Waters, Vernon Frost, Al Parker, and O.J. and I.J. McCullough, paid $29,375 (plus $1,187 in artwork) for a full-page ad saluting Wayne and the film in the March 7, 1960, issue of *Life*. Superimposed over the iconic A.Y. Owen photograph of Wayne, it stated: "An open letter to John Wayne on the occasion of the 124th anniversary of the Alamo: March 6, 1960. We have heard and read of the great award which the State of Texas, through the Headliners Club and Governor Price Daniel, has bestowed upon you; an award bearing this inscription: To John Wayne, Who has made motion picture stardom one of the very great professions; Who has made *The Alamo* an international symbol of man's undying fight for freedom. To these words we would like to add this prophecy: through your motion picture of the memorable story of the Alamo you will be reminding a world, one-half of which is enslaved, that 124 years ago,

185 joined an immortal suicide pact not to retreat or surrender when encircled by 7,000 troops of an enemy dictator and thus bought with their lives thirteen days of precious time needed by General Sam Houston to prepare for Texas' final and victorious battle for liberation. We believe with you that the world—and our own nation—needs to be reminded that freedom does not come cheap and easy." It would not be the last time *Life* would be used in the publicity campaign. (This March 7 ad would be reprinted in the April 12 edition of the *Los Angeles Examiner*.)[1186]

On March 13, 1960, a full-color photo of four blue-uniformed Mexican lancers appeared on the cover of *The American Weekly*, a Sunday newspaper supplement. Inside, a short article comically read, "... the original Alamo at San Antonio was battered beyond recognition in the fight, and Wayne had to build a new one—so his cast of thousands could knock it down all over again." Birdwell took the opportunity to hype this cover to no end: "In the most intensive pre-selling publicity campaign in picture history! Months before even a release date for John Wayne's epochal THE ALAMO had been set—the 80,000,000 readers of the nation's most popular Sunday supplement, THE AMERICAN WEEKLY—were given another powerful reminder of the EXCITEMENT, the MAGNIFICENCE, the IMPORTANCE and the S-I-Z-E of this $12,000,000 production through this dramatic full-color cover and Page Two box! And who are these 80,000,000 readers? These are the important people in our country—the pace-setters, the opinion-makers, the demand everybody is so anxious to cultivate—THE ONE-HALF OF OUR TOTAL POPULATION WITH THE MONEY WITH WHICH TO PAY FOR WHAT IT WANTS—and knows WHAT IT WANTS! You can be assured that every tool and trick in the Kit of the most dynamic array of publicity brains ever assembled to promote a motion picture will be vigorously exploited to make that want for THE ALAMO as keen, widespread, and unprecedented as the picture deserves!" (*Based on data from the Newspaper Association of America, as well as the U.S. Census Bureau, it's apparent that 80 million readers may be a slight exaggeration. Total Sunday paid newspaper circulation in 1960 was only 47 million while the total number of households in the United States was around 54 million. With a population of 179 million, this implies that three out of every four individuals over fourteen read the supplement*).[1187]

On March 16, after meeting with United Artist executives William J. Heineman, Picker, and Youngstein, Wayne announced *The Alamo* would premiere simultaneously in eleven cities on October 5: New York, Washington, D.C., Toronto, Chicago, Los Angeles, San Francisco, San Antonio, Houston, Dallas, Tokyo, and London. At the time, plans called for ten performances weekly—matinees on Wednesday, Saturday, and Sunday only—plus evenings. Although the roadshow date was tentative and specific theaters not yet determined, Wayne planned to visit each city before the premiere. Previously, Wayne had announced, on February 15, that, although the film would be ready for release as early as June, a September premiere would be held in San Antonio as it would be better business to distribute it then. Duke was reluctant to release his film in this fashion but, with UA's *encouragement*, decided in pre-production to do so. However, *Variety* stated in an article published in 1961 that UA decided to test the reserved-seat route at *Wayne's* insistence. The roadshow concept was a means to publicize a film prior to its general release. It encompassed long runs in premier venues with reserved seating (hard-tickets) at higher-than-normal prices. These increased prices could be accepted if the public felt they were justified due to higher production costs, or the high demand for the film, or its prestige status. The presentations would typically have an overture, intermission, entr'acte, and exit music. It was almost like a Broadway play—patrons could have a glass of wine or some other liquid refreshment during the intermission. A follow-up shortened general release would assure the picture would be in circulation as long as possible, thereby maximizing its box-office potential.[1188]

*(Alamo and Zulu film historian Maurice Jones—owner of John Wayne-The Alamo.com and a former cinema projectionist—offered these guidelines for properly showcasing a roadshow film: "'The Alamo', a classic roadshow film, may consist of as many as six distinct parts. Follow this guide, and you will have given our patrons a First Class presentation that they will be justifiably impressed with.")*

## 1. MUSICAL OVERTURE

*The curtain shall remain closed during the overture. An overture is common on almost all roadshow films. In the heyday of roadshow films, prints were specially made with the overture volume adjusted for the density of curtains in a given theatre. With today's untutored audiences it's a good idea to bring down the house lights slightly to let them know that the film is running. If this is not possible then the stage lights on the curtains should be brought down slightly. The house and stage lights are to be fully dimmed during the last ten seconds or so of the overture. It is critical that the curtain should not start to open before the final notes of the overture because this will cause a change in the volume and tone of the music. Exceptions to the curtain rule are for films like "West Side Story" and "My Fair Lady" which have their overtures played over a picture.*

## 2. PART ONE OF THE FEATURE

*The curtains should start to open the instant that the studio logo appears and should be fully open by the time it fades out. This means that your curtains should be capable of opening in ten seconds. If they operate a little faster than that it's not a problem. If they are significantly slower then their speed should be adjusted as much as possible. If necessary, you may start to open the curtains before the studio logo appears as long as the house lights are fully down and the overture is completed. This may give you three or four additional seconds to get the curtain open before the titles begin.*

*3. END OF PART ONE - INTERMISSION*
*The curtains should start to close a few seconds after the appearance of the intermission*
*title card. They should be fully closed by the time the card fades out. The house*
*lights should not be brought up until the curtains are fully closed. Audiences must*
*never see a blank screen. Their world will consist of two places, the showman-like*
*atmosphere of the theatre and the movie—the screen does not exist.*

*4. ENTRE ACTE MUSIC*
*The second half of the film will usually begin with music without picture and it should*
*be handled exactly like the overture. The house lights should be fully dimmed at the*
*conclusion of the Entre Acte. The length of an intermission should be between ten*
*and fifteen minutes at most. A shorter intermission is a disservice to your patrons*
*and will cut into the sale of those delectable concessions. Also, remember that it*
*takes the ladies a bit longer than the gents to do their business, so have a heart.*

*5. PART TWO OF THE FEATURE*
*Open the curtain the instant that the picture appears. Close the curtain when the last*
*title card appears on screen. Bring up the house lights slowly when the curtain is*
*completely closed.*

*6. WALKOUT MUSIC*
*If the film has walkout music, don't chop it off. Do not allow any staff members to*
*enter the auditorium until the music has finished. The concept is showmanship and*
*having ushers or usherettes dragging trashcans around the auditorium before the*
*entire audience has left is decidedly unshowman-like.*

*AS A PROJECTIONIST—PLEASE NOTE:*
*Following these simple guidelines will give your audiences the experience intended for*
*an event film and whether the film itself was good or bad, audiences will always*
*remember where they saw it and the way it was presented by you and will no*
*doubt return to see it and other films in our cinema.*
*Maurice (Mo) Jones - Former projectionist of the Celtic & Conway Cinemas,*
*Aberystwyth, Mid Wales.)*[1189]

Reports from Europe indicated American roadshow films had a particular appeal to European audiences, played longer, and had more profitable returns than any time in the past. The success of films such as *South Pacific*, *The Ten Commandments*, and *Around the World in 80 Days* generated demand for more product of that sort, a switch from previous years when they didn't want long playing times or increased admissions. More than eighty European theaters were equipped to handle 70mm film with more being developed all the time.[1190]

At the end of the month, Birdwell also placed a series of nineteen weekly ads in *Variety*. Each ad was prefaced with the statement "The World Is Talking About." and a photo of the various costumed actors in the film, bookended by photos of the Alamo. A short description of the character was also included; i.e. "Mrs. Dickinson (Joan O'Brien) who refused to leave the side of her soldier husband when the enemy stormed the Alamo compound; the sole survivor of the Alamo massacre–the woman from whose lips the world learned what happened." Each weekly issue included a quarter-page ad placed on page 4 in the lower left-hand corner of the page: 3/31 *The Alamo*, 4/07 John Wayne, 4/14 Richard Widmark, 4/21 Laurence Harvey, 4/28 Richard Boone, 5/05 Frankie Avalon, 5/12 Pat Wayne, 5/19 Linda Cristal, 5/27 Joan O'Brien, 6/02 Chill Wills, 6/09 Ken Curtis, 6/16 Jester Hairston, 6/23 Aissa Wayne, 6/30 Joseph Calleia, 7/07 Veda Ann Borg, 7/14 John Dierkes, 7/21 Hank Worden, 7/28 John Ford, 8/04 *The Alamo*.

Early in the campaign, Tom Carlile had been commissioned to write a "white paper" on *The Alamo*, including sections on *Heroes of the Alamo*, *Siege of the Alamo*, *Filming of "The Alamo"*, *Production of "The Alamo"*, and *Something About the Cast*. Written under rushed and trying circumstances, Birdwell wasn't at all pleased with the result and, on April 11-14, replied to Carlile with numerous suggestions. The results of these efforts would be a massive 140-page publicity release the likes of which had never been seen before in the industry. It is clear from his critique Birdwell wanted to tighten and emphasize various aspects of both the filming and history. The fact that Birdwell's preferences were in conflict with actual facts was irrelevant:

"In your summary of the making of *The Alamo* as a motion picture you give entirely too much credit to Al Ybarra. You would think that he and he alone made the motion picture... The bulk of all this credit should go to Wayne and James Edward Grant secondly, and then go into the various department heads including a condensed version of the Art Department's work so that Ybarra's work, as great as it was, does not monopolize the making of the picture . incorporate the names of the . men . who, under the direction of Bill Daniel, furnished the fabulous longhorn cattle . build up Bill Daniel a bit."

Birdwell had already seen the film's first assembly cut and realized there was an issue with Carlile's version of the facts: "We must eliminate certain phases of history in our summary of the historical background in order that what we have on the screen does not conflict with what we write into our program. As you know we are now using the figure 185 as the number of men who were at the Alamo because this is what is said on the screen."

He also realized the film was more than a story of the battle: "I believe the thing that is missing in the writing and the recapitulation, especially in connection with the picture itself, is some indication that there is something else to the motion picture other than just a large battle. I think that it is terribly important that we inject these other qualities: the moments of tenderness, the birthday party, the songs, laughter, the humor of Beekeeper and his love of whiskey and women, the moments of classic beauty, the artistic conceptions within the picture itself, the romance–abortive as it was–between the beautiful Flaca and Crockett. I think we need to weave the idea in about the hard-living, hard-loving and hard-fighting men and their women so we don't lead anyone to believe that we have a picture based entirely on the siege of the Alamo. It is our hope that we will be able to use this document in many ways and entice people to the theatre. I don't believe we have succeeded doing this in the first draft. This does not mean that there is not some fine writing in what you have done and much of it can be salvaged."

From the beginning, it appears Birdwell intended to publish an enormous release: "I believe it would be a good idea . to index the entire affair, with tabs that will stand out from the main copy in order that a person may turn immediately and directly to the subject matter which he may wish to explore. We plan to publish this booklet on an extensive scale, and we would like for it to be easily readable and useable. There is a possibility we may perhaps print this in offset to issue as a booklet to show exhibitors well in advance of *The Alamo*. We may include in the book stills from the picture. It is important we do a splendid job toward exciting people about our picture." Birdwell then proceeded to rip Carlile's draft to shreds: ninety-two pages submitted, ninety-two pages of corrections. In many cases, entire paragraphs were scratched out; in others, whole pages. Numbers were inflated to better support the magnificence of Birdwell's efforts. Carlile returned to the drawing board.

With the involvement of Denny Morrison, Tom Carlile, Midge Hamilton, Joanne B. Howell, Peggy Wood, Paula C. Storch, Joan Rice, and Patricia Campbell, the release book was expanded to 184 single-sided pages once someone realized they could match the number of pages in the book to the number of defenders in the Alamo. (Actually, there were 185 single pages as a photograph of Dimitri Tiomkin was included on page 154-A. Pappy Ford's tribute to *The Alamo* was printed on the inside back cover and considered page 185). In addition to adding a map of the fortress' defenses, thirty-eight photographs, and a list of cast and crew, Birdwell significantly expanded the table of contents to include the following categories: The Alamo; The Struggle for Texas Liberty; The Heroes of the Alamo; Women of the Alamo; The Siege of the Alamo; Preparation for Filming *The Alamo*; Something About the Cast; James Edward Grant; *The Alamo*–A Mammoth Enterprise; *The Ala*mo; John Wayne's Salute to Texas; and John Ford's Tribute to *The Alamo*. Director George Stevens's endorsement of the film was added to the book just before printing: "When the roll call of the great ones is made, *The Alamo* will be among those few by which the films of the future will be measured. There are images in *The Alamo* that will haunt you and inspire you for a lifetime; a glorious restoration in film of the historic Alamo epic–a classic." However, the original quote reads as follows: "When the roll call of the great ones is made, *The Alamo* will be among those few by which the films of the future will *and must* be measured. There are images in *The Alamo* that will haunt you and inspire you for a lifetime. *The Alamo is among the screen's finest literature—a classic."* No doubt, Birdwell must have had his hand in this fine-tuning; the quote was changed to be less grandiose. (By 1965, Larry Edmunds Book Store in Hollywood sold copies of the release to the public for $15 each, after paying Birdwell $4 for every copy he could find.)[1191]

Apparently, poet and biographer Carl Sandburg must have been privy to an early preview of Wayne's film as he was said to be favorably impressed. Upon learning of this, the ever-persuasive Birdwell attempted to receive permission from Sandburg to use his comment in editorial copy. The following telegram was sent to the writer: "Dear Sir, John Wayne and I were most pleased to hear of your splendid comment concerning *The Alamo*. I am appreciative that you have had a lif-long policy of never being quoted on such matters but because of the great American tradition and heritage involved in *The Alamo* I should like to come to you again and ask if you would permit us, in editorial matter only and no paid advertising, to quote you as follows, after viewing *The Alamo*:

'If anyone sees John Wayne please tell him that I, Carl Sandburg, salute him for his greatness.'

Respectfully, Russell Birdwell."

Sandburg declined.[1192]

# CHAPTER THIRTY
# "THIS, AND ONE MORE.
# NO, REALLY!"

BACK AT GOLDWYN STUDIOS, STUART GILMORE CONTINUED TO TRIM SCENES down to their proper length, and made sure the cuts were smooth and seamless. Fades and dissolves were added. Scenes and shots were tweaked or removed. Through subtle changes in rhythm and pacing, he eventually reached a point where his first assembly cut became a fine cut. "Duke would decide with my dad what scenes (would be cut)," explains Gilmore. "We'd do the first pass through the fine cut with the director in post, and you might lose ten minutes. Now, you take the movie into the projection room and run it again all the way through. And you get a feeling for the fact that hopefully it's speeded up, and the relationships are better, etc. It's like peeling an onion. You don't just cut thirty minutes out of a movie, you do it in pieces, so, you peel the onion, you don't cut it. Then you start the editing process, and, bear in mind, it's only picture-edited. Sound and music have nothing to do with the picture editing. Now, you're picture-editing, and you usually do it a reel at a time. Duke and my dad would run reel one four or five times in a projection room, and Duke would give my dad notes. Duke would take off, and my dad would make those changes in the afternoon. Then you have a choice. You can either stay with reel one and continue to fine-tune it, or you can move on to reel two. My dad always felt you should not do a fine cut of reel one, you (only) should do a pass. So you make the changes on reel one, move on to reel two, make the changes to reel two, and there were seventeen reels. S, two-and-a-half, three weeks of editing, and you've done the first pass of editing. Bear in mind, in those days, there was a picture and the 35mm magnetic track. So you would have cuts in both and then after three weeks or four weeks or however long it took to get through the seventeen reels, you'd have a second-cut screening. Now, (for example), instead of the movie being three hours, it's two-and-a-half. And the second cut always makes everyone feel a little better because, the obvious stalls and shoe leather and things that take forever on screen, they're usually trimmed or cut so that the movie plays a lot better. To fine-cut a movie, you repeat this process, reel by reel, until you get the movie down to the length that you want it. And what you're doing is you're working towards locking the picture."

Post-production is basically divided into two elements: the creative form, in which the film will actually be in; and the technical aspect. Picture lock would include the original soundtrack and "temp dubs" where more than one sound is combined on a single track. After final polishing, Gilmore moved on to audio editing. Sound effects, looping, Foley, and music were all incorporated into the assembled product. All the sync sound was included and synced correctly, matching to the locked picture, frame by frame.

Sound editors work with huge libraries of recorded sounds–libraries where one can find not hundreds, but literally thousands of different sounds to choose from. Some editors also like creating and recording their own sound effects. Sound elements such as production wild tracks, dialogue tracks, library material, and Foley effects–these are the things an editor, when creating a soundtrack, cuts and synchronizes to the picture. He then presents these to the re-recording mixer for final sound balance. They work closely with the editor, re-recording mixer and director to establish what sound effects are required throughout the production and to ensure that these effects are available from sound-effect libraries, or can be created to production requirements within tight time schedules.

Head sound engineer Jack Solomon estimated "85% of our original soundtrack is usable, just as we recorded it." The frightening bawling of cattle, the hoarse coughing of men as they walked to their battle posts in the chill morning air, crickets chirping in the evening. "All of these are sounds that usually would be eliminated from the average soundtrack," explained Solomon. "But John Wayne was unique as a director in believing that we should record the sound for this picture as it actually happened. We recorded in driving rain, we recorded when a swarm of crickets swooped down onto the set, we recorded when horses were moving around and neighing in the background, we recorded when the birds on the prairie outside were singing their fool heads off. And it's all there on the track, the kind of realistic noises of nature that have rarely been heard in any previous outdoor motion picture dramas, because nearly all of them have been removed when the major part of the soundtrack was 'looped' back at the studio." Frequently, five Mitchell cameras were recorded simultaneously on the sound truck as Bill Griffith installed a radio and walkie-talkie system to monitor activity over the sprawling location. "As a result of this efficient communication system," explained Solomon, "we had a minimum of interference in our sound truck from automobile and truck noises in the distant background."[1193]

A Foley studio is a soundproof room with a remarkably eclectic collection of fabrics, household objects, pieces of metal, small floor patches of different materials (wood, stone, gravel, sand, etc.), and hundreds of other objects used to make and record sounds to enhance whatever sound was recorded on the film set: clothes rustling, footsteps, pouring water, objects being placed on tables, etc. Foley artists precisely match the sounds they make in the studio with the locked cut, which is projected on a screen while they work. For example, they match their footsteps with the footsteps on the screen while walking on the patch of studio floor that has the right kind of surface (gravel or dirt or wood), or they create the sound of cloth rustling to match the exact movements (and type of cloth) of a character moving (sitting, standing, running, etc.) in the film.

The emotional impact of a scene can be heavily influenced by its music. Using different types of music is a simple but very emotional experience. For example, depending upon the music used, a shot of someone riding into town can be made to feel hopeful, menacing, or even triumphant. Music editors help directors achieve their musical ambitions on films, and provide a crucial link between the film and composer. They structure the soundtrack, ensuring that all the components work together. For film music to work successfully, it must be beautifully written, well performed, and appropriate to the story and setting. In addition, it must be very carefully placed within the film, so it complements the action rather than detracts from it. As Elmer Bernstein, composer of *The Magnificent Seven*'s glorious score, once said, "Music is the motor that drives a movie." Dimitri Tiomkin was a master at this and explained in several interviews, "To appreciate the effect of the music and to realize how much it adds, one should see the average movie, before and after the music is added. Not only are all the dramatic effects heightened, but in many instances the faces, voices, and even the personalities of the players are altered by the music." He further stated, "The audience doesn't consciously hear the music; it subconsciously hears it and transfers or ascribes its qualities to the person on the screen." It used to be that no one was ever supposed to hear the music in a score. Composers for the screen were warned to always keep their music "unintrusive." Tiomkin explained, "The wretched conductor used to take a can of film, run it and then apply music and the louder (it was), the more endearing it was to the producer and director. I am always unhappy when the director insists on music throughout the film. There are scenes where no music belongs, and when he wants loud music, I grieve. I tremble when this happens, wondering if I should attend the movie, sit with the audience whose ears ache, what would happen if they should recognize me?" Instead, Tiomkin wanted his music to speak to the audience; at times fun, jaunty, and amusing, at others ominous, threatening, and relentless. Always animated, melodious, and picturesque. Combining folk-like ballads, rhythmic Mexican melodies, thundering horns, "Taps", and "The Eyes of Texas," Tiomkin created a rousing, memorable, stirring score. Historian, researcher, and author Jeffrey Dane wrote, "A composer's function in the context of a movie is not to force his music upon the audience, but to infuse the music into the film by an integration between image and sound."[1194]

As *The Alamo* already included the talents of two vocalists (Avalon and Curtis), Wayne requested that Tiomkin compose a few tunes they could sing in the film. *Variety* erroneously referred to Dimi's songs as "Toss to the Lady" and "Tennessee Baby." On March 2, Avalon returned to Hollywood to record the lively and playful "Here's to the Ladies" by Tiomkin and Paul Francis Webster. (While watching the rushes, Wayne had discovered Avalon didn't have the appropriate sound he wanted while he sang that song, so, Avalon was rushed back from the East Coast to re-record exactly eighteen seconds! Wayne, Tiomkin, Grant, and eight technicians were on hand to shoot one hundred feet of film. When he finished, Avalon lingered around the studio until Wayne yelled, "What are you still doing here? Go back to Philadelphia!"). Tiomkin and Webster also collaborated on "The Green Leaves of Summer" and "Ballad of the Alamo." The latter two songs proved extremely popular as they were performed by numerous artists: "The Green Leaves of Summer" was recorded by Avalon (Chancellor-EP Ch 02031), The Brothers Four (Columbia 3-41808 single 33, 4-41809 single 45), Clebanoff Strings (Mercury), Medallion Strings (Kapp Medallion), Terry Gilkyson and The Easy Riders (Kapp), Harry Simeone Chorale (20th-Fox), Hugo Montenegro (20th-Fox), Nelson Riddle (Capital 45-34354), Mantovani (London), Nick Perito (United Artists 7 EMF 238), and Bud & Travis (Liberty), while "The Ballad of the Alamo" was recorded by Avalon, Marty Robbins (Columbia 3-41809 single 33, 4-41809 single 45), Simeone, Montenegro, Gilkyson and Bud & Travis. Even the Knightsbridge Strings (Top Rank) recorded "Here's To The Ladies." The score was published by Feist, of the Big Three combine).

Tiomkin began to score the film in March at the Goldwyn Studio, and completed his work by late May. The studio had the honor of recording three of the biggest film scores of all time. Recorded in consecutive order on six-track stereo were *Spartacus* (scored by Alex North), *The Alamo*, which was recorded between May 16-20, and *West Side Story*, which began in early June under the direction of Saul Chaplin. (On January 3, 1961, the National Labor Relations Board rejected a petition by the American Federation of Musicians, which was seeking to represent the eighty musicians, arrangers, copyists, proofreaders, and librarians who worked on *The Alamo* score. The AFM was contending that the musicians were employees of the Alamo Company, which produced the film. They later claimed the musicians were actually independent employees of Tiomkin's Erosa Music Corp. The NLRB rejected the union's argument that the

Alamo Company's agreement to pay the musicians' re-use and recording rates for future television and recording use of the score in effect created an employer-employee relationship).[1195]

Tiomkin received a flat fee for the first seventy minutes of film with a per-minute rising scale beyond that. The film ran three hours and twelve minutes, the score two hours and twenty minutes. (A recent recording of Tiomkin's complete soundtrack by The City of Prague Philharmonic Orchestra, accompanied by the Crouch End Festival Chorus, verifies the actual time length of the composer's score. However, an analysis of the original cue sheets suggests it was only two hours and one minute. The sheets suggest that Tiomkin utilized three unique orchestral instrumentation configurations to record his score: For the gentler and more intimate moments, he employed a chamber orchestra of one flute, one oboe, one clarinet, one French horn, one trumpet, acoustic guitar, harpsichord, accordion, and a small string line-up; a second larger orchestra was comprised of enlarged string forces with three French horns, three trumpets, three trombones, piano, harpsichord, accordion, and four percussion, with a small woodwind section of one flute, one oboe, two clarinets, and one bassoon; for the battle sequences, Tiomkin used a string section, nine woodwinds, four French horns, three trumpets, three trombones, one tuba, two grand pianos, and five to seven percussion. Plus a sixty-voice chorus backup directed by choirmaster Jack Halloran. Dimi recorded the entire score in just sixty-three hours).[1196]

While Tiomkin worked on the score, numerous recording labels dickered for exclusive rights to market the soundtrack album, including Victor, MGM, Kapp, Liberty, Imperial, Mercury, Coral, Chancellor, UA Records, Capital, Columbia, Dot, Verve, and Decca. It was understood that the winning company would promise Batjac-United Artists the "best exploitation which can be used in cross-ballyhooing the picture," according to Birdwell. (Columbia would eventually win the rights to the soundtrack. According to Tiomkin, consideration was given to the fact that Decca would market the *Spartacus* soundtrack, MGM *Ben-Hur*, and Victor *Exodus*). In addition to Columbia's (CL1558 –$3.98 Hi-Fi, CS-8358 – $4.98 Stereo), two other Alamo albums would be issued before the premiere: *Remember the Alamo*–Terry Gilkyson and The East Riders (Rich Dehr, Bernie Armstrong and Carson Parks), (Kapp KL-1216), and *Music From the Film The Alamo*–Tex Beneke and Orchestra (RCA Camden, CAL-655).[1197]

Wayne had previously worked with Tiomkin on *Red River*, *The High and the Mighty*, and *Rio Bravo*, and knew what the composer was capable of; as a result, Dimi was Duke's first and only choice. "I never had any other thought than to ask Dimitri Tiomkin to compose the score," said Duke. Added Tiomkin, "I used a piece of music in *Rio Bravo* called 'De Guello' which is composed for the trumpet and which (the script said) the Mexicans played during the siege of the Alamo as a way of trying to make the defenders of the Alamo anxious. And in *Rio Bravo* the men who have the town surrounded play that music. I always thought it was a most beautiful piece of music and couldn't understand why it would upset anyone. John Wayne said to me, 'We have to have that music in *The Alamo*.' I said, 'It won't upset the defenders.' He said, 'I know, but can you find different ways to use it?' I said, 'Yes,' and I used it as a lament for the dead and dying Mexican soldiers, I used it as a piece of military music just before the battle, and I used it to glorify Crockett's death. It was the biggest picture I had worked on up till then, and it gave the opportunity to really expand my repertoire. I already had a certain style, so people tell me, but *The Alamo* widened my horizons and gave me the reputation of being able to compose for epic films, which is just about all I went on to do after *The Alamo*."[1198]

Due to Tiomkin's busy schedule, he wasn't given a great amount of time to finish the score and likened a Hollywood composer to a newspaper reporter: "A director can take two years to make a picture. The musician scoring it must have his work done in ten days. He is just like a newspaper reporter, he is always fighting a deadline. Four weeks is all I was allowed to write *The Alamo* score. This old fellow Tiomkin will do it, they say to me. 'Your experience will enable you to do it.' Yes, my experience allows me to do it–working day and night. It is ruining my health and my heart. Throughout history, music has been written for money. The outfits offering the most cash got the best composers. At first it was the church, then the royal courts, society, opera, and symphony. The stage was next, and finally movies. Maybe it won't last, because it is an integral part of another art–the movies. It is not written for the ear alone. One needs the visual aspect to appreciate movie scores. I have no ambition to write 'significant' music like symphony. I want to do significant and important motion picture scores. For that is today's classical music. It is also the most financially rewarding." But Dimi wasn't complaining: "Duke Wayne is a very profound and sensitive creator. It was a real pleasure working with him. He was very helpful, telling me just what he wanted. He was not a dictator as are some directors." (Final tweaking would run all the way through September 18, 1960).[1199]

Though satisfied with his compositional efforts, Tiomkin was less than pleased with the lack of publicity he was receiving. "Hardly mentioned" at all in various advertising, Dimi complained to Milton Weiss, who passed the comment along. Birdwell was instructed to mention Tiomkin's name a bit more frequently. Price Daniel also flexed his gubernatorial muscles when he heard brother Bill might not receive appropriate credit for his efforts on the film. "I do not know what credit line the movie will contain with respect to Brother Bill," he wrote to Birdwell, "and was concerned to hear from a mutual friend that maybe it would have none at all. If his work as coordinator and in various other capacities was as satisfactory as was reported to me, I certainly think it should be credited in some manner. There will be many people, including 'yours truly' disappointed if this is not done." As he did with Tiomkin, Birdwell assured the governor that Bill would be given screen credit.[1200]

(Tiomkin would later protest Columbia failed to give him proper credit on the soundtrack album as composer of the film's score. The album sleeve didn't list him as composer, only as conductor, and the back listed him as composer along with Paul Francis Webster, who actually wrote the lyrics for four themes based on Tiomkin's score. On October 19, in a wire sent to Tiomkin's attorney Harry Sokolov, based on Dimi's demand, Columbia agreed to make a public correction pronouncement and took out a full-page ad in the trade papers, crediting Tiomkin as composer. A sticker would be placed on a future shipment of 25,000 albums to that effect and all subsequent albums would have the correct credits. Trade paper ads addressed the 23,000 albums previously distributed. Tiomkin ended up with only 50% of the publication and copyright of the score. "Whereas pay levels for most workers in pictures have risen sharply over the last decade," explained Tiomkin, "they have decreased for scorers. A decade ago the mean average pay for scoring a picture ranged between $15,000 and $40,000. Today the offers range from $5,000 to $20,000. Blame television, and here's why. Studios have learned almost all composers have written themes or scored TV films for peanuts. They did it between feature assignments and because it automatically gave scores a chance to reap coin from performing rights–something that didn't exist in theatrical pix. It was a good deal for scorers and TV. Everybody has gotten into the act. Before an indie producer rolls a camera these days, he flags a music publishing wing. So composers are caught in a two-way squeeze. They are offered less to score a picture and get no cut of pub rights.")[1201]

According to Bill Gilmore, "Post-production took six months at least. I've forgotten how long it took; (it) might (have) even took longer. So, we were back working on this film forever. I remember scoring and dubbing took forever. It was all in 70mm, special sound. The sound effects people (would) ride with Duke, work the cut picture, and he sent them his notes. So they then use that in preparing all the sound-effects tracks. Duke, the director, and my dad would run the picture with Dimitri Tiomkin, and they would decide where he was gonna write the music. And that's where Bob Tracy came in because as the music editor, Bob was the one who worked with Tiomkin. Bob would take his black and white copy of the fine cut, mark it up, and tell Dimi where it started, where it ended, the amount of footage, and give Dimi a copy of (the film) so that, when he's writing (the music), he can see the various cuts and what's happening. Once the picture is fine-cut and Duke is happy with the condition of every cut in the movie, it's turned over, what we call turning it over to sound effects and music. And they go ahead and assemble all their soundtracks." [1202]

On April 22, while Gilmore continued to work on the edit, over at Todd-AO, technicians began to create a six-track sound mix, including dialogue, score, and ambient sound effects. They used the raw stems recorded in Brackettville to create a sophisticated and rerecorded sound mix. The technicians worked most of the summer before it was complete.[1203]

The previous week, on behalf of all Kinney County citizens, Happy Shahan presented Wayne with an official proclamation from the Kinney County Chamber of Commerce. The document stated that the citizens of Kinney County thanked Wayne and Batjac for choosing their county to film *The Alamo*. Two weeks later, forty pupils from Crockett Elementary school signed a huge thirty-eight-inch by five-foot postcard requesting Wayne hold his premiere in San Antonio. On one side was a picture of a large crowd jamming Houston Stree. for the premiere. On the other was a message that boosted the Alamo City as a logical choice for the premiere and a promise of promotional support. Previously, Wayne had announced a simultaneous premiere in several cities, and, as *The Dallas Morning News* wrote, "Holding the premiere in any other city than San Antonio, where the actual Alamo is located, would be an affront to every loyal Texan, native or adopted." On hand, along with the school's buckskin-wearing, coonskin-capped students, were San Antonio mayor Kuykendall, Postmaster Dan Quill, Trinity University's president, Mrs. H. R. Hagan (president of the Houston chapter of the Daughters of the Republic of Texas), Happy Shahan, and many local civic leaders. San Antonians were urged to write to Wayne with their request. The students presented Postmaster Quill with an authentic powder horn to be mailed to Wayne. With the signatures of over three hundred residents, the postcard took $7.20 in 9¢ stamp postage! Upon delivery in Los Angeles, the card was presented to Wayne by Postmaster Otto K. Olesen, long-time friend of Quill.[1204]

Occasionally pushing the bounds of ridiculousness, Birdwell, unhampered by facts, discretion, or good taste, still could run the gamut from sublime to outrageous. To Houston DRT president Hagan, he wrote, "It was a pleasure to have talked with you on the telephone in respect to the following ideas: 1). The Daughters of the Republic of Texas, under your leadership at the next board meeting, to consider passing a resolution to send an invitation to the leaders of the Summit Powers (France, Russia, England, and the United States) to hold their next summit Meeting at the Alamo in San Antonio. It seems only fitting that the leaders of the Summit Nations, meeting for the avowed purpose of seeking freedom and justice for all, should foregather on an historic site where men of many nationalities believed so deeply in these things they gave their lives as one in the face of unbelievable odds. 2). The Daughters of the Republic of Texas, at this upcoming board meeting, to consider petitioning the United States Government to award posthumously Congressional Medals of Honor to the 185 men who together died above and beyond the call of duty in defense of freedom and liberty in the Alamo at San Antonio, Texas. It seems only fitting, also, that these men, heroes all, should posthumously have some sort of a piece of metal accorded to each of them ... to be placed in niches of honor in state and governmental places as a reminder that men who wish to be free and who, even more importantly, wish

662

others to be free, came to the Alamo from many states and many foreign lands." (The DRT eventually convened and adjourned its Waco state convention without taking any action to endorse or reject the proposal).

Birdwell had previously approached Luther Skaggs of the Congressional Medal of Honor Society with the same idea, as well as the Texas congressional delegation. William B. Macomber, Jr., Assistant Secretary of the Department of State, rejected the proposal on May 13, saying "The proposal concerning the Congressional Medal of Honor is not within the jurisdiction of the Department of State, and it would not be appropriate, therefore, for us to comment on that proposal." On May 15, Price Daniel echoed that sentiment when he wrote Birdwell, "I strongly recommend that the proposal referred to in your letter of April 18 that Mrs. Raymond H. Hagan of Houston suggest a future summit conference of major powers (including Russia) to be held in the Alamo at San Antonio should be dropped . You won't find many people who would like for Khrushchev to visit our state–much less attend a meeting in the Alamo. Sincerely Yours, Price Daniel." Four days later, Birdwell told Daniel he would drop the idea. The publicist knew there wasn't the slightest chance of having a summit meeting in San Antonio, and he also surely must have known that many of the defenders, whether they came from the United States or Mexico, were loyal Mexican citizens who only wanted to overthrow the dictatorship of Santa Anna. Neither proposal was remotely possible, but they did serve to keep Wayne's movie in the minds of prospective audiences.[1205]

Birdwell's occasional lapses in common sense weren't the only things Wayne had been putting up with; there had been flak from other directions, not all of it domestic. Throughout his entire time on location, Wayne had received numerous complaints from Mexican media about his perceived offensive and blatantly biased attitude toward the Mexican people. Under the name of "Nikita Nipongo," a *Novedades* columnist wrote that U.S. motion picture producers were "enemies of the American people" because pictures sent abroad "paint a false picture of the United States." Nipongo went on to write the American woman (on film) "is not a woman, she is a plastic doll, or a disgusting witch, or just a fool," and the "American man in U.S. movies, is comparable to a presumptuous stone block, then you add the gangsters, the boys of the old West, soldiers who kill Indians, Japanese and others of inferior races, or who confront slinky Red spies, and you have a cocktail which is equal to a vile campaign against the American people." His general comments about U.S. movies led up to a specific criticism of *The Alamo*. The columnist stated no matter how it was treated, the subject of the Texas-Mexican war was bound to "stir up ill feeling between residents on the opposite sides of the Rio Grande." Earlier that year, before the start of production, a Mexico City daily newspaper stated: "*The Alamo* is considered offensive to Mexico, and Wayne's plan to film it here is in abeyance." The *Diario De La Tarde* even went so far to say that Wayne wouldn't be permitted to produce the film in Mexico because "the plot might offend this country." The fear was that the whole tone of the film would be to place the country and its people in an unfavorable light. Officials from the Department of Cinematografia stated they wanted to review the script to make sure it wasn't objectionable. Wayne responded to the claims, "I've been so busy getting everything set for the filming of the picture, I haven't even had a chance to answer some of these phony charges. In the first place, when they see my completed picture, they won't have anything to gripe about–the scenes will be fair to everyone concerned." He angrily denied he had any plans to film in Mexico and stated Batjac had already spent $500,000 constructing a set that accommodated both interior and exterior scenes. "Why should I want to go to Mexico and spend any more money and time?" he asked. "I don't know how (that rumor) got started. I never planned to film any part of this picture in Mexico. The only connection here is that bullfighter Carlos Arruza will have a part in our picture. Actually, all this mess is being kicked up by a Communist-inspired newspaper in Mexico City that doesn't like me. The Commies don't like me, ever since I helped break their back in Hollywood." Convinced he had a fair and equitable treatment, Wayne concluded, "They will find there is nothing in the film to squawk about." Even Arruza came under attack as Mexican newspapers were panning him for even appearing in Wayne's film, which caused him great concern as he considered the charges against him "an unfair attack."[1206]

Ruben Padilla quickly came to Arruza's defense in a letter he wrote to Wayne. After an April 1 response from Birdwell that the situation was under control, Padilla expressed his feeling in reply: "Thank you very much for yours of the thirteen[h], in relation to my letter to Mr. John Wayne, in which I expressed concern about the possible Mexican reaction to the motion picture 'The Alamo' Mr. Birdwell, Carlos Arruza and I share your feeling, in the sense that Mr. Wayne has done everything possible to make 'The Alamo' an inspiring dramatization of an epic event in the Mexican-American history, presenting the Mexican aspect in a dignified, discreet manner. Our main concern is with certain reactionaries and malcontents who, since the beginning of time and throughout history, have been the calamity and scourge of patriots and historians. Several attempts by Carlos to calm, clarify, and place in the proper perspective the ends pursued by Mr. Wayne were met with derision and further abuse. These attacks continued after Carlos was interviewed by the press and on television and after perusal of the script by influential persons in Mexico City. Carlos is now in Madrid, Spain, which is as far away as he can get from the coming "rumble" in Mexico."[1207]

Padilla no doubt was referring to Jorge Ferretis, head of the Mexican Film Bureau. Ferretis said he was "tired" of American producers not following instructions of the Bureau relative to script changes. It was time that Hollywood learned Mexico was "stubbornly determined" in its stand that the country and its citizens are portrayed accurately, and not in any defamatory manner, no matter how slight. Ferretis concluded that the film still contained scenes considered "insulting" to Mexico. Undeterred, Wayne made a personal appeal to the Bureau. Arguing the film conformed to historical accuracy, he was nonetheless denied a permit to show the film in Mexico. Claiming it still contained scenes defamatory to Mexico, Ferretis countered that the film needed to eliminate those scenes and further stated the United State. would have the same reaction and refuse to grant permits if a producer took the theme of the Mexican-U.S. War of 1847 and presented Americans in an unfavorable light. United Artists even got involved in the fracas. Its local Mexican distributor arranged for a copy of the film to be imported, allegedly with cuts of various scenes that could prove to be offensive to Mexico. UA wanted Ferretis to review the film and render a final decision in the matter. Wayne even asked Miguel Aleman, friend and former president of Mexico, to sponsor the release of the film in Mexico. Aleman smiled and then told Wayne, "We never had this conversation." (On March 19, 1961, the Mexican government indicated it would not grant a permit for the film to be shown in local theaters. Ferretis denounced the film and warned that Mexico "would not tolerate movies that deform the reality of the country.")[1208]

*San Antonio Express and News* columnist Gerald Ashford had an opportunity to read a copy of *The Alamo* script given to the DRT library and took exception to those claims. "I was glad to find that the script clearly shows that the Texans had mixed motives, and that Mexicans in the interior also resisted Santa Anna," he wrote. "Besides being accurate to this extent, the screenplay . is a work of unusual cinematic quality which presents the heroes as real human beings with faults as well as virtues . the few historical inaccuracies it does contain . are not worth bothering about. There is a great final scene which should bring tears to the eyes of every Texas......."[1209]

There even was one domestic snag. Wayne was scheduled to receive an award from the Children of the American Revolution National Society on April 27. Due to scheduling issues, though, he couldn't attend, so Batjac president Bob Newman suggested that Harvey, filming in New York at the time, perhaps could fly to Washington and pick up the award for Duke. (Exhausted from his rigorous schedule, Wayne actually was in temporary seclusion and avoiding visitors, telephone calls, and interviews). Laurence agreed and flew to D.C. on April 19. Upon arrival, he was greeted with a package from Birdwell that included copies of PR stories planted on Harvey's behalf. Pleased with the results, Harvey wrote Birdwell, "Thank you so much for your kind note. I am so overwhelmed by it all that I still can't believe it, although, Lord knows, I've always paid my dues. Looking forward to seeing you again. As ever, Larry." But four days later, for whatever reason, Harvey returned to New York and notified UA he would be unable to fill in for Wayne. Furious, Birdwell found a substitute and fired off a telegram to Harvey: "Dear Larry, Am terribly surprised that you would walk out on a firm appointment in behalf of Wayne without calling me. Surely there must be some valid reason for cancelling out and thus the more surprising that you did not call me. Sincerely, Russell Birdwell."[1210]

Birdwell presented a new publicity campaign budget on April 21. Previously set at $415,000 but now reduced to $311,000, it included, among other items: $35,000 for the creation and production of newspaper ads; $20,000 for television; $25,000 for stills; and $35,000 for actors' personal tours. Birdwell also hired John Jensen to create artwork for the campaign. Jensen, concept and continuity artist during the shoot, provided four rough drawings for review. Based on the results, Birdwell paid Jensen $1,350 and required completion and delivery of the artwork in early June.[1211]

Desperate for additional funds to cover the costs of editing, musical scoring, print costs, and publicity, Batjac entered into a $700,000 loan agreement with the Bank of America, National Trust and Savings Corporation, on May 19, 1960. Secured by its film library, Batjac used as collateral its interest in *The High and the Mighty, Hondo, Island in the Sky, Man in the Vault, Ring of Fear, Big Jim McLain,* and *Gun the Man Down.* Attached to the loan agreement were two documents: Schedule A–Schedule of funds received and applied by the Alamo Company (United Artists - $2,000,000, Murchison - $1,500,000, McCullough Tool Company - $1,575,000, Batjac - $205,519.05), and Schedule B–an itemized list detailing the purpose for each dollar of the loan.[1212]

Upon receipt of temporary funding and with the publicity campaign in Birdwell's *good* hands, Wayne began to film *North To Alaska* in May. Previously referred to as *Go North, Port Fury,* and *The Alaskans, Alaska* was the second of three films Duke had contracted in 1956 to do for Fox. With locations in Lone Pine and Big Bear, California, and studio work in Century City, Wayne easily could keep tabs on what was happening with *The Alamo.*

As well he should. One of the more interesting yet amusing *Alamo* publicity ploys was the Popsicle campaign. Batjac entered into a nationwide promotional tie-up with Joe Lowe Corporation, licensors of "Popsicle." In a blatant attempt to encourage children to see the movie, ads were placed in various comics throughout the summer. During this golden age of comics, nothing could sell product placement better than monthly comic books: Twinkies, Cracker Jack, "Amazing Wrist Radios," "Genuine Nickel Silver Signet Rings–Absolutely Free!" "Check the Kind of Body YOU Want: With Charles Atlas" and. "Hey Kids! Help John Wayne Defend the Alamo!" Starting May 30, boys and girls had a chance to enter ten weekly "Alamo Heroes" contests with over "2,000 Big Prizes!" Entry blanks were available by mail or from a local ice cream vendor. Hidden picture puzzle coloring books also were used, and kids were asked to identify the hidden characters. Just color the drawing, paste on three red "sicle" balls, and mail in. Along with daily, Sunday, and trade papers, billboards also prominently featured Wayne. Duke would appear wearing a coonskin cap on the left side of the billboard with a drawing on the right side of a Popsicle popsicle: "Have a Popsicle and cool off says John Wayne star of *The Alamo*." As columnist Ivan Spear wrote, it just goes to show you, even press agents are suckers for a tie-in. Birdwell wasn't the only one to come up with wild ideas. UA announced it was going to develop the film into a television series, and Wayne was invited to a shooting contest to promote the film. He turned it down, though: "I can't really hit the side of a barn!"[1213]

On Saturday, April 30, Richard Boone presented an "Evening of Theater" at the Glendale College Auditorium. Co-sponsored by La-Cañada-Flintridge Orthopaedic Guild and the Glendale Foothill Auxiliary to benefit the pediatric ward of the new Orthopaedic Hospital, Boone offered a variety of entertainment that included a live gunfight, an Abraham Lincoln sketch from Norman Corwin's drama *The Rivalry*, selections from *Cyrano de Bergerac, MacBeth*, and *The Rainmaker*, and, to top it off, musical selections from Tiomkin's *Alamo* score and "The Ballad of Sam Houston" sung by Jester Hairston and choir. What an entertaining way to get the film and its music in front of the public.[1214]

At this time, Batjac also contracted with Avon Book Division of the Hearst Corporation to publish Steve Frazee's novelization of Grant's script. With a release date scheduled for late September, the 35¢ paperback ran 160 pages with photographs from the film prominently placed on both front and rear covers. Grant graciously endorsed Frazee's efforts: "No one book can be expected to encompass the vast canvas of John Wayne's *The Alamo*, but Steve Frazee has turned out a masterpiece!" However, in a June 23 letter to Wayne and Birdwell, Grant pointed out a few of the book's inconsistencies and/or errors: "Frazee seems to lean over backward to avoid using any of the actual scenes from the script of *The Alamo*. Structural plot points which we tell through highly dramatized scenes involving major protagonists he chooses to tell through the eyes of comparatively unimportant personalities. Frazee has the defenders hold an election–in the presence of Travis–wherein they elect Bowie commander. In our version, of course, Houston tells him to take command. (He also) has Travis threaten to burn 'The Alamo' and move the entire force to Concepcion. There are a few incidents which I know will bring forth a howl from Duke. The outstanding one is where Bowie, looking for Travis, finds him disrobing a Mexican girl of good family, whose parents are friends of Bowie. I changed some other small errors–Bonham is referred to as Colonel John Bonham. (Frazee) chose to call Travis's friend Dickerson, where we call him Dickinson. He calls Bowie's slave 'Ham.' Our research showed up with a half a dozen names and we–possibly in error–called him Jethro." (All of Grant's observations remained in the book.)[1215]

Author Lon Tinkle had previously published *13 Days to Glory* in 1958, but, in order to take advantage of the movie, the Signet book was republished in early 1960 with the new title, *The Alamo*. Again, sketches and photos from Wayne's film appeared on the book's covers. Winner of both the Texas Institute of Letters, and the Sons of the Republic of Texas "Best Texas Book of the Year" awards, Wayne agreed with J. Frank Dobie's comment that "this is a splendid book about the Alamo." Not to be outdone, Birdwell began work on a souvenir program for the roadshow. Available in both hard and soft-cover, it was written by Denny Morrison and based on Tom Carlile's "White paper." Mike Wayne and Don LaCava coordinated the program project. "Yes, Michael and I did that souvenir program," recalls LaCava. "We published it, had it printed, and I remember going back to Chicago and getting the printers to do the job for us. We worked on the design, set up the programs, and had them printed. The printers handled most of the stuff for foreign distributions." On July 8, in another one of his wild ideas, Birdwell wrote to former Prime Minister Winston Churchill to solicit his endorsement of the project: "Dear Sir, As you may know by now John Wayne has produced and directed a twelve million dollar picture entitled *The Alamo*. Based upon the great chapter in Texas early history which was made possible by seventeen men from England who were among the 185 who fought to their deaths against the seven thousand enemy troops of General Santa Anna. We are planning to issue a souvenir program with great dignity with historic scenes, and Mr. Wayne and I would be most grateful if you would consider writing a hundred word forward for this book. We would be most happy to pay a fee to any charity that you would like to name. Few people know or remember that once, just 124 years ago, seventeen men came from your great country to take their stand at the Alamo to set an example and a pattern for free men everywhere. John Wayne and I would be most grateful if we might hear from you at your earliest convenience. Respectfully, Russell Birdwell." Churchill wisely declined.[1216]

Although Wayne had previously announced an October 5 simultaneous premiere of *The Alamo* in eleven cities, actual plans had not yet been finalized. Therefore, Batjac's Bob Newman visited San Antonio on May 18 and intimated the city's premiere probably would take place the day before the first showing in Dallas and Houston. He further agreed that, despite some technical difficulties, it would be ridiculous to hold the film's premiere in any city but San Antonio. After reviewing the city's preparations, Newman continued on to New York but promised a nationwide announcement in a few weeks. In Dallas, meanwhile, Wayne faced the issue of which theater the film would be shown in. As the movie was filmed in the widescreen Todd-AO process, it was suggested that Interstate equip its 2,000-seat Palace theater downtown with the appropriate equipment. But Interstate, with the Tower theater already so equipped, demurred. That left either the Tower or Trans-Texas's Capri. With the Tower currently showing *Ben-Hur*, which would run into November, it was likely the Capri would get the booking.[1217]

On Tuesday, June 7, from the set of *North to Alaska*, Wayne announced the world premiere of *The Alamo* would be held October 24 at the Woodlawn theater in San Antonio, two days before its release in ten other cities. Plans for a major celebration were discussed by Wayne, San Antonio civic and governmental leaders, and newsmen as a part of a multi-city conference call. Two local actors who had parts in the film, Big John Hamilton and Buddy Ochoa, also were on hand in the Menger Hotel's Minuet Room for the call. Proclaimed Wayne, "It's been a long time between the inception of *The Alamo* as a motion picture and its premiere. I can think of no better place for the world premiere than San Antonio–the home of the Alamo. We understand your Chamber of Commerce has planned a wonderful program for a real Texas-sized premiere." After his announcement, Wayne admitted he needed $17,000,000 in revenue before he could break even. "I probably won't see any dough until '62," remarked Duke. Asked why the Woodlawn was chosen, he said it was the only theater that agreed to renovate itself with the necessary equipment to show the film. Woodlawn theater manager Tom Powers stated modifications would cost in excess of $30,000. (It had been thought that the Broadway theater–already equipped for Todd-AO equipment and 70mm–would host the San Antonio premiere, but, as with the Tower in Houston, the Broadway was already exhibiting *Ben-Hur*). Powers further explained the choice: "The Todd-AO camera projection angle had to be 9 degrees, and the Woodlawn booth was already throwing its film from a 7 degree angle. The Majestic, Texas, and Aztec weren't chosen because they couldn't afford to devote themselves to one long-run feature for eight to twelve months." (A painting of San Antonio's Jimmy Mesquiti with Frankie Avalon, as they appeared in the film, would be on display in the Woodlawn's lobby for the run of the show. Mesquiti, garbed in white peasant attire, is seen kneeling along-side a standing Avalon in the middle of the Village with Frankie's hand on his shoulder. Painted as if standing on Back Street behind the blacksmith's shop, Wayne's office, a set in the film named Comanderia de Policia, can be seen in the background). Chamber president Walter Corrigan then informed Wayne that tentative plans called for an old-time trail drive from Brackettville, a special Alamo breakfast, barbecue, gala, and a full-scale downtown Alamo parade with Wayne as grand marshal. Bleachers and Western false fronts would be installed all up and down Houston Street to add flavor to the parade. Along with a reproduction of Fiesta Week's "A Night in Old San Antonio," Corrigan discussed plans to promote "Alamo Airlift" through airlines serving San Antonio. He promised, "As president of the San Antonio chamber of commerce, I pledge to you one hundred percent cooperation in making this occasion one that will be long remembered by everyone. Again, may I say a hearty thank you to you, Robert Newman, Bill O'Donnell, to United Artists, Tommy Powers, Russell Birdwell, Happy Shahan, and everyone who has worked and cooperated to bring *The Alamo* to San Antonio." Although arrangements for a Houston theater weren't finalized yet, Wayne then confirmed the film would open at the Capri in Dallas the day following San Antonio's premiere where the memory of Texas exhibitor and philanthropist Robert J. O'Donnell would be honored with a special invitation-only presentation. With tickets priced at $50 in the 1,575-seat theater, all proceeds would go to a new Varsity Club building named for O'Donnell and the Blind Children's Services. The Club had already purchased a fifty by one hundred eighty-one foot lot for $21,000 and expected to spend another $50,000 for the building. A sell-out of the theater, at the highest prices ever charged for a charity event, could raise as much as $78,000 for the agency. Government officials, social leaders, and other dignitaries would attend along with Wayne. The Capri would even be spruced up with a new "waterfall" curtain, mezzanine and balcony carpeting, and a general repainting of the theater.[1218]

United Artists issued an official announcement a few days later: $100,000 had already been deposited into an "Alamo Fund" to finance the San Antonio celebration and numerous company officials would attend the premiere, including Arthur B. Krim, president; Robert S. Benjamin, board chairman; and vice-presidents Max E. Youngstein, William J. Heineman, Arnold M. Picker, Roger H. Lewis, and Robert Blumofe. Following the premiere, the film would be shown at the Cathay Circle in Los Angeles.[1219]

Now that San Antonio's date was set, Theo Weiss, former president of the chamber of commerce, was named head of a two hundred-man committee to plan the three-day celebration. Forrest Smith, National Bank of Commerce president, was named vice-chairman of the overall committee as well as chairman of a finance committee. He was asked to raise $15,000 by public subscription to underwrite part of the cost of promotion of the event. In an announcement worthy of Birdwell, Corrigan stated, "The Chamber of Commerce pressed vigorously to have the world premiere of *The Alamo* held here in the Alamo City. These two community leaders are aware of the tremendous economic impact this picture will have on our area, and they have accepted their responsibility to assist in the greatest single promotional opportunity presented to San Antonio." In addition to members from the business area, eleven representatives from the city's military community were also on the committee, including Air Force and Army reserve, retired and active duty personnel. Co-chairmen of the committee, representing Air Force, Army and civilian directorship of the events, were Lt. Gen. Edward T. Williams, commanding general of the Fourth Army; Jack Morse, San Antonio department store executive; and Maj. Gen. Robert M. Stillman, commander of Lackland Military Training center.[1220]

Weiss seconded Corrigan's comments. "The premiere committee was enlarged to include state-wide representation," Weiss explained, "because the impact of *The Alamo*'s promotion is also going to be felt in other areas of the state. The focal point is San Antonio since this is the location of the Alamo, but the promotion program and movie are going to turn interest on a whole period of Texas history and on those places where the events occurred. To predict a considerable interest in coming tourist business here as a result of the showing of this movie around the countr, is almost to make an understatement. People are going to see the Alamo in the movie. Then they are going to want to see the real Alamo and other locations of Texas history."[1221]

Even though tickets were not yet on sale, Birdwell wired Norman Levinson, the Capri's general manager, and requested six pairs of tickets for Wayne and his party just to make darn sure they had seats. In San Antonio, meanwhile, the San Antonio Chamber thoughtfully sent Peru's president an invitation to the premiere. But it took a while for the letter to arrive as it was sent by truck! Walter Meyer, who made a living selling Peruvian horses, returned to his home and delivered an Alcalde of La Villita scroll to president Dr. Manuel Prado y Ugarteche courtesy of Mayor Kuykendall. The Chamber suggested the premiere might be of more than normal interest as Wayne's wife Pilar was from Lima.[1222]

After Duke's Texas announcement, interest in the film reached a fever pitch. People just couldn't wait to see it and clamored for any bit of information they could get. Within twenty-four hours after plans for the premiere were announced, more than 1,000 people called and asked if tickets could already be reserved in advance. Producer A.C. Lyles learned firsthand just how excited people were. Lyles visited Texas to drum up interest in *Raymie*, a film he produced. But when people heard he was one of the first to actually see Wayne's film, all they wanted to know about was *The Alamo*. During a ten-day, ten-city tour, Lyles granted thirty-four television, forty-six radio, and twenty-five newspaper interviews. "I found myself making a career in Texas of just talking about *The Alamo* and John Wayne," Lyles confessed, "when the prime purpose for my trip, of course, was to do a little ballyhoo for my own film. After each radio or TV show, people would call in to ask additional questions about Wayne's picture. Several times people heard an interview on their car radio and would be waiting outside the station when I left." To show how crazy the tour was, after a TV interview in Dallas, Lyles received a call from a woman saying her club met once a month and paid as high as $25 for a guest speaker. She thought they could up the ante if he would speak at their next meeting about *The Alamo*. "It seems everybody in Texas is a personal friend of John Wayne. If I gave Wayne a list of the people who sent their regards, it would take pages." If people were this excited without even seeing the film, imagine what it would be like when it came out! Wayne was ecstatic and confident he had a winner: "I know we've got it!"[1223]

# CHAPTER THIRTY-ONE
# ON THE ROAD AGAIN

THE 1960 PRESIDENTIAL ELECTION PROVED TO BE A WATERSHED MOMENT IN the American political landscape. After a decade of Republican control, the nation would choose between Republican Vice-president Richard M. Nixon and Democrat Senator John F. Kennedy. While the struggle for civil rights and desegregation began to deeply divide the populace, and, despite the fact that the nation was experiencing an economic recession, in 1960, foreign affairs took center stage. President Eisenhower's policy of deterrence gave priority to nuclear weapons at the expense of conventional military forces; by keeping pressure on the Soviet Union, he tried to stem the tide of communist domination. His doctrine of massive retaliation relied on long-range missiles and Polaris missile submarines—an all-out attack in response to any provocation. Questioned on the use of nuclear weapons in North Korea, Eisenhower bluntly replied, "We make a hell of a lot of weapons. We spend a lot of money on them. What the hell do we make them for if we don't ever use them, if we have to?"

A moderate progressive, Eisenhower was the first to articulate the domino-theory concept as it related to the spread of communism. Unfortunately, the Cold War escalated during his presidency. Initially promising only economic and foreign aid, by the end of his second term, Eisenhower had sent over 1,000 American military advisers to Vietnam. Then, in a March 1960 meeting, Eisenhower instructed the CIA to set up a plausible Cuban government in exile, and to step up internal propaganda and intelligence gathering while training a paramilitary force of Cuban exiles in Guatemala. While no specific invasion plan had been set, he stressed the importance of finding a legitimate Cuban leader as an alternative to Fidel Castro. "In the long run," he explained, "the United States cannot allow the Castro government to continue to exist in Cuba." He also authorized deployment of a Lockheed U-2 high-altitude reconnaissance plane over Russia. On May 1, 1960, just six months before the coming election, pilot Francis Gary Powers was shot down near Sverdlovsk, an incident that had long-lasting negative effects on U.S.-U.S.S.R. relations. (The 1960 Four Power Paris Summit between Eisenhower, Soviet Premier Nikita Khrushchev, British Prime Minister Harold Macmillan, and French president Charles de Gaulle was canceled in large part because of this U-2 incident. Eisenhower refused to accede to Khrushchev's demand that he apologize for spying, and, as a result, Khrushchev refused to take part in the summit). The Soviet leader even had some leverage since his country had taken the lead in the space race by launching the Sputnik satellite.

By default, presidents inherit the foreign policies of their predecessors, and, with tensions at an all-time high, the new chief executive would have to steer the ship of state through stormy, treacherous waters. The nation had a choice—elect heir-apparent Nixon and continue Eisenhower's policies, or follow Kennedy and a return to liberalism in the "New Frontier." JFK's campaign was about age, energy, and a vision for the new decade; he would move the country out of economic stagnation an, rebuild and restore its prestige. Charismatic, young, intelligent, dynamic, and a legitimate war hero, he also campaigned on the promise he would be tougher on communism and Castro than Nixon. On the other hand, Nixon, seasoned congressman, avid anti-communist, prosecutor of Alger Hiss and experienced in foreign policy, was perceived as a candidate with no concrete political philosophy of his own. He attempted to identify himself with the popular Eisenhower and raised doubts about Kennedy's maturity, despite the fact that both he and Kennedy had first been elected to Congress in 1946. Nixon also was only four years older than JFK. Asked by *Time* magazine's Charles Mohr to name some of Nixon's contributions during his presidency, Eisenhower replied, "If you give me a week, I might think of one. I don't remember." With remarkably similar agendas, both candidates expounded on the need for a stronger America, emphasizing national security, and the threat of communism. Kennedy speechwriter Arthur Schlesinger was so dismayed by the perceived lack of substantive differences in the candidates, he felt compelled to write a pamphlet debunking them: "Kennedy or Nixon: Does It Make Any Difference?"[1224]

So, one may ask, "Why is this important?" Well, Wayne, a staunch Republican, would support whomever the party nominated to run against the Democrats, But he also wanted to insure that whoever ran won. What better way than to plant the seeds of mistrust and concern in the minds of the opposition electorate?

Birdwell and Wayne thus came up with a brilliant concept–incorporate political dialogue in cinematic advertising. In early June, the duo secretly negotiated with *Life* magazine to take out a three-page gatefold advertisement extending out from the front cover and adjoining page. Because of the text and commanding position inside the front cover, the ad had to be approved by the magazine's editorial board. *Life* had planned a July 4 special issue focusing on U.S. politics and the Democrats' upcoming national convention. Wayne's ad would be a shot across the bow of Democrat voters. Birdwell recalled, "In (Duke's) dressing room one day, I suggested an article entitled, 'There Were No Ghost writers At The Alamo.' Before I had finished outlining the article in full, Wayne interrupted and said, 'Go.' 'Go where?' 'I mean go all the way,' Duke said. I explained I wanted to take a three-page gate-fold advertisement in *Life* magazine on the eve of the Democratic convention in Los Angeles, where most, if not all, of the speeches would be ghost written, and this would cost in excess of $150,000. The Duke smiled tolerantly. He said, 'That's pretty good going and that's what I mean. Go ahead.'" In a June 9 memo, Birdwell shared the idea with his staff: "This will constitute, in my opinion, the boldest and most adventurous step that we have undertaken to project, obliquely and without commercialism, a motion picture into the national, as well as international, news stream of press and airwaves. We believe that what we have to say in these pages will leap from our advertising category into the news sections and onto the air." A serious understatement, that: the ad generated a wealth of discourse and publicity, extending to the candidates themselves. (Though the ad was placed in *Life*, the copy first appeared in *Variety* on 6/29/60–without the painting.)[1225]

The gatefold cover consisted of a color print of one of the Russell Roberts paintings used in the movie's opening credits. In yellow block letters on the lower right-hand side of the painting was *THE ALAMO*. Written in script at the bottom of the page was, "The Mission that Became a Fortress–The Fortress that Became a Shrine." Below *THE ALAMO* was written in script, "World Premiere October 1960." On the facing page, Birdwell wrote the following:

"There Were No Ghost writers At The Alamo" by Russell Birdwell. Very soon, two great political parties of the United States will nominate their candidates for president. One of these men, by vote of the people, will be assigned the awesome duties of the White House: civilian leader of the nation, commander-in-chief of all of its armed forces and keeper and director of its nuclear weaponry.

"Who are these men who seek the most formidable job, the most responsible job on earth? But more important: who is the one man who, after the political merry-go-round has stopped, will hold in his hand the gold ring of victory?

"Do we know him? Have we ever known him? Will we ever know him?

"Who has written his speeches? Who–or what board of ghostwriting strategists–has fashioned the phrases, molded the thoughts, designed the delivery, authored the image, staged the presentation, put the political show on the road to win the larger number of votes?

"Who is the actor reading the script? Or, in this moment when eternity could be closer than ever before, is there a statesman who for the sake of a vote is not all things to all men; a man who will put America back on the high road of security and accomplishment, without fear or favor or compromise; a man who wants to do the job that must be done and to hell with friend or foe who would have it otherwise; a man who knows that the American softness must be hardened; a man who knows when our house is in order no man will ever dare to trespass.

"In short, a Man!

"There is a growing anxiety among the people to have straight answers. They don't want the handiwork of the opinion molder. They have had a bellyful of payola, influence peddling, quiz show rigging, the ghostwriting of political speeches—symptoms of a pallid public morality.

"They are finished with the great deceptions.

"They wait impatiently, as the free world becomes smaller and smaller, for a return to the honest, courageous, clear-cut standards of frontier days—the days of America's birth and greatness; the days when the noblest utterances of man became unrehearsed.

"There were no ghostwriters at the Alamo. Only men. Among them Colonel David Crockett, who was 50 years old; Colonel James Bowie, 40; William Barret Travis, 26.

"These men left a legacy for all who prize freedom above tyranny, individualism above conformity. They had gone to Texas to carve out new lives. Their ranks included men from 18 states and 6 foreign nations.

"Their foe was a Mexican dictator, General Santa Anna, at the head of an army of 7,000 well-equipped, well-trained troops, who in 1836 sought to crush the growing state of that faraway land now known as Texas. Santa Anna crossed the Rio Grande River, invaded San Antonio. His first target was the Alamo, a mission built in 1718 by Franciscan Friars and manned in the year 1836 by 185 volunteer citizen-soldiers. Presumably an easy target; 185 against 7,000.

"The dictator did not realize that his enemy were not a common breed. He faced hard-living, hard-loving, hard-fighting believers in freedom.

"Let us look now at a few of them. Their own words.

"Defeated for his fourth term in the United States Congress, Crockett announced; 'You all can go to hell—I'm going to Texas.'

"And then he rode 1,500 miles on horseback to Texas, not yet a part of the United States, and, in his diary, he wrote:

"I promised to give the Texans a helping hand in their high road to freedom. Early this morning the enemy came in sight, marching in regular order and displaying strength to the greatest advantage in order to strike us with terror.

That was no go. They'll find they have to do with men who will never lay down their arms as long as they can stand on their legs.'

"In 1834, two years before Colonel Crockett rode into the Alamo with his followers 'to hit a lick against what's wrong and to say a word for what's right,' he toured the New England states as a United States Congressman and, while visiting Boston, he wrote:

"We then went up to the old battleground on Bunker's hill, where they were erecting a monument to those who fell in that daybreak battle of our rising glory. I felt as if I wanted to call them up, and ask them to tell me how to help protect the liberty they bought for us with their blood; but as I could not do so, I resolved on that holy ground, as I had done elsewhere, to go for my country, always and everywhere.'

"After entering the Alamo Colonel, Crockett wrote to his children in Tennessee: 'I hope you will do the best you can, and I will do the same. Do not be uneasy about me—I am with friends. Your affectionate father, Farewell, David Crockett.'

"As the Santa Anna hordes pounded against the mission that had become a fortress, Colonel Crockett wrote in his diary: 'We are all in high spirits though rather short of provisions for men who have appetites that could digest anything—but oppression.'

"Land was cheap in Texas in those days—it was selling for 12½ cents an acre. But the price of freedom and liberty came high. Before the Alamo fell, Crockett wrote: 'We will go ahead and sell our lives at a high price.'

"Colonel James Bowie, in words remembered by Mrs. Susanna Dickinson (she and her thre3-year-old daughter with a little Negro boy were the only survivors of the glorious disaster), said: 'I prefer to die in its ditches rather than give up a inch of Texas soil to a dictator.'

"When word of Jim Bowie's death reached his mother, she said: 'So Jim is dead. I bet they found no bullets in his back.'

Colonel William Barret Travis, the young South Carolina lawyer entrusted with command of the Alamo by General Sam Houston, in a letter to Texas's Governor Henry Smith:

"We are ill-prepared for attack, yet we are determined to sustain it as long as there is a man left. Death is preferable to disgrace. Should Bexar (San Antonio) fall, your friend will be buried beneath its ruins. I shall not surrender or retreat.'

"The situation hopeless, Colonel Travis gave his men a way out just before the final onslaught: 'Any of you who wish may leave with honor. Here on these ramparts you have bought a priceless ten days of time for General Houston. You are brave and noble soldiers. God bless you.'

"No man gave up his post. All gave their lives, after killing 1,700 and holding the enemy for thirtee3 days. The precious time bought enabled General Houston, forty-si6 days later at San Jacinto, to win Texas' liberation.

"There were no ghost writers at the Alamo. Only men."
A STATEMENT OF PRINCIPLE – JOHN WAYNE, BATJAC
PRODUCTIONS – JAMES EDWARD GRANT, AUTHOR OF *THE
ALAMO*.[1226]

Ingeniously comparing *The Alamo* to the current political campaign while
steering clear of partisanship, Birdwell attempted to cast doubts on both
candidates' qualifications. Rather than knowing the real individual, the public, he
implied, only was being told what it wanted to hear. Speeches molded by opinion
polls, sound bites tailored to generate publicity. Though not naming the candidates
specifically, there is no doubt he was referring to Kennedy. Birdwell detailed what
a president should be: fearless, battle-hardened, tenacious, uncompromising–the
implication being Kennedy was none of those. Invoking images of America's
frontier days–honesty, greatness, and courage–Birdwell cleverly reminded the
nation of Eisenhower's presidency and, by default, Nixon. Even the story of the
Alamo could be viewed as a metaphor for Nixon's war on communism.

Wayne's feelings about Nixon and communism were well documented.
While vice-president, Nixon was asked to endorse the film and, anticipating
Duke's support during the election, of course, agreed. Refusing to join twenty
other Hollywood actors drumming up support for one or another of the
opposition hopefuls, Wayne just said, "Let the Democrats spend all their money
and make a lot of noise. They haven't got a chance in November." However,
along with Helen Hayes, Mervyn LeRoy, Irene Dunne, Walter Pidgeon, Mary
Pickford, Dick Powell, Dina Merrill, Jeanette MacDonald, Gordon and Sheila
MacRae, and many others, Wayne did join "Celebrities For Nixon-Lodge," an
organization created to work for the Republican ticket within the entertainment
industry. Powell said the actors who came out for Nixon were far statelier than
those who supported Kennedy: "We're the opposite of the rat pack," he said,
referring to Sinatra's friends. "We've tried to get the most reputable movie people.
They may not be the most popular at the moment, but they have dignity and the
right image. If I were working for Kennedy, I would try to stay away from the
element that is supporting him. I'm good friends with most of them, but I think
these people hurt Kennedy with their cheap publicity." Wayne's fellow actor (and
registered Democrat) Ronald Reagan even volunteered during the campaign to
"cross the aisle" and switch to the Republican Party. In October 1960, Reagan
became vice chairman of the Southern California Democrats for Nixon. "As a
lifelong Democrat," he declared, "today I feel no Democrat can ignore that the
party has been taken over by a faction which seeks to pattern the Democratic
Party and its politics after the Labor-Socialist government of England." Like
Birdwell, Reagan attacked Kennedy's political philosophy but was less allegorical.
In a July 15 letter to Nixon, he wrote (that) under his "tousled boyish haircut

(Kennedy) is still old Karl Marx" and his New Frontier program was "nothing new in the idea of a government being Big Brother to us all."[1227]

Expressing his concerns on the spreading communist scourge, Wayne was equally blunt. "These are perilous times," Wayne explained. "The eyes of the world are on us. We must sell America to countries threatened with Communist domination. Our picture is also important to Americans who should appreciate the struggle our ancestors made for the precious freedom we enjoy." Wayne further explained his position in an article written for the thirtieth anniversary issue of *The Hollywood Reporter*: "*The Alamo* was and is a picture that should have been made, and I damn well knew it. And what effect did we want to make with it? Well, I'll tell you. I'd say that we wanted to recreate a moment in history which will show to this living generation of Americans what their country really stands for, and to put in front of their eyes the bloody truth of what some of their forebears went through to win what they had to have or die–Liberty and Freedom. These are tough days that we're living through. We are at a crossroads of history and no fooling. The tempo of events is so swift, the forces aligned against us are so ruthless, the pressures that are building so menacing that we and the free world that stands with us have reached the point where further appeasement may well mean disaster . I hope that the rallying cry of 'Remember the Alamo' will be heard again to put new heart and new faith into all the world's free peoples." Birdwell's ad reinforced those comments.[1228]

Wayne explained his reasons for the ad in a July 5 three-column interview with columnist Joe Hyams. "Because I'm an actor, I don't think I should be robbed of the right to speak. I hoped that, by taking out the ad, this way, I might prompt more motion picture companies into taking out institutional ads with a more patriotic attitude in their test. It seems to me we are limited now to a few television announcers and an occasional newspaper writer to remind us that we owe a little something to our country rather than what our country owes us in federal relief insurance, old age health and welfare benefits, and the like. Speaking as a citizen of the U.S., as a guy at the corner drug store, I think politics today is smothering the individual principles of candidates who are all bounded by party rules, so it would be very pleasant for me to find a man, a Republican or Democrat or whatever, who really speaks up and says what he thinks. In delving back into the history of the time of the Alamo, I found that men, still in their twenties, thought deeply of the problems of our country. They were the men who gave us our heritage, and I don't think we give our heritage enough careful thought. Days are moving too fast. We don't sit down and think of the real purposes and needs of our existence. I think we need to reflect on our history–to realize that, when we are aroused, we can be savage and cruel and that, in our time of need, we can carry our share of burdens as we are proving to the tune of some $70 billion dollars of foreign aid each year. Now with the political conventions upon us, it behooves us to choose a leader–a man who can stand up and tell us what he thinks is right, whether it works a hardship on us or not. We need men who will recall to the world what we Americans really are."[1229]

(Curiously, it had been stated the ad actually may have been an endorsement for Lyndon Johnson. In fact, during an NBC televised news conference at the Hotel Roosevelt where Kennedy answered charges from former president Harry Truman that the Democratic national convention was rigged, a newsman rose, waved a copy of *Life* and asked, "I have here an ad for *The Alamo* which cost $152,000. Did you read into it a veiled plug for the candidacy of Senator Lyndon B. Johnson?" Answered Kennedy, "I didn't read that into it at all." Johnson declined to campaign in the primaries and didn't *publicly* run for president during the summer. He preferred to perform his machinations behind the Senate's closed doors and initially hoped to be a compromise candidate at the convention, But, on July 5, just ten days before the convention, he finally declared his candidacy: "The next president must be able to stand against the challenge of communism. And he will have little time to learn on the job." Wayne wouldn't support Johnson and despised Kennedy, calling him a "snot-nosed kid who couldn't keep his dick in his pants." (Wayne, however, was an American through and through. After the presidential campaign was over, a reporter asked if Nixon was still Duke's man. Wayne firmly replied, "No. John F. Kennedy is my man now. He is the president of the United States."[1230]

When Frank Sinatra hired Albert Maltz, one of the Hollywood Ten, to write a screenplay for *The Execution of Private Slovik* (based on William Bradford Huie's book of the same name), Wayne said, "I disliked the book because it portrayed our military as the heavies. I never thought Sinatra was a Commie, but he hired a Commie to write a screenplay the Communists would have just loved. I wonder how Sinatra's crony, Senator John Kennedy, feels about him hiring such a man? I'd like to know his attitude because he's the one who is making plans to run the administrative government of our country." (A few nights later, Sinatra ran into Duke at a costumed charity benefit in the Moulin Rouge nightclub and called him out on his comment. Francis was dressed as an Indian squaw, while Duke, as usual, wore cowboy attire. "Now, now, Frank," said a calm Wayne out in the parking lot. "We can discuss this somewhere else." Sinatra screamed back, "I want to talk about it right now!" As Duke turned away, friends stepped in to hold back the snarling, alcohol-infused Sinatra. Wayne said, "It's a good thing some of his friends pulled him away because I'd sure hate to have flattened him." But according to other accounts, Sinatra stalked off the stage when Duke came up to the microphone. Wayne, confused, asked Frank why. Told it was about the Maltz comment, Duke asked if he wanted to talk about it. "Some other time," replied Sinatra. "Duke, we're friends, and we'll probably do pictures together. Let's forget the whole thing.") No, the ad wasn't an endorsement for Johnson, though it may have caused LBJ to throw his hat into the ring. Interestingly, on September 12, 1960, Kennedy stopped in San Antonio, signed the guest register at the Alamo and gave a campaign speech addressing Latin America and the good-neighbor policy.[1231]

Birdwell knew the ad would generate an enormous amount of publicity. *Life* printed seven million copies of the issue, its largest single run to date. Another 250,000 mailers were distributed to religious, industrial, and political leaders in addition to convention delegates and the mass communications media–print, television and radio–that covered the convention. Over 5,500 correspondents, commentators, writers, and broadcasters would be in Los Angeles. According to W.R. Wilkerson, "The perfect timing of Wayne's guided word missile now in orbit around the globe multiplies its explosive effect in stirring excitement over a forthcoming motion picture." U.S. Rep. Donald L. Jackson, a Republican from Santa Monica, even inserted the ad into the California Congressional Record. Newscasters and commentators at a large number of television stations read the ad over the air, and the London Daily Mail even reprinted its entire text. Florabel Muir's article in *LimeLight* was typical of the response: "I'm here to assert that what Wayne has to say, under Birdwell's byline, adds up to one of the greatest, most eloquent, and most significant and timely calls to the conscience of a nation that I have ever read. I said that his message is addressed to the Democratic delegates. In reality, it is a full-throated challenge to the people of America and the Free World. It echoes the spurring eloquence that sparked this nation's growth and glory in historic times of crisis, But, most of all, it is a prayer, exalted and moving, and the burden of its solemn appeal is remindful of Kipling's 'Recessional" 'Lord God of Hosts, be with us yet, Lest we forget, lest we forget' " On July 5, Birdwell ordered another 2,500 reprints of the magazine and notified his staff, "You have new lists coming with the reprints. Send them to the priority of lists... If we miss some of the minor lists, don't worry about it. After all, *Life* will have thirty-five million readers." With that many readers, the ad would be seen by almost 30 percent of the entire U.S. population![1232]

Amusingly, there were those who seemed to miss the point of the missive entirely. DRT Librarian Marg-Riette Montgomery wrote to Birdwell, "Your editorial in *Life* for July 4th is inspiring in conception and lofty in tone. But, for your own protection, it should be called to your attention that the best authority... says that the so-called David Crockett Diary is a literary hoax . original editions of all works attributed to him were authorized by him in an off-hand, cooperative manner. But they were written by the best political ghost-writers of the day. So while your point stands: There were no ghost-writers at the Alamo; it is on pretty shakey (sic) foundation. There were no ghost-writers–until after they were all ghosts." (Of course, after viewing Wayne's film she said, "The Crockett role is the best in the picture. It is very faithful to all that is known about him.")[1233]

Finally, columnist Dick West may have said it best when he wrote, "I am fairly familiar with Texas history, and I was aware that the Alamo defenders were short of guns and ammunition. But I never knew until I read Birdwell's tone poem that the poor souls had to get along without ghostwriters. Had it not been for that, they might . have held out a week or two longer. If Birdwell will search the records closely, I'll bet he also will find that there were no press agents at the Alamo (either)."[1234]

Although Birdwell and UA's Roger Lewis seemed to have resolved their differences on how to run the publicity campaign, the former still kept the *Life* ad a secret until the last minute. On June 16, buried on page nine of a thirteen-page memo to Lewis, he explained why: " Pinpointing our triple-page ad, *Life* magazine will take six columns in *The Hollywood Reporter* and *Motion Picture Daily*. If the reaction to this three-page spread is as good as *Life* expects, *Life* intends to issue a success booklet. Duke Wayne and I would have preferred to tell all of you about our three-page advertisement in *Life* in advance of its publication. We did not for the simple reason that we felt we were dealing with an idea which we wished to protect with all possible secrecy and, sometimes, in a very large organization, word leaks out. We are hopeful that the idea warranted our caution and our secrecy and are hopeful that you will understand that we took these steps in our mutual interests in behalf of *The Alamo*." Not a very resounding endorsement of Lewis or the UA publicity department.[1235]

The following month, Birdwell received a letter from Earle Wakefield, an editor at *Life*. It described comments made by Henry Luce, the magazine's founder. A co-worker wrote, "I got a chance to ask Mr. Luce what he thought of *The Alamo* gatefold and the accompanying copy, He said he was 'really impressed–and inspired' by it, and also deeply gratified by the evident impression it made on so many *Life* readers." Martin Davis, advertising director at Paramount Pictures, said he thought "the *Life* advertisement (the) most extraordinary, best thing that ever happened in advertising, (that it) set a new all time high for Hollywood, that the word of mouth had been most penetrating, that (I) had not heard one single word of dissent of any sort (and) that it was the one thing in this area that had been cheered with praiseful unanimity."' The staggering amount of publicity the ad generated even surprised Duke. "When you get back to New York," he wrote Birdwell, "please tell *Life* we expected big results from our *Alamo* ad, but we did not anticipate that it would create a continuing dividend of news and editorial impact over a six-month period–not only throughout the United States but a large part of Europe. I've been told by experts that our gatefold ad has brought us more than five million dollars worth of editorial recognition–influential, selling space in newspapers, magazines as well as over network television and radio shows. And it went even beyond this. Presidential candidates, for the first time in history, used the Alamo story in their campaigns, and the man who was elected president quoted verbatim, in a major address, our *Alamo* advertising legend first published in *Life* magazine. I wonder if even *Life* knows that the right ad with the right staging and timing can become enduring advertising literature?"[1236]

John Jensen wasn't the only artist hired to contribute to the publicity campaign. Batjac *planned* to distribute to all domestic and European UA exchanges over six hundred of Ybarra's set and scenic sketches used to design the Alamo. The sketches would be used in display exhibits to exploit the film. Western artist and sculptor George Phippen was asked to supply a variety of sketches for the souvenir program. In 1949, Phippen had settled in Prescott, Arizona, and built a studio, rapidly establishing his reputation. In his work, he meticulously researched backgrounds, elements, people, settings, and historically accurate gear to portray his subjects with as much detail as possible. Duke had heard of the artist's reputation for authenticity and invited him to the location. They became fast friends, and, as a result, Michael Wayne asked Phippen to contribute to the program. After considering his options, Phippen came up with a multi-directional approach: "A colorful early morning battle scene in front of the burning Alamo, with the trio, Mr. Wayne, Mr. Widmark, and Mr. Harvey, being spotlighted figures in the foreground." He initially planned on a portrait of Wayne in either oil or watercolor but, due to lack of time, only pen and ink drawings and two watercolors would be available. Initially, the souvenir program would be sixty-four pages long, thirty-two in black ink and thirty-two in color. As 100,000 copies from Pacific Press would cost $63,775, Wayne and LaCava wisely decided to shorten the length to thirty-six pages. (Available in both hard and soft cover, each program version was slightly different; the hard cover version, which could be purchased for just $1, had thirty-six pages and six Phippen sketches, while the soft cover version had only fourteen pages and three sketches. The Japanese version was even shorter: twelve pages and two sketches one printed in red!). When Wayne left for Africa, Phippen sent him a letter. Receiving no reply, he sent another, this time including a sketch of Wayne being eaten by man-eating lions. Wayne immediately replied by return mail! [1237]

Reynold Brown was the third artist commissioned to do artwork for the film. Birdwell asked him to paint a proposed twenty-four-sheet conception on a three-by-six-foot wooden board for $1,500. By July 25, the work was completed in Brown's garage as it was too large to fit in his house. With only one preliminary drawing, it took just fifteen days to complete—the largest movie illustration Brown ever did. (As a freelance artist, Brown provided paintings and drawings used to promote over 250 films including, coincidentally, *The Man from the Alamo*). According to Reynold's son Franz, "The layout was partially determined by movie contractual requirements. Star location and size was determined by their significance to the movie; obviously Wayne was most important. The picture is designed to draw the viewer's attention to the Crockett/Wayne character. Costumes and architecture were based on various pictures provided by the production company." Referred to as "The Last Charge at the Alamo" or "The Battle of the Alamo," the painting appeared on posters and billboards and was prominently featured in the film's promotion campaign. Upon completion, the painting was approved by Wayne, photographed, and then sent to UA's Lewis in

New York where further photographs were taken and lithographs made. Birdwell wrote to Lewis that the painting eventually should be shipped to Jim Powers, Woodlawn theater manager in San Antonio. He went on to say, "When they have finished with it, it is our hope that they will present the painting in the name of John Wayne to the Daughters of the Republic, in a fitting ceremony, so that the painting may hang in the Alamo." A copy of the letter was also sent to Mrs. T.E. McCram, the DRT's acting director, who referred it to the Alamo committee for consideration. As usual, the publicist held nothing back when he spoke of Brown's painting: "A heroics size oil painting titled 'The Last Charge at the Alamo' has just been completed on John Wayne's order by Artist Reynold Brown. Aflame with action and color, Brown's canvas, covering an area of twent0 square feet, shows the Mexican army under the dictator Santa Anna moving in for the kill on the morning of March 6, 1836. In the background is the crumbling Alamo ablaze, with attacking troops including cavalry, artillery, and lancers at close grips with the defenders. (With) heroic figures in the foreground . the artist caught the climactic moment of the battle just before the Mexican assault overpowered the mission-fortress, with the 185 beleaguered Texans slain to the last man by the 7,000 attacking troops." During the premiere, the painting was also displayed at Frost Bros., a local San Antonio high-fashion retail chain.[1238]

Birdwell also updated Lewis on the October San Antonio preparations, including the airlift of seventy-five newsmen for the premiere. "Perhaps you will recall," he wrote on June 24, "that I suggested some months ago that I wanted to fly seventy-five newspapermen into San Antonio for the world premiere—without any cost to us. This has been arranged. The San Antonio Chamber of Commerce is picking up the tab on seventy-five newspapermen, covering all transportation, hotel accommodations, and subsistence from October 22 to October 25." They would stay at the finest hotels, receive premium tickets for the premiere, and even be given commemorative Bowie knives! (Manufactured by Carvel Hall, each three-quarter-scale reproduction was fourteen and a half inches in overall length with a ten-inch chrome-plated carbon steel blade capped with a brass strip. The wooden handle was antique-stained beech).[1239]

In June, Wayne ordered cutting of the negative into its final form with a running time of 192 minutes. Although *Box Office* stated Wayne also ordered twenty prints processed immediately at a cost of $200,000, that was incorrect. "There were no prints run off in June," says Bill Gilmore. "I can assure you. The negative could have been print, and there could have been an answer print, but I don't think they ran off prints. Those are release prints. You don't make release prints until you're completely finished with the editing process, and you're literally turning the negative over to the distributor, and the distributor orders the print. There's no way we would have ordered release prints without (first) showing it to an audience. No audience saw the movie; I'm talking about an unbiased audience. I'm not talking about John Wayne and Stuart Gilmore's relatives." So what better way to generate some feedback than to have a good old-fashioned sneak preview?[1240]

A time-honored Hollywood tradition, sneak previews were legitimate test screenings attended by studio executives to gauge audience response and develop marketing strategies. They usually were scheduled on Friday or Saturday nights with only a small notice in the local paper that read "Major Studio Sneak Preview Tonight at 8:00." Admission usually was free, and secrecy was important because studios wanted genuine audience responses, unfettered by bias toward actors or genres. Given the importance of the film, a sneak preview was scheduled for Denver in early August.[1241]

With "at least" $1.3 million to spend before the movie premiered, Birdwell continued seeking ways to publicize the film. Batjac and United Artists launched a series of full-sized display ads in thirty-five leading newspapers in twelve major cities in the United State. and Canada. The ads, reaching a combined circulation of over fifty million readers, included mail-order coupons for premieres in each city. Seventy-one major newspapers in New York, Connecticut, and New Jersey, with a combined circulation of over ten million, ran Rheingold Beer display ads tying into the film; they included a life-sized photograph of Wayne and focused attention on the Rivoli premiere in New York. UA fieldmen in each territory developed local drives with exhibitors, music shops, and retail outlets. Posters, displays, streamers, sales literature, and other promotional material were sent to these outlets and focused attention on the film and regional openings. A schedule of advertising aimed at the music trade and press underscored the scope of the promotion.[1242]

In San Antonio, meanwhile, plans for the celebration were in high gear! The Chamber of Commerce sent a letter to various civic and business leaders and to heads of industry and government, encouraging them all to serve on the *Alamo* World Premiere Committee. Its theme was "rededication to the ideal of the Alamo and of tribute to the heroic stand of its defenders. The presentation of the premiere here," said committee chairman Weiss, "will focus national attention on Texas history and on the principles which motivated the Alamo heroes." By mid-July, they had already received 150 favorable replies, including Happy Shahan's. A.J. Ploch, chairman of The Bexar County Sheriff's Mounted Posse, also announced a 137-mile trail ride from Brackettville to San Antonio. Inviting all known South Texas trail ride clubs to join the event, the five-day ride expected to attract as many as 1,000 riders and would end just in time for the riders to join the downtown parade. Led by Indian scouts, the participants would be dressed in Western gear and include wagons and buckboards. Shahan planned a kick-off barbecue in Brackettville with another scheduled for the riders upon their arrival in San Antonio.[1243]

Two hundred and fifty downtown businesses were asked to put up decorations and plan promotions for the premiere with emphasis on the Alamo.

Weiss declared, "We are going to carry out the Alamo theme everywhere. Visitors will know from the moment they arrive that this is the Alamo city." Another key event would be "A Night in Old San Antonio." Located in La Villita, a restored original section of the city, the event compressed centuries of Spanish Southwestern history into a few hours presentation. The Symphony Society of San Antonio also took part in the celebration by arranging a concert conducted by Dimitri Tiomkin. Birdwell elaborated on the plans in a memo to Lewis: "During that time, there will be many colorful events: a mammoth street breakfast in front of the Alamo attended by thousands; a re-dedication in front of the Alamo; a gigantic luncheon of 'Texas Under Six Flags' with cuisine to match each nationality...." A finance committee started a fund drive to raise $15,000 in contributions from local businesses to support preparations. Other costs would be covered through the sale of $50 Gold Patron tickets for the premiere ($1.84 admission, $.16 federal and state taxes, and $48 Patron subscription). San Antonio's Municipal advertising committee even budgeted $5,000 to cover promotion costs. And the companies that contributed were as varied as their businesses: Blue Bonnet Hotel, Gebhardt Chili Powder Co, United Gas Pipe Co., Jefferson Standard Life Insurance, San Antonio Music Co., Humble Oil and Refining Co., Hertzberg Jewelry Co., Hemphill Food Center, Kelly Field National Bank, A-Alamo Rent and Sales, and Southern Steel Co. among them. Yes, the whole city was preparing for an anticipated onslaught of as many as 400,000 visitors. And it wasn't just San Antonio. Through the efforts of United Artists' Arnold Picker, Great Britain's Princess Margaret and Lord Anthony Armstrong-Jones graciously agreed to attend the London premiere at the Astoria Theatre on October 26. Naturally, Wayne wanted to show his appreciation and what better way than to give an English cowgirl a silver-studded Western saddle.[1244]

While Birdwell and Lewis seemed to have mended their fences, the relationship between Wayne and United Artists left a lot to be desired. Birdwell learned from Earle Wakefield that "it is general knowledge in the trade that Arthur Krim and Max Youngstein—mostly Max—(were) very upset with (Wayne and Birdwell)." As Batjac was an independent production company and not directly under UA's control, it was felt that if Wayne was successful, other production companies would take the same approach, thereby diluting the studio's influence, control, and profitability. By this time, numerous actors already had formed their own production companies: Wayne and Batjac, Holden and Toluca, Brando and Pennebaker, Mitchum and DRM, etc. As Wayne had shown, independents could produce films completely outside of the major studio film system. By creating their own companies, they could better control their own creative work in addition to advertising and marketing. UA was acutely aware of that. Stated Wakefield, "If Wayne and Birdwell get away with this, United Artists fears that, with rebellion from other independent producers, they will be out of the promotion and advertising business—one of their profitable mainstays. They want to stop this break in the dike." Wayne felt all along that something wasn't quite right with UA. The constant bickering, the lack of promotion, and minimal results. Now, he was furious.[1245]

On July 26, Burt Sloan called Wayne and Birdwell and complained he hadn't previously been told about a *Life* magazine article that would run in the September 19 issue and further said that UA had been planting *Alamo* stories for months. Wayne shot off a telegram the following day and blasted Sloan: "Are you kidding? Where are all those stories you said had been written and planted by United Artists and copies of which you were going to let me see? I, John Wayne, am sending this wire without Birdwell's knowledge and would like to know exactly what you and yours have been doing back there during the last six months to help *The Alamo*. Duke." Obviously, according to Duke, either no one had sent Wayne any copies of the proposed stories or nothing actually had been written. Either way, he wanted to know what the hell was going on! Birdwell fueled the fire as well with his telegram: "We planted *Life* layout many months ago, and both Duke and I have known for some weeks now that the layout was set." The gauntlet was cast, and make no doubt about it, Wayne and Birdwell were letting the studio know in no uncertain terms that going forward, they, not UA, would take charge of publicity.[1246]

Naturally, Sloane took exception to the comments and accusations and, in a letter to Lewis, outlined UA's contributions: " the biggest contribution of the (publicity) department can't be catalogued as material turned out or breaks pasted up. Our unique ingredient is a working knowledge of the unglamorous details and routine chores that underwrite any successful campaign. These are things that Birdwell does not know. To put it another way, our job has been and will be to bridge the gap between the Bird's high-fashion hokum and essential, journeyman pressagentry. Most of the Birdwell copy in its natural or raw state is plain unprintable. He doesn't understand the difference between a brochure and a feature, how to couple art with text, who uses what kind of color, what makes a serviceable lead, the difference between random background material and copy aimed for publication, how to break down the big story into separately angled pieces, how to shape special material for special markets." As a follow-up, he prepared a summary of UA activities broken down into several categories: production, post-production, columns, and syndicates. "Virtually all the production material is non-Birdwell," he wrote, "since he came on the picture towars the closing scenes. The post-production material, at worse, breaks fifty-fifty, Birdwell vs. UA. The column items are principally UA. The syndicate plants are exclusively UA."[1247]

UA was correct. Features had been published in *Look*, *Pageant*, *Coronet*, *Sixteen*, *Holiday*, *Cavalier*, *Seventeen*, *Movie Digest*, *Saturday Evening Post*, *Parade*, *The American Legion Magazine*, *This Week*, and *Junior Scholastic*. Just to whet the audience's appetite, the November 1960 issue of *Screen Stories* even had a seven-page adaptation of the script, albeit an earlier version and not the one that was eventually filmed. Twenty-one layouts and mailing pieces also had been serviced for key domestic and foreign newspapers. About $50,000 had been spent so far in movie business publication alone; another $50,000 was budgeted for after the premieres. Targeted publications included *Box Office Digest, Box Office, Film Daily, Greater Amusements, Hollywood Diary, Hollywood Reporter, Independent Film Journal, Motion Picture Daily, Motion Picture Herald,* and *Variety.* Saturation TV and radio spots would begin in late September with one-minute and three-minute trailers scheduled hourly, But what was just as important were the opportunities that *weren't* taken advantage of. In February, UA had alerted Birdwell on the importance of staging an event on Alamo Day, rather than just relying on an ornate and overly long handout with very limited potential. It didn't happen. In April, Sloane suggested to Birdwell that there were enormous possibilities in erecting an Alamo exhibit at Freedomland U.S.A. It could have been *the* exhibit that represented Texas. Again, the suggestion was never implemented. (Referred to as "Disneyland of the East," Freedomland U.S.A. was a history-themed amusement park located in the Baychester area of the Bronx. At eighty-five acres in size, it was larger than Disneyland (sixty-five acres). Its layout was in the shape of a large map of the forty-eight contiguous United States and divided into different themed areas based on the history of the United State., each with its own attractions, shops, and restaurants: Little Old New York (1850-1900), Chicago (1871), The Great Plains (1803-1900), San Francisco (1906), The Old Southwest (1890), New Orleans-Mardi Gras, and Satellite City-The Future. The park opened June 19, 1960, and, with an attendance of over two million visitors its first year, it would have been a perfect venue to advertise both Wayne's film and the Alamo).[1248]

However, Sloane was less than candid when he spoke of his lack of knowledge regarding the September *Life* spot. While on July 26, he complained he hadn't previously been told about the article, on July 27 he explained to Lewis, "You may care to know that the art was serviced to *Life* before Birdwell came on the picture, that there have been numerous UA meetings and follow-ups on this, and that, as recently as this noon, Tess Michaels sat with the *Life* people to retrieve the final selections of art and to confirm the proper identifications."[1249]

In addition to the *Life* layout, Wayne recorded a radio spot that plugged *The Alamo* and encouraged listeners to vote in the upcoming election: "This is John Wayne speaking. Ever since my school days, I've been fascinated by the legend of that handful of heroic men who saved the day for Texas at the Alamo. That's why I am so proud to have produced and appeared in *The Alamo,* an exciting page of our history re-enacted on the screen. You'll preview this new motion picture exclusively in this week's *Life* magazine......."[1250]

The underlying premise of a sneak preview was that if audience members didn't know beforehand what film they'd see, they'd have open minds and thus give honest opinions. Of course, if they knew ahead of time which film they'd see, it defeated the purpose. So, Wayne took an interesting approach to marketing the film's soundtrack album. Looking for feedback, he only invited selected musicians and music industry executives to a special screening of the film. Even Batjac's film editors weren't asked to attend. On July 29, he sent out the following telegram: "We are running a hush hush screening of John Wayne's *The Alamo* at 8p.m. on Tuesday, August 2, in Todd-AO theater at 1021 North Seward, Hollywood, for the purpose of letting you hear Dimitri Tiomkin's fabulous musical score before we make the final decision on *The Alamo* album. You are invited. I would appreciate it deeply if you would keep this screening most confidential. Please advise if you can attend . Russell Birdwell." The intent was to release the soundtrack as a double album, but, after feedback from the screening's attendees, it was decided to only issue a single album. Released by Columbia Records in both mono and stereo, only thirty-six minutes and forty-one seconds of Tiomkin's magnificent score would be heard, augmented by "The Ballad of the Alamo" by Marty Robbins and "The Green Leaves of Summer" by The Brothers Four.[1251]

Several days later, an official sneak preview was announced in Denver. Though not identified as such, everyone knew it would be *The Alamo*. And how couldn't they?

> "Friday Night at 8:30 P.M. WORLD PREMIERE "SNEAK PREVUE" at the Aladdin Theater–one show only! All seats Reserved! 12-million dollar super production Todd-AO and Technicolor in 70MM FIRST SHOWING IN THE WORLD!"[1252]

It had been in the papers for days. Not officially, of course. But everyone knew. Columnist Larry Tajiri of the *Denver Post* informed his readers several days before that the preview had to be *The Alamo* because:

-Wayne had booked a room at the downtown Brown Palace hotel.

-Batjac handled arrangements for the special showing.

-Twenty-five rooms had been reserved for Batjac and United Artists personnel from Hollywood.

-Only a film the size and importance of *The Alamo* would engender such preparations. On August 2, Birdwell sent a telegram to the mayor of Denver stating Wayne was " Looking forward to seeing you when he gets to Denver on Friday." No wonder the nine hundred-seat Fox Intermountain's Aladdin Theater was sold out by Tuesday.

The Mile High City had been used several times in the past to sneak a preview. A prototypical American city, Denver had hosted numerous Cecil B. DeMille screenings in the past, and, on September 4, 1959, MGM had chosen the Centre theater to sneak-preview *Ben-Hur*. Along with Dallas and San Diego, Denver's audience reaction was critical in reducing the original length of the film by twenty minutes. Asked why he chose Denver, Wayne replied, "I brought it to Colorado so that I could get a reaction which would be that of a representative cross-section of the American people. California is too professional, and New York too provincial." So, for that Friday, the matinee and evening screenings of the 131-minute musical comedy *Can-Can* were canceled and replaced by *The Alamo*. A real bargain, too, as reserved-seat ticket prices remained the same (Children 50¢, Students $1, Adults $1.50-$2.50). Wayne had flown into town that afternoon. Understandably nervous, he showed no outward signs as he calmly waited while the audience filed into the theater. Everyone knew they would be watching a screening of *The Alamo*; the preview cards they were given said so.[1253]

"*The Alamo* Preview, Friday, August 5, 1960. Aladdin Theatre, Denver, Colorado. (Courtesy, Mr. Robert W. Selig, executive Vice-president National Theatres & Television, Inc.)

You are the first to have seen a public showing of our Batjac Production, *The Alamo*. We have flown here to Denver for this special preview in order that we may obtain straightforward, honest, constructive comments.

WOULD YOU MIND HELPING US?

How would you classify *The Alamo*? Great, Excellent, Good, Fair.

Which scenes did you like most? 1, 2, 3, others.

Which scenes, if any, did you dislike?

What players did you enjoy most? 1, 2, 3, 4, others.

Any other comment?

Would you recommend *The Alamo* to your friend?

Age group 16-20, 20-30, 30-40, Over 40 male, female

If you wish, please sign your name and address, so I may drop you a line, Thank you very much, John Wayne. Space for name and address"

But would Wayne be there? Ah, that was the question. Wayne flew out from California that morning accompanied by Pilar, Batjac VP Bob Newman, Grant, Tiomkin, and publicists Birdwell, Midge Hamilton, Peggy Wood, and Joan Rice. Flying separately was B. Gerald Cantor, president of NT&T, which owned the Aladdin. The Denver audience erupted into a resounding roar when Duke walked out. After a few introductory remarks–thanking the audience for being there, describing his fourteen-year journey to reach this point, introducing numerous celebrities that included, among others, Mike Wayne, Bill Clothier, Bob Newman, Bob Tracy, Stuart and Bill Gilmore, Tiomkin, and Birdwell, as well as Max Youngstein, Arnold Picker, and William Heineman from UA–Duke sat down and waited for the movie to begin. Also in attendance were Web Overlander and Don LaCava from Batjac, Dave Picker, James Velde and Ralph Clark from UA, Gordon Hewitt and Roy Evans from National Theaters, Sam Norton from Cinemiracle, and Sala Hassenein from UA Theaters.[1254]

In the projection room, a dual interlocking system had been installed to accommodate the 70mm film. The term "70mm print" is misleading because the picture actually is only 65mm. The other 5mm holds the soundtrack–the magnetic track that is imprinted on the side; the soundtrack is recorded separately onto the print. But, a 70mm print was ordered *without* soundtrack for the premiere, so the film could be shown in its best possible visual manner. Along with a separate soundtrack, the interlocking system was installed to sync the sound to the picture. A projector was used to provide the picture while synchronized sound was played back on an accompanying machine. The only problem you would have is if one or the other breaks down, which, fortunately, it didn't.[1255]

As the curtains pulled back, the sounds of the overture filled the theater, followed by the audience's applause as the film's title appeared, increasing in volume, if possible, when Wayne's name followed. For 192 minutes, the audience reacted exactly as Wayne had hoped, exactly as he'd dreamed about ever since the movie had been filmed. Laughter, cheers, applause, they all reaffirmed Wayne's hard work and effort. As the crowd burst into yet another round of cheers when the film ended, Wayne took the stage again. He thanked them for their appreciation, reminded them to fill out their preview questionnaires, and left with his compadres for a press party and reception at the Brown Palace's Onyx Room. Bill Gilmore wasn't so lucky; he still had an important job to do. "I don't know what happened after the preview," recalls Bill. "I was involved with the prints and the technical side, so I certainly didn't go back to the hotel. It's very possible my dad went back with Duke, and Birdwell and Grant and whatever and they discussed some things, but I was not there. My job was to be in charge of the print, and so, as soon as it was over, I went up into the projection booth and made sure it was completely rewound and put back into the case and whatever. And I was responsible for physically getting the case back to the hotel."[1256]

Bill was correct. Duke, Grant, Stuart Gilmore, and others discussed possible changes, audience reactions, etc. Youngstein was exuberant in his praise: *The Alamo* will be "one of the biggest grossers of all time–Duke has done an amazing job." Immediate audience comments praised the spectacular battle sequences, Clothier's photography, Wayne's direction, and the acting abilities of Widmark, Harvey, and Wills. But some thought the movie was too long and should be shortened. Of course, they wouldn't officially know how the audience felt until all the preview cards arrived, but they believed they had a hit. Over the next few weeks, the cards began to flow in. They heaped praise on Harvey and Widmark. Of the 900 attendees, 394 questionnaires were returned–88 percent of the responders rated the film "Great" or "Excellent," equally split between males and females. The largest number of favorable replies came from twenty-to-thirty-year-olds, followed by thirty-to-forty-year olds. Unfortunately, those two demographic groups also returned the highest number of "Good" to "Fair" replies. UA was favorably surprised and pleased with the results, but what did it expect? The audience was skewed by those who already knew what the film would be and the actors who would be in it. Unless it was an absolute bomb (which it wasn't), it would stand to reason the replies would be favorable. Of greater concern should have been the replies *not* received. Even with an added incentive of a response from Wayne, over 50 percent of the audience didn't bother to return the questionnaire. Based on the replies, Wayne and UA decided to release the film virtually as is. Gilmore remembers "...the changes that came out of that preview were pretty standard. That's what you have a preview for–to tell you what works and what doesn't work and if there's a bad lapse somewhere. There was no huge revelation...it wasn't a disaster. The audience liked the film, it played well. And we made changes...we might have moved some things around. If there was a laugh in the wrong place, we'd fix it. But, it didn't change that much." The film ran three hours and eighteen minutes with a fifteen-minute intermission. According to Wayne, approximately eight minutes would be trimmed. Literally just frames and seconds. No "lifts," just minor trims. Batjac president Bob Newman stated the changes made were those Wayne had already decided upon before showing. And Duke promised there would be no more showings until the San Antonio premiere.[1257]

Grant was also quick to jump on the bandwagon. Convinced that *Alamo* would be a smash, he began to devise ways to cash in on the impending bonanza. In an August 1960 letter to Wayne, he suggested the concept of "cross-collateralization"–an accounting practice whereby profits in one market are offset against losses in another, or on one film versus another. He suggested offsetting dogs against the "accumulating monies of 'Alamo.'" Further, he stated, "We could make *A Walk For Nails*, we could make *Mandingo*. (Written by Grant, *Nails* was about a bank robber with a heart of gold.) It is possible we could wind up getting all the money to make *Mandingo* in a cross collaterization (sic) deal with another source than a releasing organization. Make it under an insignia other than Batjac, bring Birdwell and some theater expert in and release it ourselves. It seems to me it has to sell tickets to everybody who can still get a hard on and also to the millions who wish they still could with ads such as: *Mandingo*–The Human Breeding Farm–A Thousand dusky Virgins–Men as Stallions. Christ, we don't need Bird. I can write this sort of stuff myself and feel a slight, very slight stirring while doing so." Thank God Grant wasn't involved in this.[1258]

On August 8, the Kinney County Chamber of Commerce placed a full-page ad in *The Hollywood Reporter* praising Wayne for his efforts and thanking him for choosing Brackettville as the movie's location: "The Folks of Brackettville, Texas SALUTE and THANK John Wayne for making *The Alamo* on Brackettville soil–We believe your 12 million dollar Todd-AO Batjac Production will make the world a better and greater place for all Mankind! Come and see us again, Duke, and please bring the other great stars of *The Alamo*: Richard Widmark, Laurence Harvey and co-stars Frankie Avalon, Patrick Wayne, Linda Cristal, Joan O'Brien, Chill Wills, Joseph Calleia, Ken Curtis and guest star Richard Boone. Bring everybody–especially James Edward Grant, that colorful author, and Dimitri Tiomkin, who composed that fabulous score; William H. Clothier, that great photographer and Stuart Gilmore, who really is a genius at editing film. KINNEY COUNTY CHAMBER OF COMMERCE, Brackettville, Texas." Reading more like a promotion of the film rather than a thank-you card, the copy could very well have been written by Birdwell himself.[1259]

After filming *The Alamo*, post-production, working on *North to Alaska*, the Denver sneak preview, etc., well, Wayne was justifiably exhausted. And he still had a two-month, fourteen-city promotional tour before the San Antonio premiere. In the meantime, Grant was all set to start the screenplay for *General Sam Houston*, which would be filmed after Duke returned from Africa in 1961 where he would work on *The African Story*, later known as *Hatari!* Wayne needed a well-deserved rest and check-up so, after the preview, he checked into the Denver Scripps Clinic. No matter–Youngstein showed up in Wayne's room to discuss cuts and the publicity campaign. (Unfortunately, *Houston* never got off the ground.) But Grant was undeterred. In an August 1960 letter to Wayne, he wrote: "This project should not be slighted. Storywise, this is a better property than *Alamo* because the personal story has ups and downs and because the big action sequences are split rough (sic) the picture rather than coming in a clump. It is a better property from a marquee and casting point of view. There are parts for two big men–but more important there are parts for *three* women of stature. The casting of female names has always been a difficulty in epics–here it is solved. But most important of all–the time to strike is when the material is hot. The metal will be glowing because of the fire of *Alamo* and only a dunce would fail to have the hammer poised."[1260]

On August 11, Birdwell had a comprehensive, argumentative, and extremely long publicity/exploitation meeting with Fred Goldberg, Burt Sloane, and various UA minions. Among the major decisions made were:

1.   In addition to receiving a Bowie knife, each member of the press also would receive a huge hospitality basket of Texas-grown products including fruit, melons, etc. The knife would be put in the basket.

2.   Only the San Antonio premiere would be called World Premiere. All others would be called Los Angeles special invitational premiere, Chicago special invitational premiere, etc. The London premiere would be called the International premiere.

3.   In that the Woodlawn theater only had 1,000 seats, Goldberg suggested a second premiere for San Antonio youth VIP's. Birdwell vetoed the idea, stating it would confuse and distract from what was already planned.

4.   As of the eleventh, the Dallas premiere had not sold out. When it was suggested that the remaining tickets be purchased to assure a sell-out, Birdwell adamantly refused and stated if they did so, they might end up giving the tickets away. He reiterated his previous statement: Their policy was not to give away any houses–the sponsoring organization would buy the house and give away tickets as they saw fit. (By comparison, as of August 21, the Woodlawn had already received 23,000 advance ticket orders!)[1261]

UA's Buddy Young proposed that TV's Ed Sullivan do a remote from Texas on October 30. Failing that, he suggested Wayne say a few words during the San Antonio premiere, and Sullivan could use it on his weekly show. Birdwell refused. Young countered it would just be news coverage; again, Birdwell refused. Young then suggested Sullivan could promote the Pontiac television special. Birdwell stated the Sullivan proposal was out as they already had an agreement with Pontiac and ABC and didn't want to do anything to jeopardize it. However, as they had $250,000 invested in the special, "If we can make arrangements where we can shoot what we want to, we can let Sullivan use it after the show, if he wants to." Birdwell further suggested if they could get the entire one-hour Sullivan show, he was willing to discuss it with Pontiac.

Sloane then asked Birdwell if he would consider a Wayne appearance on *What's My Line?* Wayne wouldn't consider it, and Birdwell wouldn't let him. Said Birdwell, "Everybody is on that show. (Don't you) realize that Wayne is a big (star)? He's not just some little starlet that needs to be pushed on every little show that's available." (Due to scheduling concerns, Wayne also rejected the opportunity to be parade marshal of the Huntington Park Christmas Parade).[1262]

Birdwell said the final edit would be completed by August 24 at which time special screenings would be held for various magazines.

Somebody asked if celebrities other than Wayne would be used to promote the film. Birdwell replied it was possible but not likely. In particular, he wasn't in favor of using Boone unless (the latter was) in a group: "We are not particularly interested in tying the picture to Wayne. We want the picture to be larger than Wayne. We have tried to make the image of *The Alamo* bigger than any or all of the stars."

Throughout the meeting UA persistently brought up the television special and its lack of involvement in it. Birdwell was equally uncompromising: "Everything is in the hands of Pontiac, and we would like to leave it up to them. Take my word for it. Don't suggest Pontiac push ABC. We don't want to rock the boat." But UA wouldn't take no for an answer. Val Coleman suggested they do something to help Pontiac marshal their publicity forces to give the picture more notice. Enough was enough. After the meeting, Birdwell cornered Coleman: "You and Mr. Young don't seem to understand this situation. You're to stay away from the Pontiac show. Just leave it alone, and everything will be fine."[1263]

The following day, Birdwell's staff had additional meetings with UA's Sol Hassenein and Bill Heineman. Anxious to finalize preparations, Birdwell and Roger Lewis flew to San Antonio on the seventeenth to meet with the premiere committee. Birdwell described his hectic schedule in a letter ". Accompanied by two men from United Artists, I arrived in San Antonio at 11:47 a.m. on August 17 and, without going to my hotel room to wash my face, I went into meetings with multiple committees of the Chamber of Commerce which extended without a break until 2:30 a.m. the following day. I got up at 5:30 a.m. and caught a plane to Dallas to go through the entire performance again with committees there in connection with our opening......." In addition to an outline of daily events, the ads, schedules, group sales, unique problems associated with specific cities and front of theater decorations also were discussed. The Texas State Fair was scheduled to run in Dallas from October 8 to 23–a perfect opportunity to share information about the film–so UA planned to have a booth there complete with slides and color transparencies. Known as a "ballyhoo" setup, the booth was a perfect way to allow over three million expected Fair visitors the opportunity to buy tickets for any of the Texas premiere dates. By the twenty-sixth Lewis was back in Los Angeles and shared final San Antonio publicity plans with his team: twenty-one unique events spanning four days including receptions, parade and motorcade, luncheons, barbecue and brunch, a thirty-two-man Marine march from Gonzales, recreating the famous arrival of reinforcements, etc., capped off by the World Premiere. (Supplies for the Marines would be air-dropped by the Alamo wing of the Air Force reserve–candy bars and heel plasters!) Lewis also announced that the son of Gutzon Borglum, who had carved the Mount Rushmore Memorial, would design a medallion that would be given to foreign dignitaries. According to Lewis, " it will be a true work of art, expertly rendered, and not a mere token document or gee-gaw."[1264]

Of particular importance was Wayne's presence at the various premieres. With simultaneous openings scheduled throughout the country, it was physically impossible for him to appear at all of them. In fact, immediately after San Antonio, Duke and Pilar would fly to New York and then to London. As a result, other co-stars and actors would appear in his place: Wills in Chicago, Cristal, Harvey, and Pat Wayne in Los Angles, and so on. Boone had previously told reporter Vernon Davis that the stars would be divided into four or five groups each of which would be sent to different premiere cities. (*Variety* erroneously printed that Wayne, Widmark, and Harvey would attend the London premiere). Lewis was careful to warn his team not to share that information: "It is important that we do not in any way publicize that fact that he will not make the other two (Texas) openings. This is for your information." Obviously it wasn't public knowledge as newspapers still reported Wayne would host a barbecue and dance in a tent on the grounds of the Cathay Circle immediately after the Los Angeles premiere. Guests were even invited to wear frontier attire![1265]

In mid-March, Wayne had announced simultaneous premieres in eleven cities on October 5. Three months later, he changed the San Antonio date to October 24, two days before most of the remaining cities would have their actual premieres. Due to the wave of favorable publicity over the last several months, by the end of August three more cities were added to the premiere schedule: Montreal, Oklahoma City, and Tulsa. The premiere dates were now as follows:

October 24: San Antonio (Woodlawn)

October 25: Dallas (Capri)

October 26: Chicago (Palace), Houston (Alabama), Los Angeles (Carthay Circle), London, (Astoria), Montreal (Seville), New York (Rivoli, with a $125,000 publicity budget), Philadelphia (Midtown), San Francisco (Alexandria), Toronto (Tivoli).

November 9: Oklahoma City (State), Tulsa (Brook).

December 4: Tokyo (Tokyo Gekijo, Shibuya Pantheon and the Shinjuku Milano-Za).

December 26: Paris and Stockholm. According to Batjac president Bob Newman, the film would eventually be booked into a large portion of the 150 to 200 theaters worldwide that were equipped to handle Todd-AO projection and sound requirements. (Several of the aforementioned dates would eventually be changed).[1266]

Meanwhile, in San Antonio preparations reached a fever pitch. At an August 25 luncheon at the St. Anthony Hotel, finalized plans were presented to the Celebration Committee. Several new events, including the San Antonio Press Club reception and Annual Gridiron Show, were added to the schedule. Jim Battersby, festival arrangement director, told the crowd the four-day celebration would cost $45,000, most of which would be financed by the sale of premiere tickets. Local businesses developed their own promotions: Handy-Andy supermarket held a "Win a Lunch Date with John Wayne" contest. The lucky winner and one other person of their choice would meet Wayne and other stars, have lunch and their picture taken with them, and attend both a cocktail reception, and the World premiere. On August 28, the first official ads for tickets started to appear in newspapers. The announcement in the Sunday edition of *The New York Times* was typical: "OPENS OCTOBER 26th! MAIL ORDERS NOW! *THE ALAMO*–EXCLUSIVE ENGAGEMENT! RIVOLI." Orchestra, Loge, and Balcony ticket prices ranged from $1.50-$2.50 for matinees to $1.80-$3.50 for evening presentations. The Woodlawn was a bit less expensive: $1.25-$2.00 for matinees and $1.75-$2.50 for evenings. Of course, premiere Gold tickets ran $50! But the purchasers of such tickets were entitled to choice seats for the premiere in addition to being honored guests at the Night in Old San Antonio festivities, Alamo breakfast, rededication ceremony, and a special reception where they would meet John Wayne and other stars of the film.[1267]

In Los Angeles, even though he wouldn't attend, Wayne purchased the first $50 tickets for the invitational premiere and would pick up the tab for the supper party afterward. All the proceeds from the benefit went toward support of the Exceptional Children's Foundation and Child Guidance Center for the Mentally Retarded, which was sponsored by SHARE, Inc., a philanthropic charitable organization run by the wives of top names in the film industry. Asked why SHARE, Inc. wanted to sponsor the event, Mrs. Sammy Cahn replied, "Our committee chose *The Alamo* because its universal message of courage, selfless devotion, and inspiration is a counterpart of our own program." Advertised to appear at the benefit were the likes of Dean Martin, Janet Leigh, Tony Curtis, Lucille Ball, Peter Lawford, Milton Berle, Barbara Rush, Howard Keel, June Hutton, Guy Madison, Sheila and Gorden MacRae, Jo Stafford, Marge and Glower Champion, Hank Mancini, Anne Jeffreys, Robert Mitchum, Laraine Day, and Robert Sterling. The invitation included a personal message from Wayne: *"SHARE, INC. has become world famous for its humanitarian deeds. With fabulous parties they have raised great funds with which to carry on their noble work for mentally retarded children. The SHARE girls invite you to one of the most colorful parties–with music, dancing, cocktails, and the greatest entertainment in the world (which only SHARE,*

*INC. can produce). The party and supper will be given under a big tent on the grounds of the Carthay Circle after the invitational premiere of our picture on October 26th. You won't want to miss this tremendous SHARE, INC. treat–for which I am most grateful. Sincerely, John Wayne."*[1268]

On September 8 at a luncheon in Austin, Wayne received a Texas award for meritorious service in historic preservation from the biennial statewide Congress of Historical Heritage Organizations–the award recognized the historical contributions of Duke's film. Later that month, for the first time in over seventy-five years (and with Birdwell's encouragement), *Good Housekeeping* magazine honored a motion picture–*The Alamo*. Asked why, editor Wade H. Nichols explained, "We are motivated by a belief that this fine presentation of a great event in our history deserves special recognition." William Randolph Hearst Jr. would preside over the presentation at New York's famous 21 Club.[1269]

But everything wasn't going quite as planned. As previously announced, Tiomkin was to conduct the seventy-three-piece Symphony Society of San Antonio in an eighteen-minute excerpt from the film's score. To make sure the musicians met his level of perfection, the Oscar-winning conductor insisted upon a six-hour rehearsal, at a cost of $3,000! The society refused, the musicians refused, but Tiomkin was adamant. He considered himself a perfectionist and wouldn't go onstage unless he was positive his music would be played perfectly. The musicians took the view they were professionals as well and entirely capable of playing Tiomkin's score with ease and confidence. With a normal rehearsal time of two and one-half hours and $1,500 cost, the society proposed a five-hour limit. Musical director Victor Alessandro even rescheduled a school concert and gave up his own rehearsal time in an attempt to cooperate. Tiomkin refused. Birdwell promised to speak with the Tiomkin to broker a compromise, which he did.[1270]

In order to hype publicity even further, UA distributed a 147-page promotion kit in September that included fifty feature stories and sixty-two pieces of black and white and color art, 11x14 photos, 4x5 color transparencies with accompanying copy, all contained in a 12x15 black pebble-grained, bi-fold portfolio with large gold "A" on the cover, and the words, "*The Alamo* in Todd-AO," on the side. Copy-trans were included so that theatres could run color ads in the Sunday rotogravure section of the newspapers. Information was divided into several sections including: Facts About The Production; Profiles of the Stars; Off The Amusement Page Features; Historical Background; and Column Items and Biographies. The kits were distributed to newspapers in the premiere cities and UA fieldmen to help promote the film.[1271]

On September 12, Wayne began his barnstorming *Alamo* publicity tour: thirteen cities in thirty-one days before he returned to Los Angeles. The schedule was brutal:

698

Houston, September 12-14

Tulsa, September 15

Oklahoma City, September 16

Chicago, September 17-21

Montreal, September 22

Toronto, September 23

New York, September 24-28

Boston, September 29-30

New York, October 1-2

Philadelphia, October 3-4

Washington, D.C., October 5-6

Austin, October 7-8

Dallas, October 9-12

Los Angeles, October 13-21

San Antonio, October 22-24.

Along with Jimmy Grant, Grant's wife, and Pilar, Duke left Los Angeles early that Monday morning via American Airlines, and stopped briefly at Fort Worth's Amon Carter Field to meet the McCullough brothers and hold a short press conference. He endorsed Chill Wills ("I don't see how Chill can miss an Oscar") and encouraged reporters to help out by promoting his performance. He also praised Avalon's efforts ("I've worked with Avalon, Fabian, and Ricky Nelson, and all three are fine kids. Frankie really surprised us with his acting ability on this one"). When a reporter suggested that some felt it was impossible for an actor to act and direct simultaneously, Duke flatly replied, "I think I did a good job." He also took the opportunity to address the ongoing Mexican issue: "We give every human being his own dignity, and I don't think there will be any objection to the film in Mexico." In closing, Wayne also touched on Hollywood directors ("Otto Preminger and Stanley Kramer are 'pseudo-intellects' (who) ridiculed honor and beliefs in basic American principles"); Sinatra ("We're still the best of friends. I like Frankie very much and that entire hassle was instigated by a news reporter who didn't bother to check the facts"); and the current election ("I hope (Kennedy) follows (behind Nixon] clear through November"). Kennedy, also scheduled to arrive in Houston that morning, heard that Wayne would arrive thirty minutes ahead of him and asked Wayne to postpone his arrival. The answer was a flat no. After lunch in Fort Worth, Duke hopped aboard McCulloughs's private plane and continued to Houston to kick off the "official" tour. Both the *Houston Post* and *Chronicle* already had full-page ads announcing reserved-seat mail order prices for his film.[1272]

Wayne arrived at 3:30 p.m. and was greeted by mayor Lewis Cutor, Gov. Price Daniel, and Leon Jaworski, president of the Houston Chamber of Commerce and later of Watergate fame. While Air Force jets from Ellington Field spelled out "ALAMO" overhead, Duke received the keys to the city and a proclamation making September 12 "John Wayne Day." After a short press conference in the airport "Cloud Room," Wayne and his entourage headed into town. That evening, a dinner was held in his honor. Checking into the Rice Hotel's John Wayne Suite (formerly known as the presidential Suite), white-coated waiters rushed in and out of his room with carts full of food and drink. (The Rice Hotel also named three large new suites in honor of Texas heroes–Travis, Bowie, and Crockett.) The phone constantly rang, and Wayne constantly spoke on it. One time, as Grant, Birdwell, and Web Overlander patiently stood by, the affable Wayne talked with one caller for a few minutes and then with a fond goodbye, hung up. Asked who it was, Duke replied, "Never heard of him in my life, but he seemed to be a right nice sort of fella." Wayne then faced the usual friendly barrage of questions from local reporters:

*"Did you really spend all that money on The Alamo?"*

"When I say I spent $12 million, I'm leveling. I've got everything I own in it. I borrowed from banks and friends. Take a look at one scene, and you'll never be able to count the thousands of people."

*"Are you concerned?"*

"I'm not worried. This is a darned good picture–it's real American history, the kind of movie we need today more than ever. It'll make money for years to come." (Duke later stated the film cost $14 million, and he would have to gross $17 million before "(I) can collect anything on it." This led Red Skelton to observe, "With a budget like that, if people don't come to see the picture (Duke) won't EVER forget the Alamo!)[1273]

Wayne was extremely proud of his efforts. "Imagine," Duke told the reporters, "Dimitri Tiomkin giving up a month of his free time to re-score the music because he thought some of it might detract from scenes. I didn't even consider any other composer. Dimitri feels American freedom and puts it into music that is as American as Valley Forge. He learned the hard way how valuable freedom is." Ever courteous, Duke freshened all the reporters' drinks and even had asked

700

newspaper acquaintances if they knew local reporters or columnists. If so, would they be kind enough to drop them a line for him. "I kind of hate to walk in cold," he explained. "They don't know me."[1274]

Duke had a typically hectic schedule in Houston: a flight to Liberty, Texas, where, on behalf of the Liberty Muscular Dystrophy Research Foundation, he unveiled and rang a replica of the Liberty Bell, manufactured by the Whitechapel Bell Foundation, the same company that had made the original one in Philadelphia…a Houston Advertising Club luncheon . acceptance of the "Outstanding Texas Salesman of the Year award" from the Houston Sales Association. The latter award presented by Gov. Price Daniel before a crowd of over 4,000 people, was given to Wayne as the individual who contributed most in spreading the good name and fame of Texas. Brother Bill Daniel couldn't attend the event; he was on a worldwide tour himself, promoting the film where he'd made his acting debut.[1275]

Work already had started to convert the Alabama Theater into a Todd-AO venue. The box office, normally located in front of the theater, was moved to the side. New carpet, seats, and paint were among the refurbishments. To minimize disruption, this work took place in the evening after the last show and continued through the night until the theater re-opened the following day. It had been estimated that it would only take twenty-four hours to install the special equipment necessary to show the film, but unfortunately, the theater couldn't be finished in time. *Ben-Hur*, scheduled to play at the Tower theater for over a year, instead only ran a mere twenty-four weeks. This unforeseen slack time at the Tower, combined with the Alabama's lack of readiness, prompted Interstate Theaters to move the premiere to the Tower theater.[1276]

Two days later, after Pilar and the Grants flew back to Los Angeles, Duke and Birdwell continued on to Tulsa, their next stop. Wherever Wayne appeared, crowds were sure to show up. In fact, the largest crowd ever to welcome a motion picture celebrity showed up at the Tulsa International Airport for his arrival. The next day, Wayne drove to Oklahoma City, where he was met at the turnpike gate by Mayor Norick and taken to the Skirvin Tower Hotel in a parade. As he emerged from his limousine, he was surrounded by a crowd of screaming admirers who asked for autographs. Duke was quickly fitted with an Indian headdress, given a giant key to the city by the mayor, made an honorary colonel by Judge Kirksey Nix (a long-time friend), and presented with a massive two hundred-pound, 1,200-piece floral arrangement shaped like a large letter *A*. All the while, the crowd was serenaded by the Kiltie Band as cheerleaders from Northeast Junior High yelled in the background. As usual, Duke posed for photographs and gave interviews in his hotel suite. Asked if he had any plans to appear on television, he explained, "I'm too busy in pictures. I don't have time for TV, but, I do put in an occasional appearance." The next day at a joint luncheon of the Oklahoma City Chamber of Commerce and the National Cowboy Hall of Fame,

Wayne was honored as a "Westerner-first class" and made a lifetime member of the Hall. Following the presentation, Wayne surveyed the buildings that would eventually house the Hall of Fame and Western Heritage Center. He even gave his stamp of approval to the project by branding a "W" on a wooden concrete form as spectators looked on. "It's great to have a part in something like this," he declared. "It sure is typical of the Old West...all that wide open space."[1277]

To further promote his film, Wayne appeared on the "Ida B Show," a local OKC celebrity chat program hosted by Ida Blackburn. Telecast on KOCO Channel 5, Blackburn started her career as "Miss Ida" on the nationally syndicated kid's program "Romper Room" in 1958. Unfortunately, she should have prepped a bit more for her interview with Wayne:

Ida: "I'm with John Wayne, the noted talented actor of radio and television. Nice to have you with us, Mr. John Wayne. Or should I call you John?"

Wayne: "My talent is motion pictures most of my career. Not radio and television. But I certainly liked the way you mentioned my name, Ida."

Ida: "Well, we do see you, you know, on the features . I just had to mention that. Not only are you admired and respected in Oklahoma but all over world for, I know, not only your talent in pictures, but also as a respected individual."

Wayne: "Well, thank you, Ida."

Ida: "And, as I said, it's nice to have you with us today, and I'd like for you to give s some information to our people today about the upcoming spectacular in regards to your new movie which is *The Alamo*. And would you be so kind as to sort of give us a rundown of what the spectacular will be?"

Wayne: "Well, I think that we're very lucky in the United States that most everyone has heard about the Alamo. We have chosen for Jim Bowie in the picture, a man named Richard Widmark; to play Travis is Laurence Harvey who is a young English actor that has come up very fast in the last year. I play Crockett. We've spent fourteen years preparing this product. It took us three years to build our set. We had it prepared in time so that we could grow real shrubbery around it. We've done everything that we can to make it measure up as far as the correct size and everything of the city of San Antonio at the time of the Alamo. And, whether we maybe measure up, you'll have to find out by coming to see it November the ninth or thereafter at the State Theater here in Oklahoma."

Ida: "The actual date for the spectacular that I was mentioning over ABC network is November the fourteenth. Is that right?"

Wayne: "Oh, yes. That's right. November the fourteenth ABC came down to the location and when we finished the picture we've used around 6,000 Texans down there, so we had to do something to pay them back."

Ida: "Actually, Mr. Wayne. As I said, I don't know what to call you."

Wayne: "Well, call me Duke. That's what most people call me."

Ida: "Well, wonderful. I'd be glad to call you Duke. One of the things that I would like to know is that the actual time of the spectacular, which will be here on Channel 5 is from 8:30 to 9:30. Isn't that correct? I'm pretty sure ...."

Wayne: "In November. This is quite a little ways...."

Ida: "Yes, but with you being there and being in the spectacular and being about your movie. In fact, didn't you direct and produce this also?"

Wayne: "I directed and produced the motion picture...."

Ida: "That's what I mean."

Wayne: "But Pontiac sent their own people down to do the spectacular."

Ida: "Well, another thing. It seems to me , of course, I am very small on the scale in the way of show business, but I still have convictions about what I would like to do in my own abilities. And I'm sure you have probably found an outlet in this production and directing as to being on the other side of the fence from talent. How do you feel about that?"

Wayne: "Well, I took on the job because I felt that I had this particular subject in my heart more than anyone that I could get to direct it. I offered it to long-time mentor John Ford, and he said, 'Duke, this is something that you have been working on for a long while, and I feel you should do it yourself.' S, I took the chance, and, luckily we now know from professionals that have seen the picture that we have a fine picture. In that spectacular, Frankie Avalon, I think a lot of the teenagers will know who he is, sings. Joan O'Brien, Linda Cristal is in it. And a dear friend of Oklahoma, a name, Chill Wills is also in it. Naturally, Mr. Harvey and Mr. Widmark and myself do our little bit."

Ida: "It's just going to be one great big party."

Wayne: "It's a big family party. You're all invited."

Ida: "Wonderful. And I'm sure we'll all be looking forward to, not only the spectacular, but to the movie as well. And, we certainly do appreciate being able to talk with you, and we hope you enjoy your stay here."

Wayne: "Thank you."

How painful it must have been for Duke to sit through those type interviews with local celebrities.[1278]

On September 17, Wayne and Birdwell continued on to Chicago. For four days, Duke met local dignitaries, gave interviews, held news conferences, and conducted all the standard activities one does when promoting a film. He also gave a few choice quotes when asked about the film: "(I don't mind doubling as director) although I felt after the picture was half done that it would be pretty frightening to lose one of the stars because of sickness. Then again," he laughed, "I decided that this better be what the boys call a 'massive and important' picture when I found out how much it was going to cost." During lunch one day, Wayne discussed his apprehension on such a large project. "I went into it like a lamb, and then one night it hit me. I'm mortgaged up to my necktie, and that would have been tied up, too, except that someone gave it to me after the picture was finished.

John Ford and George Stevens are directors, too. How dare I step into their epic film class? Then one night I woke up in a cold sweat and asked myself, 'what would I have done without such experienced players as Laurence Harvey and Richard Widmark, for instance?' Ford said, 'Duke, you directed yourself better than I ever did. Stop sweating at night.'"   Wayne also expressed his views about appearing on television: "I suppose, if I had wanted to go into television, I could have made a lot of money at it. But years ago I was talking to the TV people. I decided we had been doing (in the movies) for years what they claimed they were going to do (on TV). Also I didn't care particularly to be controlled by advertising men who, I decided, didn't know the entertainment field. So I elected to stay with motion pictures. I've never been sorry. I don't think I've ever regretted turning down a movie role, either. But there have been some I accepted that I wish now I hadn't." During his time off, Wayne visited Sam Schwartz's Guildhall Galleries and purchased some new art imports. Unfortunately, in Chicago he also caught a flu bug that plagued him throughout the remainder of his tour.[1279]

It was during this tour that Wayne wound up as the first actor cast for George Stevens's all-star biblical epic, *The Greatest Story Ever Told*. According to *Variety*, "Wayne will essay the role of the Roman who scourges Jesus on the way to the cross, but ultimately becomes the first believer at the crucifixion." Dressed in a centurion's armor and toga and paid $25,000, Wayne was to look up at the cross and say, "Truly, this man was the Son of God." Not satisfied with the first take, Stevens pulled Duke aside and gently said, "Duke, what we need in this line is something more. Put a little more awe into the line." Wayne nodded, Stevens signaled the cameras to roll, and Wayne grinned and said with an exaggerated Western drawl, "Awww, truly this man was the Son of God." Everyone laughed, and this time, the third take was a charm. This incident may have never happened, but Pilar did include the story in her book, *My Life With the Duke*.[1280]

After Chicago, Wayne visited Montreal and explained, yet again, how financially important the film was to him: "This tie around my neck isn't mortgaged," he told the press, "but the rest is. The jacket and shoes and pants. The Wayne bundle and my friends' bundle are riding on this." He further detailed his investment: $1.6 million raised by mortgaging Batjac assets, $700,000 cash put up by Batjac, and a $250,000 personal note from Wayne. Duke would usually promote any local charity when in town and in Montreal, it was the United Appeal. Within an hour-and-a-half of his arrival, he visited an orphanage, toured a rehabilitation center for the handicapped, and visited the local United Artists headquarters. While there, he met a delegation of co-eds from McGill University working for UA, posed for pictures, taped three radio interviews, recorded a series of two- and three-second spots for the United Appeal, had a press and radio conference and then, led by a motorcycle escort, sped off to Dorval Airport. The next morning in Toronto, Wayne started out with an 8:00 a.m. CBC-TV interview on *Close-*

*up* with June Callwood, then met the mayor at city hall. After an Old Fort York press luncheon, he visited UA headquarters, Wood Green Community Center, University Settlement house, and East General Hospital before finally returning to his hotel. Between Toronto and Montreal, Wayne had passed out over 1,500 autograph cards! As he left the Toronto CBC building, he stopped to sign an autograph–as he had run out of cards–and a photographer asked Duke to kiss the girl who'd asked for his signature. Wayne reached for the camera and said, "What are you, a sex fiend? You kiss her, and I'll take the picture." At 8:15 that evening, he left for the Toronto airport and finally checked into his New York hotel by midnight.[1281]

So important was New York to Wayne's tour, he planned to visit there twice: September 24-28 and again on October 1-2. As usual, Wayne's schedule was hectic: interviews, press conferences, radio shows, and, on September 26, he appeared on the Jack Paar show, along with humorist-author Alexander King, comedienne Renee Taylor and singer Jack Haskell. But only two weeks into the tour, the strain of the past year was starting to take its toll. Of course, the Chicago flu bug didn't help; "I've got a helluva cold," Duke admitted. "I'm starting to fold, and I need to sleep for about thirty hours." Rest alone wasn't sufficient as Duke came down with a severe case of bronchitis; Pilar flew to New York to accompany him home, and, upon his return to Los Angeles, Wayne's physician ordered him to bed for two weeks. Wayne agreed–he was exhausted. Birdwell issued an official announcement; "On the advice of his doctors, John Wayne has been forced to cancel the remainder of his cross-country personal appearance tour on behalf of *The Alamo.* Wayne is recovering from acute bronchitis. He recently returned to Hollywood from New York for a period of treatment and rest, before attending the world premiere on October 24."[1282]

While Duke winged his way back to California, Birdwell finalized distribution of the press release book. The cost for both the two-and-a-quarter-pound book and the publicity kit was covered by the $10,000 Special Exploitation & Publicity budget. Birdwell wrote to Lewis that at 140 pages "…10,000 copies of the bible (would) cost somewhere between $8,500 and $9,500." However, as the size of the book expanded, so did the cost. Maxing out at $14,752, Birdwell had to find some way to cover it. (Another $3,500 was required for postage!) After ruminating for a while, he contacted Lewis with a suggestion. "What with the John Wayne Tour being curtailed due to Wayne's illness, I recommend that this increase in the cost of the 10,000 'bibles' be covered out of the original hypothetical budget of $42,500 which was penciled in for Wayne ($35,000) and Birdwell ($7,500) tours. Or," he said facetiously, "perhaps you have a better idea where the money can be found within the budget." As the 'bible' would be printed by Los Angeles' Magyary Printers starting September 28 at the rate of 1,500 per day, Lewis had no choice but to accept Birdwell's suggestion. Rubbing salt into the wound, Birdwell bragged, if the release response was positive, Batjac was pre-pared to finance another 100,000 copies.[1283]

There was no doubt Wayne was concerned about the film's success; it had to be if he was to pay back all the money he'd borrowed. While filming *North to Alaska*, Duke confided his financial status to co-stars Ernie Kovacs and Stewart Granger: "It's the biggest project of my life, and I'm pretty lucky to have the full support of the sovereign state of Texas. (But) I need the money. That's why I keep working so hard. I don't want you to start taking up a collection for me here on the set. But sometimes a fellow commits himself to so much that he really has to keep pumping to hold the ship afloat. I'm in that position now. I have *The Alamo* and the other assets, but, to realize their full value, I have to really stay with it—and the wait may be long." Duke later added, "My problem is I'm not a handsome man like Cary Grant—my favorite actor—who will still be handsome at sixty-five. I may be able to do a few more man-woman things before it's too late, but then what? I never want to play silly old men chasing young girls, as some of the stars are doing. I *have* to be a director—I've waited all these years to be one. *The Alamo* will tell what my future is." After all, Batjac put $1,000,000 into *The Alamo*, which is about all Batjac had. And, as Duke said, "Batjac is John Wayne."[1284]

Even the extravagant Grant tried to pitch in to help Wayne out of this fi-nancial quagmire. Mortgaged to the hilt with no cash coming in at all, there was only one thing to do—reduce Batjac's overhead until revenue from *The Alamo* was realized. Therefore, on September 24, Grant proposed wholesale changes to the corporate structure, and he spared no expense when he criticized Duke's employ-ees. With an annual operating budget of $450,000, "the...alternative is to stick a surgical knife into Batjac and let the pus out." First, Grant suggested Wayne fire Robert Weesner, Batjac's financial officer, an annual saving of $36,000: "His usefulness is nil. He runs a couple of businesses of his own under your roof, but he personally does none of the physical work of accounting." Next on his list was production manager Nate Edwards, which would save $38,000: "There can be no need for a skilled production man until, at least, a year from now. When in late '61 or early '62 we are ready to begin to start preparing to make *Sam Houston*, it is a simple matter to re-hire Edwards. Or hire a Relyea...." Once eliminated, Batjac's rented office space would be turned back to the owners. Leaving no stone unturned, he also recommended, "no more coffee shop and free telephone service for out of work actors." Grant then suggested Bob Newman's annual salary of $100,000 be charged directly to *The Alamo*. He also suggested Wayne cut his brother Bob Morrison's salary in half and force him to look for employment in television. Such savings were a good starting point, but more was needed. Grant was ruthless with his suggestions: fire all secretaries, clerks, and readers, but keep Mary St. John and George Coleman. Then sell the Batjac building and move into rented studios offices. Batjac then could operate on $75,000 to $100,000 a year.

Never one to pass up an opportunity, Grant then suggested, "Do one of my scripts immediately on your return from Africa. *Nails* with Ford if we can set it up, But a more sensible and sure fire deal would be for you to play that tough embittered cop who goes down to Mexico to kill that old bastard. It's a cinch characterization for you, and the love-story element is also a cinch because we can use care in selecting the woman and get her a match for you, agewise, if you know what I mean. It would be stupid to let this go by default so that Skouras and Hawks will cash in, but you won't." Thankfully, Wayne declined.[1285]

# CHAPTER THIRTY-TWO
# HOORAY FOR HOLLYWOOD!

IN THE WEEKS LEADING UP TO THE PREMIERE, EVERYONE WAS INVOLVED IN PRO-MOTION. While Wayne and Birdwell were involved in the publicity tour, Tiom kin took time off from his busy schedule to speak to Loyola University students on various aspects of the film's score. He also voiced an opinion on the dreaded practice of parents forcing their children to take up a musical instrument: "American kids love music … they love it more than European children . American parents are making a mistake by forcing Junior to spend unhappy hours practicing on a musical instrument when he would much rather be practicing to be a second baseman. No true artist," he continued, "ever acquired his talent by force. There are too many parents whose families, when they were young, were too poor to provide music lessons for them. Now, as parents, they insist that their kids take music lessons whether the kids like it or not. They are forcing their own musical frustrations onto their children. This is not good." But the composer also was very complimentary of American musicians. "They are unsurpassed anywhere in the world," he boasted. "Look at the ovations American symphony orchestras have received abroad! But, American musicians must be able to make a decent living. If Father can eke out only a bare existence because he is a musician, is Junior going to want to take up music for a profession?" In the weeks before the various premieres, three LP albums and nineteen single 45-rpm records were released; while they weren't major hits on the *BillBoard* Top 100, they still proved so popular that numerous artists recorded the tunes.[1286]

Wayne quickly recovered from his bronchitis and immediately worked again on his promotional activities, later admitting he'd really had bronchial pneumonia that had required twenty-four-hour nursing. News releases and telegrams were issued on a daily basis and ads touting the upcoming extravaganza appeared in all the premiere cities. In New York City alone, over 7,800 *Alamo* posters were placed in railway stations, subways, and bus terminals. The *Los Angeles Times* sponsored a contest for two reserved-seat tickets to *The Alamo*. All the five winners had to do was search the October 30 edition's classifieds–if two stars preceded their names, they won. Five others would win the Columbia soundtrack album. In Chicago, children could identify drawings of animals that appeared in the film. The first ten correct replies received a pair of tickets to the film, the next five correct entries won the Columbia ST record, the next five got a UA recording of the song, and the last five received Avon's Alamo paperback. On Friday, October 21, the lucky winner of "Queen For a Day," Mrs. Jeanne Taylor, received, from host Jack Bailey, an all-expenses paid trip to the San Antonio premiere. As a guest of Handy-Andy supermarkets, she received an original gold lamé "Alamo" hat–valued at $550–from H. Robert Exclusive Millinery. The queen and one guest would have lunch with Wayne and other stars, be treated to a cocktail reception and buffet dinner, and receive two tickets to the world premiere.

Even Linda Cristal promoted the film, albeit indirectly. In early October, along with the mayor of Monterey Park, Cristal helped dedicate Alamo Drive, a new street in the Monterey Highland development where houses ranged from $25,000 to a whopping $41,000! Pilar was no slouch, either. On October 5, in support of Cedars of Lebanon Hospital, the Cedars Valley Guild held a membership champagne dessert in the gardens of the John Wayne estate. The program included Dr. Benjamin M. Kagan's discussion on free pediatric service and comments from Leon Uris on his new book *Exodus-Revisited*. Ironically, the Guild had also planned a January 1961 fund-raising event where members would be taken to the Stanley Warner Theater in Beverly Hills for a showing of . *Exodus*.

Wayne was in competition with himself as 20th Century-Fox had launched a massive publicity campaign for *North to Alaska*. That film and its stars were featured in all types of print media, and special openings were arranged in key cities, all heralding the induction of the forty-ninth state in pre-play date promotions. Duke's co-star Fabian went on a forty-city tour and appeared on both the *Gary Moore* and *Perry Como* television shows, and Columbia Records pitched the title song sung by Johnny Horton. Fabian was more than happy to promote this film, and Duke was "very pleased" to have the young singer in *North To Alaska*. "The way it happened is interesting, and I think indicative of young Fabian's character," Wayne said. "He wanted to be in the picture, but we felt we couldn't afford his price. Then Twentieth (Century Fox) lined up a whole group of young actors for me to see and in that lineup was Fabian. When I saw him, I called him aside, and said, 'What are you doing here?' and he said, 'I want to do this movie with you. I don't care if I make any money or not. I want to be with you because Frankie Avalon told me how wonderful it is to work with you.'"[1287]

Back amid San Antonio's hoopla for *The Alamo*, UA publicity director Addie Addison arrived in town the week of October 2 to work with the chamber of commerce's premiere committee in promoting festivities. And a few days later, Tiomkin arrived and was interviewed by Carey Deckard at WOAI studios. He had previously taped an interview with KABC-TV Jimmy Baker's *Music is my Beat* program. With emphasis placed on Tiomkin's various music scores, singer Bob Grabeau sang two songs written for *The Alamo*. WOAI television station had exclusive rights to telecast the premiere from in front of the Woodlawn. As one might imagine, the impending arrival of up to one hundred newspaper, magazine, radio, and television representatives posed a huge logistics issue for the city. So a force of almost 3,500 Texans was marshaled to assist in various ways. For instance, transportation wasn't an issue as 150 cars (ten radio-equipped), ten airplanes, six trucks and buses, and a boat were available when necessary, And, in late September, letters had been mailed to World Premiere committee members requesting their cooperation in buying tickets to the premiere:

> "Dear Committee Member:
>
> Our ticket committee has set aside a limited number of these choice seats for *The Alamo* World Premiere to be held at the Woodlawn Theatre, October 24, 1960. This will be the most gala social event of many a year, and as a committee member we want to offer you the opportunity of purchasing select seats before the public sale. As you know the money raised from public subscription and the sale of premiere tickets go entirely to defray the cost of the four-day promotion including the expenses of seventy-five of the nation's top newsmen who will be flown to San Antonio as guests of our committee. Tickets for the premiere are priced at $50 each and include many of the activities for the stars and guests. Your purchase of the $50 ticket will admit you to a Night in Old San Antonio at La Villita, a street breakfast in front of the Alamo, a VIP cocktail and reception to meet the stars. In addition to your choice seat at the premiere, you will be given special parking privileges near the theater and an Alamo Patron Gold Badge. As we have only a limited number of seats available may we suggest that you send in your ticket order now . This will be truly an historic occasion and we hope to see you at the premiere celebration.
>
> Cordially, Theo F. Weiss, Chairman"

Similarly, a specific number of seats also were set aside for special guests such as the Alamo's Mrs. T. E. McCray:

"Dear Mrs. McCray:

The Alamo Premiere Committee of the San Antonio Chamber of Commerce and John Wayne cordially extend to you an invitation to be their guest at the world Premiere Reception at the St. Anthony Hotel and the World Premiere of *The Alamo* at the Woodlawn Theatre, Monday, October 24, 1960. Due to the very limited capacity of the theatre and the numerous visiting dignitaries who will attend, this invitation is extended on a personal basis and is limited to you. As all seats are reserved we will appreciate hearing from you whether you are able to accept this personal invitation.

Cordially, Theo F. Weiss, Chairman"[1288]

(The Woodlawn Theatre sat 1,042 customers. More than four hundred seats had been blocked off for Wayne's party, the stars, over seventy-five newsmen, and visiting governors and ambassadors. By early October, only two-thirds of the six hundred Gold tickets had been sold; Weiss announced that the rest would be sold on a first-come-first-served basis. As late as the morning of the premiere, tickets were still available. General admission tickets for showings after the premiere went on sale October 3 at two theaters: the Woodlawn and the downtown Texas Theater).[1289]

In New York, meanwhile, Peter Grimm, chairman of the premiere event, announced that Mrs. Albert Lasker and Arthur J. Watson, president of IBM International, were named co-chairmen of the MEDICO benefit premiere of Wayne's film. Founded in 1958 by Dr. Thomas Dooley, MEDICO (Medical International Cooperation Organization) was a nonprofit that worked to establish hospitals and clinics in newly developed areas of the world and to staff them with American physicians and para-medical personnel. The gala premiere would be attended by members of the diplomatic corps, leading figures from the field of medicine and research and social and civic dignitaries.[1290]

Despite Wayne's comments immediately following the Denver sneak preview, he decided it would be beneficial to have a few more "previews" prior to the premieres. Roger Lewis had contacted Birdwell on August 29 and suggested a private screening in New York for a banker's convention. Wayne agreed, and they settled on September 24 as Duke would be in town that day. Three preview showings for some 4,500 opinion-makers took place October 24 and 25 at the Rivoli before Wednesday's charity premiere. Of course, for some, there were strings attached. On October 21, 1960, UA's Buddy Young contacted Lester Dinoff of station WABC in New York with an interesting proposal. Although time was running short, Young offered the station five hundred seats for the October 25 2 p.m. *Alamo* preview. "In return for the seats," he wrote, "I would like to have the following on the night of the premiere. A television remote truck from your station parked in front of the (Rivoli) theater and also the use on the *Joe Franklin Show* the next morning of some movie film which we will shoot. In addition, I would like to propose that if we service you with a good enough still photo of the premiere, that you look favorably upon putting it on your 11:00 p.m. News Show. It is my feeling that any publicity you can give to the opening of *THE ALAMO* will benefit you on your upcoming show *Spirit of THE ALAMO* . Both these requests and the amount of tickets that I have offered you are flexible."[1291]

Robert Hulter, director of group sales at the Carthay Circle, arranged an October 14 screening for the Screen Director's Guild in Los Angeles, and Wayne scheduled a special showing for members of the press at the Carthay three days later. According to reports, the press corps at Carthay Circle consisted of the largest group of reporters to preview a film since *Around the World in 80 Days*. All did not go off as planned, though. A piece of film leader caught in back of the projector lens caused a slight snafu at the beginning of the second half. But, at least, Wayne was able to get another preview in before the film's official release. No wonder so many news publications were able to print official reviews on the night of the premiere.[1292]

Although celebrities, actors, foreign dignitaries, and governors all would be in San Antonio for the premiere, there was one man above all else Wayne wanted there–soon-to-be former president Dwight Eisenhower. On October 20, Wayne had sent Ike a telegram in Palm Springs: "Dear Mr. President. We are opening our picture, *The Alamo*, at the Woodlawn Theatre in San Antonio, Texas, on the evening of October 24. If you and your staff would care to attend, we will assure you that we will not make use of your presence in our publicity. We are being honored on that night with the presence of ten or twelve illustrious generals and governors and ambassadors, and I feel that you would enjoy being with them as well as seeing what we feel is the finest motion picture ever made. A telephone call or wire to me at Olympia 2-3670 in Los Angeles this week will assure our being able to make the proper arrangements. Respectfully yours, John Wayne." Duke greatly admired Eisenhower but was irate at the gentle treatment Russian Premier Khrushchev had recently received at the United Nations. "I want to go on record saying I'm proud the president of the United States is a gentleman," he told Hedda Hopper, "but I wouldn't care if he walked up and punched Khrushchev in the nose. I'd applaud and holler, 'Attaboy, Ike.' (Khrushchev) was always trying to belittle this country, to downgrade it, to smear and boast and toss out insults and to brawl and threaten. Why don't Kennedy and Nixon take this yelling braggart and boor apart? When Nixon was in Moscow, he took him on his own backyard and made him like it. I want no one running our country," he added, "who doesn't have the brains, strength, and pure guts to face any other country that wants to take its best shot at us. Why don't both our presidential candidates emphasize that this is the greatest nation in the history of the world? In science, we have the Salk vaccine to lick polio, and a breakthrough on cancer is imminent. We have the finest system of transportation and communication. And when the world was flat on its back, what brought it back? American money and American energy, our humanitarianism and our sense of social responsibility for friend and foe alik....it's God's grace to the world that there was one nation left after the last war where the spirit of brotherhood is really alive. That's us, and let's be proud and glad about it! This is a time of danger and uncertainty, granted, but all through its history our country has had crisis—some of them terrible—but it has always faced up to them and won." Unfortunately, the president wasn't able to make it, but Wayne was pleased to receive a cable that wished him success.[1293]

Later that month, several charter members of *The Alamo* family returned to Brackettville to film John Ford's *Two Rode Together*. Widmark, Cristal, Olive Carey, Ken Curtis, Jack Pennick, Danny Borzage, Bill Henry, Big John Hamilton, Cliff Lyons, extras Robert Harris and Marshall Jones, stuntmen Chuck Hayward, Chuck Roberson, "Red" Morgan, Jack Young, Bill Williams, Dean Smith, Rudy Robbins, Ed Juaregui, and crewmembers Frank Beetson Jr. and Ron Talsky—all found themselves back on Alamo Village's dusty streets. The location had changed as well—the walls of the fortress were reconfigured to create Fort Grant, a hotel built on Front Street and new signage erected to transform Old San Antone into the western town of Tascosa.[1294]

At 1:00 p.m. on October 18, trail boss A.J. Ploch called, "Wagon Ho!" and the largest, most colorful trail ride in Texas history left Brackettville on a five-and-a-half-day journey to San Antonio. Ford's crew had been on hand at Alamo Village the previous evening to entertain the riders before they headed out. The caravan included covered wagons, buckboards, carriages, and stagecoaches, with Indian and trail scouts in full-dress costume. Riders carried their own bedrolls and cooking utensils while a welcome committee and entertainment, complete with portable dance floor and band, were provided each evening. The first overnight stop was at a large roadside park between Brackettville and Cline. The second day was the longest one in the saddle with a thirty-five-mile ride to Uvalde. Thursday, the riders stopped for lunch in Knippa and pitched camp that evening on the Hobbnicker Ranch northeast of Sabinal. Friday found them in D'Hannis at noon; they spent the night at Hondo AFB. On Saturday, they traveled through

Dunlay, Castroville, and finally arrived that evening at the Ray Ellison ranch just west of San Antonio. The final twenty-five miles were covered on Sunday, October 23, and, upon their arrival, they bivouacked at Joe Freeman Coliseum. Miss San Antonio Lucille Allen then hung a large, gold-colored horseshoe around Ploch's neck and planted a welcoming kiss on his check. Tired but in good spirits, horses and riders prepared for Monday's parade. [1295]

The parade would stretch for miles and follow a circuitous route through Downtown. Forming on Alamo Street, north of Fifth, the parade would move south to Houston, west to Soledad, south on Soledad to Commerce, and then east on Commerce to South Alamo. It would then turn north to cross Alamo Plaza in front of the Alamo and move out Avenue E. to Fourth, where units would disband. Up to 1,000 horsemen and horsewoman of the Brackettville trail ride were expected to participate along with floats, military and school bands, military marching units, Charros, and a motorcade of movie stars and celebrities. [1296]

On October 22, the day after the final Kennedy-Nixon presidential debate, while Ford remained in Brackettville, the first of several special chartered planes–each a TWA Constellation–arrived in San Antonio, full of celebrities, dignitaries, and reporters. The massive Alamo Airlift had originated simultaneously in New York, Boston, Philadelphia, Washington, D.C., Chicago, Toronto, Cleveland, Denver, Seattle, Portland, Seattle, San Francisco, and Los Angeles. A record number of correspondents converged on The River City, among them Joe Hyams, *The American Weekly*; David Zeitlin, *Life*; Bob Jennings, *Time*; Thomas Pryor, *Daily Variety*; *Sheila Graham, NANA (North American Newspaper Alliance)*; Mike Connolly, *Hollywood Reporter*; Erskine Johnson, *NEA* (Newspaper Enterprise Association); Stan Delaplane, Hedda Hopper, and Louella Parsons. Major newspapers included the *Boston Globe, Philadelphia Inquirer, Chicago Tribune, Los Angeles Herald and Express, Detroit Free Press, Miami Herald, Dallas News, Denver Post, Salt Lake Tribune, St. Louis Globe-Dispatch, Cincinnati Inquirer, Atlanta Journal, Toronto Globe*, and on and on. The Los Angeles contingent left at 9:00 a.m. that morning and numbered over sixty, plus Duke, Pilar, Grant, Patrick Wayne, Linda Cristal and Chill Wills. MGM had given Harvey time off from his co-starring role with Shirley MacLaine in *The Spinster*, but he suddenly took ill and missed the premiere. Widmark was supposed to attend the premiere as well, although as previously mentioned, it took a little persuading from Pappy. [1297]

Others, such as Batjac president Bob Newman, arrived the previous week and so did Tiomkin, who on Thursday began rehearsals with the symphony orchestra. One woman was puzzled when she saw Dimi at the airport and said he must be in the movies. Tiomkin admitted he was an actor and that he was in *The*

*Alamo.* "Really?" asked the woman. "What part do you play?" Said Tiomkin, "I'm Sam Houston." Sound engineer Gordon Sawyer was there already to check out the theater's projection and sound equipment. For that, the film's first reel was test-run for selected individuals, one of whom, *San Antonio Express and News* columnist Gerald Ashford, wrote, "I want to be the first of many who will recommend (the film) for an award for the best color photography of the year. It is so perfectly done that you can even see the texture of the canvas and the brush strokes in an oil painting which is used for the first title. And the outdoor and indoor scenes are both beautiful and true to nature, like nothing I can remember." On loan from Samuel Goldwyn, Sawyer also inspected the other Texas and California theaters scheduled to show the film.[1298]

The first planes began to arrive at 8:00 a.m., more scheduled throughout the day. The United Artists' executive echelon, which flew in from New York, included Arthur Krim, Robert Benjamin, Max Youngstein, William Heineman, Robert Blumofe, and Roger Lewis. By the time Avalon's plane arrived from Philadelphia at 12:30 p.m., the airport was jammed with over five hundred youngsters, their parents and fans screaming with delight as the plane touched down. The Lockheed Electra slowly taxied across the tarmac and came to a stop. A wheeled staircase was rolled out, and as the plane's door swung open and Avalon appeared, the shako-headed, red-and-gray-uniformed Robert E. Lee High School band began to play a medley of Avalon's songs. This time, the screams were even louder, and one scribe wrote the squeals reminded him of "hog killing down on the farm." The excitement continued as Pat Hooker's Antoinette corps lined the steps to the plane and the High-Lites of the San Antonio twirling club formed a two-row reception line. With entertainment provided by mariachis, Mexican dancers, Trinity University Tigerettes, the Texas Dancing Dolls, and Willie and Teresa Champion, Avalon was made an honorary Alcalde by Mayor Kuykendall. After a brief fifteen minutes, the singer was escorted to a car for the trip into town. Scribbling a few autographs, he piled in but not before one lass threw her arms around him for a kiss.[1299]

(Although prominently featured in the film's advertising and publicity, Joan O'Brien was one of the few actors in the movie who didn't show up for the premiere. "I believe the picture will do me a lot of good," Joan admitted, "but rather than just sit around after it was finished, I took the offer of my good friend Buddy Bregman to be his soloist (at Hollywood's Moulin Rouge). In October 1959, it was predicted Bregman would marry O'Brien's co-star in *The Alamo*, Linda Cristal. In Joan's spare time that year, she also appeared in numerous television programs, including *Wagon Train, Cheyenne, The Westerner, The Islanders, Lock Up, The Deputy, The Alaskans, Perry Mason, Bachelor Father,* and *Bronco).*[1300]

Overcast skies didn't dampen the spirits of the attendees. Planes continued to land, bands played, fans cheered. Finally, after a more than two-hour delay, the plane that everyone was waiting for arrived. The pilot had previously made this announcement: "I guess by now you people would like to know where we are......Well, so would we." Reporters complained the stewardesses were so busy, they didn't get any cocktails! But, as the plane touched down, the band broke into "The Eyes of Texas" and quickly segued into "Don't Fence Me In." Three minutes later, Wayne, wearing a Western hat and Lucchese boots, appeared at the top of the stairs and waved to the crowd. The cheers were deafening. At the bottom of the stairs, Kuykendall and Postmaster Dan Quill stood on a red carpet and waited to make Duke a citizen of San Antonio and honorary Alcalde. This time, the Tigerettes served as an honor guard on the steps. Shahan was also on hand to welcome the visitors. Wayne then was given the first of many gifts he would receive over the next four days—an embroidered saddle blanket with a depiction of the Alamo on it. The gift was presented by two lovely women—Sandra Callan (Miss Mohair) and Jean Williams (Miss Wool). Pilar noticed a run in her nylons as she walked across the red carpet and borrowed a pair from *Oregonian* reporter Phyllis Lauritz "so her memorable legs might be conservatively clad for the battery of photographers (that) would record her appearance." Duke waited a few minutes for Richard Boone to arrive from Phoenix on a private plane. (Boone had changed his Paladin shooting schedule from four segments in two weeks to five segments in three weeks just so he could attend the premiere). Then, the Alamo Follow-Me girls of the Kelly AFB Beauty Queens escorted the visitors to their cars. At 5:30 p.m., Wayne's group departed the airport with Boone and Pat Wayne and headed for the hotel. Imagine Birdwell's surprise when he arrived at the St. Anthony and found another Russell Birdwell already checked in. When the latter received a wire meant for the publicist that read, "Successful planting today," the oilman asked the room clerk, "What is he in? Cotton?"[1301]

The next three days would be packed with personal appearances, receptions, luncheons, and dances, but first, a press reception was in order. In the Gunter Hotel's North Terrace room, Wayne was peppered with questions about the film, his career, how he liked working in Texas, etc. But the first thing everyone wanted to know was "How much did this film cost?" Once again, he laid out the specifics: United Artists contributed $2.5 million and had 10% interest; I.J. and O.J. McCullough, $3 million; Clint Murchison, $2.5 million; Yale Foundation, $1.5 million. Wayne put up the rest. He also said Grant would participate in 10% of Batjac's profits, and Duke would keep his word. Jim Henaghan would get his cut—2.5% up to $100,000. (Despite being mentioned in various newspaper articles, there is no evidence that the multi-billion-dollar Yale Foundation endowment fund ever actually invested in Wayne's film. Perhaps the opportunity wasn't approved, perhaps the monies were offered and rescinded.) Duke admitted he'd miscalculated production costs by $780,000, which included lab fees. "And," he added, "we couldn't have made this at a major studio. They would have wanted to change the ending." Then he talked about the state of his country: "I think we've (been) given too strong a downbeat feeling about this country. I think it's time we established first in this country and in the world that there is no fear in the country and that we're going forward." Patrick Wayne endorsed his father's feelings: "I go to school at Loyola, and these kids are all forming their opinions now of what America is and what it should be. I think this picture will give them some meaning of what America should be." Boone and Tiomkin also attended the event; the impish Dimi drew huge laughs when he constantly referred to Boone as "Houston" or "Pat."[1302]

In Gonzales, thirty-two Marine reservists of San Antonio's 14th Infantry Battalion began a seventy-one-mile, two-day forced march under full combat dress to re-enact the arrival of those who came to help the Alamo defenders. The Marines carried a silk replica of the "Come and Take It Flag" that Gonzales mayor R.H. Walker, Jr. had presented to Col. J.R. Lirette, director of the 8th Marine Corps Reserve and Recruitment District, New Orleans. He in turn presented it to the marchers as the Gonzales High School band played. Upon arrival in San Antonio, the flag would be offered as a replacement for the cotton one currently displayed. Walker called a roll of the original men with a Marine answering for each one. The Marines left Gonzales at dusk, marched all night, and arrived in Seguin in the morning. Resting during the day, they left Seguin that evening and continued thirty-seven miles to the Joe Freeman coliseum. (Capt. Harvey Mayberry, assistant inspector instructor, and M-Sgt. Spencer Kirschman had done a dry run of the march one week earlier and all they could say was, "they better keep to the shoulder of the road and march at a pretty good clip.")[1303]

Meanwhile, in San Antonio, celebrities checked into their respective hotels for some rest and a bite to eat as the remainder of the evening's schedule was fairly hectic. Several hotels scattered around downtown San Antonio, including the St. Anthony, Gunter, Granada and Menger, housed all the celebrities, dignitaries, and reporters. Some folks even stayed at Fort Sam Houston. A "Square and Round Dance" to benefit the DRT's Alamo Preservation Committee kicked off the evening's events in the massive parking lot of the Handy-Andy supermarket. Ads promised that over 10,000 vehicles could park there...a good thing as over 20,000 people showed up! With music provided by Don Pack & His Orchestra, the dance began promptly at 5:30 p.m. but Wayne, Boone, Cristal, Wills, and Pat Wayne didn't arrive until 7:30 p.m. Four large searchlights crisscrossed the evening sky and guided partygoers to the event. In the car on the way, Wayne worried about being late and kibitzed with Boone about equal billing in *The Alamo*.

It was quite a sight as police sirens blared as the motorcade made its way into the parking lot and the crowd cheered as Wayne and the other stars left their limousines. Pack played "San Antonio Rose" and a sequence from the movie's theme music as Wayne mounted the steps to the stage and shook Pack's hand. "I didn't wash my right hand for a couple of months," remembers Pack. "John Wayne was an American icon. He was a great hero of mine, so it was a real thrill to be onstage with that man. It was quite exciting for us. We'd been involved with Nashville-type celebrities, but nothing of that magnitude. It was pretty elaborate." In appreciation of his interest in the Alamo, the DRT gave Wayne a commendation for the "true historical data in this production"; he, in turn, presented a trophy to the Texas Starlets' square dance caller.

And since this was Texas, an enormous thirty-foot-long "Battle of the Alamo" cake had been baked especially for the dance. Said Handy-Andy bakery superintendent Tim Strickler, "This cake has created production problems to equal its unprecedented size. It will weigh more than 2,000 pounds–requiring a specially-reinforced structure to hold the cake." No wonder it weighed so much–it contained 220 pounds of flour, 1,009 pounds of sugar, sixty pounds of shortening, forty-five pounds of butter, 1,760 eggs, and other ingredients. Prepared in six-foot sections, each four inches deep, it required eight specialists from the bakery to complete the frosting. The battle was depicted with hundreds of miniature foot soldiers, horsemen, and artillery. Before the cutting ceremony, the cake was screened off from public view by a giant plywood covering that Boone had the honor of "blasting" away with a small cannon. Pack says the ceremony was a fiasco: "About the time they were getting ready to fire that cannon, ol' Chill Wills threw a bunch of his personal cards to the audience, who were behind barriers and, of course, they broke the barriers and ran in to get the cards. They pushed John Wayne and one of the Daughters of the Texas Republic right in the cake. They had cake all over the front of their clothes, which at that time was pretty funny." Drummer Johnny Bush remembered Wills as obnoxious and inebriated. "I think he embarrassed Wayne everywhere he went," said Bush. Duke cut the first slice with a Bowie knife and gave it to Mrs. E.R. Simmang, chairwoman of the DRT's Alamo committee. Thereafter, slices of the rest of the cake were sold to the crowd at 10¢ cents a slice. With fifteen refreshment stands offering food, beverages, two barbecued steers, wieners, tamales, Coke, Royal Crown Cola, Dr Pepper, Pepsi, Seven-Up, coffee, and ice cream , well, it was quite a feast! Proceeds from the sales of food and beverages were turned over to the DRT for care and maintenance of the Alamo. The event was broadcast live by TV and radio (local KONO-TV weatherman Bill Kelso functioned as emcee), and Wayne was mobbed by adoring fans. Sadly, his suit jacket was the evening's first casualty as it lost two buttons. Duke, Cristal, and Wills then piled into their car and headed to the last scheduled event of the evening. En route, everyone took turns trying to turn off the interior dome light that mysteriously kept blinking on and off. An exasperated Wayne finally asked the driver, "Is this car new?" "It was this morning, sir," the driver replied dryly.[1304]

While Duke was busy cutting cake, Tiomkin was busy conducting the San Antonio Symphony Orchestra in a special concert of *The Alamo Suite* at the Municipal Auditorium. In a program printed especially for the event, Tiomkin was praised for his efforts:

> "In future times when the music of today has become history, experts in their researches will certainly interest themselves in music incidental to present day films, much of it of a superior quality which all too often passes through the ears of the listener unheeded, in the absorption of the drama. Among the composers in this field, a preeminent place will be held by Dimitri Tiomkin, whose work has been associated with large numbers of important and significant motion pictures. This writer remembers with especial fondness the composer's poetic and elegant musical backgrounds for *Portrait of Jennie* and *Cyrano de Bergerac*. And one remembers as well, the unforgettable *Lost Horizons* in which Tiomkin made his first splash in the cinema world. Today a new peak in a noteworthy career has been achieved with his score for the epic film *The Alamo* which of course means so much to Texans in general and San Antonians in particular. Thus it is inevitable that the San Antonio Symphony, the orchestra that belongs to the city whose proudest historical treasure is that old tan structure in the midst of the busy town—quivering with history—shimmering under the hot sun, immersed in a haze of memory, historical overtones felt everywhere—should play the world premiere of the selection of music from the film."

Joining Tiomkin were orchestra conductor Dr. Victor Alessandro and Clifford Williams of the University of Texas, the latter conducting the premiere of his composition "Festival." Rising to the challenge of the presence of a four-time Academy Award winner, Alessandro's conducting of Dvorak's Fourth Symphony and Tchaikovsky's Symphonic Fantasy Francesca da Rimini was said to be inspired. But the evening belonged to Tiomkin. Pilar, Boone, Grant, and Pat Wayne watched him conduct the eight-movement Alamo Suite, which featured the combined fifty-person a cappella choirs of Trinity University and San Antonio College singing the vocal parts while the one hundred-piece orchestra performed the music. The Suite opened with "Prelude," followed by "De Guello," "Arrival of Davy Crockett" and "Cattle Raid." "Tennessee Babe," "The Ballad of the Alamo," and "The Green Leaves of Summer" completed the vocal section. The final section, "Attack on the Alamo," ending with a rousing "Eyes of Texas" and a standing ovation. A critic wrote, "Tiomkin conducted with a firm, authoritative style. Both the orchestra and the choruses performed nobly, with a sureness of touch that was probably a product of Tiomkin's insistence on extra rehearsals. The chorus was eminently satisfactory, enunciating precisely and blending voices in smooth unison except for 'Green Leaves' which, owing to a last-minute switch in key by Tiomkin from D to C, now and then flattened out." Tiomkin was gracious in his acceptance: "I want to thank all the Bachs, Mr. Beethoven, and Mr. Brahms for all the help they gave me in writing it. Without their help, all movie composers would be dead."[1305]

At 9:00 p.m., while Tiomkin conducted, Avalon entertained at halftime of the Trinity University-McMurry University football game along with the 110-piece Trinity band, the Trinity Tigerettes, vocalist Ron Bretz, and a Trinity ROTC drill squad performing the theme from *The Alamo*. (To those interested in such things, Trinity blanked McMurry 20-0). Avalon later admitted he was happy Wayne cut down his one song in *The Alamo* to just a few bars: "This way it doesn't interfere with the story line," said the young crooner. Rounding out the evening was the San Antonio Press Club's annual Gridiron Show at the Pearl Corral in the Pearl Brewery. Dubbed "Out of the World Premiere" and with 575 persons attending, the show was a combination roast and lampoon of Wayne, the Alamo, Lyndon Johnson, and local and national elections. Carl Atkins, head of the Drama department at San Antonio College, directed the event and WOAI-TV news director Frank McCall produced it. No subject was off-limits. They even skewered Wayne's argument with Sinatra. A displayed sign read "Frank Sinatra is handling the parking lot." Gov. Daniel, Happy Shahan, and brewery executive Aubrey Kline received special awards while Wayne was given the club's Frying Pan award and made an honorary member. The evening ended in uproarious laughter as the club satirized *The Alamo* with Wayne laughing louder than anyone. All in all, it was a perfect way to end the first day's activities.[1306]

Saturday had been cloudy with a high of 75º, and Sunday's forecast was much the same: partly cloudy and a little warmer with a high in the upper 70s–an absolutely beautiful October day in San Antone. While many slept late to recover from the previous night's activities, Duke, Cristal, Boone, and others attended a 10:00 a.m. press conference at the Gunter Hotel. Awaiting them were over one hundred national and local newsmen who touched on a variety of topics. Asked about his feud with Sinatra, Wayne explained, "Frank and I had no real problem. There was a conversation, that's all." Comparing himself to Fess Parker's earlier version of Crockett, Wayne admitted, "I can't sing." Wayne stated that *The Alamo* could contribute to building up America's image and reverse the trend of "negative thinking." It was a comment he would continually pound home: "The overwhelming majority of our population is in the middle-class," he emphasized. "Everybody has radio and TV's, there are four boats to every family, we work five days instead of six, and we get paid the sixth day anyway. There are no vacant seats at the World Series . Oh, I know the Russians have the bomb, and they're tough. They put up Sputnik, and we put up twenty—we've got one that can't stop talking back to us. This is the image of America that we should establish in our country first and then in the rest of the world, to let them know there's no fear in this country, and we're not going into any recession." The reporters applauded at the conclusion of Duke's comments. Boone agreed: "We hope that if the American people are ever called upon again to stand on principle, we can do so by remembering the people of the past with pride and follow their example." The press conference also saw Wayne criticize the presidential campaign, voice support for the Nixon-Lodge ticket, and explain historical inaccuracies in his film. He knew changes had been made for dramatic effect but said he had checked out each change with J. Frank Dobie, Lon Tinkle, and other historians, who had all agreed the changes were unimportant in relation to the overall message of the film. "It's amazing how little history and how much legend exists about the Alamo," he rationalized. "There's both good legend and bad legend, but it's hard to get exact facts about the Alamo." On a lighter note, Boone told reporters he hadn't been sure he'd even get the role of Paladin because a voice from Madison Avenue had said, "My gosh, no, he's a doctor," referring to *Medic*, his earlier TV series. Later, after viewing the pilot of *Have Gun Will Travel*, the "same voice on Madison Avenue said, 'You know, that doctor rides a horse pretty well.'" Wills continued in the same comedic vein when he bragged he could part the hair in the back of his head because of a "well-placed arrow."

Immediately afterward, Wayne and Avalon, who had missed the press conference, flew to Huntsville in O.J. McCullough's VIP private plane to appear at the fourth session of the 29th Annual Prison Rodeo. (Earlier that month, rodeo spectators were entertained by Ricky Nelson, Bo Diddley, Jimmie Rodgers, Neal Sedaka, and the always popular Dallas performer, Candy Barr).[1307]

Other *Alamo* stars, including Wills, attended that day's 11:45 a.m. brunch on the Hilton Granada Hotel's fourteenth floor, where they learned, courtesy of the master schedule of events, that "Texans traditionally have their morning steak-and-eggs about sun-up but to ease the visitors into Texas life gradually, this convivial session will start at this time and breakfast will be served as a brunch. It has been set late to give everyone time to sleep and still be there. In addition to usual breakfast items, we will be featuring our 'Hangover Bar' to get the day started off right." With nothing further scheduled until late that afternoon, the city's visitors had time for sightseeing or even a siesta. Back in Huntsville, Duke and Avalon entertained the crowd. Frankie sang a few songs; Wayne just stood up, and the people cheered. Once again, he spoke about the film's message and said, "I'm sure glad to be here, and I'm glad I have a round-trip ticket." After thanking the crowd again, Duke and Avalon flew back to San Antonio.[1308]

Back in town, the next scheduled event was a 4:30 p.m. boat ride down the peaceful San Antonio River, which gently flowed through the heart of the downtown area. Begun in 1939 and initially completed just two years later, the Riverwalk was lined with stairways to street level, footbridges, walkways, rock walls, shops, restaurants, and hotels. Tourists could wander along its banks in the shadow of skyscrapers, albeit not very tall ones. Narrow, with twists and turns, the river was spanned by forty-two bridges in just six miles. In a bend in the heart of downtown stood the Arneson River Theater. Concession stands and a projection room sat on the south bank above tiers of grass seats where 1,000 could watch performances on the stage across the river. In the evening, colorful mariachis and Mexican troubadours strolled the sidewalks, entertaining the boat's passengers. For over an hour, the Arneson featured an authentic international revue with Yolanda Almaguer, Ricardo and his Latin Holiday, and the orchestra of Mateo Camargo—an evening of Latin entertainment under the Texas stars.[1309]

At the conclusion of the boat ride, guests disembarked at the river entrance to the San Antonio Press Club for a cocktail reception. Most of the celebrities were there, including Duke, Pilar, Pat and Mike, Linda, Chill, Dimi, Boone, Grant, and Happy. Everyone was asked to sign the guest register; unfortunately, someone ripped the page with Duke's and Boone's signatures out of the book! Frankie arrived late as screaming fans tried to climb iron gates surrounding the press club. Boone didn't have much luck either; he was hit by a splintered flash bulb tossed by an overzealous fan when the actor tried to pass through the Villita street entrance. Stunned, Boone quickly changed plans and detoured to Alamo Street. Although police closely guarded the club's gates, some autograph seekers still sneaked through, and even scattered showers and dark clouds refused to dampen the crowd's spirits as fans jammed the gates looking for celebrities. Inside, Duke posed next to an Alamo/cannon ice sculpture, shook hands, and mingled with the crowd. Boone found himself surrounded by a ballet dance class while young Pat ogled another Pat—Pat Carroll, a beautiful girl in a golden cage. Rosie Flores, an Incarnate Word College art major, presented Wayne with a painting of the Alamo she had done herself. An hour later, she received a telegram. "Dear Rosie (it read): I have received many nice awards and people in this town have been very thoughtful to me, but mostly I think I appreciate your lovely painting. Thank you very much, John Wayne."[1310]

"A Night in Old San Antonio" wrapped up the evening's festivities. This annual four-day fiesta usually was held in April at La Villita, one of San Antonio's first neighborhoods. Located on the south bank of the San Antonio River,

La Villita originally had been a settlement of primitive huts to house Spanish soldiers stationed at Mission San Antonio Valero (the Alamo). Hosted by seven hundred members of the San Antonio Conservation Society, the fiesta was recreated this one night as a special tribute to Wayne and the film company. Attendance was limited to 4,000 with tickets sold at $2 each. "The visitors roamed in colorful San Antonio at the turn of the century" wrote one reporter, "with troubadours, costumed street vendors, brightly-dressed Spanish dancers, all manners of local food and beverages, and music from five nations, including a Dixie-land band." Son-of-a-gun stew, Helote, Chalupas, Bunuellos, Kolaches, and Old South ham and honey biscuits were just a few of the delicacies offered.

Only Wayne and his family dared venture out into the crowd celebrating the fiesta; after spending most of their time in the press club, the other stars left through its back entrance without even dropping in to the enjoy the fun. Duke wore a large crepe-paper yellow rose pinned to his suit's lapel. Everyone wanted to have their picture taken with him; Patty Park, Aubrey Jean Kline, Diana Serur, and Ardis June Kline had the good fortune to have their photo with him published in the *San Antonio Light*! When a woman photographer spied Duke and asked him to pose, a flash bulb exploded in mid-flash! Not a good day for flash bulbs. Three attempts were made to assist Wayne in his exit, but the mob at the Press Club wouldn't allow it. Finally, after reinforcements arrived, the Waynes left the fiesta, escorted by police in a flying wedge. Said one official, "It was necessary in view of Wayne being mobbed the previous evening at Handy-Andy's." According to chamber president Corrigan, "pieces of Mrs. Wayne's $300 gown" were torn off in the melee, and an "escorting state highway patrolman had to assist in carrying her out," but this "in no way reflects on the Conservation Society but on a small mob of kids and star-worshiping women." As another successful day's activities drew to a close, Wayne had but one thought on his mind: What would tomorrow's audience think of his film?[1311]

But before he called it a night, Wayne had one last engagement, an impromptu dinner at the mahogany, silver, and crystal Argyle Club. Only seven men, their wives, and a columnist were invited, including Bill Daniel, Shahan, and the McCullough brothers. All the wives were seated at one table, the men at another, perhaps by design, as Happy and Duke sat across from each other and patched up unspoken differences related to the filming. They had a very unusual friendship, "I was with him many places," said Shahan. "Las Vegas, Dallas, San Antonio. We had a funny relationship. We argued all the time and enjoyed every minute of it." Happy then spoke with the McCulloughs about a possible Kinney County oil deal. Daniel just sat at the end of the table and listened to all the conversations.[1312]

Monday dawned on an action-packed schedule of events: first a Frontier Street Breakfast followed by a Tribute to the Heroes of the Alamo, Texas Under Six Flags Luncheon, Alamo Premiere Celebration Parade, VIP Cocktail Party an& Reception, and finally, The World Premiere of *The Alamo*. Wow! But the forecast said partly cloudy and occasional drizzle, so Wayne could only hope the events wouldn't be rained out. No matter–the day he'd waited for finally had arrived, and he was ready. Schools let out at 2:00 p.m., so kids could watch the parade and see the stars. How neat! And that evening, after a few cocktails and with family and friends in attendance, Duke would bask in the glow of his triumph. But first things first.

At 8:00 a.m., the San Antonio Restaurant Association served a Frontier Street Breakfast on the street in front of the Alamo. With more than six hundred VIP's in attendance, the open-air, Texas-style breakfast featured pioneer dishes of the frontier era, including twenty gallons of orange juice, 1,440 eggs, fifty pounds of ham, fifty pounds of sausage, 1,500 hot rolls, 1,500 sweet rolls, and fifty gallons of coffee–all donated by the Association. Red-and-white checkered tablecloths covered seventy tables; folding chairs were filled almost to capacity. A team of six waitresses handled the buffet-style chuck wagon meal in three serving lines. At that early hour, most of the Hollywood folks were a trifle late, but Wayne, Cristal, Boone, Avalon, Pat, and Mike were there. Wills had an appearance in Dallas. Boone even passed out a few of his *Have Gun Will Travel* calling cards in exchange for his meal!

At 9:30 a.m., immediately following the breakfast, the Tribute to the Heroes of The Alamo ceremony took place. The solemn ceremony featured patrons and friends of the production, movie stars and celebrities, state, local, and national government officials, representatives of foreign countries, and members of the chamber of commerce, all standing in the rain to hear the roll call of the names of the Alamo heroes. Present were Gov. Daniel, mayor Kuykendall, Gov. Jimmy Davis of Louisiana, Lt. Gov. Garland Byrd of Georgia, Lt. Gov. William Baird of Tennessee, Lt. Gov. A.E.S. Stephens of Virginia, Lt. Gov. John W. Donahey of Ohio, Robert Haynsworth of South Carolina, Secretary of State Herbert Ladner of Mississippi, Consul General of England Henry Niblock, and Lt. Col. Joachim Vogt of Germany. All Texan patriots had been invited. In a speech, premiere chairman Weiss reminded everyone, "We firmly believe every Texan should take the opportunity to review the character and idealism which sustained the 185 men of the Alamo in a thirteen-day struggle against overwhelming odds, in the face of certain death. We should dedicate ourselves today to protection of the same ideals of liberty and freedom which, in our time, are just as dangerously threatened."

The ceremony's emotional high point was the arrival of the thirty-two Marines from Gonzales. The crowd broke into wild cheers as the Marines, led by five mounted horsemen carrying flags, marched double-time around the Houston Street corner in front of the post office. So enthusiastic was the crowd that Wayne jumped up from his chair, waved at the fans and photographers, and yelled to the crowd, "Get out of there and let 'em through!" Naturally, they obliged. The Marines then marched off to their appointed place on the grounds. Then, bareheaded in the rain with the umbrella-holding Cristal beside him, Wayne stood in silence as each defender's name was read. After the ceremony, Wayne and the other stars personally shook hands with each Marine and thanked him. Said one foot-weary leatherneck to Capt. Mayberry, "Captain, I'm sure glad you weren't mixed up in a world premiere of *Around the World in 80 Days*." Air Force reservists of San Antonio's Alamo Wing, Kelly AFB 433rd Troop Carrier Wing, were scheduled to fly over in C-119 Flying Boxcars in an aerial salute to the defenders, but it was canceled due to the weather.[1313]

In the name of the people of Texas and the Texas State Historical Survey Committee, Gov. Price Daniel then presented Alamo Medallions of Honor to ten state and foreign representatives in recognition of their area's contribution in the heroic battle. A plaque commemorating Louisianans who defended the Alamo was presented to Gov. Davis. Paxton Moore, UA advance man, noted this presentation was the first official recognition of Louisiana's part in the historic battle. When he learned details of the planned celebration, reporter Frank Gagnard of the *New Orleans Times-Picayune* facetiously suggested it would surpass even the one on November 11–South Texas Vegetable Day! Unfortunately, due to the increasingly heavy rain, Daniel asked each representative to forgo any speech. Wayne then placed a wreath of flowers on the Alamo's front door and, along with Cristal, Boone, Avalon and Pat, took a tour of the shrine and the Alamo Museum. By that time, rain was pouring, driving away many participants. Guests scurried away and looked for raincoats and umbrellas.[1314]

Next came a private cocktail reception for press, celebrities, and visiting dignitaries in the Menger's Colonial Room, immediately followed by the Texas Under Six Flags luncheon. The latter honored the six historic periods in which six different flags flew over Texas: Spain, Mexico, France, the Republic of Texas, the Confederacy, and the United States. The chamber-sponsored luncheon–a gesture of goodwill and appreciation to the visiting press and movie stars–featured food that represented each of the various periods. Once again, Rev. Peter Rogers gave an invocation that blessed the gathering, the film, and its players. The luncheon also featured numerous award and citation presentations, including two to Wayne: one on behalf of the ex-Students Association of the University of Texas, and one from the Texas Historical Survey Committee that honored

Duke for his cultural and dramatic contributions to Texas. Price Daniel presented both awards. In making the latter, the governor said, "It is impossible for any work based on history to be one-hundred-percent correct, but because of my personal knowledge of the depths to which John Wayne had gone in making this picture accurate, it is a pleasure to present him with this award." Grant received an historical literary achievement award from Trinity University of San Antonio president Dr. James Laurie. The plaque read: *To James Edward Grant, who has taken the words and deeds of the men and women of the Alamo and reverently placed them into the frame of one of the great motion pictures of all time.* "I appreciate this award," Grant said. "I'm glad to note that a Texas university recognizes the things actors say on the screen aren't dreamed up in their own little pointed heads. How I hope John Wayne doesn't fire me." Then, Rev. Father Walther Bielher, president of St Mary's University, presented Tiomkin a decree of honorary doctor of music in recognition of his numerous musical scores. It marked the first time the award had been given outside the actual confines of the university. Rounding out the presentations, Lloyd S. Simpkins, assistant to Maryland Governor J. Millard Tawes, gave Daniel a mounted silver Bowie knife. Joked the governor, "Now we'll have to make it legal again to carry these things." The knife came in handy as yet again, another Alamo-shaped cake was served.[1315]

After a short break, everyone was looking forward to the next scheduled event, the Alamo Heroes Parade. "A moving stream of color and excitement" with motorcade, floats, bands, Charros, marching units, and almost 1,000 horses and riders, the parade would stretch for miles through downtown San Antonio. Unfortunately, the weather wouldn't cooperate; if anything, it began to rain even harder. The co-chairmen Lt. Gen. E. Williams, Maj. Gen. Robert Stillman, and Jack Worse, had a tough decision to make. The safety of riders and horses on wet pavement was paramount, and, sadly, the trio decided to cancel the last public event before the premiere. Once notified, guests at the luncheon stayed for another two hours, gave interviews, and enjoyed the company of others. But one group, the members of the trail ride, was not deterred. More determined than ever, many donned rain gear, slickers, and ponchos, and slowly paraded to and around the Alamo, "in a triumphant, albeit wet, ending to their ride."[1316]

As celebrities relaxed and enjoyed the unexpected free time, others were not so fortunate. There were still a thousand last-minute details to attend to. Tuxedos pressed, dresses ironed, shoes shined. Limousines fueled and vacuumed. Thousands of balloons inflated. For the premier cocktail party, tables and chairs set up, glasses cleaned and arranged on bar countertops. Celebrities' arrival and departure schedules from various hotels were confirmed. One last rehearsal for the evening's entertainment. As the premiere would really be a "red-carpet" event, the actual red carpet was cleaned and rolled out in front of the theater. At the

Woodlawn Theater where a new screen was installed, one last sound check, one last check of the projectors. Searchlights in place outside. Wooden platform placed in front of the theater and a huge *Alamo* marquee erected. TV and radio crews that would broadcast live coverage performed sound checks and replaced faulty equipment. Cameramen from six companies shot newsreel footage day and night; their work would appear in 8,000 theaters and 150 television stations. Wayne later carried a filmed record of the premiere activities to London where it was aired by the BBC.

While local guests dressed for the cocktail reception, Widmark, Ken Curtis, and Harry Carey, Jr. drove in from Brackettville; Little John Hamilton came in from Cuero. Hamilton and Marshall Jones, Duke's lighting stand-in, were asked to escort two of Rev. Peter Rogers's friends. Many locals who'd appeared in the film purchased $50 Gold Tickets to attend the premiere; Charlie Rios, for example, bought his on the installment plan–$10 a week. Explained Rios, "My friends say, 'Hell, Charlie. You ain't in the movies,' and I just have to go to the premiere to see myself and make sure I really am in, at least, one little scene." At the other extreme was O.J. McCullough; the millionaire purchased a block of twenty-four tickets and flew in a group of his Houston friends for the premiere![1317]

While preparations were being checked and double-checked, yet another presentation was in progress. Grant was a special guest of honor at an afternoon literary session at the O. Henry House on the grounds of the Lone Star Brewing Co. Considered one of America's greatest short-story writers, O. Henry had lived in this house in 1885. As editor of his newspaper *The Rolling Stone*, he had used San Antonio as the setting for some of his most intriguing short stories such as *A Fog in Santone* and *The Higher Abdication*. Harry Jersig, president of Lone Star Brewing, gave Grant an award for literary excellence.[1318]

The last scheduled event before the premiere was a 5:30 p.m. VIP black-tie cocktail party and reception in the Anacacho Room of the St. Anthony Hotel. Over nine hundred of San Antonio's movers and shakers, celebrities, and newsmen packed the room to overflow capacity. Wayne, Widmark, Wills, Avalon, Boone, Cristal, Grant, Tiomkin, and Pat Wayne all appeared, as did Clint Murchison, the McCullough brothers, Mayor Kuykendall, Theo Weiss, oilman Glen McCarthy, United Artists and Batjac representatives, current and former military commanders from local installations, Ethel Kennedy, the presidential candidate's sister-in-law, his sister Jean Kennedy Smith, and many, many others. Duke received yet another gift: a one-of-a-kind, hand-engraved, single-action, gold-covered, pearl-handled Colt. On one side of the butt was a picture of the Alamo; on the other, the name "Duke." Everyone was decked out in their finest tuxedos and short formal and cocktail dresses. Linda Cristal had worn an array of clothes from day to day that was the envy of every woman. Every time Cristal appeared at an event she looked absolutely gorgeous. She and Pilar always wore the most beautiful of outfits: leopard-collared fur coats, jersey sheaths, hats trimmed in mink, and four-strand pearl chokers with large diamond pendants. Tonight was no exception.[1319]

Even though it continued to pour, by 6:00 p.m., fans began to line Fredericksburg Road in front of the Woodlawn Theater to await the arrivals of their stars. The streets were so crowded, spectators, decked out in raincoats, hats, and umbrellas, peered over the edge of the Woodlawn roof. Nobody knew how in the world they got up there. With searchlights splashing across the redecorated marquee, pre-premiere entertainment was provided by the busy Trinity Tiger Band; The Chordsmen, a champion choral group; 141th Infantry Drill Team, Marine Horse Color Guard; the Antonettes, a dancing group; the Alamitos, the flamenco dance and song group who appeared in the film; the San Antonio Premiere Orchestra; the Bandera Gunslingers, and the Trinity Tigerettes twirling group. At 7:00 p.m, The first guests—members of the visiting press arrivem. As they rode up in a chauffeured limousine, each was greeted with a drum roll from the band. The Gunslingers welcomed each with a fifteen-gun salute as guests walked from their limousine to the stage. The route took them up a short flight of stairs to a larger wooden platform where they were met by a bevy of dancing beauties and the evening's emcees, Tommy Reynold and Jim Wiggins. The turnout impressed Los Angeles KTLA television personality Larry Finley: "To think people would stand out in the rain for this, it's just marvelous. They wouldn't do this in Hollywood. This is absolutely the biggest turn-out of people I've seen at any premiere. And just think, it's raining, too." UA's Roger Lewis seconded that opinion: "I think the whole thing is just wonderful. The rain didn't seem to dampen anybody's ardor. Would you just look at that crowd? I have never seen (a premiere) with the cooperation and enthusiasm that we've gotten here from everyone. It's just wonderful." Due to the high humidity and inclement weather, the 10,000 balloons donated by Handy-Andy failed to float aloft. Instead, they gaily blanketed the red carpet in a cascade of color. And the kids had fun using them for punching bags![1320]

Boisterous Chill Wills was the first star to arrive. After ducking under the covered platform, he won the crowd's hearts by grabbing a microphone and yelling, "I'm going to get out here in the rain and get wet with everybody else!" With ad-libs, jokes, and songs, he became the event's unofficial master of ceremonies and probably salvaged the evening. Waving his arms, Wills cried, "We got Texas upstairs, downstairs, and all around us! I haven't been this wet since I was a baby." Some of Chill's gags were as corny as Francis the Talking Mule, a character whose voice Wills had supplied. Like most entertainers, Wills kibitzed with band members and got a huge laugh when they struck up a tune as a police car showed up. Everyone expected a limousine to follow, and, when it didn't, Chill exclaimed, "That's a swell fanfare for a cop!" Sometimes, though, excitement got the better of him. After one particularly rousing number, he thanked the band for a "helluva job." He caught himself and apologized: "I probably should not use that word, but it explains it (the band's stirring performance in the rain)." Thanks to his improvising and other entertainment, the crowd was in fine spirits. Pat Wayne then arrived, took a moment to chat with the glamorous Tigerettes, then went inside, prompting one scribe to say that it just goes to show that Texas gals were just as beautiful as those in Hollywood! Pat was quickly followed by Price and Bill Daniel, Ethel Kennedy, Linda Cristal with beaming escort Lt. Col. Bill Hunter from Fort Sam Houston, and Richard Boone. Like the other stars, Boone was greeted by the Bandera Gunslingers' fifteen-gun salute as he walked from limousine to platform. Quipped Boone, "This movie will separate the men from the boys, and I'm going in and look. I'll come out and let you know whether I'm a man or a boy!" Widmark told the crowd he hoped they enjoyed the movie. Bored beyond belief, he held his comments in check until someone asked how he liked working again in Brackettville: "Come on down and see this one," he said of filming *Two Rode Together*. "It's not nearly as cold as when you watched us making *The Alamo*." A veiled comment on his relationship with Wayne?[1321]

Avalon's arrival brought out throngs of adoring teenagers with cameras and autograph pads; no one could say whether the screams were louder for Frankie or Pat. Many teenagers even waited in front of the theater to cheer the stars after they left the theater. Every arrival brought a combination of cheers and explosions of flash bulbs. Each celebrity would quickly mount the wooden platform, say a few words into the mics, and head into the theater to escape the rain. This sometimes caused considerable confusion for the procession because other stars were being introduced and then interviewed by TV and radio crews. The always beautiful Linda Cristal exclaimed it was "the most exciting night of my life," and she would leave Bexar with a "heart full of gratefulness." Then, finally, at 8:15 p.m., the big man himself arrived: John Wayne and his lovely wife Pilar. Earsplitting cheers greeted them as they exited the limousine. Before heading inside, Wayne paused on the platform to speak to the crowd: "It's mighty wonderful of you to turn out in the rain like this," he said gratefully. "We've done the very best we could with the picture. I hope you all get to see it." Young Joe Sarli vividly recalls that evening. He and his mother had walked in the rain to the theater from their Hollywood Street home. "I remember my mom holding me up, so I could see John Wayne walk in," says Sarli, whose father, longtime rodeo band director Don Sarli, was playing saxophone with the orchestra in the lobby. "John Wayne was a big deal. It was like seeing the Beatles."[1322]

Inside, attendees presented their Gold Patron tickets to a uniformed attendant and members of the press received small 2¼ x 3-inch gold-painted metal badges that identified their respective news organizations. Lovely gowned attendants passed out souvenir programs and directed people to their seats; a balcony staircase to the left, main floor to the right. Wayne was greeted with another round of applause when he and Pilar entered the lobby. But confusion still reigned supreme as limousines dropped people off faster than ushers could accommodate them inside. People thus were packing into the lobby like sardines. But flamenco dancers and singers entertained the crowd as people waited to be seated and reporters took one last opportunity to chat with stars before the film began. Asked if he was looking forward to seeing the film, Widmark agreed and said condescendingly, "I never saw it before, you know. Been too busy." Eventually, everything was sorted out. According to the *San Antonio Express*, "the performers (outside) kept the show moving after the dignitaries arrived, and the crowd . were still cheering after the 'first call' for the premiere rang out at 8:30 p.m."[1323]

Herman Sollock managed the Woodlawn at the time and his wife Sammie recalls an interesting encounter with Duke. She had just escaped the crush of bodies in the lobby and was relaxing in her husband's office when she heard a knock on the door. Opening it, she was face-to-face with Wayne. "Herman said I could come in here and get a drink," said Duke. Herman had been advised to have some bourbon in his office just in case. "Sure enough, I gave him a little jigger," said Sammie. "And he poured a little jigger of it, swallowed that. Poured him another one, swallowed that. He was extremely nice, just wonderful, very tall." Duke thanked her, admitting, "Now I guess I can make it the rest of the time." [1324]

Once everyone was seated, each star was introduced, stood up, and made a few gracious remarks. Wayne was the last to be recognized and, once again, received a huge ovation. Finally, at 8:50 p.m., as the curtains parted, the lights began to dim, and the first strains of Tiomkin's eerie overture was heard. Chills ran up and down the spines of the audience, which broke into wild applause as the opening credits appeared on screen. With each new name, the applause grew louder until Wayne's name caused an overwhelming roar, the sound only to be repeated again when each star first appeared on screen. Local extras tried to pick themselves out in the various scenes. It was a joyous moment for Duke. With a sound system tweaked to perfection, every note, every nuance was crystal clear. It must have been an incredible movie-going experience–the sounds of marching troops, pounding hooves, flags snapping in the breeze. The explosions of cannon were thunderous, the cadence of drums resounding. The wide, curved screen enhanced the viewing experience and Clothier's camerawork was brilliant: colors as vibrant as they've ever been, the sharpness and clarity beyond description.

During intermission, Duke huddled with Murchison and the McCulloughs. Said I.J., "Well, Duke. We went down the line with you win, lose, or draw, and, by glory, from here it sure looks like we filled our hand." Duke agreed. After intermission, the audience response, if anything, was even better. The film ended at twelve minutes past midnight...a moment of awed silence, then a thunderous burst of applause and standing ovation from the cheering crowd.

He did it, by God, Duke did it! He pulled it off! And he couldn't be happier. Stars, friends, investors, and newsmen all rushed to congratulate him. The only discouraging word came from a woman who'd participated in the 137-mile trail ride; she said the movie was too long for sitting still! Wayne, Pilar, and several other celebrities returned to the St. Anthony Hotel for a post-premiere celebration. Finally, at 2:00 a.m., Wayne took the elevator to his sixth-floor suite. Tired, so hoarse he could barely speak, but happily satisfied, he ran into *Limelight*'s Florabel Muir, who observed Duke was "as fresh and smiling as a Texas bluebonnet." Wayne enjoyed a short three-hour nap before he and Pilar headed off to London, the next stop on his world premiere tour.[1325]

While Wayne was busy in San Antonio, a potential issue was averted in Hollywood when British chief censor John Trevelyan met with producers to discuss his concerns on violence and brutality in American cinema. He previously had stated that sometimes the levels were more than British audiences were willing to accept, and specifically referred to *The Alamo*, *Spartacus*, and *Ben-Hur*. Trevelyan, secretary and chief executive officer of the British Board of Film Censors, went to great lengths to explain the Board's current policies. Fortunately, *The Alamo* had been given a "U" rating, meaning it could be exhibited without restrictions. On the other hand, *Ben-Hur* was given an "A" rating, indicating children under sixteen must be accompanied by an adult. That type rating naturally wouldn't have had the same economic impact on a hard-ticket film such as *The Alamo* when compared to grind-policy flicks. *Spartacus* had not yet been reviewed, but Trevelyan said its violence caused some concern.[1326]

Tuesday morning dawned with considerable cloudiness and light rain in San Antonio. Wayne, Birdwell, Grant, and Tiomkin left town on the 7:00 a.m. flight to New York City. As Wayne winged his way toward Idlewild Airport, a special 9:00 a.m. showing of *The Alamo* took place at the Woodlawn for Brackettville riders, Marines of Gonzales, and premiere workers, followed by a noon wrap-up brunch. Sponsored by the Premiere committee and the City of San Antonio, the luncheon was held for stars and visiting newsmen who had not yet left for home. Local papers' early editions had already been printed and contained the film's first reviews as well as articles and photographs of Monday's premiere. As expected, reviews were extremely favorable. Gerald Ashford of the *San Antonio News* was unrestrained in his praise: "John Wayne's *The Alamo*, which could easily have been an anticlimax after the terrific barrage of publicity that scorched the earth ahead of its world premiere at the Woodlawn Monday night, proves to be, in fact, one of the most significant historical spectacles ever to thunder across the screen. All of the actors are excellent, and several give performances that might seriously be considered for awards. Another award might go to the superb Todd-AO color photography. Further, *The Alamo* cuts through a century-old fog of misconceptions to give a true perspective of the spirit and motives of the 180-odd men who sacrificed their lives in the old mission. The picture was researched with infinite care for accuracy, and no one but local historical hobbyists will quibble over minor departures from the record which have been deliberately decided upon for dramatic effect."[1327]

Equally complimentary was Warren Darby of the *San Antonio Express*: "In the 124 years since the Battle of the Alamo, the story…has been told innumerable times and in many versions. But it probably never has been told dramatically and vividly, and with such impact, as in *The Alamo* actor-director-producer John Wayne spent $12 million to recreate at Brackettville the San Antonio de Bexar of 1836. If audience reaction at Monday night's premiere is any criterion, it has been a brilliantly successful venture." *Denton Record-Chronicle* staff writer Bob Porter, however, was one of the first to point out some of the movie's problems: "*The Alamo* was revealed as a film of magnificent proportions dealing intimately with the lives lost in that battle. There is room for argument in some of the details of the story, but then, this is the way it is with the Alamo. For example, after being speared, Crockett's last action is the blowing up of the Alamo's magazine, a point of contention with historians. And the famous drawing of the line in the dirt by Travis is omitted. But this too is a point of contention. Of course there are flaws as could be expected of anything on this scale. Some of the acting is uneven and if ever there is danger of maudlinism (sic), it comes with the treatment of Dickinson's three year old daughter, who is too cute for words."[1328]

Ed Castillo was one of the fortunate reporters who'd had a sneak peek the previous Friday, and he incorporated that viewing into his review, writing "We probably are the only ones that saw the first half of *The Alamo* one night, and the second and final half a few nights later. We caught an early screening of the picture Friday night, left at the half to catch the Kennedy-Nixon debate, and returned Monday night to see the picture it its entirety. We are happy to report it was a pleasure to see the first half for a second time, we seemed to get even more out of it than the first time we viewed it. The last half is the payoff of the great Wayne celluloid masterpiece. It moves so fast that the 3 hrs–15 min. running time of the picture is something the theater patron doesn't even contend with. Every foot of the film keeps your interest whetted to the utmost."[1329]

When Renwicke Cary of the *San Antonio Light* wrote his review, the praise was unanimous: "John Wayne aimed *The Alamo* at the box office–wisely so–and his aim was true. He scored a bull's-eye. Wayne has brought the stirring saga of Texas' freedom fight to the screen in spectacular fashion. There are few lofty speeches and there's a minimum of soul-searching. When these things do come up, they are short and to the point. The finished product seems just right. What Wayne has done, very successfully, is to lay the emphasis upon the action. Here let us say if there be moot points about (the actor's) characterizations or about any of the movie's other historical aspects, we shall leave them to the students of Texas history. *The Alamo* was painstakingly researched for years before the cameras ever started to turn. Whatever scripting license has been taken, it must have been done consciously for dramatic effect." Great praise indeed. However, Cary also was one of the first to mention the length of the film, a portent of things to come.[1330]

When visiting columnists returned home, they couldn't have been more complimentary of their time in San Antonio:

"We used to speak of 'Southern Hospitality' . now it's 'San Antonio Hospitality.'" George Burke, *Miami Herald*.

"The story here Monday night was the Taj Mahal of all premieres." Elston Brooks, *Ft. Worth Star-Telegram*.

"Throughout the nation the interest may be centered on ... the election, but in this gem of a Texas Town, it's John Wayne's *The Alamo*." Phyllis Lauritz, *Oregonian*.

"Venice has nothing on San Antonio either as a place to walk along the river...or as a place to see outdoor theater." E.B. Radcliffe, *Enquirer*.

But the *Los Angeles Examiner*'s Vincent X. Flaherty may have used every possible adjective when he wrote, "One of the most charming cities in America and, by far the most attractive in Texas, is San Antonio...most free thinking city in Texas. This place really has something extra special on the ball...probably the most American town in the nation....Unlike any other American city...a fascinating mixture of unspoiled antiquity, modern structures and know-how."

The city couldn't have asked for a better review than that. The San Antonio Chamber of Commerce and the Municipal Advertising Bureau created publicity scrapbooks to hold all the premiere clippings. Between the two organizations, they accumulated three scrapbooks totaling 566 local, state, and national stories, and 182 photographs.[1331]

Even local merchants took advantage of the movie's promotion. Mammy's Cafeteria added a $2,500 false-front replica of the Alamo, and the main window of Sommers Drug Store was filled with an Alamo display: three pocketbook versions of *The Alamo*, three record albums based on *The Alamo* music, large Texas-sized postcards of the Alamo, and a $19.95 replica of a Bowie knife. A nearby gas station was renamed "Taylor's Livery Stable." Bales of hay were stacked outside and gas pumps were encased in wooden boxes labeled "Pure water" and "Hard cider."[1332]

As he couldn't fly nonstop to London, Wayne's party had a few hours' layover in New York on Tuesday before he left again at 8:30 p.m.; he finally arrived in London at 7:00 a.m. Wednesday, October 26. While Duke was flying to jolly old England, Chill Wills stood in for him Tuesday evening at the Dallas Capri Theater benefit premiere where he received a plaque from Gordon McLendon of the Variety Club. The committee had hoped Linda Cristal would be there as well, but it was not to be. Like in San Antonio, red carpet, music, and klieg lights were the order of the day. The festivities started at 7:15 p.m. when the Hillcrest High School band played a concert in front of the theater. Trans-Texas general manager Norm Levinson and president Earl Podolnick presented a book on the film to Dallas mayor Robert L. Thornton. The book contained the complete history of the film from planning stage to production completion. At eight o'clock, after an introduction from emcee McLendon, the Hillcrest Choir sang a selection of songs from *The Alamo* and other Texas songs. After Wills presented corsages to the Premierettes, official hostesses to the event, made a few appropriate remarks, and accepted the plaque, he also received a watch and then the film began. The Variety Club's guests for the evening were members of the Dallas and SMU Symphony Orchestras, the Dallas Civic Doormen and Ushers Association, residents of Golden Acres and Fowler Home, associates of the Lighthouse for the Blind and teachers of blind children in Dallas schools. Dallas critics were as favorably impressed as those in San Antonio had been—no superlatives were left unused. William Payne, who had filed numerous articles from Brackettville over the past year, suggested, "There was communicated from the screen that same feeling of electric drama, of seeing men and action that heretofore had been familiar only through a printed description or an artist's sketch of his conception of how these events might have appeared. The camera work is excellent . the magnificent cloud formations throughout the film, and the dawn silhouette of the Alamo after the first day's battle are superb. Dimitri Tiomkin deserves much credit for the mood created by his score . (and) the film reflects painstaking research, even to the point of using the flag of the 1824 revolution rather than the current flag of Texas or Mexico, and the dozens of types of uniforms worn by combatants on both sides." Payne also praised the acting ability of local boy Wills.[1333]

## New York

Meanwhile in New York, the curtain rose at the Rivoli Theater in Manhattan for the film's East Coast premiere. As expected, several celebrity notables were in attendance including Ina Balin, Eva Gabor, Sabrina, and Shelly Winters. Highlights of the event were broadcast world-wide by NBC Monitor, the Voice of America, and the Armed Forces Radio Network. With mostly favorable reviews, the response was so positive the theater expanded its staff to accept box office reservations for the roadshow engagement. Rose Pelswick of the *New York Journal-American* and Kate Cameron of the *Daily News* were very complimentary, and described the film as proud, moving, and excellent. In particular, Cameron pointed out the "photography is impressive (and) Clothier presents a series of tableaux that slows the action, but they are like enormous canvases painted by a master artist." Pelswick seconded the opinion: "Spectacular is the word for *The Alamo*. Wayne has done a magnificent job. Visually and dramatically, *The Alamo* is top-flight picture-making." *Newsday*'s Ben Kubasik also complimented Wayne's directorial efforts but severely questioned the film's length. "The last portion of the film is as stirring as anything ever mounted for the motion picture screen," he wrote, further praising Wayne, Widmark, and Boone's acting. But he noted, "With so many elements going for the movie, it is a wonder that Wayne...could not see that his movie's major flaw is that it takes too much time to tell. It lasts 192 minutes–plus a fifteen minute intermission–and much time is taken up with what are long, almost meaningless scenes detailing the rowdiness of Crockett's men, a simple-minded love affair between Wayne and a Mexican girl played by Linda Cristal and other such nonsense. It is almost as though Wayne...felt he had to make it worth releasing on a reserved-seat basis. On the whole, Wayne's film is exciting and worthwhile, but he would have had a more powerful, dramatic vehicle had he cut an hour out of it." Alton Cook of the *New York World-Telegram* agreed: "This picture seems likely to be transformed from intermittently halting melodrama to one of our great western dramas. Its episode nature makes pruning of the too frequent lulls a comparatively simple task."[1334]

However, movie critic Paul Beckley of the *New York Herald Tribune* was more than a little brutal when he savaged Wayne's attempt at entertainment. After discussing the merits of artistic and esthetic films versus entertainment for the sake of entertainment, Beckley questioned whether Wayne's film was entertainment or a "serious effort to make history lusty." Praising its artistic touches–men sleeping picturesquely on moonless ramparts, well-composed battle scenes–he then writes, "the total effect of Wayne's film did not for me equal the force of the sum of its parts. There are too many static segments, too many versions which do not turn out to be integral to the movie's main point . One senses a looseness, a feeling of wandering, an indecisiveness in weighing the

736

relative importance of the diverse elements of history or fiction or characterization. Nicely as many of these distractions are filmed, they tend to diminish rather than increase the tension. Since the battle scenes do not occur until the final thirty or forty minutes . one's interest begins to flag and the finale loses its impact. It wouldn't make any difference if you went for the sake or entertainment or the sake of art; this would be so."[1335]

It seemed *New York Post* critic Archer Winsten took an almost perverse pleasure in shredding the film: "Another giant has come to town…it's bigger only because it has been padded…(T)he script…sinks to almost juvenile levels at its worst and rises only to heavily educational speeches at best. Following the principles of his model and teacher, John Ford, Wayne has injected low comedy at intervals. He has utilized a couple of low comedians for the work, and it's no better here than in the latter-day John Ford, perhaps worse. Wayne…could probably make a picture of this kind in his sleep. So it should occasion no surprise at all if the action clichés are all here. *The Alamo* has the size and the photography to be a major picture. It has also the costumes and some of the performers. It hasn't got the director…because as a director, John Wayne is merely a second-hand John Ford. Those who take their history seriously and those others who demand the best of their movies will want to give *The Alamo* a wide berth." Bosley Crowther of the *New York Times* summed up most New York critics when he wrote the film was "another beleaguered blockhouse western" and "the main character in *The Alamo* is much less a convincing figure from history than he is a recreation of Mr. Wayne. As his own producer and director, Mr. Wayne has unfortunately let his desire to make a 'big' picture burden him with dialogue. His action scenes are usually vivid; his talk scenes are long and usually dull. Laurence Harvey's Colonel Travis is a solid, consistent character, though perhaps a bit too foppish. He might be good in another frame. Richard Widmark's snarling Jim Bowie is a grown-up Dead End Kid. Mr. Wills is the best man in the cast. At least he stands by tradition. He lives in a coonskin cap. And he talks a little bit like Fess Parker. You can kill his body, but you can't kill his soul. You don't feel that way about the fellow performed by Mr. Wayne." New York critic reviews spanned the entire spectrum from good to bad: *The Journal-American*, Excellent; *News*, Excellent; *Tribune*, Good to Fair; *Sun*, Good to Fair; *Mirror*, Fair; *Times*, Fair to Poor and *Post*, Poor.[1336]

The *New Yorker's* Brendan Gill wrote a savage critique of Wayne's efforts: "Not like *The Alamo*? What am I—some sort of un-American nut or something? For here is a telling of one of the great American stories, and if I accuse John Wayne, who produced and directed it and plays one of the leading roles, and his associate producer, James Edward Grant, who wrote the screenplay, of having turned a splendid chapter of our past into sentimental and preposterous flapdoodle, I'm apt to be accused in turn of deliberately downgrading Davy Crockett, Jim Bowie, and all the other brave men who died in that heroic fiasco ....."[1337]

With scathing reviews such as these, it's a wonder Wayne had any career at all after this film. The DRT's reply to such slander was quick and to the point. Although Alamo Mission chapter president Mrs. Philip Harrel felt uneasy about the film's historical accuracy, she said, "It is out of line for the New York papers to be so sarcastic." (The picture as a whole is inspiring in that) "it instills into the minds of people today that our wonderful freedom did not come by accident." Apparently everyone wasn't put off by all the criticism as on October 28, the Gramercy Boys of New York sponsored a benefit performance of the film for headliners of stage, television, and motion pictures.[1338]

## Los Angeles

While Duke had flown east, Pat Wayne, Linda Cristal, Boone, and survivors of the weekend had headed west to prepare for the Los Angeles premiere. In San Antonio, clothes for the evening had been formal gowns and tuxedos; in Hollywood, it was a Western motif—boots, jeans and chaps. Escorted by baseball's Leo Durocher, actress Shirley MacLaine came dressed as an Indian maiden. Princess Soraya, divorced wife of the Shah of Iran, was one of the few dressed in formal attire. Bleachers were erected beside the entrance way and the long walk from limousines to the Carthay Circle were lined by police, rope barriers, and more than 2,000 teenagers, screaming fans and autograph seekers. They noisily cheered the arrival of their favorite celebrities. Everybody who was anybody was there: Edd Byrnes, Dorothy Provine, Gardner McKay, Bret Halsey, Richard Long, Howard Keel, Nick Adams, Sammy Cahn, Pat Wayne (standing in for his father), Barbara Rush with husband Warren Cowan, John Smith and Luana Patten with Bob Fuller, Gloria and Mike Romanoff, Dale Wexler with newly announced fiancée Linda Cristal (who promised not to wed until after *Two Rode Together* finished filming), Yvonne De Carlo and Bob Morgan, Eve and Van Johnson, Albertina (Mrs. Dimitri) Tiomkin, Chill Wills and daughter Jill, Mr. and Mrs. Bill Castle, Gene Barry and John Russell (*Lawman*), Milton Berle, Anne Jeffreys and husband Bob Sterling, Greta Thyssen and Vic Orsatti, Helen (Greco) and Spike Jones, Jeanne and Dean Martin, Mr. and Mrs. Dennis O'Keefe, Bill Hollingsworth, Troy Donahue and Donna Needham, the Dick Shawns, Laurence Harvey and Mrs. Joan Cohn (widow of Columbia Pictures founder), Jack Entratter, Betty and David Rose, the Jackie Coopers, Mr. and Mrs. Bill Goetz, Jeff Chandler, Sherry Jackson, Gene Kelly, Fess Parker, Ben Cooper, Walter Brennan, Henry Hathaway, and Rex Allen. Once again, KTLA's Larry Finley attended the premiere and interviewed numerous celebrities as they arrived while emcee Dick Haynes introduced everyone over a loudspeaker microphone.[1339]

A huge circus tent was pitched on the lawn next to the theater where, during intermission, attendees enjoyed beer and pretzels. Afterward, the post-premiere party offered enchiladas, chili, and a ranch supper of scrambled eggs, ham, and assorted stick-to-the-ribs offerings with everything washed down with good old Texas corn liquor. Extensive radio coverage included live airings by KTLA before and after the premiere, as well as "Monitor," "Dick Strout's Hollywood," Armed Forces Radio, and a host of foreign broadcasters. (Both pre- and post-premiere events were broadcast live on Channel 5.) With music provided by Bernie Richards and his orchestra, the party lasted past 3:00 a.m. So many people wanted to be there, sponsors were forced to limit them by placing an ad in *The Hollywood Reporter*: "SRO *The Alamo. We of SHARE, INC. regret not being able to accommodate everyone who wanted to attend the premiere of The Alamo. Our deepest thanks for your generosity.* P.S. The picture will start promptly at 8 p.m."[1340]

New high-definition projection lenses had been installed at the Carthay Circle. Previously available only for theaters showing *Ben-Hur*, these lenses were designated as PV Steinheil Pan-Quinon, and utilized an advanced optical design with German "rare earth" glass material. This produced a superior screen image for field illumination, edge-to-edge sharpness, flatness of field, and unprecedented definition. The Los Angeles audience loved the film—everyone except Harvey. Holding a small British flag because "it keeps me from being lonesome," he hid out in the lobby as the film was shown, admitting, "Is there anything worse in the world than going to your own premiere? I can't stand it." Joan O'Brien also missed viewing the film but for a different reason—she was home in bed with the flu. Despite Harvey's uneasiness the premiere was a tremendous success—over $60,000 in proceeds were given to SHARE (Share Happily and Reap Endlessly), which was earmarked for the Exceptional Children's Foundation and the Child Guidance Center.[1341]

As might be expected, many Hollywood reporters were unrestrained in their praise. Harrison Carroll of the *Los Angeles Herald and Express* called it "A great action picture with sweep and pace, (and) earthy comedy to lighten its story of bravery and sacrifice." Carroll was one of the few to laud its length, writing ". the result is a tremendously exciting and inspirational film. The test is that its three and a half hours seem to pass swiftly. This is perhaps the greatest saga of battle ever put upon screen. There are some speeches about the meaning of liberty . but they are neither long nor high flung. They are in the vernacular of these frontiersmen who backed up their belief with their blood ... it is a fine thing to come across a picture that speaks out loud and firm for the great traditions of the American heritage. *The Alamo* proves that it can be done without preachment. This is a message picture in the best possible sense ...."[1342]

However, Wylie Williams of the *Citizen-News*, while recommending the actors' performances, Clothier's cinematography, and Tiomkin's musical score, cautioned potential ticket-buyers that, with "orchestral preludes and a ten-minute intermission," they face "a three and one half hour test." Philip K. Scheuer of the *Los Angeles Times* gave Wayne an "A" for effort and believed Duke had succeeded more than he had failed. Although not the last word on the subject, Scheuer felt it would be "the definitive one for a long time to come." But he also was brutally honest: "Frankly, I wish they had set out with less than an epic in mind. Either that. Or with a more fool-proof screenplay. A great deal that goes on in the first two-thirds of the film might have been scissored (sic) to advantage—not so much because it is incompetent, irrelevant, or immaterial as because it is corny."[1343]

*Limelight*'s Jack Moffitt hit the proverbial nail on the head, however, when he questioned whether Hollywood had the desire to recognize patriotic beliefs: "The public will not only 'Remember the Alamo'...but when Academy Award time comes around, it will remember John Wayne as the...(man) who has recalled this inspiring event at a time...when it is most needed. And when that time occurs, it will be inclined to ask, most pointedly, if Hollywood values freedom, courage, self-sacrifice, and democracy—for all those things are in Wayne's presentation of the epic clash that made possible the freedom of Texas and, indirectly, that of the entire Southwest."[1344]

## London

In London, Duke and Pilar prepared to attend the Astoria Theater premiere. first, however, he delivered the same message he'd voiced at every packed press conference over the past year: "*The Alamo* was and is a picture that should have been made, and I damn well knew it. The men in it are the sort of men who have made my country—who have established freedom all over the world." He went on to say that we were living through tough times, and the free world had reached a point where further appeasement may well mean disaster. After chatting a bit about his family, he was asked about the current political situation back in the States. "Senator McCarthy was a friend of mine," Wayne admitted. "I admired the work he did. Whether he went overboard or not, he was a value to my country. A number of liberals think he started a witch hunt. I think he was witch hunted." When a reporter asked if he was wealthy, Duke replied, "I have a fine family and many friends, but I am not solvent, if that is what you mean." He then left to change clothes from a dark suit with ill-fitting soft collar to his tuxedo.

While in London, Wayne's entourage stayed at the famous Savoy, but everyone wasn't pleased with the accommodations. Tiomkin complained vociferously about his room, Wayne's party was reallocated, and Dimi was satisfied: "At least now I can sleep if I get the time. Sure, I was annoyed. I think, when I come to

London, they treat me with the respect which England shows for the musician. A room with about five other boys they give me–five other *boys*! I wouldn't have cared if they were girls. Three days I haven't slept, and they expect me to share a room. Me! Tiomkin!"[1345]

In the weeks prior to the premiere, United Artists had deluged the United Kingdom with a massive *Alamo* exploitation campaign–radio, television, newspapers, magazines, window displays, music outlets, and mobile selling displays. Referring to the film's marketing, Duke said, "This is what we call penetration. And I am firmly of the opinion that *The Alamo* has received the widest and deepest penetration of any motion picture ever made." By the time Wayne arrived in town, British fans were in a frenzy.[1346]

Sponsored by Variety Tent for the benefit of the Invalid Children's Aid Association, the London premiere was hosted by members of the Royal Family and expected to raise over £5,000. As the rain poured, bobbies battled crowds of fans who swarmed the streets to get glimpses of celebrities. Heavy West End traffic briefly delayed Princess Margaret and Mr. Antony Armstrong-Jones who were expected at 7:30 p.m. When they finally did arrive, the royal couple was escorted inside the Astoria Theatre where the princess was presented with a flower bouquet from eight-year-old Kathleen Dyke. After numerous obligatory introductions Wayne eventually presented the princess with a $2,000 silver-mounted saddle flown in from Texas for the occasion. (It had been erroneously reported the saddle cost as much as $7,500.) Crafted by San Antonio master saddler Oscar Carvajal, it was fashioned from California leather on trees made in Vernal, Utah. Why not Texas leather? "It's not quite as good for saddles because of Texas' climate and method of tanning," said Carvajal, "and it's possible that water drunk by the stock affects leather quality." When Wayne told the princess it was a "real roper's saddle," she replied in typical British understatement, "Gracious me." Wayne added, "I figured, Ma'am, you did not have a western saddle. If you don't know how to ride western style, I'll be happy to give you some lessons." "How thoughtful of you, John," Megs replied. Wayne then jokingly told the audience, "If you don't know American history–for a small sum, I'll tell you who wins." When asked later about the conversation Wayne replied, "She was very pleased and asked a lot of questions about (the film)." Tiomkin added humorlessly, "In London, I meet Princess Margaret and Mr. Jones at *Alamo* premiere. I explain about beeg saddle Duke Wayne geev her, and Mr. Jones asks me if I am from TEXAS!"[1347]

Upon the couple's entrance into the Royal Circle, they were greeted by a short fanfare of trumpets sounded by the Herald Trumpeters of the Royal Artillery, followed by the national anthem. And then finally, the film began. English movie-goers loved American Westerns, and this film was no exception; as in San

741

Antonio, the film received a standing ovation. The *Guardian* printed a typical review: "In its broad and simple way, it is a good and handsome film which comes with slow deliberation to a magnificent conclusion. It would be much, much better had it been shorter by fifty minutes and stripped accordingly of those long conversations between Davy Crockett and a pretty Mexican lady. (Wayne, Widmark, and Harvey) all do well, but all of them are the victims of the film's elephantiasis." C.A. Lejuene, also of the *Guardian*, praised Wayne's efforts without any comment on the film's perceived excessive length: "Although conventional in its kind, without any of the spectacular drama of DeMille or the clean-cut, isolated passages of Ford, *The Alamo* is by no means ineffective. Some of the widescreen shots of the gathering of Mexican armies have conspicuous power, and although the dialogue is unimaginative, the acting, oddly dominated by Laurence Harvey, often gives the lines a point they do not naturally possess." Both the *Daily Mail* and the *Daily Sketch* called it "magnificent" while the *Evening Standard* thought it was "spectacular." The *Times* wrote, "There is a sweep, a rhythm, about *The Alamo*—action and battle on the screen have never been more convincingly portrayed." And the *Daily Express*, in typical British understatement, simply said "A massacre you'll enjoy. Terrific!" Although there were a few negative reviews, they didn't stop movie patrons from forming large queues to see the film.[1348]

Attendees of the premiere were given an eighty-page, red-tasseled souvenir program complete with advertisements, congratulations, and compliments from local vendors, such as Smith's Crisps, the Hyde Park Hotel, Baron of Beef Cocktail Bar, Carters Tested Seeds Limited, United Lubricants, and Taylor-Woods Hosiery and Lingerie. Included in an eight-page insert were Alamo photographs, film commentary, and an explanation by Wayne about why he made *The Alamo*: "Making *The Alamo* has been an abiding ambition for fourteen years. During that time I developed, with my staff, many specific ideas, how I believed the subject should be presented on screen. Perhaps I could have contented myself with playing one of the star roles in the picture. There are, for sure, many able men who could have been entrusted with the tasks of producing and directing and who could have brought these tasks to a successful conclusion. But this is something I wanted to do with my own Batjac company. And now I come to the real hub of the problem—organization. It was not very long after I knew that one day I would make a picture about the Alamo, and that I would play the role of David Crockett, that I began to build up my own producing company, Batjac Productions. Let me say now, and with no false modesty, that, without this organization at my back, I don't believe I ever should have had the confidence that I needed to bring off a project of the magnitude of *The Alamo*. By the same token, with this organization smoothly functioning, I never had a moment's doubt or qualm. The men and the women of Batjac have been carefully chosen over the years. I have not a moment's hesitation in telling the world that they are the best in the business. James Edward Grant is not only the author of the original story and script of *The Alamo* but has been a close and valued associate over the years. Elsewhere in this programme, we have listed the great men and women who helped make *The Alamo*; without them I would not have even attempted to do what together we were able to accomplish. A producer uniquely placed, as I was in the case of *The Alamo*, can certainly utilize his spot to see that his own ideas are put into execution. Functioning also as director, he can make certain that the scenes which he has envisioned and the story sequences which he has worked out with the writer get on the screen as planned. The case of *The Alamo* was, I point out again, a very special one, a cherished personal project, and that we were able to bring it off successfully is due more to the men and women of Batjac, and to a cast that can only be described as wonderful, than to the individual efforts of any one man."[1349]

# CHAPTER THIRTY-THREE
# "THE NOMINEES FOR BEST
# PICTURE ARE..."

BY THE TIME THE LOS ANGELES CELEBRATION ENDED AT 3:00 A.M., DUKE'S film had premiered all across the country–Houston, San Francisco, Chicago, and Philadelphia–and earned generally positive reviews with sell-out showings being the norm. In Chicago, The Palace added three extra showings to accommodate the overflow. The Carthay Circle in Los Angeles added a Thanksgiving Day matinee for the convenience of its patrons. Critics usually commended the acting, praised the action scenes, and fawned over Clothier's cinematography and Tiomkin's score. They recognized it was a "message" movie and, typically, endorsed the message: freedom, courage, liberty, sacrifice. As the reviews began to flow in the following week, they ran the spectrum from magnificent to tepid. The *Houston Post*'s Paul Hochuli thought the film would rate as many nominations as *Ben-Hur* did the previous year while Clyde Gilmore of the *Toronto Telegram* went even further and stated it would win multiple Oscars. Frank X. Tolbert of the *Dallas Morning News* told readers that his reaction was somewhere between the all-out endorsement of John Ford to "the nasty attitude of two national news magazines who are calling it 'shamelessly inaccurate' when 'it finally gets down to historical cases'...(and) 'as flat as Texas' (*Time*), and 'probably the most lavish B-picture ever made...with a silly banal script.' (*Newsweek*)." Columnist Sheila Graham erroneously reported that Wayne's Texas investors were so thrilled they offered Duke another $15 million as a floating fund for future films, while

Irv Kupcinet of the *Chicago Sun-Times* reported Wayne was so impressed with Avalon's performance, he signed him for two more films![1350]

While the majority of reviews were favorable, though, many were quick to point out the film's shortcomings. An unidentified critic thought the film was loaded with "happy homilies on American virtues and patriotic platitudes... which smack of yesteryear theatricalism rather than the realism of modern battle drama. In the second half, there is a rather embarrassing 'birthday party' passage in which the film momentarily seems on the verge of dissolving into a family musical." Referring to Wayne, the same critic stated "(Wayne is) generally playing with one expression on his face, he seems at times to be acting like a man with 12 million dollars on his conscience." Another called the film "shamelessly inaccurate (including) a seduction, an orgy, a murder (and) a battle royal in a barroom. The Mexican army, apparently in deference to the large Mexican movie market, is presented as a body of sensitive young men who look as though they all have college degrees and suffer every time they pull a trigger. And at one point, just in case the teenagers don't dig all that ancient history, Singer Avalon jumps up and belts out a little rock 'n roll." Dick Williams of the *Los Angeles Mirror* said it was too long and hampered by a slow, mostly uneventful first half. Doris Arden of the *Chicago Sun-Times* wrote it looked "more like a tribute to Cecil B. DeMille than to that of Houston, Crockett, Travis and Bowie. (Wayne) stages it rather like a lavish pageant, with scarcely a nod in the direction of realism. The heroic story has been told on a thoroughly childish level. It is long enough, however, to contain some scenes that are down-right embarrassing—including Wayne's love scene and farewell to the beauteous Linda Cristal (he appears to be playing a parody of himself)." And Mae Tinee of the *Chicago Tribune* called it an "overextended epic...sheer melodrama written with a heavy touch. There are times when Laurence Harvey...can't avoid appearing ridiculous. The film is more like an endurance contest than entertainment," but "there's little wrong with it that some judicious but liberal use of a scissors wouldn't cure."[1351]

But all the criticism wasn't confined to domestic newspapers. Even though the film wasn't shown in Mexico, Col. C. Julian Velarde, archaeologist and former historian for Mexico's National Museum of History, engaged in a war of words with *Los Angeles Mirror-News* columnist Paul Coates and took exception to several of Birdwell's comments. Velarde charged the losses sustained by the Mexican Army were closer to 500 than 1,700 and the reason why they were so high was that, on the last day of the battle, many local Mexican natives joined the Alamo defenders. Curiously, he further claimed that, with the stipulation their lives would be saved, Travis, Bowie, Crockett, and Fannin agreed to surrender and *signed* Santa Anna's terms. He also stated the reason why the surrender was never consummated was because animosities flared anew while Mexican soldiers were en route to Mexico City to have the surrender terms approved by Mexico's minister of war! While in Mexico City, *Hollywood Citizen-News* columnist

Lowell Redelings asked local residents if they knew of Wayne's film. "I hear that each Alamo defender kills seven or more Mexicans," said one suspiciously. "This is not right. Mexican soldiers are as brave as any. It makes American soldiers look very good, and we Mexican look–how do you say–stupid?" Still, there were those like Carlos Tinoco, union official and Hollywood liaison, who weren't very happy about the inability of *The Alamo* to be shown in Mexico. Tinoco had read the film's script and felt that, while censorship was a necessary evil, it shouldn't be crippling to an industry. Further, while he thought there were sections that were a bit crude, it wasn't anything that couldn't be erased with "judicious rewrites."[1352]

Some members of the industry even seemed to take a perverse joy in Wayne's predicament. As director John Huston walked through the San Francisco airport, he spotted a trade paper headline touting *The Alamo*'s financial and artistic problems. Wasting no time, Huston hoofed it to the Western Union office and sent Wayne the following wire: "Delighted at the success of your picture." Others felt that too many motion pictures, many of them unworthy of the promotion, received roadshow treatment anyway. In an article published in a convention program, Ben Marcus, chairmen of the board of Allied States Association, wrote "the problem that worries most exhibitors is the fact that distribution is being falsely carried away by the thought that any picture that has near qualifications of a spectacular must merit roadshow treatment, with the result that most exhibitors are denied the privilege of showing these pictures to their patrons while they are new and in public demand…in spite of the prior buildup given many of these pictures, results at the box-office do not always deliver the grosses that will shatter all precedents as was anticipated. (Distributors) have lulled themselves into the feeling that every picture in which they put the same effort and same production values has got to be a success. When we approach the public with special roadshow prices and do it consistently on pictures that do not warrant the hard-ticket sale, we are only fooling ourselves and kidding the public." Though not comparing *The Alamo* to films such as *Ben-Hur*, *The Ten Commandments*, and *Around the World in 80 Days*, their phenomenal success was a hard level to attain. Many distributors felt, if a film opened at a minimum number of locations for prestige purposes and then went into general release immediately thereafter, the film would be much more successful.[1353]

However, there still were some folks unconcerned about the film's length, who understood exactly what Wayne was trying to accomplish, who understood its underlying message. In a letter to the editor of the *Los Angeles Times*, Dr. Sven Wahlroos wrote, "Last Sunday my wife and I saw *The Alamo*. We were so moved by its message that we feel we must write and urge all patriotic citizens to see this magnificent film. It has been at least twenty years since movies were made as a tribute to gallantry, chivalry, and patriotism. We had lost hope of ever seeing such a movie from Hollywood again. Imagine then our pleasure on seeing the old values of honor, steadfastness and self-sacrifice brought back more beautifully than ever before. John Wayne is one of the great American actors. He is also one of the most courageous freedom-fighters this country has. My wife is a refugee from Hungary. She saw in *The Alamo* the siege of Budapest in 1944 and 1956. I am from Finland. I saw in this film a tribute to Finnish valor and to the fight for freedom of all people everywhere." This is exactly the impact Wayne had hoped to have on the film's audience.[1354]

It was clear almost from the beginning that while the public loved the film as evidenced by reserved-ticket purchases and packed houses, critics continually harped on its length. Theater owners complained this limited the number of showings per day, which, combined with reduced concession revenue, severely limited their profits. Others complained that the final show ended after the last bus of the evening; many patrons thus couldn't attend that showing due to lack of transportation. Even Birdwell noted that with the present version of the film, some New Yorkers didn't get home until well after 1:00 a.m. While the weekend business was extremely good, the mi-week take was off. The always spin-conscious publicist attributed the 70-75% capacity in the soft period to the "public interest in the presidential election." Birdwell went on to say that it was never Wayne's intention to make every date a roadshow engagement; it was necessary to feel one's way to determine a release pattern, But Duke still had a problem. The only way to make back his investment was to show the film as frequently as possible on an expensive hard-ticket basis that wasn't working. His solution? Get the film out in a 35mm general release as quickly as possible. Obviously, more theaters could show it in that format than in 70mm Todd-AO. He also decided to cut scenes that slowed down the film's pace or didn't advance an actor's characterization. The fact that some theaters were already eliminating "the birthday party" scene in reel 9B made the selection of that particular trim an easy decision. Wayne had said earlier in San Antonio, "A picture should be as long as it takes to tell the story. It's true that when you road-show a picture, people expect it to be longer. We hoped to bring in *The Alamo* at about two hours and 40 minutes, but we came in with more than three hours. I can tell you, though, that no scene was left in to give it length. Every one was to give it strength." Now, Wayne had some difficult choices to make.[1355]

After the London premiere, Duke, Pilar, and Birdwell planned to fly to Stockholm and Rome where they would continue to prime the *Alamo* publicity pump. Then, Duke would fly to Tanganyika where he would star in old friend Howard Hawks's *Hatari!* However, as the principal photography was delayed until November 28 due to casting and script issues, Duke decided on October 30 to return home. Tiomkin, however, continued with the tour; in appreciation of Hy Kanter's hard work on the score, Tiomkin took the Leo Feist publisher along on the two-week European engagement. In Paris, while attending the annual mid-winter meeting of the Societe des Auteurs, Compositeurs et Editeurs de Musique, in which he held membership, Tiomkin hosted a press party and reception before he led the Boulogne Symphony in a performance of his movie scores. In London, in an event sponsored by the London Symphony, he conducted an evening of music from both *The Alamo* and *The Sundowners* to raise money for the Allemanda Foundation Music conservatory scholarship fund. During the following month, Tiomkin traveled between Europe and the States several times to promote Wayne's film while simultaneously working on his score for *The Guns of Navarone*. On November 17, with King Paul and Queen Frederika of Greece in attendance, Tiomkin conducted the Athens' Royal Society of Music Orchestra in a special symphonic arrangement of *The Alamo*. He also visited Italy and Germany to plug the film. The end of the month found him in New York for five days of long-distance interviews and personal appearances.[1356]

Wayne always had intended to release the roadshow version of the film in 35mm for general release. The only question was, when was the appropriate time? The plan was to showcase the film as a premium event with specialized pricing for as long as possible, and then expand distribution. Based on numbers authorized by United Artists executive Seymour Poe, the studio ordered the following Technicolor prints:

Fifty-one 70mm prints (twenty-six for foreign markets)
Fifty 35mm magnetic optical prints
Four hundred fifty 35mm optical prints
Thirty 16mm prints

After Wayne returned to Hollywood he contacted Howard Hawks for advice on the film. In a 1976 interview with Peter Lehman, Hawks explained his reply: "(Duke) put (the film) out, and we were going to go make *Hatari!* He said, 'Howard, I'm going to lose every nickel I've got.' And I said, 'Well, there's one man that can help you. I got this fellow.' (Wayne) said, 'I can sell a picture if you don't try to sell it at advanced prices and reserved seats.' And then I didn't talk about it, just said cut about fifty minutes out of it. So Wayne talked to these fellows, and he said, 'Will you cut that fifty minutes out for me that you told me about?' And I said, 'Yes, but it's going to cost you a whole lot just for a new orchestration.' It cost him six or seven hundred thousand dollars. He re-cut it and made new prints and everything. But he got his money back. Didn't make any." Asked what he thought of Wayne's performance as Crockett, Hawks replied, "Oh, well. I don't think Duke can direct. The less said the better." Paul Helmick, Hawks's assistant director, recalled, "When (the film) was shown to several friends in the business, including Hawks and me, it wasn't very well thought of and Wayne knew it." Asked in 1974 what he thought of the film, Hawks replied with one word, "Bad."[1357]

Producer and agent Charles Feldman claimed, "The day after the (San

Antonio) premiere, I sat in Duke's suite from eleven in the morning until 3:30 p.m., with everyone from United Artists. I spent the entire morning and afternoon going into every phase of the picture and made practically every recommendation for the cutting of the picture. I talked Duke and Birdwell out of cutting the cattle stampede on which Duke fought me and later gave in to me; and it is still in the picture. After the long drawn-out speeches in the first part of the picture and the birthday scene in the second half are now deleted from the picture. At least forty minutes have been taken out." *(Author's note: The only problem with this statement is that Duke flew to New York the morning after the premiere and thus couldn't have met with Feldman. Perhaps the meeting was on a different day).*[1358]

Wayne told author Michael Munn he felt he was forced to make the cuts: "When we premiered the film, everyone said it was too long. I said, 'How can it be too long? It's not as long as *Gone with the Wind*, and that didn't have any action scenes at all.' It was the fucking critics. The left-wing critics on the East Coast—they still had it in for me, and they didn't like the idea I was saying the freedom from dictatorship was bought with blood. They didn't like that I was using *The Alamo* as a metaphor for America, and, although I wanted to show the Mexicans with dignity, it was a warning against anything that stole our freedom, and, yes, that included Communism. They didn't like that. They criticized my politics, not my film. So United Artists said, 'We gotta lose a half an hour.' It broke my heart cutting so much out of my picture. But I know the people liked it. They still do. People tell me they like it. That picture meant more to me—means more to me—than any other picture I made. Or will make."[1359]

Once the decision was made to trim the film's length and speed up distribution, Bill Gilmore recalls how it was done: "The picture had been turned over to Technicolor, the negative and the positive. They literally had started to make prints, and they're making 70mm prints. And we were just wrapping up the show and were ready to move on to another picture, and we got a call from the Batjac office saying that United Artists called Wayne and demanded that the picture be shortened by a half hour. So we wound up going back into the film and go into a new phase of editing, and we dropped a lot of footage; the decision was made to cut almost a half hour out of the road show version." Stuart Gilmore, Bill's father, had already gone on to another project and wasn't available and, because it was felt Bill was too young and inexperienced, Danny Mandell was brought in to do the edits. "I wasn't senior enough," says Bill. "The union wouldn't allow me to do the work since I didn't have enough time in the union. So they hired Danny Mandell, who is an Academy Award guy and he came in. All those 70mm prints were worth a fortune—they were really, really expensive. We had twenty-six reels, I think eighteen were affected. (Each) reel of film section had to be cut into the thirty-seven prints that had already been run off. And, I did all that work myself. I made a lot of overtime. Don't forget that the negative was 65mm. And the dailies were reduced from 65(mm) to 35(mm). S, we cut the film on 35mm. When the picture was turned over to negative cutting, the negative was 65(mm). So they had to be very careful, but they went ahead and cut all the 65mm film to match the 35mm cutting copy that we gave them, and they started to make prints. There was no trimming down, it was just lifts. It was more mechanical than normal editing is. I helped Danny because I knew the film, and he didn't. And we cut it down. Anytime you change picture it changes all the tracks. So then we had to go back on the dubbing stage and re-dub the picture.

"It didn't take anywhere near as long as the first time," Bill adds. "Danny came in, and he executed the shortening of the film, and the taking the lifts out and making obvious cuts for length. So when we finally cut it down to the 160 (minutes), and they cut the negative, what they did was made sections, little sections of film that would cut into the 70mm and cut it down to 160 (minutes). And there would be two or three or four pieces that would be cut into almost every reel. I think I worked out a deal with the head of production there of Batjac to do it for $100 a print. A print took four hours to do the swap; you had to go through all seventeen reels. And you had to do it in 70mm 'cause these prints were to go out in the field. You couldn't have a splice break or anything. As I remember, that's how I furnished my living room. I was working at Paramount, and I'd finish my day job, and I'd go over to (the company)Todd-AO. Every day I'd try to do one print, And, by the way, no one's alive anymore, (so) I can say it . I got so good, once I got the hang of it, I could do a print in like two hours. And $60 an hour in 1960, I did very well. My wife didn't like it, and the kids didn't like it as I was never home, but I was able to make some moonlight money. Todd-AO was where they had 70mm equipment where I could make the cuts. We then had to go back onto the dubbing stage, re-cut the sound effects, re-positioned the music. I'm not sure what else we had to do, but you do what you have to do to make it all work. And, in most cases, sometimes we used new film that had to be put into the negative. Certainly, the soundtrack didn't work on any reel."[1360]

Most, though not all, of the cuts were made in the first half of the film. *(The following comparison is between the 202-minute, 70mm Todd-AO roadshow release and the 161-minute, 35mm general release. All information has been taken from the September 14, 1960, Combined Script Continuity document)*: Elimination of Overture;

**Reel One Part A (**Scene 10): Elimination of Todd-AO title credit. The Todd-AO credit was originally superimposed over the same background painting as Grant's screenplay credit. It read "Produced in Todd-AO. Developed by the AMERICAN OPTICAL COMPANY and MAGNA." The majority of general release prints were made in 35mm CinemaScope, hence, the elimination of the Todd-AO credit. The scene number on each reel is not the same scene number that appears in the script. Each part of each reel began again with Scene 1.

**Reel One Part B** (Scenes 35-44): Elimination of the second half of Bowie's opening conversation with Jethro. Bowie confronts Travis in the street outside his room;

**Reel Two Part A** (Scenes 1-10): Elimination of Bowie being told Travis is in command, Bowie instructs volunteers, Travis sends Bonham to Goliad for help;

**Reel Two Part B** (Scenes 3-15): Elimination of "Jeffersonian" speech to Dickinson, entrance of Mrs. Dickinson bringing coffee;

**Reel Four Part B** (Scenes 26-40): Death of Emil Sand in church basement;

**Reel Five Part A** (Scenes 1-16): Smitty asks Crockett "Is he dead?" "Sort of." Crockett informs Flaca of death of Sand. She falls into Crockett's arms and cries. (Scenes 39-47): Flaca descends staircase, assists Mrs. Guye with fallen belongings from wagon;

**Reel Five Part B** (Scenes 12-14): Powder burn on Smitty's sleeve. Smitty talks about fight. (Scenes 37-40): "Pyrotechnics. What does it mean?";

**Reel Six Part A** (Scenes 32-34): "Old buck, young doe."; Intermission Reel, superimposed over a painting of adobe wall was the word "INTERMISSION." Music in background";

**Reel Seven Part B** (Scenes 10-11): Smitty log sequence. (Scenes 12-25): Bowie and Travis argument on cannon ramp. Scenes 26-30. Bonham reports on Goliad trip;

**Reel Eight Part A** (Scenes 1-6): Travis gives Dickinson's horse to Bonham;

**Reel Nine Part A** (Scenes 22-51): Scouting party discovers cattle, chased by Mexican patrol, deaths of Scotty and Estoyo, Travis sympathizes with Mrs. Estoyo;

**Reel Nine Part B** (Entire reel eliminated.) – (Scene 1): Remainder of previous scene, "There will be no more patrols...." (Scenes 2-8): Arrival of Gonzales reinforcements. (Scene 9): Mrs. Dickinson decorates birthday cake. (Scenes 10-41): Birthday party, singing/dancing; party;

**Reel Eleven Part B** (Scene 71): Beekeeper informs Crockett about Parson's injury;

**Reel Twelve Part A** (Scenes 1-9): Parson's death scene, Crockett speaks to God;

**Reel Thirteen Part A** (Scenes 1-6): Tar and feather discussion with atheist;

**Reel Fourteen Part A** (Scene 27): After Crockett is stabbed and he breaks off a portion of the lance, he staggers out of the doorway, falls back into the door and staggers out again. The first stagger out of the doorway is eliminated in the shorter version; Elimination of EXIT music.[1361]

After flying to Hollywood on November 1 to supervise the editing, Wayne announced the following day that he would remove approximately thirty minutes from his film due to "audience restlessnes". In an attempt to get the film out as soon as possible, Birdwell said the shortened version would be shown in theaters by the end of the week. It had been hoped that the revised version would be available for the next set of premieres and that it would go into existing engagements as soon as possible. According to the braggart, "At last there will be a roadshow to which the family may go without the necessity of putting a baby-sitter under long-term contract." He also said Wayne admitted he was "over sentimental" about Aissa's birthday party sequence, but, in the interest of tightening the film, it would be eliminated to improve the film. ("I guess I got carried away," Wayne admitted, "and forgot I was a producer, not just a father.") Unfortunately, not all were pleased with Birdwell's comments. UA's Roger Lewis had never gotten over his problems with the publicist and was furious that Birdwell had announced the film would be cut. He later told Birdwell, "I note that you recommend that we publicize the fact that we have cut the picture. In my opinion, this is absolute suicide–and every experience in the industry proves it. You can't tell people that they are buying the cut version even if you justify it by saying it has improved the picture. It merely plants the conviction that there was something wrong to begin with, or that they are not getting their money's worth. As long as I have any influence, we'll sell what we have–not what we haven't."[1362]

Nevertheless, during the following several weeks both 70mm and 35mm prints began arriving in numerous cities throughout the country. (A tangential benefit of 70mm releases were the long overdue reconditioning of numerous theaters to accommodate the film, including installation of new projection and sound equipment, larger screens, and refurbished lobbies). The second wave of premieres began on Wednesday, November 9, in Tulsa, Oklahoma City, Toronto, and Montreal. Although Gene Campbell, president of the OKC Press Club, had hoped to have several stars at the premiere, only Chills Wills made it. Wills had arrived several days earlier to appear on local television shows and at the Tuesday night Press Club "Election Party." In his spare time, he also put in a few guest appearances at the State Theater where the film would be shown. Profits from the evening's premiere were used to bring prominent speakers in journalism to the city and to establish a scholarship fund. Wills said he enjoyed working with Wayne "as much as in any movie I have made. I was real excited in working with Wayne. Instead of a man, I think of him as an institution."[1363]

In Toronto, the film premiered at the Famous Players Tivoli. (A benefit sponsored by the Variety Club for its Variety Village School was held the previous evening). As in other cities, festivities included a parade, costumed characters, and a four-horse Texas stagecoach owned by Col. Ted Westervelt of the Lazy JB ranch. The Texas outriders stayed at the Royal York Hotel while their horses settled for the hotel's parking garage. Eventually, the equines were moved to the Woodbine racetrack stables. After the premiere, the *Toronto Telegram*'s Clyde Gilmour wrote ho, "…No crystal ball is needed to inspire a prediction that *The Alamo* will be honored more than once when the next Academy Awards are being handed out in Hollywood." But Gerald Pratley of the *Toronto Daily Star* wasn't as kind: "As entertainment, it is some and tiresome . and padded with trivial details. Shakespeare would have soared to great heights with such a tale, but Wayne . and Grant seldom rise above the Texas dust. Wayne's direction is often clumsy, awkward, and broken. It is a pity this heroic stand which turned into such slaughter has been compromised by half-truths, distortions, (and) feeble entertainment values."[1364]

The Quebec branch of the Canadian Picture Pioneers sponsored Montreal's premiere. Held at the Seville Theatre with red carpet, floral decorations, klieg lights, and Crockett-costumed doormen, three Montreal radio stations covered the affair: CFCF and CKGM for English-language listeners and CKVL for French. Interviews were conducted before and after the presentation and were played back throughout the week following the opening.[1365]

But even less-than-favorable reviews failed to stem audience enthusiasm—they still packed the movie houses. And with the increased number of prints in general release, Wayne began seeing a corresponding increase in revenue. In cities like Chicago, where the film drew less than expected at the premium-priced Palace, it was very successful at the regularly-priced Roosevelt. Critics may not have liked the film, but audiences loved it, And some even felt the negative reviews were not indicative of the film's quality but rather, a plot against Wayne. Supposedly, Communists and their supporters were circulating the rumor that Duke's film was a "box-office flop"–even the critics said so. In 1961, screenwriter Borden Chase told reporter Thomas B. Morgan, "When *The Alamo* was coming out, the word of mouth on it was that it was a dog. This was created by the Communists to get at Wayne. Then, there were some bad reviews inspired by the Communists. Of course, I wouldn't say that all criticism of *The Alamo* was Communist inspired, but some of these movie reviewers, who are only liberals, have some best pals who are Communist–now, these reviewers don't know that the pals are Communists, and so they are influenced by them. This is why some of them said it was a dog. It's a typical Communist technique, and they were using it against Duke for what he did in MPA." The reason? Over the years Communists had destroyed such anti-Communists as Joe McCarthy and blacklisted others as well. Wayne consistently ranked among the top ten box-office draws, so now was the time to defeat the biggest flag-waver of them all. When asked about Chase's comments during his famous/infamous *Playboy* interview, all Duke could say was, "There's always a little truth in everything you hear. The Alliance thing was used pretty strongly against me in those days."[1366]

Sadly, Wayne wasn't able to enjoy the audience response as much as he could have. Unfortunately, Ward Bond, Duke's close friend and fellow actor, died of a heart attack in Dallas on November 5. Bond was in town for a Dallas Cowboys-Los Angeles Rams football game and had recently remarked he was "very tired" and wasn't feeling well of late. As a result, he had been given three weeks off from *Wagon Train* to rest and recuperate. He had a history of cardiac issues, and left the series for a short period two years earlier because of the same condition. He and his wife Maisie had checked into the Town House Motor Hotel, and Ward wanted to freshen up with a shower before the game. While on the toilet, he suffered a massive heart attack, fell against the bathroom door, and wedged it shut. Unable to open it on her own, his wife ran for help. By the time it arrived, Bond was dead. When Ken Curtis notified Pappy on location in Brackettville on *Two Rode Together*, Ford momentarily fell silent, then shouted, "Son of a bitch!" He exclaimed, "The doctor told him! The doctor told him over and over again! For months and months, he'd been warned!" Then, he looked up at Andy Devine, who was standing nearby. "You're gonna have to be my horse's ass now. Ward just died." He then called a three-minute halt in production to honor the memory of his old friend. Pappy flew to Dallas over the weekend along with Curtis and Dobe Carey, met Maisie, and arranged the transport of the body. Curtis and Dobe continued on to Los Angeles to coordinate Ward's funeral arrangements. Bond would lie in state at the chapel of the Field Photo Memorial Homes in Reseda until funeral services were held on November 7. Flags were lowered to half-mast as mourners filed past a flag-draped casket with uniformed honor guard. As Pappy flew back to Brackettville to continue filming (stand-ins would be used for Curtis and Dobe), Mary Ford attended the funeral in his absence. Pallbearers Frank McGrath, Terry Wilson, Curtis, and Duke carried the casket to the parade ground; Curtis, Dobie, and The Sons of the Pioneers sang several tunes. Wayne delivered the eulogy: "He (Bond) blew many a part by standing up and saying what he thought." (Years earlier, Bond had bought a beautiful new shotgun that a jealous Wayne asked to borrow. Ward was said to reply, "Over my dead body." However, on a hunting trip near Hemet, California, Bond acquiesced, but then Duke accidentally shot Bond in the backside. Ward explained, "Four or five of us had gone up into the San Bernardino Mountains, and Duke, who had no shotgun, borrowed my twenty-gauge. We were strung out in a line, with Wayne on a ridge above me, in brush so high, it was almost impossible to see each other. I had turned my back to the ridge and was starting down into the valley, when Duke flushed a covey of quail and let go with the shotgun. I got the charge in my shoulders, arms, and the back of my head, and, for a moment, I thought my skull was gone. I let out a yell, and Duke rushed down. I was afraid to have him take off my cap; I thought I was already dead and only dreaming of what had happened. The shock was so great I actually sat down in a bed of cactus and didn't even begin to feel those needles until I was in the hospital." Duke threw him over his shoulder and carried Bond out of the woods to a local town where they bought a quart of bourbon and poured a slug into him. Doctors then removed sixty buckshot from Bond's backside. When asked if it was his fault, Wayne said, "Sure, I shot him. How else could I tell what pattern the shells were making?" Bond got in the last laugh, though. He bequeathed Wayne the shotgun that nearly killed him.) Duke was present when Bond's ashes were scattered over the waves in the channel between San Pedro and Catalina. A provision in Ward's will instructed he should be buried at sea as "I loved lobster all my life, and I want to return the favor."[1367]

The last official *Alamo* promotional event for the year was *Pontiac Star Parade's* November 14 airing of *The Spirit of the Alamo* on ABC, pre-empting *Adventures in Paradise*. Though entertaining, many newspaper and trade papers still called it just another extended plug for the film. *Variety* praised Tiomkin's music, saying the special wasn't completely lacking in entertainment value, but other than that, it was all "drumbeat, publicity style...it was...an exploration of the $13,000,000 investment in exposed film and its meaning to anticipated distribution revenues." *The Chicago Tribune* called it "appallingly bad...a one-hour pitch...interrupted only by what might be called sub-commercials for an auto manufacturer." *UPI* opined Wayne "said everything they had to say in the first three minutes and spent the rest of the hour repeating it." But, it wasn't a total loss. Said columnist Fred Danzig, "I saw Frankie Avalon work and the girls in the audience merely applauded. I guess they were so busy remembering the Alamo that they plumb forgot to scream."[1368]

A *Box Office* editorial written by Ivan Spear questioned the value of the television promotion. On one hand, Spear stated, "the video show can be considered a gigantic trailer for the motion picture (which) will generate an additional must-see urge among ticket-buyers." On the other hand, "the postage-stamp size of the television screens failed by a country mile to do justice to the scope, photography, spectacle, and sweep that contribute so much to making *The Alamo* a milestone motion picture." Whether the telecast would stimulate or deter ticket sales was a subject of debate. Data suggests that although the film generally opened strong, after several weeks it would usually tail off to relatively normal levels. To take advantage of Wayne's popularity, some distributors resorted to counter-programming. Given the huge *Alamo* promotional campaign, theaters would program other Wayne films at the same time *The Alamo* was showing, hoping to draw in collateral interest; in some cities, an extremely upset Duke found himself in competition with *Angel and the Badman*, *Sands of Iwo Jima*, *She Wore a Yellow Ribbon*, *North to Alaska*, and even *Jet Pilot*. No wonder *The Alamo* didn't generate *Ben-Hur* revenue ($40 million its first year). In fact, *North To Alaska* turned in the biggest holdover record for any Twentieth Century-Fox release in 1960. In just over one month, the film had grossed over $2 million![1369]

A financial comparison of the film's revenue in its initial release proved extremely interesting. In Chicago, *The Alamo's* receipts during its fifth week of release amounted to $18,500 while *North To Alaska*, shown the same week, totaled over $29,500. *Butterfield 8* starring Elizabeth Taylor generated $40,000 and even *Spartacus* in its seventh week brought in $26,000 during the same time frame. In Pittsburgh, *Ben-Hur* still brought in over $21,500 after its forty-fifth week while Elvis Presley's *GI Blues* totaled $15,000! In New York, *Butterfield 8* generated $73,000 while *The World of Suzie Wong* (including stage show) brought in a massive $135,000–all during the same week! And *Exodus*, in its first week at New York's Warner Theatre, brought in a massive $49,000. (By its fourth week, *Exodus* still racked up an amazing $48,799!) So, while *The Alamo*'s returns were respectable, by no means were they on the order of what was expected. On the average, after two months, *The Alamo*'s weekly receipts declined anywhere from 25-30% from its opening week, and, in some cases, more than 50%! Regardless of its domestic return, *The Alamo* did very well in foreign markets–at the Stockholm Ritz Theatre, it outgrossed every film in the history of the house, including *Around the World in 80 Days* and *Solomon and Sheba*. Having said that, *The Alamo* still ranks #14 in the top western box-office draws of all-time (adjusted receipts) behind *Butch Cassidy and the Sundance Kid*, *How The West Was Won*, *Dances With Wolves*, *Duel in the Sun*, *True Grit* (1969), *Little Big Man*, *True Grit* (2011), *Shane*, *Unforgiven*, *Django Unchained*, *Maverick*, *Wild Wild West*, and *The Outlaw*.[1370]

In late November 1960, Duke returned to Rome to work on arrangements for *The Alamo*'s premiere at the Royal Theater the following February. However, before he arrived, he spent a weekend in New York promoting his film. Dorothy Kilgallen guessed Wayne as the *What's My Line* mystery guest after only three questions. But that was OK because he just wanted to talk about *The Alamo* anyway. He also appeared on the *Ed Sullivan Show* and taped a spot on Jack Benny's program as well. On November 14, Wayne and Birdwell left for Paris. But before they arrived, they stopped in London for a reception thrown by UA at the Savoy. John Cutts, the London correspondent for *Films and Filming*, had written a scathing review of *The Alamo*, and when Wayne was introduced to him by a publicity hack, he was furious. "Cutts?" he said as he glared at the writer. "You wrote that review, didn't you? I've got a good mind to knock your teeth in." Cutts, tall and stout, though not as tall as Duke, stood trembling as Wayne clenched his fists. "Mr. Wayne. You are perfectly at liberty to knock me down," he replied. "However, I feel I must warn you that I shall get up and hit you as hard as I can, and perhaps we shall both get rather badly bruised." Wayne, amused and impressed by the Brit's chutzpah, decided to forgive and forget. He put out his hand and, as they shook, said, "Let's forget about the whole thing." Duke got even, though. He coerced Cutts to have a shot of 108 proof Wild Turkey bourbon![1371]

Immediately upon Duke's arrival in Paris, he was asked by Brigitte Bardot's producer if Wayne would like to make a film with her. "I'd love to change my ten-gallon hat for a beret and put her in a western saddle," he said. "When do we start?" As usual, Duke took time to chat with local reporters and promote the film. Accompanied by a translator, Duke expressed his long-held desire to direct: "As a matter of fact, I've been a producer for about fifteen years. But the important thing in our business, in my mind, is to be a director because that's the creative side of our business. And I was very happy to put on the three hats in order to get this job. When I started in the business, I wanted to be a director, but they gave me so much money as an actor that I couldn't afford to quit. And this is my first opportunity to get in on the creative side of pictures." He was then asked why he chose the story of the Alamo as his first test. "Well, first you have to have a story that will attract the attention of the people who put up the money. So, we had a story about Texas, and we went to the Texas oil millionaires and talked to them. And since it was something that they felt was not only good for Texas but for their country, they went along with me."[1372]

Visits were also scheduled for Berlin, Hamburg, Madrid, and Rome where, on November 24, he would have a private audience with Pope John XXIII before continuing on to Africa. According to Maurice Zolotow, Wayne packed his pockets with the medals of St. Christopher, St. Jude, and St. Genesius before meeting the Pope. Supposedly, he told Birdwell he didn't believe in Roman Catholic Church dogma, but that all his children and wives did, and he thus thought maybe his one chance of entering the gates of Heaven was the metallurgical one. (Duke converted to Catholicism shortly before he died in June 1979). Interestingly, while in Rome, he ran into columnist Henry McLemore at a café on the Via Veneto and admitted he was very nervous about meeting the Pope as he was afraid he'd blow his lines! He also shared that Princess Margaret seemed pleased with the saddle he'd given her and said she was ten times prettier than in her photos. Wayne confessed, "The audience granted me by Pope John XXIII turned out to be hilarious and somewhat mysterious, too. His Holiness doesn't speak English. I don't speak Italian, and the Irish priest who acted as (the) interpreter laughed uproariously throughout our meeting!" Ironically, the hero of *The High and the Mighty* also couldn't get a flight to Africa. "There are all sorts of flights out of here to the place," Wayne said, "but all the seats are taken. I thought I'd have a plane to myself. Who goes to Tanganyika? Why all the rush to (get) there? You happen to know anyone who happens to sell seats to Tanganyika under the counter?"[1373]

By the end of the year, *The Alamo* had been released in twenty-four different cities, among them:

Paris, France (Richelieu and Ambassador, 12/21/60),
Boston (Gary, 12/23/60),
Buffalo (Teck, 12/23/60),
Cincinnati (Valley, 12/23/60),
Cleveland (Ohio, 12/23/60),
Pittsburgh (Warner, 12/23/60),
Washington, D.C. (Warner Uptown, 12/23/60),
Miami Beach (Roosevelt, 12/26/60),
Stockholm (Ritz, 12/26/60),

Osaka (Namba D and New O.S., 12/31/60), and
Tokyo (Milano Za, Pantheon, and Togeki). A seventy-five-foot sign of
Wayne in costume was mounted over the Pantheon marquee.

As with Wayne, several of the film's co-stars showed up at the various releases:
Avalon was guest of honor at the Washington, D.C. premiere sponsored by the
Texas Women's League, while music critics from France, Luxembourg, Belgium,
and Switzerland honored Tiomkin at a special screening in Paris. In preparation
for the continental premieres, Tiomkin's "The Green Leaves of Summer" was
released in four different languages–French, Danish, German and Italian.[1374]

Some engagements would run only six or seven weeks, others as long as
twenty-six. (Cleveland, Buffalo, and Pittsburgh were on a continuous performance
basis). Even with pre-Christmas shopping activities and bad weather, total
receipts approached almost $2 million by the end of December; by mid-January
it reached $2.5 million, But it could have been better. In Houston, two small-
time crooks robbed the Tower theatre of its nightly take. Fortunately, the night
watchman who had been tied up escaped his bonds and notified the police of an
attempted robbery. As the K-9 unit arrived, the burglars escaped with a grand
total of…$40.[1375]

Birdwell's one-year publicity contract on *The Alamo* had expired December
9, 1960. All of the film's promotional activities would now be turned over to
UA's Roger Lewis, who must have been more than pleased to see the end of
both Birdwell's massive spending spree and his novel-length, contentious
memorandums…but the publicist's involvement in the film wasn't yet finished.
Less than two weeks later, following a telephone conversation he had while
working on location in *Hatari!*, Wayne announced Birdwell would steer *The
Alamo*'s Oscar nomination campaign. The 1960 Academy Awards were thought
to be a wide-open race without any overwhelming favorite poised to sweep the
awards as did *Ben-Hur* the previous year. Given the continued praise of selected
critics within the motion picture industry and the film's strong West Coast
showing, it was only natural to expect *The Alamo* would be the recipient of such
honors, And, of course, anything Birdwell could do to "grease the skids" to a win,
so to speak, would prove beneficial.[1376]

Russell Juarez Birdwell was a veteran motion-picture publicist known for
his flamboyancy and outrageous exploitation stunts. Originally a reporter for the
Hearst newspaper syndicate, he covered Charles Lindbergh's takeoff for Paris
in 1927. In one of his many stunts after he broke into show business, Birdwell
stoked the flames of Rudolf Valentino mania by hiring an actress who, while
mysteriously dressed in black and driven by a chauffeur to the gates of Hollywood
Cemetery, would alight, place red roses on Valentino's tomb, and silently depart.
After directing a few shorts, Birdwell became director of publicity for David O.
Selznick and, in February 1939, opened Russell Birdwell and Associates with

offices in Beverly Hills and New York. His greatest success probably was the three-year nationwide search for an actress to play Scarlett O'Hara in *Gone With the Wind*, which featured endless opportunities for hype and gossip. However, his most infamous campaign featured Jane Russell's cleavage in Howard Hughes's *The Outlaw*—a film that made pin-ups ubiquitous. Hughes scandalized the industry as he flaunted the Production Code and focused on Russell's breasts. Hollywood legend says Hughes used his engineering expertise to design a cantilevered underwire bra to enhance her already-generous assets. Curved structural steel rods embedded in the brassiere's cups served to push her breasts upward and thereby emphasize her bosom even more. Said Russell, "Howard invented a bra for me. Or he tried to. It was like one of the seamless ones they have now. But I never wore it in *The Outlaw*, and he never knew. He wasn't going to take my clothes off to check if I had it on. I just told him I did." Ever tactful, Birdwell even had skywriters create two large circles in the heavens...with two dots in the center. Then he advertised, "Here are two good reasons to see *The Outlaw*." He also surreptitiously created a false campaign to have the film banned due to its sexual nature, thereby generating increased demand for its release. If he could create such a frenzied campaign for Hughes, he certainly could push *The Alamo* into the Oscar's winner circle.[1377]

Birdwell was of the publicity school that believed an Academy Award could be bought—not by cash payoffs, mind you—but through huge sums invested in relentless propaganda. Through the effective use of promotional brainwashing, voters could be persuaded to cast a winning vote for a particular film. Although it wasn't officially announced until late December, Birdwell had already notified his staff in mid-November that "Chances are we may renew on *The Alamo* account, but this will not be determined for a few days...it will now be necessary to curtail the expenses." During Wayne's European promotional trip later that month, Duke agreed Birdwell would renew his contract, but news of it had to remain quiet for a few weeks. However, immediately, upon his return to the States, Birdwell began a clandestine campaign. To give the impression he no longer worked for Wayne, Birdwell sent out 2,000 copies of the following notification to selected editors, reporters, and columnists: "All of You. Our one-year publicity and advertising assignment on John Wayne's *The Alamo* has come to an end. Your unprecedented interest in this extraordinary production has made 1960 one of the happiest business years of our lives." *(Even in his supposed termination, he couldn't help but pump up the publicity).* "The press and electronic media, in many instances, have stated that *The Alamo* has become the biggest motion picture news story of all time. For this, we thank you and John Wayne. We feel confident that the releasing company, now assuming the responsibility for advertising and publicity on *The Alamo*, will continue to maintain this news and prestige momentum. With any worthy product, an inspired and stimulating campaign must be sustained to insure the ultimate in success. We feel certain you will continue to support this splendid film achievement. John Wayne joins me and my staff in expressing our sincere thanks to you and yours. Russell Birdwell."[1378]

On December 14, in a letter to one of his associates, Birdwell laid out key dates for the campaign:

> February 2, ballots mailed for acting, directing, writing, and best picture.
> February 13, ballots mailed for art direction, cinematography, costume design, film editing, and music.
> Depending upon the category, voting ended on either February 14 or February 21. And, no matter which category one was concerned about:
> February 27, all nominations were announced.
> March 17, final ballots were mailed.
> April 3, voting ended.
> April 17, presentation of Academy Awards.

Birdwell had returned to his Beverly Hills office after spending two months in New York and Europe. While abroad, he signed affiliate public relations offices to represent his organization in London, Paris, and Rome. Now that he was back home, it was time to get serious. Given the limited time available, the endlessly resourceful Birdwell mounted a full-court press on the Academy's attention and patriotism. To win, one had to be nominated, which really wasn't that difficult. Out of a total 1960 Academy membership of 2,354 individuals, two hundred were publicists and executives for large public relations companies. Another two hundred were studio executives, one hundred were administrators, 150 were producers, 250 were writers, 150 were directors, 175 were "at large" members, 125 made short subjects, and the rest were actors. And, only 40-50 percent of the membership could really be counted on to vote. While each craft nominated its own (directors nominate directors, costume designers nominate costume designers, etc.), all Academy members voted for Best Picture nominees. Members each listed their five choices as first, second, third, fourth and fifth. According to author Peter Brown in *The Real Oscar*, studios perfected a system that limited the number of quality films in competition: "If you were a studio insider…you knew that you could put your guy first, then list four completely hopeless choices as two through five. Your man got five votes instead of one." So, that was the first step. All one had to do was to push box office over art, emotion over substance. Said Henry Rogers, founder of Rogers and Cowan Public relations and a veteran of dozens of successful Oscar campaigns, "A few hundred votes, and sometimes as few as twenty-five or fifty, one way or the other, could determine the winner. The Academy Awards are more of a popularity contest than a talent contest. Whether Hollywood likes to face up to it or not, the voter casts his ballot emotionally, and not critically. Unable to decidd which performance he feels is best, he allows his emotions to take over–he has no choice." According to a Paramount publicist,

761

"...some pictures HAVE to get an Oscar to make it in the marketplace. That's a dangerous situation. When a film has to win in order to make back its costs, some of us will have to do everything short of killing to get them." Author Raymond Chandler, famous for *The Big Sleep*, *Farewell, My Lovely*, and many others, further explained, "(The awards) are not decided by the use of whatever artistic and critical wisdom Hollywood may happen to possess. Instead, they are bally-hooed, pushed, yelled, screamed, and in every way propagandized into the consciousness of the voters so incessantly in the weeks before the final balloting that everything except the golden aura of the box office is forgotten." Of course, *The Alamo* didn't necessarily fall into that category; it had a decent script, three strong principal actors, achingly beautiful photography, magnificent battle scenes, and the public loved it. But, a little push to the Academy voters couldn't hurt.[1379]

So, on December 27, couched in an air of respectability and honor, a full-page ad appeared in *Variety*. Superimposed over a photo of the Alamo with the now iconic promotion "The Mission that Became a Fortress–The Fortress that Became a Shrine," Birdwell appealed to Hollywood's sense of tradition:

"Note: To Academy Voters –

"The industry's highest honor–its approving pat on the back for a dedicated piece of work – is summed up in the golden statuette of The Academy of Motion Picture Arts and sciences, affectionately known as Oscar.

"A few, in days gone by, have disdained this form of Hollywood Knighthood; one or two have rejected it, but these are incidents to be written off to perversity or to misguided 'showmanship.'

"Many of those who have given their hearts to this industry believe it is right and proper to speak up forthrightly about their dreams without attempting to devise an oblique or indirect approach in the hopes of winning an Oscar vote.

"If men seeking the Presidency of the United States can be understood and admired for stating frankly and uninhibitedly, 'I want your vote,' then there is no reason why men and women devoted to the fine art of film entertainment should be less timid in expressing their hopes and aspirations.

"Hollywood has many excellent productions deserving of your nominations in many categories.

"Among these productions is *The Alamo* which is representing the industry with respectability and dignity, without sacrificing its great entertainment values.

"Respectability and dignity are pretty good things to be spreading around right now; not a bad public relations contribution from Hollywood to a world that is becoming unglued.

762

"Perhaps the Oscar should say something more this year than it has ever said before.

"In 1961, through the Oscar, Hollywood can say: 'We were born of respectability and dedication and love of country and belief in our industry.'"

(This ad would be repeated in the January 9, 1961, and February 8, 1961, issues of *The Hollywood Reporter*. In fact, throughout the campaign, various ads would appear multiple times in both trade papers for maximum exposure, just not on the same day.)[1380]

With a combination of compliments, rationalization, history, and outright begging, Birdwell began an outrageous Academy Award campaign that would forever change the ways Oscars would be won and lost. In the same *Variety* issue, Birdwell pressed Oscar on all fronts and suggested *The Alamo* be nominated in fifteen categories: Best Picture, Best Director, Best Story & Screenplay, Best Actor, Best Supporting Actor, Best Supporting Actress, Best Song, Best Score, Best Cinematography–Color, Best Film Editing, Best Art Direction–Color, Best Costume Design–Color, Best Special Effects, Best Sound Recording, and Best Set Direction–Color. Under each category, Birdwell placed numerous well-chosen comments culled from the nation's newspapers:

> Best Picture ——"The greatest saga of battle ever put on the screen." Harrison Carroll, *L.A. Herald & Express*.
>
> Best Director ——"producer and director as well as star, Wayne has done a magnificent job." Rose Pelswick, *New York Journal-American*.
>
> Best Actor ——"When you get right down to cases, Richard Widmark may wrap up the Oscar." *Paul Hochuli, Houston Press*.
>
> Best Supporting Actor ——"Chill Wills is a runaway for supporting actor award. No one is near him." *Jimmy Starr, Los Angeles Herald & Express*.
>
> Best Supporting Actress ——"Three inimitable performances of Oscar dimension are contributed by the talented trinity–Linda Cristal, Joan O'Brien and Veda Ann Borg." Harold Heffernan, *NANA*.[1381]

(Birdwell's organization wasn't the only one to promote the film. UA placed an ad in the December 14 and 19 issues of *The Hollywood Reporter* that praised Tiomkin's and Webster's musical efforts: "United Artists *joins the critics in applauding* Dimitri Tiomkin's *brilliant score for* The Alamo *and congratulates* Mr. Tiomkin and Paul Francis Webster *on the unprecedented number of recordings of their big, hit song* 'The Green Leaves of Summer.'" Columbia placed its own ad in the January 3, 1961, issue of the same trade paper: "Let me write the songs of a Nation and I care not who makes its Laws! Dimitri Tiomkin did not say this–BUT HE COULD DO IT!" The ad also included endorsements from Jimmy Starr of the *LA Herald & Express* and Jack Moffitt of *Limelight*. Tiomkin's competition was thought to include: *Facts of Life, North To Alaska, The Second Time Around, Pepe,* and *Never On Sunday*).[1382]

And on and on ad nauseam, Birdwell would send a barrage of advertising the likes of which the Academy had never seen. Wayne had previously said, "Nobody should come to see this movie unless he believes in heroes." Some critics got the message, others, not so much. Said the *Southern California Prompter*, "If he is saying is what America needs is about 10 million men with the courage and determination of Davy Crockett, Jim Bowie and Colonel Travis, the point is well taken. It may also occur to some he is suggesting that the easy answer to today's complex problems is to pit this raw courage against Russia's 10 million Santa Annas, the result of which may be a worldwide Alamo, and, instead of a shrine, we may have only a cosmic incinerator full of ashes. If this is what Wayne is proposing, the defenders of the Alamo were not only brave but smarter than those who speak for them. Their fate was extinction, but this was not their purpose." Producer Samuel Goldwyn reportedly said, "If Duke wanted to send a message, he should have used Western Union." According to author Ronald Davis, Wayne admitted, "My politics interfered with the fucking critics on that one." The movie was "a damned good picture" with "nothing in it political at all." Wayne claimed that reviewers failed to understand that he wasn't for Travis and Houston and the rest of the Texans; it was *freedom* he favored. And, as Pilar says, "Duke forgot an important principle in filmmaking–people don't go to the movies to be lectured, they go to be entertained." Ken Curtis agreed: "Duke's mistake was in giving Birdwell a free hand. In fact, his mistake was in hiring Birdwell in the first place. Birdwell's greatest success was in selling Jane Russell's breasts. But selling *The Alamo* was different. We all know Duke made the film as a patriotic statement, but that wasn't the angle to sell the public. They wanted action, romance, and comedy. They didn't want to be told that if they were patriots, they would see *The Alamo*, and that's what Birdwell's publicity campaign said. It was in poor taste, and it upset–well, not so much the public–it got the media's back up. That's why I think the critics went for it in such a savage way; they were like hounds tearing a doe apart. They just didn't give it a chance." Even Harvey was aghast at the ferocity of the attacks: "The critics were most unkind about just about everything to do with the film, which I understand was something of a backlash against Wayne's politics. I mean, they absolutely tore him and the film apart. I couldn't understand why it was criticized so vehemently."[1383]

Wayne was worried. Forced to shorten his film's running time just two weeks after its initial release due to both critical and audience response, he knew his only chance to make any profit was to win an Oscar. Official recognition from the Academy would go a long way toward recouping his investment and further cementing his reputation as an industry heavyweight. according to Pilar, he, however, really didn't care if *his* work received any recognition: "He hoped William Clothier's cinematography, Dimitri Tiomkin's score, Widmark's performance, and James Grant's script would get the merit they merited." However, if Duke won not only would he receive the prestige associated with an Academy Award, the film would receive the obligatory box-office bump. What better way than to court the press and critics who vote in the pre-Oscar contest. Wayne and Birdwell couldn't be worried about the East Coast liberal press; they would focus on the Hollywood trade papers.[1384]

Still, Wayne couldn't be too disappointed with the financial returns. On January 3, 1961, while on the *Hatari!* location in Tanganyika, he received the following Western Union wire: "First six days *Alamo* Tokyo Osaka all time house records for all five theaters. Paris two theaters first week exceeds *80 Days* and *Solomon Sheba*. Stockholm first four days exceeds *Solomon Sheba* (and) *80 Days*. Domestic business excellent during holiday period inclusive seven new openings." (*The Alamo* had out-grossed every UA film in the history of the Ritz Theater in Sweden). In its first three weeks in Tokyo and Osaka, it was also the biggest early-earner of any picture in Japan's history. The Woodlawn reported "the best Christmas week ever recorded for a reserved seat attraction in San Antonio."

Previously, both Wayne and Birdwell had made the ridiculous claim that *The Alamo* would gross in the neighborhood of $100 million! Grant was so enamored with this preposterous assertion that in May 1960, he suggested Batjac "write a letter of agreement stating that I am not to receive my percentage payments faster than fifty thousand dollars per year. Done now, there can be no tax beefs later. This will give Batjac an untaxed fund that will eventually amount to an asset of millions." As the foreign returns started to roll in, Grant must have felt he had made a very wise decision.[1385]

With that type of reaction, Duke now had a decent chance to win several Oscars…*if* he had an effective promotional campaign. On January 5, 1961, Birdwell published a list of scheduled advertising for *The Hollywood Reporter*. The same ads would also appear in various issues of *Variety*. Obviously, many of the ads had already been formatted as the list referred to ads previously published in 1960.[1386]

12/29/60 – 1 full page (*Sons & Lovers* and *The Alamo*).
12/30/60 – 1 column x 7 inches (Academy invitation).
01/03/61 – 1 column x 7 inches (Academy invitation).
01/09/61 – 3 pages (Note to *Alamo* voters).
01/09/61 – 1 column x 7 inches (*Alamo* invites).
01/12/61 – 2 vertical half-pages (Starr & Hooper quotes).
01/19/61-02/02/61 – 2 column x 1 inch (Remember the Alamo).
01/23/61 – 2 horizontal half-pages (Series of quotes).

02/01/61 – 3 pages (Tombstone.").
02/02/61 – 2 column x 1 inch (Vote for *The Alamo*).
02/03/61 – 2 horizontal half-pages (Series of quotes).
02/07/61 – 1 page (page 5, American Classic).[1387]

## CHAPTER THIRTY-FOUR
## WAR OF THE WORDS

THE FOLLOWING DAY, BIRDWELL SENT A LETTER TO ROGER LEWIS, SUGGESTING UA fund the Oscar campaign for *The Alamo*. He said, in part, "As you know, John Wayne is personally picking up the tab and cost of this new (Academy Award) campaign, and I am wondering if United Artists on its own has set aside a budget in behalf of their pictures which are up for academy consideration. If so, you may be assured that we will be happy to partake of the budget and to use same in behalf of *The Alamo*. It seems like a sensible idea because if *The Alamo* receives what it deserves, United Artists, too, would be a beneficiary." Despite asking for UA's assistance, Birdwell then went on to blast the studio for not adequately supporting Wayne's film: "It has been very sad to stand by and watch *The Alamo* go into obscurity during the past few weeks....It has been my driving objective during my one year association not to let this happen to *The Alamo*... Nor have I seen any advertisements quoting Hedda Hopper that "*The Alamo* is one of the best five motion pictures of the year–a motion picture that will live for one hundred years.' Nor have I seen any advertisements that *The Alamo* is a contender for the Academy Award nomination–phrases that are being attributed to many other films including some that are being handled by United Artists." Why would Birdwell insult Lewis while at the same time asking for his support and money?[1388]

No matter. After putting up with Birdwell's arrogance, insolence, pettiness and obnoxiousness for over a year, Lewis had had enough. He could turn his cheek and ignore Birdwell's thinly veiled sarcasm, but that wasn't his style. On January 11, Lewis replied with both barrels blasting: "This is a letter I tried for over a year NOT to write, but your letter of January 6th is just a little too much to ignore or swallow ... So sit back, fasten your seat belt and let's have a little fact with our fantasy for a change." Lewis went on to refute all of Birdwell's accusations with sarcasm of his own: "This is sheer unadulterated bull, and you know it. Obviously, you feel that without your master touch, nothing good can happen. This may salve your ego, but does not square with the record... On those occasions, when someone had the temerity to protest or suggest that there might be a more practical or sensible approach, you lashed out with bitter accusation or scathing indictment...Did it or does it occur to you that perhaps you did something wrong? Do you dismiss the public response to the 'image' you projected as an unimportant detail?...I could go on and on, but I believe the record speaks for itself to anyone who cares to examine it...I must make it clear that I cannot and will not work with you on the old basis nor will I tolerate any longer the kind of assaults on the people in my organization that you have perpetuated in the past." *(For those interested in reading more of this interesting exchange, please refer to page 145 of Clark & Andersen).*[1389]

Lewis copied his reply to fifteen individuals at Batjac and United Artists. He also informed everyone that UA did not have a specific budget for *The Alamo* and that Birdwell's antics could have a negative effect on all UA Oscar-worthy productions. For that reason, Lewis added, "I am most concerned about your plans and hope you will consult with someone at Batjac before proceeding on any activities. The time for secrecy is also past..." Perhaps Birdwell took these comments to heart, but probably not. Still, his *Alamo* Oscar campaign started out respectable and relatively low-keyed, which was probably the plan: Lull the Academy into a false sense of security, then blast it with both barrels. However, with only six weeks left before all votes were cast, Birdwell remained relentless in his promotions. A new ad would appear virtually every day in the trade papers:

*December 30, 1960* ——*The Hollywood Reporter.* "*The Alamo* invited Academy Members of these branches: art directors, cinematographers, costume designers, film editors, Musicians, Set directors to be our guests at Carthay Circle. Present Academy Card at Box Office for Reserved Seats." This ad was repeated again on January 3, 1961, to give potential voters the maximum number of opportunities to view the film before they voted.

*December 31, 1960* ——*Variety.* Full-page ad. "*Sons and Lovers* and *The Alamo* (in that order). Named Top Films of 1960–By the Committee on Exceptional Films of the National Board of review of Motion Pictures, Henry Hart,

Chairman." Short, simple, factual, to the point, this ad also appeared in *The Hollywood Reporter* on December 29.

*January 4, 1961* ——*Variety's* 55th anniversary issue. A full-page ad with red *Alamo* "A" and the iconic slogan: "The Mission that Became a Fortress —— The Fortress that Became a Shrine." Again, nothing offensive or in poor taste.

*January 4* ——*Variety*. One half-page ad. "John Wayne–The public will not only 'Remember the Alamo' (as it has for 124 years) but when Academy Award time comes it will remember John Wayne as the producer, director, actor and patriot who has recalled this inspiring event in American history at a time when its example is most needed." Jack Moffitt (screenwriter). Another safe, non-controversial request for nomination.

*January 9* ——*Variety*. Two vertical half-page ads. "Hedda Hopper names *The Alamo* one of the Top Films of 1960! *The Alamo* Named Top film of 1960 by Jimmy Starr." Birdwell began to enlist the support of selected newspaper critics and columnists to endorse Wayne and the film. (This ad also appeared in the January 10 and February 9 issues of *The Hollywood Reporter*).

*January 9* ——*The Hollywood Reporter*. "*The Alamo* invites directors, producers, writers and All Academy Members with their friends to be our guests at Carthay Circle. Present Academy Card at Box Office for Reserved Seats." On January 12 and January 30, this ad would be modified to include "All Members of Industry Crafts." There would be no excuse for Academy voters to be uninformed about potential contenders. It had been said in the past that "a good deal of the Oscar balloting was not entirely fair and objective because many voters had not seen the pictures but were filling out their ballots on the basis of hearsay, friendship for contenders or for some other reasor besides their honest judgment arrived at after seeing the pictures themselves." This year, in addition to return engagements, special screenings were held at studios, in private projection rooms, and even in homes of actors and executives.[1390]

*January 13* ——*The Hollywood Reporter*. One vertical half-page ad. "John (Duke) Wayne rides tall and easy among that band of leathery men who won the West for Hollywood. After thirty years of making 150 pictures that have grossed more than 300 million dollars, Duke seems in no danger of being unhorsed by a new generation of virile young tenderfeet. Wayne has the personality and character of an old cavalry boot–weathered, tough and unpolished–and roughly handsome. And like an old boot he seems to wear better and become more highly prized with time and hard use. In contrast with his image as an unschooled, rough-hewn frontiersman, Wayne is a man of exceptional intelligence and scholarly background. 'When I came into this business I had to learn how to say 'ain't,' he said. 'Now it comes natural.' He was graduated from Glendale High with a 91% average. He wanted to go to Annapolis, but missed an appointment. He was given a scholarship by SC, where he achieved public notice as a football lineman. John Wayne summed himself up this way, win or lose: 'I am six foot four, fifty-three years old, and I have five children, four grandchildren–and I love good whiskey.'——Jack Smith *The Los Angeles Times* of May 29, 1960." Another attempt to humanize Wayne by using columnist endorsement.

Back on December 29, the New York Film Critics Award for the 1960 best picture of the year had been a tie between *The Apartment* and *Sons and Lovers*–the first time since the organization's awards were instituted in 1935 that dual honors had been awarded to an English-language film. A fairly accurate barometer of the eventual Academy Award winner, the critics also awarded dual best director honors to Billy Wilder and Jack Cardiff for the same films. Conspicuous in its absence was any mention of Wayne or *The Alamo*. Wilder took advantage of the occasion to deliver a wonderful monologue on movie critics. "(The press) can be divided into three categories," said the director. "First, there are the morons–they cover about 85 percent! These are the representatives of publications who delude themselves that because they know how many times Ginger Rogers was married or what Jayne Mansfield's dimensions are, this entitles them to explore the broader (no pun intended!) field of criticism. Secondly, there are the critics who write for the highbrow art magazine with a mass circulation of 700! They don't like anything unless it's made abroad–preferably by Ingmar Bergman. If they would only learn the Swedish language and understand what they are seeing, it would be interesting to read their comments then! And finally there are you New York critics here tonight, who really try to be constructive and who endorse American films like *The Apartment* and encourage film making in Hollywood."[1391]

The Committee on Exceptional Films of the National Board of Review of Motion Pictures awarded *Son and Lovers* as the best film of 1960. Similarly, the best picture of the year as awarded by the British Select Film Committee of the International Board of Motion Picture Reviewers was also a tie–this time between *The Angry Silence* and *Psycho*. Again, Wayne and *The Alamo* weren't mentioned. Even the Cleveland Film Critics Circle named *Spartacus* its best film of the year. Birdwell, needing to change his promotional approach if he expected to garner any interest in Duke's masterpiece, decided to steer the campaign in a more aggressive, patriotic direction by calling out the "foreign" nature of the competition. So...

*January 16 – The Hollywood Reporter.* One half-page ad. "*The Alamo* Fought and Filmed in the U.S.A." This was a direct attack against Otto Preminger and *Exodus*. Dalton Trumbo, blacklisted screenwriter from the infamous "Hollywood Ten," was involved in both *Exodus* and *Spartacus*. Birdwell would later solicit the support of Hedda Hopper, William Randolph Hearst,

Jr., and other publishers and columnists in the fight against communism. (This ad also appeared in the January 17 issue of *Variety* and the January 25 issue of *The Hollywood Reporter*).[1392]

*January 18* ——*Variety*. Two half-pages. "We Believe *The Alamo* is deserving of your nomination." Comments from Hedda Hopper, Florabel Muir, Jonah M. Ruddy. "A Picture of the Decade! One of the great motion picture of this decade, *The Alamo* relates in magnificent film terms that courage and gallantry are immortal. And for the millions and multitudes who need inspiration in the battle of life, John Wayne's superb production, *The Alamo* stands monumentally, to say as Colonel David Crockett did in 1836, 'do the best you can.' For in *The Alamo* there is faith and hope and charity." (A not-so-subtle appeal to one's character traits and beliefs, this ad tied together all three aspects of the campaign: Wayne, patriotism, and *The Alamo*. This ad also appeared in the January 23 and February 3 issues of *The Hollywood Reporter*).

*January 19* ——*The Hollywood Reporter*. Placed on virtually a daily basis between January 19 and February 13, was a simple one- by two-inch-column ad that simply said "Remember the Alamo." Interestingly, whether by accident or not, these ads were frequently placed on the same pages as those for *Exodus*.

On January 19, Birdwell enlisted the support of *Limelight*'s columnist Florabel Muir in a full-page ad to further personalize the campaign:

"This is a message about a man. Not a message in the sense that it carries any implication of hidden persuasion, for there is nothing about this man that is not open, clear, uncompromising, for all the world to see, four-square in his strength, integrity, and courage. I'm inspired to set down this appraisal by the recent announcement that once more the name of John Wayne has been included in the roster of the Ten Top Money-making Stars of Motion Pictures–and this is an unprecedented record, for no other star name has so consistently graced the list.

"This is a verdict returned annually by a grass roots poll conducted by the Quigley Publications. It is a verdict from the horse's mouth. No star makes the Top Ten by accident or favoritism. It is a direct echo from that most sensitive of all Hollywood barometers, the box office. There has to be a reason for this year after year expression by the ticket-buyers of their esteem and affection for Duke Wayne. I'll tell you what, in my opinion, the reason boils down to, John Wayne stands for something in the eyes of Hollywood and of the vast motion picture audience in this country and the world. He has come to be a symbol, an image, a label–the prototype of the American heritage. I've known The Duke. I've been a fan of his since the time many years ago when his rugged individuality flashed on the screen in the role of Johnny Ringo, the outlaw with both heart and guts who dominated John Ford's memorable award-winning film *Stagecoach*.

771

"Heart and guts have been The Duke's trademark in all the years between. Heart and guts are the main ingredients of his popular appeal. Similarly, heart and guts are the ruling influences in his private life–his relations with co-workers, associates, partners, pals. Heart and guts lie at the core of his character, his patriotism, his personal standards and ideals. These qualities have brought him to the van as a recognized, respected, and highly valued leader in the creative and professional community of Hollywood.

"Heart and guts are components of character hewn out of struggle, the basic 'priceless ingredients' of being a man. Nobody is born with them. They are manufactured out of the stuff of life and living, by the course a man chooses from day to day, by his striving and driving, by his failures probably even more than by his triumphs. Duke's leathery face, clear blue eyes, level stare, yes, and the hard fists that can carry the impact of a lean sinewy two hundred pounds–these are the trail marks footprinted by a distinguished life.

"What do they all add up to? For one thing, that Duke Wayne is a man worthy of friendship and trust. Friendship and trust persuaded a group of hardheaded Texans to lay millions on the line so that Wayne with his toil and sweat might fulfill a dream and create *The Alamo*.

"'By their works ye shall know them.' Wayne has always stood stalwart on the side of right, never compromising, never pussyfooting, never trying to straddle two sides of the fence. He is first and foremost an American with roots centuries deep, the product of pioneer forebears. In a world disturbed and menaced by the deadly new terrors of nuclear fission and the ruthless march of atheistic ideologies bent upon the destruction of our free way of life, he stands as the motion picture industry's embodiment of true Americanism. In knightly days, he would have been hailed as a champion. As Oscar time rolls around, we in Hollywood begin to give thought to our Champions. We take note, with an excusable pride, that the man who these many years has ridden high on the tide of universal acclaim is always there in the forefront, a bulwark, a symbol, and a promise. John Ford said of *The Alamo* that it is a picture that will never be forgotten. Now, after a few weeks in only sixteen of the world's theatres, it is galloping toward its fourth million in grosses. Experts predict it will eventually top fifty million. Duke Wayne has left his personal stamp no less indelibly on our industry and on the world which supports it. The people through the years have always voted 'yes' on Wayne." (This ad also appeared in the January 23 issue of *Variety*.)

The ad was a massive testimonial to Wayne's character and blatant endorsement of the actor, his film, and its message. Did Birdwell write this missive on Muir's behalf? It couldn't have been better if he had. The campaign had changed from an award for the film to an outright recommendation of Wayne for his beliefs and long illustrious career. The Southern California Motion Picture Council previously awarded *The Alamo* a Certificate of Great Merit, which story editor Tom Kane happily accepted. The American Legion voted an exceptional award of merit to Wayne as a result of the "widespread and constructive influences" of his film, while the Mexican-American Chambers of Commerce presented another merit award in the form of a plaque honoring Wayne and the film. Even the U.S. Government was getting involved. Turner Shelton, head of motion pictures for the U.S. Information Agency, said the USIA had been asked on behalf of *Alamo* to request overseas American embassies assist in "dressing up" openings by getting VIP's out for the occasion. According to Shelton, this had been done in the past for American films of "outstanding artistic, cultural, and production merit" when it was "mutually believed the motion picture would be beneficial to the U.S. interest." In Germany, the film was cited as "Specially Valuable," a category accorded to motion pictures of exceptional merit. This predicate certificate conferred special tax and other privileges upon the film, permitted both exhibitor and distributor to share in a larger net revenue and was of considerable exploitation value. *Good Housekeeping* magazine had also announced on December 29 that *The Alamo* would receive an "Award of Merit," the first time in seventy-five years a film was so honored. Tiomkin's score was the winner of the first Western Heritage Award in the musical composition category, which was perfect timing as on January 21 he was saluted on the *Music Is My Beat* program. And on January 20, Pat Wayne and Don LaCava represented Duke at the National Cowboy Hall of Fame when it selected *The Alamo* as one of its top annual award winners. Unfortunately, mention of Wayne's film was noticeably absent from the more important lists. Two days earlier, the director's Guild of America announced fourteen films eligible for "Outstanding directorial Achievement" and, although it included *The Apartment, Sons and Lovers, Psycho, Elmer Gantry, Sundowners,* and even *Sink the Bismarck,* once again, *The Alamo* was left off the list. Birdwell had to somehow deflect this lack of recognition. (Billy Wilder and assistant director Hal Polaire would win the DGA "Outstanding Achievement" award for *The Apartment*).[1393]

January 24 — *Variety*. Two full-pages. "*The Alamo* Wins in Limelight's Poll of 220 U.S. Critics. American critics Vote *Alamo* No. 1 Film of 1960" as well as best score, best song, and best color cinematography. Interestingly, Avalon came in second as top male newcomer behind George Peppard in *Home From the Hill*. Supposedly, the award was a result of coast-to-coast balloting by the nation's top daily newspaper film critics. The honor was given on January 13, just ten days before Florabel Muir's wondrous endorsement. Coincidence? One questions the timing. Birdwell now attempted to persuade Academy voters that not only was the film a financial success as evidenced by public support, but also a critical success worthy of further awards.

On January 25, Birdwell wrote Hedda Hopper, "…I sure would like to see James Edward Grant get a nomination…And it most certainly would be a lot better for a great American like Grant to walk down the aisle, with the world looking on, to pick up an Oscar instead of someone who is against our great country." An obvious reference to Trumbo. Hopper had previously mentioned in her column "We had some fine (films) this year, but none were great. Among the best: *The Sundowners, The Apartment, Sons and Lovers, The Alamo, Cimarron, Elmer Gantry, Home From the Hill, Swiss Family Robinson, The Angry Silence*. I loathed *Spartacus*, but didn't see *Exodus*."[1394]

But there were also powerful detractors, critics of Wayne's producer-director-actor stint. In a Parisian interview with James Bacon, expatriate producer Darryl Zanuck took on independent production companies and actor's agents. He said he fled Hollywood when agents started telling producers how to make movies: "I saw it coming and I knew it was time to get out. It was bad enough when actors turned producers, but now agents. It's more than I can take. There's no creativity left in (being the head of a studio). The stars or their agent want to tell you what to do. They are more interested in making a good deal than a good picture." He expanded his comments when he subsequently told Hedda Hopper: "I'm not going to work for actors. I've got a great affection for Duke Wayne, but what right has he to write, direct and produce a motion picture? What right has Kirk Douglas got? Or Widmark? Or Brando? Look at poor old Duke Wayne–he's never going to see a nickel! He put all his own money into finishing *Alamo*." Duke was furious with Zanuck's comments and took out an ad to reply in excruciating detail.[1395]

*January 25 —Variety. (January 26, 1961 —The Hollywood Reporter)*. One full-page. "John Wayne answers Darryl Zanuck. Darryl Zanuck in Paris huddled with Miss Hedda Hopper and declaimed he would not work for American actors, leaving the speculation he has preferred living and working abroad for the past three years...Miss Hopper, in her fairness as a great newspaper woman, published a portion of Wayne's reply: 'Understand Darryl Zanuck decided to 'stop working for actors' and is shedding crocodile tears for poor old Duke Wayne and his *Alamo*. Please inform him that as far as old Duke Wayne and his picture are concerned, which was made by the way in the U.S.A., it has made just under two million in three months in thirteen theatres in America and has 10,000 more play dates to go. It is breaking records of *Around the World* in such places as Tokyo, London, Paris, and Rome and will end up being one of the highest grossers of all time.'"

"Duke Wayne, now on location, has telegraphed he believes a more detailed reply to Mr. Zanuck's observations is indicated. Here it is: 'It is my hope that expatriate American producers shed no crocodile tears over poor old Duke Wayne who has thus far in a thirty-year starring career brought $300 millios into produce's' tills and plans not only to keep on doing this for producers but is doing a little bit of it for himself for a change. I speak up for myself, for my industry, and all those in it whose work I admire. The challenge to make pictures–to produce pictures–is not the divine right of self-appointed kings. It is not necessary for me to speak up for Kirk Douglas or Richard Widmark or Marlon Brando. Their great work is testimonial to the fact Hollywood is a greater and healthier place because they are in and of our industry. Nor is it necessary for me to speak up for all the great and inspired actors who are either directing or producing–or have their own production companies. But I shall speak up–because I am proud to be a member of a group of hard-working, dedicated men and women who are giving us a new and spirited industry. Producers and directors have come from every category in Hollywood–from publicity offices (Hal Wallis is a shining example); talent agencies (Harold Hecht is another shining example); from film editing (the great George Stevens, and the famed Mark Robson and Robert Wise); from the sound department (the illustrious George Sidney); from cinematography (the fabulous Jack Cardiff); from the writing ranks has come a steady flow of genius. And from the acting ranks a fresh supply of blood and energy and imagination has emerged to assist the others in keeping our industry one of the finest and most productive in the world. Zanuck won't work for actors? Following are some of the actors, or former actors, who are either producing or directing or have their own production companies, constituting the backbone of our business: Dana Andrews, Desi Arnez, James Arness, Gene Autry, Lucille Ball, Harry Belafonte, Jack Benny, Pat Boone, Charles Boyer, Marlon Brando, Yul Brynner, George Burns, James Cagney, Rory Calhoun, Gower Champion, Jeff Chandler, Gary Cooper, Joseph Cotton, Bing Crosby, Robert Cummings, Tony Curtis, Doris Day, Kirk Douglas, Howard Duff, Jose Ferrer, Mel Ferrer, Henry Fonda, Glenn Ford, George Gobel, Cary Grant, Laurence Harvey, Paul Henreid, Charlton Heston, William Holden, Bob Hope, Rock Hudson, Ross Hunter, Danny Kaye, Gene Kelly, Henry King, Alan Ladd, Burt Lancaster, Charles Laughton, Jack Lemmon, Sheldon Leonard, Jerry Lewis, Arthur Lubin, Ida Lupino, Dean Martin, Groucho Marx, James Mason, Joel McCrea, Ray Milland, Robert Mitchum, Marilyn Monroe, Robert Montgomery, Ozzie Nelson, David Niven, Edmond O'Brien, Donald O'Conner, Gail Patrick, John Payne, Gregory Peck, Dick Powell, Otto Preminger, Richard Quine, Ronald Reagan, Dale Robertson, Roy Rogers, Mickey Rooney, Rosalind Russell, Robert Ryan, Dinah Shore, Red Skelton, Frank Sinatra, Ann Sothern, Robert Stack, Rod Steiger, James Stewart, Don Taylor, Danny Thomas, Lana Turner, Raoul Walsh, Jack Webb, William A. Wellman, Orson Welles, Richard Widmark, Henry Wilcoxon, Cornel Wilde, Ed Wynn and Robert Young. I'm mighty proud to be in their company, and I am proud, too, that my producing company, Batjac, made *The Alamo*. James Edward Grant, who wrote the inspired original story and screenplay, as well as serving as associate producer on the picture, and I are extremely pleased that our efforts have been praised and that our film is heading toward the biggest gross in history. We are also pleased that an actor's producing company handed out 11,588 paychecks to American workers during September, October, November and December of 1959 when unemployment in the U.S. had reached the critical figure of four and a half million men and women out of work.'"

In private, Wayne was even more explicit: "I couldn't believe that there was such a backlash even in the industry I loved. I don't know—maybe I was being blamed for the writers who went to jail for being in contempt." As he told Pilar, "It's son of a bitches like Zanuck that made me become a producer. Who the hell does he think he is, asking what right I have to make a picture? What right does he have to make one?" Clever and convincing, Wayne's reply gave him the opportunity to wave the "Made in America" flag. Ironically, Duke's reply was wired from Africa where he was on location filming *Hatari!*[1396]

Duke wasn't the only celebrity/producer to reply to Zanuck's comments. Jerry Lewis sent an open letter to Zanuck that began "I'm sorry I read your article in Hopper's column. I have enough to do without adding irritants that become compulsive challenges which must be answered. And believe me, Mr. Zanuck, your comments truly need to be answered by someone who knows. Take my word for it. I know." Lewis then proceeded to blast Zanuck for three pages.[1397]

(Wayne got even with the producer in 1962 when he was asked to appear in Zanuck's epic masterpiece, *The Longest Day*. Duke was offered the role of Lt. Col. Benjamin Vandervoort, 82nd Airborne, in the film, but, still upset with Zanuck's *Alamo* comments, told him, "I'm really not interested in doing a picture. Pilar and I are thinking of taking a vacation." Undeterred, Zanuck sweetened the pot. Each day he would call and increase the amount he was willing to pay. Each time, Duke refused. First $25,000, then $50,000. Most other stars received just $30,000 for their cameo work. But Zanuck continued to increase his offer as he knew, if Wayne agreed to appear, other stars would line up. Finally, just to get the producer off his back, Duke said he'd do the film—for $250,000, with the stipulation that filming would be delayed if Pilar, pregnant with Ethan, gave birth. To his surprise, Zanuck agreed. Wayne admitted, "I wanted to do the film because I thought it was an important picture, and I wanted Zanuck to pay for what he'd said about me directing *The Alamo*. He paid all right, to the tune of two hundred and fifty thousand dollars. He got his money's worth anyway. What the hell. It might be highway robbery, but it serves the bastard right. I shouldn't have been that rotten, I guess…I always liked that son of a bitch. A good chess player. A good poker player. Loves pictures. Good studio boss. My idea of the kind of guy Hollywood needs, But I was goddamn mad at his attack on me. I didn't like being pitied by him or anybody. But you know, it was nice that, when I got over there on location, old Zanuck was decent to me. He was so pleasant that I kinda wished I hadn't charged him that much money. That had to be the most expensive interview a movie producer ever gave. Should teach us all to keep our mouths shut more often." Duke worked just four days—he appeared on screen a total of twelve minutes! Apparently, William Holden and Charlton Heston were also approached a few times to be in Zanuck's film, but Heston was only interested in the part Wayne filled. (In one early press release, Holden was announced to fill the part). According to Heston, "In the end, John Wayne decided he liked the part, too. The Duke was the thousand-pound gorilla, if ever there was one; Zanuck snapped him up at once...."[1398]

While Birdwell pushed *The Alamo* down the throats of Academy voters, Chill Wills decided to hire his own press agent to win him a nomination as best supporting actor–enthusiastic reviews of his performance had led Wills to believe it was justified. Better known as the voice of Francis the Talking Mule, Wills rightly assumed this might be his only chance ever to win an Oscar. Rather than use Birdwell, though, Wills decided to go with an untried, former physical education instructor for prison inmates, the notorious W.S. "Bow-Wow" Wojciechowicz. Bow-Wow, previously married to columnist Sheila Graham, felt her media contacts might aid his efforts. As usual in such campaigns, saturation advertising was the technique of choice. So, utilizing one of the film's still photos, Wills appeared in a *Variety* ad along with the customary editorial praise:

*January 26* ——*Variety.* One half-page ad. "The greatest explosion to ever come out of Texas was Chill Wills's great dramatic performance in *The Alamo*. A performance that will live as long as the Shrine of the Alamo...an acting performance that should give Chill Wills an Academy Award nomination as Best Supporting Actor!"–Jimmy Dupont, *World News Motion Picture Review.* The following day, a large photograph of Wills's *Alamo* death scene appeared in the trade papers with an even larger endorsement:

*January 27–Variety.* Full-page ad. "CHILL WILLS is Big Big Big and walks Tall all throughout *The Alamo* . Cousin Chill Wills's fine acting should walk him right into an Academy Award Oscar nomination." Earl Wilson, *New York Post* (most widely read columnist in the world).

Once again on January 30, Birdwell implored Hopper, " We need help at this eleventh hour. We truly believe Duke Wayne deserves to have *The Alamo* nominated as one of the five 'best pictures.' And I'm sure you agree. I wish you would say so–just once more before the balloting begins–February 3 to February 14."

*January 30* ——*The Hollywood Reporter.* One half-page horizontal ad. "Chill Wills Academy Award Nomination For Best Supporting Actor w/numerous endorsements.

*January 31* ——*The Hollywood Reporter.* Two-page full ad. "Paris Acclaims *Alamo* as Best American Film of 1960. *The Alamo* Is The Perfect Show. The Best

American Movie Of The Year. John Wayne Is A Sensation." This ad included reviews from Robert Sardou (UA European representative), Paris-Presse, Le Figaro, L'Aurore, Le Canard Enchaine, and France-Observateur. It didn't hurt to show the film had garnered fabulous reviews, both domestic and foreign.

On February 1, Birdwell was responsible for one of the most infamous ads ever published in an Oscar campaign. Not satisfied to focus only on Wayne and the film, he decided to personalize his approach to each and every member of the Academy. Shame, guilt, coercion, sarcasm, whatever it took. The full-page *Hollywood Reporter* ad simply consisted of a sketch of a tombstone. Engraved were the words "Hollywood–Born 1907 A.D.–Died 3000 A.D. 'When the motion picture industry's epitaph is written–what will it say? Will another civilization, coming upon the ruins, find something of worth–a spool of film spelling out a great dream? Or a sequence that merely featured a sex measurement or an innuendo that "got by" the censors? Will there be left behind, for the ages to come, an enduring screen literature that played a vital role in the twentieth century? Or do you care? The sincere and dedicated do care. This includes every man and woman who contributed to the making of *The Alamo*. They believe that the motion picture is the greatest force for good and evil the communication sphere has ever known. The sincere and dedicated throughout the industry have used it for good. They know that inexorable evolution will some day, perhaps by 3000 A.D., replace the present day magic of celluloid in a manner not yet born in the ivory towers of those devoted to the science of obsolescence. But an obituary will come, an epitaph will be written. What will it say–or, do you care?'"

Obviously, the implication was that since Wayne's film was such a masterpiece, its competition in the race not only wasn't worthy, but also contributed to the moral decline of the industry. To further influence the prospective voter, three additional full-page ads were included in the same issue: George Stevens's quotation ("When The Roll Call Is Made"), John Ford's tribute to *The Alamo* ("This is the most important picture ever made"), and a photograph of Chill Wills defending the Alamo ("Chill Wills Academy Award Nomination for Best Supporting Actor"). The ads also contained endorsements from Earl Wilson, Jimmy Starr, and Mike Connolly. Birdwell even had a banner hung across Hollywood's Sunset Boulevard with Ford's endorsement.[1399]

The industry's reaction to the ad was both intense and immediate. Numerous friends and associates continually contacted Birdwell, offering support and sharing feedback from other Oscar competitors. As one might expect, the replies were highly unfavorable. In an attempt to reply to anticipated ads, Birdwell contacted Wayne in Africa on February 3 and begged for additional financing: "Dear Duke, I underestimated fierceness, intensity and below belt fighting in Oscar sweepstakes. Need 35 thousand dollar soonest. Please advise Michael

(Wayne) and Don (LaCava) to give it to me immediately. Wish I could predict what our chances are but I can tell you with great accuracy your prestige and reputation have never been higher both in industry and country and we did the right thing in resuming campaign. *Life* magazine's special book about *Alamo* and ghostwriters ad will be issued next week, an unprecedented tribute to you and *Alamo*. Birdwell." Although Wayne had already made arrangements with United Artists to assist in covering costs of the Oscar campaign, Birdwell received his requested funds.

*February 2 —The Hollywood Reporter*. Full-page ad reprint from an article in the January 3ʰ issue. "Yes, there is an Award! *The Alamo*–Long-Range contender. In this era of long-range production-planning, with many film projects being kicked around for years before they hit the combination that brings them to fruition, John Wayne's *The Alamo* lays claim to something of a record. It took Wayne 14 years to get his property off the ground. After many ups and downs, he finally raised the money, assembled a Hollywood company of 400 and took off for Texas where he produced and directed his Oscar contender in its entirety–handing out <u>11,588 paychecks in the process. There are no awards yet for this kind of contribution to the American film industry.</u> 11,588 Americans got paychecks!" A non-so-subtle comparison to foreign competition, re; *Exodus*. And a rousing support of "Made in America!"

On February 2, the National Society of the Daughters of the American Revolution named *The Alamo* "The Best Historical Film Released in 1960." Presentation of the award would be made April 20 at Constitution Hall in Washington, D.C., before more than 4,000 delegates. It was expected that Wayne would be present to accept the award. The next day, the National Society, Children of the American Revolution, also named the film "The Best Motion Picture Reflecting American Ideals made in 1960." Later, *The Alamo* would also win the 1960 Thomas Alva Edison Foundation Award as the "best film serving the national interest." Accepted by United Artists' Arthur Krim, the award cited the film for "increasing understanding at home and abroad of the values and ideals of American tradition." Another honor for both Duke and the film, but again, not one of the more prestigious ones.[1400]

The closer it got to the day of the nomination announcement, the greater the frequency of the ads. Wojciechowicz knew that Sal Mineo (*Exodus*) and Peter Ustinov (*Spartacus*) would be Wills's main competition if Chill were nominated. So, Bow-Wow cranked up the publicity mill.

*February 2 —The Hollywood Reporter*. A two-inch full-page vertical ad. "Chill Wills. Nomination For Best Supporting Actor." Quiet and reserved, the calm before the storm.

*February 3* —*The Hollywood Reporter.* A full-page copy of an October 26, 1960, article written by Bill Roberts of *The Houston Post,* along with a photo of Wills and several endorsements from the usual cast of characters: Earl Wilson, Mike Connolly, Jimmy Starr, and Jonah Ruddy.

Some ads were short, simple, and to the point:

*February 6* —*The Hollywood Reporter.* A full-page photograph of Laurence Harvey in costume with the following: "...and Colonel Travis led all the rest."

In another piece of cross-promotion, the February 6 issue of *The Hollywood Reporter* included an ad with an article from the February 2 issue of *Variety:* "No Film in History Has ever Matched *The Alamo* Business! *Alamo* Gross \$3,187,223 in 16 Theaters."

Birdwell had already utilized press endorsements, foreign and domestic awards, readers polls, guilt, and statistics to try and prove to the Academy that Wayne and *The Alamo* were worthy of their consideration. So—why not try religion, too?

*February 6* —*The Hollywood Reporter.* "John Wayne's *The Alamo* is the best motion picture of 1960–by far! Magnificently augmented by the best original story and screen play of the year–written by James Edward Grant–*The Alamo* artistically and inspirationally outshines all other Oscar contenders. The Tiomkin music will last as long as *The Alamo* and that's a mighty long time. *The Alamo* is a memorable giant among the pygmies. Fortunately, too, here is one big film the whole family can see and enjoy." William H. Mooring. Famed nationally syndicated critic for Catholic magazines and newspapers.

The following day, an October 27, 1960, editorial from the *Los Angeles Evening Herald-Express* was re-printed in *The Hollywood Reporter:* "Has Any Film In 1960 Received Such Acclaim? An American Classic. You come away after seeing John Wayne's tremendous historical motion picture, *The Alamo,* feeling that here REALLY is an American picture made for Americans. You feel glad all over again that you're an American! A giant of film classics, you realize that here was a superproduction made by a man with a big dream (Wayne), with the story written by an American, the acting, directing and producing done by Americans. And where was it all done? In America (Texas) of course. To the people of the United States, the tragedy of the Alamo has always meant a spirit, a spirit of bravery, a spirit of never say die. 'Remember the Alamo.' There was no 'Surrender' in that glorious epic of the past, no spirit of appeasement. There was truthfulness, honesty, integrity, supreme bravery by a band of courageous warriors who could have saved their lives but instead chose death for a principle. That the film was planned originally 14 years ago and worked for diligently since then by this foremost actor who long has been known for his Americanism is all the more gratifying. That it will prove the field of American history is wide open for still more fine film classics also is of importance, not only for its entertainment, but for the effect it can have on American minds, especially the young. In a day in which we shudder at what is being tried by the leftists and Communists to indoctrinate Americans, we hope that every school child, every college young man and woman, can get the opportunity to see this magnificent color classic, *The Alamo*." Wrapping up Wayne, Americanism, Communism, Leftists, patriotism, classic films, education, and our youth all in one advertisement–what more could Birdwell ask for?

On February 9, Wayne received a full-page celebrity endorsement from two other cowboy legends: "The Beloved Dale Evans and Roy Rogers for the first time in their careers speak out concerning a motion picture . They Name *The Alamo* As 'Finest Motion Picture To Be Produced In More Than A Decade.' This is what Dale Evans and Roy Rogers said: 'We believe that *The Alamo* is the finest motion picture to be produced in more than a decade. For this reason we will visit the site of the *Alamo* location in Brackettville, Texas, to create a special production number which America will view on the Chevy Show Rodeo, February 19th, from San Antonio. We are dedicating this effort to our good friend, John Wayne, for a magnificent achievement in producing his great picture. Inspired by Dimitri Tiomkin's stirring award-worthy music, 'Ballad of the Alamo,' and 'The Green Leaves of Summer,' we humbly hope to bring to our television audience a greater awareness of American spirit and integrity as it is portrayed in this historic film.'–Dale Evans and Roy Rogers." Given the duo's popularity, Wayne couldn't have asked for better approval than this.

With his words superimposed over a photograph of the Alamo, Duke replied in kind: "Dear Dale and Roy, From all of us at *The Alamo*–deep thanks. And to our friends we urge you to see and hear the inspiring *Alamo* production number by Roy Rogers, Dale Evans, the Sons of the Pioneers, Paul Weston and his orchestra and chorus on the Chevy Show Rodeo over NBC, Sunday, February 19th at 9:00P.M.–produced and directed by Alan Handley. John Wayne."

On the same day, nominees for the Golden Globe Award, the last major award ceremony before the Oscars, were announced. The honor was bestowed by members of the Hollywood Foreign Press Association and recognized excellence in film and television, both domestic and foreign. As expected, *Spartacus, Elmer Gantry, Sons and Lovers, Inherit the Wind*, and *Sunrise at Campobello* were nominated for Best Motion Picture–Drama. (*The Apartment* was nominated as Best Motion Picture–Comedy). *The Alamo's* lone recognition was for Best Original Score. By the end of the month, the Screen Producers Guild had also announced its nominations for best film: Sixteen motion pictures including all of the usual suspects. Yet, absent once again, was *The Alamo*, But all was not lost as the California Federation of Women's Clubs would later recognize Wayne as the actor displaying the greatest courage in accepting a challenging role, and the one who has consistently avoided unfavorable publicity and association. Clothier received an award in the field of cinematography while both Wayne and United Artists were given an award to the studio and producer displaying the greatest courage in using the screen as a medium of expression in producing a picture high in social and ethical, as well as technical entertainment value.[1401]

*February 13* —*The Hollywood Reporter.* In an ad sponsored by Columbia, an editorial from the January 14, 196, issue of the *Los Angeles Herald-Express* was used to endorse Tiomkin's efforts. "Dimitri Tiomkin's *Alamo* Music Brings Honor to Industry. Music of the Films. St. Mary's University in San Antonio, Texas, has conferred a special degree upon Dimitri Tiomkin, four-time Hollywood Academy winner, for his music written for the motion pictures. The degree allots to him the title of 'Distinguished Professor of Music Honoris Causa.'" It also went on to say that Tiomkin, through his meritorious music, had contributed to the "great musical folklore of our nation. This is an interesting point on the serious writing of music for the films, and the likelihood that considerable of our good music for the future may be that which is written to illustrate moods or themes or even the plots of film classics. Tiomkin's music in *The Alamo* is great music. His 'Green Leaves of Summer' is so fascinating you find yourself humming it; you find it on the new phonograph recordings. Predictions are that *The Alamo* music may win this fine musician another Academy Award. We never know from where our greatest music is to come. Did the people of Stephen Foster's era, for instance, even though they may have reveled in his music, suspect that it would grow in stature with the passing of time?" *(Author's note: Notice the difference in tone and content between Tiomkin's advertisements and those pushed by Birdwell. Straightforward, to the point, without bombastic superlatives or hyperbole.)*

*February 21* —*The Hollywood Reporter.* A one-column advertisement with photo of Chill Wills: "Chill Wills Nomination For Best Supporting Actor."

With virtual non-stop advertising, endorsements, and begging, Birdwell felt he had done everything possible to reward Wayne with the nomination he so richly deserved. Now, all they could do was wait for the electorate to cast its votes. Would Birdwell's efforts be successful? It wouldn't be for lack of effort.

# CHAPTER THIRTY-FIVE
## "AND THE WINNER IS..."

ON FEBRUARY 28, WITH VOTING COMPLETE AND COUNTS TALLIED, NOMINATIONS for the Academy Awards were finally announced, and United Artists led the way with forty-one, including *The Apartment* (ten), *The Alamo* (seven), *Elmer Gantry* (five), *The Facts of Life* (five), *Inherit the Wind* (four), and *Exodus* (three). Though not nominated for Best Actor or Director, *The Alamo* received recognition for Best Motion Picture, Best Performance by a Supporting Actor (Chill Wills), Best Film Editing (Stuart Gilmore), Best Cinematography, Color (William H. Clothier), Best Motion Picture Score of Dramatic or Comedy Picture (Dimitri Tiomkin), Best Sound (Samuel Goldwyn Studios Sound Department, Gorden E. Sawyer, sound director; and Todd-AO Sound Department, Fred Hynes, sound director) and Best Original Song ("The Green Leaves of Summer," music by Dimitri Tiomkin, lyrics by Paul Francis Webster). Amusingly, *The Alamo*, *Pepe*, and *Spartacus* each was nominated for Best Film Editing despite the fact that each was further edited after initially hitting the screen. Pilar had tried that whole night to contact Duke in Tanganyika with the good news. When she finally reached him, the surprised Wayne told her, "In thirty years in the business, this is the greatest thing that ever happened to me." Privately, Duke was disappointed he didn't receive recognition as actor or director, nor Grant as writer. In fact, only three of the five films nominated for best film also drew nominations for best director. No matter. Seven *Alamo* nominations would translate very well at the box office. Extremely grateful for the recognition his film had received from the Academy, he placed a full-page note of appreciation in the trade papers:

783

*March 1——The Hollywood Reporter.* "John Wayne Thanks You."[1402]

Conspicuous by their absence from the list of Best Picture nominees were *Spartacus, Psycho, Never on Sunday, Exodus,* and *Butterfield 8.* Though some had waged campaigns every bit as unworthy as Birdwell, their efforts weren't as successful. Many people felt a nomination was more a result of advertising and publicity rather than artistic merit, that the awards contest was being excessively commercialized, and that votes, in effect, were being bought. while the nomination selection was a preferential or proportional process rather than a direct count tally, in the final ballots, a film had to have the most first-place votes to win. Plus, a voter could only vote for one nominee in each category. Second, third, fourth, and fifth did not add points as they did in the preferential system, so, block voting by fans of Wayne, his politics, and his film could result in a nomination.[1403]

According to columnist Ivan Spear, "If memory serves correctly, never before has there been so much tocsintitillating in efforts to win merely Academy nominations for pictures and/or the people who worked in or on them...Most of the prenomination ballyhoo took form in paid advertising space in the Hollywood tradepapers, the publishers of which should light a candle at Oscar's shrine every day from now on...*(Both "Variety" and the "Reporter" charged $250 a page for advertising and hundreds of ads appeared in their pages over the past month.)* One cannot but help wonder to what degree Academy voters are influenced by such messages or how much they follow their own judgments..." One publicist, specializing in Oscar campaigns, noted how "It's an old political theory well tested and documented that people like to vote for winners. We try to create an image that our person or picture is so far ahead of the others that he or it has to win." Referring to Birdwell, Spear wrote, "Some of his advertisements–and there was a goodly sprinkling of the aforementioned spreads among them–were adroitly conceived and effective. Others were ill-advised and blatant and, in this opinion, were more apt to alienate prospective votes than to attract them."

Dick Williams of the *Los Angeles Mirror* and Philip K. Scheuer of the *Los Angeles Times* were particularly vocal in their criticism of both the film and the campaign. Williams echoed Spear's sentiments when, on March 1, he wrote "*The Alamo,* which has campaigned with the biggest promotional drive inside the film industry, won a best picture bid, and six other nominations. But I can see nothing reprehensible in artists or productions blowing their own horns. It is done in almost every other phase of American life. Presumably, the Academy membership is still able to make up its own mind in the balloting." Scheuer even left *The Alamo* off his list of ten best films in 1960 and expressed surprise it even had won seven nominations and emerged as a contender in the Best Film category: "I find it almost impossible to understand why *Pepe* and *The Alamo* should have captured seven nominations apiece," he wrote. "They are two of the least distinguished films representative of the "art" (or even, by extension, "popular art") that have ever been shown at advanced prices on a prestige basis. In the case of *The Alamo*–which I'll grant, was made pictorially memorable in the final battle siege–I hear the frequent allegation that the whirlwind ad campaign in the local trade papers was what turned the trick. (Academy members, apparently, are supposed to be susceptible to sells, hard or soft, as anybody else)…Some nominators may have had the uneasy feeling that NOT to vote for it would be kind of un-American… What I find troubling is that judges of at least presumed works of art should be swayed, if they are, by such external political considerations–either left or right–as long as the propaganda that reaches the screen isn't the subversive kind…I still cannot understand why (withholding praise for *The Alamo*) might have been construed as a reflection on my own patriotism. For years, I have been shouting the praises of such pro-southern epics as *The Birth of a Nation* and *Gone With the Wind*, but no one has accused me of being anti-Union because of it." Never one to turn the other cheek, Birdwell published his reply in the March 6 *Hollywood Reporter*: "To Philip K. Scheuer, In confirming publicly you are a poor loser, you have also insulted the integrity of the membership of the Academy of Motion Picture Arts and Sciences, in my opinion. Russell Birdwell. P.S. Remember the Alamo!"[1404]

Claiming "the public is acutely dissatisfied with the Academy Award nominations," Williams even printed various letters he'd received, including one from a David R. Moss from West Los Angeles: "That the Academy nominations, as well as the awards themselves, are strictly commercial in every department, becomes increasingly apparent each year. *Sunrise at Campobello* was acclaimed on all sides as one of the finest productions of 1960. *The Alamo* was roasted by almost every critic in the country. But as every fool over the age of 10 could have predicted weeks ago, *Campobello*, unfortunately a big box-office flop, was ignored in the voting, while *Alamo*, on which mentor John Wayne reportedly spent well over $75,000 'buying' votes (why give the practice fancy names), was nominated as one of the top five motion pictures of 1960…Why don't they simply rename it the Academy of Motion Picture Dollar-and-Centses?" Hollywood shouldn't have been surprised at the nominees. The Academy had a long history of ignoring films worthy of recognition: *The Jazz Singer*, *Little Caesar*, *Of Human Bondage*, *Laura*, *Lifeboat*, *The Third Man*, *Death of a Salesman*, *Singing in the Rain*, *Rear Window*, *Some Like It Hot*, and *North by Northwest* all failed to achieve a Best Picture nomination![1405]

Screenwriter, producer, and gossip columnist Sidney Skolsky, who claimed to be the person who gave the nickname "Oscar" to the Academy Award, said of Wayne's film's nominations: "It appears that more people have voted for it than have seen it while *Close-Up* published an expose on the nomination process entitled "*The Alamo* Reduces Oscar To Pop Corn Shambles." (Of disputed origin,

Bette Davis claimed she named the statuette after her first husband, Harmon Oscar Nelson. The Academy's Executive Secretary, Margaret Herrick, said the award reminded her of her Uncle Oscar Pierce. Skolsky was present when Herrick made the comment and used the name in his byline. A legend was born. The statuette is officially known, though, as the Academy Award of Merit.) Humorous, sarcastic, and brutal in his comments, Skolsky not only explained in detail why the film wasn't worthy of nomination, but also shared gossip and innuendo: "The whole sheer idiocy of the selection is painfully palpable in a dozen different respects. *THE ALAMO* was ignored entirely in both 'best performance' by an actor and actress. It was not mentioned for 'best supporting actress,' but did reach the roster with Chill Wills, who played hardly more that a bit, for 'best supporting actor,' John Wayne's direction didn't get a call. It was singled out for 'best film editing,' which is something of a real horse laugh, inasmuch as more than a half-hour had to be cropped after the picture got into release. The original story and screenplay by James Edward Grant—with, of course, Wayne's collaboration—was entirely passed up. The photography by William Clothier, and the score by Dimitri Tiomkin and the song 'THE GREEN LEAVES OF SUMMER' by Tiomkin and Paul Webster, were nominated. IN A WORD, THE VOTERS WERE NOT AT ALL IMPRESSED WITH THE STORY OR THE DIRECTION OR THE PERFORMANCES, BUT THEY THOUGHT THAT *THE ALAMO* WAS 'THE BEST PICTURE' OF 1960 BECAUSE IT WAS PHOTOGRAPHICALLY PRETTY AND HAD NICE MUSIC." The article went on to say Birdwell "shoved the cornball razzle-dazzle down the Academy's throat, basing his whole approach, not on the artists merits of the picture, but instead on the fact that 'John Wayne is a fine American,' and that '*THE ALAMO* was fought and filmed in the U.S.A.'" Not satisfied to ravage Wayne and the film, Skolsky added that "There is a persistent (*unconfirmed*) rumor that a deal for $500,000 was made under the table with a certain newspaper outlet for one of the nominations." After discussing Tiomkin's (*once again, unconfirmed*) involvement in the sabotage effort of *Never On Sunday* for best song, Skolsky gave the definite implication that Birdwell knew the results of the nominations in advance as "he had his 'Thank you' ad from Wayne already at the engravers twenty-four hours before the nominations were even released."[1406]

Surprise and criticism weren't confined to newspaper columnists or trade papers. *Tonight Show* host Jack Paar reportedly asked his studio audience to "vote" on the Oscar nominations by applause. Paar began reading names of the nominees with the audience's response following. When he called out *The Alamo*, it was met with embarrassing silence, followed by laughter. Paar made a wisecrack and continued on.[1407]

While some questioned whether *The Alamo* even should have been nominated, others felt the honor justified. Hedda Hopper, always a supporter of Wayne, wrote in her column that "the Academy nominations pleased me. *The Alamo*, frowned on by liberals here, got nominated and I believe has a good chance of winning…I hope Chill Wills gets the Best Supporting Award…" Joan Williams also picked Wills to win, although she thought *The Apartment* would win for Best Picture. Yet despite all the attacks on the nomination campaigns, who was in, who wasn't, the discussion of popularity over artistic merit, how much money was spent for votes, etc., Birdwell and *The Alamo* were exactly where they wanted to be–nominated for Best Picture and considered by many a front-runner to win. In fact, Birdwell kept an unofficial running total of potential votes, which showed *The Alamo* in the lead for best picture with 372 votes as compared to its nearest rival, *The Apartment*, with ninety-eight votes. Even Wills appeared to be in the lead for supporting actor. Therefore, rather than dial back the vitriol and outright pandering, he continued his campaign in the same, albeit distasteful, vein: Attack the competition and question the Academy's integrity. In order to further hype the film, on March 6, in celebration of Alamo Day in Texas, UA booked *The Alamo* for a saturation spread in over fifty cities throughout Texas. Even cities outside of the state took part in the celebration. Baltimore set aside the same day honoring the anniversary of the battle as well as Wayne's film.[1408]

*March 8* ——*Variety*. Full-page ad. "7 Academy Award Nominations–*The Alamo*." The ad utilized the Reynolds Brown painting with the seven award categories superimposed over the print. It was actually one of the more tasteful ads used in the campaign.

*March 8* ——*Variety*. The exact same Chill Wills ad that was placed in the February 3 issue of *The Hollywood Reporter* except that now it read "Academy Award Nomination For Best Supporting Actor."

*March 9* ——*Variety*. Full-page ad. "Tiomkin, Nominated for Best Score of a Drama or Comedy." Included were seven individual endorsements from newspapers and trade magazines. A similar ad ran in the March 14 issue.

*March 10* ——*Variety*. Full-page ad. "What Will Oscar Say This Year To The World?" Repeated again in the March 15 issue and the March 14 and 16 issues of *The Hollywood Reporter*.

*March 13* ——*Variety*. Full-page ad. "It's up to Oscar."

*March 14* ——*The Hollywood Reporter*. Full-page ad. The photos and names of thirty-one actors, including Alan Ladd, James Stewart, Van Johnson, Rhonda Fleming, Elizabeth Taylor, Mickey Rooney, and Clark Gable, appeared in the ad in a checkerboard format. Below Wills's much larger photo, it read "Through the years I've supported them all and loved every minute of it. Each one deserves an Oscar. Chill Wills–Best Supporting Actor." A not-so-subtle reminder that "I voted for you. Now it's my turn."

Wayne returned from the *Hatari!* location on March 11 after stopping in London to visit Elizabeth Taylor in her hospital room. "I hadn't expected to see her," said Duke. "I called Eddie Fisher because Elizabeth and Mike Todd were so kind to me when I was ill in Japan." As he deplaned, the media asked him what he thought of his chances in the Oscar race. "This is not the first time *The Alamo* has been underdog," he replied. "We need defenders today just as they did 125 years ago this month." The movie-going public apparently already had listened because on March 15, UA announced that after switching showings to a continuous basis, the first thirty-two *Alamo* engagements racked up box office figures that topped such previous UA blockbusters as *Some Like It Hot*, *The Vikings*, and *Solomon and Sheba*. The strong attendance was attributed to deep penetration of the all-out campaign on the film plus publicity from the Oscar nomination. The thirty-two engagements consisted of sixteen in Texas, seven in Illinois, two each in Arizona, Florida, and Indiana, and one each in Colorado, Kentucky, and Ohio. Receipts were surprisingly strong, in many cases doubling the average take.[1409]

Apparently, Birdwell's nomination campaign must have been somewhat successful as UA executive Seymour Poe pointed out in the following letter to Michael Wayne: "*Alamo* is continuing to do s great job at the box office, and I thought you would be interested in certain weekend figures which are rather significant. In Minneapolis we opened on Friday and in three days grossed over $15,000. At the same theater *On The Beach* grossed $13,980 for a whole week. In Denver we grossed $13,967 on the third Friday, Saturday and Sunday compared to $12,633 during our second weekend. I think this is rather remarkable. In Kansas City our first Friday, Saturday and Sunday was $10,079. Our second Friday, Saturday and Sunday is $10,163. In Washington, D.C. our third Friday, Saturday and Sunday totaled $5,172. The same days of the fourth weekend totaled $5,884. When I see you in California, I will give you many more details all of which add up to only one thing: the picture is a smash."[1410]

On March 16, the Hollywood Foreign Press Association held its eighteenth annual Golden Globe Awards, a fairly accurate barometer of the upcoming Academy Awards. As expected, UA racked up a sizable portion of the thirty-four awards. *The Apartment* won for Best Comedy of the Year (as well as Best Comedy Actor–Jack Lemmon and Best Comedy Actress–Shirley MacLaine), while *Spartacus* won for Best Dramatic Picture of the Year, and Sal Mineo took home the Globe for Best Supporting Actor. *The Sundowners* received an award for "outstanding merit in authenticity and characterization," while the annual Samuel Goldwyn International Award for Best Foreign Film went to *Never On Sunday*. The only award *The Alamo* won was Best Original Musical Score, which Tiomkin accepted from Natalie Wood. The film's failure to win anything else was a portent of things to come.[1411]

Full-page ads from Tiomkin and both John Ford's and George Stevens's endorsements for *The Alamo* ran in rapid succession (March 20 and March 22, respectively). As would be expected, the composer's reply was more reserved and appropriate:

*March 20* ——*Variety/The Hollywood Reporter.* "Dimitri Tiomkin Thanks The Members of the Foreign Press for presenting to him The Golden Globe Award For The Best Original Musical Score–John Wayne's *The Alamo.*" Short, simple, professional.

*March 20* ——*The Hollywood Reporter.* A full-page ad. "The Big Three–Robbins-Feist-Miller Congratulates Dimitri Tiomkin and Paul Francis Webster for 'The Green Leaves of Summer.' Nominated for 'Best Song' Academy Award. Dimitri Tiomkin for The Musical Score From *The Alamo.* Nominated for 'Best Film Score' Academy Award."

*March 24* ——*Variety.* "Columbia Records congratulate DIMITRI TIOMKIN upon winning two nominations for the 1960 Academy Awards. Best Musical Score–*THE ALAMO* Best-selling Columbia album of the Original Soundtrack. Best Motion Picture Song–"THE GREEN LEAVES OF SUMMER." Music by Dimitri Tiomkin, Lyrics by Paul Francis Webster. Best-Selling Columbia single by THE BROTHERS FOUR. THE SOUNDS OF HOLLYWOOD . ON COLUMBIA RECORDS."

*March 24* ——*Variety.* One half-page vertical ad. "The music meets the challenge of the story at every turn, conveying with never-failing skill and resourcefulness the excitement and violence, the tenderness and heroism of frontier life . the work of a master." Deems Taylor (composer and music critic) Nomination Best Score–John Wayne's *The Alamo.* TIOMKIN." (This ad also appeared in the March 29 *Hollywood Reporter.*)

Meanwhile, intra-Hollywood bickering reached new level of pettiness. In the March 15 issue of the *Los Angeles Mirror*, Dick Williams had launched another all-out attack on Wayne and his campaign. Stating that the Academy was being subjected to "one of the most persistent pressure campaigns this year I have seen since covering the Oscar show thirteen years ago," he specifically referred to several of the aforementioned ads. "Almost daily in their customary reading material," he continued, "the Hollywood trade papers, *Daily Variety* and *Hollywood Reporter*–the voters are being hit with full-page ads. One of these reads: 'What will Oscar say this year to the world?' Below is a small picture of the battered fortress, the Alamo. Another ad reads: 'It's up to Oscar' and, leaving nothing to chance, lists *The Alamo* in prominent type below. The implications are unmistakable. Oscar votes are being appealed to on a patriotic basis. The impression is left that one's proud sense of Americanism may be suspected if one does not vote for *The Alamo.* This is grossly unfair. Obviously, one can be the most ardent of American patriots and still think *The Alamo* was a mediocre movie, But you'd never infer this from the advertising barrage being laid down by Russell

Birdwell, John Wayne's major-domo." He closed with a warning: "Unofficial estimates on the behind-the-scene advertising for *The Alamo* vary from $75,000 to $150,000. Certainly it has been huge. So much so that some Academy officials are deeply concerned, But they don't speak publicly about it. Wayne, obviously, takes his own advertising seriously. I wonder how many other Academy voters will also?"

Birdwell countered with an immediate seven-page reply printed in its entirety in the March 21 issue of *Variety* and simply titled: "Why this indictment of the Academy and John Wayne?"

"To Dick Williams, *Los Angeles Mirror*. On March 1, 1961, you wrote in the *Los Angeles Mirror*: '*The Alamo*, which has campaigned with biggest promotional drive inside the film industry, won a best picture bid, and six other nominations. But I can see nothing reprehensible in artists or productions blowing their own horns. It is done in almost every other phase of American life. Presumably, the Academy membership is still able to make up its own mind in the balloting.'

"*When you wrote these lines we had concluded our paid advertising campaign in the trade papers and spent $25,564.40–$6,865.53 of which was for engravings, art work and hand set type. On March 10, we resumed our advertising in the trade papers and at the time you wrote your remarks of today, March 15, we had taken only three pages of advertising in each of the trade papers: 'The Hollywood Reporter' and 'Daily Variety.'*

"On March 15, you wrote as follows: (Birdwell repeated Williams's aforementioned comments re: 'It's up to Oscar,' and 'What will Oscar say . ,' in addition to comment on patriotism and the advertising budget.)

"*What is behind-the-scene advertising? Our advertising has been placed openly in reputable motion picture trade papers. What is the hidden inference?*

"*Along with Philip K. Scheuer of the 'Los Angeles Times', you suggest very emphatically that we have conducted a campaign that to vote against 'The Alamo' is un-American. This is a gratuitous and erroneous conclusion on your part and falls into that avenue of attempting either to coerce or to intimidate the voters of the Academy. I detect a complete reversal of attitude on your part. No one questions someone's right to a change of opinion, but you have not been in a position to judge what the second phase of 'The Alamo' advertising campaign may be.*

"In your column of March 15, you state: 'One of the incongruities of the entire *Alamo* furor is this: it won a nomination as best picture, yet it did not win a nomination for best actor or actress, best director or screenplay–all key elements in insuring the perfection of any top picture.'

"*Surely you must know that within the Academy framework each individual category votes to select its own nominees. For example, actors nominate actors, writers nominate writers, directors nominate directors, and so forth until there are five nominees in each category. The various crafts and guilds nominate their fellow worker in their own particular craft or guild. There is only one category that is voted upon by the entire membership of the Academy in naming a nomination and that is the category of best motion picture of the year. I repeat, the full membership of the Academy with its secret ballot votes for the best picture and it is the only category that is nominated by the majority vote of the full membership. You have taken the same line that was published in a scandal sheet. This scandal sheet has venomously attacked Wayne and 'The Alamo' over a period of time and by following, advertently or inadvertently, the thinking of the scandal sheet you have attempted to lead your readers, in my opinion, into believing there is some loathsome stigma to be attached to the fact that 'The Alamo' failed to receive nominations in categories beyond the seven nominations it did receive. 'The Alamo' was awarded by secret ballot of the Academy, one of the highest honors that can come to a picture maker from his fellow-workers because the vote came not from a single guild or craft, but from the entire membership of the Academy.*

"On March 7, you ran a column quoting letters from your readers and one letter charged 'John Wayne reportedly spent well over $75,000 'buying votes."

*"This is a serious accusation not only against John Wayne but against the integrity of the membership of the Academy of Motion Picture Arts and Sciences, even if it is a quote from an irresponsible reader published in a responsible and reputable newspaper.*

*"In your article of March 1, you so fairly defended the right of a company to advertise, I started to send you a letter congratulating you on your editorial stand, but then suddenly realized that in congratulating you on stating that companies have the right to advertise freely and openly, it was tantamount to congratulating you on believing in God or Mother or the American home. We accept as one of our freedoms the right to advertise as we see fit and we find it bewildering to encounter criticism from a newspaper whose existence depends on advertising. I am sure none of you find fault that occasionally Ohrbach's may take one more page than the May Co. or Bullock's. In your article of today there is an implication that this is wrong. We advertise 'The Alamo' regularly in all the major city newspapers, including the Mirror, and I feel that you and your associates in the newspaper world would be rightly up in arms if someone challenged our right to advertise in newspapers, including the 'Mirro'.' You question our right to advertise 'The Alamo' openly and freely as our judgment dictates. Philip K. Scheuer also has assumed this position. Members of the Academy of Motion Picture Arts and Sciences have a secret ballot. They vote as they wish. The motion picture has the right to present its case and be heard. And, I am confident the voter will make up his own independent mind, in contrast to the thinking as expressed by yourself and Scheuer. Frankly I am baffled that a responsible representative of a newspaper enjoying the great influence and prestige that you have, would question or indict or make implications against our right to advertise a product in the accepted free enterprise system of our country, which has made possible the majority of all publications that exist today in the United States.*

*"It seems to me there is something more important at stake here than whether a film receives a nomination or an award. Do we not have a right to present our case in the paid advertising columns of reputable motion picture trade papers? And,*

*if we are questioned or maligned for presenting our picture as we see it, and as it has been accepted both in the United States and abroad as the most popular and in many instances the most artistic motion picture to have been made in many years, isn't there a possibility or a danger that someday someone or some group may question our right to advertise in your own newspaper? Your column of today, along with Philip K. Scheuer's column of March 6, trespasses, in my opinion, into an additional area of grave consequences. Both of you have singled out 'The Alamo' advertising campaign as some sort of monster. The other campaigns have scarcely been mentioned. Are you and Philip K. Scheuer trying to imply there is some point at which there should be a ceiling on our advertising thinking? Is there a department store to be condemned and ridiculed by some person or faction that would find fault at the amount of advertising that the store places in newspapers in order to present its wares to the public?*

*"Both you and Philip K. Scheuer have made these reckless charges and neither one of you have ever called me to ask for any facts concerning any phase or facet of our campaign. For some sudden reason you have switched your own editorial opinion and you have violated, in my opinion, the first trust of a newspaperman who should investigate the facts and present them accordingly. By using your 'unofficial estimates' which 'vary from $75,000 to $150,000' you have suggested to your readers and the members of the Academy that there is something overridingly sinister in these figures— said figures being untrue. Attributing this sinister implication to the amount of money spent (which is incorrect in your column) you then carry the following two lines: 'So much so that some Academy officials are deeply concerned. But they don't speak publicly about it.' In this item, a blind item, you use your important position in an attempt to strike fear in the Academy membership. If this should happen—which it will not!—you would have succeeded in keeping our picture from having a fair hearing. I still believe in freedom of the press but you and Philip K. Scheuer seem to indicate that freedom of the press, in advertising, applies to all other motion pictures with the exception of 'The Alamo.' I believe wholeheartedly that the Academy voter will decide for himself without being subjected to either your editorial influence or the influence you charge we have tried to exert through our advertising."*[1412]

No stranger to confrontation, even Duke took the opportunity to voice his displeasure with Scheuer in a letter to the *Los Angeles Times*: "Mr. Scheuer's column of March 6 posed the question that it was almost impossible to understand why *Pepe* and *The Alamo* should have captured seven nominations apiece. In his judgment he thought these were two of the least distinguished films representative of the art. With his long career as a film critic and editor, it would not seem to me that it would be surprising to him to find out that a great number of people, of certainly as renowned standing as his, have not agreed with him in their criticism of past pictures. I would like to remind Mr. Scheuer that the Academy of Motion Picture Arts & Sciences (is) an accredited organization, made up of honorable people with certain creative talents. It is quite obvious that the appreciation and commendation of their own workers is a happy reward that each of them desires. I would like to remind Mr. Scheuer that each member casting a vote for nomination is allowed a vote for the person within his own category of the Arts and Sciences, plus the right of all to vote for the best picture. I would like to point out that this is a secret ballot, and that it is processed by an accredited organization. Therefore, Mr. Scheuer's intimation that *The Alamo*, with its subject matter, coerced anyone into voting for it, seems quite ridiculous. Some fourtee4 years ago we started with the idea that we thought would make fine entertainment for the motion picture goer. We have received, by secret ballot, the highest kudos that can be paid to the people in our profession. We are sickened by his belittling the reward and honor which the Academy has bestowed upon us." Duke also sent a letter directly to the *LA Times* publisher Otis Chandler: ". I would not be this presumptuous if I did not feel he had used very unfair tactics. His opinion of our picture, his professional judgment of its worth, is his right to publish, and this is not being questioned. His irresponsibility and direct slap at the Academy voters is being questioned." But Wayne, furious at Birdwell for the tone and content of the campaign, told him to change the approach, or he was fired. Birdwell got the message; all subsequent ads were a bit less antagonistic.[1413]

*March 17* — *The Hollywood Reporter/Variety.* Full-page ad. "Oscar Will Make up its Own Mind!"

*March 23* — *Variety.* Two-page, full-page ad. A sketch of the Alamo by Frances Hernandez Cunningham with fiftee5 weekly *Variety* headlines itemizing gross revenue.

*March 24* — *Variety/The Hollywood Reporter.* A full-page ad. Sketch of an explosion in front of the Alamo chapel, with a welcome mat. This ad appears in both trade papers but with a slightly larger explosion in *Variety*.

Wills, no slouch in the promotion field, also ratcheted up his campaign and took out a two-page, full-page ad in the March 17 issue of *The Hollywood Reporter* in which he listed literally hundreds of names of fellow actors and actresses and the banner: "Win, Lose, Or Draw. You're Still My Cousins And I Love You All." He would repeat this ad on March 20 and 22 with a slightly different format. This was a dangerous tactic, and the repercussions of such a distasteful, inappropriate, and blatant appeal for votes proved catastrophic both to Wills and *The Alamo*.

On March 21, twenty-six Texas friends, including Happy Shahan, Bob O'Donnell, Big John Hamilton, Jerry McCutchin, and Phil Isley, placed an ad in *Variety* endorsing Chill Wills as "1960's Best Supporting Actor. 'The Beekeeper' Chill Wills! should be the 'O-keeper.' Signed, your 'Texas Cousins.'" At this point, it appeared both Wills and *The Alamo* were front-runners in their respective categories. Though their campaigns seemed a bit tacky, they weren't that much worse than many of the other contenders. Had publicists Birdwell and Bow-Wow Wojciechowicz maintained the status quo, Wayne and Wills probably had extremely good chances of winning. But then the shit hit the fan! On March 2, Hedda Hopper had written in her daily column that she "hoped Chill Wills would get the Oscar for best supporting role." But she rescinded her endorsement in her March 23 column: "Now I learn that Chill has sent out my name to try to influence academy voters to vote for him, and because of this he's lost my vote." (Wojciechowicz had sent letters to all Academy members that stated Hopper wanted Wills to win.) Wills immediately replied to Hopper's statement and denied any personal responsibility for the letters. He further stated the public relations efforts on his behalf had been handled by an unidentified press agent "who may have been imprudent. Although my representative may have gone too far, it is possible that Miss Hopper has also. If Miss Hopper feels that publicity on her printed endorsement of me was out of bounds, I would certainly be willing to apologize to her." *Strike one!*[1414]

On March 24, in reply to Wills's "Win, Lose, Or Draw...you're still my cousins..." ad, Groucho Marx humorously replied in *Variety* with his own ad: "Dear Mr. Chill Wills, I am delighted to be your cousin, but I voted for Sal Mineo–Groucho Marx." *Strike two!*[1415]

The same day, Bow-Wow placed an ad in *The Hollywood Reporter* of unbelievably poor taste and shameful ignorance. It boggled the mind. An enlarged image of Wills stood superimposed over a photograph of the entire cast in front of the Brackettville Alamo chapel. The copy simply read, "We of the *Alamo* cast are praying harder–than the real Texans prayed for their lives in the Alamo–for Chill Wills to win the Oscar as the Best supporting actor–Cousin Chill's acting was great. Your *Alamo* Cousins." To its credit, *Variety* refused to publish it. *Strike three!*

Hollywood was aghast, Texas was outraged, and Wayne was furious! After all he had tried to do to rein in Birdwell and his campaign of pleading and patriotism, now Wills had to pull this bone-headed stunt! He chewed out Wills big-time. "He'd been given no authority to do that," stated Wayne. "I called him up and told him that if I saw him soon, he'd better start running fast! It was in bad taste." On March 27, Wayne was forced to publish a disclaimer in the trade papers: "I wish to state that the Chill Wills ad published in the *Hollywood Reporter*, of which we had no advance knowledge, in which he wrote or permitted to be written, that 'We of the *Alamo* cast are praying harder–than the real Texans prayed for their lives in the Alamo–for Chill Wills to win the Oscar' is an untrue and reprehensible claim. No one in the Batjac organization or in the Russell Birdwell office has been a party to his trade paper advertising. I refrain from using stronger language because I am sure his intentions were not as bad as his taste.–John Wayne." Recognizing the impact this had had on Wills's chances, Wojciechowicz shouldered the blame and placed his own ad in the papers: "Notice, John Wayne, Chill Wills was in no way responsible for the *Alamo* ad which appeared in *The Reporter* on Friday. Chill Wills did not know anything whatsoever about this ad, and when he saw it he was madder than John Wayne and Birdwell together. I informed John Wayne and Birdwell after the ad appeared that I was fully responsible.–W.S. Wojciechowicz." Even Birdwell was amazed: "It was like taking a bucket of fecal matter and throwing it over a beautiful rose."[1416]

True or not, it really didn't matter–the damage was done. Whatever sympathy and support Wayne and Wills may have had vanished in the turn of a page. Some columnists felt the entire episode was a classic case of the pot calling the kettle black. Wrote Joe Hyams in the *Los Angeles Times*: "The battle between Messrs. Wayne and Wills seems to be a high point in the Hollywood battle waging around *The Alamo* which threatens to make the original scrap look like a skirmish. There are those in Hollywood, including this writer, who think that for John Wayne to impugn Chill Wills's taste is tantamount to Jayne Mansfield criticizing Sabrina for too much exposure." Sabrina (Norma Ann Sykes) was a 1950s English glamour model better known for her 41-17-36 measurements than her acting ability. She appeared in a handful of movies, her last *The Ice House* (1969), ironically as a replacement for Jayne Mansfield who had recently died in a car accident.[1417]

Columnist Skolsky hit the nail on the head: "Chill Wills…and *The Alamo* …were knocked out of the box for the Oscar by its own powerful weapon, trade advertising, and by humor, which its supporters didn't possess–or at least exhibit. It started with Groucho Marx's advertisement… But the final chill was applied to Wills by John Wayne himself. This would imply that there's a falling out of 'cousins.'" There were several good humorous remarks about Wills and *The Alamo* at the Screen Writers Guild (SWG) dinner. Comedian Mort Sahl suggested a new Oscar be awarded to Groucho for "the best ad for nomination for an academy award." Billy Wilder, director of *The Apartment*, won the SWG award for Best Picture and closed his acceptance speech by saying, "Keep praying, cousins! We hope Oscar will say the right thing this year!" Comparing the Academy Awards to a horse race between humans, journalist and reformed handicapper James Bacon humorously set the following odds: Third race: Best Picture Sweepstakes; purse worth millions added at gate: *The Apartment*, figures on previous wins, 7-5. *The Sundowners*, watch this Aussie entry, could cop, 9-5. *Elmer Gantry*, Runs well Brimstone turf, 3-1. *The Alamo*, Texas big betters may bring down odds, 5-1. *Sons and Lovers*, British entry figures long shot at best, 7-1. Fifth race: supporting actor Maturity, turf, $50,000 added. Peter Ustinov, Carries most weight field but has stamina, 2-1. Sal Mineo, Classy Italian colt, wears Israeli silks, 3-1. Peter Falk, Could murder them all at wire, 4-1. Jack Kruschen, If Lemmon entry, could share pot, 7-1. Chill Wills, Bad handling by trainers wreaked chances, 10-1.[1418]

After this, the remaining publicity campaign was somewhat anti-climatic. Thank goodness the voters would have to suffer this onslaught for only seven more days. *The Alamo* had been shown at a special eight o'clock screening at the

Director's Guild Theater on March 22, and, for those who weren't able to obtain seats, the Academy arranged for another nomination screening at the Academy Award Theater on March 27. Various ads were placed in both papers trying to salvage the damage of Wills's brainless scheme:

*March 28 —The Hollywood Reporter.* Superimposed over four photographs of Tiomkin as he conducted his orchestra, it read "Dimitri Tiomkin's Finest Motion Picture Score To Date. Nominated John Wayne's *The Alamo.* TIOMKIN."

*March 29 —The Hollywood Reporter.* A full-page ad. "Thank you, Dimitri Tiomkin and Paul Francis Webster, for THE GREEN LEAVES OF SUMMER which has rewarded us with worldwide recognition. Recorded for Columbia and to be sung at the academy presentations by THE BROTHER FOUR."

On March 29, *The Alamo* opened to general distribution in numerous Los Angeles-wide theaters and drive-ins. (In Chicago, over 61 venues showed it on a continuous run basis.) Wills, refusing to give up, appeared at several openings: the LaReina at 6:30 p.m., the Baldwin at 7:45 p.m. and the Loyola at 9 o'clock. He wasn't going down without a fight![1419]

Finally, on April 3, the last ad of the campaign was placed on the back cover of *The Hollywood Reporter:* "We the 2000 little guys and gals of Texas who worked with our Cousin Chill on the *Alamo* are pulling and praying Texas style for him to win the Oscar.–The little guys and gals of the *Alamo* committee for Cousin Chill Wills. Big John Hamilton, Chairman." But, as they say, there's no such thing as bad publicity. On April 4, the *Harvard Lampoon* published its annual poll of worst awards winners. *Butterfield 8* was named the worst film of 1960 while Eddie Fisher, who appeared in the film, was given the worst supporting actor award. The magazine said that the choice of Fisher was difficult: "In any other year he would have won easily, but this was a banner year for bad movies." Ranked behind *Butterfield 8* was *Strangers When We Meet, The Gazebo, The Ice Palace, Exodus, It Started in Naples, Pepe, Pollyanna, Because They're Young,* and *High Time.* Frank Sinatra was given the worst actor award for his performance in *Can-Can* while Eve Marie Saint won for her role in *Exodus.* Fabian took home the "Uncrossed Heart" award as the least promising actor for his performance in *North to Alaska* while *The Alamo* won "Along the Mohawk Grant" special award for the film with the most drummed up publicity. While one joke that made the rounds was "Forget *The Alamo,*" another was that, if Dalton Trumbo had written the script, it would have ended with the Mexican peons arising and slaughtering Santa Anna's army and the Yankee imperialists! After that, all that was left was the voting.[1420]

# CHAPTER THIRTY-SIX
# AFTERMATH

*"I always go to the Academy Awards each year, in case one of my friends, who is out of town, wins an Oscar and I can pick it up on his behalf. I have received awards for Gary Cooper and John Ford. But no one–including me–has ever collected one for John Wayne. That doesn't keep me tossing in bed at night. Of course, the fellows who own and operate theaters don't know that I'm not much of an actor, as they have been foolish enough to pick me as the box-office champion of the year a couple of times."* John Wayne facetiously discussing his failure to win an Oscar.

In California, spring was in full-bloom by April 17, 1961. Blue, partly-cloudy skies without torrential rain, mudslides or canyon wildfires. After several days of almost 100° temperatures, it finally dropped to a very pleasant 86°. By evening, it fell even further to around 80°, a perfect night for formal gowns and tuxedos. A Monday was picked in deference to movie theater owners because, traditionally, that evening was the poorest night of the week at the box office. But there was one major change: ABC was broadcasting the 33$^{rd}$ Annual Academy Awards from the Santa Monica Civic Auditorium, the first time ever outside of Los Angeles. For the previous several years the event had taken place at the Pantages Theater in Hollywood, but the Academy of Motion Picture Art and Sciences' board of governors now felt the venue was too small. A "2,588 seating capacity, excellent stage facilities, the availability of a large conference room for press accommodations and parking spaces for 1,500 vehicles" swayed the officials toward Santa Monica. Beside, the Pantages had cut its capacity from 2,812 to 1,512 for the current run of *Spartacus* and also had remodeled in a manner that impeded a telecast. Hollywood was in an uproar over the change in locale, and Hedda Hopper blasted the decision in her column: "While I was abroad the Academy did a sneaky thing, moved the Oscar show to Santa Monica. Said Pantages Theater wasn't big enough. How about the Chinese or the Egyptian Theaters? I'm so mad I'd like to broadcast a protest from the highest mountain. We have so little glamour any more let's cling to what's left. Is having star names in the cement of the boulevard glamour? After a three-block walk craning your neck to read names you're ready for an osteopath. And Mickey Neilan's name smack in front of Pantages is misspelled. I have an idea for the next show. Let's seat all nominees on stage so they'll be handy and the public can see our beautifully dressed women who've been nominated."[1421]

Regardless, the decision had been made, and everything was in place for the evening's activities: red carpet rolled out, searchlights activated, temporary bleachers erected to hold 1,200 spectators, But the police estimated more than 1,500 were crammed into those seats, and another 1,000 standees, ten rows deep, lined every available space. As expected, Elizabeth Taylor and Duke were fans' favorites. Unfortunately, officials forgot one small detail. A traffic jam extended, at least, a quarter mile down several streets leading to the auditorium. Thus, many attendees discovered it took, at least, two minutes to travel the last forty-four yards to the parking lot, which caused hundreds to be late. As a result, when the show began there were many empty seats. Outside, three lanes of five cars each were unloading as rapidly as possible. One of the first celebrities to arrive was Juliet Prowse at 6:25 p.m., quickly followed by Chill Wills. Wills, as nervous as a long-tailed cat in a room full of rocking chairs, was seen rushing through the lobby like his coattails were on fire. He skidded to a stop, wiped perspiration from his brow and said to a friend, "Phone me at Forest Lawn tomorrow!"

The evening opened with a five-minute medley of Oscar-winning songs performed by the Academy orchestra and conducted by Andre Previn as the audience found its seats. Upon its conclusion, Valentine Davies, president of the Academy of Motion Picture Arts and Sciences, took the podium and started the proceedings. Given that year's spirited publicity campaigns, nobody was surprised when Davies tried to lend a tone of professionalism to the event. "For over thirty years now," said Davies, "members of this academy have voted by secret ballot to select the winners. Their votes have been based on their professional appraisal of what is the best achievement in each of the various categories. The awards which will be presented here tonight represent the considered opinion of 2,300 outstanding craftsmen in this industry whose knowledge and judgment, democratically expressed, will honor our winner." Bill Miller of Price Waterhouse then made the obligatory appearance and vouched for the secrecy of the votes. Finally, it was time for the evening's emcee, comedian Bob Hope.[1422]

Hope, a nine-time perpetual host, was in rare form, skewering both nominees and attendees alike in his eight-minute monologue: "This is the historic occasion in which the members of the Academy of Motion Picture Arts and Sciences decide which actor and actress has the best press agent. No, it's a whole new thing. I didn't realize there was any campaigning at all going on until I saw my maid wearing a Chill Wills button...I wouldn't say feeling has been running high, but if *The Alamo* doesn't win, they may do it over again, live, right here." Hope then addressed the recent change in venue: "No, we're telecasting from the magnificent new Santa Monica Civic Auditorium . this is quite a departure, holding the Academy Awards in Santa Monica. That makes two towns I've lost in. We had to move the awards presentation from Hollywood. Last year the losers were throwing themselves on the freeway. But they're tempting fate to hold this Roman holiday on the shores of the ocean. Any moment, the sea will part and Otto Preminger will appear with a whip and drive us all back to the Pantages." After discussing the first Russian in space ("All this proves is that their German scientists are better than our German scientists"), he sketched the nominated films: "They've been showing some great films this year: *Exodus* ("about the Republicans"), *The Apartment* ("Sinatra's life story"), *Sons and Lovers* ("about Bing's family"), *Elmer Gantry* ("fun in the organ loft"), *Never on Sunday* ("about a Greek coffee break"), and *Butterfield 8* ("one girl's fight against American Tel and Tel"). The picture *Psycho* taught our children a valuable lesson–Never take a shower."

The previous year, Hope asked Duke, who'd presented the award for Best Director, why he wanted to direct:

"Duke, what (drove) you to become a director: the need for self-expression or a new outlet for artistic endeavors?"

"No, I wanted a chair with my name on the back."

"Well, who was your star?"

"I was."

"Your producer?"

"I was."

"You don't need a chair, you need a couch."

"A couch and that fella to talk to."

This evening's presenters were every bit as glamorous and famous as their nominated counterparts: Yul Brynner, Greer Garson, Tony Randall, William Wyler, Shirley Temple, Eva Marie Saint, Gina Lollobrigida, Bobby Darin and Sandra Dee, Danny Kaye, and Audrey Hepburn, to name a few. Duke, wearing a tuxedo complete with tails, white vest, and tie, sat in the audience as did a fingers-crossed Wills, just in front of Elizabeth Taylor and Eddie Fisher. After Hope's opening remarks, the ceremony began. The first award, presented by Janet Leigh and Tony Curtis ("Hollywood's happiest married couple"), was for Best Documentary–Feature and Best Documentary–Short Subject. This was quickly followed by a performance of the first nominated song, and presentation of the Special Effects award by Polly Bergen and Richard Widmark. After Barbara Rush and Robert Stack announced the Costume Design Award winners, the moment Wills had been waiting for all evening arrived: the award for Best Supporting Actor. As expected, Hope took the opportunity to give the nominees a little jab: "And, now we come to the moment of truth–the first award for acting. At this very instant, there are five actors in the audience being held down by their psychiatrists...and their cousins...To present the award for Best Supporting Actor, Miss Eva Marie Saint." (Shelly Winters had been expected to present the award but was a no-show). When Peter Ustinov won for his performance as Batiatus in *Spartacus*, the crowd erupted in an extended forty-second ovation. Wills, crestfallen and bitter, brushed away a tear and remained seated. When later asked about Bow-Wow and that campaign, Wills vowed to columnist Sheilah Graham, "One day I'll get even with that so-and-so if it's the last thing I do."[1423]

After the performance of the second nominated song, Paula Prentiss and Jim Hutton came on to present the award for Best Sound. This was the first award *The Alamo* had a reasonable chance of winning and...it did. Gordon Sawyer and Fred Hynes accepted Oscars on behalf of Samuel Goldwyn Studios and Todd-AO, but had to introduce themselves–the presenters didn't know who they were. Once the Short Subject and Foreign Language Awards were presented and the third nominated song performed, it came time for *The Alamo*'s next Oscar opportunity: Film Editing. Stuart Gilmore was nominated for his work on Wayne's film but unfortunately lost to Daniel Mandell and *The Apartment*. Hugh Griffith then gave Shirley Jones her Oscar for Best Supporting Actress for *Elmer Gantry*, and, after the Art Direction Award and yet another song performance, Tony Martin and gorgeous Cyd Charrise gave the award for Best Cinematography to Russell Metty and *Spartacus*. Just like Gilmore, first-time nominee William Clothier didn't win for his efforts on *The Alamo*. With just three opportunities left to win, time was running out for Duke. Tiomkin was passed over for Best Scoring of a Drama by Ernest Gold and *Exodus*. After the performance of the fifth nominated song, Steve Allen and Jayne Meadows came out to present the award for Best Song. The nominated songs had been performed by Connie Francis ("Never on Sunday"), Sarah Vaughan ("Faraway Part of Town"), Hi-Los ("Facts of Life"), The Brothers Four ("The Green Leaves of Summer"), and Jane Morgan ("The Second Time Around"). "Green Leaves" and "Second Time" were the odds-on favorites, but when "Never on Sunday" won instead, there was a noticeable lack of audience reaction before the applause started. To further heighten the dramatics, Manos Hadjidakis, composer and lyricist, wasn't even there to accept the honor. Unfortunately, UA hadn't designated anyone to pick up the award should he win. Quick to react, Hope stepped in, grabbed the award, and quipped, "This is the moment I have been waiting for."[1424]

Interspersed throughout the evening were honorary awards for Gary Cooper,

Stan Laurel, and Hayley Mills. Then, it finally came time for the major awards: Best Director (Billy Wilder for *The Apartment*), Best Screenplay (*Elmer Gantry*), Best Original Story (*The Apartment*), Best Actor (Burt Lancaster for *Elmer Gantry*), Best Actress (Elizabeth Taylor for *Butterfield 8*). By the time Audrey Hepburn announced the award for Best Film, Duke had seen the handwriting on the wall. *The Apartment* already had won five awards, *Spartacus* four, and *Elmer Gantry* three. Before announcing the Best Picture winner, Hope and Hepburn engaged in a little repartee: "Audrey, how would you like to make a picture with me? I've had an offer to remake some of the old William Powell-Myrna Loy pictures." Hepburn coyly replied, "I think you would be perfect. I could never be as good as Bill Powell was." Hepburn then announced the nominees and when she excitedly cried—"...*The Apartment*! Billy Wilder!"—all Wayne could do was smile and applaud. (*The Apartment* was the last black-and-white film to win Best Picture during an era when B&W mainstream films were still common; it didn't happen again until 1993 when *Schindler's List* won.) Pilar knew Duke was disappointed but not surprised *The Alamo* only won one award that evening. "There was a lot of jostling for the Oscars," complained Duke. "There always has been, and there always will be. But the only film that gets criticized for its Oscar campaign is *The Alamo*. Why is that? And which film won Best Picture that year? *The Apartment*. A comedy about how funny it is to let your boss use your apartment to commit adultery. *The Alamo* was about courage, justice, and freedom. Sour grapes? You bet. My politics definitely interfered with the fucking critics but, sonofabitch, after all that work I thought we'd win something. It was a damn good picture. The left-wing critics on the East Coast—they still had it in for me, and they didn't like the idea I was saying that freedom from dictatorship was brought with blood. They didn't like it that I was using the Alamo as a metaphor for America, and although I wanted to show the Mexicans with dignity, it was a warning against anything that stole our freedom, and yes, that included Communism." (Wayne shouldn't have felt too disappointed. The clergy, conservative press, and mid-America all were outraged that films about promiscuity, adultery, and prostitution were even nominated. They felt that "Hollywood appraised sex, sordidness, and the unpleasant aspects of life in higher terms than wholesome family entertainment"). But Duke also knew Birdwell's campaign had backfired. "It hurt us," he admitted. "Hurt the way the film was accepted. I made a bad error of judgment over the publicity." Production assistant Tom Kane agreed but was more specific: "The campaign was a terrible thing. Chill Wills, he hurt us. Of course he did. (His promotion) was ludicrous and reflected on our campaign. And between us, I don't think Birdwell's campaign helped us (at all). It antagonized many and cost us votes. We were up for seven awards—only won one for sound. (We) had great songs—the 'Green Leaves of Summer'—we should have won Best Picture." But Pilar was more rational. "Although Duke didn't make any profit from all his work," she said, "he had the satisfaction of having made a dream come true. And, after the deal with United Artists was finished, he could sleep better at night knowing we were solvent again."[1425]

Although *The Alamo* was not a bad effort, Duke's future was in front of the camera, not behind it. He would officially direct only one more film–*The Green Berets*. Yet another film about men, war, patriotism, and liberty, like *The Alamo*, it was panned by the critics. (*Berets* was Wayne's tribute to Army Special Forces. Filmed in 1967 prior to the height of America's involvement in Vietnam, Duke felt so strongly about the project, he turned down the World War II role of Major Reisman in *The Dirty Dozen*. According to Emanuel Levy's review of the film, Wayne said his motive was to glorify American soldiers as the finest fighting men "without going into why we are there, or if they should be there." His "compulsion" to do the movie was based on his pride of the Special Forces, determined to show "what a magnificent job this still little-known branch of service is doing." "I wasn't trying to send a message out to anybody," he reasoned, "or debating whether it is right or wrong for the United States to be in this war. What war was ever popular, for God's sake. Those men don't want to be in Vietnam anymore than anyone else." "Once you go over there," he said, "you won't be middle-of-the-road." Released June 17, 1968, less than five months after the Tet Offensive, critics of the film were brutal, but, as with *The Alamo*, the public loved it as evidenced by domestic receipts of over $24 million.)[1426]

But like Capt. Brittles in *Yellow Ribbon*, Duke wasn't going to apologize for his feelings. A patriot's patriot, Wayne felt he owed the country more than just mere entertainment. "An actor has to be more than a part of a self-contained group," he said. "We're part of a bigger world. We've got to have a sense of responsibility about that world. I figure sometime or other a man's got to take a stand for what he believes. I would want to do it the same way if I had my life to live all over again. I get a tremendous boot out of my work. I enjoy every day of it, every minute of it, it's a great challenge to a guy. I can reach millions, please millions…now I've got a controlling say in making pictures. For years I've offered suggestions and was told to shut up. It's frustrating. I will listen to anybody who wants to talk to me. I've always spent time away from the narrow, little self-contained group in which the sun rises and sets on motion pictures only. We're part of a big world and have to have a sense of responsibility about it." Duke did, and, in making *The Alamo*, he suffered the consequences.[1427]

Aissa feels her father was accepting of the film's limited success. "Within the Wayne family, we've never considered *The Alamo* a failure," she says. "We spoke about it so much during my childhood, I grew up believing it was the finest picture ever made. Although my father toiled on it on and off for ten years, and it drove him to the financial brink, I never heard him complain about how things turned out. For all the heartache and lost money it must have cost him, I think my father understood he'd given his Alamo dream his very best shot, and that this, in itself, made him a winner."[1428]

Interviewed on the set of *Hatari!*, a consigned Wayne admitted in May that his film wouldn't generate as much at the box-office as he originally expected: "The latest figure is a gross of seventeen million, and it may go higher. It's doing fantastic business in Japan, also Scandinavia and England. Over here, it's doing fine. When I left for Africa last fall, things looked pretty grim. We were blasted out of the water by some critics who I know did it because they didn't like me. The initial reserved-seat runs weren't good because we didn't have time to put on a campaign in each city. The way it looks now, we'll all make a little profit. Not much, but some. I'm happy not only because I had some of my own dough in the picture for the first time. I talked my friends into investing, too. I was sweatin' it out for those Texans who backed me. I took a chance, and I'm glad of it."[1429]

He shouldn't have felt too bad, though. Two days after the Oscars, the Daughters of the American Revolution (DAR) named *The Alamo* as best historical film of 1960. (While Birdwell picked up a plaque in Washington, D.C., Wayne accepted a citation May 23 at a special luncheon at Paramount Studios.) At the same time, the DAR, via a proclamation, took the opportunity to lambaste film, television, the stage, and show business in general: "Whereas the entertainment industry again is employing certain writers, directors and actors who have openly been defiant of our country's duly authorized investigative bodies and who serve to weaken the prestige of the U.S. by distorted themes and slanted emphases and inaccurate facts, thereby strengthening the Communist position in the ideological world (and) Whereas there has been a noticed increase in the themes of brutality, defeatism, sadism, perversion, and violence in the American theater and in the motion picture and TV industries, it is resolved the (DAR) call upon the entertainment industry to clean its own house before federal censorship becomes inevitable and it is further resolved that the (DAR) protest the downgrading of American history that distorts historic fact and maligns the character of American patriots." Only forty-four of 204 films screened by the DAR were deemed fit for family viewing. All previewed films were approved by the Production Code of the Motion Picture Association of America. Eric Johnson, president of the MPAA, was quick to defend films: "The American motion picture industry need apologize to no one for its Americanism, its patriotism and its devotion and service to the ideals of democracy and freedom in the United States and around the world. No medium over the years has done more to bring about an appreciation of the history, the principles, and the traditions of America." And Johnson wasn't alone in his sentiments. Recommended Columbia producer George Sidney, "We need unity in any fight against pseudo-critics, alleged censorship experts and vilification diehards. All these people need is an issue or fig of a story or acting not to their liking to start a barrage. And then we're off to defending ourselves again."[1430]

Generally, Academy voting was divided into two camps. One camp insisted the Oscar represented a "glitzy, high-stakes contest designed to promote stars and hustle the goods." While epics and audience favorites fell into this category, multiple Academy Awards also guaranteed a box-office bonanza. *Spartacus*, for instance, experienced a 20% increase at the box office after it won five Oscars! The other camp believed an Oscar was recognition of personal achievement, not commerce. To be nominated by one's peers was infinitely more important than winning. Well-acted character studies and niche films fell into this category. But in 1960, unfortunately, there was also a third camp: those who took offense when their patriotism was questioned. So, combine that with a liberal press, supposed fellow travelers and those who really felt there were films of higher quality in nomination...well...Wayne didn't stand a chance.[1431]

Others helped Duke recover from the Academy's snubbing of *The Alamo*. Later that month, the U.S. Marine Corps announced, in appreciation for his continued work on behalf of the Corps, that Wayne would receive its highest civilian award–the Commandant's Certificate of Appreciation. Previously, the award had only been given to large corporations and other organizations that contributed to the wartime effort. In addition to his appearances in *Sands of Iwo Jima* and *Flying Leathernecks*, Wayne always supported the Corps through recruiting films, advertising, and other efforts. It wasn't an Oscar, but it wasn't bad. And by the end of the month, *Life* published a brochure for distribution to advertising agencies, advertisers, and opinion control groups. Titled "A Statement of Principle," it was said to be "the most elaborate mailing piece of its kind in the publication's history." Because Birdwell's ad text "There Were No Ghost writers at the Alamo" had been widely quoted, the *Alamo* ad was singled out "because of its widespread reaction and infiltration."

Early June found Wayne at Harold's Club Fun Room in Reno, Nevada, when he presented a posthumous plaque to Mazie Bond, Ward's widow. Also there were Richard Boone, accepting the annual Silver Spur Award, and Pappy Ford, on break from filming his *How The West Was Won* segment in Paducah, Kentucky. Wayne, a previous Spur winner, said of Bond, "He nearly destroyed his career by attacking Communist infiltrators in Hollywood a decade ago. He was one of the first to recognize the danger, and he spoke at dinners and parties. It made him unpopular with the phony liberals and cost him many good roles. But he wouldn't be quiet."[1432]

In September, Wayne and Greer Garson were presented the Motion Picture Costumer's 1961 Figleaf Award as the actor and actress who best distinguished themselves with artistry in costumes during the year. Wayne's award, for *The Alamo*, was the highlight of the evening. John Ford made the presentation, and Maureen O'Hara was a surprise guest who introduced Ford. One month later, Wayne was named the best foreign actor at the French Victoire Awards in Paris, even though French critics were "merciless" in their review of his film. And, in December, Wayne was honored by the California department of the American

Legion. A resolution praised *The Alamo* for telling a patriotic story and returning cinema art "to the realm of sanity, honor and beauty."[1433]

While Wayne gave and received awards, meanwhile, back in Hollywood, the Academy tried to address the recent outrageous Oscar campaigns. A special committee headed by former Academy president George Seaton was charged with the responsibility of studying past campaigns and "then determine how the academy can most effectively maintain the dignity and integrity of its awards, to the benefit of our industry, in the future." As a result, the following year, the Academy distributed a statement of policy to all nominees and persons handling their publicity. Recognizing that its members need be well informed on the merits of the nominees and cast ballots only on those merits, the academy issued the following: "After a thorough study of violations of good taste in the trade paper advertising on behalf of achievements nominated for the Annual Awards in 1961, we feel that it has now become necessary to state our position in this regard to all potential nominees in 1962. We are mindful that throughout the years the great majority of those nominated, or seeking nominations, have exercised restraint in reminding the voting members of the academy of their achievements. Regrettably, however, a few resorted to outright, excessive and vulgar solicitation of votes. This becomes a serious embarrassment to the academy and our industry. In order to prevent a reoccurrence, we are hopeful that all segments of our industry will join with us in a cooperative effort to eliminate those advertising practices which are irrelevant to the honest evaluation of artistic and technical accomplishments and violate the principles under which the Academy was established. We are hesitant to set down specific rules governing advertising. Consequently, we leave the decision for this year to the good conscience of the nominees, confident that they are well aware of the differences between that which enhances and that which lessens the stature of the Academy. Whether or not a nominee has overstepped the boundaries of accepted behavior will be decided (as it has in the past) by the voting membership. This group when incensed by the tactics or taste of an incogitant nominee has a habit of demonstrating its displeasure in a most definite manner. Undesirable practices other than improper advertising have also become apparent. These, however, are not general, being limited to special organization such as the Academy can command respect only as long as its members and the nominees take unto themselves the responsibility of dignified conduct. We are hopeful that this reminder will be sufficient." Apparently it was—future campaigns were much more low-key, without the grandiose verbosity and solicitation experienced in years before.[1434]

Unfortunately, the backlash against Wayne and *The Alamo* wasn't over. *Mad*, a monthly, satirical magazine, published a withering parody of Duke's film in June 1961, that echoed many of the critic's comments. Titled "Mad visits John *Wayde* on the set of 'At the Alamo,'" the article skewered Duke, the actors, rock 'n' roll, the film, and its length. According to *Wayde*, "As we all know, the **longer** the picture nowadays, the **greater** it is. Well, we had a greatness problem right from the start. Namely, how to add three hours to an exciting half-hour assault on the Alamo by the Mexican army. One way was to pad the time with lengthy speeches about freedom. '**Republic!** I like the sound of that word, Travis. It means a place where a man can live free, and work free, and get drunk free. It means a place where a baby can shave, and a girl can dance, and a stuntman can break a leg free. Republic! Yep, those pictures I starred in made a lot of money for Republic. And that's what I'm fighting for !'" *Wayde* continued, "Another way to run a picture 3½ hours so we can charge $3.50 for reserved seats is to fill the time with events in the lives of the Alamo heroes. But rather than deal in historical facts, which would require research, we did the next best thing: we lied." Written by Larry Siegal and illustrated by Mort Drucker, the parody concluded by killing John *Wayde*. "We're going to kill John *Wayde* for making us sit through this 3½ hour **MISERY!** Next, I take my army of movie-goers, and we wipe out **Charlton Histon** for **3½ hours** of *"Ben Her."* And then we wipe out **Kirt Dougless** for **3½ hours** of **"Sparticuss."** And anybody **else** who tries pictures like **this** again!" Cruel? Definitely! Unfair? Positively. But, regrettably, that was how some of the critics felt, not only about *The Alamo*, but also the plethora of roadshow exhibitions.[1435]

In desperate needs of funds, Wayne hit the cinema trail once again. "It was a relief not having to do anything but remember my own lines," Wayne thankfully admitted. Between the monies he owed United Artists, McCullough Tool, and the Bank of America, well, the only way he was going to repay everyone was to continue acting. (Duke had previously repaid Clint Murchison while still filming *The Alamo*. Where those funds came from is anyone's guess. Perhaps his agent Charles Feldman floated Duke a loan similar to the way he did when Wayne needed money after Hawks held up his profits on *Red River*. Nevertheless, Relyea accompanied Wayne when he flew to Athens, Texas, to repay Murchison. On the way back to Brackettville, Duke told Relyea, "(Murchison's) no gambler. He's not gracious. He took my personal check. The only son of a bitch who's going to be broke is me.")[1436]

So, Duke continued to work. His next film after *North to Alaska* was *Hatari!* Filmed between early September 1960 and March 15, 1961, it wouldn't be released until the following year. Immediately after the Academy Awards, Wayne filmed a $25,000, five-day cameo as General Sherman in *How The West Was Won*. Duke had been scheduled for a second sequence in the film at his normal fee, but he offered to waive it if MGM would give one of its Elvis Presley commitments to Batjac. Unfortunately, that never materialized. Incidentally, Tiomkin was the original choice to compose the film's score but had to bow out due to eye surgery. He was replaced by Alfred Newman.[1437]

One week after *HTWWW*, Wayne appeared in *The Comancheros* for 20th

Century-Fox. Filmed between June and mid-August 1961, it completed his three-picture commitment to the studio, which allowed him to ply his talent on the open market. More importantly, it also entitled him to the full two-million dollars he was owed. He quickly signed a ten-picture, six-million dollar, non-exclusive contract with Paramount; all six million was paid up front. (Wayne received 10% of the gross receipts on *Hatari!* against a guaranteed minimum of $750,000, while on *HTWWW*, he was paid a flat $25,000.) But given the terms of his *Alamo* agreement, Wayne didn't realize anything for starring in the film. Section 3 (a) of his contract stated: "We agree to pay to you an amount equal to seven and one-half percent (7½%) of the 'gross receipts' derived from the distribution and exhibition of said photoplay." Unfortunately, section 3 (b) went on to say: "Your percentage participation shall be deferred and shall not be payable to you until such time as the first money loans (UA) and all secondary loans shall have been fully recouped and paid over to the respective parties entitled thereto." If the film didn't make enough to pay off all loans, Wayne would be paid 7½% of Batjac's net proceeds, not to exceed $100,000 per year for tax purposes. As it was, Duke only made around $13,000, the Directors Guild minimum. He estimated he'd lost over $4 million in potential earnings during all the time he put into his *Alamo* project. In later years, he rationalized, "Financially, the film really didn't fail, it made fifteen million the first time around. Of course I didn't make a cent because I made a bad goddamn deal. United Artists made a great deal of money, and I didn't make a cent. But I had it in my blood to do the picture. I know the rumors was always that it was a bomb, but listen. I've only directed two pictures, both of them did fifteen million first time around. Show me another director who's done that. It cost twelve million dollars to make, and it took in almost eight million dollars in America alone. It made at least as much again abroad. I make that at least sixteen million dollars. I don't call that a box-office failure. The critics always say it lost money. It only lost *me* money. United Artists did very well out of it. I sold all my shares in the picture to them to help pay off the debt I'd gotten myself in, and I ended up doing some work for them for free, so they were the ones who earned all the money. I wish they would re-release *The Alamo* today. There's more to that movie than my damn conservative attitude."[1438]

According to Grant, in March 1960, Wayne had been offered "a huge capital gain to sell out right now, but he is going to ride the tiger the whole way. Yours truly has a piece of the action, and I was happy with his decision, even though the sale would have brought me a sizeable bundle. (Grant was to receive "$100,000 against 10% of Batjac's profit in the project.") I feel that my piece may bring in so much money that I can afford to start drinking again and will have sense enough not to." Too bad. Coulda, shoulda, woulda. As for Wayne, "That picture lost so much money," he once said, "I can't buy a pack of chewing gum in Texas without a cosigner." He later said he made a horrible deal and should have insisted on a larger percentage of future profits. While the studio would generate a profit through re-releases, Wayne made little back other than his initial investment. Batjac remained open but inactive, and, although the staff was on full salary, the company wouldn't release another film until *McLintock!* in November 1963 which meant Wayne could cover his debt. In time, all investors were paid back either through film rentals or directly by Duke himself. By 1968, all Wayne owed was his $700,000 personal loan.[1439]

Over the years, several studios, including Columbia, Seven Arts, and Fox, expressed interest in buying Batjac's assets. Seven Arts even offered $3 million for the film library, a four-picture deal with Wayne and Batjac's percentage of *The Alamo*. The net result would have been $1 million in Wayne's pocket, but he turned the offer down. Selling Batjac was tantamount to an admission of failure. For a man who lived by the creed, "Never apologize, mister–it's a sign of weakness," selling Batjac was out of the question. He turned over control of the company to son Michael, and closed another chapter in his life. Michael would go on to produce many of his father's future films including *McLintock!*, *Cast a Giant Shadow*, *The Green Berets*, *Chisum*, *Big Jake*, *The Train Robbers*, *Cahill U.S. Marshal*, and *McQ*. (It was a wise business decision on Duke's part as by 1965, Michael estimated the market value of Batjac diversified holdings to be in excess of $10 million. In addition to its interest in films, Batjac also owned a condominium and land in Malibu, a convalescent home in Glendale, farms in Arizona, apartment houses in Pasadena, publishing companies, oil interests in California, Texas, and Louisiana, as well as numerous other interests.)[1440]

As previously discussed, it was extremely difficult to determine exactly how much money *The Alamo* actually cost. Hollywood movie studios were notorious for their creative accounting practices–costs assigned to films without regard to actual amounts. "How much is two plus two?" "How much do you want it to be?" Nearly every and any cost possible was charged against a film to keep it from being profitable. Believe it or not, despite generating hundreds of millions of dollars at the box-office, mega-hits such as *Forrest Gump*, *Spiderman*, *Return of the Jedi*, *Harry Potter and the Order of the Phoenix*, and even the *Lord of the Rings* trilogy were classified as losers. Though not anywhere near as egregious, several audits of UA's *Alamo* records showed numerous erroneous charges against Wayne's film: advertising, incorrect royalties, print overcharges, excessive overhead, foreign distribution fees. These charges still had not been satisfactorily addressed more than two years after the initial audit. The single biggest issue was UA's treatment of Todd-AO royalties. According to Batjac president Bob Newman, the royalty was always intended to be treated as an "off-the-top" charge rather than a producer's expense. While Mike Wayne admitted the contract was ambiguous on this issue, a favorable treatment would result in an additional $25,000 to the producer's share of the gross. After five years, Michael Wayne estimated all open issues still amounted to between $150,000 and $200,000. Something had to be done.[1441]

In late 1964, UA suggested it might make sense to re-issue *The Alamo*. Given the success of the 35mm re-issue of *HTWWW* following its Cinerama first run, perhaps UA felt it was time again for another Western, and, it might work out for everyone. Industry rumors at the time suggested Wayne still owed his Texas investors $1.5 million. Mike Wayne agreed with UA, but there had to be a 50/50 split of the gross this time, and all Batjac monies had to go to retire some it its debt. By this time, not only was the McCullough investment still outstanding, but Batjac also owed another $2.5 million to UA for financing *China Doll, Gun the Man Down, Legend of the Lost*, and *Escort West*. The unfortunate thing was, all those films lost money! Michael would even give up the rights to *China Doll* and *Escort West* (both Victor Mature films) if this would resolve all the outstanding accounting issues. So began the negotiations. In the interim, UA announced its 1965 schedule of releases: *Goldfinger, How To Murder Your Wife, The Greatest Story Ever Told, The Hallelujah Trail, I'll Take Sweden, What's New Pussycat, Thunderball*, and *Return of the Seven* among them. *The Alamo* was conspicuously absent.[1442]

It took over a year of haggling, but finally everyone agreed. In a November 5, 1965, meeting at the Beverly Hills Hotel, all concerned parties agreed to the following:

1). UA would cancel the *Legend of the Lost* debt; $200,000 principal plus $150,000 accrued interest.
2). UA would cancel the *Escort West* and *China Doll* debt; $100,000.
3). UA would credit *The Alamo* with $164,000–the difference between the road show and grind distribution fee on certain first-run foreign openings.
4). UA would credit *The Alamo* with $25,000 of unresolved accounting differences identified in previous audits.
5). UA agreed to release all *Alamo* security on the $700,000 completion loan, except for *McLintock!* and *The Alamo*.
6). UA agreed to buy out the I.J. McCullough interest for $1 million.

In return, UA wanted to re-issue *The Alamo* in April 1967 and have the right to put the film on television subject to Batjac's consent. In addition, it also wanted to make a television arrangement for *McLintock!* UA estimated Batjac's return on the *McLintock!* network run to be over $500,000. (Amusingly, both UA and Paramount initially refused to distribute the film as they "weren't interested in Westerns.")[1443]

By 1967, *The Alamo* was still carried on UA's books as a $2 million loser, and Batjac had had enough. For $500,000 and forgiveness of all its debt, Batjac would relinquish its 16.5% ownership; UA agreed and, on April 12, 1967, immediately reissued the film in its shortened general release format. As a condition of the sale, Batjac turned over to UA the following deliverables: the original 65mm camera negative; the 65mm protection masters; the 35mm internegative fine cut; the 35mm reversal interpositive; the original 65m negative trims and any available 70mm positive trims. However, Batjac did keep a 35mm four-track stereo 161-minute print for itself. And, believe it or not, UA either lost or discarded the original 65mm negative trims![1444]

Released earlier, it was now time for a new advertising campaign. What better way than to try and attract film-goers who had seen the movie once before: "Now! For those who missed it! Again! For those who saw it and ... and can't forget it!"; "*The Alamo* Lives Again"; "Remember IT! Remember IT!"; "...It Lives Again! *The Alamo*." The campaign worked—over $700,000 domestic and $160,000 foreign revenue was generated this go-around. It was estimated $1.2 million was realized in the re-release. Given its competition, *The Alamo* did extremely well as it had to contend with the re-release of *Gone With The Wind, Spartacus, To Kill a Mockingbird, That Touch of Mink, The Greatest Show on Earth, Snow White and the Seven Dwarfs*, and a double-bill of *The Shaggy Dog* and *The Absent-Minded Professor*. (*The Alamo* domestic rentals including re-release amounted to $7,918,776; the total all-release gross was $17.8 million or $149.0 million adjusted for inflation. According to author Fred Landesman's *The John Wayne Filmography*, the worldwide box office was in excess of $28 million. By comparison, Disney's 2004 *The Alamo* cost $145.0 million with revenue of only $25.8 million, resulting in a loss of $119.2 million. When adjusting for inflation, this means that Disney's *Alamo* lost $144.9 million, the second-largest box-office bomb of all-time. *The Alamo* was released again in 1970 on an extremely limited basis but was pulled so fast it was hardly remembered.)[1445]

In the summer of 1971, UA also licensed the film to be viewed on television. (According to the November 14, 196, edition of *Variety*, "Wayne is about ready to talk TV terms for *The Alamo*. Two million - $.") Shown in two parts on Saturday and Monday, September 18 and 20, the film was billed as a major motion picture event. "One of the big ones. John Wayne, Richard Widmark star in an 'NBC Saturday Night at the Movies' hit. See part II on Monday." "John Wayne and Richard Widmark are superb in this 'NBC Monday Night at the Movies' action attraction. It's a really big one!" At that time, most films on television were usually edited down to a maximum of two hours, including commercials. But not *The Alamo*! Part of a ninety-five picture, $115 million deal with UA, Wayne's film was shown as a two-day special event garnering a 23.0 rating its second night., An, it was ranked among the top ten movies shown on television that year. Along with the $1.2 million from the general re-release, plus television revenue, *The Alamo* was now in the black. UA eventually paid off the McCullough loan in 1969 and so ended Wayne's twenty-year journey. (Shown again in two parts, NBC would re-broadcast it on July 31 and August 3, 1973, as well as September 11 and 14 later that same year. CBS would broadcast it in its entirety on May 1, 1977.)[1446]

Three weeks after he completed *Comancheros*, Wayne was back before the camera once again, this time with John Ford in *The Man Who Shot Liberty Valance*. Wayne again received a guaranteed $750,000 against 7.5% of the gross receipts. Filmed almost entirely on the Paramount soundstage except for a few outdoor sequences at the Paramount Ranch in Agoura, California, some witnesses said Ford was unusually brutal in his treatment of Wayne—perhaps in retaliation for his treatment on the *Alamo* set. Cast member Ken Murray remembered, "it was reputed that (Ford) was particularly nasty to Wayne because Ford was upset that Duke did not use him more on *The Alamo*. Ford was a monster on the set. He was an ogre; I was scared of him." One day after Wayne made a recommendation, Ford erupted, "Jesus Christ, here I take you out of eight-day Westerns, I put you in big movies, and you give me a stupid suggestion like that!" Ford also made malicious comparisons between Wayne's football career and that of actor Woody Strode. "Duke," said Ford, "there's a real football player." He even went out of his way and taunted Wayne about how Woody had served in World War II and Duke hadn't. According to author Joseph McBride, "Ford's baiting of Wayne probably reflected his growing anger over Wayne's superior position in the industry," and Scott McBride agreed it had to do with Wayne's legendary stature: "…at this stage in their careers, Ford needed John Wayne more than John Wayne needed Ford. '(Ford) still had life,' said producer Howard Koch, 'but the Big Cowboy was really the whole thing.'" Ford's grandson Dan surmised it may also have had something to do with the growing political differences between Wayne and Pappy. Wayne was growing increasingly conservative while Ford was more and more liberal. According to Dan, "While (Ford) thought that *The Alamo* was a good story, he didn't think it was America's epic poem, and he thought Wayne's approach was too self-consciously political." (Even though it must have grated on Duke's nerves to be treated that way, he still wasn't going to do anything to offend Ford. During the filming of *Liberty Valance*, Wayne was scheduled to receive an award at the Beverly Hilton's costumed Adam and Eve ball—Duke asked Pappy to present it. According to costumer Ron Talsky, who assisted Ford that evening, "Well, they announced Mr. Ford to come out to take a bow and give Duke his… award. So Mr. Ford gets up. He has this eye patch and the room isn't well lit. Well, he trips down the two stairs momentarily, braces himself, jumps right up, and gets to the microphone. Then he announces Duke's award." Wayne, sensitive to Ford's vanity, got up, and stumbled down the stairs as well. "Everybody thought this was all in fun and they had a good laugh," explained Talsky. "The truth was that Duke did the same thing as Ford to make it look like that was what he was supposed to do all along. He did it to cover up Ford's bad sight. The audience just loved it. It was a validation. But he did this to take away the embarrassment from Ford."[1447]

Ford would go on to direct just four more films: *How The West Was Won*

(Civil War segment), *Donovan's Reef*, *Cheyenne Autumn*, and *7 Women*. None of them matched the splendor or artistic creativity of his earlier work. Wayne, on the other hand, went on to appear in twenty-six more films over the next fourteen years, eventually winning an Academy Award for Best Actor in *True Grit* which, arguably, should have been his fourth after *Sands of Iwo Jima*, *She Wore a Yellow Ribbon*, and *The Searchers*. Though respectful, never again would the two have the same close relationship as they once had. Ford's perceived treatment on the set of *The Alamo* and Wayne's subsequent punishment on *Liberty Valance* forever put an end to the mentor-student connection.

## CHAPTER THIRTY-SEVEN
## CONCLUSIONS

In the 1950s, the movie industry experienced an upheaval that shook it to its very core. Through government decree, massive entertainment companies were forced to end vertical integration by divesting themselves of their movie theater divisions. No longer could studios produce, distribute, and then exhibit their own films. Contract players were released; studio-bound actors and directors were free to ply their talents on the open market. More and more, major studios financed and distributed independently-produced films. Television debuted and brought entertainment out of movie theaters and into living rooms. As a result, movie-theater ticket sales were abysmal. So, to woo back audiences, studios developed new viewing formats that included 3-D and such widescreen processes as Cinerama (an anagram for "American"), VistaVision, SuperScope, WarnerScope, MGM Camera 65, Panavision, Super Panavision 70, Ultra Panavision 70, Super Technirama, Super Technirama 70, Techniscope, and Todd-AO. Lavish, sumptuous productions were the norm, whether they be musicals such as *An American in Paris*, *Singing in the Rain*, and *Guys and Dolls*, biblical epics like *The Ten Commandments*, *Ben-Hur*, *Quo Vadis*, and *The Robe*, spectaculars like *Around the World in 80 Days* and *The Greatest Show on Earth*, and historical epics such as *The Alamo*.

*The Alamo* is that rare film which combines popular entertainment with a social message. On one level, it is simply a classic epic that depicts a small battle in the fight for Texas independence. Wayne took the thirteen-day siege of the

813

historic fortress Alamo and condensed it into a four- or five-day story complete with humor, pathos, duty, action, and drama. Outside of Crockett, Bowie, Travis, and possibly Houston, other characters are given little if any depth. A visually elegant but highly inaccurate view of the battle, the film consists of patriotic speeches and heroic posturing interspersed with magnificent battle scenes. On another level, it's a study of autocratic, paternalistic, and democratic leadership styles vis-à-vis various types of geo-political systems. Travis–strict control, direct supervision, and adherence to policies and procedures; Crockett–a father figure worthy of loyalty and trust; and Bowie–discussion and debate.

In addition, Wayne utilized the story as a metaphor for Communism and world domination. "I'd read up on the history of our country, and I'd become fascinated with the story of the Alamo," explained Wayne. "To me it represented a fight for freedom, not just in America, but it all countries. Seeing (*Davy Crockett at the Fall of the Alamo*) was a real inspiration to me, and I guess it stuck with me until it became a passion of mine to make *The Alamo*. It's a story of freedom, and courage, and doing right in the face of adversity." Although mentioned before, this bears repeating. Asked if his film was about Communism, Wayne said, "It was, in part. But it was more than that. I hoped it would convey to people all over the free world that they owed a debt to all men who gave their lives fighting for freedom. I hope that the battle of the Alamo will remind people everywhere that the price of freedom and liberty doesn't come cheap. I was always inspired by the story because I don't know of any other moment in American history which portrays the courage of men any better. It's the courage of those men that always moved me. Since then men–and women–have shown many great acts of courage in the face of adversity. But what for me was the defining moment when men put their lives before all else, was when Travis tells all the volunteers who are on their horses and ready to withdraw from a battle they know they can't win, that they can leave the Alamo without fear of criticism or shame. And every one of those volunteers got off their horses and stood behind Travis. It's a story for all the world, but it is a special story for the patriots of America. I put my heart and soul into the picture. It said everything I felt about my country, about freedom, and about dictatorships. It was seen by those on the left as a piece of propaganda, and hell, it was. But it was also, first and foremost, a great story and a grand piece of entertainment."[1448]

Throughout numerous interviews, Wayne never hesitated to explain his desire to film this project: "That was something in my heart. The bloody truth of what some forebears went through to win what they had to have or die–liberty and freedom. This picture is America. It's the first time in my life I've been able to express what I feel about people. There is something inside everyman that tells him he needs a place he can call his own and needs the freedom to be what he feels he ought to be. You know, that's what I want to show in this picture. Every man ought to have something he thinks is worth dying for. For these men, that something was a concept of liberty."[1449]

Unfortunately, the film, laced with strong Fordian themes, bears only a slight semblance to actual facts. Its inadvertent mistakes and outright falsehoods are legendary. Supporting characters are barely fleshed out; rather than personalities, they have occupations–gambler, drinker, parson. When they die in the final assault, little loss is felt as the audience never makes a strong connection with these characters. Viewers never felt empathy for, or even sympathy with the characters because they never really knew them. Under siege for thirteen days, defenders come and go at will, seemingly without fear of attack. There was no sense of being surrounded without hope of relief. The European cannon, the raid for cattle, the church basement–the film is a series of isolated episodes connected by a very loose thread. Crockett's sacrificial death, though tragic, seems stylized because "Crockett doesn't die," Wayne does. But Wayne's intent was not to create a documentary, nor was it to educate the masses in historical accuracy. The film's atmosphere and message of dedication, sacrifice, and liberty are more important than how many soldiers are in the attacking forces, the direction the Alamo faces, or how Crockett dies.

In cinema criticism, classical auteur theory holds that a director's film reflects his personal creative vision, as if he is the primary "auteur" or author. The assumption is that his personal influence and artistic control are so great, he thus is considered the author of the film. The theory goes on to say that through lighting, camerawork, staging, and editing, the director brings the film to life and uses the film to express his thoughts and feelings on the subject matter. Supporters of the theory contend that the most cinematically successful film will bear the unmistakable stamp of the director, and, as the director oversees all visual and audio components of the film, he may be considered more the "author" of the film than the screenwriter. While not at all in the same league as auteur filmmakers such as Alfred Hitchcock, Akira Kurosawa, François Truffaut, Jean-Luc Godard, or even Howard Hawks, Wayne definitely placed his stamp on his film. Was he the primary cinematographer? No. But according to Clothier, Duke knew appropriate camera placement as well as which lens to use and how to place lighting to achieve a specific effect. Was he the main screenwriter? Not really. But he did work each night with Grant, creating and modifying scenes and dialogue and helped expand a simple "B" Western into a major epic. Did he supervise the editing process? Not exactly, but he did coordinate with Stuart Gilmore the inclusion or exclusion of every single scene and take. And, even though he received assistance from Ford and Lyons, first and foremost, Wayne was the film's director. He had the vision, he had the drive. Living and breathing the project for almost fourteen years, he was the one who pulled together the cast and crew; he was the one who had the set built; he was the one who beat the bushes to finance the film, the one who spent every single dime he owned on the film. He was the one who brought this project to fruition. So, from that perspective, he was truly the auteur.

The problem with the film, as it is with almost every film about the Alamo, is that *everybody knows how it will end.* (Except the foreign market, which explains in part why the film was so successful overseas.) Director Burt Kennedy agreed: "Three hours is a long time to tell the story of the Alamo. It would be a good 110-minute movie. It's a story that's been told so many times that it's hard to keep interest in it." Wayne's film is no different; it has a complicated plot and continually shifts from action to comedy to drama. The trick was how to hold the audience's attention and interest until the final scene. Some directors add fictitious characters and improbable scenarios, others present a straightforward telling of the tale without any attempt to explain the *why.* The astute filmmaker understands that the story of the Alamo and the struggle for freedom ars complementary to a character study of the principal performers. Most of Wayne's films were message films–perhaps not as blatant as *Alamo* or *Green Berets,* but message films nonetheless. A central theme: the strong defend the weak, a man's gotta do what a man's gotta do, stand up for what's right, rugged American individualism. As Crockett, Wayne waxed poetically when he expressed his chivalrous feelings towards women: *"You haven't seen me before tonight, but I'm offering you my services. If that fella's making you stay in Bexar, I'm ready, willing and able to provide you a transport to wherever you wanna go. And on the other hand, if you choose to stay in Bexar, I'm ready, willing and able to see that he don't bother you."* Later, Crockett's oration to Flaca personifies Wayne's beliefs: *"That's what's important. To feel useful in this old world. To hit a lick against what's wrong or to say a word for what's right, even though you get walloped for saying that word. There's right and there's wrong–you gotta do one or the other. You do the one and you're living. You do the other, and you may be walkin' around, but you're dead as a beaver hat."* As Wayne told author Lawrence Suid, if he had a goal in his movies, it was "to pass along the message of preparedness to the country. No weak nation makes treaties. It's a strong nation that gets things done, and we can't allow to become second rate." Duke's roles never changed, just the character's names, the clothes they wore and the situations they found themselves in. Which is exactly what the audience wanted and expected.[1450]

Overly long and extremely loquacious to the point of tediousness, at times, however, *The Alamo* reaches levels of resplendency, particularly in its action sequences. Corny, yes. Uneven, definitely. The film is filled with undefined characters and unnecessary skits, But that's what makes it so compelling. After all, it's John Wayne, for God's sake! Ford was the master of humorous vignettes. He would build tension to an unbearable level, then insert a scene that lets the audience catch its breath, so to speak. Sometimes too formulaic but effective nonetheless. Wayne, though, seemed to add vignettes as transitions between action sequences. They really don't move the story along, but Wayne apparently

816

considered them necessary for the film to be of a certain length, i.e., the "birthday party" or "Smitty and the log" sequences. Humor should be subordinate to the narrative. It's almost as if Wayne understood the necessity but not the concept. Having said that, the vignettes do allow the actors to flesh out their characters a bit. But Duke must be given credit–he recognized the necessity of their elimination when he had to shorten the roadshow version.

Ford advocated shooting scenes once, accepting their content, complete with mistakes and all. The natural, ordinary, and legitimate aspects of the gaffes added to the quality of his scenes. Plus, it was very difficult to edit a film when there weren't any alternate angles or cutaways to review, which was Ford's intention. Wayne tried to emulate Pappy but also knew that, once he left the location, he never could return to re-shoot scenes due to the significant costs. Besides, much of the *Alamo* set had been destroyed. Also, since Wayne had filmed hundreds of thousands of feet of footage on the chance he might want to use it, minor flubs had to be accepted. Just as dogs sometimes appeared in the background of Ford's scenes, so were mistakes included in Wayne's. Many times unplanned, they nonetheless add touches of realism to the scenes. Even Wayne's own mistakes appear: After the raid for cattle, Wayne, as Crockett, rides back into the Alamo compound, dismounts, runs to the main gate, and stumbles as he runs up the stairs.

Analyzing the film's underlying themes is enthusiastically pursued by those who want to interpret and then explain *why* Wayne made his film. Some have focused on the independent nature of Crockett's Tennesseans and thus compare them to American's desire for liberty. Others have addressed Crockett's relationship with Flaca and suggested it mirrors Wayne's relationship with Pilar. Still others have focused on the religious presence of crosses and Crockett's prayer to God. Authors Shepherd and Slatzer, in *Duke: The Life and Times of John Wayne*, viewed the film as a manifestation of not only Wayne's patriotic beliefs but also of his mi-life crisis. They thought Duke felt he was too old to be a "dashing leading man anymore. He knew he lacked the dramatic range to handle the meaty, mature roles that would be left to a man of his approaching years." In *Duke: We're Glad We Knew You*, Herb Fagen called it "a period war saga locked into the sentiment and drama of its time," while Gary Wills proposed that much of Wayne's dialogue was autobiographical, that he was trying to make sense of his own life. Further, in *John Wayne's America: The Politics of Celebrity*, Wills contends that Crockett's death, as portrayed by Wayne, "has symbolic force. It makes (his) death an assertion of will, not the obliteration of it. As Crockett blows up a building that, nonetheless survives, so his own death is transformed into a cleansing apocalyptic fire in which he will live forever." And finally, Wills asserts the "Flaca tree" scene is a mirror image of Wayne's speech at the end of Raoul Walsh's classic, *The Big Trail*, right down to the dialogue and message.[1451]

One certainly can see similarities between the two films, and all of the aforementioned observations can be supported to one extent or another. However, some may be looking too hard for symbolic rationale and explanation where none exists–seeking subtleties where none existed. Wayne was a professional; he knew his medium. He knew the message he wanted to convey and how best to do so. To look for a hidden meaning is useless; with Wayne, what you saw is what you got. He wore his beliefs on his sleeve, and you only had to spend a few minutes with him to find out exactly how he felt on any given subject. To think there were deep, hidden messages in his films is foolish. The secret to a successful presentation is to tell your audience what you're going to say, say it, then tell them what you just said. Wayne knew that and followed it to a "T." He told everyone *The Alamo* would be about freedom and liberty. The film's dialogue reinforced that theme, And, after the film was finished, he reasserted his message of sacrifice and dedication in all the publicity.

The clash between Alamo defenders and the Mexican army is personified in a running conflict among the film's three protagonists: Travis, the dandified disciplinarian; Bowie, a reckless, impetuous, Chicago-style gangster; and Crockett, the backwoods conciliatory mediator. Author Richard D. McGhee accurately describes Wayne's Crockett as "a hero of moderation, balance, and cool sanity." Crockett provides the balance between two extremes: the impulsive, action-oriented, foolhardy, knife-wielding Bowie, and the structured, humorless, egotistical Travis. And Bowie, in Grant's script, sums up these differences: "You can't help being you, Travis. And I can't help being me." In *John Wayne: Actor, Artist, Hero*, Richard McGhee writes, "Bowie has to learn to calm down, to trust authority; Travis has to learn to put people before plans, to trust his fellow man, and to realize that noble ends do not justify ignoble means; Crockett exemplifies the wisdom of these lessons. He has Travis's manners and Bowie's feelings. Wayne (as Crockett) balances the extremes."[1452]

In *Three Bad Men*, Scott Allen Nollen describes Duke's performance in exceedingly glowing terms: "His acting (which is quite convincing) sprang from such a font of sincerity that Wayne couldn't help but wax in a manner that reaches near-Shakespearean proportions. (As) to his legendary interpretation of the character of Crockett, there is no line between truth and myth, because Wayne really believed what he was saying." Although undoubtedly sincere, Nollen possibly stretches his credibility a bit by comparing Wayne to Laurence Olivier: "Both played in grand costume epics based primarily on myths, and their scripts featured 'soliloquies' ergo 'preaching.' Arguably, the sincere effort put forth by Wayne as the storybook Crockett in *The Alamo* is just as convincing as Olivier's monstrous turn as the hunchbacked villain in his 1955 adaptation of Shakespeare's very unsubtle *Richard III*." There is no doubt Wayne's portrayal is heartfelt. He had the strength of his convictions to support him. Plus, everything Duke had was riding on the success of the film–he couldn't afford *not* to be sincere. Still, there are times when it appears he walks through scenes in a detached manner.

It's obvious the pressure of being director, producer, and actor weighed heavily on his shoulders. On the screen, Wayne becomes the mythic hero, and Crockett takes on Duke's traits and personality. It's impossible to separate the two, and, at a time in our history when the country needed heroes more than ever, Wayne/Crockett fit the bill.

Harvey utilizes his dramatic acting credentials and gives an impressive performance. Though his accent floats in and out, he convincingly portrays a Southern aristocrat. Absent his "Jeffersonian" speech, his dialogue isn't weighed down by Wayne's constant theme. In his portrayal, he figuratively and literally rises above the other defenders and actors. However, Widmark walks through his role with surprisingly poor acting and ill-timed gestures. After forcibly insisting he play Bowie, he doesn't seem all that interested in the part. Much of the indifference can be attributed to his constant conflicts with Wayne. The intensity Widmark brought to Tommy Udo in the film-noir classic *Kiss of Death* is woefully lacking in *The Alamo*. Perhaps it was Wayne's direction, perhaps it was Widmark's interpretation, but his performance is unconvincing and pedestrian. And as for Chill Wills, the less said the better. Vastly undeserving of an Academy Award nomination, his portrayal of a drunken, backwoods country bumpkin is an insult to country bumpkins.

It's only in the second half of the film when *The Alamo* comes into its own. Outstanding photography, magnificent music, and spectacular battle sequences are the order of the day. Gone is the constant beating of the message drum because Wayne already had said everything he wanted to convey. Now it was time for action. Words were no longer necessary. Naturally, Grant wouldn't be Grant if he didn't add a few corny scenes: *"If your stick don't float that way,"* and *"if discussion mean what I think it do?"* But these corny scenes are offset by some truly emotional, heart-tugging segments: the figurative line in the sand and *"Not thinkin'. Just rememberin' .... "*

Is *The Alamo* a great film? No, it's not. But it's damn good! As a novice director, Wayne pulled off a herculean task and did it admirably. Wayne embodied everything it meant to be an American. He was a mythic hero, charismatic, and larger than life, personified on screen as a cowboy, soldier, sailor, Marine, industrialist, diplomat, Cossack, Texas Ranger, adventurer, and frontier legend. The roles he played represented everything that is good about our country, everything that we are, everything we aspire to be. To pull off *The Alamo* took fourteen years of his life and every penny he owned. Lesser men would have given up; those not as dedicated would have quit long ago. But not Wayne.

So, after all the time, all the research and the preproduction activity, all the costume designs and the set construction, all the interviews and casting, all the begging and pleading for financing, all the discussions and endless nights, all the script revisions, all the EVERYTHING–was *The Alamo* a success? Well, that depends on how you define success. If you define it in terms of profit and loss, dollars and cents, then no, it wasn't—at least, not for Wayne. If, however, you define success in terms of dedication, ambition, commitment, hard work, effort, and sacrifice, then yes, it was successful beyond Wayne's wildest dreams. He gave it his best, and that's all that anyone can ask. "I put my heart and soul into that picture," said Wayne. "It said everything I felt about my country, about freedom, and about dictatorships. I hoped it would convey to people all over the free world that they owed a debt to all men who gave their lives fighting for freedom. I hope that the battle of the Alamo will remind people everywhere that the price of freedom and liberty doesn't come cheap."

And as Crockett says in the film, "That's not a bad stab at putting it into words."

# APPENDIX A
## The World Premiere

As detailed elsewhere in this book, the four-day San Antonio *Alamo* premiere was a star-studded, action-packed celebration, full of celebrities, news reporters, politicians, guests, visitors and Texans. With so many interesting activities scheduled, one couldn't possibly attend them all, or even be aware of some of them. However, for those who swim in the pool of minutia, the following outlines the tentative events as listed in an August 26, 1960 letter from Roger H. Lewis, combined with timing from the master schedule.

*Saturday, October 22, 1960:*

International Airport reception for arrival of the stars–Mexican Fiesta atmosphere including bands and flamenco dancers. Presentation of Alcade (honorary mayor) certificates to every arriving visitor.

International Airport reception for "Alamo Airlift" of newswriters.

International Airport reception for visiting governors and foreign ambassadors.

Evening reception for the stars, visiting, and local press.

*Alamo* Symphony concert with San Antonio Symphony Orchestra,

Municipal auditorium, Dimitri Tiomkin, guest conductor.

San Antonio Press Club Annual Gridiron Show, Pearl Corral, John Wayne as honored guest.

_Sunday, October 23, 1960:_

"Howdy" brunch for visiting press, downtown hotel.

Ranch Bar-B-Que and party for visiting press at the Ray Ellison ranch. Located a few miles north of town near Bulverde. Entertainers will be brought from town as this isn't a dude ranch.

Evening River ride along San Antonio River Walk with mariachis and strolling troubadours.

San Antonio Press Club reception for visiting press, Press Club on the banks of San Antonio river in LaVillita. The reception will commence at the conclusion of the river ride.

Gala "Night in Old San Antonio" at picturesque La Villita (two hundred-year-old reconstructed Spanish village)–this will be a typical fiesta reminiscent of San Antonio during the days of the Alamo.

_Monday, October 24, 1960:_

Frontier Street breakfast served outdoors at historic Alamo Plaza.

The presentation to governors of seventeen states and ambassadors of six countries (including Great Britain, Germany, Denmark, Ireland and Mexico), from the Governor of Texas, of a medallion recognizing the part played by their citizens in Texas' fight for liberty. This would mark the first time in 124 years that Texas officially recognized the men of The Alamo from these places. This part of the program would be handled with the utmost dignity and solemnity, but naturally would be as photogenic and dramatic as we could arrange it without sacrificing stature.

"Texas Under Six Flags" luncheon, downtown hotel, honoring John Wayne. Award presented by Governor Price Daniel on behalf of the University of Texas ex-students association.

Arrival of Trail Riders for Brackettville.

Arrival of "Men of Gonzales." U.S. Marines of San Antonio reserve Marine battalion seventy mile, two-day forced march from Gonzales.

Giant downtown Alamo parade with trail riders, floats, Charros, military bands and marching units, governors, stars and military.

Reception and cocktail party for premiere guests and Gold patrons to meet the stars and visiting press, downtown hotel. The Alamo World Premiere committee has a special presentation for John Wayne to be made during the reception.

Mass motorcade of stars, visiting press and dignitaries to premiere from downtown hotel.

World Premiere ceremonies at Woodlawn Theater–details to be worked out by Cinema Arts, United Artists, Batjac Productions, Chamber of Commerce.

*Tuesday, October 25, 1960:*

Special morning showing of The Alamo at Woodlawn Theater for Trail riders, Men of Gonzales and premiere workers.

Wrap-up brunch for survivors of Alamo premiere. Sponsored by the Premiere committee and the City of San Antonio for stars and visiting newsmen who have not yet left the city.

## APPENDIX B
## "This is the West, Sir.
## When the legend becomes fact,
## print the legend."

With apologies to the Bard...

*"To direct, or not to direct—that is the question: Whether 'tis nobler to stand in lingering shadows and gaze upon efforts of enthusiastic youth, or to take arms against a sea of troubles whilst masticating linen white and by opposing end them?"*

Much has been written in these pages about John Ford's involvement in *The Alamo* or lack thereof. Did he show up in Brackettville on his own accord or was he invited? Was he involved in the development of the script and did he direct any actors, including Wayne? If so, which scenes? To better understand Ford's involvement, perhaps we should define exactly what a director does. Veteran Stills Photographer Louis Goldman's close proximity to the set gave him a unique perspective: "Filmmaking is above all a team effort, but the director is the one most responsible for the finished product. Consider, if you will, what a director's job entails: total concentration; the ability to keep track of an inner vision that becomes chopped up into a thousand disconnected short pieces; the leadership necessary to mold an army of technicians into a smoothly functioning unit; the talent to extract the best performances from a large and diverse cast; the strength to face constant pressure, conflict, and crisis while remaining levelheaded; and the self-assurance to prevail against dissenting opinions from powerful studio executives . . . The task is herculean but the director has the awesome power to carry it out. During a movie production many things can go wrong, causing irritating delays, but the greatest frustration for the director comes from the fact that in the realization of a deeply personal concept, much must be delegated to others."

While Goldman explained what a director does, Ford was a bit more succinct when he described the essence of a director: "A lot of people ask me what is the secret of direction. Well, there is no secret. Most of the majority—the majority of the good directors have started at the bottom. They learned their art thoroughly and when they had a chance to direct, they usually came through . . . In our day direction came by instinct. We knew the fundamentals and when we had a chance we applied those fundamentals. There is no secret about directing except good common sense. And a belief in what you are doing. The reason I think that movies have slipped is that they have directors from all walks of life, people who don't know the fundamentals. Most of the young directors are obsessed by the camera, which is a new toy. Instead of looking at their people they look at the camera. And moving it around. The camera obsesses them and they think that is the secret—it isn't. The secret is in people's faces, their eye expression, their movements."

So, given the aforementioned parameters, did Ford really direct any sequences in *The Alamo*? Well . . . maybe. Even though *The Alamo* was Wayne's vision, Ford was involved in the project from the very beginning. Recall that during a March 1948 visit to San Antonio with Wayne, Bond, Merian Cooper and Tex Hill, Ford stated Duke would play David Crockett and he (Ford) would be involved in the project. "It may be a year before *we* start shooting scenes of the Alamo picture," said Ford. One year later, Wayne confirmed Ford's involvement. Wayne would star in the film but Ford would take over the directorial reins for those sequences in which Wayne would appear. "I've got a finished script for a story I'd like to do," he said. "It's called *Alamo* . . . Jack Ford has offered to help me with it and to direct the scenes in which I appear." Keeping the project in the family, Duke even had Ford's son Pat work on a script treatment while working at Republic. Subsequently, after his acrimonious departure from Herb Yates and Republic, Wayne in an October 29, 1952, letter to Ford, stated in part, " . . . (Yates) then put out a story that I had left Republic because he wanted to make *The Alamo* in Texas and was being loyal to the Texans, and that I insisted on doing it in Panama. He knows, you know, and I know that the reason *we* are not making it in Texas is that he wouldn't put out the money.[1453]

Throughout the 1950s, while Wayne accumulated the necessary funds to support his project, Hollywood trade papers buzzed with rumors of Ford's anticipated involvement: "Wayne wants Ford to direct . . . *The Alamo*," "Wayne plans to direct *Alamo* . . . except own scenes," "John Wayne to direct *Alamo* in Fall." Interestingly, while neither Wayne nor Ford made any attempt to clarify those headlines, neither one flatly denied them either. Many major studios were reluctant to financially back Wayne's project for the simple fact that Duke wanted to direct the film himself. If they thought Ford would direct it, *or at least would be somewhat involved*, they might be more favorably disposed to fund the project. So, why deny a rumor if, by doing so, it would create funding issues? Wayne admitted, " . . . they all turned me down unless I got John Ford to direct. But this was my dream. I didn't want anyone else to direct it–not even my dear friend Jack Ford." Really? Supposedly, Ford, Hawks and Hathaway all volunteered to direct Wayne's scenes, and just before the start of production *Variety* announced Wayne had decided on Ford. As usual, Pappy denied it: "No one ever talked to me about it." Since Wayne had asked Ford for advice during pre-production activities and even traveled with him to scout possible locations, it seemed logical Ford would also be involved in the actual shoot. Similarly, by virtue of Harvey's comments, we know that Ford interviewed and approved Larry's involvement in the project. Ford bluntly told Wayne, "*We* haven't got any time. Hire the bastard." Given Ford's commanding personality and inability to defer to others, one can assume he wasn't referring to the royal *we* when he instructed Wayne to do so. In September 1959, Ford even wrote his friend Lord Killanin that "I hope to go to Texas and cast a paternal eye on Duke Wayne." Perhaps he was just commenting on his travel plans or, more likely, he had been asked to help out. This was not a spur-of-the-moment decision; it was well planned, well organized. In fact, since Ford spent fifty of the ninety-eight scheduled days on location, he wouldn't have been there all that time just to watch someone else make a movie.

In summary, then, this evidence strongly suggests Ford played more than just an advisory role in the project. He had even set up a specific *Alamo* account in John Ford Production financial records to record costs applied against the film ($2,800 from October through December 1959. Interestingly, the vice-president of JFP was . . . John Wayne). Although Wayne and Ford would frequently write each other on a variety of subjects, including future projects, there isn't any specific correspondence from Wayne asking Ford to come down on location. However, as stated in various interviews, Wayne told the stuntmen he knew Ford was coming down and he knew Ford would film numerous scenes. Pappy even stayed at a cottage in Ft. Clark as did many principal members of the cast and crew. Why would Wayne keep a room available on the off-chance Ford might show up if it wasn't really necessary? Given the astronomical budget, Wayne could ill afford to waste money on an unoccupied dwelling.

As previously mentioned, *The Horse Soldiers* wrapped up location shooting on December 6, 1958, immediately following the accidental death of stuntman Fred Kennedy. Nineteen additional days of shooting were scheduled in Los Angeles–exteriors on the Goldwyn lot, interiors at MGM. Finally the film ground to a merciful end. Wayne immediately jumped feet first into *Alamo* pre-production; Ford left for Honolulu. After an extended stay in Hawaii with time off for a rumored dalliance in Korea, Pappy's next major project was *Sergeant Rutledge* which began July 16, 1959, in Monument Valley. Though he was only on location a mere 10 days, his attention began to dwindle; was he already thinking about Wayne's film? According to grandson Dan Ford, "(Ford) worked quickly and impersonally, cutting corners wherever he could." Pappy returned again to Los Angeles to wrap up *Rutledge,* and on September 1 returned to Honolulu. He knew Wayne had scheduled *Alamo*'s start of production for early September; let the novice director get his feet wet for a few days before Ford would ride in like the cavalry and rescue the film. On September 19, he was in Brackettville and ready to assume control.

So, given the fact that Ford was more than just tangentially involved, exactly how large a directorial role did he play? The lack of any documentary evidence to support anyone's contention is surprisingly strong. Some cinematic historians believe that the overwhelming denials of Ford's involvement by many of those present should be accepted at face value. Others postulate if Ford was present while a scene was filmed, he must have directed it. Leading credence to this argument is the fact that numerous photographs show Pappy sitting in his personalized leather-engraved director's chair while that occurred. An analysis of memoirs, personal correspondence and interviews include numerous actor appreciations for his influence on their performances–but specific *scenes* are rarely mentioned.

In numerous interviews, Ford said he was only down there to help and never really directed anything. But as everyone knows, Pappy hated giving interviews, never told the truth in them anyway (according to Wayne) and said only what he thought interviewers wanted to hear. Ford was notorious for not really telling interviewers anything; he would turn questions around, deliberately mislead them, refuse to answer or give one-word replies. So, his complete denial of any involvement in Wayne's film lacks credibility.

Also, Ford's travel records reveal the length of time he was in Brackettville but unfortunately, the assistant director's daily production reports, which would show what was filmed on what day and who was present, are unavailable. It is only by peeling away the layers of the onion–matching the various scripts to the Master Shooting Schedule to travel records, photographs and personal correspondence–that we can approximate what was filmed when.

First, let's hear from the participants themselves:

**Ford**–"I was merely down there on vacation and Duke said, 'Do you mind going out and getting a shot of so-and-so?' And I did. We got some wonderful scenes–guys swimming rivers, that sort of thing–but they were all cut out."

**Clothier**–"Ford went out and shot stuff that couldn't possibly be used. It had absolutely nothing to do with the picture we were making. I don't think we used three cuts that the Old Man did."

**Cristal**–In reference to a scene with Wayne when: "(Ford) wanted to get something from me that he didn't get … but when I saw it on the screen it was there, the feeling was there, that he wanted. He *directed*."

**Michael Wayne**–"When JW decided Ford could *direct* a second unit, he gave me the job of watching over him."

There is no doubt Ford directed various actors in numerous scenes. The only question now is, what scenes were they? To answer that we need to determine when Ford was on location, when a specific scene was filmed, and was there any photographic or anecdotal evidence to suggest that he directed that particular scene? According to Ford's 1959 travel log, he was present in Brackettville on the following dates:

September 19 through September 29.
October 5 through October 19.
November 17 through November 28.
November 30 through December 12.

Utilizing the August 21, 1959, Master Shooting Schedule, the following will identify when specific scenes were filmed.

*September 4/5*: Opening shots with Mexican Army, caissons, horses, etc. Caissons crossing creek.
*September 9*: Invocation and Scene 4–Houston's arrival in Bexar; Scene 5–Houston and Travis enter hotel; Scene 15–Houston leaves Bexar.
*September 10*: Scene 6–Houston gives Travis command (filmed at Ft. Clark airplane hangar).
*September 11/12*: Scenes 16-17-18-19–Jethro and Bowie inside Bowie's room, Travis informs Bowie of his command; Scenes 50-51-52-53–Seguins ride through Bexar (omitted); Scenes 69-70–Crockett and Tennesseans arrive in town (filmed, not included); Scenes 127-128–Tennesseans leave town for Alamo.
*September 14*: Scenes 20-21-22-23–Bowie and men arrive in Alamo, Bowie speaks with Travis, flag-raising ceremony; Scene 113–Bowie encounters Gambler/morning after.
*September 15*: Scenes 59-60-61-62-63-64-65-66–Smitty and Parson view the Alamo; Scenes 45-47–Seguins ride toward Bexar (omitted); Scene 124–Tennesseans cluster around Cantina, discuss Santa Anna.
*September 16/17*: Scenes 109-110–Crockett watches refugees leave Bexar; Scene 124 (partial)–Flaca reads Crockett's letter to Tennesseans.
*September 18*: Scenes 139-140-141-142–Mexican troops arrive in Bexar.
*September 19*: Scenes 123-123A–Crockett, Flaca and Seguin discuss Santa Anna. Ford arrives in Brackettville.
*September 21*: Scene 49A–Bowie and Finn talk while working on walls; Scenes

829

62-63-64-65–Crrockett and Tennesseans meet Smitty/Parson on top of hill overlooking Alamo, and possibly Scene 333–Mexican troops starting to arrive in town.

**September 22:** Scenes 54-55-56-57–Seguins report to Travis.

By this time, the Master Shooting Schedule had been modified so significantly, it is difficult to determine exactly what was filmed when. However, once he arrived, there is neither photographic nor anecdotal evidence to suggest Ford directed any of the above-mentioned scenes. Perhaps the scenes were filmed too early for Ford's 10 a.m. wake-up call, or maybe he was just getting the feel of the set. Further, by analyzing what was filmed between September 4 and September 18, one can also determine those scenes that Ford definitely wasn't involved in.

On Wednesday, September 23, Wayne returned to the airplane hangar and continued filming.

**September 23/24:** Scenes 80, 82, 92–Crockett/Sand in hotel corridor; Scenes 81, 86, 89, 91–Interior Flaca's room; Scenes 83, 84, 88–Interior Crockett's room and corridor (omitted).

**September 25:** Scene 106–Crockett informs Flaca of Sand's death; Scene 112– Flaca writes letter for Crockett.

The following day, Wayne returned to the village set and resumed night shooting.

**September 26:** Scene 71–Patrol led by Travis and Dickinson enters Bexar; Scene 73–Travis enters Cantina.

**September 28:** Scenes 79, 90, 93, 94–Sand stops Flaca from leaving, Sand's thugs attack Crockett, Bowie helps Crockett, and possibly Scenes 72, 73, 74– Beekeeper sings, Travis speaks with Smitty, meets Crockett.

Ford left the set the next morning. Is there any evidence, then, that he directed any scenes during his time there? Yes. In all likelihood, whatever scene Ford injected himself into was probably directed by him. There are photos of him, hand on hip, in animated conversation with Harvey and Wayne in the cantina, where he provided guidance and suggestions. Further, on September 30, Widmark wrote a letter to Ford that stated, "... I want to thank you for the help that you gave me while you were here. It was a thrill for me to be *directed* by a man I've long admired." There were only three scenes that Widmark appears in while Ford was on location: Scene 94 (when Bowie assists Crockett in the street fight), Scene 49A (when Bowie speaks with Finn), and Scenes 54 through 57 (when the Seguins report to Travis). Photographs plainly show Wayne, dressed in white Guayabera shirt, giving instructions to Widmark, Joseph Calleia and both Julian and Edmundo Trevino. So, obviously, Widmark was referring to one or both of the other scenes. Cristal speaks specifically of Ford directing her in a scene filmed in the hangar: " ... he wanted me to put my hand on the side of my face and let it slide down until it went to my mouth until (Wayne) closed the door." And, don't forget the filmed-but-never-used pet bird sequence between Cristal and Lau. In an October 1 letter to Ford, Wayne confirmed Pappy's involvement: "Saw the cuts you made on the wall. They turned out great, as you know. There's a light and camera in the window waiting for your return. Sure appreciate having your shoulder to lean on." What he didn't appreciate was Ford taking over—hence the offer to direct the second unit.

So, did Ford direct any scenes in the film? Yes, most certainly, he did.

Four days later on October 5, Ford returned to the set, which makes one wonder if he'd even yet received Wayne's letter. No matter, because Wayne still was heavy into night shooting and Ford returned just in time to direct Scene 104—the church "basement" sequence that included discovery of the gunpowder and the death of Sand. Again, photographs confirm both his presence and involvement. Unfortunately, he had missed filming Scene 78 (Crockett's "Republic" speech) and Scene 95 (Crockett and Bowie's conversation in front of the cantina). Ford also missed filming of the can-can dance and feather fight scenes. Too bad—perhaps some of those shenanigans would have been better served by one who was a master of the genre. In addition, a sequence was filmed where a Tennessean (Bob Morgan) chases a young senorita out into the street and a subsequent brawl occurs that Ybarra said Ford directed.

In early October, Wayne returned again to daytime shooting. Over the course of a week, he filmed numerous scenes, including 114 (Crockett/Bowie arrive with gunpowder), 115 (Travis instructs Dennison to open gate) and 113 (Crockett leaves the Alamo after talk about Mike Fink fight). Ford directed Wayne and Widmark in Scene 120 ("pyrotechnics"). It is not known exactly when Wayne shot the scenes that included LaJean Ethridge; she was murdered Oct. 11. As mentioned, Duke learned of her death while filming at the Sabinal location with Ford, Cristal, Avalon, Worden and Boone. Although Ford was there at Sabinal, there's no evidence he was involved in Scenes 125-126—the "Flaca tree" sequence. However, in addition to photographic evidence, Avalon stated Ford did direct him and Boone in scenes 435-438 at Houston's camp (which included Avalon's crossing of a stream) and his meeting with both sentries and Houston. Boone's wife Claire also verified Ford's involvement. "Of course, Dick just did the cameo," she explained. "He did that as a favor to Duke, and *John Ford* really asked him to do it. This was the first time Duke was directing, but Ford was there a lot to help. He was particularly there on Dick's scenes, and he actually directed the scenes that Dick did." While Wayne was tied up with the Ethridge affair, Ford continued to direct on his behalf. During his time at Sabinal, Pappy also filmed the "morning patrol/Mexican cattle herd sequence." *(Author's note: It should be mentioned that it is almost impossible to cross-reference the numbers of specific scenes in the script to what was actually filmed. The latest version of the script dated October 5, 1959, listed 566 specific scenes which included eighty setups for the first and another one hundred setups for the final assault. However, photographs taken on location clearly show scenes filmed with slate numbers well in excess of #566. i.e., #813–evening dance following birthday party, #830–prelude to first Mexican assault.)*[1454]

Now finished with the Sabinal location, Wayne returned to Brackettville to continue filming. Ford had previously been given a second unit and, according to many, went out and filmed scenes that couldn't possibly be used in the film: i.e., action staged on only one side of the frame, stuntmen fighting in a corner, etc. There is also some evidence to suggest that Ford re-filmed some scenes that Wayne had previously been involved with, i.e., Wayne had directed a sequence in the film where Arruza leads a platoon of dragoons down the middle of a stream and up its back. In a continuation of the scene in which Arruza stops and speaks with a peasant family, there is photographic evidence that shows Ford directed that portion. However, the interesting aspect of this is that photographs show both portions of the sequence were filmed at the same location on two separate days. Why? Why would a film crew go back to the exact same location, to film the exact same sequence a second time? Perhaps the dailies from the first showing weren't all that great or perhaps the lab had problems when it developed the film or maybe Wayne just wanted to keep Ford busy.

Ford left Brackettville on October 19 and didn't return again until November 17. But before his departure, Wayne and Clothier filmed Mexican troops marching over hill and valley on the way to San Antonio. During Pappy's hiatus from the set, Wayne filmed the first shots fired by a limited number of Mexican troops and over the next several weeks was extremely busy shooting numerous scenes, including 180-185 (Defender patrol arrives in Alamo, whiskey barrel destroyed by "European" cannon), 139-160 (Santa Anna's surrender demand, Travis's cannon reply), 318-320 (daytime portions of the birthday party sequence), and probably 168-170C (Smitty, log and bucket of water). With more nighttime shooting scheduled during the first two weeks of November, Wayne was able to complete the entire destruction of the "European" cannon sequence and the subsequent safe return of the defenders, the evening portion of the raid for cattle sequences (including wading through Las Moras Creek and Smitty's departure), the arrival of Gonzales reinforcements, Bowie's notification of his wife's death, and the defenders' last evening before the final assault. Ford returned November 17 just in time to watch Dean Smith hurdle a horse and take out stuntman Bear Hudkins, who doubled as a Mexican horseman. He also directed the evening portion of the birthday party, including Jocko and Blind Nell's dancing sequence, which wasn't included in the film.

To show his commitment, Ford stayed on location for the remainder of principal filming except for one day. Although Wayne directed the entire cattle stampede sequence, Ford did have some tangential involvement. As seen in the film, the cattle start to stampede driven by Crockett, Bowie and the Tennesseans. They then cross Pinto Creek, run down the length of Back Street and head out onto the plain toward the Alamo. In a subsequent sequence, Ford placed a camera in a pit at ground level on a village side street between the blacksmith shop and a small house. Although footage of these cattle racing by appeared in Huberman's documentary, it wasn't used in Wayne's film. Ford was famous for ground-level shots; he'd used them as early as *The Iron Horse* (1924). When he hit on something that worked, he used it over and over again: dramatic angles, shadows, backlights, the obligatory fistfight. Pappy did direct Scene 316–Hayward's spectacular stunt fall as he is "shot" off a charging horse by Travis. Later that week, Ford also filmed the arrival of Santa Anna while Wayne handled the buildup of Mexican troops and subsequent departure of the noncombatants.

Absent internal Batjac documents (camera logs, daily PA reports, script supervisor reports, etc.), it is very difficult to determine exactly which specific assault scenes Ford directed. But on Saturday, November 21, he did direct Scene 441–Parson's death sequence. Prior to his momentary departure on November 28, Ford also filmed the short death scenes of extras Jim Brewer and David Kuykendell. Rudy Robbins was a bit more fortunate, however. Ford directed him in an extended sequence where Robbins commanded a cannon on the West wall. Unfortunately, only the last few seconds of the scene are in the film. Ford also directed a great deal of action footage on the West wall with Dean Smith and John Dierkes as well as some of the post-battle action. He later would film Roberson and Robbins's death scene as well as Harvey's. He also directed Pat Wayne when Bonham returns to the Alamo with news of Fannin's death. Though present, there is no indication Ford actually directed the filming of the destruction of the North wall and its subsequent breach; Travis' headquarters explosion; Wills's, Pyle's, Widmark's and Wayne's death scenes; the fourteen-horse jump over the palisade; the powder magazine explosion; the uncovering of Joan O'Brien, Aissa and John Henry Daniels under the blanket; or the trio's subsequent departure from the Alamo.

Finally, there is one last piece of evidence to consider. As previously mentioned, Batjac entered into a $700,000 loan agreement with the Bank of America, National Trust and Savings Corporation to cover the costs of editing, musical scoring, print costs and publicity. Attached to the loan agreement were two documents: Schedule A–Schedule of funds received and applied by the Alamo Company and Schedule B–an itemized list detailing the purpose for each dollar of the loan. Included in the $700,000 was, among other things, $55,000 for Avalon, $25,000 for Boone, $117,000 for the Erosa Music Corporation (Tiomkin), $100,000 for dubbing, $70,000 for personal property taxes and $30,000 for the lab. Interestingly, there was also a $100,000 line item for John Ford. According to Dan Ford, "(Pappy) didn't do enough to ask for money. I'm sure it was a cover," i.e., the money designated for Ford was actually being used for other expenses. However, that explanation doesn't hold up upon closer examination. At the time Batjac entered into the loan agreement it was well

833

known that Wayne's project was way, way over budget. To try and hide extra expenses under a Ford-designated category didn't make any sense. Who cared and what purpose did it serve; if the funds weren't for Ford, what were they really for? It only seems logical to assume they were for services rendered.

So, what does this all tell us? We know Ford planned to "visit" Brackettville and that Wayne was aware of it. Ruben Padilla said it was a well-known fact on the set that UA had instructed Ford to go there and help. We know the exact dates Ford was on location and that he was there when the vast majority of the scenes were filmed. We know he specifically directed numerous actors, including Wayne, in several of their scenes. We know Wayne gave Ford a second-unit camera and crew and asked him to help out. And, finally, we have numerous photographs of Ford directing specific scenes. That much is irrefutable; so why did so many deny his involvement? In particular, why did Wayne? In a BBC *Picture Parade* interview with Robert Robinson, Wayne minimized Ford's role in the production: "Well, he was certainly my mentor. And I had all of his enthusiasm and his good wishes. He came down to visit us a couple of times on the set but he was very careful to stay in the background, realizing that these people, you know, (it) might affect their performance."

Duke intimately knew every line of dialog and every foot of exposed film. He knew what he filmed; more importantly, he knew what Ford filmed. Bill Gilmore stresses that he and his dad were loyal to Wayne and Wayne alone. When editing the film, no one except Wayne told them what to include or exclude. Still, Wayne knew he was using numerous sequences Ford had shot. Not only did Duke know it, but so did anyone on the set when those scenes were filmed. And still, virtually everyone downplayed Ford's involvement, including Ford. Why? The answer is simple. Wayne, Ford, Clothier and possibly Lyons all agreed to minimize Ford's involvement through a collaboration of denial and silence. Wayne appreciated Ford's talent and intuition; Ford didn't want to jeopardize Duke's reputation. While Wayne made every creative decision in the film, regardless of Ford's input or help, Duke also wanted to make sure that everyone knew this was his film, not Ford's. The uneducated masses might wrongly assume that Ford's presence on location meant *he* directed the film, not Wayne. There is no doubt that this is Wayne's film … but Ford's stamp is all over it. Aissa Wayne emphatically points out that her father did not want the film community believing Ford had had any part of this because if the industry's movers and shakers thought so—and if the film was a success—then, obviously it was because of Pappy's involvement. Hence, the denials.

Ford knew Wayne had talent. "Duke has been able to learn a decent amount of things about filmmaking by keeping his eyes and ears open," Ford prophesized. "During a career that spanned twenty years, he was a prop assistant, an electrician, a stuntman, an extra, a bit part actor, an assistant director, a producer, and a star. I would not be surprised if one day he directed a film that will induce jaw dropping among the Hollywood establishment." And, Wayne was smart. Smart enough to know that he didn't know everything. The fact that he may have needed assistance from time to time shouldn't be considered a fault. To oversee a project of this scope would take an enormous amount of skill, talent and experience. To be successful, you surround yourself with those who have better skills than yourself and then utilize and coordinate their talents to achieve the common goal. But there is no question as to who was in charge on this set. It was Wayne. Everyone on location knew Wayne was directing the film. Ford himself conceivably would have consulted with Wayne as an uncredited co-director and while he wouldn't have asked Wayne for permission to do something, in all probability they sat up late each evening and planned the next day's activity. From a second-unit perspective, Ford was A director, not THE director. Cliff Lyons directed most of the action sequences but he wasn't THE director, either. Wayne was. Ford was on location in some sort of supporting, subordinate role to assist Wayne in the event he needed it. There were some scenes Ford definitely directed by himself, just as there were some scenes Wayne was in that Ford directed for him. When the director also is the star, every film has someone present to direct the star when he's acting. Ford would have still regarded that as a subordinate position; they just wouldn't have acted that way on the set.

Thank goodness the two had a unique relationship. As a first-time director, Duke was under tremendous scrutiny, so why not utilize the mentor-protégé relationship to his advantage? To think that Ford would be on the set for 50+ days and do nothing other than observe seems foolish. Wayne wanted and needed "backup" to a degree. The more he directed, the more comfortable he became. Filling the roles of actor, director and producer would have been an all-consuming task—even the most experienced individual would have had trouble juggling the balls. After obtaining what he needed (comfort and verification of ability), Wayne looked for a reason to minimize Ford's involvement. Hence the cover story. At some point, Ford must have realized that and decided to back away. Thus the numerous trips back and forth. It doesn't seem unreasonable to assume everyone thus agreed to spread the Ford second-unit story so the press wouldn't claim Ford directed the film. Pappy clearly understood how important it was to keep the press from jumping to that conclusion and didn't want to jeopardize Wayne's film. And, it wasn't lying—it was just the way Hollywood addressed those types of issues. Bottom line? Although this is most definitely Wayne's film, Ford played a much larger role in its production than has been previously been admitted and he directed and/or was involved in numerous scenes that made it into the film's final print. After all is said and done, Wayne and Ford's conspiracy of silence and denial was just a collaboration between two professionals to minimize any potential fallout.

# APPENDIX C
# "And the Winner is…"

"Best Picture: The Apartment – Billy Wilder,
    Nominees: The Alamo – John Wayne
        Elmer Gantry – Bernard Smith
        Sons and Lovers – Jerry Wald
        The Sundowners – Fred Zinnemann

Best Actor in a Supporting Role: Peter Ustinov (Spartacus)
    Nominees: Peter Falk (Murder, Inc.)
        Jack Kruschen (The Apartment)
        Sal Mineo (Exodus)
        Chill Wills (The Alamo)

Best Cinematography – Color: Russell Metty (Spartacus)
    Nominees: William H. Clothier (The Alamo)
        Joseph Ruttenberg, Charles Harten (Butterfield 8)
        Sam Leavitt (Exodus)
        Joseph MacDonald (Pepe)
Best Sound – Gordon Sawyer (Samuel Goldwyn SSD), Fred Hynes (Todd-AO SSD) – The Alamo
    Nominees: Gordon Sawyer (Samuel Goldwyn SSD) –
        The Apartment
        Franklin Milton (MGM SSD) – Cimarron
        Charles Rice (Columbia SSD) – Pepe
        George Groves (Warner Bros. SSD) – Sunrise at Campobello

Best Film Editing – Daniel Mandell (The Apartment)
    Nominees: Stuart Gilmore (The Alamo)
         Frederic Knudtson (Inherit the Wind)
         Viola Lawrence, Al Clark (Pepe)
         Robert Lawrence (Spartacus)

Best Music, Scoring of a Dramatic or Comedy Picture – Ernest Gold (Exodus)
    Nominees: Dimitri Tiomkin (The Alamo)
         Andre Previn (Elmer Gantry)
         Elmer Bernstein (The Magnificent Seven)
         Alex North (Spartacus)

Best Music, Original Song – "Never on Sunday" Manos Hatzidakis (Never on Sunday)
    Nominees: "The Facts of Life" Johnny Mercer (The Facts of Life)
         "Faraway Part of Town" Andre and Dory Previn (Pepe)
         "The Green Leaves of Summer" Dimitri Tiomkin, Paul Francis Webster (The Alamo)
         "The Second Time Around" Jimmy Van Heusen, Sammy Cahn (High Time)

# APPENDIX D
# Lost, Found, and Lost Again

THE TELEPHONE RANG SEVERAL TIMES BEFORE IT WAS ANSWERED.

"Hello?"

"Hi, Ron. Guess what?"

"Who is this?"

"Ron, this is Ashley. Ashley Ward. Guess what? We found it! We found a director's-cut, full-length version of *The Alamo!*"

Ron Haver couldn't believe it. Hell, no one could believe it. Everybody thought it had been lost long ago. For some, the discovery was a stroke of luck; for others, it culminated a life-long search. As per internal Batjac documents, Technicolor had initially planned to make up fifteen Todd-AO, 202-minute, 70mm prints with six-track magnetic stereo sound. Utilized only for roadshow engagements, the prints, once their bookings ended, then were sent back to UA to be edited down to a revised 161-minute cutting continuity version. They then were placed back into the normal distribution cycle. All fifteen prints supposedly had been modified by late 1961 although *Alamo* fan Peter Gustawsenit said that an original roadshow print ran in Sweden as late as 1971. And yet here was at least one excited individual on the phone who knew otherwise.

Our story begins long ago in the frozen north. Bob Bryden managed a record store in Hamilton, Ontario, and in March 1980, went to Toronto to replenish his inventory. Having some spare time one evening, he decided to visit the Cinesphere theater at Ontario Place. The Toronto Film Festival had scheduled a 70mm showing of *Cleopatra* and Bob thought it might be fun to attend. But when he phoned the theater to check show times, he was totally surprised to find out *The Alamo* would be run instead! Fox couldn't provide a print of Elizabeth Taylor's film but the UA depot in Calgary (or Edmonton) instead offered a 70mm print of Wayne's film as a replacement. Its file card said it was the 160-minute version. No matter. Bryden, a self-confessed "dyed in the wool *Alamo* fanatic and John Wayne devotee," naturally wanted to see the film again. Put yourself in his place…imagine your astonishment when you realize you're seeing the 202-minute version! Bob was flabbergasted. Virtually all alone in that giant theater, Bryden vowed to see it again, and two nights later, along with a few friends, he did just that.

Fast-forward to September 12, 1990. Lee Pfeiffer's book *The John Wayne Scrapbook* recently had been published and on page ninety-one, film historian and preservationist Haver stated that by 1979 all 70mm prints of *The Alamo* had been edited to the shorter version. (Haver, who had already restored *A Star is Born* and *The Big Trail*, had previously checked with UA offices in Los Angeles, London and Rome; they all said the same thing: they didn't have copies and no original unedited versions of *The Alamo* were still in existence. He'd even checked the original camera negative kept in the MGM/UA Hutchinson, Kansas, storage salt mine—that print had been cut as well. *Alamo* author Don Clark had discovered Reel 9B in Europe in 1980 and even obtained an 8mm print. 9B had been shown on British TV in the mid-70s and had been included with the 161-minute version for one presentation, but by the mid-80s, had been lost). According to Ashley Ward, fellow *Alamo* enthusiast and film expert, Haver called UA and was told that after a 70mm booking in Atlanta in 1979, all remaining 70mm materials from the film were scrapped. In fact, in order to send a complete print to Atlanta, UA had had to piece together odd reels from remaining prints as most existing reels were full of tears and splices. Thus, all reports suggested that after Atlanta there were no longer any complete prints. Said Haver, "The likelihood of finding an original uncut 70mm print of The Alamo (is) about the same as a man giving birth to a baby!" But Bryden knew otherwise—he'd seen one in 1980 and even written about it in his daily journal: "How thrilling it was to see "The Alamo" in its original glory." He subsequently contacted Tim Lilley, editor of *The Big Trail* (a John Wayne newsletter), and told him of his experience in that Toronto theater. Lilley contacted Ward and shortly thereafter, either Bob received a call from Ward or Ashley received a call from Bob. No matter. Ward knew exactly where and when each 70mm print had been shown and questioned Bob about his claim. By the end of their conversation, convinced of Bryden's sincerity and intrigued by his comments, Ashley asked him to continue his search for the elusive print. He also put Bob in contact with close friend David Mocniak who lived in Niagara Falls, just a short distance from Hamilton. Bryden made regular trips to The Record Store in Buffalo anyway; a visit with David was arranged. Bob also convinced David he had seen the roadshow print. Based on Ward's request, Bryden contacted Melissa Contardi of MGM/UA's Toronto office and confirmed that yes, a 70mm print of *The Alamo* had been rented to the Cinesphere theater in March 1980. In addition, UA still had two *Alamo* prints in Canada: a 35mm print in Toronto and a 70m print in Calgary. But according to Contardi, both prints were listed on her document as only 162 minutes long! Asked if the records could be wrong, she replied it was possible, but highly unlikely.

Disappointed with this information and now even questioning his own memory, Bryden phoned Ward back and told him what Contardi had said. Undeterred, Ashley decided nevertheless to rent a theater in Toronto and show whatever-length print was available; at least they could watch the 70mm Todd-AO in all its glory in an environment in which it was meant to be seen. After a bit of research, Ward also discovered that the Eglinton Theatre in Toronto still ran 70mm twin projection equipment and would be happy to book a private screening ... for a price. At $950 Canadian, it seemed a bargain. All Ward had to do was come up with the money. He called Mocniak and friends Kipp Martin and Murray Weissmann, enlisted their support, and the cost was covered. He also asked the Alamo Society's Bill Chemerka to help promote the showing but to the dismay of everyone involved, no one was interested. And since it was too late to publish an announcement in *The Alamo Journal*, the general membership thus couldn't be properly notified. However, a limited special mailing did go out to those who previously had expressed interest in the film and/or those in the Toronto area.

So, with his preliminary research done, Ward called Bryden back for a final opinion.

"What's the Eglinton Theater like?"

"Probably the finest 70mm facility in Toronto. It used to be a Cinerama theater."

"Good. We've rented it and we're all coming up to watch that print."

"You mean that even though the paperwork says it's the wrong print, on my say-so you're going to rent the biggest theater in Toronto and bring a bunch of people up here anyway?"

"Yup."

On Friday, November 23, Ward drove to Toronto and checked out the Eglinton. Stored in its projection booth were nine huge 70mm reel cases. Due to their size and number, the local projectionist said the film had to be a shorter version as there were no way these reels could hold 202 minutes of film.

The showing was scheduled for 8 o'clock that Saturday morning. Snow on the ground and single-digit temperatures would not dissuade the faithful attendees. In addition to Ward, Mocniak and wife Catherine, Martin, Weissmann and daughter Lauren, Bryden, wife Lynn and sons Grant and Calvin, this audience also included several friends: Christopher Byers, Michael Guild, Franz and Maxine Nangle, Ray Panavas, Graeme Burk and Larry Somerville. The latter recalled admission was $25 Canadian, Ward thought it was $5. So a theater designed to seat 825 people instead hosted a grand total of seventeen people–truly an exclusive, private screening. Once everyone was seated, the lights dimmed and the familiar Overture began. Ashley instructed the projectionist to crank up the sound to maximum. However, by the time the curtain opened, the audience had missed the title card! But then as the opening credits rolled, the Todd-AO credit suddenly appeared, too–the first hint that this might be more than just a standard print. The movie then began. Everybody knew that the first trimmed scene in the shortened version of *The Alamo* was the conversation between Hairston and Widmark that ended with Bowie saying, "Houston come and gone and me lyin' drunk." That moment arrived. Everyone waited with bated breath–would the scene fade to black or continue? And then ... and then ... the audience heard and saw Jethro say, "Well, your stomach, Mr. Jim, and that ague and whatnot ..." Yes!! It continued!!!!!! Doubtless, the rest of the scene's dialog was drowned out because everyone was astonished–they WERE watching Duke's original uncut version. Ashley leapt to his feet and yelled . . . (well, we really can't repeat what he yelled) . . . others stood with tears streaming down their faces . . . Bob's wife Lynn squeezed his hand . . . the room was electric. Murmurs of excitement ran through the audience. These folks still admit they really couldn't put into words how thrilled everyone was at that special moment. After all these years, the complete version of *The Alamo* in six-track discrete stereo was seen and heard once again. It wasn't perfect; the film only had 75% of its color, but it was close enough. In the words of Kipp Martin, after the viewing " . . . everyone was emotionally spent." Mocniak calls it "truly incredible" while Weissmann admits he "kept looking at the sides of the screen in order to view scenes that no one had seen in thirty years." According to Bryden, "When the 'Exit' music played, an awestruck but vindicated group of people floated into the lobby. We spent a few short hours together 'fellowshipping' 'round our discovery and then parted company, each of us resolving, I think, to do whatever we could do to see that this print was protected, preserved, restored and issued to the general public."

Once Ashley returned home to Cincinnati, he contacted Robert Harris and Haver and shared the good news. *(Harris should not be confused with another Robert Harris who appeared as an extra in The Alamo).* Haver was so excited he immediately phoned MGM/UA in Culver City. Harris, a renowned preservationist, like Haver, made a few calls and arranged to have the film placed in cold storage at the Academy of Motion Picture Arts and Sciences offices in Los Angeles. Unfortunately, it never made it there. Meanwhile, Mocniak received a call from Chemerka and relayed the highlights of the weekend while Bryden taped an interview with a Canadian radio station and discussed the rediscovery. Bob also called Ashley only to find that the phone lines had been burning–over one hundred calls concerning the rare print were made just that day. Then, when Bryden called Contardi back, she told Bryden she had also received numerous calls and that the print would be on its way back to the MGM/UA Classics Division office in Hollywood that very week. Although everyone hoped the studio would carefully restore and preserve this print, that, sadly, was not to be.

Perhaps a little technical history is now necessary. Filmed in 1959, *The Alamo* was produced on Eastman Color Negative stock utilizing the Todd-AO 65mm process and printed on 70mm positive stock. Unfortunately, both stocks were highly susceptible to fading, which proved disastrous to a film's longevity. Wayne's intent was to leave the 65mm camera negative uncut and complete, and to that end, a black-and-white protection master was made of the final edit. Unfortunately, it was out of focus and thus proved completely useless. Once the decision was made to edit the film's roadshow version down to a 161-minute general release, a fine cut was made on 35mm anamorphic dupe negative stock in addition to a 35mm anamorphic reversal interpositive. Despite best intentions, however, the original full-length camera negative was mistakenly cut, which left absolutely no record of Wayne's roadshow version. According to Harris, "Those involved in the cut were led to believe that the extant 70mm prints would be trimmed and resounded, and new printing matrices produced for the 35mm release in shorter form–but that the original negative would not be harmed or modified. However, the original negative and all protection elements, inclusive of the sixty-five separation masters, (still) were cut to conform to the new 161-minute length, (and) the trims and deletions were destroyed. Over the years, several versions of the film were distributed, including a 140-minute 35mm print shown in drive-ins. Reissued in 1967, Technicolor printed one hundred additional 35mm optical monaural dye transfer prints, using whatever leftover available 70mm and 35mm prints from 1960-1961 it could find. A 172-minute 70mm print was shown in Chicago: 161 minutes plus 11 minutes of roadshow music. The film was re-released again in both 1971 and 1979 but no new prints were struck for these releases. By now the film had been cut, hacked and spliced to pieces and bore little if any semblance to Wayne's original intent. And, if anyone wanted to see a version of Wayne's film, they had to wait for yet another re-release...or purchase a VHS tape. And, irritatingly, you never knew exactly what you might see because so many different VHS versions were out there. In 1982, Warner Home Video released the 161-minute edited version as did CBS/Fox in 1984; in 1988 Warner came back with a 155-minute version. And, in 1990, MGM/UA Home Video released a 173-minute wide-screen format version. Back in 1982, CBS/Fox Video even released a 161-minute version on CED (Capacitance Electronic Disc System). Unfortunately, by then, the RCA analog video disc playback system had become obsolete with the emergence of MCA DiscoVision, better known as the laserdisc. MGM/UA would later release a two-disc, 172-minute, Deluxe Letterbox Laser Disc edition in 1990.

(There was even thought that the film might be released in the Cinerama format. In January 1963, a new technique was developed that enabled any 70mm negative to be converted for projection on a three-panel screen while eliminating the three strips of film used in standard Cinerama photography. According to experts, transformation of a single strip of film was accomplished through an optical process in the projection. Wayne loaned a print of *The Alamo* for a test run and results were said to be "astonishing." Alas, it was not to be.)[3]

But at least the discovery in Toronto of a complete, unaltered 70mm print had been a dream come true. And after MGM/UA home video head George Feltenstein authorized the transfer, the actual reconstruction work was assigned to Rennie Johnson. "We were fortunate because the print we were working with had maintained about 70% of its original color," Johnson explained. "On some of the films I've worked on, the color had already turned to pink." Canada's climate even had helped. "Have you ever been to Toronto?" asked Harris. "There are penguins and polar bears walking down the street most of the time: That's why the color was still in the (70 mm) print." The footage was mastered by Ron Feneis at Crest National Videotape; Stephen Bookbinder at AME, Inc. performed the edit; audio restoration was engineered by Ted Hall at Digital Magnetics.

However, in its infinite wisdom, MGM/UA decided to release the film on laserdisc and VHS cassette—not a bad decision—but the execution was pitiful. A CineRank machine was used to digitally master the print but each machine could only handle 1,000-foot reels. Recall that the 70mm roadshow version consisted of 21,586 feet and seventy frames spread over twenty-seven sections? Well, so the machine could accommodate the footage, it was necessary to separate each reel into Parts A and B. To make matters worse, rather than first color-correcting the entire Toronto print (which would have been terribly expensive), MGM/UA decided to intercut missing 70mm scenes into the pre-existing 35mm tape master. According to Ward, "this created more problems than it solved. Nobody did an in-depth study of the differences between the 202-minute and the 161-minute versions. The material from the digital tape master was sourced from the 35mm anamorphic dye transfer film, which has an aspect ratio of 2.35:1. The 'missing scenes' were sourced from a faded 70mm Eastman color print, with an aspect ratio of 2.20:1. They did not match, either for color or shape purposes. (And) they overlooked the Todd-AO credit completely. Nobody still working for them knew that Todd-AO films had two sets of credits (one for roadshow and another for 35mm general release). This 'facsimile' was not an exact recreation of the roadshow version ... so it was decided to call it the 'director's cut' and release it on laserdisc and VHS cassette ... it is not a recreation of the Toronto print, and in fact, it is not a recreation of any version of the film!"

And finally, the *piece de resistance*. In an attempt to mitigate the effects of "vinegar syndrome," the Toronto print was chemically treated and stored in an un-air-conditioned warehouse in Glendale, California. At the time, film was generally made of cellulose triacetate plastic; vinegar syndrome is a film-base degradation inherent to the chemical nature of plastic. So called because of the pungent vinegar smell, such damage as shrinkage, embrittlement and buckling or channeling of the gelatin emulsion takes place in advanced stages of deterioration; heat and humidity accelerate the chemical reaction. In its ignorance, all MGM/UA did was to take a relatively clean 70mm print and destroy it. Explains Harris, "They didn't want to ruin it–it just happened–but what happened is unthinkable. The thought of this thing going is just horrible. How do you tell your kids there's no more *Alamo*? How do you tell the world you've lost a major John Wayne film?"

Coincidentally, while Rennie Johnson had been busy on the restoration, years earlier, filmmaker Brian Huberman had been working on an independent documentary on the making of Duke's film. With unprecedented access to the Wayne family as well as such surviving members of the cast and crew as Al Ybarra, Bill Clothier, Happy Shahan, Frankie Avalon, Hank Worden, Rudy Robbins, Ken Curtis and Linda Cristal, Huberman compiled a sixty-eight-minute oral and video story of Wayne's odyssey that included stills and home movies from Shahan, Bill Moody, Carroll Lewis, Yvonne De Carlo and the Pat Cumiskey family. Huberman contacted MGM to see if it might be interested in using his film and after Michael Wayne reviewed the documentary and gave it his enthusiastic endorsement, MGM contracted with Huberman for its use. (In all fairness, although Shahan and Moody signed release forms that loaned their 16mm color movies to Huberman, both were upset when they heard of the arrangement with MGM/UA. Moody said he thought the films were going to be used for educational purposes. According to Shahan, he had an agreement with Huberman that if anything "big" ever became of the documentary, they would all be in it together. In Happy's opinion, both he and Moody were "cut out" and Bill was furious about it. Brian agreed there were issues with Moody and felt that the release form adequately addressed the issues. KTLA also provided necessary video footage to Huberman.)

Asked why he made the documentary, Huberman explains, "On one level, it's not very complex. I was just the right age to be perverted by Walt Disney's *Davy Crockett*, even though I was in England at that time. Of course, American movies have colonialized the world . . . so I was definitely impacted by that. That just came at the right moment for me. And then the next thing I know–a couple of years later it felt like–*The Alamo* came out. And then in between had been *The Last Command*. My God, you couldn't get away from this stuff at that time. It was hardly esoteric material. So, that made a big impact, too. Wayne's *Alamo*, of the many versions made . . . I still hold Wayne's film the best."

Some may question why many *Alamo* actors and stuntmen didn't appear in the film's documentary. The answer is simple–MGM. Huberman explains, "Initially, I was making my film as an independent educational piece. Along the way this MGM thing raised its head so I had to re-approach everybody; they had to sign releases. At that point it became a whole different business. Legitimately, these are a lot of old guys. I think they thought it would be a nice gesture for a huge company like MGM (to) at least give them day rate. And they wouldn't. And so I had a palace insurrection and a whole bunch of them refused to be in the film. My whole goddamn film was suddenly in doubt because of this issue. I don't know what it was. I guess I committed a faux-pas by not having MGM approach them directly with the forms. Hardly done by design on my part."

The first release of MGM/UA's "Restored Original Director's Cut" came out on VHS in August 1992. Included in the two-cassette, 202-minute, wide-screen versions were *Overture*, Entr'Acte and *Exit* music, and a forty-minute abbreviated version of Huberman's documentary. Unfortunately, it could have been so much more. "Basically, I was given a free hand, any length," says Huberman. "The laserdisc (version of his documentary) was 70 minutes. And then at the same time, they had the VHS version. There physically wasn't enough space for the (longer version), so literally, I had no time at all, just to slash out some material and reduce it so it would fit the VHS. So, that's the forty-minute version. When I made the deal with MGM to put the thing on their piece, I thought with their leverage we might get to (Widmark) and, maybe have him narrate the piece. So, through their agency we approached him but his response was ridiculous. He wanted so much money it was tantamount to 'I don't want to do it.'" This release was quickly followed by a three-disc, Deluxe Letterbox laserdisc version that not only included all the features of the VHS tape but an expanded sixty-eight-minute documentary, original theatrical trailer and chapter stops that identified major restored sequences.

Over the years, the only way one could see Wayne's film in its intended version was to view the two aforementioned releases. Of course, MGM/UA continued to milk the proverbial cow by re-releasing additional versions: Deluxe Letterbox Edition–Original Uncut version, 193-minutes in 1995 and a 155-minute version in 1997. Once the DVD (digital video disc) was introduced in 1995, MGM was quick to release a wide-screen 162-minute version, complete with original theatrical trailer and abbreviated documentary. This version was re-released again in 2004.

The studio's flurry of releases and formats eventually backfired, as Bryden dryly states:

"In the late 90's or whenever laserdisc was just being phased out and DVD on its way in, I received an e-mail from no less than the head of MGM/UA home video. This communication was actually asking me if I might know where the digital master of the director's cut of *The Alamo* might be! I don't know if you can grasp the insanity of this. I'm a total civilian in the boonies of Canada and here is the general of their video division in Hollywood asking me if I know where the now-restored Alamo master tape might be!!?? I was absolutely livid. I fired back immediately. 'Are you telling me you lost it again?!' I also advised him to check with the previous employees of his laserdisc branch and/or even the VHS people who prepared the director's cut for videotape. I did not hear back from him."

Evervision Corp. even took advantage of the medium to issue a 202-minute, deluxe Letterbox DVD edition, albeit without any extras. (In all probability, this was a copy of MGM's 1993 laserdisc release.)

In 2009, Harris contacted MGM/UA and convinced the studio that if it expected to preserve the film for future generations, a total restoration was necessary. Although initially resistant, the studio agreed once Harris suggested that he output a restored negative on 35mm VistaVision film, a cheaper alternative to 65mm stock. Usually, studios would preserve their films by creating black & white separation masters of color negative productions. Though created in the longer version, they were cut and also experienced early signs of vinegar syndrome. And, the original negative was unusable to make other prints or preservation elements. So, Harris recommended that *The Alamo*'s 65mm camera negative be scanned frame by frame, then color-corrected. The print, which was now fully faded, would serve as the image basis for some, but not all, of the deleted scenes and shots. It would be re-combined via 3D warping technology with the 480i master, which is the only content for color.

According to author Robert Wilonsky, MGM initially had asked Harris if he could restore the film for home-video release. Harris replied it was possible but as the film was in such a sorry state, it was a one-shot deal: either repair it at a cost of $1,000,000, issue as a DVD and never view it again in a theater, or spend twice as much and preserve the film forever. Harris wisely chose the latter. Once fully funded, the work was expected to take from ten to twelve months. According to Harris, "MGM and a number of vendors have been very supportive . . . and are making generous contributions. Still, in order to expedite a full and proper restoration we are seeking financial support from outside sources, both corporate and private, for the remaining $1.4 million dollars." Although MGM couldn't afford to invest millions of dollars into the restoration of a single film, it did provide an initial $500,000. Its rationalization was painfully simple—why spend an exorbitant amount on one film when the same funds could be spread out over dozens of films in better shape? Once restoration was completed, two versions would be available: the original roadshow version and the general release, both with *Overture*, *Entr'Acte* and *Exit* music. Says Harris, "The most important (version) would be the theatrical event projected fully restored in 70mm or Digital Cinema in 2K or 4K. The running time would be approximately 172 minutes, replicating the visual and aural splendor of *The Alamo* as it originally premiered in San Antonio on October 24, 1960, albeit in the general release cut of the film. While the general release cut would be available for DVD and Blu-Ray, the roadshow version of the film is intended solely for the DVD and Blu-Ray home video audience. (In addition), once completed, MGM would make a restored digital cinema element or 70mm print available for special charity screenings. The print, provided in the names of major donors, with all proceeds going toward the charities involved, would include end credits containing the names of major donors, both corporate and private, which would be seen on screen and later on home video and other uses of the work …."

The initial goal was to have the project completed by March 6, 2010, but, sadly, this was to not to be as sufficient private funding never materialized. In addition, in 2014, MGM has started re-thinking its position; only time will tell whether that means additional funding or abandonment of the project. Nevertheless, time is running out because all elements soon will be lost forever. As Harris so eloquently puts it, "One of the most important ways people know of the extraordinary gift of freedom given to Texas and our nation by those who defended the Alamo is by virtue of this film. Although an imperfect representation historically, John Wayne's work brilliantly portrays that larger than life tale, capturing the hearts and creating lasting memories for all who experience this great film. We are attempting to pull this important film back from the very brink of extinction and preserve it for generations to come."

With adequate funding, an insurmountable will to succeed and a fair portion of luck, Harris is confident he can prevail.

*(Although specific references are identified in the endnotes, this appendix could not have been developed without the input and support of Bob Bryden, Don Clark, Robert Harris, Brian Huberman, Tim Lilley, David, Mocniak, Lee Pfeiffer, Ashley Ward, Robert Wilonsky, Murray Weissmann and many, many others.)*

# APPENDIX E
## The Cast and Crew

THE FOLLOWING IS A LIST OF CAST, CREW MEMBERS AND OTHER INDIVIDUALS associated with The Alamo. It should not be considered complete or all-inclusive. No attempt has been made to differentiate between "above-the-line" and "below-the-line" categories. The names have been compiled from a variety of sources and, although every attempt has been made to verify their accuracy, no assurances are given. In instances where individuals have been dismissed and replaced, both names are listed. All names and titles listed in the screen credits have been identified in capital letters with unique font. When an individual performs mutilple duties, all functions are listed (If the reader knows of any additons and/ or corrections, please feel free to contact the author. jkfarkis@earthlink.net)

### DIRECTION:
**Director:**
JOHN WAYNE

### PRODUCTION:
**Producer:**
JOHN WAYNE

**Assistant to Producer:**
MICHAEL WAYNE

**Associate Producer:**
JAMES EDWARD GRANT – ASSOCIATE PRODUCER
Michael Wayne – Associate Producer

**Assistant Director:**
ROBERT RELYEA – ASSISTANT DIRECTOR
ROBERT SAUNDERS – ASSISTANT DIRECTOR

**Second Unit Director:**
John Ford – Second Unit Director
Ray Kellogg – Second Unit Director
CLIFF LYONS – SECOND UNIT DIRECTOR

**Assistant Director – Second Unit:**
Michael Wayne – First Assistant Director
Gene DeRuelle – Second Assistant Director
Fred Hartsook – Second Assistant Director
Michael Messinger – Second Assistant Director (dismissed)
Lionel C. Place – Second Assistant Director

**Production Manager:**
George Coleman
NATE E. EDWARDS

**Unit Manager:**
THOMAS J. ANDRE

**Production Assistant:**
Thomas Kane
Burt Kennedy
Robert Morrison

**Original Screenplay:**
JAMES EDWARD GRANT

**Casting:**
Raoul A. Cortez
Bill Mayberry – Casting Director
Frank Leyva – Casting Director
Pat Paterson
Josephine Pena
Thomas Roselle – Casting Associate Director

**Stunt Coordinator:**
Cliff Lyons

**ART DEPARTMENT:**
**ART:**
**Art Director:**
ALFRED YBARRA

**Production Illustrator:**
John Jensen

**SETS:**
**Set Decoration:**
VICTOR GANGELIN

**PROPS:**
**Property Master:**
JOSEPH LABELLE
J. Frederick LaTour

**WARDROBE DEPARTMENT:**
**Costumers:**
FRANK C. BEETSON
Norman Burz
Pat Kelly
Sandra Ann Maguire
Edward McDermott
ANN PECK
Ron Talsky

**HAIR AND MAKEUP:**
**Makeup Supervision:**
WEB OVERLANDER

**Makeup:**
Layne Britton
George H. Edds Jr.
Grant R. (Bob) Keats
Raymond Lopez
Norman H. Pringle
Monty Westmore

**Hair Stylist:**
FAE M. SMITH

**SPECIAL EFFECTS:**
**Special Effects:**
Daniel Hays
LEE ZAVITZ

**ARMOURER:**
George Ross

**Main Title:**
PACIFIC TITLE & ART STUDIO

## CAMERA:

**Cinematographer:**
WILLIAM H. CLOTHIER – DIRECTOR OF PHOTOGRAPHY

**Camera Operator:**
Irwin Blanche
Walter Davis
Lou Jennings
Art Lane
Joe Rave
Robert Rhea
Jack Specht (*San Antonio Light* photographer)

**Camera Grip:**
Don McLendon

**Technicolor Color Technician:**
Alfred D. Baalas

## PRODUCTION SOUND:

**Sound:**
Harry J. Alphin
Alan Boyle
Wm. F. Flannery
Wm. L. Griffith
JACK SOLOMON – SOUND MIXER
Al Yaylian

**Sound Recording:**
FRED HYNES – SUPERVISION
GORDON SAWYER – SUPERVISON

**Sound Editor:**
DON HALL, JR.

**Additional Sound:**
Terrell Morse
James Richard
Barbara Sherman
Walter Wormell

WESTREX RECORDING SYSTEM

**PRODUCTION SUPPORT:**
**Technical Supervision:**
FRANK BEETSON
JACK PENNICK

**Transportation Director:**
Lefty Budman
George Coleman

**Drivers:**
Gabby Garcia
Pat Hustis
George A. Lucas
Jack Morgan

**Medical Staff:**
Jerry O. Parker
Fred L. Vinson

**Historical Consultant:**
J. Frank Dobie (requested name to be stricken from credits)
Lon Tinkle (requested name to be stricken from credits)

**Secretary:**
Mary St. John

**Office Personal:**
Robert Carlson
Vivie J. Hill
Hazel Gunn Jackson
Ana Lee Jamison
Lucille Martha Webb Johnson
Lillian Massoth
Olga Pena
Jamie Shahan

**Head Wrangler:**
Bill Jones

**Wranglers:**
Bill Allen
Irvin Brittmecher
Bill Daniel, Jr.
Bob Davenport
Al Delamare
Bruce Galbraith
Dub Glynn
Roy Kennedy
Frank D. Lane
Rusty McDonald
Walter Osterman
Corky Randall
Plunker Sheedy
Buddy Sherwood
Herman Siegler
Billy Winn

**Tack Repair:**
Herman Allen
Jack Allred
Mike Hawks

**Caterer:**
Rolly Harper

**Wayne Chauffeur:**
Ben Dorcy

**Wayne Physician:**
Dr. James Pittman

**Accounting:**
Mary Dora
Al Podlasky – Comptroller

**Investors:**
Batjac
I.J. McCullough
O.J. McCullough
Clint Murchison
John Dabney Murchison
United Artists
Yale Foundation
John Wayne

**Choreographer:**
Antonia Morales – Lead
Felibe de la Rosa

**Invocation:**
Father Peter Rogers O.M.I.

**Additional Crew:**
Alton Applewhite, Jr.
Frank Austin
Layne Britton
Charles Gregory Bryne
Patrick Cummings
Phil Easterly
Patrick Farrell
Julia French
George Freundlich
Adolph Froehlich
Emil Garner
Andrew Gilmore
Fidel Gonzales
Marion Harper
Erwin E. Jones
Arthur Lopez
Jeanette Marvin

Lon J. Massey, Jr.
Maudlee McDougall
Patrick J. Palmer
Albert Podaloski
George W. Reber
George Thayer
ChesterThomas
Nick Toarilas
Ralph Volkie
Henry Williams
Edith Wilson
Evard Wilson

**Location School Teachers:**
Florrie Wills
Else Sauer

# SET CONSTRUCTION:
**Ranch Owners:**
James T. "Happy" Shahan
Virginia Shahan

**Construction Foreman:**
Jose "Chato" Hernandez
Fred Latour

**Labor:**
Theodore Claire – Carpenter
Ralph Gonzales
Juan Hernandez
Severiano Hernandez
Sostenes Hernandez
Victor Jimenez
Jose Luis Rodriguez
Manuel Roman

**Painter:**
Fidel E. Gonzales

**Electrical:**
Ralph D. Owen – Gaffer (head electrician)
Kenneth E. Sheehan – Grip

**Bracketville Enterprises:**
C.C. Belcher
W.Z. Conoly
Tom Hurd
A.H. Kreiger
W.L. Moody IV
James T. "Happy" Shahan
Charles Veltmann

## LOCAL CASTING:

Texas Employment Commission:
A.V. Bonnet – Eagle Pass Branch Manager
Augustin Estrada – Eagle Pass Placement Interviewer
Travis Kuykendall – Uvalde
Pat Paterson – Val Verde County
Tom Roselle – Brackettville

## POST PRODUCTION:
### EDITORIAL:
**Film Editor:**
STUART GILMORE
Alfred D. Baala – Color Technician
Bill Gilmore – Assistant Editor

### MUSIC/SOUND:
**Music Composition and Orchestration:**
DIMITRI TIOMKIN – COMPOSER/CONDUCTOR
Paul Francis Webster – Composer

**Music Editor:**
ROBERT TRACY

**Music Recorded By:**
MURRAY SPIVACK
VINTON VERNON

**Re-Recording:**
Edwin P. Baker
Walter Gest
Willis Hawley
Roger Heman
Joseph I. Kane

L. John Myers
Raymond F. Regula
Dean Salmon
Frank Webster, Jr.
Al Weiss
W.H. Wilmarth

**Lyrics Written By:**
PAUL FRANCIS WEBSTER

**Musician – Guitar:**
Laurindo Almeida
Willie Champion

**Set Musician:**
Frank Borzage

**Orchestrator:**
Manuel Emanuel
Jimmie Haskell
George Parrish
Lucie Svehlova
Herbert Taylor

**PUBLICITY:**
**Public Relations:**
Russell Birdwell – Vice-President Advertising/Publicity Consultant
Tom Carlisle – Unit Publicist
Elena Da Vinci – Publicity (dismissed)
Hank Fine – Unit Publicist (dismissed)
Al Finestone
Jim Henaghan – Production Executive (dismissed)
Joe Hyams – Director of Publicity
Frank Phillips – Unit Publicist (dismissed)
Emily Stevens – Unit Publicist (dismissed)
Milton Weiss – Unit Publicist

**Still Photographer:**
Bernie Abramson
Roman Freulich
Louis Goldman
Wayne Miller

A.Y. Owens
Sam Shaw
Phil Stern
Dennis Stock

**Artist:**
Reynold Brown
Russell Roberts

## PRINCIPLE CAST IN ORDER OF CREDIT:

JOHN WAYNE – COL. DAVY CROCKETT
RICHARD WIDMARK – JIM BOWIE
LAURENCE HARVEY – COL. WILLIAM TRAVIS
FRANKIE AVALON – SMITTY
PATRICK WAYNE – CAPT. JAMES BUTLER BONHAM
LINDA CRISTAL – FLACA
JOAN O'BRIEN – MRS. SUE DICKINSON
CHILL WILLS – BEEKEEPER
JOSEPH CALLEIA – JUAN SEGUIN
KEN CURTIS – CAPT. ALMERON DICKINSON
CARLOS ARRUZA – LT. REYES
JESTER HAIRSTON – JETHRO
VEDA ANN BORG – BLIND NELL ROBERTSON
JOHN DIERKES – JOCKO ROBERTSON
DENVER PYLE – THIMBLERIG (THE GAMBLER)
AISSA WAYNE – LISA ANGELICA DICKINSON
HANK WORDEN – THE PARSON
BILL HENRY – DR. GRANT
BILL DANIEL – COL. NEILL
WESLEY LAU – EMIL SAND
CHUCK ROBERSON – BROWN, A TENNESSEAN
GUINN WILLIAMS – LT. "IRISH" FINN
OLIVE CAREY – MRS. DENNISON
RUBEN PADILLA – GENL. SANTA ANNA
RICHARD BOONE – GENL. SAM HOUSTON

## ADDITIONAL CAST:

Roy Ackland – Bugler
Lee Allison – Atheist
Carol Baxter aka Carol Berlin – Melinda Dennison
Danny Borzage – Tennessean
Willie "El Curro" Champion – Flamenco Guitarist

859

Teresa Champion – Flamenco Dancer
John Henry Daniels – Happy Sam
LaJean Ethridge – Mrs. Guy
Rojelio Estrada – Mexican boy luggage carrier
Manuel Farias – Mexican colonel
Rosita Fernandez – Cantina girl
Ron Gast – Houston camp guard
Fred Graham – Bearded volunteer
Big John Hamilton – Mr. Dennison
Marshall Jones – Hap/Bystander
Don LaCava – Mexican officer
Toni Wayne LaCava – Pioneer woman/Flamenco dancer
Cliff Lyons
Blas Munoz – Tamale seller
Jack Pennick – Sgt. Lightfoot
Eleno Rodriguez – Messenger
Anita Swift LaCava – Young child
Julian Trevino – Silverio Seguin
Pilar Wayne – Flamenco dancer/background
Jack Williams – Bob

**BOWIE CHAROS:**
Georges Cartes
Vincente Castro
Raul De Luna
Manuel Farias
Miguel Garza
Yndalecio Gonzales
Efrain Maldonada
Bob Moss, Sr.
Lupe Reyes
Cruz Rodriguez
Eleno Rodriguez
Ricardo Rosales
Alberto Sandoval
Guadalupe Santoya
Greg Souquet
Martin Torres
Jesse Valdez

**BOWIE MEN:**
D.E. Barentine

Abe Blankenship
F. Bode
Danny Borzage
Paul Breen
Joe Canutt
Tap Canutt
A.R. Carpenter
Ed Carter
Mickey Finn – Mickey
Gerry Fisher
Mike Goulla
Big John Hamilton
Robert H. Harris
Doug Hodges
Leroy Johnson
Elmo Jones
Wayne Kendrick
Jim Kennedy
Charles Kone
Ray Liberto
John McGuyer
J.R. Miller
Jack Miller
Ray Ochoa
Warren Rhea
George Ross
LeRoy Ryland
Pete Schneider
Ben Shirley
Don Smith
Dean Smith
George Sofge
Jack Spain
Jerry Sterner
Ted Sumerall
Alfred Taylor
Jim Walker
Dean Williams
Jack Williams
Clay Wilson
Thomas Worrell
Jim Wright

**CROCKETT TENNESSEANS:**
Lee Allison
Frankie Avalon – Smitty
Buff Brady
Jim Burk
Chuck Hayward
Tom Hennessey – Bull
John Hudkins
Eddie Juaregui
Cy Malis – Pete
Bob Morgan
Boyd "Red" Morgan
Gil Perkins – Scotty
Rudy Robbins – It Do
Chuck Roberson – Brown
Bob Rose
Denver Pyle – Thimblerig
Bill Shannon
Winner (Slim) Stevens
Ted White
Bill Williams
Chill Wills – Beekeeper
Hank Worden – The Parson

**TRAVIS REGULARS:**
Roy Ackland
Charles Akins
Harold Allgood
Jim Brewer
Estill Ezell
Karl Flenn
Fred Graham – Fred
Joe Graham
Frank Higgins
Joe Jackson
David Kuykendall – Sentry
Ronald Lee
Dave Marshall
Bryan McAfee
Doug McNealy
Don Middlebrook
C.A. Nicks

862

Dale Parsons
Jerry Phillips
Homer Pierce
Lee Roy Powell
Ed Riley
Charles Sanders
Charles Veltmann, Jr.

**HOUSTON TROOPS:**
Ken Curtis – Capt. Dickinson
Bill Daniel – Col. Neill
John Dierkes
Bill Moody III
Jack Pennick
Rudy Robbins

**STAND-INS/DOUBLES:**
Caesar Daniels – John Henry Daniels
Ray Everson – Laurence Harvey
Sheila Fine – Carol Baxter
Marshall Jones – John Wayne
Dave Marshall – Richard Widmark
Elaine Moody – Aissa Wayne
Pinni Townsend – Linda Cristal

**STUNTMEN:**
Buff Brady
Jim Burk
Joe Canutt
Tap Canutt
Tex Collins
Eddy Donno
John Richard Gill
Fred Graham
Bill Hart
Chuck Hayward
Tom Hennessey
John "Bear" Hudkins
Ed Jauregui
LeRoy Johnson
Bob Morgan
Red Morgan

Gil Perkins
Phil Rawlinson
Chuck Roberson
Bob Rose
Bill Shannon
Dean Smith
Blackie Storm
Ted White
Bill Williams
Jack Williams
Jack Young

**ADDITIONAL EXTRAS:**
Maydelle Anderson – Pioneer woman
Norman Andrews
Bill Babcock
Dorothy Baker – Pioneer woman
Buddy Bregman
Don Borzage
Daisy Boyd – Pioneer woman
Stockton Briggle
Layne Britton
Jerry Carlsen
Smokey Chisum
Alice Cromwell – Pioneer woman
Bill Cumiskey
Leona Cumiskey
Pat Cumiskey – Young boy
Tim Cumiskey – Young boy
Bill Daniel, Jr.
Caesar Daniels – Young boy
Paul Davis (Birthday party)
Jerry Derderian
Jerry Dickens
Jan Donoho
Wayne Ben Dorcy (Defender)
Dave Dunlop
Harry Froboess
Henry Garcia – Young boy
Hilda Garcia
Elizabeth Gilliland
Little John Hamilton – Houston sentry

Darrell Hansen
Carleen Hartman
Jim Henaghan, Jr.
Ray Henschel
Fran Higgins (Birthday party)
Tex Hill
Frank Hoyles (Mr. and Mrs.)
Bess Huebner – Pioneer woman
Elmo Jones
Marjory Jones
Ethal Clara Kelly
Jim Kinney
Myles Kuykendall
Elias Lara
Ron Lee
Elmer Lorenz
Eusebio Lugo
Sonny Lugo
Mario Madujano
Romain Martinez
Rusty McDonald
Charles McQuarry
Phil Medlin
James Mesquiti – Mexican peasant
Elaine Moody (Birthday party)
Al Murphy
Fred Murphy
Arthur Names
Buddy Ochoa aka Buddy Trone
Johnny Ortega
Oscar Ortiz
Will Paradeaux
Peggy Ponder
Sharyn Postell (Birthday party)
John Quehada
John Quinn – Defender
Phil Rawlinson
Charlie Rios
Dianna Roselle
Lance Roselle
Mike Roselle
Bodie Rosenow

Jose Saenz
Ernie Saftig
A.J. Schubach (Birthday party)
Diana Sue Schubach
Eve Schwartz – Pioneer woman
Lynn Seargeant – (Birthday party)
Tommy Dee Seargeant (Birthdayt party)
Chester Harvey Smith
Jack Spain
William Stephens
Winner Stevens
Hilda Stillwater – Young child
Nick Toamlas
Martin H. Torres
Edmundo Trevino – Seguin bodyguard
Frank Trevino
Elwynn Von Funk – Texican soldier
Ricci Ware – Houston sentry
Bud Whistler – Pioneer
Margenia Whistler – Pioneer
Barbara Wills White
Faye Woolf
Joe York, Jr. (Birthday party)

## ADDITIONAL NAMES (UNIDENTIFED AS CREW OR EXTRA):

Robert Albert
Lou Clothier
Al Delamore
Inez Donoho
Ronald Harris
Leland Johnson
Betty McGonagill
Bob Moss, Jr.
Roy Nelson
Betty Pena
Ruben Perez
Lou Place
George Reles
Dolores Salmon
Krys Schubach
Billy Sherman
Johnny Ward

Paul Weddell
Guy Williams
Julian Wilson

**CANTINA DANCERS:**
Yolanda Almaguer
Conjunto Antano
Nela Bernal
Ann Barrera-Morse
Violeta Cantu
Alicia Margo Cardenas
Madga Carreno
Teresa Champion
Rosita Fernandez
Maria Nela Garcia
Raquel Garcia
Theresa Ada Garcia
Maruca Gloria
Maris Luisa Gonzales
Emma Hernandez
Hilda Jiminez
Maris Luisa Martinez
Guadalupe Oriz
Vera Pedraza
Alma Reyes
Netty Rodriguez
Sylvia Rosario
Sonia Salinas
Mary "Maruca" Vidal

**PUBLICIZED POTENTIAL/POSSIBLE CAST MEMBERS:**
James Arness _ Houston
Don Barry – Travis
Alfonso Bedoya – Antonio
Theodore Bikel
Ward Bond – Bowie
Marlon Brando _ Santa Anna
Walter Brennan
Hillary Brooke – Mrs. Dickinson
Diahann Carroll
John Carroll – Thimblerig
Harry Carey, Jr. Bub

867

Chuck Conners – Bowie
Sammy Davis, Jr. – Jethro
Maria Demas
Maria Felix
Clark Gable – Travis
John Gavin – Capt. Dickinson
Charlton Heston – Bowie
William Holden – Bowie/Travis
Rock Hudson – Bowie
Burl Ives – Bee Hunter
Ben Johnson – Messenger
Burt Lancaster – Bowie
Bob Mathias
Dorothy Malone – Mrs. Dickinson
Robert Mitchum – Bowie
Audie Murphy – John W. Smith
Sondra Osborne (Miss Oklahoma 1959)
Fess Parker
Estrellita Rodriguez – Lupita
Gail Russell
Frank Sinatra – Travis
Robert Stack – Bowie
Harry Stampler
Danny Stradella
Constance Towers – Mrs. Dickinson
Blue Washington – Sam
Esperanza Wayne
Johnny Weissmuller – Crockett
Loretta Young – Mrs. Dickinson

**SPIRIT OF THE ALAMO TELEVISON PROGRAM:**
Allan Baab – Video
Kenneth Becker – Audio
Robert Boatman – Lighting Director
John Buttler – Choreographer
Joe Cates – NBC Producer
Kevin Cleary – Audio Dubbing
Ed Cosgrove – Associate Producer
Perry Cross – Producer
Hal Dasbach – KLTA Production Supervisor
Vincent Filizola – Video Recording
Greg Harney – Lighting Supervisor

Richard C. Harris – Music Editor
Hector Highton – Unit Manager
Ed Hunt – Film Cutter
Bruce Minnex – Associate Director
Jerry Pattison – Audio
John Polich – Engineering Supervisor
Ernest Rinaldi – Video Recording
Seymour Robbie – Co-Producer and Director
L.I. Salaman – Writer
Bob Saunders – Associate Director
Robert Spears – Video
Dimitri Tiomkin – Conductor and Composer
Paul Francis Webster – Lyrics
Lou Wolf – Video

Bob Quinlan – KTLA Program Manager
John Silva – KTLA Chief engineer

# BIBLIOGRAPHY

Manuscript collections:
AJW   Allen J. Wiener interview, July 18, 1995
AHS   Arizona Historical Society
AMP   Academy of Motion Picture Arts and Sciences, Margaret Herrick Collection
AF    The *Alamo* File, Daughters of the Republic of Texas Library, San Antonio, Texas
BBC   The Theodore Huff Memorial Film Society
BH    Brian Huberman, Rice University, Houston, Texas
BYU   James D'Arc, Brigham Young University
HFH   Hollywood Film History Oral History Project, Columbia Universoty
JFP   John Ford Papers, Lilly Library, Indiana University, Bloomington, Indiana
JSP   James T. "Happy" Shahan Papers, Alamo Village, Brackettville Texas
JWB   John Wayne Birthplace, Winterset, Iowa
JWF   John Wayne File, Federal Bureau of Investigation, Washington, D.C.
FTC   Frank Thompson/Craig Covner
MZP   Maurice Zolotow Papers, Humanities Research Center, University of Texas at Austin, Austin,
Texas
MBI   Michael Boldt interview
PFP   Patrick Ford Papers, Brigham Young University, Salt Lake City, Utah
RHI   Rick Hassler interview
RDP   Ronald Davis Papers, Degolyer Library, Southern Methodist University, Dallas, Texas
TTU   Texas Tech University, Southwest Special Collections Library
USC   University of Southern California

Interviews, Oral Histories and Personal Correspondence:
All interviews without an institutional affiliation were conducted by the author.
Chris Andersen
Maydelle Anderson
Pedro Armendariz, JFP
Frankie Avalon, BH
Mike Bacarella
Budd Boetticher, BH
Jim Brewer

871

Bob Bryden
B.J. Burns
Bruce Cabot, AHS
Joe Canutt
Yakima Canutt, AHS
Harry Carey Jr.
Harry Carey Jr. , JFP, RDP
Jerry Carlsen
Teresa Champion, BH
William "El Curo" Champion, BH
Don Clark
William Clothier, AHS, BH
Fourth Coates
Linda Cristal
Linda Cristal, BH, RDP
Leona Cumiskey
Pat Cumiskey
Tim Cumiskey
Rich Curilla
Ken Curtis BH, JFP
Bill Daniel, BH
John Henry Daniels
Sam Darden, BH
Zack Davis
Gene DeRuelle
Jerry Dickens
Mary Doria, BH
Roy Estrada
Scott Eyman
Barbara Ford, JFP
Dan Ford
John Ford, BBC, JFP
Patrick Ford, BYU
Billie Foust
Marty Freize
Henry Fuentes
Hilda Garcia
Bobby Gardiner
Bill Gilmore
Ralph Gonzales
Geoff Grant
John Hagner
Chuck Hall
"Little" John Hamilton
Robert Harris (extra)
Robert Harris (film restoration)
Chuck Hayward, BH, JFP
Howard Hawks, AHS, HFH
Chris Hearn
Jose Hernandez III
Mary Hernandez
John Hinnant
Bill Jensen
John Jensen, BH
Ben Johnson , AHS, RDP
Marshall Jones
Tom Kane
Burt Kennedy, BH, RDP
Alan Kreiger, Jr.
David Kuykendall

872

Don LaCava
Mrs. Ray Liberto
Ernesto Malacara
Kipp Martin
Andrew McLaglan, RDP
Don McLendon, BH
Clio Merkel
Bruce Minnex, BH, MBI
Bill Moody IV
Elaine Moody
Bob Morgan, BH
Joe Musso
Rob Newman
Joan O'Brien
Robert Oliver
Ruben Padilla Jr.
Carolyn Roos Olsen
Ruben Padilla III
Ruben Padilla Jr.
Fess Parker, BH
Gil Perkins RDP
Denver Pyle AJW, BH
Ken Pruitt
John Quinn
Robert Quinones
Jamie Shahan Rains
Robert Relyea
Rudy Robbins
Rudy Robbins, BH
Chuck Roberson, AHS, MZP
Randy Roberts
Randy Roberts, RHI
Mike Roselle
Patrick Saunders
Chuck Schoenfeld
James T. (Happy) Shahan, BH, FTC, TTU
Jamie Shahan (Rains)
Tulisha Shahan (Wardlaw)
Tully Shahan
Virginia Shahan
John (Plunker) Sheedy
Bob Shelton
Anne Siani
Dean Smith
Dean Smith, JFP
Hilda Stillwater
Susan Raney Stone
Anita LaCava Swift
Frank Thompson
Crystal Harvey Wade
Mary Virginia Pitmann Waller
Ashley Ward III
Tulisha Shahan Wardlaw
Ricci Ware
Gwen Watkins
Aissa Wayne
Gretchen Wayne
John Wayne, AHS, HFH, JFP, MZP
Michael Wayne BH
Patrick Wayne

Patrick Wayne BH
Pilar Wayne, BH
Murray Weissmann
Barbara Wills White
Ted White
Richard Widmark, CLOSEUP Radio program, March, 1997. Nigel Andrews.
Bob Williams
Jack Williams
Jack Williams, AHS
Ted White
Hank Worden, BH RDP
Tommy Worrell
Billy Winn
Al Ybarra, BH, FTC
Joe York, Jr.

Books:

*Alamo program.* Hollywood, California: Sovereign Publications, 1960.

Alexander, Linda J. *Reluctant Witness: Robert Taylor, Hollywood and Communism.* Swansboro, North Carolina: Tease Publishing, LLC, 2008.

Amaral, Anthony. *Movie Horses: Their Treatment and Training.* Indianapolis, Indiana: Bobbs-Merrill Company, Inc., 1967.

Ambrose, *Stephen E. Eisenhower: Soldier and President.* New York, New York: Simon and Schuster, 1991.

Anderson, Paul F. *The Davy Crockett Craze.* Hillside, Illinois: R&G Productions, 1996

Arness, James with James E. Wise, Jr. *James Arness, An Autobiography.* Jefferson, North Carolina: McFarland & Company, Inc., 2001.

Baxter, John A. *The Cinema of John Ford.* London: C.Tinling and Co. Ltd, 1971.

_____, *Stunt, The story of the great movie stuntmen.* Garden City, New York: Doubleday, 1974.

Bill, Tony. *Movie Speak: How to Talk Like You Belong on a Film Set.* New York, New York: Workman Publishing, 2008.

Billingsley, Kenneth Lloyd. *Hollywood Party: How Communism Seduced the American Film Industry in the 1930s and 1940s.* Rocklin, California: Forum, 1998.

Birdwell, Richard. *The Alamo.* United Artists press release. 1960.

Bishop, George. *John Wayne: The Actor, The Man.* Ottawa, Illinois: Caroline House, 1979.

Block, Alex Ben. *George Lucas's Blockbusting: A Decade-by-Decade Survey of Timeless Movies Including Untold Secrets of Their Financial and cultural Success.* New York New York: George Lucas Books, 2010.

Bogdanovich, Peter. *John Ford.* Berkeley, California: University of California Press, 1978.

_____, *Who The Devil Made It: Conversations with Legendary Film Directors.* New York, NewYork: Ballantine, 1997.

_____, *Who The Hell's In It: Conversations with Hollywood's Legendary Actors.* New York, New York: Ballantine, 2004.

_____, *Pieces Of Time.* New York, New York: Arbor House, 1985.

Boswell, John and Jay David. *Duke: The John Wayne Album: An Intimate Look at a Legend.* New York, New York: Ballantine Books, 1979.

Breivold, Scott. *Howard Hawks Interviews.* Jackson, Mississippi: University Press of Mississippi, 2006.

Bronson, Fred. *The Billboard Book Of Number One Hits.* New York, New York: Billboard Publications, 1985.

Brooker, John. *The Life and Times of John Wayne.* London: Hamlyn, 1979.

Brown, Dee. *When the Century Was Young.* Little Rock, Arkansas: August House Publishers, 1993.

Brown, Peter H. *The Real Oscar: The Story Behind the Academy Awards.* Westport, Connecticut: Arlington House, 1981.

Canutt, Yakima with Oliver Drake. *Stunt Man. The Autobiography of Yakima Canutt.* New York, New York: Walker and Company, 1979.

Carey, Harry, Jr. *Company of Heroes: My Life as an Actor in the John Ford stock Company.* Metuchen, New Jersey: The Scarecrow Press, 1994.

Carpozi, George, Jr. *The John Wayne Story.* New York, New York: Dell, 1979.

Clark, Donald and Christopher Andersen. *John Wayne's The Alamo: The Making of John Wayne's 1960 Epic Film.* Hillside, Illinois: Midwest Publishing, 1994.

Ceplair, Larry and Steven Englund. *The Inquisition in Hollywood: Politics in the Film Community 1930-1960*. Berkeley, California: University of California Press, 1983.

Conley, Kevin. *The Full Burn*. New York, New York; Bloomsbury, 2008.

Cowie, Peter. *John Ford and the American West*. New York, New York: Harry N. Abrams, Inc, 2004.

Davis, Ronald L. *John Ford: Hollywood's Old Master*. Norman, Oklahoma: University of Oklahoma Press, 1995.

_____, *Duke: The Life and Image of John Wayne*. Norman, Oklahoma: University of Oklahoma Press, 1998.

Daughters of the Republic of Texas, *The Wall of History*. San Antonio, Texas: Clark Printing Company, 2001.

DeRuelle, Gene. *It's a Funny Business: Life at the Bottom of the Food Chain*.

Dietrich, Noah. *Howard: The Amazing Mr. Hughes*. Greenwich, Connecticut: Fawcett, 1972.

Dmytryk, Edward. *It's a Hell of a Life But Not a Bad Living*. New York, New York; Times Books, 1978.

Eliot, Marc. *Reagan; The Hollywood Years*. New York, New York: Three Rivers Press, 2008.

Eyman, Scott. *Five American Cinematographers*. Metuchen, New Jersey: Scarecrow Press, 1987.

_____, *John Wayne: The Life and Legend*. Simon & Schuster, New York, New York, 2014.

_____, *Print the Legend: The Life and Times of John Ford*. Baltimore, Maryland: The Johns Hopkins University Press, 2000.

Fagen, Herb. *Duke: We're Glad We Knew You. John Wayne's Friends and Colleagues Remember His Remarkable Life*. New York, New York: Citadel Press, 1998.

Finler, Joel W. *Hollywood Movie Stills: Art and Technique in the Golden Age of the Studios*. London, United Kingdom: Titan, 2012.

Ford, Dan. The UnQuiet Man: *The Life of John Ford*. London: William Kimber, 1979.

Ford, Peter. *Glenn Ford: A Life*. Madison, Wisconsin: The University of Wisconsin Press, 2011.

Frazee, Steve. *The Alamo*. New York, New York: Avon Book Division, 1960.

Freese, Gene Scott. *Hollywood Stunt Performers: A Dictionary and Filmography, 1922-1996*. Jefferson, North Carolina: McFarland, 1998.

Fyne, Robert. *The Hollywood Propaganda of World War II*. Lanham, Maryland: The Scarecrow Press, 1997.

Gaddis, John Lewis. *Russia, The Soviet Union and The United States, An Interpretive History*. New York, New York: McGraw Hill, 1990.

_____, *The Cold War; A New History*. New York, New York: Penguin Press, 2005.

Gallagher, Tag. *John Ford: The Man and his Films*. Berkeley, California: University of California Press, 1986.

Gibbs, Nancy and Michael Duffy, *The President's Club: Inside the World's Most Exclusive Fraternity*. New York, New York: Simon and Schuster, 2012.

Goldman, Louis. *Lights, Camera, Action!* New York, New York: Harry N. Abrams, Inc.,1986.

Goldman, Michael. *John Wayne: The Genuine Article. The Unseen Archive of an American Legend*. San Rafael, California: Insight Editions, 2013.

Goldstein, Norm. *John Wayne, A Tribute*. New York, New York: Holt, Rinehart and Winston, 1970.

Grams, Jr. Martin and Les Rayburn. *The Have Gun – Will Travel Companion*. Arlington, Virginia: Kirby Lithographic Company, 2000.

Haenn, William F. *Fort Clark and Brackettville, Land of Heroes*. Chicago, Illinois: Arcadia Publishing, 2002.

Hagner, John. *Bob Rose, "The Nerviest Stuntman Ever."* Moab, Utah, 1994.

Hall, Sheldon and Steve Neale. *Epics, Spectacles and Blockbusters: A Hollywood History*. Detroit: Wayne State University Press, 2010.

Hayden, Sterling. *Wanderer*. New York, New York: W.W. Norton & Company, Inc., 1977.

Helmick, Paul. *Cut, Print, and that's a Wrap: A Hollywood Memoir*. Jefferson, North Carolina: McFarland & Co., Inc., 2001.

Hepburn, Katharine. *Me: Stories of My Life*. New York, New York: Alfred A. Knopf, 1991.

Heston, Charlton. *The Actor's Life Journals 1956-1976*. New York, New York: Pocket Books, 1978.

_____, *In the Arena: An Autobiography*. New York, New York: Boulevard Books, 1997.

Hickey, Des and Gus Smith. The *Prince; The Public and Private Life of Laurence Harvey*. London: Leslie Frewin Publishers, 1975.

Huffines, Alan C. *Blood of Noble Men*. Austin, Texas: Eakins Press, 1999.

Hughes, Howard. *Stagecoach to Tombstone*. New York, New York: I. B. Taurus, 2008.

Hurst, Richard M. *Republic Studios: Between Poverty Row and the Majors*. Lanham, Maryland: The Scarecrow Press, 2007.

875

Hutton, Paul Andrew. *A Narrative of the Life of David Crockett by Himself.* Lincoln, Nebraska: University of Nebraska Press, 1987.

Jeavons, Clyde. *A Pictorial History of War Films.* New York, New York: Citadel Press, 1974.

Joyner, C. Courtney. *The Westerners: Interviews with actors, Directors, Writers and Producers.* Jefferson, North Carolina: McFarland & Company, 2009.

Kaminsky, Stuart M. *Don Seigel: Director.* New York, New York: Curtis Books, 1974.

Kazanjian, Howard, and Chris Enss. *The Young Duke: The Early Life of John Wayne.* Guilford, Connecticut: Morris Book Publishing, 2007.

Kelly, Kitty. *His Way – The Unauthorized Biography of Frank Sinatra.* New York, New York: Bantam, 1986.

Kennedy, Burt. *Hollywood Trail Boss: Behind the scenes of the Wild, Wild Western.* New York, New York: Boulevard, 1997.

Kieskalt, Charles John. *The Official John Wayne Reference Book.* Secaucus, New Jersey: Carol Publishing, 1995.

Klinck, Richard E. *Land of Room Enough and Time Enough.* Salt Lake City, Utah: Gibbs M. Smith, Inc., 1984.

Koppes, Clayton R. and Gregory D. Black. *Hollywood Goes to War: How Politics, Profits and Propaganda Shaped World War II Movies.* Berkeley, California: University of California Press, 1990.

Landesman, Fred. *The John Wayne Filmography.* Jefferson, North Carolina: McFarland & Co, 2004.

Levy, Emanuel. *John Wayne: Prophet of the American Way of Life.* Lanham, Maryland: The Scarecrow Press, Inc., 1998.

Lilley, Tim. *Campfire Conversations: Big Trail Interviews with Some of John Wayne's Coworkers.* Akron, Ohio: Big Trail Publications, 1992.

_____, *Campfire Conversations Complete: Tim Lilley's Interviews with the coworkers of John Wayne.* Akron, Ohio: Big Trail Publications, 2010.

_____, *Campfire Conversations: Deluxe Centennial Edition.* Akron, Ohio: Big Trail Publications, 2007.

_____, *Campfire Embers: More Big Trail Interviews Of John Wayne's Coworkers.* Akron, Ohio: Big Trail Publications, 1997.

_____, *Campfire's Glow: More Big Trail Interviews Of John Wayne's Coworkers.* Akron, Ohio: Big Trail Publications, 1995.

_____, *Campfire Rekindled: More Big Trail Interviews Of John Wayne's Coworkers.* Akron, Ohio: Big Trail Publications, 1994.

_____, *The Big Trail, December 1994 Vol. XI no. 4.*

_____, *The Trail Beyond.* Volume I, December, 1999. Akron, Ohio: Big Trail Publishing, 1999.

_____, *The Trail Beyond.* Volume II, December, 2000. Akron, Ohio: Big Trail Publishing, 2000.

_____, *The Trail Beyond.* Volume III, December, 2001. Akron, Ohio: Big Trail Publishing, 2001.

_____, *The Trail Beyond.* Volume V, December, 2003. Akron, Ohio: Big Trail Publishing, 2003.

_____, *The Trail Beyond.* Volume VI, December, 2004. Akron, Ohio: Big Trail Publishing, 2004.

_____, *The Trail Beyond.* Volume VII, December, 2005. Akron, Ohio: Big Trail Publishing, 2005.

_____, *The Trail Beyond.* Volume VIII, December, 2006. Akron, Ohio: Big Trail Publishing, 2006.

_____, *The Trail Beyond.* Volume X, December, 2008. Akron, Ohio: Big Trail Publishing, 2008.

Lindley, Thomas Ricks. *Alamo Traces: New Evidence and New Conclusions.* Lanham, Maryland: Republic of Texas Press, 2003.

Lisanti, Tom. *Fantasy Femmes of Sixties Cinema: Interviews with 20 Actresses from Biker, Beach, and Elvis Movies.* Jefferson, North Carolina, McFarland & Company, Inc., 2001.

Macklin, Tony and Nick Pici. *Voices from the Set. The Film Heritage Interviews.* Lanham, Maryland: The Scarecrow Press, 2000.

MacHale, Des. *The Complete Guide to The Quiet Man.* Belfast, Ireland: Appletree Press, 2000.

Madsen, Axel. *John Huston: A Biography.* New York, New York: Doubleday, 1978.

Marx, Arthur. *Red Skelton: An Unauthorized Biography.* New York, New York: E.P. Dutton, 1979.

McBride, Joseph. *Hawks on Hawks.* Berkley, California: University of California Press, 1982.

_____, *Searching for John Ford: A Life.* New York, New York: St. Martin's Griffin, 2001.

McCarthy, Todd. *Howard Hawks: The Grey Fox of Hollywood.* New York, New York: Grove Press, 1997.

McGhee, Richard D. *John Wayne: Actor, Artist, Hero.* Jefferson, North Carolina: McFarland Classics, 1999.

McGivern, Carolyn. *John Wayne: A Giant Shadow.* Bracknell, United Kingdom: Sammon Publishing, 2000.

_____, *The Lost Films of John Wayne.* Nashville, Tennessee: Cumberland House, 2006.

McNee, Gerry. *In the Footsteps of the Quiet Man.* Edinburgh, Scotland: Mainstream Publishing, 1990.

Miller, Frank. *Leading Couples: The Most Unforgettable Screen Romances of the Studio Era*. San Francisco, California: Chronicle Books, 2008.

Mirisch, Walter. *I Thought We Were Making Movies, Not History*. Madison, Wisconsin: University of Wisconsin Press, 2008.

Mitchum, Petrine Day. *Hollywood Hoofbeats: Trails Blazed Across the Silver Screen*. Irvine, California: Bow Tie Press, 2005.

Moon, Samuel. *Tall Sheep: Harry Goulding - Monument Valley Trader*. Norman, Oklahoma: University of Oklahoma Press, 1992.

Mosley, Leonard. *Zanuck: The Rise and fall of Hollywood's Last Tycoon*. 1984. McGraw-Hill, 1985.

Munn, Michael. *John Wayne: The Man Behind the Myth*. New York, New York: New American Library, 2005.

Needham, Hal. *Stuntman*. New York, New York: Little, Brown and Company, 2011.

Nollen, Scott Allen, *Three Bad Men: John Ford, John Wayne, Ward Bond*. Jefferson, North Carolina: McFarland, 2013.

O'Hara, Maureen, with John Nicoletti. *'Tis Herself: An Autobiography*. New York, New York: Simon and Schuster, 2005.

Olsen, Carolyn Roos, with Marilyn Hudson. *Hollywood's Man who Worried for the Stars*. Bloomington, Indiana: Author House, 2008.

Pattie, Jane. *John Wayne: There Rode a Legend. China*: Western Classics, 2000.

*Pictorial History of the Second World War: A Photographic Record of all Theaters of action chronologically arranged, Vol 1*. New York, New York: Wm. H. Wise and Co., Inc., 1944.

Perry, Gerald. *John Ford Interviews*. Jackson, Mississippi: University Press of Mississippi, 2001.

Ramer, Jean. *Duke: The Real Story of John Wayne*. New York, New York: Charter, 1973.

Redfern, Nick. *Celebrity Secrets: Government Files on the Rich and Famous*. New York, New York: Paraview, 2007.

Relyea, Robert. *Not So Quiet On The Set: My Life in Movies During Hollywood's Macho Era*. New York, New York: iUniverse, Inc., 2008.

Roberson, Chuck, and Bodie Thoene. *The Fall Guy. 30 Years As The Duke's Double*. North Vancouver, British Columbia, Canada: Hancock House, 1980.

Roberts, Randy and James S. Olson. *John Wayne: American*. New York, New York: Free Press, 1995.

_____, *A Line In The Sand: The Alamo in Blood and Memory*. New York, New York: Touchstone, 2001.

Rosenberg, Bernard and Harry Silverstein. *The Real Tinsel*. London, England: Macmillan, 1970.

Rothel, David. *An Ambush of Ghosts; A Personal Guide to Favorite Western Film Locations*. Madison, North Carolina: Empire Publishing, 1990.

_____, Richard Boone, *A Knight Without Armor in a Savage Land*. Madison, North Carolina: Empire Publishing, 2000.

Schlesinger, Arthur. *Kennedy or Nixon: Does It Make Any Difference?* New York, New York: Macmillan, 1960.

Schlossheimer, Michael. *Gunmen and Gangsters: Profiles of Nine Actors who Portrayed Memorable Screen Tough Guys*. Jefferson, North Carolina" McFarland & Company, Inc., 2002.

Schoelwer, Susan Prendergast. *Alamo Images: Changing Perceptions of a Texas Experience*. Dallas, Texas: Degolyer Library and Southern Methodist University, 1985.

Server, Lee. *Robert Mitchum: "Baby, I Don't Care."* New York: St. Martin's Griffin, 2001.

Shaw, Sam. *John Wayne In The Camera Eye*. New York: Pebble Press International Inc., 1979.

Shepherd, Donald and Robert Slatzer with Dave Grayson. *Duke: The Life and Times of John Wayne*. Garden City, New Jersey: Doubleday, 1985.

Sinai, Anne. *Reach for the Top: The Turbulent Life of Laurence Harvey*. Lanham, Maryland: The Scarecrow Press, Inc, 2003.

Sinclair, Andrew. *John Ford; A Biography*. New York, New York: The Dial Press, 1979.

Sinclair, Harold. *The Horse Soldiers*. New York, New York: Dell, 1959.

Shackford, James Atkins. *David Crockett; The Man and the Legend*. Lincoln, Nebraska: University of Nebraska Press, 1984.

Skinner, Kiron, Annelise Anderson and Martin Anderson, *Reagan, A Life in Letters*, Free Press, 2004.

Smith, Dean with Mike Cox. *Cowboy Stuntman: From Olympic Gold to the Silver Screen*. Lubbock, Texas: Texas Tech University Press, 2013.

Snuggs, Ann. *Uncredited: Cliff Lyons On & Off Screen*. Crosby, Texas: Painted Word Studios, 2008.

Stack, Robert with Mark Evans. *Straight Shooting*. New York, New York: Macmillan, 1980.

Stern, Phil. *Phil Stern: A Life's Work*. New York, New York: Powerhouse Books, 2003.

Stevens, George, Jr. *Conversations with the Great Moviemakers of Hollywood's Golden Age at the American Film Institute*. New York, New York: Alfred A. Knopf, 2006.

Suid, Lawrence. *Guts and Glory: Great American War Movies*. Lexington, Kentucky: The University Press of Kentucky, 2002.

Summers, Neil. *The Unsung Heroes*. Vienna, West Virginia: The Old West Shop Publishing, 1996.

Tinkle, Lon. *13 Days to Glory*. New York, New York: McGraw-Hill, 1960.

Tinkle, Lon. *An American Original: The Life of J. Frank Dobie*. Boston, Massachusetts: Little, Brown and Company, 1978.

Thomas, Bob. *Golden Boy: The Untold Story of William Holden*. New York, New York: St. Martin's Press, 1983.

Thompson, Frank. *Alamo Movies*. Plano, Texas: Woodware Publishing, Inc., 1991.

_____, Frank T. *William A. Wellman*. Metuchen, New Jersey: The Scarecrow Press, 1983.

Tiomkin, Dimitri and Prosper Buranelli. *Please Don't Hate Me: The gay confessions of an unpredictable musician*. New York, New York: Doubleday, 1959.

Tomkies, Mike. *Duke: The Story of John Wayne*. New York, New York: Avon, 1972.

Tuska, John. *The Filming of the West*. Garden City, New York: Doubleday, 1976.

Uecker, Herbert G. *The Archaeology of the Alamo*. 2001.

Wasserman, Harvey and Norman Soloman. *Killing Our Own*. New York, New York: Delta, 1982.

Wayne, Aissa with Steve Delsohn. *John Wayne, My Father*. New York, New York: Random House, 1991.

Wayne, John. *My Kingdom for a Horse*. Proposed autobiography.

Wayne, Pilar with Alex Thorleifson. *John Wayne: My Life with the Duke*. New York, New York: McGraw-Hill, 1987.

Wilkerson, Tichi and Marcia Borie. *The Hollywood Reporter*. New York, New York: Arlington House, 1984.

Wills, Gary. *John Wayne's America*. New York, New York: Simon and Schuster, 1997.

Wise, Arthur and Derek Ware. *Stunting in the Cinema*. New York, New York: St. Martin's Press, 1973.

Woods, Robin. *Howard Hawks*. Garden City, New York: Doubleday & Co., 1968.

York, Neil Longley. *Fact As Fiction: The Horse Soldiers & Popular Memory*. Kent, Ohio: The Kent State University Press, 2001.

List of Newspapers:
Abilene Reporter-News, The, (Abilene, TX)
Ada Evening News, The, (Ada, OK)
Advertising Age, (Detroit, MI)
Advertising News of New York, (New York, NY)
Air Force Times
Albuquerque Journal, (Albuquerque, NM)
Albuquerque Tribune, The, (Albuquerque, NM)
Altoona Mirror, The, (Altoona, PA)
Alton Telegraph, (Alton, IL)
Amarillo Globe-Times, (Amarillo, TX)
Anderson Daily Bulletin, (Anderson, IN)
Anderson Herald, The, (Anderson, IN)
Appeal-Democrat, (Marysville, Yuba City, CA)
Arizona Daily Sun, (Flagstaff, AZ)
Atchison Daily Globe, (Atchison, KS)
Augusta Chronicle, The, (Augusta, GA)
Austin American, The, (Austin, TX)
Austin American Statesman, (Austin, TX)
The Austin Statesman, (Austin, TX)
Avalanche Journal, (Lubbock, TX)
The Bakersfield Californian, (Bakersfield, CA)
The Baytown Sun, (Baytown, TX)
The Bedford Gazette, (Bedford, PA)
The Bee, (Danville, VA)
The Berkshire Eagle,(Pittsfield, MA)
Biddeford Journal, (Biddeford, ME)
The Billings Gazette, (Billings, MT)
The Big Spring Daily Herald, (Big Spring, TX)
Big Spring Herald, (Big Spring, TX)
Bluefield Daily Telegram, (Bluefield, WV)

Boston Herald, (Boston, MA)
Brackett News, Brackettville, TX)
Brownsville Herald, Brownsville, TX)
The Brazosport Facts, (Brazoria County, TX)
Burlington Daily Times-News, (Burlington, NC)
The Capital Times, (Madison, WI)
Cedar Rapids Gazette, (Cedar Rapids, IA)
The Cedar Rapids Tribune, Cedar Rapids, IA)
Charleston Daily Mail, (Charleston, WV)
The Charleston Gazette, (Charleston, WV)
The Charlotte Gazette, (Charlotte, NC)
Chicago Daily News, (Chicago, IL)
Chicago Daily Tribune, (Chicago, IL)
Chicago Sun-Times, (Chicago, IL)
Chicago Tribune, (Chicago, IL)
The Chronicle-Telegram, (Elyria, OH)
The Citizen News, (Hollywood, CA)
The Citizen-News, (Hollywood, CA)
Cleveland Plain Dealer, (Cleveland, OH)
Clovis News-Journal, (Clovis, NM)
The Columbus Daily Telegram, (Columbus, OH)
Corpus Christi Caller-Times, (Corpus Christi, TX)
Corpus Christi Times, (Corpus Christi, TX)
The Corsicana Daily Sun, (Corsicana, TX)
The Coshocton, (Coshocton, OH)
The Coshocton Tribune, (Coshocton, OH)
Covina Argus Citizen, (Covina, CA)
Cumberland Evening News, (Cumberland, MD)
The Daily Courier, (Connellsville, PA)
The Daily Facts Review, (Brazoria County, TX)
The Daily Gleaner, (Fredericton, New Brunswick, Canada)
The Daily Herald, (Provo, UT)
The Daily Independent, (Ridgecrest, CA)
The Daily Journal-Gazette and Commercial Star, (Mattoon, IL)
The Daily Mirror, (London, England)
The Daily News, (Huntingdon, PA)
The Daily Reporter, (Dover, OH)
The Daily Review, (Hayward, CA)
The Daily Sun, (Flagstaff, AZ)
The Daily Texan, (Austin, TX)
Dallas Morning News, (Dallas, TX)
Del Rio Herald, (Del Rio, TX)
Del Rio News-Herald, (Del Rio, TX)
Denton Record-Chronicle, (Denton, TX)
The Denver Post, (Denver, CO)
El Paso Herald-Post, (El Paso, TX)
ENQUIRER
The Evening Independent, (Massillon, OH)
The Evening Observe, (Dunkirk, NY)
The Evening Standard, (Uniontown, PA)
Evening Times, (Cumberland, MD)
Fairbanks News-Miner, (Fairbanks, AK)
Fitchburg Sentinel, (Fitchburg, MA)
Florence Morning News, (Florence, SC)
The Fort Clark, Texas Post Return, (Brackettville, TX)
Fort Worth Star-Telegram, (Fort Worth, TX)
The Galveston Daily News, (Galveston, TX)
The Galveston News, (Galveston, TX)
The Gettysburg Times, Gettysburg, PA)
Glean Times Herald, (Kingston, Jamacia)

Graham Leader, (Graham, TX)
Greeley Tribune, (Greely, CO)
The Guardian, (England)
Hamilton Journal, (Hamilton, OH)
The Hammond Times, (Northwest IN)
The Handy-Andy Herald, (San Antonio, TX)
Herald Tribune(New York, NY)
Hollywood Citizen News, (Hollywood, CA)
Hollywood Stuntmen's Hall of Fame Newsletter, (Moab, UT)
Houston Chronicle, (Houston, TX)
The Houston Post, (Houston, TX)
Humboldt Standard, (Eureka, CA)
Hutchison News, (Hutchison, KS)
The Hutchinson News-Herald, (Hutchinson, KS)
Idaho State Journal, (Pocatello, ID)
Independent, (Long Beach, CA)
The Independent, (Long Beach, CA)
Independent Press Telegram, (Long Beach, CA)
Indiana Evening Gazette, (Indiana, PA)
The Intelligence, (Doylestown, PA)
The Inter Lake, (Kalispell, MT)
The Irish Times, (Dublin, Ireland)
Ironwood Daily Globe, (Ironwood, MI)
Island Breeze, (South Padre, TX)
Joplin Globe, (Joplin, MO)
The Kerrville Times, (Kerrville, TX)
Kerrville Mountain Sun, (Kerrville, TX)
Kingsport News, (Kingsport, TN)
Kingsport Times, (Kingsport Times, TN)
The Kinney County News, (Brackettville, TX)
The Lancaster Eagle-Gazette, (Lancaster, OH)
The Laredo Times, (Laredo, TX)
Las Vegas Daily Optic, (Las Vegas, NV)
Lationo Star y Teleguia
The Laurel Leader-Call, (Laurel, MS)
Lawrence Journal-World, (Lawrence, KS)
The Lawton Constitution, (Lawton, OK)
Leader-Times, (Kittanning, PA)
Lebanon Daily News, (Lebanon, PA)
The Lethbridge Herald, (Lethbridge, Alberta, Canada)
Lima News, (Lima, OH)
Limelight, (Hollywood, CA)
Lincoln Sunday-Journal, (Lincoln, NB)
Linton Daily Citizen, (Linton, IN)
Llano News, (Llano, TX)
Long Beach Independent, (Long Beach, CA)
Long Beach Press-Telegram, (Long Beach, CA)
Los Angeles Daily News, (Los Angeles, CA)
Los Angeles Examiner, (Los Angeles, CA)
The Los Angeles Herald and Express, (Los Angeles, CA)
Los Angeles Herald Express, (Los Angeles, CA)
Los Angeles Herald & News, (Los Angeles, CA)
Los Angeles Mirror, (Los Angeles, CA)
Los Angeles Mirror-News, (Los Angeles, CA)
The Los Angeles Times, (Los Angeles, CA)
The Lowell Sun, (Lowell, MA)
Lubbock Morn. Avalanche, (Lubbock, TX)
Madison Capitol Times, (Madison, WI)
Manitowac Herald-Times. (Manitowac, WI)
The Mexico City Daily Bulletin, (Mexico City, Mexico)

Miami Daily News-Record, (Miami, OK)
Middletown Times Herald, (Middletown, NY)
The Milwaukee Journal, (Milwaukee, WI)
The Milwaukee Sentinel, (Milwaukee, WI)
Montana Standard, (Butte, MT)
Moberly Monitor Index, (Moberly, MO)
Morning Advocate, (Baton Rouge, LA)
The Morning Herald, (Hagerstown, MD)
Muscatine Journal, (Muscatine, IA)
Nevada State Journal, (Reno, NV)
New Castle, Pa. News, New Castle, PA)
The New Mexican, (Santa Fe, NM)
New York Daily News, (New York, NY)
New York Herald, (New York, NY)
New York Herald-Tribune, (New York, NY)
New York Journal-American, (New York, NY)
New York Post, (New York, NY)
New York Times, (New York, NY)
New York World-Telegram, (New York, NY)
The Newark Advocate, (Newark, NJ)
The Newark Advocate and American Tribune, (Newark, NJ)
Newport Daily News, (Newport, RI)
The News, (Newport, RI)
The News-Palladium, (Benton Harbor, MI)
Oakland Tribune, (Oakland, CA)
Ocala Star-Banner, (Ocala, FL)
Odessa American, (Odessa, TX)
Ogden Standard-Examiner, (Ogden, UT)
The Oklahoman, (Oklahoma city, OK)
Omaha World Herald, (Omaha, NE)
Oregon Journal, (Portland, OR)
The Oregonian, (Portland, OR)
Oshkosh Northwestern, (Oshkosh, WI)
Oxnard Press Courier, (Oxnard, CA)
Pacific Star and Stripes, (Tokyo, Japan)
Paris News, (Paris, TX)
Pasadena Independent, (Pasadena,CA)
Palladium Times, (Oswego, NY)
People's Daily World, (San Francisco, CA)
Pharos-Tribune, (Logansport, IN)
The Portsmouth Herald, (Portsmouth, NH)
The Post-Register, (Idaho Falls, ID)
The Post-Standard, (Syracuse,NY)
Pottstown Mercury, (Pottstown, PA)
The Press-Courier, (Oxnard,CA)
Press-Telegram, (Long Beach, CA)
Press Telegram, (Long Beach, CA)
The Progress Index, (Petersburg, VA)
Racine Journal, (Racine, WI)
Racine Journal-Times, (Racine, WI)
Racine Sunday Bulletin, (Racine, WI)
The Raleigh Register, (Beckley, WV)
Record Chronicle, (Denton, TX)
Record-Eagle, (Traverse City, MI)
The Register News, (Mt. Vernon, IL)
Register-Star-News, (Sandusky, OH)
Reno Evening Gazette, (Reno, NV)
The Rhinelander Daily News, (Rhinelander, WI)
The Robesonian, (Lumberton, NC)
Rockford Morning Star, (Rockford, IL)

Rockford Register, (Rockford, IL)
The Rocky Mount
The Salisbury Times, (Salisbury, MD)
The Salt Lake Tribune, (Salt Lake, UT)
San Angelo Standard Times, (San Angelo, TX)
San Antonio Express, (San Antonio, TX)
San Antonio Express and News, (San Antonio, TX)
San Antonio Express-News, (San Antonio, TX)
San Antonio Light, (San Antonio, TX)
San Antonio News, (San Antonio, TX)
The San Antonian, (San Antonio, TX)
San Diego Union, (San Diego, CA)
San Mateo Times, (San Mateo, CA)
Sandusky Register, (Sandusky, OH)
The Sandusky Star-Journal, (Sandusky, OH)
The Santa Ynez Valley Journal, (Santa Barbara County, CA)
The Seguin Gazette, (Seguin, TX)
The Seguin Gazette-Enterprise, (Seguin, TX)
The Sheboygan Press, (Sheboygan, WI)
South Texas Farm & Ranch News
Star Bulletin, (Honolulu, HA)
Star-News, (Pasadena, CA)
The Stars and Stripes
Statesville Daily Journal, (Statesville, NC)
The Sun, (Flagstaff, AZ)
The Sunday Times-Signal, (Zanesville, OH)
Sunday Herald, (Utah County, UT)
Sunday World Herald, (Omaha, NE)
Syracuse Herald, (Syracuse, NY)
Syracuse Herald Journal, (Syracuse, NY)
Times-Bulletin, (Van Wert, OH)
Times-Mirror, (Loudoun County, VA)
Times-Picayune, (New Orleans, LA)
The Times Recorder, (Zanesville, OH)
Tipton Tribune, (Tipton, IN)
Trenton Evening Times, (Trenton, NJ)
Toronto Daily Star, (Toronto, Ontario, Canada)
Toronto Telegram, (Toronto, Ontario, Canada)
Tucson Daily Citizen, (Tucson, AZ)
Ukiah Daily Journal, (Ukiah, CA)
The Uvalde Leader-News, (Uvalde, TX)
Van Nuys News, (Van Nuys, CA)
Victoria Advocate, (Victoria, TX)
The Vidette Messenger, (Valparaiso, IN)
Waco Tribune-Herald, (Waco, TX)
The Washington Post, Washington, D.C.)
Waterloo Daily Courier, (Waterloo, IA)
Waterloo Evening Courier and Reporter, (Waterloo, IA)
Waterloo Sunday Courier, (Waterloo, IA)
Weirton Daily Times, (Weirton, WV)
Wichita Falls Times, (Wichita Falls, TX)
The Winchester Star, (Winchester, MA)
Winnipeg Free Press, (Winnipeg, Manitoba, Canada)
The Winona Daily News, (Winona, MN)
The Winona Republican-Herald, (Winona, MN)
The Wisconsin State Journal, (Madison, WI)
The Yuma Daily Sun, (Yuma, AZ)
The Zanesville Signal, (Zanesville, OH)

Newspaper articles and Periodicals:

Abbott, Carol. "Bill Daniel Rides Into Own in Film." *The Kerrville Times*, November 8, 1959.

Adler, Dick. "Had gun, traveled, is back in TV." *TV Guide*, September 25, 1971.

Alden, Robert. *New York Times*, October 6, 1960.

Alert, Bill. "Next Battle Of Alamo Slated For Shahan Ranch." *South Texas Farm & Ranch News*, October 3, 1958.

Allen, Nelson. "Remembering 'The Alamo.'" *San Antonio Express-News*, September 16, 1989.

Allen, Paul. "A Star Businessman, Big John was also an Actor." *San Antonio Express-News*, May 16, 2010.

Anderson, Nancy. "Another John Wayne Out There." *The Daily Gleaner*, October 31, 1979.

Andreeva, Tamara. "Hollywood's Dollar Watcher." *Glean Times Herald*, November 28, 1949.

Archerd, Armand. "Hollywood Happenings." *Times-Bulletin*, November 19, 1958.

Archerd, Army. "Just For Variety." *Variety*, January 17, 1957.

_____, "Just For Variety." *Variety*, December 13, 1957.

_____, "Just For Variety." *Variety*, January 21, 1959.

_____, "Just For Variety." *Variety*, May 14, 1959.

_____, "Just For Variety." *Variety*, August 17, 1959.

_____, "Just For Variety." *Variety*, September 17, 1959.

_____, "Just For Variety." *Variety*, September 25, 1959.

_____, "Just For Variety." *Variety*, October 9, 1959.

_____, "Just For Variety." *Variety*, October 14, 1959.

_____, "Just For Variety." *Variety*, October 20, 1959.

_____, "Just For Variety." *Variety*, November 12, 1959.

_____, "Just For Variety." *Variety*, November 18, 1959.

_____, "Just For Variety." *Variety*, November 25, 1959.

_____, "Just For Variety." *Variety*, December 7, 1959.

_____, "Just For Variety." *Variety*, December 14, 1959.

_____, "Just For Variety." *Variety*, January 6, 1960.

_____, "Just For Variety." *Variety*, February 10, 1960.

_____, "Just For Variety." *Variety*, May 12, 1960.

_____, "Just For Variety." *Variety*, May 23, 1960.

_____, "Just For Variety." *Variety*, August 9, 1960.

_____, "Just For Variety." *Variety*, August 11, 1960.

_____, "Just For Variety." *Variety*, October 24, 1960.

_____, "Just For Variety." *Variety*, October 26, 1960.

_____, "Eyes of Texas Are Upon Wayne." *Variety*, October 26, 1960.

_____, "Just For Variety." *Variety*, March 1, 1961.

_____, "Just For Variety." *Variety*, June 5, 1961.

_____, "Just For Variety." *Variety*, June 27, 1961.

_____, "Just For Variety." *Variety*, March 20, 1962.

_____, "Just For Variety." *Variety*, August 18, 1964.

_____, "Just For Variety," *Variety*, May 7, 1968.

_____, "Just For Variety," *Variety*, November 14, 1968.

Arden, Doris. "'Alamo' Lavish But Childish." *Chicago Sun-Times*, October 28, 1960.

Arneel, Gene. "Oscarcast Itself Rates No Oscar; But Bob Hope a Barbed 'Critic.'" *Variety*, April 19, 1961.

Ashford, Gerald. "Bowie Role in 'The Alamo' Still Open Despite Rumors." *San Antonio News*, January 3, 1958.

_____, "Alamo Press Agent Gets Ridiculous." *San Antonio Express and News*, April 30, 1960.

_____, "'The Alamo' Premiere Looms As A Natural for S.A." *San Antonio Express and News*, May 21, 1960.

_____, "With Gerald Ashford 'On the Aisle.'" *San Antonio Express and News*, June 4, 1960.

_____, "'Gantry' Film Is Picture worth Seeing." *San Antonio Express and News*, September 17, 1960.

_____, "Tiomkin Wins Big Ovation." *San Antonio Express and News*, October 23, 1960.

_____, "'The Alamo' Vivid Tale Of Heroes." *San Antonio News*, October 25, 1960.

Avent, G. Jeanette. "Ruben Padilla Dies; Ex-Actor, Tourism Chief." *Los Angeles Times*, June 18, 1991.

Bacon, James. "Wayne Doesn't Feel Guilty About Prices He Demands." *Waterloo Sunday Courier*, March 22, 1959.

_____, "John Ford Is Successful Director, But Rough And Gruff When Making Films." *The Gettysburg Times*, October 15, 1959.

_____, "Zanuck Fled When Agents Began Directing Producers." *Lima News*, November 6, 1960.

Bacon, Joyce. "'Alamo' Film Set Visited." *San Antonio Light*, July 16, 1959.

_____, "Shooting Started on 'Alamo.'" *San Antonio Light*, September 11, 1959.

_____, "He's Horsey Guy." *San Antonio Light*, September 30, 1959.

_____, "Frankie Avalon Doffs His White Shoes for Film Role." *San Antonio Light*, October 4, 1959.

_____, "'Alamo' Filmers in Last Stand." *San Antonio Light*, December 6, 1959.

_____, "Around the Plaza." *San Antonio Light*, August 17, 1960.

_____, "John Wayne Reveals 'I Hate Politicians.'" *Los Angeles Herald-Examiner*, November 21, 1972.

Barrett, Rona. *Rona Remembers John Wayne*, 1979.

Bart, Peter. "Lighten Up, Oscar; it's simply a tapas in a teapot." *Variety*, February 22, 1993.

Battelle, Phyllis. "Runyon Character in the Flesh." *The Lowell Sun*, June 12, 1959.

Beckley, Paul V. "The Alamo." *New York Herald-Tribune*, October 1960.

_____, "Is It Entertainment or Art?" *New York Herald-Tribune*, October 30, 1960.

Beutel, Paul. "Remember the Alamo!" *Austin American Statesman*, May 29, 1977.

Birdwell, Russell. "Interview with John Wayne." *Variety*, June 1, 1965.

Blakeley, Mike. "Alamo Village: The stuff westerns are made of." *Texas Highways*, May 1985.

Bolton, Whitney. "Glancing Sideways." *Evening Times*, October 22, 1957.

Boyle, Hal. "Only Top Box-office Star, Duke Fails To Get Oscar." *The Austin Statesman*, March 31, 1955.

_____, "Star Does 150,000 miles a Year." *The Lowell Sun*, June 26, 1958.

Brady, Thomas F. "John Ford will do a film in Ireland." *The New York Times*, May 29, 1947.

Brashears, Frances. "Powell Stars in 'Authentic' Mystery Film Opening Today." *Corpus Christi Caller-Times*, June 20, 1948.

Brooks, Elston. "Plainly Not on Wane, Wayne Visits Again." *Unknown paper*, January 30, 1960.

Buchwald, Art. *Newport Daily News*, March 26, 1958.

_____, "Stars Turn Noses Up, Aid Campaign." *Los Angeles Times*, October 22, 1960.

Buckley, Michael. "Richard Widmark (Part One.)" *Films In Review*, April 1986.

_____, "Richard Widmark (Part Two.)" *Films In Review*, May 1986.

_____, "Richard Widmark (Part Three.)" *Films In Review*, June/July 1986.

Burton, Ron. "Film Shop." *Record-Eagle*, March 13, 1957.

_____, "Omens Run Rampant At Filming." *Register-Star-News*, April 4, 1957.

Bustin, John. "Murphy Probably Out Of Alamo Production." *The Austin American*, June 10, 1959.

_____, "John Wayne Viewing Another Texas Legend." *The Austin American*, November 18, 1959.

Byers, Bill. "'Alamo's" Staff Visits Houston Before Starting a Coonhunt." *The Houston Post*, August 13, 1959.

_____, "'The Eyes of Texas' Copyright Was received by U.T. in 1936." *Houston Chronicle*, October 30, 1959.

Byrd, Sigman. "The Texas Rancher Who Will Inherit a Make-Believe City." *The Houston Chronicle*, October 15, 1958.

Caen, Herb. "Fall days in a Confident City." *Los Angeles Times*, November 14, 1960.

Cameron, Kate. "The Rivoli Presents Wayne's 'The Alamo.'" *New York Daily News*, October 27, 1960.

Canby, Vincent. *The Motion Picture Herald*, February 2, 1957.

Carlisle, Tom. "'Alamo' Memento." *New York Times*, October 4, 1959.

Carpenter, Les. "Charge Red-Tinges As Well As 'Perversion and Violence,' Eric Johnson Hits Back." *Variety*, April 20, 1961.

Carroll, Harrison. "Hollywood." *The Evening Independent*, September 7, 1951.

_____, "Behind the Scenes in Hollywood." *The Letheridge Herald*, October 8, 1953.

_____, "Hollywood." *The Evening Independent*, May 20, 1954.

_____, "Behind the Scenes in Hollywood." *The Letheridge Herald*, November 16, 1954.

_____, "Hollywood." *The Evening Independent*, March 25, 1955.

_____, "Hollywood." *The Evening Independent*, April 19, 1955.

_____, "Behind the Scenes in Hollywood." *The Letheridge Hearld*, August 9, 1955.

_____, "Behind the Scenes in Hollywood." *The Vidette Messenger*, September 25, 1956.

_____, "In Hollywood." *The Lancaster Eagle-Gazette*, April 14, 1959.

_____, "In Hollywood." *The Lancaster Eagle-Gazette*, April 28, 1959.

_____, "In Hollywood." *The Lancaster Eagle-Gazette*, September 24, 1959.

_____, "In Hollywood." *The Lancaster Eagle-Gazette*, October 27, 1959.

_____, "'Alamo Emerges as Great Motion Picture." *Los Angeles Herald and Express*, October 27, 1960.

_____, "Behind the Scenes in Hollywood." *The Vidette – Messenger*, March 24, 1961.

Cary, Renwicke. "Around the Plaza." *San Antonio Light*, March 11, 1948.

____, "Around the Plaza." *San Antonio Light*, December 16, 1957.
____, "Around the Plaza." *San Antonio Light*, November 14, 1958.
____, "Around the Plaza." *San Antonio Light*, September 2, 1959.
____, "Around the Plaza." *San Antonio Light*, September 4, 1959.
____, "Around the Plaza." *San Antonio Light*, September 8, 1959.
____, "Around the Plaza." *San Antonio Light*, September 9, 1959.
____, "Around the Plaza." *San Antonio Light*, September 14, 1959.
____, "Around the Plaza." *San Antonio Light*, September 15, 1959.
____, "Around the Plaza." *San Antonio Light*, September 16, 1959.
____, "Around the Plaza." *San Antonio Light*, October 27, 1959.
____, "Around the Plaza." *San Antonio Light*, November 4, 1959.
____, "Around the Plaza." *San Antonio Light*, November 29, 1959.
____, "Around the Plaza." *San Antonio Light*, December 4, 1959.
____, "Around the Plaza." *San Antonio Light*, December 11, 1959.
____, "Around the Plaza." *San Antonio Light*, January 3, 1960.
____, "Around the Plaza." *San Antonio Light*, January 15, 1960.
____, "Around the Plaza." *San Antonio Light*, June 13, 1960.
____, "Wayne Hits $$ Bull's-Eye." *San Antonio Light*, October 25, 1960.
____, "Around the Plaza." *San Antonio Light*, October 27, 1960.
Casstevens, David. "Texas stuntman recalls rough-and-tumble career." *Island Breeze*, November 29, 2008.
Castillo, Ed. "Behind The Scenes In Hollywood." *The Evening Independent*, November 27, 1941.
_____, "Fred Powers Opens at Lounge." *San Antonio Light*, July 7, 1953.
_____, "The Bexar Facts." *San Antonio Light*, February 17, 1955.
_____, "The Bexar Facts." *San Antonio Light*, March 18, 1955.
_____, "The Bexar Facts." *San Antonio Light*, August 26, 1955.
_____, "The Bexar Facts." *San Antonio Light*, March 5, 1957.
_____, "About Town." *San Antonio Express and News*, March 15, 1959.
_____, "About Town." *San Antonio Express and News*, August 8, 1959.
_____, "About Town." *San Antonio Express and News*, August 15, 1959.
_____, "Daniel Approves Re-Creation Of Old San Antonio." *San Antonio Express and News*, August 15, 1959.
_____, "About Town." *San Antonio News*, August 21, 1959.
_____, "About Town." *San Antonio Express and News*, August 23, 1959.
_____, "About Town." *San Antonio Express and News*, September 6, 1959.
_____, "About Town." *San Antonio Express and News*, September 12, 1959.
_____, "About Town." *San Antonio Express and News*, September 23, 1959.
_____, "About Town." *San Antonio, Express and News*, September 26, 1959.
_____, "About Town." *San Antonio Express and News*, October 4, 1959.
_____, "Slayer's Examining Trial Stars Wayne." *San Antonio Express and News*, October 17, 1959.
_____, "S.A. Flamenco Troupe Booked Solid." *San Antonio Light*, October 22, 1975.
_____, "About Town." *San Antonio Express and News*, October 24, 1959.
_____, "About Town." *San Antonio Express and News*, November 7, 1959.
_____, "Duke Goes Big With Alamo." *San Antonio Express and News*, October 27, 1960.
Cerone, Daniel. "Western Costume: Preserving Fabric of Hollywood History." *Los Angeles Times*, March 14, 1989.
Chemerka, Bill. "The Nock Volley Gun." *The Alamo Journal*, July 1986.
Chick, Fern. "Off Camera with Fern Chick." *San Antonio News*, August 4, 1960.
Christian, George. "Alamo Revisited." *The Houston Post*, November 15, 1959.
Clapp, Marjorie. "Bejar comes to Life." *San Antonio Light*, mid-December 1958.
____, "Wayne at Uvalde." *San Antonio Light*, February 22, 1959.
Coates, Paul. "Mexican Takes Issue With Press Agent for Alamo Film." *Los Angeles Mirror-News*, November 5, 1960.
Cone, Theresa Loeb. "'Peking Letter' Director Named." *Oakland Tribune*, February 11, 1958.
Connally, Sue. "Paladin Travels, Without His Gun." *Dallas Morning News*, September 8, 1959.
Connolly, Mike. "Jayne Mansfield to go West." *Star-News*, April 7, 1958.
_____, "Gary Goes for Picasso Painting." *Star-News*, April 9, 1958.
_____, "Van Cliburn Names Vocalists." *Star-News*, August 5, 1958.
_____, "Marion Davies Wants Out of Pay TV Deal." *Star-News*, October 10, 1958.
_____, "Liquid Gift From Sinatra." *Pasadena Independent*, December 11, 1958.

_____, "Sofia Loren Gets Moscow Bid." *Pasadena Independent*, January 19, 1959.

_____, "Rambling Reporter." *The Hollywood Reporter*, July 6, 1959.

_____, "Rambling Reporter." *The Hollywood Reporter*, August 28, 1959.

_____, "Crosbys Will 'Keep' Little Mary Frances." *Star-News*, October 19, 1959.

_____, "Rambling Reporter." *The Hollywood Reporter*, December 14, 1959.

_____, "Brando Hauls Bongos to 'Mutiny" Site." *Star-News*, November 4, 1960.

_____, "Rambling Reporter." *The Hollywood Reporter*, December 6, 1960.

_____, "Rambling Reporter." *The Hollywood Reporter*, April 18, 1961.

Conrad, Barnaby. "Homage To A Peerless Matador." *Sports Illustrated*, August 1, 1966.

Considine, Bob. "John Wayne: No Ham In Him." *The Independent*, February 26, 1951.

_____, "On The Line." *Anderson Daily Bulletin*, June 25, 1959.

Cook, Alton. "John Wayne's 'Alamo' Holding Out at Rivoli." *New York World-Telegram*, October 27, 1960.

Copeland, Bobby. "Cowboy Commentary." *Western Clippings*, #97, Sept/Oct 2010.

Cox, Stephen. "The Big Man of American Politics." *Liberty*, December 2008.

Crawford, Bill. "The Billboard." *The Lawton Constitution*, January 1, 1958.

Crowley, Roger. "Alamo Village." *The Westerner*, Issue 15, 1990.

Crowther, Bosley. *The New York Times*, May 11, 1940.

_____, *The New York Times*, December 26, 1947.

_____, *The New York Times*, June 25, 1948.

_____, *The New York Times*, March 4, 1949.

_____. *The New York Times*, February 3, 1951.

_____, *The New York Times*, May 31, 1956.

_____, *The New York Times*, February 1, 1957.

_____, *The New York Times*, October 27, 1960.

Dale, Bob. "Face of San Antonio." *San Antonio Express-News*, December 30, 1962.

____, "Face of San Antonio." *San Antonio Express-News*, March 28, 1965.

Daniel, Bill. "'Alamo' Movie Role Supreme Thrill For Bill Daniel." *Baytown Sun*, September 18, 1960.

____, "Bill Daniel Recounts Yarns Of Film." *The Baytown Sun*, September 11, 1960.

____, "Longhorns Star In 'Alamo.'" *The Brazosport Facts*, September 25, 1960.

Danini, Carmina. "Ponder, 81, did local theater and was a weather girl on WOAI." October 3, 2007. Mysa.com.

Danzog, Fred. "Television in Review." *Leader-Times*, November 15, 1960.

Darby, Warren. "'Alamo' Impact Powerful." *San Antonio Express*, October 25, 1960.

D'Arc, James V. "I Want Stone-Age Faces!" *American Classic Screen*, Winter 1980.

DeBlasio, Ed. "Why I Didn't Become a Nun..." *Modern Screen*, May 1959.

Dettman, Bruce. "Ernest Borgnine On 'The Last Command.'" *The Alamo Journal*, September 2005.

Dickens, Jerry. "Remember the Alamo?" *Texas Co-op Power*, March 2001.

Di Fate, Vincent. "3-D Cinema: Yesterday, Today, and Tomorrow!, part 2." *Filmfax plus*, Summer 2009.

Dolan, George. "This is Texas." *Fort Worth Star-Telegram*, February 3, 1961.

Dubois, Jules. "John Wayne Loses $500,000; Arias Asked for Accounting." *Corpus Christi Times*, May 4, 1959.

Du Brow, Rick. "Actress' New Fame Rewarded with Death." *Appeal-Democrat*, October 12, 1959.

_____, "Hollywood stars Are Investing In All Kind Of Business But Their Own." *The Lawton Constitution*, June 29, 1960.

English, Richard. "How We Almost Lost Hawaii to the Reds." *Saturday Evening Post*, February 2, 1952.

Eyman, Scott. "Looking Back: John Wayne talking to Scott Eyman." *Focus on Film*, Spring 1975.

Fidler, Jimmie. "In Hollywood." *The Chronicle - Telegram*, January 8, 1942.

____, *Nevada State Journal*, November 3, 1951.

____, *Nevada State Journal*, February 23, 1954.

____, *Nevada State Journal*, July 10, 1954.

____, *Nevada State Journal*, March 30, 1955.

____, *Nevada State Journal*, July 10, 1955.

Fields, Sidney. "Wayne Is Still Riding High." *Unknown newspaper*, June 29, 1960.

Finnigan, Joe. "Actor Made Long Trip to 'The Alamo.'" *Oakland Tribune*, December 19, 1959.

_____, "Hollywood Notes." *The Bedford Gazette*, January 7, 1960.

Flaherty, Vincent X. "John Wayne Takes $12 Million Gamble." *The Houston Post*, September 12, 1960.

_____, "Alamo Movie Seen as Anti-Red Crusade." *San Antonio Light*, October 20, 1960.

Florence, William R. "John Ford…the Duke…and Monument Valley." *Arizona Highways,* September 1981.

Foreman, Carl. "On the Wayne." *Punch,* August 14, 1974.

Fosters, Jeremy. "All the Work, None of the Credit." *The Santa Ynez Valley Journal,* July 16, 2009.

Francis, Warren. "Disney Tells How Reds Tried to Take Over Studio." *Los Angeles Times,* October 25, 1947.

Freeman, Bill. "I've Been Told." *San Antonio Express,* October 26, 1952.

Fulton, Harry. "Inside Out." *The Independent,* July 17, 1953.

Gaberseck, Carlo and Ken Stier. "In Search of Western Movie Sites: Goulding's Trading Post." *Western Clippings,* Sept/Oct 2005.

Gagnard, Frank. "On The Square." *Times-Picayune,* September 30, 1960.

Gillette, Don Carle. "Tradeviews." *The Hollywood Reporter,* January 30, 1961.

_____, "Tradeviews." The Hollywood Reporter, May 31, 1961.

Glover, William. "Search for New Roles Takes Actor To All Parts Of World." *Burlington Daily Times-News,* November 10, 1958.

Goldstein, Norm. *John Wayne: A Tribute.* 1979.

Gordon, Jack. "Wayne, on Airport Stop, Says 'Alamo' Coming in September." *Unknown newspaper,* January 31, 1960.

Gould, Helen. "Coast's Stars Succumb To The Directing Urge." *The New York Times,* July 15, 1951.

_____, "Weekend Round-Up." *The Mexico City Daily Bulletin,* No date.

Graham, Sheila. "Robert Mitchum to Star in Flynn Movie Remake." *Bluefield Daily Telegram,* April 6, 1948.

_____, "Hollywood Today." *San Antonio Express,* January 25, 1954.

_____, "Marilyn Takes Daily Walk in Sand To Keep Her Legs in Top Shape." *San Antonio Express,* August 6, 1955.

_____, "Dean Martin May Team Up With Brando in 'Young Lions.'" *Stars and Stripes,* April 23, 1957.

_____, "Pat Wayne, Son of John, Pursing His own Career." *Dallas Morning News,* September 21, 1958.

_____, "Roman Bigamy Threat Keeps Ingrid Away From Italy; Roberto Visits." *San Antonio Express,* January 7, 1959.

_____, "John Wayne, in Acapulco, Works On Script for 'The Alamo' Movie." *San Antonio Express,* January 14, 1959.

_____, "Hollywood Today." *Republic Register,* February 13, 1960.

_____, "Hollywood Today." *Rockford Register,* July 19, 1960.

_____, "Hollywood Today." *Rockford Register,* October 26, 1960.

Graham, Sheilah. "Just For Variety." *Variety,* February 27, 1952.

_____, "Just For Variety." *Variety,* October 30, 1952.

_____, "Just For Variety." *Variety,* November 17, 1952.

_____, "Just For Variety." *Variety,* December 5, 1952.

_____, "Just For Variety." *Variety,* December 18, 1952.

_____, "Just For Variety." *Variety,* December 22, 1952.

_____, "John Wayne Offers Princess Riding Lessons." *Register Republic,* November 5, 1960.

Greenfield, Peter. "Print the Fact." *Take One,* November 1977.

Greeley, Bill. "Pontiac's Projected Splurge On Original-Book Musicals Hits snags – On Other Madison Ave. Fronts." *Variety,* March 23, 1960.

Griffith, Richard. "'High Noon' Wins Praise From Eastern Critics." *Los Angeles Times,* August 5, 1952.

Gris, Henry. "Invasion from Hollywood Takes Over Utah Town." *Fairbanks News-Miner,* July 15, 1954.

Gruner, Anthony. "London report." *Box Office,* November 14, 1960.

Gualano, Michele. "Guerra played a cantina girl in 'The Alamo,'" September 6, 2010, Mysa.com.

Guild, Leo. "The Duke Throws a TV Party." *Unknown magazine,* unknown date.

Gutierrez-Mier, John. "'Alamo' Remembered Movie's cast salutes 40th anniversary." *San Antonio Express-News,* September 7, 1999.

Gwynn, Edith. "Barbara Stanwyck to be Star." *The Wisconsin State Journal,* August 30, 1948.

_____, "Hollywood." *Pottstown Mercury,* June 20, 1953.

Hagner, John. *Hollywood Stuntmen's Hall of Fame Newsletter,* Vol. 1, no. 11, 1988, Vol. 8, No. 19, Nov/Dec 1972.

Hamilton, Bob. "A Morning with the Duke." *Radio Report,* March 26, 1973.

Hamilton, Jack. "Linda Cristal: The Girl Who Travels Alone." *Look,* July 19, 1960.

_____, "John Wayne: The Big Man of the Westerns." *Look*, August 2, 1960.

_____, "All my MONEY – and all my SOUL." *Today*, October 29, 1960.

Hamilton, John C. "Obituaries." *The Seguin Gazette-Enterprise*, December 7, 1984.

Handasker, Gene. "Hollywood." *The Raleigh Register*, April 3, 1949.

Hano, Arnold. "John Wayne - His Greatest Battle." *People*, August 24, 1966.

Harris, Adam Duncan. "Extra Credits: The History and Collection of Pacific Title and Art Studio." University of Minnesota.

Harris, Radie. "Broadway Ballyhoo." *The Hollywood Reporter*, January 26, 1961.

Harrison, Paul. "In Hollywood." *Ironwood Daily Globe*, February 14, 1942.

Hearst, Jr. William Randolph. "'Alamo' Big Story." *San Antonio Light*, December 6, 1959.

Heffernan, Harold. "John Wayne at Peak Of Great Popularity." *Dallas News*, February 26, 1950.

_____, "Wealthy John Wayne Sells Luxury Yacht." *The Oregonian*, July 15, 1960.

Henaghan, Jim. "Inside John Wayne." *Cavalier Magazine*, July 1961.

Hill, Gladwin. "Tales of a Horse Opera Hot Shot." *New York Times*, November 7, 1948.

Hochuli, Paul. "'The Alamo' Likely to Grab All the Oscars." *The Houston Press*, October 25, 1960.

_____, "Even Rain Couldn't Dampen Ardor of World Premiere." *The Houston Post*, October 25, 1960.

Holleran, Scott. "Interview: Director Andrew V. McLaglen." *Box Office Mojo*, May 23, 2007.

Holloway, Ronald. "The Searchers." *Variety*, March 15, 1956.

Hopper, Hedda. "Looking at Hollywood." *Los Angeles Times*, March 1, 1945.

_____, "John Wayne Appraised as Triple Threat." *Los Angeles Times*, May 11, 1947.

_____, "Looking at Hollywood." *Los Angeles Times*, March 16, 1948.

_____, "Looking at Hollywood." *Los Angeles Times*, July 27, 1948.

_____, "Abbey Players Will Act in 'Quiet Man.'" *Los Angeles Times*, August 16, 1948.

_____, "Looking at Hollywood." *Chicago Tribune*, February 1949.

_____, "Samuel Goldwyn Jr. Joins Western Staff." *Los Angeles Times*, April 20, 1949.

_____, "John Ford Prepares Bulging Program." *Los Angeles Times*, May 30, 1949.

_____, "Argosy film Unit Moves to Republic." *Los Angeles Times*, January 6, 1950.

_____, "'Soldiers Three' Gets Strong Stellar Group." *Los Angeles Times*, August 8, 1950.

_____, "Patricia Neal Will Play Publisher Role." *Los Angeles Times*, August 24, 1950.

_____, "'Song of Ruth' Latest Biblical Project." *Los Angeles Times*, November 28, 1950.

_____, "Cortesa Will Portray Pirate with Douglas." *Los Angeles Times*, December 12, 1950.

_____, "Wayne Plans Ford Picture After Tour." *Los Angeles Times*, February 17, 1951.

_____, "Three Stars Selected for Harding Original." *Los Angeles Times*, June 26, 1951.

_____, "Douglas, Stanwyck Set for 'Clash by Night.'" *Los Angeles Times*, August 9, 1951.

_____, "Gary Cooper to Stay Out of Film Deal." *Los Angeles Times*, November 2, 1951.

_____, "Mitchum Promotes Gold Mystery Film." *Los Angeles Times*, February 6, 1952.

_____. "Looking at Hollywood." *The Winona Republican-Herald*, March 5, 1952.

_____, "Warners to Sponsor Wayne's 'Jim McLain.'" *Los Angeles Times*, March 6, 1952.

_____, "Looking at Hollywood." *The Winona Republican-Herald*, March 21, 1952.

_____, "Glenn Ford will Star for U-I and Warners." *Los Angeles Times*, August 11, 1952.

_____, "'Flight to the Islands' set for Spencer Tracey.'" *Los Angeles Times*, October 28, 1952.

_____, "In Hollywood." *The Newark Advocate and American Tribune*, July 27, 1953.

_____, "'High, Mighty' Lead Considered by Fonda." *Los Angeles Times*, August 11, 1953.

_____, "Farrow will Direct Wayne in 'Sea Chase.'" *Los Angeles Times*, August 25, 1953.

_____, "Writes From Hollywood." Altoona Mirror, October 14, 1953.

_____, "Altoona's Own Writes From Hollywood." *The Altoona Mirror*, November 12, 1953.

_____, "Richard Carlson Has Outdoor Drama Lead." *Los Angeles Times*, January 14, 1955.

_____, "Altoona's Own Writes From Hollywood." *The Altoona Mirror*, February 4, 1955.

_____, "Altoona's Own Hedda Hopper Writes From Hollywood." *The Altoona Mirror*, April 7, 1955.

_____, "Civil War Spy Story to Star Fess Parker." *Los Angeles Times*, August 19, 1955.

_____, "Kirk Douglas Invites Ava Gardner to Costar." *Los Angeles Times*, August 23, 1955.

_____, "John Wayne Daughter Plans June Wedding." *Los Angeles Times*, December 31, 1955.

_____, "John Wayne Presented Daughter by Third Wife." *Los Angeles Times*, April 1, 1956.

_____, "Jane Powell Tells Record, Film Plans." *Los Angeles Times*, April 27, 1956.

_____, *The Altoona Mirror*, June 29, 1957.

_____, "Morbid Films Ruin the Fun, Veteran Producer Groans." *Salt Lake Tribune*, August 30, 1957

_____, "The 'Secret's Out – Meet Gloris – Bright New Star." *The Salt Lake Tribune*, September 10, 1957.

_____, "Sophia's Used to Working." *Los Angeles Times*, October 6, 1957.

_____, "John Wayne Awes His Fans in Japan." *Los Angeles Times*, December 27, 1957.

_____, *The Altoona Mirror*, January 27, 1958.

_____, "Holden Offered Role in Espionage Story." *Los Angeles Times*, February 14, 1958.

_____, "Ricky Nelson Will Do Film For Hawks." *Los Angeles Times*, April 26, 1958.

_____, "Wayne Still Measures Up as Ideal Type of Western star." *Los Angeles Times*, May 25, 1958.

_____, *Tucson Daily Citizen*, July 18, 1958.

_____, "Wayne, Fess Parker in Business Deal." *Los Angeles Times*, August 4, 1958.

_____, *Lima News*, August 9, 1958.

_____, "Panama and Frank Film 'Li'l Abner.'" *Los Angeles Times*, May 5, 1959.

_____, "Grandfather Wayne To Be Father Again." *Los Angeles Times*, May 19, 1959.

_____, "Laurence Harvey, Wayne May Star." *Los Angeles Times*, July 15, 1959.

_____, *Tucson Daily Citizen*, August 10, 1959.

_____, "Connors: A Major-Leaguer." *Los Angeles Times*, September 6, 1959.

_____, *The Altoona Mirror*, November 11, 1959.

_____, "Looking at Hollywood." *The Rocky Mount*, December 8, 1959.

_____, "Paladin's My Pal." *Chicago Tribune*, December 13, 1959.

_____, "Dean Jones to Star In 'Magnificent Seven.'" *Oregon Journal*, December 20, 1959.

_____, "Richard Boone – A Happy Man." *San Antonio Express and News*, January 3, 1960.

_____, "Wayne Has Writer Grant Doing Sam Houston Story." *The Chicago Daily Tribune*, August 29, 1960.

_____, "Cinerama Films Planned." *The Times-Picayune*, October 5, 1960.

_____, "Linda Cristal Gets a Plum Movie Role." *Chicago Tribune*, October 6, 1960.

_____, "Hollywood." *Daily News*, October 21, 1960.

_____, "'The Alamo' – A Dream Comes True For Duke." *San Antonio Express and News*, October 23, 1960.

_____, "Wayne Has Mission: Arouse Patriotism." *Los Angeles Times*, October 23, 1960.

_____, "A Big One for 'Duke.'" *Unidentified newspaper*, unidentified date.

_____, "John Wayne Says 'Yes' to Movie with Bardot." *Chicago Tribune*, November 18, 1960.

_____, "Hedda Hopper." *San Antonio News*, December 2, 1960.

_____, "Moving of Oscar Site Protested." *Los Angeles Times*, December 8, 1960.

_____, "Looking at Hollywood." *Odessa American*, January 25, 1961.

_____, "Hedda Hopper." *Lima News*, January 26, 1961.

_____, "Film About Credit Card Spree Slated." *Los Angeles Times*, March 2, 1961.

_____, "Looking at Hollywood." *Odessa American*, March 30, 1961.

Hopper, Heddy, "Movie-Men Shoot 'Alamo' Film In Mexico City." *San Antonio Express*, July 18, 1951.

Hyams, Joe. "Wayne Finds It Painful To Discuss Film Salary." *Corpus Christi Times*, January 8, 1959.

_____, "New Departure in Movie Advertising." *Herald Tribune*, July 5, 1960.

_____, "Is It Really Possible to Purchase an Oscar?" *Los Angeles Times*, February 10, 1961.

_____, "Battle of 'The Alamo' Continues Hot, Heavy." *Los Angeles Times*, March 30, 1961.

Ingram, Frances. "Richard Widmark, Utter simplicity and Realism." *Films of the Golden Age*, Summer 2009.

Jackovich, Karen G. "The Children of John Wayne, Susan Hayward and Dick Powell Fear That Fallout Killed Their Parents." *People*, November 10, 1980.

Jacques, Hal. "Hollywood Gun expert Rates John Wayne as Top Tough Guy." *ENQUIRER*, unknown date.

James, T.F. "The Man Who Talks Back to John Wayne." *Cosmopolitan*, August 1960.

Jenkins, Leigh. "Courthouse turns 100." *Brackett News*, March 17, 2100.

Jennings, Dean. "John Wayne, The Woes of a Box-Office King." *Saturday Evening Post*, October 27, 1962.

Johansen, Arno. "The John Wayne Family." Independent Star-News, January 10, 1960.

Johnson, Erskine. "In Hollywood." *Miami Daily News-Record*, November 20, 1945.

_____, "Looking at Hollywood." *The Lima News*, April 19, 1946.

_____, "In Hollywood." *The Portsmouth Herald*, June 23, 1948.

_____, "In Hollywood." *Kingsport Times*, February 1, 1949.

_____. "Mayer's Daughter No. 1 Heiress?" *The Rhinelander*, September, 15, 1949.

_____, "In Hollywood." *The Zanesville Signal*, October 11, 1950.

_____, "Spike Jones Campaigns for Laughs." *The Rhinelander Daily News*, April 11, 1951.

_____, "Marilyn Monroe Says Her 'Gentlemen Prefer Blondes' Role Won't Lead to More Musicals." *The Inter Lake*, December 7, 1952.

_____, "In Hollywood." *Clovis News-Journal*, April 26, 1953.

_____, "Mitzi Gaynor Will Portray Ranch Hand." *Los Angeles Times*, July 20, 1953.

_____, "Hollywood Today!" *Sunday Herald*, July 28, 1953.

_____, "Hollywood Today." *The Altoona Mirror*, November 12, 1953.

_____, "Feature Length Dragnet Film Looms for Jack Webb." *The Independent*, November 19, 1953.

_____, "In Hollywood." *Statesville Daily Journal*, January 2, 1954.

_____, "Vacation from Marriage." *The Post-Register*, January 4, 1954.

_____, "Pass Up $100,000." *The Post-Register*, January 25, 1954.

_____, "Crosby, Hope, Lewis, Martin May Make a Movie Musical." *The Independent*, April 1, 1954.

_____, "Man About Hollywood." *The Daily Journal-Gazette and Commercial Star*, June 18, 1954.

_____, "Hollywood Today!" *Daily Herald*, July 15, 1954.

_____, "Jean Peters Denies She Is Shelving Acting Career Since Marriage to Millionaire." *Avalanche Journal*, July 18, 1954.

_____, "She is Shelving Acting Career Since Marriage To Millionaire." *The Avalanche Journal*, July 18, 1954.

_____, "In Hollywood." *The Evening Observer*, August 13, 1954.

_____, "Hollywood Today." *Corpus Christi Times*, March 10, 1955.

_____, "Hollywood Today!" *Humboldt Standard*, August 25, 1955.

_____, "In Hollywood." *Atchison Daily Globe*, October 26, 1955.

_____, "Hollywood Today." *Corpus Christi Times*, April 2, 1956.

_____, "Hollywood Today!" *The Lima News*, January 24, 1958.

_____, "Hollywood Today." *The Evening Standard*, May 26, 1958.

_____, "Hollywood Today." *Sandusky Register*, May 26, 1958.

_____, "Hollywood Today." *Humboldt Standard*, May 30, 1958.

_____, "Hollywood Today." *Humboldt Standard*, November 11, 1958.

_____, "Hollywood Today." *Corpus Christi Times*, November 22, 1958.

_____, "Hollywood Glances!" *Miami Daily News Record*, October 20, 1959.

_____, "John Wayne Finally Realizes Big Dream in 'Alamo' Film." *Los Angeles Mirror-News,* October 21, 1959.

_____, "'Alamo' Filming Ends Struggle." *Burlington Daily Times-News*, November 3, 1959.

_____, "In Hollywood." *Morning Advocate*, May 29, 1960.

_____, "In Hollywood." *Morning Advocate*, September 18, 1960.

_____, "Hollywood Today." *The Register-News*, November 25, 1960.

_____, "Richard Widmark Worried About 'German Arrogance." *Corpus Christi Times*, November 25, 1960.

_____, "Not Ghost of 'Alamo' Says Ford." *Los Angeles Mirror*, November 4, 1960.

Johnson, Grady. "John Ford: Maker of Stars." *Coronet*, December 1953.

Johnson, Leland and Charles Veltman, Jr. "When Hollywood Came to Kinney County." *Mary Immaculate*, July-August 1966.

Johnstone, Bob. "Wayne Plugs Film – Charity, Too." *Toronto Daily Star*, September 24, 1960.

Jordon, R.G. "He's Happy – Well Dug for Movie Scene on His Ranch Still Flowing." *Unknown newspaper*, unknown date.

Joyner, C. Courtney. "Andrew V. McLaglen, Director." *Wildest Westerns*, No. 5.

_____, "Glenn Ford." *Wildest Westerns*, No. 7.

Kahn, Stephen. "Will Frankie's Flame Flicker?" *Teen*, May 1960.

Keating, Micheline. "Facelifting Old Tucson." *Tucson Daily Citizen*, April 4, 1958.

_____, "Rio Bravo's Gone Guys." *Tucson Daily Citizen*, May 10, 1958.

_____, "So They want New Faces, Well - Here's Angie." *Tucson Daily Citizen*, May 17, 1958.

_____, "Making Movies At Night." *Tucson Daily Citizen*, May 24, 1958.

Keavy, Hubbard. "John Wayne Story Ideas Flood Office." *San Mateo Times*, July 15, 1954.

_____, "Screen Life in Hollywood." *San Antonio Express*, April 26, 1956.

Kelly, John. "One Marine's Moment." *The Washington Post*, February 23, 2005.

Kelton, Elmer. "Texans Lure Film Maker Wayne To Brackettville." *Del Rio News-Herald*, April 23, 1958.

Kenyon, E.E. "The Wit Parade." *The American Weekly*, January 15, 1956.

Kiefer, Steve. "Janet Leigh, Every Cowboys Sweetheart." *Wildest Westerns, A Look Back*.

Kilman, Ed. "Old City Rebuilt In Minute Detail." *Houston Post*, October 1, 1959.

_____, "Wayne Wanted Sunshine, Got Rid of Clouds Quickly." *The Houston Post*, October 2, 1959.

Kilgallen, Dorothy. "Voice of Broadway." *Trenton Evening Times*, May 3, 1960.

King, Paul. "Wayne confesses; I've been overlooked, broke and blackballed during the years." *Photoplay*, November 1973.

Kleener, Dick. "The Marque." *The News*, August 12, 1954.

Kubasik, Ben. "John Wayne's 'Alamo' Is Bold, Stirring Show." October 27, 1960.

Kluge, P.F. "First and Last a Cowboy." *Life*, January 1971.

Kountze, Denman, Jr. "Trend to 'Spectacle' Continues in Pictures." *Sunday World-Herald*, September 25, 1960.

Kroll, Jack. "John Wayne: End as a Man." *Newsweek*, June 25, 1979.

Kupcinet, Irv. "Kup's Column." *Chicago Sun-Times*, October 28, 1960.

Lackey, Jerry. "WINDMILL: South Texas ranch catered to Hollywood heavyweights." *www.sanangelo. com*

LaRoche, Clarence. "Brackettville - Country of Texas West." *San Antonio Light*, May 18, 1953.

Lauritz, Phyllis. "Colorful Junket To San Antonio Promotes Premiere Of John Wayne's Fantastic Alamo." *The Oregonian*, October 24, 1960.

Leaf, Earl. "My Fair and Frantic Hollywood." *Teen*, March 1960.

Lehman, Peter. "Howard Hawks, A Private Interview." *Wide Angle* 1:2, 1976.

Lejune, C.A. "Living for the Week-end." *The Guardian*, October 30, 1960.

Lesner, Sam. "Wayne on $12 Million Limb." *Chicago Daily News*, September 20, 1960.

Leuchtenburg, William E. "Hoover Faces the Crash." *American Heritage*, Summer 2009.

Lewis, Richard Warren. "Playboy interview: John Wayne." *Playboy*, May 1971.

Libby, Bill. "The Old Wrangler Rides Again." *Cosmopolitan*, March 1964.

Lightman, Herb A. "Filming "The Alamo" in Todd-AO." *American Cinematographer*, November 1960.

Lilley, Tim. "Convention Conversations." *The Big Trail*, Vol. XII, #1, June 1995.

_____, "Convention Conversations." *The Big Trail*, Vol. XII, #2, August 1995.

_____, "Bernie and the Duke." *The Big Trail*, Vol. XV, #4, December 1998.

_____, "I Went Through a Lot of Windows." *The Trail Beyond*, Vol. VIII.

_____, "Making Hero's out of those Cowboy Actors." *The Trail Beyond*, Vol. II.

Lisanti, Tom. "What A Dish." *Films of the Golden Age*, Summer 1999.

Lively, Ken. "Alamo Village." *The Texas Mohair Weekly and Rocksprings Record*, May 27, 1960.

Lodge, John F. "Movie Stunt Men Risk Their Lives to Thrill Millions." *Popular Science*, November 1935.

Lousarian, Ed G. "Denver Pyle: One of America's Greatest Character Actors." *Wildest Westerns*, No. 1.

Love, Syd. "Reminiscences of Life on Both Sides: Culture: Movies and bullfights are the spice of life for an 80-year-old San Diego border straddle." *Los Angeles Times*, April 23, 1990.

Lowe, Walter. "Hollywood Reconstructs Replica of Alamo." *The Times Recorder*, December 23, 1959.

Ludwig, Charles. "George Phippen's Finest Hour." *Protestant Magazine for Armed Forces Personnel*, September 1969.

Lyon, Herb. "Tower Ticket." *Chicago Daily Tribune*, September 15, 1960.

_____, "Tower Ticket." *Chicago Daily Tribune*, September 27, 1960.

Lyons, Leonard. "Duke's Choice." *The Independent*, September 15, 1955.

_____, "Scribe Lands in Isolated Sahara, but Forgets to Bring Anything to Forget!" *Independent*, January 31, 1957.

_____, "Perle Mesta Has a Ball." *San Mateo Times*, September 28, 1959.

_____, "Hoffa Has A Candidate." *San Mateo Times*, October 16, 1959.

_____, "Visiting Soviet Composers." *The Evening Standard*, November 19, 1959.

_____, "Acapulco Treats Scofflaws Hard." *Boston Herald*, September 27, 1960.

MacArthur, Bill. "That's Show Business." *Variety*, May 25, 1960.

Macklin, F. Anthony. "I Come Ready." *Film Heritage*, Summer 1975.

Mahin, John Lee and Martin Rackin. "The Horse Soldiers or Grierson's Raid." *Civil War History*, Vol. 5, 1959.

Mahony, Jim. "Behind The Scenes in Hollywood." *The Vidette-Messenger*, August 1, 1957.

Mahoney, Mary. "Lights…Camera…Action!" *Better Farms & Ranches*, September 23, 1959.

Manners, Dorothy. "Kirk Replaces Wayne." *Waterloo Daily Courier*, December 4, 1953.

_____, *Los Angeles Examiner*, May 28, 1954.

_____, "Cary, Paramount Sign." *San Antonio Light*, November 1, 1954.

_____, "Tom Ewell To Star In New Musical." *The Daily Review*, August 8, 1955.

_____, "Olympic Champion to Star in Steve Canyon Comic Strip Film." *Waterloo Daily Courier*, October 16, 1957.

_____, "She Found Work Fun at 'Alamo.'" *Unknown newspaper*, unknown date.

McCain, Nina. "John Wayne Talks Of Men at Alamo." *Unknown newspaper*, unknown date.

McDaniel, Ruel. "City Links Old and New Texas." *The Dallas News*, August 29, 1926.

McGown, Tom. "Move Makers Keep Brackettville In Action With 'Two Rode Together.'" *San Antonio Light*, November 13, 1960.

_____, "Linda Cristal Finds Golden Philosophy at Rainbow's End." *San Antonio Light*, November 16, 1960.

_____, "A Clear Mission." *Unknown newspaper*, unknown date.

McGraw, Preston. "Movie Location Houses Used By Navajos." *Las Vegas Daily Optic*, August 20, 1955.

McManus, John T. "Speaking of Movies." *Unknown newspaper*, March 13, 1944.

McLean, J. H. "Kinney Rancher, Hit by Drought, Has Faith in Future." *San Antonio Light*, July 2, 1953.

McLearn, Frank. "Broadway Nights." *The Corsicana Daily Sun*, July 30, 1937.

McLellan, Dennis. "Jack Williams, 85; stuntman known for horse-riding skills." *Los Angeles Times*, April 16, 2007.

McLemore, Henry. "Cowboy Meets Cracker At Café In Rome." *Lebanon Daily News*, December 2, 1960.

Mennhofter, Leona. "Brother Red Sez." *The Kerrville Times*, June 14, 1959.

Meroney, John. "Left in the Past." *Los Angeles Times*, February 2012.

Miers, Virgil. "Oscar, Ads and 'Alamo.'" *Unknown newspaper*, March 1, 1961.

Mike, B. "Behind the Mike." *Oregonian*, October 30, 1959.

Miller, Fred. "Miller's Grist." *Del Rio News-Herald*, February 19, 1959.

Miller, Leaford. "Bexar Facts." *San Antonio Light*, September 28, 1959.

Miller, Roger. "Filming of Horse Soldiers Impresses Author Sinclair." *Unknown paper*, November 11, 1958.

Milne, J.R. "Next to Riding in Rodeos I Like Escorting Divorcees Best." *Syracuse Herald*, February 22, 1931.

Mitchell, George J. "Ford on Ford." *Films in Review*, vol. XV, no. 6, June/July 1964.

Moffitt, Jack. "The Alamo." *Limelight*, October 27, 1960.

Morgan, Thomas B. "God and Man in Hollywood." *Esquire*, May 1962.

Morris, Frank. "Here, There and Hollywood." *Winnipeg Free Press*, November 3, 1954.

_____, "Here, There and Hollywood." *Winnipeg Free Press*, August 27, 1955.

_____, "Here, There and Hollywood." *Winnipeg Free Press*, July 26, 1958.

Mortimer, Lee. "New York Confidential." *Humboldt Standard*, August 7, 1959.

Mosby, Aline. "John Wayne Predicts Public will Forgive Parks." *The Independent*, March 23, 1951.

_____, "Hollywood Scrambles." *The Daily News*, November 18, 1953.

_____, "Jan Sterling Sheds Glamour For 'Gruesome" Role." *The Avalanche*, April 11, 1954.

_____, "Today in Hollywood." *Charleston Daily Mail*, July 8, 1954.

_____, "Latin Actress Complains of Hollywood-Enforced Diet." San Mateo Times, March 17, 1956.

_____, "Wayne Credits Star Shortage For High Pay." *San Mateo Times*, October 5, 1956.

Muir, Florabel. "Just For Variety." *Variety*, March 15, 1948.

_____, "Wayne, Birdwell Challenge Demo Convention Delegates." *Limelight*, June 30, 1960.

_____, "'Alamo' Premiere." *Limelight*, October 27, 1960.

_____, "Industry Hails Big Pictures." *Limelight*, October 27, 1960.

Musso, Joe. "Duke's Movie Knives." *Blade*, August 2007.

_____, "Found: Another Iron Mistress Knife." *Blade*, September 2011.

_____, "The Iron Mistress." *The Alamo Journal*, July 1986.

_____, "The Iron Mistress Movie that Changed KNIVES FOREVER." *Blade*, May 2002, June 2002.

Myers, Sim. "An Explosion." *The Times-Picayune*, December 19, 1959.

Nason, Richard. "Biggest Western To Cost $8,000,000." *New York Times*, July 29, 1959.

Naughton, Walter. "Dies on Hollywood." *San Antonio Light*, June 29, 1944.

Navasky, Victor S. "To Name or Not to Name." *The New York Times Magazine*. March 25, 1973.

Neff, Donald. "Kennedy Extremism Blast Hit by Anti-Red Speakers." *Los Angeles Times*, December 13, 1961.

Negri, Miguel. "John Wayne - Going, Going, Gone." *Confidential*, November 1956.

Newman, Jack. "'Big John' At Home..." *San Antonio Light*, February 13, 1977.

Noli, Luis. "Panama Holds 87 Cuban Captives." *Corpus Christi Times*, May 2, 1959.

Norman, Jerry. "Brackettville Set Gains Applause From Movie." *San Angelo Standard Times*, September 1995.

Nugent, Frank S. THE SCREEN: 'Man of Conquest,' A Spectacle-Charged Biography of Sam Houston, Reminds the Capitol of the Alamo At the Palace." *New York Times*, April 28, 1939.

_____, "Pubs, Pictures and 'Nice Soft Days' in Erie." *The New York Times*, August 5, 1951.

Oliver, Wayne. "Movie Comeback." *The Evening Independent*, June 4, 1954.

Olson, Dale. "Santa Monica Basks In Oscar's Shining Glory." *Variety*, April 18, 1961.

Parsons, Louella. "Marian Hopkins Settles Long Row With Paramount." *San Antonio Light*, November 10, 1932.

_____, "John Wayne Adds Writing to Acting." *San Antonio Light*, May 1, 1945.

_____, *The Lowell Sun*, December 28, 1945.

_____, "Wayne Will Play Role In 'Alamo.'" *The Charlotte Gazette*, November 19, 1948.

_____, "Ford to Produce 'What Price Glory." *The Charleston Gazette*, January 14, 1949.

_____, "Roz Russell, Bob Cummings in Film." *San Antonio Light*, February 23, 1949.

_____, *The Lowell Sun*, August 11, 1952.

_____, "John Wayne to Make 'The Alamo' In Mexico as Result of Dispute." *Albuquerque Journal*, November 21, 1952.

_____, "Bob Stack Gets Role of Pilot." *The Daily Review*, October 30, 1953.

_____, "MGM Makes Sentimental Casting." *The Daily Review*, January 21, 1954.

_____, "Olivia OK's Film, Summer Nuptial." *The Daily Review*, February 19, 1954.

_____, "Avedon Deserves Lead in Movie." *The Daily Review*, May 6, 1954.

_____, "Academy Award Winner Holden on Tour Around World for Studio." *Albuquerque Journal*, June 18, 1954.

_____, "Deborah Kerr Seeks Place in Cast." *The Avalanche*, October 27, 1954.

_____, "Yul Brynner, Star of 'The King and I' Signed for Film Version of Noted Play." *Lubbock Morn. Avalanche*, October 27, 1954.

_____, "Italian Beauty Excited About Deal to do Pictures Here." *The Lima News*, December 29, 1954.

_____, "Deborah Kerr and Yul Brynner To Be Co-stars in 'King and I.'" *Albuquerque Journal*, January 24, 1955.

_____, "John Wayne Plans New Deal With Warner Bros." *Chronicle-Telegram*, March 18, 1955.

_____, "Tony Curtis Figures in Swap To Co-star in Circus Thriller." *Albuquerque Journal*, June 13, 1955.

_____, "Fonda Is Choice for Aldrich Role." *The Daily Review*, August 8, 1955.

_____, "News of Keaton Film biography Kindles Nostalgia." *The Lima News*, September 1, 1955.

_____, "Vidor to Direct Joe E. Lewis Epic." *The Daily News*, October 21, 1955.

_____, "Wayne, Ford to Team Up Again." *The Daily Review*, December 7, 1955.

_____, " Dan Dailey Gets 'Wings of Eagles' Role With John Wayne for Metro." *Albuquerque Journal*, June 27, 1956.

_____, "Logan wants Mitzi in Role." *San Antonio Light*, January 31, 1957.

_____, *Kingsport Times*, March 11, 1957.

_____, "Troubled Duke To Do Harris Story." *The Daily Review*, June 4, 1957.

_____, "Hollywood," *Tipton Tribune*, October 8, 1957.

_____, "Hollywood," *Tipton Tribune*, December 14, 1957.

_____, "Bob Hope Wants Jayne Mansfield As Co-Star in Jesse James Film." *Albuquerque Journal*, January 17, 1958.

_____, "Fast Pace Set by Star." *San Antonio Light*, January 24, 1958.

_____, "Natalie's Lucky." *San Antonio Light*, February 25, 1958.

_____, "John Wayne sings to star in Hawks' 'Bull by the Tail.'" *Albuquerque Journal*, March 15, 1958.

_____, "New Story Is Brought By Columbia Studio." *Anderson Daily Bulletin*, April 5, 1958.

_____, "Rita to Do Columbia Film." *The Daily Review*, June 26, 1958.

_____, "Texans Back Film." *San Antonio Light*, July 18, 1958.

_____, "Maurice Chevalier to Play Singing Priest in New Movie." *Albuquerque Journal*, December 3, 1958.

_____, "'Peyton Place' Sequel To Be Brought To screen In Spring." *Anderson Daily Bulletin*, January 10, 1959.

_____, "Burton to Play Doctor." *San Antonio Express*, January 22, 1959.

_____, "Robert Stack Trying To Take Role With Wayne In 'Alamo.'" *Anderson Daily Bulletin*, June 12, 1959.

_____, "Another Ike star?" *San Antonio Light*, August 8, 1959.

_____, "Male Star Has Glamor." *San Antonio Light*, September 9, 1959.

_____, "Lerner and Loewe In Movie Roles." *The Cedar Rapids Gazette*, October 3, 1959.

_____, "Holden to Play Top Role In 'Suzie Wong.'" *Anderson Daily Bulletin*, October 31, 1959.

_____, "Hollywood Talk Topics." *San Antonio Light*, November, 1, 1959.

_____, "Prize for Wallis; Laurence Harvey." *Cedar Rapids Gazette*, December 30, 1959.

_____, "Movie Producer Enters New Field, He'll Publish." *Anderson Daily Bulletin*, April 2, 1960.

_____, "Hollywood Stars Are Talking About..." *San Diego Union*, June 19, 1960.

_____, "Star Coming Back." *San Antonio Light*, November 29, 1960.

_____, "Quick European Trip for Romance." *San Antonio Light*, September 4, 1961.

Pavillard, Dan. "Old Tucson Gets 'Alamo' Props." *Tucson Daily Citizen*, November 26, 1966.

Payne, William. "Wayne Rebuilding Alamo for Film."*Dallas Morning News*, April 19, 1958.

_____, "Texans Back Film." *San Antonio Light*, July 18, 1958.

_____, "Wayne Confers on Promotion For 'Barbarian and Geisha." *Dallas Morning News*, September 24, 1958.

_____, "Fortnight Film List Gains Two Pictures." *Dallas Morning News*, October 15, 1958.

_____, "Musical Revue Saluting Awards In Sportswear to Be Seen Here." *Dallas Morning News*, May 22, 1959.

_____, "Dallas Has Its Own Festival of Top Pictures." *Dallas Morning News*, June 19, 1959.

_____, "English Actor Ready For Role as Travis." *Dallas Morning News*, September 8, 1959.

_____, "Male Star Has Glamor." *San Antonio Light*, September 9, 1959.

_____, "Curtain Rises On Fair Shows." *The Dallas Morning News*, October 9, 1959.

_____, "Dallas Is Scheduled to Share Premiere Showing for 'Alamo.'" *The Dallas Morning News*, March 18, 1960.

_____, "San Antonio Invites Premiere of 'Alamo.'" *Dallas Morning News*, April 29, 1960.

_____, "Wayne Will Lift 'Alamo' Veil." *Dallas Morning News*, June 7, 1960.

_____, "Wayne Confirms Capri Theater Will Open 'Alamo' on Oct. 26." *Dallas Morning News*, June 8, 1960.

_____, "Nelson Eddy to sing At State Fair event." *Dallas Morning News*, August 24, 1960.

_____, "Variety Committee Maps Plans For 'Alamo' Benefit Premiere." *Dallas Morning News*, September 1, 1960.

_____, "Opera Underwriters Get Annual Notices." *Dallas Morning News*, September 3, 1960.

_____, "Martha Hyer to Tour Texas for New Film." *Dallas Morning News*, September 7, 1960.

_____, "John Wayne Calls 'Alamo' 'Segment of History' Movie." *Rockford Morning Star*, October 16, 1960.

_____, "Benefit Show Opens 'Alamo.'" *Dallas Morning News*, October 25, 1960.

_____, "Wayne Motion Picture Makes Alamo Siege Live." *Dallas Morning News*, October 26, 1960.

Pelswick, Rose. "Wayne Spectacular A Texas-Size Show." *New York Journal-American*, October 27, 1960.

Petersen, Clarence. "'Alamo' Loses Again-as a TV Commercial." *Chicago Tribune*, November 15, 1960.

Phillips, Marianne Ohl. "Sheena Scrapbook: When Irish Eyes are Smiling." *Tease* 1995, #3.

Praley, Gerald. "'Alamo' Takes Long Time Biting Texas Dust." *Toronto Daily Star*, November 12, 1960.

Proctor, Kay. *Los Angeles Examiner*, April 9, 1953.

Pryor, Thomas M. "Adventure, Real and Cinematic, is his Dish." *The New York Times*, June 19, 1949.

_____, "John Wayne Makes New Warner Deal." *The New York Times*, March 6, 1952.

_____, "Jaffe Agency Ties New Film Package." *The New York Times*, August 14, 1952.

_____, "Mitchum's Role Taken By Wayne." *The New York Times*, January 17, 1955.

_____, "New Movie Deal For John Wayne." *The New York Times*, October 12, 1956.

_____, "Court Opens Way For Holden Film." *New York Times*, October 14, 1958.

Quigg, Jack. "Rugged Actor John Wayne Wants to Transfer Talents." *Del Rio News-Herald*, September 15, 1948.

Quill, Gynter. "Wayne, Holden, Hudson May Be Stars In New Film on Battle of the Alamo." *Waco Tribune-Herald*, October 26, 1958.

Ratcliff, Larry. "A Texas treasure - John Wayne's 'Alamo' just part of the story for Texas' first film czar Happy Shahan." *San Antonio Express-News*, July 16, 1995.

Redelings, Lowell. "Texas Premiere As Big as State." *The Citizen News*, October 26, 1960.

Reed, Allen C. "John Ford makes another movie classic in Monument Valley." *Arizona Highways*, April 1956.

Reeves, Frank. "New 'Old City' Astonishes Passersby." *Fort Worth Star Telegram*, March 22, 1959.

Reid, Jim. "Wayne Impressed by Cowboy Shrine." *The Oklahoman*, September 17, 1960.

Reyes, Luis I. "The Duke in Hawaii." *Hawaii Magazine*, November/December 2001.

Rhoades, Frank. "The Highroad." *San Diego Union*, July 16, 1959.

_____, *San Diego Union*, December 15, 1959.

Ricketts, Sgt. Albert D. "On the Town." *Pacific Stars and Stripes*, September 13, 1954.

Rimoldi, Oscar. "What Price Glory? Audie Murphy." *Films in Review*, April, 1986.

Robb, Inez. "Wayne May Star In Film With Utah Background." *Long Beach Press-Telegraph*, September 15, 1948.

_____, "Barron Know Nothing About Our Texas Alamo." *El Paso Herald-Post*, November 6, 1959.

Roberts, Bill. "$1 Billion Houston Capital Talks John Wayne Movie." *The Houston Post*, July 16, 1959.

_____, "Town Crier." *The Houston Post*, August 11, 1959.

_____, "Big Town." *The Houston Post*, October 11, 1959.

_____, *The Houston Post*, November 4, 1959.

_____, "A Big Night in Old San Antone…" *The Houston Post*, October 25, 1960.

Roderick, Kevin. "Veteran of western films, Wills' falsetto voice silent." *Winnipeg Free Press*, December 19, 1978.

Rogers, Ray. "Showers Fail To Wash Away Premiere Glamor." *San Antonio Express*, October 25, 1960.

Rose, Bob. "Cheating Death for a Living." *Popular Mechanics*, February 1935

Rosenfield, John. "Audie Murphy And 13 Days." *Dallas Morning News*, December 13, 1958.

_____, "Parlor Debate For a Holiday." *Dallas Morning News*, December 25, 1958.

Runyon, Damon. "The Brighter Side." *San Antonio Light*, August 25, 1949.

Ryon, Art. "Teach Child to Love Music, Tiomkin Urges." *Los Angeles Times*, October 9, 1960.

Saldana, Hector. "The Alamo Turns 50." Mysanantonio.com

Schallert, Edwin. "Dramatic Story by Fulop-Miller Purchased to Star Bobby Breen." *Los Angeles Times*, May 28, 1937.

_____, "Richard Barthelmess to Become Independent Movie Producer." *Los Angeles Times*, July 10, 1937.

_____, "Drama: Ford's 'Irish' cast set." *Los Angeles Times*, May 29, 1947.

_____, "Drama: 'Devil and Miss Jones' Set as Musical; Wayne Would Direct 'Alamo.'" *Los Angeles Times*, January 28, 1950.

_____, "Submarine War Film Excellent." *Los Angeles Times*, January 10, 1951.

_____, "'Bal Tabarin' to Feature Paris Anniversary." *Los Angeles Times*, January 22, 1951.

_____, "John Wayne to Direct 'Alamo' in Fall." *Los Angeles Times*, February 21, 1951.

_____, "Actor or Not, Wayne Hits screen Jackpot." *Los Angeles Times*, March 4, 1951.

_____, "Wayne Profile: Box Office With a Chin." *Los Angeles Times*, March 4, 1951.

_____, "Allan Jones Will Star in Stage 'Guys and Dolls." *Los Angeles Times*, April 16, 1951.

_____, "Mildred Dunnock Deals Multiply." *Los Angeles Times*, June 4, 1951.

_____, "Ford, Darnell Hailed for Costarring." *Los Angeles Times*, September 27, 1951.

_____, "John Wayne Probes Red Plots in Waikiki Area." *Los Angeles Times*, August 30, 1952.

_____, "'Julius Caesar' Will Miss Next Oscar Derby." *Los Angeles Times*, November 27, 1952.

_____, "Chill Wills to Costar With Murphy." *Los Angeles Times*, March 13, 1953.

_____, "Hepburn - Wayne Deal Simmers." *Los Angeles Times*, April 6, 1953.

_____, "Karen Goes High and Mighty With Her First Role in Films." *Los Angeles Times*, April 11, 1954.

_____, "High and Mighty' Inspires Epochal Type of Premiere." *Los Angeles Times*, May 28, 1954.

_____, *Los Angeles Times*, March 8, 1955.

_____, "Wayne Plans 'Gunsmoke' Production for Arness." *Los Angeles Times*, December 17, 1956.

_____, "Air Film Previewed Aboard Navy Carrier." *Los Angeles Times*, January 25, 1957.

_____, "Wayne Subject Picked; Dancers to Be Teamed." *Los Angeles Times*, March 26, 1958.

_____, "Here We Go Again-Movies Comb World for New Queen." *Oakland Tribune*, April 1, 1959.

Schellie, Don. "Saguaro Summit Session?" *Tucson Daily Citizen*, May 4, 1960.

Scheuer, Phillip. "Gary Hits Target On Stroke Of Noon." *Los Angeles Times*, August 14, 1952.

_____, "Cinemascope Shoots 'High and Mighty.'" *Los Angeles Times*, December 6, 1953.

_____, "South American Flight Film Likely for Wayne." *Los Angeles Times*, December 25, 1953.

_____, "Free Hand Promised to Ace Film Trio by Allied Artists." *Los Angeles Times*, June 6, 1954.

_____, "'Searchers' aims, Fires - and Hits." *Los Angeles Times*, March 18, 1955.

_____, "John Wayne Signs To $2,000,000 Contract." *Los Angeles Times*, July 13, 1956.

_____, "South 'Shook Up' by Horse Soldiers." *Los Angeles Times*, December 17, 1958.

_____, "Option of $1 Puts Pair in Business." *Los Angeles Times*, February 9, 1959.

_____, "Civil War Tale Scores." *Los Angeles Times*, June 14, 1959.

_____, "'Horse Soldiers' Rich in Pictorial Excitement." *Los Angeles Times*, June 25, 1959.

_____, "U.N. to Be Extolled in Prize Playlets." *Los Angeles Times*, July 24, 1959.

_____, "John Gavin to Join Wayne in 'Alamo.'" *Los Angeles Times*, August 14, 1959.

_____, "Oscar Wilde Trial to Reach Screen." *Los Angeles Times*, December 11, 1959.

_____, "Palpitating 'Alamo' Windup Reported." *Los Angeles Times*, December 16, 1959.

_____, "As Actor, Avalon Tops With Wayne." *Los Angeles Times*, April 6, 1960.

_____, "'Alamo' Wayne Dream Realized." *Los Angeles Times*, October 27, 1960.

_____, "'Alamo" and 'Pepe' Victories Puzzle." *Los Angeles Times*, March 6, 1961.

Scott, John L. "Vera Steps Up to Stardom." *Los Angeles Times*, May 27, 1956.

_____, "Hollywood in New Link With Manila." *Los Angeles Times*, November 24, 1958.

Scott, Martin. "John Wayne." *Cosmopolitan*, November 1954.

Scott, Vernon. "Director Robert Fellows Mystery Man to Outsiders." *San Mateo Times*, August 31, 1953.

_____, "Career, Security Gone Now Says Mrs. Wayne." *Chronicle-Telegram*, October 24, 1953.

_____, "John Wayne Is Boss, but Takes Orders." *The Stars and Stripes*, November 15, 1954.

_____, "Filmland Music is Praised." *The Galveston News*, May 9, 1956.

_____, "Suspension Better Than Bad Picture, Bill Holden Claims." *The Coshocton Tribune*, March 9, 1958.

_____, "Disc Jockeys on Way Out, says KLAC Radio Station." *Ukiah Daily Journal*, April 16, 1958.

_____, "Hollywood Report." *Oxnard Press Courier*, May 16, 1958.

_____, "John Wayne Claims He Needs the Money." *The Daily Independent*, July 24, 1958.

_____, "John Wayne Claims To Be 'Poor Boy' Of Movie Idols." *The Daily Courier*, July 24, 1958.

_____, "Tennis Star Althea Gibson Excited About Movie Role." *Leader-Times*, December 8, 1958.

Shanks, Dave. "Texas' History Turns a Profit, Brackettville Is Claiming Fame." *Austin American-Statesman*, June 26, 1960.

Sharpe, Howard. "The Star Creators of Hollywood." *Photoplay*, vol. 50, no. 41, 1936.

Sharpe, Matthew. "Nock's Volley Gun – "A Fearful Discharge." *American Rifleman*, December 2012.

Shearer, Lloyd. "Are TEN TOP STARS Strangling Hollywood?" *Parade*, October 12, 1958.

_____, "Can a Hollywood actress make it on her own?" Independent Star-News, May 17, 1959.

Sherman, Sam. "The Duke of Action." *Screen Thrills Illustrated*, September 1962.

Simon, Jerome S. "Richard Widmark." *Films In Review*, January 1971.

Simpson, Gay. "Best-Dressed Report." *Dallas Morning News*, October 6, 1959.

Skolsky, Sidney. "Oscar Ads Hurt chill." *Hollywood Citizen News*, March 29, 1961.

Smith, Jack. "Wayne Plays Wayne Hard, Rides Fame Easy." *Los Angeles Times*, May 29, 1960 .

Soanes, Wood. "Curtain Calls: Leftists in Hollywood 'Face War.'" *Oakland Tribune*, February 15, 1944.

_____, "Film Studio Cling To Old Headliners." *Oakland Tribune*, August 4, 1955.

Sokolsky, George E. "These Days." *The Billings Gazette*, March 23, 1949.

Sparks, Preston. "Blast's ties to cancer unclear." *The Augusta Chronicle*, March 16, 2009.

Spears, Ivan. "Spearheads." *Box Office*, February 8, 1960.

_____, "Spearheads." *Box Office*, February 13, 1960.

_____, "Hollywood Report." *Box Office*, March 21, 1960.

_____, "Spearheads." *Box Office*, April 4, 1960.

_____, "Spearheads." *Box Office*, May 23, 1960.

_____, "Spearheads." *Box Office*, July 11, 1960.

_____, "Spearheads." *Box Office*, August 1, 1960.

_____, "Spearheads." *Box Office*, December 5, 1960.

_____, "Spearheads." *Box Office*, February 13, 1961.

Spiro, J.D. "The Annual Oscar Derby." *The Milwaukee Journal*, April 9, 1961.

Staff Writer. "2nd Press club Gridiron Show To 'Roast' personalities, Alamo." *The San Antonian*, October 13, 1960.

_____, "3-Day Film Fete." *San Antonio Light*, July 14, 1960.

_____, "11-City Simultaneous Preem For 'The Alamo.'" *Variety*, March 17, 1960.

_____, "14 Films eligible For SDG Awards." *The Hollywood Reporter*, January 19, 1961.

_____, "20th Adds 4th Film To John Wayne Pact." *Variety*, July 13, 1956.

_____, "'21' Producer Ready to Face Federal Probe." *The Kerrville Times*, November 6, 1959.

_____, "24-Sheeting 'Alamo' With Oil Painting." *Unknown newspaper*, August 8, 1960.

_____, "32 'Alamo' Continuous Runs Top Comparable Blockbusters." *The Hollywood Reporter*, March 15, 1961.

_____, "50 Planes due Here On Tour." *Paris News*, October 4, 1959.

_____, "100 Scribes Invade Texas For 'Alamo.'" *Variety*, October 19, 1960.

_____, "137-Mile Trail Ride Planned For Premiere." *San Antonio Express and News*, July 17, 1960.

_____, "165 Extras Register For Alamo Movie." *Uvalde Leader News*, August 23, 1959.

_____, "300 'Alamo' Movie Extras Needed From Uvalde." *The Uvalde Leader-News*, August 16, 1959.

_____, "400-Acre 'Alamo' Set On Texas Ranch Will Cost $1,500.000." *The Hollywood Reporter*, July 29, 1959.

_____, "400 Attend Brackettville STTC Meet." *San Antonio Express*, August 28, 1959.

_____, "400 Kiwanians Pay Tribute To Movie Greats Visiting City." *Austin American*, October 9, 1951.

_____, "900 at Cocktail Party." *San Antonio Light*, October 25, 1960.

_____, "4,000 Whoop It up At 'Night In Old S.A." *San Antonio News*, October 24, 1960.

_____, "8000 Swarm to See 'Alamo' Stars." *San Antonio Light*, October 24, 1960.

_____, "23,000 'Alamo' Tix Orders in Hometown." *Variety*, August 22, 1960.

_____, "$50,000 Hoedown Premieres 'Alamo' In Hollywood." *San Antonio News*, October 27, 1960.

_____, "$100,000 Celebration Will Launch 'Alamo.'" *Unknown newspaper*, unknown date.

_____, "$1,500,000 Town Built For 'Alamo.'" *Variety*, July 29, 1959.

_____, "$5,000,000 Budget On Batjac 'Alamo.'" *Variety*, December 11, 1957.

_____, "$9,000,000 Budget On 4 Batjac Productions For UA." *Variety*, November 12, 1956.

_____, "A.C. Lyles Parlays Peek At 'Alamo' Into Booking Bonanza For "Raymie."" *Variety*, June 23, 1960.

_____, "Academy Awards Hypo 'Spartacus' Boxoffice 25 Pct." *The Hollywood Reporter*, April 26, 1961.

_____, "Academy Roster At Record 2354." *The Hollywood Reporter*, December 5, 1960.

_____, "Academy To Study Oscar Contenders' Promotion Practices." *The Hollywood Reporter*, June 22, 1961.

_____, "Action Element Is Giving 'Alamo' Big Foreign Draw." *The Hollywood Reporter*, January 12, 1961.

_____, "Actor Chill Wills dies." *Lawrence Journal-World*, December 17, 1978.

_____, "Actor Chill Wills dies at 77." *Wisconsin State Journal*, December 17, 1978.

_____, "Actor Gets The 'Point' In Painful Performance." *Joplin Globe*, June 22, 1958.

_____, "Actor Grant Withers, 55, Is Suicide." *The Sheboygan Press*, March 28, 1959.

_____, "Actor John Wayne's Wife Is Burned On Arm In House Fire." *Ocala Star-Banner*, January 14, 1958.

_____, "Actor Ken Curtis of 'Gunsmoke' dies in his sleep." *The Stars and Stripes*, May 1, 1991.

_____, "Actor Made Plenty But it Went Fast." *The Ada Evening News*, May 20, 1953.

_____, "Actor Presents Saddle to Meg." *Omaha World-Herald*, October 28, 1960.

_____, "Actor Protests "Closed Door" Death Hearing." *The Press-Courier*, October 17, 1959.

_____, "Actress Granted Default Decree." *The Daily Herald*, December 9, 1959.

_____, "Actress In Wayne Movie Slain." *Los Angeles Times*, October 12, 1959.

_____, "Actress Olive Carey; Played in Silent Films." *The Post-Standard*, March 16, 1988.

_____, "Actress-Wife Of Larry Parks In Hospital." *The Daily Review*, March 22, 1951.

_____, "Actress' Fear Described." *San Antonio Light*, October 16, 1959.

_____, "Ad Which 150G'The Alamo' Free Plug on NBC's Kennedy Telecast." *Variety*, July 5, 1960.

_____, "Adler Buys Country Club." *Reno Evening Gazette*, October 31, 1950.

_____, "'Alamo' Activities Stirring Houston." *Box Office*, September 19, 1960.

_____, "'Alamo' Adds Three Extra Performances." *Chicago Tribune*, November 5, 1960.

_____, "'Alamo' Americans Aura Brings Tears To The Eyes OF Texas." *Variety*, October 25, 1960.

_____, "'Alamo' Built At Brackett For Production Of Major Film." *Del-Rio News-Herald*, June 25, 1958.

_____, "'Alamo' Cast Due to Visit Movie Scene." *San Antonio Express*, July 12, 1959.

_____, "Alamo Celebration Revives Texas 'Shining Hour." *The San Antonian*, October 20, 1960.

_____, "'The Alamo' City wide." *Los Angeles Examiner*, March 29, 1961.

_____, "'Alamo' Creators Honored For Filming." *The San Antonio Light*, October 25, 1960.

_____, "Alamo Dance Big Success." *The Handy-Andy Herald*, November, 1960.

_____, "Alamo Day Proclaimed." *San Antonio Light*, March 1, 1960.

_____, "'Alamo' Debut At Woodlawn." *San Antonio News*, June 7, 1960.

_____, "'Alamo' Denver Sneak." *Variety*, August 5, 1960.

_____, "'Alamo' Early High Grosser in Japan." *Variety*, January 24, 1960.

_____, "'Alamo' Editorial lauded In Herald-Express." *Variety*, October 28, 1960.

_____, "'Alamo' Facing Ban in Mexico As Nat'l Sensitivity Heightens." *Variety*, September 7, 1960.

_____, "'Alamo' Filmers in Last Stand." *San Antonio Light*, December 6, 1959.

_____, "Alamo Film Extras Sought." *San Antonio Express and News*, August 22, 1959.

_____, "Alamo Film to be Shot Near S.A." *San Antonio Express*, January 19, 1958.

_____, "'Alamo' Gets A Big Hearst Plug." *Variety*, December 11, 1959.

_____, "'Alamo' Gets Away From Post-Production Looping." *Unknown magazine*, 1960.

_____, "'Alamo' Gets Exceptional Tax-Free German Rating." *The Hollywood Reporter*, January 31, 1961.

_____, "'Alamo' Gets Okay to Use of 'Eyes of Texas.'" *San Antonio Express and News*, October 24, 1959.

_____, "'Alamo' Guns Made by Local Firm." *San Antonio Light*, October 29, 1960.

_____, "'Alamo' Guns Readied For Action." *San Antonio Express and News*, August 1, 1959.

_____, "'Alamo' Hitches 152G Ride Publicity Bandwagon Via Life Mag Ad." *Variety*, June 28, 1960.

_____, "'Alamo' Honored By Good Housekeeping." *San Antonio Light*, September 21, 1960.

_____, "'Alamo' In Multiple Chicago Booking." *The Hollywood Reporter*, March 24, 1961.

_____, "'Alamo' Invitation on Way To President of Peru." *Box Office*, June 27, 1960.

_____, "'Alamo' Makes Great Movie." *Denton Record-Chronicle*, October 25, 1960.

_____, "'Alamo' Motif Pervades Town." *Variety*, November 30, 1960.

_____, "'Alamo' Murder Trial Called for Tomorrow." *Del Rio News-Herald*, November 8, 1959.

_____, "'Alamo' N.Y. Previews." *The Hollywood Reporter*, October 26, 1960.

_____, "'Alamo' Needs $17 Mil Before Netting Profit." *Variety*, October 5, 1960.

_____, "'Alamo' Office Burns Sunday." *Del Rio News-Herald*, November 16, 1959.

_____, "'Alamo' Opens Door To 'Big' Support By Gov't Of Selected Pix Preems Abroad." *Variety*, March 23, 1961.

_____, "'Alamo' Opens, 'Share' Gains." *The Citizen News*, October 27, 1960.

_____, "Alamo Painting Given to City." *San Antonio Express and News*, October 16, 1960.

_____, "Alamo Picture Moves To Texas." *Record Chronicle*, August 26, 1951.

_____, "Alamo Picture Site Rapped." *San Antonio Express*, August 5, 1951.

_____, "'Alamo' Plea on Way." *San Antonio Light*, April 28, 1960.

_____, "Alamo Premiere Chairmen Named." *The San Antonian*, June 23, 1960.

_____, "Alamo Premiere Committee Formed." *The Recorder*, July 28, 1960.

_____, "Alamo Premiere Head cheers As Funds Reach $11,640 Mark." *The San Antonian*, September 8, 1960.

_____, "'Alamo' Premiere Is 'Riot.'" *Los Angeles Herald & News*, October 27, 1960.

_____, "'Alamo' Premiere Set Here." *San Antonio Express*, June 8, 1960.

_____, "Alamo Premiere Trail Riders Leave Brackettville Oct. 18." *Farm and Ranch News*, October 7, 1960.

_____, "Alamo Premiere Workers Shaping Up, 150 in Fold." *The San Antonian*, July 14, 1960.

_____, "'Alamo' Set Tourist Trap." *Variety*, March 2, 1960.

_____, "'Alamo' Shooting As Pontiac Special." *Variety*, October 7, 1959.

_____, "'Alamo' Sked Re-vamped For Harvey Fest Visit." *Variety*, December 7, 1959.

_____, "'Alamo' Song In 4 Tongues." *The Hollywood Reporter*, December 21, 1960.

_____, "'Alamo' Spot lighted In Celebrations." *The Hollywood Reporter*, March 6, 1961.

_____, "'Alamo' Statistician's Delight As Winds Tex Locale Lensing." *Variety*, December 16, 1959.

_____, "'Alamo' Tickets On sale Monday." *San Antonio Express and News*, October 3, 1960.

_____, "'Alamo' to Have Matinee Today." *Los Angeles Times*, November 24, 1960.

_____, "'Alamo' to Premiere In Texas October 24." *Box Office*, June 13, 1960.

_____, "Alamo Trip Program Prize." *San Antonio Light*, October 19, 1960.

_____, "Alamo Village." *This is West Texas*, November-December 1970.

_____, "Alamo Village good enough to convince some tourists it's the real thing." *The Houston Post*, September 1, 1991.

_____, "'Alamo' winds Up 82-Day, $4 Mil Location; 1000 Horses On Block." *The Hollywood Reporter*, December 16, 1959.

_____, "'Alamo' Wins Edison Award." *Variety*, March 21, 1961.

_____, "'Alamo' World Premiere Ticket Sales Brisk, One Third to go." *The San Antonian*, September 29, 1960.

_____, "Alamo's Fall, Life of Travis Told in 'The Last Command.'" *The Abilene Reporter-News*, August 7, 1955. _____, "All Invited To Share 'Alamo' Fun." *San Antonio Light*, September 4, 1960.

_____, "All Is Bliss Again for John Wayne and Wife." *Los Angeles Times*, September 8, 1958.

_____, "Almost Shot Wayne After Night Out, Wife Testifies." *Los Angeles Times*, October 21, 1953.

_____, "Along Show Row." *The Houston Chronicle*, November 22, 1959.

_____, "Americanize the Movies." *The San Antonio Light*, February 9, 1944.

_____, "An Unknown Perfection." *Star Bulletin*, April 24, 1960.

_____, "Appoint Birdwell Batjac Pub-Ad V-P On 'The Alamo.'" *Hollywood Reporter*, August 12, 1959.

_____, "Argentine Beauty Versatile Actress." *Independent Press Telegram*, October 8, 1959.

_____, "Army Architecture." *The Fort Clark, Texas Post Return*, Summer 2008.

_____, "Army Status of Lew Ayres Veiled by Ft. Lewis Officers." *Los Angeles Times*, May 20, 1942.

_____, "Around Town." *Del Rio News-Herald*, September 4, 1959.

_____, *Del Rio News-Herald*, September 6, 1959.

_____, *Del Rio News-Herald*, September 8, 1959.

_____, *Del Rio News-Herald*, September 27, 1959.

_____, "As patriotic As You Dears." *Variety*, April 26, 1961.

_____, "Athenian Honor." *Los Angeles Times*, November 17, 1960.

_____, "Avalon In 'Alamo' Gala. *The Hollywood Reporter*, December 6, 1960.

_____, "Avalon Lilt's Ladies." *Variety*, March 2, 1960.

_____, "Aviator Injured in Fall on Stairs." *Ogden Standard-Examiner*, April 16, 1926.

_____, "Award To 'Alamo.'" *The Hollywood Reporter*, December 21, 1960.

_____, "Barrymore Jr. Will Make Stage Debut In 'The Rogue' At Hollywood Theater." *The Salt Lake Tribune*, March 27, 1951.

_____, "Baseball and Cars May Outrank Acting." *San Antonio Light*, October 21, 1960.

_____, "Batjac Group Suspends." *The New York Times*, December 1, 1955.

_____, "Batjac Settles IA Pubs' Beef; Hired Flacks Get $892 each." *Variety*, March 24, 1960.

_____, "Battle of Alamo Over." *San Antonio Light*, December 15, 1959.

_____, "Beatles & 'Alamo' In Fresh Orbit." *Variety*, October 7, 1966.

_____, "Beauty in 'Alamo' Movie Killed With Hunting Knife." *San Antonio Express*, October 12, 1959.

_____, "Beauty's Disappointment Brief." *Press-Telegram*, July 20, 1959.

_____, "Bedroom scene." *Daily Herald*, October 21, 1960.

_____, "Behind Hollywood Scenes." *The Daily Facts-Review*, June 9, 1954.

_____, "Behind the Scenes in Hollywood." *The Vidette-Messenger*, May 18, 1957.

_____, "Bexar Facts." *The San Antonio Light*, August 10, 1960.

_____, "Big Quarrel Preceded Shooting Of Publisher." *Lebanon Daily News*, September 6, 1956.

_____, "Bill Daniel Named 'Alamo' Executive." *Del Rio News-Herald*, August 19, 1959.

_____, "Bill Holden Suspended." *Star-News*, March 4, 1958.

_____, "Bill Holden to Play Bowie in 'Alamo'; Wayne Will Direct." *Variety*, December 16, 1957.

_____, "Billy Wilder, George Schaefer win Directors guild Awards." *The Hollywood Reporter*, February 6, 1961.

_____, "Birdwell Ballyhooing 'The Alamo' Again." *Variety*, December 21, 1960.

_____, "Birdwell Ends 1-Year Hitch On 'The Alamo.'" *Variety*, December 12, 1960.

_____, "Birdwell Foreign Tieups." *The Hollywood Reporter*, December 20, 1960.

_____, "Birdwell Sets $1.3-Million Ad Drive For 'The Alamo.'" *Advertising News of New York*, July 8, 1960.

_____, "Birdwell Takes Prose Flight." *Variety*, February 10, 1960.

_____, "Bo Roos, Advisor of Film Stars, 69." *The New York Times*, August 13, 1973.

_____, "Body Pushes Battle For Alamo Plan." *San Antonio Light*, July 5, 1936.

_____, "Bond Recovering." *Cumberland Evening News*, October 17, 1959.

_____, "Boone Plans Gun Fight For Youngster's Matinee." *Valley Sun*, April 28, 1960.

_____, "Boone Will Holster His 'Gun' in October." *Los Angeles Times*, August 9, 1962.

_____, "Brackett Goes Into Movie Production." *Del Rio News-Herald*, January 5, 1958.

_____, "Brackettville area will remember the Alamo for a long time to come." *Better Ranches & Farms*, September 23, 1959.

_____, "Brief from Lots." *Variety*, December 25, 1957.

_____, "Brit Censor Okays 'Alamo', Questions About 'Spartacus.'" *Variety*, October 24, 1960.

_____, "British Actress To Speak Here At Guild social." *Dallas Morning News*, November 8, 1959.

_____, "British Reviewers' Bests.'" *Variety*, January 18, 1961.

_____, "Burt Kennedy Interviews John Ford." *Action*, Vol. 3, No. 5, September/October 1968

_____, "Call for 1,300 Male extras for Wayne Movie at Brackett." *Del Rio News-Herald*, July 19, 1959.

_____, "Camporre Attended By 200 Boy Scouts." *Del Rio News-Herald*, April 6, 1959.

_____, "Canal Status Is Satisfactory To Panama." *The Berkshire Eagle*, May 27, 1959.

_____, "Carlos Arruza to Fight in Macarena." *Del Rio Herald*, October 29, 1959.

_____, "Casts and Forecasts: For Youth." *Dallas Morning News*, June 25, 1960.

_____, "Cedars Valley Guild Plans Champagne Event." *Los Angeles Times*, September 25, 1960.

_____, "Celebrities of Stage, Screen, Gridiron to Attend Jewel Ball." *Dallas Morning News*, September 30, 1959.

_____, "CFWF Names Award Winners in Motion Picture Ballot." *Van Nuys News*, March 23, 1961.

_____, "Chamber to Produce World Premiere for "Alamo."" *The San Antonian*, June 9, 1960.

_____, "Channel 5 to Cover 'The Alamo' Premiere." *Los Angeles Times*, October 26, 1960.

_____, "Chatterbox - Star in a Rush." *Dallas News*, July 10, 1951.

_____, "Chicago Theaters Ban Ayres Films." *Los Angeles Times*, April 2, 1942.

_____, "Chill Wills dies at 78; film actor." *Alton Telegraph*, December 18, 1978.

_____, "Chow Call at "The Alamo."" *San Antonio Light*, December 24, 1959.

_____, "Classified Holds Key To 'Alamo' Set." *Los Angeles Times*, October 23, 1960.

_____, "Cleveland Critics Circle Votes 'Spartacus' Best.' *The Hollywood Reporter*, January 10, 1961.

_____, "Col Gets Rights to 'Alamo" LP; Tiomkin's 200G." *Variety*, August 31, 1960.

_____, "Col Record's And Tiomkin Settle Tiff." *Variety*, October 19, 1960.

_____, "Col Settles Tiomkin's Beef on 'Alamo' Credits With Correction Via Ads." *Variety*, October 26, 1960.

_____, "Cong Film May be Ford's 'Swan Song.'" *The Irish Times*, July 11, 1951.

_____, "Connie Towers deserting Clubs." *Dallas Morning News*, June 21, 1959.

_____, "Copies of 183-Page Birdwell Ballyhoo Blast For 'The Alamo' Selling For $15." *Variety*, May 13, 1965.

_____, "Cross-Complaint Filed for Divorce." *Oshkosh Northwestern*, September 11, 1959.

_____, "Daily Knave." *Oakland Tribune*, January 27, 1955.

_____, *Oakland Tribune*, February 1, 1955.

_____, "DAR Picks 'Alamo.'" *The Hollywood Reporter*, February 2, 1961.

_____, "Daring Aviator Fractures Neck." *The San Diego Union*, April 16, 1926.

_____, "Daughters of American revolution Rise rhetorically Vs. Show Biz." *Variety*, April 26, 1961.

_____, "Daughters Of Texas: Fie On N.Y. Critics." *Unknown newspaper*, November 15, 1960.

_____, "Davis Given Colonelcy By Governor." *Dallas Morning News*, November 8, 1959.

_____, "Davy Crockett Is Big Business." *Dallas Morning News*, May 31, 1959.

_____, "Days Past: Prescott's own George Phillpen, Western artist extraordinaire." *The Daily Courier*, January 22, 2012.

_____, "Deal Made By Killer Of Starlet." *San Antonio Light*, November 10, 1959.

_____, "Del Rioans At Cancer Meeting." *Del Rio News-Herald*, September 21, 1959.

_____, "Den 3 Cub Scouts Visit Alamo Set At Brackettville." *Del Rio News-Herald*, October 21, 1958.

_____, "Dennis King Joins Cronyns For New Play at the Geary." *Oakland Tribune*, August 21, 1955.

_____, "Denver Pyle, Uncle Jesse on 'Dukes of Hazzard,' Dies at 77." *The Winchester Star*, December 27, 1997.

_____, "Different "Outdoor" Picture is "Mantrap", and It Tells a Powerful Story." *The Sandusky Star-Journal*, August 21, 1926.

_____, "Digs Denver." *The Abilene Reporter-News*, May 31, 1970.

_____, "Dimitri Tiomkin Rehearses." *San Antonio Express and News*, October 22, 1960.

_____. "Dimitri Tiomkin to Speak." *Box Office*, August 29, 1960.

_____, "Distinction Of Furnishing Bakery Movie Cast during Filming At Brackettville." *San Antonio Express and News*, October 16, 1960.

_____, "Dog Saves John Wayne's Wife and Baby From Fire." *Los Angeles Times*, January 15, 1958.

_____, "Dripping Skies Fail to dampen 'Alamo' Enthusiasm." *San Antonio Express*, October 25, 1960.

_____, "'Duke' Wayne Tells Views On Nation." *Los Angeles Times*, October 21, 1960.

_____, "Duke' son: Film site not to blame in cancer." *Chronicle Telegram*, August 7, 1979.

_____, "Early Efforts Aid 'Alamo.'" *The Exhibitor*, October 12, 1960.

_____, "Easing 'Alamo' Into Grind Engagements." *Variety*, November 7, 1960.

_____, "Eight Large Cities See It Next Week." *San Antonio Express and News*, October 22, 1960.

_____, "Emma Hernandez, A Tejano Music Legend." *Latino Star y Teleguia*, February 6, 2000.

_____, "Envelope Slated On Pony Express." *Dallas Morning News*, December 28, 1959.

_____, "Esperanza Wayne Said Ready To Open Fight For Alimony." *The Progress Index*, June 8, 1954.

_____, "Every Studio is after John Wayne." *Cedar Rapids Gazette*, February 19, 1950.

_____, "Exact Replica of Alamo Being Built at Brackett For John Wayne Movie." *Uvalde Leader-News*, January 17, 1958.

_____, "Exodus' $48,799 Fourth Week In NY." *The Hollywood Reporter*, January 16, 1961.

_____, "'Exodus' $49,000 In First NY Week." *The Hollywood Reporter*, December 23, 1960.

_____, "Expected Baby Lost By John Waynes." *Los Angeles Times*, May 27, 1995.

_____, "Extensive Air Coverage For 'Alamo' Preem Here." *The Hollywood Reporter*, October 26, 1960.

_____, "Extras for 'Alamo' Still Being Signed." *Del Rio News-Herald*, August 14, 1959.

_____, "Extras Work Friday." *Del Rio News-Herald*, September 2, 1959.

_____, "'Eyes of Texas' Are Upon 'The Alamo' Cuffo; Looks Like Trouble Brewing." *Variety*, November 4, 1959.

_____, "Eyes Of Texas Will Be Upon 'Alamo' Oct 24." *Variety*, June 6, 1960.

_____, "Fabulous Fabian to Appear at Congress." *Waterloo Daily Courier*, August 31, 1959.

_____, "Face's Pretty, But Figure Her Fortune." *The Salt Lake Tribune*, December 5, 1959.

_____, "Fall Of Alamo At The Rialto." *San Antonio Light*, September 28, 1926.

_____, "Fall of Alamo To Be Filmed Near S.A." *San Antonio Express and News*, January 19, 1958.

_____, "Fallout risks told, government claims." *The New Mexican*, December 17, 1979.

_____, "Famed Matador In Special Fight Sunday." *San Antonio Express and News*, October 31, 1959.

_____, "Fiesta Noche Del Rio." *San Antonio Light*, October 21, 1960.

_____, "Fight to Delay Movie Extra's Trial Is Seen." *San Antonio Express and News*, November 7, 1959.

_____, "Figleaf Awards To Garson a& Wayne." *Variety*, September 25, 1961.

_____, "Film Alliance Asks More data on Larry Parks." *Los Angeles Times*, March 30, 1951.

_____, "Film Beauty Mulls 'Thought Travel.'" *Racine Sunday Bulletin*, September 18, 1955.

_____, "Film Boon to Cong." *Greeley Tribune*, January 19, 1954.

_____, "Film Brawler Confesses All." *The Coshocton*, August 10, 1958.

_____, "Film Capitalizes Stage's Shortcomings, says Ford." *Los Angeles Examiner*, May 3, 1925.

_____, "Film Group to Install Wayne as President." *Los Angeles Times*, March 24, 1949.

_____, "Film Hero Here to Help Cowboy Hall." *The Oklahoman*, September 16, 1960.

_____, "Film Hero Weds For Third Time." *The Billings Gazette*, November 2, 1954.

_____, "Film Notables Throng Toni Wayne's Wedding." *Los Angeles Times*, May 27, 1956.

_____, "Film Pair To Wed." *Racine Journal-Times*, October 4, 1960.

_____, "Film Role Path to Death." *Los Angeles Herald Express*, October 12, 1959.

_____, "Film Star John Wayne Takes in S.A. Rodeo." *San Antonio News*, February 18, 1959.

_____, "Film Success For Actress Means Soaking." *The Ogden Standard-Examiner*, November 9, 1958.

_____, "Film Trade Cancelled." *Dallas Morning News*, November 25, 1959.

_____, "Film Troupe Due Tomorrow." *Arizona Daily Sun*, June 14, 1955.

_____, "Filmland Yawns at Soviet Ranting." *Los Angeles Times*, May 13, 1947.

_____, "Filmster 'Won't Testify;' Parks Denied Movie Role." *The Salt Lake Tribune*, March 21, 1951.

_____, "Find 2nd Cache of Arms in Panama Rebel Hunt." *Racine Journal-Times*, April 24, 1959.

_____, "Fire Destroys Fort of Wayne's Jinx film." *Pasadena Independent*, November 16, 1959.

_____, "Fire Razes Fort Clark Film Site." *The Galveston News*, November 16, 1969.

_____, "First Big 'Alamo' Day Here." *San Antonio Express and News*, October 22, 1960.

_____, "Five-Day Party To Precede 'Alamo.'" *Variety*, August 3, 1960.

_____, "Five of Movie Company Sentenced After Brawl." *Oakland Tribune*, February 12, 1955.

_____, "Flat Broke Millionaire." *Movie Life Year Book*, # 34, 1963.

_____, "For Deanna It Was a First Kiss but for Bob it Was Almost a Last Gasp." *The Cedar Rapids Gazette*, November 27, 1955.

_____, "Ford will Direct 'The Quiet Man.'" *The New York Times*, June 1, 1937.

_____, "Foreign, U.S. Officials Accept Alamo Invites." *The San Antonian*, October 20, 1960.

_____, "Four Days of Festivities Planned Around 'Alamo' World Premiere." *Box Office*, September 5, 1960.

_____, "Frankie Avalon To Co-Star In 'Alamo.'" *Variety*, August 4, 1959.

_____, "Gail Russell—in memoriam." *The Los Angeles Times*, July 5, 2007.

_____, "Gary Cooper Critical of TV Horse Operas." *Linton Daily Citizen*, May 15, 1958.

_____, "Gavin Out of 'Alamo' As U-I Balks At Loanout Terms." *Hollywood Reporter*, September 9, 1959.

_____, "Generals See Alamo Battle Filming." *San Antonio Light*, December 10, 1959.

_____, "Gilmour, Clyde. "Cheers for The Alamo." *Toronto Telegram*, October 25, 1960.

_____, "Glen McCarthy Active in Show Biz; Plots 3-D System sans Eyeglasses; Currently Producing 3 Features." *Variety*, November 11, 1959.

_____, "Glory for John." *Screenland*, June 1950.

_____, "Goldwyn Annual Writing Awards Both For Novels." *Variety*, May 6, 1959.

_____, "Good Mag Cites 'Alamo.'" *Variety*, December 29, 1960.

_____, "Gov. Daniel Speech Making." *Brownsville Herald*, January 29, 1960.

_____, "Governor Gives Chunk of Alamo To Actor Wayne." *El Paso Herald-Post*, August 14, 1959.

_____, "Governor Gives Okay To 'Alamo' Movie Set." *Del Rio News Herald*, August 14, 1959.

_____, "Gunsmoke's Festus Dies; Also Singer With Big Bands." *The Winchester Star*, April 30, 1991.

_____, "Handy-Andy Stages 'Hoe-Down.'" *San Antonio Light*, October 21, 1960.

_____, "Happy Shahan To Committee for Premiere of Alamo." *Del Rio News-Herald*, July 17, 1960.

_____, "Harvey Will Accept Award For Wayne." *Variety*, April 20, 1960.


_____, "Has He Everything Now? How About the 'Alamo.'" *Unknown* newspaper, October 20, 1971.

_____, "Hats Mark Position." *Times-Picayne*, September 11, 1960.

_____, "Hayworth Just Invites Herself." *Dallas Morning News*, March 30, 1959.

_____, "Heavy Rains Flood Roxton In Big Area Thunderstorm." *The Paris News*, June 17, 1958.

_____, "Helen Hayes, LeRoy Head Nixon-Lodge Showbiz Campaign." *Variety*, August 17, 1960.

_____, "Hepburn, Laddie win Awards for Acting Ability." *The Lima News*, March 30, 1954.

_____, "Highest Marine Citation Awarded To John Wayne." *Box Office*, April 24, 1961.

_____, "Historic Link." *Variety*, March 13, 1961.

_____, "History Comes To Life With 'Alamo' Movie." *The Dallas Morning News*, October 23, 1960.

_____, "Hitch on 'The Alamo.'" *Variety*, December 12, 1960.

_____, "Holden Says Search For Paris Prompts World Travels." *The Rhinelander Daily News*, November 20, 1958.

_____, "Hollywood." *Billboard*, October 24, 1960.

_____, "Hollywood." *Variety*, October 4, 1961.

_____, "Hollywood Also to Have Its Battle of the Alamo." *San Antonio Express*, July 16, 1959.

_____, "Hollywood by Louella Parsons." *Middletown Times Herald*, November 19, 1948.

_____, "Hollywood doubtful actor's cancer linked to A-bomb." *The News*, August 7, 1979.

_____, "Hollywood Notables Due." *San Antonio Light*, October 5, 1951.

_____, "Hollywood Praises Courage Of Parks' Red Declaration." *The Salt Lake Tribune*, March 22, 1951.

_____, "Hollywood Sends Delegation to Mex. Film Review Fest." *Variety*, November 27, 1959.

_____, "Hollywood Stars Back Texas Town." *San Antonio Express and News*, August 19, 1961.

_____, "Honored." *San Antonio Express and News*, January 31, 1960.

_____, "Hospital Notes." *Del Rio News-Herald*, October 8, 1959.

_____, *Del Rio News-Herald*, October 27, 1959.

_____, "Houston Tower Burglars Tale 'Alamo' Receipts." *Box Office*, January 16, 1961.

_____, "How Alamo Village Came Into Being." *Alamo Village Star*, May 1961.

_____, "Hubby-Engineer Now Actor; Actress-Wife Back At Work." *Burlington Daily Times-News*, September 11, 1958.

_____, "Huge Parade Highlight Of 'Alamo' Festivity." *Box Office*, October 17, 1960. *Bayton Sun*, September 11, 1960.

_____, "Huntsville Prison Rodeo To Feature Top Entertainers." *Baytown Sun*, September 11, 1960.

_____, "Hyams Exits As Batjac Director Of Publicity." *Variety*, January 29, 1960.

_____, "IA Publicists Union Challenges Layoff of Three By Batjac." *The Hollywood Reporter*, October 7, 1959.

_____, "Independents Sign Top Stars." *Pacific Stars and Stripes*," December 7, 1958.

_____, "Inside Stuff-Music." *Variety*, October 5, 1960.

_____, "Irish Film Star Lands at Shannon." *The Irish Times*, June 7, 1951.

_____, "It's a Draw - Both Waynes Win Decree." *Long Beach Independent*, October 29, 1953.

_____, "It's as Rugged as a Year of Mondays." *Oakland Tribune,* May 30, 1954.

_____, "'Jet Pilot' In A Spin." *Variety*, November 12, 1956.

_____, "Joan O'Brien Has Formula For Success." *The Bee*, October 27, 1960.

_____, "Joan O'Brien In 'Alamo.'" *Variety*, August 20, 1959.

_____, "Joe Hyams Resigning as H-H-L Coast Flack." *Variety*, February 17, 1959.

_____, "John Gavin In 'Alamo.'" *Hollywood Reporter*, August 14, 1959.

_____, "Johnson Sees Threat of Red Base on Cuba." *Monthly Index and Democrat*, July 5, 1960.

_____, "John Wayne Abed On Medico's Orders." *Variety*, September 27, 1960.

_____, "John Wayne Abroading To Hoopla 'The Alamo.'" *Variety*, November 14, 1960.

_____, "John Wayne Admits His 'Alamo' A 'Message" Pic-Americanism." *Variety*, October 26, 1960.

_____, "John Wayne Admits Rumor Based on Family Breakup." *Salt Lake Tribune*, September 7, 1958.

_____, "John Wayne as the Last Hero." *Time*, August 8, 1969.

_____, "John Wayne deplores Film 'Filth.'" *The Citizen-News*, January 13, 1960.

_____, "John Wayne Discloses Who, How Much And How Great 'Gamble' Is On 'Alamo.'" *Variety*, October 24, 1960.

_____, *John Wayne – Duke's Own Story.* 1979.

_____, "John Wayne et al Is Sued By Publicist Henaghan." *Box Office*, January 25, 1960.

_____, "The John Wayne Family." *Parade*, January 10, 1960.

_____, "John Wayne First Casting For 'The Greatest Story.'" *Variety*, September 19, 1960.

_____, "John Wayne Gets Award From American Legion." *The Hollywood Reporter*, January 20, 1961.

_____, "John Wayne, Governor Dine." *San Antonio Light*, August 13, 1959.

_____, "John Wayne Has a Full Schedule." *Manitowoc Herald-Times*, March 8, 1948.

_____, "John Wayne has Minor Role as Son Stars in TV Drama." *Racine Journal-Times*, October 19, 1955.

_____, "John Wayne Here Sunday." *San Antonio Express and News,* August 16, 1959.

_____, "John Wayne: He's Ready For 'Role' As Director." *The Salt Lake Tribune*, March 1, 1959.

_____, "John Wayne Hurt in Fall On Marin Set." *Oakland Tribune*, January 28, 1955.

_____, "John Wayne in New York, London for Premieres." *Box Office*, October 31, 1960.

_____, *John Wayne is Dead.* 1979.

_____, "John Wayne Lashes 'Last Summer' And 'Cordura' As Poison 'Polluting The Bloodstream Of H'wood." *The Hollywood Reporter*, January 11, 1960.

_____, "John Wayne Link in Panama Plot." *Oakland Tribune*, April 23, 1959.

_____, "John Wayne Meets Texas Coin-Bags Re 'The Alamo.'" *Variety*, July 22, 1959.

_____, "John Wayne Planning All Texas 'Alamo.'" *The Dallas Morning News*, August 15, 1959.

_____, "John Wayne Remembers." *Chicago Sun-Times*, October 16, 1960.

_____, "John Wayne Says Separation Off." *San Antonio Express*, September 8, 1958.

_____, "John Wayne Sets Personal Appearances Here Tomorrow." *El Paso Herald Post*, November 24, 1953.

_____, "John Wayne Star of "High and the Mighty" - Paramount." *The Cedar Rapids Tribune*, July 8, 1954.

_____, "John Wayne Starlet Dies in Stabbing." *Press Telegram*, October 12, 1959.

_____, "John Wayne stars in epic film of heroic battle for Texas Independence." *The Emporia Gazette*, April 30, 1977.

_____, "John Wayne Takes Peruvian Beauty for Third Bride." *The Daily Courier*, November 2, 1954.

_____, "John Wayne Takes to Plane in 'High and Mighty' Film." *The Ogden Standard-Examiner*, July 4, 1954.

_____, *John Wayne the Legendary Duke.* 1979.

_____, "John Wayne: To Each his Own." Warner Bros. Press release. No date.

_____, "John Wayne To Get Texas Headliners Award For 'Alamo.'" *Variety*, January 18, 1960.

_____, "John Wayne To Receive DAR Award For 'Alamo.'" *The Hollywood Reporter*, May 17, 1961.

_____, "John Wayne to star in 'Searchers' in June." *The Los Angeles Times*, April 26, 1955.

_____, "John Wayne To Sub For Robert Mitchum." *The Hutchinson News-Herald*, January 17, 1955.

_____, "John Wayne, Wife Part." *Lowell Sun*, September 7, 1958.

_____, "John Wayne's 'Alamo.'" *Variety*, February 25, 1959.

_____, "John Wayne's Co-Stars - Victor McLaglen." *The John Wayne Film Society Journal*, Spring 2008.

_____, "John Wayne's Texas Kick." *Variety*, November 18, 1959.

_____, "John Wayne's 'The Alamo' Being Cut to 200 Minutes." *Box Office*, June 20, 1960.

_____, "John Wayne's 'The Alamo' Started." *The Kinney County News*, January 17, 1958.

_____, "John Wayne's Wife Expecting Baby." *The Winona Daily News*, October 18, 1955.

_____, "John Wayne's Wife Going to Move Out." *Los Angeles Times*, September 7, 1958.

_____, "John Waynes Expecting Baby In April." *Los Angeles Times*, October 18, 1955.

_____, "Jot Dot Malone, Stack For 'Alamo'; Murchison's $2 Mil." *The Hollywood Reporter*, July 7, 1959.

_____, "Judge Defies State; Holds Secret Trial." *Del Rio News-Herald*, October 16, 1959.

_____, "Jungle Trapper Freed of Shooting Publisher." *Times-Mirror*, September 7, 1956.

_____, "Junketing Press To 'Alamo' Bow." *Variety*, October 21, 1960.

_____, "Ken Curtis; played Festus on 'Gunsmoke.'" *Los Angeles Times*, April 29, 1991.

_____, "Kerr Longhorns To Be In Movie, 'The Three Godfathers.'" *Kerrville Mountain Sun*, March 11, 1948.

_____, "Key Witnesses Tell Story of Actress slaying." *Del Rio News-Herald*, October 18, 1959.

_____, "KTLA Fights Rain, Skunks & Rattlers To Tape 'Alamo' Spec At 65% savings." *Variety*, December 1, 1959.

_____, "KTLA Tapes Batjac 'Alamo' Party As NBC Pontiac Spec." *Variety*, November 9, 1959.

_____, "Lampoon Larrups Movie and Actors." *Madison Capital Times*, April 4, 1961.

_____, "Las Moras Creek Floods Brackett, Closing Highway 90 East OF Here." *Del Rio News-Herald*, June 17, 1958.

_____, "Leaders of Film Industry Form Anti-Red Group." *Los Angeles Times*, February 5, 1944.

_____, "League City Movie 'Stars' Set for film." *The Galveston Daily News*, October 27, 1959.

_____, "Leaves for Prison." *Del Rio News-Herald*, November 13, 1959.

_____, "Leighton Cancellation." *Dallas Morning News*, November 10, 1959.

_____, "Let's Do It Again." *Tucson Daily Citizen*, May 23, 1958.

_____, "Lew Ayres Arrives at Camp for Duty With War Objectors." *Los Angeles Times*, April 2, 1942.

_____, "Life Mag issues Brochure On 'Alamo' Gate-fold Ad." *The Hollywood Reporter*, April 28, 1961.

_____, "Light Photographer Wins Annual Headliners Award." *San Antonio Light*, January 31, 1960.

_____, "Linda Cristal, Oil Husband Break Up." *Big Spring Herald*, March 8, 1959.

_____, "Linda Cristal Sheds Oilman, Shuns Alimony." *Los Angeles Times*, December 9, 1959.

_____, "Local Seen-ry: Wool Week in S.A." *San Antonio Express*, September 3, 1959.

_____, "Localized Actions Urged To Defeat Communism." *Los Angeles Times*, March 10, 1947.

_____, "Lone Star Spread, A." *San Antonio Light*, December 29, 1958.

_____, "Louella to Be In S.A. For Premiere." *San Antonio Light*, September 25, 1960.

_____, "Love Nest Knife Killer Jailed in Del Rio." *Del Rio News-Herald*, October 12, 1959.

_____, "Majors Originated 'Outrageous Wages'; Mirisch: Stars A Calculated Risk." *Variety*, December 10, 1958.

_____, "Man Claims Blackout In Texas Slaying Of Actress." *Los Angeles Times*, October 13, 1959.

_____, "Many Today Dub Selves 'Producers' But qualify on None of Essential Realities of Title–John Wayne." *Variety*, January 15, 1964.

_____, "March from Gonzales No Lark for Marines." *The San Antonian*, October 13, 1960.

_____, "Marines' March could Be Worse." *San Antonio Express*, October 25, 1960.

_____, "Market Value of Batjac Prods. Via diversification, Mounts To $10 Mil." *Variety*, April 28, 1965.

_____, "McLaglen, Boisterous Actor, Dies." *Corpus Christi Caller-Times*, November 8, 1959.

_____, "Method and Madness of Movie Music." *Los Angeles Examiner*, October 25, 1960.

_____, "Mexican Critic says Films Enemy of U.S." *El Paso Herald-Post*, October 13, 1959.

_____, "Midas Touch." *Winnipeg Free Press*, December 5, 1960.

_____, "Miss Deibel, Actor's Son Recite Vows." *Los Angeles Times*, October 1, 1958.

_____, "Miss Deibel Betrothal Announced." *Los Angeles Times*, February 10, 1958.

_____, "Mitchum Dismissed From Movie in Row." *Long Beach Press-Telegram*, January 12, 1955.

_____, "Mitchum Fired but Denies Pushing Man into Icy Bay." *Oxnard Press-Courier*, January 13, 1955.

_____, "Mitchum Fired For Dunking Aide in Bay." *Oakland Tribune*, January 12, 1955.

_____, "Monterey Park Development Honors Alamo." *Los Angeles Times*, October 9, 1960.

_____, "More Airs For 'Alamo'." *Variety*, April 14, 1960.

_____, "More than the formula." *The Guardian*, October 29, 1960.

_____, "Moscow Hurls Sharp Criticism at Hollywood." *Los Angeles Times*, May 13, 1947.

_____, "Movie Actors Play It Cool." *The Times-Picayune*, May 24, 1960.

_____, "Movie Cannon Made in City." *San Antonio Express and News*, October 16, 1960.

_____, "Movie Casts Briton as Texas Hero." *The Salt Lake Tribune*, October 6, 1959.

_____, "Movie Extra Calls to S.A. Unlikely." *San Antonio Light*, August 23, 1959.

_____, "Movie Extras May File Here During August." *Del Rio News-Herald*, July 23, 1959.

_____, "Movie Extras Sign." *Del Rio News-Herald*, August 10, 1959.

_____, "Movie Gathers Largest Herd of Old Longhorns." *Del Rio News-Herald*, November 9, 1959.

_____, "Movie Hit." *San Antonio News*, January 24, 1961.

_____, "Movie Men Organize to Combat "Isms."" *The Sunday Times-Signal*, February 6, 1944.

_____, "Movie Producer Seeks San Antonio Scenery." *San Antonio Express*, March 9, 1948.

_____, "Movie Star Slain At Brackettville." *The Galveston Daily News*, October 12, 1959.

_____, "Movie Tickets Winner Told In Classified." *Los Angeles Times*, October 30, 1960.

_____, "Movie World's Spotlight on Alamo Premiere." *San Antonio Express*, October 21, 1960.

_____, "Movie's Sound Man Says Country Noisy." *Covina Argus Citizen*, July 31, 1958.

_____, "Movieland Briefs." *Los Angeles Times*, July 23, 1952.

_____, *Los Angeles Times*, October 13, 1952.

_____, "Movies Play Second Fiddle to Baseball for Laraine Day." *Racine Journal*, January 9, 1954.

_____, "Mules May Miss Out In Movie Actor Roles." *San Antonio Express and News*, September 12, 1959.

_____, "Music critics to Attend 'Alamo' Paris Screening." *The Hollywood Reporter*, December 13, 1960.

_____, "Musical Battle Of 'Alamo' Ends On Sweet Note." *San Antonio Express and News*, September 24, 1960.

_____, "N.Y. Group Due in S.A." *San Antonio Light*, October 25, 1959.

_____, "N.Y. Reviewers Are Like-Minded." *Variety*, January 11, 1961.

_____, "Nag Says "Neigh" To Screen Chance." *The Abilene Reporter-News*, November 9, 1958.

_____, "Nationwide Premiere clippings Hail SA Opening of Alamo Epic." *The San Antonian*, December 8, 1960.

_____, "Near the Alamo." *Abilene Reporter-News*, November 10, 1959.

_____, "'Never' Happened Before? Trophy For Tune Unclaimed." *Variety*, April 18, 1961.

_____, "New 70mm Lens For 'Alamo' run." *Unknown newspaper*, October 27, 1960.

_____, "New Alamo Rises At Brackettville." *San Antonio News*, January 16, 1959.

_____, "New Red Head on Hollywood Lot." *The San Antonio Light*, April 5, 1936.

_____, "New Star Sought for Role of Ousted Bob Mitchum." *Oakland Tribune*, January 13, 1955.

_____, "New Thunderstorms Build Up As Nueces River Rises." *Big Spring Daily Herald*, June 18, 1958.

_____, "New Wayne, Holden Offer 6 Films at $750,000 Each." *The Salt Lake Tribune*, November 25, 1958.

_____, "New York Sound Track." *Variety*, March 1960.

_____, "Newsboys Return From Alamo Visit." *Odessa American*, November 22, 1959.

_____, "Newsreels On 'Alamo' But only For Ballyhoo." *Variety*, December 9, 1959.

_____, "Night Event Set For Film Visitors." *San Antonio Light*, October 9, 1960.

_____, "NLRB Shrugs AFM 'Alamo' Protest." *Variety*, January 4, 1960.

_____, "'North To Alaska' Record Holder." *The Hollywood Reporter*, December 13, 1960.

_____, "'North to Alaska' to Get Big 20th-Fox Campaign." *Box Office*, October 3, 1960.

_____, "Obituaries." *Variety*, November 7, 1960.

_____, "Obituaries." *Variety*, November 9, 1960.

_____, "O'Brien In 'The Alamo.'" *Variety*, October 1, 1959.

_____, "Observer Likes Taylor, Lemon In Oscar Race." *Palladium Times*, March 31, 1961.

_____, "Oh - Lookee! Echos Loudly." *San Antonio Light*, November 7, 1947.

_____, "Oil Deal Shows How Movie Stars Get Rich." *The Albuquerque Tribune*, November 1, 1958.

_____, "Oldest Son of John Wayne Talks of Duke's Legacy." *Countrywide TV Guide*, June 22, 1991.

_____, "On Deck with the Duke." *International Yachtsman*, Vol. III, 1978.

_____, "Oscar on All Films Booker's Tongues as Los Angeles Year-end a Pile-Up." *Variety*, December 13, 1961.

_____, "Oscarcast moves To Santa Monica." *Variety*, November 9, 1960.

_____, "Palace Showing 'Hondo' in 3-D Opening Thursday." *Muscatine Journal*, March 20, 1954.

_____, "Paramount Tries To Stop Holden." *The Inter Lake*, September 24, 1958.

_____, "Parlay Set on Program for film Awards." Los Angeles Times, November 20, 1960.

_____, "Pedro Armendariz Hurt on Movie Set." *The Albuquerque Tribune*, July 7, 1954.

_____, "Pedro Has little Love for Horses." *The Cedar Rapids Gazette*, August 29, 1954.

_____, "Personal Appearance Tour Set by Wayne for 'Alamo.'" *Box Office*, September 5, 1960.

_____, "Picked Marines Set For Forced March." *San Antonio Express and News*, October 16, 1960.

_____, "Picture Grosses." *Variety*, December 7, 1960.

_____, "Plans Made To Make Movie Near Juarez." *El Paso Herald-Post*, March 25, 1948.

_____, "Plead for 'Alamo' In Mexico City." *Variety*, November 30, 1960.

_____, "Pope Receives Wayne." *Variety*, November 25, 1960.

_____, "Premiere Donations Continue to come In." *The San Antonian*, August 4, 1960.

_____, "Premiere to Aid Relief." *Los Angeles Times*, March 5, 1942.

_____, "Premierettes Bow At 'Alamo' Opening." *Box Office*, November 7, 1960.

_____, "Preview at San Antonio Planned for 'The Alamo.'" *Box Office*, February, 15, 1960.

_____, "Princess Margaret Meets The Cowboys." *Evening Standard*, October 28, 1960.

_____, "Princess Margaret sees 'The Alamo.'" *The Guardian*, October 28, 1960.

_____, "Private Eyes Make Mess of Wayne Job." *Syracuse Herald Journal*, July 7, 1953.

_____, "Producer Dissolves Agreement." *The Independent*, October 24, 1951.

_____, "Producer Splits With Writer On Red Quiz." *San Antonio Express*, September 27, 1951.

_____, "Producers Hit With Street-Corner Film." *Los Angeles Times*, July 9, 1957.

_____, "Producers Nominate Their List of 16 Best." *Box Office*, February 27, 1961.

_____, "Public Barred At Examining Trial In Murder." *Clovis News-Journal*, October 16, 1959.

_____, "Publicity Hit By 2 Sisters." *Amarillo Globe-Times*, October 13, 1959.

_____, "Publicity That Sticks." *The Hollywood Reporter*, December 16, 1959.

_____, "Publisher Back Home to Explain About Blonde." *The Sun*, September 12, 1956.

_____, "Publisher Says Shooting an Accident." *The Portsmouth Herald*, September 7, 1956.

_____, "Quebec CPP Sponsors 'Alamo' Bow." *Box Office*, November 28, 1960.

_____, "Quick Hi-Goodby for S.A." *San Antonio Light*, October 9, 1951.

_____, "Quick Ones." *San Antonio Express*, October 10, 1951.

_____, "Quiz Scandals Prompt CBS To Deny Autonomy To Any Packager Of Shows." *The Hollywood Reporter*, October 19, 1959.

_____, "Quotes in the News.' *Pharos-Tribune*, July 12, 1960.

_____, "Rainfall Risk in Area May Be Reduced." *Del Rio News-Herald*, November 15, 1957.

_____, "Rains Drench Del Rio Area As Rio Grande, Devil's River Crest." *Del Rio News-Herald*, June 18, 1958.

_____, "Rangers Visit Set Of 'Alamo.'" *Corpus Christi Times*, December 22, 1959.

_____, "Real Pioneers Sign for Movie." *Del Rio News-Herald*, August 24, 1959.

_____, "'Rebel Without A Cause' Opens at Cove Thursday." *Weirton Daily Times*, December 5, 1955.

_____, "Record Airlift Arranged For 'The Alamo' Premiere." *The Hollywood Reporter*, October 21, 1960.

_____, "Remembering the Alamo." *Del-Rio News Herald*, May 15, 1998.

_____, "Rep Gives 'Rio Grande' Gala Preem Deep In The Heart Of –." *Variety*, November 2, 1950.

_____, "Reporters Barred From Actress' Death Hearing." *The Bakersfield Californian*, October 17, 1959.

_____, "Republic Terms Dancer." *Variety*, October 29, 1945.

_____, "Richard Boone Pays Tribute to John Wayne as Director." *Racine Sunday Bulletin*, November 8, 1959.

_____, "Richard Boone Will Do No More Westerns When Contract Expires." *Advocate*, November 16, 1959.

_____, "River Charms Visitors." *San Antonio Light*, October 21, 1960.

_____, "Roadshow Pix Stimulate Theatre Rehabilitation." *The Hollywood Reporter*, December 8, 1960.

_____, "Roadshow Treatment Is Being Given To Too Many Pictures, says Marcus." *Box Office*, November 21, 1960.

_____, "Role Sought for Audie Murphy in 'Alamo.'" *San Antonio Express*, December 25, 1958.

_____, "Royal Society of Music In Athens Hears Tiomkin." *The Hollywood Reporter*, November 4, 1960.

_____, "'Run Silent' Bought for Submarine Film." *The Los Angeles Times*, June 10, 1955.

_____, "Russell Birdwell Takes Over 'Alamo' Pub Slot." *Variety*, December 4, 1959.

_____, "S.A. All Out For Wayne." *San Antonio Light*, October 23, 1960.

_____, "S.A. Charros to Choose Queen." *San Antonio Light*, September 3, 1959.

_____, "S.A. Hails Premiere of 'Alamo.'" *San Antonio Light*, October 25, 1960.

_____, "S.A. Salutes John Wayne on Epic World Premiere." *San Antonio Light*, October 21, 1960.

_____, "S.A. Youths In 'Alamo' Roles." *San Antonio Light*, October 4, 1959.

_____, "Saddle-Up Time in Brackettville." *San Antonio Light*, September 13, 1959.

_____, "Safety for the Stuntman." *Unknown magazine*, unknown date.

_____, "'Sam Houston' Scripter." *Box Office*, July 25, 1960.

_____, "Sam Houston' To Follow 'Alamo' On Batjac Pix Slate." *Variety*, November 17, 1959.

_____, "San Antonio." *Box Office*, August 22, 1960.

_____, "San Antonio Making Plans to Play Alamo World Premiere to the Hilt." *Del Rio News-Herald*, August 7, 1960.

_____, "San Antonio Military Leaders Help Plan 'Alamo' Premiere." *Air Force Times*, September 21, 1960.

_____, "Scandal Publisher's Shooting Accident." *Press-Telegram*, September 6, 1956.

_____, "Shahan to Sign Premiere Bid." *Unidentified newspaper*, unidentified date.

_____, "She Found Work Fun at 'Alamo.'" *Unknown newspaper*, October 23, 1959.

_____, "Shooting Accident, says Confidential Publisher." *Los Angeles Times*, September 7, 1956.

_____, "Shooting of 'Alamo' in S.A. Unlikely." *San Antonio Light*, October 9, 1951.

_____, "Showdown about the Duke." *The News*, August 8, 1979.

_____, "Signoret Passes Up 'Cheri' Role." *Dallas Morning News*, May 5, 1960.

_____, "Silver Spurs Honers Go to Boone, Ward Bond." *Reno Evening Gazette*, June 5, 1961.

_____, "Simplify Cinerama Projection Plan." *Variety*, January 30, 1961.

_____, "Sinatra vs. Wayne Not a Blow Lands." *The Oklahoman*, May 15, 1960.

_____, "Six Top Stars Missed a Bet." *Racine Journal-Times*, July 7, 1954.

_____, "Slain Starlet Goes Home For Burial." *Oakland Tribune*, October 14, 1959.

_____, "Slam Bang John Wayne Divorce Case Come to Abrupt Ending." *The Abilene Reporter-News*, October 29, 1953.

_____, "Slayer of Actress Has A Record of Assaults." *Corpus Christi Times*, October 14, 1959.

_____, "Slayer Wants To See Love Victim Last time." *Del Rio News-Herald*, October 13, 1959.

_____, "Smith Awaiting Trip to Prison." *Del Rio News-Herald*, November 10, 1959.

_____, "Smith Defense To Call Wayne." *San Antonio Express*, October 15, 1959.

_____, "Smith Pleads Guilty for 30 Years." *Del Rio News-Herald*, November 9, 1959.

_____, "'Sons and Lovers' Voted Best Film By National Board." *The Hollywood Reporter*, December 23, 1960.

_____, "'Spartacus' Gets German Tax Favor." *The Hollywood Reporter*, December 7, 1960.

_____, "'Spartacus,' 'Sons,' 'Gantry' Lead Golden Globe Nominees." *The Hollywood Reporter*, February 9, 1961.

_____, "Special 'Alamo' Premiere To Honor Bob O'Donnell." *Box Office*, June 27, 1960.

_____, "Spectacular Premieres staged for 'The Alamo.'" *Box Office*, October 31, 1960.

_____, "Squeals for Avalon." *San Antonio Light*, October 23, 1960.

_____, "Stagecoach' at Tivoli Today." *The Laredo Times*, March 26, 1939.

_____, "Stagecoach in Toronto For Premiere of 'Alamo.'" *Box Office*, November 28, 1960.

_____, "Star, Producer Seek Texas Data." *San Antonio Light*, March 10, 1948.

_____, "Star Says Film Not Obscene." *Dallas Morning News*, October 4, 1959.

_____, "Star to Visit Base." *San Antonio Light*, August 13, 1959.

_____, "Starlet dies in suspected murderer's arms." *Daily Gleaner*, October 14, 1959.

_____, "Stars Make Brief visit To Fete." *San Antonio Express*, October 24, 1960.

_____, "Stars Stud Parade List." *San Antonio Light*, October 19, 1960.

_____, "STCC MEETS at Ft. Clark." *Del Rio News-Herald*, August 28, 1959.

907

_____, "Sternly-Enforced Screen criteria; Mexico Fights Certain 'Realism'; Scripters Tread Nervous Path." *Variety*, April 26, 1991.

_____, "Studio Briefs - Janet Leigh, Van Johnson reunited After Six Years." *Los Angeles Times*, April 14, 1953.

_____, "Studio Fires Bob Mitchum." *Idaho State Journal*, January 12, 1955.

_____, "Studio says Parks' future Depends on the Public." *The Salt Lake Tribune*, March 24, 1951.

_____, "Sues for $100,000." *Nevada State Journal*, April 27, 1938.

_____, "Sunday's Bullfight Cancelled." *Del Rio Herald*, November 2, 1959.

_____, "Surprising Replica of Texas Liberty Shrine in New Locale." *Del Rio News-Herald*, March 1, 1959.

_____, "Suspect Claims Blackout." *Pasadena Independent*, October 13, 1959.

_____, "Talk Divorce." *The Albuquerque Tribune*, March 6, 1959.

_____, "Tall Men in Film." *The Independent*, August 4, 1958.

_____, "'Tall Man' Stars Clark Gable." *The Newark Advocate*, October 22, 1955.

_____, "Team to Study Urban Renewal Area." *San Antonio Express and News*, October 25, 1959.

_____, "Teen Crowd Gathers to Salute Dick Clark." *Los Angeles Times*, September 1, 1959.

_____, "Tempers Rise at J. Wayne Divorce Trial." *The Yuma Daily Sun*, October 23, 1953.

_____, "Texan (&Mexican) Pride, Plus Disputed Research, Added To 'Alamo' Logistics." *Variety*, October 7, 1959.

_____, "Texans to Put Up Half Of 'Alamo' Financing." *Box Office*, April 27, 1959.

_____, "Texas, Hollywood." *Unknown newspaper*, January 31, 1960,

_____, "Texas Honors Wayne." *Box Office*, September 12, 1960.

_____, "Texas Horse Irritated By 'Deguello.'" *Lincoln Sunday Journal*, July 6, 1958.

_____, "Texas Ready to Wage New Battle of Alamo If Wayne Does Pic in Mex." *Variety*, July 4, 1951.

_____, "Texas Town Touted as Film Mecca." *Victoria Advocate*, December 14, 1980.

_____, "Texas University Honors James Grant For 'Alamo.'" *The Hollywood Reporter*, February 1, 1961.

_____, "'The Alamo' Banned By Mexico." *San Antonio Light*, March 19, 1961.

_____, "'The Alamo' colorcast set Tuesday." *Fairbanks Daily News-Miner*, September 8, 1973.

_____, "The Alamo is rising anew." *Texas Co-op Review*, June 1958.

_____, "The Alamo Offers For Your Consideration These Academy Contenders – ." *Variety*, December 27, 1960.

_____, "'The Alamo' On Stands." *Dallas Morning News*, October 2, 1960.

_____, "'The Alamo' To Be Cut." *New York Times*, November 3, 1960.

_____, "Theatre Group Plans To Fight Communism." *The New York Times*, October 10, 1950.

_____, "The Duke Conquers All at a Press Party." *Burlington Times-News*, April 8, 1975.

_____, "The 2nd Alamo." *Houston Post*, June 12, 1960.

_____, "The San Antonian Restaurant Assn. to Donate Alamo Breakfast." *The San Antonian*, October 20, 1960.

_____, "The Things They Say About San Antonio." *Unknown newspaper*, November 23, 1960.

_____, "Things Theatrical Here at Home." *Waterloo Evening Courier and Reporter*, December 14, 1915.

_____, "Thousands Attend Square Dance Event." *San Antonio Light*, October 23, 1960.

_____, "Three Blockbusters Scoring at Goldwyn." *The Hollywood Reporter*, May 9, 1960.

_____, "Three Cities Getting 'Alamo' Continuous-Run." *The Hollywood Reporter*, December 12, 1960.

_____, "Three Conductors Give Unusual Concert." *San Antonio Light*, October 23, 1960.

_____, "Three Days of Festivities For Premiere of 'Alamo.'" *Box Office*, September 12, 1960.

_____, "Three Shaggy Fellows." *Kerrville Times*, September 1, 1959.

_____, "Ticket Rush." *Los Angeles Times*, November 24, 1960.

_____, "Tiomkin 5-Country Tour." *The Hollywood Reporter*, December 5, 1960.

_____, "Tiomkin 'Alamo' Score Wins Western Award." *The Hollywood Reporter*, January 1961.

_____, "Tiomkin: "Cleffer Rates Percentage Of Film's Profits." *Variety*, December 7, 1960.

_____, "Tiomkin Feuding With Symphony." *Dallas Morning News*, September 9, 1960.

_____, "Tiomkin, Frankie Impressive." *San Antonio Light*, October 23, 1960.

_____, "Tiomkin Going On Junket For 'The Alamo' Abroad." *The Hollywood Reporter*, November 25, 1960.

_____, "Tiomkin Host In Paris." *The Hollywood Reporter*, November 1, 1960.

_____, "Tiomkin On 'Beat.'" *Variety*, October 4, 1960.

_____, "Tiomkin to Paris Meet." *The Hollywood Reporter*, December 13, 1960.

_____, "Tiomkin TV Salute." *The Hollywood Reporter*, January 20, 1961.

_____, "Tiomkin Will Baton Benefit In London." *Variety*, September 27, 1960.

_____, "Tiomkin Will Give 'The Alamo' An Air." *The Hollywood Reporter*, August 21, 1959.

_____, "Tiomkin's 'Perfectionism' Costs Houston Smyphony (sic) 3G in Rehearsal Time." *Variety*, September 14, 1960

_____, "Today in Utah." *The Ogden Standard-Examiner*, June 24, 1954.

_____, "Today's Cover: New Star." *Oakland Tribune*, March 15, 1959.

_____, "Todd-AO Cameras on 'Alamo' Battle." *Variety*, December 30, 1959.

_____, "Top Star Wayne Takes Third Latin Bride." *The Daily Courier*, November 13, 1954.

_____, "Trail Drivers Schedule Dance." *San Antonio Light*, August 25, 1959.

_____, "Trapper's Story of How He Shot Publisher of 'Confidential' in Jungle." *Los Angeles Times*, September 6, 1956.

_____, "Trim Running Time of 'Alamo'; Playoff Strategy Being Weighed." *Unknown newspaper*, November 9, 1960.

_____, "TV a Boon For Cleffers & Curse Too, Sez Tiomkin." *Variety*, June 3, 1964.

_____, "Twin City Show Slated." *The Daily Reporter*, January 24, 1950.

_____, "Two Young Movie Stars Are Injured." *New Castle News*, August 7, 1937.

_____, "Typical John Wayne Role: 'Man Who Lives by Code.'" *El Paso Herald Post*, July 24, 1965.

_____, "UA Grabs Off Most GoldenGlobes; Curtis, Hudson Tie For 'Favorite' Honor." *Variety*, March 17, 1961.

_____, "UA Reports Big 'Alamo' Overseas." *Variety*, January 12, 1961.

_____, "UA To Drop Hardticket Policy On 'The Alamo' Next Month." *Variety*, February 8, 1961.

_____, "UCLA Student Honored as Film Group Rips Reds." *Los Angeles Times*, March 23, 1951.

_____, "Uncle Ray's Corner." *The Altoona Mirror*, June 16, 1954.

_____, "United Artists Markets 20 New Plus 007 Reissues During 1965." *Variety*, February 10, 1965.

_____, "U.S. Culture Underrated, Czarist Russian Believes." *Press-Telegram*, August 28, 1960.

_____, "Use 'Alamo' Sketches." *Variety*, September 1, 1959.

_____, "Used to Be 'Remember Alamo': Now It'll Be 'Can't Forget It,' Thanks to Big ad Push." *Advertising Age*, October 17, 1960.

_____, "Use of Legion stadium Barred to Screen Guild." *Los Angeles Times*, June 15, 1944.

_____, "Vast Traffic Snarl Slows Oscar-Goers." *Variety*, April 18, 1961.

_____, "Veteran actor Ken Curtis, was 74." *The Intelligencer*, May 1, 1991.

_____, "Veteran actor of TV, movies dies after receiving his star." *The Stars and Stripes*, December 28, 1997.

_____, "Veteran Film Star To Unsaddle Here." *The Oklahoman*, November 4, 1960.

_____, "Veteran Stunt Man Is Killed During Filming of a Movie." *Montana Standard*, December 6, 1958.

_____, "'Village' Leads L.A. Boxoffice." *The Hollywood Reporter*, December 13, 1960.

_____, "Vivid Realism Achieved." *San Antonio News-Express*, October 21, 1959.

_____, "'Wagons Ho!' for Alamo Trail Riders Tuesday Kickoff C of C World Premiere Celebration." *The San Antonian*, October 13, 1960.

_____, "Want 'Alamo' Script." *The Daily Sun*, August 6, 1959.

_____, "Warner Reveals Plans to Do 22 More 3D Pictures." *Los Angeles Times*, May 29, 1953.

_____, "Warners to Enter Wide-Screen Field." *Los Angeles Times*, May 7, 1953.

_____, "Watch Cristal." *Pageant*, June, 1960.

_____, "Wayne Beats Drums for 'Alamo.'" *Dallas Morning News*, September 13, 1960.

_____, "Wayne Bets All on 'The Alamo.'" *Los Angeles Herald Express*, December 26, 1959.

_____, "Wayne Buys First Tickets to Premiere." *Los Angeles Times*, September 1, 1960.

_____, "Wayne Captivates Younger Set on Visit to Laughlin." *Del Rio News-Herald*, August 30, 1959.

_____, "Wayne Cutting Running Time Of 'The Alamo' By 30 Minutes." *The Hollywood Reporter*, November 4, 1960.

_____, "Wayne Declares Wife's Charges Will Cost Her." *Bakersfield Californian*, October 24, 1953.

_____, "Wayne Denies Two Set For 'The Alamo.'" *The Hollywood Reporter*, July 8, 1959.

_____, "Wayne Divorce Trial May End Peacefully." *The Anderson Herald*, October 22, 1953.

_____, "Wayne Ends 'Alamo' Tour." *Box Office*, October 3, 1960.

_____, "Wayne Hires Birdwell But United Artists Pay P.A.;$175,000 Fee reported." *Variety*, December 16, 1959.

_____, "Wayne Hits Trash." *San Antonio Light*, January 12, 1960.

_____, "Wayne Honored As 'Alamo' Release Set." *San Antonio Light*, April 11, 1960.

_____, "Wayne Hurt while Filming 'Blood Alley.'" *Pacific Stars & Stripes*, January 30, 1955.

_____, "Wayne Is Sued or $102,500." *The Capital Times*, January 19, 1960.

_____, "Wayne, MacMurray Buy Into 3 Hawaii Hotels." *Variety*, August 24, 1955.

_____, "Wayne Movie Off." *The Victoria Advocate*, August 9, 1959.

_____, "Wayne On Pontiac Spec For NBC; Plug For 'The Alamo.'" *The Hollywood Reporter*, September 14, 1959.

_____, "Wayne Plans Second Epic." *Los Angeles Times*, November 17, 1959.

_____, "Wayne Plays Triple Role in "Blood Alley."" *The Brownsville Herald*, January 25, 1955.

_____, "Wayne Receives Award." *Box Office*, October 3, 1960.

_____, "Wayne Replies." *Los Angeles Times*, March 22, 1961.

_____, "Wayne Speaks Out." *Tucson Daily Citizen*, May 20, 1961.

_____, "Wayne Takes On Texas." *San Antonio Light*, September 28, 1958.

_____, "Wayne to Give Bonham His Due." *Dallas Morning News*, September 7, 1959.

_____, "Wayne to Pay $1500 For Using 'Eyes' in 'Alamo.'" *San Antonio Express*, October 30, 1959.

_____, "Wayne Again Tries For Permit To Show 'Alamo' In Mexico Key Spots." *Variety*, October 19, 1960.

_____, "Wayne-Fellows Becomes Batjac." *Los Angeles Times*, May 26, 1954.

_____, "Wayne's Alamo Is Slated In 2 Parts." *The Odessa American*, July 29, 1973.

_____, "Wayne's Dream Comes True." *San Antonio Light*, October 21, 1960.

_____, "Wayne's Movie Debut Recorded As 1926." *Indiana Evening Gazette*, June 12, 1979.

_____, "Wayne's Movie Previewed." *The Denver Post*, August 6, 1960.

_____, "Wayne's Son His Top Fan." *The Oregonian*, January 22, 1960.

_____, "Wayne's world." *San Antonio Express-News*, March 24, 2004.

_____, "Waynes Jam Alamo." *Pacific Stars and Stripes*, January 30, 1960.

_____, "Webster 'Alamo' Lyrics For Tiomkin's Score." *Variety*, September 1, 1959.

_____, "Weiss Will Head 'Alamo' Planning." *San Antonio News*, June 22, 1960.

_____, "Weldy Admits He Shot 'Confidential' Owner." *Daily Mirror*, September 6, 1956.

_____, "Welk Adds New Champagne Girl." *The Paris News*, July 22, 1959.

_____, "Were star's cancer deaths a result of bomb blast?" *Hutchinson News*, August 6, 1979.

_____, "Western Veteran Now In 'Lancer.'" *The Odessa American*, November 9, 1968.

_____, "Wet weather for most of nation." *The Columbus Daily Telegram*, June 18, 1958.

_____, "What Goes On Here." *Unknown magazine*, unknown date.

_____, "What Price Glory - Star To Appear Here." *The Independent*, February 14, 1949.

_____, "Whitman Will Star in 'Hound Dog Man.'" *Los Angeles Times*, March 10, 1959.

_____, "Who's Where." *Variety*, August 3, 1959.

_____, *Variety*, September 11, 1959.

_____, *Variety*, November 24, 1959.

_____, *Variety*, November 23, 1959.

_____, "Widmark Is Wayne Co-Star In 'Alamo.'" *Variety*, July 02, 1959.

_____, "Widmark Picked to Play James Bowie, Man of Peace." *Cleveland Plain Dealer*, November 1, 1959.

_____, "Widmark to Play in 'Alamo.'" *San Antonio Express-News*, July 21, 1959.

_____, "Wife Angry as Harrison Comes Home." *The Independent*, September 10, 1956.

_____, "Wife's Career Draws Suit Vs. Herbert Yates." *Variety*, September 26, 1956.

_____, "'Wind' Tops '67 Reissue surge Of All Majors." *Variety*, March 1, 1967.

_____, "Winding 'Alamo' Airs." *Variety*, September 16, 1960.

_____, "Win Free Tickets To See John Wayne's 'The Alamo.'" *Chicago Tribune*, October 19, 1960.

_____, "Wills Denies He's Responsible For Chill Put On Him By Hedda." *Variety*, March 24, 1961.

_____, "Wills Recalls days As Mule-skinner." *The Oklahoman*, November 8, 1960.

_____, "Wire from Wayne." *San Antonio Express*, October 25, 1960.

_____, "Witnesses Bare Quarrel Before Shooting." *The News-Palladium*, September 6, 1956.

_____, "Woman Who Lost Her Face Now a Movie Actress Again." *The Racine Journal-Times*, March 14, 1941.

_____, "'Woodstock', 'Airport' Continue Brisk Pace at Broadway B.O." Variety, April 6, 1970.

_____, "Worden Said Cowboy at 70." *Florence Morning News*, October 30, 1971.

_____, "World Premiere of 'Alamo' in S.A. Oct. 24." *San Antonio Light*, June 7, 1960.
_____, "World Premiere Trail Ride Lined Up." *The San Antonian*, July 21, 1960.
_____, "Young Actress Slain." *The Press-Courier*, October 12, 1959.
Staff Writer – no title. "Advertisement for 'The Wings of Eagles,'" *The Altoona Mirror*, February 20, 1957.
_____, *Cue*, July 3, 1954.
_____, *Films in Review*, April 1959.
_____, *Hollywood Reporter*, February 3, 1939.
_____, April 5, 1940.
_____, July 1949.
_____, August 7, 1953.
_____, January 11, 1960.
_____, *The John Wayne Film Society Journal*, Autumn 2010.
_____, *Life*, September 8, 1952.
_____, *Los Angeles Daily News*, June 2, 1953.
_____, *Morning Herald, The*, May 16, 1953.
_____, *Motion Picture Herald*, June 1949.
_____, *New York Herald*, March 19, 1959.
_____, *The New York Post*, December 18, 1945.
_____, *The New York Times*, December 17, 1945.
_____, September 21, 1944.
_____, May 7, 1953.
_____, March 19, 1959.
_____, March 31, 1956.
_____, *Parade*, August 29, 1954.
_____, *People's Daily World*, October 17, 1947.
_____, *Register-News* Picture Page, *The Register News*, February 27, 1953.
_____, *Time*, February 14, 1944.
_____, March 6, 1944.
_____, March 3, 1952.
_____, September 1953.
_____, April 6, 1959
_____, February 1, 1960.
_____, August 8, 1969.
_____, *United Artists World*, November 4, 1960.
_____, *Variety*, December 1, 1948.
_____, November 8, 1950.
_____, January 1, 1953.
_____, March 18, 1953.
_____, February 18, 1959.
Starr, Jimmy. "'Alamo' Premiere Is Texas Triumph." *Los Angeles Herald & Express*, October 26, 1960.
Stockard, Mildred. "Along Show Row." *The Houston Chronicle*, November 22, 1959.
Storms, Gay. "Smith returns to the Alamo again." *Graham Leader*, March 9, 2010.
Straach, Kathryn. "Brackettville reaches for the stars." *The Dallas Morning News*, September 10, 2000.
Stubbs, Lucille. "Personally Yours." *The Seguin Gazette*, April 8, 1964.
Sullivan, Ed. "Little Old New York." *The Morning Herald*, April 3, 1957.
Swisher, Viola. "Just For Variety." *Variety*, November 5, 1951.
_____, "Just For Variety." *Variety*, November 27, 1951.
Tajiri, Larry. "The Spectator." *The Denver Post*, August 1, 1960.
_____, "Headed By Wayne." *The Denver Post*, August 5, 1960.
_____, "The Spectator." *The Denver Post*, August 8, 1960.
Tavernier, Claude. "The Fourth Dimension of Old Age." *Cinema*, June 1969.
Thomas, Bob. "In Hollywood." *Big Spring Herald*, June 13, 1948.
_____, "In Hollywood." *Indiana Evening Gazette*, August 2, 1948.
_____, "Hollywood 'Millionaires" No Longer Pile Up Money." *The Portsmouth Herald*, December 18, 1948.
_____, "Life in Hollywood." *San Mateo Times*, March 23, 1949.
_____, "Life in Hollywood." *San Mateo Times*, July 14, 1949.
_____, "Top Moneymaker Gives Secret Of Movie Success." *The Corsicana Daily Sun*, January 2, 1951.
_____, "John Wayne Split with RKO Certain." *The Winona Republican-Herald*, November 11, 1952.

_____, "Wayne Severs Connections With Republic." *The Bee*, November, 13, 1952.

_____, "New Film Unit Clicks." *The Stars and Stripes*, December 24, 1953.

_____, "Comes Long Way." *Corpus Christi Times*, May 31, 1954.

_____, "Hollywood Phenomena." *Chester Times*, June 2, 1954.

_____, "John Wayne Has Married Three Latins." *The Bee*, December 2, 1954.

_____, "Latin Loving Habit Called Coincidence." *El Paso Herald-Post*, December 2, 1954.

_____, "In-Between Age Fails To Buffalo Natalie Wood." *Hamilton Journal*, October 13, 1955.

_____, "Duke's Happy Taking a Back Seat." *Press-Telegram*, October 19, 1955.

_____, "In Hollywood." *Fitchburg Sentinel*, October 19, 1955.

_____, "John Wayne Plays Supporting Role to Son." *Press-Telegram*, October 19, 1955.

_____, "Screen Writer's Story Is Told." *Syracuse Herald Journal*, August 1, 1956.

_____, "40 Years In Films, 3 Oscars And He's Known For One Part." *The Robesonion*, July 2, 1958.

_____, "Dean Martin Downs Belief That He Doesn't Like To Work." *Burlington Daily Times-News*, July 4, 1958.

_____, "Wayne-Hawks May Put Story Film On Wide Screen." *The News*, July 7, 1958.

_____, "Movie Lots Come Alive With New Film Activity." *The Salisbury Times*, October 2, 1958.

_____, "Fabled Studio Tycoons Fading; Top Male stars Now Take Over." *Indiana Evening Gazette*, October 7, 1958.

_____, "'Golden Dozen' Stars Rule Hollywood Now." *Press-Telegram*, October 7, 1958.

_____, "'Brand Names' Sell Movies." *Press-Telegram*, October 8, 1958.

_____, "Big Reverse In Wages At Movie Town." *Biddeford Journal*, October 15, 1958.

_____, "Martin Rackin, John Lee Mahin-Pair Of Filmland Independents." *Indiana Evening Gazette*, October 15, 1958.

_____. "Rackin, Mahin Could Write New Chapter." *The Gettysburg Times*, October 16, 1958.

_____, "In Hollywood." *The Laurel Leader-Call*, October 30, 1958.

_____, "Tall Girl Rises Up to Success." *The Lowell Sun*, October 31, 1958.

_____, "Miss Gibson Looks Good in New Role." *The Lowell Sun*, December 12, 1958.

_____, "Hoot Gibson Back in Films." *Greeley Tribune*, December 27, 1958.

_____, "Angie Dickinson Latest in Line Of Low Voiced Leading Ladies." *Waterloo Daily Courier*, March 10, 1959.

_____, "After 30 Years, John Wayne Spends Own Cash On Movie." *The News-Palladium*, October 29, 1959.

_____, "Shakespearian Actor Pops Up On 'Alamo' Set." *Big Spring Herald*, November 2, 1959.

_____, "Production Loses." *Trenton Evening Times*, May 5, 1960.

_____, "'Paladin" Is Making Movie." *Wichita Falls Times*, March 14, 1961.

Thomas, Homer. "Bullfighter's Inspiring Story." *Oakland Tribune*, December 12, 1956.

Thomas, Lynn. "19 Cakes and 40 Kisses." *Motion Picture*, January, 1960.

Thompson, Paul. "Top of the News." *San Antonio Express and News*, August 27, 1960.

Thurber, James. "State Of Humor In States." *New York Times*, September 4, 1960.

Tianen, Dave. "Beach movies were all about pretty girls." *The Milwaukee Sentinel*, November 3, 2002.

Tinee, Mae. "'The Alamo' Is Standard for Heroics." *Chicago Tribune*, October 28, 1960.

Tolbert, Frank X. "Border Scoured For 'Dobe Makers." *Dallas Morning News*, January 23, 1958.

_____. "Mr. Wayne Knew Where to Drill." *Dallas Morning News*, March 26, 1958.

_____, "Happy Sees His Adobe Washed Away." *Dallas Morning News*, June 23, 1958.

_____, "They Haul Many A Load From Fair." *The Dallas Morning* News, October 19, 1958.

_____, "From 'Ben Hur' To Brackettville." *Dallas Morning News*, July 9, 1959.

_____, "John Wayne's 'Alamo' Brings Hum Of Business to Brackettville." *Dallas Morning News*, July 10, 1959.

_____, "'Hug-Me-Tights' Are Most Popular." *Dallas Morning News*, August 18, 1959.

_____, "When Chili Willie Came to Coahuila." *Dallas Morning News*, unknown date.

_____, "1960 Plot to Take Alamo Cannon!" *Dallas Morning News*, January 27, 1960.

_____, "'Alamo' Exciting But Too Lengthy." *Dallas Morning News*, November 3, 1960.

_____, "Tolbert's Texas." *Dallas Morning News*, September 11, 1971.

Torre, Mark. "John Wayne To Make TV Debut in 1960." *Oakland Tribune*, August 7, 1959.

Turan, Kenneth. "John Wayne Bigger than Life." *The Victoria Advocate*, September 5, 1976.

Wagner, Bill. "Chapel of Alamo May Be Used for Forthcoming film." *San Antonio Evening News*, October 8, 1951.

Walsh, Maurice. "The Quiet Man." *The Saturday Evening Post*, February 11, 1933.

Walther, Ed. "Filming of 'The Alamo' Brings Stardust to Brackettville." *Daily Texan*, November 24, 1959.

Ward, Madeline. "Point staffers Skated for Film." *The Kerrville Times*, September 3, 1959.

Wayne, John. "A Picture That Had to Be Made." 30th Anniversary issue. *The Hollywood Reporter.*

_____, Letter to publisher. *Saturday Evening Post*, August 1979.

_____, "It Happened Like This." *The American Weekly*, November 28, 1954.

_____, "After Long Wait, John Is Director." *The Lima News*, September 8, 1959.

Webb, Willis. "The View from Writer's Roost." www.gilmermirror.com.

Weiler, A. H. "Random Notes on the Film Scene." *The New York Times*, June 15, 1947.

Weissmann, Dr. Murray H. "Lost Alamo Movie Found." *The Alamo Journal*, June 1999.

West, Alice Pardoe. "Behind the Scenes." *The Ogden Standard-Examiner*, March 20, 1955.

West, Dick. "There Were No 'PR' Men At The Alamo." *Sandusky Register*, September 1, 1960.

Wightman, Mary. "J. Wayne Pays Visit To Capital." *Unknown newspaper*, August 1959.

Wilkerson, W.R. "Tradeviews." *Unknown newspaper*, unknown date.

Williams, Dick. "'Alamo' Timely and Spectacular Screen Drama." *Los Angeles Mirror*, October 27, 1960.

_____, "Oscar Entries Overlook Some Top Performers." *Los Angeles Mirror*, March 1, 1961.

_____, "Readers Riled by the Oscar Nominations." Los Angeles Mirror, March 7, 1961.

_____, "Dimitri Tiomkin Says Oscar Is Losing Dignity." Los Angeles Mirror News, March 31, 1961.

Williams, Joan. "Around Town." *Los Angeles Times*, March 19, 1961.

Williams, Wylie. "'The Alamo' Story Effectively Retold." *Citizen-News*, October 27, 1960.

Willson, Morris. "The Bexar Facts." *San Antonio Light*, December 9, 1957.

_____, "The Bexar Facts." *San Antonio Light*, September 4, 1959.

_____, "The Bexar Facts." *San Antonio Light*, July 18, 1962.

_____, "The Bexar Facts." *San Antonio Light*, August 10, 1960.

_____, "The Bexar Facts." *San Antonio Light*, October 24, 1960.

_____, "The Bexar Facts." *San Antonio Light*, October 25, 1960.

_____, "The Bexar Facts." *San Antonio Light*, November 2, 1960.

Wilson, Earl. "It Happened Last Night." *Unknown newspaper*, November 24, 1958.

_____, "Debbie's Red-Faced Over Theater Incident." *Wisconsin State Journal*, June 1, 1959.

_____, "Las Vegas Hot Show Business Town Now." *The Lowell Sun*, July 16, 1959.

_____, "Lie-Ma Is Not Pronounced Leema." *The Hammond Times*, September 24, 1959.

_____, "It Happened Last Night." *Uniontown Morning Herald*, November 30, 1960

Winchell, Walter. "Montagu, Royalty Linked." *The San Antonio Light*, February 11, 1954.

_____, *Kingpost News*, January 25, 1958.

_____, "On Broadway with Walter Winchell." *The Cedar Rapids Gazette*, May 12, 1959.

_____, "Walter Winchell…of Broadway." *Lebanon Daily News*, June 4, 1959.

_____, *Syracuse Herald Journal*, October 30, 1959.

_____, "On Broadway." *San Antonio Light*, June 1, 1961.

Winsten, Archer. "'The Alamo' Arrives at the Rivoli." *New York Post*, October 27, 1960.

Woolford, Sam. "'Man of Conquest' Get Premiere." *San Antonio Light*, April 7, 1939.

Words, Damien. "Last Man Standing." *The Sunday Herald*, July 7, 2002.

Wynne, Robert. "Remember 'The Alamo' on its 30th anniversary." *San Antonio Light*, January 21, 1990.

Yokley, Ann. "Behind The Scenes Filming 'The Alamo.'" *The Quarter Horse Journal*, March 1960.

Young, Colin. "The Old Dependables." *Film Quarterly*, Fall 1969.

Zeitlin, David. "They Die On Cue For Cash." *Life*, March 26, 1965.

Ziarko, Charles. "Luster Bayless and The United American Costume Company." *Classic Images*, January 26, 2009.

Zolotow, Maurice. "Moguls turned Duke Morrison into John Wayne." *Hutchinson News*, March 14, 1970.

Zoppi, Tony. "New 'Love Affair' For John Wayne." *Dallas Morning News*, September 2, 1957.

_____, "'War Between states' Wages in Louisiana." *Dallas Morning News*, December 1, 1958.

_____, "Ageless Satchmo Provides a Thrill." *Dallas Morning News*, December 14, 1959.

_____, " Les Elgart Due Christmas Night." *Dallas Morning News*, December 16, 1959.

_____, "Dallas After Dark." *Dallas Morning News*, September 13, 1960.

Scripts:
Patrick Ford; September 21, 1948

James Edward Grant;
Prior March, 1959
May 19, 1959
June 8, 1959
June 15, 1959
June 19, 1959
July 21, 1959
August 3. 1959
September 8, 1959
September 9, 1959
September 14, 1959
September 21, 1959
September 23, 1959
October 5, 1959

Miscellaneous:
Federal Bureau of Investigation file 65-796, Hollywood Ant-Nazi League, February 1, 1941.
Hearings Regarding the Communist Infiltration of Hollywood Motion Picture Industry, Committee on Un-American Activities, House of Representatives. 1951.
Master Shooting Schedule, August 21, 1959.
National Archives and Records Administration, Records of the Office of Strategic Services. John Wayne application for employment. August 2, 1943.

Music CD:
The Alamo, recorded by The City of Prague Philharmonic Orchestra and the Crouch End Festival Chorus. Prometheus Records.

Film/Video/DVD/Laser Disc:
Carl Foreman, Words Into Images, Portraits of American Screen writers. 1981 American Film Foundation documentary
Fort Apache, Warner Bros., Turner Entertainment. 2007.
The High and the Mighty. The Batjac story.
High Noon, The Making of High Noon, Artisan Home Entertainment.
The Horse Soldiers,
How Green Was My Valley, CBS/Fox 1990. Laser disc.
Huberman, Brian. "Spirit of the Alamo."
The Quiet Man, The Making of The Quiet Man, Artisan Home Entertainment. 2002.
Thank Ya, Thank Ya Kindly. Tribute to Hank Worden, 7th Voyage Productions, 2007.

Internet:
http://backinthebronx.com.
http://cis.csuohio.edu~somos/twizone.html.
http://library.duke.edu/digitalcollections/oaaaarchives_BBB5269/
*http://oldsite.the-signal.com/?module=displaystory&story_id=47156&format=html*
http://screened.blogspot.com/2009/03/nartyrs-of-the-alamo.html.
http://www.presidency.ucsb.edu/ws/?pid=25768.
www.aintitcool.com. Angie Dickinson interview.
www.archives.gov/legislature/guide/house/chapter-22.
www.au.af.mil
http://audiemurphy.com/awards.htm.
www.b-westerns.com/villan34.htm
www.b-westerns.com/hgibson1.htm
www.bighollywood.breitbart.com. Gagliasso, Dan. "John Wayne, World War II and the Draft."
www.bloggernews.net/127668. Barrett, Simon. "Jack Young Meets His Alamo Making The Alamo."
www.boxofficemojo.com
www.brentonpriestly.com."They ain't white. Not any more. They're Comanch': Race, Racism and the Fear of Miscegenation in The Searchers."

www.CNN.com

www.cobbles.com/simpp_archive/huac_alliance.htm

www.dvdjournal.com

www.dvdverdict.com/printer/davycrockettseries.php.

http://www.eicar-international.com/definition-shooting-schedule.html

www.emanuallevy.com

www.equidblog.com.

www.express.co.uk

www.filmscriptingwriting.com

www.frankieavalon.com

www.fsmitha.com

www.gilmermirror.com

www.glamourgirlsofthesilverscreen.com

www.homestead.com/alamovillagereunion/virginiashahan.

www.IMDb.com

www.johnwayne-thealamo.com

www.lavillita.com.

www.michaelbarrier.com/ Barrier, Michael. "Interviews Fess Parker."

www.moviefanfare.com/hollywood-sneak-previews/

www.musicgames4all.com

www.nbrmp.org/features/Waynewellman.cfm/ Gallager, John. "Between Action and Cut," August 2005

www.notablebiographies.com.

www.ohenryhouse.org.

http://www.perrymasontvshowbook.com/pmb_c705.htm

http://www.pbs.org/wgbh/amex/quizshow/filmmore/transcript/index.html

www.ralphedwards/legacy/shows

www.rollanet.org. Hondo review.

www.rogerebert.suntimes.com. Rio Bravo review.

www.rogerebert.suntimes.com. The Birth of a Nation review.

www.sag.org

www.tcm.com.

www.tufts.edu/alumni/tuftonia/archives/sp00/backpage.shtml

www.tucsonweekly.com/tucson/the-cinematic-life-of-black-jack-young/Content?oid+1068423

www.umich.edu/afrommu/standifer/hairston.html

www.utahgothic.com/movies/johnwayne.html

www.widescreenmovies.org

www.widescreenmuseum.com/VistaVision.

www.westernclippings.com/bobrose_stuntmen.shtml.

www.westernclippings.com/jackwilliams_stuntmen.shtml.

http://emanuellevy.com/review/green-berets-the-2/#sthash.blok8NTW.dpuf

# ENDNOTES

INTRODUCTION

1    Frank Thompson, *Alamo Movies*, 75-6.

2    Marshall Jones interview.

3    Donald Clark and Chris Andersen, *John Wayne's The Alamo-The Making of the Epic Film*, 73; San *Antonio Light*, September 11, 1959.

4    Brian Huberman, "John Wayne's *The Alamo*," MGM, 1992, Rudy Robbins interview; Michael Munn, *John Wayne, The Man Behind the Myth*, 210.

5    *San Antonio Light*, September 11, 1959.

6    *The Kerrville Times*, November 8, 1959; *Dallas Morning News*, September 3, 1960.

7    Richard Curilla to author, July 11, 2009; Ashley Ward to author, June 24, 2011.

8    Marshall Jones interview.

9    Jim Brewer to author, April 6, 2009.

10    Rudy Robbins interview.

11    Many of the technical aspects of filmmaking addressed in this book were provided in numerous conversations with and e-mail from Richard Curilla.

CHAPTER ONE – BEGINNINGS

12    *The Alamo,* United Artists press book, 1960.

13    *The Alamo.* Dir. John Wayne. United Artists, 1960. Film, Introduction; Norman Goldstein, *John Wayne, A Tribute,* 80.

14    John Wayne biography, IMDb.com.

15    *San Mateo Times,* August 31, 1953; Maurice Zolotow, *Shooting Star,* 63.

16    Carolyn McGivern, *John Wayne: A Giant Shadow,* 77.

17    Tony Macklin and Nick Pici, *Voices from the Set: The Film Heritage Interviews,* 137.

18    Zolotow, 135; Munn, 49; Dean Jennings, "John Wayne, The Woes of a Box-Office King," *The Saturday Evening Post,* October 27, 1962, 33.

19    *Shooting Star* draft and notes, MZP.

20    Zolotow, 129-30.

21    ibid., 129; John Boswell and Jay David, *Duke: The John Wayne Album,* 47.

22    Martin Scott, "John Wayne," *Cosmopolitan,* November, 1954, 26-32; "The Wages of Virtue," *Time,* March 3, 1952, 65-69; *The Hollywood Reporter,* February 3, 1939; Howard Kazanjian and Chris Enss, *The Young Duke: The Early Life of John Wayne,* 60; John Wayne to Dr. Cory SerVass, April 27, 1979, *Saturday Evening Post,* August, 1979, 4-5.

23    *The Hollywood Reporter,* April 5, 1940; *The New York Times,* May 11, 1940; Joel W. Finler, *Hollywood Movie Stills,* 78.

24    Pilar Wayne with Alex Thorleifson, *John Wayne: My Life With The Duke,* 39.

25    Tichi Wilkerson and Marcia Borie, *The Hollywood Reporter,* 127.

26    Munn, 82; "John Wayne as the Last Hero," *Time,* August 8, 1969, 54; Dan Ford, *Pappy: The Life of John Ford,* 182.

27    *Los Angeles Times,* April 2, 1942; ibid., May 20, 1942.

28    Munn, 89.

29    Zolotow, 160; "Me? A Flag Waver?", *John Wayne - Duke's Own Story,* 60; Munn, 82; Aissa Wayne, *John Wayne: My Father,* 45-46; *Los Angeles Times,* March 26, 1946; George Bishop, *John Wayne: The Actor, The Man,* 92.

30    *The Daily Gleaner,* October 31, 1979; *The News,* August 8, 1979; *Burlington Times-News,* April 8, 1975; John Wayne interview, JFP, Courtesy The Lilly Library, Indiana University, Bloomington, Indiana.

31    *The Chronicle-Telegram,* January 8, 1942; John Ford to John Wayne, January 12, 1942, JFP; Munn, 99-100.

32    Wilkerson and Borie, 164; David Hanna, "Bittersweet Success," *John Wayne The Legendary Duke,* 31.

33    John Ford interview, JFP; Ford, 182; Munn, 88.

34    John Wayne application to Office of Strategic Services, August 2, 1943, National Archives and Records Administration, Records of the Office of Strategic Services; Dan Gaglaisso, "John Wayne, World War II and the Draft," www.bighollywood.breitbart.com/dgagl......the-draft/; *Los Angeles Times Magazine*, September 21, 2003.

35    Todd McCarthy, *Howard Hawks: The Grey Fox of Hollywood*, 335; *Los Angeles Times*, March 5, 1942; Robert Fine, *The Hollywood Propaganda of World War II*, 202.

36    Clyde Jeavons, *A Pictorial History of War Films*, 135; *Miami Daily News-Record*, November 20, 1945; Munn, 84; *San Antonio Light*, May 1, 1945.

37    Ronald L. Davis, *Duke: The Life and Image of John Wayne*, 5-6, 68; Maureen O'Hara, *Tis Herself*, 289.

CHAPTER TWO – POLITICAL REFLECTIONS I

38    Macklin and Pici, 129.

39    Davis, 5.

40    William Leuchtenburg, "Hoover Faces the Crash," *American Heritage*, Summer 2009, 72; "Depression and War," www.fsmitha.com.

41    Larry Ceplair and Steven Englund, *The Inquisition in Hollywood*, 124-28.

42    "The Last Interview with John Wayne Before his Death," *John Wayne is Dead*, 18; Macklin and Pici, 129; Scott Eyman, "Looking Back: John Wayne talking to Scott Eyman," *Focus on Film*, Spring 1975, 17-23; *The Saturday Evening Post*, October 27, 1962, 32.

43    Rona Barrett, "Rona Remembers John Wayne," *Rona Barrett's Hollywood*, 1979, 62; "Interview with John Wayne," *Playboy*, May 1971, 82.

44    "Screen Actors Guild Mission Statement," www.sag.org.

45    Clayton R. Koppes and Gregory D. Black, *Hollywood Goes to War*, 11.

46    "Record of House Select Committees, 61ˢᵗ-79ᵗʰ Congresses (1910-1946), www.archives.gov/legislature/guide/house/chapter-22.

47    *Pictorial History of the Second World War*, 7; Wilkerson and Borie, 124.

48    Koppes and Black, 33; ibid., 36.

49    ibid., viii; ibid., 16.

50    ibid., 70; ibid., 144.

51    Herb Fagen, *Duke: We're Glad We Knew You*, xxiii ; " Motion Picture Alliance for the Preservation of American Ideals- Statement of Principles," www.cobbles.com/simpp_archives/huac_alliance.htm.

52    David Hanna, "A Voice from the Right," *John Wayne, The Legendary Duke*, 37-38.

53    John Wayne, "It Happened Like This," *The American Weekly*, November 28, 1954, 12, 14.

54    *The Sunday Times-Signal*, February 6, 1944; *Los Angeles Times*, February 5, 1944.

55    *The San Antonio Light*, February 8, 1944; *Los Angeles Times*, June 15, 1944; *Oakland Tribune*, February 15, 1944.

56    *San Antonio Light*, June 29, 1944.

57    Zolotow, 237; *Unknown* newspaper, March 13, 1944.

58    *New York Times*, September 21, 1944; Zolotow, 239; *Playboy*, 88; *Time*, August 8, 1969, 55.

59    John Wayne, *My Kingdom for a Horse*, Proposed autobiography, MZP; *Playboy*, 88.

60    Wilkerson and Borie, 34; Thomas Morgan, "God and Man in Hollywood," *Esquire*, May, 1962, 74-75, 123-125; Goldstein, 113.

## CHAPTER THREE – YORK, BRITTLES AND YORKE

61    *Fort Apache*. Dir. John Ford. RKO Radio Pictures, 1948. Film, Capt. Kirby York sentiments.

62    *Ironwood Daily Globe*, February 14, 1942.

63    *New York Times*, December 17, 1945; *The New York Post*, December 18, 1945; Munn, 101; *Variety*, September 20, 1956.

64    Munn, 101, ibid., 109.

65    Randy Roberts and James S. Olson, *John Wayne American*, 282; Pilar Wayne, 48.

66    Munn,109; T. F. James, "The Man who Talked Back," *Cosmopolitan*, August, 1960, 63.

67    *Shooting Star* draft, MZP.

68    *Cosmopolitan*, 60; Paul Lansen interview.

69    *Cosmopolitan*, November, 1954, 26-32.

70    *The Lowell Sun*, December 28, 1945; Fred Landesman, *The John Wayne Filmography*, 18; Munn, 109; *Cosmopolitan*, August, 1960, 63.

71    *The Lima News*, April 19, 1946.

72    "On Deck with the Duke," *International Yachtsman*, Vol. III, 1978, 24.

73    McCarthy, 408-9; Fagen, 69; Arnold Hano, "John Wayne – His Greatest Battle," *People*, August 24, 1966, 4-7.

74    Landesman, 272-3; Scott Breivold, *Howard Hawks Interviews*, 64.

75    McCarthy, 445; Breivold, 67; Munn, 117; "Wayne Confesses," *Photoplay*, November, 1973, 16, 24, 54; John Brooker, *The Life and Times of John Wayne*, 36.

76    McCarthy, 418.

77    O'Hara, 115; Munn, 113.

78    Joseph McBride, *Searching for John Ford*, 441; Ford, 213.

79    John Ford interview, JFP; Ronald L. Davis, *John Ford: Hollywood's Old Master*, 203; ibid., 206.

80    McBride, 446.

81     ibid.

82     Munn, 115; McGivern, 173; Peter Cowie, *John Ford and the American West,* 96.

83     *Los Angeles Times,* July 27, 1948; Davis, *Ford,* 210-11; Scott Eyman, *Print the Legend: The Life and Times of John Ford,* 337.

84     *How Green Was My Valley.* Dir. John Ford. Twentieth Century Fox, 1941. Laser disc, 1990. Liner notes.

85     John Ford interview, JFP; McBride, 495.

86     *The New York Times,* November 7, 1948; ibid., June 25, 1948; Ford, 218.

87     Munn, 116; Davis, *Duke,* 134-5.

88     Harry Carey Jr. interview, JFP.

89     *The New York Times,* March 4, 1949; *Variety,* December 1, 1948; Davis, *Duke,* 138; Munn, 118; *The Los Angeles Times,* July 27, 1948.

90     Andrew Sinclair, *John Ford: A Biography,* 145-6; Eyman, *Print the Legend,* 139-140; Ford, 227-8.

91     Claude Tavernier, "The Fourth Dimension of Old Age," *Cinema,* June 1969; McBride, 460-61; Ford, 229; Davis, *Ford,* 225; Harry Carey Jr., *Company of Heroes,* 67.

92     Jon Tuska, *The Filming of the West,* 516.

93     Davis, *Ford,* 223; ibid., 230; Bill Libby, "The Old Wrangler Rides Again," *Cosmopolitan,* March 1964, 12-21.

94     McNee, *In the Footsteps of The Quiet Man,* 48; "John Wayne's Co-Stars–Victor McLaglen," *The John Wayne Film Society Journal,* Spring, 2008, 10-12; Carey Jr., 56; ibid., 63-64; Eyman, *Print the Legend,* 592, note 155; McGivern, 183.

95     Fagan, 74; Landesman, 325; *Hollywood Reporter,* July 1949; *Motion Picture Herald,* June 1949; Munn, 121; Zolotow, 235; Jack Kroll, "John Wayne: End as a Man," *Newsweek,* June 5, 1979, 76-79.

96     Zolotow, 252.

97     Chuck Roberson, with Bodie Thoene, *The Fall Guy,* 36-7.

98     Davis, *Duke,* 145; Landesman, 304-5.

99     Roberts and Olson, 319 ; Davis, *Duke,* 145; Zolotow, 145.

100    *The Washington Post,* February 23, 2005.

101    Zolotow, 235; Pilar Wayne, 56; McGivern, 199; ibid., 234; Davis, *Duke,* 147; Munn, 129; Fagen, 84-5; Lawrence Suid, *Guts and Glory: Great American War Movies,* 116.

102    "Glory for John," *Screenland,* June, 1950, 44.

103    Ford, 232; McBride, 501-2.

104    O'Hara, 137; Munn, 132.

105    Internal communication Yates, May 1, 1950, JFP; Telegram Herb Yates to John Ford, May 26, 1950; JFP, Herbert Yates to John Ford, May 3, 1950, JFP.

106 Davis, *Ford*, 240; Telegram John Ford to Herbert Yates, October 12, 1950, JFP.

107 Carey Jr., 56; ibid., 117.

108 *Life*, January, 1971.

109 Ken Curtis interview, JFP.

110 Carey Jr., 120-121; O'Hara, 3.

111 Frank Miller, *Leading Couples*, 195-98; O'Hara, 261.

112 *Variety*, November 8, 1950.

CHAPTER FOUR – POLITICAL REFLECTIONS II

113 *Los Angeles Times*, October 23, 1960; *Burlington Daily Times-News*, November 3, 1959.

114 Munn, 16; Davis, *Ford*, 220; Clark and Andersen, 3-4; ibid., 7.

115 Clark and Andersen, 9; *Cosmopolitan*, August, 1960, 63; *San Antonio Light*, November 7, 1947.

116 *San Antonio Light*, March 10 and 11, 1948.

117 *San Antonio Express*, March 9, 1948; *Los Angeles Times*, March 16, 1948; *Manitowoc Herald-Times*, March 8, 1948; *Bluefield Daily Telegram*, April 6, 1948.

118 *Kerrville Mountain Sun*, March 11, 1948; *El Paso Herald-Post*, March 25, 1948.

119 Clark and Andersen, 10; *Variety*, March 15, 1948; Patrick Ford letter, June 30, 1980, Patrick Ford Collection, L. Tom Perry Special Collections, Harold B. Lee Library, Brigham Young University, Provo, Utah.

120 ibid.; *The Alamo*, Original Screenplay Outline, September 21, 1948, Patrick Ford Collection, BYU; *Middletown Times Herald*, November 19, 1948; *Del Rio News-Herald*, September 15, 1948.

121 *The Charleston Gazette*, January 14, 1949; *Kingsport Times*, February 1, 1949.

122 *The Independent*, February 14, 1949; *San Mateo Times*, March 23, 1949; *Chicago Tribune*, February, 1949.

123 *Los Angeles Times*, April 20, 1949; *The Raleigh Register*, April 3, 1949.

124 *Los Angeles Times*, May 11, 1947.

125 *Los Angeles Times*, January 28, 1950; ibid., August 8, 1950; ibid., January 22, 1951; *Dallas News*, February 26, 1950; *The Daily Reporter*, January 24, 1950.

126 Zolotow, 275; Munn, 130-131; Davis, *Duke*, 148.

127 C. Courtney Joyner and Steve Kiefer, "Janet Leigh, Every Cowboy's Sweetheart," *Wildest Westerns, A Look Back*, 76-80; George Carpozi Jr., *The John Wayne Story*, 112.

128 Munn, 131; *The Independent*, November 19, 1953; *Corpus Christi Times*, March 10, 1955; *Variety*, November 12, 1956.

129 Zolotow, 276; Scott Eyman, *Five American Cinematographers*, 128.

130 John Lewis Gaddis, *The Cold War: A New History*, 13-23; John Lewis Gaddis, *Russia, The Soviet Union and the United States*, 156.

131  John Wayne interview, JFP.

132  *Los Angeles Times*, March 10, 1947; Kenneth Lloyd Billingsley, *Hollywood Party*, 112.

133  *Los Angeles Times*, May 13, 1947.

134  ibid.

135  Billingsley,176; Resolution dated October 16, 1947. Republican and Democratic Joint Committee of Hollywood, JFP.

136  Telegram from Special Committee of the Screen, Directors Guild to Lewis Milestone, October 20, 1947, JFP.

137  Motion Picture Chapter, Military Order of the Purple Heart resolution (undated), JFP.

138  Billingsley, 178-79.

139  ibid., 3; *People's Daily World*, October 17, 1947.

140  *Los Angeles Times*, October 25, 1947.

141  *The New York Times Magazine*, March 25, 1973.

142  Zolotow, 241.

143  Billingsley, 116.

144  *The Billings Gazette*, March 23, 1949.

145  Linda Alexander, *Reluctant Witness; Robert Taylor, Hollywood and Communism,* 221-230; Stephen Cox, "The Big Man of American Politics," *Liberty*, 43-46; *Los Angeles Times*, March 24, 1949.

146  Munn, 96-99; ibid., 125-128.

147  Zolotow, 236-242; Munn, 125.

148  *Shooting Star* draft, MZP.

149  Roberts and Olson, 337; *Playboy*, 88; *Los Angeles Herald-Examiner*, November 21, 1972.

150  Billingsley, 218.

151  Hearings Regarding the Communist Infiltration of Hollywood Motion Picture Industry, Committee on Un-American Activities, House of Representatives, 1951. 78-111.

152  *The Salt Lake Tribune*, March 24, 1951; ibid., March 21, 1951; *The Daily Review*, March 22, 1951.

153  *The Salt Lake Tribune,* March 24, 1951; ibid., March 22, 1951; *The Independent*, March 23, 1951.

154  Roberts and Olson, 346; John Wayne interview, JFP.

155  Davis, *Duke*, 143; *Saturday Evening Post*, October 27, 1962, 28-33.

156  *The Salt Lake Tribune*, March 27, 1951.

157  *Los Angeles Times*, March 23, 1951.

158  John Wayne interview, JFP.

159  *Los Angeles Times*, March 30, 1951; *The Salt Lake Tribune*, March 21, 1951.

160  Motion Picture Alliance for the Preservation of American Ideals resolution, undated, JFP.

161  *Los Angeles Times*, August 14, 1952; Howard Hughes, *Stagecoach to Tombstone*, 36.

162  *Carl Foreman: Words Into Images, Portraits of American Screenwriters*. Dir. Terry Sanders and Freida Lee Mock. American Film Foundation, 1981. Documentary.

163  *High Noon*. Dir. Fred Zinnemann. United Artists, 1952. DVD, Republic Entertainment, 2002. "The Making of High Noon."; *Los Angeles Times*, August 5, 1952.

164  *The Independent*, October 24, 1951; *Los Angeles Times*, February 6, 1952.

165  *San Antonio Express*, September 27, 1951; *Los Angeles Times*, November 2, 1951; *Nevada State Journal*, November 3, 1951.

166  *Playboy*, 90; Zolotow, 245.

167  Carl Forman, "On the Wayne," *Punch*, August 14, 1974, 240-242; Donald Shepherd, and Robert Slatzer, *Duke: The Life and Times of John Wayne*, 243.

168  *High Noon*. Dir. Fred Zinnemann. United Artists, 1952. DVD, Artisan Home Entertainment, 2002. "The Making of High Noon."

169  Munn, 124; Pilar Wayne, 55-56.

170  Kazanjian and Enss, 143; ibid., 149; *The Independent*, February 26, 1951; *Time*, August 8, 1969. 55-56.

CHAPTER FIVE – THE NOT SO QUITE MAN

171  *The Evening Independent*, September 7, 1951; *The New York Times*, August 5, 1951.

172  *Cedar Rapids Gazette*, February 19, 1950.

173  Roberts and Olson, 354.

174  *Los Angeles Times*, January 10, 1951; *The New York Times*, February 3, 1951; Landesman, 248; Munn, 135.

175  Munn, 112; Roberts and Olson, 354; Fagen, 194.

176  Maurice Walsh, "The Quiet Man," *The Saturday Evening Post*, February 11, 1933.

177  McBride, 227; McNee, 17; *Los Angeles Times*, May 28, 1937; ibid., July 10, 1937; *The New York Times*, June 1, 1937.

178  O'Hara, 102; ibid.,124; Davis, *Duke*, 159.

179  *Los Angeles Times*, March 1, 1945.

180  McNee, 26-30; Davis, *Ford*, 203; ibid., 247; *The New York Times*, June 15, 1947.

181  Ford, 210-212; *The New York Times*, December 26, 1947; McBride, 423.

182  McNee, 29; *The Big Spring Herald*, June 13, 1948; *The Portsmouth Herald*, June 23, 1948; *Indiana Evening Gazette*, August 2, 1948; *The Wisconsin State Journal*, August 30, 1948; *Los Angeles Times*, August 16, 1948.

183 McNee, 30.

184 *Los Angeles Times*, May 30, 1949; *San Mateo Times*, July 14, 1949.

185 Ford, 232; Richard M. Hurst, *Republic Studios: Between Poverty Row and the Majors*, 5–7; ibid., 15.

186 Ford, 232; John Ford interview, JFP; *Los Angeles Times*, January 6, 1950.

187 McNee, 31.

188 *Los Angeles Times*, August 24, 1950; ibid., November 2, 1950; ibid., December 12, 1950; ibid., March 3, 1951; ibid., February 17, 1951; ibid., February 21, 1951; O'Hara, 143; Des MacHale, *The Complete Guide to The Quiet Man*, 35-36.

189 *The Rhinelander Daily News*, April 11, 1951; McNee, 32; *Los Angeles Times*, April 16, 1951; Clark and Andersen, 18; *Cosmopolitan*, August, 1960, 26-32.

190 McNee, 32-33; O'Hara, 156; *The Irish Times*, June 7, 1951.

191 *The Corsicana Daily Sun*, January, 2, 1951; *Los Angeles Times*, June 4, 1951; *The Irish Times*, July 11, 1951; *Time*, March 3, 1952, 65-69; *The Quiet Man*, Dir. John Ford. Republic, 1952. DVD, Artisan Home Entertainment, 2002. "The Making of The Quiet Man."

192 *Los Angeles Times*, June 26, 1951; *The Quiet Man*, "The Making of The Quiet Man."

193 *Greeley Tribune*, January 19, 1954.

194 Gerald Perry, *John Ford Interviews*, 157-8.

195 McNee, 63-64; ibid., 67; ibid., 125; MacHale, 32; Peary, 119.

196 McNee, 126.

197 *The New York Times*, August 5, 1951; O'Hara, 164; McNee, 114.

198 Munn, 139.

199 *Los Angeles Times*, March 4, 1951; Davis, *Duke*, 159-160; Munn, 139.

200 O'Hara, 166.

201 Fagen, 61; *The Quiet Man*, "The Making of The Quiet Man."

202 Davis, *Duke*, 161; Munn, 138; O'Hara, 168.

203 Zolotow, 111-112; McNee, 103; ibid., 105; Munn, 141.

204 Sam Sherman, "The Duke of Action," *Screen Thrills Illustrated*, September, 1962, 50-57; Brooker, 16; *The Coshocton*, August 10, 1958.

205 McNee, 103.

206 *The Evening Independent*, September 7, 1951.

207 O'Hara, 153; Davis, *Duke*, 163; Munn, 141; O'Hara, 170; www.CNN.com/transcripts Larry King interview, January 2, 2003; "What Hollywood legend Maureen O'Hara doesn't dare say about 'The Duke' John Wayne," www.nationalenquirer.com/john_wayne_dirty-Secret_maureen_ohara_john_ford.

208  Munn, 142; McNee, 127.

209  ibid., 129; *Life*, September 8, 1952; McGivern, 218; Shepherd and Slatzer, 245; *Punch*, August 14, 1974, 240-242.

210  Pilar Wayne, 58; *Los Angeles Times*, August 9, 1951; Munn, 116.

211  McGivern, 75.

CHAPTER SIX – FALSE STARTS

212  Davis, *Duke*, 164.

213  *Los Angeles Times*, September 27, 1951; *Dallas News*, July 10, 1951; R.J. O'Donnell to Herbert Yates, June 21, 1951.

214  *San Antonio Express*, July 18, 1951; ibid., August 5, 1951; *Variety*, July 4, 1951.

215  *San Antonio Light*, October 5, 1951.

216  *San Antonio Evening News*, October 8, 1951; *San Antonio Light*, October 9, 1951.

217  *San Antonio Light*, October 9, 1951; *The New York Times*, October 10, 1951; *Austin American*, October 9, 1951.

218  *Record Chronicle*, August 26, 1951; *Variety*, November 2, 1950.

219  Michael Goldman, *John Wayne: The Genuine Article*, 75-76.

220  *Los Angeles Times*, February 21, 1951; "Paul Fix," www.b-westerns.com/villan34.htm.

221  Mike Tomkies, *Duke: The Story of John Wayne*, 66.

222  *The Winona Republican-Herald*, November 11, 1952; *San Antonio Express*, October 10, 1951.

223  "Quick Reviews: The High and the Mighty," www.dvdjournal.com; *The High and the Mighty*. Dir. William Wellman. Warner Bros., 1954. Film. DVD, Paramount Home Entertainment, 2005, "The Batjac Story."

224  C. Courtney Joyner, "Andrew McLaglen, Director," *Wildest Westerns*, No.5, 30-40.

225  Fagen, 88-90; ibid., 92; Davis, *Duke*, 155-57.

226  *San Mateo Times*, August 31, 1953; *Shooting Star* draft, MZP.

227  John Hayes, "The Making of The Alamo," www.widescreenmovies.org, November 6, 2009; Carolyn McGivern, *The Lost Films of John Wayne*, 11-12; *The New York Times*, March 6, 1952; *Los Angeles Times*, March 6, 1952; English, Richard. "How We Almost Lost Hawaii to the Reds," *Saturday Evening Post*, February 2, 1952, 17-19, 50, 54; "Big Jim McLain Overview," www.tcm.com/tcmdb/title.jsp?stid=68678&category=Notes.

228  *Los Angeles Times*, August 30, 1952; Emanual Levy, "Big Jim McLain-Anti-communism Propaganda,"www.emanuallevy.com; Luis Reyes, "The Duke in Hawaii," *Hawaii Magazine*, November/December 2001, 42-46; James Arness, *James Arness: An Autobiography*, 126-7.

229  Roberts and Olson, 369; Munn, 142; *The Bee*, November 13, 1952.

230  Tomkies, 68-9; Roberts and Olson, 369-370; *The Bee*, November 13, 1952; *Variety*, October 30, 1952.

231   *Variety*, December 18, 1952; ibid., December 22, 1952.

232   *Albuquerque Journal*, November 21, 1952; *The Inter Lake*, December 7, 1952; *Variety*, November 17, 1952.

233   Goldman, 66.

234   Eyman, *Print the Legend*, 414-5.

235   ibid., 414.

236   ibid.; *Variety*, December 5, 1952.

237   Telegram John Ford to Michael Killanin, July 5, 1954, JFP; Eyman, *Print the Legend*, 414; McBride, 527.

238   Ford, 250; Eyman, *Print the Legend*, 409.

239   Zolotow, 283; Noah Dietrich, *Howard: The Amazing Mr. Hughes*, 435; *Los Angeles Times*, August 11, 1952.

240   Pilar Wayne, 62-3.

241   *The Bee*, December 2, 1954; McGivern, *John Wayne*, 249; *Sunday Herald*, July 28, 1953; *Daily Herald*, July 15, 1954; *The Post-Register*, January 25, 1954.

242   *The News-Palladium*, September 6, 1956.

243   *Los Angeles Times*, September 6, 1956; ibid., September 7, 1956; *Lebanon Daily News*, September 6, 1956; *Press-Telegram*, September 6, 1956; *The Portsmouth Herald*, September 7, 1956; *Times-Mirror*, September 7, 1956; *The Sun*, September 12, 1956; *Independent*, September 10, 1956.

244   *The Lowell Sun*, August 11, 1952; *Los Angeles Times*, July 23, 1952; ibid., October 13, 1952; *The New York Times*, August 14, 1952; Davis, *Duke*, 168.

245   Shepherd and Slatzer, 208.

246   Zolotow, 288.

247   Davis, *Duke*, 169; *Variety*, March 18, 1953; *The New York Times*, May 7, 1953; Munn, 149; *The Morning Herald*, May 16, 1953; *Los Angeles Times*, November 27, 1952.

248   *Los Angeles Times*, March 13, 1953; Frank T. Thompson, *William A. Wellman*, 242; *Los Angeles Times*, April, 1951; *Daily Variety*, December, 1952.

249   Carolyn McGivern, *The Lost Films of John Wayne*, 37-39.

250   ibid., 33; ibid., 42; ibid., 44.

251   Davis, *Duke*, 170; Munn, 150; Eyman, *Focus on Film*, Spring, 1975, 17-23.

252   "Cinema: The New Pictures," *Time*, September 28, 1953; *Hollywood Reporter*, August 7, 1953; *Los Angeles Examiner*, April 9, 1953.

253   Davis, *Duke*, 171; Goldman, 67.

254   *Los Angeles Times*, April 14, 1953.

255   Vincent Di Fate, "3-D Cinema: Yesterday, Today, and Tomorrow!, part 2," *Filmfax plus*, Summer 2009.

256  *Los Angeles Times*, May 29, 1953.

257  *Countywide TV Guide*, June 22, 1991.

258  *The Independent*, July 17, 1953; *The Lima News*, March 30, 1954.

259  *Countrywide TV Guide*, June 22, 1991; "*John Wayne: To Each his Own*," Warner Bros. press release. No date.

260  C. Courtney Joyner, Ed G. Lousararian and Joseph, "Glenn Ford," Wildest Westerns, No. 7, 33-48; *Los Angeles Times*, May 7, 1953.

261  *Los Angeles Times*, April 6, 1953; Katharine Hepburn, "*Me*," 260.

262  Munn, 151; *El Paso Herald Post*, November 24, 1953; Pilar Wayne, 96-7; McGivern, *John Wayne*, 253.

263  Davis, *Duke*, 175.

264  Munn, 153.

265  McBride, 529; Tag Gallagher, *John Ford: The Man and his Films*, 535; Davis, *Ford*, 264.

266  Davis, *Duke*, 173.

267  Pilar Wayne, 94.

268  Tomkies, 72.

269  *Muscatine Journal*, March 20, 1954.

270  Roberts and Olson, 406.

271  *Los Angeles Times*, August 25, 1953; *Waterloo Daily Courier*, December 4, 1953.

CHAPTER SEVEN – "AN RKO *RADIOACTIVE* PICTURE"

272  Jack Williams interview.

273  Roberts and Olson, 237.

274  *The Abilene Reporter-News*, October 29, 1953; *Los Angeles Daily News*, June 2, 1953; *The Post Register*, January 4, 1954.

275  *Syracuse Herald Journal*, July 7, 1953; McGivern, *Lost Films*,12.

276  *The Lethbridge Herald*, October 8, 1953; *The Anderson Herald*, October 22, 1953; *The Altoona Mirror*, November 11, 1953.

277  *Long Beach Independent*, October 29, 1953.

278  *The Yuma Daily Sun*, October 23, 1953; *Los Angeles Times*, October 21. 1953.

279  *Bakersfield Californian*, October 24, 1953.

280  *San Antonio Light*, July 31, 1953; *Long Beach Independent*, October 29, 1953; *The Daily Review*, October 20, 1953; McGivern, *Lost Films*,12.

281  *Chronicle-Telegram*, October 24, 1953.

282   *The Avalanche Journal*, July 18, 1954; *The Daily Review*, February 19, 1954; *The Progress Index*,
      June 8, 1954; *The News*, August 12, 1954.

283   *The Stars and Stripes*, December 24, 1953.

284   *Statesville Daily Record*, January 2, 1954.

285   McGivern, *Lost Films*, 58; *The High and the Mighty*. Dir. William Wellman. Warner Bros., 1954.
      Film, Character descriptions from movie poster.

286   Thompson, *Wellman*, 244-5.

287   *Charleston Daily Mail*, July 8, 1954.

288   *Los Angeles Times*, August 11, 1953; December 6, 1953; *Pottstown Mercury*, June 20, 1953.

289   *Racine Journal-Times*, July 7, 1954; *The Altoona Mirror*, July 27, 1953; ibid.; October 14, 1953.

290   Lilley, "Walter Reed," *Campfire Conversations Complete*, 158.

291   *The Daily News*, November 18, 1953; *The Daily Review*, January 21, 1954; *The Cedar Rapids
      Gazette*, November 11, 1955; *Los Angeles Times*, July 20, 1953; ibid., April 11, 1954.

292   *The Avalanche*, April 11, 1954.

293   *Charleston Daily Mail*, July 8, 1954; John Gallagher, "Between Action and Cut", August 2005,
      www.nbrmp.org/features/Waynewellman.cfm.

294   *San Antonio Express*, January 25, 1954; McGivern, *Lost Films*, 83; Thompson, *Wellman*, 245.

295   *Racine Journal*, January 9, 1954.

296   Scott Holleran. "Interview: Director Andrew V. McLaglen," www.boxofficemojo.com, May 23,
      2007.

297   *The Altoona Mirror*, November 12, 1953; *The Daily Review*, October 30, 1953; Robert Stack,
      *Straight Shooting*, 57; ibid., 153-54.

298   Zolotow, 139; *The Ogden Standard-Examiner*, July 4, 1954.

299   *Los Angeles Times*, December 6, 1953.

300   *San Antonio Light*, July 31, 1953.

301   *The Cedar Rapids Tribune*, July 8, 1954; McGivern, *Lost Films*, 90-91.

302   ibid., 95; John Wayne interview, JFP.

303   *The Stars and Stripes*, November 15, 1954.

304   *Los Angeles Times*, May 28, 1954; ibid., June 6, 1954; *Los Angeles Examiner*, May 28, 1954; *Cue*,
      July 3, 1954.

305   *Pacific Stars and Stripes*, September 13, 1954.

306   *The Evening Independent*, June 4, 1954.

307   Dimitri Tiomkin and Prosper Buranelli, *Please Don't Hate Me*, 253-54; E. E. Kenyon, "The Wit
      Parade," *The American Weekly*, January 15, 1956.

308   *The Austin Statesman*, March 31, 1955; *Shooting Star* draft, MZP.

309   *Los Angeles Times*, December 25, 1953.

310   Munn, 162; *Focus on Film*, Spring, 1975, 17-23.

311   Tim Lilley, "Gregg Barton," *Campfire Conversations Complete*, 9.

312   *The Evening Independent*, May 20, 1954; *The Conqueror*, www.tcm.com; *Parade*, August 29, 1954; *Oakland Tribune*, May 30, 1954; *Corpus Christi Times*, May 31, 1954.

313   *The Independent*, April 1, 1954; *The Daily Review*, May 6, 1954; *The Daily Facts-Review*, June 9, 1954; *Albuquerque Journal*, June 18, 1954; *The Ogden Standard-Examiner*, June 24, 1954; *Nevada State Journal*, July 10, 1954; *Fairbanks News-Miner*, July 15, 1954; Davis, *Duke*, 183.

314   Lilley, "Gregg Barton," 10.

315   McGivern, *Lost Films*, 56-7.

316   *Chester Times*, June 2, 1954; *The Evening Independent*, May 20, 1954; *San Antonio Express*, September 12, 1954.

317   *The Albuquerque Tribune*, July 7, 1954; *The Post-Register*, July 8, 1954; *The Cedar Rapids Gazette*, August 29, 1954.

318   *Parade*, August 29, 1954; *Chronicle Telegram*, August 7, 1979.

319   Karen Jackovich and Mark Sennet, "The Childen of John Wayne, Susan Hayward and Dick Powell Fear That Fallout Killed Their Parents." *People*, November 10, 1980, 42.

320   Harvey Wasserman and Norman Soloman, *Killing Our Own*, 65-66.

321   "*Meeting: Discussion of Radiological Hazards Associated with a Continental Test Site for Atomic Bombs*," Atomic energy Commission, Los Alamos, New Mexico, August 1, 1950, pp. 13, 23, 24; *The New Mexican*, December 17, 1979; Jack Williams interview.

322   Wasserman and Soloman, 60.

323   *Hutchinson News*, August 6, 1979; "Did Utah Kill John Wayne?," www.utahgothic.com/movies/johnwayne.html; *The Augusta Chronicle*, March 16, 2009; *The News*, August 7, 1979.

324   *The New York Times*, March 31, 1956; Munn, 181.

325   *Los Angeles Times*, May 26, 1954; *Focus on Film*, Spring 1975, 17-23; *The High and the Mighty*, "The Batjac story."

326   *Variety*, January 15, 1964.

327   *San Mateo Times*, July 15, 1954.

328   *The Altoona Mirror*, June 16, 1954; *The Evening Observer*, August 13, 1954; *San Antonio Light*, February 17, 1955; March 18, 1955; *The Lima News*, December 29, 1954; *Los Angeles Times*, January 14, 1955; *The Abilene Reporter-News*, August 7, 1955.

329   *The Daily Courier*, November 2, 1954; Davis, *Duke*, 185; *The Billings Gazette*, November 2, 1954; *The Bee*, December 2, 1954.

330   *The Avalanche*, October 27, 1954; *Lubbock Morn. Avalanche*, October 27, 1954; *San Antonio Light*, February 11, 1954; November 1, 1954; *Nevada State Journal*, February 23, 1954; *Winnipeg*

*Free Press*, November 3, 1954; *The Letheridge Herald*, November 16, 1954; *The Daily Courier*, November 11, 1954; Roberts and Olson, 415.

331     *The Bee*, December 2, 1954; *El Paso Herald-Post*, December 2, 1954; Davis, *Duke*, 185; *San Antonio Express*, September 12, 1954.

CHAPTER EIGHT – "LET'S GO HOME, DEBBIE."

332     *The Searchers*. Dir. John Ford. Warner Bros., 1956. Film, Title song by Stan Jones.

333     *The Bee*, December 2, 1954; *The New York Times*, January 17. 1955; Lee Server, *Robert Mitchum-Baby, I Don't Care*, 282-284; *The Hutchinson News-Herald*, January 17, 1955.

334     *Oxnard Press-Courier*, January 13, 1955; *Oakland Tribune*, January 12, 1955; *Long Beach Press-Telegram*, January 12, 1955; *Idaho State Journal*, January 12, 1955.

335     Aissa Wayne, 34.

336     *Oakland Tribune*, January 13, 1955; *Los Angeles Times*, January 14, 1955; *The Brownsville Herald*, January 25, 1955; *The Daily Review*, August 8, 1955.

337     *Oakland Tribune*, January 27, 1955; ibid., January 28, 1955; ibid., February 12, 1955; *Pacific Stars & Stripes*, January 30, 1955; *The Altoona Mirror*, February 4, 1955.

338     *The Newark Advocate*, October 22, 1955.

339     *Nevada State Journal*, March 30, 1955.

340     *The Altoona Mirror*, April 7, 1955; *Oakland Tribune*, February 1, 1955.

341     *The Evening Independent*, March 25, 1955; *Chronicle-Telegram*, March 18, 1955.

342     Barbara Ford/John Ford interview, JFP.

343     Munn, 172.

344     *Albuquerque Journal*, January 24, 1955; Eyman, *Print the Legend*, 444; Davis, *Ford*, 271; *The Los Angeles Times*, March 8, 1955; ibid., April 26, 1955; *The Evening Independent*, April 19, 1955.

345     *The Laredo Times*, March 26, 1939.

346     Richard E. Klinck, *Land of Room Enough and Time Enough*, 58; Davis, *Ford*, 271; Carlos Gaberscek and Ken Stier, "In search of Western movie sites: Goulding's Trading Post (Pt. One)," *Western Clippings*, #67, Sept/Oct 2005, 15-16.

347     McBride, 289.

348     *Los Angeles Examiner*, May 3, 1925; *Cosmopolitan*, March, 1964, 12-21.

349     William Florence, "John Ford…John Wayne…and Monument Valley," *Arizona Highways*, September, 1981, 22-37; Frank Thompson, "The Wellman Westerns: An Appraisal," *American Classic Screen*, Winter, 1980, 8-15.

350     Allen Reed, "John Ford makes another movie classic in Monument Valley," *Arizona Highways*, April, 1956, 4-11; *Arizona Daily Sun*, June 14, 1955; Samuel Moon, *Tall Sheep*, 149-50.

351     Harry Carey Jr. interview, JFP.

352     *The Los Angeles Times*, June 10, 1955; *Albuquerque Journal*, June 13, 1955; *Hamilton Journal*, October 13, 1955.

353   *Nevada State Journal,* July 10, 1955; *Press-Telegram,* October 19, 1955; *Atchison Daily Globe,* October 26, 1955; *The Letheridge Herald,* August 9, 1955; *Fitchburg Sentinel,* October 19, 1955; *San Antonio Express,* August 6, 1955; *Los Angeles Times,* August 19, 1955; *Humboldt Standard,* August 25, 1955.

354   Davis, *Duke,* 205; Munn, 178; Pilar Wayne, 117; *Weirton Daily Times,* December 5, 1955.

355   Harry Carey Jr. interview, JFP.

356   *The Daily Review,* August 16, 1955; *Los Angeles Times,* May 27, 1956; John Ford interview, JFP.

357   *Racine Sunday Bulletin,* September 18, 1955; *The Twilight Zone* introduction, http://cis.csuohio.edu/~somos/twizone.html.

358   Eyman, *Print the Legend,* 444; Michael Barrier, "Fess Parker interview," www.michaelbarrier.com.

359   *Oakland Tribune,* August 4, 1955; August 21, 1955.

360   Carey Jr., 170.

361   McGivern, *John Wayne,* 265.

362   Ford, 255-9; McBride, 535.

363   ibid, 555.

364   Scott Eyman, "On and Off Poverty Row," *Take One,* November, 1977, 8-14.

365   ibid; Carey Jr.,167-68.

366   Eyman, *Print the Legend,* 405; ibid., 437; ibid., 393; O'Hara, 163-64.

367   Eyman, *Print the Legend,* 445.

368   "VistaVision," www.widescreenmuseum.com.

369   Gallagher, 460.

370   *The Searchers,* www.tcm.com, trivia.

371   *Las Vegas Daily Optic,* August 20, 1955.

372   Lilley, "Fred Libby," 127; Charles John Kieskalt, *The Official John Wayne Reference Book,* 92.

373   John Wayne interview, JFP.

374   ibid; Carey Jr., 173-74; Macklin and Pici, 135; McGivern, *John Wayne,* 264.

375   John Baxter, *The Cinema of John Ford,* 23; Brenton Priestly, "'They ain't white. Not any more. They're Comanche.' Race, Racism and the fear of Miscegenation in The Searchers," www.brentonpriestley.com.

376   Burt Kennedy, "Burt Kennedy Interviews John Ford," *Action,* vol. 3, no. 5, September/October, 1968.

377   Ken Curtis interview, JFP.

378   John Wayne interview, JFP.

379    ibid.

380    Harry Carey Jr. interview, JFP; *Take One*, November, 1977, 8-14.

381    Carey Jr.,170; ibid., 173; Munn, 176-77.

382    McGivern, *John Wayne*, 261; ibid., 263.

383    *The Victoria Advocate*, September 5, 1976; Roberts and Olson, 424.

384    *Variety*, March 14, 1956.

385    *The New York Times*, May 31, 1956.

386    *Los Angeles Times*, March 18, 1956.

387    McBride, 571.

388    Landesman, 317.

CHAPTER NINE – LOVE AND MARRIAGE

389    Pilar Wayne, 125.

390    Kazanjian and Enss, 82; *Hutchinson News*, March 14, 1979; *Indiana Evening Gazette*, June 12, 1979; Pilar Wayne, 31; *San Antonio Light*, October 10, 1960.

391    Pilar Wayne, 90-93; ibid., 117-18; *The Winona Daily News*, October 18, 1955; *The Daily Review*, October 21, 1955.

392    ; Pilar Wayne, 109.

393    ibid, 120; *Los Angeles Times*, October 18, 1955; Munn, 180.

394    *Racine Journal-Times*, October 19, 1955; *The Independent*, September 15, 1955; *The New York Times*, December 1, 1955; *The Daily Review*, December 7, 1955; *Los Angeles Times*, April 1, 1956; Tomkies, 80.

395    *Los Angeles Times*, December 31, 1955; ibid., May 27, 1956.

396    *Winnipeg Free Press*, August 27, 1955; *Los Angeles Times*, July 13, 1956; *Variety*, July 13, 1956; *San Mateo Times*, October 5, 1956.

397    *The San Diego Union*, April 16, 1926; *Ogden Standard-Examiner*, April 16, 1926; *Syracuse Herald Journal*, August 1, 1956; Sinclair, 46.

398    John Ford interview, JFP; Eyman, *Print the Legend*, 440; Peter Bogdanovich, *John Ford*, 96.

399    *The Vidette Messenger*, September 25, 1956.

400    Davis, *Ford*, 283.

401    Barbara Ford/John Ford interview, JFP.

402    O'Hara, 201; *Albuquerque Journal*, June 27, 1956.

403    Vincent Canby, *The Motion Picture Herald*, February 2, 1957; *The Altoona Mirror*, February 20, 1957; *The New York Times*, February 1, 1957; *Los Angeles Times*, January 25, 1957; Landesman, 407-8.

404    Pilar Wayne, 123; Landesman, 419-20.

405    Maureen O'Hara interview, www.moharamagazine.com.

406    Pilar Wayne, 124.

407    *Variety*, November 12, 1956; *Los Angeles Times*, December 17, 1956.

408    *The New York Times*, October 12, 1956; Wilkerson and Borie, 333; *Los Angeles Times*, December 6, 1957; *Independent*, January 31, 1957.

409    *San Antonio Light*, January 31, 1957; *The Morning Herald*, April 3, 1957; Roberts and Olson, 434; *Variety*, January 17, 1957.

410    *Register-Star-News*, April 4, 1957.

411    *Kingsport Times*, March 11, 1957; *The Stars and Stripes*, April 27, 1957; *Record-Eagle*, March 13, 1957; "Legend of the Lost; The Making of the film, *The John Wayne Film Society Journal*, Autumn, 2010, 10-11.

412    ibid; Carpozi, 130; Davis, *Duke*, 210; Pilar Wayne, 127; Tomkies, 81; McGivern, *John Wayne*, 274.

413    *The Vidette-Messenger*, May 18, 1957; *The Altoona Mirror*, June 29, 1957; Davis, *Duke*, 209; Munn, 185; Landesman, 195.

414    Aissa Wayne, 35; Pilar Wayne, 127.

415    *The Daily Review*, June 4, 1957; The Barbarian and the Geisha," www.tcm.com.

416    Pilar Wayne, 128; Davis, *Duke*, 212.

417    Axel Madsen, *John Huston*, 167-172 ; *Los Angeles Times*, December 27, 1957.

418    ibid; McGivern, *John Wayne*, 275.

419    Munn, 188.

420    *Los Angeles Times*, January 15, 1958; Davis, *Duke*, 214; *Ocala Star-Banner*, January 14, 1958; *Times-Bulletin*, November 11, 1958; *San Antonio News*, January 3, 1958.

421    Shepherd and Slatzer, 225-6; *Albuquerque Journal*, January 17, 1958; *The Altoona Mirror*, January 27, 1958; Landesman, 28; Zolotow, 298-9.

422    *The Corsicana*, December 14, 1957.

CHAPTER TEN – IT'S ABOUT TIME!

423    *San Antonio Express-News*, July 16, 1995.

424    *Brackett News*, March 17, 2011; *The Dallas News*, August 29, 1926; William F. Haenn, *Fort Clark and Brackettville: Land of Heroes*, 89; The *Dallas Morning News*, September 10, 2000.

425    *San Antonio Light*, May 18, 1963; ibid., July 2, 1953.

426    *The Houston Post*, September 1, 1991; *San Antonio Express-News*, July 16, 1995; ibid., September 7, 1999; *Fort Worth Star-Telegram*, February 3, 1961; *Victoria Advocate*, December 14, 1980.

427     Bill Moody IV interview; "Alamo Village, Built for a movie, this is now a top tourist mecca," *This is West Texas*, November-December, 1970, 20-23; Virginia Shahan interview; *San Antonio Light*, September 4, 1959.

428     ibid; *The Texas Mohair Weekly and The Rocksprings Record*, May 27, 1960.

429     "Virginia Shahan," www.homestead.com/alamovillagereunion/virginiashahan; Jamie Shahan Rains to author, October, 20, 2010.

430     *The Texas Mohair Weekly and Rocksprings Record*, May 27, 1960; Joe York, Jr. interview; Tully Shahan to author, October 21, 2010; ibid., November 18, 2010.

431     David Rothel, *An Ambush of Ghosts*, 14; B.J. Burns interview; *Austin American Statesman*, May 29, 1977; Frank Thompson and Craig Covner, Happy Shahan interview, July 1987.

432     Rothel, 14; *San Antonio Express*, October 26, 1952.

433     John Hinnant to author, October 20, 2010; Rothel, 22-23; *Fort Worth Star-Telegram*, February 3, 1961; .*Del Rio News-Herald*, April 23, 1958.

434     *Austin American Statesman*, May 27, 1977; *Dallas Morning News*, unknown date.

435     Clark and Andersen, 12-13.

436     Rob Newman interview.

437     *San Antonio Express-News*, July 16, 1995; Mike Blakely, "Alamo Village: The Stuff Westerns Are Made Of," *Texas Highways*, May 1985, 36-43; Rothel, 15; *Austin American Statesman*, May 27, 1977.

438     *Alamo Village Star*, May, 1961; *San Antonio Express-News*, September 16, 1990; Roger Crowley, "Alamo Village," *The Westerner*, Issue 15/1990, 5-10; Rothel, 15; B.J. Burns interview.

439     ibid, 23; *San Antonio Light*, August 26, 1955.

440     *Austin American Statesman*, May 29, 1977.

441     *The Vidette-Messenger*, May 18, 1957; ibid., August 1, 1957; *The Daily Review*, June 4, 1957; *The Salt Lake Tribune*, September 10, 1957.

CHAPTER ELEVEN – A BULL BY THE TAIL

442     *Rio Bravo*. Dir. Howard Hawks. Warner Bros, 1959. Film, dialog.

443     Roger Ebert, "Rio Bravo movie review and film summary, www.rogerebert.suntimes.com, July 15, 2009; Joseph McBride, *Hawks on Hawks*, 130.

444     McCarty, 532; ibid., 520; Peter Bogdanovich, *Who The Devil Made It*, 354.

445     Munn, 191; *Salt Lake Tribune*, August 30, 1957.

446     McCarthy, 540.

447     Tony Macklin, "Howard Hawks," Wide Angle 1:2, 1976, 4-57; McCarthy, 548; *The News*, July 7, 1958.

448     Munn, 264.

449     *Albuquerque Journal*, March 15, 1958; *Salt Lake Tribune*, August 30, 1957.

450   Robin Wood, *Howard Hawks*, 44.

451   McGivern, *John Wayne*, 277; Macklin, 35; *Ukiah Daily Journal*, April 16, 1958; *Star-News*, April 7, 1958; McCarthy, 554.

452   ibid; Peter Bogdanovich, *Who The Hell's In It*, 222; *Burlington Daily Times-News*, July 4, 1958.

453   *The Evening Standard*, May 26, 1958.

454   Munn, 191-2.

455   *The Sun*, May 30, 1958; *Sandusky Register*, May 26, 1958; *Wisconsin State Journal*, June 1, 1959.

456   *Humboldt Standard*, May 30, 1958; *Star-News*, April 9, 1958.

457   McCarthy, 555; *Tucson Daily Citizen*, May 17, 1958.

458   *Waterloo Daily Courier*, March 10; *Oakland Tribune*, March 15, 1959.

459   Munn, 192.

460   McCarthy, 555; *Joplin Globe*, June 22, 1958; *The Robesonian*, July 2, 1958.

461   *Tucson Daily Citizen*, April 4, 1958.

462   McCarthy, 551.

463   *The Salt Lake Tribune*, March 1, 1959; Bogdanovich, *Who The Hell's In It*, 290-1.

464   *Tucson Daily Citizen*, May 10, 1958; *Winnipeg Free Press*, July 26, 1958.

465   *Covina Argus Citizen*, July 31, 1958.

466   *The Independent*, August 4, 1958.

467   *The Abilene Reporter-News*, November 9, 1958; *Lincoln Sunday Journal*, July 6, 1958.

468   McCarty, 557-8.

469   Davis, *Duke*, 216; Munn, 192-3.

470   Peter Bogdanovich, *Who the Devil Made It*, 364.

471   *Tucson Daily Citizen*, May 23, 1958.

472   *New York Times*, March 19, 1959; Romano Tozzi, "Rio Bravo, "*Films in Review*, April 1959; "Cinema: The New Pictures," *Time*, April 6, 1959; *Variety*, February 18, 1959; *New York Herald*, March 19, 1959.

473   *The News*, July 7, 1958.

CHAPTER TWELVE – "HURRAH FOR THE BONNIE BLUE FLAG ..."

474   *The Horse Soldiers*. Dir. John Ford. United Artists, 1959. Film, "I Left My Love," song lyrics.

475   Dee Brown, *When the Century Was Young*, 189.

476   Neil Longley York, *Fact As Fiction: The Horse Soldiers & Popular Memory*, 53; ibid., 56.

477    Harold Sinclair, *The Horse Soldiers*, 7; ibid., 33; York, 62; Sally Brown to John Ford/John Wayne, November 3, 1958, JFP.

478    *The Lowell Sun*, June 12, 1959; *Kingpost News*, January 25, 1958; *Los Angeles Times*, July 9, 1957; *Oakland Tribune*, February 11, 1958; *Star-News*, October 10, 1958.

479    *Los Angeles Times*, April 26, 1958; John Lee Mahin and Martin Rackin, "The Horse Soldiers or Grierson's Raid," *Civil War History*, Vol. 5, 1959, 183-4.

480    ibid, 185; Ford, 279; *Los Angeles Times*, February 9, 1959; *Indiana Evening Gazette*, October 15, 1958.

481    John Mahin/Martin Rackin to John Ford, June 24, 1958, JFP; ibid., June 30, 1958.

482    John Mahin/Martin Rackin to John Ford, June 24, 1958, JFP.

483    *The Daily Review*, June 26, 1958; *Oxnard Press Courier*, May 16, 1958; *Linton Daily Citizen* May 15, 1958; Walter Mirisch, *I Thought We Were Making Movies, Not History*, 105; *Star-News*, August 5, 1958; *Lima News*, August 9, 1958; *Burlington Daily Times-News*, September 11, 1958; John Mahin/Martin Rackin to John Ford, June 24, 1958, JFP; ibid., June 30, 1958.

484    *Los Angeles Times*, February 14, 1958; *San Antonio Light*, February 25, 1958; *The Lowell Sun*, June 26, 1958.

485    *Star-News*, March 4, 1958; *The Coshocton Tribune*, March 5, 1958; *Newport Daily News*, March 26, 1958.

486    Bob Thomas, *Golden Boy*, 121-122.

487    *The Inter Lake*, September 24, 1958.

488    *The Salisbury Times*, October 2, 1958; *The Gettysburg Times*, October 16, 1958; *The New York Times*, October 14, 1958; *The Rhinelander Daily News*, November 11, 1958; *Burlington Daily Times-News*, November 10, 1958.

489    *The Laurel Leader-Call*, October 30, 1958; *The Lowell Sun*, October 31, 1958; *Corpus Christi Times*, November 22, 1958; *Los Angeles Times*, December 17, 1958.

490    *Leader-Times*, December 8, 1958; *The Lowell Sun*, December 12, 1958.

491    "Hoot Gibson," www.b-westerns.com/hgibson1.htm; *Greeley Tribune*, December 27, 1958.

492    *Civil War History*, Vol. 5, 1959, 184; Roberts and Olson, 444-445; Thomas, 123.

493    Ford, 279-80, 283; *The Horse Soldiers*, Mirisch Company, Detail Production Budget, October 14, 1958, JFP; *Biddeford Journal*, October 15, 1958; *The Salt Lake Tribune*, November 25, 1958; *Pacific Stars and Stripes*, December 7, 1958.

494    Ford, 280; *The Horse Soldiers*, Mirisch-Batjac Shooting Schedule, October 14, 1958, JFP; *Civil War History*, Vol.5, 184; Ford, 280-81.

495    *Unknown paper*, November 11, 1958; *Anderson Daily Bulletin*, June 25, 1959.

496    Typescript, "Six Days with Horse Soldiers," Stovall, JFP.

497    *Unknown newspaper*, November 24, 1958.

498    Thomas Lowell, 123; John Wayne interview, JFP; Bill Clothier interview, JFP.

499    *Lowell Sun*, September 7, 1958; *The Salt Lake Tribune*, September 7, 1958; *Los Angeles Times*, September 7, 1958; ibid., September 8, 1958; *San Antonio Express*, September 8, 1958; ibid., January 7, 1959; Munn, 189-90.

500    Pilar Wayne, 133-34.

501    *Rio Grande*, Dir. John Ford. Republic Pictures, 1950. Film, dialog.

502    Roberson, 227-8; *Montana Standard*, December 6, 1958; Pilar Wayne, 134; Tim Lilley, "Bob Rose," *Campfires Rekindled*, 124.

503    *Pasadena Independent*, December 11, 1958.

504    Pilar Wayne, 135.

505    *Anderson Daily Bulletin*, June 25, 1959.

506    *Los Angeles Times*, June 25, 1959.

507    *San Antonio Express*, January 14, 1959.

508    *San Antonio Light*, October 21, 1960.

CHAPTER THIRTEEN – IT'S ABOUT DAMN TIME!

509    Happy Shahan interview, April 26, 1977; Thompson and Covner, Happy Shahan interview July 1987.

510    *Salt Lake Tribune*, September 10, 1957; *Tipton Tribune*, October 8, 1957; *Dallas Morning News*, September 2, 1957; *Box Office*, September 9, 1957.

511    Jose Hernandez Jr. interview; Mary Hernandez interview; *Texas Highways*, May, 1985, 36-43; Thompson and Covner, Happy Shahan interview, July 1987; Rothel, 15.

512    *Texas Highways*, May, 1985, 36-43.

513    *Dallas Morning News*, March 26, 1958; *The Kinney County News*, January 17, 1958; The *Houston Chronicle*, October 15, 1958; *Unknown newspaper*, mid-December, 1958; *San Antonio Express and News*, March 15, 1959; *Unknown newspaper*, unknown date.

514    Rich Curilla to author, March 25, 2011; ibid., April 5, 2011; Frank Thompson and Craig Covner, Al Ybarra interview, March, 1988; Al Ybarra blueprint of Alamo and village, undated.

515    Thompson and Covner, Al Ybarra interview.

516    *San Antonio Sunday Times*, April 20, 1958; *The Houston Post*, September 1, 1991; *San Antonio Express-News*, July 16, 1995.

517    Henry Fuentes interview.

518    *The Kinney County News*, January 17, 1958; "The Alamo is Rising Anew," *Texas CO-OP Power*, June 1958, 4; *Del Rio News-Herald*, unknown date; Alan Kreiger, Jr. interview.

519    *San Antonio Express*, January 19, 1958; *Unknown newspaper*, unknown date.

520    Ralph Gonzales interview.

521    *The Dallas Morning News*, September 11, 1971.

522    *The Dallas Morning News*, January 23, 1958; *San Antonio News*, January 16, 1959; *The Times Recorder*, December 23, 1959.

523    Clark and Andersen, 29-30.

524    *San Antonio Light*, December 9, 1957; *San Antonio Express and News*, January 19, 1958; *Del Rio News-Herald*, January 5, 1958; *Uvalde Leader-News*, January 17, 1958; *The Dallas Morning News*, January 23, 1958.

525    Alan Kreiger, Jr. interview.

526    *San Antonio Light*, December 16, 1957; *New York Times*, October 4, 1959; *The Dallas Morning News*, April 19, 1958; *Anderson Daily Bulletin*, April 5, 1958; *Unknown newspaper*, June 29, 1959.

527    *The Columbus Daily Telegram*, June 18, 1958; *Big Spring Herald*, June 18, 1958; *Del Rio News-Herald*, June 18, 1958; ibid., June 17, 1958; *The Paris News*, June 17, 1958.

528    Thompson and Covner, Al Ybarra interview; *Del Rio News-Herald*, November 15, 1957.

529    *The Dallas Morning News*, unknown date.

530    Rothel, 15; *The Dallas Morning News*, October 19, 1958; *Fort Worth Star-Telegram*, February 3, 1961.

531    *Del Rio News-Herald*, June 25, 1958; Al Ybarra blueprint, March 1951.

532    *The Dallas Morning News*, September 24, 1958; October 15, 1958.

533    Bill Allert, "Next Battle of Alamo Slated for Shahan Ranch," *South Texas Farm & Ranch News*, October 3, 1958; *San Antonio Light*, September 28, 1958; *New York Journal American*, June 24, 1959.

534    *San Antonio Light*, November 14, 1958; Rich Curilla interview.

535    ibid.

536    *San Antonio Standard Times*, April 20, 1958; *The Kerrville Times*, June 14, 1959; *Fort Worth Star Telegram*, March 22, 1959; Clark and Andersen, 40; Scott Eyman, *John Wayne, The Life and Legend*, 311; ibid., 319.

537    *Del Rio News-Herald*, March 1, 1959; *Houston Post*, October 1, 1959.

538    *Waco Tribune-Herald*, October 26, 1958; Thompson and Covner, Al Ybarra Interview.

539    *Unknown magazine*; *Del Rio News-Herald*, March 1, 1959.

540    Clark and Andersen, John Wayne's *The Alamo*, 32; Richard Curilla history boards, Alamo Village.

541    Clark and Andersen, *John Wayne's The Alamo*, 33; Don Clark to author, April 25, 2011; Chuck Schoenfeld to author, November 8, 2012.

542    *San Antonio Light*, July 5, 1936; Russell Birdwell, "A News Release John Wayne's "The Alamo" (1960), 93; Elaine Davis to author, September 26, 2003; ibid., June 9, 2004; *San Antonio News-Express*, October 21, 1959.

543    *Austin American-Statesman*, June 26, 1960.

544    Alan C. Huffines, *Blood of Noble Men*, 126; Al Ybarra blueprint, March 1951; Clark and Andersen, 42.

939

545    *San Antonio Light*, December 29, 1958; *Del Rio News-Herald*, March 1, 1959; Thompson and Covner, Al Ybarra interview.

546    Tim Cumiskey interview.

547    *Dallas Morning News*, December 12, 1959; *San Antonio Light*, December 15, 1959; *Del Rio News-Herald*, March 1, 1959; *Hollywood Reporter*, December 16, 1959; *The Times Recorder*, December 23, 1959; *The Times-Picayune*, May 24, 1960.

548    *San Antonio Light*, November 4, 1958; Rich Curilla to author, June 16, 2014; B.J. Burns interview.

549    *San Angelo Standard-Times*, September, 1959; *The Houston Post*, November 4, 1959.

550    *San Antonio Light*, July 16, 1959; *New York Times*, July 29, 1959; ibid., October 4, 1959; *San Antonio Express and News*, August 23, 1959; Munn, 204.

551    *San Antonio News*, February 18, 1959; *San Antonio Light*, January 22, 1959; ibid., February 22, 1959; *Pasadena Independent*, January 19, 1959; *Variety*, February 25, 1959.

CHAPTER FOURTEEN – "BUDDY, CAN YOU SPAE A DIME?"

552    Carpozi, 143.

553    "Flat-broke Millionaire," *Movie Life Year Book*, #34, 1963, 16-22; "Wayne Confesses," *Photoplay*, November, 1973, 16, 24, 54; *People*, August 24, 1966, 4-7; *Clovis News-Journal*, April 26, 1953; "John Wayne: Another Day, Another $1,923," *Parade*, August 29, 1954; *The Ogden Standard-Examiner*, March 20, 1955; *The Los Angeles Times*, October 28, 1952; *Winnipeg Free Press*, December 5, 1960.

554    *The Albuquerque Tribune*, November 1, 1958.

555    *The Daily Independent*, July 24, 1958; *The Daily Courier*, July 24, 1958.

556    Landesman, 18, 25, 35, 84, 103, 106, 109, 118, 142, 148, 170, 172, 188, 258, 270, 274, 305, 316, 325, 351, 362, 369, 388, 395.

557    *Press-Telegram*, October 7, 1958; *Indiana Evening Gazette*, October 7, 1948; Lloyd Shearer, "Are Ten Top Stars strangling Hollywood?", *Parade*, October 12, 1958, 3-39, 41.

558    *Press-Telegram*, October 8, 1958.

559    *Parade*, October 12, 1958, 38-39, 41; *Waterloo Sunday Courier*, March 22, 1959; *Variety*, December 10, 1958.

560    Zolotow, 321; Munn, 203; ibid., 209; Fred Landesman, John Wayne to Fred Landesman, July 6, 1977.

561    *Los Angeles Times*, November 24, 1958; *The Zanesville Signal*, October 11, 1950; *American Weekly*, November 28, 1954; *The Daily Review*, August 8, 1955.

562    Aissa Wayne, 46; *Variety*, November 2, 1950; Zolotow, 302; McGivern, *John Wayne*, 283; Pilar Wayne, 136; Tomkies, 85-6.

563    *Variety*, January 21, 1959.

564    Zolotow, 164; *Glean Times Herald*, November 28, 1949.

565   *The Portsmouth Herald*, December 18, 1948; *The Lawton Constitution*, June 29, 1960; *The New York Times*, August 13, 1973.

566   *Variety*, August 24, 1955; ibid., November 5, 1951; *Reno Evening Gazette*, October 31, 1950.

567   Pilar Wayne, 45.

568   *The Ada Evening News*, May 20, 1953; Carolyn Roos Olsen, *"Hollywood's Man who Worried for the Stars,"* 71.

569   Pilar Wayne, 137-8; McGivern, *John Wayne*, 283-5; Roberts and Olson, 455.

570   Tomkies, 93-94; Davis, *Duke*, 234; Munn, 227-8; *The Cedar Rapids Gazette*, May 12, 1959.

571   McGivern, *John Wayne*, 285.

572   Olsen, 118-120; Arthur Marx, *Red Skelton: an unauthorized biography*, 241.

573   Roberts and Olson, 409.

574   Rothel, 16.

575   ibid, 17; Richard Curilla interview; Virginia Shahan interview; Aissa Wayne, 48; Tomkies, 88-89; McGivern, *John Wayne*, 298-99.

576   *Oakland Tribune*, April 23, 1959; *Variety*, May 6, 1959.

577   Nick Redfern, *Celebrity Secrets*, 49.

578   *Corpus Christi Times*, May 4, 1959.

579   Pilar Wayne, 225; *The Berkshire Eagle*, May 27, 1959; *Corpus Christi Times*, May 2, 1959; *Racine Journal-Times*, April 24, 1959; Olsen, 175-177.

580   *Variety*, December 11, 1957; ibid., May 20, 1959; ibid., July 14, 1959; ibid., July 22, 1959; ibid., July 29, 1959; *Box Office*, April 27, 1959; McGivern, *John Wayne*, 290; USC, John Wayne collection, box 3, folder 3, Bank of America loan agreement with Batjac dated May 25, 1960.

581   *The Houston Post*, July 16, 1959.

582   *Variety*, July 22, 1959; ibid., October 24, 1960; Landesman, 11, 221; Landesman, John Wayne to Fred Landesman, July 6, 1977; *San Antonio Light*, July 18, 1958; *Saturday Evening Post*, October 27, 1962, 28-33; *Esquire*, May, 1962, 74-75, 123-125.

583   USC, John Wayne Collection, box 3, folder 6, Clint Murchison to John Wayne, July 8, 1958.

584   Goldman, 73; USC, John Wayne Collection, box 3, folder 6, John Wayne to Robert Thompson, June 28, 1959; USC John Wayne Collection, box 3, folder 6, Holman Jenkens to John Wayne, June 26, 1959; Eyman, *John Wayne*, 315.

585   USC, John Wayne Collection, box 3, folder 6, Roger Davis to Walter Spradley, September 4, 1959.

586   USC, John Wayne Collection, box 3, folder 6, Clint Murchison to John Wayne, July 2, 1959.

587   USC, John Wayne collection, box 3, folder 21, George Skouras to John Wayne, July 8, 1959; Batjac Productions, Charles Feldman to John Wayne, July 16, 1959.

588   USC, John Wayne Collection, box 3, folder 21, John Wayne to George Skouras, July 11, 1959.

589    USC, John Wayne Collection, box 3, folder 21, Skouras to John Wayne, July 16, 1959.

590    ibid; Eyman, *John Wayne*, 315; *Variety*, April 30, 1959.

591    ibid.

592    USC, John Wayne collection, box 3, folder 7, John Wayne to I. J. McCullough, June 30, 1959; USC, John Wayne Collection, box 3, folder 6, John Wayne to Roger Lewis, July 30, 1959.

CHAPTER FIFTEEN – OUR PLAYERS

593    *The Rhinelander*, September 15, 1949; *The Sheboygan Press*, March 28, 1959; *Variety*, October 29, 1945.

594    Huberman, Budd Boetticher interview; *Los Angeles Times*, March 4, 1951; *The New York Times*, July 15, 1951; Ashley Ward interview.

595    *San Antonio Express*, March 9, 1948; ibid., July 18, 1951; *Bluefield Daily Telegraph*, April 6, 1948; *The Wisconsin State Journal*, August 30, 1948; *The Long Beach Press*, September 15, 1948; *The Charlotte Gazette*, November 19, 1948; *Los Angeles Times*, April 20, 1949; ibid., January 21, 1951; ibid., February 21, 1952; ibid., April 16, 1951; ibid., February 21, 1951 *The Daily Reporter*, January 24, 1950; *Dallas Morning News*, July 10, 1951; *Record-Chronicle*, August 26, 1951; *San Antonio Evening News*, October 8, 1951; *San Antonio Light*, October 9, 1951; *The Bee*, November 13, 1952; *Albuquerque Journal*, November 21, 1952; *The Daily Journal-Gazette and Commercial Star*, June 18, 1954; *The Evening Observer*, August 13, 1954.

596    *Los Angeles Times*, July 5, 2007; *Oregonian*, October 30, 1959.

597    *Variety*, November 27, 1951; *Los Angeles Times*, September 27, 1951.

598    *Waterloo Daily Courier*, October 16, 1957.

599    *The Seguin Gazette*, April 8, 1964; *The Seguin Gazette-Enterprise*, December 7, 1984; *San Antonio Light*, March 8, 1957; ibid., February 13, 1977; ibid., March 5, 1957; *San Antonio Express-News*, May 16, 2010; *San Antonio Express and News*, January 19, 1958; ibid., September 6, 1959; *Dallas Morning News*, March 26, 1959; Paula Allen, "A star businessman, Big John also an actor," www.mysa.com.

600    Oscar Rimoldi, "What Price Glory? Audie Murphy," *Films in Review*, April 1986, 215.

601    "Military decorations of Audie Murphy," http://audiemurphy.com/decorations.htm; *Los Angeles Times*, August 23, 1955; *San Antonio Express*, December 25, 1958.

602    *Dallas Morning News*, December 13, 1958; *San Antonio Express*, December 25, 1958; *The Austin American*, June 10, 1959;

603    Munn, 206; Davis, *Duke*, 224.

604    Stephen Kahn, "Will Frankie's Flame Flicker?", *Teen*, May, 1960, 16-19; www.frankieavalon.com; *Variety*, August 4, 1959.

605    Munn, 207-8; *Time*, February 1, 1960; *Albuquerque Journal*, December 3, 1958.

606    "Backpage: Jester Hairston," www.tufts.edu/alumni/tuftonia/archives/sp00/backpage.shtml; "Jester Hairston biography," www.umich.edu/afroammu/standifer/hairston.html.

607    *The Paris News*, July 22, 1959; *The Bee*, October 27, 1960; *Del-Rio News Herald*, May 15, 1998.

608    *The Salt Lake Tribune*, December 5, 1959.

609    Tom Lisanti, "Joan O'Brien, What a Dish," *Films of the Golden Age*, Summer, 1999, 45-49; *Del-Rio News Herald*, May 15, 1998; *The Hollywood Reporter*, August 20, 1959.

610    Tom Lisanti, *Fantasy Femmes of Sixties Cinema with 20 Actresses from Biker, Beach and Elvis Movies*, Joan O'Brien interview, 27-39; *Variety*, August 20, 1959; *Variety*, October 1, 1959; ibid., October 14, 1959.

611    *San Antonio Light*, November 10, 1960.

612    *San Mateo Times*, March 17, 1956; NBC press release, Fall 1967; "Linda Cristal," www.glamour-girlsofhtesilverscreen.com.

613    *The Ogden Standard-Examiner*, November 9, 1958.

614    Linda Cristal interview; Munn, 207; "Linda Cristal, The girl who travels alone," *Look*, July 19, 1960, 107-110.

615    *The Post-Standard*, March 16, 1988.

616    *The San Antonio Light*, April 5, 1936; *San Antonio Express*, April 26, 1939; *The Corsicana Daily Sun*, July 30, 1937; *New Castle, Pa. News,* August 7, 1937; *Nevada State Journal*, April 27, 1938; *The Racine Journal-Times*, March 14, 1941; *The Evening Independent*, November 27, 1941.

617    *Press-Telegram*, July 20, 1959; *Unknown paper*, unknown date; *The Lowell Sun*, July 16, 1959.

618    *Unknown paper*, August, 1959; *San Antonio Light*, August 26, 1949; *Wisconsin State Journal*, December 17, 1978; *Lawrence Journal-World*, December 17, 1978; *Alton Telegraph*, December 18, 1978; *Winnipeg Free Press*, December 19, 1978; *Dallas Morning News*, unknown date.

619    *Syracuse Herald*, February 22, 1931; *San Antonio Light*, February 23, 1949; *The Odessa American*, November 9, 1960, *Florence Morning News*, October 30, 1971, Huberman, Hank Worden interview; *Thank Ya, Thank Ya Kindly: Tribute to Hank Worden*," 7th Voyage Productions, 2007. DVD; *The Horse Soldiers*, dialog.

620    *The Abilene Reporter-News*, May 31, 1970; *The Stars and Stripes*, December 28, 1997; *The Winchester Star*, December 27, 1997.

621    Ed G. Lousararian, "Denver Pyle," *Wildest Westerns*, No. 1, 18-27; Huberman, Denver Pyle interview; Lilley, "Denver Pyle," *Campfires Rekindled*, 97-110.

622    Perry, *John Ford Interviews*, 109; *The Winchester Star*, April 30, 1991; *The Intelligencer*, May 1, 1991; *The Stars and Stripes*, May 1, 1991; *Los Angeles Times*, April 29, 1991; ibid., August 14, 1959; *Hollywood Reporter*, August 14, 1959; ibid., September 9, 1959.

623    *The Register News*, February 27, 1953; *Oakland Tribune*, December 16, 1956; *Evening Times*, October 27, 1957; Stack, 138; Barnaby Conrad, "Homage to a Peerless Matador," *Sports Illustrated*, August 1, 1966; Clark and Andersen, 54; *San Diego Union*, July 16, 1959; Robert Quinones interview.

624    "John Dierkes," www.imdb.com; *Corpus Christi Caller Times*, June 20, 1948; *The Winona Republican-Herald*, March 5, 1952; ibid., March 21, 1952.

CHAPTER SIXTEEN – THE HOLY TRINITY

625    *Variety,* February 27, 1952; ibid., December 11, 1957; ibid., October 7, 1959.

626    *Variety,* May 12, 1960; *Rockford Morning Star*, October 16, 1960.

627    *Variety,* December 13, 1957; ibid., December 16, 1957; ibid., December 25, 1957; ibid., January 8, 1958; *Dallas Morning News*, May 31, 1959; Landesman, 12.

628  Bill Kelly, "John Wayne's Last Written Interview Conducted by Bill Kelly," August 8, 1978, CD; *Dallas Morning News*, December 1, 1958.

629  *Dallas Morning News*, December 1, 1958; ibid., October 15, 1958; ibid., May 22, 1959; ibid., June 19, 1959; ibid., June 21, 1959; *San Antonio Light*, July 18, 1958; ibid., September 28, 1958; ibid., mid-December, 1958; *Waco Tribune-Herald*, October 26, 1958; *Austin American*, June 01, 1959; *Anderson Daily Bulletin*, June 12, 1959; *The Hollywood Reporter*, July 6, 1959; ibid., July 7, 1959; ibid., July 8, 1959; Munn, 204-5; *Los Angeles Times*, September 6, 1959; Charlton Heston, *The Actors Life Journals 1956-1976*, 94.

630  *San Antonio Light*, July 18, 1958; *Del Rio News-Herald*, March 1, 1959; *Variety*, February 25, 1959; Heston, 94; Davis, *Ford*, 275.

631  *Corpus Christi Times*, November 25, 1960; Gary Wills, *John Wayne's America: The Politics of Celebrity*, 204.

632  Aissa Wayne, 34; Server, 284.

633  Michael Buckley, "Richard Widmark (Part Three)," *Films in Review*, June/July 1986, 324; Richard Widmark to Phil Stern, September 30, 1959, Ashley Ward; Frances Ingram, "Richard Widmark, Utter Simplicity and Realism," *Films of the Golden Age*, Summer 2009, 73; Munn, 205.

634  Michael Buckley, "Richard Widmark (Part One), *Films In Review*, April, 1986, 222-229; ibid., May, 1986, 258-70; ibid., June/July, 1986, 322-37; *Cleveland Plain Dealer*, November 1, 1959; *Variety*, August 3, 1959; Jerome S. Simon, "Richard Widmark," *Films In Review*, January, 1971, 7.

635  Des Hickey and Gus Smith, *The Prince, The Public and Private Life of Laurence Harvey*, 34-130; Anne Sinai, *Reach for the Top*, 1-242.

636  Sinai, 246; Munn, 205-6; Hickey, 131; *Los Angeles Times*, July 15, 1959.

637  Munn, 205; *San Antonio Light*, October 27, 1960; *Esquire*, May, 1962, 74-75, 123-125.

638  *Oakland Tribune*, April 1, 1959.

639  *Lebanon Daily News*, June 4, 1959; David Rothel, *Richard Boone, A Knight Without Armor in a Savage Land*, 54, 99, 138; *Wichita Falls Times*, March 14, 1961; C. Courtney Joyner, *The Westerners*, 70; *TV Guide*, September 25, 1971; *Los Angeles Times*, August 9, 1962.

CHAPTER SEVENTEEN – GAGS, NAGS AND RAGS

640  *Hollywood Stuntmen's Hall of Fame Newsletter*, Vol.5 No. 19, Nov/Dec 1972.

641  John Hagner, *Bob Rose, The Nerviest Stuntman Ever, San Antonio Light*, November 10, 1932; Neil Summers, *The Unsung Heroes*, 3; Kevin Conley, *The Full Burn*, 1, 60; *The Santa Ynez Valley Journal*, July 16, 2009; *unknown* magazine, "Safety for the Stuntman."

642  Hal Needham, *Stuntman*. 53-4, 56-7.

643  Yakima Canutt, *Stunt Man, The Autobiography of Yakima Canutt*, 234.

644  Carey Jr., 62.

645  Ann Snuggs, *Uncredited, Cliff Lyons On And Off The Screen*, 1-8; Carey Jr., 43; McBride, 442.

646  Carey Jr., 66.

647  Roberson, 231-2.

648    Snuggs, 13-24; Dean Smith to author, September 27, 2011; Carey Jr., 62.

649    Tim Lilley, "Making Heroes out of Those Cowboy Actors," *The Trail Beyond*, Volume II, December 2000, 31-33; Snuggs, 23; Tim Lilley, "Chuck Roberson," *Campfire Conversations*, 78.

650    *Island Breeze*, November 29, 2008; Dean Smith with Mike Cox, *Cowboy Stuntman: From Olympic Gold to the Silver Screen*; 109; Eyman, *John Wayne*, 318.

651    Neil Summers, "Action Actors: Jack Williams," www.westernclippings.com/jackwilliams_stuntmen.shtml; *Los Angeles Times*, April 16, 2007.

652    Jack Williams interview; Jack Williams to author January 11, 2007.

653    Canutt, 15; Joe Canutt interview.

654    Summers, "Action Actors: Bob Rose," www.westernclippings.com/stuntmen/bobrose_stuntmen. shtml; John Lodge, "Movie Stunt Men Risk Their Lives to Thrill Millions," *Popular Mechanics*, November, 1935, 22-24; Bob Rose, "Cheating Death for a Living," *Popular Mechanics*, February, 1935, 226-230; Lilley, "Bob Rose," *Campfires Rekindled*, 126.

655    Bernard Rosenberg and Harry Silverstein, *The Real Tinsel*, 277-298; Tim Lilley, "Gil Perkins," *Campfire's Glow*, 83-4.

656    Wills, 204.

657    Lilley, "Ted White," *Campfire's Glow*, 128-9; Ted White interview.

658    Summers, "Action Actors: Chuck Roberson," www.westernclippings.com/stuntmen/chuckroberson; Lilley, "Chuck Roberson," *Campfire Conversations*, 75; *Hollywood Stuntmen's Hall of Fame*, News. Vol. 1, Number 1, Zolotow's notes, *Shooting Star*, 1.

659    Summers, "Action Actors: Chuck Hayward," www.westernclippings.com/stuntmen/chuckhayward; Lilley, "Chuck Hayward," *Campfire's Glow*, 31; Carey Jr., 126.

660    Tim Lilley, "Bill Hart," *Campfire Embers*, 53, 56.

661    *San Antonio Express and News*, September 12, 1959.

662    Ann Yokley, "Behind the Scenes Filming 'The Alamo,'" *The Quarter Horse Journal*, March, 1960, 22-25, 88; *Dallas Morning News*, July 10, 1959; *San Antonio Express and News*, August 8, 1959; "Brackettville area will remember the Alamo for a long time to come," *Better Ranches & Farms*, September 23, 1959, 4-5; *New York Times*, October 4, 1959.

663    Billy Winn interview.

664    Plunker Sheedy interview.

665    *Dallas Morning News*, July 9, 1959; *Del Rio News-Herald*, September 6, 1959; *San Antonio Express and News*, October 4, 1959.

666    *San Antonio Light*, September 13, 1959; *Del Rio News-Herald*, August 14, 1959.

667    *San Antonio Light*, September 30, 1959; *Dallas Morning News*, August 18, 1959; *The Baytown Sun*, September 11, 1960.

668    Roberson, 230-31.

669    Petrine Day Mitchum, *Hollywood Hoofbeats*. 66-7.

670     Roberson, 26.

671     Huberman, Bill Daniel interview; *Alamo* program; *Baytown Sun*, September 18, 1960; "Up That Long, Long trail," photo, *West Texas Livestock Weekly*, April 7, 1960, 2; *The Galveston Daily News*, October 27, 1959; *Variety*, June 27, 1961.

672     *San Antonio Express and News*, August 15, 1959; ibid., August 8, 1959; *Del Rio News-Herald*, August 19, 1959; ibid., November 9, 1959; *The Kerrville Times*, November 8, 1959; *Dayton Sun*, September 18, 1960; Huberman, Bill Daniel interview.

673     *Los Angeles Times*, March 14, 1989.

674     Joseph Musso to author, February 17, 2012.

675     Joseph Musso to author, November 28, 2009.

676     *El Paso Herald Post*, July 24, 1965; *Miami Daily News Record*, October 20, 1959; Fagen, 143-45; Joseph Musso to author, February 13, 2012.

677     Joseph Musso to author July 15, 16, 2010.

678     Joseph Musso to author, July 15, 2010.

679     Christopher Hearn, Various Stembridge August 1959 invoices; *San Antonio Express and News*, August 1, 1959; *San Antonio Light*, October 29, 1960; Davis, *Duke*, 223.

CHAPTER EIGHTEEN – ROOM AND BOARD INCLUDED

680     *Del Rio News-Herald*, July 23, 1959.

681     William Chemerka, "Rudy Robbins," *The Alamo Journal*, June 2007, 15-17.

682     ibid.

683     Little John Hamilton interview.

684     *The Uvalde Leader-News*, August 16, 1959.

685     Robert Harris interview.

686     Robert Relyea, *Not So Quiet On The Set*, 115; Eyman, *John Wayne*, 318.

687     Zolotow, 311.

688     Marshall Jones interview.

689     Tommy Worrell interview.

690     Jim Brewer interview.

691     *The Baytown Sun*, September 11, 1960.

692     John Henry Daniels interview; *San Antonio Light*, October 21, 1960.

693     David Kuykendall interview.

694     ibid.

695     John Quinn interview; Clark and Andersen, 38.

696  *Del Rio News-Herald*, July 19, 1959; ibid., July 23, 1959; ibid., August 10, 1959; ibid., August 16, 1959; ibid., August 23, 1959; *San Antonio Express and News*, August 22, 1959; Clark and Andersen, 38-9; *San Antonio Light*, August 23, 1959.

697  *The Baytown Sun*, September 11, 1960.

698  Hilda Garcia interview.

699  *The Baytown Sun*, September 11, 1960.

700  Maydelle Anderson interview.

701  *Del Rio News-Herald*, August 24, 1959.

702  *The Kerrville Times*, September 1, September 3, 1959.

703  *San Antonio Express and News*, August 22, 1959.

704  *Del Rio News Herald*, November 16, 1959.

705  *San Antonio Light*, January 21, 1990.

706  Jerry Dickens, "Remember the Alamo?" *Texas Co-op Power*, March 2001, 26-27.

707  Susan Raney Stone interview.

708  Don LaCava interview; *San Antonio Express and News*, August 23, 1959.

709  Lisanti, *Films of the Golden Age*, Summer 1999, 45-49.

710  "The John Wayne Family," *Dayton Daily News Parade*, January 10, 1960, 21-5, Film Wayne, 116, Davis, *Duke*, 226; Tim Lilley, "The Searchers," *The Big Trail*, Vol. XII, No. 1, June, 1995.

711  "Hank Worden interview," Ronald Davis Papers, Degolyer Library, Southern Methodist University, Dallas, Texas.

712  Huberman, Frankie Avalon interview; Ken Pruitt interview; Fred Bronson, *The Billboard Book of Number One Hits*, 62; Lynn Thomas, "19 Cakes and 40 Kisses," *Motion Picture*, January 1960, 52-55, 78.

713  Linda Cristal interview; *Independent Press Telegram*, October 8, 1959.

714  Eyman, *John Wayne*, 330.

715  Relyea, 115-126.

716  Roberson, 232.

717  *Unknown newspaper*, unknown date.

718  Jim Brewer interview.

719  Linda Cristal interview.

720  *San Antonio Light*, December 24, 1959; *San Antonio Express and News*, August 30, 1959; Rothel, *An Ambush of Ghosts*, 20.

721  Deb Slycord, "Following the in the Duke's Footsteps," *The Big Trail*, Vol. X, No. 3, October, 1993; Joan O'Brien interview.

722  *San Antonio Express and News*, October 16, 1960.

CHAPTER NINETEEN – THE PEN IS MIGHTIER THAN THE SWORD

723  Thom Hatch, *Encyclopedia Of The Alamo and the Texas Revolution*, 1, 40-1, 47, 88-90, 129-131, 161-163, 208, 210.

724  Clark and Andersen, 9-10; Patrick Ford to BYU, June 30, 1980, BYU; Dan Ford to author, January 26, 2007.

725  Clark and Andersen, 13; Don Clark to author, February 21, 2012.

726  *Cosmopolitan*, August 1960, 64.

727  Zolotow, 306.

728  *San Angelo Standard Times*, September, 1959.

729  Hurst, v-viii.

730  *Atlantic Daily Telegraph*, May 31, 1911; Thompson, *Alamo Movies*, 17-23.

731  www.rogerebert.suntimes.com; "The Martyrs of the Alamo," www.tcm.com; http://screened. blogspot.com; Thompson, *Alamo Movies*, 24-30; *Waterloo Evening Courier and Reporter*, December 14, 1915.

732  Thompson, *Alamo Movies*, 36-42.

733  Murray Weissmann, "Lost Alamo Movie Found," *The Alamo Journal*, June 1999, 17.

734  Thompson, *Alamo Movies*, 43-45; "Man of Conquest," www.tcm.com; Thomas Ricks Lindley, *Alamo Traces: New Evidence and New Conclusions*, 37-81; *San Antonio Light*, April 7, 1939; *New York Times*, April 28, 1939.

735  The Man from the Alamo," www.tcm.com; Thompson, *Alamo Movies*, 46-48; Peter Ford, *Glenn Ford: A Life*, 131.

736  "DVD Verdict Walt Disney Treasures: Davy Crockett: The Complete Televised Series," www. dvdverdict.com/printer/davycrockettseries.php; Paul F. Anderson, *The Davy Crockett Craze*, 31.

737  Anderson, 36-7.

738  "Sterling Hayden," www.tcm.com; "Sterling Hayden," www.imdb.com; Sterling Hayden, *Wanderer*, 349, 371, 378.

739  Thompson, *Alamo Movies*, 54-66.

740  *San Antonio Express and News*, October 23, 1960; *Los Angeles Mirror-News*, October 21, 1959; Roberson, 230; Bruce Dettman, "Ernest Borgnine on 'The Last Command,'" *The Alamo Journal*, September 2005, 18-19; Thompson, *Alamo Movies*, 61-62; Richard Curilla posting, Alamo Film Movie site, August 12, 2002.

741  Richard Curilla to author, March 9, 2012; The Daughters of the Republic of Texas Present *The Wall of History*; Patrick Ford Alamo treatment, BYU.

742  Patrick Ford to James D'Arc, June 30, 1980, BYU.

743  Paul Andrew Hutton, *A Narrative of the Life of David Crockett by Himself*, xxxvii; James Shackford, *David Crockett; The Man and the Legend*, 273-281.

744   Richard Curilla to author, March 9, 2012.

745   Patrick Ford interview, BYU; *The Alamo*, original screenplay outline, September 21, 1948, BYU; Ybarra interview.

CHAPTER TWENTY – PREPARATIONS

746   *San Antonio News*, October 24, 1960.

747   *Los Angeles Times*, May 19, 1959; ibid., May 27, 1959.

748   *San Antonio Express and News*, August 15, 1959; Clark and Andersen, 61.

749   *The Houston Post*, August 11, 13, 1959.

750   John Quinn to author dated December, 15, 2011.

751   *San Antonio Light*, August 13, 1959; *El Paso Herald-Post*, August 14, 1959; *San Antonio Express and News*, August 16, 1959; *Del Rio News-Herald*, August 30, 1959; *San Antonio Express*, September 3, 1959.

752   Thompson and Covner, Al Ybarra interview; Clark and Andersen, 41-2.

753   *San Antonio Express*, August 28, 1959; *San Antonio Light*, September 3, 1959.

754   Jack Williams to author, January 11, 2007; *The San Antonio Light*, September 2, 1959; Munn, 208-9; *Variety*, October 7, 1959; *Dallas Morning News*, October 23, 1960.

755   John Ford interview, JFP.

756   Relyea, 119-120.

757   *Del Rio News-Herald*, September 2 and 8, 1959.

758   Plunker Sheedy interview.

759   *San Antonio Light*, September 4, 1959; Relyea, 121-122; Robert Harris interview; Herb Lightman, "Filming "The Alamo" in Todd-AO," *American Cinematographer*, November 1960, 662-63, 699-700, 702.

760   Relyea, 123; Jim Brewer to author, December 6, 2006; Rudy Robbins interview.

761   Rich Curilla interview.

762   *Alamo* wardrobe plot, August 9, 1959; *Alamo* wardrobe/ location stills; Rich Curilla interview; *Unknown newspaper*, September, 1959.

763   Alan Kreiger Jr. interview; Zack Davis interview.

764   *The Lima News*, September 8, 1959.

765   *San Antonio Light*, September 8, 1959; ibid., September 14, 1959; ibid., September 16, 1959; Jim Brewer to author.

766   Tim Cumiskey interview; Pat Cumiskey interview.

767   Joan O'Brien interview; Relyea, 119; Jim Brewer to author, March 30, 2009.

768   *San Antonio Express and News*, August 23, 1959; September 6, 1959.

769   Ernesto Malacara interview.

770   *San Antonio Light*, August 25, 1959; *Del Rio News-Herald*, August 28, 1959; ibid., September 4, 1959; ibid., October 21, 1958; ibid., February 19, 1959; ibid., April 6, 1959; ibid., September 27, 1959; *The Kerrville Times*, June 14, 1959; *San Antonio Express*, July 12, 1959; *San Antonio News*, August 21, 1959; *Odessa American*, November 22, 1959.

771   Breivold, 132; James Edward Grant Inter-Office communication, August 4, 195, JFP.

772   Eyman, *John Wayne*, 317.

773   Lon Tinkle to Richard Curilla, April 22, 1967.

774   ibid., 316.

775   Geoffrey Shurlock to John Wayne, August 13, 1959, AMP; Analysis of Film Content, August 6, 1960, AMP.

776   Sean Anmaker, "Burt Kennedy: Writing Broadway in Arizona," November 6, 2008, www.parallax-view.org; Burt Kennedy, *Hollywood Trail Boss: Behind the Scenes of the Wild, Wild Western*, 98.

CHAPTER TWENTY-ONE – THURSDAY, SEPTEMBER 10, 1959.

777   Rich Curilla to author, May 8, 2012.

778   "Act I – The Beginning," www.filmscriptwriting.com; *The Alamo* script, August 3, 1959; author's photographic collection.

779   *Chicago Tribune*, December 13, 1959.

780   Munn, 207; Rothel, *Richard Boone*, 138; *Racine Sunday Bulletin*, November 8, 1959.

781   David Kuykendall interview; *Racine Sunday Bulletin*, November 8, 1959; *Kerrville Times*, November8, 1959.

782   "Shooting Schedule definition," www.eicar-international.com/definition-shooting-schedule.html; *The Alamo* Master Shooting Schedule, August 21, 1959.

783   *The Alamo* script, August 3, 1959; ibid., September 8, 1959; ibid., September 9, 1959.

784   Pilar Wayne, 145; McGivern, *John Wayne*, 293.

785   Munn, 211; Adrian Wooton, "Richard Widmark interview, National Film Theater, July 14, 2002, www.bfi.org.uk/features/interviews/widmark.html.

786   Relyea, 126.

787   Texas Tech University Southwest Special collections Library, Happy Shahan interview, December 10, 1975.

788   Robert Relyea interview.

789   Jamie Rains to author, December 3, 2011; Clark and Andersen, 75.

790   David Kuykendall interview.

791   Jim Brewer interview; Relyea, 126.

792   Scott Allen Nollen, *Three Bad Men: John Ford, John Wayne, Ward Bond*, 308.

793   Pilar Wayne, 135; Roberson, 228.

794   McBride, 600-01; Heran Moon to John Ford, June 14, 1959, JFP; Gallagher, 368.

795   Davis, *Ford*, 298; Colin Young, "The Old Dependables," *Film Quarterly*, Fall 1969, 8-9.

796   Davis, *Ford*, 287-8.

797   McBride, 596; Ford, 282-87; Jean Ramer, *Duke: The Real Story of John Wayne*, 152; John Wayne interview, JFP.

798   *Los Angeles Times*, May 5, 1959; *The New York Times*, July 29, 1959; *Variety*, May 14,1959; ibid., May 20, 1959; ibid., August 17, 1959; *Sunday World-Herald*, September 25, 1960.

799   Robert Relyea interview; Eyman, *John Wayne*, 322.

800   ibid., 279-281; Davis, *Duke*, 227; *Los Angeles Times*, May 5, 1959; Wills, 207; *The Altoona Mirror*, November 11, 1959; Davis, *Ford*, 301.

801   McBride, 612; Munn, 213; Sam Shaw, *John Wayne In The Camera Eye*, 84; Wills, 207; Eyman, *Five American Cinematographers*, 134.

802   Huberman, Denver Pyle interview.

803   *Corpus Christi Times*, January 8, 1959; Ramer, 154; *Anderson Daily Bulletin*, January 10, 1959.

804   Roberson, 235; *The Sunday Herald*, July 7, 2002; Grady Johnson, "John Ford: Maker of Hollywood Stars," *Coronet*, December, 1953, 133-40; Zolotow, 135.

805   Roberts and Olson, 164; Pilar Wayne, 143-44; Robert Relyea interview.

806   Howard Sharpe, "The Star Creators of Hollywood," *Photoplay*, vol. 50, no. 41, 1936, 14-15, 98-100; McBride, 613; *The Gettysburg Times*, October 15, 1959; George Mitchell, "Ford on Ford," *Films in Review*, June/July 1964, 321-32; Davis, *Duke*, 230.

807   Linda Cristal interview; Davis, *Ford*, 304-5.

808   McBride, 622.

809   Eyman, *Print the Legend*, 481; Nollen, 309.

810   Richard Widmark to Ford, September 30, 1959, JFP.

811   Zolotow, 314; Davis, *Ford*, 300.

812   Pilar Wayne, 144-145; Davis, *Duke*, 228; Davis, *Ford*, 300; Munn, 213; McGivern, *John Wayne*, 296; Rudy Robbins interview; *The Houston Post*, October 11, 1959; *The Oregonian*, January 22, 1960.

813   Tim Lilley, "Bernie and the Duke," *The Big Trail*, Vol. XV, No. 4, December, 1998.

814   Eyman, *John Wayne*, 321-22.

815   John Wayne to John Ford, October 1, 1959, JFP; John Ford 1959 travel records, JFP.

816   Lilley, John 'Bear' Hudkins," *Campfires Rekindled*, 70.

CHAPTER TWENTY-TWO – CLASH OF THE TITANS

817  *McLintock!* Dir. Andrew McLaglen. United Artists, 1963. Film, dialog.

818  Clark and Andersen, 71; Sinai, 245; Batjac press release.

819  Batjac press release; Munn, 211; *San Antonio Light,* unknown date; *The Salt Lake Tribune,* October 6, 1959.

820  *Dallas Morning News,* September 8, 1959.

821  Sinai, 247; *The Houston Chronicle,* November 22, 1959; *San Antonio Light,* unknown date; *Oakland Tribune,* December 19, 1959.

822  *The Lancaster Eagle-Gazette,* April 28, 1959; ibid., April 14, 1959; *Big Spring Herald,* March 8, 1959; *The Albuquerque Tribune,* March 6, 1959; *Humboldt Standard,* November 11, 1958.

823  Pat Cumiskey interview; *San Antonio Light,* September 9, 1959; Earl Leaf, "My Fair and Frantic Hollywood," *Teen,* March 1960, 47; *Los Angeles Times,* December 9, 1959; *Variety,* November 12, 1995; *The Cedar Rapids Gazette,* October 3, 1959; *Oshkosh Northwestern,* September 11, 1959; *Anderson Daily Bulletin,* October 31, 1959; *The Daily Herald,* December 9, 1959; "The John Wayne Family," *Parade,* January 10, 1960, 24-25.

824  *Dallas Morning News,* September 21, 1958; *Parade,* January 10, 1960, 24-25; Patrick Wayne interview.

825  *Dallas Morning News,* September 8, 1959; *Variety,* August 31, 1959.

826  *Variety,* August 31, 1959; Martin Grams, Jr. and Les Rayburn, *The Have Gun – Will Travel Companion,* 70-71; *Tucson Daily Citizen,* August 10, 1959; *Advocate,* November 16, 1959.

827  *Los Angeles Times,* September 1, 1959; *Waterloo Daily Courier,* August 31, 1959.

828  *Thank Ya, Thank Ya Kindly,* DVD.

829  David Kuykendall interview; Jerry Carlsen interview.

830  *San Antonio Light,* October 4, 1959.

831  Thomas, "19 Cakes and 40 Kisses," *Motion Picture,* January 1960, 52-55, 78; Leaf, "My Fair and Frantic Hollywood," *Teen,* March, 1960, 47; David Kuykendall interview; *Variety,* September 17, 1959.

832  *Variety,* March 24, 1960; ibid., February 17, 1959; *Hollywood Reporter,* August 12, 1959; ibid., July 7, 1959; ibid., July 29, 1959; ibid., October 7, 1959; ibid., December 14, 1959.

833  Don LaCava interview; Tom Carlisle to Phil Stern, October 15, 1959, Ashley Ward.

834  Zolotow, "Shooting Star" notes; "The John Wayne Family," *Parade,* January 10, 1960, 24-25; Davis, *Duke,* 224-225; Munn, 212.

835  Pilar Wayne, 142; McGivern, *John Wayne,* 292; Davis, *Duke,* 227.

836  Munn, 212; Huberman, Denver Pyle interview.

837  Bobby Copeland, "Cowboy commentary," *Western Clippings,* #97, Sept/Oct 2010, 35; Pilar Wayne, 141; 143; Davis, *Duke,* 233.

838  Fagen, 182, 185.

839    *The News-Palladium*, October 29, 1959.

840    Linda Cristal interview; Munn, 212; Huberman, Ken Curtis interview.

841    Eyman, *John Wayne*, 327; ibid., 330.

842    Zolotow, 314; Fagen, 137; McGivern, *John Wayne*, 295; David Kuykendall interview; *Saturday Evening Post*, October 27, 1962, 28-33.

843    Relyea, 124-5.

844    Marshall Jones interview.

845    Buckley, *Films In Review*, April, 1986, 225; Peter Bogdanovich, *Pieces Of Time*, 186; Edward Dmytryk, *It's a Hell of a Life But Not a Bad Living*, 235; Stuart Kaminsky, *Don Siegel: Director*, 209; Pilar Wayne, 145; Marshall Jones interview; Davis, *Ford*, 304; William Chemerka, "Linda Cristal," *The Alamo Journal*, September 1998, 18-19.

846    Linda Cristal interview.

847    John Quinn interview.

848    Buckley, *Films In Review*, June/July, 1986, 326; Lisanti, *Films of the Golden Age*, Summer, 2009, 73; Richard Widmark interview, CLOSEUP BBC Radio program, March 7, 1997; *The Sunday Herald*, July 7, 2002; Wills, 204.

849    Fagen, 145-46.

850    *The Milwaukee Sentinel*, November 3, 2002.

851    Rudy Robbins interview.

852    Rothel, *An Ambush of Ghosts*, 25.

853    Munn, 211.

854    Wills, 205; Fagen, 131; Carey Jr., 174; Marshall Jones interview; Jim Brewer interview.

855    Gene DeRuelle, *IT'S A FUNNY BUSINESS: Life at the Bottom of the Motion Picture Industry Food Chain*.

856    Marshall Jones interview.

857    Ted White interview.

858    Jim Brewer interview.

859    Davis, *Duke*, 225; Robert Harris interview; Tommy Worrell interview; Jerry Carlsen interview.

860    McGivern, *John Wayne*, 293; Pilar Wayne, 145; Ken Pruitt interview; Ashley Ward interview; *San Antonio Express and News*, September 23, 1959.

861    Munn, 211-212; Carey Jr., 185.

862    Eyman, *John Wayne*, 325.

863    Munn, 211; *San Antonio Light*, November 1, 1959; *Big Spring Herald*, November 2, 1959.

864    Lilley, "Bernie and the Duke," *The Big Trail*, Vol. XV, No. 4, December, 1998.

865   *The News-Palladium*, October 29, 1959; *Variety*, September 25, 1959.

866   McGivern, *John Wayne*, 291.

867   Relyea, 125-6.

868   McGivern, *John Wayne*, 294-95; Aissa Wayne, 48; Fagen, 138; Eyman, *Five American Cinematographers*, 134-135; Wills, 206; Eyman, *John Wayne*, 323.

869   *San Antonio Express-News*, July 16, 1995.

870   David Kuykendall interview; Clark and Andersen, 84.

871   Jack Hamilton, "John Wayne: The Big Man of the Westerns," *Look*, August 2, 1960, 82-87.

872   John Quinn interview.

CHAPTER TWENTY-THREE – HERE WE GO AGAIN

873   Joseph Musso to author, December 3, 2005; *The Alamo* script, October 5, 1959.

874   Eyman, *John Wayne*, 328.

875   USC, John Wayne collection, box 1, folder 10, James Edward Grant to John Wayne, October 11, 1959.

876   *Los Angeles Times*, October 12, 1959; *Appeal-Democrat*, October 13, 1959.

877   *San Antonio Light*, October 16, 1959; *The Times Recorder*, October 11, 1959; *Los Angeles Times*, October 13, 1959; Davis, *Duke*, 229.

878   Dam Cumiskey interview; Pat Cumiskey interview.

879   Jim Brewer to author, November 29, 2006.

880   Rudy Robbins interview; Lilley, "Chuck Roberson," *Campfire Conversations*, 77.

881   Lilley, "Rudy Robbins," *Campfires Rekindled*, 112; Chemerka, "Rudy Robbins," *The Alamo Journal*, June 2007, 15-17.

882   *The Houston Post*, October 2, 1959; *San Antonio Light*, September 9, 1959; ibid., July 18, 1962; ibid., October 9, 1959; *Dallas Morning News*, September 7, 1959; *San Antonio Light*, October 9, 1959.

883   Clapboard definition courtesy of Maurice Jones.

884   *The Alamo* Master Shooting Schedule, August 21, 1959.

885   Lightman, "Filming "The Alamo" in Todd-AO," *American Cinematographer*, November 1960, 662-63, 699-700, 702; Richard Curilla posting, www.johnwayne-thealamo.com/forum.

886   *Tucson Daily Citizen*, May 24, 1958.

887   "Wesley Lau," www.perrymasontvshowbook.com/pmb_c705.htm.

888   Linda Cristal interview.

889   Lilley, "Tom Hennesy," 51-64, *Campfires Rekindled*; Tim Lilley, "Campfire Rekindled," *The Big Trail*, Vol. XI, No. 4, December 1994; John Quinn interview; John Quinn to author, August 29, 2012; *American Cinematographer*, June, 1960; *The Citizen News*, October 26, 1960.

890   *San Antonio Light*, September 15, 1959.

891   *San Antonio Light*, September 11, 1959; *Latino Star y Teleguia*, February 6, 2000, 2-3; "Obituary: Ponder, 81, did local theater and was a weather girl on WOAI," www.mysa.com.

892   *San Antonio Express-News*, March 28, 1965; *San Antonio Light*, October 22, 1975.

893   Teresa Champion interview; Chemerka, Rudy Robbins," *The Alamo Journal*, June 2007, 15-17.

894   Teresa Champion interview.

895   Huberman, Willie Champion interview; Teresa Champion interview; *San Antonio Light*, December 11, 1959; Michele Gualano, "Guerra played a cantina girl in 'The Alamo,'" mysa.com; Alan Kreiger, Jr. interview.

896   *San Antonio Express and News*, August 23, 1959; *San Antonio Light*, September 9, 1959; ibid., September 28, 1959; *Del Rio News-Herald*, September 21, 1959; *Dallas Morning News*, September 30, 1959; ibid., October 6, 1959; Davis, *Duke*, 226; Lilley, "Convention Quartet," *Campfire Conversations: Deluxe Centennial Edition*, 185.

897   *Houston Post*, June 12, 1960; *Unknown newspaper*, unknown date.

898   Eyman, *John Wayne*, 324.

899   Alan Kreiger, Jr. interview.

900   Rich Curilla interview.

901   ibid.

902   Interview with Billie Foust.

903   *Variety*, October 9, 1959; Phil Stern to John Wayne, October 3, 1959, Ashley Ward.

904   Phil Stern to Jim Henaghan, October 17, 1959, Ashley Ward.

905   Richard Widmark to Phil Stern, October 23, 1959, Ashley Ward.

906   Phil Stern, *Phil Stern: A Life's Work,* 120-121.

907   Tom Carlisle to Phil Stern, undated, Ashley Ward.

908   Clark and Andersen, 77; Teresa Champion interview; *The Hollywood Reporter*, August 21, 1959; *Variety*, September 1, 1959.

909   Relyea, 127-8; *Del Rio News-Herald*, October 8, 1959; *San Antonio Express and News*, November 7, 1959; Robert Relyea interview.

910   DeRuelle.

911   John Quinn interview; John Quinn interviewed by Rich Hassler.

912   *San Mateo Times*, October 16, 1959; *Syracuse Herald Journal*, October 30, 1959.

CHAPTER TWENTY-FOUR – MURDER IN SPOFFORD

913   *The Evening Independent*, October 12, 1959; *The Galveston Daily News*, October 12, 1959; *Del Rio News-Herald*, October 13, 1959; ibid., October 12, 1959; *The Press-Courier*, October 12,

1959; *San Antonio Express*, October 12, 1959; *San Marco Times*, October 11, 1959; *Daily Gleaner*, October 14, 1959; *Press Telegram*, October 12, 1959.

914   *Amarillo Globe-Times*, October 13, 1959; *Oakland Tribune*, October 14, 1959; *Pasadena Independent*, October 13, 1959.

915   *The Oneonta Daily Star*, October 23, 1959.

916   *Corpus Christi Times*, October 14, 1959.

917   *San Antonio Express*, October 15, 1959; Huberman, Sam Darden interview; *The Bakersfield Californian*, October 17, 1959.

918   *The Press-Courier*, October 17, 1959; Carpozi, 152; *Clovis News-Journal*, October 16, 1959.

919   *Del Rio News Herald*, November 8, 1959; ibid., October 16, 1959; ibid., October 18, 1959.

920   *San Antonio Express and News*, October 17, 1959; *The San Antonio Light*, October 17, 1959; ibid., January 31, 1960; Carpozi, 153-54.

921   *San Antonio Express and News*, October 17, 1959.

922   *Del Rio News-Herald*, November 9, 1959; ibid., November 10, 1959; ibid., November 13, 1959; San Antonio Express and News, November 7, 1959; *San Antonio Light*, November 10, 1959.

923   *Los Angeles Herald Express*, October 12, 1959.

924   Jim Brewer interview.

925   Crystal Harvey Wade interview; Gwen Watkins interview.

926   Crystal Harvey Wade interview.

927   *San Antonio Light*, October 11, 1959.

928   Eyman, *Print the Legend*, 480; Little John Hamilton interview.

929   Chemerka, "Linda Cristal," *The Alamo Journal*, September 1998, 18-19; Linda Cristal interview; Davis, *Duke*, 225.

930   Relyea, 123.

931   Mary Virginia Pittman-Waller interview.

932   Linda Cristal interview.

933   Mary-Virginia Pittman Waller interview.

934   *Del Rio News-Herald*, September 16, 1959; ibid., September 29, 1959; ibid., October 8, 1959; ibid., October 27, 1959; ibid., November 16, 1959; ibid., December 3, 1959; *unknown newspaper*, October 13, 1959; *San Antonio Light*, December 15, 1959; "Jack Young Meets his Alamo Making The Alamo," www.bloggernews.net/127668; "The Cinematic Life of Black Jack Young," www.tucsonweekly.com/tucson/the-cinematic-life-of-black-jack-young.

935   Joe Canutt interview.

936   "By the way department," *The Alamo News*, July, 1983, 4, 16.

937   Roberson, 234.

938    Eyman, *Print the Legend*, 480; Munn, 213; Bogdonavich, 145; Robert Relyea interview; Thompson and Covner, Al Ybarra interview; Lilley, "Bill Hart," *Campfire Embers*, 59; Don LaCava interview; *Oregon Journal*, December 20, 1959; *Los Angeles Mirror*, November 4, 1960; *Rewgon Journal*, December 20, 1959.

939    Patrick Saunders to author, September 12, 2014.

940    George Stevens, "*Conversations with The Great Moviemakers of Hollywood's Golden Age*," 240-41; Joe York Jr. interview.

941    David Kuykendall interview.

942    Davis, *Ford*, 301; John Wayne to John Ford, October 1, 1959, JFP; McBride, 614 .

943    Pilar Wayne, 145-6; Munn, 206; Aissa Wayne, 44; *Dallas Morning News*, May 5, 1960; Munn, 206; *The Bedford Gazette*, January 7, 1960; *Pacific Stars and Stripes*, January 30, 1960.

944    Fagen, 41; Jim Henaghan, "Inside John Wayne," *Cavalier*, July 1961, 22-24, 67-73.

945    *The Houston Post*, October 2, 1959; Clark and Andersen, 89.

946    *San Antonio Express and News*, August 8, 1959; Clark and Andersen, 89.

947    Rudy Robbins interview; Rudy Robbins to author, November 22, 2005; ibid., October 16, 2006; Tommy Worrell interview.

948    John Quinn interview.

949    Robert Relyea interview; Smith, 119.

950    *San Antonio Express and News*, September 26, 1959

951    Huberman, Michael Wayne interview; Marshal Jones interview.

952    Munn, 211; Hickey, 131; Fagen, 145.

953    *San Antonio Express and News*, October 25, 1959.

954    Munn, 214; Tim Cumiskey interview; John Henry Daniels interview; Elaine Moody interview; John Quinn interview; Susan Raney Stone interview.

955    *Dallas Morning News*, October 4, 1959; *San Antonio Light*, December 15, 1959; Teresa Champion interview.

CHAPTER TWENTY-FIVE – "GOOD MORNING MR. WAYNE."

956    John Henry Daniels to author, August 6, 2006.

957    Aissa Wayne, 44; Aissa Wayne interview; Elaine Moody interview; Barbara Wills White interview.

958    John Henry Daniels interview; *Mary Immaculate*, July-August 1966, 25-28.

959    Pat Cumiskey interview; Dan Cumiskey interview.

960    Hilda Garcia interview.

961    ibid; Barbara Wills White interview.

962    Hilda Garcia interview.

963  *Anderson Daily Bulletin*, April 2, 1960; *San Antonio Light*, November 29, 1960.

964  *San Antonio Light*, October 4, 1959.

965  Jim Brewer interview.

966  Maydelle Anderson interview; *San Antonio Light*, August 10, 1960; *Box Office*, August 22, 1960.

967  Tommy Worrell interview; *Times-Picayne*, September 11, 1960.

968  Ray Campi interview; Robert Harris interview.

969  Jim Brewer interview.

970  Huberman, Don McLendon interview.

971  Don Clark interview; Alamo Village 1998 reunion, Virginia Shahan interview.

972  Tim Lilley, "Tombstone Nuggets," *The Trail Beyond*. Vol. V, December 2003, 58.

973  Joe Canutt interview.

974  Relyea, 121.

975  Smith, 122-123.

976  Roberson, 233-234; Smith, 113.

977  Smith, 119.

978  Rich Curilla interview.

979  Tommy Worrell interview; *Variety*, October 7, 1959.

980  Fourth Coates interview.

981  Tim Lilley, "The Chess Player," *The Trail Beyond*, Vol. X, December 2008, 63-65; *Variety*, October 20, 1959.

982  Lilley, "John 'Bear' Hudkins," *Campfires Rekindled*, 75-76; Davis, *Duke*, 229; Shaw, 104; Lilley, "Jack Williams," *Campfire Conversations: Deluxe Centennial Edition*," 173; Rothel, *An Ambush of Ghosts*, 26-27.

983  *The Houston Chronicle*, November 22, 1959; Relyea, 124.

984  Hickey, 102, 114, 137, 171; Sinai, 1, 43, 68, 81, 114, 128, 178, 225, 249, 298.

985  Eyman, *John Wayne*, 325.

986  Lisanti, *Fantasy Femmes of Sixties Cinema*, 31; Sinai, 248; Munn, 210-11.

987  Hickey, 132-33; Lisanti, *Fantasy Femmes of Sixties Cinema*, 27-39; Linda Cristal interview; David Kuykendall interview.

988  Joan O'Brien interview.

989  Roberts and Olson, 466; Lilley, "Harry Carey Jr.," *Campfire Conversations*, 21.

990   Lilley, "Making Heroes out of Those Cowboy Actors," *The Trail Beyond Trail*, Vol. II, December 2000, 34; Tim Cumiskey interview.

991   DeRuelle.

992   Joe Canutt interview.

993   Teresa Champion interview; Jerry Dickens, "Remember the Alamo?" *Texas Co-op Power*, March 2001, 26-27.

994   Clark and Andersen, 88-9; Haenn, 124; "Army Architecture," *The Fort Clark, Texas Post Return*, Winter 2009, Vol. 2, No. 3, 3.

995   Lilley, "Walter Reed," *Campfire's Glow*, 110.

996   Roberson, 49, 203, 235-238; Lilley, "Bob Morgan," *Campfire Conversations*, 55-64.

CHAPTER TWENTY-SIX – "NOT THAT CLOSE!"

997   Goldman, Louis. *Lights, Camera, Action!*, 13-14, 38-41; Huberman, Don McLendon interview.

998   Joan O'Brien interview.

999   *Del Rio Herald*, October 29, November 2, 1959; *San Antonio Express and News*, October 31, 1959; *The Rocky Mount*, December 8, 1959; *Dallas Morning News*, November 25, 1959; *San Diego Union*, December 15, 1959; *Los Angeles Times*, June 18, 1991; Ruben Padilla Jr. interview; Ruben Padilla III interview.

1000   *San Antonio Express and News*, October 24, 1959; *San Antonio Express*, October 30, 1959; *Houston Chronicle*, October 30, 1959; *Variety*, November 4, 1959.

1001   *The Lima News*, January 24, 1958.

1002   *Corpus Christi Caller-Times*, November 8, 1959; *Dallas Morning News*, October 9, 1959; *San Antonio Express and News*, October 25, 1959.

1003   *Humboldt Standard*, August 7, 1959; *San Antonio Light*, August 8, 1959; *Paris News*, October 4, 1959.

1004   Clark and Andersen, 85-6; *Alamo* file, Burt Sloane to Fred Goldberg, October 21, 1959, DRT.

1005   *Variety*, December 9, 1959; *Alamo* file, Val Coleman to Burt Sloane, March 23, 1960, DRT.

1006   Marshall Jones interview; Clark and Andersen, 86; Lightman, "Filming "The Alamo" in Todd-AO," *American Cinematographer*, November 1960, 662-63, 699-700, 702.

1007   Mathew Sharpe, "Nock's Volley Gun – "A Fearful Discharge," *American Rifleman*, December 2012; William Chemerka, "The Nock Volley Gun," *The Alamo Journal*, July 1986, 5-8.

1008   Robert Harris interview; Lilley, *Campfire Conversations Complete*, 82.

1009   Tim Lilley, "I Went Through a Lot of Windows," *The Trail Beyond*, Volume VIII, December 2006, 41; Jack Williams to author, January 27, 2007.

1010   *Los Angeles Times*, April 23, 1990; Ruben Padilla Jr. interview; Ruben Padilla III interview.

1011   John Henry Daniels to author, August 23 and 31, 2006.

1012   Tim Lilley, "Dimitri Tiomkin," *The Big Trail*, Vol. II, No. 2, August, 1985; *Films in Review*, November, 1951.

1013   Dave Epstein, "Backstage with Film Music Composer," *Etude*, February 1953, 19; Roberson, 238; Lilley, "Chuck Roberson," *Campfire Conversations*, 78.

1014   Robert Harris interview; Richard Curilla provided the thought-provoking explanation of this missing scene; Jim Brewer interview.

1015   Teresa Champion interview.

1016   Rudy Robbins interview; Robert Harris interview; Maydelle Anderson interview; Jerry Dickens, "Remember the Alamo?" *Texas Co-op Power*, March 2001, 26-27.

1017   Robert Harris interview.

1018   Huberman, Bruce Minnex interview; Bruce Minnex interview by Mike Boldt; Clark and Andersen, 85.

1019   Snuggs, 20.

1020   Snuggs, 13; Lilley, "John 'Bear' Hudkins," *Campfires Rekindled*, 71; Lilley, "Dean Smith," *Campfire Conversations Complete*, 86; Alamo Village 1998 reunion, Dean Smith; Alamo Society meeting, Dean Smith; Smith, 119.

1021   *The Brazosport Facts*, September 25, 1960; Alamo Village 1998 reunion, Bill Daniel; *American Cinematographer*, June, 1960.

1022   *San Antonio Express and News*, October 23, 1960.

1023   Lon Tinkle, *An American Original: The Life of J. Frank Dobie*, 229-30.

1024   Thompson, *Alamo Movies*, 77; Rudy Robbins to author, October 10, 12, 2006; *San Antonio Express and News*, October 23, 1960; Chemerka, "Rudy Robbins," *The Alamo Journal*, June 2007, 15-17.

1025   *San Antonio Express and News*, October 24, 25, 1959; *San Antonio Light*, October 25, 1959; ibid., October 27, 1959; *The Galveston Daily News*, October 26, 1959; *Lancaster Eagle-Gazette*, October 27, 1959; *Cumberland Evening Times*, October 17, 1959; *Star-News*, October 19, 1959; *Dallas Morning News*, November 8, 1959; *The Houston Post*, November 15, 1959; Rich Curilla.

1026   *The Hollywood Reporter*, September 14, 1959; *Variety*, October 7, 1959; ibid., March 23, 1960; ibid., advertisement , January 6, 1960; *Los Angeles Examiner* TV Weekly guide, Nov. 13-19, 1960; Landesman, 12.

1027   *Variety*, December 1, 1959; ibid., November 9, 1959; *Oakland Tribune*, August 7, 1959; "'Alamo' Gets Away From Post-Production Looping," Alamo Village scrapbook, 1960; USC, John Wayne Collection, Joseph Cates to Paul Wilson, August 6, 1959.

1028   "The Spirit of the Alamo," NBC Pontiac special, November, 1960; Bruce Minnex interview by Mike Boldt; David Kuykendall interview.

1029   Tinkle, 230-31; Bruce Minnex interview by Mike Boldt; USC, John Wayne Collection, box 3, folder 15, Lon Tinkle to John Wayne, November 3, 1959.

1030   Tim Cuminsky interview.

1031   USC, John Wayne Collection, box 3, folder 15, "The John Wayne Show" outline, August 5, 1959.

1032   *Unknown magazine*; USC, John Wayne Collection, box 3, folder 15, R.W. Emerick to Wayne, December 7, 1959; Gene DeRuelle to author, May 24, 2013.

1033   USC, John Wayne Collection, box 3, folder 15, "The John Wayne Show" outline, August 5, 1959; ibid., Joe Cates to John Wayne, August 7, 1959.

1034   *The Kerrville Times*, November 6, 1959; www.pbs.org/wgbh/amex/quizshow/filmore/transcript/index.html; *The Hollywood Reporter*, October 19, 1959.

1035   Lilley, "Mug Shots," *The Trail Beyond*, Vol III, December 2001, 77-83.

1036   "Army Architecture: Built to Last," *The Fort Clark, Texas Post Return*, Vol. 2 No.1, Summer 2008, 3.

1037   Robert Relyea to author dated May 5, 2010; ibid., May 11,1 2010.

1038   *The Galveston News*, November 16, 1959; *Pasadena Independent*, November 16, 1959; *Del Rio News-Herald*, November 16, 1959.

1039   Bruce Minnex interview by Mike Boldt; Robert Relyea interview.

1040   Clark and Andersen, 80.

1041   Robert Relyea interview; Don LaCava interview; Don Clark to author November 29, 2012; Carpozi, 148.

1042   Shaw, 20-21.

1043   *Variety*, December 16, 1959; ibid., December 4, 1959; ibid., December 7, 1959; ibid., January 29, 1960; Russell Birdwell interview, Zolotow notes, *Shooting Star*.

1044   *San Mateo Times*, September 28, 1959.

1045   Smith, 125-26.

1046   Robert Quinones interview.

1047   *Austin American*, November 18, 1959; *Los Angeles Times*, November 17, 1959; ibid., December 11, 1959; *Variety*, November 17, 1959; ibid., November 18, 1959; ibid., November 11, 1959; *San Antonio Light*, September 4, 1961.

1048   Maydelle Anderson interview; Barbara Wills White interview; Elaine Moody interview; Tim Cumiskey interview; Rudy Robbins interview.

1049   Don Clark posting, www.johnwayne-thealamo.com/forum; Anita Swift interview; Don LaCava interview; Clark and Andersen, 86-87; Pilar Wayne, 146; *The Bedford Gazette*, January 7, 1960.

1050   Bruce Minnex interview with Mike Boldt.

1051   Tommy Worrell interview.

1052   *Los Angeles Times*, April 23, 1990.

1053   Alamo Village 1998 reunion, Bill Daniel; ibid., Joan O'Brien interview.

1054   *Unknown newspaper*, unknown date.

1055   Aissa Wayne interview.

1056   Chuck Hayward interview, JFP.

1057   John Baxter, *Stunt, The story of the great movie stuntmen*, 219.

1058  Amaral, Anthony, *Movie Horses: Their Treatment and Training*, 15-16.

1059  Amaral, 124-5.

1060  Amaral, 23-4, 42.

1061  Needham, 126-7; Amaral, 118.

1062  Huberman, John Jensen interview; McBride, 346; Clark and Andersen, 88; *Los Angeles Mirror*, November 4, 1960.

1063  Huberman, Denver Pyle interview.

1064  Rothel, *An Ambush of Ghosts*, 22.

1065  "Photographing Life; A.Y. Owen Captured America's Moments," *Oklahoma Today*, November – December 1991, Vol. 41, No. 6; Clark and Andersen, 94; A.Y. Owen to Don Clark, December 31, 1962.

1066  Thompson, *Alamo Movies*, 8.

1067  Lindley, 192; Schoelwer, Susan Prendergast, *Alamo Images: Changing Perceptions of a Texas Experience*, 115.

1068  Huberman documentary; J. Frank Dobie, "In The Shadow Of History," www.ttp://digital.library.unt.edu/ark:/67531/metadc38858/m1/20/

1069  Davis, *Duke*, 226; Happy Shahan interview; December 10, 1975; Richard Curilla posting, Alamo Forum.

1070  Huberman, Rudy Robbins interview.

1071  Clark and Andersen, 95; Huberman, Rudy Robbins interview; *Cosmopolitan*, August, 1960, 60-63.

1072  Marianne Ohl Phillips, "Shenna Scrapbook," *Tease*, #3, 42-51.

1073  Huberman, Rudy Robbins interview.

1074  *American Cinematographer*, June, 1960.

1075  Munn, 210; Lilley, "Ted White," *Campfire Conversations, Deluxe Centennial Edition*, 165; Clark and Andersen, 94; *Tease*, #3, 42-51; *Campfire Conversations*, 77.

1076  Ted White interview.

1077  *Tease*, #3, 1995, 42-51.

1078  "Army Architecture, 1886 Mess Halls," *The Fort Clark, Texas Post Return*, Vol. 3, No. 2, Fall 2009; *San Antonio Light*, December 24, 1959; *Variety*, October 7, 1959.

CHAPTER TWENTY-SEVEN – THE OLD MAN AND THE SCENE.

1079  Lilley, "The Call Sheet," *The Trail Beyond*, Volume II, December 2000, 53.

1080  Jim Brewer to author, February 13, 2013; Brewer interview; John Ford 1959, travel records, JFP.

1081  David Kuykendall interview.

1082 Rudy Robbins interview.

1083 Lilley, "Tombstone Nuggets," *The Trail Beyond*, Vol. V, December 2003, 57; Davis, *Duke*, 228.

1084 Lilley, "Gil Perkins," *Campfires Glow*, 91.

1085 ibid.

1086 *Boston Herald*, November 11, 1959.

1087 Denver Pyle interview; Lilley, "Denver Pyle," *Campfires Rekindled*,101-103.

1088 Baxter, *Stunt*, 185; Richard Curilla interview; *American Cinematographer*, June, 1960.

1089 Smith, 120.

1090 *American Cinematographer*, June, 1960.

1091 *San Antonio Light*, December 6, 1959; *The Houston Press*, October 25, 1960; *New York Herald-Tribune*, October, 1960; *New York Times*, October 27, 1960; *Daily Texan*, November 24, 1959; Munn, 214-15; Zolotow, 320-1; Ashley Ward; Munn, 213-14.

1092 "Convention Conversations," *The Big Trail*, Vol. XII, No. 2, August, 1995; Tim Cumiskey interview.

1093 Joe Canutt interview.

1094 Robert Harris interview.

1095 Richard Hatch, *My Black Hollywood: Jester Hairston and the Legacy of the Spirituals.*

1096 DeRuelle.

1097 Tim Cumiskey interview; Marshall Jones interview; Joe Canutt interview.

1098 Eyman, *John Wayne*, 328.

1099 Roberts, Randy and James Olson, *A Line in the Sand*, 267; Clark and Andersen, 77; *Graham Leader*, March 9, 2010.

1100 Relyea, 121.

1101 Robert Harris interview; David Kuykendall interview.

1102 Smith, 118.

1103 Patrick Wayne interview; Wise, Arthur and Derek Ware, *Stunting in the Cinema*, 69; Dean Smith interview; Clark and Andersen, 97.

1104 *The Times-Picayune*, December 19, 1959; *Variety*, November 27, 1959; ibid., December 14, 1959; *Los Angeles Times*, December 9, 1959.

1105 Lilley, "Gil Perkins," *Campfire's Glow*, 92; Joe Canutt interview.

1106 ibid.

1107 *Life*, March 26, 1965; Eyman, *John Wayne*, 323.

1108 *San Antonio Light*, December 6, 1959.

1109  Chuck Hayward interview, JFP; Chuck Roberson interview, JFP; Jack Williams, interview, JFP; Lilley, "Making Heroes out of Those Cowboy Actors," *The Trail Beyond*, Vol. II, December 2000, 28-51; Jim Burk interview, JFP Jack Williams letter to author, January 22, 2007; ibid., February 7, 2007.

1110  Zolotow, 334; Davis, *Duke*, 228.

1111  *Variety*, December 11, 1959; *San Antonio Light*, December 6, 1959.

1112  Richard Hatch, letter from Hairston to wife.www.johnwayne-thealamo.com/forum; *San Antonio Light*, December 4, 1959.

1113  *San Antonio Light*, December 6, 1959.

1114  Richard Curilla posting, www.johnwayne-thealamo.com/forum.

1115  Joe Canutt interview; "John Wayne's *The Alamo*"; Huberman, Bob Morgan interview; Thompson, *Alamo Movies*, 77-8.

1116  David Kuykendall interview; Clark and Andersen, 96.

1117  Huberman, John Jensen interview; ibid., Bob Morgan interview.

1118  Huberman, John Jensen interview.

1119  *San Antonio Light*, December 10, 1959; Russell Birdwell to John Wayne, December 8, 1959, JFP.

1120  Richard Curilla to author, March 25, 2013.

1121  Alamo Village 1998 reunion, Dean Smith; Richard Curilla posting, www.johnwayne-thealamo.com/forum; Smith, 127-29.

1122  Lilley, "I Went Through a lot of Windows," *The Trail Beyond*, VIII. December 2006, 40-48.

1123  Richard Curilla posting, www.johnwayne-thealamo.com/forum.

1124  Hubermann, Ken Curtis interview; Ken Curtis to Don Clark, February 20, 1981, courtesy Don Clark, *Alamo II* Newsletter, April 1981; John Quinn interview.

1125  Jerry Lackey, "WINDMILL: South Texas ranch catered to Hollywood heavyweights," www.gosanangelo.com; Virginia Shahan interview.

1126  Clark and Andersen, 96.

1127  Richard Curilla interview; Richard Curilla to author, March 25 thru 28, 2013.

1128  Rudy Robbins interview, Alamo Village 1998 reunion, Rudy Robbins; *Spirit of the Alamo* documentary.

1129  Clark and Andersen, 96-7.

1130  Richard Curilla to author, April 1, 2013.

1131  Joe Musso, "Movies that Changed Knives Forever," *Blade*, May 2002, 19-20; ibid., June 2003, 43; ibid., July 2002, 102; ibid., September 2011, 34.

1132  Joseph Musso, "'The Iron Mistress,'" *The Alamo Journal*, July 1986, 9-11; Joseph Musso to author, January 16, 2007; Joseph Musso, "Duke's Movie Knives," *Blade*, August 2007, 112-13.

1133  *Playboy*, 82.

1134  Jester Hairston journal.

CHAPTER TWENTY-EIGHT – THE ABBY SINGER

1135  Tony Bill, *Movie speak: How to Talk Like You Belong on a Film Set*, 2.

1136  Aissa Wayne, 44-45; Aissa Wayne interview; John Henry Daniels interview; Munn, 214.

1137  Jose Hernandez III to author, May 25, 2004; Joan O'Brien interview.

1138  "Notes," www.tcm.com/the-alamo/notes.

1139  *ENQUIRER*, unknown date.

1140  Clark and Andersen, 100; "Marine Recruitment Spot from set of The Alamo" www.johnwayne-thealamo.com; *Corpus Christi Times*, December 22, 1959.

1141  Eyman, *John Wayne*, 321-22.

1142  Munn, 212.

1143  *San Antonio Express and News*, January 3, 1960; *Los Angeles Herald Express*, December 26, 1959; Rothel, *Richard Boone*, 138; *Dallas Morning News*, December 14, 1959; ibid., December 16; *Variety*, December 14, 1959; Davis, *Duke*, 225; Jane Pattie, *John Wayne There Rode A Legend*, 247; *The Cedar Rapids Gazette*, December 30, 1959; *Morning Advocate*, September 18, 1960; *San Antonio Light*, October 23, 1960; Nollen, 306-7; Munn, 204.

1144  USC, John Wayne Collection, box 1, folder 10, James Grant to John Wayne, December 2, 1959.

1145  USC, John Wayne Collection, box 1, folder 10, James Grant to John Wayne, December 4, 1959.

1146  *Los Angeles Times*, December 16, 1959; *Box Office*, February 13, 1960.

1147  *Variety*, February 10, 1960; *Box Office*, February 8, 1960.

1148  *Variety*, December 16, 1959; *The Hollywood Reporter*, December 16, 1959; *San Antonio Light*, December 15, 1959; *Variety*, December 18, 1959; ibid., January 6, 1960.

1149  *Cosmopolitan*, August, 1960, 60-65.

1150  Marty Freize interview; Roberts and Olson, 447; *Tucson Daily Citizen*, November 26, 1966.

1151  *San Antonio Express and News*, December 14, 1959.

1152  Clark and Andersen, 103; USC, John Wayne collection, box 3, folder 15, Henry Fownes, Jr. to John Wayne, May 18, 1959.

1153  Clark and Andersen, 104; Eliot, Marc, *Reagan: The Hollywood Years*, 332-334.

1154  *Variety*, January 29, 1960; *Alamo* file, Burt Sloane to U.A. staff, February 9, 1960, DRT.

1155  *Alamo* file, Marg-Riette Montgomery to Russell Birdwell, January 19, 1960, DRT.

1156  Russell Birdwell to Price Daniel, January 18, 1960; *Alamo* file, Russell Birdwell to Buck Hood, January 21, 1960, DRT.

1157  *Alamo* file, Marg-Riette Montgomery to Russell Birdwell, January 27, 1960, DRT.

1158  *Motion Picture*, January, 1960, 52-55, 78; *Parade*, January 10, 1960; *Texas Co-op Power*, February, 1960; Leaf, "My Fair and Frantic Hollywood," *Teen*, March, 1960, 47; Kahn, "Will Frankie's Flame Flicker?", May, 1960, 16-19; "Hollywood Goes European," *Playboy*, November, 1959, 43-45.

CHAPTER TWENTY-NINE – "THIS, AND ONE MORE."

1159  Zolotow's notes, *Shooting Star*.

1160  Eyman, *John Wayne*, 331.

1161  Russell Birdwell publicity bulletin; "The Alamo," The Film Daily, January 27, 1960; *Register Republic*, February 13, 1960; Fagen, 133.

1162  Buck Houghton, *What a Producer Does*, 166-175; Breivold, 133; *Los Angeles Times*, April 6, 1960.

1163  *The Hollywood Reporter*, January 11, 1960; *San Antonio Light*, January 12, 1960; *The Citizen-News*, January 13, 1960.

1164  Craig Covner to author, November 9, 2008.

1165  Extra Credits: The History and Collection of Pacific Title and Art Studio. Thesis submitted by Adam Duncan Harris, University of Minnesota, 10, 15.

1166  ibid. 87-91.

1167  Clark and Andersen, 110-11; *Morning Advocate*, May 29, 1960.

1168  Clark and Andersen, 41; Don Clark to author, April 25, 2011.

1169  *Unknown newspaper*, unknown date.

1170  *San Antonio Light*, January 15, 1960; *Dallas Morning News*, January 27, 1960; *Variety*, March 2, 1960; *Fort Worth Star-Telegram*, February 3, 1960.

1171  Rothel, *An Ambush of Ghosts*, 34.

1172  ibid., 31-34; Pat Wayne to author, June 21, 2008; *Sunday World-Herald*, September 25, 1960; John Wayne to Ned Huthmacher, March 6, 1978.

1173  *San Antonio Express and News*, August 19, 1961.

1174  *Llano News*, April 26, 1973; *Unknown* newspaper, October 20, 1971.

1175  *Variety*, January 6, 1959; ibid., January 18, 1960; ibid., October 26, 1960; *Cavalier Magazine*, July 1961, 22-24, 67-73; Ramer, 167-8; *The Capital Times*, January 19, 1960; *Box Office*, January 25, 1960.

1176  *Unknown newspaper*, unknown date; Davis, *Ford*, 301.

1177  *Brownsville Herald*, January 29, 1960; *San Antonio Express and News*, January 31, 1960; *Unknown newspaper*, January 31, 1960.

1178  Alamo Day Proclamation, March 6, 1960; *San Antonio Light*, March 1, 1960; *Variety*, February 10, 1960; *Box Office*, April 4, 1960.

1179  Burt Sloane to Fred Goldberg, February 15, 1960, author's collection.

1180  Don LaCava interview; *Variety*, February 10, March 9, 1960.

1181  McGivern, *John Wayne*, 298.

1182  AMP, George Stevens Papers, 165-f.1750, Insurance Service Bureau, Robert Thom to Robert Newman, April 3, 1962.

1183  John Wayne to Fred Landesman, July 6, 1977, courtesy of Fred Landesman; *Variety*, March 9, 1960; *Trenton Evening Times*, May 5, 1960.

1184  USC, John Wayne collection, box 3, folder 21, File Alamo audit.

1185  USC, John Wayne collection, box 1, folder 10, James Grant to John Wayne, December 12, 1960; ibid., December 13, 1960.

1186  "An Open Letter to John Wayne . . . ," *Life*, March 7, 1960, 8; *Box Office*, February 1, 1960.

1187  No. 2 Russell Birdwell *Alamo* publicity bulletin.

1188  *Variety*, March 17, 1960; February 8, 1961; *Box Office* February 15, 1960; Sheldon Hall and Steve Seale, *Epics, Spectaculars and Blockbusters*, 44; *Dallas Morning News*, March 18, 1960.

1189  Maurice Jones to author, October 11, 2104.

1190  *Box Office*, March 21, 1980.

1191  Russell Birdwell to Tom Carlile, April 12, 1960, courtesy of Bill Jweid; ibid., April 14, 1960; Tom Carlile white paper, undated, courtesy Bill Jweid; Clark and Andersen, 128; AMP, George Stevens Papers, 299-f.3461, Russell Birdwell to George Stevens, October 5, 1960; ibid., October 11, 1960; *Variety*, May 13, 1965.

1192  Western Union telegram, Russell Birdwell to Carl Sandburg, October 5, 1960, AMP.

CHAPTER THIRTY – THIS, AND ONE MORE. NO, REALLY!"

1193  "'Alamo' Gets Away From Post-Production Looping," Alamo Village scrapbook, 1960.

1194  *Etude*, February, 1953, 19, 60-61; *Films in Review*, 1951; Jeffrey Dane, "Remembering Dimitri Tiomkin," www.in70mm.com; *Los Angeles Examiner*, October 25, 1960.

1195  *The Hollywood Reporter*, May 9, 1960; *Star Bulletin*, April 24, 1960; *Variety*, January 4, 1961.

1196  *Variety*, April 14, 1960; ibid., Oct 5, 1960; ibid., August 31, 1960; ibid., May 25, 1960; ibid., March 2, 1960; *The Alamo* sound track recorded by the City of Prague Philharmonic Orchestra, 2010; The Alamo Company cue sheets, September 30, 1960.

1197  *Variety*, August 11, 1960; ibid., August 31, 1960; ibid., October 5, 1960.

1198  Munn, 215-6.

1199  *San Antonio Light*, October 23, 1960; *Variety*, September 16, 1960; *Los Angeles Mirror News*, March 30, 1961; *The Galveston News*, May 9, 1956.

1200  Clark and Andersen, 112, 115-6.

1201  *Variety*, October 19, 26 and December 7, 1960; June 3, 1964.

1202  Bill Gilmore interview.

1203  Ashley Ward to author, June 28/30, 2013.

1204  Clark and Andersen, 114; *San Antonio Light*, April 11, 1960; ibid., April 28, 1960; *Dallas Morning News*, April 29, 1960; *Unidentified newspaper*, unidentified date; *The San Antonian*, June 9, 1960.

1205  *Box Office*, May 23, 1960; *San Antonio Express and News*, April 30, 1960; Clark and Andersen, 116; *Tucson Daily Citizen*, May 4, 1960; *Alamo* file, Russell Birdwell to Mrs. H. Raymond Hagen, April 18, 1960, DRT.

1206  *Dallas Morning News*, August 15, 1959; *San Antonio Express and News*, August 15, 1959; ibid., November 9, 1959; *The Victoria Advocate*, August 9, 1959; *Daily Sun*, August 6, 1959; *El Paso Herald Post*, October 13, 1959.

1207  Clark and Andersen, 118.

1208  *Variety*, September 7, 1960; ibid., October 19, 1960; ibid., November 30, 1960; *Boston Herald*, September 27, 1960; *San Antonio Light*, March 19, 1961.

1209  *San Antonio Express and News*, June 4, 1960.

1210  Clark and Andersen, 114; *Variety*, April 20, 1960; *Trenton Evening Times*, May 3, 1960.

1211  Clark and Andersen, 114.

1212  USC, John Wayne collection, box 3, folder 3, Bank of America loan agreement with Batjac dated May 25, 1960.

1213  Landesman, 244; Clark and Andersen, 114-5; "'Alamo' Popsicle ad," *Laugh* comic book, August, 1960, 7. "Popsicle ad," http://library.duke/edu/digitslcollections/oaaaarchives_BBB5269/; *Cleveland Plain Dealer*, May 21, 1960; *San Diego Union*, June 19, 1960; *Box Office*, August 1, 1960.

1214  *Valley Sun*, April 28, 1960.

1215  USC, John Wayne Collection, box 1, folder 10, James Edward Grant to John Wayne and Russell Birdwell, June 23, 1960.

1216  Steve Frazee, *The Alamo*; Lon Tinkle, *13 Days to Glory*; Don LaCava interview; Clark and Andersen, 119; *Dallas Morning News*, October 2, 1960.

1217  *San Antonio Express and News*, May 21, 1960; *Dallas Morning News*, June 7, 1960.

1218  *San Antonio Light*, June 7, 1960; *San Antonio News*, June 7, 1960; *Dallas Morning News*, June 8, 1960; ibid., June 25, 1960; ibid., August 24, 1960; ibid., September 1, 1960; ibid., September 7, 1960; *San Antonio Express*, June 8, 1960; *Variety*, June 6, 1960; *Box Office*, June 27, 1960; *San Antonio Express and News*, August 27, 1960; ibid., September 17, 1960; *Variety*, January 6, 1960; *The San Antonian*, June 9, 1960.

1219  *Box Office*, June 13, 1960.

1220  *San Antonio News*, June 22, 1960; *The San Antonian*, June 23, 1960; *Air Force Times*, September 21, 1960; *Box Office*, October 17, 1960.

1221  *Unknown newspaper*, unknown date.

1222  *Box Office*, June 27, 1960.

1223  *Variety*, June 23, 1960; ibid., May 23, 1960; *The San Antonio Light*, June 13, 1960.

CHAPTER THIRTY-ONE – ON THE ROAD AGAIN

1224   Arthur Schlesinger, *Kennedy or Nixon: Does It Make Any Difference?* 35-42; Stephen Ambrose, *Eisenhower: Soldier and President*, 525.

1225   Clark and Andersen, 116; *Box Office*, July 11, 1960; *Variety*, June 29, 1960; *Variety*, June 1, 1965.

1226   Russell Birdwell, "There were no ghost writers at the Alamo," Tri-fold statement of principle, *Life*, July 4, 1960, 1-3.

1227   Nancy Gibbs and Michael Duffy, The *President's Club: Inside the World's Most Exclusive Fraternity*, 103, 105, 106, 109, 122, 127, 128, 130, 142, 143, 198; Kiron Skinner, Annelise Anderson and Martin Anderson, *Reagan, A Life in Letters*, 704; *Los Angeles Times*, October 22, 1960.

1228   *Pharos-Tribune*, July 12, 1960; *San Antonio Light*, October 23, 1960; *Variety*, August 17, 1960; John Wayne, "A Picture That Had to Be Made," 30th Anniversary issue. *The Hollywood Reporter*.

1229   *Herald Tribune*, July 5, 1960.

1230   *Variety*, June 1, 1965.

1231   *Mohenty Index and Democrat*, July 5, 1960; John F. Kennedy: " Remarks of Senator John F. Kennedy, the Alamo, San Antonio, TX," September 12, 1960. Online by Gerhard Peters and John T. Woolley, *The American Presidency Project*; Kitty Kelley, *His Way: The Unauthorized Biography of Frank Sinatra*, 273; *Saturday Evening Post*, October 27, 1962, 28-33; Munn, 217; *The Oklahoman*, May 15, 1960.

1232   *Variety*, June 28, 1960; *Variety*, July; Clark and Andersen, 118; *Limelight*, June 30, 1960; *Advertising News of New York*, July 8, 1960.

1233   *Alamo file*, Marg-Riette Montgomery to Russell Birdwell, July 1, 1960, DRT; *San Antonio Light*, March 5, 1961,

1234   *Sandusky Register*, September 1, 1960.

1235   Clark and Andersen, 118.

1236   ibid., 123; *Life* Tri-fold *Alamo* Statement of Principle brochure.

1237   *The Daily Courier*, January 28, 2012; *Protestant Magazine for Armed Forces Personnel*, September, 1969; Clark and Andersen, 123; *Alamo* souvenir program, Sovereign Publications, 1960; *Variety*, September 16, 1959.

1238   *Alamo* file, Russell Birdwell to Roger Lewis, August 4, 1960, DRT; *Alamo* file, Franz Karl Brown to Steve Beck, December 11, 1987, DRT; Clark and Andersen, 123; *Alamo* file, Russell Birdwell to Roger Lewis, August 8, 1960, DRT; *San Antonio Express and News*, October 16, 1960.

1239   Clark and Andersen, 119; *San Antonio Light*, August 17, 1960.

1240   *Box Office*, June 20, 1960; Bill Gilmore interview.

1241   "Hollywood Sneak Previews," Bob Campbell, www.moviefanfare.com/hollywood-sneak-previews/.

1242   *The Exhibitor*, October 12, 1960.

1243   *The San Antonian*, July 14, 1960; ibid., July 21, 1960; *San Antonio Light*, July14, 1960; *Del Rio News-Herald*, July 17, 1960; *The Recorder*, July 28, 1960; *Variety*, August 3, 1960.

1244  *Del Rio News-Herald*, August 7, 1960; Clark and Andersen, 120; *The San Antonian*, August 4, 1960; ibid., September 8, 1960.

1245  Clark and Andersen, 123-4.

1246  ibid., 124.

1247  Burt Sloane to Roger Lewis, July 7, 1960, author's collection; ibid., July 28, 1960.

1248  "Freedomland, the true history," http://backinthebronx.com; *Advertising Age*, October 17, 1960.

1249  Clark and Andersen, 124.

1250  ibid., 129.

1251  ibid., 125; Alamo Sound track, Columbia, Cl 1558.

1252  *Denver Post*, August 4, 1960.

1253  ibid., August 8, 1960; *New York Times*, September 4, 1960.

1254  *Denver Post*, August 5, 1960.

1255  *Variety*, August 5, 1960.

1256  Bill Gilmore interview.

1257  Clark and Andersen, 126; Bill Gilmore interview; *Variety*, August 9, 1960; *The Denver Post*, August 6, 1960; *Variety*, August 9, 1960.

1258  USC, John Wayne Collection, box 1, folder 10, James Edward Grant to John Wayne, August 1960.

1259  *The Hollywood Reporter*, August 8, 1960.

1260  USC, John Wayne Collection, box 1, folder 10, James Grant to John Wayne, August 16, 1960; *Variety*, August 9, 1960; ibid., August 11, 1960; *Box Office*, July 25, 1960.

1261  *Variety*, August 22, 1960.

1262  Clark and Andersen, 128.

1263  Meeting notes, U.A. and Russell Birdwell, August 11, 1960, author's collection.

1264  Clark and Andersen, 126; August 26, 1960 United Artists meeting minutes, author's collection; *Box Office*, September 26, 1960.

1265  August 26, 1960 United Artists meeting minutes, author's collection; *San Diego Union*, September 4, 1960; *Variety*, September 28, 1960; *San Antonio News*, August 4, 1960.

1266  *Variety*, August 22, 1960; *San Antonio Express and News*, October 22, 1960.

1267  *Box Office*, September 5, 1960; *San Antonio Light*, October 6, 1960.

1268  *The New York Times*, August 28, 1960; *San Antonio Light*, August 28, 1960; ibid., September 4, 1960; *Los Angeles Times*, September 1, 1960; *Variety*, October 11, 1960; *The Times-Picayune*, October 5, 1960.

1269  *San Antonio Light*, September 21, 1960; *Box Office*, September 12, 1960; ibid., October 3, 1960.

1270  *Dallas Morning News*, September 9, 1960; *Variety*, September 14, 1960.

1271  *Box Office*, September 12, 1960; Clark and Andersen, 128.

1272  *Dallas Morning News*, September 13, 1960; *Box Office*, September 5, 1960; *Chicago Daily Tribune*, October 4, 1960.

1273  *Chicago Sun-Times*, October 16, 1960.

1274  *Chicago Daily Tribune*, August 29, 1960; *The Dallas Morning News*, September 3, 1960; Clark and Andersen, 129; *Variety*, October 5, 1960; *Press-Telegram*, August 28, 1960.

1275  *Box Office*, September 26, 1960.

1276  ibid., September 19, 1960; ibid., October 17, 1960.

1277  Clark and Andersen, 129; *The Oklahoman*, September 16, 1960; ibid., September 17, 1960; *The Houston Post*, September 12, 1960.

1278  You-Tube, John Wayne interview.

1279  *Sunday World-Herald*, September 25, 1960; *Chicago Daily News*, September 20, 1960.

1280  *Variety*, September 19, 1960; Pilar Wayne, 160.

1281  *Toronto Daily Star*, September 24, 1960.

1282  *Chicago Daily Tribune*, September 27, 1960; ibid., September 15, 1960; McGivern, *John Wayne*, 301; *Box Office*, October 3, 1960; *Variety*, September 27, 1960.

1283  Clark and Andersen, 126, 129, 131; *New York Times*, October 6, 1960.

1284  *The Oregonian*, July 15, 1960; *Rockford Register*, July 19, 1960; *Los Angeles Times*, May 29, 1960; Jack Hamilton, "All my Money – and all my Soul," *Today*, October 29, 1960, 8-10.

1285  USC, John Wayne collection, box 1, folder 10, James Edward Grant to John Wayne, September 24, 1960.

CHAPTER THIRTY-TWO – HOORAY FOR HOLLYWOOD!

1286  *Los Angeles Times*, October 9, 1960.

1287  *Box Office*, August 29, 1960; ibid., October 3, 1960; *Los Angeles Times*, October 9, 1960; ibid., September 25, 1960; ibid., October 23, 1960; ibid., October 30, 1960; Clark and Andersen, 132; *Unidentified newspaper*, unidentified date; *Chicago Tribune*, October 19, 1960; *San Antonio Light*, October 19, 1960.

1288  *Box Office*, October 3, 1960; ibid., October 10, 1960; *Alamo* file, Theo Weiss to committee members, October 31, 1960, DRT; *Alamo* file, Theo Weiss to Mrs. T. E. McCray, September 29, 1960, DRT; *Variety*, October 19, 1960; ibid., October 4, 1960.

1289  "Alamo Premiere Trail Riders Leave Brackettville Oct. 18," *Farm and Ranch News*, October 7, 1960; *The San Antonian*, September 29, 1960; *San Antonio Express and News*, October 2, 1960.

1290  Batjac publicity bulletin, October 10, 1960, author's collection.

1291  *Alamo* file, Buddy Young to Lester Dinoff, October 21, 1960, DRT.

1292  *The Hollywood Reporter*, October 26, 1960; *Variety*, October 24, 1960; Clark and Andersen, 129.

1293   Clark and Andersen, 132; *Los Angeles Times*, October 21, 1960; *Daily News*, October 21, 1960.

1294   Alamo Village History Boards, Richard Curilla to author, April 14, 2004.

1295   "Alamo Premiere Trail Riders Leave Brackettville Oct. 18," *Farm and Ranch News*, October 7, 1960; *The San Antonian*, October 13, 1960.

1296   *San Antonio Light*, October 19, 1960.

1297   ibid., September 25, 1960; *Variety*, October 21, 1960; *The Hollywood Reporter*, October 2, 1960; *San Antonio Express and News,* October 22, 1960.

1298   *San Antonio Express and News*, October 22, 1960; *San Antonio Express*, October 24, 1960.

1299   *San Antonio Light*, October 23, 1960.

1300   *The Bee*, October 27, 1960.

1301   *San Antonio Express and News*, October 22, 1960; *The Oregonian*, October 24, 1960; *Mexico City Daily Bulletin*, no date; *Variety*, October 26, 1960.

1302   *Variety*, October 24, 1960.

1303   *San Antonio Express and News*, October 16, 1960.

1304   *San Antonio Light*, October 21, 1960, ibid., October 23, 1960; *The Handy-Andy Herald*, November, 1960; *San Antonio Express-News*, March 24, 2004.

1305   *San Antonio Express and News*, October 23, 1960; *San Antonio Light*, October 23, 1960; Clark and Andersen, 134; USC, San Antonio Symphony, Alamo program, No. 3 – October 22, 1960, Dimitri Tiomkin *Alamo* scrapbook.

1306   *The San Antonian*, October 13, 1960; *Variety*, October 26, 1960.

1307   *San Antonio Light*, October 24, 1960; *San Antonio News*, October 24, 1960; *San Antonio Express*, October 24, 1960; *Baytown Sun*, September 11, 1960.

1308   Clark and Andersen, 134; *Alamo* file, Master Schedule of Events World Premiere of *Alamo*, DRT.

1309   *San Antonio Light*, October 21, 1960.

1310   *San Antonio Express*, October 25, 1960; *San Antonio Light*, November 2, 1960.

1311   *San Antonio Light*, October 9, 1960; ibid., October 24, 1960; ibid., October 30, 1960; "History," www.lavillita.com; Walter Corrigan to Mrs. W.S. Hamlin, October 27, 1960, San Antonio Conservation Society Foundation Library.

1312   *The Houston Post*, October 25, 1960; *San Antonio Light*, January 21, 1990.

1313   *San Antonio Express*, October 25, 1960, ibid., October 20, 1960; *The San Antonian*, October 20, 1960.

1314   *The Times-Picayune*, September 30, 1960; *San Antonio Light*, October 24, 1960.

1315   *Alamo* file, Master Schedule of Events World Premiere of *Alamo*, DRT; *San Antonio Light*, October 25, 1960; T*he Hollywood Reporter*, February 1, 1961.

1316   *Variety*, October 25, 1960; San Antonio Express, October 25, 1960.

1317   *San Antonio Light*, October 24, 1960.

1318   www.ohenryhouse.org.

1319   *San Antonio Light*, October 25, 1960.

1320   ibid.

1321   *The Houston Post*, October 25, 1960.

1322   *The Citizen News*, October 26, 1960; *Los Angeles Herald & Express*, October 25, 1960; *The San Antonian*, October 20, 1960; ibid., October 13, 1960; *San Antonio Express*, October 21, 1960; ibid., October 25, 1960; *San Antonio Light*, October 24, 1960.

1323   Clark and Andersen, 137.

1324   *San Antonio Express-News*, March 24, 2004.

1325   *Limelight*, October 27, 1960; *San Antonio Light*, October 25, 1960.

1326   *Variety*, October 24, 1960.

1327   *San Antonio Light*, October 21, 1960; Clark and Andersen, 139; *San Antonio News*, October 25, 1960.

1328   *San Antonio Express*, October 25, 1960; *Denton Record-Chronicle*, October 25, 1960.

1329   *San Antonio Express and News*, October 27, 1960.

1330   *San Antonio Light*, October 25, 1960.

1331   *Unknown newspaper*, November 23, 1960; *The San Antonian*, December 8, 1960.

1332   *Variety*, November 30, 1960.

1333   *Dallas Morning News*, October 26, 1960; ibid., October 25, 1960; *Box Office*, November 7, 1960.

1334   *Newsday*, October 27, 1960; *New York World-Telegram*, October 27, 1960; *New York Daily News*, October 27, 1960; *New York Journal-American*, October 27, 1960; *Box Office*, October 31, 1960; ibid., November 7, 1960.

1335   *New York Herald Tribune*, October 30, 1960.

1336   *Variety*, October 28, 1960.

1337   Zolotow, 318.

1338   *New York Post*, October 27, 1960; *New York Times*, October 27, 1960.

1339   *Los Angeles Herald & Express*, October 27, 1960; *Racine Journal-Times*, October 4, 1960; *Chicago Tribune*, October 6, 1960.

1340   *The Hollywood Reporter*, October 26, 1960; *The Citizen News*, October 27, 1960; *San Antonio News*, October 27, 1960.

1341   *Unknown newspaper*, October 27, 1960; *Los Angeles Times*, October 26, 1960; Clark and Andersen, 138; *Star News*, November 4, 1960.

1342   *Los Angeles Herald and Express*, October 27, 1960.

1343  *Citizen-News*, October 27, 1960; *Los Angeles Times*, October 27, 1960.

1344  *Limelight*, October 27, 1960; *Variety*, October 28, 1960.

1345  *Daily Herald London*, October 21, 1960.

1346  *United Artists World*, November 4, 1960; *Limelight*, October 27, 1960.

1347  *Omaha World-Herald*, October 28, 1960; *Uniontown Morning Herald*, November 30, 1960; *Republic Register*, November 5, 1960; *Diary*, November 28, 1960; *Evening Standard*, October 28, 1960.

1348  *The Guardian*, October 29, 1960; ibid., October 30, 1960; ibid., October 27, 1960; ibid., October 28, 1960; *San Antonio Express and News*, December 30, 1962; *United Artists World*, November 4, 1960; *Box Office*, November 14, 1960; Royal Gala Premiere programme of *The Alamo* at the Astoria Cinema, Charing Cross Road, October 27, 1960.

1349  ibid.

CHAPTER THIRTY-THREE – "THE NOMINEES FOR BEST PICTURE ARE ... "

1350  *The Houston Post*, October 25, 1960; *Toronto Telegram*, October 25, 1960; *Rockford Register*, October 26, 1960; *Chicago Sun-Times*, October 28, 1960; *Dallas Morning News*, November 3, 1960; *Chicago Tribune*, November 6, 1960; *Los Angeles Times*, November 24, 1960.

1351  "Film Reviews," *Unknown magazine*, unknown date; *Los Angeles Mirror*, October 27, 1960; *Chicago Sun-Times*, October 28, 1960; *Chicago Tribune*, October 28, 1960; *Unknown magazine*, unknown date.

1352  *Los Angeles Mirror-News*, November 5, 1960; *Variety*, April 26, 1961.

1353  *Los Angeles Times*, November 14, 1960; *Box Office*, November 21, 1960.

1354  Emanuel Levy, *John Wayne: Prophet of the American Way of Life*, 318; *Los Angeles Times*, March 8, 1961.

1355  Clark and Andersen, 139; *Unknown newspaper*, November 9, 1960; *The Hollywood Reporter*, November 4, 1960.

1356  *San Antonio Light*, November 25, 1960; *The Hollywood Reporter*, November 1, 1960; ibid., November 4, 1960; ibid., November 25, 1960; *Variety*, September 27, 1960; *Billboard*, October 24, 1960; ibid., December 5, 1960; ibid., December 13, 1960.

1357  Breivold, 192; Paul A. Helmick, *Cut, Print, and that's a Wrap: A Hollywood Memoir*, 146; Stevens, 127; Munn, 297.

1358  Davis, *Duke*, 231-2.

1359  Munn, 220.

1360  Bill Gilmore interview.

1361  Scene by scene comparison of roadshow and general release version.

1362  *New York Times*, November 3, 1960; *Unknown newspaper*, November 9, 1960; Clark and Andersen, 139-40; *Chicago Tribune*, November 18, 1960; *The Hollywood Reporter*, November 4, 1960.

1363  *The Oklahoman*, November 4, 1960; ibid., November 8, 1960; *The Hollywood Reporter*, December 8, 1960.

1364   *Toronto Daily-Star*, November 9, 1960; November 12, 1960; *Box Office*, November 28, 1960.

1365   *Box Office*, November 28, 1960.

1366   *Los Angeles Times*, November 24, 1960; *Playboy*, May, 1971, 88.

1367   *Variety*, November 7, 1960; ibid., November 9, 1960; ibid., June 5, 1961; Nollen, 313-15; *The Saturday Evening Post*, October 27, 1962, 28-33; Michael Schlossheimer, *Gunmen and Gangsters: Profiles of Nine Actors who Portrayed Memorable Screen Tough Guys*, 78; Tim Lilley, *The Trail Beyond*, Vol. VII, December 2005, 42.

1368   *Variety*, November 14, 1960; *Chicago Tribune*, November 15, 1960; *Leader-Times*, November 15, 1960; *Los Angeles Times*, November 17, 1960.

1369   *The Hollywood Reporter*, December 16, 1960.

1370   *Box Office*, December 5, 1960; *Variety*, December 7, 1960; *The Hollywood Reporter*, December 23, 1960; ibid., January 16, 1961.

1371   Zolotow Shooting Star draft, 618; *Films and Filming*, December, 1960. Vol. 7 no. 3, pg. 32-33.

1372   You-Tube, John Wayne interview.

1373   *Lebanon Daily News*, December 2, 1960; *Variety*, November 14, 1960; ibid., November 25, 1960; Zolotow, 322-23; *San Antonio News*, December 2, 1960; *The Hollywood Reporter*, December 6, 1960.

1374   *The Hollywood Reporter*, December 6, 13 and 21, 1960.

1375   *Box Office*, January 16, 1961; *The Hollywood Reporter*, December 12, 1960; ibid., January 19, 1961; ibid., December 13, 1960; ibid., January 12, 1961.

1376   *Variety*, December 21, 1960.

1377   Michael Thornton, "The siren with the two greatest assets in Tinseltown: Behind the sex-goddess image of Jane Russell was a very different woman." http://www.dailymail.co.uk/femail/article-1362040.

1378   *Variety*, December 12, 1960, ibid., December 21, 1960; Clark and Andersen, 143.

1379   Peter H. Brown, *The Real Oscar*, 16, 63, 72, 144; *The Hollywood Reporter*, December 5, 1960; ibid., December 20, 1960.

1380   *Variety*, December 27, 1960; *The Hollywood Reporter*, January 9, 1961; ibid., February 8, 1961.

1381   *Variety*, December 27, 1960.

1382   *The Hollywood Reporter*, December 19, 1960, January 3, 1961.

1383   *Southern California Prompter*, October 1960; Pilar Wayne, 148; Davis, *Duke*, 232; Munn, 218, 220.

1384   Pilar Wayne, 148-9.

1385   USC, John Wayne Collection, box 1, folder 10, James Edward Grant to John Wayne, August 1960.

1386   *Variety*, January 24, 1960; *San Antonio News*, January 24, 1961.

975

1387   Clark and Andersen, 143; USC, John Wayne Collection, box 3, folder 12, Western Union telegram from Seymour Poe to Wayne, January 3, 1961; *Variety*, January 12, 1961.

CHAPTER THIRTY-FOUR – WAR OF THE WORDS

1388   Clark and Andersen, 144.

1389   Clark and Andersen, 145.

1390   *The Hollywood Reporter*, January 30, 1961.

1391   *The Hollywood Reporter*, January 26, 1961.

1392   *Variety*, January 11, 1961; ibid., January 18, 1961; *The Hollywood Reporter*, January 16, 1961; ibid., January 25, 1961; ibid., December 23, 1960; ibid., January 10, 1961.

1393   *Variety*, December 29, 1960; ibid., March 23, 1961; *San Antonio News*, January 20, 1961; *The Hollywood Reporter*, December 21, 1960; ibid., January 1961; ibid., January 31, 1961; ibid., December 7, 1960; ibid., January 19, 1961; ibid., January 20, 1961; ibid., February 6, 1961.

1394   *Odessa American*, January 25, 1961.

1395   *Lima News*, November 6, 1960; Clark and Andersen, 147.

1396   Pilar Wayne, 150; Munn, 226.

1397   *Lima News*, January 26, 1961.

1398   Munn, 237; Fagen, 154; Davis, *Duke*, 245; Pilar Wayne, 159; Leonard Mosley, *Zanuck: The Rise and Fall of Hollywood's Last Tycoon*, 327; Charlton Heston; *In the Arena: An Autobiography*, 270; Tim Lilley, "The Longest Day," *The Trail Beyond*, Vol. VI, December 2004, 42-59.

1399   Clark and Andersen, 146.

1400   *The Hollywood Reporter*, February 2, 1961; *Variety*, March 21, 1961.

1401   *The Hollywood Reporter*, February 9, 1961; *Box Office*, February 27, 1961; *Van Nuys News*, March 23, 1961.

CHAPTER THIRTY-FIVE – "AND THE WINNER IS ..."

1402   *Variety*, March 1, 1961.

1403   *Hollywood Citizen News*, March 29, 1961.

1404   *The Milwaukee Journal*, April 9, 1961; *Box Office*, February 13, 1961; *Los Angeles Times*, February 10, 1961; ibid., March 6, 1961; *Los Angeles Mirror*, March 1, 1961.

1405   *Los Angeles Mirror*, March 7, 1961.

1406   *Los Angeles Times*, March 6, 1961; *Close-Up*, March 9, 1961.

1407   *Unknown newspaper*, March 1, 1961.

1408   *The Hollywood Reporter*, March 6, 1961; *Los Angeles Times*, March 2, 1961; ibid., March 19, 1961; Clark and Andersen, 147.

1409   *Variety*, March 13, 1961; ibid., March 1, 1961; *The Hollywood Reporter*, March 15, 1961; *The Vidette-Messenger*, March 24, 1961.

1410   USC, John Wayne collection, box 3, folder 12, Seymour Poe to Michael Wayne, March 20, 1961.

1411   *Variety*, March 17, 1961.

1412   *Variety*, March 21, 1961.

1413   Clark and Andersen, 148; *Los Angeles Times*, March 22, 1961.

1414   *Variety*, March 24, 1961; *Odessa American*, March 30, 1961.

1415   *Variety*, March 24, 1961.

1416   Davis, *Duke*, 233.

1417   *Los Angeles Times*, March 30, 1961; "Sabrina (Norma Ann Sykes)," www.imdb.com; "Sabrina," Wikipedia.org; Munn, 227.

1418   *Hollywood Citizen News*, March 29, 1961; *The Palladium Times*, March 31, 1961.

1419   *Los Angeles Examiner*, March 29, 1961; *The Hollywood Reporter*, March 24, 1961.

1420   *Madison Capital Times*, April 4, 1961.

CHAPTER THIRTY-SIX – AFTERMATH

1421   *Star-News*, April 81, 1961; *Los Angeles Times*, November 20, 1960; ibid., December 8, 1960; *Variety*, November 9, 1960.

1422   *Variety*, April 18, 1961; *The Hollywood Reporter*, April 18, 1961.

1423   *The Hollywood Reporter*, April 18, 1961; Damien Bona, "Oscar Films: 75 years of Bribes, Lies and Overkill." http://memorialwebsites.legacy.com/DamienCBona/Subpage.aspx?mod=5&ID=30859&new=1#sthash.sjvQ3kSc.dpuf

1424   *Variety*, April 18 and 19, 1961.

1425   Munn, 218, 220, 227; Aissa Wayne, 50; Pilar Wayne, 151; McGivern, *John Wayne*, 306; Tom Kane interview; *The Hollywood Reporter*, May 31, 1961.

1426   "The Green Berets," http://emanuellevy.com/review/green-berets-the-2/#sthash.blok8NTW.dpuf

1427   Proposed John Wayne autobiography, MZP.

1428   Aissa Wayne, 50.

1429   *Tucson Daily Citizen*, May 20, 1961.

1430   *The Hollywood Reporter*, May 17, 1961; *Variety*, April 20, 1961; ibid., April 26, 1961.

1431   *Variety*, February 22, 1993; *The Hollywood Reporter*, April 26, 1991.

1432   *Box Office*, April 24, 1961; *Reno Evening Gazette*, June 5, 1961; *The Hollywood Reporter*, April 28, 1961.

1433   *Variety*, September 25, 196; ibid., October 4, 1961; *San Antonio Light*, June 1, 1961; *Los Angeles Times*, December 13, 1961.

1434   *The Hollywood Reporter*, June 22, 1961; *Variety*, December 13, 1961.

1435  Larry Siegel and Mort Drucker, "Mad visits John Wayne on the set of 'At the Alamo,'" *Mad*, June, 1961, 45-48.

1436  Munn, 218.

1437  Landesman, 154; *Variety*, March 20, 1962.

1438  Hall and Neale, 161; Munn, 221; Alex Ben Block, *George Lucas's Blockbusting*, 421.

1439  Tomkies, 90; McGivern, *John Wayne*, 304-5; Munn, 221; Davis, *Duke*, 233; Fagen, *John Wayne*, 134; Davis, *Duke*, 239-40; Landesman, 73, 135-36, 153; USC, John Wayne Collection, box 1, folder 10, James Edward Grant to Perry Leiber, March 22, 1960; USC John Wayne Collection, box 3, folder 20, John Wayne Alamo contract, September 1, 1959; Eyman, *John Wayne*, 319; John Wayne to James Edward Grant, July 20, 1959, JFP; *Variety*, May 7, 1968.

1440  *Variety*, April 28, 1965.

1441  USC, John Wayne Collection, box 3, folder 2, The Alamo Distribution Report, September 30, 1961; USC, John Wayne Collection, box 3, folder 21, 10, Interdepartment Communication, Michael Wayne to file, July 31, 1962; USC, John Wayne Collection, box 3, folder 22, The Alamo Survey of Roadshow Engagements to March 28, 1964.

1442  *Variety*, February 10, 1965.

1443  USC, John Wayne Collection, box 3, folder 17, Michael Wayne file correspondence, November 6, 1965; *Variety*, January 13, 1964; *Variety*, August 18, 1964.

1444  Ashley Ward, 'John Wayne's The Alamo – A Status Report." November 24, 1990; *Variety*, October 7, 1966.

1445  Eyman, *John Wayne*, 344; Landesman, 12; *Variety*, March 1, 1967; ibid., April 6, 1970; *The Odessa American*, July 29, 1973; *Fairbanks Daily News Miner*, September 8, 1973; *The Emporia Gazette*, April 30, 1977.

1446  *New York Daily News*, September 20, 1971; Eyman, *John Wayne*, 344; Clark and Andersen, 143; *Variety*, November 14, 1968.

1447  Davis, *Ford*, 307-8; McBride, 630; Ford, 287; McBride, *Print the Legend*, 488; Fagen, 142, 146.

CHAPTER THIRTY-SEVEN – CONCLUSIONS

1448  Munn, 16; ibid., 216.

1449  Roberson, 229; Davis, *Duke*, 224.

1450  Alamo script; Suid, 247; Davis, *Duke*, 230.

1451  Shepherd and Slatzer, 252; Fagen, 133; Wills, 205-6, 215, 226.

1452  McGhee, *John Wayne: Actor, Artist, Hero*, 199.

APPENDIX E: "THIS IS THE WEST, SIR. WHEN THE LEGEND BECOMES FACT, PRINT THE LEGEND."

1453  Louis Goldman, *Lights*, 13-14, 66; *Dallas News*, February 26, 1950; *Los Angeles Times*, January 28, 1950; ibid., August 8, 1950; ibid., January 22, 1951.

1454  Rothel, *Richard Boone*, 54.

# INDEX

## A

984

# R

# S

# NOT THINKIN'...

# JUST REMEMBERIN'...

## The Making of John Wayne's

## THE ALAMO

*John Farkis*

BearManor
Media

Albany, Georgia

Published in the USA by
BearManor Media
P.O. Box 71426
Albany, GA 31708
www.BearManorMedia.com

ISBN-10: 1-59393-796-2
ISBN-13: 978-1-59393-796-6

Printed in the United States of America